MACHINE LEARNING

Proceedings of the Sixteenth International Conference (ICML '99)

Edited by

Ivan Bratko
Faculty of Computer and Information Sciences
University of Ljubljana, Ljubljana, Slovenia and
Jožef Stefan Institute
Ljubljana, Slovenia

Sašo Džeroski
Jožef Stefan Institute
Ljubljana, Slovenia

Bled, Slovenia

June 27–30, 1999

MORGAN KAUFMANN PUBLISHERS
San Francisco, California

CIP-Kataložni zapis o publikaciji
Narodna in Univerzitetna knjižnica, Ljubljana

681.3.001.7(063)(082)

INTERNATIONAL Conference on Machine Learning (16 ; 1999 ; Bled)
Machine learning : Proceedings of the Sixteenth International Conference (ICML '99), Bled, Slovenia, June 27–30, 1999 / edited by Ivan Bratko and Sašo Džeroski. – San Francisco : M. Kaufmann, 1999

ISBN 1-55860-612-2

1. Gl. stv. nasl. 2. Bratko, Ivan 3. Džeroski, Sašo. –I. ICML '99
glej International Conference on Machine Learning (16 ; 1999 ; Bled)
99442688

Production, design, and type provided by Professional Book Center, Denver, Colorado. Order of papers and manufacturing management provided by the conference organization.

Cover image, photograph of Bled, Slovenia, courtesy of Marjan Smerke, Jožef Stefan Institute, Ljubljana, Slovenia.

Morgan Kaufmann Publishers, Inc.
Editorial Office:
340 Pine St., 6th Floor
San Francisco, CA 94104
http://www.mkp.com

ISBN 1-55860-612-2

ISSN 1049-1910

Printed in Slovenia by Tiskarna OPTIMA

02 01 00 99 4 3 2 1

Po mnenju Ministrstva za znanost in tehnologijo št. 415-01-29/99, z dne 2.3.1999
spada zbornik ICML-99 med proizvode, za katere se plačuje 5% davek od prometa proizvodov.

According to the opinion of the Ministry of Science and Technology of the Republic of Slovenia no. 415-01-29/99 of March 2, 1999, the ICML-99 Proceedings fall within the category of products to which a sales tax of 5% applies.

Contents

Preface

This volume contains the accepted technical papers and invited papers of the Sixteenth International Conference on Machine Learning (ICML'99), held June 27–30, 1999, at Bled, Slovenia. A total of 152 papers from 30 countries were submitted to the conference. Of these, 54 papers were accepted after a rigorous review process. Each submitted paper was sent to three members of the Program Committee for review. The majority of reviews were done by the Program Committee members themselves, and some by other reviewers appointed by the committee members. However, in any case, the committee members checked and approved all the reviews. About 45% of the papers, which received mixed recommendations, were discussed further by the corresponding reviewers. In the process, three reviews were obtained for each of 150 papers; we had four reviews and two reviews respectively for the remaining two papers. The quality of reviewing and the criteria set by the reviewers were generally very high, following the tradition of high standards established by the ICML conference series.

The program of ICML'99 consisted of three invited talks, oral and poster presentations of the accepted technical papers, five accompanying ICML workshops on specialized topics, and six tutorials. The conference was co-located with the ILP'99 Workshop (Inductive Logic Programming Workshop, Bled, June 24–26, 1999). The proceedings of ILP'99, edited by Sašo Džeroski and Peter Flach were published by Springer-Verlag. On June 27, ILP'99 and ICML'99 had a joint invited talk by Ross Quinlan and a joint poster session where all the papers accepted at ILP'99 and ICML'99 were presented.

Many people contributed in various ways to the ICML'99 conference. We would especially like to thank:

- The authors of the submitted papers who made it possible to maintain the high technical standard of papers presented at ICML conferences.
- The three invited speakers: John Anderson, William Cohen, and Ross Quinlan.
- The Advisory Committee for their suggestions regarding the Program Committee, invited speakers, workshops, tutorials and other topics, and encouraging remarks.
- The members of the Program Committee for their efforts in carefully evaluating the submitted papers, and to the following reviewers in addition to Program Committee members: Carolyn Allex, Sarabjot S. Anand, David Andre, Vicente Ruiz de Angulo, Riccardo Bellazzi, Francesco Bergadano, Hendrik Blockeel, Marko Bohanec, Michael Bowling, Peter Brockhausen, Maurice Bruynooghe, Cristopher H. Bryant, Enric Celaya, David Cohn, James Cussens, Chris Drummond, Werner Dubitzky, Tina Eliassi-Rad, Nicola Fanizzi, Stefano Ferilli, João Gama, Daishi Harada, Stefan Haustein, Arvid Holme, Robert Holte, Thorsten Joachims, Alipio Jorge, Dimitar Kazakov, Joerg Kindermann, Mathias Kirsten, Ralf Klinkenberg, Willi Kloesgen, Stefan Kramer, Daniel Kudenko, Matjaž Kukar, Francesca Alessandra Lisi, Huan Liu, Suresh Manandhar, Steve Moyle, Kevin Murphy, Andrew Ng, Gerhard Paass, Vassilis Papavassiliou, Rupert Parson, Dave Patterson, Johann Petrak, Bernhard Pfahringer, Jan Ramon, Marko Robnik-Šikonja, Giovanni Semeraro, Maria Eduarda Silva, Valentina Tamma, Rupert Tang, Georgios Theocharous, and Luis Torgo.
- All the sponsors (listed below), and especially the general sponsor HERMES SoftLab for their generous support.
- The members of the Organizing Committee Tanja Urbančič (Local chair), Dunja Mladenić (Workshops chair), Blaž Zupan (Tutorials chair), Damjan Demšar and Darko Zupanič; special thanks to Tanja for her enthusiasm and care in organizing so many details involved in such a conference.
- The management and staff of the Albatross Congress Tourist Agency, Bled, and the Center for Knowledge Transfer in Information Technologies, Jožef Stefan Institute, Ljubljana, for their organizational support.

- The organizers of the ICML workshops and the presenters of the tutorials.
- The Jožef Stefan Institute for providing the organizational infrastructure.
- Marilyn Alan and Denise Penrose of Morgan Kaufmann Publishers and the staff of Professional Book Center for their collaboration in this project.

Ivan Bratko and Sašo Džeroski,
ICML'99 Program Co-chairs

Acknowledgments

We acknowledge the financial support of the following sponsors:

- HERMES SoftLab, Ljubljana, Slovenia, General sponsor
- DaimlerChrysler Research and Technology Center, Palo Alto, CA, USA
- Jerovšek Computers, Ljubljana, Slovenia
- Jožef Stefan Institute, Ljubljana, Slovenia
- Microsoft Research, Redmond, WA, USA
- MLNET-II. ESPRIT IV Project 29288, Network of Excellence in Machine Learning
- Slovenian Ministry of Science and Technology, Ljubljana, Slovenia
- TEMIDA, Ljubljana, Slovenia
- TSE Trade, Ljubljana, Slovenia

We also acknowledge the support of the following:

- Faculty of Computer and Information Sciences, University of Ljubljana, Ljubljana, Slovenia
- Slovenian Artificial Intelligence Society

Advisory Committee

Luc De Raedt
Thomas G. Dietterich
Douglas Fisher
Pat Langley
Ramon Lopez de Mantaras
Tom Mitchell
Leslie Pack Kaelbling
Stuart Russell
Lorenza Saitta
Jude Shavlik
Derek Sleeman

Organizing Committee

Tanja Urbančič (Chair)
Damjan Demšar
Sašo Džeroski
Dunja Mladenić (Workshop Chair)
Blaž Zupan (Tutorial Chair)
Darko Zupanič

Program Committee

Agnar Aamodt
David W. Aha
Husein Almuallim
Chris Atkeson
Shumeet Baluja
Andrew Barto
Pavel Brazdil
Eric Brill
Claire Cardie
Mark Craven
Gerald DeJong
Kenneth De Jong
Luc De Raedt
Thomas G. Dietterich
Pedro Domingos
Floriana Esposito
Usama Fayyad
Claude-Nicolas Fiechter
Johannes Fuernkranz
Diana Gordon
H. Altay Guvenir
David Heckerman
Leslie Pack Kaelbling
Dennis Kibler
Ron Kohavi
Igor Kononenko
Miroslav Kubat
Nada Lavrač
Michael L. Littman
Sridhar Mahadevan
Donato Malerba
Stan Matwin
Dunja Mladenić
Raymond Mooney
Katharina Morik
Hiroshi Motoda
Stephen Muggleton
Enric Plaza i Cervera
Foster Provost
Stuart Russell
Lorenza Saitta
Claude Sammut
Michèle Sebag
Jude Shavlik
Ashwin Srinivasan
Richard Sutton
Prasad Tadepalli
Sebastian Thrun
Carme Torras
Paul Utgoff
Manuela M. Veloso
Paul Vitanyi
Stefan Wrobel
Gerhard Widmer
Blaž Zupan

Organizational Support

The Albatross Congress Tourist Agency, Bled

Center for Knowledge Transfer in Information Technologies, Jožef Stefan Institute, Ljubljana

Best Paper Award

During the reviewing process, each of the three Program Committee members responsible for a paper also had the opportunity to recommend that paper for the Best Paper Award. The ICML'99 Best Paper award went to

- *Least-Squares Temporal Difference Learning* by Justin A. Boyan

This paper was selected by vote by the members of the Program Committee. The following eight submitted papers that received best reviews in the review process were nominated for the vote:

- *Lazy Bayesian Rules: A Lazy Semi-Naive Bayesian Learning Technique Competitive to Boosting Decision Trees,* by Zijian Zheng, Geoffrey I. Webb, and Kai Ming Ting
- *Policy Invariance Under Reward Transformations: Theory and Application to Reward Shaping,* by Andrew Y. Ng, Daishi Harada, and Stuart Russell
- *Hierarchical Optimization of Policy-Coupled Semi-Markov Decision Processes,* by Gang Wang and Sridhar Mahadevan
- *Discriminant Trees,* by João Gama
- *Active Learning for Natural Language Parsing and Information Extraction,* by Cynthia A. Thompson, Mary Elaine Califf, and Raymond J. Mooney
- *Transductive Inference for Text Classification using Support Vector Machines,* by Thorsten Joachims
- *Large Margin Trees for Induction and Transduction,* by Donghui Wu, Kristin P. Bennett, Nello Cristianini, and John Shawe-Taylor
- *Least-Squares Temporal Difference Learning,* by Justin A. Boyan

Tutorials

Case Based Reasoning (Agnar Aamodt)

Inductive Logic Programing Made Easy (Luc De Raedt)

Hierarchical Reinforcement Learning (Thomas G. Dietterich)

Grammatical Inference: Learning Syntax from Sentences (Colin de la Higuera and Laurent Miclet)

Machine Discovery (Pat Langley)

Reinforcement Learning (Richard Sutton)

Workshops

Recent Advances in Meta-Learning and Future Work
(organized by Christophe Giraud-Carrier and Bernhard Pfahringer)

Machine Learning in Text Data Analysis
(organized by Dunja Mladenić and Marko Grobelnik)

Machine Learning in Game Playing
(organized by Johannes Fuernkranz and Miroslav Kubat)

Machine Learning in Computer Vision
(organized by Tatjana Zrimec)

From Machine Learning to Knowledge Discovery in Databases
(organized by Ivan Bruha and Marko Bohanec)

CONTRIBUTED PAPERS

Associative Reinforcement Learning using Linear Probabilistic Concepts

Naoki Abe*
Theory NEC Laboratory, RWCP†
c/o NEC C & C Media Research Laboratories
4-1-1 Miyazaki, Miyamae-ku
Kawasaki 216-8555 JAPAN
E-mail: abe@ccm.cl.nec.co.jp

Philip M. Long
Department of Computer Science
National University of Singapore
Singapore 119260, Republic of Singapore
Email: plong@comp.nus.edu.sg

Abstract

We consider the problem of maximizing the total number of successes while learning about a probability function determining the likelihood of a success. In particular, we consider the case in which the probability function is represented by a linear function of the attribute vector associated with each action/choice. In the scenario we consider, learning proceeds in trials and in each trial, the algorithm is given a number of alternatives to choose from, each having an attribute vector associated with it, and for the alternative it selects it gets either a success or a failure with probability determined by applying a fixed but unknown linear success probability function to the attribute vector. Our algorithms consist of a learning method like the Widrow-Hoff rule and a probabilistic selection strategy which work together to resolve the so-called exploration-exploitation trade-off. We analyze the performance of these methods by proving bounds on the worst-case *regret*, or how many less successes they expect to get as compared to the ideal (but unrealistic) strategy that knows the target probability function. Our analysis shows that the worst-case (expected) regret for our methods is almost optimal: the upper bounds grow with the number m of trials and the number n of alternatives like $O(m^{3/4}n^{1/2})$ and $O(m^{4/5}n^{2/5})$, and the lower bound is $\Omega(m^{3/4}n^{1/4})$.

*This author is also affiliated with the Department of Computational Intelligence and Systems Sciences, Interdisciplinary Graduate School of Science and Engineering, Tokyo Institute of Technology, 4259 Nagatsuta, Midori-ku, Yokohama 226 JAPAN.

†Real World Computing Partnership

1 INTRODUCTION

We consider the problem of maximizing the total number of successes while learning about a probability function determining the likelihood of a success. In particular, we consider the case in which the probability function is represented by a linear function of the attribute vector associated with each action/choice. In the scenario we consider, learning proceeds in trials and in each trial, the algorithm is given a number of alternatives to choose from, each having an attribute vector associated with it, and for the alternative it selects it gets either a success or a failure, where the probability of success is determined by applying a fixed but unknown linear function to the attribute vector. The goal of a learner is to select alternatives so as to maximize the total number of successes in a given number of trials, resolving the so-called exploration-exploitation trade-off along the way.

The learning model considered in this paper is applicable to many important real world problems. A good example is the problem of maximizing the effectiveness of internet banner ads. The internet banner ad is distinguished by the property that an interested user can click on it and obtain more information. One goal of an internet ad server might be to display those ads that are likely to yield higher click rates, and learning the ad preference function should further this goal.[1] It is reasonable to suppose that the click probability

[1] Although higher click rates are desirable, it is not generally considered to be the sole measure of an ad's effectiveness, and an ad server might have constraints on its choices. For a more detailed formulation of the ad server problem, we refer the reader to [1].

can be approximated by a linear function of logical combinations of various attributes associated with the users, the environment, and the ads (such as age, sex, the domain, ad genres, etc.); of course, a number of such logical combinations can be thought of as additional attributes. Whenever the server has a slot to display a banner ad, it is to select one from among a number of alternative ads each of which is associated with an attribute vector. Importantly, these attribute values for the candidate ads can change over time depending on the user and environment attributes. All of these features are captured in our model.

The problem considered here is in a class of problems referred to as *associative reinforcement learning* [9, 8]. Our theoretical model is related to a number of models from the literature [12, 4, 7, 2]. It is most closely related to the on-line evaluation model [12], which in turn is an extension of the apple tasting model[2] [7]. In the on-line evaluation model, the actual real-valued payoff was represented by a linear function of the attributes associated with the alternatives. In the model we study in this paper, the probability of getting the larger of two binary-valued payoffs is assumed to be linear in the attributes, and the learner only finds out the payoff instead of the probability of success. In many applications, including the ad placement problem, this is all the information that is available. The model of this paper can also be thought of as an extension of the bandit problem [4] (where an algorithm repeatedly must choose from among a row of slot machines) in which the success probability is dictated by a linear function of the attributes associated with the alternatives, and the attributes of the alternatives presented to the learner at each trial may change over time.

In this paper, we propose two methods for this problem and theoretically analyze their performance. Our methods, which are based on methods proposed and analyzed in [12], consist of two components; the learning method and the selection strategy. The learning method we use is the Widrow-Hoff rule with the step size set as a function of various parameters of the problem. Our selection strategies are most likely to pick the alternative with the best predicted success probability, but pick other alternatives for exploration as well, with probabilities determined by a function of those parameters. Our theoretical analysis is in terms of the worst-case (expected) regret, that is how many less successes a method is expected to obtain as compared to the optimal selection strategy that knows the success probability function a priori, on a least favorable sequence of attribute vectors and for a worst-case success function (more details are given below). We consider a worst-case sequence of attribute vectors since independence assumptions seem inappropriate for modeling applications like the ad placement problem. We have proved upper bounds and almost matching lower bounds for our methods. Our upper bounds grow with the number m of trials and the number n of alternatives like $O(m^{3/4}n^{1/2})$ and $O(m^{4/5}n^{2/5})$, and the lower bound is $\Omega(m^{3/4}n^{1/4})$.

2 FRAMEWORK

Now let us spell out our framework in more detail. We assume learning proceeds in trials. In each trial t, the learning algorithm must choose from among n alternatives. Before making this choice, it is given feature vectors $\vec{x}_{t,1}, \dots, \vec{x}_{t,n}$, one for each alternative. We will refer to the number of features as d. Then, possibly using randomization, it outputs its choice, which will formally be a number between 1 and n, and which we will refer to as a_t. To finish the trial, the algorithm receives z_{t,a_t}, a $\{0, 1\}$-valued quantity indicating whether this choice resulted in failure (0) or a success (1).

We will assume that the total number of trials m in the learning process is finite and known to the algorithm ahead of time. This is just to simplify the analysis: as was the case in [7], if our algorithms replace each dependency of a parameter on m with the same dependency on the trial number t, nearly the same analysis yields almost the same bounds.

We will assume that there is an unknown coefficient vector $\vec{v} \in \mathbf{R}^d$ such that, for all trials t and alternatives i, $\mathbf{Pr}(z_{t,i} = 1) = \vec{v} \cdot \vec{x}_{t,i}$. We will make the benign assumption that all $\vec{x}_{t,i}$'s encountered during the learning process have the property that $\vec{v} \cdot \vec{x}_{t,i} \in [0, 1]$. This assumption would be satisfied for example if there was a default probability of success (which can be represented in our framework using a feature that always has the same value) that was adjusted somewhat by the specifics of the feature vectors.

If one designs algorithms and analyzes them using the assumption that the algorithm knows a priori that the length of the feature vectors and the length of the coefficient vector are at most 1, one can apply known techniques to modify the algorithms and their analysis to cope with the case in which these lengths are greater

[2]Study of a stochastic generalization of that model which is closely related to our model was mentioned as an open problem in [7].

than 1 and they are unknown (see e.g. [5, 6]). To avoid uninteresting clutter in our analysis, we will assume that the algorithms know a priori that the length of these are at most 1.

We say that $\langle \vec{x}_{t,i} \rangle_{t,i}$ (i.e. the collection of all feature vectors encountered during some run of a learning algorithm) and $\vec{v}$ are *admissible* if all of their lengths are at most 1 and $\vec{v} \cdot \vec{x}_{t,i}$ is always in $[0, 1]$. In this case, we also say that the run is admissible.

We say that the worst case regret of a learner A is at most $f(m, n)$ if for *any* admissible run of A of length m with each trial consisting of n alternatives, the expected number of successes of A, $\sum_{t=1}^{m} \mathbf{E}(z_{t,a_t})$, is at most $f(m, n)$ less than the expected number of successes of the ideal strategy, namely $\sum_{t=1}^{m} \max_i \mathbf{E}(z_{t,i})$, where $\mathbf{E}(\cdot)$ is expectation with respect to all the randomization in the learning process.

We will assume that $m \geq n$, since in practice m should be relatively large, and it is not hard to see that the trivial upper bound of m is within a constant factor of optimal for $m < n$.

3 ALGORITHMS

Define the clipping function π by letting $\pi(x)$ be the element of $[0, 1]$ that is closest to x.

3.1 Algorithm A

Our first algorithm is distinguished by the property that each alternative *not* estimated to be the best by the current hypothesis is picked with probability roughly inversely proportional to how much worse it is predicted to be as compared to the alternative that appears to be best. We will refer to this algorithm as A. It sets $\kappa = m^{3/4}\sqrt{n}/2$, $\alpha = 1/\sqrt{m}$, and $\vec{w}_1 = (0, ..., 0)$. On the tth trial, the algorithm

- for each alternative i, calculates its estimate $\hat{y}_{t,i} = \pi(\vec{w}_t \cdot \vec{x}_{t,i})$ of the probability of success for alternative i on this trial,
- sets $g_t \in \{1, ..., n\}$ to be some alternative that maximizes $\hat{y}_{t,g_t}$, i.e. that its current hypothesis suggests is the most likely to lead to success,
- for each alternative i other than the alternative g_t that appears to be the best, sets the probability $p_{t,i}$ of choosing alternative i to be

$$p_{t,i} = \frac{1}{n + 4\kappa(\alpha - \alpha^2)(\hat{y}_{t,g_t} - \hat{y}_{t,i})}$$

- gives the rest of the probability to g_t, i.e., sets $p_{t,g_t} = 1 - \sum_{i \neq g_t} p_{t,i}$,
- chooses a_t randomly according to $p_{t,1}, ..., p_{t,n}$,
- receives $z_{t,a_t} \in \{0, 1\}$ from the environment (where for all i, $\mathbf{Pr}(z_{t,i} = 1) = \vec{v} \cdot \vec{x}_{t,i}$; let us refer to $\vec{v} \cdot \vec{x}_{t,i}$ as $y_{t,i}$)
- sets $\vec{w}_{t+1} = \vec{w}_t + \alpha(z_{t,a_t} - \vec{w}_t \cdot \vec{x}_{t,a_t})\vec{x}_{t,a_t}$.

3.2 Algorithm U

The next algorithm we propose, which we will refer to as U, is simpler than A in that it picks the not-apparently-best alternatives with equal probability; however, it takes a bigger step when a not-apparently-best alternative is chosen. In particular, it sets $\kappa = m^{4/5}n^{2/5}$, $p = \sqrt{n}/(3\kappa)^{1/4}$, $\alpha = (1/2)n^{1/3}/(p\kappa)^{2/3}$, $\beta = 1/(2\kappa^{2/3})$, and $\vec{w}_1 = (0, ..., 0)$. On the tth trial, the algorithm

- for each alternative i, calculates its estimate $\hat{y}_{t,i} = \pi(\vec{w}_t \cdot \vec{x}_{t,i})$ of the probability of success for alternative i on this trial,
- sets $g_t \in \{1, ..., n\}$ to be some alternative that maximizes $\hat{y}_{t,g_t}$, i.e. that its current hypothesis suggests is the most likely to lead to success,
- flips a biased coin, and
  - with probability p,
    * chooses a_t uniformly from at random from $\{1, ..., n\}$,
    * receives $z_{t,a_t} \in \{0, 1\}$ from the environment, and
    * sets $\vec{w}_{t+1} = \vec{w}_t + \alpha(z_{t,a_t} - \vec{w}_t \cdot \vec{x}_{t,a_t})\vec{x}_{t,a_t}$, and
  - with probability $1 - p$,
    * sets $a_t = g_t$,
    * receives $z_{t,a_t} \in \{0, 1\}$ from the environment, and
    * sets $\vec{w}_{t+1} = \vec{w}_t + \beta(z_{t,a_t} - \vec{w}_t \cdot \vec{x}_{t,a_t})\vec{x}_{t,a_t}$.

4 UPPER BOUNDS

In this section, we analyze the algorithms presented in Section 3. Following [6, 12] our analysis will proceed by using the squared distance between the hypothesis coefficient vector $\vec{w}_t$ and the target coefficient vector $\vec{v}$ as a "measure of progress".

4.1 Preliminaries

Our first progress lemma follows directly from the analysis in [6].

Lemma 1 ([6]) *For any $\vec{v}, \vec{w}_{\text{old}}, \vec{x} \in \mathbf{R}^n, z, \alpha \in \mathbf{R}$ for which $||\vec{x}|| \leq 1$, and $0 < \alpha < 1/2$, if $y = \vec{v} \cdot \vec{x}$, and $\vec{w}_{\text{new}} = \vec{w}_{\text{old}} + \alpha(z - \hat{y})\vec{x}$, then*

$$\begin{aligned} &||\vec{w}_{\text{new}} - \vec{v}||^2 - ||\vec{w}_{\text{old}} - \vec{v}||^2 \\ &\leq -(\alpha - \alpha^2/2)(\vec{w}_{\text{old}} \cdot \vec{x} - z)^2 \\ &\quad +(\alpha + \alpha^2/2 + \alpha^3/3)(y - z)^2. \qquad (1) \end{aligned}$$

Straightforward application of calculus leads to the following variant.

Lemma 2 *For any $\vec{v}, \vec{w}_{\text{old}}, \vec{x} \in \mathbf{R}^n, z, \alpha \in \mathbf{R}$ for which $||\vec{x}|| \leq 1$, $0 < \alpha < 1/2$, and $z \in [0, 1]$, if $y = \vec{v} \cdot \vec{x}$, and $\vec{w}_{\text{new}} = \vec{w}_{\text{old}} + \alpha(y - \hat{y})\vec{x}$, then*

$$\begin{aligned} &||\vec{w}_{\text{new}} - \vec{v}||^2 - ||\vec{w}_{\text{old}} - \vec{v}||^2 \\ &\leq -(\alpha - \alpha^2/2)(\pi(\vec{w}_{\text{old}} \cdot \vec{x}) - z)^2 \\ &\quad +(\alpha + \alpha^2/2 + \alpha^3/3)(y - z)^2. \end{aligned}$$

Proof: Define $f : \mathbf{R} \to \mathbf{R}$ to be the right hand side of (1), viewed as a function of $\vec{w}_{\text{old}} \cdot \vec{x}$; i.e., for all u,

$$f(u) = -(\alpha - \alpha^2/2)(u - z)^2 + (\alpha + \alpha^2/2 + \alpha^3/3)(y - z)^2.$$

Then

$$f'(u) = -2(\alpha - \alpha^2/2)(u - z).$$

If $u \geq 1$, then since $\alpha - \alpha^2/2 > 0$,

$$f'(u) \leq -2(\alpha - \alpha^2/2)(1 - z) \leq 0,$$

since z is at most 1. Thus, f is maximized, subject to $u \geq 1$, when $u = 1$.

If $u \leq 0$, then

$$f'(u) \geq (\alpha - \alpha^2/2)z \geq 0$$

since z is at least 0. Thus, f is maximized, subject to $u \leq 0$, when $u = 0$.

Overall, we have that $f(\pi(u)) \geq f(u)$, and putting this together with Lemma 1 completes the proof. □

In our next lemma, we assume that z is generated randomly according to $\vec{v} \cdot \vec{x}$, and the progress is given in terms of how well $\vec{w}_{\text{old}} \cdot \vec{x}$ approximates this probability.

Lemma 3 *For any $\vec{v}, \vec{w}_{\text{old}}, \vec{x} \in \mathbf{R}^n, \alpha \in \mathbf{R}$ for which $||\vec{x}|| \leq 1$, $0 < \alpha < 1/2$, if $y = \vec{v} \cdot \vec{x} \in [0, 1]$, $\hat{y} = \pi(\vec{w}_{\text{old}} \cdot \vec{x})$, and if $z \in \{0, 1\}$ is chosen randomly so that $\mathbf{Pr}(z = 1) = y$ and $\vec{w}_{\text{new}} = \vec{w}_{\text{old}} + \alpha(z - \hat{y})\vec{x}$, then*

$$\begin{aligned} &\mathbf{E}(||\vec{w}_{\text{new}} - \vec{v}||^2 - ||\vec{w}_{\text{old}} - \vec{v}||^2) \\ &\leq -(\alpha - \alpha^2/2)(\hat{y} - y)^2 + \alpha^2 + \alpha^3/3. \end{aligned}$$

Proof: Applying Lemma 2,

$$\begin{aligned} &\mathbf{E}(||\vec{w}_{\text{new}} - \vec{v}||^2 - ||\vec{w}_{\text{old}} - \vec{v}||^2) \\ &\leq y(-(\alpha - \alpha^2/2)(1 - \hat{y})^2 \\ &\quad +(\alpha + \alpha^2/2 + \alpha^3/3)(1 - y)^2) \\ &\quad +(1 - y)(-(\alpha - \alpha^2/2)\hat{y}^2 \\ &\quad +(\alpha + \alpha^2/2 + \alpha^3/3)y^2). \end{aligned}$$

Let $r = \hat{y} - y$. Then

$$\begin{aligned} &\mathbf{E}(||\vec{w}_{\text{new}} - \vec{v}||^2 - ||\vec{w}_{\text{old}} - \vec{v}||^2) \\ &\leq y(-(\alpha - \alpha^2/2)(1 - (y + r))^2 \\ &\quad +(\alpha + \alpha^2/2 + \alpha^3/3)(1 - y)^2) \\ &\quad +(1 - y)(-(\alpha - \alpha^2/2)(y + r)^2 \\ &\quad +(\alpha + \alpha^2/2 + \alpha^3/3)y^2). \end{aligned}$$

Simplifying yields

$$\begin{aligned} &\mathbf{E}(||\vec{w}_{\text{new}} - \vec{v}||^2 - ||\vec{w}_{\text{old}} - \vec{v}||^2) \\ &\leq -(\alpha - \alpha^2/2)r^2 + (\alpha^2 + \alpha^3/3)y(1 - y), \end{aligned}$$

which, since $y \in [0, 1]$, completes the proof. □

4.2 Analysis of Algorithm A

The following theorem is our main result about algorithm A.

Theorem 4 *The worst case regret of A is at most $(2 + o(1))n^{1/2}m^{3/4}$. That is, on any admissible run of algorithm A, if $\mathbf{E}(\cdot)$ represents the expectation with respect to all the randomization in the learning process,*

$$\sum_{t=1}^{m} \max_i \mathbf{E}(z_{t,i}) - \sum_{t=1}^{m} \mathbf{E}(z_{t,a_t}) \leq (2 + o(1))n^{1/2}m^{3/4},$$

where $o(1)$ denotes a quantity whose limit as m goes to infinity is 0.

The proof of Theorem 4 makes use of the following lemma. The proof of this lemma uses ideas from the proof of [12, Theorem 11]; however, in addition to modifying that proof to apply to our problem, we have also simplified and refined it.

Lemma 5 *On any admissible run of algorithm A, on any trial t, if $\mathbf{E}(\cdot)$ represents the expectation with respect to all the randomization in the learning process,*

$$\max_i y_{t,i} - \mathbf{E}(z_{t,a_t}) \leq \kappa \mathbf{E}(||\vec{w}_t - \vec{v}||^2 - ||\vec{w}_{t+1} - \vec{v}||^2) + \frac{n}{2\kappa(\alpha - \alpha^2)} + \kappa(\alpha^2 + \alpha^3/3).$$

Proof: Choose an admissible run of algorithm A, and fix some trial t. Let progress $= \mathbf{E}(||\vec{w}_t - \vec{v}||^2 - ||\vec{w}_{t+1} - \vec{v}||^2)$ and best $= \max_i y_{t,i}$ and drop the subscript t from all notation. Choose b so that $y_b = \max_i y_i$.

Applying Lemma 3,

$$\begin{aligned}
&\text{best} - \mathbf{E}(z_a) - \kappa \text{ progress} \\
&\leq \left(\sum_{i=1}^n p_i(y_b - y_i)\right) \\
&\quad -\kappa\left(\sum_{i=1}^n p_i((\alpha - \alpha^2/2)(\hat{y}_i - y_i)^2 - \alpha^2 - \alpha^3/3)\right) \\
&= \left(\sum_{i=1}^n p_i(y_b - y_i - \kappa(\alpha - \alpha^2/2)(\hat{y}_i - y_i)^2)\right) \\
&\quad +\kappa(\alpha^2 + \alpha^3/3).
\end{aligned}$$

Using calculus, one can see that, for each $i \neq b$, $\sum_{i=1}^n p_i(y_b - y_i - \kappa(\alpha - \alpha^2/2)(\hat{y}_i - y_i)^2)$ is maximized, as a function of y_i, when $y_i = \hat{y}_i - \frac{1}{2(\alpha - \alpha^2/2)\kappa}$. Substituting and simplifying, we get

$$\begin{aligned}
&\text{best} - \mathbf{E}(z_a) - \kappa \text{ progress} \\
&\leq \left(\sum_{i \neq b} p_i(y_b - \hat{y}_i)\right) + \frac{1 - p_b}{4\kappa(\alpha - \alpha^2/2)} \\
&\quad -p_b\kappa(\alpha - \alpha^2/2)(\hat{y}_b - y_b)^2 + \kappa(\alpha^2 + \alpha^3/3).
\end{aligned}$$

Again using calculus, one can see that the bound above, as a function of y_b, is maximized when $y_b = \hat{y}_b + \frac{1 - p_b}{2p_b\kappa(\alpha - \alpha^2/2)}$. Once again substituting and simplifying, we get

$$\begin{aligned}
&\text{best} - \mathbf{E}(z_a) - \kappa \text{ progress} \\
&\leq \left(\sum_{i \neq b} p_i(\hat{y}_b - \hat{y}_i)\right) + \frac{1 - p_b}{4\kappa(\alpha - \alpha^2/2)} \\
&\quad + \frac{(1 - p_b)^2}{4p_b\kappa(\alpha - \alpha^2/2)} + \kappa(\alpha^2 + \alpha^3/3).
\end{aligned}$$

For all $i \in \{1, ..., n\}$, let $u_i = \hat{y}_g - \hat{y}_i$. Then the above implies that

$$\begin{aligned}
&\text{best} - \mathbf{E}(z_a) - \kappa \text{ progress} \\
&\leq \left(\sum_{i \neq b} p_i((\hat{y}_g - u_b) - \hat{y}_i)\right) + \frac{1 - p_b}{4\kappa(\alpha - \alpha^2/2)} \\
&\quad + \frac{(1 - p_b)^2}{4p_b\kappa(\alpha - \alpha^2/2)} + \kappa(\alpha^2 + \alpha^3/3) \\
&= \left(\sum_{i \neq b} p_i(\hat{y}_g - \hat{y}_i)\right) - (1 - p_b)u_b + \frac{1 - p_b}{4\kappa(\alpha - \alpha^2/2)} \\
&\quad + \frac{(1 - p_b)^2}{4p_b\kappa(\alpha - \alpha^2/2)} + \kappa(\alpha^2 + \alpha^3/3) \\
&= \left(\sum_{i \notin \{b,g\}} p_i u_i\right) - (1 - p_b)u_b + \frac{1 - p_b}{4\kappa(\alpha - \alpha^2/2)} \\
&\quad + \frac{(1 - p_b)^2}{4p_b\kappa(\alpha - \alpha^2/2)} + \kappa(\alpha^2 + \alpha^3/3) \\
&\leq \left(\sum_{i \neq g} p_i u_i\right) - u_b + \frac{1}{4\kappa(\alpha - \alpha^2/2)} \\
&\quad + \frac{1}{4p_b\kappa(\alpha - \alpha^2/2)} + \kappa(\alpha^2 + \alpha^3/3).
\end{aligned}$$

Substituting into the p_b in the denominator, we get

$$\begin{aligned}
&\text{best} - \mathbf{E}(z_a) - \kappa \text{ progress} \\
&\leq \left(\sum_{i \neq g} p_i u_i\right) - u_b + \frac{1}{4\kappa(\alpha - \alpha^2/2)} \\
&\quad + \frac{n + 4\kappa(\alpha - \alpha^2/2)u_b}{4\kappa(\alpha - \alpha^2/2)} + \kappa(\alpha^2 + \alpha^3/3) \\
&= \left(\sum_{i \neq g} p_i u_i\right) + \frac{n + 1}{4\kappa(\alpha - \alpha^2/2)} + \kappa(\alpha^2 + \alpha^3/3).
\end{aligned}$$

Substituting into the remaining p_i's, we get

$$\begin{aligned}
&\text{best} - \mathbf{E}(z_a) - \kappa \text{ progress} \\
&\leq \left(\sum_{i \neq g} \frac{u_i}{n + 4\kappa(\alpha - \alpha^2/2)u_i}\right) + \frac{n + 1}{4\kappa(\alpha - \alpha^2/2)} \\
&\quad +\kappa(\alpha^2 + \alpha^3/3) \\
&\leq \frac{n}{2\kappa(\alpha - \alpha^2/2)} + \kappa(\alpha^2 + \alpha^3/3),
\end{aligned}$$

completing the proof. □

Proof of Theorem 4: Assume without loss of generality that $m > 1$. For each t, let $\text{best}_t = \max_i y_{t,i}$. Applying Lemma 5, on each trial t,

$$\text{best}_t - \mathbf{E}(z_{t,a_t}) \leq \kappa \mathbf{E}(||\vec{w}_t - \vec{v}||^2 - ||\vec{w}_{t+1} - \vec{v}||^2)$$

$$+\frac{n}{2\kappa(\alpha-\alpha^2/2)}+\kappa(\alpha^2+\alpha^3/3),$$

and therefore

$$\begin{aligned}&\sum_{t=1}^{m}(\text{best}_t-\mathbf{E}(z_{t,a_t}))\\ &\le \kappa\mathbf{E}(\sum_{t=1}^{m}(\|\vec{w}_t-\vec{v}\|^2-\|\vec{w}_{t+1}-\vec{v}\|^2))\\ &\quad+\frac{nm}{2\kappa(\alpha-\alpha^2/2)}+\kappa(\alpha^2+\alpha^3/3)m\\ &=\kappa\mathbf{E}(\|\vec{w}_1-\vec{v}\|^2-\|\vec{w}_{m+1}-\vec{v}\|^2)\\ &\quad+\frac{nm}{2\kappa(\alpha-\alpha^2/2)}+\kappa(\alpha^2+\alpha^3/3)m\\ &\le \kappa(1+(\alpha^2+\alpha^3/3)m)+\frac{nm}{2\kappa(\alpha-\alpha^2/2)}.\end{aligned}$$

Substituting the values of κ and α and simplifying yields

$$\sum_{t=1}^{m}(\text{best}_t-\mathbf{E}(z_{t,a_t}))\le\left(\frac{24\sqrt{m}-4-1/\sqrt{m}}{12\sqrt{m}-6}\right)m^{3/4}\sqrt{n},$$

completing the proof. □

4.3 Analysis of Algorithm U

The following is our main result about U.

Theorem 6 *The worst case regret of U is at most $5n^{2/5}m^{4/5}$. That is, on any admissible run of algorithm U, if $\mathbf{E}(\cdot)$ represents the expectation with respect to all the randomization in the learning process,*

$$\sum_{t=1}^{m}\max_i \mathbf{E}(z_{t,a_t})-\sum_{t=1}^{m}\mathbf{E}(z_{t,a_t})\le 5n^{2/5}m^{4/5}.$$

The proof of Theorem 6 makes use of the following lemma.

Lemma 7 *On any admissible run of algorithm U, on any trial t, if $\mathbf{E}(\cdot)$ represents the expectation with respect to all the randomization in the learning process,*

$$\begin{aligned}&\max_i y_{t,i}-\mathbf{E}(z_{t,a_t})\\ &\le\kappa\mathbf{E}(\|\vec{w}_t-\vec{v}\|^2-\|\vec{w}_{t+1}-\vec{v}\|^2)+p\\ &\quad+\frac{n}{4(\alpha-\alpha^2/2)\kappa p}+\frac{1}{4(\beta-\beta^2/2)\kappa}\\ &\quad+(\alpha^2+\alpha^3/3)pk+(\beta^2+\beta^3/3)\kappa.\end{aligned}$$

Proof: Choose an admissible run of U, and fix some trial t. Let progress $=\mathbf{E}(\|\vec{w}_t-\vec{v}\|^2-\|\vec{w}_{t+1}-\vec{v}\|^2)$ and best $=\max_i y_{t,i}$ and drop the subscript t from all other notation. Choose b so that $y_b=\max_i y_i$.

Clearly, best$-\mathbf{E}(z_a)\le(1-p)(y_b-y_g)+p$, and applying Lemma 3, we have

$$\begin{aligned}\text{progress}\ \ge\ &(p(\alpha-\alpha^2/2)/n)(y_b-\hat{y}_b)^2+\\ &(1-p)(\beta-\beta^2/2)(y_g-\hat{y}_g)^2\\ &-(1-p)(\beta^2+\beta^3/3)-p(\alpha^2+\alpha^3/3)\end{aligned}$$

so

$$\begin{aligned}&\text{best}-\mathbf{E}(z_a)-\kappa\text{ progress}\le\\ &(1-p)(y_b-y_g)+p-(\kappa p(\alpha-\alpha^2/2)/n)(y_b-\hat{y}_b)^2\\ &-(1-p)\kappa(\beta-\beta^2/2)(y_g-\hat{y}_g)^2\\ &+(1-p)\kappa(\beta^2+\beta^3/3)+p\kappa(\alpha^2+\alpha^3/3).\end{aligned}$$

The RHS of this inequality is maximized, as a function of y_b, when $y_b=\hat{y}_b+(1-p)n/(2\kappa p(\alpha-\alpha^2/2))$, and so

$$\begin{aligned}&\text{best}-\mathbf{E}(z_a)-\kappa\text{ progress}\\ &\le(1-p)(\hat{y}_b-y_g)+p+\frac{(1-p)^2n}{4\kappa p(\alpha-\alpha^2/2)}\\ &\quad-(1-p)\kappa(\beta-\beta^2/2)(y_g-\hat{y}_g)^2\\ &\quad+(1-p)\kappa(\beta^2+\beta^3/3+p\kappa(\alpha^2+\alpha^3/3).\end{aligned}$$

The RHS of this inequality is maximized, as a function of y_g, when $y_g=\hat{y}_g-\frac{1}{2\kappa(\beta-\beta^2/2)}$, which implies

$$\begin{aligned}&\text{best}-\mathbf{E}(z_a)-\kappa\text{ progress}\\ &\le(1-p)(\hat{y}_b-\hat{y}_g)+p+\frac{(1-p)^2n}{4\kappa p(\alpha-\alpha^2/2)}\\ &\quad+\frac{(1-p)}{4\kappa(\beta-\beta^2/2)}+(1-p)\kappa(\beta^2+\beta^3/3)\\ &\quad+p\kappa(\alpha^2+\alpha^3/3).\end{aligned}$$

Finally, the definition of $\hat{y}_g$ implies that $\hat{y}_g\ge\hat{y}_b$, so

$$\begin{aligned}&\text{best}-\mathbf{E}(z_a)-\kappa\text{ progress}\\ &\le p+\frac{(1-p)^2n}{4\kappa p(\alpha-\alpha^2/2)}+\frac{(1-p)}{4\kappa(\beta-\beta^2/2)}\\ &\quad+(1-p)\kappa(\beta^2+\beta^3/3)+p\kappa(\alpha^2+\alpha^3/3),\end{aligned}$$

completing the proof. □

Proof of Theorem 6: Assume without loss of generality that $m>1$. For each t, let best$_t=\max_i y_{t,i}$. Applying Lemma 7,

$$\sum_{t=1}^{m}(\text{best}_t-\mathbf{E}(z_{t,a_t}))$$

$$\leq \kappa \mathbf{E}(\sum_{t=1}^{m}(||\vec{w}_t - \vec{v}||^2 - ||\vec{w}_{t+1} - \vec{v}||^2)) + pm$$
$$+ \frac{nm}{4(\alpha - \alpha^2/2)\kappa p} + \frac{m}{4(\beta - \beta^2/2)\kappa}$$
$$+ (\alpha^2 + \alpha^3/3)pkm + (\beta^2 + \beta^3/3)\kappa m$$
$$= \kappa \mathbf{E}(||\vec{w}_1 - \vec{v}||^2 - ||\vec{w}_{m+1} - \vec{v}||^2) + pm$$
$$+ \frac{nm}{4(\alpha - \alpha^2/2)\kappa p} + \frac{m}{4(\beta - \beta^2/2)\kappa}$$
$$+ (\alpha^2 + \alpha^3/3)pkm + (\beta^2 + \beta^3/3)\kappa m$$
$$\leq \kappa + pm$$
$$+ \frac{nm}{4(\alpha - \alpha^2/2)\kappa p} + \frac{m}{4(\beta - \beta^2/2)\kappa}$$
$$+ (\alpha^2 + \alpha^3/3)pkm + (\beta^2 + \beta^3/3)\kappa m.$$

Substituting the values of α and β, and applying the fact that each is at most $1/2$, we get

$$\sum_{t=1}^{m}(\text{best}_t - \mathbf{E}(z_{t,a_t})) \leq \kappa + pm + \frac{mn^{2/3}}{(\kappa p)^{1/3}} + \frac{m}{\kappa^{1/3}}.$$

Substituting the value of p, we get

$$\sum_{t=1}^{m}(\text{best}_t - \mathbf{E}(z_{t,a_t})) \leq \kappa + \frac{2m\sqrt{n}}{\kappa^{1/4}} + \frac{2m}{\kappa^{1/3}}.$$

Substituting the value of κ completes the proof. □

5 LOWER BOUNDS

Our lower bound will be proved using a reduction from the *bandit problem* (see [4]). In the instance of the bandit problem that we need for our application, an algorithm is confronted with a row of K slot machines. Each time a slot machine is played it either pays off or doesn't. Each slot machine pays off with some probability that is unknown to the algorithm, and each time the algorithm plays some slot machine, that random outcome is independent of the other plays. The algorithm makes a sequence of T choices of which machine to play, and each time it plays some machine, it finds out whether that machine pays off. Randomized algorithms are allowed. The goal is to maximize the total number of the T plays that pay off. We will make use of the following technical lemma.

Lemma 8 ([3]) *There is a constant $\gamma > 0$ such that, for any algorithm B for the bandit problem, for any $T \geq K \geq 2$, if a slot machine $i \in \{1, ..., K\}$ is chosen uniformly at random, and*

- *the probability that slot machine i pays off is set to $p_i = \frac{1}{2} + \frac{1}{4}\sqrt{\frac{K}{T}}$, and*
- *the probability that all other slot machines pay off is set to $1/2$, then*

if $z_1, ..., z_T$ is the random sequence of outcomes obtained by applying B to those slot machines

$$\mathbf{E}\left(p_i T - \sum_{t=1}^{T} z_t\right) \geq \gamma\sqrt{KT}.$$

We apply this in our lower bound argument.

Theorem 9 *There is a constant $\gamma > 0$ such that, for any algorithm L for associative reinforcement learning of probabilistic linear functions, the worst case regret of L is at least $\gamma m^{3/4} n^{1/4}$. That is, for any number m of trials and any number n of alternatives per trial such that $m \geq n \geq 2$, there is a sequence $\langle \vec{x}_{t,i} \rangle_{t,i}$ of feature vectors and a coefficient vector $\vec{v}$ such that, if $a_1, ..., a_m$ are the (random) choices arising from L, $\langle \vec{x}_{t,i} \rangle_{t,i}$, and $\vec{v}$, and $z_{1,a_1}, ..., z_{m,a_m}$ is the corresponding random sequence of success/failure events, then*

$$\sum_{t=1}^{m}(\max_i \vec{v} \cdot \vec{x}_{t,i}) - \mathbf{E}(z_{t,a_t}) \geq \gamma m^{3/4} n^{1/4}.$$

Proof: Let $r = \lfloor \sqrt{mn}/4 \rfloor$, and divide the first $r\lfloor m/r \rfloor$ trials into $\lfloor m/r \rfloor$ stages with r trials each. In each of these stages, we simulate an instance of the bandit problem as follows.

We set the number of features d to be $n\lfloor m/r \rfloor + 1$. For simplicity, we number features from 0. Feature 0 has a value of $\sqrt{1/2}$ for all alternatives on all trials. During the jth stage, the value of the $((j-1)r+i)$th feature of the ith alternative is also $\sqrt{1/2}$, and all other features have a value of 0. For example, the sequence of trials (alternatives with their feature values) for $n = 2$ is shown in Figure 1.

Once we've fixed feature vectors as above, any algorithm A for associative reinforcement learning of probabilistic linear functions from m trials gives rise to a sequence $B_1, ..., B_{\lfloor m/r \rfloor}$ of algorithms for the bandit problem with r plays as follows. One views the state of the algorithm A at the beginning of the jth stage as a random input (i.e. as randomization), and then the decisions made by algorithm A during the jth stage as those of a randomized algorithm for solving the bandit problem. Note that, within some stage j, the probabilities associated with choosing some alternative are the

$$
\begin{array}{ll}
\text{Stage 1} & \left\{ \begin{array}{ll}
\text{Trial 1} & \left\{ \begin{array}{cccccc} \sqrt{1/2} & \sqrt{1/2} & 0 & 0 & 0 & 0 \;\ldots \\ \sqrt{1/2} & 0 & \sqrt{1/2} & 0 & 0 & 0 \;\ldots \end{array} \right. \\
\vdots & \qquad\qquad\vdots \\
\text{Trial } r & \left\{ \begin{array}{cccccc} \sqrt{1/2} & \sqrt{1/2} & 0 & 0 & 0 & 0 \;\ldots \\ \sqrt{1/2} & 0 & \sqrt{1/2} & 0 & 0 & 0 \;\ldots \end{array} \right.
\end{array} \right. \\
\text{Stage 2} & \left\{ \begin{array}{ll}
\text{Trial } r+1 & \left\{ \begin{array}{cccccc} \sqrt{1/2} & 0 & 0 & \sqrt{1/2} & 0 & 0 \;\ldots \\ \sqrt{1/2} & 0 & 0 & 0 & \sqrt{1/2} & 0 \;\ldots \end{array} \right. \\
\vdots & \qquad\qquad\vdots \\
\text{Trial } 2r & \left\{ \begin{array}{cccccc} \sqrt{1/2} & 0 & 0 & \sqrt{1/2} & 0 & 0 \;\ldots \\ \sqrt{1/2} & 0 & 0 & 0 & \sqrt{1/2} & 0 \;\ldots \end{array} \right.
\end{array} \right. \\
\vdots &
\end{array}
$$

Figure 1: The sequence of trials for $n = 2$ used in the lower bound proof.

same throughout that stage, and furthermore that the results during stages before stage j provide no information about the probabilities of success during stage j.

Now we set the coefficients of the target linear function as follows. First, we set $v_0 = \sqrt{1/2}$. For each stage j, choose i_j uniformly at random from $\{1, ..., n\}$. Then for each stage j, set $v_{(j-1)r+i_j} = (\sqrt{2}/4)\sqrt{n/r}$, and $v_{(j-1)r+i} = 0$ for all $i \neq i_j$. With this coefficient vector and the feature vectors as described above, the probability of success for i_j during the jth stage is $1/2 + \sqrt{n/r}/4$ and for all other alternatives, this probability is $1/2$.

The length of the feature vectors and the coefficient vector are at most 1. Furthermore, applying Lemma 8, there is a constant $\gamma' > 0$ such that $\mathbf{E}(\sum_{t=1}^{m} \text{best}_t - z_{t,a_t}) \geq \gamma' \lfloor m/r \rfloor \sqrt{rn}$, where this expectation is with respect to the random choice of $\vec{v}$ as well as the randomness of the learning process. This implies that there exists a choice for $\vec{v}$, such that, for that fixed $\vec{v}$, $\sum_{t=1}^{m}(\max_i \vec{v} \cdot \vec{x}_{t,i}) - \mathbf{E}(z_{t,a_t}) \geq \gamma' \lfloor m/r \rfloor \sqrt{rn}$. Substituting the value of r and simplifying completes the proof. □

6 CONCLUSION

We have presented two algorithms for associative reinforcement learning of linear probabilistic concepts, and shown that they are nearly optimal with respect to a worst-case theoretical model of the problem.

One way in which our analysis can be straightforwardly extended is to measure the length of the feature vectors and coefficient vector with norms other than the usual Euclidian norm. Learning algorithms which yield loss bounds in terms of other norms have lemmas similar to Lemma 1 known about them [10, 11], so combining our techniques with these lemmas should yield other algorithms for associative reinforcement learning of linear probabilistic concepts, and corresponding regret bounds for them.

Acknowledgements

We thank Wee Sun Lee and Atsu Nakamura for their comments on an earlier version of this paper.

Naoki Abe was supported in part by the Grant-in-Aid for Scientific Research on Priority Areas (Discovery Science) 1998 of the Ministry of Education, Science, Sports and Culture, Japan. Phil Long was supported by National University of Singapore Academic Research Fund Grant RP960625.

References

[1] N. Abe and A. Nakamura. Learning to optimally schedule internet banner advertisements. *Proceedings of the 16th International Conference on Machine Learning*, 1999.

[2] N. Abe and J. Takeuchi. The 'lob-pass' problem and an on-line learning model of rational choice. *Proceedings of the 1993 Conference on Computational Learning Theory*, pages 422–428, 1993.

[3] P. Auer, N. Cesa-Bianchi, Y. Freund, and R.E. Schapire. Gambling in a rigged casino: the adversarial multi-armed bandit problem. Technical Report NC-TR-98-025, Neurocolt, 1998. Preliminary version in FOCS'95.

[4] D. A. Berry and B. Fristedt. *Bandit Problems.* Chapman and Hall, New York, 1985.

[5] N. Cesa-Bianchi, Y. Freund, D. Haussler, D. P. Helmbold, R. E. Schapire, and M. K. Warmuth. How to use expert advice. *Journal of the Association for Computing Machinery*, 44(3):427–485, May 1997.

[6] N. Cesa-Bianchi, P. M. Long, and M. K. Warmuth. Worst-case quadratic loss bounds for prediction using linear functions a nd gradient descent. *IEEE Transactions on Neural Networks*, 7(3):604–619, 1996.

[7] D. P. Helmbold, N. Littlestone, and P. M. Long. Apple tasting and nearly one-sided learning. *Proceedings of the 33rd Annual Symposium on the Foundations of Comput er Science*, 1992.

[8] L.P. Kaelbling. Associative reinforcement learning: A generate and test algorithm. *Machine Learning*, 15(3):299–320, 1994.

[9] L.P. Kaelbling. Associative reinforcement learning: Functions in k-dnf. *Machine Learning*, 15(3):279–298, 1994.

[10] J. Kivinen and M. K. Warmuth. Additive versus exponentiated gradient updates for linear prediction. *Information and Computation*, 132(1):1–63, 1997.

[11] J. Kivinen and M. K. Warmuth. Relative loss bounds for multidimensional regression problems. *Advances in Neural Information Processing Systems*, pages 287–293, 1998.

[12] P. M. Long. On-line evaluation and prediction using linear functions. *Proceedings of the 1997 Conference on Computational Learning Theory*, pages 21–31, 1997.

*? Gittins index — sensitive to choice of learning interval. Best for short intervals. Justification assumes perfect choices.

Learning to Optimally Schedule Internet Banner Advertisements

Naoki Abe*
NEC C & C Media Research Laboratories
4-1-1 Miyazaki, Miyamae-ku
Kawasaki 216-8555 JAPAN
Tel: +81-44-856-2143
E-mail: abe@ccm.cl.nec.co.jp

Atsuyoshi Nakamura
NEC C & C Media Research Laboratories
4-1-1 Miyazaki, Miyamae-ku
Kawasaki 216-8555 JAPAN
Tel: +81-44-856-2143
E-mail: atsu@ccm.cl.nec.co.jp

Abstract

We have developed a method which learns to schedule internet banner advertisements so as to maximize the average click-through rate, while adhering to the requirements imposed by contracts with the advertisers such as a minimum guaranteed number of impressions. We focus on the problem of adaptively scheduling advertisement display probabilities as a function of a single attribute such as a search keyword. Our learning algorithm is based on an efficient solution of a special class of linear programming problems called the 'transportation problem,' and also embodies a number of measures to address the exploration-exploitation trade-off and an efficient attribute clustering method to help reduce the dimensionality. Our experimental results verify the advantage of our linear programming based approach, as well as the effect of various additional measures we incorporate into our method.

1 INTRODUCTION

Banner advertisement on the Internet is a new form of advertisement which, by allowing the users to click on the banner of their choice and obtain information and conveniences, provides a type of interactive service that was not possible with any conventional form of advertisement. With the internet and electric commerce becoming widely used, internet advertisement is attracting attention as an important source of both information and revenue. It is a fast growing industry which is expected to grow to a 50 billion dollar market in the U.S. alone, by the year 2000.

As the importance and volume of internet advertisement (or simply internet ad) industry grow, the need for an intelligent and adaptive scheduling method for internet ads has become acute, which, based on the past behavior of users, learns to display ads that will yield the highest possible click-through rate. Such a scheduling method would benefit both the advertisers and users, as it allows the advertisers to direct ads to more targeted populations, and the users to enjoy a greater convenience. It should also help the internet providers and advertising agents increase their ad revenues. Currently, typical payments are based on the number of impressions (although payments based on the number of click-throughs exist also) and are in the range of 20 to 50 dollars per thousand impressions. Higher click-through rates should contribute to raising these prices.

There are several difficult issues that must be dealt with, however, before a satisfactory method for this problem can be realized. One of these issues is that, due to the requirements imposed by typical advertisement contracts (such as minimum guaranteed numbers of impressions), straightforward learning methods like neural nets are not well-suited for this problem, as they tend to only display popular advertisements. Another challenging issue is the exploration-exploitation trade-off, namely that of resolving the trade-off between displaying ads that help the system learn about the users behavior versus those that bring more immediate rewards (clicks). Finally, the usually large cardinality of the attribute space poses a problem, both in terms of the data sparseness for the estimation of click-through rates and computational efficiency.

In this paper, we focus on the adaptive ad scheduling problem in which the ad display scheduling is determined as a (probabilistic) function of a single attribute, such as a keyword entered to a WWW search engine or the URL address of the page being browsed, and propose a learning method that successfully deals with all of the above issues. The learning engine we developed has the following characteristics: (1) It provides a computationally efficient scheduling

*Both authors contributed equally to this work.

method, by formulating the constrained click maximization problem as a special class of linear programming problems called the 'Transportation problem' and making use of an efficient method for this class. (2) Within the above linear programming formulation, it embodies several measures to deal with the exploration-exploitation trade-off, which depending on the exact condition of the application, can be selectively applied. These include the use of Gittins index in place of the estimated click-through rates in the objective function, the use of an interior point method for linear programming as a semi on-line learning method to allow gradual convergence, and a lower bounding technique which designates a certain portion of the display probabilities to all ads. (3) It employs an efficient clustering algorithm, which clusters those attributes having similar click-through rate statistics and thereby improves upon the accuracy of click-through rate estimates, as well as help ease the computational complexity of the linear programming problem by reducing its dimensionality. We believe these features of our method distinguish it from other existing approaches to adaptive targeting of internet advertisement, such as SelectCast of Aptex [A] and ClickBoosters of DoubleClick [D], although the details of these methods are not published.

We ran large-scale simulation experiments in order to demonstrate the effectiveness of the proposed method. The results of our experiments verify the following: (1) The approach based on the transportation problem manages to display all advertisements as required by the contracts while increasing the total click-through rate significantly. (2) Various measures for the exploration-exploitation trade-off improve the basic method based on linear programming in terms of the total click-through rate achieved. Relative merits and demerits of alternative measures were found to be dependent on the learning interval and the campaign length. (3) Clustering of the attributes improves the total click-through rate. (4) The computational requirement of our method is small enough to render it practical.

Some of the proposed measures for the exploration-exploitation trade-off, especially the method using Gittins index, were found to be effective only for relatively small learning intervals. Various efficiency measures we devised thus turn out to be essential for the most effective application of our method in an actual internet advertisement scheduling.

2 THE PROBLEM AND METHOD

2.1 The Problem Formulation

In what follows we formalize the banner advertisement scheduling problem, assuming for readability that the single attribute in question is a search keyword. Suppose there are m banner advertisements, $A_1, ..., A_m$, and n keywords $W_1, ..., W_n$. Suppose also that there is a contract for each of the m advertisements, which determines the total number of promised (minimum) number of impressions in a given period of time (a campaign session) and possibly a set of rental and suppressed keywords. Here, a keyword W_i can be rented out to a particular ad A_j for a specified percentage, in which case for that portion of the occurrences of W_i, A_j is to be displayed. It is also possible that one wishes to suppress a particular advertisement A_j on a keyword W_i. In this case, displaying A_j when w_i is input is to be avoided as much as possible.

A campaign session is a sequence of a number of trials, usually in hundreds of thousands or millions, where each trial consists of the following steps. First, one of the n keywords is input to the system. Here we assume that the keywords are input according to a fixed distribution. Then, the scheduler is to display one of the m ads, chosen according to its current display probability distribution over the ads. The user either clicks on the ad banner or not, and this is recorded. Here we assume that this process is dictated by the conditional probability $P(click|A_j, W_i)$, which is fixed but unknown to the scheduler.

At a fixed interval (usually once every several thousand trials or so), the scheduler 'learns' – that is, it updates its ad display probabilities, using the accumulated click through statistics. The goal of a scheduler is to maximize the total number of clicks obtained in the course of a campaign session, while adhering to the contracts. The challenge lies in the resolution of the so-called exploration-exploitation trade-off, namely it must schedule its display probabilities so that it first learns enough about the click rates[1] for ad keyword pairs, and then maximize the number of clicks it gets, using the acquired estimates for the click rates.

2.2 Click maximization as Transportation Problem

We first set aside the estimation (exploration) problem and address the constrained maximization problem – the problem of maximizing the total number of clicks while ensuring the minimum number of impressions for each advertisement, assuming that accurate click rate estimates are given.

Assume that the click through rate for ad A_j when keyword W_i is input is $c_{i,j}$. Assume further that each keyword W_i is input with probability k_i and each ad A_j should be displayed with probability h_j in order to see that the minimum impression requirement is satis-

[1] We use the phrases 'click-through rate' and 'click rate' interchangeably.

fied for each ad. Now we wish to determine the display probability $d_{i,j}$ for each ad A_j on each keyword W_i so as to maximize the total click rate. This can be formalized as the following linear programming problem.

Maximize

$$\sum_{i=1}^{n}\sum_{j=1}^{m} c_{i,j} k_i d_{i,j} \qquad (1)$$

Under the Conditions

$$\sum_{i=1}^{n} k_i d_{i,j} = h_j \qquad (j = 1, ..., m) \qquad (2)$$

$$\sum_{j=1}^{m} d_{i,j} = 1 \qquad (i = 1, ..., n) \qquad (3)$$

$$d_{i,j} \geq 0 \qquad (i = 1, ..., n, j = 1, ..., m) \qquad (4)$$

In words, we are to maximize the total expected number of clicks (1) subject to the constraints that each ad A_j gets displayed with probability h_j (2) and the $d_{i,j}$ form probability vectors for each of the n keywords (3,4). Here note that the constraints in (2) are equalities rather than inequalities and the h_j are assumed to to sum to unity. This is because it is almost as undesirable to allocate too many impressions for a particular ad as it is to have too few.

By putting $x_{i,j} = k_i d_{i,j}$ one can see that this problem is equivalent to the so-called Hitchcock style transportation problem [D63]. Since the true values of the keyword input probabilities k_i and click rates $c_{i,j}$ are unknown, we use their estimations from the past data. Within this formulation, rental keywords can be handled as follows. For example, if A_j has rented out x % of keyword W_i, then we change Condition (4) for these i, j to the following

$$d_{i,j} \geq x/100. \qquad (5)$$

Also, if W_i is to be suppressed for A_j, $c_{i,j}$ can be set to -1 so that any positive display probability would contribute negatively to the objective function being maximized.

Once we put $x_{i,j} = k_i d_{i,j}$, the above linear programming problem can be represented as $A\vec{x} = \vec{d}$, where A and $\vec{x}, \vec{d}$ are as showin in Figure 1. (Note that only non-zero entries in A are shown in the figure.)

A is an $(m + n) \times mn$ matrix having a special form involving a small number of non-zero entries. In fact, its rank can be shown to be $m+n-1$ and hence so is the size of its basis. It is furthermore possible to efficiently determine whether a given set B of $m+n-1$ variables constitutes a basis or not. In particular, letting G_B be the graph having B as the node set and with the vertex set

$$E_B = \{(x_{i_1,j_1}, x_{i_2,j_2}) : i_1 = i_2 \text{ or } j_1 = j_2\}$$

a set of variables B of size $m + n - 1$ can be shown to form a basis if and only if G_B contains no cycle. Using this property, a simplex method can be implemented requiring only a table of size mn instead of a matrix of size $mn(m + n)$. We refer the interested reader to [D63] for details.

2.3 Estimating the click rates via clustering

In the setting of keyword directed ad scheduling, the number of keywords is normally in the thousands or hundreds, even if we collect the infrequently input ones together as 'all others.' Thus, especially near the beginning of a campaign period when the data are sparse, the click rate estimates are highly unreliable and the solution of the above linear programming problem may be led astray. As a possible remedy for this problem, we formulate the click rate estimation problem as the estimation of a conditional probability model of the form:

$$P(click|A_j, W_i) = P(click|A_j, Z_k); W_i \in Z_k$$

where the Z_k's constitute partitions of the set of keywords ($Z_x \cap Z_y = \emptyset$ for $x \neq y$, $\bigcup_{k=1}^{l} Z_k = \{W_1, ..., W_n\}$). Via the Z_k's, the model also specifies which cluster each keyword belongs to, which is to be estimated from data. Hence, keyword clustering falls out, so to speak, as a side effect of estimating the above model. Since the aforementioned linear programming problem has dimension mn, where m is the number of ads and n is the number of keywords, clustering of the keywords should contribute greatly to the reduction of dimensionality and hence the computational complexity, in addition to the improvement of estimation accuracy.

For estimating the above model, we devised an efficient estimation method based on an information criterion known as AIC(Akaike's Information Criterion) [SIK86]. We also tried using MDL(Minimum Description Length principle) [R78], but it turned out that AIC worked better for our purpose, which we will discuss later. Our clustering method stipulates that the best model is the probability model P minimizing the sum of I(P) =LL(P)+PT(P), where LL(P) is the (maximum) minus log likelihood of the model and PT(P) is the penalty term representing the number of free parameters in the model. The minus log likelihood of a model, as its name implies, is the minus logarithm of the likelihood (probability) the model gives to the data. So the minus log likelihood for P with the probability parameters $P(click|A_j, Z_k)$ is

$$\begin{aligned}\mathrm{LL}(P) \;=\; \sum_{Z\in P}\sum_{j=1}^{m} &-(C_{Z,j}\log P(click|A_j, Z_k) \\ &+(D_{Z,j} - C_{Z,j})\log(1 - P(click|A_j, Z_k)))\end{aligned}$$

$$A = \left[\begin{array}{cccc} \overbrace{1\,1\cdots1}^{n} & \overbrace{}^{n} & & \overbrace{}^{n} \\ & 1\,1\cdots1 & & \\ & & \cdots & \\ & & & 1\,1\cdots1 \\ 1 & 1 & & 1 \\ \ \ 1 & \ \ 1 & & \ \ 1 \\ \ \ \ddots & \ \ \ddots & \ddots & \ \ \ddots \\ \quad 1 & \quad 1 & & \quad 1 \end{array}\right]\begin{array}{l}\left.\vphantom{\begin{array}{c}1\\1\\1\\1\end{array}}\right\} m \\ \left.\vphantom{\begin{array}{c}1\\1\\1\\1\end{array}}\right\} n\end{array}, \quad \vec{x} = \begin{bmatrix} x_{1,1} \\ \vdots \\ x_{n,1} \\ x_{1,2} \\ \vdots \\ x_{n,2} \\ x_{1,m} \\ \vdots \\ x_{n,m} \end{bmatrix}, \quad \vec{d} = \begin{bmatrix} h_1 \\ h_2 \\ \vdots \\ h_m \\ k_1 \\ k_2 \\ \vdots \\ k_n \end{bmatrix}$$

Figure 1: Constrained click maximization as Transportation problem ($A\vec{x} = \vec{d}$).

where $D_{Z,j}$ is the number of displays (or impressions) for the cluster ad pair Z, A_j and $C_{Z,j}$ is the number of clicks for the same pair. It is well-known and straightforward to verify that this is maximized by letting $P(click|A_i, Z_k) = \frac{C_{Z,j}}{D_{Z,j}}$, so the *maximum* log likelihood for a given *partition* P is given as follows.[2]

$$\begin{aligned} \mathrm{LL}(P) &= \sum_{Z \in P} \sum_{j=1}^{m} -(C_{Z,j} \log \frac{C_{Z,j}}{D_{Z,j}} \\ &\quad + (D_{Z,j} - C_{Z,j}) \log \frac{D_{Z,j} - C_{Z,j}}{D_{Z,j}}) \end{aligned}$$

The penalty term is the number of free (probability) parameters in a model, and is simply

$$\mathrm{PT}(P) = m|P|.$$

Since exact maximization is not computationally feasible, we have devised an efficient algorithm which we call CLUSTER+, shown in Figure 2, which efficiently finds a reasonably good model based on a greedy heuristic.[3] This algorithm starts with the finest partition in which each keyword constitutes its own cluster, and keeps merging the pair of keywords which reduces the value of the objective function I by the greatest amount. Doing this straightforwardly would involve calculating the decrease in I that would result by merging each of $O(n^2)$ pairs at each iteration. CLUSTER+ avoids doing so by memorizing, for each cluster p, that cluster mdp(p) which would yield the greatset decrease in I if merged with p, and the amount by which I decreases, mda(p), and updating them appropriately at each iteration. In particular, at each iteration, or when a new merge takes place, CLUSTER+ updates its information in terms of mdp(p) and mda(p) as follows: if mdp(p) has been merged then it need be updated by calculating the decrease in I for all other current clusters, but for all other clusters, their values need only be compared with the decrease in I that would result from merging with the new cluster.

2.4 Using Gittins Index in the Objective Function

As a measure to address the issue of exploration-exploitation trade-off, we import the idea of Gittins Index[G88] from the Bayesian theory of Bandit problems[BF85], and use them in place of the click rate estimates in the objective function to be maximized in the linear programming formulation. The bandit problem consists of a series of choices out of a given set of 'arms' of a bandit, each having a fixed but unknown success probability, and the goal is to maximize the total expected number of successes (or rewards), normally with the successes obtained far in the future geometrically discounted. (More precisely, the total discounted reward is written as $\sum_{i=1}^{\infty} \gamma^{i-1} \cdot t_i$, where $t_i = 1$ if the i-th trial is a success and 0 otherwise, and γ is a constant between 0 and 1.)

It is known (by a theorem due to Gittins and Jones) that the strategy of always picking an arm with the maximum 'Gittins Index' is Bayes optimal, in the sense that it maximizes the expected discounted rewards. Gittins index is defined for the statistics associated with each arm, a pair (α, β) consisting of the number of successes and number of failures for that arm, and tends to take a larger value for arms with a smaller number of trials, if the empirical success probabilities are the same. In this way, maximizing the Gittins Index is designed to automatically resolve the exploration-exploitation trade-off.

[2] We use P to ambiguously denote the partition or the probability model including the associated probability parameters.

[3] A related clustering method, for the problem of estimating a model of word co-occurrence, was proposed by Li and Abe [LA98]. Here we propose an improved efficient algorithm for a related problem of estimating a conditional probability model.

Algorithm CLUSTER+

Input: $\{(D_{i,j}, C_{i,j}) : i = 1, ..., n, j = 1, ..., m\}$
Output: A partition P of $\{1, ..., n\}$
    $P = \{\{1\}, ..., \{n\}\}$
    For all $(i, j) \in [n] \times [m]$
        $D_{\{i\},j} = D_{i,j},\ C_{\{i\},j} = C_{i,j}$
    For all $p_1 \in P$
        $\text{mdp}(p_1) = \arg\max_{p_2 \in P} (\text{I}(\{p_1, p_2\}) - \text{I}(\{p_1 \cup p_2\}))$
        $\text{mda}(p_1) = \text{I}(\{p_1, \text{mdp}(p_1)\}) - \text{I}(\{p_1 \cup \text{mdp}(p_1)\})$ $= \max_{p_2} (I \{p_1, p_2\} - I(p_1 \cup p_2))$
    Repeat
        $p_1^* = \arg\max_{p_1 \in P} \text{mda}(p_1)$
        If $\text{mda}(p_1^*) \le 0$ return P
        $p_2^* = \text{mdp}(p_1^*)$
        $P = P \cup \{p_1^* \cup p_2^*\} - \{p_1^*, p_2^*\}$
        For $j = 1$ to m
            $D_{p_1^* \cup p_2^*, j} = D_{p_1^*, j} + D_{p_2^*, j},\ C_{p_1^* \cup p_2^*, j} = C_{p_1^*, j} + C_{p_2^*, j}$
        For all $p_1 \in P$
            If $(p_1 = p_1^* \cup p_2^*)$ or $(\text{mdp}(p_1) = p_1^*$ or $p_2^*)$ then
                $\text{mdp}(p_1) = \arg\max_{p_2 \in P} (\text{I}(\{p_1, p_2\}) - \text{I}(\{p_1 \cup p_2\}))$
            Else
                $\text{mdp}(p_1) = \arg\max_{p_2 \in \{\text{mdp}(p_1), p_1^* \cup p_2^*\}} (\text{I}(\{p_1, p_2\}) - \text{I}(\{p_1 \cup p_2\}))$
            $\text{mda}(p_1) = \text{I}(\{p_1, \text{mdp}(p_1)\}) - \text{I}(\{p_1 \cup \text{mdp}(p_1)\})$
    End Repeat

Figure 2: An efficient clustering algorithm based on a greedy heuristic.

Gittins Index for an arm with associated statistics (α, β), written $G(\alpha, \beta)$, equals the probability p such that if there were another arm with *known* success probability p then taking either arm (and doing everything the optimal way after that) would lead to the same expected total rewards. If we let $R(\alpha, \beta, p)$ denote the total expected rewards under this situation with one arm having statistics (α, β) and the other having known success probability p, then we have

$$\begin{aligned} R(\alpha, \beta, p) &= \max(\frac{p}{1-\gamma}, \\ &\quad \frac{\alpha}{\alpha+\beta}(1 + \gamma R(\alpha+1, \beta, p)) \\ &\quad + \frac{\beta}{\alpha+\beta}\gamma R(\alpha, \beta+1, p)) \end{aligned}$$

Thus Gittins Index $G(\alpha, \beta)$ equals that p such that

$$\frac{p}{1-\gamma} = \frac{\alpha}{\alpha+\beta}(1+\gamma R(\alpha+1, \beta, p)) + \frac{\beta}{\alpha+\beta}\gamma R(\alpha, \beta+1, p) \tag{6}$$

Such a value can be approximately calculated using dynamic programming with a reasonable amount of computation time, by approximating the indices for sufficiently large values of α and β by the corresponding success probability (click rate in our case) estimates. In practical applications it is usual to pre-calculate and store the values of indices for small enough values of α and β. Here we use Gittins Index to modify the target function being maximized in the earlier linear programming formulation, i.e., maximize

$$\sum_{i=1}^{n}\sum_{j=1}^{m} G(C_{i,j}, D_{i,j} - C_{i,j}) k_i d_{i,j}$$

instead of $\sum_{i=1}^{n}\sum_{j=1}^{m} c_{i,j} k_i d_{i,j}$, where $C_{i,j}$ and $D_{i,j}$ are the number of clicks and displays for the pair i, j, respectively.

2.5 Semi On-line Learning using an Interior Point Method

As another method to deal with the exploration-exploitation trade-off, we propose to make use of an interior point method (the affine scaling method in particular) for linear programming in a semi on-line fashion. That is, rather than fully optimizing at each learning interval, we use it to increment the previous solution by applying a small number of iteration steps at a time. The idea is that by converging more slowly to the optimum feasible solution, we ensure that enough exploration is done at early stages. The affine scaling method is an interior point method which is simpler than Karmarker's method but is known to work efficiently in practice. It works by applying at each iteration a linear (affine) transformation (represented by matrix $D^{(k)}$) to its current solution to move it to a constant vector to ensure that the next point will be an interior point (and similarly modifying the objective function and constraints by the same transformation), and then moving along the gradient of the objective function, scaled by a constant α. (More precisely, $x^{(k+1)} = x^{(k)} + \alpha D^{(k)} d^{(k)}$) where $d^{(k)}$ is the gradient normalized to have size 1.)

Here note that we use the affine scaling method to first find a feasible solution by minimizing a modified objective function $H(x) = MC(x) - F(x)$ for some large constant M where $C(x)$ attains minimum (zero) if and only if x is feasible, and $F(x)$ is the true objective function to be maximized. This way, the feasible solution from the previous learning iteration, which is not necessarily a feasible solution with respect to the current updated statistics, can be used as an initial point to speed up the minimization of $H(x)$, as it is likely to be *nearly* feasible. We refer the interested reader to [Y97], for example, for the details of this method. In our experiments, we set α to be 0.9 and applied 10 steps at each learning iteration.

2.6 Lower Bounding

Another, perhaps more straightforward, method to address the issue of the exploration-exploitation trade-off is to bound the display probabilities from below within the linear programming formulation, so that no advertisement will receive zero display probabilities. In particular, we propose to add the following constraint

$$d_{i,j} \geq 1 \Big/ \left(2m\sqrt{D_{i,j}+1}\right) \qquad (7)$$

for each pair of ad A_j and keyword W_i, where $D_{i,j}$ is the number of times A_j has been displayed on W_i. The rationale behind this bound is that the display probability for each pair is lower bounded by an amount that is proportional to the estimation error of the corresponding click rate. Note that the click rate estimation, for each ad-keyword pair, reduces to the estimation of a bias p of a coin. Noting that the standard deviation of the frequency of heads of such a coin is $\sqrt{Np(1-p)}$, we see that the estimation error is proportional to $1/\sqrt{N}$, where N is the sample size.

3 EMPIRICAL PERFORMANCE EVALUATION

3.1 Experimental Set-up

We conducted large-scale simulation experiments to evaluate the effectiveness of the proposed method. In our experiments, a probability model of the users was constructed, which specifies a conditional click rate for each ad and keyword pair, and used this model to simulate the click-through behaviors. The model was constructed in the following fashion. First we decided on the number of ads and the number of keywords. In most of our experiments, we used a model with 32 ads and 128 keywords, which are divided into 32 clusters each containing 4 keywords. Within each cluster, the keyword input distribution was set to be in proportions of 1 : 2 : 3 : 4. The click rates were calculated as follows: (1) Determine the basic click rate pattern (p_j for $j = 1, ..., 32$) according to the following table.

j	0	1-14	15-30	31
p_j	0.13	0.05	0.09	0.01

(2) For each ad, randomly pick a multiplicative scaling factor a_j uniformly from $[0, 1]$. (3) For each cluster ad pair, Z_h, A_j, randomly pick an additive cluster noise, clnoise(h, j), uniformly from $[-0.02, 0.02]$. (4) For each keyword ad pair, Z_h, A_j, pick an additive noise, noise(i, j), uniformly from $[-0.005, 0.005]$. (5) Finally, for each cluster Z_h, for each keyword $W_i \in Z_h$ and ad A_j, calculate the click rate $c_{i,j}$ as

$$c_{i,j} = a_j(p_{\text{index}(j,h)} + \text{clnoise}(h,j) + \text{noise}(i,j))$$

Here 'index(j, h)' is set to be the remainder of dividing $j + h$ by m, so that the basic click rate pattern is translated (by one) for each cluster.

In each of the experiments reported here, we averaged over 5 campaign runs with each run consisting of 1,000,000 trials, using the above model, and with learning interval set at one of 3,125, 6,250, 12,500 or 25,000 trials. We set the desired number of impressions to be identical for all the ads and we did not use any rental or suppressed keywords for simplicity.

3.2 The effect of the linear programming approach

First we verified the effect of the linear programming approach by comparing its performance against that of two simple methods. One is the 'random selection' method, which always picks an ad uniformly at random, and the other is the 'maximum selection' method, which always picks the ad with the maximum estimated click rate for any keyword. The linear programming approach was enhanced with the 'lower bounding' technique described in the previous section, and the learning interval was set at 3,125.

Figure 3 plots how the total click rate varies with each of the three methods. One can see that the maximum selection method obtains the highest click rate of all three methods, but it suffers from the shortcoming that only popular ads get shown, as is depicted in Figure 4 which shows (one tenth of) the number of impressions and the number of clicks for each ad. It is therefore not a practical method in the presence of contracts. One can see from these figures that the linear programming approach provides a balanced method

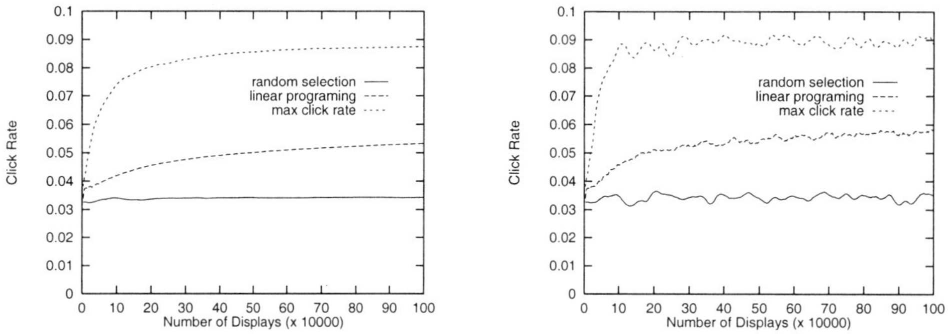

(a) Cumulative click rate (b) Instantaneous click rate

Figure 3: The total click rate of three methods.

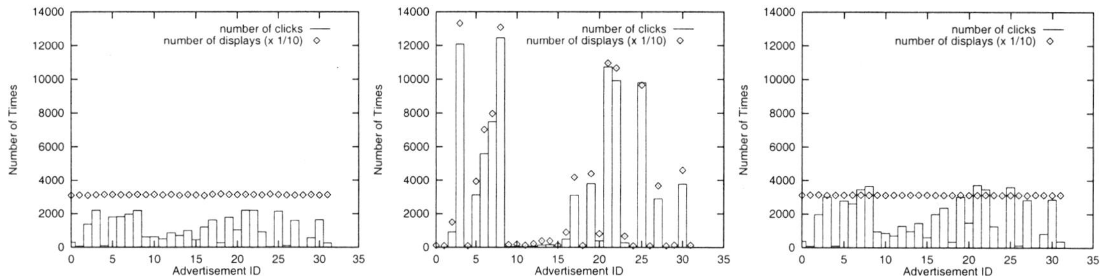

(a) The random sel. method (b) The maximum sel. method (c) Linear programming method

Figure 4: (One tenth of) the number of impressions and number of clicks for each advertisement.

which displays all the ads equally (as desired by the contracts of this experiment) and yet achieves a significantly higher click rate as compared, for example, to the random selection method.

It would be interesting to compare the performance of this method with other learning techniques that have been used for this problem, but the details of commercially available methods are not available and performance comparison is difficult to conduct. Also typical learning methods such as neural networks are not 'balanced' in the sense just explained, and thus a direct comparison is not necessarily meaningful.

3.3 The effect of various trade-off measures

Figure 5 plots the total click rate for our linear programming method when it is combined with each of the additional measures we propose, Clustering, Gittins Index, Interior point method, and Lower bounding, as well as the nothing-added (vanilla) version. Here the learning interval was set at 3,125. The graph on the left shows the cumulative click rate, while the one on the right shows the instantaneous click rate (averaged over the past 250,000 trials).

The same general tendency is found for each of the four additional measures – that in the beginning the click rate tends to be lower than the vanilla version (except the interior point method), but as the session progresses the instantaneous click rate quickly takes over and eventually the total cumulative click rate is improved by a significant margin. Note here that a session in these experiments consisted of a million trials, which correspond to the amount of transactions in a week or less at any major internet provider. Table 1 summarizes the final (cumulative and instantaneous) click rate achieved by each of these methods, where we indicate the 95 per cent confidence interval (2 standard deviations) for each figure. It is clear that each of the four measures beat the vanilla version with a statistically significant margin. As for the relative ordering among the four measures with respect to the overall performance, the results of these experiments stop short of being statistically significant.

Note here that our methods attain, in the best case, the final cumulative click rate of 5.3 % and instantaneous rate of 6.2 %. As compared with the random selection method with 3.4 % click rate, these results represent approximately 56 % (77 %) increase in the cumulative (instantaneous) click rate.[4]

[4] For reference, we note that Aptex reports up to 50 % increase in click rate over keyword and topic matching methods and 25 % over aggregated results of matching and

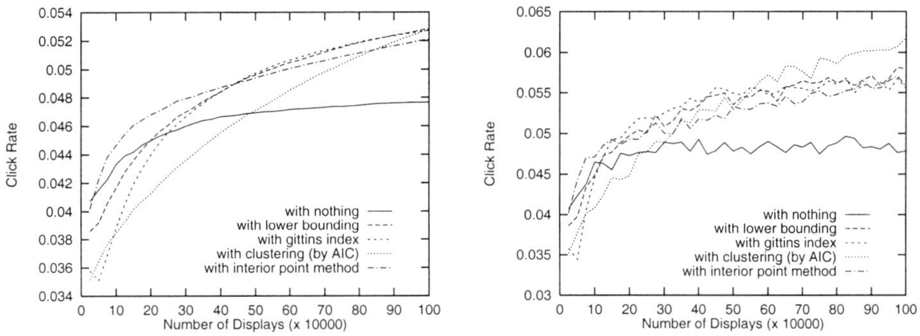

(a) Interval:3125, Cumulative click rate (b) Interval:3125, Instantaneous click rate

Figure 5: The effect of various measures on click rate

Final click rate	Cumulative	Instantaneous
Vanilla	4.77 % (± 0.13)	4.78 % (± 0.24)
Clustering	5.28 % (± 0.09)	6.18 % (± 0.43)
Gittins Index	5.27 % (± 0.10)	5.55 % (± 0.31)
Interior point	5.21 % (± 0.06)	5.58 % (± 0.22)
Lower Bounding	5.29 % (± 0.23)	5.79 % (± 0.31)

Table 1: Final cumulative/instantaneous click rate (%) achieved by each of the five methods. (Learning interval 3,125.)

Next, we examine the relative sensitivity of the four measures to the learning interval. Figure 7 plots how the total click rate changes for four different learning intervals, 3125, 6250, 12500 and 25000. It is immediately noticeable that Gittins Index is extremely sensitive to the learning interval – for short intervals its effect is very good while for longer intervals it actually degrades the performance of the vanilla version. This is attributable to the fact that Gittins index is calculated based on the assumption that at each trial the *optimal* choice is made, and hence is better suited for an *on-line* method, rather than a *batch* method. In contrast, the semi on-line interior point method and the lower bounding method seem to be relatively insensitive to the learning interval. The characteristic of the clustering method is that although it is slowest at improving the click rate it eventually reaches the highest instantaneous click rate overall, as indicated by the slope of these curves. All in all, we conclude that the relative merits of the various additional measures are dependent on the exact conditions of an application, such as the learning interval and the campaign length. When the learning interval is long, either the interior point method or the lower bounding seem to be the methods of choice, while with short learning intervals, Gittins index might be preferred. When the campaign length is long, clustering may do the best.

general rotation technique. DoubleClick claims that ClickBoosters achieves 10-40 % increase in click rate [A, D].

Incidentally, it was found that while our clustering method based on AIC was effective, the analogous method based on MDL actually degraded the performance in terms of click rate in our experiments. (See Figure 6.) As MDL is known to perform well for the pure *estimation* problem (often better than AIC), it is interesting that in the current setting involving both exploration and exploitation, AIC works much better.

3.4 Computational efficiency issues

Here we report on the computation time measurements we made on the proposed methods, using a SUN ULTRA 2 workstation (CPU:300MHz, Memory:256MB). Table 2 summarizes the results. Note that Gittins index and the lower bounding method were omitted from consideration since they had almost no effect on computation time.

#Ad×#Kw	32×128	64×256	128×512	256×1024
Transport	1.45	18.69	215.16	3224.19
Affine	5.59	44.20	476.28	4483.89
Speed-up	3.86	2.36	2.21	1.39
CLUSTER+	3.25	35.15	408.18	5240.79
CLUSTER	21.80	332.16	5833.28	—
Speed-up	6.71	9.45	14.29	—

Table 2: Computation time (in seconds) of various methods on SUN ULTRA 2(CPU:300MHz, Memory:256MB)

The learning method, using the solution for the transportation problem, was found to be quite efficient with running time (with the clustering off) 3 minutes and 35 seconds for a problem of size 128×512, and 53 minutes and 44 seconds for 256×1024. Provided that the number of keywords is somehow reduced by putting low frequency words together in a pre-processing phase, this method should be practical.

We also compared the computational efficiency of the

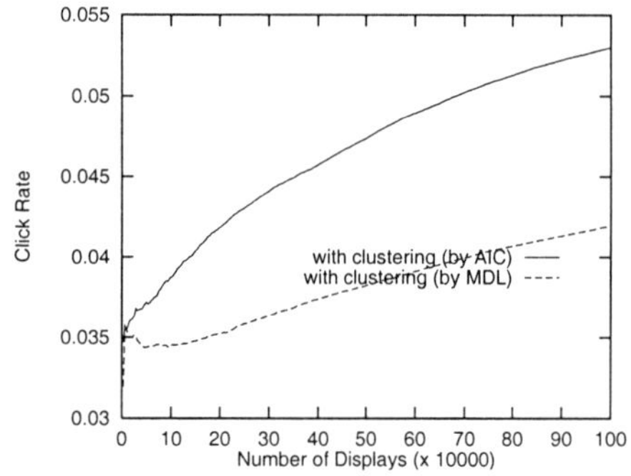

(a) Learning interval:3125, Cumulative

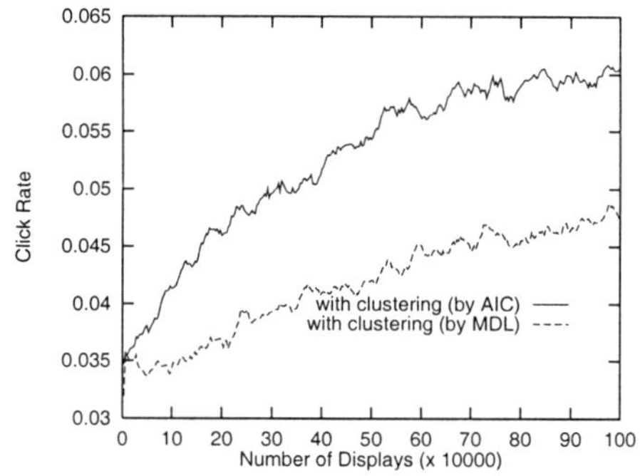

(b) Learning interval:3125, Instantaneous

Figure 6: Comparison between MDL and AIC

algorithm we employ for the transportation problem with the affine scaling method. As summarized in Table 2, the formulation as a transportation problem helps cut the computation time by as much as 4-fold, though the speed-up ratio becomes smaller for larger problems. Finally, we compared the computational requirement of our clustering algorithm CLUSTER+, with a more naive version (CLUSTER) of the algorithm, which compares *all* cluster pairs to determine the pair with the most decrease in the I-value in each iteration. It was found that the efficiency measures devised in CLUSTER+ are quite effective, and are more so for larger sized problems.

4 CONCLUDING REMARKS

Our simulation experiments have verified the effectiveness of the proposed method, both in terms of the improvement achieved in the click through performance and computational feasibility. We have incorporated our learning method in an actual internet advertisement delivery server [LNAKK99], and are planning to conduct experiments on an actual internet site to further evaluate its performance in the near future. Other important research issues include the following: (1) Combining the various measures proposed in the paper to further boost the performance of our method; (2) Taking advantage of a hierarchical decomposition of the attribute space (such as directories of URL's) in order to enhance the computational efficiency; (3) Extending the learning method to make use of general attributes, such as advertisement and user features.

Acknowledgements

We thank the following people involved in the internet ad server project for numerous comments and support: Mr. Shimojima, Mr. Sugawa, Mr. Hiroya, Dr. Koseki, Dr. Kamba, Mr. Langheinrich, Dr. Takada, Dr. Doi and Dr. Goto, all of NEC Corporation.

References

[A] Aptex Software Inc., SelectCast for Ad Servers, http://www.aptex.com/products-selectcast-ads.htm.

[BF85] D. A. Berry and B. Fristedt, Bandit Problems, Chapman and Hall, 1985.

[D] DoubleClick Inc., DART Advertisement System. http://www.doubleclick.com.

[D63] G. B. Dantzig, Linear Programming and Extensions, Princeton University Press, Princeton, New Jersey, 1963.

[G88] J. C. Gittins, Multi-armed Bandit Allocation Indices, John Wiley and Sons, Chichester, 1988.

[LA98] H. Li and N. Abe, Word clustering and disambiguation based on co-occurrence data. *Proceedings of COLING-ACL*, 1998.

[LNAKK99] M. Langheinrich, A. Nakamura, N. Abe, T. Kamba, and Y. Koseki, Unintrusive Customization Techniques for Web Advertising, Proceedings of The 8th International World Wide Web Conference, May 1999.

[R78] J. Rissanen, Modeling by Shortest Data Description, Automatica, 1978, Vol. 14, pp. 37-38.

[SIK86] Y. Sakamoto, Y. Ishiguro, and M. Kitagawa, Akaike Information Criterion Statistics, Reidel, 1986.

[Y97] Y. Ye. Interior Point Algorithms: Theory and Analysis (Wiley-Interscience Series in Discrete Mathematics and Optimization). John Wiley & Sons, 1997.

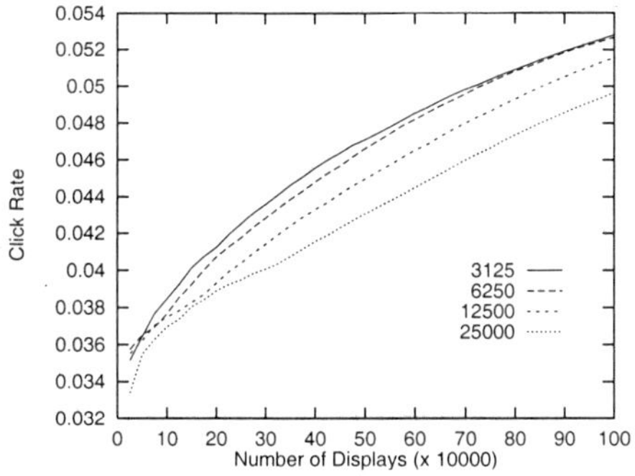

(a) Clustering, Cumulative click rate

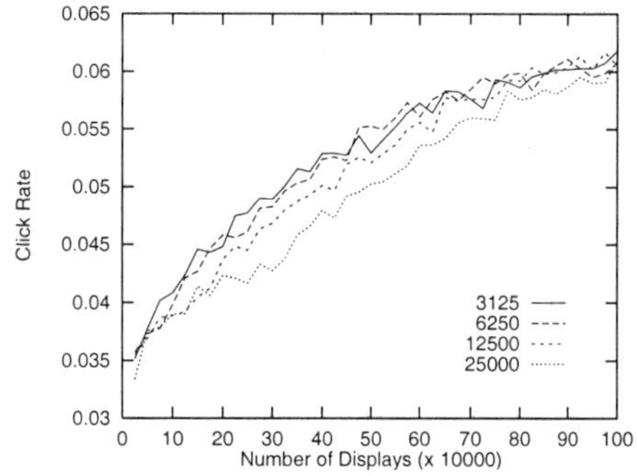

(a) Clustering, Instantaneous click rate

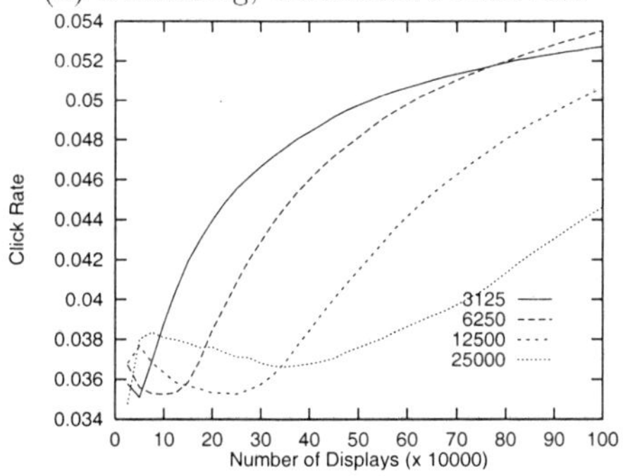

(b) Gittins index, Cumulative click rate

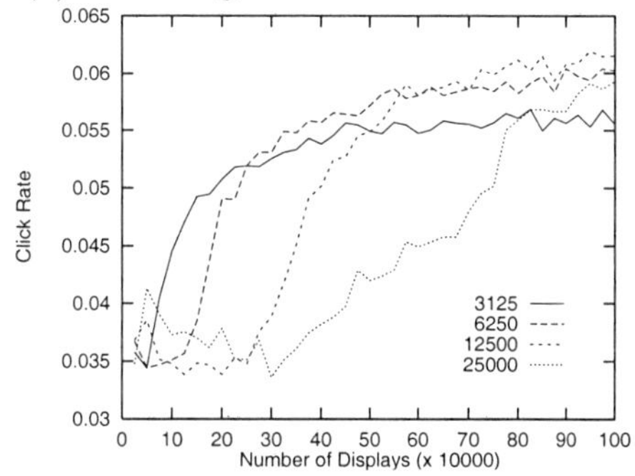

(b) Gittins index, Instantaneous click rate

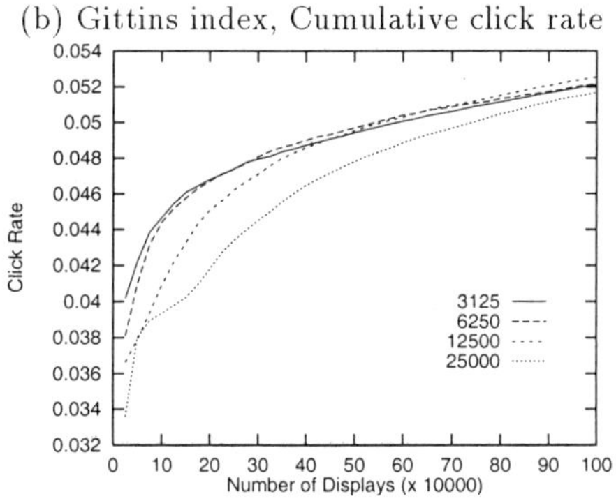

(c) Interior point method, Cumulative click rate

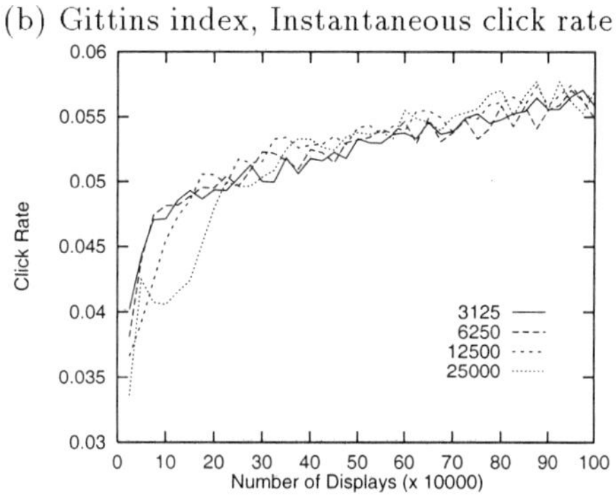

(c) Interior point method, Instantaneous click rate

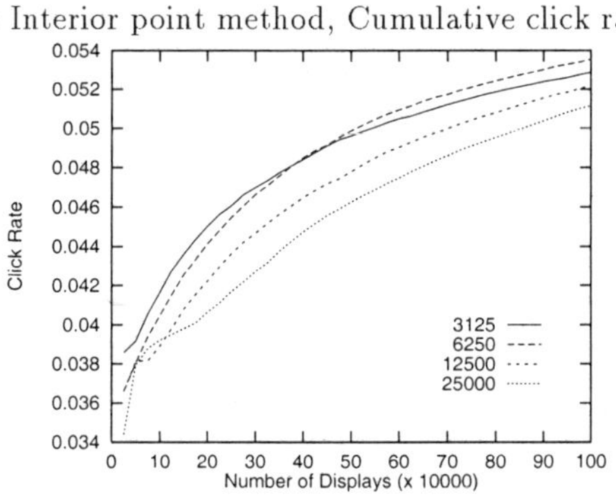

(d) Lower bounding, Cumulative click rate

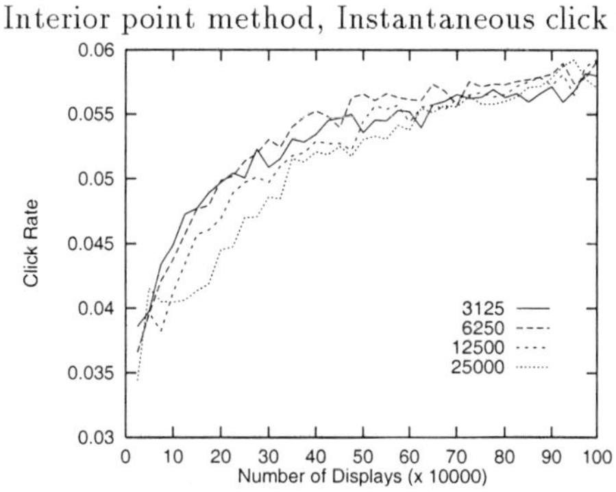

(d) Lower bounding, Instantaneous click rate

Figure 7: The effect of learning interval on click rate

A Minimum Risk Metric for Nearest Neighbor Classification

Enrico Blanzieri
ITC-IRST
via Sommarive, Povo 38050 Trento Italy
blanzier@itc.it

Francesco Ricci*
ITC-IRST
ricci@sodalia.it

Abstract

Nearest Neighbor is a well-known algorithm extensively studied by the Pattern Recognition and Machine Learning communities and widely exploited in Case Based Reasoning applications. The notion of metric is central to Nearest Neighbor's working and different feature weighting metrics have been proposed in order to increase its performance. In this work we present an original Probability Based Metric, i.e. a metric for classification tasks that relies on estimates of the posterior probabilities, called Minimum Risk Metric (MRM). MRM is optimal but it optimizes directly the finite misclassification risk whereas the Short and Fukunaga Metric minimize the difference between finite risk and asymptotic risk. An experimental comparison of MRM with Short and Fukunaga Metric, Value Difference Metric, and Euclidean–Hamming metrics on benchmark datasets shows that MRM outperforms the other metrics and performs comparably to the Bayes Classifier based on the same probability estimates. The results suggests that MRM can be useful in applications were the retrieval of a nearest neighbor is required (e.g. Case Based Reasoning).

1 Introduction

Nearest Neighbor (NN) algorithms are a well-known and intensively studied class of techniques for the solution of Classification and Pattern Recognition problems. Nowadays NNs are widely exploited in the retrieval phase of almost the totality of the Case Based Reasoning (CBR) systems. Such systems emphasize more the retrieving of a neighbor than the classification accuracy but, as was recently shown by Bellazzi et al. [BMP98], the performance of a CBR system can be improved by driving the retrieval with the information of same relevant classification in the case space, i.e. reducing the retrieval problem to a classification task. In this prospective the problem of improving the classification accuracy for NN algorithms appears to be relevant.

The NN classification procedure is straightforward: Given a set of classified points in an input space, a new point is assigned to the known class of the nearest one with respect to a metric defined on the input space. Many researchers [SF80, SF81, SW86, CMSW92, AG90, AG92, HT95, Fri94, RA95, RA98, CH97, WMA97] focused their attention on the use of local metrics, i.e. metrics that vary depending on the position of the points in the input space, in order to outperform systems based on global metrics. The claim appears to be controversial. On one hand the local metrics generate classifiers that are more sensitive to the local changes of the data and hence more accurate. On the other hand global metrics have fewer parameters and consequentially the classifiers are computationally lighter and less prone to the effect of noisy data. The critical point seems to be the grade of locality of the metric: choosing the 'right' locality in different areas of the input space should lead to better description of the separating surfaces.

Some of the proposed local metrics rely their effectiveness on the optimization of a given criterion and ultimately on the estimation of some probabilities. In this direction Short and Fukunaga [SF81] presented an initial work in the case of continuous multidimen-

* Present Address:Sodalia, via Zambra 1, 38100 Trento Italy

sional input space. They proposed to minimize the expected value of the difference between the misclassification error of a two-classes NN classifier with a finite number of samples and the misclassification error hypothetically achievable with an infinite sample. In order to achieve this goal they expressed the optimal local metric in terms of a linear estimation of posterior probabilities. More recently, and in the instance based learning context, many proposals of nominal feature metrics also involve probability estimation [SW86, CMSW92, CS93, WD95]. In these cases the estimation is performed computing frequencies of value occurrences. Finally, in the work by Wilson and Martinez [WM97] the estimation of probabilities provides an unifying framework for treating both linear (continuous or discrete) and nominal features. Their heterogeneous distances take advantage of the contemporary elaboration of the two kind of features.

Among the metrics based on probability estimation the one proposed by Short and Fukunaga has the strongest theoretical foundation. In their original proposal it was used only for numeric features problems but it is possible to extend it to nominal or heterogeneous features by considering different and more general probability estimators. In fact, in spite of the centrality of the probability estimation in such type of metrics, little or no attempt has been made to exploit the advanced nonparametric density estimation techniques developed by the applied statistics community [Sco92] and their possible extensions to nominal features.

From our point of view the approach of constructing metrics via combination of well-known probability estimators and optimal metrics presents several advantages.

The resulting metrics have a clear analytical expression and motivation. For example the metric proposed by Short and Fukunaga minimizes the difference between asymptotic and finite risk. That makes these metrics amenable to analytical study.

They can be computed using standard density estimation techniques. The issue of the choice of the right degree of locality (bandwidth selection) can rely on the solutions proposed for the choice of the bandwidth in the nonparametric density estimation models.

Finally, they can be defined on uniformly data sets with both numeric and nominal attributes. In real–world databases both continuous and nominal features can be found at the same time. The problem can be tackled in different ways:

- Ordering. Ordering and numbering the values of the nominal features and applying a continuous metric like the Euclidean one. In general this approach introduces fictitious neighborhood.
- Discretization. Discretizing the numeric values and applying a nominal metric, e.g. Hamming or Value Difference Metric [SW86]. With the discretization some information is inevitably lost and parameters of the discretization can be critical.
- Combination. Combining two metrics, a nominal and a numeric, obtaining an heterogeneous metric, e.g. Euclidean and Hamming. The heterogeneous metric is hard to adapt in a consistent way and performs poorly, as Wilson and Martinez have shown [WM97].

The metric based on probability estimation provides a natural unifying framework for dealing with both the kind of features. While the techniques of ordering, discretization and combination listed above can be used for probabilities estimation the optimality of the metric still relies on theoretical arguments.

Our initial hypothesis was that better performances should be achieved by combining Short and Fukunaga metric with more sophisticated and powerful probability estimators. This combination produced unexpected poor experimental results and outperforming of the more standard metrics were obtained only by explicit restricting the scope of application (locality) of the metric or cross–validating the estimator. This led us to a deeper analysis of the optimality condition underlying Short and Fukunaga metric and eventually to the definition of an alternative metric.

In this work we propose a Minimum Risk Metric (MRM) that relies is effectiveness on a different and simpler optimality condition than the one suggested by Short and Fukunaga. In fact MRM minimizes directly the finite misclassification risk. In order to test the effectiveness of the approach we run experiments on 29 benchmark datasets and compare the classification accuracies of Short and Fukunaga Metric and MRM with the performances of other metrics available in the literature. Moreover the accuracies of both these probability based metrics are compared to the results of the Bayes Classifiers (i.e. the classifier that assign to the example to the class with highest probability) based on the same probability estimates.

The work is organized as follows: section (2) describes Short and Fukunaga approach and presents other metrics studied in the work, in particular subsection (2.4) briefly presents the Minimum Risk Metric and its optimality criterium; section (3) describes the adopted probability estimators; section (4) presents the experimental results and finally, sections (5) draws conclusions and future directions.

2 Metrics

In this section we will briefly present the four families of metrics studied in this work.

2.1 Short and Fukunaga Metric (SF2)

Short and Fukunaga [SF81] were the first to derive a NN optimal metric relying on probabilistic considerations. In their work they consider a two-class pattern recognition task. Let $x = (x_1, \ldots, x_n), y = (y_1, \ldots, y_n)$ be two examples in $[0,1]^n$. Let $r(x,y) = p(c_1|x)p(c_2|y) + p(c_2|x)p(c_1|y)$ be the finite 1-nearest neighbor error rate at x(i.e., the probability of misclassifying x by the 1-nearest neighbor rule given that the nearest neighbor of x using a particular metric is at y) and $r^*(x) = 2p(c_1|x)p(c_2|x)$ (Cover and Hart[CH67]) be the asymptotic 1-nearest neighbor error rate (i.e., the probability of misclassifying x by the 1-nearest neighbor rule, given a hypothetically infinite design set). Short and Fukunaga show that minimizing the expectation $E[(r(x,y) - r^*(x))^2]$ is equivalent to minimizing $E[(p(c_1|x) - p(c_1|y))^2]$,so the best local metric is:

$$d(x,y) = |p(c_1|x) - p(c_1|y)| \tag{1}$$

We shall call this metric SF2. Short and Fukunaga approximate at the first order $|p(c_1|x) - p(c_1|y)| \simeq |\nabla p(1|x)^T(x-y)|$ and therefore their metric in the original formulation can be applied only to numeric features and in a local restriction.

Myles and Hand in [MH90] generalize the metric to a multiclass problem and introduce the following two:

$$sf2(x,y) = \sum_{i=1}^{m} |p(c_i|x) - p(c_i|y)| \tag{2}$$

$$sfm(x,y) = \sum_{i=1}^{m} p(c_i|x)|p(c_i|x) - p(c_i|y)| \tag{3}$$

where the classes c_i are numbered from 1 to m. We shall still call the first metric SF2, and SFM the second. It is easy to prove that on a two classes classification problem SF2 and SFM coincide. Myles and Hand use the same technique introduced by Short and Fukunaga to approximate $|p(c_i|x) - p(c_i|y)|$.

2.2 Value Difference Metric (VDM)

Another very common metric based on probabilistic consideration is the VDM introduced by Stanfill and Waltz [SW86] and used exclusively on input spaces with nominal attributes. Let $x = (x_1, \ldots, x_n)$ and $y = (y_1, \ldots, y_n)$ be two examples in $\prod_{j=1}^{n} F_j$, and $|F_j|$ is finite. The the VDM metric is defined as follow:

$$\begin{aligned} vdm(x,y) &= \sum_{j=1}^{n} \left(\sqrt{\sum_{i=1}^{m} \left(\frac{N(x_j,c_i)}{N(x_j)} \right)^2} \right. \\ &\quad \left. \sum_{i=1}^{m} \left(\frac{N(x_j,c_i)}{N(x_j)} - \frac{N(y_j,c_i)}{N(y_j)} \right)^2 \right) \end{aligned}$$

where $N(x_j, c_i)$ is the number of examples that have value x_j for the j-th attribute and are in class c_i, and $N(x_j)$ is the number of examples that have value x_j for the j-th attribute. If probabilities are estimated with frequencies VDM can also be written in the following form:

$$\begin{aligned} vdm(x,y) &= \sum_{j=1}^{n} \left(\sqrt{\sum_{i=1}^{m} (p^2(c_i|x_j)} \right. \\ &\quad \left. \sum_{i=1}^{m} (p(c_i|x_j) - p(c_i|y_j))^2 \right) \end{aligned}$$

VDM has no clear justification and seems to assume attributes independence. It is easy to conceive an ill-formed dataset where all the $p(c_i|x_j)$ are equal (for example the parity bit class) and therefore VDM is not able to distinguish among the classes. Nevertheless VDM, and a set of modified versions [CMSW92, CS93, WM97], works quite well on real data sets. Moreover, Wilson and Martinez extended VDM to instances with numeric attributes [WM97]. They essentially discretize the numeric attributes (DVDM) and then smooth the histogram estimation of $p(c_i|x_j)$ by averaging (IVDM). They also suggest an Heterogeneous VDM that combines an Euclidean metric for numeric features with a VDM (HVDM). The version of VDM we adopted in our experiments is the version without weighting factors and with the absolute values:

$$vdm(x,y) = \sum_{j=1}^{n} \sum_{i=1}^{m} |p(c_i|x_j) - p(c_i|y_j)| \tag{4}$$

2.3 Heterogeneous Euclidean–Overlap Metric (HEOM)

HEOM introduced by Wilson and Martinez [WM97], is the combination of the Euclidean metric and the

Hamming metric. Basically HEOM is an heterogeneous distance function that uses different attributes distance functions on different kinds of attributes. If $x = (x_1, \ldots, x_n)$ and $y = (y_1, \ldots, y_n)$ are two examples then $HEOM(x, y) = \sqrt{\sum_{j=1}^{n} d_j(x_j, y_j)^2}$ where $d_j(x_j, y_j)$ is the Hamming distance if the j-th feature is nominal and the Euclidean distance if numeric. The numeric features are normalized using the range.

2.4 Minimum Risk Metric

Minimum Risk Metric (MRM) is a very simple metric that directly minimizes the risk of misclassification.

Given a point x of class c_i and a nearest neighbor y the finite risk of misclassifying x is given by $p(c_i|x)(1 - p(c_i|y))$. The total finite risk is the sum of the risks extended to all the different classes and is given by $r(x, y) = \sum_{i=1}^{m} p(c_i|x)(1 - p(c_i|y))$. The approach of Short and Fukunaga and followers is to subtract the asymptotic risk $r^*(x, y)$ and minimizing $E(r(x, y) - r^*(x, y))$. Instead we propose to minimize directly the risk $r(x, y)$ and that leads to a straightforward metric:

$$mrm(x, y) = r(x, y) = \sum_{i=1}^{m} p(c_i|x)(1 - p(c_i|y)). \quad (5)$$

r(x, x) > 0

3 Probability Distribution Estimation

The presence of the conditional probabilities $p(c_i|x)$ in both SF2 metric and MRM requires consistent estimates $\hat{p}(c_i|x)$ and this section illustrates the probability estimation techniques used in the experiments. The estimates can be done directly or applying the Bayes theorem

$$p(c_i|x) = \frac{p(x|c_i)p(c_i)}{p(x)} = \frac{p(x|c_i)p(c_i)}{\sum_{k=1}^{|C|} p(x|c_k)p(c_k)} \quad (6)$$

reducing to the problem of estimating $p(x|c_k)$ and $p(c_k)$.

In the present work we carried on experiments with two different estimators. One is the Naïve Bayes Estimator that is the estimator that is implicit in the Naïve Bayes Classifier. It is a natural estimator for nominal feature and it can be extended to the numeric ones by discretization. The others one the Gaussian Kernel Estimator is a non–parametric density estimator and, in its original formulation, uses a Euclidean metric. In order to extend the density estimation technique to nominal features the Euclidean metric is simply substituted by HEOM and the density are supposed to replace the probability in the expression of the metrics.

3.1 Naïve Bayes Estimator

The simplest probability estimates are the occurrence frequencies. In this way is possible to estimate $p(c_i)$ with $\hat{p}(c_i) = \frac{N(c_i)}{N}$ where $N(c_i)$ is the number of cases that are in the c_i class and N is the sample size. Unfortunately, probability estimates based on frequencies performs poorly if the sample size is small (basically the probabilities result understimated) and so they can be improved adopting the Laplace–corrected estimate or equivalently incrementing artificially the sample size [Mit97]. Following the first possibility leads to the estimate $\hat{p}(x_j|c_i) = \frac{N(c_i)+f}{N+fn_j}$ where n_j is the number of values of the j-th attribute and $f = 1/N$ is a multiplicative factor [DP97].

Asserting the feature independence hypothesis leads to the estimates:

$$\hat{p}(x|c_i) = \prod_{j=1}^{n} \hat{p}(x_j|c_i) = \prod_{j=1}^{n} \frac{N(x_j, c_i) + f}{N(c_i) + fn_j}$$

which, substituted in the equation (6) are the estimates that are used in the Naïve Bayes Classifier approach:

$$\hat{p}(c_i|x) = \frac{\prod_{j=1}^{n} \frac{N(x_j,c_i)+f}{N(c_i)+fn_j} \frac{N(c_i)}{N}}{\sum_{k=1}^{|C|} \prod_{j=1}^{n} \frac{N(x_j,c_k)+f}{N(c_k)+fn_j} \frac{N(c_k)}{N}} \quad (7)$$

3.2 Gaussian Kernel Estimator

A broad class of nonparametric density estimators is represented by the multivariate fixed kernel estimator [Sco92]:

$$\hat{f}(\bar{x}) = \frac{1}{N} \sum_{l=1}^{n} \frac{1}{h(\bar{x}, \bar{x}_l)^n} K\left(\frac{\bar{x} - \bar{x}_l}{h(\bar{x}, \bar{x}_l)}\right) \quad (8)$$

where n is the dimension of the input space, h is the bandwidth and $K(t)$ is the kernel function. The bandwidth $h(\bar{x}, \bar{x}_l)$ can be fixed overall the input space or it can vary. Depending on whether the bandwidth h depends on the probe point $\bar{x}$ or on the sample point $\bar{x}_l$, the estimators can be divided in two wide groups: *balloon* estimators and *sample point* estimators.

The Gaussian Kernel Estimator is an example of *sam-*

ple point estimator with fixed bandwidth.

$$\hat{f}(\bar{x}) = \frac{1}{N(2\pi)^{n/2}} \sum_{l=1}^{N} \frac{\sqrt{|W|}}{h^n} e^{-\frac{1}{2}\left(\frac{\|\bar{x}-\bar{x}_l\|_W}{h}\right)^2} \quad (9)$$

where W is a positive definite diagonal matrix, and

$$\| \bar{x} - \bar{x}_l \|_W = \sqrt{(\bar{x} - \bar{x}_l) W (\bar{x} - \bar{x}_l)^T} = \sqrt{\sum_{j=1}^{n} w_{jj} (\bar{x} - \bar{x}_i)^2}$$

$$\sqrt{|W|} = \prod_{j=1}^{n} w_{jj}$$

therefore $\| \cdot \|_W$ is an Euclidean weighted metric and $w_{jj} = \frac{1}{\hat{\sigma}_j}$ with j ranging over the dimensions of the input space. In this case the optimal bandwidth is $h = \left(\frac{4}{n+2}\right)^{\frac{1}{n+4}} N^{-\frac{1}{n+4}}$.

The estimate $\hat{f}(\bar{x}|c_k)$ takes into account only the samples that belong to class c_k.

4 Experimental Results

The metrics were tested on 28 databases downloaded from the Machine Learning Databases Repository at UCI and on two new databases (Derma and Opera). Derma collects data of images for the diagnosis of skin cancer collected at Santa Chiara Hospital in Trento, Italy and Opera contains the results of a cognitive pragmatics experiment [BB96]. The results on one of the UCI database (Imports-85) was afterwards excluded from the experimentation for a wrong choice of the target. The 29 databases contains continuous, nominal and mixed features. The main characteristics of the databases are presented in tab. 1. We extended to mixed feature databases the estimate of the Naïve Bayes Estimator by discretizing the numeric features and the estimate of the Gaussian Kernel Estimator by substituting the Euclidean Metric with HEOM. We normalized the numeric features with their range and use ten intervals for all the discretizations. The unknown values were simply ignored during the computation. The experimental technique is a 10-fold cross–validation and as a significance test we adopted the paired t-test ($p < 0.05$).

The central experiments measure the classification accuracies of of the 1-NN algorithm with SF2 metric (Eq. 2) and MRM (Eq. 5) obtained using Naïve Bayes Estimator (Eq. 7) and the Gaussian Kernel Estimator (Eq. 9). The accuracies are compared to the ones of DVDM (Eq. 4), HEOM (Sec. 2.3) and IVDM (Sec. 2.2) and of the Bayes Classifier based on the same estimators. The application of SF2 can be restricted to h neighbors with respect to the metric HEOM. When the metrics are computed on the whole training set $h = N$ holds. Some of the experiments are led adopting as h the cross-validated value h_{CV}. We also cross–validate the used estimator. When this is the case the estimator is indicated as Est_{CV}. Both the cross–validations are carried on with a 10-fold cross–validation on each training partition.

Table 1: The databases used in the experimentation.

Data Set	Instances	Classes	Features: Number	Features: Cont./Symb.	Unknown
Annealing	798	6	38	9C 29S	yes
Audiology(stan.)	200	24	69	69S	yes
Breast-cancer	286	2	9	4C 5S	yes
Bridges	108	6	11	9C 2S	yes
Bridges(dis.)	108	6	11	11S	yes
Credit Screening	690	2	15	6C 9S	yes
Derma	152	2	44	44C	no
Flag	194	8	28	10C 18S	no
Glass	214	7	9	9C	no
Hepatitis	155	2	19	6C 13S	yes
Horse-Colic	300	2	27	7C 20S	yes
House-Votes-84	435	2	16	16S	yes
Ionosphere	351	2	34	34C	no
Iris	150	3	4	4C	no
Led+17noise	200	10	24	24S	no
Led	200	10	7	7S	no
Liver Disorders	345	2	6	6C	no
Monks-1	432	2	6	6S	no
Monks-2	432	2	6	6S	no
Monks-3	432	2	6	6S	no
Opera	1216	5	9	9S	no
Pima	768	2	8	8C	no
Post-operative	90	3	8	1C 7S	yes
Promoters	106	2	57	57S	no
Sonar	208	2	60	60C	no
Soybean(large)	307	19	35	35S	yes
Soybean(small)	47	4	35	35S	no
WDBC	569	2	32	32C	no
zoo	101	7	16	16S	no

4.1 HEOM and Value Difference Metrics results

A first series of experiments refers to the metrics HEOM, DVDM, IVDM and HVDM. Accuracy results are reported in Tab. 2. Tab. 3 reports the significative differences information that is not present in the previous table. The reading of the Tab. 3 is as follows: When, on a given dataset, a metric performs significantly better than another one, the symbol of the latter compares in the column of the former. All the metrics of the VDM family appears to outperform the HEOM but they are not clearly one better of the other. This results seems to partially contradict what observed by Wilson and Martinez.

Table 3: Significative differences ($p < 0.05$) of the Tab. 2. Example of reading: IVDM performs significatively better than DVDM on sonar dataset.

Data Set	VDMs: IVDM (I)	VDMs: HVDM (H)	DVDM (D)	HEOM (E)
anneal	E	E	I	
audiology	E	E		
breast-cancer				
bridges1				H
bridges2				
crx				
derma				
flag		E	I	
glass	D	D		
hepatitis				
horse-colic				
house-votes-84			H	H
ionosphere				
iris				
led				
led17	E	E		
liver				
monks-1				
monks-2	E	E		
monks-3	E	E		
opera				
pima-indians-diabetes				H
post-operative				
promoters	E	E		
sonar	D			
soybean-large				
soybean-small				
wdbc				
zoo				

4.2 Short and Fukunaga Metric

Preliminary results showed a substantial equivalence between SF2 and SFM and therefore we choose the simpler one. The Tab. 4 presents the classification accuracies of SF2 metric with different estimators (Naïve , Gaussian Kernel, and the cross–validated one) with different grades of locality. The application of the SF2 is restricted to the h nearest neighbors with respect to the HEOM metric. The problem of the locality of the SF2 metrics appears to be critical. In fact, Tab. 5 shows how an unrestricted application of the metric leads to very poor results when compared with DVDM and HEOM. The Tab. 4 shows a sharp increasing of the performances when cross–validation of the estimator, of the locality, or of both of them are performed. Finally Tab. 6 shows how the SF2 metric based on cross–validation outperforms significatively DVDM and HEOM. In particular the metric with both estimator and locality cross-validated is never worse of them and outperforms DVDM in 4 datasets and HEOM in 8 datasets. Experiments not reported here have shown that SF2 often performs worse of the Bayes Classifier based on the same estimation.

Table 5: Significative differences ($p < 0.05$) between SF2 metrics with Naïve and Kernel estimators and DVDM and HEOM.

Data Set	SF2 $h = N$: Naïve (N)	SF2 $h = N$: Kernel (K)	DVDM (D)	HEOM (E)
anneal	E			
audiology				
breast-cancer				
bridges1				
bridges2	D E			
crx				N
derma				
flag	E		K	
glass				K N
hepatitis				
horse-colic			N	
house-votes-84			N	N
ionosphere		D E		
iris				
led				
led17	E			
liver			N	N
monks-1		D E	N	
monks-2	E		K N	K
monks-3				K
opera				
pima-indians-diabetes			K	K
post-operative			N	
promoters	E			
sonar		D		N
soybean-large			K	
soybean-small				
wdbc			N	N
zoo				

4.3 Minimum Risk Metric

The Tab. 7 shows classification accuracies achieved by the MRM and by the Bayes Classifier based on the same probability estimate. The results are almost coincident and that does not surprise given the definition of the Bayes Classifier. The significative differences between the best ones and the metric DVDM and HEOM are shown in Tab. 8. The monks datasets appear to be a hard task probably as a consequence of the assumption of the independence among features that underlies the Naïve Estimator. The MRM outperforms DVDM and HEOM more convincingly than SF2 and without any local restriction (compare with Tab. 6). Finally, Tab. 9 reports the significative differences between the best of all the metrics presented. The MRM based on Naïve estimator does not differ from its version with the cross–validated estimator. Both of them, with the exception of monks datasets, outperforms SF2 with cross-validated estimator and cross-validated locality and the IVDM.

Table 2: Classification accuracies in percentage for different metrics. In bold the significative differences ($p < 0.05$) within the couples IVDM/HVDM and DVDM/HEOM.

Data Set	IVDM	HVDM	DVDM	EH
anneal	97.4 ± 1.33	**99.1 ± 1.03**	**98.4 ± 0.98**	95.4 ± 2.59
audiology	80.5 ± 7.24	80.5 ± 5.98	**80.5 ± 5.98**	72.5 ± 11.3
breast-cancer	66.4 ± 6.92	68.2 ± 8.21	64.3 ± 10.0	65.4 ± 8.54
bridges1	61.1 ± 7.97	59.3 ± 11.1	62.3 ± 16.9	65.9 ± 13.9
bridges2	62.1 ± 20.0	59.3 ± 19.0	59.3 ± 19.0	55.5 ± 17.2
crx	79.7 ± 2.36	80.5 ± 5.21	79.5 ± 4.06	81.7 ± 3.36
derma	80.0 ± 12.6	73.0 ± 12.6	74.8 ± 13.4	78.1 ± 10.6
flag	57.4 ± 12.3	**66.6 ± 8.75**	**64.0 ± 8.34**	55.8 ± 12.9
glass	72.5 ± 12.5	69.7 ± 9.32	62.1 ± 11.1	**71.1 ± 11.8**
hepatitis	82.6 ± 10.1	80.0 ± 9.94	82.0 ± 10.8	80.7 ± 11.8
horse-colic	85.6 ± 5.67	85.6 ± 7.70	86.6 ± 7.53	84.6 ± 4.76
house-votes-84	93.7 ± 3.10	93.0 ± 2.45	93.0 ± 2.45	92.3 ± 3.82
ionosphere	**87.4 ± 3.38**	35.9 ± 4.75	88.8 ± 4.75	87.1 ± 2.81
iris	94.6 ± 5.25	96.6 ± 4.71	92.6 ± 4.91	95.3 ± 5.48
led	66.5 ± 13.5	66.5 ± 13.5	66.5 ± 13.5	68.0 ± 12.9
led17	57.5 ± 12.5	59.5 ± 11.8	**59.5 ± 11.8**	39.0 ± 9.06
liver	63.9 ± 8.07	59.4 ± 11.5	64.3 ± 8.22	63.7 ± 7.82
monks-1	78.0 ± 13.4	78.0 ± 13.4	78.0 ± 13.4	71.5 ± 7.54
monks-2	92.6 ± 8.39	92.6 ± 8.39	**92.6 ± 8.39**	57.1 ± 7.21
monks-3	100. ± 0.00	100. ± 0.00	**100. ± 0.00**	79.3 ± 8.43
opera	49.0 ± 4.78	49.0 ± 4.78	49.0 ± 4.78	49.0 ± 4.84
pima-indians-diabetes	70.5 ± 4.47	68.4 ± 4.28	70.8 ± 3.31	71.7 ± 3.15
post-operative	63.3 ± 14.8	63.3 ± 13.9	62.2 ± 14.9	57.7 ± 22.7
promoters	89.7 ± 10.1	89.7 ± 8.17	**89.7 ± 8.17**	80.1 ± 9.42
sonar	85.0 ± 8.84	81.6 ± 6.42	76.9 ± 6.15	**87.0 ± 7.19**
soybean-large	92.1 ± 4.08	90.2 ± 5.80	90.2 ± 5.80	91.1 ± 5.13
soybean-small	100. ± 0.00	100. ± 0.00	100. ± 0.00	100. ± 0.00
wdbc	95.2 ± 2.19	95.7 ± 2.50	94.9 ± 3.02	95.2 ± 2.34
zoo	95.0 ± 7.00	95.0 ± 7.00	95.0 ± 7.00	96.0 ± 5.16

Table 4: Classification accuracies in percentage of the metrics SF2 with Naïve , Kernel and cross-validated estimator with different localities. Bold means a significative ($p < 0.05$) difference between the locally restricted and unrestricted metrics.

	Naïve		Kernel		Est_{CV}	
Data Set	$h = N$	$h = h_{CV}$	$h = N$	$h = h_{CV}$	$h = N$	$h = h_{CV}$
anneal	97.3 ± 2.17	97.9 ± 1.88	96.2 ± 2.88	**97.9 ± 1.47**	97.3 ± 2.17	97.9 ± 1.88
audiology	76.5 ± 6.25	77.5 ± 8.57	76.0 ± 8.43	76.0 ± 10.2	75.5 ± 7.24	75.5 ± 10.1
breast-cancer	60.4 ± 11.7	63.5 ± 9.48	**68.9 ± 5.11**	64.3 ± 8.65	65.7 ± 6.44	62.8 ± 9.85
bridges1	65.8 ± 13.4	64.9 ± 9.95	64.9 ± 9.95	60.9 ± 12.7	64.9 ± 14.5	64.0 ± 8.55
bridges2	70.4 ± 17.9	71.4 ± 19.2	66.6 ± 17.2	66.7 ± 19.1	69.5 ± 19.5	70.5 ± 20.8
crx	78.2 ± 4.32	80.4 ± 2.57	82.3 ± 2.53	82.4 ± 4.75	81.4 ± 4.03	80.8 ± 2.88
derma	74.1 ± 17.4	78.1 ± 13.1	74.8 ± 11.3	73.5 ± 11.8	72.1 ± 15.7	77.5 ± 14.2
flag	63.8 ± 6.58	59.8 ± 10.1	50.0 ± 9.75	**58.9 ± 8.16**	63.8 ± 6.58	59.8 ± 10.1
glass	61.7 ± 14.1	**69.2 ± 11.9**	58.8 ± 14.2	**73.0 ± 10.9**	56.0 ± 11.9	**68.7 ± 11.4**
hepatitis	82.6 ± 6.43	88.5 ± 8.72	82.6 ± 9.27	83.9 ± 7.93	82.0 ± 6.31	**88.5 ± 8.72**
horse-colic	79.3 ± 9.78	**83.6 ± 6.74**	82.6 ± 8.86	84.3 ± 6.85	79.6 ± 11.3	83.3 ± 7.20
house-votes-84	86.4 ± 3.66	**93.0 ± 3.78**	90.5 ± 6.44	93.9 ± 3.67	90.5 ± 6.44	93.7 ± 3.44
ionosphere	87.7 ± 6.13	86.5 ± 3.35	93.4 ± 3.29	92.5 ± 4.50	**93.4 ± 3.29**	89.4 ± 4.28
iris	93.3 ± 5.44	95.3 ± 5.48	92.0 ± 5.25	94.6 ± 6.88	92.0 ± 5.25	95.3 ± 5.48
led	68.5 ± 15.4	68.5 ± 15.4	68.5 ± 15.9	71.5 ± 17.9	68.5 ± 15.9	69.0 ± 14.4
led17	58.5 ± 10.8	58.0 ± 8.23	48.0 ± 13.3	43.5 ± 7.83	58.5 ± 10.8	58.0 ± 8.23
liver	63.4 ± 8.17	66.6 ± 10.7	55.6 ± 10.1	59.4 ± 12.7	62.2 ± 7.36	62.3 ± 12.5
monks-1	65.9 ± 11.4	76.1 ± 10.5	100. ± 0.00	100. ± 0.00	100. ± 0.00	98.1 ± 3.40
monks-2	68.5 ± 11.3	**91.1 ± 7.33**	46.7 ± 5.16	**56.4 ± 7.68**	68.5 ± 11.3	**91.1 ± 7.33**
monks-3	99.7 ± 0.73	100. ± 0.00	99.7 ± 0.73	99.7 ± 0.73	99.7 ± 0.73	100. ± 0.00
opera	49.2 ± 4.63	48.4 ± 4.41	48.9 ± 4.81	48.5 ± 4.78	49.0 ± 4.90	48.6 ± 4.74
pima-indians-diabetes	70.5 ± 4.74	70.3 ± 3.55	65.2 ± 4.66	**70.3 ± 3.17**	67.1 ± 5.94	70.3 ± 3.55
post-operative	47.7 ± 17.4	56.6 ± 18.4	53.3 ± 19.4	53.3 ± 17.9	47.7 ± 17.4	55.5 ± 16.5
promoters	90.3 ± 9.23	88.5 ± 7.81	85.6 ± 11.9	83.8 ± 12.4	89.4 ± 8.60	88.5 ± 7.81
sonar	77.9 ± 7.34	**87.0 ± 7.19**	86.0 ± 7.34	89.3 ± 5.57	86.0 ± 7.34	86.0 ± 7.74
soybean-large	88.2 ± 7.60	92.4 ± 4.94	87.5 ± 5.76	90.5 ± 5.64	88.2 ± 7.60	92.4 ± 4.94
soybean-small	100. ± 0.00	100. ± 0.00	100. ± 0.00	100. ± 0.00	100. ± 0.00	100. ± 0.00
wdbc	92.2 ± 2.35	**95.4 ± 2.36**	94.0 ± 2.21	**96.3 ± 2.53**	94.0 ± 2.21	94.7 ± 2.01
zoo	96.0 ± 5.16	96.0 ± 5.16	97.0 ± 4.83	96.0 ± 5.16	96.0 ± 5.16	96.0 ± 5.16

Table 7: Classification accuracies in percentage of Minimum Risk Metric with different estimators and $h = N$ and Bayes Classifier based on the same estimates.

Data Set	Naïve Bayes	MR Naïve	Kernel Bayes	MR Kernel	Est_{CV} Bayes	MR Est_{CV}
anneal	97.6 ± 1.61	97.6 ± 1.61	76.4 ± 3.96	76.4 ± 3.96	97.6 ± 1.61	97.6 ± 1.61
audiology	76.5 ± 7.47	76.5 ± 7.47	49.0 ± 8.09	47.0 ± 9.77	76.5 ± 7.47	76.5 ± 7.47
breast-cancer	73.4 ± 7.16	73.4 ± 7.16	72.7 ± 6.02	72.7 ± 6.02	72.3 ± 6.58	72.3 ± 6.58
bridges1	63.0 ± 11.0	63.0 ± 11.0	52.9 ± 12.6	54.6 ± 14.4	63.0 ± 11.0	63.0 ± 11.0
bridges2	69.6 ± 19.0	69.6 ± 19.0	71.1 ± 15.3	71.1 ± 15.3	69.3 ± 17.8	69.3 ± 17.8
crx	83.9 ± 1.73	83.9 ± 1.73	62.0 ± 6.02	62.0 ± 6.02	83.9 ± 1.73	83.9 ± 1.73
derma	77.4 ± 17.9	77.4 ± 17.9	75.5 ± 15.8	75.5 ± 15.8	70.8 ± 16.8	70.8 ± 16.8
flag	61.8 ± 7.83	61.8 ± 7.83	55.3 ± 11.9	55.8 ± 11.7	61.8 ± 7.83	61.8 ± 7.83
glass	66.8 ± 13.6	66.8 ± 13.6	49.0 ± 13.6	49.5 ± 14.5	66.8 ± 13.6	66.8 ± 13.6
hepatitis	87.1 ± 7.88	87.1 ± 7.88	81.4 ± 8.62	81.4 ± 8.62	87.1 ± 7.88	87.1 ± 7.88
horse-colic	83.6 ± 7.44	83.6 ± 7.44	84.0 ± 7.16	84.0 ± 7.16	83.6 ± 7.44	83.6 ± 7.44
house-votes-84	90.5 ± 4.30	90.5 ± 4.30	92.1 ± 4.47	92.1 ± 4.47	91.4 ± 5.21	91.4 ± 5.21
ionosphere	91.1 ± 3.42	91.1 ± 3.42	71.5 ± 5.04	71.5 ± 5.04	91.1 ± 3.42	91.1 ± 3.42
iris	95.3 ± 5.48	95.3 ± 5.48	95.3 ± 4.49	95.3 ± 4.49	94.6 ± 5.25	94.6 ± 5.25
led	**78.5 ± 11.5**	72.5 ± 14.5	**78.0 ± 13.1**	68.0 ± 15.3	**77.0 ± 13.3**	72.5 ± 14.5
led17	67.0 ± 9.18	67.0 ± 9.18	41.0 ± 9.06	42.0 ± 9.18	67.0 ± 9.18	67.0 ± 9.18
liver	71.3 ± 9.85	71.3 ± 9.85	60.5 ± 9.07	60.5 ± 9.07	71.3 ± 9.85	71.3 ± 9.85
monks-1	75.0 ± 7.79	66.2 ± 15.0	97.9 ± 2.54	97.9 ± 2.54	97.9 ± 2.54	97.9 ± 2.54
monks-2	66.8 ± 7.51	67.1 ± 7.49	67.1 ± 7.49	67.1 ± 7.49	67.1 ± 7.49	67.1 ± 7.49
monks-3	97.2 ± 2.40	97.2 ± 2.40	98.1 ± 2.40	98.1 ± 2.40	98.1 ± 2.40	98.1 ± 2.40
opera	57.3 ± 4.19	58.0 ± 3.70	**56.7 ± 3.52**	56.1 ± 3.32	57.8 ± 4.16	58.0 ± 3.70
pima-indians-diabetes	75.1 ± 4.76	75.1 ± 4.76	68.6 ± 3.19	68.6 ± 3.19	75.1 ± 4.76	75.1 ± 4.76
post-operative	64.4 ± 17.9	64.4 ± 17.9	71.1 ± 19.0	71.1 ± 19.0	71.1 ± 19.0	71.1 ± 19.0
promoters	90.4 ± 6.38	90.4 ± 6.38	85.6 ± 11.9	85.6 ± 11.9	90.4 ± 6.38	90.4 ± 6.38
sonar	78.3 ± 8.15	78.3 ± 8.15	67.3 ± 7.27	67.3 ± 7.27	78.3 ± 8.15	78.3 ± 8.15
soybean-large	92.5 ± 4.62	92.5 ± 4.62	79.4 ± 6.10	79.4 ± 6.10	92.5 ± 4.62	92.5 ± 4.62
soybean-small	100. ± 0.00	100. ± 0.00	100. ± 0.00	100. ± 0.00	100. ± 0.00	100. ± 0.00
wdbc	93.8 ± 2.22	93.8 ± 2.22	75.9 ± 6.63	75.9 ± 6.63	93.8 ± 2.22	93.8 ± 2.22
zoo	96.0 ± 5.16	96.0 ± 5.16	92.0 ± 7.86	90.0 ± 8.17	96.0 ± 5.16	96.0 ± 5.16

Table 9: Significative differences ($p < 0.05$) between MRM with Naïve Estimator, MRM with cross–validated estimator, SF2 metric with cross-validated estimator and cross-validated locality and IVDM.

	MRM $h = N$		SF2 $h = h_{CV}$	IVDM (I)
Data Set	Naïve (M_N)	Est_{CV} (M_{CV})	Est_{CV} (E^*_{CV})	
anneal				
audiology				
breast-cancer	E^*_{CV} I	E^*_{CV} I		
bridges1				
bridges2				
crx	E^*_{CV} I	E^*_{CV} I		
derma	M_{CV}			
flag				
glass				
hepatitis				
horse-colic				
house-votes-84				
ionosphere				
iris				
led				
led17	E^*_{CV} I	E^*_{CV} I		
liver	E^*_{CV}	E^*_{CV}		
monks-1		M_N I	M_N I	M_N
monks-2			M_N M_{CV}	M_N M_{CV}
monks-3			M_N M_{CV}	M_N M_{CV}
opera	E^*_{CV} I	E^*_{CV} I		
pima-indians-diabetes	E^*_{CV} I	E^*_{CV} I		
post-operative		E^*_{CV}		
promoters				
sonar			M_N M_{CV}	
soybean-large				
soybean-small				
wdbc				
zoo				

Table 6: Significative differences ($p < 0.05$) between SF2 with cross-validated estimators and DVDM and HEOM.

	SF2 Est_{CV}			
Data Set	$h = N$ (E_{CV})	$h = h_{CV}$ (E^*_{CV})	DVDM (D)	HEOM (E)
anneal	E	E		
audiology				
breast-cancer				
bridges1				
bridges2	E	D E		
crx				
derma				
flag	E			
glass		D		E_{CV}
hepatitis		E		
horse-colic			E_{CV}	
house-votes-84				
ionosphere	D E			
iris				
led				
led17	E	E		
liver				
monks-1	D E	D E		
monks-2	E	E	E_{CV}	
monks-3	E	E		
opera				
pima-indians-diabetes				E_{CV}
post-operative	D			
promoters	E	E		
sonar	D	D		
soybean-large				
soybean-small				
wdbc				
zoo				

Table 8: Significative differences ($p < 0.05$) between Minimum Risk Metric with Naïve Estimator and cross–validated estimator with DVDM and HEOM.

	MRM $h = N$			
Data Set	Naïve (M_N)	Est_{CV} (M_{CV})	DVDM (D)	HEOM (E)
anneal	E	E		
audiology				
breast-cancer	D E	D E		
bridges1				
bridges2	D E	E		
crx	D	D		
derma				
flag				
glass		D		
hepatitis		E		
horse-colic				
house-votes-84				
ionosphere	E	E		
iris				
led				
led17	D E	D E		
liver	D E	D E		
monks-1		D E	M_N	
monks-2	E	E	M_N M_{CV}	
monks-3	E	E	M_N M_{CV}	
opera	D E	D E		
pima-indians-diabetes	D E	D E		
post-operative	E	E		
promoters	E	E		
sonar		D		M_N M_{CV}
soybean-large				
soybean-small				
wdbc				
zoo				

5 Conclusions

The experiments show that the metric based on the observation by Short and Fukunaga works only if locally restricted. That is surprising given the theoretical optimality of the metric and further investigations are required to clarify this point. In fact, in the original formulation of Short of Fukunaga the locality is not necessary for the optimality argument but only because they adopt a linear approximation of the probability. Nevertheless the combination of cross–validated locality and cross-validated estimator leads to a metric that outperforms VDM and HEOM. The resulting metric is computationally heavy and it is outperformed by the Bayes Classifier based on the same probability estimate.

The Minimum Risk Metric that we introduced in this paper does not require local restrictions, its performances are comparable to the Bayes Classifier, its analytical form is simple and well founded, and finally, equipped with a simple Naïve Estimator, outperforms the other metrics. The accuracy is equivalent to the one achieved by the Naïve Bayes Classifier that proved to be in general a good classifier, therefore MRM appears to be relevant whenever the retrieval of a neighbor is required. For this reasons MRM seems particularly suitable for Case Based Reasoning application when a relevant classification of the cases is available.

References

[AG90] David W. Aha and Robert L. Goldstone. Learning attribute relevance in context in instance-based learning algorithms. In *Proceedings of the Twelfth Annual Conference of the Cognitive Science Society*, pages 141–148, Cambridge, MA, 1990. Lawrence Earlbaum.

[AG92] David W. Aha and Robert L. Goldstone. Concept learning and flexible weighting. In *Proceedings of the Fourteenth Annual Conference of the Cognitive Science Society*, pages 534–539, Bloomington, IN, 1992. Lawrence Earlbaum.

[BB96] E. Blanzieri and M. Bucciarelli. The evaluation of the communicative effect.

In *XVIII Cognitive Science Conference*, pages 501–506, San Diego, California, 1996.

[BMP98] R. Bellazzi, S. Montani, and L. Portinale. Retrieval in a prototype-based case library: A case study in diabetes therapy revision. *Lecture Notes in Computer Science*, 1488:64–??, 1998.

[CH67] T. M. Cover and P. E. Hart. Nearest neighbor pattern classification. *IEEE Transactions on Information Theory*, 13:21–27, 1967. [Reprinted in [Das91]].

[CH97] C. Cardie and N. Howe. Improving minority class prediction using case-specific feature weight. In *Proceedings of the Fourteenthn International Conference on Machine Learning*, pages 57–65. Morgan Kaufmann, 1997.

[CMSW92] R. H. Creecy, B. M. Masand, S. J. Smith, and D. L. Waltz. Trading MIPS and memory for knowledge engineering. *Communication of ACM*, 35:48–64, 1992.

[CS93] Scott Cost and Steven Salzberg. A weighted nearest neighbor algorithm for learning with symbolic features. *Machine Learning*, 10:57–78, 1993.

[Das91] B. V. Dasarathy, editor. *Nearest Neighbor (NN) Norms: NN Pattern Classification Techniques.* IEEE Computer Society Press, Los Alamitos, CA, 1991.

[DP97] Pedro Domingos and Michael Pazzani. On the optimality of the simple bayesian classifier under zero-one loss. *Machine Learning*, 29:103–130, 1997.

[Fri94] Jerome H. Friedman. Flexible metric nearest neighbour classification. Technical report, Stanford University, 1994. Available by anonymous FTP from playfair.stanford.edu.

[HT95] Trevor Hastie and Robert Tibshirani. Discriminant adaptive nearest neighbour classification. In U.M.Fayad and R.Uthurusamy, editors, *KDD-95: Proceedings First International Conference on Knowledge Discovery and Data Mining*, 1995.

[MH90] J. P. Myles and D. J. Hand. The multiclass metric problem in nearest neighbour discrimination rules. *Pattern Recognition*, 23(11):1291–1297, 1990.

[Mit97] T. Mitchell. *Machine Learning.* McGraw-Hill, 1997.

[RA95] Francesco Ricci and Paolo Avesani. Learning a local similarity metric for case-based reasoning. In *International Conference on Case-Based Reasoning (ICCBR-95), Sesimbra, Portugal, Oct. 23-26*, 1995.

[RA98] Francesco Ricci and Paolo Avesani. Data compression and local metrics for nearest neighbor classification. *IEEE Transactions on Pattern Analysis and Machine Intelligence*, 1998. In press.

[Sco92] D. W. Scott. *Multivariate Density Estimation: Theory , Practice, and Visualization.* John Wiley, New York, 1992.

[SF80] R. D. Short and K. Fukunaga. A new nearest neighbour distance measure. In *Proceeding of the 5th IEEE International Conference on Patter Recognition*, pages 81–86, Miami beach, FL, 1980.

[SF81] R. D. Short and K. Fukunaga. The optimal distance measure for nearest neighbour classification. *IEEE Transactions on Information Theory*, 27:622–627, 1981.

[SW86] Craig Stanfill and David Waltz. Toward memory-based reasoning. *Communication of ACM*, 29:1213–1229, 1986.

[WD95] Dietrich Wettschereck and Thomas G. Dietterich. An experimental comparison of the nearest neighbor and nearest hyperrectangle algorithms. *Machine Learning*, 19:5–28, 1995.

[WM97] D. Randall Wilson and Tony R. Martinez. Improved heterogeneous distance functions. *Journal of Artificial Intelligence Research*, 11:1–34, 1997.

[WMA97] Dietrich Wettschereck, Takao Mohri, and David W. Aha. A review and comparative evaluation of feature weighting methods for lazy learning algorithms. *AI Review Journal*, 11:273–314, 1997.

Local Learning for Iterated Time Series Prediction

Gianluca Bontempi
Iridia
Université Libre de Bruxelles
1050 Bruxelles - Belgium
http://iridia.ulb.ac.be
e-mail: gbonte@ulb.ac.be

Mauro Birattari
Iridia
Université Libre de Bruxelles
1050 Bruxelles - Belgium
http://iridia.ulb.ac.be
e-mail: mbiro@ulb.ac.be

Hugues Bersini
Iridia
Université Libre de Bruxelles
1050 Bruxelles - Belgium
http://iridia.ulb.ac.be
e-mail: bersini@ulb.ac.be

Abstract

We introduce and discuss a local method to learn one-step-ahead predictors for iterated time series forecasting. For each single one-step-ahead prediction, our method selects among different alternatives a local model representation on the basis of a local cross-validation procedure. In the literature, local learning is generally used for function estimation tasks which do not take temporal behaviors into account. Our technique extends this approach to the problem of long-horizon prediction by proposing a local model selection based on an iterated version of the PRESS leave-one-out statistic. In order to show the effectiveness of our method, we present the results obtained on two time series from the Santa Fe competition and on a time series proposed in a recent international contest.

1 INTRODUCTION

The use of local memory-based approximators for time series analysis has been the focus of numerous studies in the literature (Farmer & Sidorowich, 1987; Yakowitz, 1987). Memory-based approaches do not estimate a global model of the dynamic process underlying the time series but defer the processing of data until a prediction is explicitly requested. A database of observed values is stored in memory and the prediction is derived from an interpolation based on a neighborhood of the current state (*locally weighted regression*). These methods have been recently grouped under the denomination of *lazy learning* methods (Aha, 1997). A key issue in local learning is the selection of the local model structure which will have the best generalization performance given a set of sparse and noisy data (*bias/variance* dilemma). Under the assumption that data is described locally by a linear model, enhanced linear statistical procedures can be used to validate the local approximator. One example is the PRESS (Predicted Sum of Squares) statistic (Myers, 1994): this statistic returns the leave-one-out cross-validation error of a linear model as a by-product of the least-squares regression. As a consequence, the performance of a local linear model can be assessed with no additional computational burden, making easier the task of selecting the best local approximator. Once the most promising structure in cross-validation is selected, the local model returns the prediction.

The goal of the paper is to present a method for long term prediction based on the iteration of a one-step-ahead local learning predictor. Forecasting the value of a time series multiple steps ahead requires either a *direct* prediction of the desired value or the *iteration* of a one-step-ahead estimator. In order to emulate the system, a direct predictor often requires higher functional complexity than a one-step-ahead predictor. On the other hand it is more difficult for a one-step-ahead model to deal with the problem of accumulation of errors due to the iteration (Farmer & Sidorowich, 1987). The novelty of our approach consists in defining an iterated formulation of the PRESS leave-one-out statistic as a criterion for local model selection in multiple-step-ahead forecasting. We will show how the iterated PRESS outperforms a non iterated criterion, by assessing the generalization performance of a one-step predictor on a horizon longer than a single step, yet preserving nice properties of computational efficiency. To our knowledge there are no methods in local modeling literature which adopt cross-validation methods for iterated time series prediction. This technique makes local learning an effective alternative to state-of-the-art iterated techniques like recurrent neural networks approaches which are typically based on time consuming tuning procedures (e.g. back propagation through time (Rumelhart *et al.*, 1986) or real-time recurrent learning (Williams & Zipser, 1989)).

2 ITERATED AND DIRECT METHODS FOR PREDICTION

A time series is a sequence of measurements φ^t of an observable φ at equal time intervals. The Takens theorem (Packard *et al.*, 1980) implies that for a wide class of deterministic systems, there exists a *diffeomorphism* (one-to-one differential mapping) between a finite window of the time series $\{\varphi^{t-1}, \varphi^{t-2}, \ldots, \varphi^{t-m}\}$ (*lag vector*) and the state of the dynamic system underlying the series. This means that in theory it exists a multi-input single-output mapping (*delay coordinate embedding*) $f : R^m \to R$ so that:

$$\varphi^{t+1} = f(\varphi^t, \varphi^{t-1}, \ldots, \varphi^{t-m+1}) \quad (1)$$

where m (*dimension*) is the number of past values taken into consideration. This formulation returns a state space description, where in the m dimensional space the time series evolution is a trajectory, and each point represents a temporal pattern of length m.

A model of the mapping (1) can be used for two objectives: *one-step* prediction and *iterated* prediction. In the first case, the m previous values of the series are assumed to be available and the problem is equivalent to a problem of function estimation. In the case of iterated prediction, the predicted output is fed back as an input to the following prediction. Hence, the inputs consist of predicted values as opposed to actual observations of the original time series. A prediction iterated for k times returns a *k-step-ahead* forecasting. However, iterated prediction is not the only way to perform *k-step-ahead* forecasting. Weigend (Weigend, 1996) classifies the methods for k-step-ahead prediction, according to two features: the horizon of the predictor and the horizon of the training criterion. He enumerates three cases:

1. the model predicts k steps ahead by iterating a one-step-ahead predictor (Eq. 1) whose parameters are optimized to minimize the error on one-step-ahead forecast (one-step-ahead training criterion)

2. the model predicts k steps ahead by iterating a one-step-ahead predictor whose parameters are optimized to minimize the error on the iterated k-step-ahead forecast (k-step ahead training criterion)

3. the model performs a direct forecast at time $t+k$: $\varphi^{t+k} = f^k(\varphi^t, \varphi^{t-1}, \ldots, \varphi^{t-m+1})$

Methods of class 1 have low performance in long horizon task. This is due to the fact that they are essentially models tuned with a one-step-ahead criterion and therefore they are not able to take temporal behavior into account. Methods like recurrent neural networks (Williams & Zipser, 1989) are an example of class 2. Their recurrent architecture and the associated training algorithm (temporal backpropagation) are more able to handle the time-dependent nature of the data. Direct methods of class 3 often require high functional complexity in order to emulate the system. An example of combination of local techniques of type 1 and 3 is provided by Sauer (Sauer, 1994). In the next section we will present our local technique as a member of the second class of predictors.

3 A LOCAL METHOD FOR ITERATED PREDICTION

We propose a locally weighted regression method to estimate a one-step-ahead predictor trained and selected according to a k-step-ahead criterion. Typically, the data analyst who adopts a local regression approach, has to take a set of decisions related to the model (e.g. the number of neighbors, the kernel function, the parametric family, the distance metric). However, in local learning literature different methods exist which automatically select the adequate configuration (Atkeson *et al.*, 1997; Birattari *et al.*, 1999) by adopting tools and techniques from the field of linear statistical analysis. The most important of these tools is the PRESS statistic which is a simple, well-founded and economical way to perform *leave-one-out* cross-validation and to assess the performance in generalization of local linear models. By assessing the performance of each linear model, alternative configurations can be tested and compared in order to select the best one in terms of expected prediction.

Our method adopts the local learning procedure by replacing the one-step-ahead criterion for model selection, represented by the *conventional PRESS*, with a k-step-ahead criterion, defined as *iterated PRESS*. This criterion is used to select the best structure of a one-step-ahead estimator with the aim of capturing the long term dynamics underlying the available set

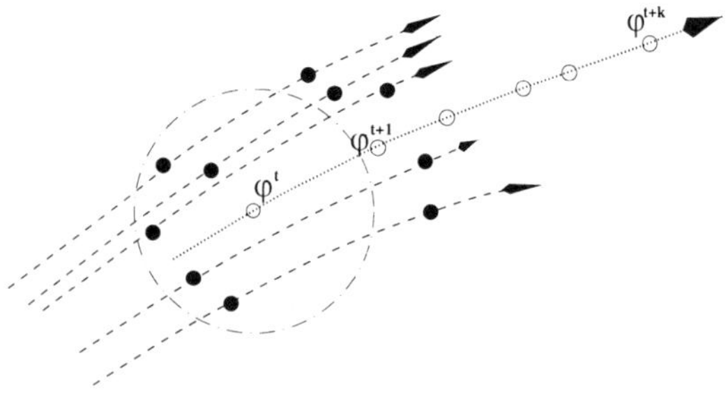

Figure 1: Local modeling in the embedding space

of observations. In this paper we will present experiments where the method is used to select query-by-query (i.e. at each time step) the best number of neighbors by keeping fixed the shape of the regression kernel (tricube) and the distance metric (euclidean). However, this approach can be extended to the selection of any desired model features, such as the set of regressors or the degree of the local approximator (Bersini *et al.*, 1998). Our local learning procedure can be summarized as follows:

1. The available realization of the time series is described in terms of a dataset D_N of N ordered pairs (x_i, y_i), where x_i is a temporal pattern of length m, and the concatenation of x_i and the scalar y_i is a temporal pattern of length $m+1$. Following this formulation, the current state is itself described by a pattern $\bar{x}$ of length m.
2. The one-step-ahead predictor is a local estimate of the mapping $f : \Re^m \rightarrow \Re$ from the dataset D_N. The estimate is performed by a locally weighted regression which selects the neighbors of $\bar{x}$ in the input space $\Re^m$.
3. The k-step-ahead prediction is performed by iterating a one-step-ahead estimator.
4. The local model is selected in a space of alternative model configurations, each characterized by a different number of neighbors.
5. The prediction ability of each alternative model is assessed by an iterated formulation of the cross-validation PRESS statistic (k-step-ahead criterion).

The basic idea of cross-validation for local modeling is represented in Fig. 1 which plots a time series in the embedding space. The open circles denote the current state φ^t and its unknown future values φ^{t+1} and φ^{t+k} while the dashed lines are a set of n observed trajectories in the neighborhood of the current state. Conventional cross-validation consists in assessing the accuracy of the local predictor by repeating n times the following procedure: the ith trajectory is removed, a one-step-ahead prediction of the removed trajectory is computed with the observations of the ith trajectory set aside and finally the leave-one-out error is obtained by comparing the prediction with the real value. The iterated PRESS generalizes this procedure by returning the leave-one-out error along the ith trajectory in the case of a prediction iterated for $k > 1$ steps. In the next section we will show how the analytic expression of the iterated statistic can be derived from the one-step-ahead leave-one-out PRESS formula.

3.1 THE CONVENTIONAL AND ITERATED PRESS STATISTIC

For a more concise formulation and a simpler graphical illustration, some simplifications are required. First, we present the case of a local model where the neighbors are weighted according to a rectangular kernel. Second, we discuss only the one-dimensional case (i.e. model in Eq. (1) with $m = 1$: $\varphi^{t+1} = f(\varphi^t)$), leaving the general case in the appendix. Furthermore, given a generic regressor r, the notation in bold characters $\boldsymbol{r}$ stands for a vector where a constant value 1 is appended to the value r in order to consider the offset term in the regression. Denote the values of the series at time t and $t+1$ with the variables $x = \varphi^t$ and $y = \varphi^{t+1}$, respectively. Suppose that the value of the series at time t is $\varphi^t = \bar{x}$, that a set of n neighbors $\{x_i\}_{i=1}^n$ of the current state is selected and that a linear regression is used to model locally the data. Let $e_{xy}(i)$ $i = 1 \dots n$ be the residual of the linear model and $e_{xy}^{cv}(i)$ the leave-one-out residual

$$e_{xy}^{cv}(i) = y_i - \hat{y}_{-i} = y_i - \boldsymbol{x}_i^T \beta_{xy}^{-i} \tag{2}$$

that is the difference between the real value of the mapping and the prediction $\hat{y}_{-i}$ in x_i of the linear model estimated with the ith point aside (see Fig. 2).

Results in linear statistical analysis say that a simple relation (PRESS statistic) exists between $e_{xy}(i)$ and $e_{xy}^{cv}(i)$ that is

$$e_{xy}^{cv}(i) = \frac{e_{xy}(i)}{1 - h_{ii}} \tag{3}$$

where h_{ii} is the ith diagonal element of the *Hat* matrix (see Appendix). Once the vector $e_{xy}^{cv}(i)$ is available,

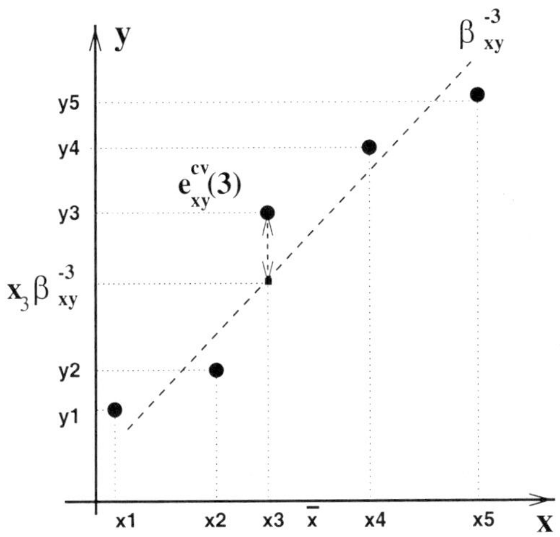

Figure 2: Conventional Press in the input-output space $X \to Y$;

it is possible to compute a leave-one-out measure (e.g. the mean squared error) of the performance of the local model for a single step prediction. Unfortunately, this index gives no hints about the expected performance of this model when used for iterated prediction. In fact, it is based on the representation of the time series as an input-output static mapping and it cannot take into account the behavior of the model as a dynamic process. To this aim it is necessary to compute a k-step-ahead criterion in order to measure the quality of the prediction on a longer horizon.

Here, we present an iterated formulation of the PRESS statistic for the horizon $k = 2$. Notice that an iterated prediction from time t to time $t+2$ is the composition of two predictions: $\hat{\varphi}^{t+1} = \hat{f}_t(\varphi^t)$ and $\hat{\varphi}^{t+2} = \hat{f}_{t+1}(\hat{\varphi}^{t+1})$ with $\hat{f}_t$ local model of the embedding (1) at time t.

Denote the values of the series at time t, $t+1$ and $t+2$ with the variables $x = \varphi^t$, $y = \varphi^{t+1}$ and $z = \varphi^{t+2}$, respectively. Hence, the prediction problem is analogous to the estimation of a composed mapping $z = g(h(x))$ whose components are $z = g(y)$ and $y = h(x)$ (see Fig. 3). Let β^{-i}_{yz} be the vector of the regression parameters estimated on the set $\{(y_i, z_i)\}_{i=1}^n$ with the i-th sample aside and let $e^{cv}_{yz}(i)$ be the leave-one-out residual of the mapping g. We will define the *iterated cross-validation residual* for $k = 2$ as

$$e^{it}_{xz}(i) = z_i - (\hat{\boldsymbol{y}}_{-i})^T \beta^{-i}_{yz} \qquad (4)$$

that is, the difference between the $k = 2$ steps ahead real value and the iteration of two one-step leave-one-out predictions.

We illustrate the idea in Fig. 3. Here we have $n = 5$ triples $\{(x_i, y_i, z_i)\}_{i=1}^5$ and we want to estimate the iterated cross-validation residual in $x_i = x_3$.

According to Eq. (2), $e^{cv}_{xy}(3)$ is the difference between y_3 and $\boldsymbol{x}_3^T \beta^{-3}_{xy}$, and $e^{cv}_{yz}(y_3)$ is the difference between z_3 and $(\hat{\boldsymbol{y}}_{-3})^T \beta^{-3}_{yz}$. From (2) and (4), the iterated cross-validation residual $e^{it}_{xz}(3)$ is the difference between z_3 and the regression value $(\hat{\boldsymbol{y}}_{-3})^T \beta^{-3}_{yz}$ where $\hat{y}_{-3} = y_3 - e^{cv}_{xy}(x_3)$ obtained by shifting y_3 by the error $e^{cv}_{xz}(3)$ incurred at the previous step. The formula of the iterated PRESS for a generic dimension m and a generic horizon k is derived in the Appendix.

The iterated cross-validation error returns an estimate of the performance of an iterated one-step estimator from time t to time $t+k$. As far as long horizon predictions are required, this statistic returns richer information than the simple one-step PRESS statistic and allows more reliable local model selection for iterated prediction.

4 EXPERIMENTS AND FINAL CONSIDERATIONS

The iterated PRESS approach has been applied both to the prediction of a *real-world* data set (A) and to a computer generated time series (D) from the *Santa Fe Time Series Prediction and Analysis Competition.* The A time series has a training set of 1000 values and a test set of 10000 samples: the task is to predict the continuation for 100 steps, starting from different points. The D time series has a training set of 100000 values and a test set of 500 samples: the task is to predict the continuation for 25 steps, starting from different points.

We adopt a local learning iterated prediction method where the selection of neighbors is made according to the iterated PRESS. The horizon of the iterated criterion is $h = 5$ for the series A and $h = 25$ for the series D. The number of neighbors is limited to range from 4 to 12 for both series. We adopt for the series A an embedding model having the same dimension $m = 16$ proposed in (Sauer, 1994) and for the series D an embedding model with $m = 20$ as reported in (Zhang & Hutchinson, 1994). Each prediction of the local model, inclusive of the modeling phase, takes about one second of computation on a Pentium machine.

Table 1 compares the NMS (Normalized Mean Squared) prediction errors on the A test set of the local

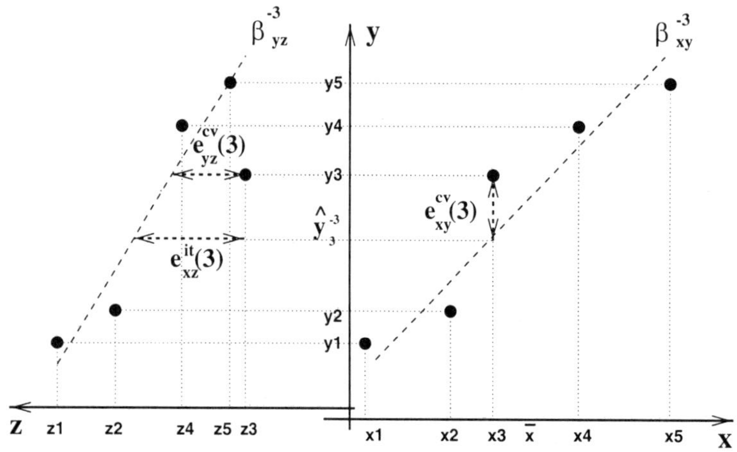

Figure 3: Iterated Press in the composed space $X \rightarrow Y \rightarrow Z$

Table 1: NMSE of the predictions for time series A

Test data	Non iter. PRESS	Iter. PRESS	Sauer	Wan
1-100	0.350	0.029	0.077	0.055
1180-1280	0.379	0.131	0.174	0.065
2870-2970	0.793	0.055	0.183	0.487
3000-3100	0.003	0.003	0.006	0.023
4180-4280	1.134	0.051	0.111	0.160

Table 2: RMSE of the predictions for time series D

Test data	Non iter. PRESS	Iter. PRESS	Zhang Hutchinson
0-24	0.1255	0.0492	0.0665
100-124	0.0460	0.0363	0.0616
200-224	0.2635	0.1692	0.1475
300-324	0.0461	0.0405	0.0541
400-424	0.1610	0.0644	0.0720

predictor (iterated and non iterated) with the performance statistics reported by Sauer (Sauer, 1994) and Wan (Wan, 1994). Sauer used a combination of iterated and direct local linear models with a fixed number of four neighbors on a data set obtained by interpolating the original one. Wan used a recurrent network (FIR-network) with one input unit, two layers of 12 hidden units each, and one output unit. The architecture was trained with temporal backpropagation, and according to Wan, a training run typically took over night on a Sun Sparc2.

Table 2 compares the local RMS (root mean squared) errors on the series D with the results obtained by (Zhang & Hutchinson, 1994). Zhang and Hutchinson adopted a combination of multilayer perceptrons for iterated and direct predictions which were trained on a Connection Machine for a total period of about 100 hours.

The iterated approach has been applied also to the prediction of a time series proposed in the competition of the *International Workshop on Advanced Black-box techniques for nonlinear modeling* (Leuven, Belgium; 1998). The data set[1] consists of 2000 values and the task is to predict the continuation for the next 200 steps (see Fig. 4). Two predictions submitted by the authors with different embedding orders ($m = 20$ and $m = 24$) ranked second and fourth, respectively (Suykens & Vandewalle, 1998).

[1]see http://www.esat.kuleuven.ac.be/sista/workshop/

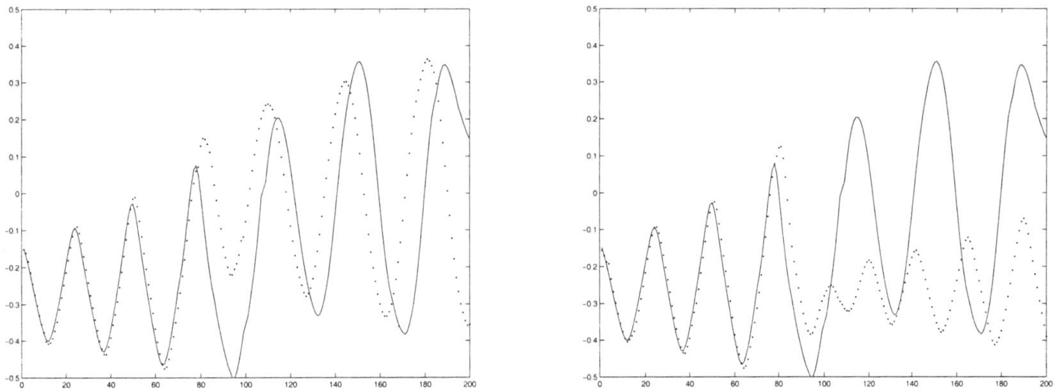

Figure 4: Predictions performed by the iterated PRESS predictor for the Leuven time series competition (full line: to be predicted, dotted: prediction): a) embedding order m=20 ($NMSE = 0.0475$) b) m =24 ($NMSE = 0.0667$)

The experiments show that for long horizons the iterated PRESS can improve the performance of the local approach based on the conventional leave-one-out cross-validation. At the same time it emerges that in iterated tasks the local approach is able to outperform complex nonlinear architectures at a reduced computational cost.

Appendix

The PRESS leave-one-out formula for a linear regression model with X input matrix $[n, m+1]$ and y output vector $[n, 1]$ is derived in (Myers, 1994) as

$$\begin{aligned} e^{cv}_{xy}(i) &= y_i - \mathbf{x}_i^T \beta_{xy}^{-i} = \\ &= y_i - \mathbf{x}_i^T [P + \frac{P\mathbf{x_i}\mathbf{x}_i^T P}{1-h_{ii}}] X_{-i}^T y_{-i} = \\ &= y_i - \mathbf{x}_i^T P X_{-i}^T y_{-i} - \frac{h_{ii}\mathbf{x}_i^T P X_{-i}^T y_{-i}}{1-h_{ii}} = \\ &= \frac{(1-h_{ii})y_i - \mathbf{x}_i^T P X_{-i}^T y_{-i}}{1-h_{ii}} = \\ &= \frac{(1-h_{ii})y_i - \mathbf{x}_i^T P (X^T y - \mathbf{x}_i y_i)}{1-h_{ii}} = \\ &= \frac{(1-h_{ii})y_i - \hat{y}_i + h_{ii} y_i}{1-h_{ii}} = \frac{e_{xy}(i)}{1-h_{ii}} \end{aligned} \tag{5}$$

where $P = (X^T X)^{-1}$, h_{ii} is the diagonal element of the Hat matrix $H = XPX^T$, $\mathbf{x}_i^T$ is the i-t row of X, $\hat{y}_i = \mathbf{x}_i^T P X^T y$ is the prediction of the linear regression, $e_{xy}(i) = \hat{y}_i - y_i$ is the residual and β_{xy}^{-i} denotes the vector $[m+1, 1]$ of least-squares coefficients computed with the ith data point aside. Note that the derivation of the PRESS formula in (5) makes use of the following equivalence $X_{-i}^T y_{-i} + \mathbf{x}_i y_i = X^T y$.

We derive now the iterated PRESS formula for a problem of prediction from time t to time $t+k$ having m as embedding order . Let $\bar{\mathbf{x}}$ be the embedding vector at time t and $\mathbf{x}_i$ a neighbor of $\bar{\mathbf{x}}$. Consider the trajectory in the m dimensional state space passing through $\mathbf{x}_i$: let $\mathbf{y}_i$ the embedding vector $k-1$ steps ahead with respect to x_i and z_i the value of the series k steps later than $\mathbf{x}_i$. The k-iterated leave-one-out residual at time t in the ith point is defined as the value of the leave-one-out regression β_{yz}^{-i} computed in the point $\mathbf{y}_i$ previously shifted of the vector $\boldsymbol{\delta}_i$ of errors cumulated in the $k-1$ previous steps. Then the iterated PRESS formula is derived as follows:

$$\begin{aligned} & e^{it}_{xz}(i) = z_i - (\mathbf{y}_i - \boldsymbol{\delta}_i)^T \beta_{yz}^{-i} = \\ & = z_i - \mathbf{y}_i^T [P + \frac{P\mathbf{y}_i\mathbf{y}_i^T P}{1-h_{ii}}] Y_{-i}^T z_{-i} + \\ & + \boldsymbol{\delta}_i^T [P + \frac{P\mathbf{y}_i\mathbf{y}_i^T P}{1-h_{ii}}] Y_{-i}^T z_{-i} = \\ & = \frac{e_{yz}(i) + \boldsymbol{\delta}_i^T[(1-h_{ii}) + P\mathbf{y}_i\mathbf{y}_i^T] P Y_{-i}^T z_{-i}}{1-h_{ii}} = \\ & = \frac{e_{yz}(i) + \boldsymbol{\delta}_i^T[(1-h_{ii}) + P\mathbf{y}_i\mathbf{y}_i^T] P (Y^T z - \mathbf{y}_i z_i)}{1-h_{ii}} = \\ & = \frac{e_{yz}(i) + \boldsymbol{\delta}_i^T[(1-h_{ii}) P Y^T z]}{1-h_{ii}} + \\ & + \frac{\boldsymbol{\delta}_i^T[-(1-h_{ii}) P\mathbf{y}_i z_i + P\mathbf{y}_i\mathbf{y}_i^T P Y^T z - P\mathbf{y}_i\mathbf{y}_i^T P\mathbf{y}_i z_i]}{1-h_{ii}} = \\ & = \frac{e_{yz}(i) + \boldsymbol{\delta}_i^T[(1-h_{ii}) P Y^T z - P\mathbf{y}_i z_i + P\mathbf{y}_i \hat{z}_i]}{1-h_{ii}} = \\ & = \frac{e_{yz}(i) + \boldsymbol{\delta}_i^T[(1-h_{ii})\beta_{yz} - P\mathbf{y}_i e_{yz}(i)]}{1-h_{ii}} \end{aligned}$$

where we used the following equivalences: $P = (Y^T Y)^{-1}$, $Y_{-i}^T z_{-i} + \mathbf{y}_i z_i = Y^T z$, $\mathbf{y}_i^T P Y^T z = \hat{z}_i$, $e_{yz}(i) = z_i - \hat{z}_i$, $\mathbf{y}_i^T P \mathbf{y}_i z_i = h_{ii}$ and $\beta_{yz} = P Y^T z$.

Acknowledgements

The work of Gianluca Bontempi was supported by the European Union TMR Grant FMBICT960692. The work of Mauro Birattari was supported by the FIRST program of the Région Wallonne, Belgium.

References

Aha D. W. 1997. Editorial. *Artificial Intelligence Review*, **11**(1–5), 1–6.

Atkeson C. G. , Moore A. W. & Schaal S. 1997. Locally weighted learning. *Artificial Intelligence Review*, **11**(1–5), 11–73.

Bersini H. , Birattari M. & Bontempi G. . 1998. Adaptive memory-based regression methods. *Pages 2102–2106 of: Proceedings of the 1998 IEEE International Joint Conference on Neural Networks.*

Birattari M. , Bontempi G. & Bersini H. 1999. Lazy learning meets the recursive least-squares algorithm. *In:* Kearns M. S. , Solla S. A. & Cohn D. A. (eds), *Advances in Neural Information Processing Systems 11.* Cambridge: MIT Press.

Farmer J. D. & Sidorowich J. J. 1987. Predicting chaotic time series. *Physical Review Letters*, **8**(59), 845–848.

Myers R. H. 1994. *Classical and Modern Regression with Applications.* second edition edn. Boston, MA: PWS-KENT Publishing Company.

Packard N. H. , Crutchfeld J. P. , Farmer J. D. & Shaw R. S. 1980. Geometry from a time series. *Physical Review Letters*, **45**(9), 712–716.

Rumelhart D. E. , Hinton G. E. & Williams R. K. 1986. Learning representations by backpropagating errors. *Nature*, **323**(9), 533–536.

Sauer T. 1994. Time series prediction by using delay coordinate embedding. *Pages 175–193 of:* Weigend A. S. & Gershenfeld N. A. (eds), *Time Series Prediction: forecasting the future and understanding the past.* Harlow, UK: Addison Wesley.

Suykens J. A. K. & Vandewalle J. (eds) 1998. *Nonlinear Modeling: Advanced Black-Box Techniques.* Kluwer Academic Publishers. Chap. The K. U. Leuven Time Series Prediction Competition, pages 241–251.

Wan E. A. 1994. Time series prediction using a connectionist network with internal delay lines. *Pages 195–217 of:* Weigend A. S. & Gershenfeld N. A. (eds), *Time Series Prediction: forecasting the future and understanding the past.* Harlow, UK: Addison Wesley.

Weigend A. S. 1996. Time Series Analysis and Prediction. *Chap. 12, pages 395–449 of:* P. Smolensky M. C. Mozer & Rumelhart D. E. (eds), *Mathematical Perspectives on Neural Networks.* Lawrence Erlbaum Associates.

Williams R. & Zipser D. 1989. A learning algorithm for continually running fully recurrent neural networks. *Neural Computation*, **1**, 270–280.

Yakowitz S. 1987. Nearest-neighbour methods for time series analysis. *Journal of Time Series Analysis*, **8**(2).

Zhang X. & Hutchinson J. 1994. Simple architectures on fast machines: practical issues in nonlinear time series prediction. *Pages 219–241 of:* Weigend A. S. & Gershenfeld N. A. (eds), *Time Series Prediction: forecasting the future and understanding the past.* Addison Wesley.

Instance-Family Abstraction in Memory-Based Language Learning

Antal van den Bosch
ILK / Computational Linguistics
Tilburg University
The Netherlands
Antal.vdnBosch@kub.nl

Abstract

Memory-based learning appears relatively successful when the learning data is highly disjunct, i.e., when classes are scattered over many small families of instances in instance space, as in many language learning tasks. Abstraction over borders of disjuncts tends to harm generalization performance. However, careful abstraction in memory-based learning may be harmless when it preserves the disjunctivity of the learning data. We investigate the effect of careful abstraction in a series of language-learning task studies, and a small benchmark-task study. We find that when combined with feature weighting or value-distance metrics, careful abstraction, as implemented in the new FAMBL algorithm, can equal the generalization accuracies of pure memory-based learning, while attaining fair levels of memory compression.

1 INTRODUCTION

Memory-based learning (Stanfill and Waltz, 1986; Aha, Kibler, and Albert, 1991; Aha, 1997) has been studied for some time now as an approach to learning language processing tasks. It is found by various studies to be successful, attaining adequate to excellent generalization accuracies on realistic, complex tasks as different as hyphenation, semantic parsing, part-of-speech tagging, morphological segmentation, and word pronunciation (Daelemans and Van den Bosch, 1992; Cardie, 1994; Cardie, 1996; Daelemans et al., 1996; Van den Bosch, 1997). Recent studies (Van den Bosch, 1997; Daelemans, Van den Bosch, and Zavrel, 1999) provide indications that forgetting (parts of) task instances during learning tends to hinder generalization accuracy of the trained classifiers, especially when these instances are estimated to be exceptional. Learning algorithms that do not forget anything about the learning material, i.e., pure memory-based learning algorithms, are found to obtain the best accuracies for the tasks studied when compared to decision-tree or edited memory-based learning algorithms.

However, these findings still leave room for the hypothesis that abstraction of a more careful type may be an equal alternative to pure memory-based learning. The topic of this paper is to perform empirical tests on language learning tasks to collect indications for the efficacy of careful abstraction in memory-based language learning, in comparison with pure memory-based learning.

The paper is structured as follows. Section 2 summarises methods for abstraction in memory-based learning; it reviews existing approaches, and presents FAMBL, a new memory-based learning algorithm that abstracts carefully by merging (families of) instances in memory. In Section 3 a number of memory-based learning algorithms performing careful abstraction are applied to six realistic large-scale language learning tasks. The section also briefly discusses to what extent language learning tasks differ from typical benchmark tasks. In Section 4, the efficacy of careful generalization over families of instances is discussed.

2 BACKGROUND: ABSTRACTION IN MEMORY-BASED LEARNING

Memory-based learning, also known as instance-based, example-based, lazy, case-based, exemplar-based, locally weighted, and analogical learning (Stanfill and Waltz, 1986; Aha, Kibler, and Albert, 1991; Salzberg, 1991; Kolodner, 1993; Aha, 1997; Atkeson, Moore, and Schaal, 1997), is a class of supervised inductive learning algorithms for learning classification tasks. Memory-based learning treats a set of labeled (pre-classified) training instances as points in a multi-dimensional feature space, and stores them as such in an *instance base* in memory (rather than performing some abstraction over them). New (test) instances are classified by matching them to all instances in the instance base, calculating with each match the *distance* between the new instance and a memory instance. The memory instances with the smallest distances are collected, and the classifications associated with these nearest neighbors are merged and extrapolated to assign a classification to the new instance.

Early work on the k-NN classifier pointed at advantageous properties of the classifier in terms of generalization accuracies, under certain assumptions, because of its reliance on full memory. However, the trade-off downside of full memory is computational inefficiency of the classification process, as compared to parametric classifiers that do abstract from the learning material. Therefore, several early investigations were performed into *editing* methods: finding criteria for the removal of instances from memory (Hart, 1968; Gates, 1972) without harming classification accuracy. Other studies on editing also explored the possibilities of detecting and removing noise from the learned data, so that classification accuracy might even improve (Wilson, 1972; Devijver and Kittler, 1980).

The renewed interest in the k-NN classifier from the late 1980s onwards in machine learning (Stanfill and Waltz, 1986; Aha, Kibler, and Albert, 1991; Salzberg, 1991) caused several new implementations of ideas on criteria for editing, but also other approaches to abstraction in memory-based learning emerged. Now, three types of careful abstraction in memory-based learning may be distinguished: (1) **Editing** (Hart, 1968; Wilson, 1972; Aha, Kibler, and Albert, 1991): removing instances according to a classification-related utility threshold they do not reach; (2) **Oblivious (partial) decision-tree abstraction** (Daelemans, Van den Bosch, and Weijters, 1997): compressing instances in the instance base into decision-tree paths; and (3) **Carefully merged instances** (Salzberg, 1991; Domingos, 1996): merging multiple instances in single generalized instances (or hyperrectangles). While individual instances are usually represented by propositional conjunctions of atomic feature values, merged instances can be conjunctions of *disjunctions of* feature values as in NGE (Nested Generalized Exemplars) (Salzberg, 1991), or rules with wildcards as in RISE (Rule Induction from a Set of Exemplars) (Domingos, 1996).

As noted in the introduction, recent studies have shown that editing in memory-based learning (1) and decision-tree induction (2), applied to language learning tasks, yield lower generalization accuracies as compared to pure memory-based learning tasks. We have argued earlier, supported by empirical evidence, that this is due to the fact that both methods tend to ignore small disjuncts (Daelemans, Van den Bosch, and Zavrel, 1999). In contrast, merging instances as in NGE and RISE is specifically designed to preserve disjuncts when appropriate. The experiments described in this paper are performed to investigate whether algorithms of this type indeed are able to maintain the level of accuracy of pure memory-based learning on langauge learning tasks. Apart from performing experiments with RISE and NGE, we introduce FAMBL, a new algorithm that combines some of the ideas that also underly NGE and RISE.

2.1 FAMBL: MERGING INSTANCE FAMILIES

FAMBL, for *FAMily-Based Learning*, is a new algorithm that constitutes an alternative approach to careful abstraction over instances. A first account of FAMBL is given in Van den Bosch (1999). In the current paper, we report on extended studies with FAMBL, among which a comparitive study on standard machine learning benchmark tasks. The core idea of FAMBL is to transform an instance base into a set of *instance family expressions.* An instance family expression is a hyperrectangle, but the procedure for merging instances differs from that in NGE or in RISE. First, we outline the ideas and assumptions underlying FAMBL. We then describe the learning algorithm.

The value of k in k-NN classification determines how many of nearest neighbours are used for extrapolating their (majority) classification to a new instance. Fixing k ignores the fact that an instance is often surrounded in instance space by a number of instances of the same class that may well be larger or smaller than k. We refer to such variable-sized set of same-class nearest neighbours as an instance's *family.* The number and sizes of families in a data set reflect the *disjunctivity* of the data set: the degree of scatteredness of classes into clusters. Many types of language data appear to be quite disjunct (Daelemans, Van den Bosch, and Zavrel, 1999).

Figure 1 illustrates how FAMBL determines the fam-

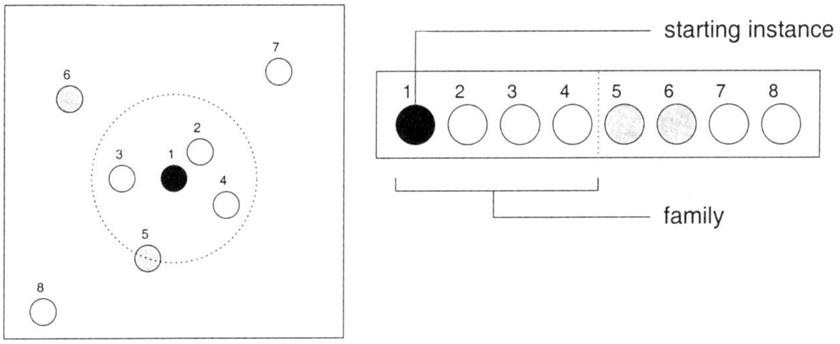

Figure 1: An example of a family in a two-dimensional instance space (left). The family, at the inside of the dotted circle, spans the focus instance (black) and the three nearest neighbours labeled with the same class (white). When ranked in the order of distance (right), the family boundary is put immediately before the first instance of a different class (grey).

ily of an instance, using a simple two-dimensional example instance space. All nearest neighbours of a randomly-picked starting instance (marked by the black dot) are searched and ranked in the order of their distance to the starting instance. Although there are five instances of the same class in the example space, the family of the starting instance contains only three, since its fourth-nearest instance is of a different class. Once a family is determined, FAMBL converts it to a *family expression*, by merging all instances belonging to that family simultaneously. When merged instances differ in values at a feature, the resultant family expression lists both values as disjunctions at that feature. In contrast with NGE, (i) family expressions are created in one operation, rather than incrementally; (ii) a family is abstracted only once and is not merged later on with other instances or family expressions.

The FAMBL algorithm has a learning component and a classification component. The learning component, in which all families in an instance base are determined and converted to expressions, is composed of two stages: a *probing* stage and a *family extraction* stage. The probing stage is a preprocessing stage to the actual family extraction as outlined above. The reason for preprocessing is visualized in Figure 2. The random selection of instances to be a starting point for family creation can be quite unfortunate. When, for example, the middle instance in the left part of Figure 2 is selected first, a seven-instance family is formed with relatively large within-family distances. Moreover, three other instances that are actually quite close to members of this big family become isolated and are necessarily extracted later on as single-instance families. The situation in the right part of Figure 2 displays a much more desirable situation, in which the space is more evenly divided between only two families instead of four.

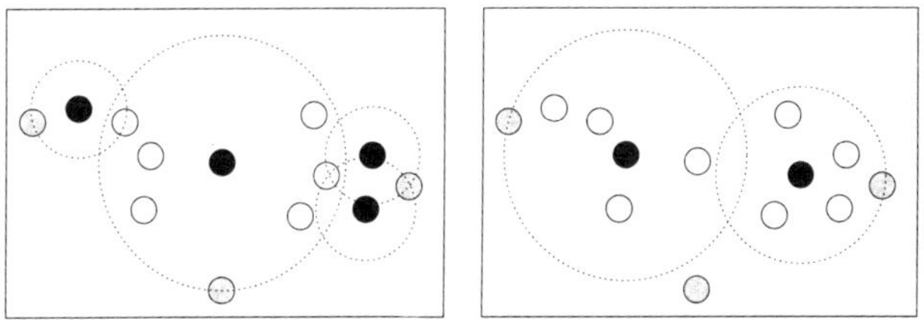

Figure 2: Illustration of the need for the preprocessing stage in FAMBL. The left figure shows a large family surrounding the middle starting-point instance (black dot), forcing the remaining three instances to be their own family. The right figure shows the same space, but with two other starting points, displaying a more evenly divided space over two families. White-dot instances are of the same class as the starting points; grey-dot instances have a different class.

In the probing stage, all families are extracted randomly and straightforwardly, while records are maintained of (i) the size of each family, and (ii) the average distance between the starting instance of each family and the other instances in the family. When all instances are captured in families, the mean and the median of both records are computed, and *both medians are used as threshold values for the second, actual family extraction phase.* This means that in the family extraction phase, no family is extracted that has more members than the probed median number of members, and no family is extracted that has an average distance from the starting instance to the other family members larger than the probed median value. Thus, the actual family extraction phase applies ex-

Procedure FAMBL FAMILY-EXTRACTION PHASE:

Input: A training set TS of instances $I_{1...n}$, each instance being labeled with a family-membership flag set to $FALSE$

Output: A family set FS of family expressions $F_{1...m}$, $m \leq n$

$i = f = 0$

1. Randomize the ordering of instances in TS
2. While not all family-membership flags are $TRUE$, Do
   - While the family-membership flag of I_i is $TRUE$ Do increase i
   - Compute NS, a ranked set of nearest neighbors to I_i with the same class as I_i, among all instances with family-membership flag $FALSE$. Nearest-neighbor instances of a different class with family-membership flag $TRUE$ are still used for marking the boundaries of the family.
   - Compute the number of members in the new virtual family: $|NS| + 1$
   - Compute the average distance of all instances in NS to I_i: $A_{NS,I}$
   - While $((|NS + 1| > M_1)OR(A_{NS,I} > M_2))$ Do remove the most distant family member to I in NS
   - Set the membership flags of I_i and all remaining instances in NS to $TRUE$
   - Merge I_i and all instances in NS into the family expression F_f and store sthis expression along with a count of the number of instance merged in it
   - $f = f + 1$

Figure 3: Schematized overview of the family-extraction phase in FAMBL.

tra careful abstraction, under the assumption that it is better to have several medium-sized, adjacent families of the same class than one big family overlapping the medium ones except for some adjacent boundary instances that get isolated.

Figure 3 summarizes the procedure followed by the actual family extraction stage. In short, family extraction is performed by repeatedly selecting a starting point, which is an instance that is not merged yet into a family, and building a family around it. This procedure repeats until all instances are in a family.

After learning, the original instance base is discarded, and further classification is based only on the set of family expressions yielded by the family-extraction phase. Classification in FAMBL works analogously to classification in pure memory-based learning, and classification in NGE: a match is made between a new test instance and all stored family expressions. When a family expression records a disjunction of values for a certain feature, matching is perfect when one of the disjunctive values matches the value at that feature in the new instance. Merged feature-value counts are summed for each feature-value match, to be used in case of ties: when two or more family expressions of different classes match equally well with the new instance, the expression is selected with the highest summed occurrence of matched features. When the tie remains, the class is selected that occurs the most frequently in the complete family expression set.

We conclude our description of the FAMBL algorithm by noting that FAMBL allows for the inclusion of informational abstraction in the form of feature-weighting, instance-weighting and value-difference metrics. For comparisons with other algorithms, as described in the next section, we have included these metrics as options in FAMBL.

3 EFFECTS OF CAREFUL ABSTRACTION IN LANGUAGE LEARNING AND BENCHMARK TASKS

As stated in the introduction, our primary goal is to investigate the effects of careful instance-family abstraction in memory-based learning of language processing tasks. In this section we report on experiments in which FAMBL, RISE, and NGE, in comparison with the pure memory-based learning algorithm IB1 (Aha, Kibler, and Albert, 1991; Daelemans and Van den Bosch, 1992), are applied to six language learning tasks, measuring the effects of their careful abstraction on generalization accuracy. First, we briefly introduce the six tasks investigated in this study. Table 1 lists the numbers of instances, feature values, and classes of the data sets of the selected six tasks.

Grapheme-phoneme conversion (henceforth referred to as GP) is the mapping between the spelling of a word and its phonemic transcription. We define the task as the mapping of fixed-sized instances representing parts of English words to a class representing the phoneme of the instance's middle letter. An example instance and its classifications is "_ _ h e a r t s _", mapping to class /A:/, which denotes an elongated short 'a'-sound to which the middle letter 'a' maps. The data used in the experiments described here are derived from the CELEX lexical data base of English (Baayen, Piepenbrock, and van Rijn, 1993).

Grapheme-phoneme conversion combined with stress assignment (henceforth GS) is similar to the GP task, but differs in two respects: (i) the windows only span seven letters, and (ii) the class represents a combined phoneme and a stress marker. Except for the data (derived from CELEX), the task is the same as the NETtalk task (Sejnowski and Rosenberg, 1987). See Van den Bosch (1997) for more details.

Morphological segmentation (henceforth MS) is the segmentation of words into labeled morphemes. Each instance represents a window snapshot of a word of nine letters. Its class represents the presence or absence of a morpheme boundary immediately before the middle letter. If present, it also encodes the type of morpheme starting at that position. See Van den Bosch, Daelemans, and Weijters (1996) for more details.

Base-NP chunking (henceforth NP) is the segmentation of sentences into non-recursive NPs. Veenstra (1998) used the Base-NP tag set as presented in (Ramshaw and Marcus, 1995): *I* for inside a Base-NP, *O* for outside a Base-NP, and *B* for the first word in a Base-NP following another Base-NP. See Veenstra (1998) for more details, and Daelemans, Van den Bosch, and Zavrel (1999) for a series of experiments on the particular data set also used here.

PP attachment (henceforth PP) is the attachment of a PP in the sequence VP NP PP (VP = verb phrase, NP = noun phrase, PP = prepositional phrase). The data consists of four-tuples of words, extracted from the Wall Street Journal Treebank. From the original data set, used by Ratnaparkhi, Reynar, and Roukos (1994), Collins and Brooks (1995), and Zavrel, Daelemans, and Veenstra (1997), Daelemans, Van den Bosch, and Zavrel (1999) took the train and test set together to form the particular data also used here.

Part-of-speech tagging (henceforth POS) is the disambiguation of syntactic classes of words in particular contexts. We assume a tagger architecture that processes a sentence from a disambiguated left to an ambiguous right context , as described in (Daelemans et al., 1996). The data set for the part-of-speech tagging task, extracted from the LOB corpus, contains 1,046,151 instances.

It was not possible to run experiments with both RISE and NGE on the maximal data set sizes (cf. Table 1) due to the large processing and memory demands of their current implementations, in relation to the computational resources available[1]. Therefore, we divided our experiments in three batches, which are described in Subsections 3.1, 3.2, and 3.3:

- In Subsection 3.1, experiments are described that deal with a 10% subset selection of the GP dataset. All algorithms (including RISE and NGE) are involved, using several combinations of feature weighting, instance weighting, and value distance metrics for the case of IB1 and FAMBL.
- In Subsection 3.2, FAMBL with gain-ratio feature weighting, RISE, and IB1 with gain-ratio feature weighting are applied to growing data sets of the GP, GS, and MS tasks, from 0.1% subsets via 1% and 10% portions to the full data sets. These experiments provide indications of the differences between RISE and FAMBL.
- In Subsection 3.3, FAMBL and IB1 are applied to the full-sized six data sets.

To make the link between language learning and machine learning in general more specific, we also report on a series of experiments in which FAMBL is applied to a number of well-known benchmark tasks, in Subsection 3.4. The results of these analyses specifically serve to show the difference in data characteristics between language learning and typical benchmark tasks.

3.1 CAREFUL ABSTRACTION VERSUS IB1 ON A GRAPHEME-PHONEME SUBSET

First, we performed a series of experiments concerning the application of a range of careful-abstracting methods to grapheme-phoneme conversion (GP). From an original instance base of 77,565 word-pronunciation pairs extracted from the CELEX lexical data base of English (Baayen, Piepenbrock, and van Rijn, 1993) we created ten equal-sized data sets each containing 7,757 word-pronunciation pairs. Using windowing and partitioning of this data in 90% training and 10% test instances, ten training and test sets are derived containing on average 60,813 and 6761 instances, respectively. These are token counts; in the training sets, 54,295 instance types occur (on average). One experiment consists of applying one algorithm to each of the ten training sets, and a test on each of the respective test sets. Apart from the careful abstractors RISE, NGE, and FAMBL, we include the pure memory-based learning algorithm IB1(-GR) (Aha, Kibler, and Albert, 1991; Daelemans and Van den Bosch, 1992) in the comparison. Each experiment yields (i) the mean generalization accuracy, in percentages correctly classified test instances, (ii) a standard deviation on this mean, and (iii) a count on the number of items in memory, i.e., (generalized) instances. Table 2 lists these

[1]Experiments were run on a dual-Pentium II 300 MHz machine, running Solaris, with 512 Mb of RAM.

TASK	# FEAT.	# VALUES OF FEATURE 1	2	3	4	5	6	7	8	9	10	11	# CLASS	# DATA SET INSTANCES
GP	9	42	42	42	42	41	42	42	42	42			61	675,745
GS	7	42	42	42	41	42	42	42					159	675,745
MS	9	42	42	42	42	41	42	42	42	42			2	573,544
PP	4	3,474	4,612	68	5,780								2	23,898
NP	11	20,231	20,282	20,245	20,263	86	87	86	89	3	3	3	3	251,124
POS	5	170	170	498	492	480							169	1,046,151

Table 1: Specifications of the six investigated language learning tasks: numbers of features, values per feature, classes, and instances.

experimental outcomes for all algorithms tested. As some of these algorithms use (combinations of) metrics for weighting or value-distance estimation: gain ratio (GR) (Quinlan, 1993), class-prediction strength (CPS, or CPS with Laplace correction as in RISE), or value-difference metrics (MVDM, or SVDM in RISE), we have marked the use of such metrics explicitly in the table.

ALGORITHM	METRICS GR	CPS	VDM	GEN. ACC. (%)	±	# MEMORY ITEMS
FAMBL	x		x	89.0	0.6	31,948
IB1	x		x	88.9	0.6	54,294
RISE		x	x	88.9	0.6	20,252
IB1	x			88.8	0.6	54,294
FAMBL	x			88.8	0.6	35,141
FAMBL			x	88.0	0.7	34,052
IB1			x	87.9	0.7	54,294
IB1				78.1	0.8	54,294
FAMBL				72.3	0.8	31,889
NGE		x		61.8	0.9	25,627

Table 2: Overview of generalization accuracies and memory usage obtained with pure memory-based learning and careful abstraction methods.

The results indicate a group of five best-performing algorithms that, in pair-wise comparisons using one-tailed t-tests, do not perform significantly different: (i) FAMBL with GR and MVDM, (ii) IB1 (with GR and MVDM), (iii) RISE (with CPS and SVDM), (iv) IB1 (with GR), and (v) FAMBL (with GR). A general property of this group is that it contains all algorithms that employ GR feature weighting.

Within the group of five best-performing algorithms, two are careful abstractors: RISE and FAMBL. As compared to the 54,295 instance types that are all stored in pure memory-based learning, RISE obtains an item compression of 62.7%. FAMBL with GR and MVDM compresses less: 41.2%. NGE with its default CPS exemplar weighting performs significantly worse than the unweighted IB1 and FAMBL, and also worse than FAMBL with CPS. This suggests that using CPS in isolation hampers performance on the GP task, while the incrementality of NGE is an additional cause for its low performance on this task.

3.2 COMPARING FAMBL, RISE, AND IB1 ON GROWING DATA SETS

It is conceivable that data set size matters in the differences between careful abstractors and pure memory-based learning. Adding more instances to a data set may alter the average number, size and within-family distance of the disjuncts in that data set. The outcome of careful abstraction may be affected by this change at a different scale than it may affect pure memory-based learning. In this subsection we report on experiments in which the careful abstractors FAMBL with GR weighting, RISE, and the pure memory-based learning algorithm IB1 with GR weighting, are applied to data sets of increasing size, of the three morpho-phonological tasks GP, GS, and MS (the other tasks could not be performed with RISE due to their high numbers of feature values, and the dependency of RISE on storing SVDM matrices in memory).

From each dataset, we extracted three smaller datasets, containing 1/1000th, 1/100th, and 1/10th of the words in the original data set, respectively. Each data set and the complete data sets themselves were used in a 10-fold CV experiment with IB1-IG, FAMBL, and RISE. RISE was not applied to the full data sets due to the computational limitations mentioned earlier.

The generalization accuracies yielded by the three learning algorithms on the three tasks are listed in Table 3. On a global level, they show that generaliza-

TASK	PORTION (%)	GENERALIZATION ACCURACY (%) IB1-GR	FAMBL-GR	RISE
GP	1/1000	63.1 ± 4.3	63.1 ± 4.3	55.0 ± 7.0
	1/100	79.1 ± 1.3	79.3 ± 1.4	80.2 ± 1.4
	1/10	88.8 ± 0.6	88.8 ± 0.6	88.9 ± 0.6
	1/1	97.4 ± 0.1	97.4 ± 0.1	—
GS	1/1000	52.0 ± 7.3	52.0 ± 7.3	46.2 ± 6.7
	1/100	69.6 ± 1.7	69.6 ± 1.7	72.8 ± 1.3
	1/10	81.8 ± 0.8	81.7 ± 0.8	82.3 ± 0.8
	1/1	93.5 ± 0.2	93.2 ± 0.2	—
MS	1/1000	77.5 ± 6.1	77.1 ± 5.6	85.5 ± 5.1
	1/100	87.3 ± 1.2	86.7 ± 1.2	89.9 ± 1.1
	1/10	93.0 ± 0.4	92.7 ± 0.4	93.4 ± 0.3
	1/1	98.0 ± 0.1	97.8 ± 0.1	—

Table 3: Overview of average generalization accuracies obtained with IB1-GR, FAMBL-GR and RISE on increasing portions of the GP, GS, and MS data sets. Generalization accuracy denotes the percentage of correctly classified test instances. '—' means that the experiment could not be performed.

TASK	PORTION (%)	# MEMORY ITEM COMPR. FAMBL-GR	RISE
GP	1/1000	0.0	2.9
	1/100	22.8	44.4
	1/10	35.2	62.7
	1/1	50.7	—
GS	1/1000	0.0	7.3
	1/100	19.1	38.8
	1/10	26.1	49.1
	1/1	35.7	—
MS	1/1000	14.4	23.9
	1/100	27.8	37.7
	1/10	47.7	49.5
	1/1	53.7	—

Table 4: Overview of average reduction in the number of stored memory items (families or rules) by FAMBL-GR and RISE, respectively, on increasing portions of the GP, GS, and MS data sets. '—' means that the experiment could not be performed.

tion accuracies do not differ much between algorithms at each data set size. There is reason to believe that RISE, when trained and tested on the full data sets, would perform similarly to the other three algorithms. One-tailed t-tests indicate that RISE has a significant advantage over the other algorithms on some reduced data sets (it is significantly better with $p < 0.01$ than the second-best algorithm in the 1/100th GS task, with $p < 0.05$ in the 1/100th MS task, and with $p < 0.01$ in the 1/10th MS task). The overall best performances are obtained with IB1-IG on the complete data sets (cf. next subsection).

Table 4 lists the memory item compression levels (in percentages) obtained by the two careful abstractors as opposed to IB1-IG. The unit of counting is the abstract notion of memory item, which is an instance type (not instance token) in IB1-IG, a family expression in FAMBL and a rule in RISE. First, larger data sets allow for more compression. All careful abstractors are able to reduce the number of generalized instances (families, rules, end nodes) further, relative to the total number of instance types, when the number of training instances increases: apparently, more of the learning material can be merged together when more data of the same task is available. Second, RISE compresses more than FAMBL on the tested data set sizes. This is at the cost of considerably longer learning times (in the order of 10 to 100 times longer than those of FAMBL), due to the possibly large number (in observed practice, between 5 and 15) of wrapped rule induction cycles needed to arrive at the final rule set.

3.3 COMPARING FAMBL AND IB1 ON SIX FULL-SIZED LANGUAGE LEARNING TASKS

For each task, FAMBL with GR feature weighting is compared with IB1 with GR feature weighting (i.e., FAMBL's pure memory-based counterpart). Table 5 lists the generalization accuracies obtained in these comparisons, on the five tasks. The results of IB1-GR on GS, NP, PP, and POS are reproduced from (Daelemans, Van den Bosch, and Zavrel, 1999). IB1-GR is significantly more accurate than FAMBL on the MS, GS, and PP tasks. Nevertheless, at least for the MS and GS tasks, the reported differences of a few tenths of percentages are negligible from a language-engineering standpoint. Still, the results show that FAMBL's careful abstraction is just not careful enough on these tasks.

We also monitored for all experiments the number of families that FAMBL probed and extracted. Table 6 displays these results averaged over the ten experiments performed on each task. The table also displays the percentage of compression over the number of memory items (instance types vs. family expressions), reported for the probing stage as well as the family stage.

In the extraction phase, compression (the percentage

TASK	IB1-GR %	±	>FAMBL?	FAMBL-GR %	±
GP	97.4	0.1		97.3	0.1
GS	93.5	0.2	**	93.2	0.2
MS	98.0	0.1	***	97.8	0.1
NP	98.1	0.1		98.0	0.1
PP	83.5	1.2	**	81.8	1.1
POS	97.9	0.1		97.8	0.0

Table 5: Generalization accuracies (percentages correctly classified test instances, with standard deviations) of IB1-GR and FAMBL on the six language learning tasks. Asterisks denote the outcomes of one-tailed t-tests, denoting a significantly better accuracy of IB1-IG compared to FAMBL. '**' denotes $p < 0.01$; '***' denotes $p < 0.001$.

TASK	PROBING STAGE #	% ITEM COMPR.	EXTRACTION STAGE #	% ITEM COMPR.
GP	31,224	90.5	162,954	50.7
GS	37,457	83.2	153,441	31.0
MS	18,783	93.4	131,776	53.7
NP	5238	97.7	59,376	72.4
PP	157	99.3	6414	70.1
POS	11,397	98.0	140,488	75.1

Table 6: Measurements on FAMBL output during the probing stage (left) and the family extraction stage (right) on each of the six learning tasks, of the number of families and the item compression compared to the original instance base.

reduction on the number of items in memory, from instances in pure memory-based learning to family expressions) ranges from 31.0% with the GS task to 75.1% with POS, which is considerable. The lowest compression is obtained with GS, on which FAMBL did not outperform IGTREE. This suggests that the GS task data has properties that FAMBL is less prepared to handle adequately. We have two working hypotheses on what these properties might be: First, the GS data is very disjunct: FAMBL detects a relatively high number of families during probing and family extraction. The random selection of starting points for family extraction, although heuristically patched with the preprocessing of the probing phase, may still lead to unwanted effects with such high disjunctivity. Second, as is the case with IB1, FAMBL tends to blur *feature interaction*: it allows the combination of feature values that never occurred in that constellation in the learning material, while for some tasks, including GS, this generalization may be unwanted.

3.4 FAMBL AND BENCHMARK TASKS

By design, FAMBL, augmented with GR feature weighting, may have a bias to language-like data. Only a small part of typical benchmark data sets is language-related, so a direct reference to well-known benchmark tasks cannot be made. To make the difference between language data and typical benchmark data more explicit, we applied FAMBL to a selection of benchmark tasks with symbolic feature values from the UCI repository (Blake, Keogh, and Merz, 1998), using 10-fold cross-validation experiments. Table 7 shows the average results from FAMBL-GR's probing phase on the number of probed families and the clusteredness of the data. Clusteredness is defined as the number of families per class, averaged over classes, weighted by their frequency. The difference in data set sizes is obvious: benchmark data sets are usually much smaller than the language data sets. Much less families are probed with the benchmark data, and furthermore, classes are scattered in much less disjunct clusters (families) with the benchmark data as compared to the language data, the PP data set being an exception.

TASK	DATA SET SIZE	# PROBED FAMILIES	CLUSTER-EDNESS
GP	675,745	31,224	1908
MS	573,544	18,783	8435
GS	675,745	37,457	1693
NP	251,124	5238	2413
PP	23,898	157	78
POS	1,046,152	11,397	479
audiology	226	72	7
kr vs kp	3,198	137	69
mushroom	8,124	23	11
nursery	12,961	682	198
soybean-l	683	90	9
splice	3,190	334	128
tic-tac-toe	958	161	84
votes	435	38	19

Table 7: Comparison of data set size, average numbers of probed families, and clusteredness, between the language data and a selection of UCI benchmark data, as measured in FAMBL's probing phase (averaged over 10-fold cross validation experiments).

Table 8 lists the average generalization accuracies produced by IB1-GR, FAMBL-GR, and FAMBL-GR-MVDM, a variation of FAMBL that combines GR feature weighting and the MVDM value difference metric (Cost and Salzberg, 1993), on the selected UCI benchmark data sets. We have added the generalization accuracies obtained by C4.5 and C4.5RULES (Quinlan, 1993), with default parameter settings, on the same data sets. Both C4.5 and C4.5RULES employ GR feature weighting, as a means to decide on feature test ordering, and both represent non-careful abstraction.

	GENERALIZATION ACCURACY (%)				
TASK	IB1-GR	FAMBL-GR	FAMBL-GR-MVDM	C4.5	C4.5-RULES
audiology	79.3	79.3	79.8	78.0	78.4
kr vs kp	97.7	97.1	97.3	99.5	99.6
mushroom	100.0	100.0	100.0	100.0	100.0
nursery	94.7	94.6	98.6	97.8	98.3
soybean-l	91.8	91.8	93.9	91.2	92.0
splice	91.9	86.6	94.4	94.0	92.8
tic-tac-toe	89.5	85.7	91.8	84.7	98.9
votes	93.8	94.3	94.3	95.9	95.5

Table 8: Average (10-fold) generalization accuracies of IB1-GR, FAMBL-GR, FAMBL-GR-MVDM, C4.5, and C4.5RULES, on eight UCI benchmark tasks.

In view of the earlier discussions on running significance tests on algorithmic performance differences obtained from applications to benchmark tasks (Salzberg, 1997; Dietterich, 1998), we do not intend to base any claims on the outcomes of such tests; we merely state that the performances of FAMBL-GR and FAMBL-GR-MVDM are mostly at the level of at least one of the generalization accuracies of IB1-GR, C4.5 or C4.5RULES for each of the data sets. A notable deviation is that FAMBL-GR performs significantly worse than all other algorithms on the 'splice' (gene splicing point detection) task, according to one-tailed t-tests with $p < 0.05$. FAMBL-GR-MVDM performs better on 'splice', and displays quite favorable performance on other tasks ('nursery'; 'soybean-l') as well. In sum, FAMBL appears to be applicable in a successful manner to at least some benchmark data sets, but more empirical work is needed to chart the causes of the differences found, and to elicit the general areas of applicability of FAMBL.

4 DISCUSSION

We have reported on the application of careful-abstraction methods in memory-based learning that abstract over families of instances, to language learning tasks and a small selection of non-linguistic benchmark tasks. In a first study, on learning grapheme-phoneme conversion from a moderately-sized data set, we found that the careful abstractors RISE and FAMBL were able to equal the generalization accuracy of their pure memory-based counterpart IB1-GR. All best-performing algorithms implement (combinations of) weighting metrics. In a second case study on the morpho-phonological tasks GP, GS, and MS, we saw that when data set size increases, careful abstractors can abstract more while keeping up with the performance of pure memory-based learning. In the third case study we applied the pure memory-based learning algorithm IB1-GR and the careful abstractor FAMBL-GR to a range of language learning tasks. FAMBL performed close to IB1-GR, equalling it on three tasks. Closer analyses are needed to determine what factors cause the slight disadvantage of FAMBL on the other three tasks GS, MS, and PP. From a language-engineering perspective, FAMBL offers adequate generalization accuracy on all six tasks, adding computationally interesting memory compression.

In a broader machine-learning context, our study suggests that careful abstraction over families of instances may be applicable to non-linguistic learning tasks as well, but more empirical work in this direction is needed. Currently, benchmark repositories hardly host non-linguistic data sets that mimic essential characteristics of language learning tasks (high disjunctivity, large data sets), although in real domains such data may exist: medical diagnosis may be an example. We envisage a large-scale study in which artificial data sets are generated according to a range of carefully-selected parameters (governing at least data set size and disjunctivity). Data may then be simulated along a continuum from low-disjunctive data to mimicking language data, in order to get a better understanding of which properties of language data favor the use of memory-based learning.

Acknowledgements

This research was done in the context of the "Induction of Linguistic Knowledge" (ILK) research programme, supported partially by the Netherlands Organization for Scientific Research (NWO). The author wishes to thank Walter Daelemans, the other members of the Tilburg ILK group, and the anonymous reviewers for their comments. Pedro Domingos (RISE) and Dietrich Wettschereck (NGE) are thanked for kindly granting permission to use their software.

References

Aha, D. W. 1997. Lazy learning: Special issue editorial. *Artificial Intelligence Review*, 11:7–10.

Aha, D. W., D. Kibler, and M. Albert. 1991. Instance-based learning algorithms. *Machine Learning*, 6:37–66.

Atkeson, C., A. Moore, and S. Schaal. 1997. Locally weighted learning. *Artificial Intelligence Review*, 11(1–5):11–73.

Baayen, R. H., R. Piepenbrock, and H. van Rijn. 1993. *The CELEX lexical data base on CD-ROM*. Linguistic Data Consortium, Philadelphia, PA.

Blake, C., E. Keogh, and C.J. Merz. 1998. UCI repository of machine learning databases, http://www.ics.uci.edu/~mlearn/mlrepository.html.

Cardie, Claire. 1994. *Domain Specific Knowledge Acquisition for Conceptual Sentence Analysis*. Ph.D. thesis, University of Massachusets, Amherst, MA.

Cardie, Claire. 1996. Automatic feature set selection for case-based learning of linguistic knowledge. In *Proc. of Conference on Empirical Methods in NLP*. University of Pennsylvania.

Collins, M.J and J. Brooks. 1995. Prepositional phrase attachment through a backed-off model. In *Proc. of Third Workshop on Very Large Corpora*, Cambridge.

Cost, S. and S. Salzberg. 1993. A weighted nearest neighbour algorithm for learning with symbolic features. *Machine Learning*, 10:57–78.

Daelemans, W. and A. Van den Bosch. 1992. Generalisation performance of backpropagation learning on a syllabification task. In M. F. J. Drossaers and A. Nijholt, editors, *Proc. of TWLT3: Connectionism and Natural Language Processing*, pages 27–37, Enschede. Twente University.

Daelemans, W., A. Van den Bosch, and A. Weijters. 1997. IGTree: using trees for compression and classification in lazy learning algorithms. *Artificial Intelligence Review*, 11:407–423.

Daelemans, W., A. Van den Bosch, and J. Zavrel. 1999. Forgetting exceptions is harmful in language learning. *Machine Learning*, 11(1–3):11–43.

Daelemans, Walter, Jakub Zavrel, Peter Berck, and Steven Gillis. 1996. MBT: A memory-based part of speech tagger generator. In E. Ejerhed and I.Dagan, editors, *Proc. of Fourth Workshop on Very Large Corpora*, pages 14–27. ACL SIGDAT.

Devijver, P. A. and J. Kittler. 1980. On the edited nearest neighbor rule. In *Proceedings of the Fifth International Conference on Pattern Recognition*. The Institute of Electrical and Electronics Engineers.

Dietterich, T. G. 1998. Approximate statistical tests for comparing supervised classification learning algorithms. *Neural Computation*, 10(7).

Domingos, P. 1996. Unifying instance-based and rule-based induction. *Machine Learning*, 24:141–168.

Gates, G. W. 1972. The reduced nearest neighbor rule. *IEEE Transactions on Information Theory*, 18:431–433.

Hart, P. E. 1968. The condensed nearest neighbor rule. *IEEE Transactions on Information Theory*, 14:515–516.

Kolodner, J. 1993. *Case-based reasoning*. Morgan Kaufmann, San Mateo, CA.

Quinlan, J.R. 1993. *C4.5: Programs for Machine Learning*. Morgan Kaufmann, San Mateo, CA.

Ramshaw, L.A. and M.P. Marcus. 1995. Text chunking using transformation-based learning. In *Proc. of Third Workshop on Very Large Corpora*, pages 82–94, June.

Ratnaparkhi, A., J. Reynar, and S. Roukos. 1994. A maximum entropy model for prepositional phrase attachment. In *Workshop on Human Language Technology*, Plainsboro, NJ, March. ARPA.

Salzberg, S. 1991. A nearest hyperrectangle learning method. *Machine Learning*, 6:277–309.

Salzberg, S. L. 1997. On comparing classifiers: Pitfalls to avoid and a recommended approach. *Data Mining and Knowledge Discovery*, 1(3).

Sejnowski, T. J. and C. S. Rosenberg. 1987. Parallel networks that learn to pronounce English text. *Complex Systems*, 1:145–168.

Stanfill, C. and D. Waltz. 1986. Toward memory-based reasoning. *Communications of the* ACM, 29(12):1213–1228, December.

Van den Bosch, A. 1997. *Learning to pronounce written words: A study in inductive language learning*. Ph.D. thesis, Universiteit Maastricht.

Van den Bosch, A. 1999. Careful abstraction from instance families in memory-based language learning. *Journal for Experimental and Theoretrical Artificial Intelligence*. conditionally accepted.

Van den Bosch, A., W. Daelemans, and A. Weijters. 1996. Morphological analysis as classification: an inductive-learning approach. In K. Oflazer and H. Somers, editors, *Proceedings of the Second International Conference on New Methods in Natural Language Processing, NeMLaP-2, Ankara, Turkey*, pages 79–89.

Veenstra, J. B. 1998. Fast NP chunking using memory-based learning techniques. In *Proceedings of BENELEARN'98*, Wageningen, The Netherlands.

Wilson, D. 1972. Asymptotic properties of nearest neighbor rules using edited data. *Institute of Electrical and Electronic Engineers Transactions on Systems, Man and Cybernetics*, 2:408–421.

Zavrel, J., W. Daelemans, and J. Veenstra. 1997. Resolving PP attachment ambiguities with memory-based learning. In M. Ellison, editor, *Proc. of the Workshop on Computational Language Learning (CoNLL'97)*, ACL, Madrid.

Least-Squares Temporal Difference Learning

Justin A. Boyan
NASA Ames Research Center
Moffett Field, CA 94035
jboyan@arc.nasa.gov

Abstract

TD(λ) is a popular family of algorithms for approximate policy evaluation in large MDPs. TD(λ) works by incrementally updating the value function after each observed transition. It has two major drawbacks: it makes inefficient use of data, and it requires the user to manually tune a stepsize schedule for good performance. For the case of linear value function approximations and $\lambda = 0$, the Least-Squares TD (LSTD) algorithm of Bradtke and Barto (Bradtke and Barto, 1996) eliminates all stepsize parameters and improves data efficiency.

This paper extends Bradtke and Barto's work in three significant ways. First, it presents a simpler derivation of the LSTD algorithm. Second, it generalizes from $\lambda = 0$ to arbitrary values of λ; at the extreme of $\lambda = 1$, the resulting algorithm is shown to be a practical formulation of supervised linear regression. Third, it presents a novel, intuitive interpretation of LSTD as a *model-based* reinforcement learning technique.

1 BACKGROUND

This paper addresses the problem of approximating the value function V^π of a fixed policy π in a large Markov decision process (Bertsekas and Tsitsiklis, 1996; Sutton and Barto, 1998). This is an important subproblem of several algorithms for sequential decision making, including optimistic policy iteration (Bertsekas and Tsitsiklis, 1996) and STAGE (Boyan and Moore, 1998). $V^\pi(x)$ simply predicts the expected long-term sum of future rewards obtained when the process starts in state x and follows policy π until termination. This function is well-defined as long as π is proper, i.e., guaranteed to terminate.[1]

For small Markov chains whose transition probabilities are all explicitly known, computing V^π is a trivial matter of solving a system of linear equations. However, in many practical applications, the transition probabilities of the chain are available only implicitly—either in the form of a *simulation model* or in the form of an agent's actual experience executing π in its environment. In either case, we must compute V^π or an approximation thereof (denoted $\tilde{V}^\pi$) solely from a collection of trajectories sampled from the chain. This is where the TD(λ) family of algorithms applies.

TD(λ) was introduced in (Sutton, 1988); excellent summaries may now be found in several books (Bertsekas and Tsitsiklis, 1996; Sutton and Barto, 1998). For each state on each observed trajectory, TD(λ) incrementally adjusts the coefficients of $\tilde{V}^\pi$ toward new target values. The target values depend on the parameter $\lambda \in [0, 1]$. At $\lambda = 1$, the target at each visited state x_t is the "Monte-Carlo return," i.e., the actual observed sum of future rewards $R_t + R_{t+1} + \cdots + R_{\text{END}}$. This is an unbiased sample of $V^\pi(x_t)$, but may have significant variance since it depends on a long stochastic sequence of rewards. At the other extreme, $\lambda = 0$, the target value is set by a sampled one-step lookahead: $R_t + \tilde{V}^\pi(x_{t+1})$. This value has lower variance—the only random component is a single state transition—but is biased by the potential inaccuracy of the lookahead estimate of V^π. The parameter λ trades off between bias and variance. Empirically, intermediate values of λ seem to perform best (Sutton, 1988;

[1] For improper policies, V^π may be made well-defined by the use of a discount factor that exponentially reduces future rewards; however, for simplicity we will assume here that V^π is undiscounted.

Sutton and Barto, 1998).

TD(λ) has been shown to converge to a good approximation of V^π when *linear architectures* are used, assuming a suitable decreasing schedule of stepsizes for the incremental weight updates (Tsitsiklis and Roy, 1996). Linear architectures—which include lookup tables, state aggregation methods, CMACs, radial basis function networks with fixed bases, and multi-dimensional polynomial regression—approximate $V^\pi(x)$ by first mapping the state x to a feature vector $\boldsymbol{\phi}(x) \in \Re^K$, and then computing a linear combination of those features, $\boldsymbol{\phi}(x)^\mathsf{T}\boldsymbol{\beta}$. Figure 1 gives a convenient form of TD(λ) that exploits this representation.

On each transition, the algorithm computes the scalar one-step TD error $R_t + (\boldsymbol{\phi}(x_{t+1}) - \boldsymbol{\phi}(x_t))^\mathsf{T}\boldsymbol{\beta}$, and apportions that error among all state features according to their respective *eligibilities* $\mathbf{z}_t$. The eligibility vector may be seen as an algebraic trick by which TD(λ) propagates rewards backward over the current trajectory without having to remember the trajectory explicitly. Each feature's eligibility at time t depends on the trajectory's history and on λ: $\mathbf{z}_t = \sum_{i=t_0}^{t} \lambda^{t-i}\boldsymbol{\phi}(x_i)$, where t_0 is the time at which the current trajectory started. In the case of TD(0), only the current state's features are eligible to be updated, so $\mathbf{z}_t = \boldsymbol{\phi}(x_t)$; whereas in TD(1), the features of all states seen so far on the current trajectory are eligible, so $\mathbf{z}_t = \sum_{i=t_0}^{t} \boldsymbol{\phi}(x_i)$.

To what weights does TD(λ) converge? Examining the update rule for $\boldsymbol{\delta}$ in Figure 1, it is not difficult to see that the coefficient changes made by TD(λ) after an observed trajectory $(x_0, x_1, \ldots, x_L, \text{END})$ have the form $\boldsymbol{\beta} := \boldsymbol{\beta} + \alpha_n(\mathbf{d} + \mathbf{C}\boldsymbol{\beta} + \boldsymbol{\omega})$, where

$$\mathbf{d} = \mathrm{E}\{\sum_{i=0}^{L} \mathbf{z}_i R_i\}; \quad \mathbf{C} = \mathrm{E}\{\sum_{i=0}^{L} \mathbf{z}_i \left(\boldsymbol{\phi}(x_{i+1}) - \boldsymbol{\phi}(x_i)\right)^\mathsf{T}\}; \tag{1}$$

and $\boldsymbol{\omega}$ = zero-mean noise. The expectations are taken with respect to the distribution of trajectories through the Markov chain. It is shown in (Bertsekas and Tsitsiklis, 1996) that $\mathbf{C}$ is negative definite and that the noise $\boldsymbol{\omega}$ has sufficiently small variance, which together with the stepsize conditions mentioned above, imply that $\boldsymbol{\beta}$ converges to a fixed point $\boldsymbol{\beta}_\lambda$ satisfying $\mathbf{d} + \mathbf{C}\boldsymbol{\beta}_\lambda = \mathbf{0}$. In effect, TD($\lambda$) solves this system of equations by performing stochastic gradient descent on a potential function $||\boldsymbol{\beta} - \boldsymbol{\beta}_\lambda||^2$. It never explicitly represents $\mathbf{d}$ or $\mathbf{C}$. The changes to $\boldsymbol{\beta}$ depend only on the most recent trajectory, and after those changes are made, the trajectory and its rewards are simply forgotten. This approach, while requiring little computation per iteration, wastes data and may require sampling many trajectories to reach convergence.

One technique for using data more efficiently is "experience replay" (Lin, 1993): explicitly remember all trajectories ever seen, and whenever asked to produce an updated set of coefficients, perform repeated passes of TD(λ) over all the saved trajectories until convergence. This technique is similar to the batch training methods commonly used to train neural networks. However, in the case of linear function approximators, there is another way.

2 THE LEAST-SQUARES TD(λ) ALGORITHM

The Least-Squares TD(λ) algorithm, or LSTD(λ), converges to the same coefficients $\boldsymbol{\beta}_\lambda$ that TD(λ) does. However, instead of performing gradient descent, LSTD(λ) builds explicit estimates of the $\mathbf{C}$ matrix and $\mathbf{d}$ vector (actually, estimates of a constant multiple of $\mathbf{C}$ and $\mathbf{d}$), and then solves $\mathbf{d} + \mathbf{C}\boldsymbol{\beta}_\lambda = \mathbf{0}$ directly. The actual data structures that LSTD(λ) builds from experience are the matrix $\mathbf{A}$ (of dimension $K \times K$, where K is the number of features) and the vector $\mathbf{b}$ (of dimension K):

$$\mathbf{b} = \sum_{i=0}^{t} \mathbf{z}_i R_i \qquad \mathbf{A} = \sum_{i=0}^{t} \mathbf{z}_i \left(\boldsymbol{\phi}(x_i) - \boldsymbol{\phi}(x_{i+1})\right)^\mathsf{T} \tag{2}$$

After n independent trajectories have been observed, $\mathbf{b}$ is an unbiased estimate of $n\mathbf{d}$, and $\mathbf{A}$ is an unbiased estimate of $-n\mathbf{C}$. Thus, $\boldsymbol{\beta}_\lambda$ can be estimated as $\mathbf{A}^{-1}\mathbf{b}$. As is standard in least-squares algorithms, Singular Value Decomposition is used to invert $\mathbf{A}$ robustly (Press *et al.*, 1992). The complete LSTD(λ) algorithm is specified in Figure 2.

When $\lambda = 0$, LSTD(0) reduces precisely to Bradtke and Barto's LSTD algorithm, which they derived using a more complex approach based on regression with instrumental variables (Bradtke and Barto, 1996). At the other extreme, when $\lambda = 1$, LSTD(1) produces the same $\mathbf{A}$ and $\mathbf{b}$ that would be produced by supervised linear regression on training pairs of {state features $\mapsto$ observed Monte-Carlo returns} (see (Boyan, 1998) for proof). Thanks to the algebraic trick of the eligibility vectors, LSTD(1) builds the regression matrices *fully incrementally*—without having to store the trajectory while waiting to observe the eventual outcome. When trajectories through the chain are long, this provides significant memory savings over linear regression.

TD(λ) for approximate policy evaluation:

Given: • a *simulation model* for a proper policy π in MDP X;
- a *featurizer* $\boldsymbol{\phi} : X \to \Re^K$ mapping states to feature vectors, $\boldsymbol{\phi}(\text{END}) \stackrel{\text{def}}{=} \mathbf{0}$;
- a parameter $\lambda \in [0, 1]$; and
- a sequence of *stepsizes* $\alpha_1, \alpha_2, \ldots$ for incremental coefficient updating.

Output: a coefficient vector $\boldsymbol{\beta}$ for which $V^\pi(x) \approx \boldsymbol{\beta} \cdot \boldsymbol{\phi}(x)$.

Set $\boldsymbol{\beta} := \mathbf{0}$ *(or an arbitrary initial estimate)*, $t := 0$.
for $n := 1, 2, \ldots$ **do**: {
  Set $\boldsymbol{\delta} := 0$.
  Choose a start state $x_t \in X$.
  Set $\mathbf{z}_t := \boldsymbol{\phi}(x_t)$.
  while $x_t \neq$ END, **do**: {
    Simulate one step of the process, producing a reward R_t and next state x_{t+1}.
    Set $\boldsymbol{\delta} := \boldsymbol{\delta} + \mathbf{z}_t\big(R_t + (\boldsymbol{\phi}(x_{t+1}) - \boldsymbol{\phi}(x_t))^{\mathsf{T}}\boldsymbol{\beta}\big)$. /* *inner product* */
    Set $\mathbf{z}_{t+1} := \lambda \mathbf{z}_t + \boldsymbol{\phi}(x_{t+1})$.
    Set $t := t + 1$.
  }
  Set $\boldsymbol{\beta} := \boldsymbol{\beta} + \alpha_n \boldsymbol{\delta}$.
}

Figure 1: Ordinary TD(λ) for linearly approximating the undiscounted value function of a fixed proper policy.

LSTD(λ) for approximate policy evaluation:

Given: a *simulation model*, *featurizer*, and λ as in ordinary TD(λ).
(No stepsize schedules or initial estimates of $\boldsymbol{\beta}$ are necessary.)

Output: a coefficient vector $\boldsymbol{\beta}$ for which $V^\pi(x) \approx \boldsymbol{\beta} \cdot \boldsymbol{\phi}(x)$.

Set $\mathbf{A} := \mathbf{0}$, $\mathbf{b} := \mathbf{0}$, $t := 0$.
for $n := 1, 2, \ldots$ **do**: {
  Choose a start state $x_t \in X$.
  Set $\mathbf{z}_t := \boldsymbol{\phi}(x_t)$.
  while $x_t \neq$ END, **do**: {
    Simulate one step of the chain, producing a reward R_t and next state x_{t+1}.
    Set $\mathbf{A} := \mathbf{A} + \mathbf{z}_t(\boldsymbol{\phi}(x_t) - \boldsymbol{\phi}(x_{t+1}))^{\mathsf{T}}$. /* *outer product* */
    Set $\mathbf{b} := \mathbf{b} + \mathbf{z}_t R_t$.
    Set $\mathbf{z}_{t+1} := \lambda \mathbf{z}_t + \boldsymbol{\phi}(x_{t+1})$.
    Set $t := t + 1$. solve $A\beta = d$. Don't invert A.
  }
  Whenever updated coefficients are desired: Set $\boldsymbol{\beta} := \mathbf{A}^{-1}\mathbf{b}$. /* *use Singular Value Decomposition* */
}

Figure 2: A least-squares version of TD(λ) (compare Figure 1). Note that $\mathbf{A}$ has dimension $K \times K$, and $\mathbf{b}$, $\boldsymbol{\beta}$, $\mathbf{z}$, and $\boldsymbol{\phi}(x)$ all have dimension $K \times 1$.

The computation per timestep required to update $\mathbf{A}$ and $\mathbf{b}$ is the same as least-squares linear regression: $O(K^2)$, where K is the number of features. LSTD(λ) must also perform a matrix inversion at a cost of $O(K^3)$ whenever $\boldsymbol{\beta}$'s coefficients are needed—typically, once per complete trajectory. (If updated coefficients are required more frequently, then the $O(K^3)$ cost can be avoided by *recursive least-squares* (Bradtke and Barto, 1996) or Kalman-filtering techniques (Bertsekas and Tsitsiklis, 1996, §3.2.2), which update $\boldsymbol{\beta}$ on each timestep at a cost of only $O(K^2)$.) LSTD(λ) performs more computation per observation than incremental TD(λ), which updates the coefficients using only $O(K)$ computation per timestep. However, LSTD(λ) offers several significant advantages:

- Least-squares algorithms "extract more information from each additional observation" (Bradtke and Barto, 1996) and would thus be expected to converge with fewer training samples.
- TD(λ)'s convergence can be slowed dramatically by a poor choice of the stepsize parameters α_n. LSTD(λ) eliminates these parameters.
- TD(λ)'s performance is sensitive to the initial estimate for $\boldsymbol{\beta}_\lambda$. LSTD($\lambda$) does not rely on an arbitrary initial estimate.
- TD(λ) is also sensitive to the ranges of the individual features. LSTD(λ) is not.

Section 4 below presents experimental results comparing the data efficiency of gradient-based and least-squares-based TD learning.

3 LSTD(λ) AS MODEL-BASED LEARNING

Surprisingly, the move from a gradient-based to a least-squares-based update rule for TD(λ) turns out to be mathematically equivalent to a move from a model-free to a model-based reinforcement learning algorithm. This equivalence provides interesting new intuitions about the space of temporal difference learning algorithms, and as such forms an important part of this work's contribution.

To begin, let us restrict our attention to the case of a small discrete state space X, over which V^π can be represented and learned exactly by a lookup table. A classical model-based algorithm for learning V^π from simulated trajectory data would proceed as follows:

1. From the state transitions and rewards observed so far, build in memory an *empirical model* of the Markov chain. The sufficient statistics of this model are
   - a vector $\mathbf{n}$ recording the number of times each state has been visited;
   - a matrix $\mathbf{C}$ recording the observed state-transition counts: $\mathbf{C}_{ij}$ = how many times x_j was seen to directly follow x_i; and
   - a vector $\mathbf{s}$ recording, for each state, the sum of all one-step rewards observed on transitions leaving that state.
2. Whenever a new estimate of the value function V^π is desired, solve the linear system of Bellman equations corresponding to the current empirical model. Writing $\mathbf{N} = \mathbf{diag}(\mathbf{n})$, the solution vector of V^π values is given by

$$\mathbf{v} = (\mathbf{N} - \mathbf{C})^{-1}\mathbf{s}. \qquad (3)$$

This model-based technique contrasts with TD(λ), a model-free approach to the same problem. TD(λ) does not maintain any statistics on observed transitions and rewards; it simply updates the components of $\mathbf{v}$ directly. In the limit, assuming a lookup-table representation, both converge to the optimal V^π. The advantage of TD(λ) is its low computational burden per step; the advantage of the classical model-based method is that it makes the most of the available training data. The empirical advantages of model-based and model-free reinforcement learning methods have been investigated in, e.g., (Sutton, 1990; Moore and Atkeson, 1993; Atkeson and Santamaria, 1997).

Where does LSTD(λ) fit in? In fact, for the case of $\lambda = 0$, it precisely duplicates the classical model-based method sketched above. The assumed lookup-table representation for $\tilde{V}^\pi$ means that we have one independent feature per state: the feature vector $\boldsymbol{\phi}$ corresponding to state 1 is $(1, 0, 0, \ldots, 0)$; corresponding to state 2 is $(0, 1, 0, \ldots, 0)$; etc. Referring to the algorithm of Figure 2, we see that LSTD(0) performs the following operations upon each observed transition:

$$\mathbf{b} := \mathbf{b} + \boldsymbol{\phi}(x_t)R_t \quad \mathbf{A} := \mathbf{A} + \boldsymbol{\phi}(x_t)(\boldsymbol{\phi}(x_t) - \boldsymbol{\phi}(x_{t+1}))^\mathsf{T} \qquad (4)$$

Clearly, the role of $\mathbf{b}$ is to sum all the rewards observed at each state, exactly as the vector $\mathbf{s}$ does in the classical technique. $\mathbf{A}$, meanwhile, accumulates the statistics $(\mathbf{N} - \mathbf{C})$. To see this, note that the outer product in Eq. 4 is a matrix consisting of an entry of $+1$ on the single diagonal element corresponding to state x_t; an entry of -1 on the element in row x_t, column x_{t+1}; and all the rest zeroes. Summing one such sparse matrix for each observed transition gives $\mathbf{A} \equiv \mathbf{N} - \mathbf{C}$. Finally, LSTD(0) performs the inversion $\boldsymbol{\beta} := \mathbf{A}^{-1}\mathbf{b} = (\mathbf{N} - \mathbf{C})^{-1}\mathbf{s}$, giving the same solution as in Equation 3.

Thus, when $\lambda = 0$, the $\mathbf{A}$ and $\mathbf{b}$ matrices built by LSTD(λ) effectively record a model of all the observed transitions. What about when $\lambda > 0$? Again, $\mathbf{A}$ and $\mathbf{b}$ record the sufficient statistics of an empirical Markov model—but in this case, the model being captured is one whose single-step transition probabilities directly encode the multi-step TD(λ) backup operations. That is, the model links each state x to all the downstream states that follow x on any trajectory, and records how much influence each has on estimating $\tilde{V}^\pi(x)$ according to TD(λ). In the case of $\lambda = 0$, the TD(λ) backups correspond to the one-step transitions, resulting in the equivalence described above. The opposite extreme, the case of $\lambda = 1$, is also interesting: the empirical Markov model corresponding to TD(1)'s backups is the chain in which each state x leads directly to absorption, and $\boldsymbol{\beta}$ then simply computes the average Monte-Carlo return at each state. In short, if we assume a lookup-table representation for the function $\tilde{V}^\pi$, we can view the LSTD(λ) algorithm as performing these two steps:

1. It implicitly uses the observed simulation data to build a Markov chain. This chain compactly models all the backups that TD(λ) would perform on the data.

2. It solves the chain by performing a matrix inversion.

The lookup-table representation for $\tilde{V}^\pi$ is intractable in practical problems; in practice, LSTD(λ) operates on states only via their (linearly dependent) feature representations $\phi(x)$. In this case, we can view LSTD(λ) as implicitly building a *compressed* version of the empirical model's transition matrix $\mathbf{N} - \mathbf{C}$ and summed-reward vector $\mathbf{s}$:

$$\mathbf{b} = \boldsymbol{\Phi}^\mathsf{T}\mathbf{s} \qquad \mathbf{A} = \boldsymbol{\Phi}^\mathsf{T}(\mathbf{N} - \mathbf{C})\boldsymbol{\Phi} \tag{5}$$

where $\boldsymbol{\Phi}$ is the $|X| \times K$ matrix representation of the function $\boldsymbol{\phi} : X \to \Re^K$. From the compressed empirical model, LSTD(λ) computes the following coefficients for $\tilde{V}^\pi$:

$$\boldsymbol{\beta}_\lambda = \mathbf{A}^{-1}\mathbf{b} = (\boldsymbol{\Phi}^\mathsf{T}(\mathbf{N} - \mathbf{C})\boldsymbol{\Phi})^{-1}(\boldsymbol{\Phi}^\mathsf{T}\mathbf{s}). \tag{6}$$

Ideally, these coefficients $\boldsymbol{\beta}_\lambda$ would be equivalent to the *empirical optimal* coefficients $\boldsymbol{\beta}^*_\lambda$. The empirical optimal coefficients are those that would be found by building the full uncompressed empirical model (represented by $\mathbf{N} - \mathbf{C}$ and $\mathbf{s}$), using a lookup table to solve for that model's value function ($\mathbf{v} = (\mathbf{N} - \mathbf{C})^{-1}\mathbf{s}$), and then performing a least-squares linear fit from the state features $\boldsymbol{\Phi}$ to the lookup-table value function:

$$\boldsymbol{\beta}^*_\lambda \stackrel{\text{def}}{=} (\boldsymbol{\Phi}^\mathsf{T}\boldsymbol{\Phi})^{-1}(\boldsymbol{\Phi}^\mathsf{T}\mathbf{v}) \doteq (\boldsymbol{\Phi}^\mathsf{T}\boldsymbol{\Phi})^{-1}\boldsymbol{\Phi}^\mathsf{T}(\mathbf{N} - \mathbf{C})^{-1}\mathbf{s}. \tag{7}$$

It can be shown that Equations 6 and 7 are indeed equivalent for the case of $\lambda = 1$, because that setting of λ implies that $\mathbf{C} = \mathbf{0}$ (thus $(\mathbf{N} - \mathbf{C})^{-1}$ is diagonal and commutes). However, for the case of $\lambda < 1$, solving the compressed empirical model does not in general produce the optimal least-squares fit to the solution of the uncompressed model.

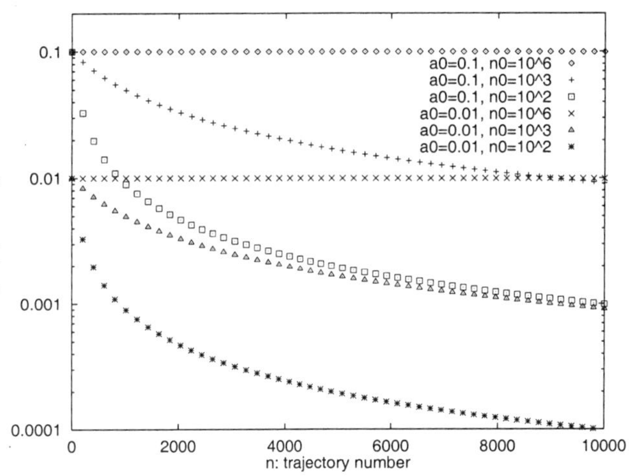

Figure 3: The six different *stepsize schedules* used in the experiments with TD(λ). The schedules are determined by Equation 8 with various settings for a_0 and n_0.

4 EXPERIMENTAL COMPARISON OF TD(λ) AND LSTD(λ)

This section reports experimental results comparing TD(λ) and LSTD(λ) on the simple Markov chain illustrated in Figure 4. The chain consists of 13 states, and we seek to represent its value function compactly as a linear function of four state features as shown. This domain's optimal V^π function is exactly linear in these features: the optimal coefficients $\boldsymbol{\beta}^*_\lambda$ are $(-24, -16, -8, 0)$. This condition guarantees

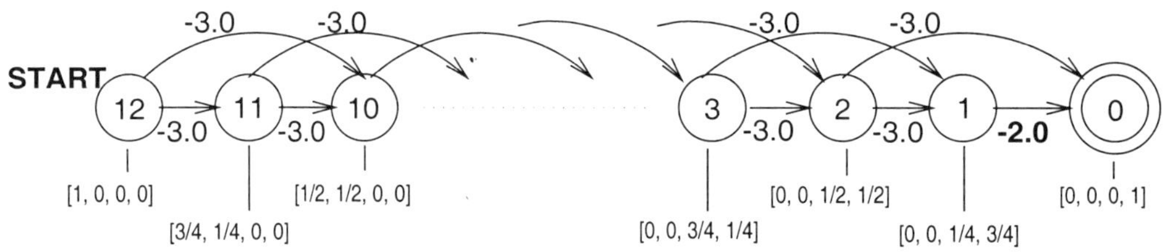

Figure 4: A 13-state Markov chain. Each state is represented by four features as shown. In states 2–12, each outgoing arc is taken with probability 0.5.

that LSTD(λ) will converge with probability 1 to the optimal β^*_λ for any setting of λ.

TD(λ) is also guaranteed to converge to the optimal V^π, under the additional condition that an appropriate schedule of stepsizes is chosen. The following three criteria on the schedule (α_n) are sufficient: $\alpha_n \geq 0 \ \forall n$; $\sum_{n=1}^{\infty} \alpha_n = \infty$; and $\sum_{n=1}^{\infty} \alpha_n^2 < \infty$. Our experiments use schedules that satisfy these criteria, having the following form:

$$\alpha_n \stackrel{\text{def}}{=} a_0 \frac{n_0 + 1}{n_0 + n} \qquad n = 1, 2, \ldots \tag{8}$$

The parameter a_0 determines the initial stepsize, and n_0 determines how gradually the stepsize decreases over time. Each TD(λ) experiment was run with six different stepsize schedules, corresponding to the six combinations of $a_0 \in \{0.1, 0.01\}$ and $n_0 \in \{10^2, 10^3, 10^6\}$. These six schedules are plotted in Figure 3, from which it can be seen that they fall into a typical range of learning rates used in applications of gradient descent.

Comparative results are given in Figures 5 and 6. Figure 5 focuses on the case of $\lambda = 0.4$, comparing the learning curve for LSTD(λ) against those of all six schedules of TD(λ). Each point plotted represents the average of 10 trials. The plot shows clearly that for $\lambda = 0.4$, LSTD(λ) learns a good approximation to V^π in fewer trials than any of the TD(λ) experiments, and performs better asymptotically as well.

Figure 6 graphically summarizes six learning-curve plots similar to Figure 5, corresponding to varying λ over the range $\{0, 0.2, 0.4, 0.6, 0.8, 1.0\}$. The results may be summarized as follows:

- Across all values of λ, LSTD(λ) learns a good approximation to V^π in fewer trials than any of the TD(λ) experiments, and performs better asymptotically as well.
- The performance of TD(λ) depends critically on the stepsize schedule chosen. LSTD(λ) has no tunable parameters other than λ itself.
- Varying λ has a relatively small effect on LSTD(λ)'s performance.

5 CONCLUSIONS AND FUTURE WORK

We have argued, both from the experimental results above and from the deep connection to model-based reinforcement learning presented in Section 3, that the least-squares formulation of TD learning makes better use of simulation data than TD(λ). Further experiments are needed to determine when to prefer one algorithm over the other as a practical matter. If a domain has many features and simulation data is available cheaply, then incremental methods such as TD(λ) may have better real-time performance than least-squares methods (Sutton, 1992). On the other hand, some reinforcement learning applications have been successful with very small numbers of features (e.g., (Singh and Bertsekas, 1997; Boyan and Moore, 1998)), and in these situations LSTD(λ) should be superior.

LSTD(λ) has been successfully applied in the context of STAGE, a reinforcement learning algorithm for combinatorial optimization (Boyan, 1998). An exciting possibility for future work is to apply LSTD(λ) in the context of approximation algorithms for general Markov decision problems. LSTD(λ) provides an alternative to TD(λ) for the inner loop of optimistic policy iteration (Bertsekas and Tsitsiklis, 1996), and should thereby enable good control policies to be discovered with fewer trial simulations.

Acknowledgments

Thanks to Andrew Moore and Jeff Schneider for helpful comments. This work was supported by a NASA GSRP fellowship while the author was at CMU.

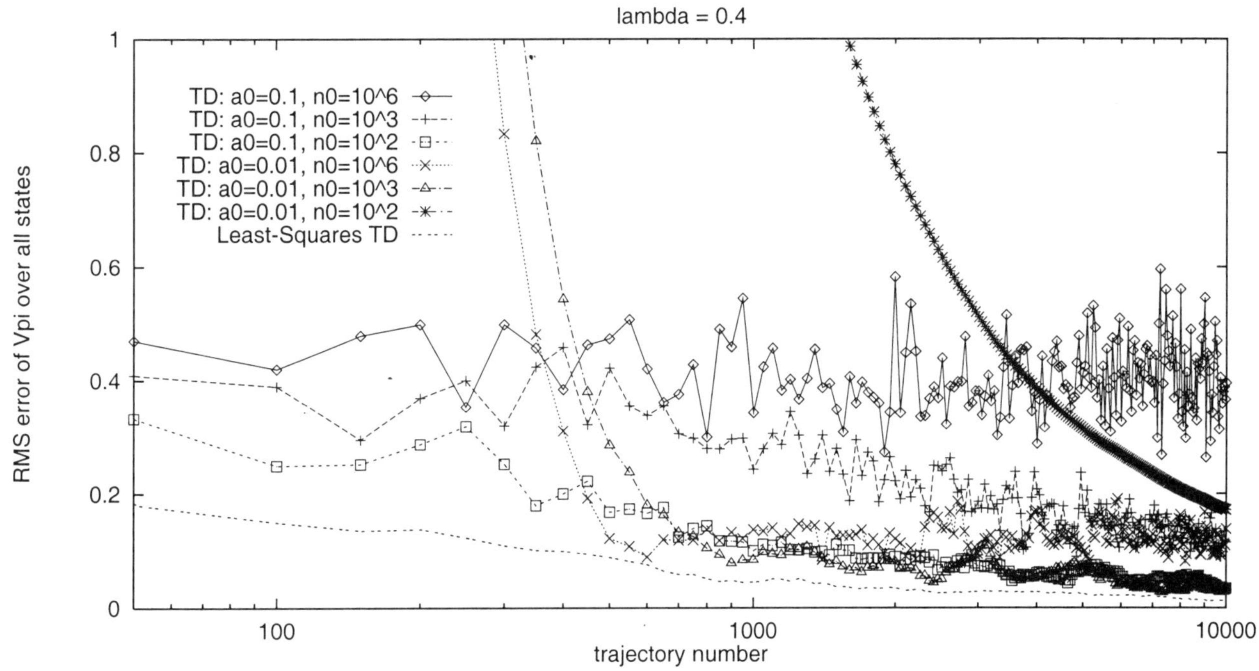

Figure 5: Performance of TD(0.4) and LSTD(0.4) on the sample domain. Note the log scale on the x-axis. All points plotted represent the average of 10 trials.

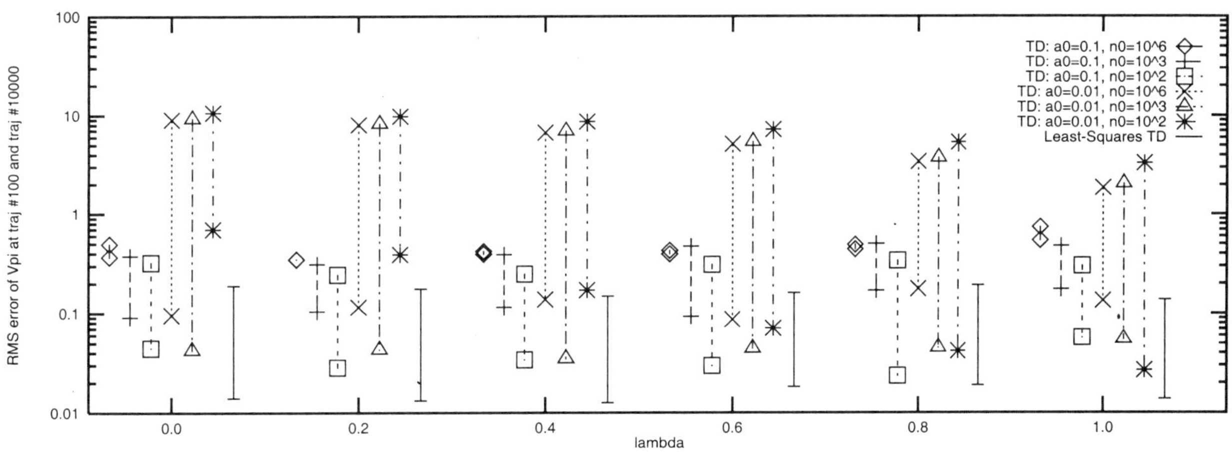

Figure 6: Summary of results at six settings of λ. At each setting, seven algorithms are compared: TD(λ) (with six different stepsize schedules) and LSTD(λ). The plotted segment shows the mean RMS value function approximation error after 100 trajectories (top of segment) and 10,000 trajectories (bottom of segment). Note the log scale on the y-axis. LSTD(λ) is best in all cases.

References

[Atkeson and Santamaria, 1997] C. G. Atkeson and J. C. Santamaria. A comparison of direct and model-based reinforcement learning. In *International Conference on Robotics and Automation*, 1997.

[Bertsekas and Tsitsiklis, 1996] D. Bertsekas and J. Tsitsiklis. *Neuro-Dynamic Programming.* Athena Scientific, Belmont, MA, 1996.

[Boyan and Moore, 1998] J. A. Boyan and A. W. Moore. Learning evaluation functions for global optimization and Boolean satisfiability. In *Proceedings of the Fifteenth National Conference on Artificial Intelligence (AAAI)*, 1998.

[Boyan, 1998] J. A. Boyan. *Learning Evaluation Functions for Global Optimization.* PhD thesis, Carnegie Mellon University, 1998.

[Bradtke and Barto, 1996] S. J. Bradtke and A. G. Barto. Linear least-squares algorithms for temporal difference learning. *Machine Learning*, 22(1/2/3):33–57, 1996.

[Lin, 1993] L.-J. Lin. *Reinforcement Learning for Robots Using Neural Networks.* PhD thesis, Carnegie Mellon University, 1993.

[Moore and Atkeson, 1993] A. W. Moore and C. G. Atkeson. Prioritized sweeping: Reinforcement learning with less data and less time. *Machine Learning*, 13:103–130, 1993.

[Press *et al.*, 1992] W.H. Press, S.A. Teukolsky, W.T. Vetterling, and B.P. Flannery. *Numerical Recipes in C: The Art of Scientific Computing.* Cambridge University Press, second edition, 1992.

[Singh and Bertsekas, 1997] S. Singh and D. Bertsekas. Reinforcement learning for dynamic channel allocation in cellular telephone systems. In M. C. Mozer, M. I. Jordan, and T. Petsche, editors, *NIPS-9*, page 974. The MIT Press, 1997.

[Sutton and Barto, 1998] R. S. Sutton and A. G. Barto. *Reinforcement Learning: An Introduction.* MIT Press, 1998.

[Sutton, 1988] R. S. Sutton. Learning to predict by the methods of temporal differences. *Machine Learning*, 3, 1988.

[Sutton, 1990] R. S. Sutton. Integrated architectures for learning, planning, and reacting based on approximating dynamic programming. In *Proceedings of the Seventh International Conference on Machine Learning.* Morgan Kaufmann, 1990.

[Sutton, 1992] R. S. Sutton. Gain adaptation beats least squares. In *Proceedings of the 7th Yale Workshop on Adaptive and Learning Systems*, pages 161–166, 1992.

[Tsitsiklis and Roy, 1996] J. N. Tsitsiklis and B. Van Roy. An analysis of temporal-difference learning with function approximation. Technical Report LIDS-P-2322, MIT, 1996.

Learning to Ride a Bicycle using Iterated Phantom Induction

Mark Brodie and Gerald DeJong
Department of Computer Science
Beckman Institute
University of Illinois at Urbana-Champaign
Urbana, IL 61801
m-brodie@cs.uiuc.edu and dejong@cs.uiuc.edu

Abstract

We build upon our work on iterated phantom induction and the work of Randløv and Alstrøm on applying reinforcement learning to the challenging control task of learning to ride a bicycle. Last year phantom induction was demonstrated on a nonlinear but non-dynamical task. The bicycle domain is a dynamical system whose next state is a function of the current state and control inputs. Randløv and Alstrøm demonstrated this task was learnable using Sarsa(λ) with shaping. Our approach integrates domain knowledge into the learning process in a flexible way. By taking advantage of what a domain theory expert can easily express, our system learns to ride in a few dozen examples rather than the thousands required by the system of Randløv and Alstrøm. We also show that the two inputs, shifting the rider's center of mass and deflecting the handlebars, are not needed simultaneously for learning. Our system learns to ride using either input alone. By extending phantom induction into the space of dynamical systems we demonstrate the applicability of our learning technique to an important and difficult class of problems.

1 INTRODUCTION

Last year we introduced a machine learning approach called *iterated phantom induction* (Brodie and DeJong, 1998) which allows qualitative domain knowledge to be easily incorporated into machine learning algorithms. We tested the approach on a simple problem in a simulated air-hockey environment and obtained encouraging results. We were interested in extending the approach to more complicated problems and also comparing it with other machine learning techniques, particularly reinforcement learning.

In an impressive piece of work (also last year), Randløv and Alstrøm demonstrated how reinforcement learning could be applied to the task of riding a simulated bicycle. They used the Sarsa(λ)-algorithm to learn how to balance the bicycle, and then applied the technique of *shaping* to learn to ride the bicycle to a goal location. Despite the complexity of the task, they were able to achieve successful results (Randløv and Alstrøm, 1998).

Although their results are impressive, they are far from optimal. Many thousands of trials were required for successful performance. Yet we know that people usually learn to ride a two-wheeler in no more than a few dozen relatively brief attempts. Clearly humans bring a great deal of prior experience and understanding to the task. Perhaps this forms a strong bias which allows us to quickly learn a successful bicycle-riding policy.

How can this gulf in performance be bridged by a machine learning system? A clue can be obtained from Randløv and Alstrøm's use of shaping, which was needed to accelerate the learning process. Shaping adds a substantial bias to their learning system by implicitly encoding domain knowledge. However they subscribe to shaping grudgingly and seem almost apologetic for the need of it: "[shaping] is a price to be paid for faster learning: We [Randløv and Alstrøm] must give up the tabula rasa attitude that is one of the attractive aspects of basic reinforcement learning".

We believe that this reverence for tabula rasa learning is terribly misguided. The key to complex concept learning is how much, not how little, we can bias the

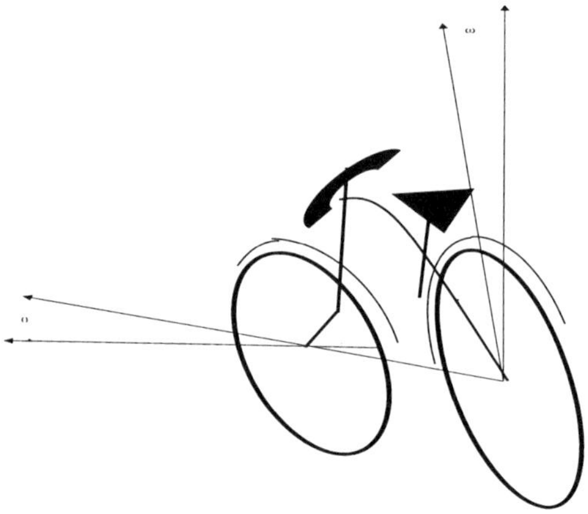

Figure 1: The Bicycle

learner. Requiring the system to discover aspects of the concept that are already confidently known wastes valuable training examples. Incorporating as much prior domain knowledge as possible into the machine learning system reduces the load carried by the training examples, allowing the system to concentrate on learning what is not already known.

In this paper we demonstrate how iterated phantom induction, a systematic approach to integrating prior knowledge into a machine learning system, yields much improved learning performance in the challenging bicycle domain of Randløv and Alstrøm. The approach efficiently integrates the constraints inherent in the prior knowledge with the constraints imposed by the training examples. We show that balanced riding can be quickly learned using either handlebar manipulation (with no weight-shifting) or shifting weight (with no handlebar manipulation - "no-hands" riding).

2 THE DOMAIN

Randløv and Alstrøm very kindly made their bicycle simulator available to us.

The bicycle (see Figure 1) is described by 5 variables:

θ - the angle between the front wheel direction and the bicycle frame direction due to the deflection of the handlebars.

ω - the tilt angle of the bicycle from vertical.

$\dot{\theta}$, $\dot{\omega}$ - the handlebar and tilt angular velocities.

$\ddot{\omega}$ - the tilt angular acceleration.

The system has two possible control actions:

d - the displacement of the center of mass.

T - the torque to apply to the handlebars.

For further details of the bicycle simulator please see Randløv and Alstrøm, 1998.

2.1 DIFFERENCES

We made some changes to the bicycle simulator:

1. Randløv and Alstrøm used both control inputs: displacement of the center of mass and applying torque to the handlebars. We use only one control input. We experimented using first only displacement of the center of mass and secondly only handlebar manipulation. Our results show that either control can be used on its own to successfully balance the bicycle.

2. Randløv and Alstrøm discretized their control inputs rather coarsely. Although there is some work in reinforcement learning which deals with continuous actions (Kimura and Kobayashi, 1998; Williams 1992), discretization is usually useful to avoid explosion of the size of the state space. Our control input is a continuous variable. This approach is considerably more natural and offers greater flexibility in the type of behavior that can be realized.

3. When controlling the handlebars, Randløv and Alstrøm's system learned directly what torque to apply. Our approach learns a "goal" angle θ_g for the handlebars. The torque is computed using a conventional PD controller (Franklin et al, 1986): $T = P * (\theta_g - \theta) - D * \dot{\theta}$. By learning to achieve θ_g the system in effect learns to control the torque. We use $P = 50$ and $D = 5$; different values can be used provided that P is about an order of magnitude larger than D.

3 THE ALGORITHM

Iterated phantom induction is a form of *explanation-based control* (DeJong, 1994). The learning system maintains both a *decision strategy* and a *decision criterion.* The system passively observes the world until the decision criterion is satisfied. The decision strategy is then invoked, the system makes a decision, and observes the outcome of its decision in the world. If the decision fails to yield the desired outcome, domain knowledge is employed to explain the observed world behavior. The observed error - the difference between the desired outcome and the observed outcome - is then propagated through the explanation, resulting in a characterization of the decision error for the decision that was made. From this decision error and the actual decision a *"phantom decision"* is produced. This phantom decision represents the decision that the system believes, after the fact, it should have made, instead of the actual decision it did make. These phantom points are employed as if they were actually observed successful training examples. A new decision strategy is generated using induction on the collection of phantom decisions, and this process is iterated.

In the bicycle domain the iterated phantom induction algorithm takes the following form ($\vec{b} = (\theta, \dot{\theta}, \omega, \dot{\omega}, \ddot{\omega})$ represents the state of the bicycle and f_j is the current strategy):

1. Set $j = 0$ and initialize f_0 arbitrarily.
2. Start a trial by setting the bicycle in an upright position and randomly perturbing the tilt angle.
3. Set $i = 1$.
4. Observe the behavior of the bicycle. The decision is set to zero until the decision criterion is satisfied.
5. When the decision criterion is satisfied, compute a control decision using the current strategy: $c_i = f_j(\vec{b_i})$.
6. Observe the behavior of the bicycle as a result of taking decision c_i. Compute the estimated decision error Δc_i.
7. Set $i = i + 1$ and return to Step 4.
8. At the end of each trial - the bicycle either falls over or balances for 1000 seconds - a collection of phantom points $(\vec{b_i}, c_i + \Delta c_i)_i$ has been accumulated. This collection is added to the set of training points.
9. Set $j = j + 1$.
10. Generate a new strategy f_j from the set of training points.
11. Return to Step 2.

The decision criterion we adopt in Step 4 is that if $|\omega|$ exceeds a threshold value of 0.01, a control action is taken. The decision criterion remains fixed; only the decision **strategy** f_j is learned.

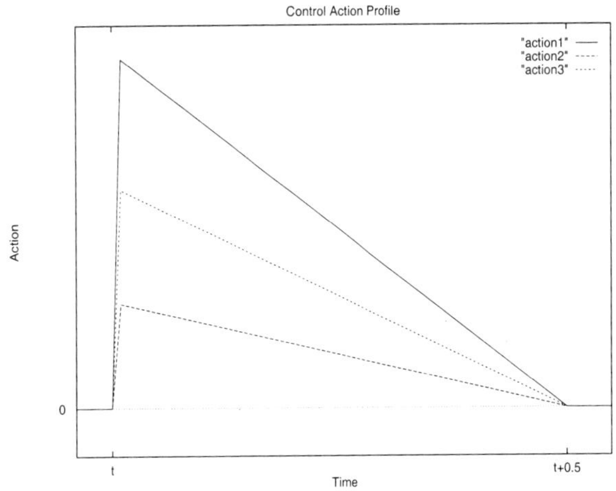

Figure 2: Three Typical Control Actions. A control action decreases to zero over a time interval of 0.5 seconds. The system's decision strategy computes the height of the triangle as $c = f_j(\vec{b})$.

The form of a control action is shown in Figure 2. The control is set at the chosen value $c = f_j(\vec{b})$ and then decreased to zero over a time interval of 0.5 seconds. During this interval no further action is taken. This profile was chosen to avoid the destabilizing effects of instantaneously changing the control.

Domain knowledge is used in Step 6 to compute the estimated decision error Δc. $c + \Delta c$ represents what the system believes would have been the correct decision. We explain in detail how this is done in Section 5 below.

Step 10 is performed using linear regression with cubic polynomials. Based on our previous work (Brodie and DeJong, 1998) other induction methods could also be used.

4 DOMAIN THEORY

The domain theory embodies information that we prefer the learning system not spend examples to acquire. Different experts may well provide distinct theories; it is not important precisely which is used. The important characteristics of a domain theory are for the representations to be as *natural*, *correct*, and *specific* as possible.

By *natural* we mean that the expert should be able to readily express his/her prior knowledge. It makes little sense to force the expert to significantly develop or modify his/her domain understanding for the sole purpose of informing the learning system. By *correct* we mean that the expert-supplied representations should not systematically contradict the learning system's experience. If the domain theory contradicts the pattern emerging from the examples, many more examples will ultimately be consumed, because the system must both counteract the information of the domain theory and then discover and confirm the true underlying pattern. Finally, a domain theory that is more *specific* than another requires fewer examples to flesh out to a usable predictive form.

4.1 REPRESENTATION OF DOMAIN THEORY

Domain knowledge is described using the notation of qualitative processes (Forbus, 1984). Let a and b be variables with particular time profiles $a_0(t)$ and $b_0(t)$. Suppose we would like b to follow a different profile $b_1(t)$ such that $b_1(t) > b_0(t)$, i.e. we would like to increase b. If one way of achieving this is by increasing a, i.e. make a follow a profile $a_1(t)$ such that $a_1(t) > a_0(t)$, we write $(Q^+ \quad a \quad b)$. Similarly we write $(Q^- \quad a \quad b)$ to mean that decreasing a will increase b.

Statements of this form are qualitative expressions of human knowledge about the domain. They can be regarded as approximations to the more precise knowledge given by the differential equations that describe the behavior of the world. The advantages of using qualitative statements rather than the differential equations include:

(i) It is easier to perform inference. Given a chain $(Q^{+/-} \quad a_1 \quad a_2)$, $(Q^{+/-} \quad a_2 \quad a_3)$, ..., $(Q^{+/-} \quad a_{n-1} \quad a_n)$ of qualitative relationships, it is obvious that the relationship between a_1 and a_n is Q^+ if the number of minus signs in the chain is even, otherwise it is Q^-. The knowledge expressed by the differential equations can be much more difficult to utilize.

(ii) They are less vulnerable to unmodeled dynamics. The differential equations may not accurately model some aspect of the domain (e.g. friction). Qualitative statements are less vulnerable to this problem because they are much less precise and make much weaker claims about the world. For example, even if we cannot precisely model friction we can certainly make accurate qualitative statements about the effect of friction in the world.

(iii) The differential equations may simply be unavailable for a variety of reasons. Qualitative domain knowledge is usually easy to obtain from human experts.

4.2 USE OF DOMAIN THEORY

After a decision $c = f_j(\vec{b})$ is taken, the system estimates what it thinks the correct decision $c + \Delta c$ would have been. It then places a "phantom" training point at $(\vec{b}, c + \Delta c)$.

If the domain knowledge were perfect, Δc could be computed exactly, and $c + \Delta c$ would coincide with the correct decision c^*. Since real-world knowledge is always imperfect, Δc can only estimate $c^* - c$, the true but unknown decision error.

Previous work (Brodie and DeJong, 1998) has shown that the iterated phantom induction algorithm converges provided that: (i) Δc and $c^* - c$ have the same sign; (ii) $|\Delta c|$ is a monotonic function of $|c^* - c|$, i.e. $|c^* - c_1| \leq |c^* - c_2| \Rightarrow |\Delta c_1| \leq |\Delta c_2|$. Requirement (i) ensures that c will always be moved in the correct direction; if c^* lies above/below c, then $c + \Delta c$ will be placed above/below c. Requirement (ii) ensures that bad decisions are moved by larger amounts than good decisions.

Note that if $e(c)$ is any function satisfying requirements (i) and (ii), then so does $\Delta c = m * e(c)$ for any $m > 0$. We call m the *scale factor*; it is a parameter to the algorithm and we are free to choose its value. The value of the scale factor affects only the **rate** of convergence.

Domain knowledge is used to construct a function $e(c)$ satisfying requirements (i) and (ii). We divide this task into two parts: computing the **sign** of $e(c)$, and computing the **magnitude** $|e(c)|$.

5 BICYCLE DOMAIN THEORY

We now describe the domain theory used in the bicycle domain. We do not claim that this theory is optimal or ideal. It simply represents human knowledge that our system is able to take advantage of.

We divide the domain theory into "directional knowledge" (used to determine the sign of $e(c)$) and "magnitude knowledge" (used to compute $|e(c)|$).

5.1 DIRECTIONAL KNOWLEDGE

A relationship between ω and each control input is needed in order to determine in which direction the control needs to be changed to bring about a desired change in ω. This is achieved by first obtaining a general relationship between ω and θ. This is then combined with specific relationships between the control inputs and θ to obtain relationships between the control inputs and ω.

First, it is clearly the case that $(Q^+ \quad \dot{\omega} \quad \omega)$ and $(Q^+ \quad \ddot{\omega} \quad \dot{\omega})$.

Next we establish a relationship between θ, the angle of deflection of the handlebars, and $\ddot{\omega}$. If θ is constant, the bicycle rides around in a circle. Circular motion generates a centrifugal force F acting along the line joining the bicycle to the center of the circle. If θ is increased, the circle becomes smaller, increasing the magnitude of the centrifugal force, i.e. $(Q^+ \quad \theta \quad F)$. Since this force acts in the direction opposite to the tilting bicycle, $(Q^- \quad F \quad \ddot{\omega})$.

From the above facts it can be inferred that $(Q^- \quad \theta \quad \omega)$. This general statement will be combined with specific knowledge about each control input c to infer a conclusion of the form $(Q^{+/-} \quad c \quad \omega)$, where c represents either displacement of the center of mass or handlebar manipulation.

5.1.1 Center of Mass Displacement

Let d represent the control action of displacing the center of mass of the rider. By conservation of momentum the bicycle tilts in the opposite direction. Hence $(Q^- \quad d \quad \omega)$.

If ω increases, the bicycle tilts over at a larger angle. This increases the deflection of the handlebars, so $(Q^+ \quad \omega \quad \theta)$.

Combining these facts with the knowledge given previously gives

$$(Q^+ \quad d \quad \omega).$$

This appears to contradict the previously stated relationship $(Q^- \quad d \quad \omega)$. The contradiction is resolved by noticing that $(Q^- \quad d \quad \omega)$ holds instantaneously after the center of mass is shifted, while $(Q^+ \quad d \quad \omega)$ holds over a longer period of time as the effect of shifting the center of mass permeates through the complex dynamics of the bicycle to affect ω.

$(Q^+ \quad d \quad \omega)$ asserts the common-sense observation that, if the bicycle starts falling over, the rider, to restore the bicycle back towards a balanced position, should shift his/her weight in the same direction as he/she wants ω to change.

5.1.2 Handlebar Manipulation

When the rider turns the handlebars to try achieve an angle of θ_g, we clearly have $(Q^+ \quad \theta_g \quad \theta)$.

Combining this with the knowledge given previously gives

$$(Q^- \quad \theta_g \quad \omega).$$

This asserts the (possibly counter-intuitive) observation that if the bicycle starts falling over, the rider should turn the handlebars in the direction of the fall. This increases the centrifugal restoring force, causing ω to move in the opposite direction, correcting the fall.

Thus the system can infer relationships of the form $(Q^{+/-} \quad c \quad \omega)$, where c represents either displacement of the center of mass or handlebar manipulation. This allows it to determine in which direction a control action should be changed in order to bring about a desired change in ω.

In this example we developed the domain theory using our own knowledge of bicycle-riding. In a more complex domain human experts might need to be consulted to obtain the necessary relationships. It is important to note that the qualitative language in which the domain theory is expressed is quite natural for domain experts and does not require any knowledge of the machine learning method to be used.

5.2 MAGNITUDE KNOWLEDGE

For simplicity we will assume that the control action c occurs when ω crosses the threshold on the positive side. For $\omega < 0$ symmetry can be used.

The consequences of a control action c fall into three cases (see Figure 3):

1) ω falls below the threshold and rises again.

2) ω falls below the threshold and continues to fall.

3) ω does not fall below the threshold.

(There is a fourth possibility: ω falls below the threshold and remains there indefinitely. This is the optimal result; action c does not need to be changed, so $\Delta c = 0$.)

In Cases 1-3 it is clear whether the behavior of ω should be increased or decreased (Case 1 - decrease, Case 2 - increase, Case 3 - decrease). The previously derived relationship $(Q^{+/-} \quad c \quad \omega)$ then determines whether c should be increased or decreased. Thus requirement (i) is satisfied: if c^* lies above/below c, then $c + \Delta c$ will be placed above/below c. We now show how the magnitude $|e(c)|$ is computed to satisfy requirement (ii).

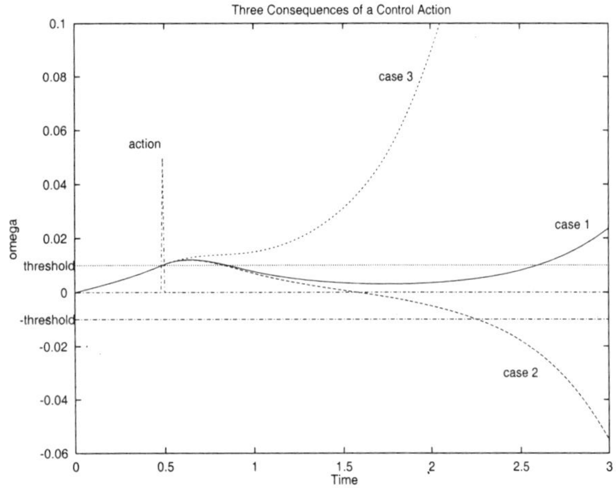

Figure 3: A control action can have three consequences: (1) ω falls below the threshold and rises again. (2) ω falls below the threshold and continues to fall. (3) ω does not fall below the threshold. The "action" spike on the graph indicates when the control action occurred. In cases 1 and 2 another control action (not shown) will be taken when ω exceeds the threshold again.

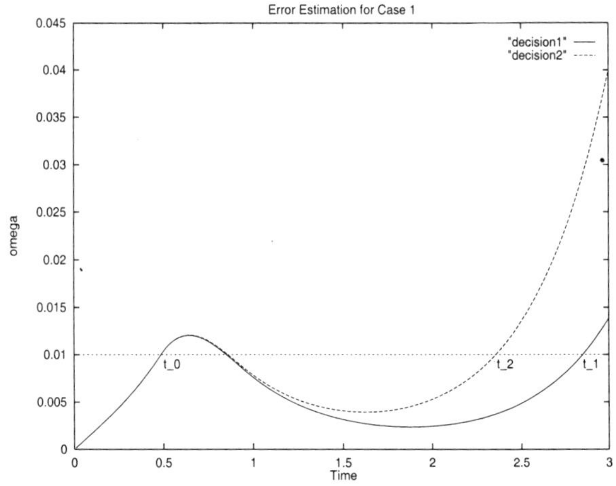

Figure 4: Error Estimation in Case 1. The error of the decision taken at time t_0 is estimated as $1/\Delta t$, where Δt is the time interval from t_0 until ω exceeds the threshold again.

5.2.1 Cases 1 and 2

Consider the two curves in Figure 4, both examples of Case 1. A control decision was taken at time t_0, but the value of the decision differed, resulting in two distinct trajectories which exceed the threshold again at t_1 and t_2. The optimal decision at t_0 would result in ω staying below the threshold for the longest possible time after t_0. Since $t_1 > t_2$, it can be concluded that decision1 is a better decision than decision2.

In general, although the true error of a control decision c is unknown, we know that it is inversely related to $\Delta t = t - t_0$, where t_0 is when the decision is taken and t is when ω exceeds the threshold again. This means that if we choose $|e(c)| = 1/\Delta t$, requirement (ii) is satisfied: $|c^* - c_1| \leq |c^* - c_2| \Rightarrow |e(c_1)| \leq |e(c_2)|$, so bad decisions will be moved by larger amounts than good decisions.

The same approach applies to Case 2. (The sign of $e(c)$ will be opposite in Case 2 to that of Case 1, because we want ω to increase instead of decrease, but the magnitude is computed the same way.)

In Cases 1 and 2 another control action will be taken when ω exceeds the threshold again. (This action is not shown in Figures 3 or 4.) The behavior of the bicycle after this next control action affects only the error estimate for that action, and has no effect on the error estimate for the action at time t_0.

We observe also that since Δt is definitely larger than two timesteps, $\exists A$ such that $e(c) \leq A \; \forall c$. This will be useful in Case 3 below.

5.2.2 Case 3

Here the value of ω continues to rise and does not fall back below the threshold, i.e. the bicycle falls over (see Figure 3). In this case c should be changed so as to decrease ω, determining, as before, in which direction to move c.

To compute $|e(c)|$, we note that any decision that results in Case 1 or Case 2 is a better decision than any decision which results in Case 3. So $|e(c)|$ when Case 3 occurs needs to be larger than $|e(c)|$ for Cases 1 and 2. We use $|e(c)| = A + 1/\Delta t$, where Δt is the length of time from taking the action until the bicycle falls over. This ensures that requirement (ii) is satisfied.

That completes the explanation of how domain knowledge is used to create phantom decisions from actual decisions.

6 RESULTS

6.1 CENTER OF MASS DISPLACEMENT

Results when the system controls the bicycle using only displacement of the center of mass are shown

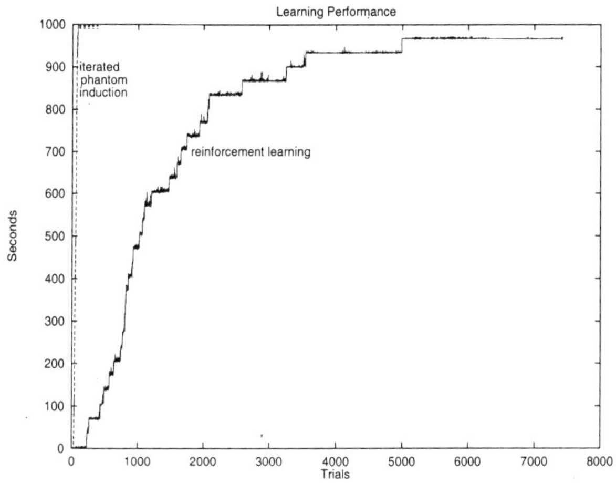

Figure 5: Comparison of iterated phantom induction with reinforcement learning. Both curves are the average of 40 runs. After the system has learned the task, 1000 seconds are used in calculation of the average. (We stopped running iterated phantom induction after 400 trials.)

in Figure 5, which compares them to Randløv and Alstrøm's results by also plotting the reinforcement learning curve from Figure 2 of Randløv and Alstrøm, 1998. A scale factor of $m = 0.05$ was used for iterated phantom induction.

Iterated phantom induction learns the task perfectly (i.e. the average of all 40 runs is 1000 seconds) in less than 100 trials. Randløv and Alstrøm's reinforcement learning system required 8000 trials to achieve this. It is clear that the introduction of domain knowledge has had a powerful effect on the learning performance - about 2 **orders of magnitude** in this case.

Figure 6 shows the paths followed by the bicycle during a typical learning run. Only the top ($y > 2600$) and bottom ($y < 30$) portions of the xy plane are shown. In the early trials at the bottom of the figure the bicycle falls over quite quickly. However performance soon improves and a number of longer paths can be seen exiting the lower figure. These are trials in which the bicycle balances for 1000 seconds. The end of these paths is shown in the top portion of Figure 6. Note that the bicycle is travelling almost directly in a straight line.

Figure 7 shows the center of mass results with three different scale factors: $m = 0.005$, $m = 0.05$, and $m = 0.5$. Performance in all three cases is considerably better than Randløv and Alstrøm's system. When $m = 0.005$, the algorithm makes good progress ini-

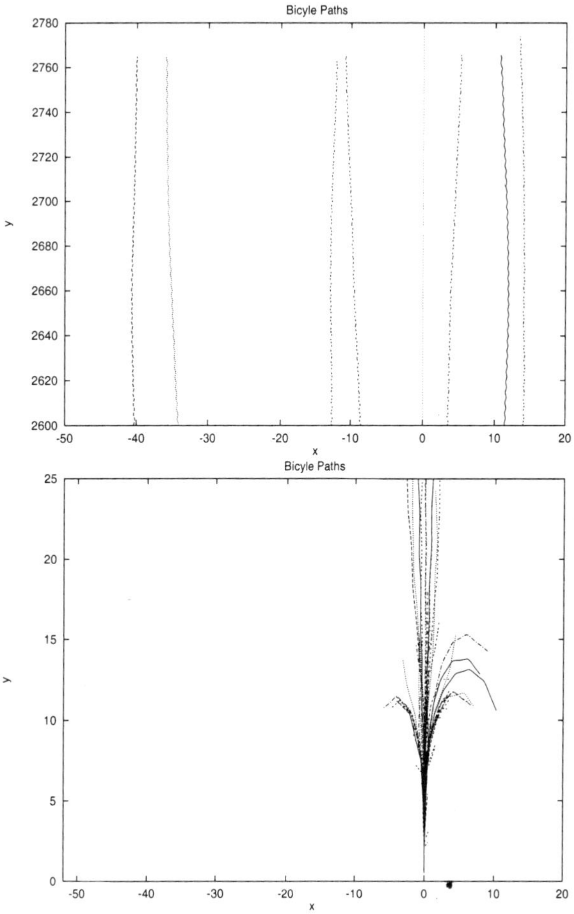

Figure 6: The first 75 trials of a typical learning run seen from above. The paths exiting the top of the lower figure are 7 trials which balance for 1000 seconds. The ends of these paths are shown in the upper figure. Compare with Figures 3 and 4 of Randløv and Alstrøm.

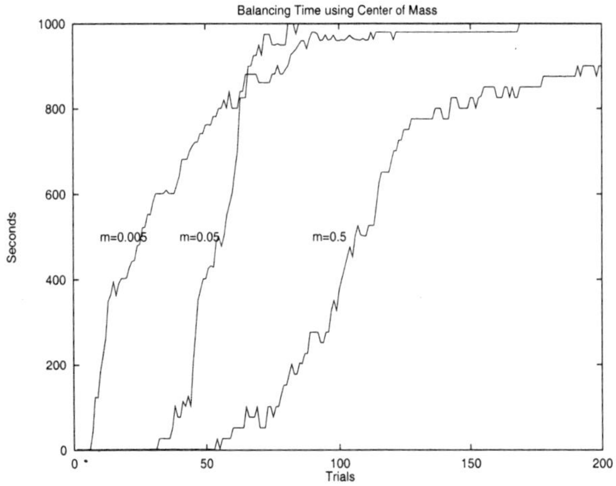

Figure 7: Number of seconds the bicycle balances as a function of the number of trials, using the center of mass as control. Average of 40 runs for three different scale factors. (After the system has learned the task, 1000 seconds are used in calculation of the average.)

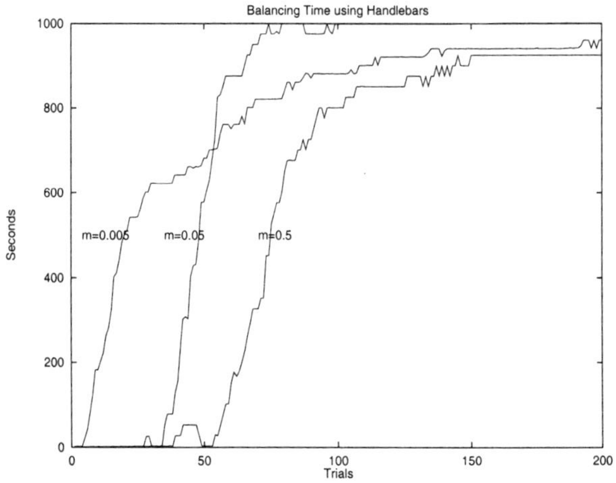

Figure 8: Number of seconds the bicycle balances as a function of the number of trials, using manipulation of the handlebars as control. Average of 40 runs with three different scale factors. (After the system has learned the task, 1000 seconds are used in calculation of the average.) Compare with Figure 7 above.

tially but soon the rate of convergence slows down. If $m = 0.5$, the algorithm converges slowly. The intermediate value $m = 0.05$ yields fastest convergence.

6.2 HANDLEBAR MANIPULATION

Results are similar when the system controls the bicycle using only manipulation of the handlebars. Figure 8 shows results for the same three scale factors. Once again they all learn much faster than Randløv and Alstrøm's system, and the intermediate value $m = 0.05$ yields the best results. Further discussion of the role of m can be found in Brodie and DeJong, 1998.

7 RELATED WORK

Iterated phantom induction exploits domain knowledge to learn a difficult control concept represented by a numeric function. Work in reinforcement learning (Sutton and Barto, 1998) and instance-based learning (Atkeson, 1990; Ram and Sanamaria, 1997) has similar objectives. Shaping (Randløv and Alstrøm, 1998), eligibility traces (Loch and Singh, 1998), and state aggregation (Uther and Veloso, 1998) can all be viewed as efforts to extend the applicability of reinforcement learning to more complex problems by using domain knowledge to reduce the exploration of the state space. In these and other approaches the human expert must express his/her knowledge in the form of the learning bias internal to the system. The use of a system's learning bias as a programming language can be awkward and limiting, and the effects of changing the bias can be difficult to predict.

The explanation-based approach makes it easy for the expert to express his/her domain knowledge in a way that the learning system can directly exploit. Although in hierarchical reinforcement learning (Dietterich, 1998) the bias is also explicitly input and is flexible and expressive, once stated it is static and not subject to inferential refinement as allowed by the explanation-based approach.

Neural nets can be viewed as forming approximations to numeric functions. Two notable approaches that support the incorporation of explicit background knowledge are KBANN (Shavlik and Towell, 1990) and EBNN (Thrun and Mitchell, 1993). The distinguishing feature of iterated phantom induction is that the knowledge is used to adjust the observed data, so that training is based not on the actual examples but on phantom examples. The domain knowledge does not directly affect the hypothesis-generation process.

8 CONCLUSION

While few would disagree that the incorporation of domain knowledge is the key to effective machine learning, the vast majority of current machine learning research ignores the issue of prior knowledge. The need for knowledge is obvious, but the mechanism by which knowledge can be flexibly and effectively incorporated is not.

Previously we have advanced iterated phantom induction as a general mechanism by which domain knowledge can be integrated into the learning process. Domain knowledge is employed to transform observed training examples into a more informative set of phantom examples. Conventional machine learning can then be performed, benefiting from both the examples and the domain knowledge.

In our previous work phantom induction was limited to nondynamical systems. In these the long-term behavior of the system is straightforwardly connected to the input decisions and so the learning problem is simplified. In nonlinear dynamical systems the state of the system can depend in a subtle way on the interactions between the input and the current state of the system. Such systems can be very difficult to predict for any length of time, and chaotic and uncontrollable behavior can arise. A task solution necessarily embodies constantly monitoring the system and shepherding it away from undesirable situations as they develop. This is the case in the bicycle control domain.

Here we have shown how the iterated phantom induction algorithm can be extended to the nonlinear dynamical system of riding a bicycle. Our system learns much more quickly than the only other learning system that has been demonstrated to achieve this challenging task. Iterated phantom induction works by using human domain knowledge expressed in a natural way to transform the observed training examples. This allows promising hypotheses to be preferentially explored while most poor hypotheses are not even entertained. The result is an efficient learning algorithm with wide applicability to challenging tasks.

Acknowledgements

This research was sponsored by the Office of Naval Research under grant N00014-94-1-0684.

We are also indebted to Jette Randløv for her invaluable assistance in providing the code for the bicycle simulator and the data from their results.

References

Atkeson, C. (1990) Memory Based Techniques for Task-level Learning in Robots and Smart Machines. In *1990 American Control Conference.* San Diego: 2815-2819.

Brodie, M. and DeJong, G. (1998) Iterated Phantom Induction: a Little Knowledge Can Go a Long Way. In *Proceedings of the Fifteenth National Conference on Artificial Intelligence.* AAAI Press, Menlo Park, CA: 665-670.

DeJong, G. (1994) Learning to Plan in Continuous Domains. *Artificial Intelligence* 65: 71-141.

Dietterich, T. (1998) The MAXQ Method for Hierarchical Reinforcement Learning, In *Proceedings of the Fifteenth International Conference on Machine Learning.* Morgan Kaufmann, San Francisco, CA: 118-126.

Forbus, K. (1984) Qualitative Process Theory. *Artificial Intelligence* 24: 85-168.

Franklin, G., Powell, J. and Emami-Naeini, A. (1986) Feedback Control of Dynamic Systems. Addison Wesley, Reading, MA.

Kimura, H. and Kobayashi, S. (1998) An Analysis of Actor/Critic Algorithms using Eligibility Traces: Reinforcement Learning with Imperfect Value Functions. In *Proceedings of the Fifteenth International Conference on Machine Learning.* Morgan Kaufmann, San Francisco, CA: 278-286.

Loch, J. and Singh, S. (1998) Using Eligibility Traces to Find the Best Memoryless Policy in Partially Observable Markov Decision Processes. In *Proceedings of the Fifteenth International Conference on Machine Learning.* Morgan Kaufmann, San Francisco, CA: 323-331.

Ram, A. and Sanamaria, J. (1997) Continuous Case-Based Reasoning. *Artificial Intelligence* 90(1-2): 35-77.

Randløv, J. and Alstrøm, P. (1998) Learning to Drive a Bicycle using Reinforcement Learning and Shaping. In *Proceedings of the Fifteenth International Conference on Machine Learning.* Morgan Kaufmann, San Francisco, CA: 463-471.

Shavlik, J. and Towell G., (1990) An Approach to Combining Explanation-Based and Neural Learning Algorithms. In *Readings in Machine Learning, J. Shavlik and T. Dietterich, Editors.* Morgan Kaufmann: San Mateo: 828-839.

Sutton, R. and Barto, A. (1998) Reinforcement Learning: An Introduction. MIT Press, Cambridge, MA.

Thrun, S. and Mitchell, T. (1993) Integrating Inductive Neural Network Learning and Explanation-Based

Learning. In *Thirteenth International Joint Conference on Artificial Intelligence.* Chambery, France: Morgan Kaufmann. p. 930-936.

Uther, W. and Veloso, M. (1998) Tree Based Discretization for Continuous State Space Reinforcement Learning In *Proceedings of the Fifteenth National Conference on Artificial Intelligence.* AAAI Press, Menlo Park, CA: 769-775.

Williams, R. (1992) Simple Statistical Gradient Following Algorithms for Connectionist Reinforcement Learning. In *Machine Learning* 8(3): 229-256.

Sonar-Based Mapping With Mobile Robots Using EM

Wolfram Burgard[1] **Dieter Fox**[2] **Hauke Jans**[1] **Christian Matenar**[1] **Sebastian Thrun**[2]
[1]Department of Computer Science
University of Bonn
D-53117 Bonn, Germany
[2]Computer Science Department
Carnegie Mellon University
Pittsburgh, PA 15213

Abstract

This paper presents an algorithms for learning occupancy grid maps with mobile robots equipped with range finders, such as sonar sensors. Our approach employs the EM algorithm to solve the concurrent mapping and localization problem. To accommodate the spatial nature of range data, it relies on a two-layered representation of maps, where global maps are composed from a collection of small, local maps. To avoid local minima during likelihood maximization, a softmax version of the M step is proposed that is gradually annealed to the exact maximum. Experimental results demonstrate that our approach is well suited for constructing large maps of typical indoor environments using sensors as inaccurate as sonars.

1 Introduction

Learning maps with mobile robots has frequently been recognized as one of the most fundamental problems in mobile robotics [CW90, KBM98]. This is because the map learning problem, often referred to as *concurrent mapping and localization*, is a chicken-and-egg problem. If the pose (we use the term *pose* to refer to a robot's x-y location and its heading direction θ) of the robot was always known during mapping—which is actually assumed by the majority of work in the field—building maps is relatively easy, and there is a large number of approaches that work well. On the other hand, if a map was available, determining the robot's poses at any time is relatively straightforward, as methods exist that even work reliably if the environment is non-stationary (e.g., densely populated by people) [BAC+98, FBTC98]. In map learning, however, neither the robot's poses nor the map is known initially—so both must be estimated from data. Unfortunately, errors in odometry (wheel encoders) amplify over time. For example, small rotational error can have a huge effect on the robot's x-y-location later in time. This makes it difficult to estimate poses while learning maps.

In the past, the problem of map learning has been tackled by a great number of researchers (see e.g., [CL85, Cho96, CKK95, Elf87, Elf89, KB91, Mat90, Mor88, Ren93, SK97]). Some recent methods, such as the *metric* approaches described in [GN97, LM97, TGF+98], have successfully been applied for learning maps up to 80 by 25 m^2 in size. However, they are closely married to *laser range finders*, a highly accurate and quite expensive sensor technology. Other methods, such as the *topological* approaches described in [Sha98, TFB98], rely on *landmarks* to build maps. They work with less accurate sensors (such as sonars), but they are forced to throw away almost all sensor data, except for extremely scarce landmark data. For example, they cannot exploit the width of a corridor to disambiguate different corridors. Some of the largest topological maps (80 by 25 m^2) have been learned using the algorithm in [TFB98]. However, it has only been demonstrated to work with pre-defined landmarks. It is remarkable, however, that most successful approaches to date use statistical techniques for map learning.

The approach proposed here builds directly on our previous work [TFB98, TGF+98]. As there, the map learning problem is phrased as a maximum likelihood estimation problem, and EM is applied for finding a local maximum in likelihood space. The algorithm proposed here differs in several aspects, crucial for its scalability. First, *small, local maps* are generated from short sequences of sensor data, exploiting the fact that in the short term odometry errors are typically small and can be neglected. These local maps replace the landmarks in [TFB98], thereby overcoming the reliance on manually labeled landmark locations. More importantly, our approach relaxes an independence assumption made in [TFB98] by a weaker one. Our previous approach represented maps in the E-step by a single, global grid; and each grid cell was estimated *independently* of other grid cells. While this is unproblematic if the robot approximately knows its position (in which case the mapping step is identical to occupancy grids [Elf87, Elf89, Mor88, Thr98]), this independence assumption leads to highly ambiguous maps when the robot is uncertain, which makes it difficult to localize the robot with sonar sensors. Here we replace these flat maps using a two-layered representation. Our algorithm replaces the single map by a collection of local maps, annotated with their pose distributions. This approach maintains dependencies between different grid cells within each local map. It enables us to use conventional metric Markov localization [BAC+98, BFHS96, BDFC98] (see also [KCK96, KS96, NPB95, SK95]) in the E-step. As a result, our new algorithm inherits all advantages of the EM approach and simultaneously is able to operate on raw proximity information without relying on pre-defined landmarks. Our approach makes EM applicable to learning maps of typical indoor environments of mobile robots equipped with sonar sensors, or other low-resolution proximity sensors.

Empirical results, described in this paper, illustrate that our approach succeeds in learning large-scale maps purely based on sonar measurements. To demonstrate its robustness, experiments with amplified odometric noise illustrate that our approach is applicable even under significant odometric errors.

2 Statistical Foundations

2.1 Models

We formulate the problem of concurrent mapping and localization as a statistical *maximum likelihood estimation problem* [TFB98]. To generate a map, we assume that a robot is given a stream of sensor data, denoted.

$$d = \{o^{(1)}, u^{(1)}, o^{(2)}, u^{(2)}, \ldots, o^{(T)}, u^{(T)}\}, \tag{1}$$

where $o^{(t)}$ stands for an *observation* that the robot made at time t (e.g., using its sonar sensors), and $u^{(t)}$ for an odometry reading that characterizes the action executed between time t to time $t+1$. T denotes the total number of time steps in the data. Without loss of generality, we assume that the data is an alternated sequence of actions and observations.

In statistical terms, the problem of mapping can be posed as the problem of finding the most likely map given the data. A *map*, denoted $m = \{m_{x,y}\}_{x,y}$, is an assignment of "properties" $m_{x,y}$ to each x-y-location in the world. In topological approaches to mapping, the properties-of-interest are usually locations of landmarks [CKK95] or, alternatively, locations of significant places [KB91, Cho96]. Metric approaches, on the other hand, usually use the location of obstacles as properties-of-interest [CL85, Mor88, LM97]. Here we follow the metric approach.

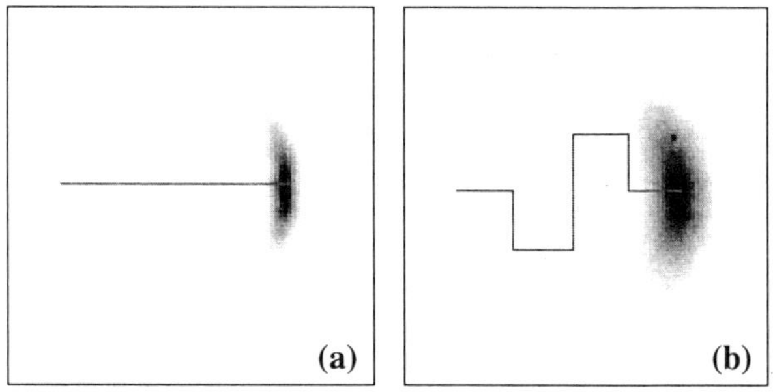

Figure 1: Motion model. The grayly shaded area shows the pose distribution (projected into 2D) after the motion command indicated by the solid line.

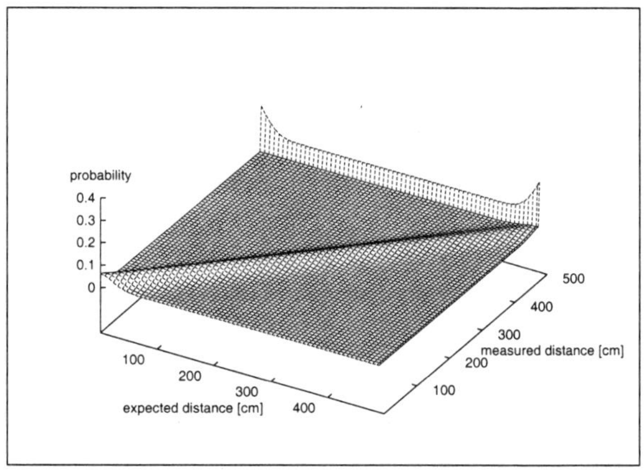

Figure 2: Perception model for ultrasound sensors. Probability of measuring a certain distance given the expected distance according to the model of the environment.

Our approach assumes that the robot is given three basic, probabilistic models, one that describes robot motion, one that models robot perception, and an inverse model of robot perception.

- **The motion model**, denoted $P(\xi' \mid u, \xi)$, describes the probability that the robot's pose is ξ', if it previously executed action u at pose ξ. Here ξ is used to refer to a pose (the x-y-location of a robot together with its heading direction θ). Our motion model assumes independent bounded and normally distributed errors in the length of the distance traveled as well as in the rotation carried out. Figure 1 illustrates the

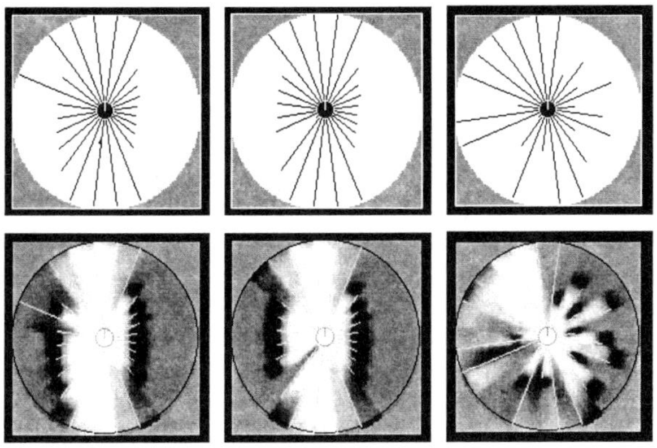

Figure 3: Inverse perceptual models: The top row shows raw sensor data, the bottom row shows a likelihood field (local map): the brighter a pixel, the higher its likelihood for being unoccupied. The inverse perceptual model has been learned from hand-labeled data, using artificial neural networks.

motion model, by showing the probability distribution for ξ' upon executing different motion actions. The images show projections of the tree-dimensional state space of the robot onto the x-y-plane.

- **The perception model**, denoted as $P(o \mid m, \xi)$, models the likelihood of observing o in situations where both the world m and the robot's pose ξ are known. For sonar sensors, as used throughout our experiments, this model is shown in Figure 2. Shown there is the probability of a sonar reading (vertical axis) as a function of the *correct* distance (determined using ray tracing) and the measured distance. The graph in Figure 2 has been generated from several millions of raw sonar readings (see [FBT98, Fox98]). It is the result of fitting a model consisting of a mixture of of a linear-Gaussian (centered around the correct distance), a Geometric distribution (modeling overly short readings) and a Dirac distribution (modeling max-range readings) to this data.

- **The inverse perception model** is denoted as $P(m \mid o, \xi)$. While the inverse perception model can be derived from the perception model using Bayes rule, it is computationally convenient to have an explicit inverse model for mapping. Here we use a model previously described in [Thr98], which applies neural network learning to compute the likelihood of occupancy from sonar scans. Figure 3 shows examples.

These three quantities, i.e., the given set d of data, the motion model $P(\xi' \mid u, \xi)$, and the perception model $P(o \mid m, \xi)$ form the statistical basis of our approach.

2.2 The Map Likelihood Function

Following [TFB98], the problem of mapping is the problem of finding the most likely map m^* given the data

$$m^* \quad = \quad \underset{m}{\operatorname{argmax}}\, P(m \mid d). \tag{2}$$

As shown there, the probability $P(m \mid d)$ can be rewritten as

$$P(m \mid d) = \lambda \int \dots \int \prod_{t=1}^{T} P(o^{(t)} \mid m, \xi^{(t)}) \prod_{t=1}^{T-1} P(\xi^{(t+1)} \mid u^{(t)}, \xi^{(t)})\, d\xi^{(1)}, \dots d\xi^{(T)}. \tag{3}$$

We are only interested in maximizing $P(m \mid d)$, hence the normalizer λ can safely be dropped. The remaining expression is a function of the data d, the perceptual model $P(o \mid m, \xi)$, and the motion model $P(\xi' \mid u, \xi)$. Maximizing this expression is equivalent to finding the most likely map.

2.3 EM for Learning Maps

Computing the *global* maximum of (3) is computationally challenging. The currently best-known solutions perform hill climbing in likelihood space. Following [TFB98], our approach uses the EM algorithm [DLR77, MK97] for maximizing likelihood. EM is a hill-climbing routine in likelihood space, which alternates two steps, an *expectation step* (E-step) and a *maximization step* (M-step). In the context of robot mapping, these steps correspond roughly to a localization step and a mapping step (see also [KS96, SK97]):

1. In the E-step, the robot computes probabilities $P(\xi \mid m, d)$ for the robot's poses ξ at the various points in times, based on the currently best available map m (in the first iteration, there will be no map).

2. In the M-step, the most likely map is determined by maximizing $\underset{m}{\operatorname{argmax}}\, P(m \mid \xi, d)$, using the location estimates computed in the E-step.

The E-step corresponds to a localization step with a fixed map, whereas the M-step implements a mapping step which operates under the assumption that the robot's locations (or, more precisely, probabilistic estimates thereof) are known. Iterative application of both rules leads to a refinement of both, the location estimates and the map.

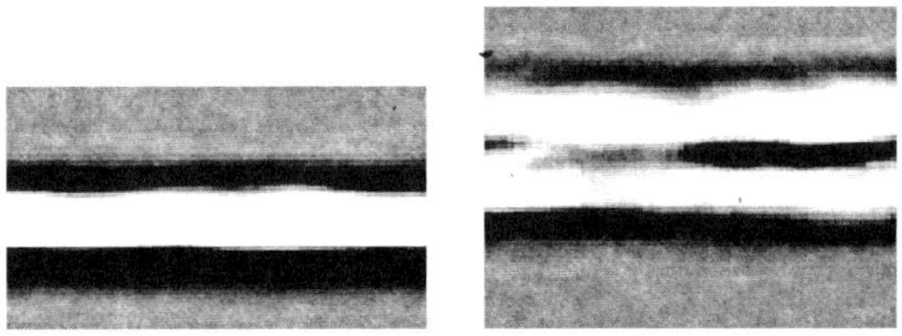

Figure 4: Local map (left) and misleading global map (right), generated by convolving the local map with a bimodal pose distribution. Such maps occur during optimization, when the robot has not yet determined its position. They make Markov localization fail. Our approach, hence, maintains the local maps during EM, and builds the global map only at the end.

3 Two-layered Map Representations

In our previous work, maps were represented by flat grids. Each grid cell represented the posterior probability of it containing a landmark. Unfortunately, this is problematic when applying EM to maps constructed by proximity sensors. Figure 4 illustrates why: Suppose the robot's sensor readings suggest a map like the one shown on the left side of Figure 4, but it has two distinct hypotheses as to where it might be. Integrating a single global map (which involves convolution with the robot's uncertainty) may yield the map shown on the right side of Figure 4. While for each individual map pixel, this map *correctly* estimates the likelihood of occupancy, the map as a whole is not usable: In some areas, it shows 3 walls, instead of 2; in others, the corridor appears to be twice as wide. Such maps are plainly not usable for localization with proximity sensors, as any specific sensor scan will not fit well anywhere into such maps. The situation is even worse when the robot is more globally uncertain, in which case the resulting maps often do not contain any visible structure.

This effect, which in fact is a consequence of the independence assumption in occupancy grids [Mor88], can be avoided by adopting a richer [JM98], layered representation. Our approach represents the world by a collection of small, local maps annotated by their location. Formally, a map m is a conjunction of N small maps, denoted $m_{[i]}$, annotated by a coordinate transform, denoted $\xi_{[i]}$:

$$m = \{\langle m_{[i]}, \xi_{[i]}\rangle\}_{i=1,\ldots,N} \tag{4}$$

We will refer to $\xi_{[i]}$ as the *pose* of the i-th local map (poses of maps are essentially the same as robot poses). For brevity, let us write

$$M_{[i]} := \langle m_{[i]}, \xi_{[i]}\rangle \tag{5}$$

and hence

$$m = \{M_{[i]}\}_{i=1,\ldots,N} \tag{6}$$

By representing maps in two layers, we eliminate the problems arising from using a single, monolithic map. This is because local maps are not convolved with their pose distribution; instead, the pose distribution is represented explicitly.

Our layered map representation requires a new definition of the perceptual model $P(o \mid m, \xi)$. Our approach makes the following conditional independence assumption:

$$P(M_{[i]} M_{[j]} \mid o, \xi) = P(M_{[i]} \mid o, \xi)\, P(M_{[j]} \mid o, \xi) \tag{7}$$

for all $i \neq j$. Clearly, this assumption is only approximately correct, but it is necessary to keep the computation manageable and in practice seems to work well (it only introduces errors in regions where local maps overlap, which results in overly confident estimates). The independence assumption allows us to extend our perceptual model to maps represented in layers:

$$\begin{aligned}
&P(o \mid \xi, m)\\
&= P(o \mid \xi, \bigotimes_{i=1}^{N} M_{[i]})\\
&= \frac{P(\bigotimes_{i=1}^{N} M_{[i]} \mid o, \xi) P(o \mid \xi)}{P(\bigotimes_{i=1}^{N} M_{[i]} \mid \xi)}\\
&= \frac{\prod_{i=1}^{N} P(M_{[i]} \mid o, \xi) P(o \mid \xi)}{\prod_{i=1}^{N} P(M_{[i]} \mid \xi)}\\
&= \frac{1}{P(o \mid \xi)^{(N-1)}} \prod_{i=1}^{N} \frac{P(M_{[i]} \mid o, \xi) P(o \mid \xi)}{P(M_{[i]} \mid \xi)}\\
&= \frac{1}{P(o \mid \xi)^{(N-1)}}\\
&\quad \prod_{i=1}^{N} \frac{P(o \mid M_{[i]}, \xi) P(M_{[i]} \mid \xi)}{P(o \mid \xi)} \frac{P(o \mid \xi)}{P(M_{[i]} \mid \xi)}\\
&= \frac{1}{P(o \mid \xi)^{(N-1)}} \prod_{i=1}^{N} P(o \mid \xi, M_{[i]})
\end{aligned} \tag{8}$$

Here the expressions $P(o \mid \xi, M_{[i]})$ are computed as described in Section 2, using the learned sensor model shown in Figure 2b. The term $P(o \mid \xi)^{(N-1)}$ represents the probability of observing o given the position ξ of the robot. This probability is a constant, since it is independent of the map. In the subsequent analysis, it will be subsumed in other normalizers and hence be dropped from consideration at this point.

As Equation (8) shows, our approach computes the likelihood of observations separately in all maps, and then combines the resulting density multiplicatively. In practice, maps which cannot overlap with the robot's position can be safely eliminated, thereby speeding up the computation while not affecting the final result.

4 Mapping

We are now ready to present the map learning algorithm. In a first pre-processing phase, our algorithm extracts local maps from the data d. It then applies EM, iterating localization (E-step) and local map alignment (M-step). Finally, a single global map is generated from the result of EM.

Figure 5 illustrates the difference between our past approach [TFB98, TGF+98], and the one presented here. Previously, EM was used to directly generate the most likely map, which works well for landmarks, but purely for proximity sensors (such as sonars). Our new approach uses an intermediate, two-layered representation, in which EM is used to estimate the position of many local maps.

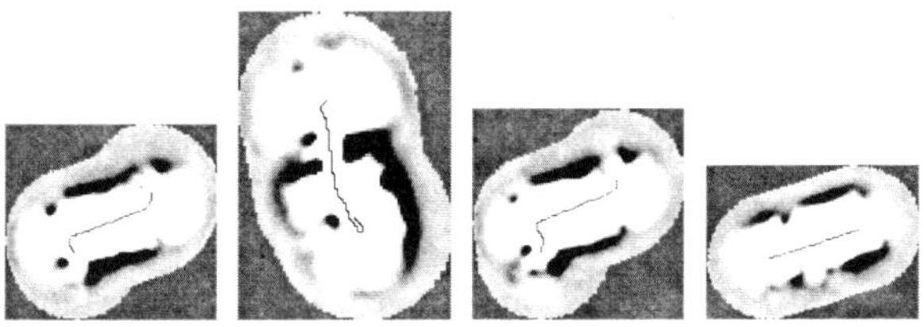

Figure 6: Examples of local maps, annotated by robot trajectories. These maps have been constructed from sonar measurements.

4.1 Pre-Processing

First, our approach generates the local maps $m_{[i]}$. This is done using conventional occupancy grid mapping [Elf87, Mor88, YLS+98], exploiting the fact that odometric errors can typically be neglected in the short range. In our current implementation, a new map is generated after every 5 meter of robot travel, during which the accumulated odometry error can be safely neglected. As mentioned above, our current implementation applies Backpropagation networks and Bayes rule to estimate the probability of occupancy in regions covered by the robot's sensors [Thr98]. Odometric errors are not corrected when building local maps. Figure 6 shows examples of such local maps. Local maps are computed only once in the beginning.

4.2 The E-Step

The E-step uses the current-best map m along with the data to compute probabilities $P(\xi^{(t)} \mid d, m)$ for the robot's poses at times $t = 1, \ldots, T$. With appropriate assumptions, $P(\xi^{(t)} \mid d, m)$ can be expressed as the normalized product of two terms

$$P(\xi^{(t)} \mid d, m) = \eta \underbrace{P(\xi^{(t)} \mid o^{(1)}, \ldots, o^{(t)}, m)}_{:=\alpha^{(t)}} \underbrace{P(\xi^{(t)} \mid u^{(t+1)}, \ldots, o^{(T)}, m)}_{:=\beta^{(t)}} \quad (9)$$

Here η is a normalizer that ensure that the left-hand side of Equation (9) sums up to one (see [TFB98] for a mathematical derivation). Both terms, $\alpha^{(t)}$ and $\beta^{(t)}$, as defined in (9), are computed separately, where the former is computed forward in time and the latter is computed backwards in time. Notice that $\alpha^{(t)}$ and $\beta^{(t)}$ are analogous to those in the alpha-beta algorithm [RJ86].

The computation of the α-values and the β-values are modified versions of *Markov localization*, using multiple (local) maps. Markov localization has recently been used with great success for robot localization in *known* environments by various researchers [BAC+98, KCK96, KS96, NPB95, SK95].

Computing the α-Values: Initially, the robot is assumed to be at the center of the global reference frame and $\alpha^{(1)}$ is given by a Dirac distribution centered at $(0, 0, 0)$:

$$\alpha^{(1)} = P(\xi^{(1)} \mid o^{(1)}, m) = \begin{cases} 1, & \text{if } \xi^{(1)} = (0,0,0) \\ 0, & \text{if } \xi^{(1)} \neq (0,0,0) \end{cases} \quad (10)$$

All other $\alpha^{(t)}$ are computed recursively:

$$\alpha^{(t)} = \eta\, P(o^{(t)} \mid \xi^{(t)}, m)\, P(\xi^{(t)} \mid o^{(1)}, \ldots, u^{(t-1)}, m) \quad (11)$$

where η is again a probabilistic normalizer. The rightmost term of (11) can be transformed to

$$P(\xi^{(t)} \mid o^{(1)}, \ldots, u^{(t-1)}, m) = \int P(\xi^{(t)} \mid u^{(t-1)}, \xi^{(t-1)})\, \alpha^{(t-1)}\, d\xi^{(t-1)} \quad (12)$$

Substituting (12) into (11) yields a recursive rule for the computation of all $\alpha^{(t)}$ with boundary condition (10). See [TFB98] for a more detailed derivation.

Computing the β-Values: The computation of $\beta^{(t)}$ is completely analogous but takes place backwards in time.

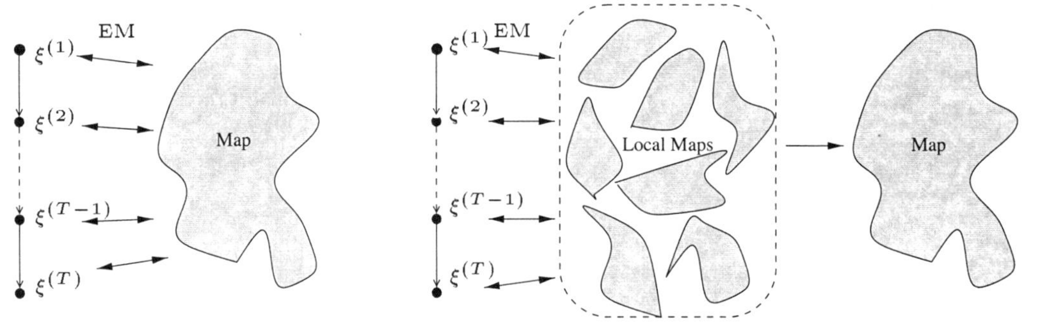

Figure 5: EM using a flat map representation (left) and using our new two-layered representation (right). In the layered approach, EM is applied for aligning small, local maps, which after the optimization are projected into a single, global map.

The initial $\beta^{(T)}$, which expresses the probability that the robot's final pose is ξ, is uniformly distributed, since $\beta^{(T)}$ does not depend on data. All other β-values are computed in the following way:

$$\beta^{(t)} = \eta \int P(\xi^{(t+1)} \mid u^{(t)}, \xi^{(t)}) \; P(o^{(t+1)} \mid \xi^{(t+1)}, m) \; \beta^{(t+1)} \; d\xi^{(t+1)} \quad (13)$$

The derivation of the equations are analogous to that of the computation rule for α-values and can be found in [TFB98]. The result of the E-step, the products $\alpha^{(t)}\beta^{(t)}$, are estimates of the robot's locations at the various points in time t.

4.3 The M-Step with Deterministic Annealing

The M-step calculates the most likely poses of the local maps. Let $t_{[i]}$ be the index of the first data point in the i-th local map. In the most generic setting, the M-step calculates

$$\begin{aligned} \xi_{[i]} &= \operatorname*{argmax}_{\xi} P(\xi^{(t_{[i]})} \mid d, m) \\ &= \operatorname*{argmax}_{\xi} \alpha^{(t_{[i]})} \; \beta^{(t_{[i]})} \end{aligned} \quad (14)$$

Unfortunately, this approach is problematic in practice. EM is a hill climbing method, which only converges to *local* maxima. If the odometric error is large, the initial map will be erroneous, and subsequent iterations of EM might not be able to recover.

The danger of getting stuck in a local maximum can be reduced significantly by a modified M-step. Instead of keeping track of the most likely model, our approach generates a distribution over models that slowly converges to the most likely one. More specifically, the M-step generates a distribution over poses, denoted μ:

$$\mu(\xi_{[i]}) \quad = \quad \eta \; \left(\alpha^{(t_{[i]})} \beta^{(t_{[i]})}\right)^{\frac{1}{\theta}} \quad (15)$$

Here η is a (different) normalizer that ensures that the probabilities integrate to 1. The parameter θ is a control parameter in $(0, 1]$ which will, in analogy to the rich literature on annealing, be referred to as *temperature*. Equation (15) is a version of the softmax function [Now91]. When $\theta = 1$, the full distribution over all poses is retained. When $\theta = 0$, our approach is equivalent to (14). To accommodate the fact that the E-step generates a distribution over maps, rather than a single map only, the expression $P(o \mid \xi, M_{[i]})$ in Equation (8) has to be substituted by

$$\int P(o \mid \xi, \langle m_{[i]}, \xi_{[i]} \rangle) \;\; \mu(\xi_{[i]}) \;\; d\xi_{[i]} \quad (16)$$

In our approach, θ is initialized with 1 and annealed towards zero using an exponential cooling schedule. The effect of the annealed softmax function in the E-step is to avoid early commitment to a single map. Instead, one can think of our approach as moving from density estimation (over the pose parameters in the map) to maximum likelihood estimation. The reader should notice that our approach is not the first to employ annealing to avoid local maxima in EM [HPJ99, Ros98].

Both the E-step and the M-step are alternated until convergence (using a criterion like a threshold on the minimum amount of change). In practice, less than 7 iterations sufficed in all our experiments.

4.4 Post-Processing

To come up with a single global map of the environment, the local maps $m_{[i]}$ are integrated based on their final poses $\xi_{[i]}$. This is done using Bayes rule, following the standard approach to building occupancy maps, as described in [Mor88, Thr98].

More specifically, let $\langle x, y \rangle$ be arbitrary coordinates of a grid cell in the global map. Let $\langle x_{[i]}, y_{[i]} \rangle$ specify the same location in the local coordinate system if the i-th local map $m_{[i]}$, which is easily obtained by applying the coordinate transformation induced by $\xi_{[i]}$. Let us furthermore use the indicator function

$$I_{\langle x,y \rangle \in m_{[i]}} \tag{17}$$

to indicate whether the local map $m_{[i]}$ covers the coordinate $\langle x, y \rangle$. Then the occupancy of $\langle x, y \rangle$ in global coordinates is given by:

$$P(occ_{x,y} \mid d) = P(occ_{x,y} \mid \bigotimes_{i=1}^{N} \langle m_{[i]}, \xi_{[i]} \rangle) = \tag{18}$$

$$1 - \left(1 + O(occ) \prod_{i: I_{\langle x,y \rangle \in m_{[i]}}} \frac{m_{[i],\langle x_{[i]}, y_{[i]} \rangle}}{1 - m_{[i],\langle x_{[i]}, y_{[i]} \rangle}} O(occ)^{-1} \right)^{-1}$$

where

$$O(occ) = \frac{P(occ)}{1 - P(occ)}. \tag{19}$$

$P(\text{occ})$ is the *prior* for the occupancy of a grid cell (it vanishes when set to 0.5), and $m_{[i],\langle x_{[i]}, y_{[i]} \rangle}$ denotes the likelihood for occupancy at $\langle x_{[i]}, y_{[i]} \rangle$ in the i-th local map. The derivation of (19) is completely analogous to the familiar occupancy grid approach, which is used to construct the local maps in the pre-processing phase). It can be found in [Thr98].

5 Experimental Results

Our approach was evaluated using various data sets collected in two indoor environments. Here we show results for two of them, one collected in the University of Bonn, and one at Carnegie Mellon University. The first is difficult because of the large number of offices, which makes it challenging to produce a straight corridor. The other contains a cycle—which is more challenging to map than non-cyclic environments [GN97, LM98]. All data has been collected using RWI B21 robots (RHINO at the University of Bonn and AMELIA at Carnegie Mellon University), equipped with 24 Polaroid sonar sensors with 15° opening angle (main cone). The reader may notice that building maps from sonar data is more difficult than building maps with high-precision laser range finders, due to their limited resolution and accuracy. Most previous approaches that successfully mapped circular environments required laser range finders (see e.g., [GN97, LM97, TGF+98]).

In our implementation, we used grids to represent probability densities, with a spatial resolution of 15 cm and an angular resolution of 2 degrees. The "tricks" described in [TFB98] were applied to keep the computation manageable.

Figure 7 shows on the left side a synthetic map of the first environment, along with the robot's path. To understand the best possible map that can be built from sonar sensors in this environment, we initially provided the robot with a correct map and used Markov localization to localize the robot. As reported in [BDFC98, GBFK98], this approach yields accurate position estimates even for ultrasound sensors. We then built a new map using the previously corrected position estimates. This map is shown on the right side of Figure 7. It can be viewed as the best possible result for EM.

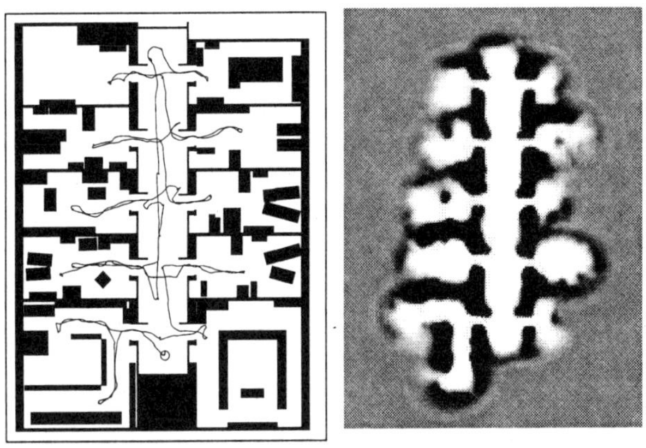

Figure 7: CAD-map of the first testing environment (left). Desks and tables are below the height of the sonars. Occupancy grid map constructed using the CAD map for localization (right). This map reflects the best possible outcome of EM.

To elucidate the scaling properties of our new algorithm, we artificially added random noise to the robot's odometry. Figure 8 shows in the upper row maps generated with different levels of artificial noise added. Here the raw odometry is insufficient to generate meaningful maps. These results are similar to those one would expect when using a low-accuracy robot, or when operating robots under less optimal conditions (e.g., on dirty surfaces that promote slippage). The lower row of this figure shows the resulting maps after applying our method. While in fact

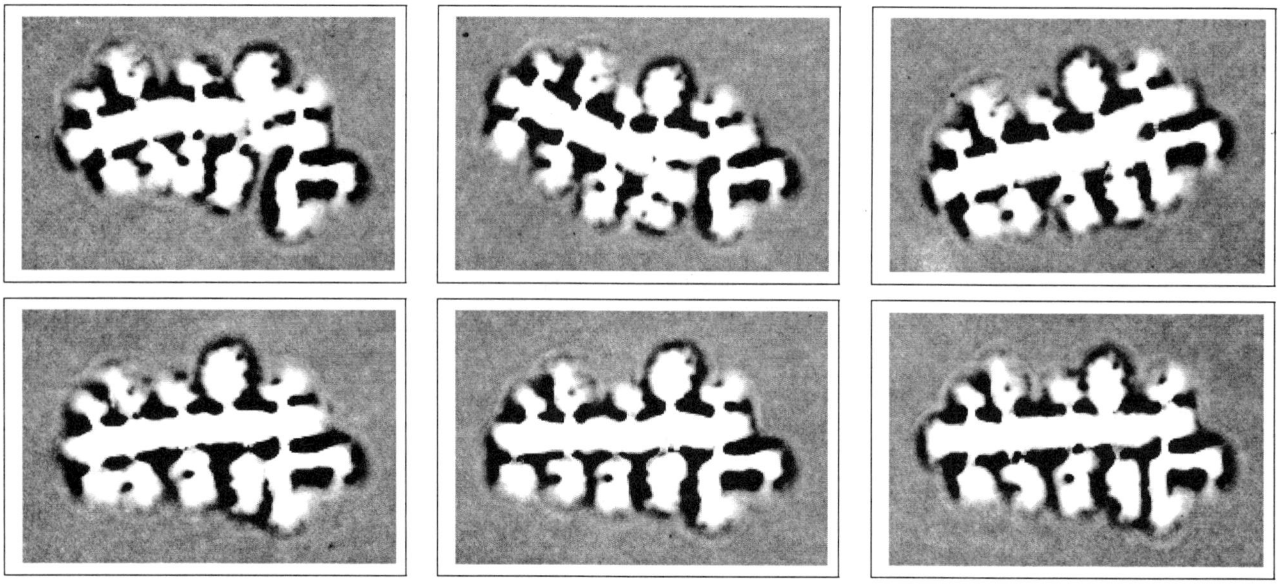

Figure 8: Maps of the first testing environment. The maps in the upper row been generated by adding different levels of noise to the odometry data. The lower row contains the maps obtained as output from applying EM.

our sonar data is insufficient to completely compensate the noise, our approach nevertheless generates maps that are basically sufficient for navigation.

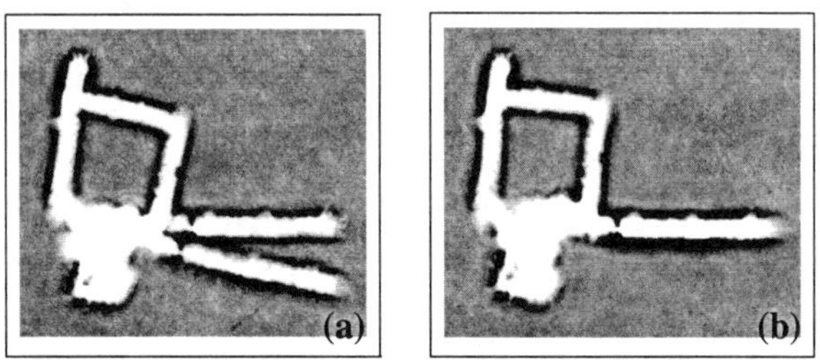

Figure 9: Maps built in Wean Hall of Carnegie Mellon University, (a) using raw odometry, and (b) using our new algorithm. These maps are comparable to those generated by our previous EM method, but without reliance on manually labeled reference positions.

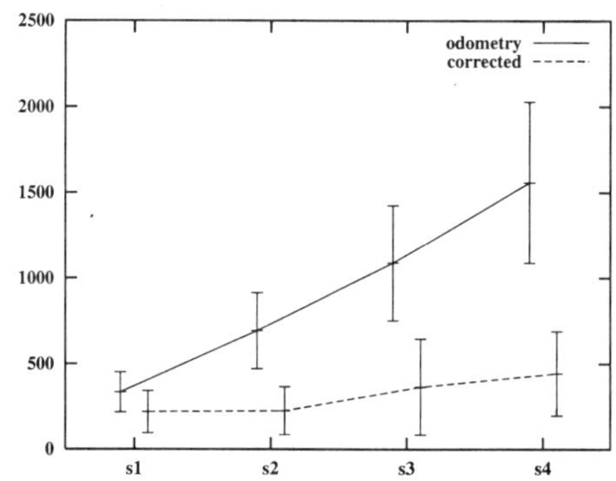

Figure 10: Square error of manually determined reference positions before and after mapping for different levels of random noise added to the odometry data. The error bars represent the 95% confidence interval.

Figure 9 shows similar results for the second environment. Here the robot is asked to map a cyclic environment. Odometric error induces an angular error of approximately 25°. The map shown in Figure 9b is highly accurate, demonstrating that our approach can handle circular environments.

To evaluate our approach quantitatively, we again used a data file which was corrected using a CAD-map of the environment. From this data file we chose several data points and computed the relative distances of the corresponding x-y-locations in the map. We then added noise to the data and applied our mapping system to compute a map. After mapping we measured the deviation of these relative distance from those in the reference map and computed the overall error consisting of the sum of squared differences. Figure 10 shows the average error before (top solid curve) and after (bottom dashed graph) mapping, for different levels of odometric noise. As is to be expected, mapping significantly reduces the error in x-y-space.

These experiments highlight some of the maps we have built over the last months. They are not as large as previously published maps (see e.g., [TFB98, TGF+98]), but they do not rely on high-accuracy laser sensors, and they do not require pre-defined landmarks. The results presented here demonstrate that the basic EM approach can be applied to a much wider array of scenarios than previously suspected.

6 Conclusion

This paper has presented a statistical method for map learning for robots equipped with low-resolution range finders such as sonars. Our approach builds on a previously developed method which uses EM for searching the most likely map. It uses a new two-layered representation of maps during EM. This way, it is able to operate on raw proximity data and does not require any pre-defined landmarks. Maps are learned in two stages: first, small, local maps are learned under the assumption that odometry is locally correct. EM is then applied to integrate these local maps, using Markov localization and the layered representation of maps. To avoid local maxima, a softmax function is applied during the M-step, and deterministic annealing is used to slowly move from density estimation to likelihood maximization. Experimental results demonstrate that our approach is well suited for constructing maps using sensors as inaccurate as sonars, without relying on human assistance.

Acknowledgment

The authors would like to thank Thomas Hofmann and various members of CMU's Robot Learning Lab for useful suggestions and comments.

This research is sponsored in part by NSF (CAREER Award IIS-9876136) and DARPA via TACOM (contract number DAAE07-98-C-L032), and Rome Labs (contract number F30602-98-2-0137), which is gratefully acknowledged. The views and conclusions contained in this document are those of the authors and should not be interpreted as necessarily representing official policies or endorsements, either expressed or implied, of NSF, DARPA, TACOM, Rome Labs, or the United States Government.

References

[BAC+98] W. Burgard, A.B., Cremers, D. Fox, D. Hähnel, G. Lakemeyer, D. Schulz, W. Steiner, and S. Thrun. The interactive museum tour-guide robot. In *Proceedings of the AAAI Fifteenth National Conference on Artificial Intelligence*, 1998.

[BDFC98] W. Burgard, A. Derr, D. Fox, and A.B. Cremers. Integrating global position estimation and position tracking for mobile robots: The dynamic markov localization approach. In *Proceedings of the IEEE/RSJ International Conference on Intelligent Robots and Systems (IROS '98)*, 1998.

[BFHS96] W. Burgard, D. Fox, D. Hennig, and T. Schmidt. Estimating the absolute position of a mobile robot using position probability grids. In *Proceedings of the Thirteenth National Conference on Artificial Intelligence*. AAAI Press/MIT Press, August 1996.

[Cho96] H. Choset. *Sensor Based Motion Planning: The Hierarchical Generalized Voronoi Graph*. PhD thesis, California Institute of Technology, 1996.

[CKK95] E. Chown, S. Kaplan, and D. Kortenkamp. Prototypes, location, and associative networks (plan): Towards a unified theory of cognitive mapping. *Cognitive Science*, 19:1–51, 1995.

[CL85] R. Chatila and J.-P. Laumond. Position referencing and consistent world modeling for mobile robots. In *Proceedings of the 1985 IEEE International Conference on Robotics and Automation*, 1985.

[CW90] I.J. Cox and G.T. Wilfong, editors. *Autonomous Robot Vehicles*. Springer Verlag, 1990.

[DLR77] A.P. Dempster, A.N. Laird, and D.B. Rubin. Maximum likelihood from incomplete data via the em algorithm. *Journal of the Royal Statistical Society, Series B*, 39(1):1–38, 1977.

[Elf87] A. Elfes. Sonar-based real-world mapping and navigation. *IEEE Journal of Robotics and Automation*, RA-3(3):249–265, June 1987.

[Elf89] A. Elfes. *Occupancy Grids: A Probabilistic Framework for Robot Perception and Navigation*. PhD thesis, Department of Electrical and Computer Engineering, Carnegie Mellon University, 1989.

[FBT98] D. Fox, W. Burgard, and S. Thrun. Active markov localization for mobile robots. *Robotics and Autonomous Systems*, 25(3-4):195–207, 1998.

[FBTC98] D. Fox, W. Burgard, S. Thrun, and A.B. Cremers. Position estimation for mobile robots in dynamic environments. In *Proceedings of the AAAI Fifteenth National Conference on Artificial Intelligence*, 1998.

[Fox98] D. Fox. *Markov Localization: A Probabilistic Framework for Mobile Robot Localization and Navigation*. PhD thesis, Dept of Computer Science, Univ. of Bonn, Germany, 1998.

[GBFK98] J.-S. Gutmann, W. Burgard, D. Fox, and K. Konolige. An experimental comparison of localization methods. In *Proceedings of the IEEE/RSJ International Conference on Intelligent Robots and Systems (IROS '98)*, 1998.

[GN97] J.-S. Gutmann and B. Nebel. Navigation mobiler Roboter mit Laserscans. In *Autonome Mobile Systeme*. Springer Verlag, Berlin, 1997. In German.

[HPJ99] T. Hofmann, J. Puzicha, and M. Jordan. Learning from dyadic data. In *Advances in Neural Information Processing Systems 11 (NIPS)*, Cambridge, MA, 1999. MIT Press.

[JM98] H. Jans and Ch. Matenar. Korrektureverfahren zum verbesserten Kartenbau mobiler Roboter. Master's thesis, Dept. of Computer Science, Univ. of Bonn, Germany, 1998. In German.

[KB91] B. Kuipers and Y.-T. Byun. A robot exploration and mapping strategy based on a semantic hierarchy of spatial representations. *Journal of Robotics and Autonomous Systems*, 8:47–63, 1991.

[KBM98] D. Kortenkamp, R.P. Bonasso, and R. Murphy, editors. *AI-based Mobile Robots: Case studies of successful robot systems*, Cambridge, MA, 1998. MIT Press.

[KCK96] L.P. Kaelbling, A.R. Cassandra, and J.A. Kurien. Acting under uncertainty: Discrete bayesian models for mobile-robot navigation. In *Proceedings of the IEEE/RSJ International Conference on Intelligent Robots and Systems*, 1996.

[KS96] S. Koenig and R. Simmons. Passive distance learning for robot navigation. In L. Saitta, editor, *Proceedings of the Thirteenth International Conference on Machine Learning*, 1996.

[LM97] F. Lu and E. Milios. Globally consistent range scan alignment for environment mapping. *Autonomous Robots*, 4:333–349, 1997.

[LM98] F. Lu and E. Milios. Robot pose estimation in unknown environments by matching 2d range scans. *Journal of Intelligent and Robotic Systems*, 1998. to appear.

[Mat90] M. J. Matarić. A distributed model for mobile robot environment-learning and navigation. Master's thesis, MIT, Cambridge, MA, January 1990. also available as MIT AI Lab Tech Report AITR-1228.

[MK97] G.J. McLachlan and T. Krishnan. *The EM Algorithm and Extensions*. Wiley Series in Probability and Statistics, New York, 1997.

[Mor88] H. P. Moravec. Sensor fusion in certainty grids for mobile robots. *AI Magazine*, pages 61–74, Summer 1988.

[Now91] S. J. Nowlan. *Soft competitive adaption: neural network learning based on fitting statistical mixtures*. PhD thesis, Carnegie Mellon University, 1991.

[NPB95] I. Nourbakhsh, R. Powers, and S. Birchfield. DERVISH an office-navigating robot. *AI Magazine*, 16(2):53–60, Summer 1995.

[Ren93] W.D. Rencken. Concurrent localisation and map building for mobile robots using ultrasonic sensors. In *Proceedings of the IEEE/RSJ International Conference on Intelligent Robots and Systems*, pages 2129–2197, Yokohama, Japan, July 1993.

[RJ86] L.R. Rabiner and B.H. Juang. An introduction to hidden markov models. In *IEEE ASSP Magazine*, 1986.

[Ros98] K. Rose. Deterministic annealing for clustering, compression, classification, regression, and related optimization problems. *Proceedings of IEEE*, D, November 1998.

[Sha98] H. Shatkay. *Learning Models for Robot Navigation*. PhD thesis, Computer Science Department, Brown University, Providence, RI, 1998.

[SK95] R. Simmons and S. Koenig. Probabilistic robot navigation in partially observable environments. In *Proceedings of IJCAI-95*, pages 1080–1087, Montreal, Canada, August 1995. IJCAI, Inc.

[SK97] H Shatkay and L. Kaelbling. Learning topological maps with weak local odometric information. In *Proceedings of IJCAI-97*. IJCAI, Inc., 1997.

[TFB98] S. Thrun, D. Fox, and W. Burgard. A probabilistic approach to concurrent mapping and localization for mobile robots. *Machine Learning*, 31:29–53, 1998. also appeared in Autonomous Robots 5, 253–271.

[TGF+98] S. Thrun, J.-S. Gutmann, D. Fox, W. Burgard, and B. Kuipers. Integrating topological and metric maps for mobile robot navigation: A statistical approach. In *Proceedings of the AAAI Fifteenth National Conference on Artificial Intelligence*, 1998.

[Thr98] S. Thrun. Learning metric-topological maps for indoor mobile robot navigation. *Artificial Intelligence*, 99(1):21–71, 1998.

[YLS+98] B. Yamauchi, P. Langley, A.C. Schultz, J. Grefenstette, and W. Adams. Magellan: An integrated adaptive architecture for mobile robots. Technical Report 98-2, Institute for the Study of Learning and Expertise (ISLE), Palo Alto, CA, May 1998.

Hierarchical Models for Screening of Iron Deficiency Anemia

Igor V. Cadez
Dept. of Information
and Computer Science
University of California
Irvine, CA 92697, U.S.A.
icadez@ics.uci.edu

Christine E. McLaren
Division of Epidemiology
Dept. of Medicine
University of California
Irvine, CA 92697, U.S.A.
cmclaren@uci.edu

Padhraic Smyth
Dept. of Information
and Computer Science
University of California
Irvine, CA 92697, U.S.A.
smyth@ics.uci.edu

Geoffrey J. McLachlan
Dept. of Mathematics
University of Queensland
Brisbane, Australia
gjm@maths.uq.edu.au

Abstract

We investigate the problem of classifying individuals based on estimated density functions for each individual. The problem is similar to conventional classification in that there is labelled training data, but different in that the underlying measurements are not feature vectors but histograms or density estimates. We describe a general framework based on probabilistic hierarchical models for modelling such data and illustrate how the model lends itself to classification. We contrast this approach with two other alternatives: (1) directly defining distance between densities using a cross-entropy distance measure, and (2) using parameters of the estimated densities as feature vectors for a standard discriminative classification framework. We evaluate all three methods on a real-world medical diagnosis problem. The hierarchical modeling and density-distance approaches are most accurate, yielding cross-validated error rates in the range of 1 to 2%. We conclude by discussing the relative merits of each approach, including the interpretability of each model from a clinical diagnostic viewpoint.

1 INTRODUCTION AND BACKGROUND

Anemia, a reduction in the circulating red cell mass that may diminish the oxygen-carrying capacity of the blood, is a common medical problem. For diagnostic evaluation of anemia and monitoring the response to therapy, blood samples from patients are routinely analyzed to determine the volume of the red blood cells (RBCs) and the amount of hemoglobin, the oxygen-transporting protein of the red cell. In this context it would be highly cost-effective to have the ability to perform automated low-cost accurate diagnostic screening of blood-related disorders using RBC measurements. Many anemia-related diseases manifest themselves via fundamental changes in the univariate volume (V) distribution and the univariate hemoglobin concentration (HC) of RBCs.

Automated techniques have been recently developed which can simultaneously measure both volume and hemoglobin concentration of RBCs from a patient's blood sample. Flow cytometric blood cell counting instruments (Technicon H*1, H*2, H*3; Bayer Corporation, White Plains, NY) make measurements using a laser light scattering system to provide the red cell volume distribution, hemoglobin concentration, and joint red cell volume and hemoglobin concentration distributions. The data we will describe in this paper was generated by such a machine. Typically it takes in about 40,000 blood cells and produces a plot of both the univariate histogram of the V distribution and univariate HC distribution. In addition, it provides a bivariate histogram (on a grid of about 100×100 cells) of the joint V-HC distribution. Figure 1 shows a two-dimensional histogram of the RBC counts in V-HC space for a healthy individual (control) and for an iron deficient patient. This particular pair of individuals have very similar histograms, making them difficult to discriminate.

Existing diagnostic techniques based on such measurements are largely limited to simple visual examination of such plots and approximate estimates of abnormality based on the skewness or shift of the histogram in various directions in the bivariate space. While this general approach will capture those patients whose dis-

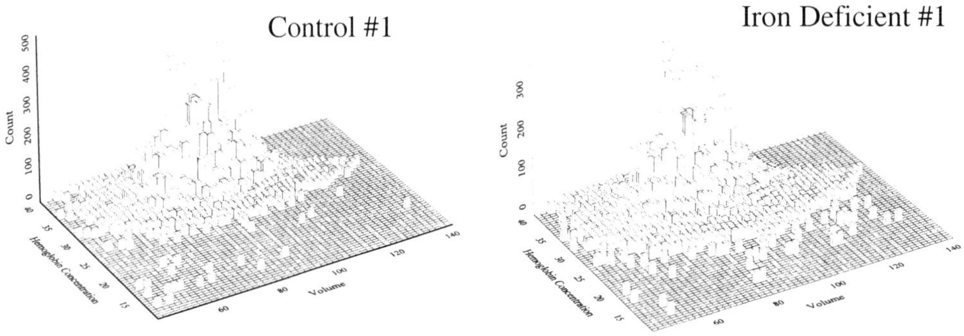

Figure 1: Two-dimensional V-HC histograms of the raw data RBC counts for a Control subject and a subject with Iron Deficient Anemia.

tributions are very clearly far removed from the normal pattern, it is relatively insensitive to more subtle changes and is also likely to be relatively insensitive to differential diagnosis among different diseases.

In this paper we will focus on the problem of learning a classification model from the data for the purposes of automated diagnostic screening in a clinical environment. We will concentrate on discrimination between two classes: healthy individuals and individuals with iron defiency anemia. Section 2 will discuss the learning aspects of the problem in general and make connections with relevant prior work. In Section 3 we introduce the notion of a probabilistic hierarchical model for this problem. This is a general framework for modeling data sets where there are multiple levels of variation in the data (here we have variation at the individual subject level as well as at the RBC level). We will show that with relatively large amounts of data at the lowest level of the hierarchy (as we have here, with 40,000 RBCs in two-dimensions per subject), that there exists a relatively efficient closed form approximation to the full Bayesian solution. In Section 4 we outline how the Expectation-Maximization (EM) algorithm is used to learn densities from the binned and truncated data. Section 5 discusses two alternative methods for classification: (1) a distance-based approach to classification based on pairwise directed divergence between two densities, and (2) a standard discriminative framework using a classification tree. In Section 6 we compare the empirical classification performance (using cross-validation) of the hierarchical approach with the afore-mentioned alternatives. Section 7 contains a discussion of the merits of the different approaches, including suggestions on how this framework, focusing in particular on the interpretability of the learned models.

In terms of related prior work McCallum et al (1998) and Heskes (1998) used hierarchical models to improve classification and regression performance, but in the more standard manner of using feature vectors rather than densities. Hierarchical models are also widely used throughout applied statistics (e.g., see Gelman et al (1995) for a Bayesian perspective). However, we are not aware of any published work in the machine learning, pattern recognition, or statistics literature on using hierarchical models specifically for classifying density functions; in this context, the contribution here is novel. In the context of screening for iron deficiency using RBCs, McLaren and colleagues in a series of papers (McLaren, Brittenham, & Hasselblad, 1986; McLaren et al., 1991; McLaren, 1996) have demonstrated that the distribution of RBC volume can be accurately modeled as a mixture of log-normal density functions. In this paper we extend this work to bivariate V-HC measurements, explicitly model the data-generating process via a hierarchical model, and evaluate the methodology in terms of classification accuracy via cross-validation.

2 A MACHINE LEARNING DESCRIPTION OF THE PROBLEM

Consider a slightly more general description of the problem described above. We have N individuals and each individual belongs to one and only one of K groups, $\{c_1, \ldots, c_K\}$. For each individual i, $1 \leq i \leq N$, in turn we have measurements on a set of n_i "lower-level objects" from that individual (for the RBC problem these lower-level objects are the individual red blood cells). Each of the lower-level objects is itself characterized by a feature-vector (for each patient we have a set of 2-dimensional counts, coming from the the RBCs analyzed by the machine). This type of multi-level structure is not unique to the RBC problem, there are numerous instances of similar scenarios which arise in many practical learning applications, e.g., identifying an individual based on multiple facial images; based on multiple spoken words; based on multiple passages of text written by the individual, and so forth.

This type of data presents two general problems in a learning context:

1. What is an appropriate classification procedure or model for assigning a new individual (described in terms of their RBC measurements) to one of the K classes?, i.e., what should be the structure of a model which relates the multiple RBC measurements to the class labels?

2. Having defined the general structure, how can we learn such a model from data?

One simple approach is to reduce the multiple measurements for each individual to a standard feature vector of fixed dimensionality. For example, we could take the mean of the V and HC measurements across all 40,000 of an individual's RBCs (or perhaps the variance, or both, or some other summary statistics). However, we don't know in advance whether these features will be discriminative or not and so this approach has somewhat of an ad hoc flavor to it.

A powerful idea in this context is the notion of a *generative probabilistic model* for the data. A generative model is a model which in a sense can "generate" or "simulate" the observed data from each class, compared to a discriminative model which need only characterize the differences between classes. A generative model is particularly relevant in the clinical context of

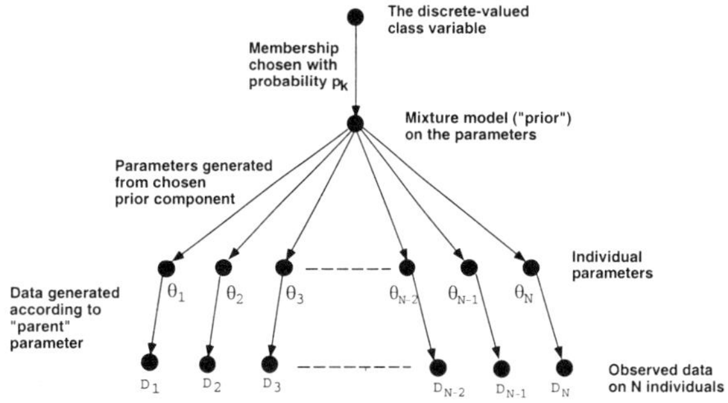

Figure 2: A graphical depiction of the hierarchical model for RBC generation.

the RBC problem, where the natural mode of presenting the data to a physician is in the form of a joint distribution. In other words it is the language of joint distributions which forms the existing basis for characterization and description of blood-related diseases given the V and HC measurements.

Let $f(V, HC|\theta_i)$ be the probability density function for the joint variation of V and HC where θ_i is the set of parameters for the model f. Based on prior knowledge of the physical mechanisms of RBC generation and evolution, the functional form of f can be well-determined as being a mixture of log-normal density functions; we will return to this point in Section 4. Thus, assuming the form of f is known, it remains to estimate the parameters θ_i for individual i. We can use standard density estimation techniques (such as EM, e.g., McLachlan and Krishnan, 1997) for this density estimation problem.

Thus, we can reduce the problem of learning from multiple measurements to that of learning from densities, since the density function in principle accurately describes all of the information contained in the original sample. At this point it is not clear yet what we have gained, since it is still not obvious how to model and classify individuals given their density functions, i.e., we are still not in the realm of more familiar classification modeling. In the next section we outline how the hierarchical modeling framework naturally and elegantly will allow us to model both similarities and differences among individuals based on their density functions.

3 HIERARCHICAL MODELS FOR CLASSIFYING DENSITY FUNCTIONS

3.1 A GENERATIVE HIERARCHICAL MODEL

Consider the following generative model for red blood cell (RBC) production for individuals:

1. Choose an individual randomly from the overall population, call this individual i.

2. Assign this individual i to class c_k with probability p_k, $1 \leq k \leq K$, (for the RBC problem we have two classes, $K = 2$, Controls and Iron Deficient).

3. Choose parameters θ_i for individual i using a prior density function $\pi_k(\theta_i)$ on parameters for class k (thus, each class has a density function π_k describing the variation in *parameters* for that class). In general terms, the parameters describing the mixture distributions will be the mixing proportions, means, variances, and covariances for each class.

4. Generate observations (data) D_i for this individual (namely, n_i multivariate measurements, such as V-HC measurements on the individual's red blood cells), conditioned on the parameters θ_i, i.e., we have a data-generating model $p(D_i|\theta_i)$.

Figure 2 summarizes the overall framework graphically. In fact, from a probabilistic viewpoint this is a formal graphical model for the problem and we can read off the relevant conditional independence relations. For example, the data set D_i for any individual i is independent of all other data sets conditioned on the parameters θ_i which generated data D_i. The hierarchical model is quite plausible as a generative mechanism for the RBC data. Homogeneity within a class (Control or Normal) is captured by the assumption that the *parameters* of the density functions for individuals belonging to that class (namely the θ_i's) are themselves parametrized by a common class density function. It is in this parameter space that we will perform classification: if there is relatively little overlap between the different class densities in parameter space, then accurate classification should be possible.

Figure 3 illustrates the general concept of how we model variability in parameter space. Here we have fitted each individual at the RBC level with a two-component mixture density function (full details in

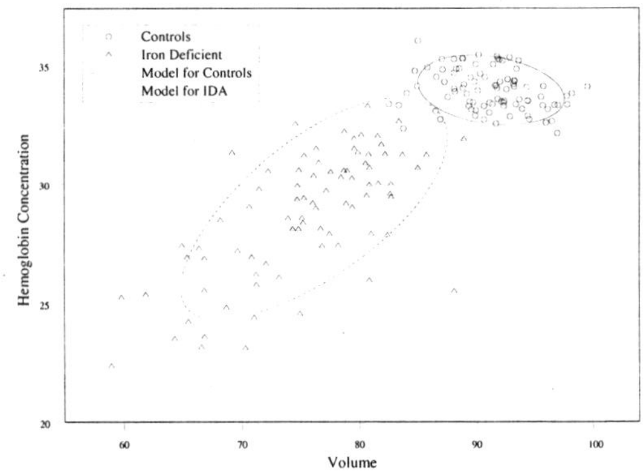

Figure 3: Scatter plot of the estimated mean parameters for individuals from the Iron Deficient and Control groups, with Gaussian "parameter variation models" superposed.

Section 4). Figure 3 is a scatter plot of the location of the estimated two-dimensional V-HC bivariate mean for the larger (in probability mass) of the two components in the fitted density function for each individual. The Controls and the Iron Deficient individuals are given different symbols. Furthermore, we have fit a Gaussian model to the parameters of each class (the covariance ellipses of these components are shown); these correspond to the "prior" density functions $\pi_k(\theta)$ on the parameters for class c_k.

3.2 INTERPRETATION OF THE MODEL

This type of hierarchical model setup is common in Bayesian statistics. In the Bayesian framework, the densities $\pi_k(\theta)$ on parameters are (naturally) referred to as priors. In fact in a full Bayesian analysis we would put another level of priors in the model, but as we shall see this is not necessary for accurate classification of the RBC data.

For our problem, since we have K different classes, the "marginal prior" on parameters is a mixture model of the form:

$$\pi(\theta|\phi) = \sum_{k=1}^{K} p(c_k)\pi_k(\theta|\phi_k) \tag{1}$$

where the $p(c_k)$ are the prior probabilities on each class ($\sum_k p(c_k) = 1$), and the $\pi_k(\theta|\phi_k)$ are "component priors" on the parameters θ in a class k and θ here is a parameter *vector*. For example, if we have univariate measurements at the RBC level which we wish to model by a Gaussian density function for each individual, then we would have $\theta = \{\mu, \sigma\}$. π_k would then be a bivariate density function on μ and σ representing the way μ and σ vary within class k. Let ϕ represent the overall set parameters which describe the prior on θ, and let ϕ_k be the parameters for component k of the prior. This appears to be quite a reasonable and parsimonious description of a generative mechanism for the data. For example, in Figure 3, we can see both systematic within- and between-class variability for the means (the μ's).

We note in passing that this mixture-based hierarchical model has broad applicability in machine learning beyond the specific medical diagnosis problem presented here. For example, in Cadez and Smyth (1999) it is shown how this model provides a general framework for probabilistic clustering of individuals based on sequence and trajectory data.

3.3 LEARNING THE PRIOR PARAMETERS Φ FROM LABELED DATA

Given a set of RBC measurements from N individuals, denote the data by $D = \{D_1, \ldots, D_N\}$, where D_i is the set of measurements on blood cells for the ith individual, $1 \leq i \leq N$. Conditioned on the parameters, and given the hierarchical graphical model of Figure 2, the likelihood of the data can be written as:

$$p(D|\theta_1, \ldots, \theta_N, \phi) = \prod_{i=1}^{N} p(D_i|\theta_i). \tag{2}$$

If we don't know the parameters θ_i (as will be the case in practice), we get the *marginal likelihood* as a function of the priors ϕ:

$$L(\phi) = p(D_i|\phi) = \int_{\theta} p(D_i|\theta_i)\pi(\theta_i|\phi)d\theta_i \tag{3}$$

Given that we have fairly large numbers of blood cells and are fitting a relatively parsimonious bivariate model to their distribution, it seems reasonable to assume that the integral above will be peaked around $\hat{\theta}$ where θ is the maximum a posteriori (MAP) value relative to the prior $p(\theta_i|\phi)$. (If we further assume that this prior is relatively flat in this part of parameter space, then the MAP and maximum likelihood values will be very close). We will simply denote the value around which the integral is peaked as $\hat{\theta}$.

Furthermore, assume that our data are labelled, i.e., we know which of the K classes each individual belongs to. The generalization to unlabelled, or partially labeled data is straightforward and useful (Cadez and Smyth, 1999), but is not discussed in this paper. Thus, we can focus on estimating ϕ_k, the parameters describing θ conditioned on membership in class k. For simplicity of notation let us assume temporarily that we only have data from class k, and that $D = \{D_1, \ldots, D_N\}$ is the data for the kth class of individuals. Let $\hat{\theta}_i$ be the estimated density parameters for the ith individual in this class, $1 \leq i \leq N$. We have that

$$\begin{aligned}
\arg\max_{\phi_k} p(\phi_k|D) &= \arg\max_{\phi_k} p(D|\phi_k)p(\phi_k) \\
&= \arg\max_{\phi_k} \left(\prod_{i=1}^{N} p(D_i|\phi_k) \right) p(\phi_k) \\
&= \arg\max_{\phi_k} \left(\prod_{i=1}^{N} \int_{\theta_i} p(D_i|\theta_i)\pi_k(\theta_i|\phi_k)d\theta_i \right) p(\phi_k) \\
&\approx \arg\max_{\phi_k} \left(\prod_{i=1}^{N} p(D_i|\hat{\theta}_i)\pi_k(\hat{\theta}_i|\phi_k) \right) p(\phi_k) \\
&= \arg\max_{\phi_k} \left(\prod_{i=1}^{N} \pi_k(\hat{\theta}_i|\phi_k) \right) p(\phi_k).
\end{aligned} \tag{4}$$

This equation is simply a likelihood times a prior, under a conditional independence assumption for the data given the model. In other words, to find the MAP value for ϕ, we can just first find the $\hat{\theta}$'s for each individual, and then find the ϕ_k's which maximize the MAP expression above, given a parametric density model for $\pi_k(\theta|\phi_k)$. If the prior $p(\phi_k)$ is relatively flat, it reduces to maximum likelihood estimation of the ϕ_k parameters based on the $\hat{\theta}_i$ "observations," $1 \leq i \leq N$.

For the RBC data, we will be fitting 2-component bivariate log-normal mixtures to the original measurements: this will result in roughly 2 means and 3 covariance parameters per component, for a total of $2(2 + 3) + 1 = 11$ independent parameters in total, i.e., each $\hat{\theta}_i$ will be an 11-dimensional vector. Details on how these parameters are fit at the individual level will be provided in Section 4.

3.4 CLASSIFICATION GIVEN THE FITTED MODEL

Assume that we have estimated all the parameters of the hierarchical model as described above. Now consider a new individual for whom we have RBC measurements, say D_{N+1}. We would like to know the class probabilities for this individual:

$$p(c_k|D_{N+1}) \propto p(D_{N+1}|c_k)p(c_k)$$

$$= \left(\int p(D_{N+1}|\theta_{N+1}) \pi_k(\theta_{N+1}|c_k) d\theta_{N+1} \right) p(c_k)$$
$$\propto p(D_{N+1}|\hat{\theta}_{N+1}) \pi_k(\hat{\theta}_{N+1}|c_k) p(c_k)$$
$$\propto \pi_k(\hat{\theta}_{N+1}|c_k) p(c_k). \quad (5)$$

Thus, based again on the MAP approximation, the posterior class probabilities have a very simple intuitive form: find the parameters $\hat{\theta}_{N+1}$ to fit the RBC data for the unclassified individual, and use Bayes' rule to classify these parameters relative to the prior $\pi_k(\theta|\phi_k)$ (in the equation above, $\pi_k(\theta|c_k)$ is the same as $\pi_k(\theta|\phi_k)$).

Thus, we have arrived at a method for performing probabilistic classification given the hierarchical model, as well as determining how that model can be learned from labelled data. To summarize, the procedure is as follows:

Training: For each class k, $1 \leq k \leq K$:

1. Estimate density function parameters $\hat{\theta}_i$ for each individual i labelled as class k,
2. Estimate the parameters ϕ_k of the "prior component" $\pi_k(\theta|\phi_k)$ using the estimated θ_i's,
3. Estimate the mixture weights in the prior, $p(c_k)$ (e.g., simply as the proportion of individuals belonging to class k).

Classification: For a new unlabelled individual, with observed data D_{N+1}:

1. Estimate the density parameters $\hat{\theta}_{N+1}$ for this individual
2. Find the maximum (over k) of $p(c_k|D_{N+1})$ as described in Equation 5.

4 DENSITY MODELING AT THE RBC LEVEL

4.1 THE FUNCTIONAL FORM OF THE RBC DENSITY MODEL

The first step in modeling the data is to characterize the two-dimensional V-HC distribution. It can be shown that the marginal volume distribution of a single population of RBC is theoretically lognormal. The lognormality comes from the biological mechanism governing the manner by which cells are produced (McLaren, Brittenham, and Hasselblad; 1986). At each "production step" cells divide and have normal variations in their respective volumes. Since the process is repetitive and the effect is multiplicative (i.e., cells divide), the resulting distribution is lognormal. For iron-deficient subjects, the argument follows that the RBC density can be well-approximated as a two-component log-normal mixture (McLaren, et al. , 1991; McLaren, 1996). Specifically, there are two biological processes that are constantly occurring in a body: 1) red blood cells are produced in the bone marrow; 2) these cells are extruded into the bloodstream and die after about 120 days. For a healthy individual a single population of red blood cells is produced with a mean cell volume and mean hemoglobin concentration within the normal range. In iron deficiency anemia the red blood cells that are produced have decreased volume and hemoglobin, below normal for that of a healthy individual. Thus with development of the disease, gradually, a second subpopulation of red blood cells begins to emerge and over a period of time, the relative ratio of subpopulations of red cells changes. We model both subpopulations using full unconstrained covariance matrices.

4.2 IMPLEMENTATION OF MIXTURE MODELING OF RBC COUNT DATA

The actual values of volumes and hemoglobin concentrations are not observed for each blood cell since they are quantized. In addition, the counts outside the measurable range are also missing. Estimation from binned and truncated data has been studied in McLachlan and Jones (1988) and McLachlan and Jones (1990) in connection with fitting univariate volume distributions of RBCs. The theoretical results in the cited papers only handle the one-dimensional case. The extension to multiple dimensions is relatively straightforward but care must be taken with numerical implementation (see Cadez et al, 1999 for details). The workhorse of the fitting procedure is the EM algorithm (McLachlan and Krishnan, 1997). For this problem the M-step does not have a closed-form solution as is the case when fitting mixture models to non-binned data. The main quantities that need to be evaluated at each EM step are now integrals over the bins (McLachlan and Jones, 1988).

Extending the McLachlan and Jones (1990) procedure to the bivariate case directly leads to a rather slow EM algorithm In the results presented here we used a heuristic initialization method which resulted in reducing the computation time for EM by about a factor of 100 (see Cadez et al, 1999, for more details). A sub-sample of data points (3000 in the results here) are drawn from the histogram counts assuming a uniform distribution in each bin. This uniform assump-

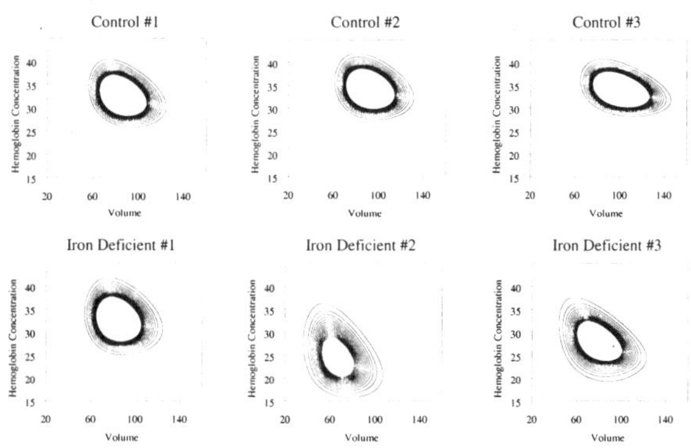

Figure 4: Contour plots from estimated density estimates for three typical Control patients and three typical Iron Deficient Anemia patients. The lowest 10% of the probability contours are plotted to emphasize the systematic difference between the two groups.

tion is clearly incorrect since the true densities will be smoothly varying in practice, however, the assumption is fine as a rough guess for initialization. EM is then run to convergence on the simulated sample. The resulting density is then used as a starting point for the version of EM which uses all of the binned/truncated data and performs numerical integration over each bin during each EM step. This reduces the number of iterations of the full EM algorithm drastically while not affecting the accuracy of the solution as the convergence criterion is defined by the full (but slow) algorithm. It is guaranteed to return a local maximum of the likelihood function for binned and truncated data. The process is repeated 10 times with different randomly chosen subsamples to avoid poor local maxima.

Figure 4 shows the densities which were fit to the histogram data by applying this EM mixture modeling procedure to 3 individuals from each class, in terms of the lower 10 percent probability contours of the estimated mixture density One can see that there are differences between the two classes, as well as specific within-class variation.

5 ALTERNATIVE CLASSIFICATION TECHNIQUES

We compared three qualitatively different approaches to classifying RBC data:

- The generative hierarchical modeling approach (described earlier),

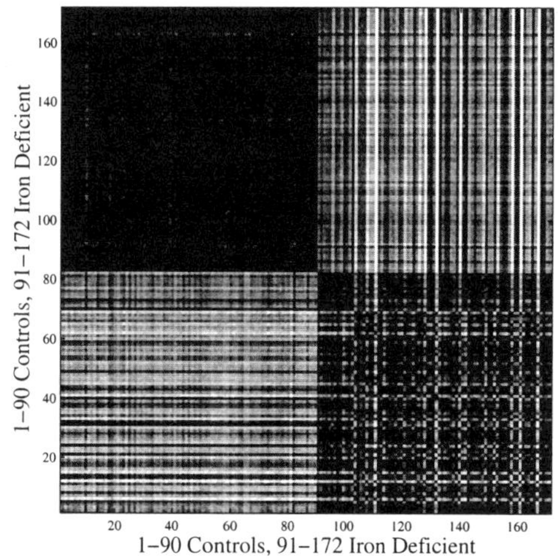

Figure 5: Matrix of Kullback-Leibler divergence scores for the fitted RBC density models.

- A non-parametric approach based on density distance and multidimensional scaling (MDS), described in Section 5.1, and,
- Discriminative classification using the C5.0 and CART classification tree algorithms (Quinlan, 1997; Breiman et al (1984)), described in Section 5.2.

5.1 DENSITY DISTANCE USING K-L DIVERGENCE AND MULTIDIMENSIONAL SCALING (MDS)

The idea here is to define a distance measure directly between the *densities* themselves, and to completely avoid modelling parameters in parameter-space. A well-known distance measure between two densities is the Kullback-Leibler (K-L) distance, defined as the cross-entropy $\int p(\theta) \log \frac{p(\theta)}{q(\theta)} d\theta$. This is not a metric, but is strictly positive unless $p = q$ everywhere. It can be made symmetric by defining the *K-L divergence* as

$$\mathrm{D}(p, q) = \frac{1}{2} \left(\int p(\theta) \log \frac{p(\theta)}{q(\theta)} d\theta + \int q(\theta) \log \frac{q(\theta)}{p(\theta)} d\theta \right) \quad (6)$$

The K-L divergence provides a well-defined notion of density distance. For a subset of the Control and Iron Deficient individuals for whom we have RBC data, we fitted densities to each as described in Section 4 and calculated the pairwise K-L divergence between each pair of individuals. The resulting distance matrix is shown in Figure 5. The separation of the two groups is

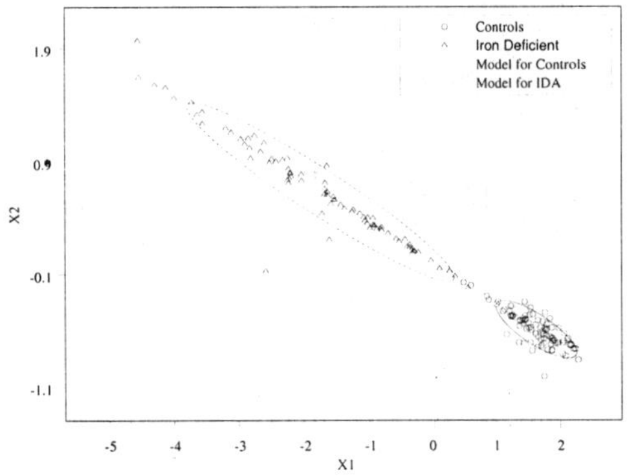

Figure 6: Kullback-Leibler matrix of pairwise density distance scores embedded in a two-dimensional vector space using the MDS technique with fitted Gaussian covariance ellipses for each class.

very clear from the block-diagonal structure of the matrix (darker pixels in the image correspond to smaller K-L values, i.e., the densities are more similar). Furthermore, there appears to be a systematic difference in the two groups in that the Controls (the upper left block) is much more homogeneous (in terms of density distances) than the Iron Deficient group (lower right block) which has greater variability in terms of pairwise distances (i.e., there is greater spread among the densities). This is consistent with Figure 3 where the spread in *component means* is lower for Controls than for Iron Deficient subjects.

The K-L matrix is useful for exploratory analysis but does not easily lend itself to classification in the standard manner. To define a classifier using this data we use multidimensional scaling (MDS) to approximate the distance matrix in a vector space (Borg and Groenen, 1997). MDS places each individual (a row or column from the matrix) in a d-dimensional space such that the pairwise matrix distances between points are preserved as closely as possible in the Euclidean vector space. Based on analysis of the fit versus dimensionality, we determined that the best number of dimensions for MDS for this data was 2. The resulting MDS-derived vector space, showing the individuals positioned to reflect as closely as possible their KL divergences, is shown in Figure 6.

With MDS as a tool to embed RBC densities into a vector space with a well defined notion of "distance." We then use a Gaussian mixture-model classifier in this vector space to classify the "points" (representing individuals) in this space.

5.2 DISCRIMINATIVE CLASSIFICATION

We also consider a standard discriminative classifier to classify the fixed-length parameter vectors obtained from the density modeling of Section 4. We chose classification trees as a typical method for discriminative classification using the C5.0 and CART algorithms. The decision tree approach is the most direct approach of the three methods for classification and has the advantage of being relatively interpretable from a clinical viewpoint.

We also use the discriminative approach on "ad hoc" features estimated directly from the histogram, Thus, no attempt is made to model the density of the RBCs but instead an individual's histogram is summarized by a vector of 4 simple features, namely, the univariate mean and standard deviation for each of V and HC, as estimated from the histogram. The tree algorithm is then used to learn a classification model in this 4-dimensional space. This approach has the advantage of being considerably simpler than any of the aforementioned classification methods and we will refer to it as the Baseline method in the rest of the paper.

6 EXPERIMENTAL METHODOLOGY AND RESULTS

6.1 EXPERIMENTAL METHODS FOR COMPARING CLASSIFIERS

Data collection for this study was completed during 1995. A reference sample group of healthy individuals was recruited from staff physicians and hospital employees at the Western Infirmary, Glasgow, Scotland. Patients included in the study were seen on the wards and in the outpatient clinics and referred to the hospital laboratories for a complete blood count. The results described here are based on the 90 Control and 82 Iron Deficient subjects in the study.

Each of the three methods begins with the EM estimates of the parameters $\hat{\theta}_i$ for each individual i, $1 \leq i \leq N$. These estimates are obtained by fitting a two-component log-normal mixture density using EM as described in Section 4. Each set of parameters $\hat{\theta}_i$ has an associated class label (Control or Iron Deficient) for individual i.

For each of the three methods we performed 100 cross-validation runs, where in each run the data were divided into a randomly chosen training set of 80% of the data and a test set consisting of the remaining 20%. Overall performance for each method is reported as the mean and standard deviation of classification accuracy on the test sets over the 100 runs. Note that the parameter estimation (the running of EM to determine the $\hat{\theta}_i$'s) is completely independent of any other data or class labels; it is a purely unsupervised procedure performed on each individual's RBC measurements.

The hierarchical model takes the 11-dimensional parameters and constructs two density models for the parameters, one for Controls and one for Iron Deficient. We experimented with two different density models for the parameters:

1. **"11-Parameters":** here we modeled all of the parameters with a Gaussian mixture model, and used block covariance matrices which allowed covariance between all 4 means and between the 3 independent covariance parameters for each RBC component.

2. **"9-Parameters":** here we re-parametrized some of the parameters to reflect a more natural scale for modeling. We modeled both the log-odds of the component weights and the log of the eigenvalues of the covariance matrices as Gaussian. We again used a two-component Gaussian mixture model with block diagonal covariance matrix allowing covariance between the 4 means, covariance between the 2 log-eigenvalues for each RBC component, and allowing the log-odds of the weight to be independent of the other parameters.

On the training data, for each cross-validation run, we performed a further "internal" cross-validation run to automatically determine whether a single Gaussian or a 2-component Gaussian mixture provides the best fit (using 20 runs of cross-validated likelihood), i.e., each $\pi_k(\theta)$ is itself modeled as either a 1 or 2-component Gaussian mixture. The motivation for this last internal cross-validation is to allow the model to automatically choose a reasonable structure for the "prior" in parameter space.

For the KL-divergence/MDS method, we project the training data as before using the KL/MDS technique described earlier and then use an internal cross-validation strategy (similar to that described above) to build a Gaussian mixture model for each class in the MDS space, using the training data. Classification is then performed on the projected test data points using this Gaussian mixture model.

6.2 EXPERIMENTAL RESULTS

Table 1 summarizes the mean cross-validated error rates and standard errors across the different methods. The discriminative algorithms (C5.0 and CART) were run on the 11 original parameters, the 9 rescaled parameters, and the 4 "Baseline" features. For both trees, the lowest error rate was obtained with the histogram-based Baseline features, followed by the 9 rescaled parameters, and then the 11 original parameters. The KL-MDS method and the Hierarchical method (with either 9 or 11 features) had lower error rates than any of the discriminative tree methods (usually on the order of a factor of 2 lower). The 11-parameter hierarchical error rate of 1.65% corresponds to about a 65% decrease in error rate from the error rate of 4.65% of CART on the same features and about a 54% decrease in error rate from the 3.62% error rate of C5.0 on the same 11 features. Thus, for this particular problem, the hierarchical model and the KL-MDS method appear superior in terms of classification accuracy.

For routine clinical classification of RBC data, the decision tree approaches are attractive since the operation of the classifier can be explained in simple "rule-like" terms to a clinician. However, if clinicians wished to rank subjects based on likelihood of iron deficiency (for example), the hierarchical model approach may be the most useful given its probabilistic basis. In addition, the hierarchical model is intrinsically interesting from a medical research viewpoint. It provides a basis for a complete characterization of blood disorders in H-VC space both in terms of typicality and variability of individuals within each group, as well as full characterization of group differences.

7 CONCLUSIONS

We investigated the problem of automated screening of blood samples of individuals for the purpose of detecting iron deficiency anemia. The problem is more complex than the typical machine learning classification problem since each individual must be classified based on a bivariate histogram (rather than a feature vector). Three different techniques for classifying the individual densities were proposed: (1) a probabilistic hierarchical model, (2) embedding pairwise KL distances between densities in a vector space, and (3) direct discrimination of density or histogram parameters using a classification tree. All methods were accurate in the 96 to 99% range in the cross-validation experiments, with density-based methods outperform-

Table 1: Means and standard deviations of the cross-validated classification error for each of the different classification models across 100 runs.

Method	Features	Mean Error Rate (%)	Standard Deviation
C5.0	Baseline	3.32	2.92
	9-Parameters	3.53	2.87
	11-Parameters	3.62	2.92
CART	Baseline	3.47	3.17
	9-Parameters	4.09	3.34
	11-Parameters	4.65	3.43
KL-MDS		1.97	2.05
Hierarchical	9-Parameters	1.90	1.94
	11-Parameters	1.65	2.06

ing simpler discriminative methods. We conclude that accurate low-cost automated screening of subjects for iron deficiency, using V-HC count data, appears quite feasible.

Acknowledgments

The contribution of CMcL to this paper has been supported in part by grants from the National Institutes of Health (R43-HL46037 and R15-HL48349) and a Wellcome Research Travel Grant awarded by the Burroughs Wellcome Fund. The contributions of IC and PS have been supported in part by the National Science Foundation under Grant IRI-9703120. We thank Thomas H. Cavanagh for providing laboratory facilities. We are grateful to Dr. Albert Greenbaum for technical assistance.

References

Breiman, L., Friedman, J., Olshen, R. A., and Stone, C. J. (1984) *Classification and Regression Trees*, Belmont, CA: Wadsworth Press.

Borg, I. and Groenen, P. (1997) *Modern Multidimensional Scaling: Theory and Application*, New York: Springer.

Cadez, I., Smyth, P., McLachlan, G. J., McLaren, C. E. (1999) 'Maximum likelihood estimation of mixture densities for binned and truncated multivariate data,' Technical Report 99-13, Information and Computer Science, UC Irvine, March 1999.

Cadez, I., Smyth, P. (1999) 'Probabilistic clustering using hierarchical models,' Technical Report 99-16, Information and Computer Science, UC Irvine, March 1999.

Gelman, A., Carlin, J., Stern., H., and Rubin, D.B. (1995) *Bayesian Data Analysis*, New York: Chapman and Hall.

Heskes, T. (1998), 'Solving a huge number of similar tasks: a combination of multi-task learning and hierarchical Bayesian modeling,' in *Machine Learning, Proceedings of the Fifteenth International Conference (ICML'98)*, J. Shavlik (ed.), San Francisco: Morgan Kaufmann, 233-241.

Jones, P. N., McLachlan, G. J. (1990) 'Maximum Likelihood Estimation from Grouped and Truncated Data with Finite Normal Mixture Models,' *Applied Statistics-Journal of the Royal Statistical Society Series C*, 39(N2):273-282.

McCallum, A., Rosenfeld, R., Mitchell, T., Ng A.Y. (1998) 'Improving text classification by shrinkage in a hierarchy of classes,' in *Machine Learning, Proceedings of the Fifteenth International Conference (ICML'98)*, J. Shavlik (ed.), San Francisco: Morgan Kaufmann.

McLachlan, G. J. and Jones, P. N. (1988) 'Fitting mixture models to grouped and truncated data via the EM algorithm,' *Biometrics*, 44(2):571-8.

McLachlan, G. J., and Krishnan, T. (1997) *The EM Algorithm and Extensions*, New York: John Wiley and Sons.

McLaren, C. E., Brittenham, G. M., Hasselblad, V. (1986) 'Analysis of the volume of red blood cells: application of the expectation-maximization algorithm to grouped data from the doubly-truncated lognormal distribution,' *Biometrics*, 42(1):143-58.

McLaren, C. E. (1996) 'Mixture models in haematology: a series of case studies,' *Statistical Methods in Medical Research*, 5(2):129-53.

McLaren, C. E., Wagstaff, M., Brittenham, G. M., Jacobs, A. (1991) 'Detection of Two-Component Mixtures of Lognormal Distributions in Grouped, Doubly Truncated Data: Analysis of Red Blood Cell Volume Distributions,' *Biometrics*, 47(2):607-22.

Quinlan, J. R. (1997) 'Using C5.0: An Informal Tutorial,' Sydney, Australia: Rulequest Research.

Combining Error-Driven Pruning and Classification for Partial Parsing

Claire Cardie, Scott Mardis, and David Pierce
Department of Computer Science
Cornell University
Ithaca, NY 14853
cardie, mardis, pierce@cs.cornell.edu

Abstract

We present a new approach to partial parsing of natural language texts that relies on machine learning methods. The approach combines corpus-based grammar induction with a very simple pattern-matching algorithm and an optional constituent verification step. The grammar induction algorithm acquires a set of rules for each level of linguistic analysis using a new technique for error-driven pruning of treebank grammars. The constituent verification step employs standard inductive learning techniques as an additional precision-enhancing device. We evaluate the approach on four partial parsing data sets and find that performance is very good (over 93% precision and recall) for applications that require or prefer fairly simple constituent bracketing. As the complexity of the partial parsing task increases, however, our approach lags the performance of competing approaches. We explain these differences in terms of the knowledge sources employed by each method and describe a number of features that make the approach attractive for large-scale, practical NLP applications.

1 Introduction

Partial natural language parsers provide a shallow analysis of the syntactic relationships that exist in a sentence. Figure 1, for example, compares one possible partial parse of a sentence with its full syntactic analysis as provided in the Penn Treebank Wall Street Journal (WSJ) corpus (Marcus *et al.*, 1993). Partial parsers produce a fairly flat parse tree in comparison to their full-parse counterparts, omitting some levels of linguistic analysis or leaving them for subsequent modules of the natural language processing (NLP) system. Nevertheless, the linguistic relationships that can be identified by partial parsers are rich enough to support a number of large-scale natural language processing applications including information extraction, phrase identification in information retrieval, named entity identification, and a variety of text-mining operations. In addition, partial parsers are typically very fast when compared to full parsers.

Many shallow parsers (e.g. Abney (1996), Hobbs *et al.* (1997)) rely on finite-state pattern-matching techniques to recognize all syntactic and semantic entities in a sentence (Roche and Schabes, 1997b). Parsing proceeds in stages: Each stage can be viewed as a finite-state transducer that regroups or relabels the tokens or constituents produced in preceding levels. The initial stages perform relatively simple tasks including tokenization, part-of-speech tagging, and simple noun phrase identification; all linguistic relationships that require higher-level attachment decisions are identified in subsequent stages and rely on output from earlier levels.

The patterns, or grammars, that drive each stage of processing traditionally have been designed manually (e.g. Voutilainen (1993), Bourigault (1992)). Also, it has been difficult to directly compare partial parsing techniques since most were evaluated by hand on a small test set. Recent work, however, has attempted the automatic acquisition of partial parsers and their evaluation on a large test corpus annotated with correct parses by an impartial third party. Ramshaw and Marcus (1998), for example, applied transformation-based learning (Brill, 1995) to the problem of noun phrase chunking, a basic step for most partial parsers.

Full parse:

```
(S  (NP-SBJ South Korea)
    (VP registered
        (NP (NP a trade deficit) (PP of (NP $101 billion)))
        (PP-TMP in (NP October)) ,
        (S-ADV (VP reflecting (NP (NP the country) 's economic sluggishness)))) .)
```

Partial parse:

$[_{\text{Subject}}$ $[_{\text{NP}}$ South Korea]] $[_{\text{V}}$ registered] $[_{\text{Object}}$ $[_{\text{NP}}$ a trade deficit]] of $[_{\text{NP}}$ \$101 billion] in $[_{\text{NP}}$ October], $[_{\text{V}}$ reflecting] $[_{\text{NP}}$ the country]'s $[_{\text{Object}}$ $[_{\text{NP}}$ economic sluggishness]].

Figure 1: Comparison of a Full vs. a Partial Syntactic Parse for the Sentence: *South Korea registered a trade deficit of \$101 billion in October, reflecting the country's economic sluggishness.* The partial parse marks the subject, verb, direct object, and noun phrase information only.

Their noun phrase bracketer learns a set of transformation rules. Each transformation updates the noun phrase bracketings associated with a single word based on local features, such as neighboring words, part-of-speech tags, and bracket boundaries. To identify base noun phrases in a novel text, the learned transformations are applied, in order, across the entire document. Argamon *et al.* (1998) developed a variation of memory-based learning (Stanfill and Waltz, 1986) for two partial parsing tasks — base noun phrase identification and verb-object recognition. During training, their MBSL algorithm saves the entire raw training corpus, which has been annotated with parts of speech, and noun phrase and verb-object brackets. Generalization of the implicit partial parsing rules in the training corpus occurs at application time — MBSL searches the novel text for tag sequences or combinations of tag subsequences (tiles) that occurred during training in a similar context.

This paper presents a new approach to partial parsing that relies on machine learning methods. The approach is implemented in a shallow parser called Empire[1] that combines corpus-based grammar induction with a very simple pattern-matching algorithm and an optional constituent verification step. The grammar induction algorithm acquires a set of rules for each level of linguistic analysis using a new technique for error-driven pruning of treebank grammars (Cardie and Pierce, 1998). In addition, we add a constituent verification step that employs standard inductive learning techniques as a precision-enhancing device.

We evaluate our approach on four data sets that comprise two partial parsing tasks — base noun phrase identification and verb-object identification. We find that the performance of our treebank approach is very good (over 93% precision and recall) for applications that require or prefer fairly simple constituent bracketing. As the complexity of the partial parsing task increases, however, the treebank approach lags the performance of competing methods. We explain these differences in terms of the knowledge sources employed by each method. Nevertheless, our approach has a number of features that make it attractive for large-scale, practical NLP applications:

- both the grammar induction algorithm and the pattern-matching parser are exceedingly simple;
- the parser is very fast, operating in time linear in the length of the text when the constituent verification phase is not used;
- the learned grammars can be easily modified for use with corpora that differ from the training texts;
- the approach is very flexible in that it allows system developers to choose a performance metric (e.g. precision, recall, F-measure) with which to tune the grammar that best supports the goals of the larger NLP application.

The next section provides a definition for, and examples of, the two partial parsing tasks. Sections 3 and 4 describe and evaluate the basic grammar induction approach. Section 5 presents the optional constituent verification step. Section 6 evaluates the entire approach. We compare Empire with related work in Section 7.

[1]The name refers to our focus on empirical methods for development of the system.

2 Base Noun Phrase and Verb-Object Identification

We focus on two shallow parsing tasks: base noun phrase identification and verb-object identification. In this work we define a *base noun phrase* (base NP) to be a simple, nonrecursive noun phrase — a noun phrase that does not contain other noun phrase descendants. In the partial parse of Figure 1, for example, *a trade deficit of $101 billion* and *the country's economic sluggishness* are too complex to be base NPs; instead, they contain four simpler noun phrases, each of which is considered a base NP: *a trade deficit*, *$101 billion*, *the country*, and *economic sluggishness*. For base NP identification then, the goal of Empire is to take a sentence as input and produce a version of the sentence in which all base NPs are bracketed.

Verb-object (VO) recognition amounts to identifying the main verb and direct object head of each clause in a sentence. Verb-object identification is performed on a tag sequence in which the base noun phrases have already been identified. Here the goal for Empire is to bracket potential verb-object constituents starting with the main verb token and ending with the base noun phrase that contains the object token: *South Korea* [$_{\text{VO}}$ *registered a trade deficit*] *of $101 billion in October,* [$_{\text{VO}}$ *reflecting the country's economic sluggishness*]. Following the application of the parser, a small set of rules is applied to the verb-object "constituent" bracket to extract the verb and object. The above verb-object bracketing, for example, would produce the following output where *registered/deficit* and *reflecting/sluggishness* are the verb-object pairs: *South Korea* [$_{\text{VO}}$ [$_{\text{V}}$ *registered*] *a trade* [$_{\text{O}}$ *deficit*]] *of $101 billion in October,* [$_{\text{VO}}$ [$_{\text{V}}$ *reflecting*] *the country's economic* [$_{\text{O}}$ *sluggishness*]].

3 Grammar Induction

Figure 2 depicts Empire's approach to shallow parsing using the base noun phrase relationship as a running example. To learn to identify a particular linguistic relationship, REL, Empire requires a corpus that has been annotated with brackets indicating that relationship. More specifically, we assume that the training corpus is a sequence of elements (either words or constituents) $e_1, e_2, \ldots$, along with a set of annotations or brackets $b_{(i_1,j_1)}, b_{(i_2,j_2)}, \ldots$, where $b_{(i,j)}$ indicates that elements i through j represent an instance of REL: [$_{\text{REL}}$ $e_i, \ldots, e_j$].

The goal of the training phase is to create a grammar for REL based on the training corpus:

1. *Run all required lower levels of Empire to assign a tag, t_i, to each element e_i in the training corpus.* For the base NP relationship, this amounts to assigning a part-of-speech tag to every token in the corpus. Verb-object recognition, on the other hand, requires both part-of-speech and base NP information: Each element in the training corpus is assigned either an NP label (for sentence elements recognized as base NPs) or a part-of-speech tag (for all tokens outside of base NPs).

2. *Extract from each* REL $b_{(i,j)}$ *in the training corpus its sequence of tags $t_i, \ldots, t_j$ to form a grammar.* In Figure 2, for example, the first base NP in the corpus, [$_{\text{NP}}$ *it*], produces the tag-sequence rule ⟨PRP⟩; verb-object rules contain both part-of-speech and NP tags.

3. *Remove duplicate rules from the grammar.*

The resulting grammar can then be used to identify the linguistic relationship in a novel text in the application phase.

1. *Run all required lower levels of the parser* to assign tags $t_1, t_2, \ldots$ to the elements $e_1, e_2, \ldots$ in the input text.

2. *Proceed through the tagged text from left to right,* at each point matching the rules against the remaining tags $t_i, t_{i+1}, \ldots$ in the text.

3. If there are multiple rules that match beginning at t_i, *use the longest matching rule R.* Continue matching at $t_{i+|R|}$.

With the rules stored in an appropriate data structure, this greedy "parsing" of constituents is very fast. Unfortunately, grammars extracted in this fashion pick up many "bad" rules due to noise in the training data (including annotation errors, part-of-speech tagging errors, and genuine ambiguities). As a result, it has become common practice to assign probabilities to the rules based on their frequency of occurrence and then use a probabilistic parser to apply the grammar to unseen text (Charniak, 1996). Our grammar induction framework employs a much simpler solution: we include a pruning phase to eliminate bad rules from the grammar and retain the longest-match heuristic.

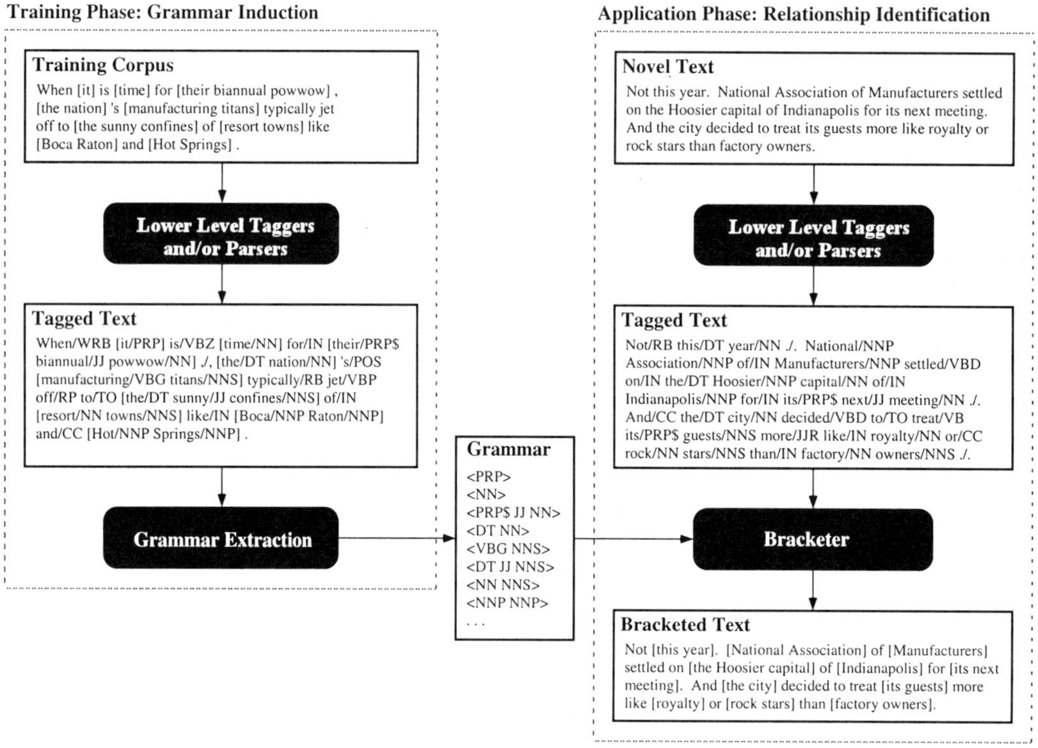

Figure 2: Shallow Parsing in Empire. The base noun phrase relationship is used as an example.

3.1 Error-Driven Pruning

Empire's grammar pruning procedure is shown in Figure 3. First, we divide the training corpus into two parts: an extraction corpus and a pruning corpus. The initial grammar for the linguistic relationship is derived from the extraction corpus as described above. Next, the pruning corpus is used to evaluate the grammar and produce a ranking of the rules in terms of their utility in identifying the linguistic relationship. More specifically, we use the rule set and the longest match heuristic to find all instances of the relationship in the pruning corpus. Performance of the rule set is measured in terms of labeled precision (P):

$$P = \frac{\text{\# of correct proposed RELs}}{\text{\# of proposed RELs}}$$

We then assign to each rule a score that denotes the "net benefit" achieved by using the rule during parsing of the pruning corpus. The benefit of rule r is given by $B_r = C_r - E_r$ where C_r is the number of RELs correctly identified by r, and E_r is the number of precision errors for which r is responsible. Alternatively, a frequency-based benefit measure can be employed: We scale B_r by the rule frequency to prune low-frequency

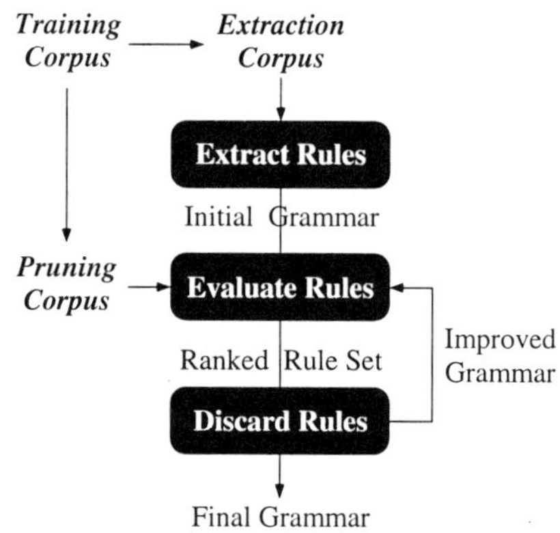

Figure 3: Error-Driven Pruning of Treebank Grammars

low-precision rules before high-frequency rules with the same precision.

The benefit scores from evaluation on the pruning corpus are used to discard the worst rules from the grammar. In the experiments below, we use two types of pruning. Each iteration of *threshold pruning* discards rules whose score is less than a predefined threshold T; it halts when all rules have a score above T. *In-*

cremental pruning discards the N worst rules in each iteration and then selects the grammar that yields either the maximum precision or the maximum recall on the pruning data, depending on the goals of the NLP application.

For a more detailed description of error-driven pruning, see Cardie and Pierce (1998). The notion of "pruning" inductive hypotheses has been explored previously in machine learning. Quinlan (1987), for example, presents several methods for simplifying decision trees using reduced-error pruning and a separate test set. If Empire's partial parsing approach is viewed as a very simple instantiation of case-based learning, then our pruning technique most resembles instance editing algorithms that discard training instances with poor classification accuracies (e.g. IB3 (Aha *et al.*, 1991)).

4 Evaluation of Error-Driven Pruning

Data Sets. In spite of the definitions in Section 2, there can be substantial differences in how base noun phrase and verb-object relationships can be encoded in any corpus. As a result, we created two data sets for each linguistic relationship, one data set that reflects a simple implementation of each relationship, and one that incorporates additional linguistic complexities. All are derived from the Penn Treebank WSJ corpus. In the Complex Base NP data set, each base NP corresponds to a non-recursive noun phrase in the Treebank parse. In particular, this data set is meant to duplicate the data used in Ramshaw and Marcus (1998) except for our handling of possessives. The Simple Base NP data set further simplifies Treebank base NPs that contain: (1) nominal conjunctions, (2) prepositions, (3) possessives, or (4) leading and trailing adverbs and verbs.

In the Complex Verb-Object data set, there is a verb-object pair for every verb and direct object component in the Treebank parse. In particular, if the object is a conjunctive phrase, the data set encodes separate verb-object pairs for each component of the conjunction. The Simple Verb-Object data set is meant to duplicate the Argamon *et al.* (1998) data and: (1) simplifies direct objects that are conjunctions or appositives, (2) simplifies conjunctive verbs, (3) simplifies ditransitives, and (4) omits objects marked by verb particles and copular verbs. By evaluating on both data sets for each linguistic task, we can explore the effect of linguistic relationship complexity on parser accuracy.

Methodology. All experiments are performed on the 25 sections of the WSJ portion of the Penn Treebank II corpus. Performance is measured in terms of precision (P) and recall (R):

$$P = \frac{\text{\# of correct proposed RELs}}{\text{\# of proposed RELs}}$$

$$R = \frac{\text{\# of correct proposed RELs}}{\text{\# of RELs in the annotated text}}$$

All results are averages using five-fold cross-validation at the document level; the same fold divisions are employed across all experiments. All experiments use the original (Treebank) segmentation for sentences and tokens.

For both base NP and verb-object recognition, part-of-speech tags were generated using Mitre's version of the Brill tagger (Brill, 1995). For verb-object identification, Empire itself identifies the base noun phrases. The threshold pruning experiments use $T = 1$; the incremental pruning experiments use $N = 3$ for verb-objects and $N = 10$ for base NPs. The verb-object experiments use recall-based pruning; incremental pruning for verb-objects uses the frequency-based benefit measure and threshold pruning employs the standard benefit measure.[2]

Results. Table 1 summarizes the performance of the Empire parser on both the Complex and Simple corpora for each linguistic relationship using incremental and threshold pruning. The first row of results for each data set shows the performance of the initial, unpruned grammars. The next two rows show the performance of the automatically pruned rule sets. As expected, the initial rule set performs quite poorly. For base NPs, both automated approaches provide significant increases in recall and precision. Note also the relatively small difference between the threshold and incremental pruning methods. For some applications, the minor drop in performance for threshold pruning may be worth the decrease in training time. For the remainder of the paper, we will use threshold pruning for base NP experiments.

For verb-object identification, the pruning results are less consistent. Both methods substantially increase precision; the finer-grained incremental pruning also increases recall. Threshold pruning, however, provides mixed results. For verb-object recognition, there are a few high-frequency, low-precision rules and the coarser

[2]The frequency-based benefit measure and threshold pruning with $T = 1$ are not compatible since all rule benefits would be below 1.

Table 1: Evaluation of Error-Driven Pruning for Base NP Identification and Verb-Object Recognition (P = precision; R = recall)

Linguistic Relationship	Simple Corpus	Complex Corpus
Base NP		
unpruned	.221P/.457R	.183P/.353R
threshold pruning	.920P/.932R	.870P/.896R
incremental pruning	.932P/.934R	.893P/.905R
Verb-Object		
unpruned	.199P/.863R	.209P/.681R
threshold pruning	.661P/.612R	.650P/.719R
incremental pruning	.569P/.895R	,619P/.789R

threshold pruning is not consistent in its handling of them: Results vary widely on a per-fold basis depending on whether these rules survive pruning. For the remainder of the paper, we will use incremental pruning for verb-object experiments.

Table 1 also clearly indicates the effects of linguistic relationship complexity. As expected, results for the Complex base NP data set are much lower than those for the Simple corpus (-5%P/-3.6%R). Since the two data sets share about 91% of their NPs, this performance drop is caused by problems introduced in the remaining 9%, of which possessives account for 3.6%; conjunctions, 2.3%; and NPs with leading and trailing adverbs and verbs, 2.4%. Analysis of the errors indicates that ambiguities introduced by allowing conjunctions and adverbs/verbs appear to be more difficult than those introduced by possessives.

Although the verb-object task is more difficult than the base NP task it subsumes, the results for the Simple and Complex verb-object data sets appear to contradict the expected trend — there is a large drop in recall (-10.6%) for the Complex verb-objects, but precision increases by 5%. One reason for this is that verb-object pairs with copular verbs are identified in both experiments but are considered errors for the simple data set. In addition, the complex data set yields many more rules (typically longer rules to handle conjunctions and appositives) that are low-frequency, but high-precision. Because of Empire's longest match heuristic, these long rules prevent Empire from identifying some erroneous verb-objects that would be selected by shorter, less accurate rules.

For two of the four data sets, our results can be compared to those obtained in evaluations of other approaches to partial parsing on the Penn Treebank. We ran an evaluation using as test data, the same sections of the Treebank as previous experimenters; the results are in Table 2.[3] Our results on Complex Base NP corpus lag the best published results (Ramshaw and Marcus, 1998) by 3-4%. Note, however, that we make no use of context or lexical (word-level) information; the best results on this data set were obtained using transformation-based learning, which employs both. By controlling for lexicalization in transformation-based learning, Empire performs more comparably (-1.2%P/-0.2%R). Empire also falls short of the best results to date on the Simple Verb-Object corpus. Argamon *et al.* (1998), however, make use of context to determine verb-object brackets. We address this issue for Empire in the next section.

Table 2: Direct Comparison to Previous Work (P = precision; R = recall). Base noun phrases were evaluated on section 20 of the WSJ corpus. Verb-object recognition was tested on section 00 of the WSJ.

Base NPs	
Ramshaw and Marcus (R&M)	.931P/.935R
Argamon *et al.*	.916P/.916R
R&M (no lexical information)	.901P/.902R
Empire (incremental pruning)	.889P/.900R
Verb-Objects	
Argamon *et al.*	.771P/.898R
Empire (incremental pruning)	.610P/.935R

[3] To match the conditions of the Argamon *et al.* evaluation, these tests were performed using the tags directly from the treebank rather than from the Mitre/Brill tagger.

Table 3: Sample Verb-Object Constituent Verification Case for *Many traders predict the U.S. currency will remain stuck in the near term.* VB refers to a base form verb; NN is a singular noun; MD is a modal verb.

Sentence Elements	Attribute	Value
	tag-prev2	nil
[$_{NP}$ Many traders]	tag-prev1	NP
[$_{VO}$ [$_{V}$ predict] [$_{NP}$ the U.S. [$_{O}$ currency]]]	verb-tag	VB
	object-tag	NN
will	tag-fol1	MD
remain	tag-fol2	VB
stuck in ...		
	Class:	**bad**

5 Constituent Verification

Although the role of context and lexicalization has not been fully explored for shallow parsing, both are known to improve the performance of a number of language learning tasks. The accuracy of Empire's shallow parsing algorithm is therefore likely to improve if context and lexical information can be suitably exploited. This section describes one method for extending Empire to incorporate context and lexicalization without sacrificing the overall simplicity of the shallow parsing approach. We use standard inductive learning techniques in a *constituent verification* step to evaluate the correctness of each proposed linguistic relationship: Those deemed correct will remain in the bracketed output of the shallow parser; those deemed incorrect are discarded. This post-processing stage is clearly a precision-enhancing device: For cascaded partial parsers, it is important that each level of analysis be as accurate at possible. In addition, some NLP applications will benefit more from output that has high precision and reasonable recall (e.g. identification of linguistic relationships for information retrieval) than the converse.

We have examined three machine learning algorithms for constituent verification: decision tree induction using C4.5 (Quinlan, 1992), an unweighted k-nearest neighbor (K-NN) classifier (e.g. IB1 (Aha *et al.*, 1991)), and a K-NN classifier that uses the value-difference metric as the similarity measure (Stanfill and Waltz, 1986). The goal of the training phase is to produce a set of training cases, each of which describes one proposed linguistic relationship and its context. A sample verb-object constituent verification case is shown in Table 3. Each case is a set of six features: the tags for the two elements that precede and that follow the bracket; and tags for the main verb and direct object head. A similar case representation is used for base NPs. Note that the current case representation contains no lexical information — the actual word tokens that comprise the bracket and its context are not included in the cases. It should be clear, however, that lexical information is easy to incorporate — in addition to the tags used in the current representation, cases would also include the token that represents the element. Finally, each training case has a class label ("good" or "bad") indicating the correctness of the proposed relationship.

Training instances are created automatically from the pruning corpus. For the K-NN variations, the value for k is learned automatically during training; during testing, we use a simple majority vote to determine the class label.

Table 4 shows the performance of the three learning algorithms using 10-fold cross validation on data sets of 1000 cases derived from each of the linguistic relationship corpora. In terms of relative accuracy, the three learning algorithms perform comparably on each data set.[4] Since the goal for constituent verification is to increase precision, however, we hypothesize that the learning algorithm with best combination of a high accuracy and low false positive rate would provide the greatest improvement in precision for the partial parsing tasks: the K-NN+VDM alternative has this property for the data sets studied here. We also believe that classification for constituent verification can be improved by controlling the characteristics of the training set — the training data for both linguistic tasks is skewed w.r.t. class distribution; no attempt

[4] χ^2 and two-tailed t tests indicate that K-NN and K-NN+VDM outperform C4.5 ($p \leq .10$) for the Simple Base NP corpus; K-NN+VDM outperforms K-NN and C4.5 ($p \leq .10$) for the Simple Verb-Object corpus; and K-NN+VDM outperforms K-NN and C4.5 ($p \leq .10$) for the Complex Verb-Object corpus.

Table 4: Performance of Inductive Learning Algorithms for Constituent Verification. Results are shown in terms of accuracy (% correct) with standard deviations. False positive rates are provided in *italics*.

Data Set	C4.5	K-NN	K-NN + VDM
Simple Base NP	90.5 ± 2.2	91.9 ± 2.6	91.6 ± 1.8
false positive rate	*7.4*	*8.1*	*6.8*
Complex Base NP	86.7 ± 3.3	87.4 ± 2.9	87.0 ± 2.1
false positive rate	*10.3*	*12.3*	*9.0*
Simple Verb-Object	68.6 ± 5.2	68.1 ± 4.7	70.6 ± 4.9
false positive rate	*19.0*	*24.4*	*19.4*
Complex Verb-Object	74.1 ± 2.5	73.7 ± 4.0	75.9 ± 3.1
false positive rate	*15.9*	*22.0*	*15.5*

was made to balance the data sets for the experiments reported here.

6 Combining Pruning and Constituent Verification

Table 5 shows the effect of constituent verification on base NP and verb-object identification. For these experiments, the learning algorithms for constituent verification were trained on 1000 cases derived from the associated pruning corpus. As hypothesized, the increase in precision is greatest for the K-NN+VDM variation. The results also show that constituent verification is a more effective way to integrate context and improve precision for verb-object identification than for base NP identification: For both the Simple and Complex verb-object data sets, more precision was gained than recall lost (+12.0% precision vs. -9% and -6% recall, respectively). Constituent verification provides much smaller precision gains for base NP recognition. One explanation is that the skewed training data for constituent verification limited performance. It is also likely that accurate verb-object identification simply requires more context, e.g. to distinguish direct objects from subjects of subordinate clauses as in the examples below. In preliminary experiments, however, we find for all of the partial parsing data sets that the precision-recall tradeoff can be further manipulated by controlling the balance of "good" and "bad" cases in the training set: As the percentage of "good" cases is decreased, precision rises and recall falls.

In spite of the addition of context, Empire still falls below the best reported results on the verb-object task: Even after re-training Empire using perfect tags (to match the Argamon *et al.* (1998) training procedure), precision remains about 6 precision points lower at the same level of recall (72.5P/87.5R). Only by assuming both perfect tags and perfect NPs can Empire surpass their results. We would expect to recover some of this discrepancy by replacing the longest-match heuristic with one that chooses the best combination of possible bracketings. For base NP identification, precision gains are modest, leaving Empire still shy of Argamon *et al.*'s results.

We conclude this section with an example of the constituent verification step in action: Table 6 shows a proposed verb-object pair that is correctly discarded (on the left) and the top-ranked case retrieved in response to the test case (on the right).

7 Related Work and Conclusions

In the evaluation sections above, we compared Empire to two other machine learning methods that have been applied to partial parsing — Ramshaw and Marcus's transformation-based bracketer and Argamon *et al.*'s MBSL. In addition to differences in recall and precision, the methods also vary in other ways. For example, the transformation-based bracketer requires the most training time, with one pass through the training data for each candidate template for each new transformation. Empire needs only a handful to a few hundred passes for pruning (for threshold and incremental pruning, respectively), while MBSL trains in a single pass over the training data. In terms of runtime speed, the Empire longest-match bracketer is the fastest, using a quick linear time algorithm. The transformation-based bracketer can be equally fast, provided that the transformations are precompiled into a single finite-state transducer (Roche and Schabes, 1997a). Empire's increase in running time for constituent verification depends on the learning algorithm used. We

Table 5: Effect of Constituent Verification (P = precision; R = recall)

Data Set	No Constituent Verification	Constituent Verification Using C4.5	K-NN	K-NN+VDM
Simple Base NP	.920P/.932R	.922P/.925R	.920P/.931R	.928P/.919R
Complex Base NP	.870P/.896R	.879P/.877R	.872P/.893R	.896P/.830R
Simple Verb-Object	.569P/.895R	.678P/.750R	.655P/.796R	.690P/.806R
Complex Verb-Object	.619P/.789R	.727P/.701R	.692P/.758R	.741P/.728R

Table 6: Sample Verb-Object Constituent Verification Case for ... *said they* ... in *Two Japanese scientists said they discovered an antibody that....* In the case representation, VBD is a past tense verb; PRP is a personal pronoun; VO is a verb-object pair; IN is a preposition or subordinating conjunction. The right-hand column shows the top-ranked retrieved case.

Test Case Sentence Elements	Case Representation Attribute	Value	Retrieved Case Sentence Elements
	tag-prev2	nil	
[$_{NP}$ Two Japanese scientists]	tag-prev1	NP	[$_{NP}$ Clinton Gas Systems Inc.]
[$_{VO}$ [$_{V}$ **said**] [$_{NP}$ [$_{O}$ **they**]]]	verb-tag	VBD	[$_{VO}$ [$_{V}$ **said**] [$_{NP}$ [$_{O}$ **it**]]]
	object-tag	PRP	
[$_{VO}$ [$_{V}$ discovered] [$_{NP}$ an antibody]]	tag-fol1	VO	[$_{VO}$ [$_{V}$ received] [$_{NP}$ a contract]]
that ...	tag-fol2	IN	from ...
			Class: bad

believe MBSL to be the slowest bracketer, comparing multiple tiling covers to score each potential NP. In addition, the runtime space burden for MBSL is very large because the memory-base stores the entire training corpus. In contrast, the transformation-based and Empire bracketers store only a few hundred to a few thousand transformation or grammar rules at runtime (for verb-object and base NP recognition, respectively).[5]

Finally, Empire's main training product — a tag-sequence grammar — can be modified for new genres of text without retraining. This level of portability is impossible with MBSL, which creates no explicit constituent grammar; and adding or deleting transformations to handle new text genres would likely yield unpredictable results with the transformation-based bracketer. In Empire, individual rules can easily be removed from or added to the grammar.

[5]Daelemans *et al.* (1999) present a learning algorithm for base NP chunking that is similar to MBSL in its memory-based approach. Their results, however, are not comparable to those reported here: They measure performance in terms of the number of words correctly bracketed rather than measuring the number of completely correct noun phrase brackets.

In conclusion, we presented a new approach to partial parsing of natural language texts that combines error-driven pruning of treebank grammars and an optional classsification-based constituent verification step. In an evaluation on four data sets, we find that error-driven pruning provides substantial increases in recall and precision over the unpruned rule sets; constituent verification provides additional increases in precision, but works especially well for the more complex partial parsing tasks. The approach also has a number of attractive features: the grammar induction algorithm and the pattern-matching parser are exceedingly simple; the parser is very fast; the learned grammars can be easily modified for use with corpora that differ from the training texts. In addition, the approach is very flexible in that it allows system developers to choose a performance metric with which to tune the grammar that best supports the goals of the larger NLP application.

Furthermore, we believe that the treebank approach to grammar acquisition may be general enough to tackle other natural language learning tasks including the acquisition of patterns for information extraction and for higher-level text-mining operations. It might also be applied to tasks outside of natural language processing applications including learning simple languages for agent communication or in grammar-based biology problems.

Finally, we believe that there are a number of extensions and improvements that could be made to obtain additional performance gains at the possible expense of some added complexity: The naive longest-match heuristic can be replaced by a dynamic programming algorithm that considers all combinations of constituent brackets; machine learning algorithms could be used to correct, rather than discard, erroneous bracketings; lexicalized features can be added to the case representation; the constituent verification phase could be incorporated directly into the pruning algorithm; training data for constituent verification can be better balanced with respect to positive and negative instances.

Acknowledgments. This work was supported in part by NSF Grants IRI–9624639 and GER–9454149. We thank Mitre for providing their part-of-speech tagger.

References

(Abney, 1996) Abney, Steven. 1996. Partial Parsing via Finite-State Cascades. In *Workshop on Robust Parsing*. 8–15.

(Aha *et al.*, 1991) Aha, D.; Kibler, D.; and Albert, M. 1991. Instance-Based Learning Algorithms. *Machine Learning* 6(1):37–66.

(Argamon *et al.*, 1998) Argamon, S.; Dagan, I.; and Krymolowski, Y. 1998. A Memory-Based Approach to Learning Shallow Natural Language Patterns. In *Proceedings of the 36th Annual Meeting of the ACL and COLING-98*. Association for Computational Linguistics. 67–73.

(Bourigault, 1992) Bourigault, D. 1992. Surface Grammatical Analysis for the Extraction of Terminological Noun Phrases. In *Proceedings, COLING-92*. 977–981.

(Brill, 1995) Brill, Eric 1995. Transformation-Based Error-Driven Learning and Natural Language Processing: A Case Study in Part-of-Speech Tagging. *Computational Linguistics* 21(4):543–565.

(Cardie and Pierce, 1998) Cardie, C. and Pierce, D. 1998. Error-Driven Pruning of Treebank Grammars for Base Noun Phrase Identification. In *Proceedings of the 36th Annual Meeting of the ACL and COLING-98*. Association for Computational Linguistics. 218–224.

(Charniak, 1996) Charniak, E. 1996. Treebank Grammars. In *Proceedings of the Thirteenth National Conference on Artificial Intelligence*, Portland, OR. AAAI Press / MIT Press. 1031–1036.

(Daelemans *et al.*, 1999) Daelemans, W.; Bosch, A.van den; and Zavrel, J. 1999. Forgetting Exceptions is Harmful in Language Learning. *Machine Learning* 11(1–3):11–43.

(Hobbs *et al.*, 1997) Hobbs, J.; Appelt, D.; Bear, J.; Israel, D.; Kameyama, M.; Stickel, M.; and Tyson, M. 1997. FASTUS: A Cascaded Finite-State Transducer for Extracting Information from Natural-Language Text. In E. Roche and Y. Schabes, editors, *Finite-State Language Processing*. MIT Press, Cambridge, MA. 383–406.

(Marcus *et al.*, 1993) Marcus, M.; Marcinkiewicz, M.; and Santorini, B. 1993. Building a Large Annotated Corpus of English: The Penn Treebank. *Computational Linguistics* 19(2):313–330.

(Quinlan, 1987) Quinlan, J. R. 1987. Simplifying Decision Trees. *International Journal of Man-Machine Studies* 27:221–234.

(Quinlan, 1992) Quinlan, J. R. 1992. *C4.5: Programs for Machine Learning*. Morgan Kaufmann, San Mateo, CA.

(Ramshaw and Marcus, 1998) Ramshaw, Lance A. and Marcus, Mitchell P. 1998. Text chunking using transformation-based learning. In *Natural Language Processing Using Very Large Corpora*. Kluwer. Originally appeared in WVLC95, 82–94.

(Roche and Schabes, 1997a) Roche, E. and Schabes, Y. 1997. Deterministic part-of-speech tagging with finite-state transducers. In Roche, E. and Schabes, Y., editors, *Finite-State Language Processing*. MIT Press. Chapter 7, 205–239.

(Roche and Schabes, 1997b) Roche, E. and Schabes, Y., editors, 1997. *Finite-State Language Processing*. MIT Press, Cambridge, MA.

(Stanfill and Waltz, 1986) Stanfill, C. and Waltz, D. 1986. Toward Memory-based Reasoning. *Communications of the ACM* 29:1213–1228.

(Voutilainen, 1993) Voutilainen, A. 1993. NPTool, A Detector of English Noun Phrases. In *Proceedings of the Workshop on Very Large Corpora*. Association for Computational Linguistics. 48–57.

AdaCost: Misclassification Cost-sensitive Boosting

Wei Fan
Computer Science
Columbia University
New York, NY 10027
wfan@cs.columbia.edu

Salvatore J. Stolfo
Computer Science
Columbia University
New York, NY 10027
sal@cs.columbia.edu

Junxin Zhang
Computer Science
Columbia University
New York, NY 10027
jzhang@cs.columbia.edu

Philip K. Chan
Computer Science
Florida Institute of Technology
Melbourne, FL 32901
pkc@cs.fit.edu

Abstract

AdaCost, a variant of AdaBoost, is a misclassification cost-sensitive boosting method. It uses the cost of misclassifications to update the training distribution on successive boosting rounds. The purpose is to reduce the cumulative misclassification cost more than AdaBoost. We formally show that AdaCost reduces the upper bound of cumulative misclassification cost of the training set. Empirical evaluations have shown significant reduction in the cumulative misclassification cost over AdaBoost without consuming additional computing power.

1 Introduction

Recently, there has been considerable interest in cost-sensitive learning [15, 8, 7, 17, 6, 2]. Turney [15, 16] discusses learning tasks sensitive to the costs of misclassification among others. We are interested in reducing *misclassification cost.* It can be either constant for each type of misclassification or conditional on a specific example under different types of misclassification. In troubleshooting systems, for example, there is usually a fixed cost in producing one type of wrong diagnosis. In fraud detection systems, however, undetected frauds with high transaction amounts are obviously more costly. In this paper, we propose AdaCost, a variant of AdaBoost, that reduces both fixed and variable misclassification costs more significantly than AdaBoost.

Freund and Schapire's AdaBoost [4] learns a highly accurate voted ensemble of many "weak" hypotheses. Typically, each hypothesis outputs both a prediction and a confidence for this prediction. Each hypothesis is trained on the same data set yet with a different distribution. Different hypotheses are produced in different rounds of boosting. At each round, AdaBoost increases the weights of wrongly classified training instances and decreases those of correctly predicted instances. AdaBoost allows for an arbitrary initial distribution. For classification error, each example is given an equal weight. To reduce cumulative misclassification costs, costly examples can be given higher weights. AdaBoost reduces the weighted error for this initial distribution. Schapire, Singer and Singhal [11] gave different weights for false positives and false negatives to apply AdaBoost in text-filtering. Karakoulas and Shawe-Taylor [5] applied a similar approach. However, misclassification cost is not used in AdaBoost's weight updating rule. In AdaCost, the weight updating rule increases the weights of costly wrong classifications more aggressively, but decreases the weights of costly correct classifications more conservatively. This is accomplished by introducing a misclassification cost adjustment function into the weight updating formula. Under this updating rule, the weights for expensive examples are higher and the weights for inexpensive examples are comparatively lower. Each weak hypothesis correctly predicts more expensive examples for such a distribution. The final voted ensemble will also correctly predict more costly instances.

The focus of this paper is on both theoretical issues and empirical evaluations. In Section 2, we describe AdaCost and derive a reasonable upper bound on the misclassification cost. We also discuss the choices of the cost adjustment function β and the hypothesis weight α to reduce this upper bound. In Section 3, we evaluate AdaCost against AdaBoost on both real world credit card fraud detection and publicly available data sets. In Section 2.6, we discuss an alternative to AdaCost.

- Given: $\mathcal{S} = \{(x_1, c_1, y_1), \ldots, (x_m, c_m, y_m)\}$; $x_i \in \mathcal{X}, c_i \in \mathbb{R}^+, y_i \in \{-1, +1\}$.
- Initialize $D_1(i)$ (such as $D_1(i) = c_i / \sum_j^m c_j$).
- For $t = 1, \ldots, T$:
  1. Train weak learner using distribution D_t.
  2. Compute weak hypothesis $h_t : \mathcal{X} \rightarrow \mathbb{R}$.
  3. Choose $\alpha_t \in \mathbb{R}$ and $\beta(i) \in \mathbb{R}^+$.
  4. Update
  $$D_{t+1}(i) = \frac{D_t(i)\exp\Big(-\alpha_t y_i h_t(x_i)\boxed{\beta(i)}\Big)}{Z_t}$$
  where $\beta(i) = \beta\Big(\text{sign}(y_i h_t(x_i)), c_i\Big)$ is a cost-adjustment function. Z_t is a normalization factor chosen so that D_{t+1} will be a distribution.
- Output the final hypothesis:
$$H(x) = \text{sign}(f(x)) \text{ where } f(x) = \left(\sum_{t=1}^{T} \alpha_t h_t(x)\right)$$

Figure 1: AdaCost

2 AdaCost Algorithm

2.1 Difference from AdaBoost

We follow the generalized analysis of AdaBoost by Schapire and Singer [9]. The algorithm is shown in Figure 1. Let $\mathcal{S} = ((x_1, c_1, y_1), \ldots, (x_m, c_m, y_m))$ be a sequence of training examples where each *instance* x_i belongs to a *domain* $\mathcal{X}$, each *cost factor* c_i belongs to the *non-negative real domain* $\mathbb{R}^+$, and each *label* y_i belongs to a finite *label space* $\mathcal{Y}$. In this paper, we focus on binary classification problems in which $\mathcal{Y} = \{-1, +1\}$. h is a weak hypothesis. It has the form $h : \mathcal{X} \rightarrow \mathbb{R}$. The sign of $h(x)$ is interpreted as the predicted label and the magnitude $|h(x)|$ is the "confidence" in this prediction. Let t be an index to show the round of boosting and $D_t(i)$ be the weight given to (x_i, c_i, y_i) at the t-th round. $0 \le D_t(i) \le 1$ and $\sum D_t(i) = 1$. α_t is a chosen parameter as a weight for weak hypothesis h_t at the t-th round. We assume $\alpha_t > 0$. $\beta(\text{sign}(y_i h_t(x_i)), c_i)$ is a cost adjustment function with two arguments: $\text{sign}(y_i h_t(x_i))$ to show if $h_t(x_i)$ is correct, and the cost factor c_i.

The difference between AdaCost and AdaBoost is the additional cost adjustment function $\beta(\text{sign}(y_i h_t(x_i)), c_i)$ in the weight updating rule (highlighted by a box in Figure 1). Where it is clear in context, we use either $\beta(i)$ or $\beta(c_i)$ as a shorthand for $\beta(\text{sign}(y_i h_t(x_i)), c_i)$. Furthermore, we use β_+ when $\text{sign}(y_i h_t(x_i)) = +1$ and β_- when $\text{sign}(y_i h_t(x_i)) = -1$. For an instance with a higher cost factor, $\beta(i)$ increases its weights "more" if the instance is misclassified, but decreases its weight "less" otherwise. Therefore, we require $\beta_-(c_i)$ to be non-decreasing with respect to c_i, $\beta_+(c_i)$ to be non-increasing, and both are non-negative. Karakoulas and Shawe-Taylor [5] have also introduced a similar parameter β into the weight updating formula: if $y = +1$ then $\beta = 1$, if $y = -1$, then $\beta = v$ ($v < 1$). Their intuition is different from our approach. In their approach, positives are given a "fixed" higher weight than negatives. The weight updating rule will increase the weights of false negatives ($+1$ predicted as -1) more than false positives (-1 predicted as $+1$). However, it will also decrease the weights of true positives more than true negatives. Two related but different cost-sensitive boosting approaches for tree classifications are proposed by Ting and Zheng [14]. Their approaches apply to situations where the costs change very often. The solution is to repeatedly use the same induced model yet with different misclassification costs at classification. Our proposal applies to situations where misclassification costs are relatively stable. In the first approach, they modify the classification procedures of AdaBoost by calculating the expected misclassification cost for every class and choosing the predicted class with the lowest expected cost for a given instance. In the second approach, they completely change the weight updating rule. The rule replaces an instance's weight with the misclassification cost if it is misclassified; otherwise the current weight is retained. They didn't provide a training misclassification cost upper bound.

2.2 Training Misclassification Cost Upper Bound

Before studying how to reduce the training misclassification cost, we derive an upper bound on the cumulative training misclassification cost.

Lemma 1
Let $f'(x) = \sum_{t=1}^{T} \alpha_t h_t(x) \beta\Big(sign(y h_t(x)), c\Big)$ *and* $H'(x) = sign(f'(x))$. *If* $\forall c, \beta_-(c) \ge \beta_+(c)$, *the following is true:*

$$\forall x \in \mathcal{S} \left(H'(x) = y \implies H(x) = y\right)$$

Proof: By definition of $H'(x)$ and $f'(x)$:

$$H'(x) = y \iff$$

$$yf'(x) = y\sum_{t=1}^{T}\alpha_t h_t(x)\beta\Big(\text{sign}(yh_t(x)), c\Big) > 0 \quad (1)$$

The righthand side of (1) can be rewritten as a sum of the correct and wrong portions of predictions by the weak hypotheses:

$$y\sum_{t_+}\alpha_{t_+}h_{t_+}(x)\beta_+ + y\sum_{t_-}\alpha_{t_-}h_{t_-}(x)\beta_- > 0 \quad (2)$$

Since $\beta_- \geq 0, \beta_+ \geq 0$ and $\alpha_t > 0$ (the requirements by AdaCost), in Eq (2),

$$y\sum_{t_+}\alpha_{t_+}h_{t_+}(x)\beta_+ > 0 \text{ and } y\sum_{t_-}\alpha_{t_-}h_{t_-}(x)\beta_- \leq 0$$

The Lemma requires that $\beta_- \geq \beta_+ > 0$, the following must be true because we have decreased the votes of the wrong portion of predictions in Eq (2).

$$\begin{array}{lcl} y\sum_{t_+}\alpha_{t_+}h_{t_+}(x)\beta_+ & + & y\sum_{t_-}\alpha_{t_-}h_{t_-}(x)\beta_+ \\ & \geq & \\ y\sum_{t_+}\alpha_{t_+}h_{t_+}(x)\beta_+ & + & y\sum_{t_-}\alpha_{t_-}h_{t_-}(x)\beta_- \end{array} \quad (3)$$

Combining Eqs (2), (3) and definition of $f(x)$ (defined in Figure 1) gives the following:

$$\beta_+(yf(x)) = y\sum_{t_+}\alpha_{t_+}h_{t_+}(x)\beta_+ + y\sum_{t_-}\alpha_{t_-}h_{t_-}(x)\beta_+ > 0 \quad (4)$$

$\beta_+ > 0$ and (4) implies

$$yf(x) > 0 \quad (5)$$

By definition of $H(x)$ and $f(x)$, (5) shows that $H(x) = y$. ■

Lemma I shows that for every example correctly classified by $H'(x)$, it is also correctly classified by $H(x)$. The difference of $H(x)$ from $H'(x)$ is that $H(x)$ has no $\beta\Big(\text{sign}(yh_t(x)), c\Big)$ terms.

Theorem 1 *The following holds for the upper bound of the training cumulative misclassification cost.* $[\![\pi]\!]$ *returns 1 if predicate* $\pi = true$ *or 0 otherwise.*

$$\sum c_i[\![H(x_i) \neq y_i]\!] \leq d\prod_{t=1}^{T} Z_t,\ d = \sum c_j$$

Proof: From Lemma I, we know that

$$\sum c_i[\![H(x_i) \neq y_i]\!] \leq \sum c_i[\![H'(x_i) \neq y_i]\!] \quad (6)$$

By unraveling the update rule (extended and modified from the proof of Theorem I in Schapire and Singer [9]), we have that

$$\begin{aligned} D_{T+1}(i) &= \frac{D_1(i)\exp(-\sum_t \alpha_t y_i h_t(x_i)\beta(i))}{\prod_t Z_t} \\ &= \frac{D_1(i)\exp(-y_i f'(x_i))}{\prod_t Z_t} \end{aligned} \quad (7)$$

Moreover, if $H'(x_i) \neq y_i$, then $y_i f'(x_i) \leq 0$ implying that $\exp(-y_i f'(x_i)) \geq 1$. Thus,

$$[\![H'(x_i) \neq y_i]\!] \leq \exp(-y_i f'(x_i)) \quad (8)$$

Combining Eqs (6),(7), (8) and $D_1(i) = c_i/\sum_j^m c_j$ gives the stated bound on cumulative misclassification cost since

$$\begin{aligned} \sum c_i[\![H(x_i) \neq y_i]\!] &\leq \sum c_i \cdot \exp(-y_i f'(x_i)) \\ &= \sum_i (\prod_t Z_t)(\frac{c_i}{D_1(i)})D_{T+1}(i) \\ &= d\prod_{t=1}^{T} Z_t,\ d = \sum c_j \end{aligned}$$

■

The reason to require $\beta_- \geq \beta_+$ in Lemma I is clear. It removes the cost adjustment function β and the true label y terms from $H'(x)$ to generate the final hypothesis $H(x)$. This is important since neither the cost c nor the label y is available during testing. Additionally, Lemma 1 shows that $H(x)$ is more accurate than $H'(x)$. Moreover, for a particular example, $\beta_- \geq \beta_+$ guarantees that the weight updating rule will increase the weight more for wrong classifications than decreasing the weight for correct predictions. The requirements of non-decreasing $\beta_-(c_i)$ and non-increasing $\beta_+(c_i)$ force the weak learner to give more attention to more "costly" examples.

2.3 Choosing α_t

One consequence of Theorem 1 is that, to reduce training cost, we should seek to minimize Z_t at each round of boosting in the choice of α_t. We derive two choices for α_t following an estimation method by Freund and Schapire [4] and a numerical method by Schapire and Singer [9] and Karakoulas and Shave-Taylor [5]. We omit the round index t. For weak hypothesis h with range [-1,+1] and cost adjustment function $\beta(i)$ in the range [0,+1], the choice of α is

$$\alpha = \tfrac{1}{2}\ln\frac{1+r}{1-r} \text{ where } r = \sum D(i)u_i,\ u_i = y_i h(x_i)\beta(i) \quad (9)$$

Since $u_i \in [-1, +1]$, the following inequality holds.

$$Z = \sum D(i)e^{-\alpha u_i} \leq \sum D(i)\left(\frac{1+u_i}{2}e^{-\alpha} + \frac{1-u_i}{2}e^{\alpha}\right)$$

By zeroing the first derivative of the right hand side, we have the choice of α in formula (9). For this choice of α, $Z \leq \sqrt{1-r^2} \leq 1$. The above proof is extended from the estimation method given by Schapire and Singer [9].

Corollary 1 *Assuming h_t has range [-1,+1] and $\beta(i)$ has range [0,+1]. α_t is chosen as in formula (9). The training cumulative cost of H is at most:*

$$d\prod_{t=1}^{T}\sqrt{1-r_t^2}$$

where $r_t = \sum_i D_t(i) y_i h_t(x_i)\beta(i)$ and $d = \sum_j c_j$

The upper bound on misclassification cost is actually reduced when $Z_t = \sqrt{1-r^2} < 1$. This estimation for Z is pessimistic and not tight. The exact range of u is $\{-\beta_-, \beta_+\}$. It is hard to find a general and tight analytical upper bound for Z if u is taken as $\{-\beta_-, \beta_+\}$ and it would still be an estimation.

A general numerical solution is given by:

$$Z'(\alpha) = \frac{dZ}{d\alpha} = -\sum_i D(i) u_i e^{-\alpha u_i} = 0 \qquad (10)$$

Since $Z''(\alpha) > 0$, $Z'(\alpha)$ can have at most one zero. A detailed analysis of this formula without the cost factor β is given by Schapire and Singer [9]. In practice, we can use the estimation method to find a candidate for α and use numerical methods to improve.

If $\alpha_t < 0$ during learning, we can reverse the sign of h_t. Thus, we use $h'_t = -h_t$ and $\alpha'_t = -\alpha_t$.

2.4 Example

We show the intuition behind AdaCost by an example from the breast cancer data set (Section 3). $((p_2, \ldots, p_{10}), y)$ is the schema and $y \in \{m, b\}$. The cost factor for instances with label m is 1 or otherwise 0.33. $h_1(x)$ is the same for both AdaBoost and AdaCost. One rule says "if $p_3 = 1$ then b" with confidence 0.972. So, $((4,1,1,3,1,5,2,1,1), m)$ is misclassified as b. D_1 of this item is .002849. AdaBoost generates $\alpha_{AdaBoost_1} = 1.48027$ and changes the example's distribution to .013. AdaCost calculates $\alpha_{AdaCost_1} = 1.481265$ and updates the distribution to .033. At round 2, the weak hypotheses produced by AdaBoost and AdaCost are different. $h_{AdaBoost_2}(x)$, has a rule "if $p_3 = 1 \wedge p_9 = 1$ then m" with 0.99 confidence that applies to the item and $\alpha_{AdaBoost_2} = 1.026$. Hence, the example is still misclassified as b. On the other hand, $h_{AdaCost_2}(x)$ has a default rule "if the instance is not classified as b, then it is m" with a confidence of 0.99. The weight is $\alpha_{AdaCost_2} = 2.11$. Therefore, the prediction by AdaCost at round 2 is m, since $1.481265 * 0.972 < 2.11 * 0.99$. The obvious reason is that AdaCost increases the weight of this instance more than AdaBoost by introducing the cost adjustment function β into the weight updating rule. The weight updating rule of AdaCost gives more weight to misclassifications with true label m since it is 3 times as "expensive" as b.

2.5 Applying Cost to other Boosting Algorithms

The addition of a cost adjustment function β into the weight updating formula doesn't violate the assumptions of AdaBoost. It can be introduced to the variations of the original AdaBoost. We show by two examples. For Schapire and Singer's AdaBoost.MH [10] (a multi-class multi-label ranking AdaBoost algorithm), the cost adjustment function can be defined as $\beta\Big(\text{sign}\big(Y_i\{l\}h_t(x_i, l)\big), c_i(l)\Big)$. $c_i(l)$ is the cost factor that document x_i is not categorized as label l. For Schapire and Singer's AdaBoost.MR [10] (a multi-class multi-label preference ranking AdaBoost algorithm), we can design $\beta\Big(\text{sign}\big(h_t(x_i, l_0) - h_t(x_i, l_1)\big), c_i(l_0, l_1)\Big)$ where $c_i(l_0, l_1)$ is the cost factor to mistakenly prefer l_0 over l_1. (The symbols presented by the original authors are used above without explanation.)

2.6 Alternative Method

An alternative weight updating formula is:

$$D_{t+1}(i) = \frac{\boxed{\beta} D_t(i)\exp\Big(-\alpha_t y_i h_t(x_i)\Big)}{Z_t} \qquad (11)$$

The difference here from Figure 1 is that β is outside of the exponent. β is a non-decreasing function of the cost factor c, such as $\beta(c) = c$. The following holds for the upper bound of training cumulative cost: $\sum c_i [\![H(x_i) \neq y_i]\!] \leq d\Big(\prod_t^{T-1} Z_t\Big)\Big(\sum_i \frac{D_T(i)}{\beta^{T-1}}\exp(-\alpha_T y_i h_i(x_i))\Big)$, $d = \sum c_i$. It can be easily proved by unraveling the weight updating rule (12) and using the techniques in the proof of Theorem 1. In order to reduce misclassi-

Table 1: Data Set Summary

$\mathcal{S}$	Data	Data Size	Testing Size	Positive%
1	hypothyroid	3163	CV	4.77
2	boolean	32768	CV	13.34
3	dis	2800	972	4.63
4	crx	690	CV	44.5
5	breast cancer	699	CV	34.5
6	wpbc	198	CV	23.74
7	chase	40K*10	40K*10	≈ 20

fication cost, we will choose α_t in the first $T-1$ rounds to minimize Z_t and in the last round minimize $\sum_i \frac{D_T(i)}{\beta^{T-1}}\exp(-\alpha_T y_i h_i(x_i))$. Since $u_i = y_i h_i, u_i \in [-1,+1]$, we can use the estimation and numerical methods to choose both $\alpha_t (1 \le t \le T-1)$ and α_T.

3 Experiment

3.1 Set up

Data Set: We used seven data sets to evaluate the performance of AdaCost against AdaBoost in reducing cumulative misclassification cost. Table 1 lists their summary statistics. Five of the data sets were downloaded from the UCI Machine Learning Database. "boolean" is an artificial data set. It has 15 boolean variables. The instance is positive if any 4 or 5 variables are true, or otherwise it is negative. The last data set is a real world credit card fraud detection data set from Chase Bank. It contains .5M transaction records spanning a period of a whole year. It was provided for our research on fraud and intrusion detection [12]. Information on the schema can be found in [13].

Cost Factor: For a simplified cost model in the credit card business [13], there is an overhead $\$ovrhd$ to challenge a fraud. For any transaction with a transaction amount lower than the overhead, that is, $\$amt \le \$ovrhd$, the authorization system will simply authorize it. The bank loses all $\$amt$ for all frauds of this kind (yet another cost of doing business). We assign them a cost factor $c = 0$, since these transcations may not contribute to learning a fraud model for a fixed $\$ovrhd$.

We can therefore save money by catching frauds with $\$amt > \$ovrhd$. We lose $\$amt$ if they are not detected. We still lose $\$ovrhd$ even if they are caught. It implies that by leaving a fraud undetected, we will lose ($\$amt - \$ovrhd$) more. For legitimate transactions mistakenly labelled as frauds, we will lose $\$ovrhd$. Let fn, fp and tp represent the predicates of *false negative, false positive* and *true positive.* For example, $fp(i) = true$ if the i-th example is a false positive. The total cost to be minimized is formulated by:

$$\sum_{i:fn(i)} \$amt_i + \sum_{j:fp(j)} \$ovrhd + \sum_{k:tp(k)} \$ovrhd \qquad (12)$$

If we don't detect any frauds, we lose $\sum_{i:p(i)} \$amt$ (p returns *true* for fraud). We call this quantity *Maximal Loss.* If every fraud is detected, we still lose $\sum_{i:p(i)} \$ovrhd$. This is named *Least Loss.* Our goal is to minimize the total cost formula (12). Logically, we can assign a cost factor c of $\$amt - \$ovrhd$ to frauds and a factor c of $\$ovrhd$ to non-frauds. This reflects how the prediction errors will add to the total cost of a hypothesis. Since the overhead $\$ovrhd$ is not known to us, we chose to set $\$ovrhd \in \{60, 70, 80, 90\}$ to run four sets of experiments. We believe that these choices are realistic approximations to the real overhead. Detailed information on credit card cost model can be found in [13].

We do not have any "business-oriented" misclassification cost models for the remaining data sets. Instead, we varied the cost ratio R of positive vs. negative from 2 to 9.

We normalized each c_i to $[0,1]$ for all data sets. The cost adjustment function β is chosen as: $\beta_-(c) = 0.5 \cdot c + 0.5$ and $\beta_+(c) = -0.5 \cdot c + 0.5$.

Training and Testing: In the credit card business, due to normal billing cycles, there is a two-month delay for data to be used to train a detection system applied to current transactions. We mirror this constraint by using one month data for training and data from two months later for testing. Our data set allowed us to form 10 such pairs of training and testing sets. For the other six data sets, we used 10-fold CV to average the results or used the specific testing data provided.

Weak Learner: We used Cohen's RIPPER [3] as the "weak" learner. We chose it because RIPPER provides an easy way to change the distribution of the training set. Since using the training set alone usually overly estimates the accuracy of a rule set, we used the Laplace estimate to generate the confidence ($|h(x)|$) for each rule [1]. RIPPER is cost-insensitive. We make it cost-sensitive, called cRIPPER, by supplying it with a distribution that is linear in the cost of each instance ($D_1(i) \propto c_i$).

Calculating α_t: Both AdaBoost and AdaCost were run to the 50th round. We carefully engineered the bisection search algorithm with the first candidate α calculated by formula (9). The second point was searched with an exponential step increment. To avoid numerical errors introduced when adding a small number to a much bigger number, we used a vector v to compute $Z'(\alpha) = -\sum_i D(i)u_i e^{-\alpha u_i}$. For simplicity, we allow the index of v to be negative. The k-th element of the vector adds up ($w_i = -D(i)u_i e^{-\alpha u_i}$), if $10^{k-1} \leq |w_i| \leq 10^k$. We add every element in the vector starting from the smallest index (to avoid addition errors) to calculate Z'.

3.2 Results

We are interested in comparing cRIPPER (as a baseline), AdaCost and AdaBoost in several dimensions. First, for each data set and each cost model, we determine which algorithm has achieved the lowest cumulative misclassification cost and how many cases AdaCost is the clear winner. Second, we also seek to know, quantitatively, the difference in cumulative misclassification cost of AdaCost from AdaBoost and the baseline cRIPPER. It is interesting to measure the significance of these differences in terms of both reduction in misclassification loss and percentage of reduction. Additionally, we also want to see for all data sets and all cost models, how many of the times AdaCost has a lower cumulative cost than AdaBoost for all corresponding rounds of boosting. Finally, we are interested to know if AdaCost consumes more computing power. We grouped the results into two groups: the six data sets excluding Chase credit card and the Chase credit card alone.

Six Data Sets All the results are summarized in Table 2 and Figure 2. We use *percentage cumulative loss* (or $\%l$) to compare across data sets. $\%l$ is defined as $\frac{cumulative\ loss}{max\ loss}$, where *max loss* is the total loss when every instance is misclassified. Table 2 lists $\%l$ for cRIPPER (cRpr), $\%l$ at the end of 50th round for AdaBoost (Bst) and AdaCost (Cst) for six data sets excluding Chase credit card. The data sets are numbered from 1 to 6. The information on each data set can be found in Table 1. The second column is the R or cost ratio chosen to go from 2 to 9. The last two columns list the difference of $\%l$ in both plain subtraction and percentage (parenthesized). $(C-B)(\%)$ includes values for $\%l_{AdaCost} - \%l_{AdaBoost}$ as well as $\frac{\%l_{AdaCost} - \%l_{AdaBoost}}{\%l_{AdaBoost}}$. $(C-P)(\%)$ lists similar values for AdaCost versus cRIPPER. We keep one decimal point significant digit for all results. When AdaCost is the best performer, it is highlighted in bold font.

In 42 (88% of 48) cases, AdaCost achieved the lowest misclassification loss. AdaBoost had the best performance in 5 (10% of 48) cases. AdaCost and AdaBoost tied at 1 run. The absolute reduction by AdaCost from AdaBoost (as shown in $(C-B)(\%)$ column) in these six data sets ranges from 0.1% (data set 1 or hypothyroid with ratio $R=7$) to 14.6% (data set 6 or wpbc with ratio $R=3$). The percentage increase goes from 2% (data set 4 or crx with ratio $R=6$) to 57% (data set 2 or boolean with ratio $R=3$). The improvements are clear. The difference of AdaCost from cRIPPER (as shown in column $(C-P)(\%)$) are even greater. The last row μ for every data set is the average percentage loss for all chosen cost ratios R.

We have plotted the individual error and error ratio points for these six data sets in Figure 2. Each point in the left figure is the ratio of AdaCost vs. AdaBoost, in other words, $\frac{\%l_{AdaCost}}{\%l_{AdaBoost}}$. We have drawn the points for all 8 ratios and all 50 boosting rounds. To avoid overlapping of these points, the boosting round t was given a random adjustment in the range of $[-0.45, +0.45]$. The majority of the points are below the "Ratio=1" line which means that in an overwhelming majority of cases, AdaCost has lower cost than AdaBoost. The figure on the right plots the same information in a different way where the value of each individual misclassification cost is shown. The majority of points are above the "$y=x$" line which also means that AdaCost clearly has lower cumulative cost.

Chase Credit Card The results are plotted in Figures 3 and 4. Figure 3 shows the average reduction of 10 months in percentage cumulative loss (defined as $\frac{cumulativeloss}{maximalloss-leastloss} * 100\%$) for AdaBoost and AdaCost for all 50 rounds and 4 overheads. We can clearly see that there is a consistent reduction of AdaCost over AdaBoost for all 400 ($= 50*2*4$) runs. The absolute amount of reduction is over 3%. We also observe that the speed of reduction by AdaCost is quicker than that of AdaBoost in all 4 figures. The speed is the quickest in the first few rounds. This means that in practice, we may not need to run AdaCost for many rounds.

Figure 4 plots the ratio of cumulative cost by AdaCost and AdaBoost. The figures are similar to those in Figure 2. We have plotted the results of all 10 pairs of training and test months over all rounds and overheads. Most of the points are below the "Ratio=1" line in the left drawing and above the "y=x" line in the right drawing, both implying that AdaCost has lower cumulative loss in an overwhelming number of cases.

Table 2: Percentage Cumulative Loss by cRIPPER, AdaBoost and AdaCost for Six Data Sets

$\mathcal{S}$	R	cRpr	Bst	Cst	(C-B)(%)	(C-P)(%)
1	2	1.4	1.6	1.2	**-0.4(-25)**	**-0.2(-16)**
	3	1.8	2.0	1.6	**-0.3(-17)**	**-0.2(-10)**
	4	2.1	2.2	1.8	**-0.4(-16)**	**-0.3(-12)**
	5	2.5	2.7	2.2	**-0.4(-16)**	**-0.3(-11)**
	6	3.2	3.0	2.5	**-0.6(-19)**	**-0.7(-23)**
	7	3.1	2.8	2.7	**-0.1(-3)**	**-0.4(-13)**
	8	3.0	3.1	2.7	**-0.4(-12)**	**-0.3(-10)**
	9	3.0	3.2	2.5	**-0.7(-23)**	**-0.5(-17)**
	μ	2.5	2.6	2.2	**-0.4 (-16.0)**	**-0.4(-14.2)**
2	2	13.8	10.5	3.3	**-7.2(-69)**	**-10.6(-76)**
	3	14.2	11.6	5.0	**-6.6(-57)**	**-9.2(-65)**
	4	15.4	10.9	6.9	**-4.0(-37)**	**-8.5(-55)**
	5	14.7	11.4	7.3	**-4.1(-36)**	**-7.4(-50)**
	6	13.9	9.3	8.1	**-1.3(-13)**	**-5.8(-42)**
	7	19.5	9.6	8.5	**-1.1(-11)**	**-11.0(-57)**
	8	18.0	9.6	8.3	**-1.3(-14)**	**-9.6(-54)**
	9	18.3	11.0	8.1	**-3.0(-27)**	**-10.2(-56)**
	μ	16.0	10.5	6.9	**-3.6 (-34.1)**	**-9.1(-56.7)**
3	2	2.3	2.6	2.0	**-0.6(-24)**	**-0.3(-14)**
	3	4.1	3.5	3.1	**-0.4(-12)**	**-1.0(-25)**
	4	5.0	4.3	4.3	0.0(0)	**-0.7(-14)**
	5	6.2	4.9	4.4	**-0.5(-10)**	**-1.8(-29)**
	6	6.5	7.0	5.5	**-1.5(-21)**	**-1.0(-15)**
	7	7.6	8.0	6.7	**-1.2(-15)**	**-0.9(-11)**
	8	6.7	7.6	6.1	**-1.5(-20)**	**-0.6(-9)**
	9	7.8	10.1	7.1	**-3.0(-30)**	**-0.7(-9)**
	μ	5.8	6.0	4.9	**-1.1 (-18.2)**	**-0.9(-14.9)**
4	2	14.0	10.5	5.4	**-5.1(-48)**	**-8.6(-61)**
	3	11.7	12.4	12.1	**-0.3(-3)**	0.4(4)
	4	11.1	11.2	11.3	0.1(1)	0.2(2)
	5	9.7	9.9	10.0	0.1(1)	0.3(3)
	6	9.8	7.4	7.3	**-0.1(-2)**	**-2.5(-25)**
	7	8.5	8.1	4.9	**-3.2(-39)**	**-3.6(-42)**
	8	8.1	10.6	8.7	**-2.0(-19)**	0.6(7)
	9	7.7	11.1	8.9	**-2.2(-20)**	1.2(15)
	μ	10.1	10.2	8.6	**-1.6 (-15.5)**	**-1.5(-14.8)**
5	2	4.4	3.2	1.7	**-1.4(-45)**	**-2.7(-61)**
	3	3.7	3.4	1.8	**-1.6(-46)**	**-1.9(-51)**
	4	3.8	4.8	3.1	**-1.8(-37)**	**-0.7(-19)**
	5	4.1	4.6	4.2	**-0.4(-9)**	0.1(2)
	6	3.5	3.6	2.2	**-1.4(-39)**	**-1.3(-38)**
	7	3.5	3.2	3.2	**-0.1(-2)**	**-0.3(-9)**
	8	3.3	3.5	2.2	**-1.4(-38)**	**-1.1(-34)**
	9	3.2	3.1	3.0	**-0.1(-3)**	**-0.2(-7)**
	μ	3.7	3.7	2.7	**-1.0 (-27.6)**	**-1.0(-27.7)**
6	2	35.8	43.7	34.0	**-9.7(-22)**	**-1.8(-5)**
	3	38.9	35.1	20.5	**-14.6(-42)**	**-18.4(-47)**
	4	36.7	33.5	35.7	2.1(6)	**-1.0(-3)**
	5	35.0	34.5	22.6	**-12.0(-35)**	**-12.4(-35)**
	6	31.2	18.7	11.1	**-7.6(-41)**	**-20.1(-64)**
	7	28.6	28.6	28.8	0.1(1)	0.2(1)
	8	24.6	24.8	25.1	0.4(2)	0.5(2)
	9	25.5	27.1	25.7	**-1.4(-5)**	0.2(1)
	μ	32.0	30.8	25.4	**-5.3 (-17.3)**	**-6.6(-20.6)**

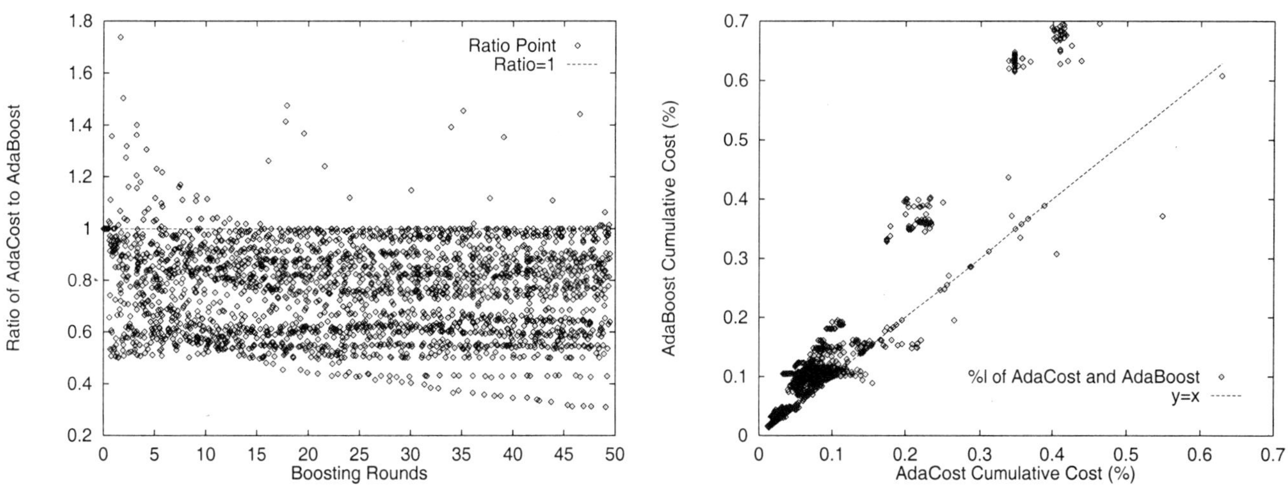

Figure 2: Cumulative Loss Ratio and Loss of AdaCost and AdaBoost for Six Data Sets

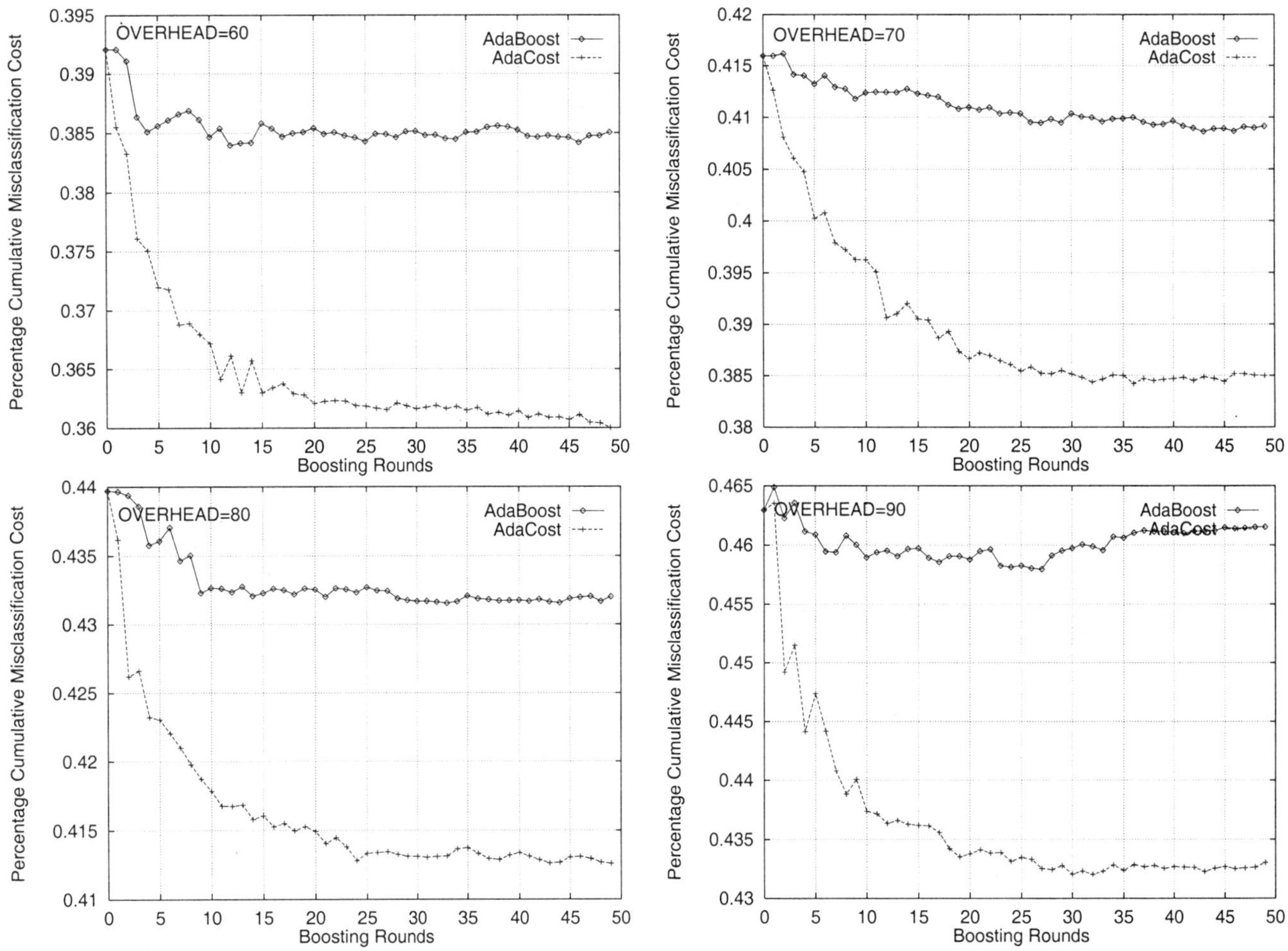

Figure 3: Cumulative Loss Ratio of AdaCost and AdaBoost for Chase Credit Card Data Set

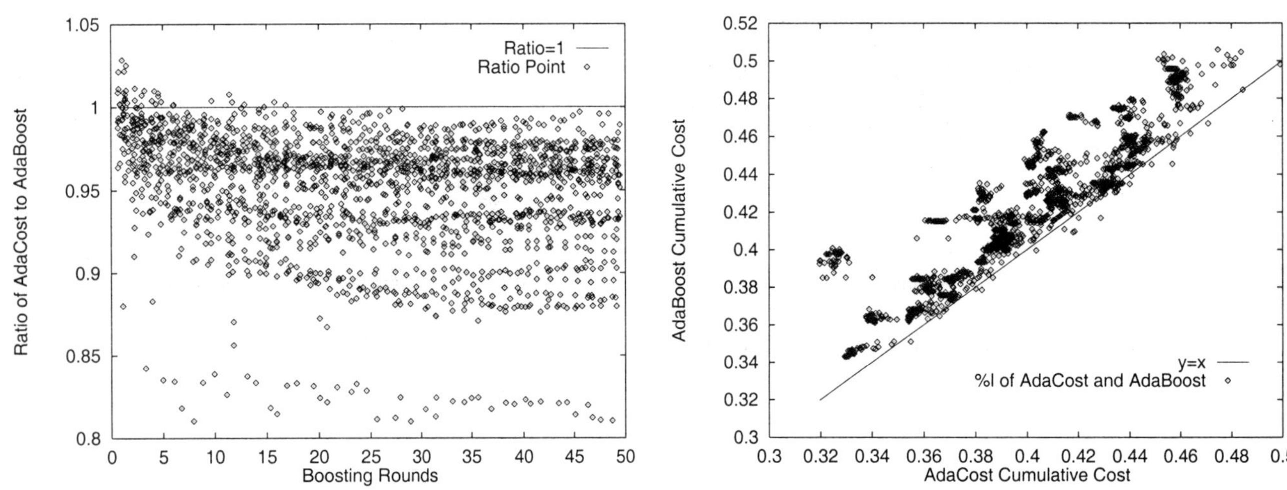

Figure 4: Cumulative Loss Ratio and Loss of AdaCost and AdaBoost on Chase Credit Card

4 Conclusion

This paper has raised an interesting question: can we improve AdaBoost based on a cost model? We have studied the problem of reducing misclassification cost using boosting methods and proposed the AdaCost algorithm. The intuition is that in addition to assigning high initial weights to costly examples, the weight updating rule should also take cost into account and increase the weights of costly misclassification more but decrease the weights of costly correct classification less. Based on Freund, Schapire and Singer's previous work, we have formally proved the upper bound of training cumulative misclassification cost and discussed the choice of α. We also attempted to apply AdaCost to other variants of AdaBoost.

We have empirically evaluated AdaCost and AdaBoost on seven data sets using both real world and artifical cost models and we have observed that AdaCost shows a consistent and significant reduction in misclassification cost over AdaBoost and it doesn't consume more computing power on average. One interesting experiment we have done, but not included in this paper, is to compare AdaBoost and AdaCost with a uniform initial distribution. In other words, we set $D(i) = \frac{1}{m}$. Chase credit card data was used in this study. The results show that AdaBoost reduces classification error significantly but doesn't reduce misclassification cost much. On the other hand, there is a significant reduction in misclassification cost by AdaCost. This experiment has, to some extent, provided additional evidence for the "benefits" of introducing cost into the weight updating rule.

Acknowledgments

This research is supported in part by grants from DARPA (F30602-96-1-0311) and NSF (IRI-96-32225 and CDA-96-25374). Our work has benefitted from in-depth discussions with Robert Schapire and Yoram Singer of AT&T Research Labs.

References

[1] K. Ali and M. Pazzani. (1996). Error Reduction through Learning Multiple Descriptions. *Machine Learning, 24(3)*, 173-202.

[2] P. Chan and S. Stolfo. (1998). Towards Scalable Learning with Non-Uniform Class and Cost Distributions: A Case Study in Credit Card Fraud Detection. In *Proc. Fourth Int'l Conf on Knowledge Discovery and Data Mining*, New York, New York. pp.164-168.

[3] W. Cohen. (1995). Fast Effective Rule Induction. In *Proc. Twelfth Int'l Conf on Machine Learning*, pp. 115-123, Morgan Kaufman.

[4] Y. Freund and R. Schapire. (1997). A decision-theoretic generalization of on-line learning and an application to boosting. *Journal of Computer and System Sciences*, 55(1):119-139.

[5] G. Karakoulas and J. Shawe-Taylor. (1998). Optimizing classifiers for imbalanced training sets. *NIPS* 1998

[6] N. Lavrac, D. Gamberger and P. Turney. (1996). Cost-sensitive feature reduction applied to a hybrid genetic algorithm. In *Proc of the Seventh Int'l Workshop on Algorithmic Learning Theory*, Sydney, Australia, pp 127-134.

[7] M. Pazzani, C. Merz, P. Murphy, K. Ali, T. Hume and C. Brunk. (1994). Reducing misclassification costs: Knowledge-intensive approaches to learning from noisy data In *Proc of the Eleventh Int'l Conf on Machine Learning*, pp:217-225, New Brunswick, New Jersey.

[8] F.J. Provost and T. Fawcett. (1997). Analysis and visualization of classifier performance: Comparison under imprecise class and cost distributions. In *Proc of the Third Int'l Conf. on Knowledge Discovery and Data Mining.*

[9] R. Schapire and Y. Singer. (1998). Improved boosting algorithms using confidence-rated predictions. In *Proceedings of the Eleventh Annual Conf on Computational Learning Theory.*

[10] R. Schapire and Y. Singer. (1998). BoosTexter: A system for multiclass multi-label text categorization. at `www.research.att.com/~schapire`.

[11] R. Schapire,Y. Singer and A. Singhal. (1998). Boosting and Rochhio applied to text filtering. In *SIGIR'98.*

[12] S. Stolfo, A. Prodromidis, S. Tselepsis, W. Lee, W. Fan and P. Chan. (1997). JAM: Java Agents for Meta-learning over Distributed Databases. In *Prod. Third Intl. Conf. Knowledge Discovery and Data Mining.*

[13] S. Stolfo, W. Fan, W. Lee, A. Prodromidis and P. Chan. (1997). Credit Card Fraud Detection Using Meta-learning: Issues and Initial Results. In *AAAI-97 Workshop on Fraud Detection and Risk Management.*

[14] K.M. Ting and Z. Zheng. (1998). Boosting Trees for Cost-Sensitive Classifications. In *Machine Learning: ECML-98: 10th European Conf on Machine Learning*, (pp. 190-195). Chemnitz, Germany:Springer.

[15] P. Turney. Cost-sensitive Learning Bibliographies. `ai.iit.nrc.ca/bibliographies/cost-sensitive.html`

[16] P. Turney. Types of Cost. at `ai.iit.nrc.ca/bibliographies/cost-types.html`

[17] P. Turney. (1995). Cost-sensitive classification: Empirical evaluation of a hybrid genetic decision tree induction algorithm. In *Journal of Artificial Intelligence Research*, 2:369-409.

Abstracting from Robot Sensor Data using Hidden Markov Models

Laura Firoiu
Computer Science Dept., LGRC
University of Massachusetts at Amherst
Amherst, MA 01003-4610
lfiroiu@cs.umass.edu

Paul R. Cohen
Computer Science Dept., LGRC
University of Massachusetts at Amherst
Amherst, MA 01003-4610
cohen@cs.umass.edu

Abstract

This work is the first step of a larger effort aimed at learning logical descriptions from robot sensory data. These representations are more compact than sensory traces and will support logical reasoning. We view the robot's experiences as trajectories through an unknown state space. The robot receives information about the state of the world through its sensors. We present a technique to automatically extract atomic propositions from these sensors. Our assumption is that a state means that something is invariant in the world, and that this invariance is reflected in some constant sensor values, or constant functions of sensor values. Our task is then to find the states and their invariant characterization. We employ a hidden Markov model to find the states and their distributional characterization. From the probability distributions of the sensor values in states we then create atomic propositions that describe the states. The transformation of atomic propositions into predicates should be straightforward given sensor models that specify the arguments of these predicates, but this has yet to be implemented.

Keywords: Abstraction learning, Hidden Markov Model, Minimum Message Length

1 Introduction

We are interested in learning without supervision elements of logical representations of experiences. The experiences in question are generated by robots interacting with their environments. Just as human infants bootstrap their sensorimotor experiences into a conceptual structure and language [Man92], so we want our robot to learn ontologies and language through interaction. Previous work has focused on learning *sensory prototypes*, which represent robot interactions in terms of how the interactions appear to the sensors [OSC99, RC98]. For example, driving toward a wall and bumping into it is represented as a decreasing series of sonar values followed by the bump sensor going high. While sensory prototypes support some kinds of reasoning (e.g., predicting that the bump sensor will go high) they do not contain explicit elements that represent the robot, the wall, and the act of driving; and so do not support reasoning about the roles of entities in experiences [CL99]. This work takes the first step from sensory prototypes to logical representations. Logical representations have two advantages:

- Because they contain terms that denote the entities in a scene and the relationships between them, logical representations such as "push(robot, object)" are compact, and easily support planning and other reasoning. The sensory prototype of pushing objects does not support these easily [SOC99].

- Abstraction can be over predicates and properties of entities, rather than over patterns in sensory traces. For instance, the extensional category of pushable objects is the set of elements i such that the robot has experienced "push(robot,i)" in the past. Given the extensional category, one can imagine learning the intensional concept of pushable object, the properties that make objects pushable. Neither kind of categorization is feasible given only sensory prototypes.

If logical representations are so advantageous, why not build them into our robots, that is, make them part of the robots' innate endowment? The reason is that we want to explain how sensorimotor activity produces thought—classification, abstraction, planning, language—as it does in every human infant. So we start with sensors and actions, and in this paper we explain how elements of a logical representation might be learned from these sensorimotor beginnings.

The representations are "passive" in the sense that, currently, they are not used by any problem solving system. These representations do not specify what to do in a certain situation or predict what will happen if an action is taken. In the absence of supervision and a problem solving task, we need a criterion for good representations to guide the learning process. We chose the principle of minimum description length. Experiences are represented as sequences of states, where each state is characterized by atomic propositions that denote true facts about that state. Our algorithm identifies the states and the atomic propositions that minimize these descriptions.

The representation of experiences as sequences of states corresponds with our intuition that experiences unfold through several relatively static stages. At least for simple robot activities, the robot's world tends to remain in the same state over some periods of time, so we expect the state sequences to be simple. For example, the experience of moving toward an object has some well defined parts: accelerating, approaching, being near the object. Ideally our learning algorithm would learn a state description for each part.

Dividing an experience into states is the first step in the process of learning logical representations of experiences. We want to identify these states and ground them in patterns of sensor values. A technique that fits our task very well is hidden Markov model (HMM) induction. The assumption behind the HMM is that the data sequence is produced by a source that evolves in a state space and at each time step outputs a symbol according to the probability distribution of the current state.

We identify the experience stages with the states of an HMM induced from all the data collected during a batch of experiences. These states are characterized by, or grounded in, stable probability distributions over sensor values. They form a single vocabulary for all experiences, so similar stages can be identified across experiences.

The second step in the process of learning logical representations is to find atomic propositions that denote facts in the current state. Since the states found by the HMM are characterized by probability distributions, the atomic propositions must be derived from them. We define the atomic propositions simply as disjunctions of the most likely sensor values according to these distributions. For example, the characterization of "accelerate" is given by some positive values of the acceleration sensor and by the velocity sensor varying within a range of values. A representation of an experience is a sequence of states described by these atomic propositions.

Each representation has a cost that reflects both the size of all its atomic propositions and states, and how well they describe the raw data. The latter criterion has two components, precision ($a \vee b$ is less precise than a) and accuracy. We minimize this cost heuristically by applying a state splitting technique during the HMM induction process. States are split and the resulting model re-trained as long as the description cost decreases.

The incremental HMM induction technique is similar with Andrew McCallum's "utile distinction memory" [McC92]. The main difference is that in the "utile distinction memory" algorithms, state splitting is driven by an "active" criterion, that of predicting utility (reward).

The creation of atomic propositions grounded in sensor values is similar with the creation of features in Luc Steels' work on perceptually grounded meaning creation [Ste96] [1]. Both atomic propositions and features are defined over regions in sensor space, and are created "as needed" by the induction algorithm. As in the work of Andrew McCallum, the key difference lies in the task of the learning algorithm. While our goal is to find a minimum cost description of experiences in an unsupervised manner, the features are induced with the "active" goal of discriminating a set of given objects. In Luc Steels' work the agent knows that the objects are distinct, while in our work the agent does not know that experiences and their stages might be qualitatively distinct.

2 The Sensor Vector

The robot receives data in the format of time-series of sensor values. From the forty or so sensors of the

[1] We thank the anonymous reviewer for pointing us to this work.

Pioneer 1 robot, we selected six that we consider relevant for describing the twelve experiences in our experiment. The experiences were all similar: the robot went towards two cups, one blue and one red, and then either hit or passed the cups. The sensors we selected are: translational velocity, contact, and for each color, visual area and visual distance. An example of a sensor time series from an experience can be seen in figure 1.

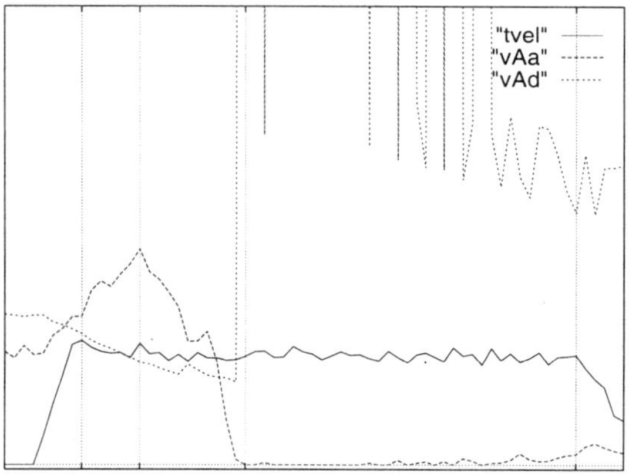

Figure 1: Sequence of sensor values for pushing an object, where the sensors are: translational velocity (tvel), blue visual area (vAa) and blue visual distance (vAd). We can identify five stages of the experience: accelerate towards blue object, approach object with approximately constant velocity, pass object, constant move with no object in view, decelerate.

While we can easily see in figure 1 the different stages of the experience, the "jittery" sensor values can bias the state induction algorithm towards frequent state changes. We correct this bias with one of our own: in a stable world, sensor values remain constant or change in a regular, not jittery, way. One way to introduce this bias is to smooth the sensor time series. We go one step further, fitting lines piecewise to the time series. These lines fragment the experience into stages in which the derivatives of sensor values are constant. The fitting algorithm works as follows:

1. A graph is constructed such that:
   - there is a node for each known point on the curve (time stamp);
   - there is one arc between any two distinct nodes; the arc points to the node with higher time stamp; the weight of the arc is the mean square error of the regression line fitted to the curve fragment defined by the two nodes (time stamps);
2. Dijkstra's shortest path algorithm is applied to the graph thus constructed; the resulting path defines a piecewise linear fit with the property that the sum over the individual fragments of the mean square error is minimized.

An example of such a fit is shown in figure 2.

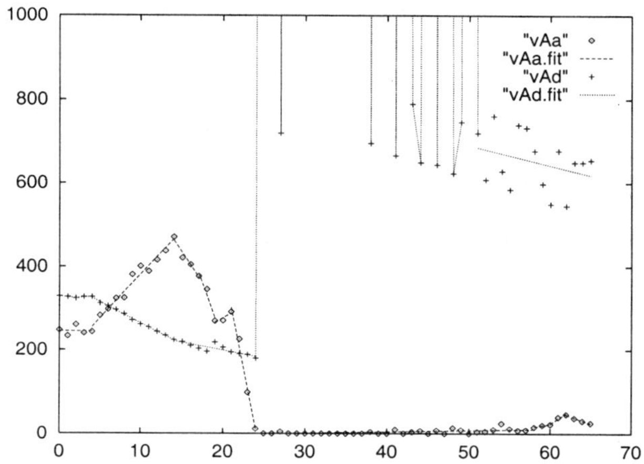

Figure 2: Piecewise fit of the sensors visual A area (vAa) and visual A distance (vAd) for one of the experiences.

A more refined and realistic definition of state is that arbitrary functions of sensors—not just linear fits—are constant in states. We plan to learn such functions in the future.

3 Hidden Markov Models

A discrete hidden Markov model [Rab89] is defined by a set of states and an alphabet of output symbols. Each state is characterized by two probability distributions: the transition distribution over states and the emission distribution over the output symbols. A random source described by such a model generates a sequence of output symbols as follows: at each time step the source is in one state; after emitting an output symbol according to the emission distribution of the current state, the source "jumps" to a next state according to the transition distribution of its current state. Since the activity of the source is observed indirectly, through the sequence of output symbols, and the sequence of states is not directly observable, the states are said to be "hidden". A continuous HMM emits symbols from a continuous space, according to probability densities instead of probability distributions. For either discrete or continuous HMMs, efficient dynamic programming algorithms exist that:

- induce the HMM that maximizes (locally) the probability of emitting the given sequence (the Baum-Welch algorithm)
- find the state sequence that maximizes the probability of the given sequence, when the model is known (the Viterbi algorithm).

While a continuous HMM appears more appropriate for our domain (the robot's sensors return continuous values) we chose discrete HMMs because our simple method of inducing atomic propositions works readily for probability distributions but not for probability densities. Since the sensors return continuous values, we must discretize them. Each sensor variable is discretized individually with a unidimensional Kohonen map [Koh95]. Each continuous input value is mapped to one unit and the resulting symbols are the map units.

The hidden Markov model definition can be readily extended to the multidimensional case, where a vector of symbols is emitted at each step, instead of a single symbol. The assumption that allows this immediate extension is conditional independence of variables given the state. Thus we can learn state descriptions based on vectors of sensor values.

4 State characterization with atomic propositions

A single HMM is learned for a batch of robot experiences, and each experience is represented by its most likely state sequence (Viterbi path) through the HMM. By representing its experiences with an HMM, the robot adds to its knowledge about the world. Specifically, the states in the model support recognition of stages of experiences and of similar experiences.

But these states do not explicitly represent the *scene elements*—physical objects, activities, spatial relations and so on—that correspond to what the robot is doing at the times the states occur. States are just stable probability distributions over sensory inputs, thus they contain only implicit information about scene elements. To represent scene elements explicitly, the robot must first create representation elements that denote them, that is solve the perceptual grounding problem [Har90]. We take a first step toward such representations by creating atomic propositions, which are logical representation elements denoting simple facts about the scenes experienced by the robot.

To characterize an HMM state by a set of logical propositions, we replace for each sensor the probability distributions over its values with logical descriptions of the distributions. These descriptions are disjunctions of possible sensor values. As such, propositions are simple facts of the form "sensor S takes values x or y". These propositions enable the construction of more complex representations as we describe later.

When inducing a proposition from a probability distribution over a sensor's values, we assume that if the distribution has a low entropy, then some constant process affects the sensor. In this case the atomic proposition is defined only for the most likely sensor values.

An example of a proposition based on the distribution of the translational velocity (t_vel) sensor is:

> distribution:
> .0 .0 .0 .0 .0 0.14 0.33 0.44 0.08 0.01
> atomic proposition:
> *t_vel_5_6_7_8*

We consider that all the values in the proposition definition are equally likely to occur in a state in which the proposition holds. Thus, the proposition is defined as a generalization of the distribution from which it was derived to the uniform distribution over the covered values. This crude generalization reduces the proliferation of propositions and allows identification of common propositions across states. In the example above, the covered values are 5 through 8. Because the velocity varies over a contiguous range of values [2], we interpret this proposition to mean that the robot either accelerates or decelerates. The interpretation is clarified when the acceleration sensor [3] is considered as well. To the robot, this proposition "means" only a pattern of its sensor values.

Given a sensor model that describes the kind of information a sensor returns, we can transform these propositions into predicates. For example, if the translational velocity sensor returns the translational velocity property of the constant *robot*, then the proposition *t_vel_5_6_7_8* becomes the predicate

[2] By discretizing with a unidimensional Kohonen map, the topology of the original real-valued space is preserved.

[3] Positive values of acceleration (corresponding in this experiment to discrete values greater than 2) indicate acceleration.

t_vel_5_6_7_8(robot). The implicit assumption in our sensor model is that during an experience, a sensor returns information about the same object. This means that the constant *object* in the predicate *vis_A_2_3(object)* that holds at one time step (state) during the experience, is the same as the constant *object* in the predicate *vis_A_1_2(object)* that holds at the next time step of the same experience, although *vis_A_2_3*(·) and *vis_A_1_2*(·) are different predicates. Although these predicates do not immediately add information beyond that implicit in the atomic propositions, they allow structured representations at the next abstraction levels.

This is the current extent of our work on transforming propositions into predicates, although it is the focus of our future work. The remainder of this section describes a criterion for inducing atomic propositions.

4.1 HMM state splitting

A limitation of HMM induction algorithms is that the number of states must be known in advance. Often, there are either too few states and the resulting propositions are too vague (for example a sensor can take any value) or there are too many states and propositions, such that the representation of experiences becomes long and not intelligible. Since we consider good representations to be "short" representations, our algorithm splits states as required to minimize the size of these representations, as measured[4] by a cost function. We designed the cost function according to the minimum message length (MML) principle [OH94], as a measure of the information needed to re-generate the original data (the time series of the experience). As in the MML paradigm, there are two pieces of information the robot must store:

1. its model; in our case the model is the collection of states, atomic propositions and state characterizations;
2. the encoding of each experience within the model;

The cost function is a sum of two components, one for each item above. The first is the cost of the model, which is a measure of the length of the model description. The second is the data cost, which is a measure of the size of all the experience encodings. The two cost components are described in more detail in section 4.2.

[4] The cost function is not the exact length of the encoded information, but a measure of it. For example we ignore string delimiters or the exact number of bits when defining the cost of encoding a number n as $log(n)$.

The state induction algorithm proceeds by recursively splitting states and re-training the resulting HMM until the cost cannot be improved:

1. initialization: the HMM has only one state
2. iterate while cost is decreasing:
   - for each state, compute the cost resulting from splitting the state
   - select the state that yields the largest cost reduction and split it

? use Hofmann ?

By choosing to split the state that yields the largest cost reduction at the current iteration, the cost is minimized heuristically. We cannot attempt to minimize cost globally, because an exhaustive search of all the splitting possibilities is exponential in the final number of states, and the HMM fitting algorithm is guaranteed to find only a local maximum, anyway.

State splitting stops because the two components of the cost functions are inversely proportional and the cost reaches a minimum.

4.2 The cost function

The model component of the cost function measures the size of the description of atomic propositions and states. An atomic proposition is described by enumerating the values it covers. We define its cost as: *# covered_values ∗ log(# all_sensor_values)*. ← *
The description of a state s_i has two parts:

- the codes for the next states, according to its transition probability distribution; these codes are used in the encoding of experiences [5] as follows: if the current state is s_i and the next state is s_j, then the optimal code for s_j, given s_i, has $-log(prob(s(t)|s(t-1)))$ bits; considering s_i a random source and s_j the emitted symbol, this code has the property that the expected length of the encoding of one symbol equals the entropy of the source; a theorem of Shannon (see [vdL97]) states that no code can achieve a lower expected symbol encoding length then the entropy[6]

[5] Although these codes appear in the redescription of experiences, they must be specified in the model description because otherwise the encoded experiences cannot be decoded.

[6] We do not know what this optimal code is — it might not exist — but for our cost function, we need to know only its length.

* #all_sensor_values:
discrete values after K-means clustering
?

- its characterization with atomic propositions; this cost is defined as: $\#\ propositions\_in\_state * log(\#\ all\_propositions)$

The cost of the model is the sum of the costs of the descriptions of propositions and states.

The data component of the cost function is the sum of the costs of the individual experiences. Recall that an experience is encoded as the most likely state sequence in the HMM induced from a batch of experiences, and further that the probability distributions over sensor values within each state are replaced by sets of logical propositions. These propositions generalize over the distributions from which they were derived and lose information that was present in the distributions. Consequently, the propositions may be inaccurate, meaning they specify incorrect sensor values, or imprecise, meaning they specify a range of sensor values. Suppose, for example, a propositional characterization of an HMM state says "translational velocity is 2, 3, or 4." If the robot's translational velocity in the state is actually 5, then the proposition is inaccurate. If translational velocity is 3, then the proposition is imprecise.

To re-generate a time series of sensor values from logical state descriptions, one would have to store additional information, either for specifying one of the covered values when the proposition is not precise, or for correcting errors when the proposition does not hold at that time step.

The cost of an individual experience is defined to include both the size of its encoding as a state sequence within the model and the additional information required for correcting the description, if necessary. Specifically, the cost is a sum over all time steps of:

1. the length of encoding with the optimal code the current state $s(t)$, given the previous state $s(t-1)$, that is $-log(prob(s(t)|s(t-1)))$

2. the length of encoding the sensor values at the current time step, given the current state; for each sensor this component of the cost is one of the following:

   - the precision cost: if the proposition that characterizes the state for this sensor covers the current value, then the cost is the entropy of the proposition; for example, for $t\_vel\_5\_6\_7\_8$ the cost is $log(4)$ because the exact value must be specified out of four equally likely possibilities; this cost reflects the precision of the proposition definition: a proposition over only one value is extremely precise and has zero cost

   - the error cost: if the current value is not covered, for example the value is 9 and the proposition is $t\_vel\_5\_6\_7\_8$, then the cost is that of specifying the exact sensor value, namely $log(\#\ all\_sensor\_values)$

5 Experiment

In twelve similar experiences, the robot was oriented toward a group of two cups, then it received the command to go for roughly 80 time steps (approximately 8 seconds). From each experience, sequences of sensor values were collected for six sensors. The contact sensor takes value 1 when either the robot gripper bumpers or beams sense an object. The translational velocity sensor takes values between 0 and 250. The visual area and visual distance sensors for channels A and C detect blue and red objects, respectively. The visual sensors return information only about the largest object (of the corresponding color) in the visual field. These are six of roughly forty sensors on board the Pioneer 1 robot. We selected these by hand because we do not know yet how select them algorithmically.

The result of the state splitting process for one experience is shown in figure 3. The final number of HMM states for this experiment is 6. Different experiments were run by varying the duration of HMM training or the regime. The training regime refers to the way the HMM is re-trained after a state is split: either the emission probabilities of all states are re-adjusted, or training is restricted to only the two states that resulted from the split. The results shown in figure 3 are from an "all states" training experiment. This training regime seems to give better results, because the search for a model is not constrained to the space of probability distributions of two states only, and thus a better HMM may be found.

The sequence of states and the defined propositions that describe the experience in figure 3 are:

- state 3 can be interpreted as "accelerate with ob-

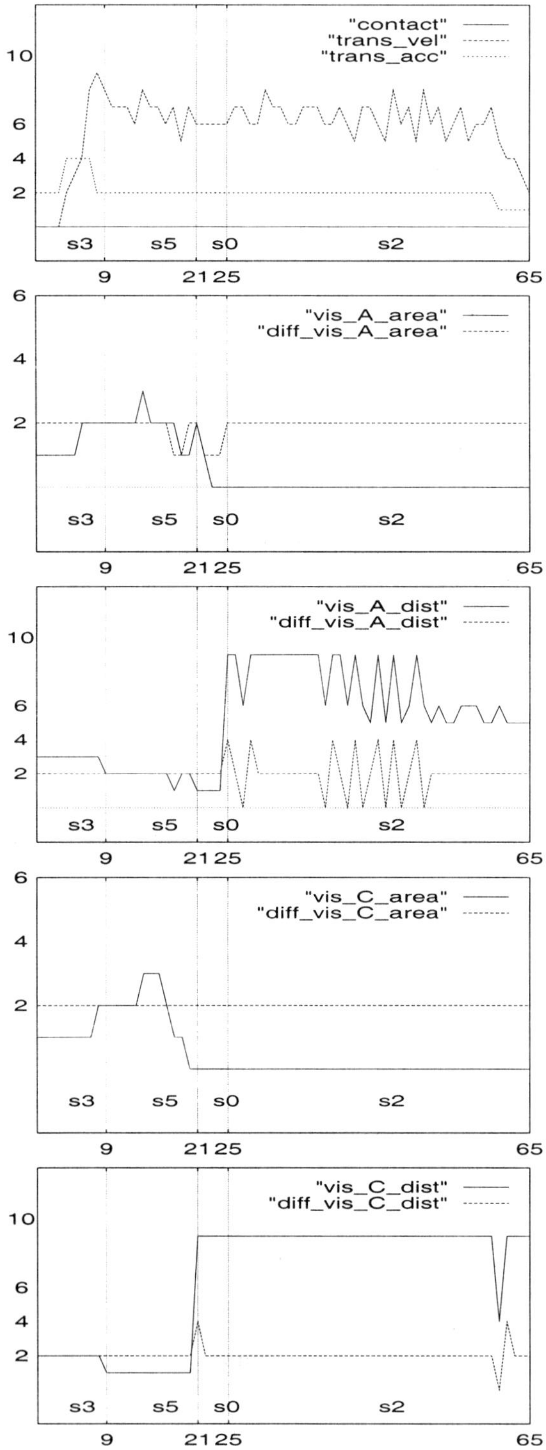

Figure 3: Partitioning of an experience into stages: a contiguous sequence of a state defines a stage. The plots have time on the x-axes and the discretized values of the selected sensors on the y-axes.

ject A and object C in view":

contact.0	*t_vel*.0.1.2.3.4.6.7.8.9	*t_acc*.2_4
vis_A_area.0_2	*diff_vis_A_area*.2	
vis_A_dist.3_5	*diff_vis_A_dist*.2	
vis_C_area.1	*diff_vis_C_area*.2	
vis_C_dist.4	*diff_vis_C_dist*.2	

The "accelerate" predicate can be mapped to the two propositions "*t_vel*.0.1.2.3.4.6.7.8.9" and "*t_acc*.2_4"; the two objects are inferred from the visual sensor propositions.

- State 5 can be interpreted (albeit with a slight difference discussed below) as "steady-go with two objects in view":

contact.0	*t_vel*.5_8	*t_acc*.2
vis_A_area.1_4	*diff_vis_A_area*.2_3	
vis_A_dist.2_3	*diff_vis_A_dist*.2	
vis_C_area.0_3	*diff_vis_C_area*.2	
vis_C_dist.1_4	*diff_vis_C_dist*.2	

The "steady-go" predicate comes from "*t_vel*.5_8" and "*t_acc*.2". There is a slight difference between what is happening during this stage of the experience and the propositional definition of s_5. In the plot of *vis_C_area* in figure 3 we notice that the object C disappears, as the *vis_C_area* sensor goes from 2-3 to 0 and *vis_C_dist* goes from 1 to 9 (the highest value). While the propositions *vis_C_area*.0_3 and *vis_C_dist*.1_4 capture a change in the perception of object C, their counterparts (the slopes of their linear fits) *diff_vis_C_area*.2 and *diff_vis_C_dist*.2[7] imply no change of perception. Due to the discretization process (*diff_vis_C_dist* and *diff_vis_C_area* have constant value 2 throughout s_5), the proposition is slightly inaccurate.

- State 0 cannot be so easily interpreted. In the context of the experience in figure 3 it means "pass object A", but the proposition description makes it a transition state (it also lasts only for 3 time steps in this experience):

contact.0_1	*t_vel*.0.5.6.7.8
	t_acc.2
vis_A_area.0_2	*diff_vis_A_area*.0_2
vis_A_dist.0.1.6.9	*diff_vis_A_dist*.0.2.4
vis_C_area.0.2.3.4.5.6.7.8	*diff_vis_C_area*.1_4
vis_C_dist.0.1.9	*diff_vis_C_dist*.2

[7]The discrete value 2 corresponds to a unit in the Kohonen map with value 0.

The propositions *vis_A_area.*0_2 and *diff_vis_A_area.*0_2 support the "pass object A" interpretation, but the propositions *vis_C_area.*0.2.3.4.5.6.7.8 and *vis_C_dist.*0.1.9 introduce an "uncertain object C in view". In reality, object C was passed during the previous stage and now is out of view. While not erroneous, the propositions are imprecise.

- State 2 is easily interpreted as "go or decelerate with no objects in view":

*contact.*0	*t_vel.*0_8	*t_acc.*0_2
*vis_A_area.*0	*diff_vis_A_area.*2	
*vis_A_dist.*5.6.9	*diff_vis_A_dist.*0.2.4	
*vis_C_area.*0	*diff_vis_C_area.*2	
*vis_C_dist.*9	*diff_vis_C_dist.*2	

While the fragmentations of experiences seem meaningful in most cases, the state characterization by propositions does not always correspond to what is happening during the stages. For example, as discussed above, our interpretation of state s_0 is slightly different from its propositional characterizations. The costs of the inaccuracies and imprecisions in the definition of this state seem to be out-weighted by the reductions in the description length and it is not split.

Transforming the state sequences of the 12 experiences into regular expressions we obtain:

$s_3^+ s_5^+ s_4^+ s_0^+ s_2^+$ (2)
$s_3^+ s_5^+ s_4^+ s_0^+$ (1)
$s_3^+ s_5^+ s_4^+ s_1^+$ (2)
$s_3^+ s_5^+ s_4^+ s_0^+ s_1^+$ (1)
$s_3^+ s_5^+ s_4^+ s_0^+ s_1^+ s_0^+ s_1^+ s_0^+$ (1)
$s_3^+ s_5^+ s_4^+ s_1^+ s_2^+$ (1)
$s_3^+ s_5^+ s_0^+ s_2^+$ (1)
$s_3^+ s_5^+ s_4^+ s_0^+ s_2^+ s_0^+$ (2)
$s_3^+ s_5^+ s_4^+ s_0^+ s_1^+ s_0^+$ (1)

The numbers in parentheses indicate how many experiences have the same regular expression. We notice that almost all sequences start with the pattern $s_3^+ s_5^+ s_4^+$. This shows that an extension of the learning process toward generalizations over state sequences will decrease the cost of the descriptions.

6 Conclusions and Future Work

During the first year of an infant's life, she apparently develops increasingly rich and efficient representations of her environment (Mandler calls this process *redescription* [Man92]). We have shown how to redescribe multivariate time series of sensor values as rudimentary logical descriptions, by creating new objects that are associated with parts of the world at different abstraction levels. The objects at one level are grounded in, or mapped to, objects at the previous level. Because both memory and time are finite resources, the criterion of minimum description must govern the process. In this work we tried to apply these ideas at the lowest levels of abstractions, by creating atomic propositions grounded in probability distributions over raw sensor values (physical level). The results are generally good: the fragmentation of experiences into states and their corresponding propositional characterizations appear most times to conform with our interpretation of the experience stages. But sometimes they do not conform, as in the case of state s_0 in the example in the previous section. The main reason for the mixed results is that the criterion that drove the learning process is purely descriptional: only "passive" descriptions are minimized. There is no special reinforcement signal to differentiate the states and there is no reasoning involved for explaining the differences between experiences or for predicting the evolution of an experience. If the agent also reasons based on its internal representation then the minimization principle will promote representation elements that simplify not only the "passive" descriptions but the "active" descriptions (computations) as well, that is the derivation of explanations and predictions. Our next goal is to create, starting from the obtained propositions, elements of representations (predicates and formulas) that explain the difference between experiences like "push object" and "pass object", or explicitly state that the robot will hit the object if it continues to move on its path.

Acknowledgements

This research is supported by DARPA/AFOSRF and DARPA under contracts No. F49620-97-1-0485 and No. N66001-96-C-8504. The U.S. Government is authorized to reproduce and distribute reprints for governmental purposes notwithstanding any copyright notation hereon.The views and conclusions contained herein are those of the authors and should not be interpreted as necessarily representing the official policies or endorsements either expressed or implied, of the or the U.S. Government.

References

[CL99] Paul R. Cohen and Mary Litch. What are contentful mental states? Dretske's theory of mental content viewed in the light of robot learning and planning algorithms. Submitted to the *Sixteenth National Conference on Artificial Intelligence*, 1999.

[Har90] S. Harnad. The symbol grounding problem. *Physica D*, 42:335–346, 1990.

[Koh95] Teuvo Kohonen. *Self-Organizing Maps.* Springer, 1995.

[Man92] Jean M. Mandler. How to build a baby: II. Conceptual primitives. *Psychological Review*, 99(4):587–604, 1992.

[McC92] R. A. McCallum. First results with utile distinction memory for reinforcement learning. Technical Report 446, Computer Science Department, University of Rochester, NY, 1992.

[OH94] J. J. Oliver and D. Hand. Introduction to minimum encoding inference. Technical Report 4-94, Statistics Dept., Open University, September 1994. TR 95/205 Computer Science, Monash University.

[OSC99] Tim Oates, Matthew D. Schmill, and Paul R. Cohen. Identifying qualitatively different experiences: Experiments with a mobile robot. Submitted to the *Sixteenth International Joint Conference on Artificial Intelligence*, 1999.

[Rab89] Lawrence R. Rabiner. A tutorial on Hidden Markov Models and Selected Applications in Speech Recognition. *Proceedings of the IEEE*, 77(2):257–285, 1989.

[RC98] Michael Rosenstein and Paul R. Cohen. Concepts from time series. In *Proceedings of the Fifteenth National Conference on Artificial Intelligence*, pages 739–745. AAAI Press, 1998.

[SOC99] Matthew D. Schmill, Tim Oates, and Paul R. Cohen. Learned models for continuous planning. In *Proceedings of Uncertainty 99: The Seventh International Workshop on Artificial Intelligence and Statistics*, pages 278–282, 1999.

[Ste96] Luc Steels. Perceptually grounded meaning creation. 1996.

[vdL97] Jan C. A. van der Lubbe. *Information Theory.* Cambridge University Press, 1997.

Q (MORIK)
Why use these methods? Morik et al tried something similar, and rejected it for a simpler numeric approach

Making Better Use of Global Discretization

Eibe Frank and Ian H. Witten
Department of Computer Science
University of Waikato
Hamilton, New Zealand
{eibe, ihw}@cs.waikato.ac.nz

Abstract

Before applying learning algorithms to datasets, practitioners often globally discretize any numeric attributes. If the algorithm cannot handle numeric attributes directly, prior discretization is essential. Even if it can, prior discretization often accelerates induction, and may produce simpler and more accurate classifiers.

As it is generally done, global discretization denies the learning algorithm any chance of taking advantage of the ordering information implicit in numeric attributes. However, a simple transformation of discretized data preserves this information in a form that learners can use. We show that, compared to using the discretized data directly, this transformation significantly increases the accuracy of decision trees built by C4.5, decision lists built by PART, and decision tables built using the wrapper method, on several benchmark datasets. Moreover, it can significantly reduce the size of the resulting classifiers.

This simple technique makes global discretization an even more useful tool for data preprocessing.

1 Introduction

Algorithms that transform numeric attributes into discrete ones are useful for several reasons. Most importantly, they enable learning schemes that can only handle nominal attributes to process numeric data. But this is not the only situation where they are useful. Often, it is worthwhile to discretize even if the learning scheme is able to process numeric data directly—as can most schemes that learn decision trees or lists. There are two reasons for this. First, discretization accelerates learning because nominal attributes are generally processed faster than numeric ones (Catlett, 1991)—assuming, of course, that the discretization itself is accomplished quickly. Second, it reduces the likelihood of overfitting by narrowing the space of possible hypotheses that the learning scheme can investigate, thereby lowering the chance of finding a complex hypothesis that fits the training data particularly well just by chance. The resulting classifiers are often significantly less complex and sometimes more accurate than classifiers learned from the raw numeric data.

Catlett (1991) presents a supervised method for global discretization and discusses the speed-up that can be achieved by applying it before building a decision tree.[1] His method is improved by Fayyad and Irani (1993), who show how to prevent the discretization from becoming too fine-grained by using the minimum description length principle to determine the appropriate granularity. Dougherty, Kohavi and Sahami (1995) compare several supervised and unsupervised methods and conclude that Fayyad and Irani's method produces the most accurate classifiers. Kohavi and Sahami (1996) extend the comparison to include three new methods, and corroborate this result.[2]

The trouble with global discretization, as it is normally used, is that the learning algorithm cannot take advantage of the ordering information implicit in numeric attributes because it treats the different discretized val-

[1] Note, however, that he sorts the data for each attribute at each node of the decision tree. This can be avoided by careful book-keeping: it is only actually necessary to sort the data once for each attribute.

[2] Neither of these two comparisons include ChiMerge, a theoretically well-founded discretization method based on the chi-squared test (Kerber, 1992).

ues as though they were completely independent. For example, if the decision-tree inducer C4.5 (Quinlan, 1992) decides to split on a pre-discretized attribute, it generates a multiway branch. In contrast, internal discretization implicitly takes advantage of ordering information by using successive binary splits instead.

However, there is a very simple transformation of discretized data that preserves the ordering information in a form that learners can use. This paper investigates the effect of this transformation on common classification models. Using a set of benchmark datasets from the UCI repository, we show that it often leads to more accurate decision trees, decision lists, and decision tables. In addition, it significantly reduces the size of these classifiers in several domains.

Section 2 describes the transformation and gives examples of its application. Section 3 applies decision-tree, decision-list, and decision-table inducers to the datasets with numeric attributes globally discretized, both with and without the transformation, and compares the results. The decision-tree and decision-list inducers are also applied to the raw datasets, using internal discretization. Section 4 discusses related work, and Section 5 gives some concluding remarks.

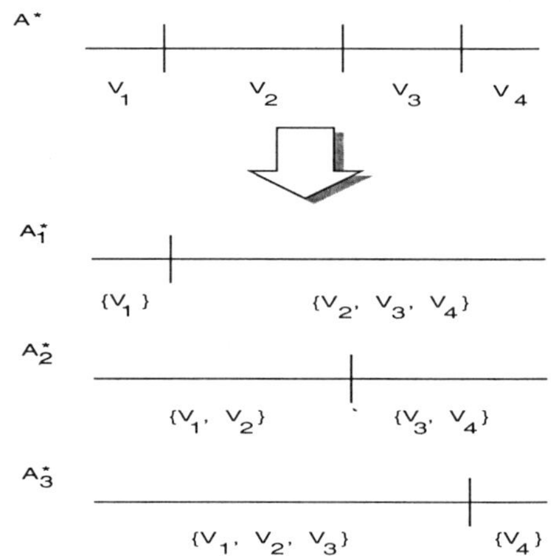

Figure 1: Transformation of a discretized attribute with four values into three binary attributes

2 Using Ordering Information in Discretized Attributes

Global discretization transforms a numeric attribute A into an attribute A^* with values $\{V_1, V_2, \ldots, V_n\}$, where each value V_i of the new attribute represents a range of numeric values of the original attribute. Virtually all supervised learning schemes treat discretized attributes in the same way as nominal ones. This means that potentially useful information is discarded—in other words, the learning algorithm is being deprived of valuable domain knowledge—for the fact is that discretized attribute values should be treated as ordered entities. In most learning schemes this loss is completely unnecessary: the ordering information can be exploited in decision trees, lists and tables without any change to the learning algorithm itself.

2.1 Decision Trees

Consider a decision tree learner that constructs trees with univariate tests. During learning, it has to select tests for each node of the tree structure, given the data present at that node. Exploiting the ordering information implicit in a discretized attribute A^* simply amounts to investigating tests of the form $A^* \leq V_i$ instead of $A^* = V_i$. Although this seems to imply that the inner workings of the learning scheme have to be changed to enable it to deal with ordered attributes of this type, the problem can be avoided by transforming the attributes before applying the learning scheme.

For each discretized attribute with n values, $n-1$ boolean ones are introduced, one for each of the attribute's first $n-1$ values, and the original discretized attribute is discarded. The ith boolean attribute represents the test $A^* \leq V_i$ (Figure 1). Figure 2b shows the effect of applying Fayyad and Irani's (1993) discretization method in conjunction with this transformation on a pruned decision tree produced by C4.5 (Quinlan, 1992) for the ionosphere dataset. The tree produced by C4.5 on the raw dataset, using its standard method of internal discretization, is shown in Figure 2a for comparison. As we will see in Section 3, the tree in Figure 2b is significantly more accurate than that of Figure 2a; it is also significantly smaller and more accurate than the tree built from the discretized data without applying the transformation.

Another way of interpreting this strategy is that it provides a way of combining *global* and *local* information during learning. The discretization method preselects candidate cutpoints based on global information, while the learner decides which of these cut-points is most appropriate in the current local context.

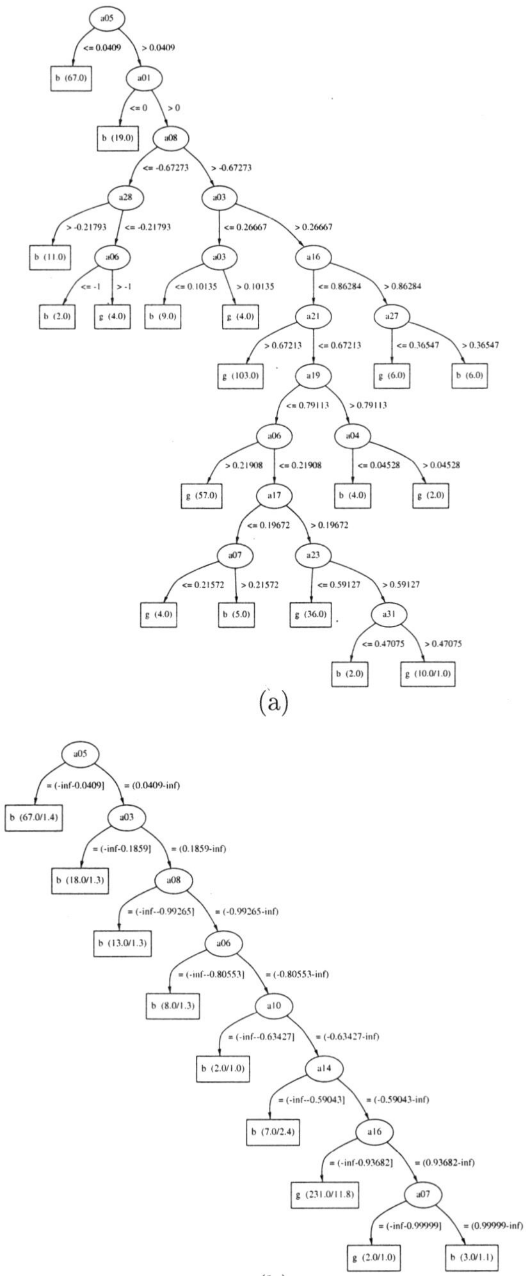

Figure 2: Decision tree for (a) raw, and (b) discretized and transformed ionosphere dataset

2.2 Decision Lists

Decision lists (Rivest, 1987) can also take advantage of ordering information. A decision list is an ordered set of rules. During classification, a test instance is assigned to the class of the first rule whose premise it satisfies. The premise of each rule consists of a conjunction of attribute-value tests. For nominal attributes, these tests have the form $A = V_i$. The ordering information implicit in discretized attributes can easily be exploited by applying tests of the form $A^* \leq V_i$. Again, the learning algorithm does not have to be changed to allow this type of test to be included: the attribute transformation of Section 2.1 can be used instead.

2.3 Decision Tables

Decision tables, like decision lists, are sets of rules. A decision table enumerates all possible combinations of attribute-value tests for a selected set of attributes, together with a class assignment for each combination. The size of the table increases exponentially with the number of attributes included: more specifically, if n_j is the number of values for attribute j, the table contains $\prod_j n_j$ rows. This means that the instance space becomes very fragmented when many attributes, with many possible values, are included in the table. The learning problem is to find a small subset of attributes, each with a small number of possible values, while maintaining high accuracy on the training data.

Decision tables can be constructed for numeric data if it is discretized *a priori*.[3] However, a discretized attribute may be only partially informative when used in conjunction with other attributes. In that case, if the discretization is too fine-grained, the instance space can become overly fragmented, resulting in suboptimal performance. The problem is easily solved by applying the transformation discussed in Section 2.1. If an attribute is partially informative, only those binary attributes derived from the original discretized attribute that are relevant in the current context will be included in the decision table, thereby minimizing fragmentation.

3 Experimental Evaluation

In this section, we will see that significantly more accurate decision trees, lists, and tables can be produced by exploiting the ordering information implicit

[3] Kohavi's (1995) method does handle numeric attributes, but only in a very limited way.

Table 1: Datasets used for the experiments

Dataset	Size	Numeric	Nominal	Classes
anneal	898	6	32	5
australian	690	6	9	2
autos	205	15	10	6
balance-scale	625	4	0	3
breast-w	699	9	0	2
german	1000	7	13	2
glass (G2)	163	9	0	2
glass	214	9	0	6
heart-c	303	6	7	2
heart-h	294	6	7	2
heart-statlog	270	13	0	2
hepatitis	155	6	13	2
horse-colic	368	7	15	2
hypothyroid	3772	7	22	4
ionosphere	351	34	0	2
iris	150	4	0	3
labor	57	8	8	2
lymph	148	3	15	4
pima-indians	768	8	0	2
segment	2310	19	0	7
sick	3772	7	22	2
sonar	208	60	0	2
vehicle	846	18	0	4
vowel	990	10	3	11
waveform	5000	40	0	3
zoo	101	1	15	7

in discretized numeric attributes. All results are based on the 26 UCI benchmark datasets listed in Table 1, each of which contains at least one numeric attribute. Fayyad and Irani's (Fayyad & Irani, 1993) discretization method was employed throughout.

3.1 Decision Trees

We begin with decision trees, and compare pruned trees generated by C4.5[4] in three different ways. First, trees are built from the discretized data transformed using the procedure described in Section 2.1 (ORD). Second, they are built directly from the discretized data (DISC). Third, they are built by C4.5 from the raw data (RAW).

The results are listed in Table 2. This shows the percentage of correct classifications, averaged over ten ten-fold cross-validation runs, along with the standard deviation of the ten. Also shown is the average tree size measured by the number of nodes in it. The same folds were used for each scheme. In all experiments with discretization, the training data was discretized separately for each fold—otherwise the cross-validation estimates would be optimistically biased (Kohavi & Sahami, 1996).

Results for DISC and RAW are marked with ∘ if they show significant improvement over the corresponding results for ORD, and with • if they show significant degradation. Throughout, we speak of results being "significantly different" if the difference is statistically significant at the 1% level according to a paired two-sided t-test, each pair of data points consisting of the estimates obtained in one ten-fold cross-validation run for the two learning schemes being compared.

Table 3 shows how the different methods compare with each other. Each entry indicates the number of datasets for which the method associated with its column is significantly more accurate than the method associated with its row.

As Table 3 shows, it is clearly advantageous to make use of the ordering information in discretized attributes. ORD is significantly more accurate than DISC on six datasets (second row, first column), whereas the inverse is never true (first row, second column). It is interesting to see that ORD and RAW are almost neck and neck in terms of accuracy: ORD is more accurate on four datasets, RAW on five. It is also apparent that RAW builds more accurate trees than DISC in eight cases, whereas the reverse is true in only two. This is consistent with the results of Quinlan (Quinlan, 1996), who found that RAW has a strong advantage over DISC in terms of accuracy. As Table 2 and Table 3 show, this advantage largely vanishes when the ordering information is exploited.

Table 3 also shows that the trees built by ORD are generally smaller than those built by DISC: the former builds significantly smaller trees for twelve datasets and significantly larger ones for only three. The advantage of using ORD is even more pronounced when compared to RAW. On sixteen datasets ORD generates smaller trees, and larger ones on only four.

3.2 Decision Lists

As explained in Section 2.2, decision lists can exploit ordering information in the same way as decision trees. The empirical results presented here were obtained using the rule learner PART, which has been shown to perform comparably to other state-of-the-art rule learning methods (Frank & Witten, 1998).

Tables 4 and 5 summarize results obtained using the

[4]In all our experiments we used C4.5 Revision 8 (Quinlan, 1996).

Table 2: C4.5: Percentage of correct classifications and size of trees, with standard deviations, for ordered (ORD), discretized (DISC), and raw data (RAW)

	Accuracy			Size		
Dataset	ORD	DISC	RAW	ORD	DISC	RAW
anneal	98.8±0.2	98.8±0.1	98.7±0.3	46.9±0.7	51.3±1.1 •	48.0±1.4
australian	86.5±0.3	86.0±0.5	85.5±0.7 •	21.1±1.7	22.6±2.2	32.5±3.2 •
autos	75.9±2.4	74.5±1.8	80.0±2.5 ◦	76.2±2.9	101.5±4.6 •	62.4±2.2 ◦
balance-scale	75.7±0.9	75.5±0.9	77.6±0.9 ◦	33.6±2.3	41.3±2.1 •	82.2±2.9 •
breast-w	95.4±0.4	95.0±0.5	94.9±0.4	18.1±1.3	20.5±1.2 •	24.6±1.3 •
german	72.2±0.8	71.8±0.7	71.1±1.1	90.6±4.9	89.1±7.2	124.4±6.0 •
glass (G2)	77.4±2.5	77.4±2.4	78.1±1.8	14.1±0.7	11.8±0.8 ◦	23.7±1.6 •
glass	70.2±2.0	72.0±1.2	68.2±2.4	28.5±1.1	37.1±1.1 •	45.5±1.3 •
heart-c	77.3±1.8	77.8±1.3	76.7±1.7	33.2±2.1	31.4±2.0 ◦	43.5±2.5 •
heart-h	79.3±1.0	79.3±1.0	79.8±0.8	9.0±1.8	9.1±1.9	10.8±0.9
heart-statlog	81.4±1.3	81.5±1.4	78.3±1.9 •	24.1±2.1	23.9±2.0	34.9±2.6 •
hepatitis	78.5±1.3	79.3±2.3	79.7±1.2	10.7±1.8	10.7±1.7	17.8±1.2 •
horse-colic	85.3±0.3	85.3±0.3	85.4±0.3	8.5±0.7	8.5±0.7	8.7±0.7
hypothyroid	99.5±0.0	99.2±0.1 •	99.5±0.0	23.2±0.4	46.6±1.3 •	27.9±0.3 •
ionosphere	93.0±0.4	89.8±1.2 •	89.4±1.3 •	17.4±0.5	25.1±2.1 •	27.1±0.9 •
iris	93.7±1.1	92.9±0.9 •	94.4±0.6	6.1±0.3	6.5±0.5	8.3±0.5 •
labor	78.0±3.4	77.5±3.3	77.2±4.1	6.5±0.5	6.4±0.5	7.0±0.8
lymph	74.9±2.0	75.8±2.0	75.8±2.9	25.5±1.3	25.6±1.3	27.7±1.2 •
pima-indians	73.9±0.8	73.8±1.0	74.5±1.4	25.3±2.1	23.6±2.1	42.3±4.1 •
segment	96.0±0.3	94.1±0.3 •	96.7±0.3 ◦	88.0±1.7	336.7±9.4 •	82.0±2.6 ◦
sick	97.8±0.1	97.8±0.1	98.7±0.2 ◦	29.1±0.7	32.2±0.9 •	48.7±2.1 •
sonar	76.0±2.2	76.0±2.2	75.0±3.0	28.5±1.6	28.5±1.6	28.0±0.8
vehicle	70.3±1.0	69.7±1.2	72.8±1.1 ◦	122.2±2.0	200.7±5.4 •	139.4±5.0 •
vowel	78.5±0.9	76.2±0.7 •	79.6±1.3	298.4±14.4	370.4±10.4 •	216.2±7.1 ◦
waveform	77.0±0.6	74.7±0.4 •	75.3±0.7 •	651.2±12.2	628.2±15.7 ◦	590.1±9.9 ◦
zoo	91.1±1.2	90.8±1.5	91.1±1.2	15.1±0.3	16.6±0.5 •	15.2±0.4

Table 3: Results of paired t-tests (p=0.01) for C4.5: number indicates how often method in column significantly outperforms method in row

	Accuracy			Size		
	ORD	DISC	RAW	ORD	DISC	RAW
ORD	–	**0**	**5**	–	**3**	**4**
DISC	**6**	–	8	**12**	–	8
RAW	**4**	2	–	**16**	13	–

same experimental procedure as in Section 3.1. ORD denotes results obtained by running PART on the discretized and transformed data—thereby incorporating ordering information in the learning process—and DISC stands for PART run on the discretized data directly. Results for PART using the raw numeric data are included as RAW.

Table 5 shows that, just as with decision trees, decision lists built from the discretized and transformed data are preferable to those generated from the discretized data directly. ORD is significantly more accurate than DISC on five datasets, whereas DISC is never significantly better than ORD. ORD is also generally the better choice when the number of rules is a critical factor. It produces significantly fewer rules than DISC on ten datasets, and significantly more on only two.

The situation is less clear-cut when ORD is compared to RAW. In four cases, PART builds significantly more accurate classifiers from the raw data than from the discretized and transformed data. In only one case is the decision list significantly more accurate for the latter type of data. Size is also not necessarily an argument for applying pre-processing. In several cases—for example waveform, vowel, vehicle, and segment—RAW generates significantly fewer rules than ORD.

Table 4: PART: Percentage of correct classifications and size, with standard deviations, for ordered (ORD), discretized (DISC), and raw data (RAW)

Dataset	Accuracy			Size		
	ORD	DISC	RAW	ORD	DISC	RAW
anneal	98.6±0.2	98.7±0.4	98.4±0.3	15.4±0.5	16.8±0.4 •	14.6±0.5
australian	84.8±0.5	84.6±0.6	84.3±1.2	21.6±1.3	21.3±1.2	30.5±1.5 •
autos	73.5±3.0	71.8±2.3	74.5±1.1	20.2±0.4	23.6±0.8 •	20.5±1.0
balance-scale	77.0±0.8	77.5±0.7	82.3±1.2 ∘	13.4±0.7	14.4±1.0	38.7±1.2 •
breast-w	95.4±0.5	95.3±0.7	94.9±0.4	11.2±0.6	9.7±0.7 ∘	10.0±0.7 ∘
german	71.0±1.3	71.3±0.9	70.0±1.4	57.6±1.7	58.7±1.8	69.6±1.3 •
glass (G2)	77.7±2.5	79.5±2.2	80.0±4.0	5.0±0.0	5.6±0.5 •	6.8±0.4 •
glass	70.6±2.1	70.9±1.8	69.8±2.3	11.5±0.5	12.6±0.5 •	15.2±0.8 •
heart-c	79.6±1.5	80.5±1.7	78.1±1.6	15.9±0.7	15.8±0.8	19.3±0.8 •
heart-h	79.8±1.5	79.8±1.5	80.4±1.6	7.7±0.5	7.8±0.6	8.9±0.9 •
heart-statlog	82.1±0.9	82.1±0.9	78.9±1.3 •	13.9±0.9	14.0±0.7	17.7±1.1 •
hepatitis	80.0±2.8	79.8±3.6	80.2±1.9	7.4±0.8	7.3±0.8	8.3±0.7
horse-colic	83.9±1.0	83.9±1.0	84.4±0.8	7.4±0.7	7.4±0.7	9.7±0.8 •
hypothyroid	99.4±0.1	99.4±0.1	99.5±0.1	8.2±0.4	14.2±0.4 •	10.4±0.5 •
ionosphere	91.4±1.3	89.9±0.7 •	90.6±1.3	7.7±0.5	10.0±0.5 •	7.6±0.5
iris	93.7±1.0	92.7±0.8 •	93.7±1.6	3.6±0.5	4.5±0.5 •	4.0±0.5
labor	76.0±4.0	75.8±4.1	77.3±3.9	3.7±0.5	3.7±0.5	3.6±0.5
lymph	76.9±2.1	77.7±3.1	76.5±2.7	10.8±0.6	10.8±0.6	11.7±0.7
pima-indians	73.5±0.8	73.4±1.3	73.6±0.5	22.2±2.7	22.4±1.7	7.3±0.5 ∘
segment	96.1±0.3	93.6±0.4 •	96.6±0.3 ∘	31.0±0.8	59.3±2.5 •	27.5±0.7 ∘
sick	97.8±0.1	97.9±0.0	98.6±0.1 ∘	15.1±0.7	14.9±0.9	19.1±0.9 •
sonar	77.1±3.7	77.2±3.5	76.5±2.3	12.5±0.5	12.5±0.5	7.5±0.7 ∘
vehicle	71.1±0.9	68.2±1.7 •	72.4±0.8 ∘	60.7±1.6	65.3±1.8 •	33.2±1.2 ∘
vowel	77.7±1.0	75.3±0.9 •	78.1±1.1	93.5±2.1	116.4±0.8 •	66.0±1.4 ∘
waveform	77.3±0.5	76.6±0.6	78.0±0.5	283.0±4.3	263.9±4.4 ∘	87.9±2.4 ∘
zoo	92.2±1.2	92.0±1.1	92.2±1.2	8.0±0.0	8.0±0.0	8.0±0.0

Table 5: Results of paired t-tests (p=0.01) for PART: number indicates how often method in column significantly outperforms method in row

	Accuracy			Size		
	ORD	DISC	RAW	ORD	DISC	RAW
ORD	–	**0**	**4**	–	**2**	**7**
DISC	**5**	–	8	**10**	–	10
RAW	**1**	2	–	**11**	9	–

3.3 Decision Tables

For our experiments on decision tables, we employed a learning algorithm that uses the wrapper method in conjunction with a best first search for selecting the attributes in the table (Kohavi, 1995). Our implementation of the wrapper employs leave-one-out cross-validation and a stopping criterion of five consecutive fully expanded non-improving nodes in the search space.

Table 6 and Table 7 show the results. The size of a decision table is measured by the number of entries in it. Only combinations of attribute-value tests that cover at least one instance of the training data are counted as entries.

Table 7 shows that ORD produces more accurate tables than DISC on seven datasets. Unlike decision trees and lists, however, for decision tables there is a dataset (glass) for which ORD is significantly less accurate—although the relative difference in accuracy is rather small. Table 7 also shows that ORD generates significantly smaller tables than DISC for eight datasets, and significantly larger ones for only two. Moreover, on one of these two datasets (waveform) it is also significantly more accurate, indicating that there are some discretized attributes in this dataset that are only partially informative, and therefore omitted from the table built by DISC. As discussed in Section 2.3, ORD successfully reduces the fragmentation of the instance space, sometimes with a positive effect on accuracy

Table 6: Decision tables: Percentage of correct classifications and size, with standard deviations, for ordered (ORD) and discretized (DISC) data

	Accuracy		Size	
Dataset	ORD	DISC	ORD	DISC
anneal	99.3±0.2	98.6±0.1 •	46.8±2.1	119.8±4.6 •
australian	85.1±0.9	85.2±0.8	43.7±7.8	45.9±7.5
autos	77.4±1.1	77.5±1.8	77.6±1.7	77.6±3.9
balance-scale	78.1±0.5	74.5±0.9 •	41.6±5.5	42.7±5.6
breast-w	95.3±0.5	94.7±0.7	32.7±3.3	46.1±6.4 •
german	71.6±0.9	71.6±0.8	122.7±21.6	120.4±21.4
glass (G2)	78.2±2.0	77.9±1.8	11.7±1.0	11.9±0.7
glass	68.1±1.2	69.6±0.7 ○	23.5±3.4	36.8±2.1 •
heart-c	78.5±2.0	78.6±1.7	37.3±4.2	42.8±6.5 •
heart-h	79.6±1.0	79.6±1.1	14.6±1.6	15.0±1.8
heart-statlog	82.6±1.4	82.5±1.3	21.5±4.7	21.6±4.8
hepatitis	80.4±2.9	80.2±2.3	39.1±5.2	36.8±4.7
horse-colic	82.7±0.8	82.7±0.8	62.0±8.1	62.0±8.1
hypothyroid	99.6±0.1	99.4±0.0 •	72.7±2.7	69.2±5.5
ionosphere	89.5±1.3	89.6±1.2	22.9±1.4	28.4±1.4 •
iris	93.2±0.8	92.7±0.5 •	4.9±0.5	5.5±0.5 •
labor	83.3±3.6	83.8±3.6	10.7±1.1	10.7±1.0
lymph	74.3±2.4	74.9±1.8	27.1±3.0	25.7±3.1
pima-indians	73.5±0.8	74.0±1.3	44.9±7.0	41.4±8.6
segment	94.3±0.4	92.1±0.5 •	143.0±11.2	302.0±11.6 •
sick	97.6±0.1	97.6±0.1	92.8±7.0	71.6±9.1 ○
sonar	73.7±2.3	73.5±2.5	35.4±2.5	35.0±2.5
vehicle	68.2±1.4	65.1±0.7 •	89.1±7.0	100.2±9.5
vowel	70.2±1.1	70.7±1.6	354.6±14.6	355.3±7.3
waveform	76.7±0.4	73.7±0.6 •	423.3±18.4	270.3±56.0 ○
zoo	91.4±1.5	90.0±1.4	12.7±0.4	15.7±0.4 •

Table 7: Results of paired t-tests (p=0.01) for Decision tables: number indicates how often method in column significantly outperforms method in row

	Accuracy		Size	
	ORD	DISC	ORD	DISC
ORD	–	1	–	2
DISC	7	–	8	–

(anneal, iris, segment).

Note that the time complexity of learning decision tables with best first search is not linear in the number of attributes.[5] Hence ORD can be significantly slower than DISC, depending on the number of attributes generated by the transformation. For C4.5 and PART the time complexity is linear, and the difference between ORD and DISC is roughly proportional to the average number of values in the discretized attributes. This difference is usually negligible compared to the time needed for the discretization, which involves sorting the training instances once for each numeric attribute.

[5]However, there are fast algorithms for learning decision tables that are linear in the number of attributes (Kohavi & Sommerfield, 1998).

4 Related Work

Work on methods for global discretization has already been discussed in Section 1. However, there is another line of research, concerned with the combination of global and local information in the learning process, that is closely related to the work presented in this paper.

Pazzani (1998) introduces the notion of globally predictive tests for rule learning systems. In order to incorporate them into rules, he introduces a bias that forces the learning scheme to choose only those tests that are globally predictive. A test is defined to be globally predictive of a certain class if the probability of observing this class after the test has been performed is greater than the prior probability of the class. On some datasets this restriction significantly increases accuracy; however, on others the effect is detrimental. Therefore the afore-mentioned bias is weakened by allowing locally predictive rules, but only if they are significantly more accurate than the globally predictive alternatives. This combination significantly increases accuracy on three out of fifteen datasets, and never significantly decreases it. It is also claimed that this procedure improves the comprehensibility of the resulting rule sets, although this claim is not validated by experiments.

Vilalta *et al.* (1997) argue that C4.5rules (Quinlan, 1992) uses a kind of global data analysis to combat the fragmentation problem in C4.5's decision trees. Each of the rules derived from a decision tree is pruned individually using all the available training data—in other words, tests are deleted from a rule if this makes the rule more globally predictive.

5 Conclusions

This paper introduces a simple transformation of discretized attributes that allows learning schemes for decision trees, lists, and tables to make full use of the ordering information present in those attributes. Implemented as a pre-processing step that takes place after discretization but before applying the learning scheme, it can be used in conjunction with existing learning algorithms without any modifications being necessary.

The empirical results we have presented show that the transformation is indeed useful when used in conjunction with decision trees produced by C4.5, decision lists produced by PART, and decision tables produced using the wrapper method. Compared to using the discretized data directly, it significantly increases the accuracy of the classifiers in several cases, rarely decreasing it. (In our experiments, a significant decrease occurred only once.) Moreover, classifiers are generally significantly smaller if the transformation is applied.

In decision trees and lists, the same effect can be achieved by coding discretized attributes as integers. In this case, if the generated classifier is to be comprehensible for the user, it should be post-processed by replacing the artificial integer-valued tests with tests on values of the original numeric attribute. The same kind of integer coding can also be used to exploit ordering information in instance-based learning algorithms. Of course, if a learning scheme supports ordered attributes directly, any transformation is superfluous: the effect is achieved by declaring discretized attributes to be of type "ordered". Whichever way it is done, our experiments show that it pays to give the learning scheme the opportunity to exploit the ordering information in discretized attributes.

References

Catlett, J. (1991). On changing continuous attributes into ordered discrete attributes. In Kodratoff, Y. (Ed.), *Proceedings of the European Working Session on Learning* (pp. 164–178). Berlin: Springer-Verlag.

Dougherty, J., Kohavi, R. & Sahami, M. (1995). Supervised and unsupervised discretization of continuous features. In *Proceedings of the 12th International Conference on Machine Learning* (pp. 194–202). Morgan Kaufmann.

Fayyad, U. M. & Irani, K. B. (1993). Multi-interval discretization of continuous-valued attributes for classification learning. In *Proceedings of the 13th International Joint Conference on Artifical Intelligence* (pp. 1022–1027). Morgan Kaufmann.

Frank, E. & Witten, I. H. (1998). Generating accurate rule sets without global optimization. In *Proceedings of the 15th International Conference on Machine Learning* (pp. 144–151). San Francisco, CA: Morgan Kaufmann.

Kerber, R. (1992). Discretization of numeric attributes. In *Proceedings of the 10th National Conference on Artificial Intelligence* (pp. 123–128). Menlo Park, CA: AAAI Press/MIT Press.

Kohavi, R. (1995). The power of decision tables. In Lavrac, N. & Wrobel, S. (Eds.), *Machine Learning: ECML-95* (pp. 174–189). Berlin: Springer-Verlag.

Kohavi, R. & Sahami, M. (1996). Error-based and entropy-based discretization of continuous features. In *Proceedings of the Second International Conference on Knowledge Discovery and Data Mining* (pp. 114–119). Menlo Park: AAAI Press.

Kohavi, R. & Sommerfield, D. (1998). Targeting business users with decision table classifiers. In *Proceedings of the 4th International Conference on Knowledge Discovery and Data Mining.* AAAI Press.

Pazzani, M. J. (1998). Learning with globally predictive tests. In *Proceedings of the 1st International Conference on Discovery Science*. Springer-Verlag.

Quinlan, J. (1992). *C4.5: Programs for Machine Learning.* Los Altos, CA: Morgan Kaufmann.

Quinlan, J. (1996). Improved use of continuous attribute in C4.5. *Journal of Artificial Intelligence Research*, *4*, 77–90.

Rivest, R. L. (1987). Learning decision lists. *Machine Learning*, *2*, 229–246.

Vilalta, R., Blix, G. & Rendell, L. (1997). Global data analysis and the fragmentation problem in decision tree induction. In *Proceedings of the 9th European Conference on Machine Learning* (pp. 312–327). Heidelberg: Springer-Verlag.

See "BROWN BOOST" : COLT 99

The alternating decision tree learning algorithm

Yoav Freund
AT&T Labs
180 Park Avenue
Florham Park, NJ, 07932, USA

Llew Mason
Department of Systems Engineering
Australian National University
Canberra, ACT, 0200, Australia

Abstract

The application of boosting procedures to decision tree algorithms has been shown to produce very accurate classifiers. These classifiers are in the form of a majority vote over a number of decision trees. Unfortunately, these classifiers are often large, complex and difficult to interpret. This paper describes a new type of classification rule, the *alternating decision tree*, which is a generalization of decision trees, voted decision trees and voted decision stumps. At the same time classifiers of this type are relatively easy to interpret. We present a learning algorithm for alternating decision trees that is based on boosting. Experimental results show it is competitive with boosted decision tree algorithms such as C5.0, and generates rules that are usually smaller in size and thus easier to interpret. In addition these rules yield a natural measure of classification confidence which can be used to improve the accuracy at the cost of abstaining from predicting examples that are hard to classify.

1 INTRODUCTION

The AdaBoost algorithm [7, 16] has recently proved to be an important component in practical learning algorithms. Two of the most successful combinations have been boosting decision trees and boosting stumps [6, 1, 13, 8] . Stumps are the simplest special case of decision trees which consist of a single decision node and two prediction leaves.

Boosting decision trees learning algorithms, such as CART [2] and C4.5 [14], yields very good classifiers. The software package C5.0[1] is one of the best packages that combines (a variant of) AdaBoost with C4.5. Unfortunately, the classifiers generated by C5.0 using boosting are often large and thus hard to interpret.

In this paper we suggest a new combination of decision trees with boosting that generates classification rules that are often smaller and easier to interpret then the rules that are generated by using C5.0 with boosting. We introduce a new representation for classifiers which we call *alternating decision trees* (ADTrees). This representation generalizes both voted-stumps and decision trees in a natural way. We show how boosting can be used as a method for learning ADTrees from data (Kearns and Mansour in [9] analyze decision tree learning algorithms as boosting algorithms. Their work suggests an algorithm similar to the one presented here).

ADTrees are similar to *option trees* first described by Buntine in [3] and further developed by Kohavi et. al. in [10]. Option trees were shown to provide significant improvements in classification error compared to single decision trees. The results reported in [10] are comparable to bagged decision trees. Our goal here is to learn a structure similar to option trees using boosting and thus achieve better performance levels. Our experiments show that the performance of this learning algorithm is similar to that of C5.0 with boosting. The question of improving the comprehensibility of trained classifiers have been previously studied by Craven [4], Domingos [5], and Margineatu and Dietterich [11].

One of the nice features of alternating decision trees is that they give, in addition to a classification, a measure of confidence which we call the classification *margin*.

[1] C5.0 was written by Ross Quinlan and is available commercially from Rulequest Research: `http://www.rulequest.com/`.

This measure of confidence has been analyzed in prior work [15]. In this work we give some new evidence for the validity and usefulness of interpreting classification margins as measures of confidence.

The paper is organized as follows. In Section 2 we describe alternating decision trees and show how they can be represented as weighted votes of simple prediction rules. In Section 3 we describe how AdaBoost is used to learn ADTrees. In section 5 we describe some experiments we have performed with the new algorithm. We conclude with a summary and a description of current work in Section 6.

2 ALTERNATING DECISION TREES

In this section we give a new semantics for representing decision trees and then show how this semantics can be extended to represent general alternating decision tree classifiers. In addition we show how alternating tree classifiers can be represented as a majority vote over very simple prediction rules. Recall that AdaBoost generates rules that *are* majority votes over simpler, so called "weak" rules. By representing alternating trees as such votes we make it easy to use AdaBoost to learn alternating trees from data.

We give a formal description of alternating trees in Figure 2. For our intuitive explanation we use a sequence of simple examples given in Figure 1. Consider first the decision tree in Figure 1(a). This is a simple decision tree with two decision nodes and three prediction leaves. The tree defines a binary classification rule which maps instances of the form $(a, b) \in R^2$ into one of two classes denoted by -1 and $+1$ (in this paper we restrict ourselves to binary classification problems.) In Figure 1(b) we give a different representation of the same classification rule. In this representation each decision node is replaced by two nodes: a *prediction node* (represented by an ellipse), and a *splitter node* (represented by a rectangle). The decision node is identical to what we had before, while the prediction node is associated with a *real valued* number. As in decision trees, an instance is mapped into a *path* along the tree from the root to one of the leaves. However, *unlike* decision trees, the classification that is associated with the path is *not* the label of the leaf, instead, it is the sign of the sum of the predictions along the path. For example, the classification of the instance $a = b = 0.5$ is $\text{sign}(0.5-0.7-0.2) = \text{sign}(-0.4) = -1$. It is easy to check that the two trees define the same classification rule. It is also clear that many different trees of the second type can represent the same tree of the first type.

We call the second representation an "alternating tree" representation for the obvious reason that it consists of alternating layers of prediction nodes and splitter nodes. So far we have described how standard decision trees can be represented as alternating trees. Before we describe general decision trees we show how alternating trees can be represented as a vote over simple prediction rules.

We think of the tree in Figure 1(b), as consisting of a root prediction node and two units of three nodes each: a decision node and the two prediction nodes that are its children (this structure is very similar to decision stumps, but the numbers associated with the leaves are real number, rather than just $+1$ or -1). It is now a simple transition to rewrite the classification rule described in Figure 1(b) as a weighted majority vote. We associate with each of the decision nodes a simple rule of the following form:

```
if(precondition) then
     if(condition) then output p1
     else output p2
else output 0
```

Specifically, with the decision nodes in Figure 1(b) we associate the following two rules:

```
r1(a,b)=                  |   r2(a,b)=
if(always) then           |   if(a<4.5) then
  if(a<4.5) then          |     if(b>1) then
       output -0.7        |          output +0.4
  else output +0.2        |     else output -0.2
else output 0             |   else output 0
```

By combining these two rules with the constant prediction associated with the root node we can rewrite the classification rule represented by the decision tree as: `sign(0.5 + r1(a,b) +r2(a,b))`. We refer to these rules as *base rules*.

It is clear that through this transformation we can represent any standard decision tree as a sum of base rules each of which corresponds to one of the decision nodes in the tree. In general **`precondition`** is the conjunction of conditions that lead to a given decision node, **`condition`** is the decision associated with the node and **`p1, p2`** are the predictions associated with the two children of the decision node.

We proceed now to show how we generalize standard decision trees to general alternating decision trees that give a much more flexible semantics for representing

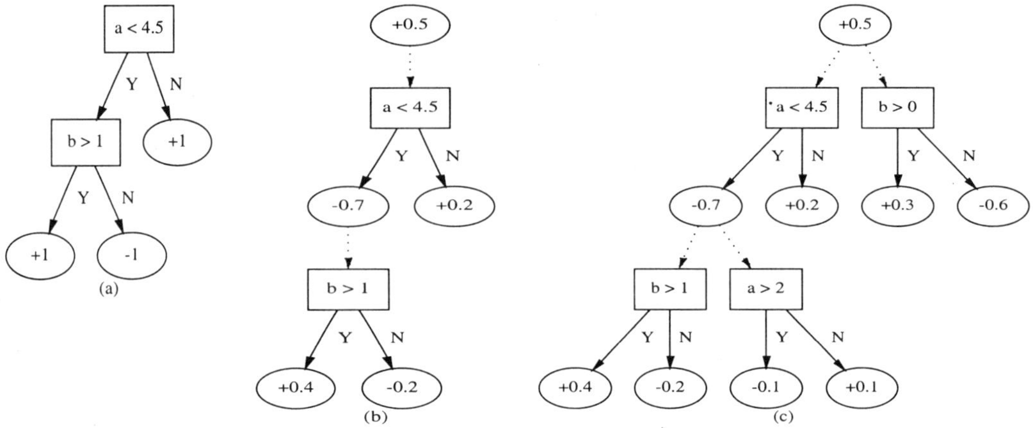

Figure 1: Tree-based classifiers: (a) a decision tree, (b) the same decision tree represented as an alternating tree. (c) a general alternating tree.

1. A *base condition* is a boolean predicate over instances. We use $\wedge$ to denote conjunction (AND), $\neg$ to denote negation (NOT) and **T** to denote the constant predicate that is always true. We use $\mathcal{C}$ to denote a set of base conditions.
2. A *precondition* is a conjunction of base conditions and negations of base conditions.
3. A *base rule* r is a mapping from instances to real numbers which is defined in terms of a precondition c_1, a base condition c_2, and two real numbers a and b. The base rule maps each instance to a *prediction* that is defined to be a if $c_1 \wedge c_2$, b if $c_1 \wedge \neg c_2$ and 0 if $\neg c_1$.
4. An *alternating decision tree* is a mapping from instances to real numbers which is defined in terms of a set of base rules. The set of base rules must obey the two following two conditions:
   (a) The set must include a base rule for which both the condition and the pre-condition are **T**. The a value of this rule is the prediction associated with the root of the tree.
   (b) A base rule r with precondition d can be in the set only if the set includes a rule r' with precondition c_1 and condition c_2 such that $d = c_1 \wedge c_2$ or $d = c_1 \wedge \neg c_2$. d corresponds to the prediction node that is the direct parent of r.

   The alternating tree maps each instance to a real valued *prediction* which is the sum of the predictions of the base rules in its set. The *classification* of an instance is the sign of the prediction.

Figure 2: A formal definition of alternating trees as weighted votes of simple rules

classifiers.[2]

Standard decision trees define a partition of the instance space into disjoint regions. Most algorithms for learning decision trees work by iteratively splitting one of the parts in two. Each part can be split at most once. In other words, only leaf nodes can be split. In *general* alternating decision trees we allow each part to be split multiple times. Returning to our example, we observe that in the alternating tree described in Figure 1(b) each predictor node has at most one splitter node attached to it. In Figure 1(c) we add two splitter nodes to this decision tree and get an example of a general alternating tree.

A general alternating tree defines a classification rule as follows. An instance defines a *set of* paths in the alternating tree. As in standard decision trees, when a path reaches a decision node it continues with the child which corresponds to the outcome of the decision associated with the node. However, when reaching a prediction node, the path continues with *all* of the children of the node. More precisely, the path splits into a *set* of paths, each of which corresponds to one of the children of the prediction node. We call the union of all

[2]Strictly speaking, any ADTree classifier can be represented by a standard decision tree. However, the decision tree can be exponentially larger.

the paths reached in this way for a given instance the *"multi-path"* associated with that instance. The sign of the sum of all the prediction nodes that are included in a multi-path is the classification which the tree associates with the instance. As examples consider the following two instances: if $a = 1$ and $b = 0.5$ then the classification is $\text{sign}(0.5 + 0.3 - 0.7 - 0.2 + 0.1) = \text{sign}(0.1) = +1$, if $a = 5$ and $b = 1$ then the classification is $\text{sign}(0.5 + 0.2 + 0.3) = \text{sign}(1.0) = +1$. In both cases the classification is $+1$, however, we can think of the second prediction as more confident then the second. We'll return to this point later.

From our description of the alternating decision trees it is clear that they are generalization of decision trees. It is not hard to see that they also generalize voted stumps. These correspond to alternating trees with exactly three layers: a root, a set of decision nodes, and the predictor nodes associated with these decision nodes. Finally, voted decision trees are also a special case of alternating decision trees, they correspond to alternating trees in which only the root prediction node has more than one child.

The representation of alternating decision trees as a majority vote over base rules is a direct extension of the representation that was described above for simple decision trees. The formal definition of alternating trees in this form is given in Figure 2.

3 BOOSTING ALTERNATING DECISION TREES

As shown in the previous section, alternating trees can be defined as a sum of simple base rules. As a result, it is a simple matter to apply any boosting algorithm to the problem of learning alternating decision trees from examples. The only special thing here is that the set of base rules (sometimes called "weak hypotheses") that are considered at each stage is not constant but increases as the tree is grown.

As our base rules generate predictions that can be *any* real valued number we use the version of AdaBoost suggested by Schapire and Singer [16] which extends the original AdaBoost algorithm of Freund and Schapire [7] that allows the base rules to make real valued prediction. In addition, Singer and Schapire give formulas for calculating the best predictions for a given partition of the input space. We use these formulas to choose the value of a and b for the base rules.

We fix a set of base conditions. In the experiments described here we use only inequality conditions that

Note: This alg. may add an extra child to an internal node.

Initialize Set $\mathcal{R}_1$ to consist of the single base rule whose precondition and condition are both $\mathbf{T}$, and whose first prediction value is

$$a = \frac{1}{2} \ln \frac{W_+(\mathbf{T})}{W_-(\mathbf{T})} .$$

Do for $t = 1, 2, \ldots, T$

1. For each base precondition $c_1 \in \mathcal{P}_t$ and each condition $c_2 \in \mathcal{C}$ calculate

$$Z_t(c_1, c_2) = 2\Big(\sqrt{W_+(c_1 \wedge c_2) W_-(c_1 \wedge c_2)} + \sqrt{W_+(c_1 \wedge \neg c_2) W_-(c_1 \wedge \neg c_2)}\Big) + W(\neg c_2) .$$

? ¬c1

2. Select c_1, c_2 which minimize $Z_t(c_1, c_2)$ and set $\mathcal{R}_{t+1}$ to be $\mathcal{R}_t$ with the addition of the rule r_t whose precondition is c_1, condition is c_2 and two prediction values are:

$$a = \frac{1}{2} \ln \frac{W_+(c_1 \wedge c_2)}{W_-(c_1 \wedge c_2)}, \qquad b = \frac{1}{2} \ln \frac{W_+(c_1 \wedge \neg c_2)}{W_-(c_1 \wedge \neg c_2)}$$ (*)

3. Set $\mathcal{P}_{t+1}$ to be $\mathcal{P}_t$ with the addition of $c_1 \wedge c_2$ and $c_1 \wedge \neg c_2$.

4. Update the weights of each training example according to the equation

$$w_{i,t+1} = w_{i,t} e^{r_t(\mathbf{x}_i) y_i}$$

(Note that if $r(\mathbf{x}_i) = 0$ the weight is not changed.)

Output the classification rule that is the sign of the sum of all the base rules in $\mathcal{R}_{T+1}$:

$$\text{class}(\mathbf{x}) = \text{sign}\left(\sum_{t=1}^{T} r_t(\mathbf{x})\right) .$$

Figure 3: An application of AdaBoost to learning alternating decision trees.

compare a single feature with a constant. This set of base rules is sufficiently restricted that it is feasible to enumerate all possible base rules that can be added to a given tree for a given training set.

The learning algorithm is described in Figure 3. We introduce some notation used in the figure.

- The training set is denoted $(\mathbf{x}_1, y_1), \ldots, (\mathbf{x}_m, y_m)$ where $\mathbf{x}_i \in R^d$ and $y_i \in \{-1, +1\}$.
- The set of base conditions (inequalities comparing a single feature and a constant) is denoted by $\mathcal{C}$.

(*) What if $W_+ = 0$ or $W_- = 0$?

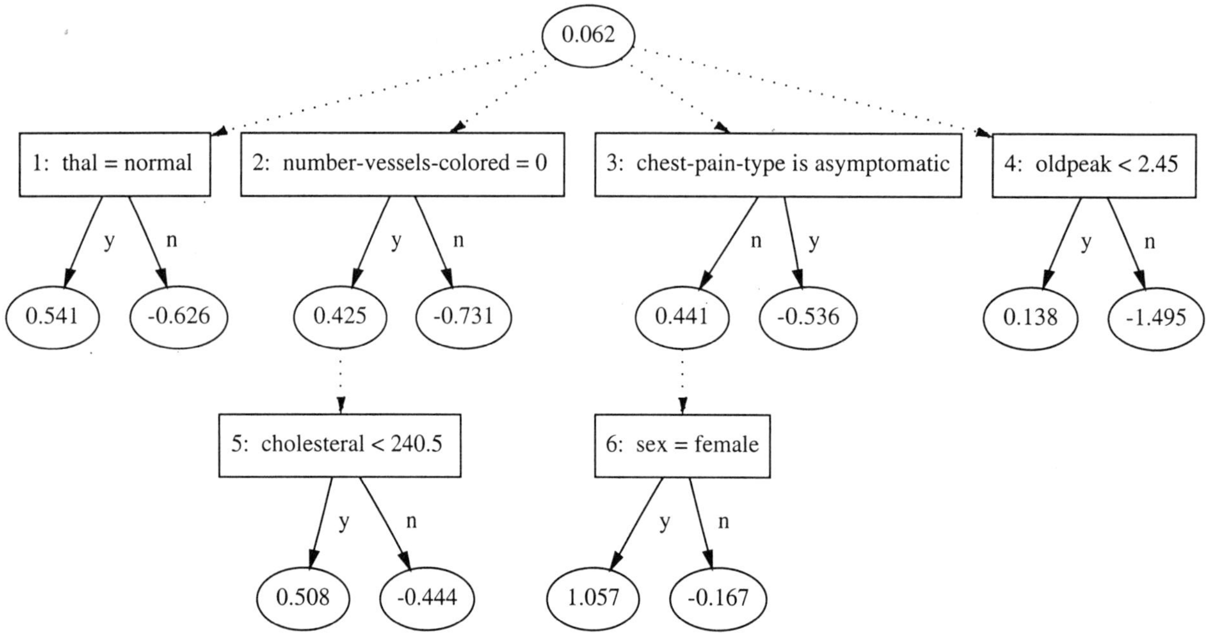

Figure 4: An alternating decision tree learned for the cleve data set (negative numbers correspond to predicted sickness).

A base rule is denoted by r and we use $r(\mathbf{x})$ to denote the real value that the rule associates with the instance $\mathbf{x}$.

- The algorithm maintains two sets, a set of preconditions and a set of rules. The symbols $\mathcal{P}_t$, $\mathcal{R}_t$ correspond to these two sets on boosting iteration t. The initial precondition set is $\mathcal{P}_1 = \{\mathbf{T}\}$.
- The algorithm associates a positive weight with each training example, we denote by $w_{i,t}$ the weight of example number i on boosting iteration t the initial weights are $w_{i,0} = 1$ for all examples $1 \le i \le m$.
- The notation $W(c)$ represents the total weight of the training examples which satisfy the predicate c. Similarly, we use $W_+(c), W_-(c)$ to denote the total weight of those examples that satisfy c and are labeled $+1$ or -1 respectively (i.e. $W(c) = W_+(c) + W_-(c)$).

The algorithm starts by finding the best constant prediction for the entire data set. This prediction is placed at the root of the tree. It then grows the tree iteratively, adding one base rule at a time. The added base rule corresponds to a subtree with a decision node as its root and two prediction nodes as the leaves. This subtree is added as a child of a predictor node which might or might not be a leaf node.

In this description we have not specified how to choose when to *stop* the boosting process. In other words, how to choose T. In fact, it is still unclear what is the best way for choosing T. In the experiments described in this paper we used cross-validation to make this choice.

The algorithm described here has some similarities to well studied learning algorithms such as C4.5 and CART. Similarly to those algorithms it proceeds in a greedy way, adding one decision rule at a time by finding the best split to expand the current tree. However, there are several important differences, among them:

- Decision nodes can be added at any location in the tree, not just the leaves.
- The splitting criterion is different, it is the weighted error of the added rule, rather than the GINI index (CART) or the information gain (C4.5).

4 INTERPRETING ALTERNATING DECISION TREES

In this section we argue for the interpretability and robustness of the alternating tree representation.

To demonstrate our interpretation, we consider the alternating tree presented in Figure 4. This tree is the result of running our learning algorithm for six iterations on the `cleve` data set from Irvine. This is a data set of heart-disease diagnostics for which the goal is to discriminate between sick and healthy people[3] In our mapping positive classification correspond to healthy and negative to sick.

This alternating tree, which consists of six decision nodes, achieves an average test error of 17%. Compare this to the classification rule that is generated by boosting C5.0 (see Table 1 at the end of the paper) which achieves a average test error of 20%. This last rule consists, on the average, of 446 decision nodes! We claim that the fact that the description of the alternating tree classifier is so much smaller makes it easier to read and to interpret. Of course, the structure of the alternating tree is more complex than that of a decision tree. However, as we shall now argue, interpreting an alternating tree is not harder, and may be even easier, than interpreting a decision tree with the same number of decision nodes.

Our main argument for the interpretability of alternating trees rests on the fact that the contribution of each decision node can be understood in isolation. Summing these contributions generates the prediction and the classification. Consider the example in Figure 4. Considering in isolation each of the decision nodes we observe that a cholesterol level higher than 240.5 and an asymptomatic chest pain are both predictors of heart problems. This is indicated by the fact that they both generate negative contributions to the prediction sum. We can easily interpret the meaning of all the decision nodes in the tree in a similar way.

After gleaning the meaning of each decision node in isolation we can analyze the interactions of the nodes. Parallel decision nodes, such as the four nodes in the first level, represent little or no interaction. In other words, the fact that the `thal` test is normal increases the likelihood that the person is healthy irrespective of the `number of vessels colored` or the type of chest pain. This is the type of association of indicators that is represented by voted decision stumps or by naive Bayes classifiers. Note that in order to represent the same information in a standard decision tree we would need a decision tree with 4 levels, each level to test for one of the indicators. Such a tree would have $2^4 - 1 = 15$ decision nodes instead of four. Indeed, the decision tree that C5.0 generates for this data set is large and has a high error rate.

In contrast to the independence of the decision nodes in the first level, the significance of the two decision nodes in the second level depends on the evaluation of their ancestral decision nodes. Specifically, regarding the node `sex = female` the fact that a patient is a male appears to be more predictive of a heart problem when their chest pain is symptomatic then in the population in general. This implies that only when the chest pain is asymptomatic it is worthwhile to check the patients gender. The decision-tree structure can represent dependences between indicators, which cannot be represented by voted stumps.

The root of the tree is associated with the fixed (unconditional) contribution of 0.062. This small positive number indicates that (according to this training set) there are slightly more healthy people then sick. This means that before testing any feature value we should predict "healthy" (but with low confidence).

All the contributions are summed in order to give the final prediction, and this prediction is thresholded to give the classification. This means that if we test the conditions given in the tree serially, we accumulate evidence for or against the health of the person as we proceed. If at some intermediate point during this process we have a sum whose absolute value is large, and the total contribution of all of the (untested) prediction nodes is small, [4] then we don't need to continue our computation - the current sign of the sum cannot change. Even if it is theoretically possible for the sign to change, it might require that most of the future tests will give contribution in the direction opposite to the sign of the current sum, which is unlikely. We thus think about the absolute value of the sum as a measure of confidence of the classification, and call it the classification *margin*. This interpretation is further justified by the theoretical analysis of margins in Schapire et. al. [15]. In Section 5 we show some empirical evidence that strengthens this interpretation and suggests how it can be quantified and used.

---

[3] provided, through David Aha, by the V.A. Medical Center, Long Beach and Cleveland Clinic Foundation: Robert Detrano, M.D., Ph.D.

[4] This situation is less likely to occur in our small example in which all of the contributions, other than that of the root, are large. However, it is a common occurrence in larger trees.

The fact that each decision node has a limited influence on the prediction adds to the robustness of this representation. In some situations we cannot evaluate some of the decision nodes. This might be because some feature values are unknown (a common occurrence in the UCI dataset) or because we are pressed for time. In such situations we can do well by considering only the reachable decision nodes whose associated predictions are large. This will degrade the accuracy only slightly because the influence of the ignored nodes is usually not sufficient to change the classification. The indices printed in the left side of the decision nodes in Figure 4 indicate the boosting iteration on which the nodes were added. In general, lower indices correspond to more influential nodes that were added earlier in the boosting process.

5 EXPERIMENTS AND RESULTS

In order to examine the practical performance of the alternating decision tree algorithm described in the previous section we ran experiments on a collection of nineteen data sets taken from the UCI machine learning repository [12]. To simplify matters, we restricted ourselves to binary classification problems only.

The three learning algorithms that we compared were:

- C5.0 (with and without boosting),
- StumpBoost: our boosting algorithm restricted to generate trees with a single layer of decision nodes.
- ADTree: our boosting algorithm run without restrictions.

We tested C5.0 by averaging over 10 runs of 10 fold cross-validation.

On the smaller data sets ADTree quickly overfits the data, as can be seen in the `cleve data` set in Figure 5. For this reason we had to carefully choose when to stop the boosting process. To choose this number of iterations we did 10-fold cross validation within the training set in each of our experiments. We chose as the stopping time the iteration in which the validation error was minimized. We then reran the algorithm on the whole training set and stopped it at the chosen iteration to generate the classifier that we tested on the held-out data set. Because of this time-consuming method for choosing the stopping iteration we tested our algorithm using 3 runs of 10-fold cross validation.

Figure 5 shows two typical learning curves for ADTree and StumpBoost. For the data set `cleve` both algorithms reach their best performance after less then ten boosting iterations. After more iterations the training error continues to decrease but the test error increases. To overcome this overfitting behavior, early stopping of the boosting algorithm is critical.The `kr-vs-kp` data set is much larger, which is probably the reason that there is almost no difference between the training and test errors. Here we see that ADTree reaches a very small error after about 50 iterations while the error of StumpBoost remains large even after 200 iterations. This is a case in which the larger capacity of ADTree gives it an advantage.

Table 1 summarizes the results from all the data sets. For each data set the number of examples and features is listed along with the average size of the generated classifier and average test error (with standard error) for each classifier tested. Note that *C5.0* refers to C5.0 without boosting (i.e. a single decision tree) and *C5.0 + Boost* refers to C5.0 with 10 rounds of boosting. For the C5.0 results, the size represents the average of the total number of decision nodes, summed over the ten trees. For StumpBoost and ADTree, the size is the average number of boosting rounds which is equal to the number of decision nodes.

For the sake of comparison, we summarize our results in two scatter plots (Figure 6.) We see that the performance of C5.0+boost is very close to the performance of our algorithm. With a slight advantage to C5.0+boost. We see that in some of the smaller data sets StumpBoost outperforms both C5.0 and ADTree, the reason for that probably being that it is less prone to overfitting.

Comparing the size of the classifiers we find that, in all but three cases, the classifiers generated by alternating tree algorithm are much smaller then those generated by C5.0 with boosting.

One interesting feature of these experimental results is that, in general, when C5.0 performed significantly better than StumpBoost, so did ADTree and when StumpBoost performed significantly better than C5.0, so did ADTree. This demonstrates the ability of alternating decision trees to represent both voted sums and decision trees.

Surprisingly, in some of the data sets the best method is C5.0 without boosting. This method has the lowest test error in `house-votes-84`,`hypo1`, `hypothyroid`, `sick-euthyroid` and `dis` and the tree size is small. We have no explanation for this behavior.

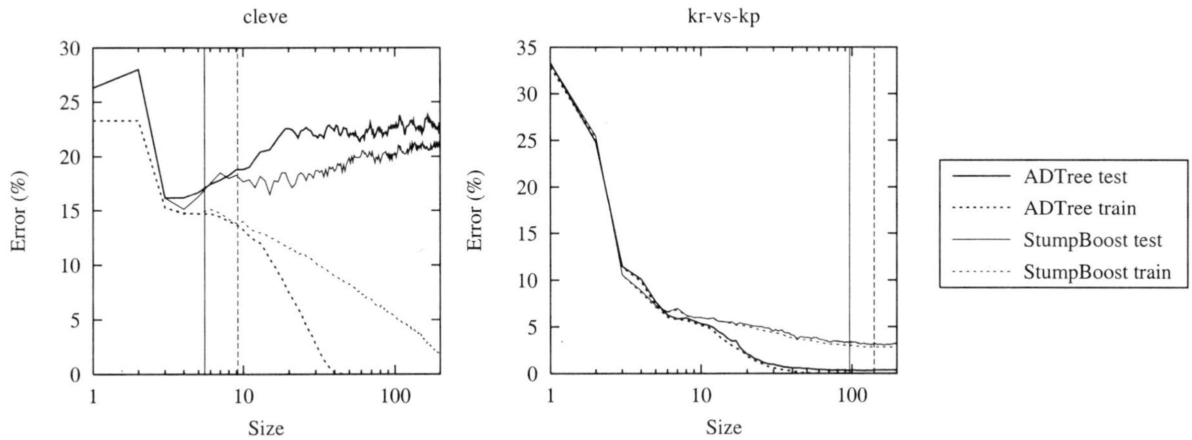

Figure 5: Averaged train and test error curves for ADTree and StumpBoost on the `cleve` and `kr-vs-kp` data sets. The average stopping points for ADTree and StumpBoost are marked with solid vertical lines and dashed vertical lines respectively.

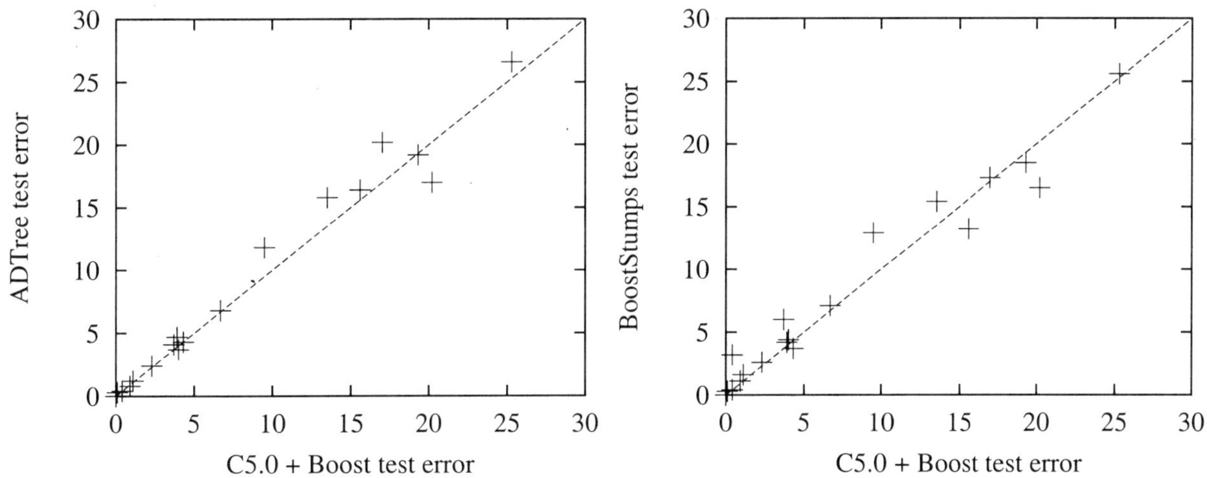

Figure 6: Average test error of C5.0 + Boost versus ADTree (left) and C5.0 + Boost versus StumpBoost (right) on all of the examined data sets.

We explored several statistics in an attempt to quantify the relation between the absolute value of the prediction and the probability that the classification is correct. From our preliminary studies, we found a graphical representation for measuring and possibly using this relationship. Two Examples are given in Figure 7. Each graph represents the conditional probability that the label is positive (which we denote by p) given the value of the prediction (denoted s). As expected, p is close to 1 when $s > 0$ and is close to 0 when $s < 0$ (otherwise, by definition, the error would be large). However, note that when s is far from zero, the conditional probability is even closer to zero and to 1 respectively. This means that when s is far from zero (i.e. the classification margin is large) we can classify the instance much more reliably then when s is close to zero (small classification margin). This gives experimental justification to interpreting the classification margin as a measure of confidence.

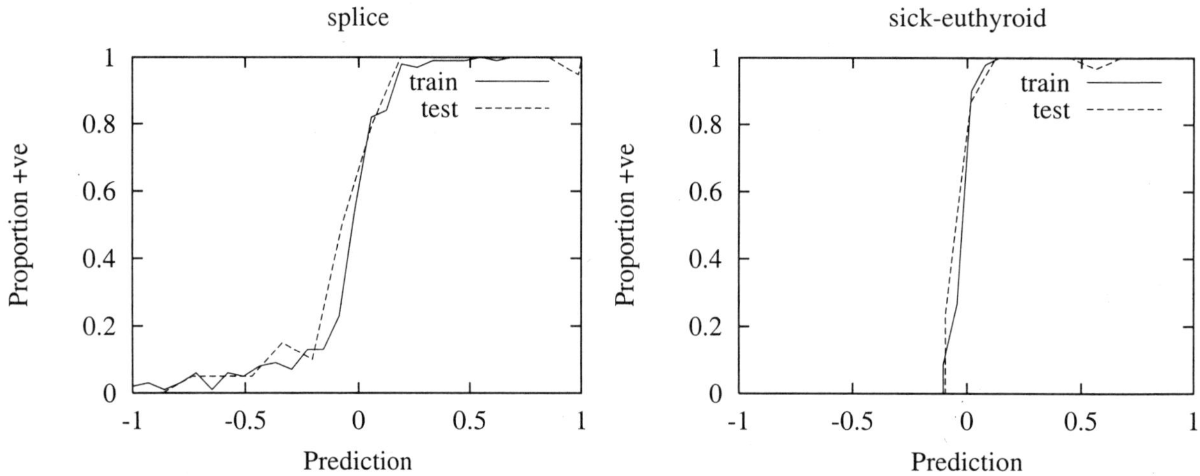

Figure 7: Calibration graphs for the `splice` and `sick-euthyroid` data sets for train and test after 100 rounds of ADTree.

In addition to justifying our interpretation, the calibration graphs can potentially be used to improve our performance situation where our classification rule is allowed to abstain from predicting on some fraction of the test examples. For the `splice` data set after 100 rounds of boosting we can chôose to abstain when $-0.2 \leq s \leq 0.2$, which would reduce the test error from 6.3% to 1% at the cost of abstaining on 22.5% of the data (for one particular train/test split). Similarly for the `sick-euthyroid` data set abstaining when $-0.063 \leq s \leq 0.063$ reduces the test error from 3.2% to 1.7% at the cost of abstaining on 10% of the data.

6 CONCLUSIONS

We have described a new representation for classification rules that is interpretable and robust. We have shown how boosting can be used to learn this type of rules. The new learning algorithm combines, in a simple fashion, decision trees and boosting. In our experiments we show that the error performance of the new algorithm is close to that of C5.0 with boosting. Lastly, we gave some preliminary experimental justification to the interpretation of the absolute real-valued prediction that is generated by the alternating decision tree as a measure of classification confidence.

In the near future we plan to further research the use of calibration graphs to decide when to abstain from prediction. We plan to integrate a new boosting algorithm which is more robust against noise than AdaBoost (to be described in a separate paper). Lastly, we plan to explore ways for speeding up the algorithm, especially for large data sets.

References

[1] Leo Breiman. Bias, variance, and arcing classifiers. Technical Report 460, Statistics Department, University of California at Berkeley, 1996.

[2] Leo Breiman, Jerome H. Friedman, Richard A. Olshen, and Charles J. Stone. *Classification and Regression Trees*. Wadsworth & Brooks, 1984.

[3] Wray Buntine. Learning classification trees. *Statistics and Computing*, 2:63–73, 1992.

[4] Mark W. Craven. *Extracting Comprehensible Models from Trained Neural Networks*. PhD thesis, University of Wisconsin-Madison, 1996. Also appears as UW Technical Report CS-TR-96-1326.

[5] Pedro Domingos. Knowledge acquisition from examples via multiple models. In *ml97*, pages 98–106, 1997.

[6] Yoav Freund and Robert E. Schapire. Experiments with a new boosting algorithm. In *Machine Learning: Proceedings of the Thirteenth International Conference*, pages 148–156, 1996.

[7] Yoav Freund and Robert E. Schapire. A decision-theoretic generalization of on-line learning and an application to boosting. *Journal of Computer and System Sciences*, 55(1):119–139, August 1997.

[8] Jerome Friedman, Trevor Hastie, and Robert Tibshirani. Additive logistic regression: a statistical view of boosting. Technical Report, 1998.

		C5.0	C5.0 + Boost	Stump Boost	ADTree	C5.0	C5.0 + Boost	Stump Boost	ADTree
Data Set	Examples & Features	Size	Size	Size	Size	Test Error	Test Error	Test Error	Test Error
labor	57 : 16	4.3	61.0	27.6	43.3	19.9 ± 0.8	15.6 ± 0.8	13.2 ± 1.0	16.4 ± 3.4
promoters	106 : 57	16.6	134.6	133.8	309.5	22.4 ± 1.1	9.5 ± 0.8	12.9 ± 1.8	11.8 ± 2.1
hepatitis	155 : 20	9.8	197.8	47.9	42.5	21.0 ± 0.4	17.0 ± 0.4	17.3 ± 0.3	20.2 ± 0.6
sonar	208 : 60	14.3	197.7	463.1	338.1	25.6 ± 0.8	19.3 ± 0.7	18.5 ± 2.2	19.2 ± 0.6
cleve	303 : 13	27.2	446.8	9.2	5.5	27.2 ± 0.5	20.2 ± 0.5	16.5 ± 0.8	17.0 ± 0.6
ionosphere	351 : 34	13.8	216.8	51.3	299.3	10.3 ± 0.3	6.7 ± 0.2	7.1 ± 0.6	6.8 ± 0.3
house-votes-84	435 : 16	5.8	292.2	9.1	10.2	3.3 ± 0.1	4.0 ± 0.1	4.4 ± 0.3	3.7 ± 0.2
vote1	435 : 16	10.9	360.8	19.6	9.1	4.9 ± 0.2	4.3 ± 0.1	3.7 ± 0.3	4.3 ± 0.2
credit	690 : 15	18.3	770.2	31.1	160.3	14.3 ± 0.3	13.5 ± 0.2	15.4 ± 0.5	15.8 ± 0.0
breast-cancer	699 : 9	12.4	346.3	48.3	135.7	5.4 ± 0.1	3.9 ± 0.1	4.2 ± 0.7	4.7 ± 0.5
pima-indians	768 : 8	22.4	821.8	56.8	14.5	25.5 ± 0.2	25.3 ± 0.3	25.6 ± 0.2	26.6 ± 0.2
kkn	1000 : 16	7.0	50.1	10.1	5.3	0.1 ± 0.0	0.1 ± 0.0	0.3 ± 0.1	0.3 ± 0.2
hypo1	2514 : 29	6.9	235.4	33.0	23.0	0.2 ± 0.0	0.4 ± 0.0	0.4 ± 0.0	0.4 ± 0.0
hypothyroid	3163 : 25	6.6	567.9	58.7	6.5	0.7 ± 0.0	0.9 ± 0.0	1.1 ± 0.0	0.8 ± 0.0
sick-euthyroid	3163 : 25	13.3	1153.0	34.2	49.7	2.0 ± 0.0	2.3 ± 0.0	2.6 ± 0.1	2.4 ± 0.1
splice	3190 : 60	109.5	2637.0	94.8	318.8	4.2 ± 0.0	3.7 ± 0.0	6.0 ± 0.1	4.1 ± 0.1
kr-vs-kp	3198 : 36	29.2	849.4	141.4	96.3	0.6 ± 0.0	0.4 ± 0.0	3.2 ± 0.0	0.4 ± 0.1
dis	3772 : 29	14.2	629.4	129.0	118.4	1.0 ± 0.0	1.1 ± 0.0	1.6 ± 0.0	1.2 ± 0.1
agaricus-lepiota	8124 : 22	22.0	51.7	42.4	14.8	0.0 ± 0.0	0.0 ± 0.0	0.0 ± 0.0	0.0 ± 0.0

Table 1: Summary of results for a collection of binary classification problems from the UCI database.

[9] Michael Kearns and Yishay Mansour. On the boosting ability of top-down decision tree learning algorithms. In *Proceedings of the Twenty-Eighth Annual ACM Symposium on the Theory of Computing*, 1996.

[10] Ron Kohavi and Clayton Kunz. Option decision trees with majority votes. In *Machine Learning: Proceedings of the Fourteenth International Conference*, pages 161–169, 1997.

[11] Dragos D. Margineantu and Thomas G. Dietterich. Pruning adaptive boosting. In *Machine Learning: Proceedings of the Fourteenth International Conference*, pages 211–218, 1997.

[12] C. J. Merz and P. M. Murphy. UCI repository of machine learning databases, 1998. www.ics.uci.edu/~mlearn/MLRepository.html.

[13] J. R. Quinlan. Bagging, boosting, and C4.5. In *Proceedings of the Thirteenth National Conference on Artificial Intelligence*, pages 725–730, 1996.

[14] J. Ross Quinlan. *C4.5: Programs for Machine Learning*. Morgan Kaufmann, 1993.

[15] Robert E. Schapire, Yoav Freund, Peter Bartlett, and Wee Sun Lee. Boosting the margin: A new explanation for the effectiveness of voting methods. *The Annals of Statistics*, 26(5):1651–1686, October 1998.

[16] Robert E. Schapire and Yoram Singer. Improved boosting algorithms using confidence-rated predictions. In *Proceedings of the Eleventh Annual Conference on Computational Learning Theory*, pages 80–91, 1998. To appear, *Machine Learning*.

Discriminant Trees

João Gama
LIACC, FEP University of Porto
R. Campo Alegre 823
4150 Porto, Portugal
jgama@ncc.up.pt

Abstract

In a previous work, we presented system *Ltree*, a multivariate tree that combines a decision tree with a linear discriminant by means of constructive induction. We have shown that it performs quite well, in terms of accuracy and learning times, in comparison with other multivariate systems like *LMDT*, *OC1*, and *CART*. In this work, we extend the previous work by using two new discriminant functions: a *quadratic discriminant* and a *logistic discriminant*. Using the same architecture as *Ltree* we obtain two new multivariate trees *Qtree* and *LgTree*. The three systems have been evaluate on 17 UCI datasets. From the empirical study, we argue that these systems can be shown as a composition of classifiers with low correlation error. From a bias-variance analysis of the error rate, the error reduction of all the systems in comparison to a univariate tree, is due to a reduction on both components.

1 Introduction

The standard algorithm to grow a decision tree selects, at each decision node, the attribute that minimizes or maximizes some merit-criterion. These kinds of trees are denoted as *univariate trees* because at each node they perform a test on a single attribute. *Multivariate trees* allows decisions on the basis of a combination of attributes. In previous work [Gam97b, Gam97a] we presented system *Ltree*, a multivariate decision tree that combines a decision tree with a linear discriminant function by means of constructive induction. From the empirical evaluation on twenty-one datasets from the UCI repository [MM98] when compared with well known univariate and multivariate systems, like *C4.5* [Qui93], *CART* [BFOS84], *LMDT* [UB91], and *OC1* [MKS94] we concluded that the proposed methodology works quite well. On the datasets used, *Ltree* never performs significantly worse than the other multivariate trees, and it was almost always significantly faster. Here we extend the previous work of *Ltree*, by using the same architecture but different attribute constructors. In *Ltree* the attribute constructor is a *linear discriminant* function. It assumes that the attributes follow a normal distribution and equal covariance matrices for all classes. *Linear discriminant* does not guarantee to minimize the classification error. Especially there is no guarantee that the hyper planes separate the classes in the separable case. The advantage is that a useful solution is obtained in both separable and non separable case. Among discriminant functions two methods relax the assumptions of *linear discriminant*. The *quadratic discriminant* that builds quadratic decision surfaces and does not assume equal covariance matrices, and the *logistic discriminant* that builds also linear decision surfaces, but can deal with non-normal distributions and different covariance matrices. We have extended the attribute constructor operator in *Ltree*. Using a *quadratic discriminant* function, we obtain *Qtree*, and using a *logistic discriminant* function, we obtain *LgTree*. The expectation is to improve *Ltree*. This paper describes the methodologies and performs an empirical evaluation of the three systems.

The rest of the paper is organized as follows. In the next section we present the discriminant functions used. In section 3 explains the method used to merge a discriminant function into a regular decision tree giving a multivariate decision tree. In section 4 we review previous work in the area of multivariate decision trees. In section 5 we perform a comparative empirical evaluation of the three systems, and compare to the *state-of-the-art* in decision trees: C5.0 [Qui98]. The last section presents the conclusions of the paper.

2 Discriminant functions

Pattern recognition and machine learning literature [DH73, Mit97] presents several approaches to the problem of learning classifiers. Most of them in a probabilistic setting. Suppose that $P(C_i|\vec{x})$ denotes the probability that example $\vec{x}$ belongs to class i. The zero-one loss is minimized if, and only if, $\vec{x}$ is assigned to the class C_k for which $P(C_k|\vec{x})$ is maximum [DH73]. Formally, the class attached to example $\vec{x}$ is given by the expression:

$$argmax_i \; P(C_i|\vec{x}) \tag{1}$$

Any function that computes the conditional probability $P(C_i|\vec{x})$ is denoted by *discriminant function.* Given an example $\vec{x}$, the Bayes theorem provides a method to compute $P(C_i|\vec{x})$:

$$P(C_i|\vec{x}) = \frac{P(C_i)P(\vec{x}|C_i)}{P(\vec{x})} \tag{2}$$

$P(\vec{x})$ can be ignored, since it is the same for all the classes, and does not affect the relative values of their probabilities. Although this rule is optimal, its applicability is reduced due to the large number of conditional probabilities required to compute $P(\vec{x}|C_i)$. To overcome this problem several assumptions are usually made. Depending on the assumptions made we get different discriminant functions leading to different classifiers. In this work we study three somewhat different discriminant functions, leading to different classifiers: the *linear discriminant*, the *quadratic discriminant*, and the *logistic discriminant.*

2.1 Linear discriminant classifier

A linear discriminant function is a linear composition of the attributes where the sum of squared differences between class means is maximal relative to the internal class variance. To minimize the number of misclassifications, the Bayes criterion assigns an object to the most probable class. Equations 1 and 2 can be rewritten as: $argmax_i \; P(C_i)P(\vec{x}|C_i)$.

Assuming that the attribute vectors for examples of class C_i are independent and follow a certain probability density function f_i, a new point $\vec{x}$ is then assigned to that class for which the probability density function $f_i(x)$ is maximized. One common assumption is that the distributions are *normal* with different means but the same covariance matrix for all the classes [DG84, MST94]. This means that the points for each class are distributed in a cluster centered at the theoretical mean for the class μ_i, of ellipsoid shape described by the (theoretical) covariance matrix Σ. In this case the boundary separating two classes is a hyper-plane and it passes through the mid-point of the two centers [MST94]. Suppose the prior probability of class C_i is $P(C_i)$ and that $f_i(x)$ is the normal probability density function of $\vec{x}$ in class C_i. The joint probability of observing class i and example x is $P(C_i)*f_i(x)$. The logarithm of this probability is [DG84, MST94]:

$$log(P(C_i)) + x^T\Sigma^{-1}\mu_i - \frac{1}{2}\mu_i^T\Sigma^{-1}\mu_i \tag{3}$$

To find the *a posteriori* class probabilities for a *query point*, the exponential is taken of the discriminant and the resulting quantities normalized to sum to unity. Thus the posterior class probabilities $P(C_i|\vec{x})$ are given by:

$$P(C_i|\vec{x}) = exp[log(P(C_i)) + x^T\Sigma^{-1}\mu_i - \frac{1}{2}\mu_i^T\Sigma^{-1}\mu_i] \tag{4}$$

In practice the population parameters μ_i and Σ are unknown and have to be estimated from the sample. The linear discriminant function is estimated using the sample estimates $\overline{x}_i$ and the pooled covariance matrix S_{pooled}. The linear discriminant builds hyper-planes of the form:

$$H_i = \alpha_i + x^T\beta_i \tag{5}$$

where

$$\beta_i = S_{pooled}^{-1}\bar{x}_i \;\; and \;\; \alpha_i = log(P(C_i)) - \frac{1}{2}\bar{x}_i^T S_{pooled}^{-1}\bar{x}_i \tag{6}$$

A common problem appears when the S_{pooled} matrix is singular or near singular. This can happen for example, if one attribute is constant in one class or along all the dataset. One solution to the singular matrix, is the use of *Singular Value Decomposition* (SVD) [PTVF92] to compute S^{-1}. SVD is numerically stable and is a tool for detecting sources of collinearity. This last aspect can be used as a method for reducing the features of each linear combination.

The number of hyper-planes can be reduced by one, normalizing the coefficients α and β of each hyper-plane by subtracting the corresponding coefficients of the last hyper-plane, as suggested in [MST94].

Linear discriminant is a one step procedure, since it does not make a recursive partition of the input space.

The advantage of this kind of systems is their ability to generate decision surfaces with arbitrary slopes. Also it works often well even if multivariate normality is not satisfied [Rip96]. The linear discriminant does not necessarily minimize the classification error. Especially there is no guarantee that the hyper planes separate the classes in the separable case, but a useful solution is obtained in both the separable and the non-separable case [MST94]. It is a parametric approach: it is assumed that classes can be separated by hyper-planes, and the problem is to determine the coefficients of the hyper-plane. Although parametric approaches are often viewed as being an arbitrary imposition of the model assumptions to the data, discriminant functions are stable with respect to small variations on the training set [Bre96]. This is due to the small number of free parameters: $(\#Classes - 1) \times (\#Attributes + 1)$.

2.2 Quadratic discriminant classifier

The quadratic discriminant is similar to the linear discriminant but does not assume equal covariance matrices for each class. In this case equation 3 is rewritten as:

$$log(P(C_i)) - \frac{1}{2}log(det(\Sigma_i)) - \frac{1}{2}(x - \mu_i)^T \Sigma_i^{-1} (x - \mu_i) \tag{7}$$

that is the quadratic discriminant for class C_i. Given a query example, the value of the quadratic discriminant of each class is calculated for this example and the class with largest discriminant is chosen. To find the posteriori class probabilities explicitly, the exponential is taken of the discriminant and the resulting quantities normalized to sum to unity. Thus the a posteriori class probabilities $P(C_i|x)$ are given by:

$$P(C_i|x) = exp[log(P(C_i)) - \tfrac{1}{2}log(det(\Sigma_i)) - \tfrac{1}{2}(x-\mu_i)^T\Sigma_i^{-1}(x-\mu_i)]$$

As in the previous case the population parameters μ_i and Σ_i are unknown and have to be estimated from the sample. The discriminant function is estimated using the sample estimates $\overline{x}_i$ and the covariance matrices S_i. As in the case of *linear discriminant* we use the *Singular Value Decomposition* [PTVF92] technique to compute S_i^{-1}.

In [MST94] the authors refer that quadratic discriminant is robust to small deviations from normality. The general form of the decision boundaries are not linear. Not only the attributes are weighted but also their second powers and crossproducts, giving terms like: $2a_1^2 + 7a_1a_2 + ...$ [WK91]. Geometrically, this represents a separating boundary that is a quadratic hyper-surface, rather than a hyper-plane. The quadratic discriminant does not assume equal covariance matrices as linear discriminant. However the number of parameters to be estimated becomes $\#Classes \times \#Attributes \times (\#Attributes + 1)/2$, that can be problematic especially for small or moderate sized datasets.

2.3 Logistic discriminant classifier

The *Logistic discriminant classifier* operates by choosing a hyper plane to separate the classes as well as possible, but the criterion for a good separation is different from the one followed in the case of the *linear discriminant classifier*. The latter optimizes a quadratic cost function whereas the former maximizes the conditional likelihood. The method is only partially parametric, as the probability density functions for the classes are not modeled, but rather the ratio between them. For a q class problem, one class is taken as reference class, and there are $q - 1$ sets of parameters for each class relative to the reference class. Given an example $\vec{x}$ and a set of $q - 1$ vectors β of coefficients, the conditional class probability for the reference class C_q and the class probability for class C_i $(i \neq q)$, take the forms:

$$P(C_q|x) = \frac{1}{\sum_{j=1,...,q-1} exp(\beta_j \vec{x})} \tag{8}$$

$$P(C_i|x) = \frac{exp(\beta_i \vec{x})}{\sum_{j=1,...,q-1} exp(\beta_j \vec{x})} \tag{9}$$

Given independent samples from the q classes, the conditional likelihood for the set of vectors β is defined to be:

$$L(\beta_1, ..., \beta_{q-1}) = \prod_{\vec{x} \in C_1} P(C_1|\vec{x}) \prod_{\vec{x} \in C_2} P(C_2|\vec{x}) ... \prod_{\vec{x} \in C_q} P(C_q|\vec{x})$$

The parameter estimates are the values that maximizes this likelihood [MST94]. The optimization problem (to find the parameter estimates that maximize the likelihood) is solved using an iterative procedure. The linear discriminant provides the initial set of parameters. These are refined using a gradient descent. The Newton-Raphson iterative procedure [PTVF92] is used because the derivatives of the likelihood are easy to obtain.

Given a *query example* the $q-1$ vectors β of coefficients are evaluated for this example. The method assigns this example to the class for which the posterior is greatest or to the reference class if all the posteriors are negative.

The logistic discriminant and linear discriminant are very similar. The major differences between the two may occur when the attributes have very non-normal distributions with very dissimilar covariances [MST94]. At each iteration, logistic discriminant requires computing the Hessian, that is a symmetric square matrix with $(\#Classes - 1) \times (\#Attributes + 1)$ rows. Each term requires a summation over all the examples. For large problems this could be a very time consuming process.

3 Multivariate Trees

In this section we explain how to merge a discriminant function into a decision tree. We follow the schema of *Ltree* [GB99] to grow a multivariate tree. At each decision node, a linear discriminant function is built using the examples that fall at this node. For each of those examples, new attributes are computed as the projection of the example over each hyper plane build by the linear discriminant function. If one of this new attributes is chosen by the splitting-criteria, then this corresponds to an oblique decision surface, because the attribute is the instantiation of a linear discriminant function. The algorithm behind *Ltree* used to grow a decision tree is similar to many others, except that it contains the ability to build new attributes as well as dealing with different number of attributes at each node. Our decision tree algorithm follows the basic algorithm of *C4.5*, but all the data-structures are dynamic. *Ltree*, *Qtree*, and *LgTree* use this base decision tree algorithm. Only the attribute constructor changes. Figure 1 presents the basic algorithm we use to built a multivariate tree. It is referred as *Mtree*. The input parameter $\Im$ is a discriminant function leading to the different multivariate trees referred. At each iteration, a constructive step occurs. The discriminant function $\Im$ builds the hyper planes on the basis of the set of examples D at this node. The instance space is reconstructed by projecting the examples in D over the hyper planes. The extended dataset is denoted by D'. In the following we describe the basic decision tree algorithm.

3.1 Constructing new attributes

At each decision point, *Mtree* computes new attributes dynamically. New attributes are linear combinations of all ordered attributes of the examples that fall at this decision node. To build new attributes the system considers at each decision point, a varying number of classes. Taking into account class distribution at this node, *Mtree* only considers those classes for which the number of examples exceeds the double of the number of attributes[1]. All the examples of this node are extended with the new attributes. Each new attribute is given by the projection of the example over the $hyperplane_i$. The projection is computed as the dot product of the example vector $\mathbf{x}$ by the coefficients of the $hyperplane_i$. Because class distribution varies along the tree, the number of new attributes is variable. Two different nodes (also at the same level) may have different number of attributes. As the tree grows and the classes are discriminated, the number of new attributes decreases. New attributes are propagated down the tree. This is one of the most innovative features of *Mtree*.

3.2 Splitting Criterion

By default *Mtree* uses *Gain Ratio* [Qui93] as the splitting criterion. A test on a *nominal* attribute will divide the data into as many subsets as the number of values of the attribute. A test on a *continuous* attribute will divide the data into two subsets: $attribute\_value > cutpoint$ and $attribute\_value \leq cutpoint$. To determine the *cut point*, we follow a process similar to C4.5 [Qui93].

3.3 Pruning

Pruning is considered to be the most crucial part of the tree building process at least in noisy domains. Deeper nodes reflect too much the training set (overfitting) and increase the error due to the variance of the classifier. The process that we use is similar to the *Error-Based* pruning followed in C4.5. Because any *Mtree* use more powerful attributes the problem of overfitting is more relevant. As such the confidence level is by default 10%. Also we use a *smoothing* process to classify an example. The class that is assigned to an example takes into account the path from the root to the leaf, and is often different from the majority class of the examples that fall in one leaf. The estimates of leaf error-rate take this into account. Another difference is that *Mtree* does not have the ability of grafting a branch onto the place of the parent node, as C4.5 does.

[1]This done so as not to underfit the concept, following Breiman et al. [BFOS84]

Input: A data set D, a discriminant function $\Im$
Output: A decision Tree

Function Mtree(D, $\Im$)
    If stop criteria(D) = TRUE
        return a Leaf with class probability distribution
    Construct the hyper planes using $\Im(D)$.
    Generate the extended dataset D' by projecting
            each example in D over the hyper planes.
    Choose the attribute that maximizes splitting criterion on D'
    For each partition of examples based on chosen attribute values
            Generate a subtree $Tree_i$ = Mtree(D'_i, $\Im$)
    return Tree as a decision node based on chosen attribute,
            storing $\Im(D)$ and descendants $Tree_i$
End

Figure 1: General algorithm for Multivariate Decision Trees

3.4 Missing Values

At learning time, if an example has a missing value on the test attribute, a fractional example is passed through all the descendent branches. When using a tree as classifier, the example to be classified passes down through the tree. At each node a test is performed, and if the value of the tested attribute is not known the normal procedure cannot choose the path to follow. Since a decision tree constitutes a hierarchy of tests, the *unknown problem* has special relevance on this type of classifiers. Any *Mtree* passes the example down all branches of the node where the unknown attribute value was detected, following. Each branch outputs a probability class distribution. The output is a combination of the different class distributions that sum up to 1.

3.5 Classifying new Examples

To be applied as a predictor any *Mtree* stores, at each node, the discriminant function generated. When classifying a new example, the example traverses the tree in the usual way, but at each decision node it is extended by the insertion of the attributes generated by projecting the example over the hyper planes generated by the discriminant function.

4 Related Work

In [BFOS84], Breiman et al. suggest the use of linear combination of attributes instead of using a single attribute. *CART* searches explicitly for a set of coefficients that minimize the partition-merit criterion defined by the user. Only instances for which no values are missing are used for training. Each instance is normalized by centering each value of each feature at its median and then dividing by its range. The algorithm incorporated in CART cycles through the attributes at each step, searching for an improved linear combination split.

After the final linear combination is determined, it is converted to a split test on the original non-normalized features. *CART* performs a *Sequential Backward Elimination* that starts with all the features in the linear combination and tries to remove the feature that will cause the smallest decrease of the partition-merit criterion. It continues removing features until a stopping criterion is met.

Similar to *CART*, *OC1* [MKS94], uses a hill-climbing search algorithm. Beginning with the best axes-parallel split, it randomly perturbs each of the coefficients until there is no improvement in the impurity of the hyper-plane. As in *CART*, *OC1* adjusts the coefficients of the hyper-plane individually finding a local optimal value for each coefficient at a time. The innovation of OC1 is a randomization step used to get out of local minima. OC1 uses an *error complexity pruning* using a separate pruning set. The *missing values* are replaced, before learning, by the mean of the attribute. *OC1* generates binary trees. The implementation that we have used in the comparative study accepts numerical attributes only.

Linear Machine Decision Tree (LMDT) of Brodley and Utgoff [BU95], uses a different approach. Each internal node in a LMDT tree is a set of linear discriminant functions that are used to classify an example. The training algorithm repeatedly presents examples at each node until the linear machine converges. Because convergence cannot be guaranteed, *LMDT* uses heuristics to determine when the node has stabilized. Trees generated by *LMDT* are not binary. The number of descendants of each decision node is equal to the number of classes that fall at this node.

The *FACT* system [LV88] recursively partition the input space using a linear discriminant function. The number of descendents of each node is equal to the number of classes. This system has results similar to *CART*, but achieves this with lower running times. Mangasarian [MSW90], presents a system that uses *linear programming* to compute the coefficients of each multivariate test.

There are several differences between any *Mtree* and other multivariate trees like *CART*, *OC1*, and *LMDT*.

With respect to the number of hyper planes, *OC1*, as *CART*, searches for only one hyper plane, regardless the number of classes. The search is guided to minimize the impurity function, that is also the attribute selection criterion. In *LMDT*, the number of hyper planes is equal to the number of classes, while in *Mtree* this is equal to the number of classes minus one. The search for the hyper planes in *Mtree* is guided by the quadratic error. Each hyper plane corresponds, by projection, to one new attribute, but one is chosen only if it also minimizes the entropy function. At each node, only one of the generated hyper planes, is eventually chosen. But all are propagated down through the tree and could be, eventually, chosen in deeper nodes. In *Mtree*, *OC1*, and *CART*, a multivariate test produces a binary split, while in *LMDT* the number of descendents is equal to the number of classes.

With respect to the method for determining the hyper planes, *CART*, *OC1* and *LMDT* use a gradient descent approach, while *Mtree*[2] uses an analytical algorithm. This aspect is relevant for learning time, and is the explanation for the comparative fast performance of *Mtree*.

5 Empirical Evaluation

In a previous work, we have compared *Ltree* versus other multivariate trees [GB99] namely *CART*, *LMDT*, and *OC1*. We have verified that, in real datasets, *Ltree* has advantages with respect to both *error rate* and *learning time*. In this work, we are interested in comparison between different attribute constructors. As such we only evaluate *Ltree*, *Qtree*, and *LgTree*. The *state-of-art* in decision trees *C5.0* is used as reference.

[2]Except in *LgTree*.

5.1 Evaluation design

We have chosen 17 datasets from the UCI repository. The choice of datasets was restricted by the criteria that all the attributes are ordered with few missing values. The evaluation methodology was designed as follows. To estimate the error rate of an algorithm on a given dataset we use 10 fold stratified cross validation. To minimize the influence of the variability of the training set, we repeat this process ten times, each time using a different permutation of the dataset. The final estimate is the mean of the error rates obtained in each run of the cross validation. To apply pairwise comparisons, we guarantee that, in all runs, all algorithms learn and test on the same partitions of the data.

Table 1 presents the results. For each pair algorithm-dataset we present the mean error rate and the standard deviation. For each dataset, the best result is presented in boldface. To have statistical confidence in the differences, we have performed *paired t-tests* with the significance level set to 99%. A +(−) sign means that this error rate is significantly better than the error rate of *C5.0*.

5.2 Discussion

On these datasets, all the three multivariate trees study here, show a significant improve of performance, both in terms of *error rate* and *tree size* when compared against the univariate tree.

With respect to the *error rates* *LgTree* performs significantly better than *Ltree* on four datasets, and worse in two. With respect to the number of leaves the differences are more relevant: *LgTree* produce statistically smaller trees in 7 datasets. Only on two cases *Ltree* produces smaller trees. *Ltree* and *LgTree* use exactly the same representation language. The difference between them is the *search* bias. *Qtree* is able to define more complex decision surfaces. The constructive schema used in *Mtree*, implies that the new attributes built at lower nodes in the tree contain terms that correspond to attributes previously built. In the case of *Qtree* this corresponds to having terms that are also quadratic terms in the quadratic function. Attributes build at lower nodes draw very complex decision sur-

Table 1: Error rates of C5.0 versus *Ltree*, *Qtree* and *LgTree*

Dataset	*Examples*	*Classes*	*C5.0*	*Ltree*	*Qtree*	*LgTree*
Australian	690	2	14.17 ±0.7	13.92 ±0.6	14.28 ±0.7	**13.56** ±0.5
Balance	625	3	22.34 ±0.8	+ 6.65 ±0.8	+ 6.43 ±0.7	+ **6.27** ±0.5
Breast(W)	699	2	5.30 ±0.5	+ **3.32** ±0.4	+ 4.13 ±0.3	+ 3.59 ±0.3
Cleveland	303	2	22.21 ±1.5	+ 17.19 ±0.7	20.90 ±1.1	+ **16.19** ±0.4
Diabetes	768	2	25.70 ±1.0	25.60 ±0.7	27.30 ±1.3	+ **24.25** ±0.6
German	1000	2	28.53 ±0.9	+ 25.29 ±0.4	27.08 ±1.0	+ **23.82** ±0.4
Glass	214	6	33.26 ±2.2	+ **29.93** ±2.1	31.35 ±2.8	32.05 ±2.4
Heart	270	2	21.64 ±1.9	+ 16.78 ±0.9	+ 19.81 ±1.1	+ **15.96** ±1.1
Hepatitis	155	2	20.82 ±2.1	**18.26** ±1.9	18.62 ±1.9	20.56 ±2.8
Ionosphere	351	2	10.47 ±1.1	11.20 ±0.7	+ **8.34** ±0.5	11.23 ±0.9
Iris	150	3	5.01 ±1.0	+ 3.40 ±0.5	+ **2.07** ±0.6	+ 3.40 ±1.0
Satimage	6435	6	13.50 ±0.2	+ **11.79** ±0.2	+ 12.28 ±0.2	+ 12.18 ±0.3
Segment	2310	7	**3.15** ±0.3	3.41 ±0.3	− 4.22 ±0.2	3.32 ±0.2
Sonar	208	2	**24.71** ±1.2	25.88 ±2.4	26.03 ±2.3	26.13 ±2.4
Vehicle	846	4	26.82 ±1.1	+ 21.27 ±1.3	+ **15.88** ±0.9	+ 21.85 ±1.3
Waveform	2581	3	24.89 ±0.6	+ 16.88 ±0.6	+ 17.45 ±0.4	+ **14.87** ±0.5
Wine	178	3	7.12 ±0.9	+ 2.17 ±0.8	+ **0.50** ±0.4	+ 1.24 ±0.7
Mean of Error Rates			18.22	14.88	15.10	14.73
Mean of Leaves			51.0	23.1	20.2	20.7

faces. The effect is that the *variance* of the classifier grows.

Learning time is also a dimension to consider when analyzing learning algorithms. To run the experiences reported here, and taking the time of *C5.0* as reference $\mathcal{T}$, *Ltree* requires $2.4\mathcal{T}$, *Qtree* requires $3.1\mathcal{T}$, and *LgTree* $10.8\mathcal{T}$.

5.3 Error Correlation

Ali and Pazzani [AP96] have shown that a desirable property of an ensemble of classifiers is *diversity.* They use the concept of *error correlation* as a metric to measure the degree of diversity in an ensemble. Their definition of *error correlation* between two classifiers is defined as the probability that both make the same error. Because this definition does not satisfy the property that the correlation between an object and itself should be 1, we prefer to define the error correlation between two classifiers as the conditional probability of the two classifiers make the same error given that one of them makes an error. This definition of *error correlation* lies in the interval [0 : 1] and the correlation between one classifier and itself is 1. Formally:

$$\phi_{ij} = p(\hat{f}_i(x) = \hat{f}_j(x) | \hat{f}_i(x) \neq f(x) \vee \hat{f}_j(x) \neq f(x)). \tag{10}$$

The discriminant functions can be used as classifiers by them selves. Also, turning off the constructive step in the decision tree, it works as an univariate tree. We can see the constructive architecture of *Mtree* as a method for combining classifiers. The table 2 presents the average of the error correlation between the decision tree and the three discriminant functions. This

Table 2: Error Correlations

	Linear	Quadratic	Logistic
Univariate Tree versus	33%	27%	31%

results provide evidence that the decision tree and any discriminant function make uncorrelated errors, that is each classifier make errors in different regions of the instance space. This is a desirable property for combining classifiers.

5.4 Bias-Variance decomposition

The *Bias-Variance* decomposition of the error rate [KW96] is a useful tool to understand the behavior of learning algorithms. Using the decomposition proposed in [KW96] we have analyzed the error decomposition of *C5.0* and all *Mtree* on the datasets under study. To estimate the bias and variance, we first split the data into training and test sets. From the training set we obtain ten bootstrap replications used to

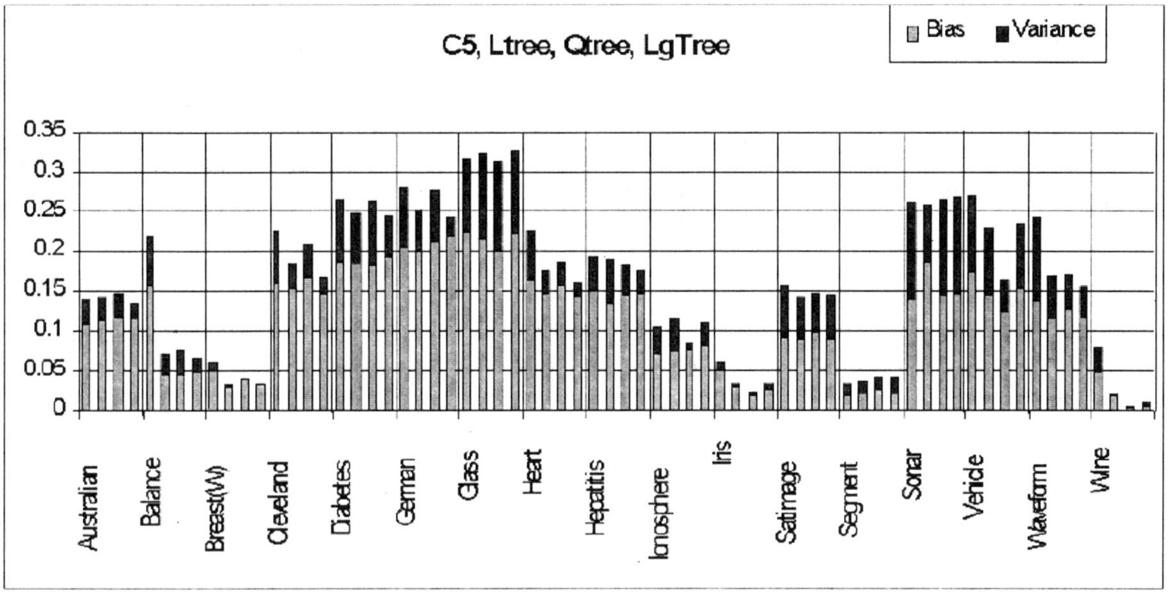

Figure 2: The Variance and the Bias components in C5.0, Ltree, Qtree and LgTree. For each dataset the results are shown in this order.

build ten classifiers. We ran the learning algorithm on each of the training sets and estimate the terms of the *variance* and *bias* using the generated classifier for each point x in the evaluation set E. All the terms were estimated using frequency counts.

Figure 2 presents, for each dataset, a comparison between all algorithms. On most datasets, we verify that any *Mtree* is able to reduce, in comparison with C5.0, both components. For example, the average error reduction verified in *Ltree* is in 52% due to reduction in *variance* and 47% due to the reduction in bias. The algorithm with lower bias is *Qtree*, and with lower variance is *LgTree*.

6 Conclusions

The main feature of *Mtree* is the use of constructive induction. When building the tree, new attributes are computed as combinations of previous ones. All new attributes are *continuous* and are propagated downward the tree. New attributes built at lower nodes contain terms based on attributes built higher up. The number of new attributes is variable along the tree, including for two nodes at the same level, decreasing for lower level nodes. This schema allows building very complex decision surfaces, mainly when using a quadratic function as constructive operator. At each decision node, *Mtree* performs two inductive steps. The first one consists on building the discriminant function, the second one consists on applying the decision tree criteria. In the first step the discriminant decision rule is not used. All the decisions are delayed to the second step. In problems with numerical attributes, attribute combination extends the representational power and relaxes the language bias of univariate decision tree algorithms. *Mtree* combines a decision tree known to have low bias but high variance with a discriminant function known to have low variance but high bias. This is the desirable composition of algorithms, and it is confirmed by the low error correlation between the components. In comparison to a univariate tree, all *Mtree* algorithms reduce the bias and the variance components of the error rate. However, it should be possible to apply a variance reduction method, like *bagging* [Bre96], to *Mtree*. We intend to explore this aspect in a future work.

Acknowledgements

Thanks to Dr. Bob Henery, from the University of StrathClyde, for making available the FORTRAN code of the discriminant classifiers. Our discriminants were rewritten in C, and closely follow those provided by Dr. Henery. Gratitude to the financial support given by the FEDER and PRAXIS XXI projects, project ECO and METAL and the Plurianual support of LIACC. Also thanks to P.Brazdil, Alipio Jorge and colleagues from LIACC.

References

[AP96] Kamal M. Ali and Michael J. Pazzani. Error reduction through learning multiple descriptions. *Machine Learning*, 24:173–202, 1996.

[BFOS84] L. Breiman, J. Friedman, R. Olshen, and C. Stone. *Classification and Regression Trees*. Wadsworth International Group., 1984.

[Bre96] L. Breiman. Bias, variance, and arcing classifiers. Technical report 460, Statistics Department, University of California, 1996.

[BU95] Carla E. Brodley and Paul E. Utgoff. Multivariate decision trees. *Machine Learning*, 19:45–77, 1995.

[DG84] W. Dillon and M. Goldstein. *Multivariate Analysis, Methods and Applications*. J. Wiley and Sons, Inc., 1984.

[DH73] R.O. Duda and P.E. Hart. *Pattern Classification and scene analysis*. New York, Willey and Sons, 1973.

[Gam97a] J. Gama. Oblique linear tree. In P. Cohen and X. Liu, editors, *Advances in Intelligent Data Analysis-Reasoning about Data*. LNCS 1280, Springer Verlag, 1997.

[Gam97b] J. Gama. Probabilistic linear tree. In D. Fisher, editor, *Machine Learning, Proceedings of the 14th International Conference*. Morgan Kaufmann, 1997.

[GB99] J. Gama and P. Brazdil. Linear tree. *to appear in Intelligent Data Analysis*, 3(1), 1999.

[KW96] Ron Kohavi and David H. Wolpert. Bias plus variance decomposition for zero-one loss functions. In L. Saitta, editor, *Machine Learning, Proceedings of the 13th International Conference*. Morgan Kaufmann, 1996.

[LV88] W. Loh and N. Vanichsetakul. Tree-structured classification via generalized discriminant analysis. *Journal of the American Statistical Association*, 1988.

[Mit97] Tom Mitchell. *Machine Learning*. MacGraw-Hill Companies, Inc., 1997.

[MKS94] S. Murthy, S. Kasif, and S. Salzberg. A system for induction of oblique decision trees. *Journal of Artificial Intelligence Research*, 1994.

[MM98] C.J. Merz and P.M. Murphy. UCI repository of machine learning databases, 1998.

[MST94] D. Michie, D.J. Spiegelhalter, and C. Taylor. *Machine Learning, Neural and Statistical Classification*. Ellis Horwood, 1994.

[MSW90] O. Mangasarian, R. Setiono, and W. Wolberg. Pattern recognition via linear programming: theory and applications to medical diagnosis. In T. Coleman and Y. Li, editors, *SIAM*, 1990.

[PTVF92] W. Press, S. Teukolsky, W. Vetterling, and B. Flannery. *Numerical Recipes in C: the art of scientific computing 2 Ed.* University of Cambridge, 1992.

[Qui93] R. Quinlan. *C4.5: Programs for Machine Learning*. Morgan Kaufmann Publishers, Inc., 1993.

[Qui98] R. Quinlan. Data mining tools See5 and C5.0. Technical report, RuleQuest Research, 1998.

[Rip96] Brian D. Ripley. *Pattern Recognition and Neural Networks*. Cambridge University Press, 1996.

[UB91] P. Utgoff and C. Brodley. Linear machine decision trees. Coins technical report, 91-10, University of Massachusetts, 1991.

[WK91] S. Weiss and C. Kulikowski. *Computer systems that learn-Classification and prediction methods from Statistics, Neural Nets, Machine Learning and Expert systems*. Morgan Kaufmann Publishers, Inc., 1991.

Experiments with noise filtering in a medical domain

Dragan Gamberger
Rudjer Bošković Institute
Bijenička 54
10000 Zagreb, Croatia
Dragan.Gamberger@irb.hr

Nada Lavrač
Jozef Stefan Institute
Jamova 39
1000 Ljubljana, Slovenia
Nada.Lavrac@ijs.si

Ciril Grošelj
University Medical Centre Ljubljana
Zaloška 7
1000 Ljubljana, Slovenia

Abstract

The paper presents a series of noise detection experiments in a medical problem of coronary artery disease diagnosis. The following algorithms for noise detection and elimination are tested: a saturation filter, a classification filter, a combined classification-saturation filter, and a consensus saturation filter. The distinguishing feature of the novel consensus saturation filter is its high reliability which is due to the multiple detection of potentially noisy examples. Reliable detection of noisy examples is important for the analysis of patient records in medical databases, as well as for the induction of rules from filtered data, representing genuine characteristics of the diagnostic domain. Medical evaluation in the problem of coronary artery disease diagnosis shows that the detected noisy examples are indeed noisy or non-typical class representatives.

1 INTRODUCTION

Effective noise handling is one of the most difficult problems in inductive machine learning. The prediction accuracy and applicability of induced rules significantly depend on appropriate noise handling procedures. Noise usually means random errors in training examples (erroneous attribute values and/or erroneous classification). In this work we use the term noise in a broader sense of outliers [17] denoting all examples that do not follow the same model as the rest of the data. This definition "includes not only erroneous data but also *surprising* veridical data" [10], including non-typical class representatives.

A *target concept* of a given problem domain is defined as the source of all possible correct examples. An inductive learning task is to find a good representation of the target concept in a selected hypothesis language. This representation is called a *target theory*. The main property of a target theory is that it should be correct for all the correct domain examples. A domain may consist of instances of a single concept, a set of subconcepts, a main concept and some subconcepts, etc. These domain characteristics together with the restrictions of the used hypothesis language may cause that in some cases a target theory may have the form of a single theory description, a set of subtheory descriptions or a main theory description and its exceptions [6].

In an ideal inductive learning problem, the induced hypothesis H is indeed a target theory that will 'agree' with the classifications of training examples E and will thus perform as a perfect classifier on yet unseen instances. In practice, however, it frequently happens that data given to the learner contain various kinds of errors, either random or systematic. Random errors are usually referred to as *noise*. Therefore, in most real-life problems the success of machine learning very much depends on the learner's noise-handling capability, i.e., its ability of appropriately dealing with noisy data. Although noise in training examples may be due to erroneous attribute values and erroneous class labels, machine learning algorithms usually treat noisy examples as being mislabeled.

It should be noted again that the term noise used in this work does not refer only to errors in the data. As opposed to the standard terminology, the term noise is here used as a synonym for outliers: it refers to errors (incorrect examples) as well as exceptions (correct examples representing some relatively rare subconcept of the target concept). The reasoning behind this decision is that, from the point of view of induction, exceptions have the same effect on the induction process as erroneous examples themselves. Distinguishing exceptions from noise and hypothesis generation including the representation of exceptions have been studied also by other authors, for example [16, 3].

Detection and elimination of noisy examples from the training set helps in the induction of the target hypothesis - a hypothesis induced from noiseless data will be less complex and more accurate when classifying unseen cases. In contrast to the so-called noise tolerant procedures for noise handling, such as rule truncation and tree pruning [14, 15], this work is concerned with the explicit detection and elimination of noisy data in data preprocessing. This work upgrades the earlier work of the authors on Occam's razor applicability for noise detection and elimination [7, 8]. The approach is based on the observation that the elimination of noisy examples, in contrast to the elimination of examples for which the target theory is correct, reduces the CLCH value of the training set (CLCH stands for the Complexity of the Least Complex correct Hypothesis). This noise detection algorithm is called the *saturation filter*, since it employs the CLCH measure to test whether the training set is saturated, i.e., whether it can be used to induce a stable target theory. Recently, an alternative approach to explicit noise detection and elimination has been suggested [1]. The basic idea of this noise elimination algorithm, called a *classification filter* in this paper, is to use one or more learning algorithms (that may but do not have to include explicit noise handling) to create classifiers that serve as filters for the training data. The experimental results published in [1] provide evidence that classification filters can successfully deal with noisy data.

In this work, a problem of diagnosis of coronary artery disease [9] is used to perform a series of noise detection experiments. Included are the experiments with our rule learner ILLM (Inductive Learning by Logic Minimization) [5] used without its noise handling capability, the saturation filter used with ILLM, the classification filter with ILLM as the incorporated classifier, and two novel approaches: a combination of noise filtering approaches called the *combined classification-saturation filter* and the *consensus saturation filter* with various consensus levels which employ different ways of n-fold saturation filtering, aimed at increasing the reliably of noisy example detection.

2 NOISE FILTERING ALGORITHMS

Four noise filtering algorithms are presented, aimed at the detection and elimination of noisy training examples: our noise filtering algorithm (here called the saturation filter, [7, 8]), the noise filtering algorithm by Brodley and Friedl (here called the classification filter, [1]) and two new algorithms that combine the two approaches to noise filtering.

2.1 SATURATION FILTER

Our approach to noise filtering has its theoretical foundation in the saturation property of training data [8]. The algorithm, described in detail in [7], is outlined here for the sake of completeness.

Suppose that a complexity measure c is defined and that for any hypothesis H its complexity $c(H)$ can be determined. Based on this complexity measure, for a training set E one can determine the complexity of the least complex hypothesis correct for all the examples in E; this complexity, denoted by $g(E)$ is called the CLCH value (Complexity of the Least Complex Hypothesis, correct for all the examples in E).

In [8] we have shown that if E is noiseless and saturated (containing enough training examples to find a correct target hypothesis), then $g(E) < g(E_n)$, where $E_n = E \cup \{e_n\}$ and e_n is a noisy example for which the target hypothesis is not correct. The property $g(E) < g(E_n)$ means that noisy examples can be detected as those that enable CLCH value reduction. The approach in an iterative form is applicable also when E_n includes more than one noisy example.

It must be noted that the saturation property of a training set is the main theoretical condition for the presented filter. In practice many domains have a restricted number of training examples and hence we may assume that these domains do not satisfy the saturation condition. Notice, however, that the described algorithm is applicable without changes also in this case. The reason is that for some subconcept of the domain there may still be enough training examples so that this subpart of the domain is saturated; hence, a subtheory description is induced by the learner whereas all other examples are eliminated since the learner will treat them as being erroneous or expections of the subtheory description being learned [6].

The greatest practical problem of the saturation filter is the computation of the CLCH value $g(E)$ for a training set E. In rule-based induction, the hypothesis complexity measure $c(H)$ can be defined as the number of attribute value tests (literals) used in the hypothesis H. In this case, the corresponding $g(E)$ value can be defined as the minimal number of literals that are necessary to build a hypothesis that is correct for all the examples in E.

Suppose that the training set is contradiction free (there are no examples that differ only in their class value), and that the set of literals L defined in the hypothesis language is sufficient for finding a hypothesis H which is correct for all examples in E. Then the necessary and sufficient condition for a subset $L' \subseteq L$ to have this same property is that for every possible example pair, such that the first example in the pair is a positive example from E and the second one is negative, there must be at least one literal in L' which covers the pair. A literal covers a pair if it is true for the positive and false for the negative example in the pair. This fact enables that the $g(E)$ value defined by the minimal number of literals can be computed by any minimal covering algorithm over the set of example pairs. In this work, the ILLM heuristic minimal covering algorithm, presented here as Procedure 1 in Figure 1, is used. The advantages of this approach are: $g(E)$ computation does not require the actual construction of a hypothesis and the $g(E)$ value can be determined relatively fast. This approach presents the heart of the saturation noise filtering method used in this work.

The procedure starts with the empty set of selected literals L' (step 1) and the set U' of yet uncovered example pairs equal to all possible pairs of one positive and one negative example from the training set (step 3), for which in (step 2) weights $v(e_i, e_j)$ have been computed. The weight of a pair is high if the pair is covered by a small number of distinct literals from L. The meaning of this measure is that for a pair with a high weight it will be more difficult to find an appropriate literal which will cover this pair than for a pair with a small weight.

Each iteration of the main algorithm loop (steps 4 – 11) adds one literal to the minimal set L' (step 9). At the same time, all example pairs covered by the selected literal are eliminated from U' (step 10). The algorithm terminates when U' remains empty. In each iteration we try to select the literal which covers a maximal number of 'heavy' example pairs (pairs with high weight). This is achieved so that a pair (e_a, e_b) is detected which is covered by the least number of literals (step 5). At least one of the literals from the set L_{ab} with literals that cover this pair (step 6), must be included into the minimal set L'. To determine this literal, for each of them weight $w(l)$ is computed (step 7) and the literal with the maximal weight is selected (step 8). The weight of a literal is the sum of the weights of example pairs that are covered by the literal.

Procedure 1: MINIMAL COVER
Input: U (set of example pairs), L (set of literals)
Output: L' (minimal set of literals)
(1) $L' \leftarrow \emptyset$
(2) **for** every $(e_i, e_j) \in U$ compute weights
$v(e_i, e_j) = 1/z$, where z is the number of literals $l \in L$ that cover (e_i, e_j)
(3) $U' \leftarrow U$
(4) **while** $U' \neq \emptyset$ **do**
(5) select (e_a, e_b)
$(e_a, e_b) \in U'$: $(e_a, e_b) = arg\ max\ v(e_i, e_j)$,
where max is over all $(e_i, e_j) \in U'$
(6) $L_{ab} \leftarrow \{l \mid l \in L$ covering $(e_a, e_b)\}$
(7) **for** every $l \in L_{ab}$ compute
$w(l) = \sum v(e_i, e_j)$, where sum is over all $(e_i, e_j) \in U'$ covered by l
(8) select literal l_s: $l_s = arg\ max\ w(l)$,
where max is over all $l \in L_{ab}$
(9) $L' \leftarrow L' \cup \{l_s\}$
(10) $U' \leftarrow U' \setminus \{$all (e_i, e_j) covered by $l_s\}$
(11) **end while**

Figure 1: Heuristic minimal covering algorithm.

Algorithm 1 in Figure 2 presents the saturation filter. It begins with the reduced training set E' equal the input training set E (step 1) and an empty set of detected noisy examples A (step 2). The algorithm supposes that the set of all appropriate literals L for the domain is defined. U represents a set of all possible example pairs where the first example in the pair is from the set of all positive training examples P' in the reduced set E', and the second example is from the set N' of all negative examples in the reduced training set E'. The algorithm detects one noisy example per iteration. The base for noise detection are weights $w(e)$ which are computed for each example e from E'. Initially all $w(e)$ values are initialized to 0 (step 6). At the end, the example with maximum weight $w(e)$ is selected (step 17). If the maximum $w(e)$ value is greater than the parameter ε_h predefined value then the corresponding training example is included into the set A

Algorithm 1: *SaturationFilter*(E)
Input: E (training set), L (set of literals)
Parameter: ε_h (noise sensitivity parameter)
Output: A (detected noisy subset of E)

(1) $E' \leftarrow E$
(2) $A \leftarrow \emptyset$
(3) **while** $E' \neq \emptyset$ **do**
(4) find U, set of all possible example pairs for examples in E'
(5) call **Procedure 1** to find minimal L', $L' \subseteq L$ so that $\forall (e_i, e_j) \in U \ \exists \ l \in L'$ with the property l covers (e_i, e_j)
(6) initialize $w(e) \leftarrow 0$ for all $e \in E'$
(7) **for** every $l \in L'$ **do**
(8) $P^* \leftarrow \emptyset$, $N^* \leftarrow \emptyset$
(9) **for** every $(e_i, e_j) \in U$
(10) **if** (e_i, e_j) covered by l and no other literal from L' **then**
(11) $P^* \leftarrow P^* \cup \{e_i\}$, $N^* \leftarrow N^* \cup \{e_j\}$
(12) **end for**
(13) **if** $P^* = \emptyset$ **then** $L' \leftarrow L' \setminus \{l\}$ and **goto** step 6
(14) **for** every $e \in P^*$ **do** $w(e) \leftarrow w(e) + \frac{1}{|P^*|}$
(15) **for** every $e \in N^*$ **do** $w(e) \leftarrow w(e) + \frac{1}{|N^*|}$
(16) **end for**
(17) select example e_s: $e_s = arg\ max\ w(e)$, where max is computed over all $e \in E'$
(18) **if** $w(e_s) > \varepsilon_h$ **then**
(19) $A \leftarrow A \cup \{e_s\}$
(20) $E' \leftarrow E' \setminus \{e_s\}$
(21) **else** exit with generated sets A and E'
(22) **end while**

Figure 2: Saturation filter.

(step 19) and eliminated from the reduced training set E' (step 20). The new iteration of noise detection begins with this reduced training set (steps 3–22). The algorithm terminates when in the last iteration no example has $w(e)$ greater than ε_h. Noisy examples in A and the noiseless E' are the output of the algorithm.

Computations in each iteration begin with the search for the minimal set of literals L' that cover all example pairs in U (calling Procedure 1 in step 5). A pair of examples is covered by a literal l if the literal is evaluated *true* for the positive example and evaluated *false* for the negative example in the pair. This step represents the computation of the $g(E')$ value. Next, a heuristic approach is used to compute weights $w(e)$ that measure the possibility that the elimination of an example e would enable $g(E')$ reduction. Weights $w(e)$ are computed so that for every literal l from L', minimal sets of positive (P^*) and negative examples (N^*) are determined, such that if P^* or N^* are eliminated from E' then l becomes unnecessary in L'. This is done in a loop (steps 9–12) in which every example pair is tested if it is covered by a single literal l. If such a pair is detected (step 10) then its positive example is included into the set P^* and its negative example into the set N^* (step 11). Literal elimination from L' presents the reduction of the $g(E')$ value. If a literal can be made unnecessary by the elimination of a very small subset of training examples, then this indicates that these examples might be noisy. In steps 14 and 15, the $w(e)$ weights are incremented only for the examples which are the members of the P^* and N^* sets. The weights are incremented by the inverse of the total number of examples in these sets. Weights are summed over all literals in L'. Step 13 is necessary because of the imperfectness of the heuristic minimal cover algorithm. Namely, if some $l \in L'$ exists for which there is no example pair that is covered only by this literal (i.e., for which either $P^* = \emptyset$ or $N^* = \emptyset$), this means that L' is actually not the minimal set because $L' \setminus \{l\}$ also covers all example pairs in U. In such case L' is substituted by $L' \setminus \{l\}$.

The presented saturation filter uses the parameter ε_h that determines noise sensitivity of the algorithm. The parameter can be adjusted by the user in order to tune the algorithm to the domain characteristics. Reasonable values are between 0.25 and 2. For instance, the value 1.0 guarantees the elimination of every such example by whose elimination the set L' will be reduced for at least one literal. Lower ε_h values mean greater sensitivity of the algorithm (i.e., elimination of more examples): lower ε_h values should be used when the domain noise is not completely random, and when dealing with large training sets (since statistical properties of noise distribution in large training sets can have similar effects). In ILLM the default values of ε_h are between 0.5 and 1.5, depending on the number of training examples in the smaller of the two subsets of E: the set of positive examples P or the set of negative examples N. Default values for the saturation filter's noise sensitivity parameter ε_h are: 1.5 for training sets with 2–50 examples, 1.0 for 51–100 examples, 0.75 for 101–200 examples, and 0.5 for more than 200 examples.

Algorithm 2: $ClassificationFilter(E)$
Input: E (training set)
Parameter: n (number of subsets, typically 10)
Output: A (detected noisy subset of E)
(1) form n disjoint almost equally sized subsets E_i, where $\cup_i E_i = E$
(2) $A \leftarrow \emptyset$
(3) **for** $i = 1, \ldots, n$ **do**
(4) form $E_y \leftarrow E \setminus E_i$
(5) induce H_y based on examples in E_y (using some inductive learning system)
(6) **for** every $e \in E_i$ **do**
(7) **if** H_y incorrectly classifies e **then** $A \leftarrow A \cup \{e\}$
(8) **end for**
(9) **end for**

Figure 3: Classification filter.

Algorithm 3: $ConsensusSaturationFilter(E)$
Input: E (training set)
Parameter: n (number of subsets, typically 10)
Parameter: v (consensus level, typically $n-1$)
Output: A (detected noisy subset of E)
(1) form n disjoint almost equally sized subsets E_i, where $\cup_i E_i = E$
(2) $A \leftarrow \emptyset$
(3) **for** $i = 1, \ldots, n$ **do**
(4) form $E_y \leftarrow E \setminus E_i$
(5) $A_i \leftarrow SaturationFilter(E_y)$
(6) **end for**
(7) **for** every $e \in E$ **do**
(8) $c \leftarrow 0$
(9) **for** $i = 1, \ldots, n$ **if** $e \in A_i$, $c \leftarrow c + 1$
(10) **if** $c \geq v$, $A \leftarrow A \cup \{e\}$
(11) **end for**

Figure 4: Consensus saturation filter.

2.2 CLASSIFICATION FILTER

The n-fold cross-validation method is a substantial part of this filtering algorithm. The classification filter (Algorithm 2, shown in Figure 3) begins with n equal-sized disjoint subsets of the training set E (step 1) and the empty output set A of detected noisy examples (step 2). The main loop (steps 3–9) is repeated for each training subset E_i. In step 4, subset E_y is formed which includes all examples from E except those in E_i. Set E_y is used as the input for an arbitrary inductive learning algorithm that induces a hypothesis (a classifier) H_y (step 5). Those examples from E_i for which the hypothesis H_y does not give the correct classification are added to A as potentially noisy examples (step 7).

2.3 COMBINED CLASSIFICATION-SATURATION FILTER

A combined classification-saturation algorithm is very similar to the original classification filtering approach. The only difference is that saturation filtering is used for every subset E_y in order to eliminate noise from E_y. The intention of this modification is the induction of more appropriate hypotheses H_y and more reliable noise detection based on these. The combined classification-saturation filter algorithm is the same as the classification filter with added saturation-based filtering between its steps 4 and 5.

2.4 CONSENSUS SATURATION FILTER

The n-fold cross-validation method is also a substantial part of the consensus saturation filtering algorithm (Algorithm 3, shown in Figure 4). Like in the combined classification-saturation filter, subset E_y is constructed (step 4) and noise eliminated from it by a saturation filter. In contrast to the combined classification-saturation filter, this reduced E_y is not used for hypothesis induction. Instead, detected noise is simply saved in the set A_i (step 5). When the procedure is performed for all E_i subsets, then n generated A_i sets are used to determine the elements of the output set A (steps 7–11). Since the same example e occurs in $n-1$ of E_y subsets, in an ideal case the same noisy example may occur in $n-1$ sets A_i. In this situation, detected by counter c (steps 9–11), example e is added to the output noisy set A (step 10), since the consensus of all A_i sets is reached. In practice we may allow that an example is detected as noisy and added to A also in cases when it is included in less than $n-1$ sets A_i. Parameter v with values less than $n-1$(e.g., $n-2$, $n-3$) enables this possibility.

3 EXPERIMENTAL EVALUATION

3.1 DOMAIN DESCRIPTION: DIAGNOSIS OF CORONARY ARTERY DISEASE

Coronary artery disease (CAD) is a result of diminished blood flow through coronary arteries due to stenosis or occlusion. The consequence of CAD is an impaired function of the heart and possible necrosis of the myocardium (myocardial infarction).

The dataset, collected at the University Medical Center, Ljubljana, Slovenia, includes 327 patients (250 men and 77 women, mean age 55 years). Each patient had performed clinical and laboratory examinations including ECG during rest and exercise, myocardial perfusion scintigraphy and finally the coronary angiography that provides for the actual diagnosis of coronary artery disease. In 229 patients, CAD was confirmed by angiography, and for 98 patients it was not confirmed. The patients' clinical and laboratory data are described by 77 attributes. This dataset was previously used for inducing diagnostic rules by a number of machine learning algorithms [9, 11].

3.2 EXPERIMENTAL DESIGN AND RESULTS

According to the standard 10-fold cross-validation procedure, the original data set was partitioned into 10 folds with 32 or 33 examples each. Training sets are built from 9 folds, leaving one fold is a test set. Let G denote the entire set of training examples, T_i is an individual test set (consisting of one fold), and G_i the corresponding training set ($G_i \leftarrow G \setminus T_i$, composed on nine folds). In this way, 10 training sets G_0 - G_9, and 10 corresponding test sets, T_0 - T_9, were constructed. Every example occurs exactly once in a test set, and 9 times in training sets.

Different noise detection procedures were used on the training sets and after the elimination of potentially noisy examples and hypothesis generation the prediction accuracy was measured on the test sets. The hypothesis was always constructed with the same algorithm so that the differences in the obtained prediction accuracy reflect only the differences in noise detection. The used rule construction algorithm was the ILLM (Inductive Learning by Logic Minimization) system used without its noise handling capability. The ILLM rule learning algorithm is similar to the AQ15 and CN2 covering algorithms for rule construction [2, 4].

In the first test we used ILLM (without its noise handling capability) to induce rules on complete G_0 - G_9 training sets. On the test sets T_0 - T_9 we measured the number of prediction errors: on the average, there were 5.5 prediction errors per test set. This corresponds to the 83.1% average prediction accuracy. This result, presented in the first row (A) of Table 1, presents the baseline for comparing the quality of different noise elimination algorithms. The average number of eliminated training examples is 0 because no noise elimination has been used. Generated rules are complete and consistent with all training examples in corresponding training sets.

In all other experiments instead of G_0 - G_9, reduced training sets G'_0 - G'_9 were used as the input to inductive learning. Reduced training sets G'_i were obtained by the elimination of noisy examples, $G'_i \leftarrow G_i \setminus A$, where A represent noisy set outputs of different filtering algorithms for G_i as input training sets.

3.2.1 Saturation Filter

By using the saturation filter presented in Section 2.1 with the ε_h parameter set to 1.0, the average prediction error was 3.6 examples per test set, which corresponds to the 89.0% average prediction accuracy. The result is presented in the second row (S) of Table 1. Compared to the results in row A this is a substantial improvement. This result was obtained by an average elimination of 30.2 examples per iteration, which represents about 10% of the training sets. A comparison to prediction results obtained by other authors, using very different machine learning methods, which are all between 86.6% and 89.7% [11], indicates that 10% of detected and eliminated noise seems to be realistic. Both the prediction accuracy and the number of eliminated examples demonstrate that saturation filtering can be used as an effective noise handling mechanism.

3.2.2 Classification Filter

Using the classification filter, described in Section 2.2, with parameter $n = 10$ for noise detection, in average 4.7 prediction errors per test set were made. This corresponds to the 85.6% average prediction accuracy. This result, presented in the third row (C) of Table 1, represents an improvement in accuracy when compared to the result of row A although it is not as good as the result obtained by the saturation filter (row S). Nevertheless, this result is important because the classification filter is computationally much simpler than the saturation filter. Additionally, according to [1], the use of simple voting mechanisms based on the results of filtering by different learning approaches (not neces-

Algorithm	Predict. err.		Accuracy	Elimin. ex.	
A	5.5	(3.03)	83.1 %	0	
S	3.6	(1.96)	89.0 %	30.2	(2.78)
C	4.7	(1.64)	85.6 %	52.6	(4.58)
CS	3.6	(1.71)	89.0 %	36.5	(4.34)
S9	4.2	(1.48)	87.2 %	12.5	(2.46)
S8	3.6	(1.17)	89.0 %	17.5	(2.12)
S7	3.6	(1.35)	89.0 %	19.8	(2.20)

Table 1: Average number of prediction errors (with standard deviation in parentheses), average prediction accuracy, and average number of eliminated examples (with standard deviation in parentheses) for different noise detection algorithms: A - ILLM without noise handling, S - saturation filter, C - classification filter, CS - combined classification-saturation filter, S9,S8,S7 - consensus saturation filters with varied levels of consensus.

sarily only inductive learning approaches) can further improve the reliability of this noise detection process. This possibility was not investigated in this work.

The average number of eliminated examples per training set was 52.6. This means that the classification filter practically detected every fifth training example as potentially noisy. This shows a weakness of the classification filter: it is non-selective. Too many examples are detected as being potentially noisy.

3.2.3 Combined Classification-Saturation Filter

Results obtained with noise filtering performed by the combined classification-saturation filter (see Section 2.3, n=10, ε_h = 1.0) are presented in CS row of Table 1. The measured average error was 3.6 examples representing the 89.0% average accuracy. It can be concluded that the combination of the two different noise detection algorithms is advantageous only in comparison with the classification filtering approach. The combined approach namely resulted in the average of 36.5 detected and eliminated potentially noisy examples per training set. Although this number is smaller than the one for the classification filter (row C with 52.6 examples) it seems that non-selectiveness is an inherent characteristic of classification filtering when a single classifier is used.

3.2.4 Consensus Saturation Filter

The relative success of the classification filter, which enables significant prediction accuracy improvement using a learning algorithm without noise handling, stimulated a series of experiments in which we tried to test if a mechanism similar to the one used in the classification filter could improve the results of saturation filtering. In all the experiments parameter n was set to 10 and ε_h=1.0, while changing the consensus level v. With a default value v = 9 the average number of eliminated examples per training set was only 12.5 and the average number of prediction errors on test sets was 4.2 (presented in S9 row of Table 1).

This result is important since a satisfactory prediction accuracy was achieved by the elimination of a very small number of training examples. When compared with saturation filtering itself (row S) we see that by requiring the consensus of filtering in 10-fold validation, lower prediction accuracy (87.2% instead of 89.0%) was achieved by a significantly smaller average number of eliminated examples (12.5 instead of 30.2).

The described consensus filtering approach seems to be a reliable noise detection algorithm. A further proof of this claim is the following: from the total of 125 examples eliminated by the consensus filter (row S9), 124 of them were detected also by the combined classification-saturation filter (row CS) which, however, eliminated 365 examples in total.

Requiring consensus in 10-fold validation results in noise detection of high specificity. However, the decreased prediction accuracy indicates that the algorithm's sensitivity is too low. This can be the consequence of a too high consensus level (in order to declare an example to be potentially noisy, the example had to be tagged as potentially noisy in all subsets in which it occurs, i.e., in 9 subsets).

The algorithm's noise sensitivity can easily be increased by decreasing the consensus level v. In this way, relaxed consensus filters can be constructed. Rows S8 and S7 present results obtained by setting the consensus levels to 8 and 7, respectively. In both cases the increase in sensitivity resulted in the increase of the achieved prediction accuracy. Good prediction accuracy of 89.0%, as in cases S and CS, is obtained by relaxed consensus filtering but with significantly fewer potentially noisy examples eliminated.

3.3 MEDICAL EVALUATION

The results of described experiments suggest that consensus saturation filtering (with consensus level 9, row S9 of Table 1) presents a reliable tool for the detection of examples that are indeed noisy. In order to test the practical usefulness of noise detection by the consensus saturation filter, we applied the described approach to the whole coronary artery disease dataset of 327 examples. In this case the training sets G_0 - G_9 were used as 10 training subsets for the consensus filter. In total 15 potentially noisy examples were detected. This is in accordance with the result obtained for G_0 - G_9 sets for which the average value of eliminated examples was 12.5.

The detected examples were shown to a domain expert for evaluation. In order to make the task more difficult to the expert, we formed a set of 20 examples consisting of 15 examples detected as noisy by the consensus saturation filter, and additional 5 randomly selected non-noisy examples. The expert analyzed the group of these 20 examples as a whole. Out of these 20 examples, 13 were of class non-confirmed (11 detected potentially noisy and 2 other examples of class non-confirmed), and 7 were of class confirmed (4 detected potentially noisy examples and 3 other examples of class confirmed).

In the class non-confirmed the expert recognized 11 cases as being outliers, and these examples were exactly those selected by the noise detection algorithm. For 8 of these 11 cases the problem was a high grade of stenosis of coronary arteries, very close to the predefined value that distinguishes between patients with confirmed and non-confirmed coronary artery disease. Other 3 cases represented patients who did not have actual coronary heart disease problems but rather problems due to recent miocardial infarction, functionally malfunctioning by-pass, and valve disease.

For the class confirmed the expert detected 4 potentially noisy cases three of which were selected also by the noise detection algorithm and one of the randomly selected cases of this class. For all 4 cases the detected grade of stenosis was very close to the border line between the two classes. Additionally, for one patient the values of measured parameters were detected as non-typical due to the improper level of stress during measurements.

The expert has also analyzed four diagnostic parameters MAIN (main coronary artery), LAD (left anterior descendens), LCX (left circumflex) and RCA (right coronary artery). Each of these parameters has values between 0 and 3 and denotes the level of stenosis or occlusion in the corresponding artery. The value 0 denotes no stenosis, value 1 up to 50%, value 2 corresponds to 50%–75%, and value 3 represents more than 75% of stenosis or occlusion. Average values of these parameters are computed for all non-confirmed class cases and 11 non-confirmed class cases selected as noise, as well as for all confirmed class cases and 4 confirmed class cases selected as noise. Results are presented in Table 2. It can be noticed that for all four parameters, noisy non-confirmed cases have higher average values than those computed for the whole class. On the contrary, for the confirmed class, for all four parameters noisy examples have lower average values than average values for the whole class of 229 cases.

	non-confirmed cases		confirmed cases	
	all	11 noisy	all	4 noisy
MAIN	0.01	0.09	1.53	0.50
LAD	0.29	0.73	2.15	0.75
LCX	0.10	0.45	1.31	0
RCA	0.15	0.18	1.38	0

Table 2: Average values for 4 diagnostic parameters.

The analysis shows that, except for a few patients who did not have actual coronary heart disease problems, most of cases detected as noise represent a special group of patients whose coronary angiography results are very close to the border line between the two classes CAD confirmed and not-confirmed. By a slight change of the definition of class confirmed these cases can change their class value, therefore it is clear that they are non-typical training cases. Their elimination from the training set, as well as the elimination of patients who did not have actual coronary heart disease problems and patients with improperly measured parameters, is reasonable if one wants to induce diagnostic rules uncovering characteristic properties of patients with CAD.

4 CONCLUSION

Explicit noise detection and elimination turns out to be a very useful and important step in data preprocessing for any inductive learning algorithm. Namely, the detection and filtering of potentially noisy examples is itself an important result that may be useful in practice for data cleansing.

Standard deviations, presented as parenthesized numbers in Table 1, show that the differences of achieved prediction accuracies by different noise filtering algorithms are not significant. On the other hand, most of the differences in the numbers of eliminated noisy examples are significant and represent genuine characteristics of the presented noise filtering algorithms.

It is interesting that a simple classification filtering approach, based on an iterative application of a machine learning algorithm (without noise handling) by itself enables an improvement of the prediction accuracy. However, in the coronary artery disease diagnostic domain, best prediction accuracies were achieved by the approaches which include saturation filtering. The proposed consensus saturation filter is an interesting combination: it eliminates only a small number of potentially noisy examples, with a very high probability of actually being noisy. This property may turn out to be decisive for a broader applicability of noise detection algorithms. The experiments suggest that a relaxed consensus saturation filter (see row S8 in Table 1) represents a very good solution to the problem of noise filtering.

Acknowledgement

We are grateful to Matjaž Kukar from the Faculty of Computer and Information Sciences, University of Ljubljana, for his help and involvement in the evaluation of the results of this study.

References

[1] Brodley, C.E. & Friedl, M.A. (1996). Identifying and eliminating mislabeled training instances. In *Proc. of the 13th National Conference on Artificial Intelligence*, 799–805. AAAI Press.

[2] Clark, P. & Niblett, T. (1989). The CN2 induction algorithm. *Machine Learning* **3**: 261–283.

[3] Dimopoulos, Y. and Kakas, A (1995) Learning non-monotonic logic programs: Learning exceptions. In N. Lavrač and S. Wrobel, editors, Proc. of the 8th European Conference on Machine Learning, volume 912 of Lecture Notes in Artificial Intelligence, 122–137. Springer-Verlag, 1995.

[4] Fürnkranz, J. (1999). Separate-and-conquer rule learning. *Artificial Intelligence Review* **13**(1): 3–54.

[5] Gamberger, D. (1995). A minimization approach to propositional inductive learning. In *Proc. of the 8th European Conference on Machine Learning*, 151–160. Springer, Berlin.

[6] Gamberger, D. & Lavrač, N. (1996). Noise detection and elimination applied to noise handling in a KRK chess endgame. In *Proc. of the 6th International Workshop on Inductive Logic Programming*, 59–75. Springer, Berlin.

[7] Gamberger, D., Lavrač, N. & Džeroski, S. (1996). Noise elimination in inductive concept learning: A case study in medical diagnosis. In *Proc. of the 7th International Workshop on Algorithmic Learning Theory*, 199–212. Springer, Berlin.

[8] Gamberger, D. & Lavrač, N. (1997). Conditions for Occam's razor applicability and noise elimination. In *Proc. of the 9th European Conference on Machine Learning*, 108–123. Springer, Berlin.

[9] Grošelj, C., Kukar, M., Fetich, J. & Kononenko, I. (1997). Machine learning improves the accuracy of coronary artery disease diagnostic methods. *Computers in Cardiology* **24**: 57–60.

[10] John, G.H. (1995). Robust decision trees: Removing outliers from data. In *Proc. of the 1st Int. Conference on Knowledge Discovery and Data Mining*, 174–179. AAI Press.

[11] Kukar, M., Grošelj, C., Kononenko, I. & Fetich, J. (1997). An application of machine learning in the diagnosis of ischaemic heart disease. In *Proc. of the 6th Conference on Artificial Intelligence in Medicine Europe*, 461–464. Springer, Berlin.

[12] Lavrač, N., Gamberger, D. & Džeroski, S. (1995). An approach to dimensionality reduction in learning from deductive databases. In *Proc. of the 5th International Workshop on Inductive Logic Programming (ILP-95)*, 337–354. Katholieke Universiteit Leuven Scientific Report.

[13] Lavrač, N., Gamberger, D. & Turney, P. (1998). A relevancy filter for constructive induction. *IEEE Intelligent Systems* **13**: 50–56.

[14] Mingers, J. (1989). An empirical comparison of pruning methods for decision tree induction. *Machine Learning* **4**(2): 227–243.

[15] Quinlan, J.R. (1993). *C4.5: Programs for Machine Learning.* Morgan Kaufmann, San Mateo, CA.

[16] Srinivasan, A., Muggleton, S. & Bain, M. (1992). Distinguishing exceptions from noise in non-monotonic learning. In *Proc. of the 2nd Int. Workshop on Inductive Logic Programming.* Tokyo, ICOT TM-1182.

[17] Weisberg, S. (1985). *Applied Linear Regression.* John Wiley & Sons.

Learning User Evaluation Functions for Adaptive Scheduling Assistance

Melinda T. Gervasio and **Wayne Iba** and **Pat Langley**
Institute for the Study of Learning and Expertise
2164 Staunton Court, Palo Alto, California 94306
{gervasio,iba,langley}@isle.org

Abstract

In this paper, we describe INCA, an adaptive, advisable assistant for crisis response. The system lets users guide the search toward particular schedules by giving high-level, operational advice about the solutions desired. Because traces of user interactions provide information regarding the user's preferences among schedules, INCA can draw on machine learning techniques to construct user models that reflect these preferences. We characterize the modeling task as that of learning a weight vector for a linear evaluation function that will lead to the same pairwise preferences between schedules as the user. INCA adapts to individual users by adjusting the weights on its evaluation function using a perceptron-type learning algorithm. To evaluate the system's adaptive capabilities, we designed an experiment involving four types of synthetic users that differed in their evaluation functions and in the level of advice they provide. We present experimental results showing that INCA achieves better performance with more specific advice and with learning, even on users with evaluation functions that have nonlinearities or unobservable factors.

1 INTRODUCTION

In recent years, there has been a growing interest in personalized software as the need has increased for systems that can tailor their behavior to different individuals. For example, the World Wide Web now has electronic commerce sites that suggest new purchases based on a user's past buying behavior, portals that choose banner ads depending on the links a user follows, and travel planners that suggest default choices based on user-specified preferences. Many of these systems use simple heuristics or require a laborious initial phase of user profile construction to achieve personalization. In contrast, an *adaptive user interface* (Langley, 1999) uses traces of its interactions with users to automatically build a model that influences the system's behavior to better suit the user's preferences. In this paper, we present one such system, INCA, an adaptive scheduling assistant that learns user evaluation functions over schedules by extracting preference information from the schedules a user chooses during interaction with the system.

INCA is a mixed-initiative system designed to aid human users in crisis response. The primary focus of our work thus far has been *urgency*, a defining theme of crisis. We have addressed this issue through the use of case-based reasoning techniques to provide initial candidate solutions (Iba et al., 1998), as well as through the application of machine learning to better predict a user's schedule modifications (Gervasio et al., 1998), both of which lead to more efficient construction of high-quality solutions. In this paper, we extend our work on adaptive assistance within a new framework that allows advisable interaction with INCA. By letting users interact with the system at higher levels of abstraction, this new framework lets them more effectively guide the development of a crisis response.

Users provide guidance in the form of *advice* that directs INCA in its search through a highly underconstrained solution space. The advice users give and the choices they make while interacting with the system implicitly define an evaluation function over solutions. For example, if a user directs INCA to modify a solution to improve its value along some dimension and then accepts the modified solution, then the user is indicating a preference for the new solution over the old one. This presents an opportunity to adapt to individual user preferences by examining interaction traces and inducing user models that approximate these preferences. In this paper, we describe an approach that learns evaluation functions over schedules by applying a perceptron-type learning algorithm to pairwise preferences that are drawn from such interaction traces.

We begin by providing an overview of INCA's interactive response process in our application domain of hazardous material incidents. We then discuss the motivations for higher-level interaction and present our new framework for advisable scheduling assistance. In the following section, we lay the groundwork for our learning experiments by presenting INCA's basic learning algorithm and discussing the representation of the examples and the schedule evaluation function. After this, we present our design for an experiment intended to test our hypotheses on the effects of adaptation, given different types of user evaluation functions and different levels of advice. The results, which we discuss in the succeeding section, support our hypotheses that both learning and more specific advice would improve performance. We conclude the paper by discussing related research and summarizing our plans for future work on adaptive assistance.

2 HAZMAT INCIDENT RESPONSE WITH INCA

INCA is a *case-based*, *interactive*, and *adaptive* computational assistant for crisis response. It uses a case library of previous solutions to seed the problem-solving process with an initial candidate plan and schedule, which lets users develop high-quality responses more quickly (Iba et al., 1998). As a mixed-initiative system, INCA benefits from the invaluable input of human users while letting them retain ultimate control over the decision-making process. And by adapting to different individuals, the system can increase the efficiency of the response process by tailoring its assistant behavior to user preferences (Gervasio et al., 1998). In this paper, we focus primarily on the adaptive nature of INCA and secondarily on the new kinds of interaction introduced by the advisable framework.

We have applied INCA to HAZMAT, a synthetic domain for hazardous materials incidents that we developed using the 1996 North American Emergency Response Guidebook (Transport Canada et al., 1996) and manuals of standard operating procedures for several fire departments. Figure 1 depicts the interactive crisis response process with INCA. Problem solving is triggered by an incident alarm, where an incident consists of a spill and possibly a fire involving some material with hazardous properties such as toxicity, corrosiveness, and flammability. Incidents vary in the type and amount of material involved, the location of the incident, and the characteristics of the spill and any fire. The alarm drives INCA to retrieve a solution to a similar incident from its case library, which

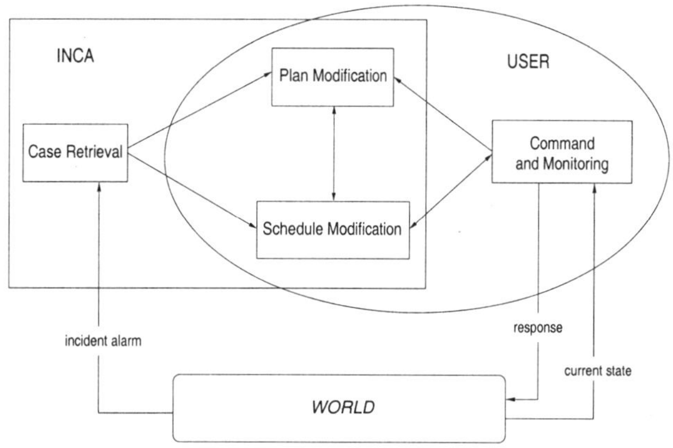

Figure 1: Interactive Crisis Response with INCA

it uses to seed the interactive planning and scheduling phases of crisis response. The primary purpose of planning is to choose a set of actions or jobs, *any* subset of which may be allocated resources during the scheduling phase. Different actions are appropriate for different incidents, with each action addressing particular aspects of a HAZMAT problem and requiring some minimum set of resources. During scheduling, decisions are made regarding the jobs to schedule and, for each job, the number of resources to allocate, the particular resources to use, a duration, and start time.

Scheduling in INCA is complicated by the fact that actions may be allocated a variable number of resources and assigned arbitrary durations. Allocating more resources to an action will result in greater effects, but at the cost of greater resource consumption that will constrain the other actions and their impact on the situation. For example, assigning all available personnel to combat the fire will extinguish the fire more quickly but will delay stopping the spill, which will result in the release of more hazardous material into the environment. Similarly, scheduling more actions that address a particular aspect of the incident will minimize the negative consequences along that dimension, but possibly at the cost of greater negative consequences along another one. The resulting underconstrained scheduling problem makes automation particularly difficult, calling for an interactive system such as INCA and presenting the opportunity for learning user models that support more productive interaction.

3 ADVISABLE INTERACTION

In previous versions of INCA, a user could only change the retrieved solution at the level of schedule modification operations: adding an action to the schedule, deleting a scheduled action, changing the duration of an action, shifting the start time of an action, or switching an action to a different resource. This type of interaction lets users make the exact changes they desire, but it can also be quite tedious—something of particular concern in time-constrained crisis domains. We decided that more efficient interaction might be achieved if we instead let INCA generate several candidate schedules and have the user choose among them, basically shifting more of the scheduling responsibility to the system. The problem remains, however, that autonomous scheduling is particularly difficult in this underconstrained domain. Our solution was to let the user guide the search for a desirable solution by providing particular types of advice, as dictated and supported by the characteristics of the solution space. This makes INCA an instance of what Myers (1996) calls *advisable planning systems.*

3.1 CHARACTERISTICS OF THE SOLUTION SPACE

A primary characteristic of the solution space for hazardous materials incident response is that it is highly underconstrained. There are many possible solutions for each problem and various ways of evaluating them, with different parameters being more important for particular problems and different users. For example, in a large spill involving a highly toxic chemical in a heavily populated area, the priority in evacuating the inhabitants to safety will probably be on speed rather than cost. In a large fire, where there is a severe shortage of resources, more emphasis may be placed on suppressing the fire near occupied buildings than on stopping the leak.

Although the underconstrained nature of the solution space and the complexity of the objective function make automation difficult, there are also characteristics that suggest a feasible method of navigation. First, we can define a direct relationship between particular parameters of solution quality and the methods for modifying a schedule. Second, we can define a direct relationship between the method for improvement along a particular parameter and the actions themselves. These two properties help shape the kinds of advice INCA can easily operationalize and suggest the framework for our advisable system.

3.2 LEVELS OF ADVICE

The first level of advice involves directing INCA's attention to improve a solution along a particular parameter. We can characterize a solution in terms of its effects on a situation (i.e., its achievement of the problem goals) as well as in terms of its cost (e.g., time taken to reach the goal, number of resources used). In the case of crisis response, as with most real-world problems, we are interested in both—we want to evaluate solutions in terms of their impact on the situation as well as on their cost of execution. However, in our initial implementation, we decided to focus on the former, using our HAZMAT simulator to project the effects of a solution on the environment.

The simulator tracks the development of the spill, the fire, and the fire and health hazards in terms of the amounts and derivatives of various quantities. By comparing the simulation of a response on the incident with the simulation of an unabated situation, we can come up with a measure of performance improvement along the different parameters. For example, if the amount spilled in the unabated situation was s_u, while the amount spilled with a response was s_a, then the improvement in the amount spilled is $1 - s_u/s_a$.

Thus, an improvement percentage of 1.00 would signify an instantaneous stoppage of the spill, while 0.00 reveals that the response had no effects whatsoever. The simulator keeps track of a total of fifteen parameters, which we can distill into three improvement percentages corresponding to spill improvement, fire improvement, and hazard improvement. At the first level, the user can thus provide INCA with three types of parameter advice: improve spill handling, improve fire handling, or improve hazard handling.

The second level of advice involves indicating the particular modification method to achieve the desired improvement. As stated earlier, there is a direct relationship between the parameter being improved and the schedule modification methods. A choice of improvement parameter constrains the modification methods that may be applied. In our case, the three schedule quality parameters we have defined correspond to the same four schedule modification methods. Specifically, to improve a schedule along any parameter, INCA can either add a new action, assign more resources to a scheduled action, increase the duration of a scheduled action, or start a scheduled action earlier. Applying any of these modifications on a relevant action is guaranteed not to degrade the quality of the schedule with respect to the chosen parameter.

The third level of advice involves specifying the action or job on which to apply the chosen modification method to achieve the desired improvement. An action is relevant to a particular parameter if it affects that parameter. Thus, a given parameter and modification method define a fixed set of actions over which the next decision must be made. For example, if the user directs INCA to improve fire handling by adding an action, then the only relevant choices are those unscheduled actions that affect the fire, such as extinguishment and fire suppression. But if improvement is to be achieved by means of shifting an action earlier, then the only relevant actions are those scheduled actions that do not already start immediately.

The fourth, and final, level of advice involves variable instantiation—that is, specifying particular resources, start times, and durations for a job. Providing advice at this level is equivalent to INCA's original mode of interaction in which users were required to specify the particular schedule modifications they wanted.

3.3 VARIABLE-LEVEL INTERACTION

The basic interaction loop involves the user choosing a schedule from among the current candidates and giving INCA direction on how to improve the solution by providing advice at each level. However, at any level, the user may defer all remaining decisions to INCA by choosing the *ANY* option. With the user's advice, INCA then generates a set of candidates for the next cycle, continuing in this manner until the user is satisfied with one of the current solutions. In keeping with the urgent nature of crisis response, we constrain INCA to a fixed amount of computational resources on each cycle. Thus, more specific advice lets INCA expend more resources in exploring a smaller area of the search space, potentially finding solutions it may not have found with more abstract advice.

In terms of Myers's (1996) three-level taxonomy of advice, parameter specification is a form of *evaluational advice*, which "encompasses constraints on some metric defined for the overall plan." Method specification is a form of *strategic advice*, which "consists of recommendations on how goals and actions are to be accomplished." Finally, action specification and variable instantiation may be seen as forms of *task advice*, which "designates specific goals to be achieved and actions to be performed." As in Myers's work on advisable planning, our objective in incorporating advice taking into INCA was to enable users to more effectively influence the problem-solving process.

4 ADAPTIVE INTERACTION

The traces of user interactions with INCA provide a ready source of training data for adaptation and previous versions of the system used such traces to learn to predict the schedule modification operations a user would choose next (Gervasio et al., 1998). The idea was that, by accurately predicting a user's actions, INCA can facilitate the response development process. We can extend this work within the current framework by using similar inductive learning techniques to predict the particular advice a user will give in the current situation, based on the user's previous behavior.

However, the current advisable interaction framework also provides an opportunity to explore a new learning task. INCA currently employs a weighted linear evaluation function over schedules. If we let c be a particular candidate schedule, and s_c, f_c, and z_c be its spill, fire, and hazard improvement, as defined earlier, then INCA's evaluation function is $I(c) = w_s s_c + w_f f_c + w_z z_c$, where w_p is a weight associated with parameter p. We can thus characterize INCA's task of adapting to a user as that of learning a weight vector $\langle w_s, w_f, w_z \rangle$ that will lead it to prefer (i.e., rank higher) the same schedules as the user. More concretely, if we let the target function (i.e., the user's evaluation function) be U, then we can say that INCA models the user perfectly if $\forall_{c_1,c_2} U(c_1) > U(c_2) \rightarrow I(c_1) > I(c_2)$.

Cast in this manner, INCA's learning task becomes very similar to that of Roger et al.'s Adaptive Route Advisor (1999), which seeks to discover user preferences over alternative driving routes. Drawing from that work, we decided to use a differential perceptron, which learns over sets of examples indicating pairwise preferences—in our case, preferences between schedules. That is, each example is an ordered pair (c_1, c_2), where $U(c_1) > U(c_2)$, and INCA's training task is to find an evaluation function that will minimize the number of examples over which it prefers the wrong candidate.

Without requiring the user to rank every set of candidate schedules, we can still obtain these pairwise preferences from a user's interactions with INCA. In the advisable framework, the user indicates a preference for a particular schedule over all other candidates when he directs the system to improve that schedule. Given that the user has so far had j interactions with INCA in developing a response for a particular problem and now chooses the ith candidate in a set of n candidates, we can extract $n-1+j$ pairwise preferences—specifically, $n-1$ examples capturing the information that the user preferred the ith candidate over the $n-1$ other candidates in the set, and j examples denoting the user's preference of this ith candidate over all the candidates chosen in the j previous interactions.

INCA uses a batch update scheme, adjusting the perceptron weights once per epoch. Let E be that subset of a set of examples X where I prefers the wrong candidate (i.e., $E = \{(c_1, c_2) \in X | I(c_1) \leq I(c_2)\}$), and let p_c be the value of parameter p for candidate c. Then the differential perceptron update rule will increase the weight associated with p by the amount $\eta_p \sum_{(c_1,c_2)\in E}(p_{c_1} - p_{c_2})$, where η_p is the learning rate associated with p.[1] Intuitively, INCA will move towards the correct preference by increasing the weight for a parameter if that parameter had a higher value for the preferred candidate than for the non-preferred

[1] To speed convergence, we use adaptive learning rates, where each parameter has its own learning rate determined by the current indicated change on its associated weight as well as the direction and magnitude of previous recent changes (Jacobs, 1988).

candidate, and by decreasing it if it had a lower value instead. In standard perceptron training fashion, INCA iterates through its training examples until it makes no more errors or it has gone through more than some maximum number of epochs.

5 ADAPTATION EXPERIMENTS

To evaluate INCA's adaptive capabilities, we developed a variety of synthetic users to test our hypotheses about the effects of evaluation functions and advice on adaptation. While we might expect INCA to adapt to users with evaluation functions similar to its own, we also believe that INCA will be able to tailor its behavior to users with evaluation functions of different forms. Furthermore, we expect that more specific advice during scheduling will, in some sense, provide "better" examples and thus enable INCA to adapt more quickly.

5.1 USER EVALUATION FUNCTION

We designed three types of synthetic users to test our hypothesis on INCA's ability to adapt to different individuals. Type 1 users had evaluation functions of the same form as INCA's weighted linear combination over the spill, fire, and hazard improvement measures. They differed only in the specific weights they attached to each parameter. We created five Type 1 users, each with a randomly generated weight vector. Type 2 users also used a linear evaluation function but this function included three additional features (unknown to INCA) that measured, respectively, the number of scheduled jobs, the number of resources used, and the duration of the schedule. We created three Type 2 users, whose weight distribution varied between the known and unknown features. Specifically, these three users had a weight ratio between known and unknown features of 1:1, 1:3, and 3:1 respectively. Type 3 users used some nonlinear combination of the original three features, and we created three such users with different nonlinear evaluation functions. Specifically, if we let s be the spill improvement, f the fire improvement, and z the hazard improvement, the first Type 3 evaluation function was sfz; the second was $\sqrt[3]{sfz}$; and the third was sf^{1-z}.

5.2 LEVEL OF ADVICE

We created one more user type to evaluate our hypothesis on advice. By default, our synthetic users provide only the highest level advice, namely that of instructing INCA to improve the schedule along *ANY* parameter. User Type 4 was a variant of User Type 1 who differed only in that it gave advice at the parameter level, specifying the parameter along which improvement was desired. Specifically, a Type 4 user requests

Table 1: Average Number of Interactions, Candidates, and Examples Generated for Different User Types During Problem Solving

User Type	interactions/ problem	candidates/ interaction	examples/ problem set
1	7.58	16.04	757.12
2	5.00	15.77	384.20
3	5.65	18.79	629.67
4	5.86	5.15	219.08
all	6.02	13.94	497.52

improvement along that parameter which has the potential to contribute the most to the overall schedule evaluation, given that user's evaluation function. If we let p be the current improvement measure for a particular parameter (spill, fire, hazard), then the amount of potential improvement associated with p is $w_{pu}(1-p)$, where w_{pu} is the user's weight on feature p.

5.3 TRAINING REGIMEN

Learning was carried out online using the perceptron training algorithm presented earlier, with random initial weights and the maximum number of epochs set to 100.[2] After each interaction, new examples were extracted from the current set of candidates and the user's choice, and these were were added to the set of all examples. INCA was then retrained on the whole set, starting with the final set of weights from the previous training episode.

To control for the effects of problem sequence on learning and of specific problems on performance, each user was trained five times using five different problem sets, each consisting of a sequence of five randomly generated problems. That is, each user responded to twenty-five different problems broken up into five separate training sequences, with the problems and sequences constant across all users. Also, problem solving was always started with an empty schedule. On average, each response to a problem required 6.02 interactions, with each interaction resulting in an average of 13.94 candidates. Each problem set also generated an average of 497.52 examples over the course of solving all five problems in the set. Table 1 provides a more detailed breakdown by user type. The baselines were determined by running INCA's default evaluation function (which assigns equal weights to the parameters) over the same five problem sets.

[2]The adaptive learning rates η_p were initialized to 0.01 for each parameter p, with $\kappa = 0.1$, $\phi = 0.5$, and $\theta = 0.7$.

Table 2: Predictive Errors for Different User Types, Averaged Over All Users and Problem Sets

User	Baseline		With Learning	
Type	mean	std. err.	mean	std. err.
1	10.59	1.61	4.24	0.40
2	5.49	0.95	6.11	1.08
3	10.48	2.11	6.76	1.20
4	1.12	0.48	0.83	0.43

Table 3: Rank Error for Different User Types, Averaged Over All Users and Problem Sets

User	Baseline		With Learning	
Type	mean	std. err.	mean	std. err.
1	1.93	0.36	0.63	0.08
2	0.82	0.13	0.92	0.15
3	2.34	0.49	1.39	0.26
4	0.07	0.04	0.05	0.03

5.4 PERFORMANCE MEASURES

The objective of adaptation in INCA is to learn to present the user with those candidate schedules that he finds desirable. As discussed earlier, one measure of the quality of a user model is how well its induced preferences over a set of schedules mimic those of the user's. Recall that learning is applied on a set of examples derived from interaction with a user U, with each example being an ordered pair (c_1, c_2), where $U(c_1) > U(c_2)$ and INCA is in error if $I(c_1) \leq I(c_2)$. The *predictive error* of a hypothesis I on a set of examples X, where it makes errors on the subset $E \subseteq X$, is thus defined simply as $|E|/|X|$.

We can measure the effects of learning in an online fashion by testing the current user model after every interaction on the set of new examples generated from that interaction, *prior* to retraining. This achieves the necessary separation between training and testing, since INCA is always evaluated on examples it did not see during learning. If we let e_j be the number of errors INCA makes on the x_j *new* examples generated from interaction j, then we can calculate INCA's predictive error over a problem set involving n interactions as $(\sum_{j=1}^{n} e_j)/(\sum_{j=1}^{n} x_j)$. We can similarly establish the baseline predictive error by summing the errors INCA makes using its default evaluation function and dividing by the total number of examples, the only difference being that, since no training is involved, testing may be done after all the examples are generated.

A second measure of model goodness is based on the rank r of the candidate a user chooses. INCA presents the set of candidates in ranked order, depending on their value according to its current evaluation function. Thus, if INCA had a perfect user model, the user would always choose the highest ranked schedule (i.e., $r = 1$) in the set of candidates the system presents. As before, we can measure the effects of learning in an online fashion by looking at the immediate result of an interaction, prior to retraining. More concretely, let r_j be the rank of the candidate the user chooses at interaction j, where the new candidates were ordered according to the current model. Then INCA's *rank error* over a set of interactions J is defined as $(\sum_{j \in J}(r_j - 1))/|J|$, with perfect models having a rank error of zero. We can again establish the baseline in a similar fashion by using INCA's default evaluation function and summing the relative ranks of the chosen candidates, and then dividing by the total number of interactions.[3]

In summary, our two independent variables were user type (evaluation function) and level of advice, and our two dependent variables for measuring performance were predictive error on pairwise preferences and rank error on the user's chosen candidates. Our two primary hypotheses were that online learning would lead to better performance, and that adaptation would be easier (i.e., performance would be better) on users who provided more specific advice. A secondary hypothesis was that adaptation would be more difficult (i.e., performance would be worse) on users with complex evaluation functions.

6 EXPERIMENTAL RESULTS

The results of our experiment are summarized in Tables 2 and 3, with the error for each user type averaged over all the problem sets and the different users for that type (i.e., twenty-five data points for Types 1 and 4, fifteen for Types 2 and 3). In general, the results support all our hypotheses regarding the benefits of learning and more specific advice. Predictive error (Table 2) was significantly lower with learning for all but User Type 2 (where there was no significant difference), and rank error (Table 3) was also significantly lower except for User Types 2 and 4 (where there were again no significant differences), thus supporting our hypothesis that learning would improve performance

[3]With a variable number of candidates at each interaction, an alternative would be to look at some normalized ranking. However, because of the difficulty of graphically displaying many candidates and the additional cognitive load this presents to human users, we feel that absolute rank is a better measure of performance.

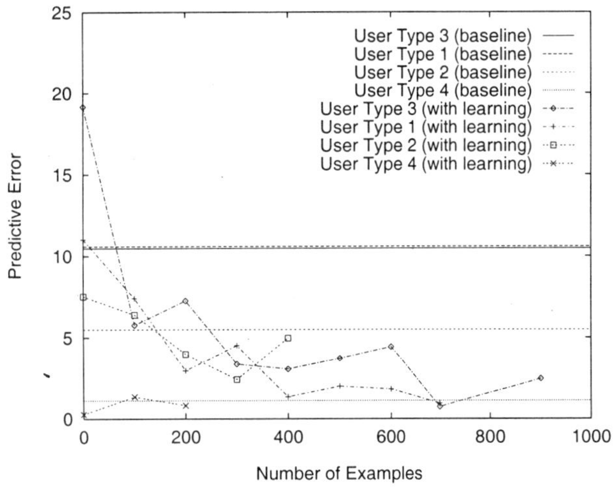

Figure 2: Online Learning Curves Showing Decrease in Predictive Error with Number of Training Examples

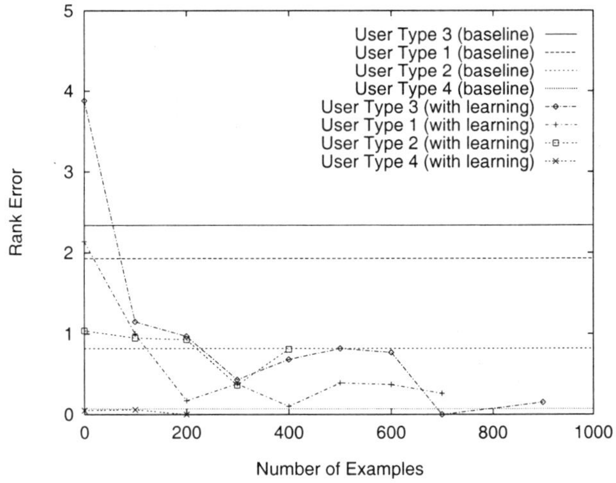

Figure 3: Online Learning Curves Showing Decrease in Rank Error with Number of Training Examples

over the baseline.[4] Errors were also lower when users provided more specific advice (Type 4 vs. Type 1). However, the Type 4 baselines were also much lower, so all we can conclude is that more specific advice simplifies the learning problem and results in better overall performance. The results also support our secondary hypothesis that adaptation will be more difficult on users with more complex evaluation functions (Types 2 and 3).

The results on users with different evaluation functions (Types 2 and 3) provide some insight into the difficulties that can arise when the assumptions of the perceptron algorithm are not met. In particular, target functions with additional features unknown to INCA (Type 2) were more difficult to learn than nonlinear functions using only known features (Type 3). A deeper investigation into the results with Type 2 users reveals that performance with learning was worst with the second user, who gave 75% weight to the unknown features. Performance was best with the third, who gave only 25% weight to these features. This satisfies the intuition that INCA will adapt better to users who do not place too much weight on features unknown to the system when evaluating schedules.

Recall that the results reported in Tables 2 and 3 are averaged over the course of online learning. We expect that, while both types of error may be high early on, they will gradually decrease as more examples are gathered and the system undergoes more training. An alternative, and perhaps more informative, summary of the results are the learning curves shown in Figures 2 and 3, which reveal that, under all conditions, the predictive error and rank error tended to decrease as the number of training examples increased.[5] Consistent with the results presented in Tables 2 and 3, the curves show the least improvement for User Type 2. They also highlight the fact that the baseline errors for User Type 4 were very low to begin with, leaving so little room for improvement that the resulting non-significant decrease in rank error was not surprising.

The experimental results generally support our hypothesis that learning will enable INCA to successfully adapt to different users, as shown by a decrease in predictive error of pairwise preferences over all users, and a decrease in the rank error on the user's chosen candidates. In deploying a system such as INCA, we would not want to overwhelm the user with all possible candidates at each interaction, as was done here to avoid confounding factors. Thus, predictive error—which measures the global goodness of a hypothesis—is particularly important, as lower errors along this dimension should translate to greater ability to choose the correct top candidates for presentation to the user. In addition, because schedules are complex entities, we might expect a scheduling assistant to be able to display only one schedule at a time. This makes low rank error particularly important, as it would mean displaying the preferred candidate sooner rather than later, thereby saving valuable time in urgent crisis situations.

[4]All differences presented are significant (paired t-test, $p < 0.05$) unless stated otherwise.

[5]Because different users and problem sets will lead to different numbers of examples, we ended the plot once there were less than 80% of the maximum number of data points available (i.e., we required at least twenty data points over which to average for User Types 1 and 4, and twelve for Types 2 and 3). Using the number of interactions instead of the number of examples leads to learning curves that exhibit similar patterns.

7 RELATED WORK

Much of the earlier work on personalization has been in the realm of computer-aided instruction (e.g., Self, 1974; Clancey, 1979; Sleeman & Smith, 1981). In these systems, detailed student models are built for the purpose of determining level of expertise and selecting lessons to address deficiencies in a student's knowledge while utilizing what he already knows. The system controls the interaction and the goal is to ensure that a student acquires particular skills. In contrast, adaptive computational assistants such as INCA are designed only to aid users during problem solving, the goal being to facilitate the development of a solution while letting users retain control of the process. INCA thus develops user models for the purpose of anticipating a user's choices or identifying a user's preferred solutions. In addition, while the unobtrusive acquisition of user models is highly desirable for computational assistants, tutoring systems are necessarily proactive and can probe specific areas of a student's knowledge to develop better models.

More recently, there has been work on adaptive user interfaces (Langley, 1999)—systems that, like INCA, learn user models for the purpose of modifying their behavior to better reflect user preferences. Most of these systems have focused on the task of recommending items such as news stories (Lang, 1995), music (Shardanand & Maes, 1995), web pages (Pazzani & Billsus, 1997), and movies (Basu et al., 1998) that are consistent with user preferences. Our system differs in that its suggestions are more complex structures (schedules) that entail the generation of candidate solutions aside from rating those solutions. In this sense, INCA is more similar to adaptive interfaces such as CLAVIER (Hinkle & Toomey, 1994), which suggests configurations for autoclave loading; Hermens & Schlimmer's (1994) form-filling assistant, which suggests default field values for standard forms; and CAP (Dent et al., 1992), a calendar assistant that suggests meeting times and rooms when scheduling appointments. While CLAVIER uses case-based reasoning techniques to retrieve and adapt a previous solution to solve a new problem, INCA learns an evaluation function over solutions to guide the search for and ranking of candidates for a new problem within a mixed-initiative framework. And while the form-filling assistant and CAP learn separate models for the individual components of a solution, INCA learns a single predictive model over schedules.

As stated earlier, INCA borrows the differential perceptron algorithm used by the Adaptive Route Advisor (Rogers et al., 1999). Aside from the difference in application domain, the two systems vary in their approach towards finding a solution. The Route Advisor always presents an optimal solution according to its current user model, with exploration of the solution space to generate training examples achieved by tweaking the weights (e.g., by placing all the weight on number of turns to generate a route with a minimal number of turns). In contrast, because of the highly underconstrained nature of its solution space, INCA always presents a set of sub-optimal candidates and relies on user advice to guide the search for better solutions, while also extracting training examples based on the candidate a user chooses at each interaction. INCA performs online learning, and there has been a significant body of work on this topic in the computational learning theory community. Much of that work has addressed simplified decision tasks and has focused on proving theoretical bounds on weighted majority algorithms and various extensions (e.g., Littlestone & Warmuth, 1984; Freund & Schapire, 1997), in contrast to our focus on practical performance in complex problem-solving domains. However, we may still be able to gain insight and direction from their results in our continued search for simple, efficient learning algorithms.

Most earlier work on learning for scheduling has focused on improving the performance of autonomous systems by applying learning techniques to generate higher quality solutions (e.g., Eskey & Zweben, 1990; Zhang & Dietterich, 1995; Schneider et al., 1998) or to generate them more efficiently (e.g., Gratch & Chien, 1993). An exception is CABINS (Miyashita & Sycara, 1995), an assistant for job-shop scheduling that acquires optimization preferences by learning the user's preferred repairs on schedules. CABINS is a case-based system that stores repair cases, which it uses to direct an iterative schedule repair procedure in future situations. The user model is thus embodied in these cases, which are gathered during a knowledge acquisition phase wherein the user directs CABINS to try particular repairs, rates the resulting schedule as acceptable or unacceptable, and assigns salience values (i.e., weights) to the case features. In contrast, INCA's user model takes the form of a linear evaluation function over schedules, which the system uses to order the candidate schedules it presents to the user. INCA also extracts its training examples unobtrusively from its interactions with the user during problem solving.

8 FUTURE WORK

The work described in this paper provides some validation of our work on adaptive, interactive systems, but there is much room for further investigation. INCA currently lets the user direct improvement only with respect to the outcome of the solution. We are currently extending INCA's advice-taking capability by incorporating parameters that measure schedule properties, such as the ones employed by User Type 2. This has, in turn, required the identification and inclusion of additional schedule modification methods to achieve improvement along the new dimensions. In providing the user with more options, however, we must be careful not to introduce too many—otherwise, we risk cognitive overload. In addition, increasing the number of parameters complicates INCA's learning task.

We chose to use a simple linear evaluation function and a perceptron-type algorithm because we wanted to achieve fast adaptation. However, as seen in the results with User Type 2, this simplicity may prevent INCA from adapting to user types that are not that unlikely. Using more sophisticated representations and learning methods may solve this problem, but probably at the cost of slower adaptation and infeasible online learning. A possible hybrid approach might use online learning to learn a good approximate user model quickly during problem-solving, and then to use more expressive representations and more powerful learning techniques offline to acquire more accurate models of user preferences.

In this paper, we demonstrated INCA's ability to adapt to a variety of synthetic users but, ultimately, we are interested in its ability to adapt to human users. Thus, we plan to run experiments with actual users to evaluate INCA's adaptation capabilities as well as to better understand the space of real user preferences. An interesting empirical issue is whether linear functions with a small number of features are in fact adequate for useful adaptation, which would obviate the need for more complex representations and learning algorithms. We expect that as we continue to investigate different ways in which computational assistants can adapt to individual users, we will be able to better identify the different kinds of adaptations possible and the approaches that make them feasible.

Another avenue for future work involves taking advantage of user advice to more directly manipulate the weights on the schedule evaluation function. Currently, INCA only trains on the preferences implied by the particular schedule a user chooses from a set of candidates. However, a user's advice to improve the schedule along a particular parameter may also be used to directly increment the weight associated with that feature. We might also let the user indicate a willingness to sacrifice some improvement along a particular parameter, which would lead to decrementing the weight associated with that feature.

INCA is part of an ongoing project to develop adaptive computational assistants for crisis response. We recently replaced the system's automated case retrieval and interactive planning with a new planning module that employs conversational case-based reasoning (Muñoz-Avila et al., in press). In the near future, we also plan to begin development of information-gathering assistants, which would actively seek out information that the user needs to make decisions, and also filter incoming information to present the user with relevant information in a timely fashion. Both revisions open up new opportunities for adaptation, such as tailoring the case retrieval's ranking mechanism to order cases by user preference and learning the types of information a user requests when making particular decisions. Also, although we have studied adaptation within the application domain of hazardous material incidents, we believe that our approach will also prove useful elsewhere. In particular, we expect similar benefits from advisability and adaptation in domains where optimization rather than satisfaction is the key issue, and we are exploring other domains to identify areas that may benefit from adaptation to user preferences.

9 SUMMARY

In this paper, we presented INCA's advisable interaction framework, in which users can give advice at variable levels of specificity to guide the search toward desirable solutions. This new framework provided the opportunity to apply a perceptron-type learning algorithm to adapt the schedule evaluation function to different users. We drew on synthetic users with distinct types of evaluation functions and advice strategies to experimentally investigate INCA's ability to adapt to different individuals. The results support our hypotheses that performance would improve with learning and with more specific advice, as measured by the error in predicting users' pairwise preferences and the rank error on users' chosen candidate solutions. The current interest in personalization, and the trend toward mixed-initiative systems that assist rather than replace human users, present exciting new opportunities for applying machine learning in real-world domains, making it increasingly important to develop and evaluate adaptive, interactive computational assistants such as INCA.

Acknowledgments

This work was supported by the Office of Naval Research under Grant N000014-96-1-1221.

References

Basu, C., Hirsh, H., & Cohen, W. (1998). Recommendation as classification: Using social and content-based information in recommendation. *Proceedings of the Fifteenth National Conference on Artificial Intelligence* (pp. 714–720).

Clancey, W. J. (1979). Dialogue management for rule-based tutorials. *Proceedings of the Sixth International Joint Conference on Artificial Intelligence.*

Dent, L., Boticario, J., McDermott, J, Mitchell, T., & Zaborowski, D. (1992). A personal learning apprentice. *Proceedings of the Tenth National Conference on Artificial Intelligence* (pp. 96–103).

Eskey, M. & Zweben, M. (1990). Learning search control for constraint-based scheduling. *Proceedings of the Eighth National Conference on Artificial Intelligence* (pp. 908–915).

Freund, Y. & Schapire, R. E. (1997). A decision-theoretic generalization of on-line learning and an application to boosting. *Journal of Computer and System Sciences*, 55(1):119–139.

Gervasio, M. T., Iba, W., & Langley, P. (1998) . Learning to predict user operations for adaptive scheduling. *Proceedings of the Fifteenth National Conference on Artificial Intelligence* (pp. 721–726).

Gratch, J. & Chien, S. (1993). Learning effective control strategies for deep-space network scheduling. *Proceedings of the Tenth International Conference on Machine Learning* (pp. 135–142).

Hermens, L. A. & Schlimmer, J. C. (1994). A machine-learning apprentice for the completion of repetitive forms. *IEEE Expert* 9:28–33.

Hill, W., Stead, L., Rosenstein, M., & Furnas, G. (1995). Recommending and evaluating choices in a virtual community of use. *Proceedings of CHI-95: The ACM SIGCHI Conference on Human Factors in Computing Systems*

Hinkle, D., & Toomey, C. (1994). CLAVIER: Applying case-based reasoning to composite part fabrication. *Proceedings of the Sixth Conference on Innovative Applications of Artificial Intelligence* (pp. 55–62).

Iba, W., Gervasio, M. T., Langley, P., & Sage, S. (1998). Evaluating computational assistance for crisis response. *Proceedings of the Twentieth Annual Meeting of the Cognitive Science Society.*

Jacobs, R. A. (1988). Increased rates of convergence through learning rate adaptation. *Neural Networks* 1(4):295–308.

Lang, K. (1995). NewsWeeder: Learning to filter netnews. *Proceedings of the Twelfth International Conference on Machine Learning* (pp. 331–330).

Langley, P. (1999). User modeling in adaptive interfaces. *Proceedings of the Seventh International Conference on User Modeling.*

Littlestone, N. & Warmuth, M. K. (1994) The weighted majority algorithm. *Information and Computation* 108:212–261.

Miyashita, K. & Sycara, K. (1995) CABINS: A framework of knowledge acquisition and iterative revision for schedule improvement and reactive repair. *Artificial Intelligence* 76:337–426.

Muñoz-Avila, H., Hendler, J. A., & Aha, D.W. (in press) Conversational case-based planning. *Review of Applied Expert Systems.*

Myers, K. L. (1996) Advisable planning systems. In Tate, A. (Ed.), *Advanced Planning Technology*, (pp. 206–209). Menlo Park: AAAI Press.

Pazzani, M. & Billsus, D. (1997). Learning and revising user profiles: The identification of interesting web sites. *Machine Learning* 27:313–331.

Rogers, S., Fiechter, C.-N., & Langley, P. (1999). An adaptive interactive agent for route advice. *Proceedings of the Third International Conference on Autonomous Agents.*

Schneider, J. G., Boyan, J. A., & Moore, A. W. (1998). Value function based production scheduling. *Proceedings of the Fifteenth International Conference for Machine Learning* (pp. 522–530).

Self, J. A. (1974). Student models in CAI. *International Journal of Man-Machine Studies* 6:261–276.

Shardanand, U. & Maes, P. (1995). Social information filtering: Algorithms for automating "word of mouth". *Proceedings of the CHI-95 Conference.*

Sleeman, D. H. & Smith, M. J. (1981). Modelling student's problem solving. *Artificial Intelligence* 16:171–187.

Transport Canada, the U.S. Department of Transportation, and the Secretariat of Communications and Transportation of Mexico. *1996 North American Emergency Response Guidebook.*

Zhang, W. & Dietterich, T. (1995). A reinforcement learning approach to job-shop scheduling. *Proceedings of the Fourteenth International Conference on Artificial Intelligence.*

On some misbehaviour of back-propagation with non-normalized RBFNs and a solution

Attilio Giordana
Dipartimento di Scienze e Tecnologie Avanzate
Universià di Torino
c.so Svizzera 185, 10149 Torino (ITALY)
attilio@al.unipmn.it

Roberto Piola
Gruppo IH Srl
via Bonsignore 4, 10131 Torino (ITALY)
piola@di.unito.it

Abstract

The quadratic error gradient descent is widely used for learning weights in neural networks. The method is simple to apply, but in some cases it hides pitfalls which must be carefully considered. In this article we will prove for the Radial Basis Function Networks the existence of attractors in the quadratic error space which can entrap the gradient descent with dramatic consequences. More specifically, we show that, depending on the initial values of the weights and on the distribution of the learning instances, it is possible that the radial functions shrink under the action of the Δ-rule reaching a degenerated state, in which the width is null, so that convergency is prevented. Sufficient conditions for the manifestation of this anomalous behavior are formally stated. Moreover, an experimental analysis on two case studies is reported. We show that reducing the learning rates (the usual trick when the network degenerates) does not help. The obtained results apply also to back-propagation variants. At last, we present a modification of the basic algorithm that can help in obtaining a convergent behavior.

Keywords: *RBFN degeneration, back-propagation.*

1 INTRODUCTION

Radial Basis Function Networks (RBFNs) (Poggio and Girosi, 1990; Moody and Darken, 1989), are gaining popularity both as classifiers and as general approximators for continuous functions. The reasons for their success are several. First of all they are universal function approximators (Park and Sandberg, 1993), which benefit by learning algorithms based on pseudo-inverse matrix calculus (Poggio and Girosi, 1990) and clustering algorithms (Wilpon and Rabiner, 1985), faster than the back-propagation commonly used for training other feed forward networks inspired to the multilayer perceptron (Rumelhart and McClelland, 1986). Second, they exhibit interesting properties with respect to incremental learning: in a RBFN it is possible to locally modify the network without unlearning the knowledge encoded in other regions (Blanzieri and Katenkamp, 1996). Third, they exhibit symbolic properties (Trespet al., 1993; Baroglio et al., 1996; Giordana et al., 1993), which can be exploited in many ways. For instance, they can be constructed using a symbolic learning algorithm such as a decision or a regression tree (Baroglio et al., 1996), or can easely encode a propositional knowledge base supplied by an expert.

For these last two reasons, RBFNs have been frequently used for applications where the classical learning method based on the pseudo inverse matrix can not be applied immediately, and the simpler approach of using the Δ-rule in order to perform the quadratic error gradient descent has been preferred. Moreover, it also happens that performing the quadratic error gradient descent leads to more accurate final results than the pseudo-inverse matrix method. In our experience, when the Δ-rule is applied on a network synthesized using the k-means clustering algorithm and the pseudo-inverse matrix algorithm, the network error can still be reduced. The reason is that the RBF centers and widths computed by the k-means are not optimal for the classification or regression task the network is used for, so that the Δ-rule can find better values for them.

However, the gradient descent hides some pitfalls that we intend to discuss here. Recently, Gori and Bianchini (Bianchini et al., 1995; Bianchini and Gori, 1996) proved that when the weights of a RBFN range between 0 and 1, the quadratic error surface has a unique minimum, so that the gradient descent will lead to an optimal approximation; this is the case found in classification problems.

Here, we will show that in the case of weights in an unrestricted range, as it necessarily happens approximating a generic continuous function, there exist conditions in which radial functions continue to shrink, under the action of the Δ-rule, until their amplitude reduces to zero, with dramatic consequences. These conditions are easy to meet when on-line learning is applied, as frequently done in robotic applications. Nevertheless, they can be also verified applying off-line learning, when a weight must change sign. This anomalous behavior of error gradient descent will be referred to as *degenerative behavior.*

The paper is organized as follows: Section 2 briefly introduces RBFNs and describes how the gradient descent method can be applied. Section 3 formally characterizes the conditions entailing a degenerative behavior for the Δ-rule. The result is extended to some variants of back-propagation in Section 4 and some heuristic solutions are suggested in Section 5. Two case studies are described in Section 6, whereas Section 7 derives the conclusions.

2 GRADIENT DESCENT IN RBFNs

In this section we will briefly introduce the Radial Basis Function Networks and we will overview their properties. The general form for RBFNs, introduced in (Moody and Darken, 1989), corresponds to a weighted sum of radial functions:

$$\hat{f}(\vec{x}) = \sum_j w_j R_j(\vec{x}) \tag{1}$$

where $\hat{f}(\vec{x})$ is the approximation of a scalar function $f(\vec{x})$ defined in a vectorial space $\mathcal{X}$ and $\vec{x}$ denotes a point in $\mathcal{X}$. Expression (1) describes a two layer neural network where the hidden layer corresponds to the set of radial functions $R_j(\vec{x})$ and the output layer corresponds to a single neuron performing the weighted sum of the hidden layer outputs.

The formal mathematical framework has been set up by Poggio and Girosi (Poggio and Girosi, 1990) which showed that (1) corresponds to a development in term of Green's functions provided that the basis function $R(\vec{x})$ is properly chosen.

Networks of this kind are known to be universal function approximators (Moody and Darken, 1989; Park and Sandberg, 1993) and can be trained using the well known Δ-rule performing the quadratic error gradient descent (Moody and Darken, 1989; Weymaere and Martens, 1991; Bianchini et al., 1995; Blanzieri and Katenkap, 1996). Given a training set L, where each element $p \in L$ is a pair $\langle \vec{x}_p, f(\vec{x}_p)\rangle$ linking a point $\vec{x}_p$ in the domain $\mathcal{X}$ to the corresponding value $f(\vec{x}_p)$ in the co-domain, the quadratic error of a function approximator is defined as:

$$\mathcal{E} = \sum_p \mathcal{E}_p = \frac{1}{2}\sum_p \left(f(\vec{x}_p) - \hat{f}(\vec{x}_p)\right)^2 \tag{2}$$

Any parameter λ in a RBFN can be trained by iterating the Δ-rule:

$$\lambda(T+1) = \lambda(T) + \Delta_T\lambda\ ; \quad \Delta\lambda = -\eta \sum_p \frac{\partial \mathcal{E}_p(T)}{\partial \lambda} \tag{3}$$

In equation (3), $\mathcal{E}_p(T)$ is the error on pattern p made by the network after training for T epochs, and $0 < \eta < 1$ the *learning rate.* Rule (3) is said an *off-line* learning rule because it updates the network parameters after accumulating the error on whole all set L. Nevertheless, in many practical applications, such as robotics, the *on-line* version of the Δ-rule is frequently used where L consists of a possibly infinite sequence of examples, each one used only once, and the network parameters are updated of an amount

$$\Delta_p\lambda = -\eta \frac{\partial \mathcal{E}_p}{\partial \lambda} \tag{4}$$

every time a new example p is available. By doing so, the learned knowledge is exploited immediately. However, this process does not follow exactly the error gradient descent so that convergency is no longer guaranteed, in general (Rumelhart and McClelland, 1986).

Assuming that the $R_j(\vec{x})$ in (1) are Gaussian functions of the form $R_j(\vec{x}) = e^{-((\vec{x}-\vec{c}_j)/\sigma_j)^2}$, computing the derivative in (3) with respect to σ_j and w_j, yelds the values for $\Delta_T w_j$ and $\Delta_T \sigma_j$ at each epoch T:

$$\Delta_T w_j = \eta_w \sum_p \delta(\vec{x}_p) e^{-\left(\frac{r_j(\vec{x}_p)}{\sigma_j}\right)^2}; \tag{5}$$

$$\Delta_T \sigma_j = \eta_\sigma \sum_p \delta(\vec{x}_p) e^{-\left(\frac{r_j(\vec{x}_p)}{\sigma_j}\right)^2} \frac{w_j}{\sigma_j}\left(\frac{r_j(\vec{x}_p)}{\sigma_j}\right)^2 \tag{6}$$

being $\delta(\vec{x}_p) = f(\vec{x}_p) - \hat{f}(\vec{x}_p)$ the error on the example $\vec{x}_p$ at the epoch T, and $r_j(\vec{x}_p)$ the distance $|\vec{x}_p - \vec{c}_j|$ of $\vec{x}_p$ from the center $\vec{c}_j$ of R_j. The rule for training the centers $\vec{c}_j$ can be obtained in a similar way.

For on-line learning, expression (4) takes the simpler form:

$$\Delta_p w_j = \eta_w \delta(\vec{x}_p) e^{-\left(\frac{r_j(\vec{x}_p)}{\sigma_j}\right)^2}; \tag{7}$$

$$\Delta_p \sigma_j = \eta_\sigma \delta(\vec{x}_p) e^{-\left(\frac{r_j(\vec{x}_p)}{\sigma_j}\right)^2} \frac{w_j}{\sigma_j} \left(\frac{r_j(\vec{x}_p)}{\sigma_j}\right)^2 \tag{8}$$

3 GRADIENT DESCENT DEGENERATIVE BEHAVIOR

As it has been shown by Bianchini et al. (1995), when a RBFN encodes a boolean function the quadratic error function does not have local minima so that performing the error gradient descent a global minimum is always reached. Here we will show that in the general case of a RBFN encoding a scalar function, there exist attractors capable of entrapping the gradient descent. In this case, the involved radial functions continue to shrink tending to a width $\sigma = 0$. This problem holds both in the cases of on-line and off-line learning.

3.1 LEARNING ON-LINE

Let us analyze the evolution of a RBFN (1) where the radial functions are Gaussian and on-line learning (7) is applied.

We will first obtain an analytical expression describing the trajectory followed by the gradient descent in the plane $\langle \sigma, w \rangle$, when trained on-line with a sequence of examples all falling at the same distance r from the center $\vec{c}$ of a given Gaussian R. Afterwards we will state the conditions sufficient for R evolving into a degenerated function with $\sigma = 0$.

Theorem 1 *Let R be a Gaussian function belonging to a RBFN, and let, moreover, σ_0 be the width of R and w the corresponding weight. Given an infinite training sequence L, such that each element $\langle \vec{x}_p, f(\vec{x}_p) \rangle \in L$ falls at the same distance r from the center $\vec{c}$ of R, the trajectory followed by the gradient descent is a line described by the equation:*

$$w(\sigma, r) = \pm\sqrt{\frac{\alpha}{2r(\vec{x})^2}(\sigma^4 - {\sigma_0}^4) + {w_0}^2}\ , \quad \alpha = \eta_w/\eta_\sigma. \tag{9}$$

Proof 1 *Consider the ratio $\frac{\Delta_p w}{\Delta_p \sigma}$. According to (7), we will have:*

$$\frac{\Delta_p w}{\Delta_p \sigma} = \alpha \frac{\sigma}{w} \left(\frac{\sigma}{r(\vec{x}_p)}\right)^2 \tag{10}$$

When η_w and η_σ become infinitesimal, the equation (9) tends to the differential equation $\frac{dw}{d\sigma} = \alpha \frac{\sigma}{w} \left(\frac{\sigma}{r(\vec{x}_p)}\right)^2$ that has the general solution:

$$w^2 = \frac{\alpha\sigma^4}{2r(\vec{x})^2} + C\ ; \quad w = \pm\sqrt{\frac{\alpha\sigma^4}{2r(\vec{x})^2} + C} \tag{11}$$

being C a constant to be determined.
Equation (10) describes the generic evolution of w in dependency of σ for a generic Gaussian function when trained with a sequence of learning events all of them falling at the same distance r from the center of R.

By requiring that a trajectory $w(\sigma)$ goes through the point $\langle w_0, \sigma_0 \rangle$, corresponding to the initial status of R, the constant C can be determined as a function of $r(\vec{x})$. Then, posing $w = w_0$ and $\sigma = \sigma_0$ in equation (10) and solving with respect to C, the following relation is obtained:

$$C = {w_0}^2 - \frac{\alpha}{2}\frac{{\sigma_0}^4}{r^2} \tag{12}$$

Substituting this expression for C into (10), the thesis follows.

The family of trajectories obtained for different values of r in equation (8) are described in Figure 1. We observe that there exists a critical distance r_c such that the corresponding trajectory goes through the Origin $\langle \sigma = 0, w = 0 \rangle$. Every trajectory corresponding to $r < r_c$ crosses the σ axis ($w = 0$). On the contrary, for each $r > r_c$ there exist two symmetric trajectories, corresponding to the positive and negative sign in equation (8), respectively, each one meeting horizontally the w axis ($\sigma = 0$) without ever trespassing the σ axis. This means that, if the minimum error corresponds to a value for w laying in the opposite side of the σ axis, with respect to w_0, $\delta(\vec{x})$ remains always negative (when $w_0 > 0$) or positive (when $w_0 < 0$) until the w axis is met. Then, the radial function R will degenerate into a function of width $\sigma = 0$.

More formally, the relation between the initial status $\langle w_0, \sigma_0 \rangle$ of R and the value of r_c is obtained by requiring that the trajectory (8) goes through the Origin $\langle w = 0, \sigma = 0 \rangle$:

$$r_c = \pm\sqrt{\frac{\alpha}{2}\frac{{\sigma_0}^2}{w_0}} \tag{13}$$

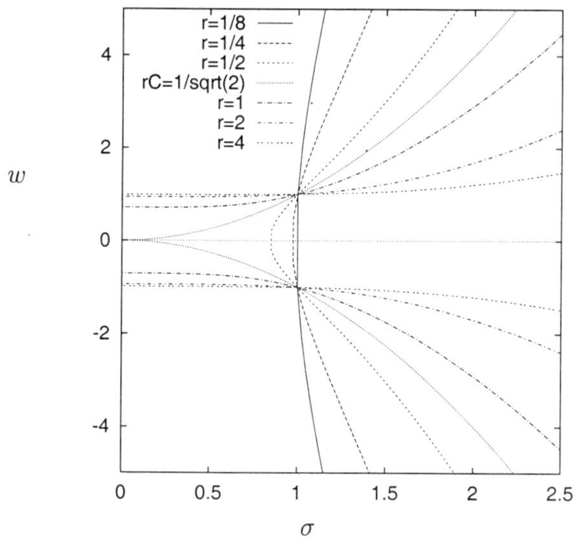

Figure 1: Family of trajectories for different values of r. The initial values for σ and w are $\sigma_0 = 1$ and $w_0 = -1$, whereas the error $\delta(\vec{x})$ is supposed to be always positive.

Afterwards the conditions for a degenerative behavior are stated by the following theorem:

Theorem 2 *Given a Gaussian radial function R of initial width σ_0 and weight w_0, and an infinite learning sequence L, if every example $\langle \vec{x}, f(\vec{x}) \rangle \in L$ falls at a distance $r(\vec{x}) > r_c$ from the center c of R and the sign of the error $\delta(\vec{x})$ is always opposite to the one of w_0, then the width of R will definitively tend to 0.*

Proof 2 *Let us consider a sequence of examples all at the same distance $r_1 > r_c$. Posing $\sigma = 0$ in (8) and solving with respect to w, we find the solution:*

$$w = \pm\sqrt{{w_0}^2 - \frac{\alpha}{2r^2}{\sigma_0}^2} \tag{14}$$

where the positive solution corresponds to a positive value of w_0, and the negative one to a negative w_0. Moreover, according to (9), $(dw/d\sigma)_{\sigma=0} = 0$.

Afterwards, we observe that starting with a $w_0 < 0$, if the error $\delta(\vec{x})$ is positive, it will be $\Delta w > 0$ and $\Delta\sigma < 0$, so that the gradient descent will follow upward the trajectory laying in the region of the plane $\langle \sigma, w \rangle$ where $w < 0$. In a symmetric way, it will follow the trajectory downward in the region where w is positive when $w_0 > 0$ and $\delta(\vec{x}) < 0$.

Consider now an infinite sequence of examples each falling at a different distance $r(\vec{x}) > r_c$. According to the hypothesis made, every learning step will move the value of σ and w along a trajectory which will end in $\sigma = 0$, so that, the resultant trajectory will necessarily end in $\sigma = 0$, with a value of $w \neq 0$, concordant with the sign of w_0, and with $(dw/d\sigma)_{\sigma=0} = 0$.

Theorem 2 states only sufficient conditions for degenerative behavior. In fact also learning sequences containing examples falling at distance $r < r_c$ and/or exhibiting error $\delta(\vec{x})$ of sign concordant with w_0 can still produce a degenerative behavior. Anyhow, without precisely characterizing the learning sequence is not possible to predict the kind of behavior it will produce.

3.2 LEARNING OFF-LINE

Consider now the case of off-line learning: the value of $\Delta\sigma$ and Δw at each epoch is obtained as a sum of the elementary contributions $\Delta_p\sigma$, $\Delta_p w$ according to (6). In other words, the corresponding step in the plane $\langle \sigma, w \rangle$ is obtained as vectorial composition of the elementary steps corresponding to the single learning examples.

From this observation it is immediate to conclude that, if every example $\langle \vec{x}_p, f(\vec{x}_p) \rangle$ falls at a distance $r(\vec{x}_p) > r_c$ from the center of the radial function R, then the gradient descent will follow a trajectory which will end up in a degenerative status, provided that learning is not stopped earlier.

Weaker conditions can still produce a degenerative behavior, but little is possible to say without entering into the details of the specific learning set.

As a representative case, we will consider the learning problem, as simple as possible, of approximating a function $y = f(x)$ with a RBFN, where $f(x)$ is an horizontal straight line $y = k$ and the RBFN kernel set consists of a single unidimensional RBF with fixed center[1]. Using a Gaussian RBF $r(x) = e^{-(x/\sigma)^2}$, the considered network is fully described by:

$$\hat{f}(x) = we^{-(x/\sigma)^2} \tag{15}$$

Suppose $k < 0$ (say $k = -1$) and initially $w_0 > 0$. We observe that perfect approximation is obtained when $w = k$ and $\sigma = \infty$. In practice, the approximation is satifying with w slightly greater than k and σ very large.

[1]the condition on the center is not limiting: since the center does not change anyway during the learning because of the symmetries in the learning set

Figure 2(a, b, c), describes in the plane $\langle w, \sigma \rangle$ the evolution of the gradient descent for different values of the learning rate for w and σ. The network parameter changes at each iteration of the Δ-rule are represented as vectors $\langle \Delta w(t), \Delta\sigma(t) \rangle$ originating in the point $w(t), \sigma(t)$.

In this way, the evolution of a network starting with an initial assignment $\langle w_0, \sigma_0 \rangle$ is described by the flow line originating in $\langle w_0, \sigma_0 \rangle$. We can see that, for $w_0 \gg 0$ and $w_0 > \sigma_0$ the flow lines tend to cross the w axis vertically, i.e. exhibit the degenerative behavior theoretically foreseen. The phenomenon depends upon the ratio $\alpha = \eta_w/\eta_\sigma$: increasing α, it mitigates.

On the contrary, we observe that increasing the dimensionality of the problem, the phenomenon get worse, as it can be predicted from the theoretical analysis. As an example figure 2 (d) reports the case for a two-dimensional case in which the target function is a plane $z = k$.

As an alternative view of the phenomenon, Figure 3 shows the trajectories followed by the gradient descent on the error surface drawn in dependency of w and σ. The degenerative behavior occurs only when the setting of the learning rate and the start point are such that the descent path falls in the attractor basin. We can see clearly that the simple reduction of both learning rates by the same factor produces the same trajectory.

4 GRADIENT DESCENT VARIANTS

The results obtained in the previous section also hold for some popular variants of the gradient descent algorithm. More specifically, the momentum method (Sarkar, 1995), the resilent back-propagation RPROP (Riedmiller and Braun, 1993) and the conjugate gradient method (Sarkar, 1995), incur in the degenerative behavior as well.

Conjugate gradient

The conjugate gradient method (Sarkar, 1995) tries to speed up the learning process avoiding to recompute too frequently the derivatives defining the error gradient. This is done according to the following strategy: after the gradient direction has been computed, the learning algorithm follows it until a local minimum is reached. Then the gradient is computed again and another sequence of learning steps follows.

On the field view of Figure 2, this means that, starting from a point in the weight space, the direction of the arrow in that point will be followed until a minimum of the error is reached. Many gradient vectors point in the direction of the degeneration line $\sigma = 0$.

Resilient back-propagation (RPROP)

The essence of this method (Riedmiller and Braun, 1993) consists in maintaining an individual learning step size for each parameter, increasing it when the direction of the gradient does not change dramatically from epoch to epoch and reducing it when the sign of the derivatives changes. From Figure 2, we can see that there are regions in which the sign of the derivatives (the direction of the gradient along the axis) does not change, and RPROP is driven to the border $\sigma = 0$ with increasing speed.

Momentum

In the momentum method, the changes at every learning step are increased by an inertial term that is proportional to the previous update. Like the case for RPROP, since the direction of the gradient is not inverted in the basin of attraction of $\sigma = 0$, the learning process is driven to the degenerative behavior even faster than regular back-propagation.

5 AN AD HOC Δ-RULE VARIANT: ALGORITHMIC Δ^*

A simple method for avoiding the degenerative behavior is to modify the Δ-rule in such a way that the parameters σ_j cannot tend to 0 in a finite time. This can be achieved by modifying the the gradient descent algorithm as in the following Algorithm Δ^*:

At each learning step:

1. For each radial function R_j, compute $\Delta\sigma_j$ and Δw_j according to (3).

2. if $|\Delta\sigma_j| < \vartheta \cdot \sigma_j$, i.e., if its absolute value does not exceed the current value of σ multiplied by a parameter, $0 < \vartheta < 1$, then set $\sigma_j = \sigma_j + \Delta\sigma_j$ (regular gradient descent); otherwise, set $\sigma_j = \sigma_j + Sign(\Delta\sigma_j)\vartheta \cdot \sigma_j$.

As algorithm Δ^* slows down the radial function narrowing as long as their width approach to zero, the degenerative condition cannot be reached in a finite time. However, even this strategy avoids the degeneration, it will not always converge to a satisfactory approximation of the target function.

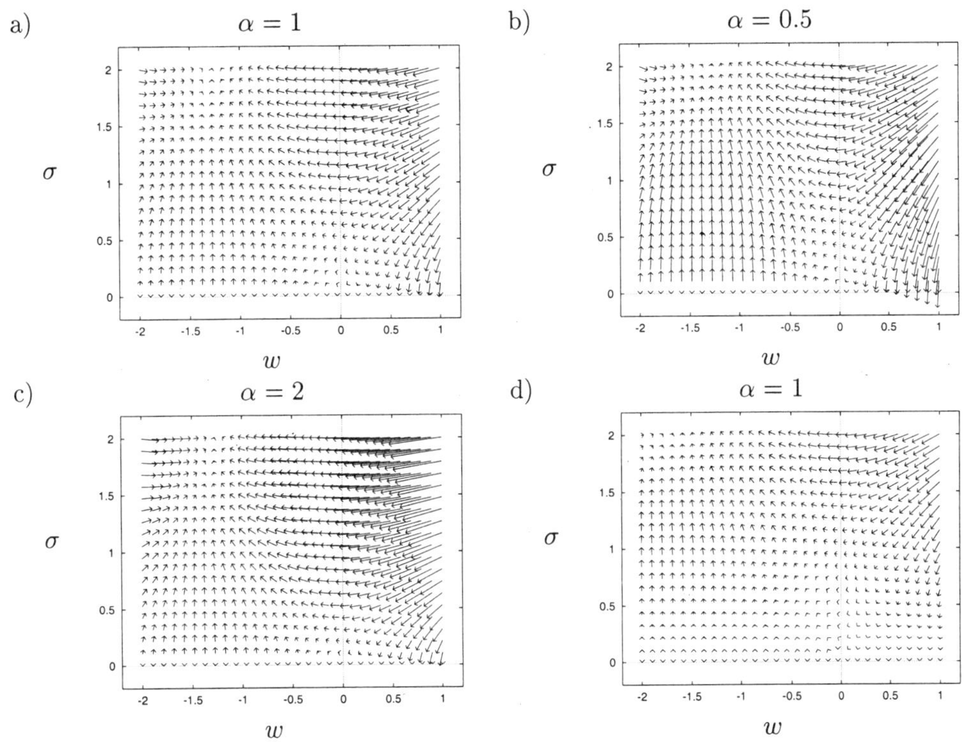

Figure 2: The field of the gradient of the error with different ratios between the learning rates; the task at hand was the toy problem of learning an horizontal line (a,b,c) and a plane (d) with a single gaussian kernel.

6 EVALUATION ON TWO CASE STUDIES

In this section, the degenerative behavior we formally predicted will be demonstrated on two case studies. In the first case, a RBFN based on Gaussian units has been used for approximating a target function starting with initial conditions which were predicted to fall in degenerative behavior by the theoretical analysis. The network has been synthesized using the k-means clustering algorithm in order to determine the centers and the width for the radial functions, and the initial weight values have been set to a value laying on the opposite side of the plane $z = 0$ with respect to the corresponding value of the target function. Afterwards the quadratic error gradient descent was performed, training weights and widths until the network reached a stable configuration.

On the contrary, the second case study is a classical benchmark for neural networks (the Mackey-Glass time series) and the degenerative behavior has not explicitly sought, but naturally occurred with many values for η.

6.1 EXPERIMENT ONE: TARGETING A FUZZY CONTRoLLER

The first case study was to learn the target function described in Figure 4a, with a RBFN consisting of 5 Gaussian Radial Functions initialized in order to generate the output described in Figure 4b.

The target function in Figure 4a was encoded in a fuzzy controller, which was used for generating a learning set of 1600 uniformly distributed examples.

Even if, considering the strong similarity between the generator of the function and the learner, the task was considered extremely easy, the basic gradient descent always ended up in a configuration generating an output like the one described in Figure 4c.

On the contrary, the modified algorithm Δ^* was able to learn a reasonable approximation using the *off-line* learning strategy, but provided worse results using the *on-line* one, as it is emerges from the RMS-error time evolution reported in Figure 5. The explanation for this behavior is that, using a learning set randomly sampled, after some learning steps, the radial functions become so narrow that they are no more activated by any example, so that the learning process stops.

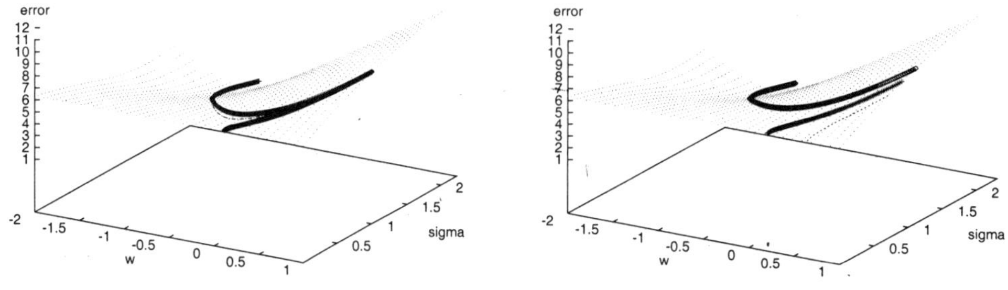

a) b)

Figure 3: Paths of the gradient descent on the error surface (off-line case): (a) Starting from the same initial condition with different learning rates; the two trajectories converging to $w = -1, \sigma \leq 2$ were generated with $\eta_w = \eta_\sigma = 0.01$ (thick line) and with $\eta_w = 0.01, \eta_\sigma = 0.011$ (thin one); the diverging line was produced with $\eta_w = 0.01, \eta_\sigma = 0.012$ and $\eta_w = 0.001, \eta_\sigma = 0.0012$. (b) Starting from different initial settings, the thin line diverges as well.

As a comparison of the two algorithms with respect to the degenerative behavior, Table 1 reports the minimum, average and maximum width detected for the gaussian functions after training in different conditions. From the reported data, it appears that, even if the approximation is not always good, the Δ^* algorithm doesn't produce degenerated units.

Table 1: Results with the artificial domain of five gaussian units: the minimal, average and maximal width of the units are reported against the learning method used. All results except the one marked with an asterisk come after 1000 epochs of back-propagation with $\eta_\sigma = \eta_w = 0.1$; the marked result come with $\eta_\sigma = 0.1, \eta_w = 0.3$. Symbol D represents the number of degenerated units.

Alg.	ϑ	σ_{min}	σ_{avg}	σ_{max}	D	RMS
Initial		0.780	0.780	0.780		1.106
	—	0.033	0.047	0.064		0.935
off-line	0.1	0.042	0.047	0.065		0.935
	0.01	1.674	2.469	2.709		0.222
(*)	0.01	1.647	2.243	2.428		0.171
	—	**0.0**	0.381	1.164	**3**	
on-line	0.1	0.245	5.231	13.173		0.257
	0.01	1.6744	2.469	2.709		0.312

6.2 EXPERIMENT TWO: PREDICT THE MACKEY-GLASS SERIES

The Mackey-Glass chaotic series is generated by the differential equation:

$$\dot{x} = \frac{0.2x(t-\tau)}{1 + x^{10}(t-\tau)} - 0.1x(t) \tag{16}$$

with $x(t < 0) = 0$, $x(0) = 1.2$ and $\tau = 17$. The classical learning problem is to forecast $x(t+84)$ when given $x(t)$, $x(t-6)$, $x(t-12)$, $x(t-18)$.

Table 2: Results with the Mackey-Glass time-series: the minimal, average and maximal width of the units are reported against the learning method used. All results come after 1000 epochs of back-propagation with $\eta_\sigma = \eta_w = 0.1$.. The network contained 384 hidden units.

Alg.	ϑ	σ_{min}	σ_{avg}	σ_{max}	D	RMS
Initial		0.075	0.168	0.300		0.829
	—	**0.0**		4.498	**127**	
on-line	0.1	0.046	0.760	6.301		0.068
	0.01	0.065	1.605	5.753		0.040
	—	**0.0**		0.513	**21**	
off-line	0.1	0.006	0.178	0.482		0.040
	0.01	0.027	0.178	0.395		0.039

In the experiment we used a RBFN initialized with a symbolic learner (Baroglio et al., 1996) and we trained the network with a sequence of 1000 examples.

The results obtained learning both *off-line* and *on-line* with the basic gradient descent and with the Δ^* al-

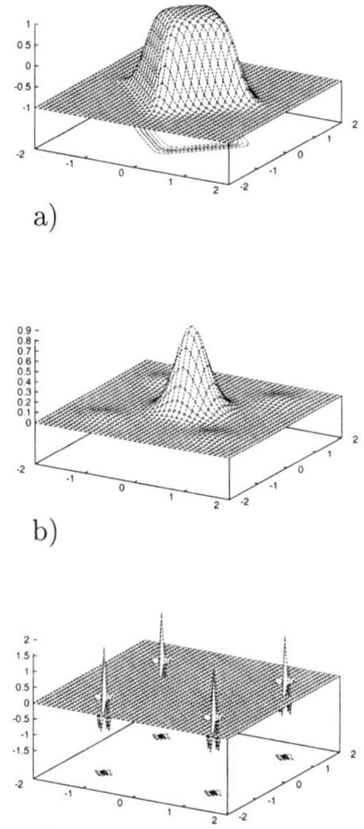

Figure 4: The target function (a) used in the first case study, (b) the output initially generated by the RBFN used as approximator, (c) the output function produced by the degenerated RBFN after performing the quadratic error gradient descent.

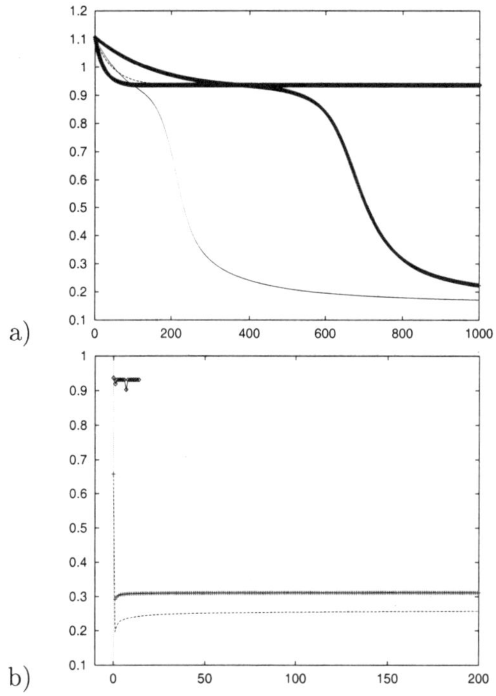

Figure 5: Results for the Fuzzy controller targeting problem; (a)off-line learning: all lines except the last one have learning rates $\eta_w = \eta_\sigma = 0.1$ The bold line ending above 0.9 is without using algorithm Δ^*; the dashed line (ending above 0.9 and mostly superimposed with the previous one) is with $\vartheta = 0.1$; the bold line converging at 0.2 is with $\vartheta = 0.01$; the dotted line with $\vartheta = 0.01$, $\eta_w = 0.3, \eta_\sigma = 0.1$; (b) on-line learning: the truncated line is without the Δ^* algorithm; the thick one with $\vartheta = 0.01$ and the thin one with $\vartheta = 0.1$

gorithms are shown in Table 2 and confirm the ones obtained for the first case study. The network converges to a very good approximation using algorithm Δ^* and an off-line learning strategy. The behavior of the on-line learning strategy is unsatisfactory also in this case. The Δ^* algorithm did not produce degenerated units under any learning condition, whereas basic gradient descent did.

7 CONCLUSIONS

In this paper, we presented a formal analysis of the error gradient descent evolution in Radial basis function Networks, and we proved the existence of some anomalies we must be aware of when we apply this appealing learning method. Even if the theoretical results have been obtained for Gaussian radial functions, the same results can be easely obtained also for other kinds of bell-shaped radial functions. The conjecture is that the same problem holds for every kind of admissible radial function (Poggio and Girosi, 1990).

Our results do not contradict those of (Bianchini et al., 1995) because their results apply to classification tasks with some assumptions about the separability of the target classes, while we addressed a regression task with no restrictions on the target function.

The conclusion is that the error gradient descent cannot be applied without care, even if, under specific conditions, can be useful and produces excellent results.

References

C. Baroglio, A. Giordana, M. Kaiser, M. Nuttin, and R. Piola. Learning controllers for industrial robots.

Machine Learning, 23:221–249, 1996.

M. Bianchini, P. Frasconi, and M. Gori. Learning without local minima in radial basis function networks. *IEEE Trans. on Neural Networks*, 6(3):749–756, 1995.

M. Bianchini and M. Gori. Optimal learning in artificial neural networks: a review of theoretical methods. *Neurocomputing*, 13(5):191–211, 1996.

E. Blanzieri and P. Katenkamp. Learning radial basis function networks on-line. In L. Saitta, editor, *13th International Conference on Machine Learning*, pages 37–45, Bari, Italy, July 1996. Morgan Kaufmann.

A. Giordana, M. Kaiser, and M. Nuttin. Robot controller synthesis: How to reduce costs. In *Proceedings of the Workshop on Learning Robots*, Torino, October 1993.

J. Moody and C. Darken. Fast learning in networks of locally tuned units. *Neural Computations*, 1(2):281–294, 1989.

J. Park and I.W. Sandberg. Approximation and radial-basis-function networks. *Neural Computation*, 5(3):305–316, 1993.

T. Poggio and F. Girosi. Networks for approximation and learning. *Proceedings of the IEEE*, 78(9):1481–1497, September 1990.

M. Riedmiller and H. Braun. A direct adaptive method for faster backpropagation learning: The RPROP algorithm. In *IEEE International Conference on Neural Networks*, volume 1, pages 588–593, San Francisco, CA, 1993. The IEEE press.

D. E. Rumelhart and J. L. McClelland. *Parallel Distributed Processing : Explorations in the Microstructure of Cognition, Parts I & II.* MIT Press, Cambridge, Massachusetts, 1986.

D. Sarkar. Methods to speed up error backpropagation learning algorithm. *ACM Computing Surveys*, 27(4):519–542, December 1995.

V. Tresp, J. Hollatz, and S. Ahmad. Network structuring and training using rule-based knowledge. n S. J. Hanson, J.D. Cowan, and C.L. Giles, editors, *Advances in Neural Information Processing Systems 5 (NIPS-5)*, pages 871–878. Morgan Kaufmann, 1993.

N. Weymaere and J.P. Martens. A fast and robust learning algorithm for feedforward neural networks. *Neural Networks*, 4, 1991.

J.G. Wilpon and L.R. Rabiner. A modified k-means clustering algorithm for use in isolated work recognition. *IEEE transactions on acoustics, speech and signal processing*, ASSP-33:587–594, Jun 1985.

Boosting a Strong Learner: Evidence Against the Minimum Margin

Michael Harries
School of Computer Science and Engineering,
University of New South Wales,
Sydney 2052, Australia
mbh@cse.unsw.edu.au

Abstract

Boosting is a method by which an ensemble of classifiers can be assembled with, generally speaking, much improved results over individual classifiers and other ensemble methods. It works by re-weighting the training set after each classifier is induced, so that misclassified training instances are given increased weight in the subsequently induced classifier. The focus on misclassified instances has meant that boosting cannot continue if the learning system creates a classifier that fits the data. This article presents a simple boosting-like method for fitted decision trees with empirical results very similar to boosting. This provides an alternative view of the reasons for performance improvements due to boosting, and provides a further counter example for minimum margin as an explanation for boosting performance.

1 INTRODUCTION

Ensemble methods for improving classification accuracy have recently become a focus for the machine learning community. These methods combine learned classifiers to form a meta-classifier with improved classification accuracy. The best known approaches are *Bagging* (Breiman, 1986) and, more recently *Boosting* (Freund and Schapire, 1997; Schapire and Singer, 1998). In bagging, classifiers are induced from random samples drawn, with replacement, from the original training data. In boosting, classifiers are induced from a series of training set distributions. The distribution is changed after each classifier is induced such that misclassified instances carry more weight.

Boosting is designed for use with *weak* learners, those that achieve more than 50% and less than 100% accuracy on the training set, and has proven very successful, particularly in combination with decision trees (Freund and Schapire, 1996; Quinlan, 1996a; Quinlan, 1996b; Breiman, 1999; Bauer and Kohavi, 1999; Dietterich, 1998). The accuracy of boosting is particularly surprising as with decision trees it frequently fully fits the training data, and creates a very complex combined classifier, yet appears not to over-fit. Attempts to understand the success of boosting include margin analysis (Schapire, Freund, Bartlett, and Lee, 1997; Brieman, 1997) , and casting it as a form of additive logistic regression (Friedman, Hastie, and Tibshirani, 1998).

This paper presents an alternative boosting-like method that does not use misclassification yet achieves similar accuracy to AdaBoost on C4.5. It shows, empirically, that re-weighting in boosting need not rely upon misclassified instances. It confirms that fitting the training data does not necessarily imply over-fitting. It also provides another (Quinlan, 1999; Grove and Schuurmans, 1998) counter example to the use of minimum margin as an explanation for ensemble generalization performance, and in particular, AdaBoost performance.

We proceed with a brief review of AdaBoost, then present an alternative *fitted* boosting algorithm, fBoost, and implementation. The new method is evaluated empirically, and we conclude by discussing implications for Boosting overall.

2 ADABOOST

AdaBoost (here we refer to AdaBoost.M1 (Freund and Schapire, 1997)) applies a classifier learning system to a succession of adaptively altered distributions of the

Table 1: AdaBoost:M1

AdaBoost

Input: n training instances x_i with labels y_i. Maximum trials, T. Base learner, H.

Initialization: All training instances begin with weight $w_i = 1/\mathrm{n}$.

Repeat for T trials:

- Induce classifier, h_j, using weighted training data and H.
- ϵ_j = weighted error for h_j on the training data. If $\epsilon_j > 1/2$, discard h_j and stop boosting. (If $\epsilon_j = 0$, then h_j gets infinite weight.)
- Classifier weight, $w_j = log\frac{\epsilon_j}{1-\epsilon_j}$
- Re-weight training instances:
  if $h_j(x_i) \neq y_i$ then, $w_{i+1} = w_i/(2\epsilon_j)$
  else, $w_{i+1} = w_i/2(1-\epsilon_j)$

Unseen instances are classified by voting the ensemble of classifiers h_j with weights w_j.

dataset in order to learn an ensemble of classifiers. After each classifier is induced, all instances in the training set are re-weighted so that the total weight of misclassified instances sum to 1/2 the total weight of the training set. The ensemble is applied to unseen instances by applying a weighted vote from the learned classifiers. Table 1 shows AdaBoost in more detail.

AdaBoost appears to work by allocating a high weight to initially incorrectly classified instances. As boosting continues, those items that have been well classified receive less weight, then are eventually misclassified, which leads to them subsequently receiving higher weights. This is elegant, and focuses attention on regions of the attribute space that are difficult to classify.

An alternative, ad hoc, boosting algorithm, ARC-x4 (Breiman, 1999), was designed to demonstrate that AdaBoost is an example of a broader class of methods that Adaptively Reweight and Combine (ARC). ARC-x4 has a similar accuracy to AdaBoost (Breiman, 1999) (Bauer and Kohavi, 1999), but uses a different weighting scheme. This scheme also relies upon misclassifications. After each trial, instances are given a new weight $1 + e(x)^4/N$ where $e(x)$ is the sum of misclassifications made on instance x in the past, and N is a normalisation constant. We focus our subsequent discussion on AdaBoost.

Theoretical results for AdaBoost (Freund and Schapire, 1997) guarantee that AdaBoost will improve the accuracy with which a *weak* learner classifies the training set. The results for AdaBoost far outstrip this simple goal. While boosting leads to improved results for all weak learners, boosting with decision trees (such as C4.5 (Quinlan, 1993), and CART (Breiman et al., 1984)) gives close to the lowest achievable test set error rates quickly and without tuning parameters (Breiman, 1999). Indeed, while boosting with decision tree learners frequently leads to ensembles that *fit* the training data, additional boosting trials after this point continue to improve results on unseen test data (Schapire et al., 1997; Breiman, 1997; Schapire and Singer, 1998).

An ensemble of classifiers can be characterized by its minimum margin. Suppose that the total weight of classifier votes is first normalized to one. For a given example, the margin is the difference between the weight of votes correctly classifying that example and the maximum weight of votes for any incorrect label. This number falls between one and minus one. The minimum margin is the worst such margin in the training set. Schapire et al. (1997) proposed the minimum margin as an explanation for the performance of AdaBoost. They showed both that AdaBoost operates to further increase the minimum margin after the ensemble fits the training data, and that large minimum margins on training data result in an improved bound on generalization error.

A practical difficulty faced when using AdaBoost with decision trees is that a single classifier can often achieve 100% accuracy on the training data. In this case, boosting halts and the 100% accurate classifier is given infinite voting weight. The rest of the ensemble is effectively discarded. In addition, any further improvements in accuracy that might have resulted from additional boosting are lost. In other words, although AdaBoost has been shown to have interesting properties beyond improving the classifier accuracy on training data, it is restricted to learning with methods that don't fully fit the data.

This article investigates boosting with a *strong* base learner, that is, with a learner that fits the training data with 100% accuracy[1].

3 FBOOST

fBoost is an algorithm designed to emulate boosting with a decision tree learner that *fits* the training data

[1] Where possible.

Table 2: fBoost algorithm

fBoost
Input: n training instances x_i with labels y_i. Trials, T. Base decision tree learner (no pruning), H.
Initialization: All training instances begin with a weight w_i of 1/n. Repeat for T trials

- Induce classifier, h_j, using weighted training instances and H.
- Re-weight training instances:

$$w_{i'} = \frac{w_i}{W_i(h_j)L(h_j)}$$

Where: $w_{i'}$ is the new weight for x_i; $W_i(h_j)$ is the total weight of instances falling into the same leaf of the most recent classifier; and $L(h_j)$ is the number of leaves in classifier h_j.

Unseen instances are classified by voting the ensemble of classifiers h_j with equal weight.

with 100% accuracy. As there are no misclassifications, an alternative re-weighting scheme is necessary. The scheme used is designed to force a broad range of the possible models to be explored on the presumption that much of the AdaBoost performance is due to the broad distribution of classifiers in the ensemble. The algorithm reweights instances to ensure that each instance is covered by a broad range of decision tree leaves (or conjunctive rules), ranging from well populated to poorly populated, ideally with minimal overlap.

Table 2 shows the fBoost algorithm. A training set of size n, and a number of trials, T, are required as input. The base learner, H, must fit the training data if possible. Associated with each item in the training set is a weight, initialized to $1/n$.

At each iteration of the fBoost algorithm, a hypothesis, h_j, is induced from the training data. Whereas AdaBoost uses training set misclassifications to change the importance (or weight) of each instance, fBoost uses information from the hypothesis. Each instance is re-weighted according to the size of the decision tree leaf (or rule) of the most recent hypothesis, h_j, in which it falls. All instance weights are multiplicatively updated so that each leaf of the most recent hypothesis would have the same total weight.

Classification is by applying an equally weighted vote from all classifiers in the ensemble.

3.1 IMPLEMENTATION

The implementation of the fBoost strong learner is based on C4.5 release 8[2]. This software is able, with minor modifications, to directly utilize instance weights for learning. All pruning was disabled.

On some datasets it is not possible to create a decision tree that fully fits the training data. There are two main reasons for this:

- **Identical data instances:** There may be identical data instances with differing class labels.
- **Unknown attribute values:** C4.5 uses a heuristic approach to deal with unknown attribute values. In cases where a decision node makes a test on an attribute with some missing values, instances with the missing values are added to both sub-trees. Each version of the instance receives a portion of the total instance weight. Under some circumstances, this makes finding pure leaves very difficult.

fBoost deals with any resulting impure leaves by treating them as if split into pure daughter leaves. If an unsplitable node has 10 instances, 5 of each class, each instance will be re-weighted by 1/5. This scheme was chosen to minimise the impact of impure leaves on the re-weighting scheme and to simplify implementation.

It should also be noted that fBoost accentuates problems with very small weights in AdaBoost. In AdaBoost, the minimum possible instance weight is bounded by

$$\frac{2^{-t}}{n}$$

where t is the number of trials, and n is the number of training instances. In fBoost, the minimum possible weight is bounded by

$$\frac{1}{n}\prod_t \frac{1}{W_{max}(h_k)L(h_k)}$$

where k is the trial number, h_k is the classifier from trial k, $W_{max}(h_k)$ is the largest leaf weight in classifier h_k, and $L(h_k)$ is the number of leaves in classifier h_k.

As previously noted by Bauer and Kohavi (1999) combinations of very small and very large instance weights

[2]Ross Quinlan kindly provided his version of C4.5 altered for boosting (Quinlan, 1996a) which was then further altered.

can lead to problems with floating point calculations of entropy. We minimise the impact of this problem by running fBoost for only a limited number of trials. An alternative would be to bound each weight to a given minimum.

4 EVALUATION

We report three different evaluations of fBoost. These include: An evaluation of accuracy in comparison with C4.5, Bagging and AdaBoost; A comparison of relative instance weights for AdaBoost and fBoost; A decomposition of the error terms into bias and variance for C4.5, AdaBoost and fBoost.

We begin with the comparison on accuracy.

4.1 ACCURACY

fBoost was evaluated in competition with C4.5, bagged C4.5, and AdaBoosted C4.5 on a representative set 27 datasets from the UCI repository[3]. These datasets, described in Appendix A, cover a broad range of sizes, attribute types, and class labels. C4.5 was run with default settings. All ensemble learners were run with 10 trials. Each classifier was evaluated on each dataset with ten randomized repetitions of a ten fold cross-validation.

Table 3 shows relative results, comparing C4.5 with Bagged C4.5, with AdaBoosted C4.5, and with fBoost on each dataset. The first column shows the percentage error rate achieved by C4.5 on each dataset, and the standard error in brackets. The second column shows the results for Bagged C4.5, both as an percentage error and relative to C4.5 alone. The third column shows the results for AdaBoosted C4.5 both as percentage and relative error. The fourth column shows results for fBoost, again with both percentage and relative errors.

The geometric mean of the ratios, in Table 3, show that fBoost gets an improvement of 17.2% over C4.5 alone. This compares well with Bagging with a 10% improvement and AdaBoost with an 18.3% improvement. The difference between fBoost and AdaBoost was not significant (paired t-test).

The results for fBoost and AdaBoost are very similar. fBoost beats C4.5 on 22 of the 27 datasets. AdaBoost beats C4.5 on 21 of the 27 datasets. In addition, four of the five datasets upon which fBoost does less well

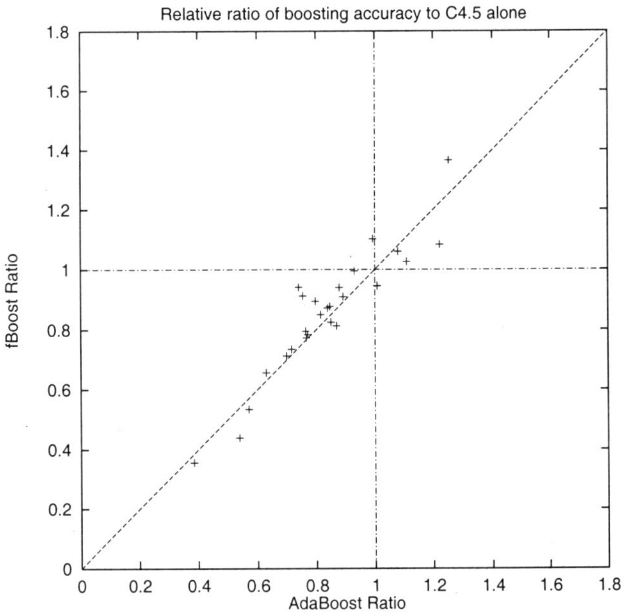

Figure 1: Relative Ratios

than C4.5 are also datasets upon which AdaBoost does poorly. Figure 1 shows the correlation between methods graphically. This figure also shows the proportion of domains for each method that beat C4.5; all points within the box bounded by $x = 1$ and $y = 1$ indicate that both methods beat C4.5.

fBoost might be expected to benefit if larger regions of attribute space can be identified by the learning system as this broadens the range of rules that might cover a given instance[4]. One way to do this is to permit C4.5 to use sub-setting; this allows tests on a discrete attribute to group discrete values into a single node, thus reducing fragmentation due to discrete attributes. With sub-setting turned on, fBoost achieved a 19.2% improvement over C4.5, and AdaBoost achieved an 18.6% improvement. Again, this difference is not significant.

As previously noted, it is not always possible to learn a classifier that completely fits the training data. This occurred on the datasets phoneme, anneal, colic, hepatitis, soybean, and splice, and was due to attributes with unknown values. Colic was particularly problem-

[3]These datasets were previously used by Quinlan (1996a; Quinlan, 1996b; Quinlan, 1999) .

[4]AdaBoost would also benefit, but not as much, as it can express hypotheses with impure rules, which gives it a much broader range of possible rules that cover each instance.

Table 3: Comparative results.

Dataset	C4.5 Average Err (%)	Bagged C4.5 Average Err (%)	Ratio	AdaBoost C4.5 Average Err (%)	Ratio	fBoost Average Err (%)	Ratio
anneal	7.65 (0.18)	5.85 (0.17)	0.764	4.81 (0.10)	0.629	5.02 (0.11)	0.656
audiology	22.53 (0.30)	19.74 (0.40)	0.876	16.11 (0.18)	0.715	16.54 (0.40)	0.734
auto	19.30 (0.67)	21.16 (0.65)	1.096	16.76 (0.32)	0.869	15.69 (0.24)	0.813
breast-w	5.33 (0.19)	4.32 (0.13)	0.810	4.09 (0.16)	0.766	4.12 (0.14)	0.772
chess	9.03 (0.25)	8.87 (0.25)	0.982	4.87 (0.18)	0.539	3.96 (0.14)	0.439
colic	15.01 (0.14)	14.90 (0.08)	0.993	18.79 (0.41)	1.252	20.51 (0.39)	1.366
credit-a	14.36 (0.23)	13.49 (0.18)	0.939	15.93 (0.19)	1.109	14.74 (0.26)	1.026
credit-g	28.86 (0.18)	26.19 (0.14)	0.907	29.07 (0.36)	1.007	27.31 (0.27)	0.946
diabetes	25.09 (0.19)	24.81 (0.26)	0.989	27.08 (0.30)	1.079	26.59 (0.14)	1.060
glass	32.99 (1.00)	27.06 (0.62)	0.820	25.45 (0.64)	0.771	25.87 (0.51)	0.784
heart-c	23.02 (0.42)	22.45 (0.40)	0.976	21.41 (0.50)	0.930	22.89 (0.48)	0.995
heart-h	22.29 (0.32)	21.07 (0.23)	0.945	22.47 (0.44)	1.008	21.06 (0.38)	0.945
hepatitis	21.08 (0.33)	18.51 (0.40)	0.878	16.79 (0.48)	0.797	18.85 (0.66)	0.894
hypo	0.49 (0.01)	0.44 (0.02)	0.908	0.41 (0.02)	0.850	0.40 (0.02)	0.825
iris	4.80 (0.18)	5.60 (0.25)	1.166	5.87 (0.25)	1.222	5.20 (0.28)	1.083
labor	19.00 (1.34)	14.50 (0.75)	0.763	14.33 (0.82)	0.754	17.33 (0.59)	0.912
letter	11.98 (0.05)	7.68 (0.04)	0.641	4.62 (0.02)	0.385	4.26 (0.03)	0.356
lymphography	21.94 (0.72)	20.90 (0.60)	0.953	19.27 (0.62)	0.878	20.63 (0.52)	0.940
phoneme	19.46 (0.09)	18.82 (0.08)	0.967	16.30 (0.12)	0.838	16.96 (0.05)	0.872
segment	3.29 (0.06)	2.75 (0.05)	0.836	1.88 (0.04)	0.571	1.76 (0.05)	0.534
sick	1.32 (0.01)	1.17 (0.04)	0.885	1.01 (0.03)	0.764	1.05 (0.03)	0.795
sonar	27.37 (0.44)	23.17 (0.57)	0.847	20.24 (0.57)	0.740	25.74 (0.50)	0.941
soybean	8.33 (0.21)	7.87 (0.16)	0.944	6.79 (0.20)	0.815	7.08 (0.14)	0.850
splice	5.99 (0.05)	5.60 (0.09)	0.935	5.34 (0.05)	0.891	5.45 (0.05)	0.909
vehicle	27.21 (0.49)	25.83 (0.35)	0.949	23.03 (0.40)	0.846	23.87 (0.31)	0.877
vote	4.95 (0.12)	4.60 (0.18)	0.929	4.91 (0.21)	0.993	5.45 (0.18)	1.102
waveform	27.40 (0.64)	20.83 (0.84)	0.760	19.13 (0.60)	0.698	19.50 (0.40)	0.712
Geometric Mean			0.900		0.817		0.828

atic as missing attribute values in combination with the fBoost updating scheme led to classifiers that misclassified larger and larger numbers of instances. In all of these domains the classification trees were relatively large compared to the size of the training set. Omitting these datasets gives a fBoost a 17.3% improvement over C4.5 and AdaBoost a 15.9% improvement. It is interesting that removing these datasets did not particularly improve the fBoost result but made the AdaBoost result worse; this suggests that AdaBoost (with C4.5) does well on these *difficult* datasets.

One might also question how competitive fBoost is for a larger number of trials. After 20 iterations, AdaBoost achieves a 23.1% improvement over C4.5 and fBoost achieves a 20.7% improvement. This result omits the phoneme dataset, as the fBoost image for 20 iterations exceeded 128Mb. (Omitting the difficult datasets gives results: AdaBoost 24.6% improvement, fBoost 23.0% improvement.)

4.2 RELATIVE WEIGHTS

The similarity of results for the fBoost and AdaBoost algorithms suggest that the weight update mechanism in fBoost might indirectly simulate that of AdaBoost. We tested this hypothesis by logging the final instance weights for both AdaBoost and fBoost on each dataset after 10 trials.

Each sub-figure in Figure 2 shows the results for a single dataset, and relates the AdaBoost and fBoost final weights for each training instance. The X-axis represents the log of AdaBoost weights, and the Y-axis represents the log of fBoost weights.

A number of interesting observations can be drawn from this figure. Instances with high weights in AdaBoost frequently have high weights in fBoost, but the converse is not true. This is not surprising as the fBoost algorithm puts high weights on instances that are frequently represented by small decision tree leaves. This criteria captures instances that would be misclassified in the AdaBoost framework, and hence would be weighted highly by AdaBoost. In addition, the fBoost algorithm places large weights on instances that would be correctly classified by AdaBoost, but that are still associated in fBoost with relatively small leaf weights. The effect is consistent over all the datasets.

Another observation is that the weights in AdaBoost are stratified after 10 trials, whereas they appear to be uniformly distributed for fBoost. In addition, the expectation that fBoost would have a much smaller minimum weight is confirmed, with a minimum fBoost weight of the order of 10^{-16}, and a minimum AdaBoost weight of the order of $10^{-7.5}$.

The fBoost and AdaBoost algorithms share some similarities in the distribution of instance weights resulting from their individual weighting schemes. Nonetheless, the differences in both weight distribution and magnitude are large enough to conclude that fBoost does not merely simulate the AdaBoost algorithm.

4.3 BIAS-VARIANCE

Another way to characterise classification methods is to divide the error on a given dataset into bias and variance. For repeated learning on randomly selected training sets, and a fixed test set, bias is that portion of errors that regularly occurs on the same test items, and variance is the remainder[5].

A previous study of bias and variance concluded that the higher accuracy of AdaBoost over Bagging in many domains was due to a reduction of bias. AdaBoost was also found to frequently have higher variance than Bagging (Bauer and Kohavi, 1999).

The goal of this experiment was to further characterise the difference between AdaBoost and fBoost in terms of bias and variance. We calculated bias and variance using methods due to Kohavi and Wolpert (1996) and methodology drawn from Bauer and Kohavi (1999).

Following this method, we selected datasets with more than 1,000 items. Only seven of the datasets available met this criteria. For each of these, a training set size was chosen that maximised the test set size, while ensuring that meaningful learning could take place[6]. Appendix B shows the datasets selected and the training set sizes.

The process used was as follows: Each dataset was partitioned into two subsets; one of twice the size of the training sets, from which training sets would be randomly selected, and the other was used as a fixed test set. Ten randomly selected training sets were provided to each learning system, and the resulting classifiers applied to the test set. Bias and variance were calculated from the errors on the fixed test set. To ensure an accurate estimate, this process was repeated three times for each dataset. This method provides a similar estimated error to using holdout error estimation

[5]Noise in the training data will be included in the bias term.

[6]For those datasets also used in Bauer and Kohavi (1999) we used the same training set size.

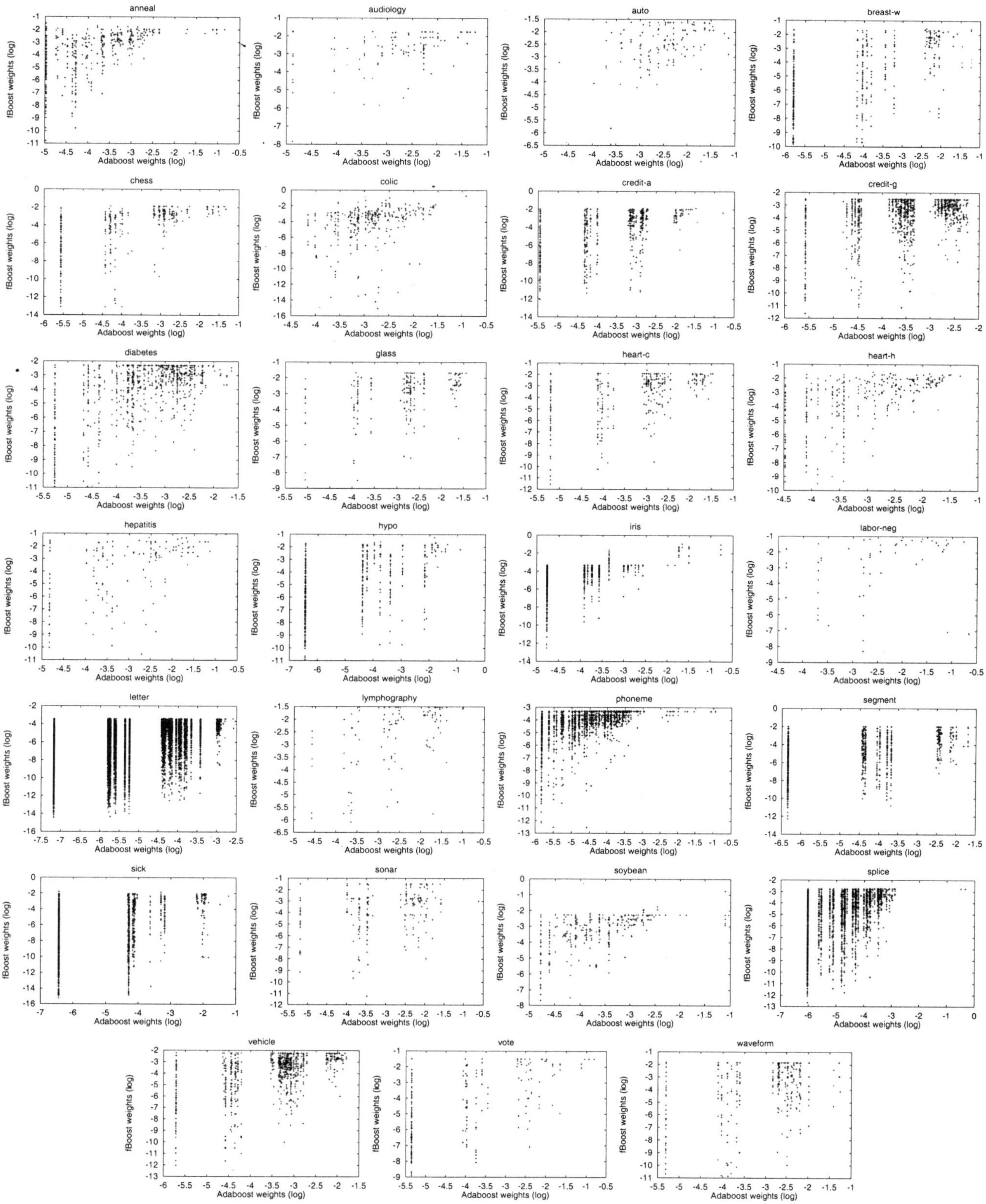

Figure 2: Relative instance weights for AdaBoost and fBoost after ten trials on each dataset. The x-axis is the log of the AdaBoost weight. The y-axis is the log of the fBoost weight.

repeated 30 times (Bauer and Kohavi, 1999).

Table 4 shows the bias-variance results for C4.5, AdaBoosted C4.5, and fBoost. For comparison purposes, the raw bias/variance figures for the boosting methods have also been expressed as ratios to the C4.5 bias/variance. While the number of datasets is too small to draw general conclusions, a number of observations can be made.

Both boosting methods improve bias over C4.5 in all cases, although the improvement is marginal on the sick, and credit-g datasets. Both boosting methods improve the variance for all but the hypo dataset. On average, AdaBoost and fBoost improve bias by 23%, and 24% respectively, and improve variance by 24%, and 28% respectively.

The geometric mean of bias improvements over C4.5 for both AdaBoost and fBoost is very similar, with a difference in ratios of only 1%. The geometric means for variance differ slightly, with fBoost getting a 4% greater improvement than AdaBoost.

These differences between AdaBoost and fBoost in bias and variance are not significant (paired t-test).

5 DISCUSSION

It is remarkable that we have been able to achieve AdaBoost-like performance (at least for 10 trial boosting) by the simple mechanism of repeatedly over-fitting the training data with a substantially different re-weighting mechanism.

As previously noted, AdaBoost performance has been explained (Schapire et al., 1997; Breiman, 1997) in terms of improving the minimum margin. fBoost (where possible) completely fits the training set. Correspondingly, all training instances will be correctly classified by all classifiers, and the ensemble will have a minimum margin of one. Additional trials will not affect the margin level. Hence, margin analysis cannot be used as an explanation for the success of fBoost, which shows that margin analysis cannot account for the improvement in accuracy due to the use of ensembles. Previous work has also shown holes in the minimum margin approach (Grove and Schuurmans, 1998; Quinlan, 1999).

Most work in boosting assumes the use of weak classifiers that only provide a class prediction. Schapire and Singer (1998) extend AdaBoost for weak classifiers that provide a confidence measure for each prediction. Their analysis has a number of relations to the current work.

fBoost shows that the focus of AdaBoost on misclassification is not necessary. This is implicitly recognized by Schapire and Singer. While they do not state that the new formulations of AdaBoost can be applied with a *strong* base learner, this appears to be the case.

Schapire and Singer also generalize minimum margin results for boosting with confidence based predictions. If the fBoost leaf size were to be considered a measure of confidence, this enhanced definition of margin might well be applicable to fBoost.

6 CONCLUSION

Boosting has been restricted to learning with *weak* learners. This article presented a new boosting-like method which learns with a *strong* learner, and has empirically demonstrated AdaBoost-like performance.

A number of implications can be drawn from this:

- the emphasis on misclassification in boosting is not necessary,
- boosting can take place with a *strong* learner, and finally,
- fitting the data need not imply over-fitting the data.

In addition, the basic minimum margin analysis cannot explain fBoost performance. This casts further doubt on the use of the minimum margin as a general explanation for ensemble accuracy.

Acknowledgements

The author is grateful to the anonymous reviewers for their insightful comments and suggestions; to Waleed Kadous for extensive discussions of the material and paper; and to Ross Quinlan, Andrew Mitchell and Virginia Wheway for their comments and suggestions on earlier drafts of the paper.

This work was supported by the Australian Research Council.

References

Bauer, E. and Kohavi, R. (1999). An empirical comparison of voting classification algorithms: Bagging, boosting, and variants. *Machine Learning*. (to appear).

Table 4: Bias/Variance Decomposition

Dataset	C4.5		AdaBoost				fBoost			
	Bias	Var	Bias	Var	Bias Ratio	Var Ratio	Bias	Var	Bias Ratio	Var Ratio
credit-g	17.99	15.21	17.69	13.72	0.98	0.90	17.51	11.81	0.97	0.78
hypo	0.37	0.35	0.29	0.43	0.78	1.23	0.23	0.43	0.62	1.23
letter	7.69	12.74	4.20	6.43	0.55	0.50	3.90	5.93	0.51	0.47
phoneme	14.56	10.91	12.16	10.56	0.84	0.97	13.09	10.23	0.90	0.94
segment	3.34	3.96	2.28	2.35	0.68	0.59	2.24	2.31	0.67	0.58
sick	1.35	1.07	1.29	0.83	0.96	0.78	1.33	0.84	0.99	0.79
splice	4.80	6.67	3.44	4.02	0.72	0.60	3.74	3.62	0.78	0.54
Geometric Mean					0.77	0.76			0.76	0.72

Breiman, L. (1986). Bagging predictors. *Machine Learning*, 24:123–140.

Breiman, L. (1997). Arcing the edge. Technical Report 486, Statistics Department, University of California.

Breiman, L. (1999). Bias, variance, and arcing classifiers. *Machine Learning*. (to appear).

Breiman, L., Friedman, J., Olshen, R., and Stone, C. (1984). *Classification and Regression Trees*. Chapman and Hall.

Dietterich, T. G. (1998). An experimental comparison of three methods for constructing ensembles of decision trees: Bagging, boosting, and randomization. (unpublished manuscript).

Freund, Y. and Schapire, R. E. (1996). Experiments with a new boosting algorithm. In *Proceedings Thirteenth International Conference on Machine Learning*, pages 148–156, San Francisco. Morgan Kaufmann.

Freund, Y. and Schapire, R. E. (1997). A decision theoretic generalization of on-line learning and an application to boosting. *Journal of Computer and System Sciences*, 55:119–139.

Friedman, J., Hastie, T., and Tibshirani, R. (1998). Additive logistic boosting: a statistical view of boosting. Technical report, Stanford University, Department of Statistics.

Grove, A. J. and Schuurmans, D. (1998). Boosting in the limit: Maximizing the margin of learned ensembles. In *Proceedings Fifteenth National Conference on Artificial Intelligence*, pages 692–699. AAAI press.

Kohavi, R. and Wolpert, D. H. (1996). Bias plus variance decomposition for zero-one loss functions. In *Proceedings Thirteenth International Conference on Machine Learning*, pages 275–283, San Francisco. Morgan Kaufmann.

Quinlan, J. R. (1993). *C4.5: Programs for Machine Learning*. Morgan Kaufmann, San Mateo.

Quinlan, J. R. (1996a). Bagging, boosting, and C4.5. In *Proceedings Thirteenth National Conference on Artificial Intelligence*, pages 725–730. AAAI press.

Quinlan, J. R. (1996b). Boosting first order learning. In *Algorithmic Learning Theory*, LNAI 1160. Springer-Verlag.

Quinlan, J. R. (1999). Miniboosting decision trees. *Journal of AI Research*. (to appear).

Schapire, R. E., Freund, Y., Bartlett, P., and Lee, W. S. (1997). Boosting the margin: A new explanation for the effectiveness of voting methods. In *Proceedings of the Fourteenth International Conference on Machine Learning*.

Schapire, R. E. and Singer, Y. (1998). Improved boosting algorithms using confidence-rated predictions. In *Proceedings of the Eleventh International Conference on Computational Learning Theory*.

A Datasets

Name	Cases	Classes	Attributes	
			Continuous	Discrete
anneal	898	6	9	29
audiology	226	6	-	69
auto	205	6	15	10
breast-w	699	2	9	-
chess	551	2	-	39
colic	368	2	10	12
credit-a	690	2	6	9
credit-g	1,000	2	7	13
diabetes	768	2	8	-
glass	214	6	9	-
heart-c	303	2	8	5
heart-h	294	2	8	5
hepatitis	155	2	6	13
hypo	3,772	5	7	22
iris	150	3	4	-
labor	57	2	8	8
letter	20,000	26	16	-
lymph	148	4	-	18
phoneme	5,438	47	-	7
segment	2,310	7	19	-
sick	3,772	2	7	22
sonar	208	2	60	-
soybean	683	19	-	35
splice	3,190	3	-	62
vehicle	846	4	18	-
vote	435	2	-	16
waveform	300	3	21	-

B Datasets in Bias Variance Analysis

Name	Cases	Training Size
credit-g	1,000	300
hypo	3,772	1000
letter	20,000	5000
phoneme	5,438	1500
segment	2,310	500
sick	3,772	1000
splice	3,190	800

Detecting Motifs from Sequences

Yuh-Jyh Hu[1], Suzanne Sandmeyer[2], and Dennis Kibler[1]
Information and Computer Science Department[1]
Biological Chemistry Department, College of Medicine[2]
University of California, Irvine
yhu@ics.uci.edu, sbsandme@uci.edu, kibler@ics.uci.edu

Abstract

The problem of multiple global comparisons of families of biological sequences has been well-studied. Fewer algorithms have been developed for identifying local consensus patterns or motifs in biological sequences. These two important problems have different biological constraints and, consequently, different computational approaches. The difficulty of finding the biologically meaningful motifs results from the variability in (1) the bases at each position in the motif, (2) the location of the motif in the sequence and (3) the multiplicity of motif occurrences within a given sequence. In addition the short length of many biologically significant motifs and the fact that motifs gain biological significance only in combinations, makes them difficult to determine using standard statistical methods. In this paper we introduce our own approach, DMS, which combines multiple objective functions with an improved iterative sampling search method. We compare the main approaches for finding motifs and test the effectiveness of the various algorithms by comparing them on ten real domains and fourteen artificial domains. The main advantage of DMS is that it is better able to find shorter motifs.

1 Introduction

Genome projects are generating large data sets of genomic sequence data. However, the size and speed of acquisition of these data sets exceeds the pace of experimental analyses and interpretations. In 1996, with the international collaboration of over 100 laboraties, the yeast genome was completely sequenced. It has 12 million base pairs (bps) and about 6,000 genes. To the surprise of biologists, the biological functions of only about 2,000 genes were known. The functions of another 2,000 genes could be inferred by comparison. The functions of the remaining 2,000 genes, called orphans, are unknown. Recently the complete genome (approximately 100 million bps) of a multi-celled animal (*C. elegans*) was sequenced. Within a few years the sequencing of the human genome (approximately 3 billion bps) is anticipated. Once the genome and genes have been determined, there are two essential questions to be answered: 1) What is the function of each gene, and 2) When are genes expressed?

The first question has been heavily studied and primarily depends on both experimental tests of gene activities and predictions of gene activity base on structure. Computationally, the most successful way of characterizing a gene has been based on probabilistic models, usually via some instantiation of Hidden Markov Models (HMMs). HMMs work well for this problem since they provide a global model which allows insertions, deletions, and substitutions. These capabilities match the intuition that similar genes have had a common evolutionary history and the evolution process involves insertions, deletions and changes to the base pairs.

The second question has been less well studied and has a very different character. Biologists have determined that the control or regulation of gene expression is primarily determined by relatively short sequences in the region surrounding a gene. These sequences vary in length, position, redundancy, orientation, and bases. Insertions and deletions are uncommon in regulatory motifs. These qualities prohibit the simple application of HMMs.

Several methods have been developed for detecting patterns shared by functionally related biosequences (Helden *et. al.*, 1998; Hertz & Stormo, 1995; Hertz *et. al.*, 1990; Bailey & Elkan, 1995; Lawrence *et. al.*, 1993; Hughey and Krogh, 1996; Eddy, 1995). We review these methods according to their representations, objective functions, and search strategies.

In addition, we present a new approach called DMS to detect motifs from sequences. DMS extends previous work by combining multiple objective functions with an improved iterative sampling technique. The performance of our algorithm and several others are compared on ten problems taken from the biological literature. Each of these problems consists of a set of biological sequences with known motifs. To further understand the limitations and value of these programs, we also compared the programs on fourteen artificial problems, which were designed to mimic real data.

2 Characteristics of Motif-finding Problem

Fundamentally gene regulation is determined by chemical reactions which are, in turn, controlled by the shape and electrostatic charges of the molecules involved. One such instance of this is the interaction between regulatory proteins and their target binding site. The significance of this is that this can lead to a coordination of regulation via a combination of motifs. Unfortunately this information is not typically available. We expect that the local shape of a binding or receptor site will be primarily determined by the bases involved, acknowledging the fact that non-local base changes can affect local shape.

There are a number of consequences that we can expect from this view. These consequences are supported by the structure of known motifs.

- Patterns are relatively short since they only define a local shape.
- Patterns are not defined by an exact sequence of bases, and variation is allowed. Typically the variation is represented via a probability matrix.
- The precise location of the receptor site may not be important, as the goal of the receptor site is to bind to another molecule.
- Multiple occurrences of a receptor site may be important since each occurrence would give a molecule a greater chance of finding the binding site and since bound molecules may interact, modifying the structure and the binding properties.
- Insertion and deletions are less likely to occur than base variation, as this would have a drastic effect on the conserved features of the receptor.
- The pattern or motif should be common to most of these sequences in a family and uncommon in the entire genome. It is essential that not all genes are expressed, but only a selected few. Also there may be multiple ways of turning on a gene, so it is not required that the motif occur in every sequence in a given family.

These characteristics make the problem somewhat ill-defined. The terms of "common", "pattern", and "most" require precise definitions. While various definitions are possible, which best corresponds to the underlying biological problem is unclear.

In any case these characteristics make the problem computationally difficult. For example, a typical problem would be: given 30 DNA sequences, each of length 800, find a common pattern of length 8. Let us simplify the problem, as many algorithms do, and assume the pattern occurs exactly once in each sequence. This means that there are approximately 800^{30} potential locations for a motif candidate.

3 Issues in Motif-Finding Algorithms

There are three main interrelated computational issues: the representation of a pattern, the definition of the objective function, and the search strategy. While we examine the algorithms on computational grounds, the final, gold-standard is how well the algorithm does at predicting motifs.

3.1 Representation

As the primary DNA sequences are described by a double-stranded string of nucleic bases {A,C,G,T}, the most basic pattern representation is the exact base string. Due to the complexity and flexibility of the motif binding mechanism, there is rarely any motif that can be exactly described by a string of nucleic bases. To obtain more flexibility, the IUPAC code was designed, which extends the expressiveness of the simple base string representation by including all disjunctions of nucleotides. In this language there is a new symbol for each possible disjunction, e.g. W represents A or T.

A more informative pattern representation is a probability matrix in which each element reflects the importance of the base at a particular position. Such matrices can be easily translated into the IUPAC code, while the converse is not true. These matrices are often transformed from the observed occurrence frequencies. One limitation of probability matrices is that correlation or dependence between positions are not represented.

3.2 Objective Function

The purpose of an objective function is to approximate the biological meanings of the patterns in terms of a mathematical function. The objective function are heuristics. Once the objective function is determined, the goal is to find those patterns with high objective function value. Different objective functions have been derived from the background knowledge, such as the secondary structures of homologous proteins, the relation between the energetic interactions among residues and the residue frequencies, etc (Stormo, 1990; Lawrence *et. al.*, 1993). Objective functions based on the information content or its variants were proposed (Hertz *et. al.*, 1990; Lawrence *et. al.*, 1993). Others evaluate the quality of the pattern by its likelihood or by some other measures of statistical significance (Bailey & Elkan, 1995; Helden *et. al.*, 1998). In addition, some define the pattern as a model of a probabilistic sequence generator and evaluate the model by the probability that the given sequence data is generated by the model (Hughey and Krogh, 1996; Eddy, 1995).

Even though there are many different objective functions currently used, it is still unclear what is the most appropriate object function or the best representation for patterns that will correspond to biological significant motifs. More likely, additional knowledge will need to be incorporated to improve motif characterization. In the final analysis, the various algorithms can only produce candidate motifs that will require biological experiments to verify.

3.3 Search Strategy

If one adopts the exact string representation, then one can exhaustively check every possible candidate. However this approach is only able to identify short known motifs or partial long motifs (Helden *et. al.*, 1998). Therefore, the primary representation used is a probability matrix (Harr *et. al.*, 1983; Staden, 1984; Hertz *et. al.*, 1990; Lawrence *et. al.*, 1993; Bailey and Elkan, 1995). Once one accepts a probability matrix as the representation, then there is no possibility for an exhaustive search. Initial approaches started with hill-climbing strategies, but these typically fell into local optimum. Standard approaches to repairing hill-climbing, such as beam and stochastic search, were tried next. The current approaches involve a mixture of sampling and stochastic iterative improvement. This avoids the computational explosion and maintains or improves the ability to find motifs (Lawrence *et. al.*, 1993; Bailey and Elkan, 1995).

4 The DMS Algorithm

DMS adopts the probability matrix representation for motifs. The user provides a family of sequences and how many motifs he would like returned. The system returns that number of motifs, ranked by a significance measure, which will be defined.

The probability matrix representation has been used in various pattern identification problems (Harr *et. al.*, 1983; Staden, 1984; Hertz *et. al.*, 1990; Lawrence *et. al.*, 1993). It is usually built from the base frequency of example biosequences. For example, in the NIT regulatory family (Helden, *et al.*,1998) which contains 7 members, a possible 6-base motif matrix is illustrated in Figure 1. The normalized matrix is also shown in this figure.

Based on the normalized motif matrix, we could calculate the match score of any 6-base sequence by dividing the sum of the values for each position of the motif. For example, given a 6-base sequence, GATAAG, its match score is $\frac{0.86+1+1+1+1+1}{6}$. The success of these analyses confirms the fact that the frequencies of bases at positions within sites are related to the importance of the bases to the functioning within the sites (Stormo, 1988). The challenge is to find a matrix that well represents the motif in terms of the objective function.

We propose a new motif-finding algorithm, DMS. Unlike other approaches, DMS uses multiple types of objective functions, the motif consensus quality, the motif multiplicity significance and the motif coverage. The consensus quality is only used to guide the search for well-conserved motif candidates, the motif multiplicity significance reflects the value of multiple copies of motifs, and the motif coverage addresses the importance of a motif's being commonly shared by a given family of sequences.

The consensus quality of a matrix is derived from the entropy, the lower the entropy, the better conserved the motif. The entropy is calculated from the probability that each base occurs at each position in the motif, Pm_{base}. More precisely, the entropy for a particular column n in the matrix is given by:

$$E_n = -\sum_{i=b_1}^{b_4} Pm_i \lg Pm_i$$

where $b_1..b_4$ are the bases A, G, C, T. If the bases are uniformly distributed over a position, then the maximum value of 2 is obtained. If only a single base appears in a position then the minimum value of 0 is obtained. Thus we define the consensus quality of column n as:

$$C_n = 2 - E_n$$

The final consensus quality of a matrix b, is defined as the average of all position quality.

$$con(b) = \frac{1}{W}\sum_{n=1}^{W} C_n$$

where W is the width of the motif.

The multiplicity significance is derived from the measure of precision as defined in the information retrieval

A	0	7	0	7	7	0		A	0.00	1.00	0.00	1.00	1.00	0.00
G	6	0	0	0	0	7	normalized to	G	0.86	0.00	0.00	0.00	0.00	1.00
C	1	0	0	0	0	0		C	0.14	0.00	0.00	0.00	0.00	0.00
T	0	0	7	0	0	0		T	0.00	0.00	1.00	0.00	0.00	0.00

Figure 1: A 6-base Motif Matrix Example

paradigm. It is simple and empirically effective. We define the multiplicity significance of a motif b as:

$$mul(b) = \frac{occ_S(b)}{occ_G(b)}$$

where $occ_S(b)$ is b's occurrences in S, $occ_G(b)$ is b's occurrences in genome.

The motif coverage is defined as the ratio of the number of the sequences containing b to the total number of sequences given, i.e.:

$$cov(b) = \frac{cont_S(b)}{|S|}$$

where $cont_S(b)$ is the number of sequences in S that contain b, and $|S|$ is the total number of sequences in S.

Given a set of N biosequences, DMS carries out an iterative improvement search strategy that attempts to find a user-defined number, d, of matrices that maximize the consensus quality defined above. These d matrices are motif candidates. DMS then ranks these motifs according to a merit measure based on the combination of the consensus quality, the multiplicity significance and the motif coverage. Given the d motifs, we first normalize the consensus quality, the multiplicity significance and the motif coverage of each motif b, using the maximum value, as defined below :

$$Con_{normal}(b) = \frac{con(b)}{MAX(con)}$$
$$Mul_{normal}(b) = \frac{mul(b)}{MAX(mul)}$$
$$Cov_{normal}(b) = \frac{cov(b)}{MAX(cov)}$$

where $MAX(con)$ is the maximum consensus quality of the d motifs, $MAX(mul)$, the maximum multiplicity significance of the d motifs, and $MAX(cov)$, the maximum motif coverage of the d motifs.

We assign the equal weight to every measure discussed above and propose a final merit measure of a motif b defined as :

$$Merit(b) = \frac{1}{\frac{1}{3}\left(\frac{1}{Con_{normal}(b)} + \frac{1}{Mul_{normal}(b)} + \frac{1}{Cov_{normal}(b)}\right)}$$

The value of merit reflects the synergy of the consensus quality, the multiplicity significance and the motif coverage. There are three steps in DMS which are detailed in the following subsections.

4.1 Translation: Subsequences into Matrices

If we knew the motif location(s) in every sequence, we could start with a probability matrix corresponding to these positions. As this is unknown, we begin by allowing each subsequence of length W to be a candidate motif. We convert this particular subsequence into a probability matrix in two steps, adopting an idea from (Bailey and Elkan, 1995). First we fix the probability of every base in the subsequence to some value $0 < X < 1$, and assign probabilities of the other bases according to $\frac{1-X}{4-1}$ (4 nucleic bases). Following Bailey and Elkan, we set X to 0.5. This gives us a set of seed probability matrices to be used as starting points for iterative improvement. Since motifs should occur in most sequences, we can select a random subset of the sequences and only generate candidate starting points from this subset.

4.2 Determining Possible Motif Occurrences

Rather than making the common assumption that each motif occurs only once per sequence, we allow for the possibility that a motif may occur multiple times in a single sequence. For each matrix and each sequence, we find the position that maximizes the match score. Now we set the threshold for deciding if a motif occurs at any position as the mean of match scores. Finally we add to the list of motif positions any position whose match score is greater than this threshold. This process defines a set of potential motif positions. Once these motif positions are defined, the seed probability matrices are no longer used.

4.3 Finding and Ranking Motif Candidates

After the likely motif positions are determined, DMS performs an iterative optimization procedure to find the motif probability matrix. Unlike current approaches that search all possible positions within a sequence, DMS only considers the potential motif positions determined in the previous step. This strategy significantly constrains the search space. For initialization, a randomly selected motif position from the potential positions in each sequence forms the initial probability matrix.

A sequence is then chosen at random for optimization. DMS optimizes the information content of the matrix by checking every potential motif position within the selected sequence. The position that gains the highest information content is chosen to update the matrix. The process is repeated until no improvement is noted. In each optimization cycle, the order of sequences is randomly shuffled. The randomization in each trial cycle is important to remove implicit biases, such as the order of the sequences, that can be harmful in search algorithms (Hampson and Kibler, 1996). At this point, in each sequence, the subsequence that contributes to the last updated matrix is determined. We then compute the mean of the match scores of the subsequences that form the matrix, and isolate all subsequences with a match score over the mean as possible motif repeats in each sequence. All these motif repeats in sequences are used to form the final motif matrix.

The same procedure is performed on all matrices to produce the motif candidates. Finally, DMS ranks the motif candidates according to its significance measure. Unlike other algorithms that use a probabilistic representation, DMS sets a threshold which defines whether or not a subsequence is a motif. This permits DMS to use the merit measure for ranking motifs. Other algorithms cannot directly apply the same merit measure.

A pseudocode description of matrix optimization procedure is given in Figure 2.

5 History/Related Work

We review some of the methods developed for the detection of the motifs. These methods were selected since they have been well-developed, are freely available over the internet, and represent a spectrum of different approaches.

CONSENSUS (Hertz *et. al.*, 1990; Hertz and Stormo, 1995) were pioneers in using computer search algorithms for identifying motifs. Their algorithms assume that there is exactly one occurrence per string and uses a beam search method with an information content evaluation function. The algorithms are somewhat limited in that they find a single motif (and variants) from a set of sequences and may lodge in local optima.

The Gibbs sampler (Lawrence *et. al.*, 1993) uses a probabilistic matrix to describe motifs, and adopts a search strategy based on random, iterative sampling. It is capable of finding multiple motifs in sequences when the number of occurrences of each motif in each sequence is known (Bailey & Elkan, 1995). It is computationally expensive and has difficulty learning short motifs.

The MEME algorithm (Bailey & Elkan, 1995) is a development of the Expectation Maximization (EM) algorithm introduced by Lawrence and Reilly, 1990. Similar to the Gibbs sampler, it uses a probabilistic representation. By repeatedly applying EM, MEME finds a matrix with maximum likelihood. MEME works particularly well on longer sequences. A potential limitation is that MEME performs less well on shorter patterns, as indicated by trials on real and artificial data.

Helden *et. al.* designed a simple, fast algorithm that detects over-represented oligonucleotides within sequences (Helden *et. al.*, 1998). This method exhaustively counts all oligonucleotide occurrences in the sequences, and estimates their statistical significance. This work highlighted the value of using multiplicity in identifying motifs with biological significance. However final identification of the motif is done manually using the program's output. To maintain the simplicity of the string representation, this approach sacrifices the expressiveness of probability matrices, making it less powerful in finding motifs with a large amount of variability.

We summarize the main design features of the various algorithms in Table 1.

6 Experiments on Real Domains

Recall that our goal is to describe the motif(s) that determines when a gene is expressed. From the literature, Helden *et. al.* defined ten families of genes that contain a number of known and probably unknown motifs. The known motifs for each family of yeast genes define ten learning tasks for evaluating the various motif algorithms. These families are listed in Table 2. Also recall that the (transcriptional) regulation of a yeast gene is primarily determined by motifs in the upstream region. As in the Helden study, we used the 800 bp upstream region of each ORF. These data are available from Saccharomyces Genome Database at Stanford[1].

We ran all the motif finding algorithms above on these regulatory families except for the Helden algorithm, since his results were published. Except for DMS, none of the algorithms we tested provides any ranking information in its output. As they all adopt the matrix as the representation, and the matching threshold is implicit in the programs, our objective is to test whether they can identify the published motifs based on other

[1] http://genome-www.stanford.edu/Saccharomyces

```
Given: a set of biosequences, B
       A random subset of B, S
       the width of motif, W
Return: a set of ranked motif candidates, C

Step 1. Translation
        For each subsequence s in B Do
          Translate s into candidate probability matrix m via:
          m(i,base) = .50 if base occurs in position i
                    = .17 otherwise

Step 2. Determine possible motif positions
        For each sequence s in S Do
          Find highest match scoring subsequence in s
        Compute the mean of the highest match scores in S
        For each sequence s in S Do
          Set Potential Positions to those with match
          score >= mean

Step 3. Find and rank motif candidates
        Randomly choose a Potential Position in each sequence
        to initialize matrix M
        Repeat
          Randomly pick a sequence s in S
          Check if M's quality can be improved by using a
          different Potential Position in s
          Update matrix M
        Until no improvement in M's quality
        Compute the mean of match scores of subsequences
        contributing to M
        For each sequence ŝ in S Do
          Isolate motif repeats to those with match score >= mean
        Form the final matrix FM with all repeats in S
        Put FM in C
Sort all motif candidates in C according to significance
Return C
```

Figure 2: Pseudocode of DMS

Table 1: Characteristics of Motif-Finding Algorithms

Algorithm	Search Strategy	Objective Function	Representation
CONSENSUS	beam search	information content	frequency matrix
Gibbs	stochastic hill-climbing	ratio of pattern probability to background probability	probabilistic matrix
MEME	EM variant	likelihood	probabilistic matrix
Helden	exhaustive	statistical significance assuming binomial distribution	base string
DMS	stochastic hill-climbing	information content and significance	probabilistic matrix

Table 2: Ten regulatory families and the associated published motifs

Family	Size	published motifs
NIT	7	GATAAG
MET	11	TCACGTG AAAACTGTGG
PHO	5	GCACGTGGG GCACGTTTT
PDR	7	TCCGCGGA
GAL	6	CGGNNNNNWNNNNNCCG
GCN	38	RRTGACTCTTT
INO	10	CATGTGAAWT
HAP	8	CCAAY
YAP	16	TTACTAA
TUP	25	KANWWWWATSYGGGGW

controllable parameters, e.g., the motif width and the number of motifs desired. Because of the variation in strategies of the algorithms, we allowed each algorithm to construct 100 motifs from each family. As biological experimentation is complex, expensive, and subject to noise, the literature typically only publishes the IUPAC code for regulatory motifs. Consequently we needed to construct a way to credit the algorithms that determined a probability matrix. Also the biological published motif contain some noise, We adopted the following procedure for determining a match. From each probability matrix we constructed a consensus pattern. If this consensus pattern matched the published motif in 80% of the positions of the motif, we counted this as a correct match. A base in the consensus sequence was allowed to match a disjunction of bases (as described by the IUPAC code) if the disjunction contained the base.

The experimental results are presented in Table 3. Column 2 to 5 shows whether the algorithm successfully identified the motifs. A "*" means the motifs(s) was successfully found, a "Δ" shows the motif(s) was contained in a longer pattern, and a blank indicates a failure.

In these trials, CONSENSUS did not find the GATAAG motif in the NIT family, which was reported by Helden *et. al.*. The algorithm requires setting several parameters whose influence is unclear. There may be some settings which permit the motif to be found. Moreover CONSENSUS failed to identify the published motifs in GCN, HAP, YAP and TUP regulatory families. Gibbs sampler found the published motifs in each family except the motifs in the HAP family, and the less conserved GCACGTTTT motif in PHO family. Gibbs is very sensitive to the setting of the expected number of motif occurrences. Wrong settings may hinder Gibbs sampler from isolating the correct motifs. MEME also identified all the published motifs except for the motifs in the HAP family, but it is also sensitive to whether to allow multiple appearances of a motif in any sequence or not. For example, allowing multiple appearances of a motif in any sequence prohibits MEME from detecting the target motif in the TUP family. In addition, MEME tended to detect longer elements even if we set it to find short motifs. Some of the shorter patterns are contained in longer ones, such as the motifs in the NIT family, the YAP and the MET. DMS identified all the published motifs in all regulatory families.

7 Experiments on Artificial Domains

The primary standard is how effectively these algorithms identify the reported motifs on real domains. However, as the biologists do not always have a complete idea of these regulatory families, and the collection of data sets is not extensive at the moment, it is useful to use synthetic domains to evaluate the various algorithms. While we have tried to maintain fidelity with real domains, we also had the ability to create motifs with known and controllable properties.

As the size of the families varied from 5 to 38 in the real domains, we used artificial families with sizes of 10 to 40 sequences. For the most part in real domains, the various algorithms did well at finding large motifs, but as the motif got shorter, the difficulty of finding them became higher. Consequently we created test sets with motif widths varying from 4 to 8 bases. The background sequences were generated either at random or by randomly shuffling real upstream regions from the yeast genome, e.g., the sets of 38 sequences are derived from the GCN family. To insert the motif into a sequence, we used four probabilities.

1. P_0 the probability of no artificial motif in a sequence
2. P_1 the probability of one artificial motif in a sequence,
3. P_2 the probability of two artificial motifs in a sequence,
4. P_B the probability of the preferred bases in the motif,

These fourteen artificial regulatory families are described in Table 4. The results are presented in Table 5, where we used the same test methodology as in the real domains. First, this data reinforces the conclusions from the experiments on real data, namely that CONSENSUS is unable to deal with variability in the motifs and that the stochastic search process of Gibbs only occasionally, but not always, lets it find the motif. MEME, which performed well on long motif patterns, failed to find the small seeded small motifs. On the other hand, DMS found all the seeded motifs.

8 Conclusions

Finding local consensus patterns in biosequences, i.e., motifs, is a very different problem than finding global alignments. We have reviewed the computational design of the leading approaches for finding motifs and provided the first empirical comparison of these on a common set of real and artificial problems. We have also introduced our own algorithm DMS for finding motifs, which combines many of the aspects of previous algorithms. This algorithm incorporated some novel constraints on the search that increases speed significantly without losing its ability to find motifs. On the chosen real domains, DMS and MEME performed nearly equivalently and much better than the

Table 3: Results of ten regulatory families

Family	CONSENSUS	Gibbs	MEME	DMS
NIT		*	Δ	*
MET	*	*	Δ	*
PHO	*	missed GCACGTTTT	*	*
PDR	*	*	*	*
GAL	*	*	*	*
GCN		*	*	*
INO	*	*	*	*
HAP	*			*
YAP		*	Δ	*
TUP		*	*	*

Table 4: 14 artificial regulatory families and the seeded motifs

	Family Size	Seq Length(bps)	Motif	P_0	P_1	P_2	P_B
1	10	800	CGCAA	0.0	0.8	0.2	1.0
2	10	800	CGTTT	0.0	0.8	0.2	1.0
3	38	800	CGCAA	0.0	0.8	0.2	1.0
4	38	800	CAGACA	0.0	0.8	0.2	1.0
5	38	800	CAGTC	0.0	0.8	0.2	0.9
6	38	800	CAGACA	0.0	0.8	0.2	0.9
7	38	800	CAGTCA	0.2	0.6	0.2	0.9
8	38	800	GTGTGTT	0.2	0.6	0.2	0.9
9	38	800	GCGAATT	0.2	0.6	0.2	0.9
10	38	800	CACGATA	0.2	0.6	0.2	0.9
11	40	500	CCCT	0.0	1.0	0.0	1.0
12	40	500	WCKGMCWG	0.0	1.0	0.0	1.0
13	40	500	WCTSACTG	0.0	1.0	0.0	0.9
14	40	500	WCTSACTG	0.0	1.0	0.0	0.8

Table 5: Results of 14 artificial families

Family	CONSENSUS	Gibbs	MEME	DMS
1		*		*
2		*		*
3				*
4		*	Δ	*
5				*
6		*		*
7				*
8				*
9				*
10				*
11				*
12		*	*	*
13		*	*	*
14				*

alternative algorithms. We believe that the DMS algorithm is superior at finding short motifs and that conclusion was supported by artificial experiments with seeded, variable, short motifs.

This research is part of a larger system that begins with collecting genes expression patterns using an Affymetrix gene-chip machine. Genes are then grouped into families with similar expression patterns via a new clustering algorithm. This affords us an automatic way to acquire families of similarly regulated genes. When DMS is run on these clusters, it has rediscovered know regulatory motifs and suggested additional motifs.

9 References

Bailey, T. and Elkan, C. (1995) "Unsupervised Learning of Multiple Motifs in Biopolymers Using Expectation Maximization", Machine Learning, 21, p51-80.

Eddy, S. (1995) "Multiple Alignment using Hidden Markov Models", in Proceedings of International Conference on Intelligent Systems for Molecular Biology, p114-120.

Hampson, S. and Kibler, D. (1996) "Large Plateaus and Plateau Search in Boolean Satisfiability Problems: When to Give Up Searching and Start Again", In DIMACS Series in Discrete Mathematics and Theoretical Computer Science, 26, p437-455.

Harr, R., Haggstrom, M. and Gustaffson, P. (1983) "Search Algorithm for Pattern Match Analysis of Nucleic Acid Sequences", Nucleic Acids Res., 11, p2943-2957.

Helden, J. V., Andre, B, and Collado-Vides, J. (1998) "Extracting Regulatory Sites from the Upstream Region of Yeast Genes by Computational Analysis of Oligonucleotide Frequencies", Journal of Molecular Biology, 281, p827-842.

Hertz, G., Hartzell III, G. and Stormo, G. (1990) "Identification of Consensus Patterns in Unaligned DNA Sequences Known to be Functionally Related", Computer Applications in Biosciences, Vol 6, No 2, p81-92.

Hertz, G. and Stormo, G. (1995) "Identification of Consensus Patterns in Unaligned DNA and Protein Sequences: A Large-Deviation Statistical Basis for Penalizing Gaps", in Proceedings of the 3rd International Conference on Bioinformatics and Genome Research, p201-216.

Hughey, R. and Krogh, A. (1996) "Hidden Markov Models for Sequence Analysis: extension and analysis of the basic method", Computer Applications in Biosciences, Vol 12, No 2, p95-107.

Lawrence, C., Altschul, S., Boguski, M., Liu, J., Neuwald, A. and Wootton, J. (1993) "Detecting Subtle Sequence Signals: A Gibbs Sampling Strategy for Multiple Alignments", SCIENCE, Vol 262, p208-214.

Lawrence, C. and Reilly, A. (1990) "An Expectation Maximization (EM) Algorithm for the Identification and Characterization of Common Sites in Unaligned Biopolymer Sequences", Protein: Structure Function and Genetics, 7, p41-51.

Staden, R. (1984) "Computer Methods to Locate Signals in Nucleic Acid Sequences", Nucleic Acids Res., 12, p505-519.

Stormo, G. (1988) "Computer Methods for Analyzing Sequence Recognition of Nucleic Acids", Annual Review of Biophysic and Biophysical Chemistry, 17, p241-263.

Distributed Robotic Learning: Adaptive Behavior Acquisition for Distributed Autonomous Swimming Robot in Real-World

Daisuke Iijima Wenwei Yu Hiroshi Yokoi and Yukinori Kakazu
Lab. of Autonomous Systems Eng.
Hokkaido University
N-13, W-8, Kita-ku, Sapporo 060-8628, Japan

Abstract

This paper proposes the construction of a "strong" autonomous mobile robot, which can acquire environment oriented behavior through learning, as a distributed autonomous system. It is thought that such a system has many advantages over other systems in terms of adaptability to the environment and so on. However, the potential of this type of system has yet to be demonstrated in experiments under real-world conditions. We conducted an experiment to determine whether a distributed autonomous swimming robot could acquire target-approaching behavior on a water surface. The experimental conditions were set in order to reproduce the unstableness and uncertainty of the real world. Therefore, control of the robot was difficult, and it took many repetitions before the target behavior was acquired. In this study, we attempted to produce fast learning by introducing oscillation action patterns suitable for providing motion through water. As a result, the robot acquired the active target-approaching behavior using only local learning even if partial fault has occurred, and the behavior was almost the same as that in the centralized control.

1 INTRODUCTION

Until now, most research on autonomous mobile robots (AMRs) has been performed on robots constructed so as to be capable of a certain range of movements within their environment; e.g., a two-wheel drive robot is capable of forward, backward, left, and right motion on flat ground (Floreano and Mondada, 1994; Tani, 1996). However, successfully performed motion under such conditions does not guarantee the ability to perform similar movements in the real world as such robots would come to a standstill if either a wheel was broken or the ground become uneven. On the other hand, a great deal of this type of research is performed using computer simulations (Sims, 1994; Yokoi, Mizuno, Takita and Kakazu, 1994). Thus, the problem of the gap between the simulated world and the real world is raised. We consider that an AMR should possess at least the following functions in order to ensure its "autonomy":

(a) a function that enables it to adopt its motion to changes in its environment

(b) a function that enables it to satisfy its own energy requirements

(c) a function that enables it to recover any troubles

We define a robot capable of the above functions as a "strong" AMR, and distinguish it from robots that are designed to move easily within a well-known environment, that is, "weak" AMRs.

A distributed autonomous robotic system (DARS) could provide the answer to the construction of a "strong" AMR because DARS offers the following advantages:

(I). Plenty of action variation originated from redundant actuator group (it guarantees the realization of (a))

(II). The compensatory ability for the lost functions based on the redundant system structure (it guarantees the realization of (c))

(III). The minimum programming cost because of the identical unit structure.

(IV). The good efficiency of the action learning because of not so large number of the learning parameter and the mutual influence between individual units.

(V). The easy expansion / the reduction of the system scale by changing the number of unit.

Accordingly, this paper proposes the construction of an AMR as a DARS. As we believed that testing of this robot should be performed under real-world conditions, a water environment was chosen because it reproduced the unstableness and uncertainty that are characteristic of the real world. Thus, we constructed a distributed autonomous swimming robot that was also to float on the water surface (Iijima, Yu, Yokoi and Kakazu, 1998) (see below section 3). Moreover, on adaptive oscillator method (AOM), based on energy management, was proposed as the general decision-making mechanism in this robot in order that it could be satisfy the above mentioned requirement (b) for an AMR (see below section 5). This study also sought to clarify whether the proposed system could satisfy requirements (a) and (c) for an AMR. Thus, the experiment performed tested the capability of the robot to autonomously acquire target approaching behavior (see below section 4).

In a previous study, we prepared an enormous state space in which to test the learning capabilities of robots under uncontrolled conditions. However, we adopted the AOM without any consideration of learning efficiency; thus, the real time necessary for a single learning trial was unsuitable.

Therefore, in this study, in order to investigate real-world learning within a shorter time frame, we preset the oscillating action patterns which were shown to be effective in enabling floating objects to move in a watery environment, as the elementary action patterns. As a result, the desired action sequence was obtained within a reasonable period, even if partial fault has occurred (see below section 6). Furthermore, the behavior acquired by the distributed system was compared with that acquired by a centralized system on the basis of a replay experiment. Similar environment-oriented behavior was observed in both systems.

2 ROBOT CONTROL ON A WATER SURFACE

In the past, the following problems in controlling a robot on the water surface have been observed (Iijima et al., 1998):

- As fluid force and inertia dominate in the environment, even a slight motion would cause the robot to continue in that direction at a decreasing velocity
- The flow state differs between the walls and corners of the pool and the center of the pool
- Near the wall of the pool, the dynamic characteristics of the robot are different because of the friction between the robot and the wall

Here, the fluid force is the force of waves and flows produced by the robot itself, while inertia is the momentum which causes the robot to continue to move a certain period after it has generated some force.

The control algorithm for these problems should be constructed so as to provide not only the dynamic characteristics of the robot but also the nonlinearity depending on the environment.

3 DISTRIBUTED AUTONOMOUS SWIMMING ROBOT

Figures 1 and 2 show the distributed autonomous swimming robot which consists of several round floats linked together to form a two-dimensional structure. In this robot, each float is a single, identical agent, and the robot proposed in this study is comprised of three such agents. Because each agent has an actuator attached to one side, a dummy float is required at one end of the chain of agents. Being thus constrained, each agent can move only with cooperation between itself and its neighboring agents.

Fig.1: Whole view of the swimming robot (3 Agents)

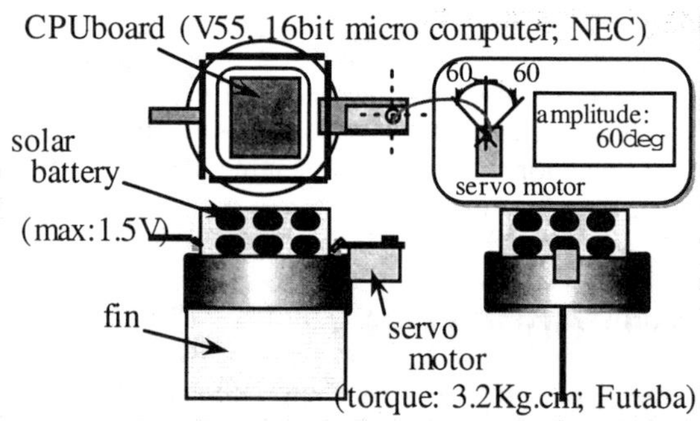

Fig.2: Construction of the agent

Each agent has a CPU located inside the float, four sensors (solar batteries) arranged in a square on the float, and an actuator (servo motor) which is suited at the point of connection between the agents. Furthermore, each agent can exchange local information it has gathered using 2-channel serial ports. In the future, the solar batteries will also serve to make the robot self-sufficient in terms of power supply. However, the amount of power produced by them at present isn't enough to drive the robot; therefore, the robot is actually driven by battery cells.

4 TASK - TARGET APPROACHING -

The task assigned to the robot in the behavior acquiring experiment is to approach a light source, as illustrated in Fig. 3A. Having sensed the presence of a light source that was set in the 2.6m× 2.6m pool, the robot was required to learn how to move toward the light source by the cooperation of its component agents. In experiments, the number of steps in each trial were unlimited, and the trial only stopped when the robot reached the goal as shown in Fig. 3B. The starting area of the robot was the same corner in each trial. There were, however, slight differences in the direction of the robot and in the water current. The target was always placed in the corner diagonally opposite the robot.

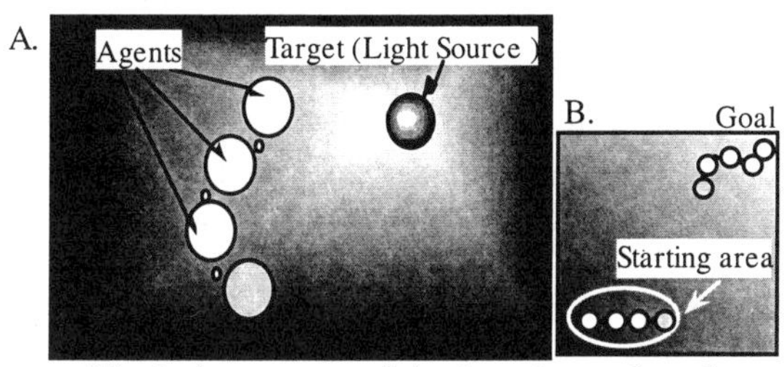

Fig.3: A, concept of the learning task and B, the starting and the completed states

5 DECISION MAKING METHOD

As reported in our previous papers (Iijima et al., 1998), the adaptive oscillator method was adopted as the decision-making method for the DARS. In order for the swimming robot to acquire the behavior necessary to complete its task, this method was also applied in the present study. This proposed method can be expressed as

$$g(\sum_n k_n \frac{d^n}{dt^n} y^n) + f(S) = e, \quad \cdots\cdots\cdots\cdots (1)$$

where

y : solution of equation(1), i.e., action that agent outputs

k_n : coefficient toward differentiated y^n, the weight of n-dimensional value

$g()$:function to transform outputs of the differential calculator term

S : input vector including all sensory inputs and decision-making factors (the energy acquired by the outputted action of AOM is also component of this input vector)

$f()$:function to transform all external inputs

e : internal energy where the agent keeps the value constant

In equation (1), the first term on the left side is a differential calculating term that enables the system to reflect the effects of long-term, high-dimensional derivatives because it is constructed as an AR (autoregressive)-related model. Hence, the system's next action is determined according to time sequential data involving the effect on inertia. On the other hand, the second term on the left side is an external-effect-inputted-term, and the right side of the equation is the internal energy of the agent. Thus, it is assumed that energy management can be realized through a comparison of the external energy and internal energy levels. In addition, in this system it is also desirable that all parameters and functions are autonomously adjusted through the learning process.

In this study, an oscillation pattern based on a sine function was assigned to the action of the robot. In the case that this equation can represent a sine function, it is thought that the differential calculating term is transformed as follows. That is, in the term, y is replaced with x, instead, the whole this term is y. After that, k_1 is 1, k_2 is 0, k_3 is -1/3!, k_4 is 0, k_5 is 1/5!, $\cdots$. Thus, we have the following equation:

$$y = x - \frac{x^3}{3!} + \frac{x^5}{5!} - \frac{x^7}{7!} \cdots$$
$$= \sin x \quad \cdots\cdots\cdots\cdots (2)$$

Equation (2) is a sine function. In a previous study, we introduced a TD (temporal difference)-based NN learning scheme into this decision-making method (Iijima et al., 1998). However, little progress was made in the learning process within a reasonable real time. Thus, in the present study we employed Q-learning (Watkins and Dayan, 1993), which is an approximate dynamic programming method in that it only performs value updating based on current experience, while decision making is based on local information. This fast step-by-step value updating and decision making can reduce the sequential effect of the watery environment to a rational level. If the learning environment is based on the Markov Decision Process (Christman and Littman, 1995), it can be guaranteed that learning will proceed continuously, then consequently, resulting in the successful acquisition of target-approaching behavior.

6 EXPERIMENTS

6.1 EXPERIMENTAL SETTINGS

To build a Q-table, it is necessary to divide the sensory input received by the agents into states. Further, for efficient learning, it is desirable that the number of such states is as small as possible. In this experiment, we defined a sensing state as follows. As shown in Fig. 4, we first numbered the left, front, right and rear sensors on each agent as 1, 2, 3 and 4, respectively. The sensor which received the largest input represented the state for that agent. In this way, the number of states for each agent was restricted to four. Thus, as shown in Fig. 4, if sensor 3 receives the largest input, the state for that agent is 3 (hereafter expressed as S:3). It is unclear whether this compression way of the sensing state is most appropriately, but we regarded it as the most basic idea. The state for the robot model is expressed as a combination of the states of the three agents.

On the other hand, it is also desirable that action patterns are design so as to make the robot learn easily. Here, action patterns should be defined so as to enable the robot to move straight forward or backward, forward and to the right or left, and backward and to the right or left if all agents cooperate in selecting the appropriate action (about this appropriate action, see below Fig. 9). For this purpose, in this study, we preset a oscillating action pattern, especially based on a sine function, which were shown to be effective in enabling floating objects to move in a watery environment, as the elementary action patterns.

Twelve elementary action patterns, generated by synthesizing the patterns shown in Fig. 5, were preset in each agent. Effective motion was made possible through the combination of these elementary action patterns. Variations in the action pattern could be achieved by varying the center angle of the oscillation and the phase. The amplitude was set from -30 to +30 degrees, three center angles were set at -30, 0, +30 degrees, and four phases were set at 0, $\pi/2$, π, and $3\pi/2$. Thus, from Fig. 5, if the oscillation center angle of the chosen action is +30 degrees and the phase of the action is π, the action would be represented by actions 3-* and *-4 (hereafter expressed as A:3-4). Executing term of each oscillation motion per one action is two periods.

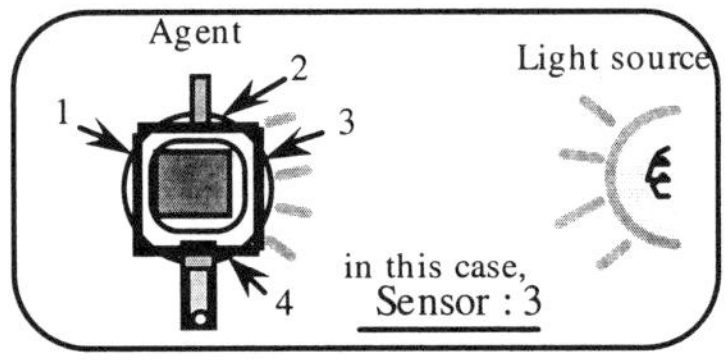

Fig. 4 : Definition of sensing states

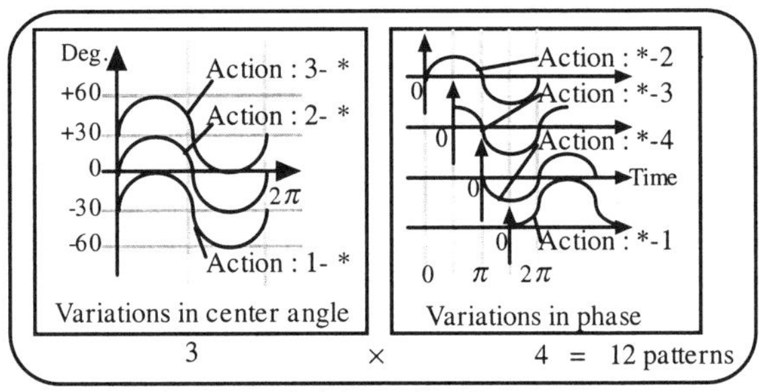

Fig.5 : Definition of action patterns

To update the Q-value, equation (3) is used. For action selection, the Boltzmann exploration dependent on equation (4) was implemented. Here, x_t and a_t are the state and the action of the robot at time t, and $Q(x_t, a_t)$ is the Q-value at that time. α is the learning rate and is set on 0.1, and γ is the discounting rate and is set in 0.95, as a general setting. T is the thermal parameter which decides the randomness of the action and r_t is the reward value. In the present experiments, when the robot reached the goal, r_t was given as 100.

$$\Delta Q(x_t, a_t) = \alpha(r_t + \gamma \max_b Q(x_{t+1}, b) - Q(x_t, a_t)), \qquad \text{(3)}$$

$$P(a \mid x) = \frac{\exp(Q(x,a)/T)}{\Sigma \exp(Q(x,a)/T)}. \qquad \text{(4)}$$

The Q-value was constructed as follows. In order to construct a distributed control system, it is necessary for each agent to observe the state of its neighboring agents. It is thought that each agent should know as much as possible about the state of its neighboring agents in order to guarantee controllability. However, the state space will increase dramatically as the number of attributes observed increase. In this study, we constructed the Q-value using only the sensing states of the neighboring agents (it should be noted that agent 2 has two neighbors, while agent 1 and 3 have only one neighbor each). Consequently, the Q-value is set as follows:

$$Q((\underset{Agent:left}{Sensor_t}, \underset{Agent:self}{Sensor_t}, \underset{Agent:right}{Sensor_t}), Action_t)$$

The size of the state space of the Q-table obtained from this setting is $((4 \times 4 \times 4) \times (3 \times 4)) = 768$ states. This state space size falls within the processing capabilities of our experimental robot. As it was judged preferable that the thermal parameter T should be $\fallingdotseq 2.0$ in the experiments using robots with centralized control, we implemented in the case $T = 2.0$, and in the twice case $T = 4.0$.

6.2 EXPERIMENTAL RESULTS

A dark bold line in Fig. 6 shows the number of steps needed to reach to the light source in 200 trials. From the initial to about the one-hundredth trial, the robot needed an average of 40 steps to reach the goal, though a considerable difference can be observed between cases. After 100 trials, the number of steps needed to complete the task became relatively stable at about 15 steps.

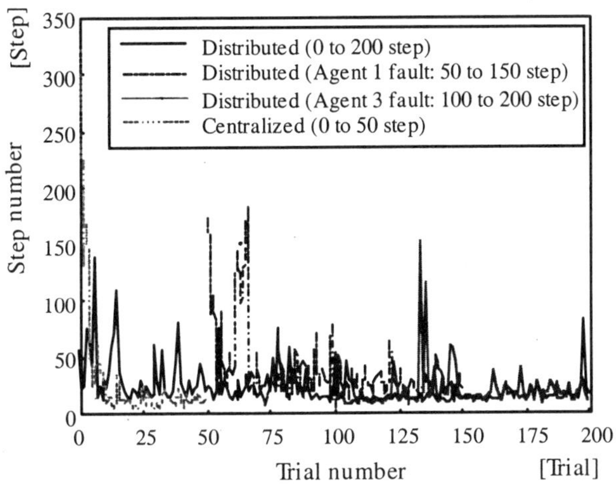

Fig.6 : The number of steps needed to reach the light source

Fig. 7 shows the acquired action patterns and the history of selection probabilities of each action pattern.

The upper part of the figure shows two patterns which enabled the robot to reach the goal. These two action patterns were acquired within about 20 trials from the start of the experiment. The procedure by which the goal was reached was as follows. First, by performing certain actions, the robot arrived in the condition shown in the upper left portion of the figure, referred to as condition 1. In this condition, the sensing states of the robot's three constituent agents (1, 2, and 3) can be expressed as [S:3, S:3, S:3]. The condition shown in the upper portion of the figure (referred to as condition 2) can be expressed as [S:3, S:3, S:2]. If the robot arrived in either condition, the robot could reach the goal by alternatively making right turns (from condition 1) and moving forward and slightly to the left (from condition 2).

Next, looking at the Fig.7 with attending about the connections of each acquired actions, we can observe the process that the action selection probability was reinforced from the action pattern with high expected value to approach to the goal state. Moreover, each reinforced action pattern also influences the selection probability of former patterns. These results confirmed the expected pattern of Q-learning.

The selection probability of the action patterns when the robot's sensing state was [S:3, S:3, S:3] or [S:3, S:3, S:2] increased 100 % at an early stage of the experiment. The selection probability of the action pattern when the robot's sensing state was [S:2, S:1, S:1] increased markedly, and the action pattern became quite decisive after about 130 trials when the robot aimed at the two stable states as subgoals. Sensing states of [S:1, S:1, S:1] and [S:4, S:1, S:1] both achieved selection probabilities of 100 % after about 180 trials. And it took over 200 trials for robot's with sensing states of [S:4, S:1, S:4] and [S:2, S:1, S:4] to reach a 100 % selection probability.

Fig. 8 shows the complete behavior pattern that results from the combination of these acquired action patterns. If the robot was located at the corner of the pool that was diagonally opposite the goal, the robot was seen to move in such a manner as to place itself in either condition 6 or 7. From these conditions the robot maneuvered itself through the various conditions, as shown by the arrows, until it reached its goal.

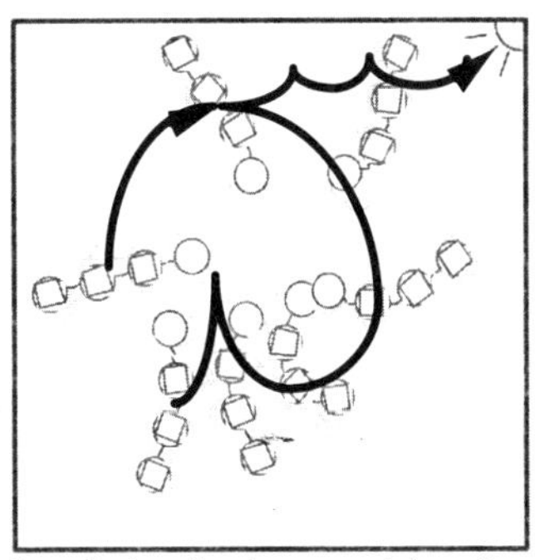

Fig.8: Complete behavior by transitional action patterns

6.3 FAULT-TOLERANCE EXPERIMENTS

Fault-tolerance tests ware also performed. In this experiments, one agent was technically "broken", that is, the agent lost its mobile ability and communicative ability. Two case were studied. In the first experiment, agent 3 (see Fig. 1) was "broken", after 100 trials. In this case, considerably smooth target-approaching behavior was realized in next few trials. The robot reached the goal at about 20 steps after 100 trials learning (see Fig. 6).

In the second experiment, the agent 1 (see Fig. 1) was "broken" after 100 trials, however the robot could hardly reach the goal. This shows the fact that, when the environmental oriented behavior is formed, each agent in DARS plays different role. It may need greater real time which is critical to the real world application to recover from the fault caused by agent 1. So that we decide to perform the environment that the fault happens before the task behavior was completely formed, by shifting the broken point to 50 trials. As the result, the robot ultimately can reach the goal at 30-40 steps after another 100 trials.

6.4 REPLAY EXPERIMENTS OF ACQUIRED ACTIONS

Replay tests of acquired behavior in above experiments were performed using each Q-table. The robot had to reach each goal as it was switched on in turn. The results of these tests were compared with those of a test in which a robot with centralized control performed the same tasks. Because the centralized control experiment was only aimed to be compared, we gave the learning parameters little artifice so as to be learned the objective behavior faster, as shown in Table 1 and Fig. 9. On the Q-value setting, action pattern in $t-1$ step was added to the sensor state so that learning progressed more smoothly, and action patterns were specialized within 6 patterns by which the robot could move successfully. A result of 50 trials centralized control experiment is also shown in Fig. 6.

Table 1: Experimental conditions in centralized control

Sensing states	4 (agent 2's sensor 1, agent 1's sensor 2, agent 2's sensor 3, agent 3's sensor 4
Action patterns	6 (refer to Fig. 7)
Q-value setting	$Q((Action_{t-1}, Sensor_t), Action_t)$
Q-table size	$(6 \times 4) \times 6 = 144$
Each parameter value	$\alpha = 0.1, \gamma = 0.95, T = 1.7$

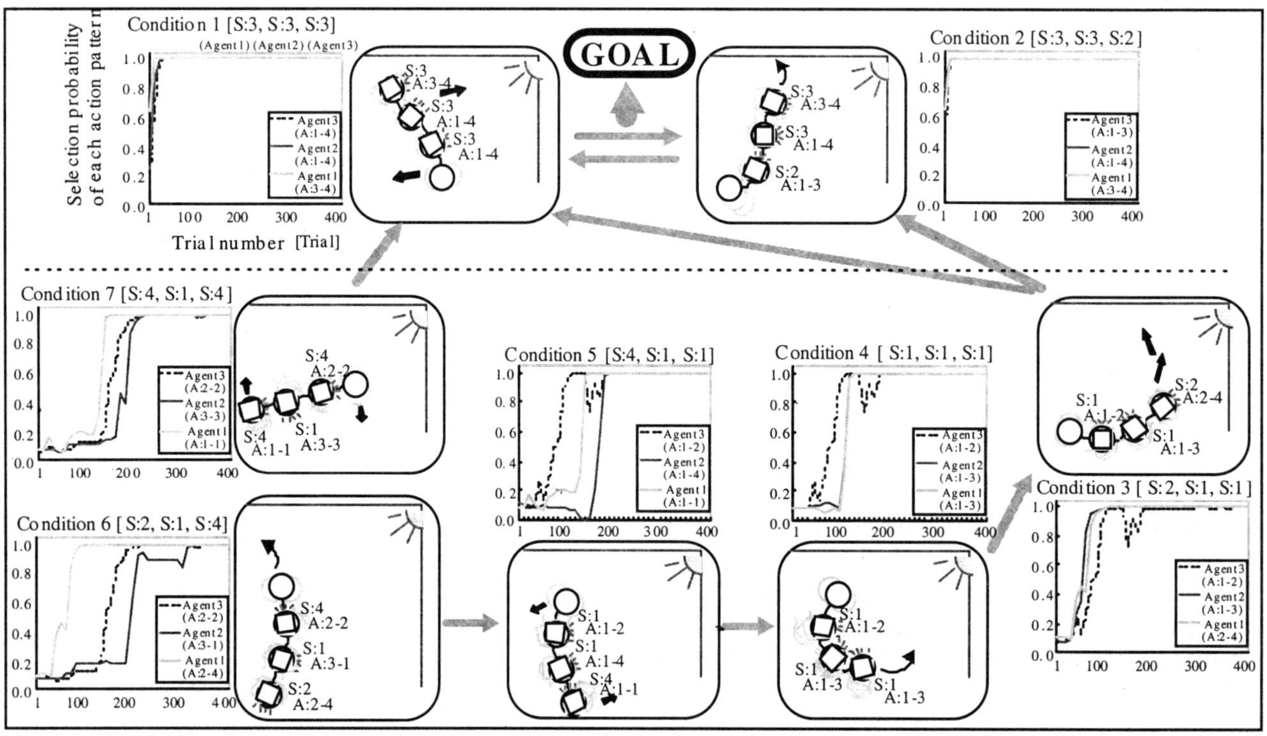

Fig.7 : Acquired action patterns and the history of selection probabilities of each acquired action pattern

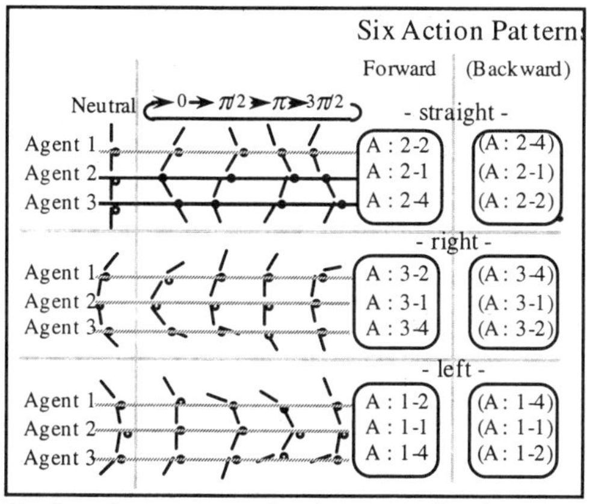

Fig.9 : 6 action patterns for the centralized control experiment

6.5 RESULT OF REPLAY EXPERIMENT

Fig. 10 shows a comparison of the robot's behavior of the two controlling methods including two partially broken cases. Pictures were made by the coordinates of the center of the robot which were processed by a tracking vision system. The target light sources were in the following order: the lower left, upper right, lower right, and upper left of the pool. The initial position of the robot was in the upper right of the pool.

From these figures, we can see that the distributed autonomous robot system acquired the target-approaching behavior equally as efficiently as did the robot with centralized control, even if partial fault has occurred.

7 DISCUSSIONS

With regard to learning efficiency, in this study, we found that behavioral learning was achieved within a relatively short time because of the effect of the oscillation action patterns which had been preliminarily introduced. Fig. 7 shows that the most quickly acquired action pattern was learned within about 20 trials, and that even the most slowly acquired pattern was acquired within about 200 trials. Converting that into time, it took about 5 hours until the convergence of the learning because each step took about 4 seconds and there were a total of 4259 steps in the 200 trials. However, in our previous study, the attainment of behavioral learning took over one week. Thus, the current result shows a great improvement, and suggests the possibility of real-time learning by distributed robots.

Major questions concerning distributed autonomous controlled systems are whether the whole system can obtain behavior as a whole robot by the learning based on the local information, and whether the system can complete

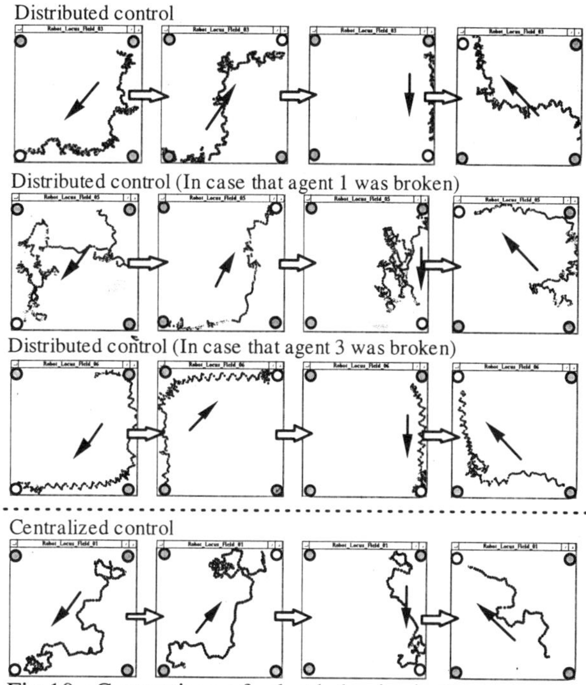

Fig.10 : Comparison of robot behavior in the replay experiment

an objective if any troubles has occurred partially. Fig. 9 shows that, on the basis of the replay experiments, such behavior can be acquired by robots with distributed control as efficiency as that acquired by robots with centralized control, and such behavior can be realized even if one agent has broken.

Moreover, we verified that acquired actions could be adapted to the environment. The acquired behavior in these experiments was not autonomously acquired behavior, however, the generation of behavior from elementary actions and sensing states is also significant the real-world applications. Although, some unexpected action patterns (e.g., the robot used the wall of the pool to aid in propulsion) occurred in the target-approaching sequence, we consider these action patterns to be the result of adaptive learning rather than uncertain patterns with a harmful effect on the search process. As the range, by which the goal could be approached in this experiment was narrow, some specialized action patterns were needed to enable the target to be reached. Actually, the action patterns acquired in case of agent 1's fault ware not action patterns which used friction of the wall. So, the robot often couldn't readily reach the goal. Our experiment clearly demonstrated that the action patterns by which the robot could approach the goal gradually but steadily were generally more suitable to the environment than those action patterns by which the robot could directly approach the goal in less steps but which often resulted in it coming to a standstill.

Additionally, from the selection probabilities of the actions performed when the sensing state was [S:2, S:1, S:1], [S:1, S:1, S:1], and [S:4, S:1, S:1], it is certain that in the relatively early trials, agent 3 chose the action [A:1-2] when its own sensing state was [S:1] and its neighbor's state was also [S:1]. Then, as the trial proceeded other agents were affected by this pattern. Consequently, the action pattern which led to the transition from condition 4 ([S:1, S:1, S:1]) to condition 3 ([S:2, S:1, S:1]) was reinforced; that is, the robot in condition 4 took condition 3 as a sub-goal. After this step, the action pattern for the robot in condition 5 was learned. Thus, the ability to learn at a local level, and the interaction of locally acquired learning, characteristics which were excepted from this system (see section 1), were verified by real-world experiments.

Finally, we have to mention two lessons we learned by the study. First, the oscillation action patterns were basically effective for the fast learning of this kind of robots. Second, from the result of 50-trial centralized control experiment, we learned that it is effective to include previous action (or sensing) information as action decision attribute. These manually decided state space and action space coding schemes took great effect in the current stage of learning. We expected that these elements can also be automatically learned or obtained, therefore, to lead to faster and more appropriate action learning.

8 RELATED WORKS

This study is related to the research of fish or eel like robot. Grillner et al. studies the control of eel like fish. In their research, they applied the mechanism of neural oscillator in eel like fish to engineering, but there is not yet real-world application. As the research on autonomous under water vehicles (AUVs) in real-world, there is study about ROBO-TUNA (Tuohy, Leonard, Bellingham, Patrikalakis, and Chryssostomidis, 1996). They approached a under water navigation problem with physical fish like robot. Their trial of navigation used map information, moreover, their focus of research isn't distributed control. Although there were many studies treating the robot navigation problem as application problems of learning algorithms (Lin, 1993), study by distributed approach is still rare. Canudas et al are challenging a navigation problem for train-like vehicles in nuclear power station(Canudas, NDoudi and Micaelli, 1997). Their approach is similar to our research as regards the structural mechanism, but on processing algorithm, they don't use any learning methods. Hirose has developed a distributed modular-type snake-like robot, "Active Cord-Mechanism" (ACM) (Hirose, 1993), which is structurally similar to our work. ACM has many modular units, by which high flexibility is realized, but their research focused on the bio-mechanisms. About research how multi-robot behave cooperatively by coordination, Kitano et al. approached to a robot soccer problem(Kitano, Asada, Kuniyoshi, Noda, Osawa, and Mathubara, 1997). However, their work didn't address the mechanically constrained robot.

9 CONCLUSIONS

In order to develop an autonomous system capable of adaptive decision-making in the real world, we constructed a distributed autonomous swimming robot that was able to learn target-approaching behavior through the cooperation of its constituent components. For this purpose, we introduced oscillation action patterns as elementary actions to AOM. A simple Q-learning process was adopted as the learning method. As a result, the robot acquired environment-oriented action patterns (by which to actively approach its targets)similar to the acquired action patterns observed in robots with centralized control. Consequently, it was demonstrated that a DARS can acquire collective target-approaching behavior, even if partially fault has occurred. We also observed mutual influence between individual agents, which is a characteristic we had expected to find in distributed autonomous systems. In future, we aim at the construction of an algorithm that can enable the autonomous acquisition of more efficient action patterns and that can make more use of time series information.

References

Floreano, D., and Mondada, F., (1994). Automatic Creation of an Autonomous Agent: Genetic Evolution of a Neural Network Driven Robot, From Animals to Animats, Third International Conference on Simulation of Adaptive Behavior (SAB94) In Cliff, D., Husbands, P., Meyer, J.-A., and Wilson, S. (Eds.), MIT Press, 421-430.

Tani, J., (1996). Model-based Learning for Mobile Robot Navigation from the Dynamical Systems Perspective, IEEE Trans. on System, Man and Cybernetics Part B (Special Issue on Robot Learning), 26(3), 421-436.

Sims, K. (1994). Evolving 3D Morphology and Behavior by Competition, Artificial Life IV Proceedings, R. Brooks and P.Maes (Eds.), MIT Press, 28-39.

Yokoi, H., Mizuno, T., Takita, M., Kakazu, Y., (1994). Amoeba Like Grouping Behavior for Autonomous Robots Using Vibrating Potential Field (Obstacle Avoidance on Uneven Road), Distributed Autonomous Robotic Systems 2, Springer, 209-219.

Iijima, D., Yu,W., Yokoi, H., Kakazu, Y.,(1998). Autonomous Acquisition of Adaptive Behavior for a Distributed Floating Robot Based on the AHC Method. Intelligent Engineering Systems through Artificial Neural Networks, 8, ASME Press, 537-542.

Watkins, C.J.C.H. and Dayan,P.,(1993)., Technical Note:Q-Learning, R.S. Sutton (Eds.), Reinforcement Learning, Kluwer Academic, 55-68.

Christman , L., Littman , M., (1995). Hidden State and Short-Term Memory, Presentation at Reinforcement Learning Workshop, Machine Learning Conference.

Grillner, S., Wallen, P., and Brodin, L., (1991). Neural Network Generating Locomotor Behavior in Lamprey: Circuitry, Transmitters, Membrane properties, and Simulation., Annu. Rev. Neurosci., 14: 169-199.

Tuohy, S. T., Léonard, J. J., Bellingham, J. G., Patrikalakis, N. M., and Chryssostomidis, C. (1996). Map Based Navigation for Autonomous Underwater Vehicles, International Journal of Offshore and Polar Engineering, 6(1).

Lin, L., J., (1993). Scaling Up Reinforcement Learning for Robot Control, Proc. of the Tenth International Conference on Machine learning (ML93), 182-196.

Canudas de W., C., NDoudi-L., A., D., and Micaelli, A., (1997). Nonlinear Control for a Train-like Vehicle, The International Journal of Robotic Research, 16(3), 300-319.

Hirose, S., (1993). Biologically Inspired Robots (Snake-like Locomotor and Manipulator). Oxford University Press.

Kitano, H., Asada, M., Kuniyoshi, Y., Noda, I., Osawa, E., and Mathubara H., (1997). ROBOCUP: A Challenge Problem of AI, AI Magazine, 18: 73-85.

Transductive Inference for Text Classification using Support Vector Machines

Thorsten Joachims
Universität Dortmund, LS VIII
44221 Dortmund, Germany
joachims@ls8.cs.uni-dortmund.de

Abstract

This paper introduces Transductive Support Vector Machines (TSVMs) for text classification. While regular Support Vector Machines (SVMs) try to induce a general decision function for a learning task, Transductive Support Vector Machines take into account a particular test set and try to minimize misclassifications of just those particular examples. The paper presents an analysis of why TSVMs are well suited for text classification. These theoretical findings are supported by experiments on three test collections. The experiments show substantial improvements over inductive methods, especially for small training sets, cutting the number of labeled training examples down to a twentieth on some tasks. This work also proposes an algorithm for training TSVMs efficiently, handling 10,000 examples and more.

1 Introduction

Over the recent years, text classification has become one of the key techniques for organizing online information. It can be used to organize document databases, filter spam from people's email, or learn users' newsreading preferences. Since hand-coding text-classifiers is impractical — or at best costly — in many settings, it is preferable to learn classifiers from examples. It is crucial that the learner be able to generalize well using little training data. A news-filtering service, for example, requiring a hundred days' worth of training data is unlikely to please even the most patient users.

The work presented here tackles the problem of learning from small training samples by taking a *transductive* [Vapnik, 1998], instead of an inductive approach. In the inductive setting the learner tries to induce a decision function which has a low error rate on the whole distribution of examples for the particular learning task. Often, this setting is unnecessarily complex. In many situations we do not care about the particular decision function, but rather that we classify a *given set of examples (i.e. a test set) with as few errors as possible.* This is the goal of transductive inference.

Some examples of transductive text classification tasks are the following. All have in common that there is little training data, but a very large test set.

Relevance Feedback : This is a standard technique in free-text information retrieval. The user marks some documents returned by an initial query as relevant or irrelevant. These compose the training set of a text classification task, while the remaining document database is the test set. The user is interested in a good classification of the test set into those documents relevant or irrelevant to the query.

Netnews Filtering : Each day a large number of netnews articles is posted. Given the few training examples the user labeled on previous days, he or she wants today's most interesting articles.

Reorganizing a document collection : With the advance of paperless offices, companies start using document databases with classification schemes. When introducing new categories, they need text classifiers which, given some training examples, classify the rest of the database automatically.

This paper introduces *Transductive Support Vector Machines* (TSVMs) for text classification. They substantially improve the already excellent performance of SVMs for text classification [Joachims, 1998, Dumais et al., 1998]. Especially for very small training sets, TSVMs reduce the required amount of labeled training data down to a twentieth for some tasks. To facilitate the large-scale transductive learning needed for text classification, this paper also proposes a new algorithm for efficiently training TSVMs with 10,000 examples and more.

2 Text Classification

The goal of text classification is the automatic assignment of documents to a fixed number of semantic categories. Each document can be in multiple, exactly one, or no category at all. Using machine learning, the objective is to learn classifiers from examples which assign categories automatically. This is a supervised learning problem. To facilitate effective and efficient learning, each category is treated as a separate binary classification problem. Each such problem answers the question of whether or not a document should be assigned to a particular category.

Documents, which typically are strings of characters, have to be transformed into a representation suitable for the learning algorithm and the classification task. Information Retrieval research suggests that word stems work well as representation units and that for many tasks their ordering can be ignored without losing too much information. The word stem is derived from the occurrence form of a word by removing case and flection information [Porter, 1980]. For example "computes", "computing", and "computer" are all mapped to the same stem "comput". The terms "word" and "word stem" will be used synonymously in the following.

This leads to an attribute-value representation of text. Each distinct word w_i corresponds to a feature with $TF(w_i, x)$, the number of times word w_i occurs in the document x, as its value. Figure 1 shows an example feature vector for a particular document. Refining this basic representation, it has been shown that scaling the dimensions of the feature vector with their *inverse document frequency* $IDF(w_i)$ [Salton and Buckley, 1988] leads to an improved performance. $IDF(w_i)$ can be calculated from the document frequency $DF(w_i)$, which is the number of documents the word w_i occurs in.

$$IDF(w_i) \doteq log\left(\frac{n}{DF(w_i)}\right) \tag{1}$$

Here, n is the total number of documents. Intuitively,

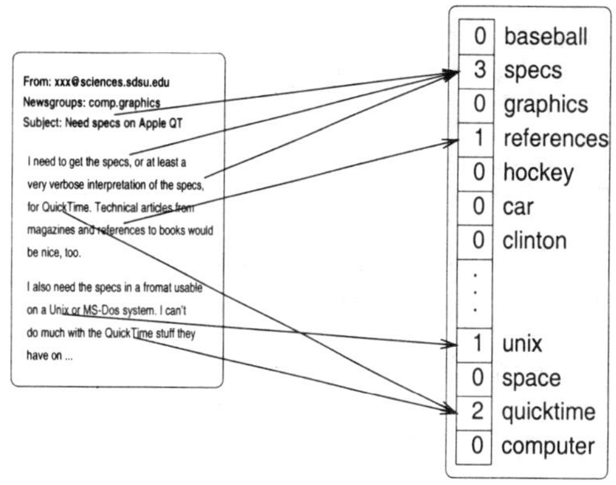

Figure 1: Representing text as a feature vector.

the inverse document frequency of a word is low if it occurs in many documents and is highest if the word occurs in only one. To abstract from different document lengths, each document feature vector $\vec{x}_i$ is normalized to unit length.

3 Transductive Support Vector Machines

The setting of transductive inference was introduced by Vapnik (see for example [Vapnik, 1998]). For a learning task $P(\vec{x}, y) = P(y|\vec{x})P(\vec{x})$ the learner L is given a hypothesis space H of functions $h : X \longrightarrow \{-1, 1\}$ and an i.i.d. sample S_{train} of n training examples

$$(\vec{x}_1, y_1), (\vec{x}_2, y_2), ..., (\vec{x}_n, y_n) \tag{2}$$

Each training example consists of a document vector $\vec{x} \in X$ and a binary label $y \in \{-1, +1\}$. In contrast to the inductive setting, the learner is also given an i.i.d. sample S_{test} of k test examples

$$\vec{x}_1^*, \vec{x}_2^*, ..., \vec{x}_k^* \tag{3}$$

from the same distribution. The transductive learner L aims to selects a function $h_L = L(S_{train}, S_{test})$ from H using S_{train} and S_{test} so that the expected number of erroneous predictions

$$R(L) = \int \frac{1}{k} \sum_{i=1}^{k} \Theta(h_L(\vec{x}_i^*), y_i^*) dP(\vec{x}_1, y_1) \cdots dP(\vec{x}_k^*, y_k^*)$$

on the test examples is minimized. $\Theta(a, b)$ is zero if $a = b$, otherwise it is one. Vapnik [Vapnik, 1998] gives bounds on the relative uniform deviation of training error

$$R_{train}(h) = \frac{1}{n}\sum_{i=1}^{n}\Theta(h(\vec{x}_i), y_i) \tag{4}$$

and test error

$$R_{test}(h) = \frac{1}{k}\sum_{i=1}^{k}\Theta(h(\vec{x}_i^*), y_i^{true}) \tag{5}$$

With probability $1-\eta$

$$R_{test}(h) \leq R_{train}(h) + \Omega(n, k, d, \eta) \tag{6}$$

where the confidence interval $\Omega(n, k, d, \eta)$ depends on the number of training examples n, the number of test examples k, and the VC-Dimension d of H (see [Vapnik, 1998] for details).

This problem of transductive inference may not seem profoundly different from the usual inductive setting studied in machine learning. One could learn a decision rule based on the training data and then apply it to the test data afterwards. Nevertheless, to solve the problem of estimating k binary values $y_1^*, ..., y_k^*$ we need to solve the more complex problem of estimating a function over a possibly continuous space. This may not be the best solution when the size n of the training sample (2) is small.

What information do we get from studying the test sample (3) and how can we use it? The training and the test sample split the hypothesis space H into a finite number of equivalence classes H'. Two functions from H belong to the same equivalence class if they both classify the training and the test sample in the same way. This reduces the learning problem from finding a function in the possibly infinite set H to finding one of finitely many equivalence classes H'. Most importantly, we can use these equivalence classes to build a structure of increasing VC-Dimension for *structural risk minimization* [Vapnik, 1998].

$$H'_1 \subset H'_2 \subset \cdots \subset H' \tag{7}$$

Unlike in the inductive setting, we can study the location of the test examples when defining the structure. Using prior knowledge about the nature of $P(\vec{x}, y)$ we can build a more appropriate structure and learn more quickly. What this means for text classification is analyzed in section 4. In particular, we can build the structure based on the margin of separating hyperplanes on both the training and the test data. Vapnik shows that with the size of the margin we can control the maximum number of equivalence classes (i. e. the VC-Dimension).

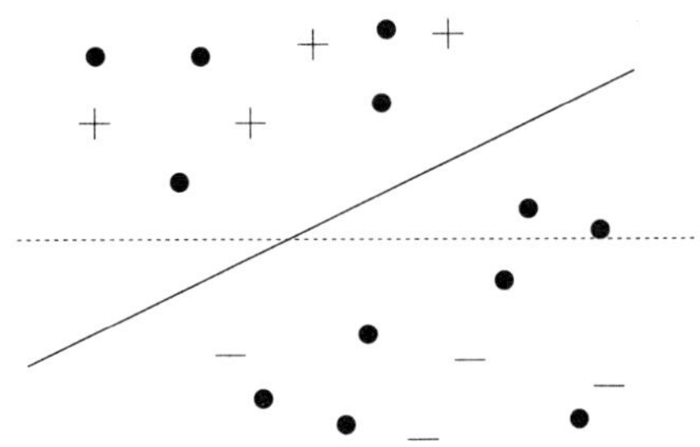

Figure 2: The maximum margin hyperplanes. Positive/negative examples are marked as +/−, test examples as dots. The dashed line is the solution of the inductive SVM. The solid line shows the transductive classification.

Theorem 1 ([Vapnik, 1998])
Consider hyperplanes $h(\vec{x}) = sign\{\vec{x}\cdot\vec{w}+b\}$ as hypothesis space H. If the attribute vectors of a training sample (2) and a test sample (3) are contained in a ball of diameter D, then there are at most

$$N_r < exp\left(d\left(\frac{n+k}{d}+1\right)\right), d = min\left(a, \left[\frac{D^2}{\rho^2}\right]+1\right)$$

equivalence classes which contain a separating hyperplane with

$$\forall_{i=1}^{n}\left|\frac{\vec{w}}{||\vec{w}||}\cdot\vec{x}_i+b\right| \geq \rho \qquad \forall_{j=1}^{k}\left|\frac{\vec{w}}{||\vec{w}||}\cdot\vec{x}_j^*+b\right| \geq \rho$$

(i.e. margin larger or equal to ρ). a is the dimensionality of the space, and $[b]$ is the integer part of b.

Note that the VC-Dimension does not necessarily depend on the number of features, but can be much lower than the dimensionality of the space. Let's use this structure based on the margin of separating hyperplanes. Structural risk minimization tells us that we get the smallest bound on the test error if we select the equivalence class from the structure element H'_i which minimizes (6). For linearly separable problems this leads to the following optimization problem [Vapnik, 1998].

OP 1 (Transductive SVM (lin. sep. case))
Minimize over $(y_1^*, ..., y_n^*, \vec{w}, b)$:

$$\frac{1}{2}||\vec{w}||^2$$

subject to:

$$\forall_{i=1}^{n}: y_i[\vec{w}\cdot\vec{x}_i+b] \geq 1$$
$$\forall_{j=1}^{k}: y_j^*[\vec{w}\cdot\vec{x}_j^*+b] \geq 1$$

Solving this problem means finding a labelling $y_1^*, ..., y_k^*$ of the test data and a hyperplane $< \vec{w}, b >$, so that this hyperplane separates both training and test data with maximum margin. Figure 2 illustrates this. To be able to handle non-separable data, we can introduce slack variables ξ_i similarly to the way we do with inductive SVMs.

OP 2 (Transductive SVM (non-sep. case))
Minimize over $(y_1^*, ..., y_n^*, \vec{w}, b, \xi_1, ..., \xi_n, \xi_1^*, ..., \xi_k^*)$:

$$\frac{1}{2}||\vec{w}||^2 + C\sum_{i=0}^{n}\xi_i + C^*\sum_{j=0}^{k}\xi_j^*$$

subject to:

$$\forall_{i=1}^{n} : y_i[\vec{w} \cdot \vec{x}_i + b] \geq 1 - \xi_i$$
$$\forall_{j=1}^{k} : y_j^*[\vec{w} \cdot \vec{x}_j^* + b] \geq 1 - \xi_j^*$$
$$\forall_{i=1}^{n} : \xi_i > 0$$
$$\forall_{j=1}^{k} : \xi_j^* > 0$$

C and C^* are parameters set by the user. They allow trading off margin size against misclassifying training examples or excluding test examples. How this optimization problem can be solved efficiently is the subject of section 4.1.

4 What Makes TSVMs Especially well Suited for Text Classification?

The text classification task is characterized by a special set of properties. They are independent of whether text classification is used for information filtering, relevance feedback, or for assigning semantic categories to news articles.

High dimensional input space:
When learning text classifiers one has to deal with very many (more than 10,000) features, since each (stemmed) word is a feature.

Document vectors are sparse:
For each document, the corresponding document vector $\vec{x}_i$ contains few entries that are not zero.

Few irrelevant features:
Experiments in [Joachims, 1998] suggest that most words are relevant. So aggressive feature selection has to be handled with care, since it can easily lead to a loss of important information[1].

[1]This does not mean that aggressive feature selection cannot be beneficial for certain learning algorithms or certain tasks (see [Yang and Pedersen, 1997][Mladenič, 1998]).

	nuclear	physics	atom	parsley	basil	salt	and
D1	**1**						**1**
D2	1	1	1				1
D3			1				1
D4				1	1		1
D5				1		1	1
D6					**1**	**1**	**1**

Figure 3: Example of a text classification problem with co-occurrence pattern. Rows correspond to documents, columns to words. A table entry of 1 denotes the occurrence of a word in a document.

Arguments from [Joachims, 1998] show that SVMs are especially well-suited for this setting, outperforming conventional methods substantially while also being more robust. Dumais et al. [Dumais et al., 1998] come to similar conclusions. TSVMs inherit most properties of SVMs so that the same arguments apply to TSVMs as well.

But how can TSVMs be any better? In the field of information retrieval it is well known that words in natural language occur in strong co-occurrence patterns (see [van Rijsbergen, 1977]). Some words are likely to occur together in one document, others are not. For examples, when asking the search engine Altavista about all documents containing the words `pepper` and `salt`, it returns 327,180 web pages. When asking for the documents with the words `pepper` and `physics`, we get only 4,220 hits, although `physics` is a more popular word on the web than `salt`. Many approaches in information retrieval try to exploit this cluster structure of text (see [van Rijsbergen, 1977]). And it is this co-occurrence information that TSVMs exploit as prior knowledge about the learning task.

Let's look at the example in figure 3. Imagine document *D1* was given as a training example for class *A* and document *D6* was given as a training example for class *B*. How should we classify documents *D2* to *D4* (the test set)? Even if we did not understand the meaning of the words, we would classify *D2* and *D3* into class *A*, and *D3* and *D4* into class *B*. We would do so even though *D1* and *D3* do not share any informative words. The reason we choose this classification of the test data over the others stems from our prior knowledge about the properties of text and common text classification tasks. Often we want to classify documents by topic, source, or style. For these type of classification tasks we find stronger co-occurrence patterns within categories than between

Algorithm TSVM:

Input:	– training examples $(\vec{x}_1, y_1), ..., (\vec{x}_n, y_n)$
	– test examples $\vec{x}_1^*, ..., \vec{x}_k^*$
Parameters:	– C,C^*: parameters from OP(2)
	– num_+: number of test examples to be assigned to class +
Output:	– predicted labels of the test examples $y_1^*, ..., y_k^*$

$(\vec{w}, b, \vec{\xi}, \_) := solve\_svm\_qp([(\vec{x}_1, y_1)...(\vec{x}_n, y_n)], [], C, 0, 0)$;

Classify the test examples using $< \vec{w}, b >$. The num_+ test examples with the highest value of $\vec{w} * \vec{x}_j^* + b$ are assigned to the class + ($y_j^* := 1$); the remaining test examples are assigned to class – ($y_j^* := -1$).

$C_-^* := 10^{-5}$; // some small number

$C_+^* := 10^{-5} * \frac{num_+}{k - num_+}$;

while(($C_-^* < C^*$) || ($C_+^* < C^*$)){ // Loop 1

  $(\vec{w}, b, \vec{\xi}, \vec{\xi}^*) := solve\_svm\_qp([(\vec{x}_1, y_1)...(\vec{x}_n, y_n)], [(\vec{x}_1^*, y_1^*)...(\vec{x}_k^*, y_k^*)], C, C_-^*, C_+^*)$;

  while($\exists m, l : (y_m^* * y_l^* < 0) \& (\xi_m^* > 0) \& (\xi_l^* > 0) \& (\xi_m^* + \xi_l^* > 2)$) { // Loop 2

    $y_m^* := -y_m^*$; // take a positive and a negative test

    $y_l^* := -y_l^*$; // example, switch their labels, and retrain

    $(\vec{w}, b, \vec{\xi}, \vec{\xi}^*) := solve\_svm\_qp([(\vec{x}_1, y_1)...(\vec{x}_n, y_n)], [(\vec{x}_1^*, y_1^*)...(\vec{x}_k^*, y_k^*)], C, C_-^*, C_+^*)$;

  }

  $C_-^* := min(C_-^* * 2, C^*)$;

  $C_+^* := min(C_+^* * 2, C^*)$;

}

return($y_1^*, ..., y_k^*$);

Figure 4: Algorithm for training Transductive Support Vector Machines.

different categories. In our example we analyzed the co-occurrence information in the test data and found two clusters. These clusters indicate different topics of $\{D1, D2, D3\}$ vs. $\{D4, D5, D6\}$, and we choose the cluster separator as our classification. Note again that we got to this classification by studying the location of the test examples, which is not possible for an inductive learner.

The TSVM outputs the same classification as we suggested above, although all 16 dichotomies of $D2$ to $D5$ can be achieved with linear separators. Assigning $D2$ and $D3$ to class A and $D3$ and $D4$ to class B is the maximum margin solution (i.e. the solution of optimization problem OP1). We see that the maximum margin bias reflects our prior knowledge about text classification well. By analyzing the test set, we can exploit this prior knowledge for learning.

4.1 Solving the Optimization Problem

Training a transductive SVM means solving the (partly) combinatorial optimization problem OP2. For a small number of test examples, this problem can be solved optimally simply by trying all possible assignments of $y_1^*, ..., y_k^*$ to the two classes. However, this approach become intractable for test sets with more than 10 examples. Previous approaches using branch-and-bound search [Wapnik and Tscherwonenkis, 1979] push the limit to some extent, but still lag behind the needs of the text classification problem. The algorithm proposed next is designed to handle the large test sets common in text classification with 10,000 test examples and more. It finds an approximate solution to optimization problem OP2 using a form of local search.

The key idea of the algorithm is that it begins with a labeling of the test data based on the classification of an inductive SVM. Then it improves the solution by switching the labels of test examples so that the objective function decreases. The algorithm takes the training data and the test examples as input and outputs the predicted classification of the test examples. Besides the two parameters C and C^*, the user can specify the number of test examples to be assigned to class +. This allows trading-off recall vs. precision (see section 5.2). The following description of the algorithm covers only the linear case. A generalization to non-linear hypothesis spaces using kernels is straightforward.

The algorithm is summarized in figure 4. It starts with training an inductive SVM on the training data and classifying the test data accordingly. Then it uniformly increases the influence of the test examples by incrementing the cost-factors C^*_- and C^*_+ up to the user defined value of C^* (loop 1). The algorithm uses unbalanced costs C^*_- and C^*_+ to better accomodate the user defined ratio num_+. While the criterion in the condition of loop 2 identifies two examples for which changing the class labels leads to a decrease in the current objective function, these examples are switched.

The function *solve_svm_qp* refers to quadratic programs of the following type.

OP 3 (Inductive SVM (primal))
Minimize over $(\vec{w}, b, \vec{\xi}, \vec{\xi}^*)$:

$$\frac{1}{2}||\vec{w}||^2 + C\sum_{i=1}^{n}\xi_i + C^*_-\sum_{j:y^*_j=-1}\xi^*_j + C^*_+\sum_{j:y^*_j=1}\xi^*_j$$

subject to: $\forall_{i=1}^{n} : y_i[\vec{w}\cdot\vec{x_i} + b] \geq 1 - \xi_i$
$\forall_{j=1}^{k} : y^*_j[\vec{w}\cdot\vec{x_j} + b] \geq 1 - \xi^*_j$

This optimization problem can be solved in its dual formulation using SVM^{light} [Joachims, 1999][2]. Especially designed for text classification, SVM^{light} can efficiently handle problems with many thousand support vectors, converges fast, and has minimal memory requirements. Let's finally look at an algorithmic property of the algorithm before evaluating its performance empirically in section 5.

Theorem 2 *Algorithm 1 converges in a finite number of steps.*

Proof: To prove this, it is necessary to show that loop 2 is exited after a finite number of iterations. This holds since the objective function of optimization problem OP2 decreases with every iteration of loop 2 as the following argument shows. The condition $y^*_m y^*_l < 0$ in loop 2 requires that the examples to be switched have different class labels. Let $y^*_m = 1$ so that we can write

$$\frac{1}{2}||\vec{w}||^2 + C\sum_{i=0}^{n}\xi_i + C^*_-\sum_{j:y^*_j=-1}\xi^*_i + C^*_+\sum_{j:y^*_j=1}\xi^*_i$$

$$= \frac{1}{2}||\vec{w}||^2 + C\sum_{i=0}^{n}\xi_i + ... + C^*_+\xi^*_m + ... + C^*_-\xi^*_l + ...$$

$$> \frac{1}{2}||\vec{w}||^2 + C\sum_{i=0}^{n}\xi_i + ... + C^*_-(2-\xi^*_m) + ... + C^*_+(2-\xi^*_l) + ...$$

$$= \frac{1}{2}||\vec{w}||^2 + C\sum_{i=0}^{n'}\xi_i + ... + C^*_-\xi^{*'}_m + ... + C^*_+\xi^{*'}_l + ...$$

It is easy to verify that the constraints of OP2 are fulfilled for the new values of y^*_m, y^*_l, $\xi^{*'}_m$, and $\xi^{*'}_l$ (potentially, after setting negative $\xi^{*'}_m$ or $\xi^{*'}_m$ to zero). The inequality holds due to the selection criterion in loop 2, since $\xi^{*'}_m = max(2 - \xi^*_m, 0) < \xi^*_l$ and $\xi^{*'}_l = max(2 - \xi^*_l, 0) < \xi^*_m$. This means that loop 2 is exited after a finite number of iterations, since there is only a finite number of permutations of the test examples. Loop 1 also terminates after a finite number of iterations, since C^*_- is bounded by C^*. □

5 Experiments

5.1 Test Collections

The empirical evaluation is done on three test collection. The first one is the Reuters-21578 dataset[3] collected from the Reuters newswire in 1987. The "ModApte" split is used, leading to a corpus of 9,603 training documents and 3,299 test documents. Of the 135 potential topic categories only the most frequent 10 are used, while keeping all documents. Both stemming and stop-word removal are used.

The second dataset is the WebKB collection[4] of WWW pages made available by the CMU text-learning group. Following the setup in [Nigam et al., 1998], only the classes `course`, `faculty`, `project`, and `student` are used. Documents not in one of these classes are deleted. After removing documents which just contain the relocation command for the browser, this leaves 4,183 examples. The pages from Cornell University are used for training, while all other pages are used for testing. Like in [Nigam et al., 1998], stemming and stop-word removal are not used.

The third test collection is taken from the Ohsumed corpus[5] compiled by William Hersh. From the 50,216 documents in 1991 which have abstracts, the first 10,000 are used for training and the second 10,000 are

[2] Available at http://www-ai.cs.uni-dortmund.de/svm_light

[3] Available at http://www.research.att.com/~lewis/reuters21578.html

[4] Available at http://www.cs.cmu.edu/afs/cs/project/theo-20/www/data

[5] Available at ftp://medir.ohsu.edu/pub/ohsumed

	Bayes	SVM	TSVM
earn	78.8	91.3	95.4
acq	57.4	67.8	76.6
money-fx	43.9	41.3	60.0
grain	40.1	56.2	68.5
crude	24.8	40.9	83.6
trade	22.1	29.5	34.0
interest	24.5	35.6	50.8
ship	33.2	32.5	46.3
wheat	19.5	47.9	54.4
corn	14.5	41.3	43.7
average	35.9	48.4	60.8

Figure 5: P/R-breakeven point for the ten most frequent Reuters categories using 17 training and 3,299 test examples. Naive Bayes uses feature selection by empirical mutual information with local dictionaries of size 1,000. No feature selection was done for SVM and TSVM.

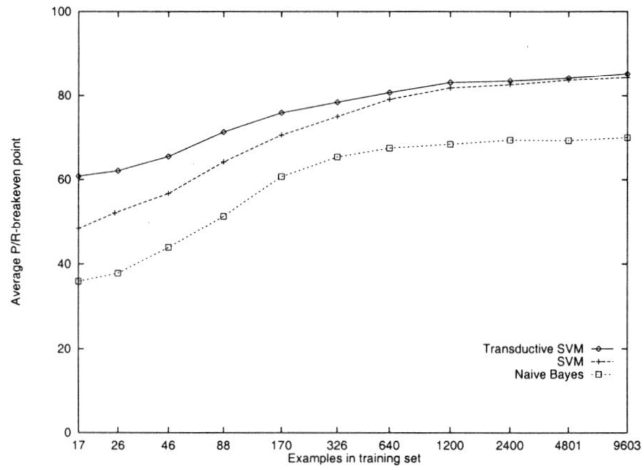

Figure 6: Average P/R-breakeven point on the Reuters dataset for different training set sizes and a test set size of 3,299.

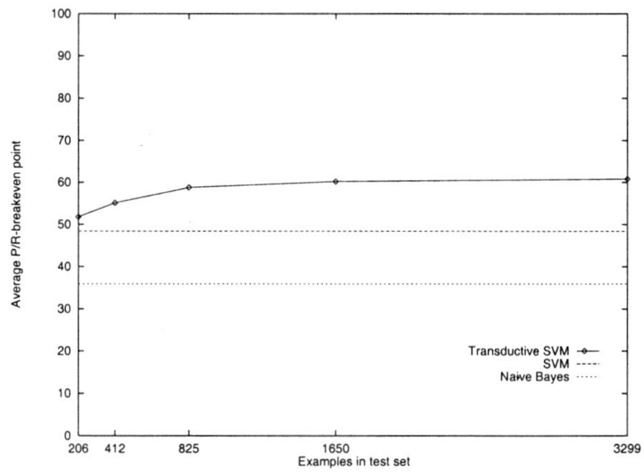

Figure 7: Average P/R-breakeven point on the Reuters dataset for 17 training documents and varying test set size for the TSVM.

used for testing. The task is to assign documents to one or multiple categories of the 5 most frequent MeSH "diseases" categories. A document belongs to a category if it is indexed with at least one indexing term from that category. Both stemming and stop-word removal are used.

5.2 Performance Measures

Since for both the Reuters dataset and the Ohsumed collection documents can be in multiple categories, the *Precision/Recall-Breakeven Point* is used as a measure of performance. The P/R-breakeven point is a common measure for evaluating text classifiers. It is based on the two well know statistics *recall* and *precision* widely used in information retrieval. Precision is the probability that a document predicted to be in class "+" truly belongs to this class. Recall is the probability that a document belonging to class "+" is classified into this class (see [Raghavan et al., 1989]). Both can be estimated from the contingency table.

Between high recall and high precision exists a trade-off. The P/R-breakeven point is defined as that value for which precision and recall are equal. The transductive SVM uses the breakeven point for which the number of false positives equals the number of false negatives. For the inductive SVM and the Naive Bayes classifier the breakeven point is computed by varying the threshold on their "confidence value".

5.3 Results

The following experiments show the effect of using the transductive SVM instead of inductive methods. To provide a baseline for comparison, the results of the inductive SVM and a multinomial Naive Bayes classifier as described in [Joachims, 1997, McCallum and Nigam, 1998] are added. Where applicable, the results are averaged over a number of random training (test) samples.

Figure 5 gives the results for the Reuters dataset. For training sets of 17 documents and test sets of 3,299 documents, the transductive SVM leads to an improved performance on all categories, raising the av-

	Bayes	SVM	TSVM
course	57.2	68.7	93.8
faculty	42.4	52.5	53.7
project	21.4	37.5	18.4
student	63.5	70.0	83.8
average	46.1	57.2	62.4

Figure 8: Average P/R-breakeven points for the WebKB categories using 9 training and 3957 test examples. Naive Bayes uses a global dictionary with the 2,000 highest mutual information words. No feature selection was done for the SVM. Due to the large number of words, the TSVM used only those words which occur at least 5 times in the whole sample.

	Bayes	SVM	TSVM
pathology	39.6	41.8	43.4
Cardiovascular	49.0	58.0	69.1
Neoplasms	53.1	65.1	70.3
Nervous System	28.1	35.5	38.1
Immunologic	28.3	42.8	46.7
average	39.6	48.6	53.5

Figure 9: Average P/R-breakeven points for the Ohsumed categories using 120 training and 10,000 test examples. Here, Naive Bayes uses local dictionaries of 1,000 words selected by mutual information. No feature selection was done for the SVM. The TSVM again uses all words that occur at least 5 times in the whole sample.

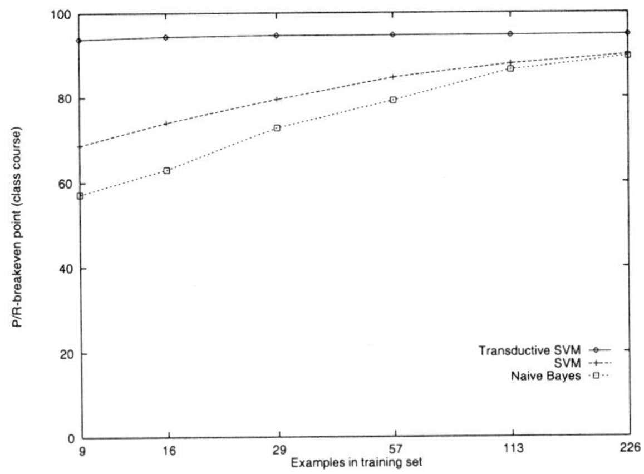

Figure 10: Average P/R-breakeven point on the WebKB category `course` for different training set sizes.

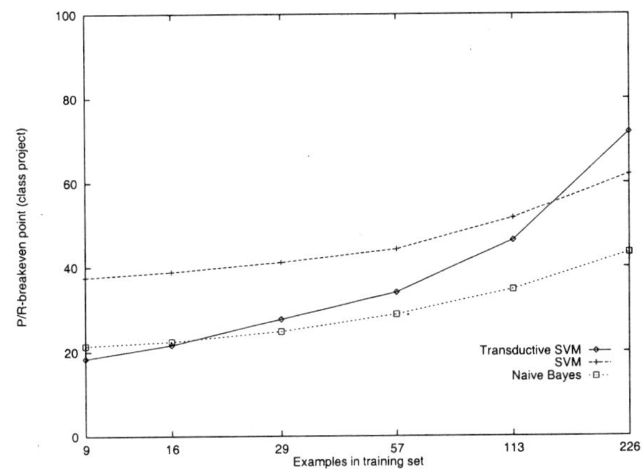

Figure 11: Average P/R-breakeven point on the WebKB category `project` for different training set sizes.

erage of the P/R-breakeven points from 48.4 for the inductive SVM to 60.8. These averages correspond to the left-most points in figure 6. This graph shows the effect of varying the size of the training set. The advantage of using the transductive approach is largest for small training sets. For increasing training set size, the performance of the SVM approaches that of the TSVM. The influence of the test set size on the performance of the TSVM is displayed in figure 7. The bigger the test set, the larger the performance gap between SVM and TSVM. Adding more test examples beyond 3,299 is not likely to increase performance by much, since the graph is already very flat.

The results on the WebKB dataset are similar (figure 8). The average of the P/R-breakeven points increases from 57.2 to 62.4 by using the transductive approach. Nevertheless, for the category `project` the TSVM performs substantially worse, while the gain on the category `course` is large. Let's look at this in more detail. Figures 10 and 11 show how the performance changes with increasing training set size for `course` and `project`. While for `course` the TSVM nearly reaches its peak performance immediately, it needs more training examples to surpass the inductive SVM for `project`. Why does this happen?

First, `project` is the least populous class. Among 9 training examples, there is only one from the `project` category. But more importantly, a look at the project pages reveals that many of them give a description of the project topic. My conjecture is that the margin along this "topic dimension" is large, and so the TSVM tries to separate the test data by topic. Only when there are enough project pages with different topics in the training set, the generalization along the project topic is ruled out. Most course pages at Cornell, on the other hand, do not give much topic information besides the title, but rather link to assignments, lecture notes etc. So the TSVM is not "distracted" by large margins along the topics.

The results in figure 9 for the Ohsumed collection complete the empirical evidence given in this paper, also supporting its point.

6 Related Work

Previously, Nigam et al. [Nigam et al., 1998] proposed another approach to using unlabeled data for text classification. They use a multinomial Naive Bayes classifier and incorporate unlabeled data using the EM-algorithm. One problem with using Naive Bayes is that its independence assumption is clearly violated for text. Nevertheless, using EM showed substantial improvements over the performance of a regular Naive Bayes classifier.

Blum and Mitchell's work on co-training [Blum and Mitchell, 1998] uses unlabeled data in a particular setting. They exploit the fact that, for some problems, each example can be described by multiple representations. WWW-pages, for example, can be represented as the text on the page and/or the anchor texts on the hyperlinks pointing to this page. Blum and Mitchell develop a boosting scheme which exploits a conditional independence between these representations.

Early empirical results using transduction can be found in [Vapnik and Sterin, 1977]. More recently, Bennett [Bennett, 1999] showed small improvements for some of the standard UCI datasets. For ease of computation, she conducted the experiments only for a linear-programming approach which minimizes the L_1 norm instead of L_2 and prohibits the use of kernels. Connecting to concepts of algorithmic randomness, [Gammerman et al., 1998] presented an approach to estimating the confidence of a prediction based on a transductive setting.

7 Conclusions and Outlook

This paper has introduced Transductive Support Vector Machines for text classification. Exploiting the particular statistical properties of text, it has identified that the margin of separating hyperplanes is a natural way to encode prior knowledge for learning text classifiers. By taking a transductive instead of an inductive approach, the test set can be used as an additional source of information about margins.

Introducing a new algorithm for training TSVMs that can handle 10,000 examples and more, this work presented empirical results on three test collections. On all data sets the transductive approach showed improvements over the currently best performing method, most substantially for small training samples and large test sets.

There are still a lot of open questions regarding transductive inference and SVMs. Particularly interesting is a PAC-style model for transductive inference to identify which concept classes benefit from transductive learning. How does the sample complexity behave for both the training and the test set? What is the relationship between the concept and the instance distribution? Regarding text classification in particular, is there a better basic representation for text, aligning margin and learning bias even better? Besides questions from learning theory, more research in algorithms for training TSVMs is needed. How well does the algorithm presented here approximate the global solution? Will the results get even better, if we invest more time into search? Finally, the transductive classification implicitly defines a decision rule. Is it possible to use this decision rule in an inductive fashion and will it perform well also on new test examples?

8 Acknowledgements

Many thanks to Katharina Morik for comments on this paper and to Tom Mitchell for the discussion. Thanks also to Ken Lang for providing some of the code. This work was supported by the DFG Collaborative Research Center on Statistics "Complexity Reduction in Multivariate Data" (SFB475).

References

[Bennett, 1999] Bennett, K. (1999). Combining support vector and mathematical programming methods for classification. In Schölkopf, B., Burges, C., and Smola, A., editors, *Advances in Kernel Methods - Support Vector Learning*. MIT-Press.

[Blum and Mitchell, 1998] Blum, A. and Mitchell, T. (1998). Combining labeled and unlabeled data with co-training. In *Annual Conference on Computational Learning Theory (COLT-98)*.

[Dumais et al., 1998] Dumais, S., Platt, J., Heckerman, D., and Sahami, M. (1998). Inductive learning algorithms and representations for text categorization. In *Proceedings of ACM-CIKM98*.

[Gammerman et al., 1998] Gammerman, A., Vapnik, V., and Vowk, V. (1998). Learning by transduction. In *Conference on Uncertainty in Artificial Intelligence*, pages 148–156.

[Joachims, 1997] Joachims, T. (1997). A probabilistic analysis of the Rocchio algorithm with TFIDF for text categorization. In *Proceedings of International Conference on Machine Learning (ICML)*.

[Joachims, 1998] Joachims, T. (1998). Text categorization with support vector machines: Learning with many relevant features. In *European Conference on Machine Learning (ECML)*.

[Joachims, 1999] Joachims, T. (1999). Making large-scale svm learning practical. In Schölkopf, B., Burges, C., and Smola, A., editors, *Advances in Kernel Methods - Support Vector Learning*. MIT-Press.

[McCallum and Nigam, 1998] McCallum, A. and Nigam, K. (1998). A comparison of event models for naive bayes text classification. In *AAAI/ICML Workshop on Learning for Text Classification*. AAAI Press.

[Mladenič, 1998] Mladenič, D. (1998). Feature subset selection in text learning. In *European Conference on Machine Learning (ECML)*, Springer LNAI.

[Nigam et al., 1998] Nigam, K., McCallum, A., Thrun, S., and Mitchell, T. (1998). Learning to classify text from labeled and unlabeled documents. In *Proceedings of the AAAI-98*.

[Porter, 1980] Porter, M. (1980). An algorithm for suffix stripping. *Program (Automated Library and Information Systems)*, 14(3):130–137.

[Raghavan et al., 1989] Raghavan, V., Bollmann, P., and Jung, G. (1989). A critical investigation of recall and precision as measures of retrieval system performance. *ACM Transactions on Information Systems*, 7(3):205–229.

[Salton and Buckley, 1988] Salton, G. and Buckley, C. (1988). Term weighting approaches in automatic text retrieval. *Information Processing and Management*, 24(5):513–523.

[van Rijsbergen, 1977] van Rijsbergen, C. (1977). A theoretical basis for the use of co-occurrence data in information retrieval. *Journal of Documentation*, 33(2):106–119.

[Vapnik, 1998] Vapnik, V. (1998). *Statistical Learning Theory*. Wiley.

[Vapnik and Sterin, 1977] Vapnik, V. and Sterin, A. (1977). On structural risk minimization or overall risk in a problem of pattern recognition. *Automation and Remote Control*, 10(3):1495–1503.

[Wapnik and Tscherwonenkis, 1979] Wapnik, W. and Tscherwonenkis, A. (1979). *Theorie der Zeichenerkennung*. Akademie Verlag, Berlin.

[Yang and Pedersen, 1997] Yang, Y. and Pedersen, J. (1997). A comparative study on feature selection in text categorization. In *International Conference on Machine Learning (ICML)*.

Efficient Non-Linear Control by Combining Q-learning with Local Linear Controllers

Hajime Kimura*
Tokyo Institute of Technology
gen@fe.dis.titech.ac.jp

Shigenobu Kobayashi
Tokyo Institute of Technology
kobayasi@dis.titech.ac.jp

Abstract

This paper presents a new approach to reinforcement learning (RL) to solve a non-linear control problem efficiently in which state and action spaces are continuous. In real-world applications, an approach combining discrete RL methods with linear controllers is promising since there are many non-linear control problems that can be decomposed into several local linear-control tasks. We provide a hierarchical RL algorithm composed of local linear controllers and Q-learning, which are both very simple. The continuous state-action space is discretized into an array of coarse boxes, and each box has its own local linear controller as an abstract action. The higher-level of the hierarchy is a conventional discrete RL algorithm that chooses the abstract actions. Each linear controller improves the local control policy by using an actor-critic method. The coarse state-space discretization is a quite simple way to cope with the curse of dimensionality, but often gives rise to non-Markovian effects. In our approach, the local linear controllers make up for these undesirable effects. The algorithm was applied to a simulation of a cart-pole swing-up problem, and feasible solutions are found in less time than those of conventional discrete RL methods.

1 Introduction

Many DP-based reinforcement learning (RL) algorithms approximate the value function and give a greedy policy with respect to the learned value function. Theoretical results guarantee that several DP-based algorithms will find optimal policies (e.g. [Watkins et.al 92], [Jaakkola et al. 93], [Tsitsiklis et al. 97], etc.) and a great deal of effort has been made on the techniques to approximate value functions (e.g., CMAC, Neural-Net [Lin 93]). However, it is too expensive to fit highly accurate value functions, particularly in continuous state-action spaces. To overcome this problem, several techniques are proposed (e.g., Parti-game [Moore 95], Coarse grids +environment models +search techniques [Davies et al. 98], interpolation on a coarse grid [Davies 96]). On the other hand, it is shown that a local gradient-ascent search over stochastic policy-space is possible without explicitly computing value or gradient estimates [Williams 92], [Kimura et al. 95], [Kimura et al. 98]. That is to say, the DP-based RL methods have features of a global search in terms of optimality and computational expense, and the gradient RL methods have a feature of a local search. This paper presents a new model-free approach that bridges a gap between DP-based methods and local gradient-ascent methods.

In real-world applications, an approach combining discrete RL methods with linear controllers is promising since there are many non-linear control problems that can be decomposed into several local linear control tasks. Based on this principle, we provide a new algorithm with the key ideas including:

- A hierarchical RL method composed of Q-learning and local linear controllers, which are both very simple.
- Generalization techniques for continuous state-action spaces: *coarse discretization* for the high-level of the hierarchy, and *local continuous-vector* representation for the low-level linear controllers.
- A policy improvement algorithm for the local linear controllers with imperfect value functions.

The coarse state-space quantization is a quite simple

* Interdisciplinary Graduate School of Science and Engineering, Tokyo Institute of Technology, 4259 Nagatsuta Midori-ku Yokohama 226–8502 JAPAN.

way to cope with the curse of dimensionality. But in many cases, it often gives rise to undesirable non-Markovian effects. In our approach, local linear controllers, which use a continuous-vector for the local state representation, make up for these effects.

Although hierarchical algorithms can often yield sub-optimal solutions, there are significant benefits in learning efficiency, search space, and re-use of knowledge [Singh 92], [Kaelbling 93], [Dietterich98], [Sutton et al. 98], [Parr et al. 98]. In general, the low-level of the hierarchy is composed of learning control modules that represent subtasks or abstract actions. Each subtask is defined in terms of termination conditions, and the low-level module is to find a local optimal policy. The RL techniques for discrete semi-Markov decision processes (SMDPs) would be applied to learning of the high-level module that selects a low-level modules as abstract action. In our approach, the low-level modules correspond to linear controllers.

Actor-critic methods [Barto et al. 83] are often used for learning on the linear controllers [Gullapalli 92], [Doya 96]. Generic actor-critic methods can be classified into a local gradient-ascent method with respect to policy space by using learned value functions. But in our hierarchy, the linear controllers cannot hold accurate value functions on account of practical limitations on the computational resources. Fortunately, it is shown that an actor-critic algorithm using eligibility traces in the actor can improve its stochastic policy even though the estimated value function is inaccurate [Kimura et al. 98]. We take advantage of this method for the local policy improvement.

This paper is structured as follows. First, we review the basic notion of RL and control problems in continuous state dynamic systems. In Section 3 we introduce the generalization techniques for continuous state-action spaces and the hierarchical algorithm combining Q-learning with linear controllers. Section 4 presents behavior of the algorithm through simulations of a cart-pole swing-up task. In Section 5, we summarize the paper and discuss some directions of combining other methods for future work.

2 Problem Formulation

2.1 Markov Decision Processes

At each discrete time t, the agent observes x_t containing information about its current state, select action a_t, and then receives an instantaneous reward r_t resulting from state transition in the environment. In general, the reward and the next state may be random, but their probability distributions are assumed to depend only on x_t and a_t in Markov decision processes (MDPs), in which many reinforcement learning algorithms are studied. In MDPs, the next state y is chosen according to the transition probability p^a_{xy}, and the reward is given randomly according to the expectation r^a_x. but the agent does not know p^a_{xy} and r^a_x ahead of time. The objective of reinforcement learning is to construct a policy that maximizes the agent's performance. A natural performance measure for infinite horizon tasks is the cumulative discounted reward:

$$V_t = \sum_{k=0}^{\infty} \gamma^k \, r_{t+k} \, , \tag{1}$$

where the discount factor, $0 \leq \gamma < 1$ specifies the importance of future rewards, and V_t is the value on time t. In MDPs, the value can be defined as:

$$V^{\pi}(x) = E_{\pi} \left[\sum_{k=0}^{\infty} \gamma^k \, r_k | x_0 = x \right] \, , \tag{2}$$

where E_π denotes the expectation assuming the agent always uses stationary policy π. The objective in MDPs is to find an optimal policy that maximizes the value of each state x defined by Equation 2. In MDPs, The optimal value of taking action a in state x, denoted $Q^*(x,a)$, satisfies the Bellman equations for all x and a:

$$Q^*(x,a) = r^a_x + \gamma \sum_y p^a_{xy} \max_{a'} Q^*(y,a') \tag{3}$$

2.2 A Non-Linear Control Problem

We are given learning control of non-linear dynamic systems in which :

- State and action spaces are continuous and multidimensional.
- The task could be decomposed into several local linear or bang-bang control tasks.
- The agent does not know dynamics of the environment ahead of time.

Throughout the paper, we use a cart-pole swing-up task for the example.

3 Combining Q-learning with Local Linear Controllers

3.1 Hierarchical Decomposition

In our approach, the agent adopts hierarchical state representation. The higher-level of the hierarchy uses discrete representation of the state variables by coarse quantization. Representative points are situated at the center of the grid's boxes. Each box has its own local linear controllers as discrete abstract actions, that is, the controllers in a particular box are differently initialized.

Assume that given a n-dimensional state input $(x_1, x_2, \cdots x_n)$ and the corresponding box (B_i) with the representative point at $(b_1^i, b_2^i, \cdots b_n^i)$, then the low-level linear controller gets a local continuous input

$$C = (c_1, c_2 \cdots c_n) = (x_1 - b_1^i, x_2 - b_2^i, \cdots, x_n - b_n^i) \ . \ (4)$$

Figure 1 shows an example of the state representation in which the state space is two-dimensional.

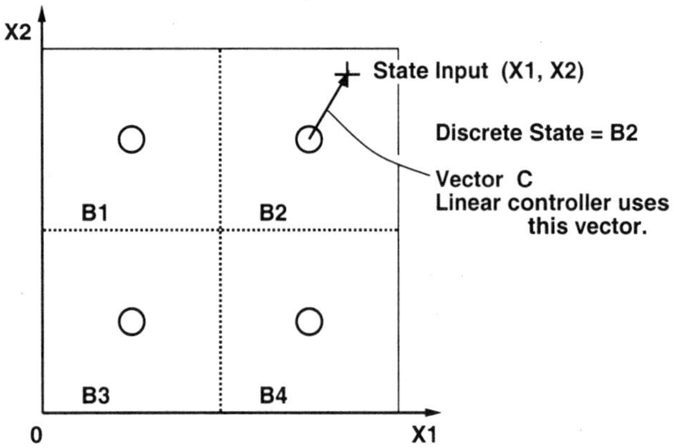

Figure 1: An example of the hierarchical state representation in a 2-dimensional task. Small circles at the center of the grid's boxes denote its representative points.

3.2 Event-driven Decision Making

In dynamic control, an optimal policy often selects the same action (or holds similar continuous action) for a certain period of time. Then, uniform regions are likely to exist in the state space where all of the states have the same (or similar) optimal action. In our approach, the coarse grids approximate the uniform regions. The high-level decision maker selects abstract action each time when the continuous state input is going across the boundary of the box, or a certain period of time passes. This model of abstract action can be seen as an extension of Markov options [Sutton et al. 98] in which the policy is given by linear control and the termination condition is given by the boundary of the box.

Figure 2 helps to define the big-steps that the high-level learner takes. If all the linear controllers hold stationary policy, the high-level learner is to solve a semi-Markov decision problem.

When a linear controller (option) o is taken, then primitive actions are selected according to its linear control rule π^o until the next decision making occurs on the high-level hierarchy. In this paper, we will use the following notation based on [Sutton et al. 98]. Let $\pi^o(x)$

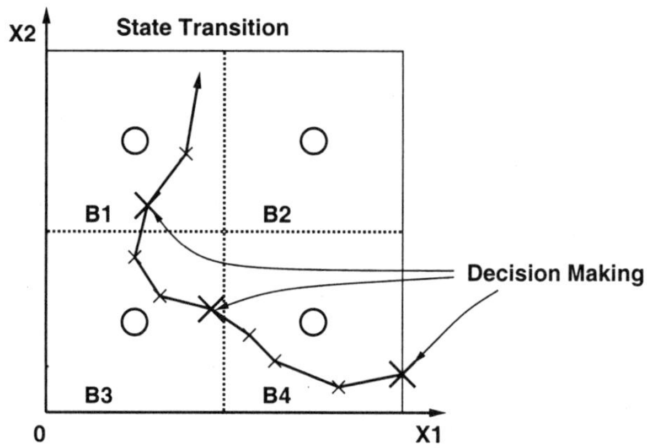

Figure 2: The big-steps on the high-level learner. This modeling is closely related to semi-Markov decision processes (SMDPs). The high-level decisions are only allowed at events which occur whenever the state transition goes across the boundary of the box, or a certain period of time passes.

be the primitive action taken in state x according to o. Assume that current o terminates at next time step according to the probability $T(x, a)$, where $a = \pi^o(x)$. Then, we can define the optimal option-value function recursively by

$$\begin{aligned} Q^*(x, o) &= r_x^a + \gamma(1 - T(x, a)) \left(\sum_y p_{xy}^a Q^*(y, o) \right) \\ &\quad + \gamma T(x, a) \left(\sum_y p_{xy}^a \max_{o'} Q^*(y, o') \right), (5) \end{aligned}$$

where $a = \pi^o(x)$. If all states x, y are discrete and π^o is stationary, then Equation 5 can be solved by Intra-Option value learning [Sutton et al. 98]. Unfortunately, the state spaces are continuous and it is too expensive to learn the accurate value function. In the next section, we will present a new method that uses Q-values averaged in the coarse regions.

3.3 A Learning Algorithm

Figure 3 gives an overview of the hierarchical algorithm. The high-level decision maker accumulates Q-values using tables with one entry for each box-option pair. In this case, each box-option value (or box value) $Q(B_i, o)$ and $V(B_i)$ represent approximation of averaged values weighted by the visiting frequency over the coarse regions, i.e., $V(B_i) \simeq \sum_{x \in B_i} U^\pi(x) V^\pi(x)$, and $Q(B_i, o) \simeq \sum_{x \in B_i} U^\pi(x) Q^*(x, o)$, where B_i denotes the box, $U^o(x)$ denotes the probability of occupying state x under the policy π. The learner also accumulates state value $V(B_i)$. Unfortunately, this value function does not satisfy Bellman equations in

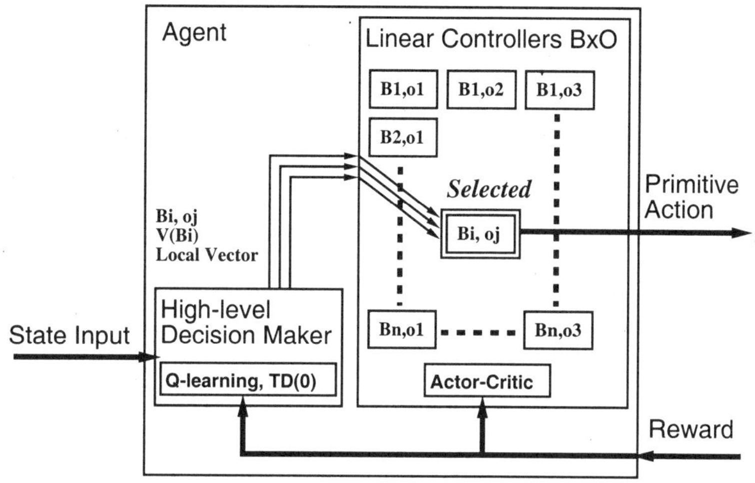

Figure 3: The hierarchical structure of the algorithm. $B_1, B_2, \cdots B_i \cdots B_n$ denote the state boxes, and every small rectangle labeled "B_*, o_*" denotes a linear controller. In this figure, a particular box B_i has three controllers which are differently initialized.

the strict sense. However, we try to provide a good approximation algorithm.

Assume that the agent selects o_t at time t in the region $B(t)$ and makes next decision at time $t+k+1$ in the region $B(t+k+1)$. Then we approximate values at each time by:

$$\begin{aligned} E\{V_t^\pi\} &\simeq E\{r_t + \gamma r_{t+1} + \gamma^2 r_{t+2} \cdots + \gamma^k r_{t+k}\} \\ &\quad + \gamma^{k+1} V(B(t+k+1)), \\ E\{V_{t+1}^\pi\} &\simeq E\{r_{t+1} + \gamma r_{t+2} + \gamma^2 r_{t+3} \cdots + \gamma^{k-1} r_{t+k}\} \\ &\quad + \gamma^k V(B(t+k+1)), \\ &\vdots \\ E\{V_{t+k}^\pi\} &\simeq E\{r_{t+k}\} + \gamma V(B(t+k+1)). \end{aligned}$$

We approximate the value of the box B_i according to averaging these values:

$$V(B_i) = \frac{1}{k+1}\left(V_t^\pi + V_{t+1}^\pi \cdots + V_{t+k}^\pi\right). \quad (6)$$

Then, the TD-error for $V(B)$ in the high-level module is given by

$$\text{TD-error} = \frac{1}{k+1}\left(\sum_{i=0}^{k} r_{t+i} \sum_{j=0}^{i} \gamma^j\right) + \frac{1}{k+1}\left(\sum_{i=0}^{k} \gamma^{i+1}\right) V(B(t+k+1)) - V(B(t)). \quad (7)$$

This result leads us to the learning algorithm for the high-level module.

A Learning Method for High-Level Module: To estimate box values, the algorithm updates by

$$V(B(t)) \leftarrow V(B(t)) + \alpha_v \text{ (TD-error)}, \quad (8)$$

where α_v is a learning coefficient, and TD-error is given by (7). Similarly, the box-option value is updated by

$$\begin{aligned} Q(B(t), o_t) &\leftarrow Q(B(t), o_t) \\ &+ \alpha_v \left[\frac{1}{k+1}\left(\sum_{i=0}^{k} r_{t+i} \sum_{j=0}^{i} \gamma^j\right)\right. \\ &+ \frac{1}{k+1}\left(\sum_{i=0}^{k} \gamma^{i+1}\right) \max_{o'} Q(B(t+k+1), o') \\ &- \left. Q(B(t), o_t)\right]. \end{aligned} \quad (9)$$

Although this algorithm is ad hoc, it works very well for two reasons:

1. Policies that are greedy for Q-functions are optimal if the Q-functions are a certain degree of approximation [Singh et al. 94], [Heger 96].
2. In our approach, learning in the linear controllers makes up for undesirable effects.

A Learning Method for Linear Controllers: The high-level decision maker selects one of $B \times O$ linear controllers according to some exploration strategy, where B denotes the number of the state boxes, O is the number of possible options per each box. When the state input vector is n-dimensional, the linear controllers have $n+1$ parameters $W = (w_1, w_2, \cdots w_{n+1})$ per dimension of the output vector.

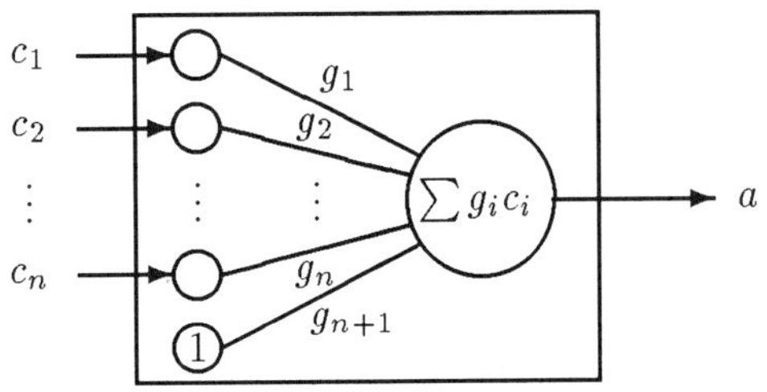

Figure 4: An instanceof the linear controller. g_i denotes a feedback gain which is characterized by w_i according to $g_i = w_i + N(0, \sigma^2)$. The controller learns w_i to achieve good control.

The controllers learn W to make good control. A linear controller o determines its state feedback-gain parameters $(g_1, g_2, \cdots g_{n+1})$ as to the control rule π^o by using W, . After that, primitive actions are selected according to π^o until the termination of the option. The linear controllers adopt an actor-critic architecture to learn feedback-gain parameters. The actor-critic provides continuous action as the feedback-gain, and makes use of $V(B_i)$ for the critic. The output of the critic is too coarse to calculate value gradient from the learned value function, because the approximation function $V(B_i)$ is flat in the same state region. Therefore we adopt a slightly modified actor-critic algorithm using eligibility traces in the actor [Kimura et al. 98], that can improve its policy even though the estimated value function is inaccurate.

Figure 4 shows an instance of the actor-critic algorithm in which the action is of one dimension. In the beginning of the option, the actor selects its feedback-gain parameters $(g_1, g_2, \cdots g_{n+1})$ according to $g_i = w_i + N(0, \sigma^2)$ for all $i = 1, 2, \cdots n+1$, where $N(0, \sigma^2)$ denotes the normal distribution. At each time step $t < t + i \leq t + k$, primitive actions are selected until the termination of the option according to

$$a = c_1 g_1 + c_2 g_2 + \cdots + c_n g_n + g_{n+1} \,, \qquad (10)$$

where $C = (c_1, c_2, \cdots c_n)$ is the local continuous vector at the time $t + i$ as shown in Equation 4. When the option terminates at time $t+k+1$ in the region $B(t+k+1)$, all linear controllers updates according to

$$\begin{aligned} Trace_i &\leftarrow Trace_i + (g_i - w_i) \\ w_i &\leftarrow w_i + \alpha_{ac}\,(\text{TD-error})\,Trace_i \\ Trace_i &\leftarrow \frac{1}{k+1}\Big(\sum_{j=0}^{k} \gamma^{j+1}\Big)\,Trace_i \end{aligned}$$

,where $Trace_i$ denotes an eligibility trace on w_i, and α_{ac} is a coefficient of learning. TD-error is shown in Equation 7. The eligibility of w_i corresponds to $(g_i - w_i)$ that is similar to *Gaussian unit* [Williams 92] and Gullapalli's *neural reinforcement learning unit for continuous action* [Gullapalli 92].

Initial feedback-gain parameters are all set to zero, except that the linear controllers in the same state region have different initial offsets of the primitive actions, i.e., every w_{n+1} are different. Owing to this initializing, the agent can execute various actions even if the linear controllers do not move the parameters at all.

4 Applying to a Cart-Pole Swing-Up Task

The behavior of this algorithm is demonstrated through a computer simulation of a cart-pole swing-up task. We modified the cart-pole problem described in [Barto et al. 83] so that the action is taken to be continuous.

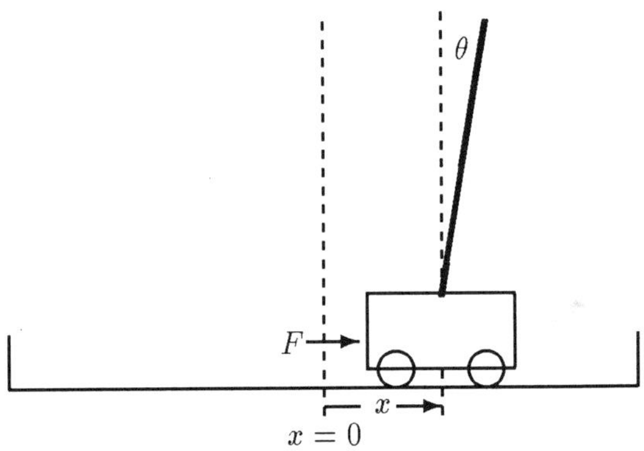

Figure 5: A simulation model of the cart-pole task.

4.1 Details of the Cart-Pole Simulation

The dynamics are modeled by

$$\ddot{\theta} = \frac{g \sin\theta + \cos\theta\left(\frac{-F - m\ell\dot{\theta}^2 \sin\theta + \mu_c sgn(\dot{x})}{M+m}\right) - \frac{\mu_p \dot{\theta}}{m\ell}}{\ell\left(\frac{4}{3} - \frac{m\cos^2\theta}{M+m}\right)} \,,$$

$$\ddot{x} = \frac{F + m\ell\left(\dot{\theta}^2 \sin\theta - \ddot{\theta}\cos\theta\right) - \mu_c sgn(\dot{x})}{M+m} \,,$$

where $M = 1.0$(kg) denotes mass of the cart, $m = 0.1$(kg) is mass of the pole, $2\ell = 1$(m) is the length of the pole, $g = 9.8(m/sec^2)$ is the acceleration of gravity, F(N) denotes the force applied to cart's center of mass, $\mu_c = 0.05$ and $\mu_p = 0.01$ are coefficient of friction of the pole and the cart respectively. In this simulation, we use discrete-time system to approximate these equations, where $\Delta t = 0.02$sec. At each discrete time step, the agent observes $(x, \dot{x}, \theta, \dot{\theta})$, and controls the force F. The agent can execute action in arbitrary range, but the possible action in the cart-pole system is constrained to lie in the range $[-10, 10](N)$. When the agent chooses an action which does not lie in that

range, the action F is saturated. The system begins with $(x, \dot{x}, \theta, \dot{\theta}) = (0, 0, 3.0, 0)$. When the cart collides with the end of the track $(-3.0 \leq x \leq 3.0)$, the cart rebounds from the bumper with a coefficient of rebound 0.2. The agent receives a reward (penalty) signal of
(a) -1 when the pole falls over $\pm 0.8\pi$ (rad),
(b) -4 when the cart bounces at the end of the track,
(c) -3 when $\dot{\theta} < -10$ or $10 < \dot{\theta}$ (rad/sec),
(d) $+1$ when $-0.133\pi < 0.133\pi$ and $-2 < \dot{\theta} < 2$ (rad/sec).

Note that the domain shown here differs from traditional cart-pole tasks in that the environment has no termination condition.

4.2 Implementation

In this experiment, the state space is normalized as $(x, \dot{x}, \theta, \dot{\theta}) = (\pm 3.0 \text{ m}, \pm 10 \text{ m/sec}, \pm \pi \text{ rad}, \pm 10 \text{ rad/sec})$ into $(\pm 0.5, \pm 0.5, \pm 0.5, \pm 0.5)$. The agent discretizes the normalized state space evenly into $3 \times 3 \times 5 \times 5 = 225$ or $3 \times 3 \times 6 \times 6 = 324$ boxes, and attempts to store in each box $V(B_i)$ and $Q(B_i, o)$. Each linear controller accumulates five feedback-gain parameters $w_1, w_2, \cdots w_5$, for the continuous-state input is 4-dimensional. On each state box, the high-level decision maker selects one of 3 (or 4) options. When 3 options are within the box, the initial parameters are set to $w_5 = -1/3$, $w_5 = 0$, $w_5 = 1/3$ respectively. When 4 options are within the box, the initial parameters are set to $w_5 = -3/8$, $w_5 = -1/8$, $w_5 = 1/8$, $w_5 = 3/8$ respectively. In the linear controllers, an action a is generated by Equation 10, where the normal distribution follows $\sigma = 0.5$. Then the force F is executed according to $F = a \times 20$.

The high-level hierarchy makes decision each time when the continuous state input moves to a different box or the state input keeps within the same box for 2 seconds (100 steps). It uses ϵ-greedy exploration strategy, that is, choosing greedy options with probability 0.99^k, where k is the period of time steps on the previous option. The learning rate α_v is set to 0.3 in 3x3x6x6 boxes or to 0.1 in 3x3x5x5 boxes. The learning coefficient of the actor-critic is set to $\alpha_{ac} = 0.01$. The discount rate is set to $\gamma = 0.98$.

4.3 Simulation Results

Figure 6, 9, 12, and 15 show the on-line performance with using different grids and different number of abstract actions. The performance measure is the occupancy rate of the current state in which the system gives positive reward. The rate is calculated by using 20 independent runs. The results show that the proposed methods achieved learning to gain positive rewards. However, Q-learning-only methods in which linear controllers do not learn (i.e., $\alpha_{ac} = 0$) couldn't learn it at all. It is clear that learning on linear controllers has these effects. The increase of the performance with $3 \times 3 \times 5 \times 5$ boxes is better than with $3 \times 3 \times 6 \times 6$ boxes. One reason for this is an effect of decreasing the number of boxes by the coarse discretization. The other is that the location of the boundaries of the boxes fits for this task fortuitously. Since the agents retained the exploration strategy for all learning steps, the performance could not approach to one. Figure 7, 10, 13 and 16 show examples of trajectories on learned greedy policies after 7,200,000 steps (40 hours on simulation time). The policies were feasible, but no agent could obtain optimal swing-up behavior. The reason is that the growth of swing-up behavior is slowed down for decreasing in opportunity of swing-up, because the agent makes progress in keeping the pole vertical.

Figure 8, 11, 14 and 17 show the corresponding state-action flow respectively. The behavior seems to be a mixture of bang-bang control and linear control. Around $\theta = 0$, we should notice that a bang-bang control rule was found by the algorithms with $3 \times 3 \times 6 \times 6$ boxes whereas a linear control rule was found by the algorithms with $3 \times 3 \times 5 \times 5$ boxes. Anyway, the algorithm founds preferable solutions.

Figure 18 and 19 show the on-line performance of conventional Q-learning using 3x3x10x5 and 3x3x12x6 boxes, which are just twice the boxes. The performance is slightly better than that of Q-learning only in Figure 6, 9, 6 and 9, but they could not learn the control to keep the pole standing. The results show that the task is not trivial.

5 Discussion

Evaluation: We cannot conclude superiority of the proposed method, because the complexity of our approach is obviously larger than that of conventional Q-learning in the experiment. The experiment shows that the learning of the local linear controllers can make up for lack of control ability in the high-level decision maker.

Effects of the Partitioning Location: In our test cases, different discretizations led the algorithms to learning quite different control rules, especially around $\theta = 0$. These things make it clear that the shape and location of the quantized regions have great effects on the performance. Joint use of variable-grid methods (e.g. parti-game [Moore 95]), would be needed for generating discrete representation rather than the use of the fixed grid.

Time Intervals of High-level Decision Making: In our approach, time intervals of decision making on

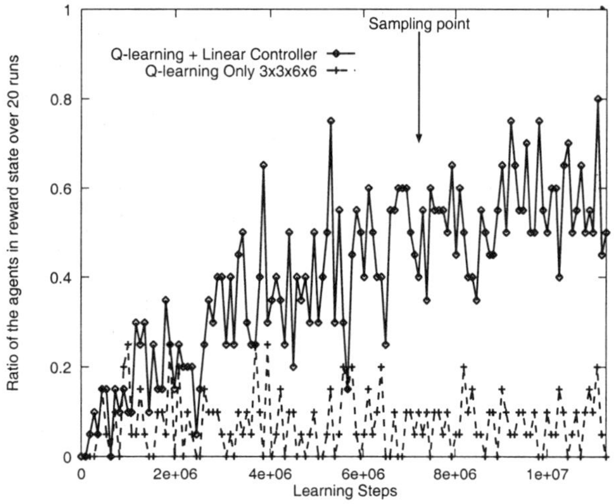

Figure 6: On-line performance using 3x3x6x6 grids and 4 abstract actions.

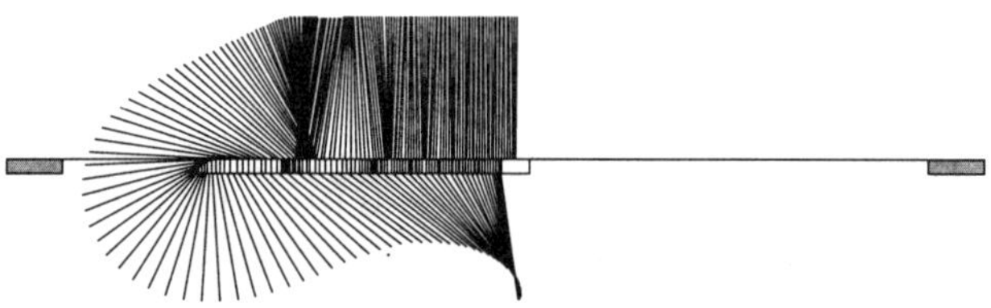

Figure 7: An example of swing-up behavior on 3x3x6x6 grids and 4 actions.

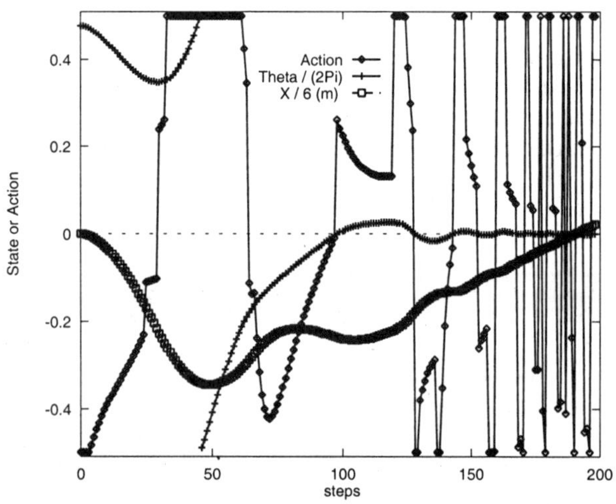

Figure 8: Detail of the behavior.

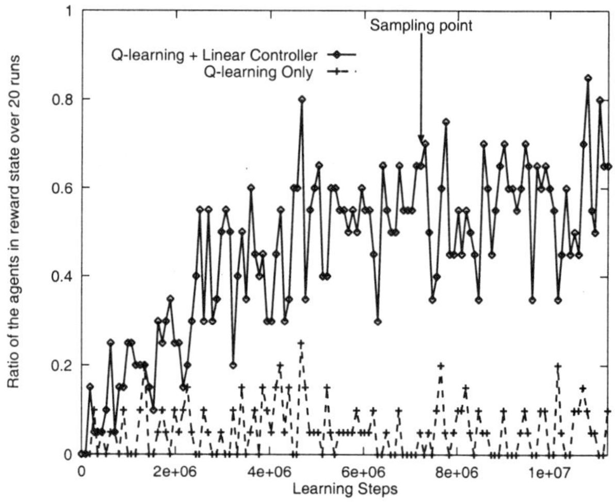

Figure 9: On-line performance using 3x3x6x6 grids and 3 abstract actions.

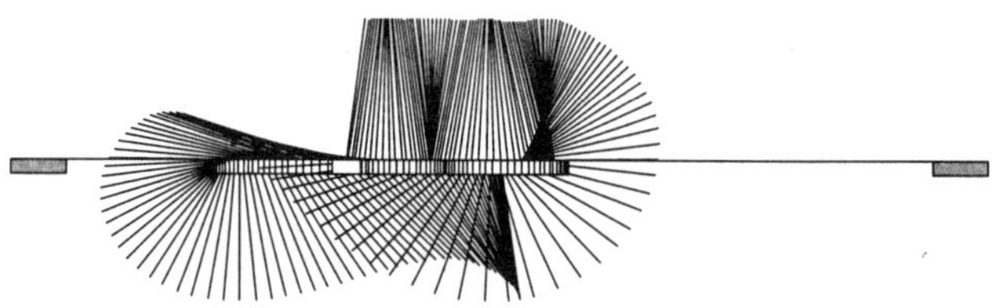

Figure 10: An example of swing-up behavior on 3x3x6x6 grids and 3 actions.

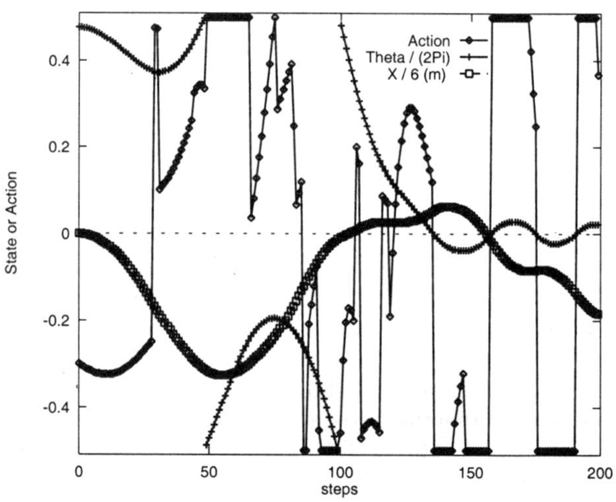

Figure 11: Detail of the behavior.

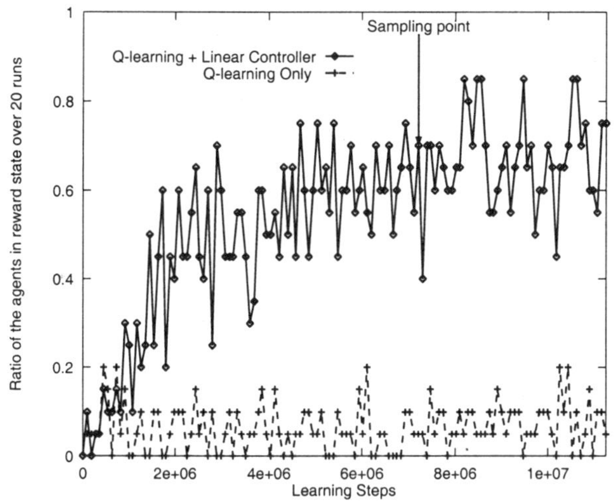

Figure 12: On-line performance using 3x3x5x5 grids and 4 abstract actions.

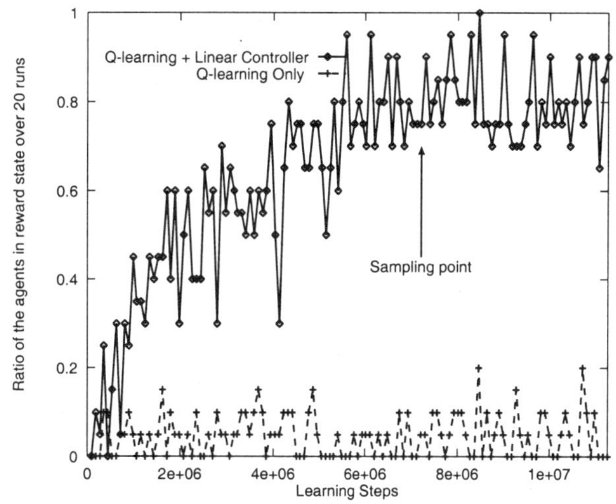

Figure 15: On-line performance using 3x3x5x5 grids and 3 abstract actions.

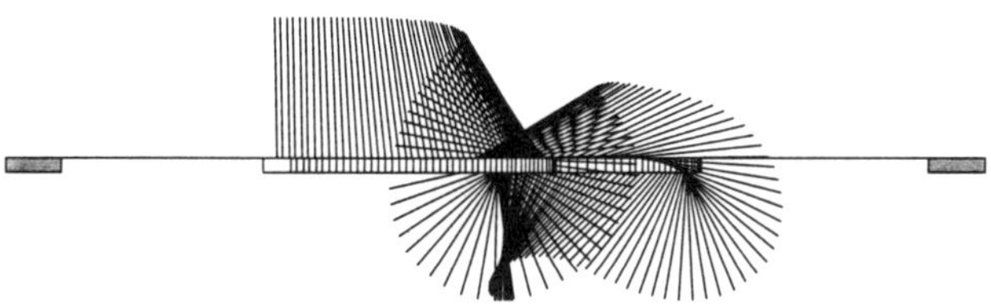

Figure 13: An example of swing-up behavior on 3x3x5x5 grids and 4 actions.

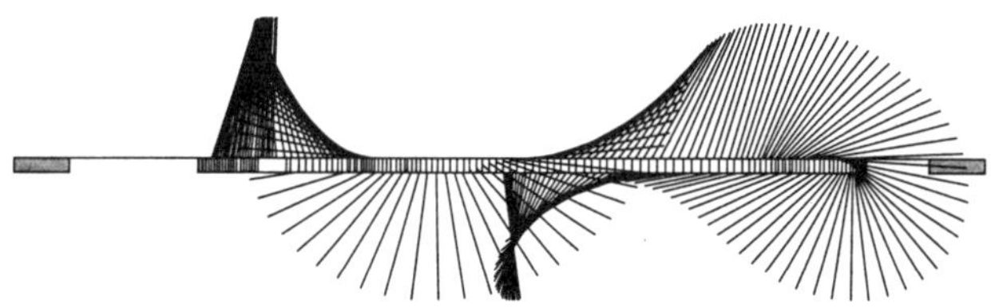

Figure 16: An example of swing-up behavior on 3x3x5x5 grids and 3 actions

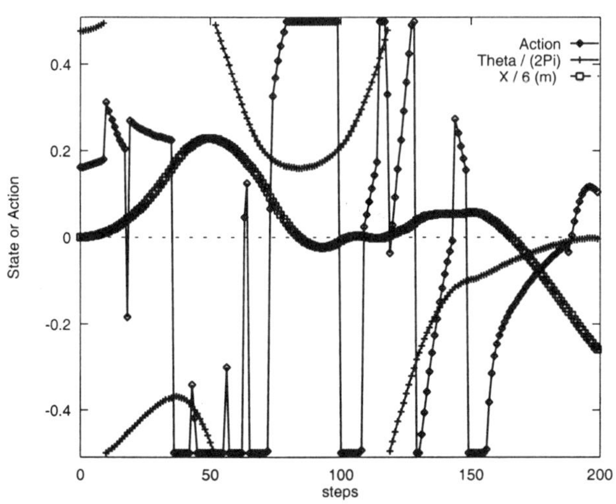

Figure 14: Detail of the behavior.

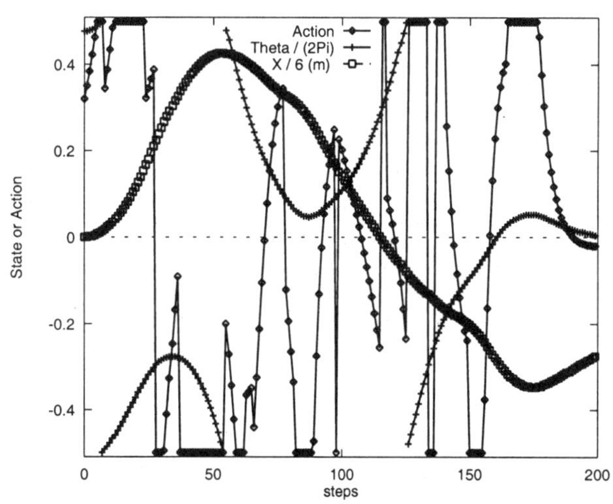

Figure 17: Detail of the behavior.

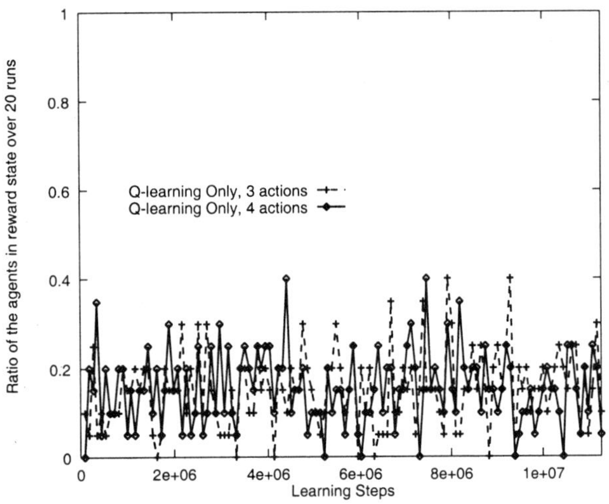

Figure 18: On-line performance of conventional Q-learning using 3x3x10x5 grids and 3 (or 4) abstract actions. It is just twice as many as the boxes in Figure 12 and 15.

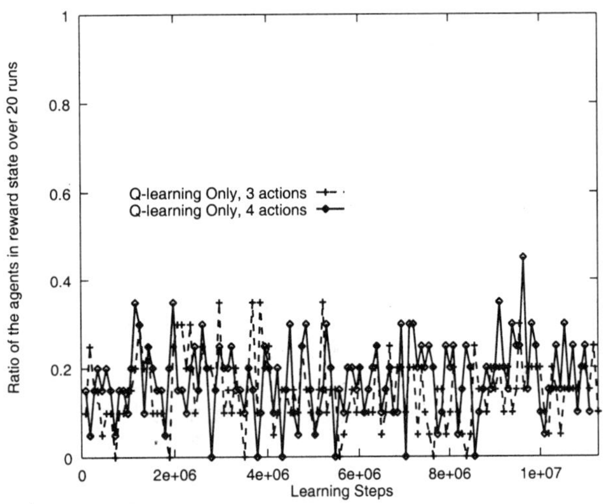

Figure 19: On-line performance of conventional Q-learning using 3x3x12x6 grids and 3 (or 4) abstract actions. It is just twice as many as the boxes in Figure 6 and 9.

the high-level hierarchy are mostly owing to the size of the state boxes. It can be seen as an adaptive choice of time intervals in continuous-time domains [Pareigis 98] [Buckland et al. 93].

Learning with Extremely Coarse Value Approximation: Many DP-based (RL) algorithms are motivated by a desire for finding highly accurate value functions. However, it costs too much memory to approximate such functions in many cases. In contrast, our approach does not stick to finding accurate value functions, because the policy can be improved by a gradient-ascent search without explicitly computing value estimates. However, shown in the experiments, it costs many experiences instead of the memory required in DP-based methods.

Combining with Model-based Methods: Since the proposed algorithm in this paper is a model-free and memory-less method, many model-based methods can make use of it easily. It is interesting to note that [Davies et al. 98] proposed a model-based approach that uses environment models to make up for the poor ability of the value function approximation.

6 Conclusions

This paper presented a hierarchical RL algorithm composed of Q-learning and local linear controllers to solve a non-linear control problem in which state and action spaces are continuous. It is a hybrid method between DP-based value estimation and policy improvement by gradient-ascent without value estimation. The continuous state-action space is discretized into an array of coarse boxes, and roughly the high-level hierarchy estimates the value functions over the discrete space to find a globally preferable policy. The local linear controllers are to improve the policy by stochastic gradient-ascent. This method does not need to fit accurate value functions, therefore it may be promising to overcome the curse of dimensionality. The algorithm was applied to a simulation of a cart-pole swing-up problem, and better solutions are found than those of traditional discrete RL methods.

Acknowledgements

We would like to thank reviewers for many helpful comments and suggestions.

References

[Barto et al. 83] Barto, A. G., Sutton, R. S. and Anderson, C. W.: Neuronlike Adaptive Elements That Can Solve Difficult Learning Control Problems, *IEEE Transactions on Systems, Man, and Cybernetics*, vol. SMC-13, no.5, September/October 1983, pp. 834-846.

[Buckland et al. 93] Buckland, K. M. and Lawrence, P. D.: Transition Point Dynamic Programming, *Advances in Neural Information Processing Systems 6*, pp. 639–646 (1993).

[Davies 96] Davies, S.: Multidimensional Triangulation and Interpolation for Reinforcement Learning, *Advances in Neural Information Processing Systems 9*, pp. 1005-1011 (1996).

[Davies et al. 98] Davies, S., Ng, A. Y. & Moore, A.: Applying Online Search Techniques to Continuous-State Reinforcement Learning, *15th National Conference on Artificial Intelligence*, pp. 753–760 (1998).

[Dietterich98] Dietterich, T. G.: The MAXQ Method for Hierarchical Reinforcement Learning, *Proceedings of the 15th International Conference on Machine Learning*, pp. 118–126 (1998).

[Doya 96] Doya, K. : Efficient Nonlinear Control with Actor-Tutor Architecture, *Advances in Neural Information Processing Systems 9*, pp. 1012–1018 (1996).

[Gullapalli 92] Gullapalli, V.: Reinforcement Learning and Its Application to Control, *PhD Thesis*, University of Massachusetts, Amherst, COINS Technical Report 92-10 (1992).

[Heger 96] Heger, M.: The Loss from Imperfect Value Functions in Expectation-Based and Minimax-Based Tasks, *Machine Learning, 22,*, pp. 197–225 (1996).

[Jaakkola et al. 93] Jaakkola, T., Jordan, M. I. & Singh, S. P.: On the Convergence of Stochastic Iterative Dynamic Programming Algorithms, *Neural Computation 6*, pp.1185–1201 (1993).

[Kaelbling 93] Kaelbling, L. P.: Hierarchical Learning in Stochastic Domains: Preliminary Results, *Proceedings of the 10th International Conference on Machine Learning*, pp. 167–173 (1993).

[Kaelbling et al.96] Kaelbling, L. P., & Littman, M. L., & Moore, A. W.: Reinforcement Learning: A Survey, *Journal of Artificial Intelligence Research*, Vol. 4, pp. 237–277 (1996).

[Kimura et al. 95] Kimura, H., Yamamura, M. and Kobayashi, S.: Reinforcement Learning by Stochastic Hill Climbing on Discounted Reward, *Proceedings of the 12th International Conference on Machine Learning*, pp. 295–303 (1995).

[Kimura et al. 98] Kimura, H. & Kobayashi, S.: An Analysis of Actor/Critic Algorithms using Eligibility Traces: Reinforcement Learning with Imperfect Value Function, *15th International Conference on Machine Learning*, pp.278–286 (1998).

[Lin 93] Lin, L. J.: Scaling Up Reinforcement Learning for Robot Control, *Proceedings of the 10th International Conference on Machine Learning*, pp. 182–189 (1993).

[Lin et al. 96] Lin, C. J. and Lin, C. T.: Reinforcement Learning for An ART-Based Fuzzy Adaptive Learning Control Network, *IEEE Transactions on Neural Networks*, Vol.7, No. 3, pp. 709-731 (1996).

[Moore 95] Moore A. W. & Atkeson, C. G.: The Partigame Algorithm for Variable Resolution Reinforcement Learning in Multidimensional State-spaces, *Machine Learning 21*, pp. 199-233 (1995).

[Pareigis 98] Pareigis, S.: Adaptive choice of grid and time in reinforcement learning, *Advances in Neural Information Processing Systems 10*, pp. 1036–1042 (1998).

[Parr et al. 98] Parr, R. & Russell, S.: Reinforcement Learning with Hierarchies of Machines, *Advances in Neural Information Processing Systems 10*, pp. 1043–1049 (1998).

[Singh 92] Singh, S. P.: Transfer of Learning by Composing Solutions of Elemental Sequential Tasks, *Machine Learning 8*, pp. 323-339 (1992).

[Singh et al. 94] Singh, S. P. and Yee, R. C.: An Upper Bound on the Loss from Approximate Optimal-Value Functions, *Machine Learning, 16*, pp. 227-233 (1994).

[Singh 96] Singh, S. P., & Sutton, R.S.: Reinforcement Learning with Replacing Eligibility Traces, *Machine Learning 22*, pp. 123-158 (1996).

[Sutton 88] Sutton, R. S.: Learning to Predict by the Methods of Temporal Differences, *Machine Learning 3*, pp. 9-44 (1988).

[Sutton 90] Sutton, R. S.: Reinforcement Learning Architectures for Animats, *Proceedings of the 1st International Conference on Simulation of Adaptive Behavior*, pp. 288-295 (1990).

[Sutton et al. 98] Sutton, R. S. & Barto, A.: Reinforcement Learning: An Introduction, *A Bradford Book*, The MIT Press (1998).

[Sutton et al. 98] Sutton, R. S., Precup, D. & Singh, S.: Intra-Option Learning about Temporary Abstract Actions, *Proceedings of the 15th International Conference on Machine Learning*, pp. 556–564 (1998).

[Tsitsiklis et al. 97] Tsitsiklis, J. N., & Roy, B. V.: An Analysis of Temporal-Difference Learning with Function Approximation, *IEEE Transactions on Automatic Control*, Vol.42, No.5, pp. 674–690 (1997).

[Watkins et.al 92] Watkins, C. J. C. H., & Dayan, P.: Technical Note: *Q*-Learning, *Machine Learning 8*, pp. 55-68 (1992).

[Williams 92] Williams, R. J.: Simple Statistical Gradient Following Algorithms for Connectionist Reinforcement Learning, *Machine Learning 8*, pp. 229-256 (1992).

Tractable Average-Case Analysis of Naive Bayesian Classifiers

Pat Langley*(langley@isle.org)
Stephanie Sage (sage@isle.org)
Institute for the Study of Learning and Expertise
2164 Staunton Court, Palo Alto, CA 94306 USA

Abstract

In this paper we present an average-case analysis of the naive Bayesian classifier, a simple induction algorithm that performs well in many domains. Our analysis assumes a monotone 'M of N' target concept and training data that consists of independent Boolean attributes. The analysis supposes a known target concept and distribution of instances, but includes parameters for the number of training cases, the number of irrelevant, relevant, and necessary attributes, the probability of each attribute, and the amount of class noise. Our approach differs from most previous average-case analyses by introducing approximations to achieve computational tractability. This lets us explore the behavioral implications for larger training and attribute sets than the earlier exact analyses, and experimental studies show that the analysis makes very accurate predictions despite its use of approximations. In closing, we suggest promising directions for future research on the average-case analysis of induction.

1 Introduction and Motivation

Typical theoretical analyses of machine learning focus on worst-case results, including those in the 'probably approximately correct' framework (Haussler, 1990). Although this approach lets analysts obtain quite general, distribution-free results, it also means their predictions of learning rate are much slower than those observed in practice. As a result, the link between theory and experiment in machine learning has become tenuous, leading some researchers to explore other paths.

An alternative approach involves the *average-case* analysis of specific induction algorithms on domains with known characteristics. For example, Pazzani and Sarrett (1992) report early results of this sort for a conjunctive learning method, and similar studies have been done for decision stumps (Iba & Langley, 1992), the naive Bayesian classifier (Langley, Iba, & Thompson, 1992), 1-nearest neighbor (Langley & Iba, 1992), and k-nearest neighbor (Okamoto & Nobuhiro, 1997). Each analysis produced predictions about the effect of domain characteristics, averaged over different training sets, that fit experimental data very closely.

However, this theoretical accuracy came with a price. For even simple methods like naive Bayes and nearest neighbor, the calculations needed to predict behavior could take drastically longer than actually running experiments with synthetic data, even when the latter averaged over many training sets. The difficulty resulted from the analyses' reliance on the exact calculation of probabilities for all possible combinations of events. For many induction methods, the number of such events grows exponentially with the number of attributes and size of the training set. This meant that theoretical predictions were only possible for small domains and early parts of the learning curve.

In this paper, we present a more tractable approach to the average-case analysis of induction algorithms. We demonstrate the framework with a new treatment of the naive Bayesian classifier, both because of the growing interest with this simple yet powerful method (e.g., Domingos & Pazzani, 1997) and because our earlier results were especially problematic in computational terms. The new analysis uses many of the same techniques as the previous one, but it introduces approx-

*Also affiliated with the DaimlerChrysler Research & Technology Center, Palo Alto, and the Center for the Study of Language and Information at Stanford University.

imations based on the normal distribution that let us calculate means and variances for the sums and differences of quantities, rather than reasoning about the probabilities of their explicit combinations.[1] The result is a tractable average-case analysis of naive Bayes that, as experimental studies reveal, remains accurate despite its use of approximations.

2 A Brief Review of Naive Bayes

Although it has a long history in pattern recognition (Duda & Hart, 1973), the naive Bayesian classifier first appeared in the machine learning literature as a straw man against which to compare more sophisticated methods (e.g., Cestnik, Konenenko, & Bratko, 1987). Only gradually did researchers become aware of its potential, but now it is widely recognized as a viable and robust approach to supervised induction.

Before beginning the analysis, we should review the manner in which naive Bayes operates. The method represents each class with a single probabilistic summary, each having an associated class probability or base rate, $p(C)$, which specifies the probability that one will observe a member of class C. Every description also includes an associated conditional probability distribution for each attribute. For symbolic domains, on which we will focus here, one typically stores a discrete distribution for each attribute in a description, with each $p(v|C)$ term specifying the probability of value v given an instance of class C.

To classify a new instance I, which is simply a conjunction of attribute values $\bigwedge v_j$, the naive Bayesian classifier applies Bayes' theorem to determine the probability of each description given the instance, giving

$$P(C_i|I) = \frac{P(C_i)P(I|C_i)}{P(I)} = \frac{P(C_i)\prod_{j=1}^{J} P(v_j|C_i)}{\sum_{k=1}^{K} P(C_k)\prod_{j=1}^{J} P(v_j|C_k)} ,$$

where K is the number of classes, J is the number of attributes, and $P(v_j|C_k)$ is the conditional probability for the observed value of attribute j given the class C_k. The product of conditional probabilities comes from the assumption that attributes are independent given the class, which greatly simplifies the computation of the class scores and eases the induction process. After calculating $P(C_i|I)$ for each class, the algorithm assigns the instance to the class with the highest overall score or probability.

Although the above formulation of naive Bayes is the traditional one, we can express the score for each class in another form that is more tractable for analytical purposes. The basic idea is that, if we are concerned only with predictive accuracy, we can invoke any monotonic transformation that does not affect the *ordering* on class scores. One transformation involves removing the denominator, which is the same for each class, and another involves taking the logarithm of the numerator. Together, these produce a new score

$$\mathcal{S}_C = logP(C) + \sum_{atts} logP(v_j|C) .$$

In fact, this form is often used in practice (e.g., Langley & Sage, 1994), since it is efficient to calculate and reduces round-off errors due to small fractions. The new score $\mathcal{S}_C$ is no longer a probability, but is quite sufficient to predict the most probable class.

We should also discuss the estimation of probabilities in this expression. The typical implementation of naive Bayes stores an overall count n, one count k_C for each class, and one count c_j for each attribute value given the class. During training, the induction algorithm increments the overall count on each training instance, increments the class count for each example of that class, and increments the class-specific count for each attribute value that appears in the instance. During performance, the classifier uses these counts to estimate probabilities, giving

$$\mathcal{S}_C = log\left(\frac{k_C}{n}\right) + \sum_{atts} log\left(\frac{c_j}{k_C}\right) .$$

However, if the algorithm has not seen a particular class or an attribute value for some class during learning, a slight problem arises because a count is zero.

Clark and Niblett (1988) dealt with this issue by checking for zero counts and using $\frac{1}{n}$ as the probability when this occurred. A more common approach is to assume 'uniform priors' over both the classes and the values for each attribute, which can be achieved by using the same initial count for each attribute-value pair and their sum for the class count.[2] A common decision is

[1]Golea and Marchand (1993) report an average-case analysis of perceptron learning that also incorporates normal approximations, but their work includes other ideas from statistical mechanics that make it inaccessible to the machine learning community.

[2]The size of these counts reflects the degree to which one believes the prior probabilities they produce, with higher initial counts taking more training data to overcome them. The same approach underlies Cestnik and Bratko's (1991) *m estimate* for balancing prior beliefs and experience.

to initialize counts to 1 for each value, which we will also assume in our analysis. Moreover, since we assume Boolean attributes, we will set the initial count for each class to 2, and since we assume two classes, we will use 4 as the initial total count. This results in prior probabilities of $\frac{1}{2}$ for both classes and for each value given a class.

These decisions about how to initialize counts require a slight revision of the score for each class. Moreover, our assumption that attributes are Boolean lets us store only one count c_j for each attribute, for when it is present in an instance (i.e., has value TRUE). When the attribute is absent from an instance (i.e., has value FALSE), we can simply use $k_C - c_j$ as the count. We can reflect this in the score by separating the contribution for features that are present and absent, giving

$$\begin{aligned} \mathcal{S}_C &= log\left(\frac{k_C+2}{n+4}\right) + \sum_{atts} log\left(\frac{c_j+1}{k_C+2}\right) \\ &+ \sum_{atts} log\left(\frac{k_C-c_j+1}{k_C+2}\right) . \end{aligned}$$

We can also remove the denominator $n+4$ in the first term, since it is the same for both classes. This modified form of the class score will play a central role in our average-case analysis of naive Bayes.

3 Analysis of Classification Accuracy

We will assume that the target concept C is a monotone function of r relevant Boolean attributes that returns TRUE if q or more of these r attributes are present and returns FALSE otherwise. Thus, for a '3 of 5' concept, any instance that has three, four, or five features present is a positive example of the concept. We further suppose that there are i irrelevant Boolean attributes that play no role in the target concept, giving $r+i$ total Boolean features, each of which occurs with probability $P(A)$. We further posit that attributes are independent of each other. For now, we also assume that both training and test data are noise free, though we will return to this issue later.

Given this information, we want to predict the probability $A(n)$ of classifying a test case correctly after naive Bayes has seen n training instances. We can partition this accuracy measure into two components, one dealing with positive test cases and the other with negative test cases. Both terms involve summing over different types of test cases that differ in the number j out of i irrelevant attributes that are present in the case and in the number s out of r relevant attributes that are present. This gives us the expression

$$A(n) = \sum_{j=0}^{i}\sum_{s=q}^{r} T_{j,s}\mathcal{A}^{+}_{j,s}(n) + \sum_{j=0}^{i}\sum_{s=0}^{q-1} T_{j,s}\mathcal{A}^{-}_{j,s}(n) ,$$

where $T_{j,s}$ is the probability of encountering a test case with exactly j out of i irrelevant attributes and exactly s out of r relevant attributes, $\mathcal{A}^{+}_{j,s}(n)$ is the probability of correctly classifying such a test case, and $\mathcal{A}^{-}_{j,s}(n)$ is the analogous term for a negative instance.

Let us first consider the probability of encountering a given type of test case. Because each attribute occurs independently with probability $P(A)$, the number of irrelevant attributes j that appear in a test case follows a binomial distribution with probability of success $P(A)$, as does the number of relevant attributes s that it contains. Taken together, this gives

$$T_{j,s} = B(j,i,P(A)) \cdot B(s,r,P(A)) ,$$

where

$$B(k,r,p) = \binom{r}{k} p^k (1-p)^{r-k} .$$

We multiply the binomial expressions $B(j,i,P(A))$ and $B(s,r,P(A))$ because these two probabilities are independent, with the j irrelevant attributes and the s relevant ones occurring in exactly $\binom{i}{j}$ and $\binom{r}{s}$ different ways, respectively.

Now we can focus on the predictive accuracy $\mathcal{A}^{+}_{j,s}(n)$ for a positive test case in which j irrelevants and s relevants are present. For this, we must average over the various concept descriptions that naive Bayes will acquire from different training sets. We can decompose the accuracies after n training cases into weighted sums of accuracies $A^{+}_{j,s}(k)$ and $A^{-}_{j,s}(k)$ for different numbers of positive instances, giving

$$\mathcal{A}^{+}_{j,s}(n) = \sum_{k=0}^{n} P(c_+ = k) A^{+}_{j,s}(k)$$

and

$$\mathcal{A}^{-}_{j,s}(n) = \sum_{k=0}^{n} P(c_+ = k) A^{-}_{j,s}(k) ,$$

where $P(c_+ = k)$ is the probability that exactly k out of n training instances are positive. Since each training case is independent of the others, the number k follows a binomial distribution, so that we have

$$P(c_+ = k) = B(k,n,P(C)) ,$$

where $P(C)$ is the probability that any given instance will be positive.

Let us now consider the accuracy on a positive test case with j irrelevant attributes and s relevant attributes present, given that naive Bayes has observed k out of n positive training cases. Recall that, for each test case, the Bayesian classifier produces a score for the positive class, which we will call $\mathcal{S}$, and a score for the negative class, which we will call $\bar{\mathcal{S}}$. For a positive test case, the expected accuracy is precisely the probability that $\mathcal{S} > \bar{\mathcal{S}}$. We can restate this relation by defining the difference between these two scores $d = \bar{\mathcal{S}} - \mathcal{S}$, which lets us compute the accuracy $A^{+}_{j,s}(k)$ as the probability $P(d \leq 0)$, to which we now turn.

4 Analysis of Class Scores

As explained earlier, our previous average-case analysis of naive Bayes was computationally intractable because it used the binomial distribution to compute the exact probability for every possible combination of counts for classes and attributes. However, one of the key results in statistics states that, given a reasonable number of samples, one can approximate a binomial distribution with mean μ and variance σ^2 using a normal distribution with the same parameters. Another key idea is that a linear combination of normally distributed variables will also follow a normal distribution. And given a normally distributed variable, one can convert its values into the standard normal distribution $\Phi(x)$, which has a mean of zero and variance of one, and for which one can easily compute the area for any interval.

We will take this latter approach to compute $P(d \leq 0)$, assuming that d follows a normal distribution by reasoning we will explain shortly. This assumption lets us convert d's values into the standard normal form $\Phi(x)$ by subtracting its mean and dividing by its variance, which gives

$$P\left(\frac{d-\mu_d}{\sqrt{\sigma_d^2}} \leq x\right) = \Phi(x) \ .$$

If we let x be $-\mu_d/\sqrt{\sigma_d^2}$, then we have

$$A^{+}_{j,s}(k) = P(d \leq 0) = \Phi\left(\frac{-\mu_d}{\sqrt{\sigma_d^2}}\right) \ ,$$

which we can compute for different values of μ_d and σ_d^2 by approximating the area under the standard normal distribution for a given number of positive training cases k. For each negative test case, we have the same scores s (for the positive class) and $\bar{s}$ (for the negative class), but the expected accuracy on such instances equals the probability that $\bar{\mathcal{S}} > \mathcal{S}$. This occurs when the difference $d > 0$, which is exactly the opposite of the situation we considered above. Thus, we can express the accuracy on negative test cases as

$$A^{-}_{j,s}(k) = P(d > 0) = 1 - \Phi\left(\frac{-\mu_d}{\sqrt{\sigma_d^2}}\right) \ ,$$

which we can again calculate by approximating the area under the standard normal distribution.

However, we have yet to characterize μ_d and σ_d^2, the relevant terms for positive test cases, using more primitive expressions. We can assume that the variable d follows a normal distribution if we can express it as the difference of two other normally distributed variables, say the negative score $\bar{\mathcal{S}}$ and the positive score $\mathcal{S}$. We can also rewrite its mean and variance using those for its components, which gives $\mu_d = \mu_{\bar{\mathcal{S}}} - \mu_{\mathcal{S}}$ and $\sigma_d^2 = \sigma_{\bar{\mathcal{S}}}^2 + \sigma_{\mathcal{S}}^2$.

We can treat the scores $\mathcal{S}$ and $\bar{\mathcal{S}}$ as normally distributed provided we assume they are both sums of variables that are themselves normally distributed. Recall that earlier we expressed the score $\mathcal{S}$ for each class as the sum of logarithms for observed counts, storing only one count c for each Boolean attribute to reflect the number of times it has been present in instances of that class. We can compute the other count, for the number of times it was absent, as $k - c$. We can also decompose the score into different terms for irrelevant and relevant attributes, giving

$$\begin{aligned}\mathcal{S} &= (1-i-r)\cdot log(k+2) \\ &\quad + \sum_{w=0}^{j} log(c_w+1) + \sum_{x=j+1}^{i} log(k-c_x+1) \\ &\quad + \sum_{y=0}^{s} log(c_y+1) + \sum_{z=s+1}^{r} log(k-c_z+1) \ ,\end{aligned}$$

where the first term represents influence from the count for the class, the second from the counts for the j irrelevant attributes present in the test case, the third from the counts for the $i-j$ irrelevant attributes that are absent, and the last two terms from the analogous counts for the s relevant attributes that are present and the $r-s$ ones that are absent. The added constants 1 and 2 come from our earlier decisions about how to initialize various counts.

Again, note that for attributes absent from the test case, the score uses the count for the class *minus* the count for the attribute, since this specifies the number of times it has not been observed. As mentioned earlier, we assume that the count for each attribute is initialized to 1, which conveniently means the minimum log will be 0, but which also agrees with common practice about setting uniform priors. Similarly, we assume that the total count is initialized to 4 and that the count for each class is initialized to 2, since there are two possible values for each attribute.

The counts for each attribute follow a binomial distribution, which means we can approximate them with a normal distribution for large training sets. However, the score uses not the counts themselves but rather a logarithmic transformation of the counts, which clearly does *not* follow a binomial. Nevertheless, since each attribute is independent, the central limit theorem tells us that we can use a normal curve to approximate their distribution. Moreover, we can reexpress the mean and variance for this distribution using the means and variances of the score S's components, giving us

$$\mu_S = (1 - i - r) \cdot log(k+2) + j \cdot \mu_\star + (i-j) \cdot \mu_{\bar\star} + s \cdot \mu_\circ + (r-s) \cdot \mu_{\bar\circ}$$

and

$$\sigma_S^2 = j \cdot \sigma_\star^2 + (i-j) \cdot \sigma_{\bar\star}^2 + s \cdot \sigma_\circ^2 + (r-s) \cdot \sigma_{\bar\circ}^2 ,$$

where $\mu_\star$ is the mean of the log counts for each irrelevant attribute present in the test case, $\mu_{\bar\star}$ is the mean for each irrelevant attribute absent from the test case, $\mu_\circ$ and $\mu_{\bar\circ}$ are the analogous terms for relevant attributes, and the σ^2 terms specify the variances for the various situations.

We must still calculate the means and variances for the log counts of irrelevant and relevant attributes. We do not know any closed-form expressions for these quantities, but we can compute them from their definitions for a given number of positive training cases k. In particular, for any variable x we have $\mu_x = \sum xP(x)$, and we know that the probability of each possible log value is the same as the probability for its corresponding count. Thus, we have

$$\mu_\star = \sum_{m=0}^{k} log(m+1) \cdot B(m, k, P(A_\star|C)) ,$$

where $P(A_\star|C)$ is the probability that an irrelevant attribute will appear in a positive instance. The mean for irrelevant attributes not present in the test case is

$$\mu_{\bar\star} = \sum_{m=0}^{k} log(k-m+1) \cdot B(m, k, P(A_\star|C)) ,$$

since the two differ only in their contributions to the overall score and not in their probabilities. The analogous expressions for relevant attributes, $\mu_\circ$ and $\mu_{\bar\circ}$, are identical except that they replace the conditional probability $P(A_\star|C)$ with the term $P(A_\circ|C)$.

Similar reasoning lets us determine the variances for the different log counts. For any variable x, we have $\sigma_x^2 = [\sum x^2 P(x)] - [\mu_x]^2$. Again, since we know the probability of each possible log value from the probability for its corresponding count, we have

$$\sigma_\star^2 = \left(\sum_{m=0}^{k} log(m+1)^2 \cdot B(m, k, P(A_\star|C)) \right) - \mu_\star^2$$

as the variance for an irrelevant attribute that is present in a positive instance and

$$\sigma_{\bar\star}^2 = \left(\sum_{m=0}^{k} log(k-m+1)^2 \cdot B(m, k, P(A_\star|C)) \right) - \mu_{\bar\star}^2$$

as the variance for an irrelevant feature that is not present in a positive instance. Again, the variances for relevant attributes, $\sigma_\circ^2$ and $\sigma_{\bar\circ}^2$, are the same except that they replace $P(A_\star|C)$ with $P(A_\circ|C)$.

For the negative class, we can decompose the mean $\mu_{\bar s}$ and variance $\sigma_{\bar s}^2$ in the same manner. We will not give details here, but note only that the means and variances for irrelevant and relevant attributes are identical, except that they replace k with $n-k$, $P(A_\star|C)$ with $P(A_\star|\bar C)$, and $P(A_\circ|C)$ with $P(A_\circ|\bar C)$. Combined with the expansion for μ_s and σ_s^2, this lets us complete our calculation of the positive accuracy $P(d \le 0) = A_{j,s}^+(k)$ and the analogous calculation for the negative accuracy $A_{j,s}^-(k)$.

5 Analysis of Component Terms

Our remaining unknown terms include the conditional probability of an attribute given a class and the probabilities of the classes themselves, $P(C)$ and $P(\bar C)$. Recall that we know the distribution of instances for the domain, which is determined by the given probability $P(A)$ that each attribute will occur in an arbitrary instance. Since we assume these attributes are independent, we know that the number of attributes present in an instance follows a binomial distribution with probability of success $P(A)$. However, we are concerned here with q of r concepts, so we care only about those instances with q or more relevant attributes present out of the r possible. Thus, we have

$$P(C) = \sum_{u=q}^{r} B(u, r, P(A))$$

as the probability of observing a positive instance, which takes the binomial form because there can be different ways for u out of r relevant attributes to be present. And since we have only two classes, we know that $P(\bar{C}) = 1 - P(C)$.

Because the naive Bayesian classifier stores counts for each predictive attribute, we must also calculate the probability $P(A_\circ|C)$ that a relevant attribute will occur in an arbitrary positive instance for a q of r target concept. From Bayes' rule, we have

$$P(A_\circ|C) = \frac{P(A_\circ) \cdot P(C|A_\circ)}{P(C)} ,$$

and since $P(C|A_\circ)$ assumes at least one relevant attribute is present, we need only another $q - 1$ out of $r - 1$ attributes present to ensure a positive instance. Thus, we can replace this term with a binomial summation, giving

$$P(A_\circ|C) = \frac{P(A_\circ)}{P(C)} \cdot \sum_{k=q-1}^{r-1} B(k, r-1, P(A)) .$$

Similarly, we can specify the probability $P(A_\circ|\bar{C})$ that a relevant attribute will occur in an arbitrary negative instance using the analogous expression

$$P(A_\circ|\bar{C}) = \frac{P(A_\circ) \cdot P(\bar{C}|A_\circ)}{P(\bar{C})} .$$

The conditional term $P(\bar{C}|A_\circ)$ also assumes at least one relevant feature is present, so we have

$$P(A_\circ|\bar{C}) = \frac{P(A_\circ)}{P(\bar{C})} \cdot \sum_{k=0}^{q-2} B(k, r-1, P(A)) .$$

since a negative instance can occur only if we have no more than $q - 2$ relevants out of the $r - 1$ remaining.

Finally, we must express the probabilities that an irrelevant attribute $A_\star$ will appear in an arbitrary positive and in a negative instance. However, the definition of an irrelevant attribute implies that its values are completely independent of the class. This means that $P(A_\star|C) = P(A_\star|\bar{C}) = P(A_\star)$, so that we can use each irrelevant attribute's probability $P(A)$ directly in our various calculations.

We can extend the framework to handle class noise by modifying the definitions of three basic terms: $P(C)$, $P(A_\circ|C)$, and $P(A_\circ|\bar{C})$. A common definition of class noise involves the corruption of class names (i.e., replacing the actual class with its opposite) with a certain probability $0 \leq z \leq 1$. As Iba and Langley (1992) have noted, the probability of the class after introducing corrupted values is

$$\begin{aligned} P'(C) &= (1-z)P(C) + z(1-P(C)) \\ &= P(C)[1-2z] + z \quad , \end{aligned}$$

since there exists a $P(C)$ probability that the class was actually present and a $1 - z$ probability it was not corrupted, as well as a $1 - P(C)$ probability that it was not present and a z probability that corruption has made it seem present.

For an irrelevant attribute $A_\star$, the conditional probability $P(A_\star|C)$ is unaffected by class noise and remains equal to $P(A)$, since the attribute is still independent of the class. However, the situation for relevant attributes is more complicated. In particular, we must reexpress the (corrupted) conditional probability of a relevant attribute $A_\circ$ given the (corrupted) class C as

$$\begin{aligned} P'(A_\circ|C) &= \frac{P'(A_\circ \wedge C)}{P'(C)} \\ &= \frac{(1-z)P(A_\circ \wedge C) + zP(A_\circ \wedge \bar{C})}{P'(C)} , \end{aligned}$$

where the terms in the numerator are the pre-noise conditional probabilities and the denominator is the noisy class probability given above. We can use similar reasoning to express the post-noise probability of a relevant attribute given the negative class $\bar{C}$ as

$$\begin{aligned} P'(A_\circ|C) &= \frac{P'(A_\circ \wedge \bar{C})}{P'(\bar{C})} \\ &= \frac{(1-z)P(A_\circ \wedge \bar{C}) + zP(A_\circ \wedge C)}{P'(\bar{C})} , \end{aligned}$$

where $P'(\bar{C}) = 1 - P'(C)$. We then replace the original terms for $P(C)$, $P(A_\circ|C)$, and $P(A_\circ|\bar{C})$ with their corrupted analogues in earlier parts of the analysis in order to determine the effect of class noise on the naive Bayesian classifier.

6 Implications for Learning Behavior

The equations in the previous section provide a formal description of naive Bayes' behavior, but their implications are not obvious. However, we can use the analysis to make average-case predictions about the algorithm's accuracy under different domain characteristics. Because the analysis introduces normal approximations to the binomial and relies on the central limit theorem, the predictions will not be perfect, but their accuracy should increase with the number of

Cross-over between 3 of 3 and 5 of 5 predicted by theory

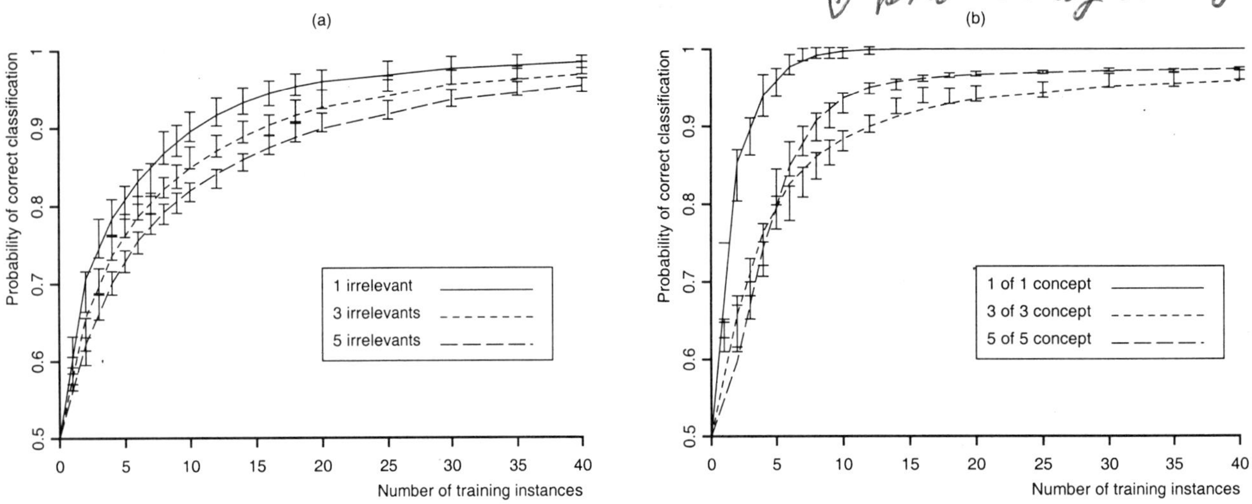

Figure 1: Theoretical and experimental learning curves for naive Bayes when (a) the domain involves a '2 of 2' target concept and varying numbers of irrelevant attributes, and (b) for a domain with one irrelevant attribute and a conjunctive target concept with varying numbers of relevant features. The error bars represent 95% confidence intervals for the experimental curves.

training cases and attributes. Moreover, because the analysis is tractable computationally, we can examine larger training and attribute sets than in our previous average-case treatment of the naive Bayesian classifier.

In addition to making theoretical predictions, we collected experimental learning curves for naive Bayes on 100 randomly generated training sets. Each curve reflects the average classification accuracy over these runs on a single noise-free test set that includes all possible instances. In each case, we bound the mean accuracy with 95% confidence intervals to show the degree to which our predicted learning curves fit the observed ones. These empirical results provide an important check on both our reasoning and the ability of the analysis to predict behavior despite its simplifying approximations.

Figure 1 (a) shows the effect of irrelevant attributes on naive Bayes' rate of learning when the training data contains no noise. In this study, we used $P(A) = \frac{1}{2}$ as the probability for each attribute and a '2 of 2' target concept, while we varied both the number of training cases and the number of irrelevant attributes. As typical with learning curves, the accuracies begin low and gradually improve with the size of the training set. The effect of irrelevants also agrees with our intuitions, in that it degrades the learning rate gracefully and does not alter asymptotic accuracy, which is 100 percent on conjunctive concepts (Domingos & Pazzani, 1997). Moreover, the predicted and observed learning curves are in close agreement, even for very small training sets where we expected divergence due to our use of approximations.

Figure 1 (b) presents the corresponding effect of relevant attributes on learning rate, again in the absence of noise. Here we used a single irrelevant attribute in all conditions, but we varied the number of training cases and the number of relevant features in a conjunctive target concept. As before, we used $P(A) = \frac{1}{2}$ for each attribute, which causes class distributions to become ever more skewed as one adds relevant features. Intuition suggests that this should make more complex concepts more difficult to master and, indeed, the '1 of 1' concept has the highest learning rate. But the analysis predicts that, over most of their learning curves, accuracy will be higher for a five-attribute conjunction than for one with three attributes. The empirical results confirm this surprising phenomenon, matching the predictions closely enough to reflect a crossover between curves around the fifth training instance.[3]

Another interesting question concerns the effect of q, the number of necessary attributes in a q of r concept, which we could not address in our earlier study because it was limited to conjunctive concepts. Figure 2 (a) shows the learning curves for target concepts with five relevant attributes when $q = 3$, $q = 4$, and $q = 5$.

[3]The same effect occurs if one increases the number of both relevant and irrelevant attributes but holds constant their ratio, though the crossover occurs at a later point.

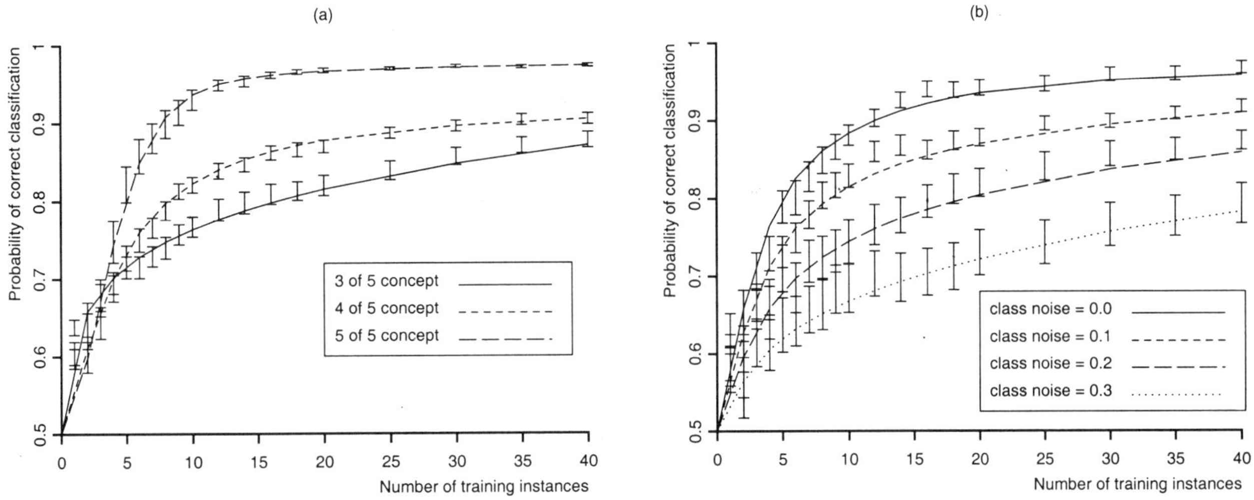

Figure 2: Theoretical and experimental learning curves for naive Bayes when the domain involves one irrelevant attribute and (a) a q of r target concept with different values for q, as well as (b) a '3 of 3' concept with varying levels of class noise.

Intuition suggests that concepts with the highest and lowest q values should be easiest to learn, since relevant features will be easier to identify when they are more nearly criterial. The analysis predicts this effect over most of the learning curves, and again the experimental curves match the analytic ones quite well. We have not shown curves for $q = 1$ and $q = 2$, since they are identical to those for $q = 5$ and $q = 4$, respectively.

The presence of noise is another complicating factor that makes induction difficult. Figure 2 (b) illustrates the effect of class noise on the learning rate for naive Bayes, given a '3 of 3' target concept and one irrelevant feature. To support more direct correspondence among different noise levels, we omitted noise from the test set, which normalizes accuracies and eases comparison. Both the theoretical and experimental curves match the intuition that learning rate should slow with class noise, but this time the predictions do not fit the observations quite as well as before, showing there can be a cost to introducing approximations for the sake of efficiency.

7 Concluding Remarks

In this paper, we have presented an improved average-case analysis of the naive Bayesian classifier, an induction algorithm that has become increasingly popular in recent years. The treatment generalized our earlier analysis by extending it to arbitrary 'M of N' concepts. But more important, the new analysis was much more tractable, in computational terms, than its predecessor, which let us make predictions about naive Bayes' behavior on larger training sets and on domains with more attributes. The price of this improved computational efficiency was a reliance on normal approximations to the binomial distribution, which meant our ability to fit experimental results became an empirical question.

To explore the implications of the analysis, we plotted the predicted behavior of the algorithm as a function of the number of training instances, the amount of noise, and the number of irrelevant, relevant, and necessary attributes, finding graceful degradation as these parameters varied. As a check on our analysis, we ran the algorithm on synthetic training and test sets with the same characteristics. In general, we found excellent fits between the theoretical predictions and observed behavior, which lends support to our use of approximations to make the analysis tractable.

One issue we have not addressed is the sensitivity of our analysis to its underlying assumptions. We know that naive Bayes often behaves well even when the predictive attributes are not completely independent given the class (Domingos & Pazzani, 1997), but this does not mean that the analysis will accurately predict its learning curve under such conditions. In our future work, we should run experiments with domains that violate the independence assumption to varying degrees, as Pazzani and Sarrett (1992) did for their analysis of conjunctive learning. They reported good fits to observed learning curves despite strong dependencies, and we anticipate similar results for naive Bayes.

ATKINSON, BOWER & CROTHIER 1965

We also hope to extend our approach to the average-case analysis of other induction algorithms like nearest neighbor, which Langley and Iba (1993) analyzed for conjunctive concepts, and k-nearest neighbor, which Okamoto and Nobuhiro (1997) analyzed for 'M of N' concepts. These analyses provided useful insights but were limited to small training and attribute sets due to computational intractability, which our approximate approach should remedy. Techniques for the induction of determinations (Kohavi, 1994; Langley, 1996), which rely on feature selection to construct simple tables for classification, also seem amenable to average-case analysis. Since they select or reject features over the entire training set, such methods should be easier to analyze than more complex schemes for decision-tree and rule induction.

A final direction for future research involves using average-case analysis to better understand the behavior of naive Bayes and other algorithms in natural domains. For any natural data set, we can estimate $P(C)$, $P(A)$, and $P(A|C)$, and we know the number of training cases and attributes. We do not know the number of relevant attributes, the noise level, or the exact target concept, but experimental learning curves provide constraints that we can use to select among alternative settings for parameters from the average-case model. This would require extending the analysis to handle non-Boolean attributes and a broader range of target concepts, but the result would be a much stronger connection between the theoretical and empirical branches of machine learning, bringing the field closer to becoming a true science of the artificial.

Acknowledgements

Thanks to Mostefa Golea for showing us that tractable average-case analyses of induction were possible, to Seishi Okamoto and Nobuhiro Yugami for discussions that rekindled our excitement in the topic, and to Claude-Nicolas Fiechter for advice about the standard normal and for crucial checks on our reasoning.

References

Cestnik, B., & Bratko, I. (1991). On estimating probabilities in decision-tree pruning. *Proceedings of the 1991 European Working Session on Learning* (pp. 138–150). Porto, Portugal: Springer-Verlag.

Cestnik, G., Konenenko, I, & Bratko, I. (1987). ASSISTANT-86: A knowledge-elicitation tool for sophisticated users. In I. Bratko & N. Lavrac (Eds.) *Progress in machine learning.* Sigma Press.

Clark, P., & Niblett, T. (1989). The CN2 induction algorithm. *Machine Learning*, *3*, 261–284.

Duda, R. O., & Hart, P. E. (1973). *Pattern classification and scene analysis.* New York: John Wiley & Sons.

Domingos, P., & Pazzani, M. (1997). On the optimality of the simple Bayesian classifier under zero-one loss. *Machine Learning*, *29*, 103–130.

Golea, M., & Marchand, M. (1993). On learning perceptrons with binary weights. *Neural Computation*, *5*, 767–782. Use stat. Mechanics - overkill

Haussler, D. (1990). Probably approximately correct learning. *Proceedings of the Eighth National Conference on Artificial Intelligence* (pp. 1101–1108). Boston: AAAI Press.

Iba, W., & Langley, P. (1992). Induction of one-level decision trees. *Proceedings of the Ninth International Conference on Machine Learning* (pp. 233–240). Aberdeen, Scotland: Morgan Kaufmann.

Kohavi, R. (1994). The power of decision tables. *Proceedings of the 1995 European Conference on Machine Learning* (pp. 174–189). Heraklion, Crete.

Langley, P. (1996). Induction of condensed determinations. *Proceedings of the Second International Conference of Knowledge Discovery and Data Mining* (pp. 327–330). Portland: AAAI Press.

Langley, P., & Iba, W. (1993). Average-case analysis of a nearest neighbor algorithm. *Proceedings of the Thirteenth International Joint Conference on Artificial Intelligence* (pp. 889–894). Chambery, France.

Langley, P., Iba, W., & Thompson, K. (1992). An analysis of Bayesian classifiers. *Proceedings of the Tenth National Conference on Artificial Intelligence* (pp. 223–228). San Jose, CA: AAAI Press.

Langley, P., & Sage, S. (1994). Induction of selective Bayesian classifiers. *Proceedings of the Tenth Conference on Uncertainty in Artificial Intelligence* (pp. 399–406). Seattle, WA: Morgan Kaufmann.

Okamoto, S., & Yugami, N. (1997). An average-case analysis of the k-nearest neighbor classifier for noisy domains. *Proceedings of the Fifteenth International Joint Conference on Artificial Intelligence* (pp. 238–243). Yokohama, Japan: Morgan Kaufmann.

Pazzani, M., & Sarrett, W. (1992). A framework for average-case analysis of conjunctive learning algorithms. *Machine Learning*, *9*, 349-372.

Learning Hierarchical Performance Knowledge by Observation

Michael van Lent and John Laird
Artificial Intelligence Lab
University of Michigan
1101 Beal Ave.
Ann Arbor, MI 48109-2110
{vanlent,laird}@umich.edu

Abstract

Developing automated agents that intelligently perform complex real world tasks is time consuming and expensive. The most costly part of developing these agents is extracting knowledge from human experts and encoding it in a form useable by automated agents. Automated learning from a sufficiently rich and focused knowledge source can significantly reduce the cost of development by automating the knowledge acquisition and encoding process. Learning by observation is particularly well suited to learning hierarchical performance knowledge for tasks that require realistic, human-like behavior. Our learning by observation system, called KnoMic (Knowledge Mimic), uses a supervised learning algorithm that reads observation traces of an expert performing a task and generates production rules that an agent can use to perform the same task. Results of our efforts to learn performance knowledge with KnoMic in the tactical air combat domain and the computer game Quake II are reported.

1. INTRODUCTION

Frequently the most time consuming and costly part of developing intelligent agents is the acquisition and hand coding of task performance knowledge in an appropriate knowledge format, such as production rules. Knowledge acquisition often involves lengthy interviews with human experts, thousands of hours hand-programming and debugging, and frequent demonstrations to allow the experts to verify the final agent behavior. The experts are required to organize and communicate their knowledge to the programmers and the programmers are required to learn the details of the task, effectively becoming experts themselves.

One approach to improving the efficiency of knowledge acquisition is to use an unsupervised machine learning system that learns to perform the task without relying on an expert. Unfortunately, the knowledge required for performance tasks tends to be complex, and learning it solely through unsupervised experiments in the task environment can be more costly than the original knowledge acquisition process (when it is possible at all). Furthermore, the resulting performance knowledge, if successful, may not behave as humans do, which limits its usefulness in some types of tasks such as training. A second approach is to develop a supervised learning system that uses an expert to provide a more focused source of knowledge, such as instruction or observation. Supervised learning doesn't require the expert to learn a new tool or programming language and doesn't require the programmer to learn the task. Furthermore, the resulting performance knowledge is based on an expert's behavior and allows different experts to generate different styles of performance. Finally, a well-chosen form of expert input can minimize the need for the expert to organize and communicate his or her knowledge.

Input to the KnoMic (Knowledge Mimic) system consists of observations of an expert performing the task and annotations. Based on this, KnoMic learns the knowledge necessary for an intelligent agent to perform the task. Each observation used by KnoMic consists of a temporal sequence of the sensor inputs from the environment, any actions taken by the expert, and annotations indicating active goals. The system can learn on-line, using these observations as they are generated, or the observations can be stored and used to learn off-line. The sensor inputs and actions are represented as attribute/value pairs with each pair consisting of a symbolic attribute (sensor or action name) and a numeric or symbolic value. A programmer develops the interface between the environment and KnoMic, which should mimic the interface between the environment and the expert. KnoMic is designed to work in complex domains with real time behavior requirements, external and durative actions, non-determinism, and other complexities.

Like design tasks and analysis tasks, performance tasks represents a class of problems for machine learning. In a performance task, the intelligent agent performs actions in a constantly changing environment to achieve or maintain a collection of goals. Such agents have also been termed Teleo-Reactive (Benson, 1996). We've identified five properties that allow performance agents to be effective in the types of task we are interested in. Our performance agents are:

1. reactive
2. able to perform durative actions
3. directed by a hierarchical goal decomposition
4. able to create persistent internal state features
5. able to modify behavior based on task parameters

Many performance tasks, such as flying a plane or playing a computer game, require the agent to be reactive enough to respond to changes in the environment in real-time. These tasks frequently require the agent to take actions that must be performed over multiple time steps. An example of a durative action is "turn left until flying due west." To successfully perform it's task, the agent's behavior and responses need to be directed towards achieving the task goals. These goals are usually best represented by a hierarchical decomposition where lower level goals represent steps in the achievement of the higher level goals. Persistent internal state features provide the agent with a context of it's past sensing to insure the current behavior is consistent. Finally, the agent should also be able to use the same knowledge to perform the task in a variety of ways based on task parameters provided at run time.

In the next section, three earlier supervised learning systems that learn by observation are described. Section three describes the format of the performance knowledge generated by KnoMic. The KnoMic system, described in the fourth section, combines many of the strengths of the systems described in section two while overcoming some of their weaknesses. The fifth section provides examples and evaluation of the knowledge generated by KnoMic within a tactical air combat domain.

2. RELATED RESEARCH

The KnoMic system described in this paper is preceded by three significant research efforts in the area of learning by observation, behavioral cloning (Bain, 1995; Sammut, 1992), OBSERVER (Wang, 1996; Wang, 1995), and TRAIL (Benson, 1996; Benson 1995). KnoMic can be viewed as an attempt to combine aspects of these three research efforts to create a system that can learn performance knowledge that satisfies all five agent properties.

2.1 BEHAVIORAL CLONING

Sammut, Hurst, Kedzier and Michie have used behavioral cloning to learn the knowledge necessary to fly a Cessna along a specific flight plan within the Silicon Graphics flight simulator. Behavioral cloning applies the C4.5 induction algorithm to situation/action examples taken from observations of a expert to build decision trees that decide which actions to take based on the sensor input. A human expert, whose behavior is to be cloned, flies a strictly defined flight plan 30 times. Recording the sensor inputs and the value of each control approximately 20 times a second creates an observation log of each flight. These observation logs form a large set of training examples with the sensor inputs as the attributes and the controls as the class values. Behavioral cloning uses this set of training examples to induce decision trees that classify the appropriate control values (or actions) based on the sensor inputs. These decision trees can then be used to mimic the expert's behavior and fly the plane by setting each control to the value specified by applying the current sensor inputs to the decision tree.

The flight plan is divided into seven stages and a separate decision tree is learned for each control in each stage. Since each stage is a different aspect of the task, such as takeoff and fly to an altitude of 2,000 feet, the expert's responses to the same sensor inputs differ according to the goal of the current stage and a separate decision tree is needed for each stage. Splitting the observation logs into stages adds a goal directed aspect to behavioral cloning although there is no support for hierarchical goal decomposition.

The behavioral cloning system learns 28 decision trees that effectively control the four controls over seven stages of the flight plan. Using these decision trees as performance knowledge, an intelligent agent can take off, follow the defined flight plan and land in a manner very similar to the expert being cloned. One of the most impressive aspects of behavioral cloning is its effectiveness in a complex domain. The flight simulator domain is non-deterministic, includes a large set of complex sensors and durative actions, exhibits standard and homeostatic goals, the observations contain noise and the nature of the domain requires rapid reactions to input. By using a number of small decision trees, behavior cloning splits the knowledge into many, rapidly processed structures, which allows the agent to react quickly.

While behavioral cloning has been successfully applied to a complex, real world domain, behavior cloning's performance knowledge doesn't support all five agent properties mentioned above. The major weakness of behavioral cloning is that it doesn't include any theory for automatically dividing the task into separate phases according to the expert's goals. Even when the division is done by hand, behavioral cloning doesn't support a hierarchical decomposition of goals. Also, decision trees don't support any persistent internal state features and learning a separate decision tree for each control limits behavioral cloning's ability to represent interactions between actions. Another weakness of decision trees is than they can't easily handle task parameters, such as flight plans. It is impossible to learn generally useful decision trees that apply to multiple flight paths.

2.2 OBSERVER

The OBSERVER system learns STRIPS style operators (Fikes, 1971) using a learning method similar to version spaces. Xuemei Wang developed OBSERVER and applied it to a process-planning domain, in which the task is to generate a plan to produce machine parts meeting a set of specifications. For each operator OBSERVER creates and refines a most specific set of operator preconditions S(Op), a most general set of operator preconditions G(Op) and a set of operator effects E(Op). OBSERVER initially learns S(Op) and E(Op) in a learning by observation phase. Then a second, unsupervised learning phase is used to improve S(Op) and E(Op) and to learn G(Op). When S(Op) and G(Op) match then the operator's preconditions are assumed to be correct.

An advantage of the OBSERVER system over behavioral cloning is the more expressive performance knowledge format learned by OBSERVER. The STRIPS style operators, learned by OBSERVER, include complexities such as negated preconditions and conditional actions. While the operators are more difficult to learn, they give the agent the ability to create persistent state features and can better deal with task parameters. Additionally, the operator effects, which are learned as part of each operator, predict how applying the operator will change the current state. These effects provide the predictive knowledge necessary to evaluate the outcome of proposed plans.

The OBSERVER system is described in the context of a design task that isn't as complex as the performance tasks demonstrated by behavioral cloning. One weakness of the STRIPS style operators is that they represent high level, discrete actions more easily than fine-grained, durative actions needed for highly reactive agents in tasks such as flight simulation. Since the design task contains no noise or non-determinism, OBSERVER can and does generate knowledge based on a single observation. In more complex domains, this will result in incorrect or over specific operators. While the STRIPS operators do support hierarchical goals, OBSERVER doesn't use this goal knowledge in its learning process. Goal knowledge is very useful when learning operator effects as the goal focuses the learning algorithm on a set of features the operators are trying to achieve.

2.3 TRAIL

Scott Benson's TRAIL system combines a learning algorithm and a planning algorithm to create teleo-operators for autonomous agents. The learning algorithm can use traces of both undirected exploration by the agent and performance directed by an expert. From these traces TRAIL learns the pre-conditions and effects of STRIPS-like operators called teleo operators (TOPs). A planning algorithm uses these teleo operators to create plans that can be converted into teleo reactive trees (Benson, 1996) that perform the task.

TRAIL uses an inductive logic programming approach to learn TOPs based on positive and negative examples taken from the traces. The behavioral traces include knowledge of which TOP the expert is performing at each time step. Positive instances are steps where the actions performed eventually achieved the TOP's post-conditions. Negative instances include the time steps with actions that didn't achieve the post-conditions. TRAIL's learning algorithm generates a set of pre-conditions that includes all positive instances and no negative instances. TOP effects are learned by detecting features with values that have changed when the expert is finished with the TOP.

TRAIL has been applied to complex domains, including a flight simulation similar to behavioral cloning. Agents using the knowledge learned by TRAIL are reactive, can handle durative actions and modify their behavior based on task parameters. However, the are not able to create persistent internal state features and the TOPs learned are not hierarchical. Also, TRAIL creates plans without considering the expert's behavior, which can result in agents that don't behave in the same fashion as the experts.

3. PERFORMANCE KNOWLEDGE

The performance knowledge in KnoMic is represented using a specialized form of Soar's production rule format. The rules implement a hierarchy of operators with sub-operators representing steps in the completion of the high level operator (see Figure 1). Each operator is implemented by three types of production rules; operator selection rules, conditional action rules and goal achievement rules. Currently, each operator has a single operator selection rule that tests a conjunctive set of

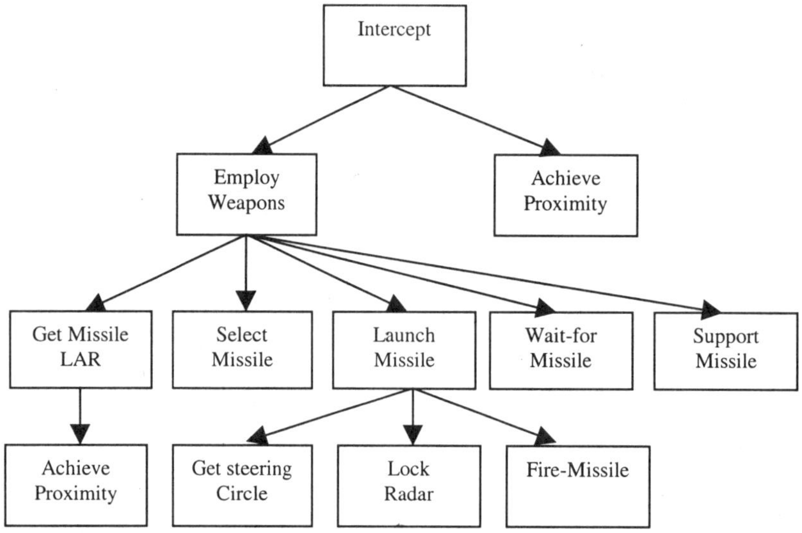

Figure 1: The operator hierarchy for the intercept portion of the tactical air combat task.

operator pre-conditions and selects the operator as the active operator at it's level of the hierarchy. Plans to allow multiple pre-condition rules that implement pre-conditions in disjunctive normal form are being implemented. Operator pre-conditions can test external sensors, internal state features and the names of the operators active at higher levels of the hierarchy. Action rules test external sensors and the active operators and issue action commands for the agent to perform in the external environment. For example, the action/value pair `^heading 90` would cause the plane being controlled to turn to a heading of 90 degrees from due north. Since each operator has separate action rules, different operators can select the values of their actions differently to achieve their specific goal; much like behavior cloning's different decision trees for different phases of the task. In some cases, the action's value is taken from one of the features tested in the rule's conditions. For example, a production might test the direction of an enemy then use as the value of an action to turn towards that enemy. This type of application rule is said to "pass through" the value of a sensor input to an action command.

Each operator has one or more rules that represent a set of conditions in disjunctive normal form that indicates when the operator's goal has been achieved (see Figure 2). When the goal achievement conditions have been, met, the operator terminates. Goal achievement features frequently represent relationships between sensor inputs in the domain. For example, a takeoff operator's goal conditions might test that the plane's current altitude is equal to the flight plan's cruising altitude. By representing the achievement explicitly, the goal of this operator can be incorporated in future rules rather than relearning the relationship between altitude and cruising altitude each time. Also, goal features are likely to represent concepts familiar to the expert, making the learned rules easier to understand.

```
sp {racetrack*propose*fly-to-racetrack
   (state <s> ^name racetrack
              ^top-state <ts>)
   (<ts> -^achieved-racetrack)
-->
   (<s> ^operator <o> +)
   (<o> ^name fly-to-racetrack)
   }

sp {fly-to-racetrack*apply*heading
   (state <s> ^operator <o>
              ^top-state <ts>)
   (<ts> ^waypoint.bearing <he>)
   (<o> ^name fly-to-racetrack
       -^desired-heading)
-->
   (<o> ^desired-heading <he>)
   }

sp {fly-to-racetrack*achieved
   (state <s> ^operator.name fly-to-
racetrack
              ^mission <m>
              ^top-state <ts>)
   (<ts> ^parameter <p>
        ^waypoint.range <= <r>)
   (<p> ^waypoint-achieved-range <r>)
   (<m> -^achieved-racetrack)
-->
   (<m> ^achieved-racetrack <ar>)
   }
```

Figure 2: Sample pre-conditions, action and goal achievement productions for the fly-to-racetrack operators.

The details of if and when the goal achievement feature is removed are an important aspect of the task performance knowledge. In many cases it is important for a performance agent to remember that a goal has been achieved even if the goal conditions are no longer true. For example, the goal condition of a `Takeoff` operator might be that the plane has reached the cruising altitude. Once this goal is achieved, the agent should remember that `Takeoff's` goal has been achieved so that `Takeoff` won't be reselected if the agent changes the altitude to something other than the cruising altitude. Therefore, goal achievement features can be persistent or non-persistent. Persistent goal achievement features remain on the internal state after the goal conditions are no longer matched. Non-persistent goal achievement features are removed from the state when the goal conditions no longer match. Furthermore, a persistent goal achievement feature can be removed as an action of a later operator. KnoMic classifies operators according to the persistence of their goal-achieved features. One-time operators have persistent goal features that are never removed by a later operator. Initialization operators that fire once at the beginning of a task are examples of one-time operators. Repeatable operators have persistent goal achievement features that can be removed by later operators. Examples of repeatable operators will be presented later in the context of the tactical air combat domain. Finally, operators with non-persistent goal achievement features deal with homeostatic goals that must be maintained once achieved. While flying to a specific waypoint, an operator might set the plane's heading to point in the waypoint's direction. Once the plane is pointing towards the waypoint, the operator's goal is achieved and the operator is unselected. If the plane's heading deviates from that direction, the operator's goal is no longer true, the goal-achieved feature would be retracted and the operator would again become active to get the plane pointing in the correct direction and re-achieve the goal. Thus the operator maintains the plane's heading pointing towards the waypoint.

At any given time, one operator at each level of the hierarchy can be selected as active. An operator is selected when the pre-conditions in the operator selection rule are matched. As KnoMic generates operator pre-conditions, it ensures that the pre-conditions of the operators at each level of the hierarchy are mutually exclusive to avoid operator conflicts. Once selected, the operator action rules and/or sub-operators perform actions to achieve the operator's goal conditions. An operator remains active until it's goal conditions are achieved or its pre-conditions are no longer met. When the goal conditions are achieved, the goal-achieved feature is added to the system's internal state and the operator is unselected.

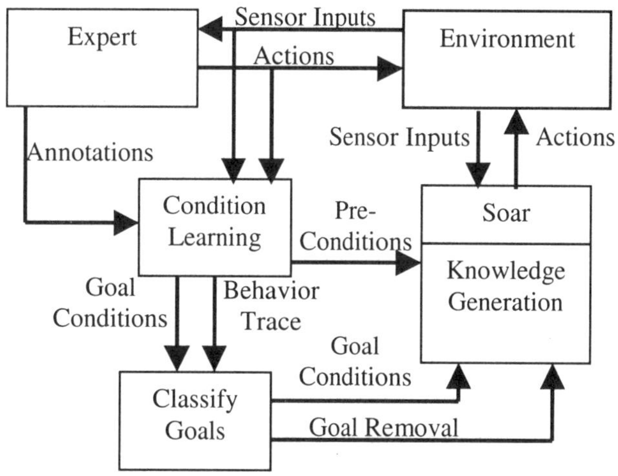

Figure 3: The KnoMic system.

Using the RETE algorithm, the Soar architecture can determine which productions match very quickly allowing the agent to be very reactive. In experiments in a tactical air combat domain and with the computer game Quake II, KnoMic agents react to sensor inputs 10-20 times a second. The operator hierarchy described above naturally supports hierarchical goal decomposition while the persistent goal achievement features gives KnoMic agents the ability to create internal state features. Unlike STRIPS, KnoMic operators may be applied over a series of time steps, making it possible for operators to have durative actions and for higher level operators to remain active while their sub-operators are selected. The "pass-through" action values support task parameters by passing the parameter values through to the actions that perform the task. Thus, if one task parameter is `patrol_altitude=20,000 feet`, then a pass-through action production could easily pass this value through to the `desired_altitude=20,000 feet` action. Finally, the explicit goal achievement condition specifies the intended effects of each operator that could be used by a planning algorithm to generate new behavior in novel situations.

4. KnoMic

The KnoMic system consists of three components that observe the interactions between the expert and the environment (or simulator) and communicate among themselves to generate performance knowledge (see Figure 3). The Soar architecture then acts as the execution architecture of the intelligent agent using the learned knowledge to perform the task. The condition learning component compares the expert system's behavior to the current performance knowledge and generalizes operator and goal conditions in situations where the performance knowledge doesn't match the expert's behavior. The goal classification component uses the learned goal conditions and the expert's behavior to classify each goal feature as persistent or non-persistent and to build any necessary goal removal operators. The conditions and goal classifications are passed to the knowledge generation component, which simply formats the conditions into Soar production rules. An intelligent agent can then use the Soar architecture to perform the task using this new performance knowledge. KnoMic is described here in the context of a combat flight simulation domain.

4.1 OBSERVATION TRACES

An expert's interaction with the environment while performing a task can be viewed as a loop of communication. An interface with the environment sends sensor information to the expert in the form of instruments (altitude dial, air speed indication...), the view from the cockpit window and perhaps sounds from a radio. The expert reacts to this information by sending actions to the environment interface in the form of changes to aircraft controls (flight stick, throttle...) or keypresses and mouse movements that represent aircraft controls in a simulation. The interface performs the actions in the environment and the sensor information sent to the expert changes to reflect the effects these actions have on the current situation of the agent in the environment.

For KnoMic, the information passed between the expert and the environment is translated into a symbolic form. Thus, where the expert perceives a needle pointing to 320 on the airspeed indicator, KnoMic perceives a `^vehicle.speed` sensor feature with a value of 320. For each relevant sensor displayed for the expert, KnoMic receives a corresponding sensor input feature. Similarly, for each action the expert can take, KnoMic is provided with a symbolic action/value command such as `^air_speed=300 knots`. Sensor input features are also used to represent static domain constants such as mission parameters (`cruising_altitude=2,000 feet`) and vehicle properties (`turn_rate=12.4 deg/sec`). When reading an observation trace, KnoMic makes an initial pass to record which sensor inputs are static (value never changes during the trace) and which are dynamic (value changes during the trace). As described later, this distinction is used by the condition learning component. Creating the symbolic sensor inputs and actions requires a programmer with a limited amount of task knowledge.

As the expert performs the task, changes in the sensor inputs and action commands issued by the expert create a trace of the expert's behavior. As mentioned previously, the expert annotates the observation log with the operators and sub-operators currently active at each level of the operator hierarchy. A graphical operator hierarchy display has been built to aid the expert in specifying which operators are active while performing the task. Before beginning the task, the expert can use the graphical editor to organize an operator hierarchy. While the task is underway, the expert can click on the operators he or she is currently performing to specify which operators are active. In our experience, developing an operator hierarchy is a much easier task than developing the productions to implement the hierarchy. Furthermore, debugging these agents consists almost exclusively of correcting production conditions and actions. The operator hierarchy maybe be extended through the addition of new operators, but it is rarely modified.

4.2 CONDITION LEARNING

For each operator, the condition learning component must select the operator's pre-conditions, action conditions, and goal conditions. To successfully perform realistic, complex tasks, operator conditions must include negated conditions (tests for the absence of an attribute/value pair), tests that the value of an attribute is within a numeric range and comparisons between the values of two attributes (equal, greater than, less than). A simple specific-to-general learning algorithm is used to learn all three types of conditions. This algorithm initially creates a most specific set of conditions and then generalizes that set based on further observation traces.

When learning an operator's pre-conditions, the expert's annotations allow KnoMic to identify points in the observation trace where an operator is selected. The record of changes to the sensor attribute/value pairs and knowledge of the operators already learned allows KnoMic to determine the external and internal state of the agent at the point of operator selection. When the first operator selection is observed, KnoMic initializes the operator's pre-conditions to include a condition for every feature in the agent's state (a maximally specific set of conditions). Furthermore, if a dynamic attribute/value pair has the same value as a static attribute/value pair then an additional condition will be created that tests that the two attributes have the same value (greater than and less than tests can't be learned for pre-conditions). Thus, if when an operator O1 is first observed to be selected, the agent's state consists of the dynamic attribute/value pairs D1=3, D2=99, and D3=52 and the static task parameter S1=3 then the initial preconditions for O1 would be D1=3, D2=99, D3=52, S1=3, and S1=D1. When subsequent selections of the same operator are observed, KnoMic can generalize these conditions in three ways. First, if an attribute isn't present as part of an attribute/value pair for the subsequent selection, then all pre-conditions that test that attribute are removed. Second, if the attribute is still present but has a different numeric value, then the existing condition will be generalized to test a range of values which includes the new value. Thirdly, if static and dynamic attribute/values pairs have different values then any conditions that require them to be equal are dropped. Thus, if the agent's state is D1=5, D2=95 and S1=3 the second time O1 is observed to be selected then the new pre-conditions for O1 would be D1=3-5, D2=95-99 and S1=3. It is currently possible for KnoMic to learn overgeneral pre-conditions. In most cases, operators with disjunctive pre-conditions cause this. Although KnoMic can't currently learn disjunctive operator pre-conditions, a method for correcting overgeneralization by splitting pre-conditions into disjunctive rules is being implemented.

Goal conditions and action conditions are learned by the same algorithm with one modification. When learning goal and action conditions, KnoMic biases the features considered to include only those internal and external features that have recently changed. This is based on the heuristic that when an operator goal is achieved or a conditional action is performed, some recent change in the agent's state must have triggered that change in behavior. Since the action rules and goal achievement rules only fire when their associated operator is selected, the operator pre-conditions already provide testing of the static context. The action and goal conditions only need to test for changes within this context (i.e. the recent changes). Biasing the learning algorithm to only consider features that have recently changed focuses the condition selection on changes that may have triggered the agent's behavior and avoids re-testing the pre-conditions. For example, if a plane's altitude reaches 2,000 feet immediately before the `Takeoff` operator is terminated in every observation, a goal conditions for `Takeoff` will naturally be `altitude= 2,000`. If the `cruising_altitude=2,000` parameter is also present, then another condition will test `altitude=cruising_altitude`. By examining the value previous to a recent change, KnoMic's learning algorithm can also detect that dynamic attribute/value pairs recently became less than or greater than static inputs and build these conditions as well. Some highly dynamic sensors might change every time step of the observation trace. KnoMic detects these frequently changing sensors and doesn't include them as conditions unless they are part of a static/dynamic comparison condition. The recent-change bias has been successful in both the tactical air combat and Quake II domains.

4.3 GOAL CLASSIFICATION

The goal classification component classifies each operator as a maintain operator, one-time operator or repeatable operator as described in Section 2. Once this classification is made, the persistence of each goal achievement feature is determined and new operators are created to remove the repeatable operator's goal achievement features when necessary. Goal features are classified by examining the expert's behavior and determining when each operator's goal conditions change from true to false. If the expert immediately reselects the operator every time that operator's goal conditions are no longer true, then KnoMic hypothesizes that the expert is using the operator to maintain the truth of the goal conditions. In this case, the operator is classified as a maintain operator and its goal feature is marked as non-persistent. If the operator isn't reselected when the goal conditions become untrue, then the operator either needs to be executed only once (a one-time operator) or is reselected only under certain conditions (a repeatable operator). In either case, the goal-achieved feature is persistent. If the operator is reselected at a later time, it is classified as repeatable, and the situations in which the operator is reselected are used to learn the pre-conditions of a goal feature removal operator.

4.4 SOAR ARCHITECTURE

The Soar architecture uses the sensor inputs and the performance knowledge to generate actions that perform the task. At a simple level, the Soar architecture compares the performance knowledge rules to the current symbolic sensor inputs. At the top level of the hierarchy, the operator with matching selection conditions is selected. Once an operator is selected, its application rules and/or sub-operators are selected and applied until the goal conditions are achieved. Once the goal is achieved, a goal feature is generated and the operator is unselected so a new operator can be selected and applied. Operators can also be unselected if the situation changes such that their pre-conditions no longer match. A full description of the Soar architecture (Laird, 1987) is not necessary to understand how the performance knowledge learned by KnoMic is used. Once the performance knowledge is correctly learned, an intelligent agent, using Soar, can replace the human expert and perform the task in the style of the human.

5. EXPERIMENTAL RESULTS

The KnoMic system, as described above, is fully implemented and has been connected to the ModSAF battlefield simulator used in the TacAir-Soar project (Jones, 1999) and to the computer game Quake II. With the ModSAF simulator, eighty-seven sensor values are converted to symbolic inputs including the plane's position and velocity, radar information, mission parameters, waypoints and a waypoint computer. Twenty output actions are available including flight controls, radar controls weapon controls and various miscellaneous controls. The interface with Quake II has 7 symbolic sensor inputs and 5 output actions.

The sensor inputs and output actions used by KnoMic were originally developed as part of the TacAir-Soar project and have been incorporated unchanged. A Human Interface Panel (HIP) has been implemented and connected to the system so that KnoMic can learn task knowledge based on observations of a human expert controlling a plane in ModSAF. KnoMic can also learn by observing hand coded intelligent agents as they control the plane in ModSAF or play Quake II. The results presented in this section are based on experiments with KnoMic learning from the hand coded TacAir-Soar agents. This is particularly interesting, as comparing the rules learned by KnoMic to the hand coded rules is an effective way of evaluating the effectiveness of the KnoMic system. Performance knowledge has also been successfully learned in Quake II although those experiments are not presented here.

Human experts will be less precise in their performance of tasks, which will cause more variations between the observations. In some cases this additional noise may help the system generalize out irrelevant conditions but in general, learning from observations of human experts is expected to be more difficult. Variations in human behavior such as delays between receiving input and taking actions and performance errors will introduce noise into the observation traces. However, early experiments with the racetrack portion of the air combat task have shown that KnoMic can learn correct, functional rules based on observations of humans.

5.1 THE AIR COMBAT TASK

The knowledge learned in the experiments with the ModSAF simulator performs the air combat task based on observations of the micro TacAir-Soar agent. The micro TacAir-Soar agent is a reduced version of the full TacAir-Soar agent and is used in research and teaching situations. To perform the air combat task, TacAir-Soar takes off and flies to a specified waypoint. Once the waypoint is reached the plane flies a patrol pattern, called a racetrack, until an enemy plane is detected on radar. When the enemy plane is detected the agent engages the enemy plane, selects and fires missiles and, once the threat is eliminated, returns to flying the racetrack pattern. The hand coded micro TacAir-Soar agent uses approximately 250 production rules to perform the air combat task.

The racetrack pattern involves flying at a specific heading (the racetrack heading parameter) until a specific distance away from the specified waypoint is reached (the racetrack distance parameter) and then flying back to the waypoint. The racetrack waypoint, heading and distance are specified as mission parameters (static sensor inputs).

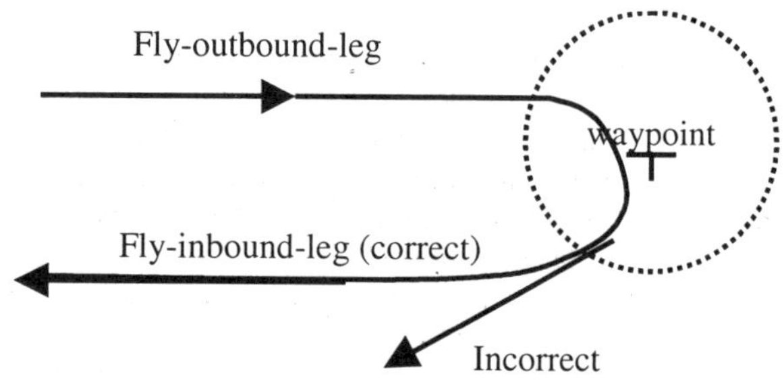

Figure 4: The agent flies the outbound leg towards the waypoint and then turns to fly the inbound leg (searching for inbound enemies) once the waypoint range is less than 3000 meters.

The operator annotations, which are based on the hand-coded operator hierarchy, divide the task into five top level operators, init-agent, create-agent, wait-to-start-vehicle, init-plane and execute-mission. The execute-mission operator has two sub-operators, racetrack and intercept. The racetrack operator has three sub-operators, fly-to-racetrack; fly-inbound-leg and fly-outbound-leg while under intercept are 11 operators in a four level hierarchy.

One aspect of the racetrack pattern demonstrates why persistent features are necessary. Consider the case where the KnoMic agent is flying towards the waypoint and must change heading to the racetrack direction parameter once the plane is close enough to the waypoint (see Figure 4). What should happen in this situation is that the fly-outbound-leg operator achieves it's goal (i.e. the waypoint range is less than the waypoint achieved range parameter), generates a goal feature and terminates. Fly-outbound-leg's goal feature is a pre-condition of fly-inbound-leg so fly-inbound-leg is selected and an application rule fires immediately to turn the plane to the racetrack direction parameter. If fly-outbound-leg's goal feature is non-persistent, then once the waypoint range again becomes greater than the achieved parameter, the goal feature is removed and fly-inbound-leg is unselected since its pre-conditions are no longer satisfied. The agent effectively forgets it is flying the inbound leg and never completes its turn to fly in the racetrack direction. However, if the goal feature is made persistent then it is not removed when the waypoint range becomes greater than the achieved parameter and the turn is completed correctly. Note that fly-outbound-leg's persistent goal feature will have to be removed by a goal feature removal operator before fly-outbound-leg can be reselected.

5.2 PERFORMANCE KNOWLEDGE FOR RACETRACK

Figure 5 displays the results of KnoMic's learning over three observations of the racetrack portion of the air

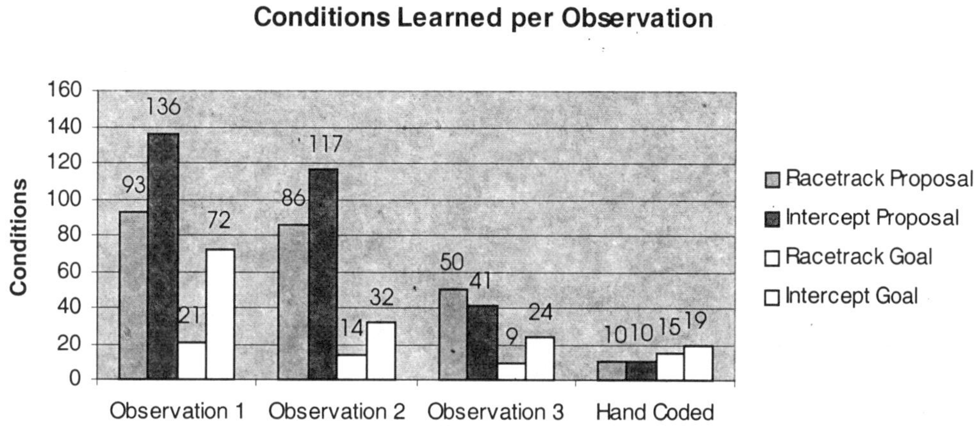

Figure 5: The results of KnoMic's learning over a series of three observations of the TacAir-Soar agent performing the racetrack task. The fourth data set represents the hand-coded micro TacAir-Soar agent.

combat task. After three or four observations KnoMic has generated rules that takeoff and fly the racetrack pattern correctly. Three quarters of the rules for the intercept part of the task are correct while the other quarter need to be corrected by hand. Since KnoMic's learning algorithm is specific-to-general, the rules learned are initially over specific (too many conditions) and as subsequent observations are made the rules are generalized. After the first observation, conditions have been learned for the 91 rules that implement the 22 operators required for the air combat task. Altogether, the rules have 229 operator pre-conditions and 93 goal conditions. After the second observation 26 pre-conditions and 20 goal conditions have been removed through generalization. The starting conditions for the third observation are slightly different than the first two allowing for greater generalization and 112 pre-conditions and 13 goal conditions are removed. While the performance knowledge is functional, it does contain a number of extraneous conditions that are not present in the hand-coded productions. Almost all of these conditions are unnecessary but not incorrect in that they won't cause the learned agent to behave differently than the hand-coded agent. Many of the rules learned by KnoMic bear a striking similarity to the hand-coded rules in the TacAir-Soar system. Approximately 75% of the rules learned by KnoMic have hand-coded counterparts. The similarity between the learned knowledge and the hand-coded knowledge suggests that programmers and experts will easily understand knowledge generated by KnoMic if it ever needs to be examined.

5.3 EFFICIENCY OF LEARNING BY OBSERVATION VS. HAND-CODING

Although the performance knowledge learned for the racetrack portion and most of the intercept portion of the task is correct and functional, KnoMic is only useful if it generates the knowledge more efficiently than hand coding. To test this we compared the time required for KnoMic to generate the performance knowledge for the racetrack portion of the task to the time taken by each of four programmers. The ModSAF simulator can be run up to ten times faster than real time, which decreases the time KnoMic spends observing and doesn't affecting the knowledge generated. As shown in Figure 6, when run at ten times real time KnoMic requires 3 minutes to start the simulator, 2 minutes for each observation, 2 minutes to generate the task knowledge and 2 minutes to demonstrate the final behavior for a total time of 15 minutes. If run at real time this increases to approximately 50 minutes. By comparison, the fastest human programmer required 50 minutes to learn the racetrack task and 75 minutes to program the performance knowledge. The slowest human had programmed half the required performance knowledge after 400 minutes. This experiment demonstrates that KnoMic is likely to generate performance knowledge more efficiently than that generated by human programmers.

6. Future Research

The current focus of research with the KnoMic system is to correct and expand learning system so that the entire air combat task is correctly learned. A number of the operators in the intercept portion of the task set internal timers and are unselected when the timers expire. Adding timer sensors and actions to the observation trace allows KnoMic to learn these operators but it requires the human expert to explicitly set timers in the interface. While KnoMic can correctly learn conjunctive operator pre-conditions, disjunctive pre-conditions can't currently be learned. Also conjunctive operator goal conditions won't be learned correctly if all the conditions in the conjunction don't become true at the same time. Due to

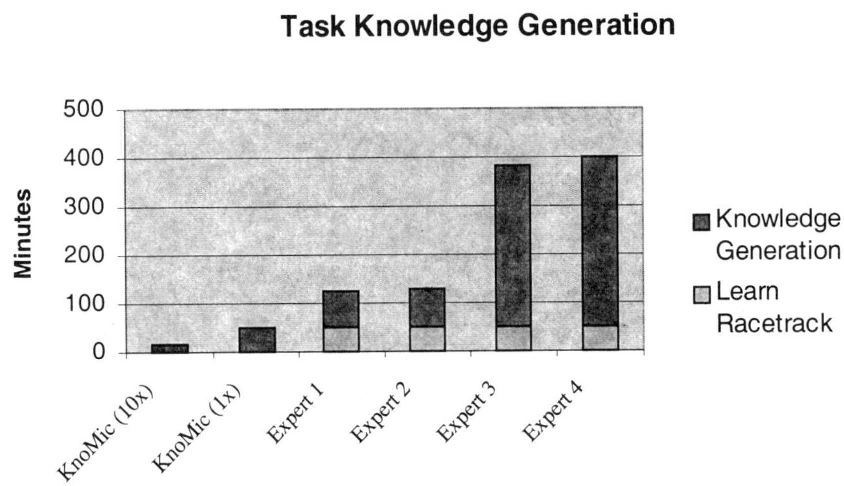

Figure 6: Time KnoMic and four experts spent generating the performance knowledge for the racetrack task. The 10x KnoMic learned from observations run at 10 times real time while the 1x observations were in real time.

the bias towards using recently changed inputs as goal conditions KnoMic only learns the last condition in the conjunction to become true. Possible solutions include relaxing the bias and including a small amount of domain knowledge that suggests combinations of inputs that are likely to be tested together.

To date KnoMic has only been applied to observations of hand-coded intelligent agents, as opposed to human experts. Variations in human behavior such as delays between sensing and actions and performance errors will likely introduce noise into the observation traces. Although the few experiments that have been performed are promising, it is likely that KnoMic's learning algorithm will need to be more noise tolerant before it can learn from human experts. One possibility is to integrate other systems that use different supervised knowledge sources such as instruction.

Acknowledgement

This research was supported under contract N61339-97-K-008 from the Defense Advanced Research Projects Agency (DARPA).

References

Bain, M. and Sammut, C (1995). A framework for behavioral cloning. in S. Muggleton, K. Furakawa, and D. Michie (Eds.), Machine Intelligence 15. Oxford University Press.

Benson, S. S. (1996). Learning Action Models for Reactive Autonomous Agents. PhD thesis, Stanford University, Computer Science Dept., 1996.

Benson, S.S. and Nilsson, N.J. (1995). Reacting, Planning and Learning in an Autonomous Agent. in S. Muggleton, K. Furakawa, and D. Michie (Eds.), Machine Intelligence 14. Oxford University Press.

Fikes, R.E. and Nilsson, N.J. (1971). STRIPS: a new approach to the application of theorem proving to problem solving. Artificial Intelligence 2(3,4):189-208.

Jones, R. M., Laird, J. E., Nielsen, P. E., Coulter, K. J., Kenny, P.. and Koss, F. V. (1999). Automated Intelligent Pilots for Combat Flight Simulation. AI Magazine, 20(1):27-41.

Laird, J. E., Newell, A. and Rosenbloom, P.S. (1987). Soar: An architecture for general intelligence. Artificial Intelligence 33:1-64.

Sammut, C., Hurst, S., Kedzier, D. and Michie, D. (1992). Learning to Fly. in D. Sleeman (Ed.) Proceedings of the Ninth International Conference on Machine Learning, Aberdeen: Morgan Kaufmann, 385-393.

Wang, X. (1995). Learning by Observation and Practice: An Incremental Approach for Planning Operator Acquisition. in Proceedings of the 12th International Conference on Machine Learning.

Wang, X. (1996). Learning Planning Operators by Observation and Practice. PhD thesis, Carnegie Mellon University, Computer Science Dept., 1996.

leave noise in
remove noisy cases
correct noisy cases ←

POLISHING:
propose changes to attribute values
make SOME of them.
Avoid introducing even more noise

Correcting Noisy Data

Higher classification accuracy
smaller trees
Irrelevant attributes:
adjust only attributes used for classification
post-polishing

Choh Man Teng
cmteng@cse.unsw.edu.au

School of Computer Science and Engineering
University of New South Wales
Sydney NSW 2052 Australia

Abstract

Inductive learning aims at constructing a generalized description of a given set of data, so that future similar instances can be classified correctly. The performance on this task depends crucially on the quality of the data. We investigate here an approach to handling noise in the training data by identifying possible noisy attributes and/or class in each instance, and replacing such values with more appropriate ones. The resulting data set would preserve much of the original information, but conform more to the ideal noise-free case. A classifier built from this corrected data should have a higher predictive power. We make use of the interdependence among attributes and between the attributes and the class to predict the value of one attribute using the rest of the attributes together with the class value. These predictions serve as candidates for possible adjustments to a training instance that has been misclassified. We selectively adjust some of the attribute values accordingly to obtain a better fit of the polished instance to the classifier. Preliminary experimentation suggests that this is a viable approach to noise reduction and correction.

1 INTRODUCTION

Inductive learning aims at constructing a generalized description of a given set of data, so that future similar instances can be classified correctly. The performance of this task depends crucially on the quality of the data. When noise is present, the classifier built from this data would be less accurate a description of the target concept and thus be of a lower utility. Unfortunately it is inevitable that noise exists in real world data sets, due to clerical error, faulty measuring devices, and the like. Thus, noise handling is a major issue in machine learning systems.

The standard approach to coping with noise is to avoid overfitting, so that the classifier does not build overly complicated structures just to fit the noise [Quinlan, 1987; Clark and Niblett, 1989]. These classifiers are robust and the noisy instances are retained as part of the data set. Another approach tackles the problem from the input end, and eliminates from the data set instances that are suspect of noise according to certain evaluation mechanisms [John, 1995; Brodley and Friedl, 1996; Gamberger *et al.*, 1996]. A classifier is then built using only the retained instances. Similar ideas can be found in robust regression and outlier detection techniques in statistics [Rousseeuw and Leroy, 1987].

In removing noisy instances from the data, there is a tradeoff between the amount of information available for building the classifier and the amount of noise retained in the data set. We investigate a third approach, namely, correcting the noisy instances rather than eliminating them. The resulting data set would preserve much of the original information, but conform more to the ideal noise-free case. A classifier built from this corrected data should have a higher predictive power.

The rest of the paper is organized as follows. The basic methodology of the noise correction procedure we call *polishing* is described in Section 2. In Section 3 we outline the setup for experimental evaluation, and the preliminary results are reported in Sections 4 and 5. Additional discussion follows in Section 6, and we conclude in Section 7.

2 BASIC METHODOLOGY

The naive Bayes classifier assumes that the attributes are conditionally independent given the target class. It has often been pointed out that this assumption is a gross over-simplification of the actual relationship between the attributes; hence the word "naive" [Mitchell, 1997, for example]. Extensions to the naive Bayes classifier have been introduced to loosen the independence criterion [Kononenko, 1991; Langley *et al.*, 1992], but some have also investigated alternative explanations for the success of this classifier [Domingos and Pazzani, 1996].

Controversy aside, most would agree attribute dependence is exhibited in a wide variety of settings. The idea behind polishing is very simple. Instead of assuming conditional independence, we exploit the interdependence between attributes, as well as between the attributes and the target class. We assume that there is some pattern of relationship among the different components of a data set. Just as we can predict the target concept by examining the attribute values, we can turn the process around and use the target class value together with some attributes to predict the value of another attribute. Note that except for totally irrelevant attributes, each attribute would at least be related to some extent to the target class even if not to another attribute. This idea is related to structured induction [Shapiro, 1987], where classifiers for individual attributes are built from a set of other attributes.

In a noisy instance, some of the attributes and/or class have inappropriate values. We can increase the classification accuracy by polishing the data; that is, by changing some of the incorrect attribute or class values back to their non-noisy values. If the combination of the target class and a subset of the attributes is a good predictor of the value of the remaining attributes, we then have a way of determining which attributes or class are noisy in a particular instance.

This is obviously an idealization of the procedure. In practice, the prediction is far from perfect, and incorporating every predicted change into an instance would probably introduce more errors than it fixes. Thus, we adopt a conservative adjustment strategy: we would like to alter the data as little as possible, while still achieving some level of improvement. In the following sections we will investigate experimentally how we can make polishing work, and to what extent it works. But first let us look at the polishing mechanism more closely.

2.1 PROCEDURE

Given a training set, we try to identify suspect attributes and classes and replace their values according to a polishing procedure. The barebones description of polishing is given in Figure 1. `Polishing` makes use of a procedure `flip` to recursively try out different combinations of attribute changes. The function `classify`(*Classifiers*, x_j, c) returns the number of classifiers in the set *Classifiers* which classify the instance x_j as belonging to class c.

Each polishing run consists of two stages. In the *prediction phase*, for each attribute we perform a 10-fold cross validation on the data with this attribute as the target and the original class participating as an attribute in its place. In other words, the attribute to be predicted and the original class swap roles. For each attribute, the data set is partitioned in a way to achieve a similar distribution of the attribute-turned-class in all folds. The list of attribute-value pairs predicted for each training instance serves as the recommended changes we would try out in the next phase.

In the *adjustment phase*, we selectively change some of the attribute/class values of an instance in order to obtain a better fit of the polished instance to the classifier. First we perform a 10-fold cross validation on the given training set. For each of the instances that has been misclassified, we try to tweak the attributes and the class so that the instance can be classified uniformly and correctly by the classifiers generated during the cross validation. The only allowable tweaks are the changes from the list of attribute-value pairs nominated during the prediction phase, plus the class value suggested by the classifiers for this particular instance. The rationale behind this is that the pattern of relationship among the attributes and the class would be preserved to a certain extent even in the face of noise, and thus the predicted values are more likely to be the correct ones.

Note that we do not indiscriminately replace all the attribute values with the predicted. We tweak only those instances that were misclassified in the first place, and for these instances we try to keep the number of changes to a minimum, preferring those attributes with a higher classification accuracy during the prediction phase. As we will see, this has the consequence that even though there may be an increase in classification accuracy, a lot of the noise remains uncorrected.

When no combination of attribute value replacement is capable of correcting the classification, we replace the class value of the instance with the one predicted

```
Polishing(OldData, NewData, votes, changes, cutoff)
Input  OldData:  (possibly) noisy data
       votes:  #classifiers that need to agree
       changes:  max #changes per instance
       cutoff:  size of attribute subset considered
Output NewData:  polished data

  for each attribute a_i
    AttList_i ← ∅;
    tmpData ← swap a_i and class c in OldData;
    10-fold cross-validation of tmpData;
    for each instance x_j misclassified
      new ← value of a_i predicted for x_j;
      AttList_i ← AttList_i ∪ {⟨j, new⟩};
    end
  end

  NewData ← ∅;
  AttSorted ← attributes sorted
              in ascending order of |AttList_i|;
  Classifiers ← classifiers from 10-fold
              cross-validation of OldData;
  for each instance x_j
    for k from 0 to changes
      adjusted ← flip(j, votes, k, cutoff);
      if adjusted then break;
    end
    if (not adjusted) and (∃class c s.t.
       classify(Classifiers, x_j, c) ≥ votes)
    then
      class of x_j ← c;
      NewData ← NewData ∪ {x_j};
    end
  end

flip(j, votes, k, cutoff)
Input  j:  index of the instance to be adjusted
       votes:  #classifiers that need to agree
       k:  #changes yet to be made
       cutoff:  size of attribute subset considered
Output true/false: whether a change has been made
        (also modifies NewData)

  if k = 0 then
    if classify(Classifiers, x_j, class of x_j) ≥ votes
    then
      NewData ← NewData ∪ {x_j};
      return true;
    end
    else return false;
  else for i from 0 to cutoff
    a_i' ← AttSorted[i];
    if ⟨j, new⟩ ∈ AttList_i' then
      attribute a_i' of x_j ← new;
      adjusted ← flip(j, votes, k − 1, i − 1);
      if adjusted then return true;
      reset a_i' of x_j;
    end
  end
  return false;
```

Figure 1: Polishing

by the largest number of classifiers if there is enough agreement between them. The assumption here is that a wrong replacement in the attributes is less harmful than a wrong replacement in the target class, since there are usually a lot more attributes than class, and the effect of assigning an individual attribute a wrong value might not always be noticeable, while a wrong class assignment is definitely counter-productive.

2.2 ADJUSTMENT HEURISTICS

In the prediction phase we collect all the nominated changes to the attributes of each instance, and in the adjustment phase we selectively replace some of the attribute/class values with the suggested ones. There are several considerations we need to bear in mind when trying to correct the data. While the suggested values from the prediction phase might be the correct ones to use, they can also be spurious and the use of these values can instead increase the amount of noise in the data set even further. This is especially true for attributes which, through no fault of their own, bear little relationship to the others and thus the prediction of their values is of poor accuracy.

One way to alleviate this problem is to sort the list of attributes according to the accuracy of their classification during the prediction phase, and try replacing the more accurately predicted attributes first whenever applicable. Another concern is that we do not know the number of noisy attributes and/or class in each instance. We try to make as few changes as possible so as to minimize the risk of introducing additional noise into the data.

A third consideration is the criterion of accepting a classification. The 10 classifiers obtained from the 10-fold cross validation of the training data are used to determine the classification. Since these classifiers are built based on noisy data, they might not be a very accurate evaluation mechanism, even when the test instance does not contain noise.[1] Thus we do not necessarily require every single classifier to agree on the classification to accept it as correct. Rather, we determine a reasonable threshold by approximating it with the maximum number of classifiers that agree on the most instances.

In summary, when there are multiple combinations of changes that would fix the classification error, we prefer the one with the fewest number of changes and involving attributes that have been the most accu-

[1]Otherwise, we wouldn't have the need to improve their performance, would we?

rately predicted. In addition, we allow for some slight disagreement between the classifiers in determining whether an instance is considered to have an "acceptably correct" classification. The polished data set such produced can then be used to generate a classifier for future use.

3 EXPERIMENTAL SETUP

In this section we outline the way the experiments were conducted. We used the decision tree builder c4.5 [Quinlan, 1993] as the underlying machinery for classification.

3.1 DATA SETS

Six data sets from the UCI Repository of machine learning databases [Murphy and Aha, 1998] were used. Below we briefly describe some of the characteristics of these data sets. Where separate training and test sets exist at the repository, we combined the two into a single data set. All the attributes are nominal (or ordered), and attributes for identification purposes only were ignored.

mushroom This data set consists of 8124 instances of mushrooms. There are 22 attributes describing the physical characteristics of each instance, and the target concept is the edibility of the mushroom.

soybean The soybean data set consists of 683 instances. There are 35 attributes describing the appearance and climatic conditions. The target concept classifies each instance into having one of 19 diseases.

LED-24 This data set describes the LED display of a digit. The target concept is one of the ten digits (0...9), and the attributes are the 7 LED components plus 17 irrelevant attributes with randomly generated values. The data set we generated contains 1000 instances.

vote This data set contains 435 voting records of the House of Representatives in the United States in 1984. The 16 attributes corresponds to issues voted on in the House, and the target concept is the political party affiliation (republican or democrat) of the members.

audiology The audiology data set consists of 226 instances. There are 69 attributes, each corresponding to a property or condition of the case, and the target concept consists of 24 possible audiological diagnostics of the instances.

promoters This data set consists of 106 sequences of 57 nucleotides, and the target concept is whether a gene sequence is a "promoter" (a section of a sequence at which gene expression is initiated).

The characteristics of the data sets are summarized in Table 1. We also give the baseline classification accuracy of c4.5 on these data sets when no noise has been added.

Table 1: Summary of Data Sets

Data Set	Size	#Attributes	#Classes	c4.5 Accuracy
mushroom	8124	22	2	100.0%
soybean	683	35	19	92.1%
LED-24	1000	24	10	100.0%
vote	435	16	2	94.7%
audiology	226	69	24	78.0%
promoters	106	57	2	75.6%

LED-24 is an artificial data set, but it has the advantage that we know exactly the structure of the data set and the relationship between the attribute and class values. This proved to be quite useful for the analytical exercises in Section 5.

3.2 NOISE

We divided each data set into 10 (almost) equal parts. For each run, 9 parts of the data were used for training, and the tree generated from the polished data was used to classify the reserved 1 part of test data. The training set was artificially corrupted by introducing random noise into the attributes as well as the class. A noise level of $x\%$ means that the value of each attribute and the target class is assigned a random value approximately $x\%$ of the time, with each alternative value being approximately equally likely to be selected. The actual percentages of noise in the various components of the data sets are given in Table 2.

The actual percentage of noise is always lower than the theoretical noise level, as sometimes the random assignment would pick the original value. Note that, however, even if we exclude the original value from the random assignment, the extent of the effect of noise is still not uniform across all components. Rather, it is dependent on the number of possible values in the attribute or class. As the noise is evenly distributed among all values, this would have a much smaller effect

Table 2: Noise Characteristics of Data Sets at Various Noise Levels. An instance, attribute value, or class value is considered noisy if the respective component differs from that of the original instance.

Data Set	Noise Level	Instances with Noise	Attribute Noise	Class Noise
mushroom	0%	0.0%	0.0%	0.0%
	10%	91.0%	7.4%	5.1%
	20%	99.2%	15.0%	10.1%
	30%	100.0%	22.4%	15.3%
	40%	100.0%	29.9%	20.7%
soybean	0%	0.0%	0.0%	0.0%
	10%	94.7%	5.6%	8.8%
	20%	99.7%	11.3%	17.3%
	30%	100.0%	16.7%	29.1%
	40%	100.0%	22.5%	38.1%
LED-24	0%	0.0%	0.0%	0.0%
	10%	93.4%	5.2%	8.2%
	20%	99.6%	10.0%	19.2%
	30%	100.0%	14.9%	26.2%
	40%	100.0%	20.3%	35.8%
vote	0%	0.0%	0.0%	0.0%
	10%	81.6%	6.5%	5.3%
	20%	97.7%	13.0%	10.3%
	30%	99.5%	20.0%	16.6%
	40%	100.0%	26.6%	16.3%
audiology	0%	0.0%	0.0%	0.0%
	10%	100.0%	5.2%	8.8%
	20%	100.0%	10.4%	19.9%
	30%	100.0%	15.3%	27.9%
	40%	100.0%	21.1%	38.9%
promoters	0%	0.0%	0.0%	0.0%
	10%	99.1%	7.6%	6.6%
	20%	100.0%	14.3%	10.4%
	30%	100.0%	22.2%	13.2%
	40%	100.0%	29.9%	29.2%

on attributes with a large number of possible values than those that have, say, only two possible values.

3.3 EVALUATION MEASURES

We made use of several metrics for gauging the effects of polishing. First we looked at the classification accuracy and tree size of the decision trees built from the polished data. Then we compared the original noise-free data, the noise-added data, and the polished data to determine the change in the amount of noise attributable to polishing. We also looked at whether the correct value of a noisy attribute or class was indeed the nominated one obtained during the prediction phase of polishing. For convenience, we will use the term "attribute" to refer to both attributes and class when they are treated equally. Below we will discuss the preliminary experimental results obtained.

4 TREE ACCURACY AND STRUCTURE

The classification accuracy of the decision trees built from data sets with various noise levels, with and without polishing, is summarized in Table 3. Differences that are significant at the 0.05 level using a one-tailed paired t-test are marked with an $*$.

Decision trees built from the polished data performed as least as well as the decision trees built from the uncorrected data in all but two categories (soybean at 0%, and audiology at 10% noise levels). At the lower noise levels (0–10%), the differences in classification accuracy were not significant, which could partly be due to the fact that the accuracy was close to 100% for a few data sets in both the polished and unpolished cases. At the intermediate noise levels (20–30%), the improvements using the polished data were significant for most categories. At the highest noise level tested (40%), the results were more mixed. The differences were significant for four of the six data sets.

Grouping by data sets, improvements for soybean, LED-24, audiology and promoters were more significant. The mushroom data set fared well at some noise levels, but vote seemed to be immune to polishing and did not show any significant improvement at almost all levels. The most dramatic improvements were obtained with LED-24 and promoters at the higher noise levels. We will investigate possible reasons for these behaviors in Section 5 when we look at the actual changes made in the data sets.

The average tree size for each category is also shown in Table 3. In all but one category (mushroom at 30% noise level), the polished data gave rise to trees at least as small as the ones built from the unpolished data, sometimes with a fairly substantial reduction in size. Polishing seems to be able to remove some of the irregularities in the data, allowing a more compact tree to be built from the more uniform data.

5 PROXIMITY TO THE ORIGINAL DATA

Next we dug into the data sets and performed a count of the errors removed as well as introduced (separately) by polishing. We devised three different metrics for measuring the proximity of the polished data to the original noise-free data, and the relevant figures are summarized in Table 4. We will introduce the three metrics in Sections 5.1, 5.3, and 5.4 respectively. Some

Table 3: Classification accuracy (with standard deviation) and tree size without and with polishing. An * indicates a significant difference in classification accuracy at the 0.05 level.

Data Set	Noise Level	Accuracy ± Standard Deviation without	Accuracy ± Standard Deviation with		Tree Size without	Tree Size with
mushroom	0%	100.0 ± 0.0%	100.0 ± 0.0%		30.6	30.6
	10%	99.9 ± 0.1%	100.0 ± 0.0%		214.3	173.5
	20%	99.7 ± 0.4%	99.9 ± 0.1%	*	268.3	228.5
	30%	99.0 ± 0.7%	99.3 ± 0.6%	*	338.7	414.6
	40%	98.6 ± 0.5%	98.7 ± 0.5%		535.2	439.4
soybean	0%	92.1 ± 2.0%	91.9 ± 2.3%		95.1	94.5
	10%	86.2 ± 4.9%	88.9 ± 3.0%		156.9	123.2
	20%	83.0 ± 3.3%	85.2 ± 4.5%	*	202.3	192.5
	30%	72.2 ± 6.1%	76.3 ± 4.1%	*	278.5	243.3
	40%	50.7 ± 8.4%	55.0 ± 4.6%	*	328.8	299.6
LED-24	0%	100.0 ± 0.0%	100.0 ± 0.0%		19.0	19.0
	10%	100.0 ± 0.0%	100.0 ± 0.0%		78.2	48.1
	20%	92.3 ± 4.3%	97.6 ± 2.1%	*	193.4	87.9
	30%	76.2 ± 4.7%	90.6 ± 4.1%	*	336.0	157.4
	40%	49.0 ± 5.9%	67.8 ± 5.7%	*	491.6	323.6
vote	0%	94.7 ± 2.0%	94.7 ± 2.5%		14.5	4.9
	10%	94.7 ± 2.5%	95.0 ± 3.0%		17.8	12.7
	20%	94.0 ± 2.1%	95.7 ± 2.4%	*	20.8	10.0
	30%	92.9 ± 3.2%	94.2 ± 3.6%		43.3	25.6
	40%	92.4 ± 3.1%	92.9 ± 3.0%		27.1	18.7
audiology	0%	78.0 ± 7.7%	78.4 ± 8.5%		50.5	47.9
	10%	73.0 ± 7.9%	72.6 ± 5.7%		66.6	60.6
	20%	67.8 ± 8.0%	70.4 ± 5.8%	*	90.5	89.1
	30%	55.3 ± 11.7%	60.6 ± 8.3%	*	127.4	115.0
	40%	33.6 ± 11.7%	47.3 ± 4.4%	*	143.3	131.6
promoters	0%	75.6 ± 13.5%	76.7 ± 17.3%		21.1	11.8
	10%	73.0 ± 12.5%	81.6 ± 12.7%	*	21.8	15.0
	20%	65.9 ± 9.0%	82.1 ± 9.7%	*	28.2	12.2
	30%	55.6 ± 10.3%	70.9 ± 9.5%	*	32.2	16.2
	40%	60.3 ± 10.3%	64.8 ± 11.1%	*	31.8	30.2

of these metrics are inapplicable when the amount of noise is 0% or when the number of changes made by polishing is 0. These entries are marked with an * in the table.

5.1 REDUCTION IN OVERALL NOISE

An obvious metric to use would be the difference in the amount of noise in the data set before and after polishing. Let n_i and m_i respectively be the number of correct adjustments (from noisy to non-noisy values) and incorrect adjustments (from non-noisy to noisy values) made to the i-th attribute by the polishing procedure. Let t_i be the total number of instances with a noisy value in the i-th attribute. The net percentage reduction in noise averaged over all attributes is given by

$$NR = \frac{1}{k} \sum_{1 \leq i \leq k} \frac{n_i - m_i}{t_i},$$

where k is the total number of attributes (skipping over attributes with $t_i = 0$). The values for *NR* are shown in the column *Net Reduction* in Table 4.

The *NR* score can range from $-\infty$ to $+\infty$, a negative score indicating that more noise has been introduced into than removed from the data set, while a positive score indicates the opposite. Note that in most categories the net percentage reduction, although positive, was not very large. There are a number of excuses for this phenomenon. Recall that even if an instance contained noise, it was tweaked during the adjustment phase only if it could not be classified correctly by the trees originally built using the noisy data in a 10-fold cross validation. We can get an idea of how much noisy data could slip through without being flagged as requiring adjustment, by comparing the classification accuracy without polishing to the actual percentage of instances with noise. Except for the 0% noise level, the percentage of noisy instances was close to 90 or 100%

Table 4: Net percentage reduction in noise, percentage of changes that are correct, and percentage of noise correctly identified during the prediction phase. Ill-defined entries are marked with an $*$.

Data Set	Noise Level	Net Reduction	Correct Change	Noise Predicted
mushroom	0%	*	*	*
	10%	7.4%	69.6%	76.5%
	20%	6.8%	76.6%	73.6%
	30%	13.4%	80.0%	69.7%
	40%	4.2%	69.6%	64.6%
soybean	0%	*	0.0%	*
	10%	7.7%	65.5%	83.2%
	20%	4.0%	88.8%	77.0%
	30%	0.0%	48.6%	69.8%
	40%	0.8%	68.8%	65.6%
LED-24	0%	*	*	*
	10%	9.1%	29.1%	63.6%
	20%	2.1%	28.9%	61.5%
	30%	-2.6%	30.4%	60.0%
	40%	-6.3%	32.1%	57.3%
vote	0%	*	0.0%	*
	10%	1.6%	26.9%	74.1%
	20%	5.3%	47.2%	69.2%
	30%	2.0%	30.6%	65.0%
	40%	4.9%	56.6%	60.2%
audiology	0%	*	0.0%	*
	10%	6.7%	72.2%	92.6%
	20%	4.5%	91.1%	89.7%
	30%	3.1%	83.1%	87.1%
	40%	2.6%	84.6%	85.2%
promoters	0%	*	0.0%	*
	10%	-23.4%	15.8%	26.9%
	20%	-16.9%	14.0%	25.6%
	30%	-7.5%	12.7%	26.2%
	40%	-3.2%	17.1%	27.6%

(Table 2). However, for most categories, the classifier was able to maintain a fairly high classification accuracy without polishing (Table 3). For example, at the 40% noise level, every instance in the mushroom data set contained some noise, but only 1.4% was misclassified. Thus, we can expect a large proportion of the noisy data to go undetected during polishing and therefore was never subjected to adjustment at all.[2]

One of the reasons why the accuracy did not decrease as rapidly as the increase in the amount of noise might be that some of the attributes were not very relevant to the classification. Noise introduced into these attributes would not have as much of an impact. Thus, even though the majority of instances contained at least one noisy value, for most of these instances the classification was not affected, and thus we would not even attempt to adjust their values. Together with our conservative bias towards minimizing the number of adjustments made to each instance, the fairly low percentage reduction in the overall noise is somehow expected in the polishing setting.

[2]Note that the two criteria for correct classification are not exactly the same, as an instance only needs to be classified correctly by one particular tree in cross validation, while it is evaluated against all 10 trees generated from the (10-fold) cross validation in polishing.

5.2 ANOMALY: LED-24

A more disturbing observation is that for LED-24 at the 30–40% noise levels, and for promoters at all noise levels, the amount of noise *increased* after polishing (negative *NR* scores), while their corresponding classification accuracy improvements were among the highest of all data sets. We have two explanations for this phenomenon, and we will verify them using the LED-24 data set. The refined figures for the three metrics of Table 4 are given in Table 5. For comparison, the entries for LED-24 in Table 4 were reproduced in the columns marked *All*.

5.2.1 Irrelevant Attributes

LED-24 contains only 7 "real" attributes, and the other 17 attributes were assigned randomly generated values. We cannot reasonably expect to be able to deal with "noise" in an attribute with random values. By excluding these 17 spurious attributes from the calculation, we obtained the figures shown in the columns *7 Attributes:+Class* in Table 5. The *NR* values showed a marked increase from the ones computed using all 24 attributes. Note that the irrelevant attributes did not have to be removed from the data set before polishing; they were just excluded from the calculation of the metric *NR*.

Thus, we are improving the accuracy of the relevant attributes at the expense of the irrelevant attributes. This arguably can be defended by saying that the relevant attributes are the only ones that really matter. After all, ideally the irrelevant attributes would not enter into consideration by the classifier. However, a procedure that does not put more noise into the irrelevant attributes would still be preferable. One solution might be to limit the adjustments to only those attributes that are actually examined by the classifier. Or we might borrow an idea from the post-pruning of decision trees: after locating an appropriate combination of adjustments for an instance, we can try to remove as many adjustments as possible without altering the classification of the instance. This might limit the spurious changes, as removing these changes should not affect the classification.

5.2.2 Adjustments Towards an Alternative

The other explanation for the low *NR* value of LED-24 has to do with the design of the adjustment procedure. We prefer to change the attribute values rather than the class value, and a change in the latter is considered only when no appropriate combination of attribute changes can be found. Thus, when the class value contains noise, the adjustment procedure would first try to change the attribute values to fit the incorrect class value. The tweaks in the attributes might indeed be the correct ones associated with the altered class value, but in the eyes of our simple counting mechanism, the changes are for the worse as we are introducing additional changes that are not in the original data set. We can expect this effect to be more prominent in data sets where a small number of attributes are highly predictive of the class value, as then only a few tweaks to these attributes would be enough to fit the altered class value.

In the context of LED-24, we can check this hypothesis as we know the structure of this artificial data set. Preliminary examination of the polished data seemed to support the hypothesis. An instance with a changed class value was often prescribed attribute value changes that would move the instance "closer" to the changed class rather than to the original class. Here the distance was measured by the number of differences between the 7 relevant attributes of two instances.

To verify this hypothesis, we applied the metrics of Table 4 only to the portion of the data set whose class values had not been tampered with. These figures are reported in the columns *7 Attributes:-Class* in Table 5. The *NR* values increased to a level not seen in Table 4 for any data sets, but they are more in accord with the extent of improvement in the classification accuracy of LED-24 (Table 3).

We suspect these problems affected all data sets to some extent (perhaps in particular also promoters), but in the other cases it is not as easy to check into the data, as we do not know the underlying structure of the real life data sets.

Thus, the *NR* metric might not be very informative. In particular, we need a better way to assess the amount of noise in a data set. Rather than insisting on the original class value and penalizing any deviation from the original instance, we should reward changes towards fitting the altered class.

5.3 PERCENTAGE OF CORRECT ADJUSTMENTS

Another metric we used was the percentage of adjustments that were correct, in the sense that the corresponding values in the original noise-free data were restored. Let n_i and m_i be as in Section 5.1. The percentage of correct adjustments averaged over all attributes is given by

$$CA = \frac{1}{k} \sum_{1 \leq i \leq k} \frac{n_i}{n_i + m_i},$$

where k is the total number of attributes (skipping over attributes with zero changes). The values for *CA* are shown in the column *Correct Change* in Table 4.

Unlike the *NR* metric which is expected to have a fairly low value for most data sets, the *CA* metric can have values that range from 0 to 100%. A *CA* value of 50% indicates that the attributes are adjusted correctly half of the time and incorrectly the other half of the time, thus with no net change in the overall amount of noise. We would therefore like to see *CA* values greater than 50%, and the higher the value the better. The data sets mushroom, soybean, and audiology had fairly high *CA* values, indicating that the adjustment procedure was correcting the noisy values quite often. However, LED-24, vote, and promoters had *CA* values well below 50%.

The *CA* metric suffers from the same problems as *NR*. It can be affected by irrelevant attributes, and it does not take into account that the "incorrect" changes might make an instance fit the altered class rather than the original class. The problematic categories seemed to match those we encountered with *NR*. Similar to the situation for *NR*, for the LED-24 data set, there was a substantial improvement in the *CA* values when we considered only the 7 relevant attributes, in particular when we also excluded those instances with noisy class values (Table 5).

5.4 CORRECTLY IDENTIFIED NOISE DURING PREDICTION

One data set that consistently scored low on almost all the metrics we have considered so far is vote. At most noise levels, there was not much significant improvement in classification accuracy, the *NR* values were quite small, and the *CA* values were below 50%. This

Table 5: Statistics for subsets of the LED-24 data set. "All" includes the whole data set. "7 Attributes:+Class" considers only the 7 relevant attributes. "7 Attributes:-Class" in addition excludes all those instances with noisy class values.

Noise Level	Net Reduction			Correct Change			Noise Predicted		
	All	7 Attributes		All	7 Attributes		All	7 Attributes	
		+Class	-Class		+Class	-Class		+Class	-Class
0%	*	*	*	*	*	*	*	*	*
10%	9.1%	26.7%	44.7%	29.1%	72.8%	100.0%	63.6%	97.2%	97.9%
20%	2.1%	18.5%	36.8%	28.9%	70.3%	98.6%	61.5%	91.0%	97.7%
30%	-2.6%	11.0%	26.0%	30.4%	65.2%	94.3%	60.0%	83.0%	89.0%
40%	-6.3%	3.1%	13.6%	32.1%	58.3%	85.6%	57.3%	81.4%	81.9%

prompted us to question the quality of the attribute value nominations available in the first place. In the column *Noise Predicted* in Table 4, we report on the percentage of noisy attribute values in the training set that were correctly identified together with a correct nominated value in the prediction phase.

This value provides an upper bound for how well the adjustment phase can fare, in terms of the metrics we have defined. If a correct attribute value is not on the predicted list, we can hardly make the correct adjustment for it. The percentage of noise correctly predicted was reasonable for almost all data sets, including vote, but not for promoters. We have noted that promoters and LED-24 exhibited similar patterns: high classification accuracy improvement, but negative *NR* scores, and below 50% *CA* scores. Isolating the relevant attributes for LED-24 resulted in a jump in the percentage of noise predicted (Table 5), and we might expect a similar increase for promoters.

The poor results for vote, despite the high percentage of noise predicted, suggests that the weakness was in the adjustment phase of polishing (as opposed to the prediction phase), and in Section 6 we will discuss some desirable extensions. Another possible explanation is that although the percentage of noise predicted was reasonably high, the predictions might not include the most relevant attributes. We need to develop more informative metrics for measuring the various components affecting the performance of polishing, in order to achieve a better understanding of the mechanism.

6 FURTHER THOUGHTS

The analysis of the polished data sets generated during the experimental evaluation and the discrepancies between this and the classification accuracy pointed us to some desirable extensions, both in the polishing procedure and in the evaluation metrics. The prediction phase seems to be adequate, correctly identifying a fair percentage of the noise. There are a number of ways the adjustment phase can be improved. At the moment there is no provision for changing *both* the attribute and class values in the same instance. The mechanism only allows for adjusting either a set of attributes or failing that, the class value alone. Obviously this would miss at least part of all those instances in which both the attribute and class values have been corrupted. We would need to sort out a more comprehensive desirability ordering of the adjustments, and the associated heuristics.

We may also try to "re-polish" the polished data, and see if the data set can be progressively refined. While this might identify additional noise in the data, we can also expect that more and more of the data are *not* adjusted in successive iterations, as the data become more and more uniform. As we have observed, the majority of noisy instances were not adjusted at all, and this proportion is likely to rise with re-polishing. A related problem is whether we can use a more stringent criterion so that more instances would be subjected to adjustment, without overfitting the data to the trees we have at hand. Perhaps trees with a coarser structure (more heavily pruned) would be a better basis for polishing.

Another dimension of improvement is to develop a better evaluation metric for analyzing the performance of polishing. Classification accuracy is a very practical measure, as this is what we would be concerned about with future unseen instances. However, as we have discussed, the measures for determining the actual noise difference in the data might miscount some of the desirable changes as undesirable. Note that in the case of the LED-24 data set, we only tested the hypothesis that the adjustments were made towards fitting the altered class value. In general, however, there might be more than one combination of attribute settings that can result in the same classification, and the adjustments could well have been made to fit not the original combination, but an alternative but nonetheless correct combination. A more involved metric to determine the error count might be the difference between the polished instance with its nearest neighbor in the original data set, not necessarily the instance it was obtained from.

7 CONCLUSION

The experimental evaluation suggests that polishing is a promising approach to not only identifying the noise in the data, but also correcting it. Trees built from polished data resulted in higher classification accuracy and smaller tree size in many cases. Merely counting the changes in the polished data, however, did not produce very satisfactory scores in a number of cases, and we attribute this partly to the evaluation metrics themselves, which do not fully capture the essential information.

The major drawback of polishing is the time complexity involved. We need to build many trees with each of the attributes as the target class, as well as search over a potentially very long list of predicted changes for the appropriate adjustments. Another weakness is that the procedure is restricted to only nominal attributes, which limits its applicability.

Polishing assumes that the attributes are somehow related to each other and to the target class. We would expect it to perform poorly with two classes of attributes: those that are irrelevant for the classification task, and those that are independent of the other attributes. As discussed in Section 5.2.1, we might minimize changes made to the irrelevant attributes by limiting adjustments to only those attributes deemed predictive by the classifier, or by "post-pruning" the adjustments so that only the essential changes are retained.

In the LED-24 data set, there are 17 irrelevant attributes, and all attributes are conditionally independent given the target class. However, a substantial improvement in classification accuracy could still be obtained, suggesting that the relationship between each (relevant) attribute and the target class might be strong enough in some cases to achieve reasonable classification results. Experimenting with a larger variety of data sets and noise levels and developing more informative evaluation metrics would help us better understand the generality and characteristics of polishing.

Acknowledgement

I would like to thank Uroš Pompe for showing me pictures of Slovenia, and Ross Quinlan for pointing me in the right direction. This research was supported by the Australian Research Council A49801208.

References

[Brodley and Friedl, 1996] Carla E. Brodley and Mark A. Friedl. Identifying and eliminating mislabeled training instances. In *Proceedings of the Thirteenth National Conference on Artificial Intelligence*, 1996.

[Clark and Niblett, 1989] P. Clark and T. Niblett. The CN2 induction algorithm. *Machine Learning*, 3(4):261–283, 1989.

[Domingos and Pazzani, 1996] Pedro Domingos and Michael Pazzani. Beyond independence: Conditions for the optimality of the simple Bayesian classifier. In *Proceedings of the Thirteenth International Conference on Machine Learning*, pages 105–112, 1996.

[Gamberger *et al.*, 1996] Dragan Gamberger, Nada Lavrač, and Sašo Džeroski. Noise elimination in inductive concept learning: A case study in medical diagnosis. In *Proceedings of the Seventh International Workshop on Algorithmic Learning Theory*, pages 199–212, 1996.

[John, 1995] George H. John. Robust decision trees: Removing outliers from databases. In *Proceedings of the First International Conference on Knowledge Discovery and Data Mining*, pages 174–179, 1995.

[Kononenko, 1991] Igor Kononenko. Semi-naive Bayesian classifier. In *Proceedings of the Sixth European Working Session on Learning*, pages 206–219, 1991.

[Langley *et al.*, 1992] P. Langley, W. Iba, and K. Thompson. An analysis of Bayesian classifiers. In *Proceedings of the Tenth National Conference on Artificial Intelligence*, pages 223–228, 1992.

[Mitchell, 1997] Tom M. Mitchell. *Machine Learning*. McGraw-Hill, 1997.

[Murphy and Aha, 1998] P. M. Murphy and D. W. Aha. UCI repository of machine learning databases. University of California, Irvine, Department of Information and Computer Science, 1998. `http://www.ics.uci.edu/~mlearn/MLRepository.html`.

[Quinlan, 1987] J. Ross Quinlan. Simplifying decision trees. *International Journal of Man-Machine Studies*, 27(3):221–234, 1987.

[Quinlan, 1993] J. Ross Quinlan. *C4.5: Programs for Machine Learning.* Morgan Kaufmann, 1993.

[Rousseeuw and Leroy, 1987] Peter J. Rousseeuw and Annick M. Leroy. *Robust Regression and Outlier Detection.* John Wiley & Sons, 1987.

[Shapiro, 1987] Alen D. Shapiro. *Structured Induction in Expert Systems.* Addison-Wesley, 1987.

An Accelerated Chow and Liu Algorithm: Fitting Tree Distributions to High-Dimensional Sparse Data

PROBABILISTIC TREE models (undirected)

inference $O(n)$ worst case; $O(n \log n)$ average
learning $O(n^2)$

Marina Meilă
Center for Biological and Computational Learning
Massachusetts Institute of Technology
Cambridge, MA 02142, USA
mmp@ai.mit.edu

Abstract

Chow and Liu introduced an algorithm for fitting a multivariate distribution with a tree (i.e. a density model that assumes that there are only pairwise dependencies between variables) and that the graph of these dependencies is a spanning tree. The original algorithm is quadratic in the dimension of the domain, and linear in the number of data points that define the target distribution P. This paper shows that for sparse, discrete data, fitting a tree distribution can be done in time and memory that is typically subquadratic in the number of variables and the size of the data set. The new algorithm, called the **acCL** algorithm, achieves speed ups of several orders of magnitude in the experiments.

1 Introduction

[Chow and Liu, 1968] introduced an algorithm for fitting a multivariate distribution with a tree, i. e. a density model that assumes that there are only pairwise dependencies between variables and that the graph of these dependencies is a spanning tree. Recently, the interest in this algorithm, hitherto called the CL algorithm, has been revived by the introduction of several probabilistic models that extend the spanning tree model. The mixture of trees of [Meilă and Jordan, 1998] is a mixture model in which each component is a spanning tree with a possibly different topology over the set of variables. The TANB (Tree Augmented Naive Bayes) model of [Friedman et al., 1997] is a mixture of trees designed for classification.

Trees enjoy many properties that make them attractive as modeling tools: they are intuitively appealing, have low complexity and yet a flexible topology, have efficient and simple algorithms for sampling and inference. Moreover, trees are one of the few classes of graphical models for which structure search is tractable [Heckerman et al., 1995]. The CL algorithm finds the structure and parameters of the tree T that best fits a given distribution P as measured by the Kullback-Leibler (KL) divergence

$$KL(P\,||\,T) \;=\; \sum_x P(x) \log \frac{P(x)}{T(x)} \qquad (1)$$

The algorithm uses the mutual information I_{uv} under P between each pair of variables u, v in the domain. When P is an empirical distribution obtained from and i.i.d. set of data, the computation of all the mutual information values takes time quadratic in the number of variables n and linear in the size of the dataset N. This time is acceptable for many problems but becomes prohibitive when the dimension n of the domain becomes large.

For example, in information retrieval, the data points are documents and the variables are words from a vocabulary. A document is represented as a binary vector with a component equal to 1 for each word v that is present in the document and a 0 component for each of the non-appearing words. The number N of documents in the data set is of the order of 10^3 – 10^4 and so is the vocabulary size. This means that fitting a tree to the data requires $n^2 N \sim 10^9 - 10^{12}$ counting operations. But this domain has a particularity: each document contains only a relatively small number of words (of the order of 10^2) and therefore most of the components of its binary vector are 0. This property is called data *sparsity*.

The present paper shows how to take advantage of

sparsity to improve on the time and memory requirements of the CL algorithm in order to allow the use of tree density models for higher dimensional domains. This improvement can be carried over to learning mixtures of trees or TANB models. One idea is to compare mutual informations between pairs of variables **without actually computing them** when this is possible. A second idea is to exploit the sparsity of the data to speed up the computation of the sufficient statistics. Combining the two will result in an algorithm that typically is jointly subquadratic in N and n w.r.t. both running time and memory. This algorithm, that we call **accelerated CL** algorithm (**acCL**) will be presented and analyzed in the rest of this paper.

2 Fitting a tree to a distribution

We start by introducing the tree distribution and the notation that will be used throughout the paper. For more detail the reader is recommended to consult [Chow and Liu, 1968, Meilă and Jordan, 1998, Meilă-Predoviciu, 1999]. Let V denote the set of variables of interest, $|V| = n$. Let v be a variable in V, r_v its number of values (it is assumed that all the variables are discrete), x_v a particular value of v and x an n-dimensional vector representing an assignment to all the variables in V.

Tree distributions. We use trees as graphical representations for families of probability distributions over V that satisfy a common set of independence relationships encoded in the tree topology[1]. V are the tree's vertices; E denotes its edge set. Edges show direct dependencies, or, more precisely, the absence of an edge between two variables signifies that they are independent, given all the other variables in V. Now we define a probability distribution T that is *conformal* with a tree. Let us denote by T_{uv} and T_v the marginals of T:

$$T_{uv}(x_u, x_v) = \sum_{x_{V-\{u,v\}}} T(x_u, x_v, x_{V-\{u,v\}})$$
$$T_v(x_v) = \sum_{x_{V-\{v\}}} T(x_v, x_{V-\{v\}}).$$

Let $\deg v$ be the *degree* of vertex v, e.g. the number of edges incident to $v \in V$. The distribution T is conformal with the tree (V, E) if it can be factored as:

$$T(x) = \frac{\prod_{(u,v)\in E} T_{uv}(x_u, x_v)}{\prod_{v\in V} T_v(x_v)^{\deg v - 1}} \tag{2}$$

[1]We shall call a graph that has no cycles a *tree*. Note that in the graph theory literature, our definition corresponds to a *forest*.

The distribution itself will be called a tree when no confusion is possible.

The CL algorithm Let us now turn to learning trees from data. The observed data are denoted by $\mathcal{D} = \{x^1, x^2, \ldots, x^N\}$, where each x^i represents a vector of observations for all the variables in V. Learning a tree in the Maximum Likelihood framework means finding T^{opt} that satisfies

$$T^{opt} = \operatorname*{argmax}_T \sum_{i=1}^{N} \log T(x^i) \tag{3}$$

This problem is a special case of the more general task of fitting a tree to a distribution P by minimizing $KL(P\,||\,T)$. The fact that the tree model is factorable allows for an efficient and elegant algorithm for solving the latter problem, owed to Chow and Liu [Chow and Liu, 1968]. The algorithm is briefly described here.

The algorithm is based on the fact that all the information about a distribution P that is necessary to fit a tree is contained in its *pairwise marginals* $P_{uv}(x_u, x_v) = \sum_{x_{V-\{u,v\}}} P(x_u, x_v, x_{V-\{u,v\}})$. If the distribution is an empirical distribution defined by a data set $\mathcal{D}$, computing these marginals from data takes $\mathcal{O}(n^2 N)$ operations.

Further, to find the tree structure, given by its set of edges E, one has to compute the mutual information between each pair of variables in V under the target distribution P

$$I_{uv} = \sum_{x_u x_v} P_{uv}(x_u, x_v) \log \frac{P_{uv}(x_u, x_v)}{P_u(x_u) P_v(x_v)}, \quad u, v \in V, u \neq v. \tag{4}$$

Since V has n variables, there are $n(n-1)/2$ mutual informations to be computed. After that, the optimal tree structure E is found by a *Maximum Weight Spanning Tree* (MWST) algorithm using I_{uv} as the weight for edge $(u, v), \forall u, v \in V$. The MWST can be found in several ways [Cormen et al., 1990, Tarjan, 1983, Fredman and Tarjan, 1987]. Here we use the Kruskal algorithm [Cormen et al., 1990], which is essentially a greedy algorithm. The candidate edges are sorted in decreasing order of their weights (i.e. mutual informations). Then, starting with an empty E, the algorithm examines one edge at a time (in the order resulting from the sort operation), checks if it forms a cycle with the edges already in E and, if not, adds it to E. The algorithm ends when $n-1$ edges have been added to E; in this process $n_K \geq n-1$ edges are examined.

The time required by the Kruskal algorithm is $\mathcal{O}(n^2 \log n)$ corresponding to the time necessary to sort the $n(n-1)/2$ mutual informations. The Kruskal algorithm is not the fastest MWST algorithm, but it has the advantage to be compatible with the accelerating method that is proposed here. All the other known MWST algorithms have a running time at least proportional to the number of candidate edges. In this case, they will be at least quadratic in n, having only a $\log n$ advantage over the Kruskal algorithm.

Once the tree is found, its marginals T_{uv}, $(u,v) \in E$ are exactly equal to the corresponding marginals P_{uv} of the target distribution P.

$$T_{uv}^{opt} \equiv P_{uv} \text{ for } (u,v) \in E \tag{5}$$

In conclusion, the running time of the CL algorithm is dominated by the computation of the pairwise marginals and is

$$\mathcal{O}(n^2(N + \log n)). \tag{6}$$

3 Assumptions

Here are presented the assumptions underlying the accelerated CL algorithm. Of the four assumptions, only the sparsity assumption is essential; we shall see later on that the first two can be relaxed.

Binary variables. All variables in V take values in the set $\{0,1\}$. When a variables takes value 1 we say that it is "on", otherwise we say it is "off". Without loss of generality we can further assume that a variable is off more times than it is on in the given dataset.

The target distribution P is derived from a set of observations of size N. Let us denote by N_v the number of times variable v is on in the dataset and by N_{uv} the number of times variables u and v are simultaneously on. We call each of the latter events a *cooccurrence* of u and v. The marginal P_{uv} of u and v is given by

$$\begin{aligned} N.P_{uv}(1,1) &= N_{uv} & (7)\\ N.P_{uv}(1,0) &= N_u - N_{uv} & (8)\\ N.P_{uv}(0,1) &= N_v - N_{uv} & (9)\\ N.P_{uv}(0,0) &= N - N_v - N_u + N_{uv} & (10) \end{aligned}$$

All the information about P that is necessary for fitting the tree is summarized in the counts N, N_v and N_{uv}, $u,v = 1,\ldots,n$ that are assumed to be non-negative. From now on we will consider P to be represented by these counts. In the rest of this paper, for simplicity, the counts will be considered to be integers. But the reader should note that this condition can be dropped if necessary (as, for example, if the data points are "weighted" by real numbers).

Sparse data. Let us denote by $0 \le |x| \le n$ the number of variables that are on in observation x. Further, define s, the *sparsity* of the data by

$$s = \max_{i=1,N} |x^i| \tag{11}$$

If, for example, the data are documents and the variables represent words from a vocabulary, then s represents the maximum number of distinct words in a document. The time and memory requirements of the accelerated CL algorithm that we are going to introduce depend on the sparsity s. The lower the sparsity, the more efficient the algorithm. From now on, s will be assumed to be a constant and $s << n,\ N$.

Data/dimension ratio bounded The ratio of the number of data points N vs. the dimension of the domain n is bounded. $\frac{N}{n} \le R$. This is a technical assumption that is plausible for large n and N.

4 The accelerated CL algorithm

First idea: Comparing mutual informations between binary non-cooccurring variables Let us focus on the pairs u,v that do not cooccur, i.e. for which $N_{uv} = 0$. For such a pair, the mutual information is

$$\begin{aligned} I_{uv} &= \qquad (12)\\ &= \frac{1}{N}\{-(N-N_u)\log(N-N_u) - (N-N_v)\log(N-N_v)\\ &\quad + (N-N_u-N_v)\log(N-N_u-N_v) + N\log N\} \end{aligned}$$

Knowing that N is fixed for the dataset, it follows that I_{uv} in the 0 cooccurrence case is function of 2 variables: N_v and N_u. Let us fix u (and consequently N_u) and analyze the variation of the mutual information w.r.t. N_v:

$$\frac{\partial I_{uv}}{\partial N_v} = \log \frac{N - N_v}{N - N_u - N_v} > 0 \tag{13}$$

It follows that if $N_{uv} = 0$ then the mutual information I_{uv} is monotonically increasing with N_v for a fixed u. Put in other terms, for a given variable u and any two variables v, v' for which $N_{uv} = N_{uv'} = 0$

$$N_v > N_{v'} \text{ implies that } I_{uv} > I_{uv'}.$$

This observation allows us to partially sort the mutual informations I_{uv} for non-cooccurring pairs u, v,

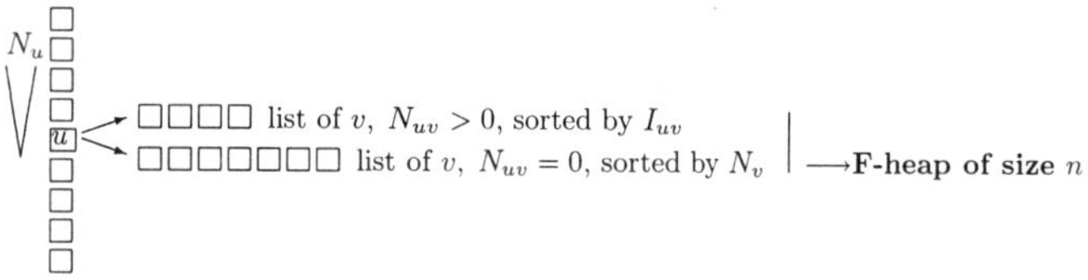

Figure 1: The data structure that supplies the next candidate edge. Vertically to the left are the variables, sorted by decreasing N_u. For a given u, there are two lists: $C(u)$, sorted by decreasing I_{uv} and (the virtual list) $V_0(u)$ sorted by decreasing N_v. The maximum of the two first elements of these lists is is inserted into an F-heap.The overall maximum of I_{uv} can then be extracted as the maximum of the F-heap.

without computing them. First, we have to sort all the variables by their number of occurrences N_v. We store the result in a list L. This gives an ordering "$\succ$" for all the variables in V.

$$v \succ u \;\Leftrightarrow\; N_v > N_u \tag{14}$$

For each u, we define the list of variable following u and not cooccurring with it:

$$V_0(u) \;=\; \{v \in V,\; v \prec u,\; N_{uv} = 0\} \tag{15}$$

This list is sorted by decreasing N_v and therefore, implicitly, by decreasing I_{uv}. Since the data are sparse, most pairs of variables do not cooccur. Therefore, by creating the lists $V_0(u)$, a large number of the mutual informations are partially sorted. Before showing how to use this construction, let us examine an efficient way of computing the N_{uv} counts when the data are sparse.

Second idea: computing cooccurrences in a list representation Let $\mathcal{D} = \{x^1, \dots x^N\}$ be a set of observations over n binary variables. If $s << n$ it is efficient to represent each observation in $\mathcal{D}$ as a list of the variables that are on in the respective observation. Thus, data point $x^i, i = 1, \dots N$ will be represented by the list $xlist^i = \text{list}\{v \in V | x^i_v = 1\}$. The space required by the lists is no more than sN and much smaller than the space required by the binary vector representation of the same data (i.e. nN).

Now, note that the total number N_C of cooccurrences in the dataset $\mathcal{D}$ is

$$N_C \;=\; \sum_{v \succ u} N_{uv} \;\leq\; \frac{1}{2} s^2 N. \tag{16}$$

Indeed, each data point x contains at most s variables that are on, therefore contributing at most $s(s-1)/2$ cooccurrences to the sum in (16).

For the variables that cooccur with u, a set of *cooccurrence lists* $C(u)$ is created. Each $C(u)$ contains records (v, I_{uv}), $v \prec u, N_{uv} > 0$ and is sorted by decreasing I_{uv}. To represent the lists $V_0(u)$ (that contain many more elements) we use their "complements" $\overline{V_0}(u) = \{v \in V,\; v \prec u,\; N_{uv} > 0\}$. $\overline{V_0}(u)$ contains the same variables as $C(u)$ but no mutual informations, and is sorted by decreasing N_v. Accessing any $V_0(u)$ sequentially (in decreasing order of the [not computed] I_{uv}) is done by traversing the list L starting at the successor of u, skipping the variables contained in $\overline{V}_0(u)$.

It can be shown [Meilă-Predoviciu, 1999] that computing all the cooccurrence counts and constructing the lists $C(u), \overline{V}_0(u),\; u \in V$ takes an amount of time proportional to the number of cooccurrences N_C up to a logarithmic factor, namely

$$\mathcal{O}(s^2 N \log(s^2 N/n)). \tag{17}$$

Compare this value with $\mathcal{O}(n^2 N)$ which is the time to compute P_{uv} in the CL algorithm to see that (if the logarithmic factor is ignored) the present method replaces the dimension of the domain n by s the number of variables observed to be on in the expression of the running time. The memory requirements for the lists are also at most proportional to N_C, hence $\mathcal{O}(s^2 N)$.

Putting it all together: the acCL algorithm and its data structures. So far, we have efficient methods for computing the cooccurrences and for partially sorting the mutual informations. What we aim for is to create a mechanism that will output the edges (uv) in the decreasing order of their mutual information. If this is achieved, then the Kruskal algorithm can be used to construct the optimal tree.

We shall set up this mechanism in the form of a *Fibonacci heap* (F-heap) [Fredman and Tarjan, 1987] called *vheap* that contains an element for each $u \in V$, represented by the edge with the highest mutual information among the edges (uv), $v \prec u$. The maximum over this set will obviously be the maximum over the mutual informations of all the possible edges not yet eliminated. The record in *vheap* is of the form (c, u, v, I_{uv}), with $v \prec u$ and I_{uv} being the key used for sorting. Once the maximum is extracted, the used edge has to be replaced by the next largest (in terms of I_{uv}) edge in u's lists.

To perform this latter task it easy now: for each

u we have the lists $C(u)$ and $V_0(u)$. All we have to do is to compute I_{uv_0} with v_0 being the head of $V_0(u)$. By comparing I_{uv_0} with the mutual information of the head of $C(u)$ we find $\max_{v \prec u} I_{uv}$. This value, together with its corresponding u, v, N_{uv} forms the record that is inserted in the F-heap. Every time an edge (u, v, N_{uv}, I_{uv}) is inserted in *vheap*, v is deleted from $C(u)$ or respectively $V_0(u)$. The data structures involved in this process are schematically shown in figure 1 (b). Now the Kruskal algorithm can be used to construct the desired spanning tree.

Algorithm **acCL**

Input variable set V of size n
dataset $\mathcal{D} = \{xlist^i,\ i = 1, \ldots N\}$
1. compute N_v for $v \in V$;create L, list of variables in V sorted by decreasing N_v
2. compute cooccurrences N_{uv}; create lists $C(u)$, $\overline{V}_0(u),\ u \in V$
3. create *vheap*
for $u \in vlist$
$v = \underset{\text{head}C_u, \text{head}V_0(u)}{\text{argmax}} I_{uv}$
insert (c, u, v, I_{uv}) in *vheap*
4. E = **Kruskal**(*vheap*); store $c = N_{uv}$ for the edges (uv) added to E
5. for $(uv) \in E$
compute the probability table T_{uv} using N_u, N_v, N_{uv} and N.

Output T

Running time The algorithm takes: $\mathcal{O}(sn)$ for computing $N_v, v \in V$, $\mathcal{O}(n \log n)$ for sorting the variables, $\mathcal{O}(s^2 N \log(s^2 N/n))$ for step 2, $\mathcal{O}(n)$ for step 3[2], $\mathcal{O}(n_K \log n + N_C)$ for the Kruskal algorithm (n_K is the number of edges examined by the algorithm, $\log n$ is the time for an extraction from *vheap*, N_C is an upper bound for the number of elements in the lists $\overline{V}_0$ whose elements need to be skipped occasionally when we extract variables from the virtual lists V_0), $\mathcal{O}(n)$ for creating the the $n - 1$ probability tables in step 5. Summing these terms we obtain the upper bound for the running time of the acCL algorithm as

$$\mathcal{O}(n \log n + sn + s^2 N \log \frac{s^2 N}{n} + n_K \log n). \tag{18}$$

If we ignore the logarithmic factor this simplifies to

$$\tilde{\mathcal{O}}(sn + s^2 N + n_K). \tag{19}$$

[2]Plus the time to skip some elements of $\overline{V}_0(u)$ if necessary. This time is accounted for by the bound for step 4.

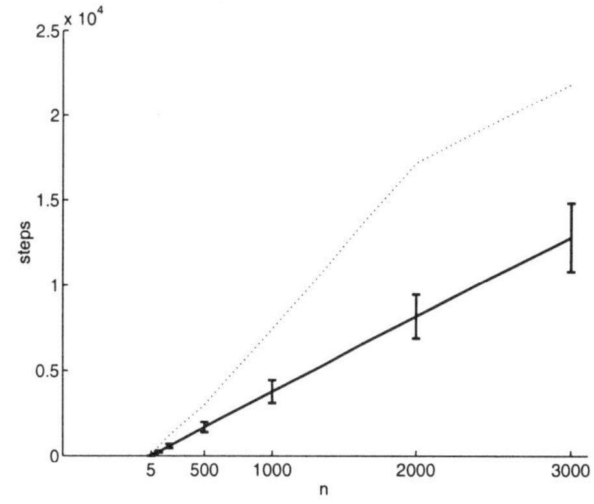

Figure 2: The mean (full line), standard deviation and maximum (dotted line) of Kruskal algorithm steps n_K over 1000 runs plotted against $n \log n$. n ranges from 5 to 3000. The edge weights were sampled from a uniform distribution.

For constant or bounded s, the above bound is a polynomial of degree 1 in the three variables n, N and n_K. But we know that n_K the total number of edges inspected by Kruskal's algorithm has the range $n - 1 \leq n_K \leq \frac{n(n-1)}{2}$. Hence, in the worst case the above algorithm is quadratic in n. However, there are reasons to believe that in practice the dependence of n_K on n is subquadratic. Random graph theory implies that if the distribution of the weight values is the same for all edges, then Kruskal's algorithm should take a number of steps proportional to $n \log n$ [West, 1996]. This result is sustained by experiments we have conducted: we ran Kruskal algorithm on sets of random weights over domains of dimension up to $n = 3000$. For each n, 1000 runs were performed. Figure 2 shows the average and maximum n_K plotted versus $n \log n$. The curves display a close to linear dependence.

Memory requirements Besides the memory for data and results, we need $\mathcal{O}(N_C)$ to store the cooccurrences and the lists $C(u), \overline{V}_0(u)$ and $\mathcal{O}(n)$ for L, *vheap* and the Kruskal algorithm. Hence, the additional space used by the acCL algorithm is $\mathcal{O}(s^2 N + n)$.

5 Generalization to discrete variables of arbitrary arity

This section will show how the Chow and Liu algorithm can be accelerated in discrete domains where the variables can take more than two values. We shall assume that a variable $v \in V$ takes r_v values, $2 \leq r_v \leq r_{MAX}$. The algorithm that we are going to develop is a simple extension of the acCL algorithm. Therefore, we shall present only the ideas that lead to extension and the modifications to the acCL algorithm that they imply.

First we redefine the data sparsity: in the forthcoming we shall assume that for each variable exists a special value that appears with higher frequency than all the other values. This value will be denoted by 0, without loss of generality. For example, in a medical domain, the value 0 for a variable would represent the "normal" value, whereas the abnormal values of each variable would be designated by non-zero values. An occurrence for variable v will be the event $v \neq 0$ and a cooccurrence of u and v means that u and v are both non-zero in the same data point. We define $|x|$ as the number of non-zero values in observation x. The sparsity s will be the maximum of $|x|$ over the data set, as before.

It is anticipated that the high frequency of the 0 values will help accelerate the tree learning algorithm. As before, we shall represent only the occurrences explicitly, creating thereby a compact and efficient data structure. Moreover, we shall demonstrate that presorting mutual informations for non-cooccurring variables in this case can be done in the same way as for binary variables.

Computing cooccurrences Following the previously introduced idea of not representing 0 values explicitly, each data point x will be replaced by the list $xlist$ of the variables that occur in it: $xlist = \text{list}\{(v, x_v), v \in V, x_v \neq 0\}$.

A cooccurrence will be represented by the quadruple (u, x_u, v, x_v), $x_u, x_v \neq 0$. Counting and storing cooccurrences can be done in the same time as before and with a proportionally larger amount on memory, required by the additional need to store the (non-zero) variable values.

Instead of one cooccurrence count N_{uv} we shall now have a two-way contingency table N_{uv}^{ij}. Each N_{uv}^{ij} represents the number of data points where $u = i, v = j$, $i, j \neq 0$. This contingency table, together with the marginal counts N_v^j (defined as the number of data points where $v = j$, $j \neq 0$) and with N completely determine the joint distribution of u and v (and consequently the mutual information I_{uv}). Constructing the cooccurrence contingency tables multiplies the storage requirements of this step of the algorithm by $\mathcal{O}(r_{MAX}^2)$ but does not change the running time significantly.

Presorting mutual informations Our goal is to presort the mutual informations I_{uv} for all $v \prec u$ that do not cooccur with u. We show that this can be done exactly as before. The derivations below will be clearer if they are made in terms of probabilities; therefore, we use the notations:

$$P_v(i) = \frac{N_v^i}{N}, \quad i \neq 0; \quad P_{v0} \equiv P_v(0) = 1 - \sum_{i \neq 0} P_v(i) \tag{20}$$

The above quantities represent the (empirical) probabilities of v taking value $i \neq 0$ and 0 respectively. Entropies will be denoted by H.

A "chain rule" expression for the entropy of a discrete variable. The entropy H_v of any multivalued discrete variable v can be decomposed in the following way:

$$\begin{aligned} H_v &= \\ &= -P_{v0} \log P_{v0} - \sum_{i \neq 0} P_v(i) \log P_v(i) \\ &= \underbrace{-P_{v0} \log P_{v0} - (1 - P_{v0}) \log(1 - P_{v0})}_{H_{v0}} - (1 - P_{v0}) \\ &\quad \underbrace{\sum_{i \neq 0} \frac{P_v(i)}{(1 - P_{v0})} \log \frac{P_v(i)}{(1 - P_{v0})}}_{-H_{\overline{v}}} \\ &= H_{v0} + (1 - P_{v0}) H_{\overline{v}} \end{aligned} \tag{21}$$

This decomposition represents a sampling model where first we choose whether v will be zero or not, and then, if the outcome is "non-zero" we choose one of the remaining values by sampling from the distribution $P_{v|v \neq 0}(i) = \frac{P_v(i)}{1 - P_{v0}}$. H_{v0} is the uncertainty associated with the first choice, whereas $H_{\overline{v}} \equiv H_{v|v \neq 0}$ is the entropy of the outcome of the second one. The advantage of this decomposition for our purpose is that it separates the 0 outcome from the others and "encapsulates" the uncertainty of the latters in the number $H_{\overline{v}}$.

The mutual information of two non-cooccurring variables is $I_{uv} = H_u - H_{u|v}$. The second term, the conditional entropy of u given v is

$$H_{u|v} = P_{v0} H_{u|v=0} + \sum_{j \neq 0} P_v(j) \underbrace{H_{u|v=j}}_{0} \tag{22}$$

The last term in the above formula is 0 because, for any non-zero value of v, the condition $N_{uv} = 0$ implies that u has to be 0. Let us now develop $H_{u|v=0}$ using the decomposition in equation (21).

$$H_{u|v=0} = H_{u0|v=0} + (1 - P_{u=0|v=0}) H_{u|u \neq 0, v=0} \tag{23}$$

Because u and v are never non-zero in the same time, all non-zero values of u are paired with zero values of v. Consequently $Pr[u = i|u \neq 0, v = 0] = Pr[u = i|u \neq 0]$ and $H_{u|u \neq 0, v=0} = H_{\overline{u}}$. The term $H_{u=0|v=0}$ is the entropy of a binary variable whose probability is $Pr[u = 0|v = 0]$. This probability equals

$$Pr[u = 0|v = 0] = 1 - \frac{1 - P_{u0}}{1 - P_{v0}} \quad (24)$$

Note that in order to obtain a non-negative probability in the above equation one needs $1 - P_{u0} \leq P_{v0}$, a condition that is always satisfied if u and v do not cooccur. Replacing the previous three equations in the formula of the mutual information, we get

$$\begin{aligned} I_{uv} &= P_{u0} \log P_{u0} - P_{v0} \log P_{v0} \quad (25) \\ &= +(P_{u0} + P_{v0} - 1) \log(P_{u0} + P_{v0} - 1) \end{aligned}$$

This expression, remarkably, depends only on P_{u0} and P_{v0}. Taking its partial derivative with respect to P_{v0} yields

$$\frac{\partial I_{uv}}{\partial P_{v0}} = \log \frac{P_{v0} + P_{u0} - 1}{P_{v0}} < 0 \quad (26)$$

a value that is always negative, independently of P_{v0}. This shows the mutual information increases monotonically with the "occurrence frequency" of v given by $1 - P_{v0}$. Note also that the above expression for the derivative is a rewrite of the result obtained for binary variables in (13).

We have shown that the acCL algorithm can be extended to variables taking more than two values by making only one (minor) modification: the replacement of the scalar counts N_v and N_{uv} by the vectors N_v^j, $j \neq 0$ and, respectively, the contingency tables N_{uv}^{ij}, $i, j \neq 0$.

6 Experiments

The following experiments compare the speed of the acCL algorithm w.r.t the traditional Chow and Liu method under controlled conditions on artificial data.

The binary domain dimension n varies from 50 to 1000. Each data point has a fixed number s of variables being on. The sparsity s takes the values 5, 10, 15 and 100. The small values were chosen to gauge the advantage of the accelerated algorithm under extremely favorable conditions. The larger value will help us see how the performance degrades under more realistic circumstances. The data were generated from an artificially constructed non-uniform, non-factored distribution. For each pair n, s a set of 10,000 points was created.

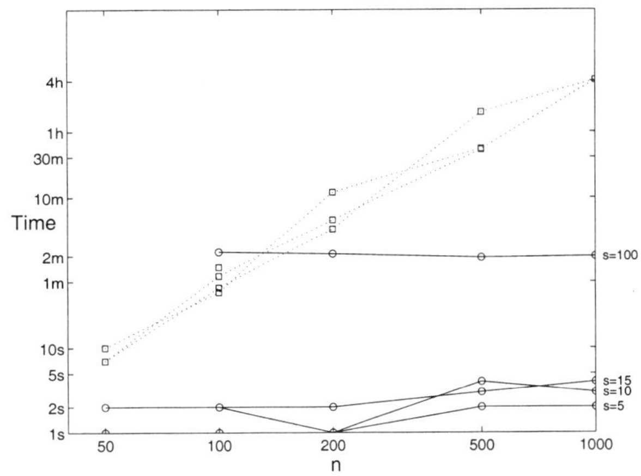

Figure 3: Real running time for the accelerated (full line) and traditional (dotted line) CL algorithms versus number of vertices n for different values of the sparsity s.

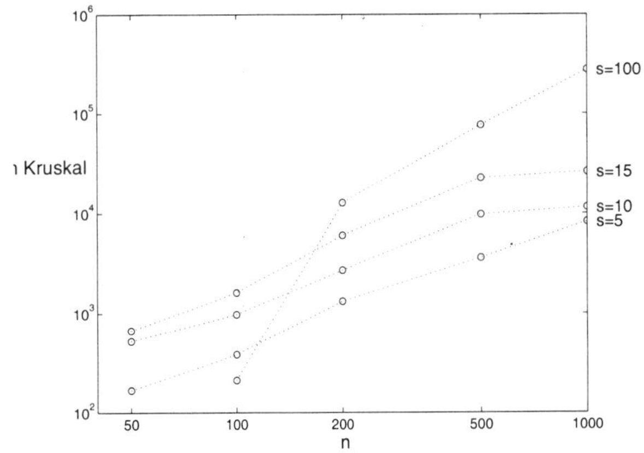

Figure 4: Number of steps of the Kruskal algorithm n_K versus domain size n measured for the acCL algorithm for different values of s.

Each data set was used by both CL and acCL to fit one tree distribution and the running times were recorded and plotted in figure 3. The improvements over the traditional version for sparse data are spectacular: learning a tree over 1000 variables from 10,000 data points takes 4 hours by the traditional algorithm and only 4 seconds by the accelerated version when the data are sparse ($s = 15$). For $s = 100$ the acCL algorithm takes 2 minutes to complete, improving on the traditional algorithm by a factor of "only" 120.

Note also that the running time of the accelerated algorithm seems to be almost independent of the dimension of the domain. On the other side, the number of steps n_K (figure 4) grows with n. This implies that the bulk of the computation lies with the steps preceding the Kruskal algorithm proper. Namely, that it is in computing cooccurrences and organizing the data that most of the time is spent. Figure 3 also confirms that the running time of the traditional CL algorithm grows quadratically with n and is independent of s.

7 Concluding remarks

This paper has presented a way of taking advantage of sparsity in the data to accelerate the tree learning algorithm. The method achieves its performance by exploiting characteristics of the data (sparsity) and of the problem (the weights represent mutual informations) that are external to the Maximum Weight Spanning Tree algorithm proper. The algorithm obtained is worst case $\tilde{\mathcal{O}}(sn + s^2N + n^2)$ but typically $\tilde{\mathcal{O}}(sn + s^2N)$ a significant asymptotic improvement over the $\mathcal{O}(n^2N)$ of the traditional algorithm. Throughout the paper we have assumed that s is constant and small. If s is large, then the acCL algorithm degrades to a traditional CL algorithm. If s varies, then the formulas provided will allow one to establish the corresponding growth rates.

The algorithm extends to non-integer counts, hence being applicable to the much richer class of mixtures of trees as well. It has been shown empirically that a very significant part of the algorithms' running time is spent in computing cooccurrences. This prompts future work on learning statistical models over large domains to focus on the efficient computation and usage of the relevant sufficient statistics. Work in this directions includes the structural EM algorithm [Friedman, 1998] and its variant [Friedman and Getoor, 1999] as well as the A-D trees of [Moore and Lee, 1998]. The latter are closely related to our representation of the pairwise marginals P_{uv} by counts. In fact, our representation can be viewed as a "reduced" A-D tree that stores only pairwise statistics. Consequently, when an A-D tree representation is already computed, it can be exploited in steps 1 and 2 of the acCL algorithm. But constructing the whole A-D tree for the data set is considerably more demanding computationally than computing the cooccurrence counts alone. The works of [de Marcken, 1998, Steeg, 1997] on discovering dependencies in subquadratic time propose heuristic methods aimed at modeling very high dimensional domains that are not sparse.

Acknowledgements

I am indebted to Paul Viola for suggesting this topic and to David Karger for many stimulating discussions along the way.

References

[Chow and Liu, 1968] Chow, C. K. and Liu, C. N. (1968). Approximating discrete probability distributions with dependence trees. *IEEE Transactions on Information Theory*, IT-14(3):462–467.

[Cormen et al., 1990] Cormen, T. H., Leiserson, C. E., and Rivest, R. R. (1990). *Introduction to Algorithms.* MIT Press.

[de Marcken, 1998] de Marcken, C. G. (1998). Dependency detection in subquadratic time.

[Fredman and Tarjan, 1987] Fredman, M. L. and Tarjan, R. E. (1987). Fibonacci heaps and their uses in improved network optimization algorithms. *Jounal of the Association for Computing Machinery*, 34(3):596–615.

[Friedman, 1998] Friedman, N. (1998). The Bayesian structural EM algorithm. In *Proceedings of the 14th Conference on Uncertainty in AI*, pages 129–138. Morgan Kaufmann.

[Friedman et al., 1997] Friedman, N., Geiger, D., and Goldszmidt, M. (1997). Bayesian network classifiers. *Machine Learning*, 29:131–163.

[Friedman and Getoor, 1999] Friedman, N. and Getoor, L. (1999). Efficient learning using constrained sufficient statistics. In *Proceedings of the 7th International Workshop on Artificial Intelligence and Statistics AISTATS-99.*

[Heckerman et al., 1995] Heckerman, D., Geiger, D., and Chickering, D. M. (1995). Learning Bayesian networks: the combination of knowledge and statistical data. *Machine Learning*, 20(3):197–243.

[Meilă and Jordan, 1998] Meilă, M. and Jordan, M. I. (1998). Estimating dependency structure as a hidden variable. In Jordan, M. I., Kearns, M. J., and Solla, S. A., editors, *Neural Information Processing Systems*, number 10, pages 584–590. MIT Press.

[Meilă-Predoviciu, 1999] Meilă-Predoviciu, M. (1999). *Learning with Mixtures of Trees.* PhD thesis, Massachusetts Institute of Technology.

[Moore and Lee, 1998] Moore, A. W. and Lee, M. S. (1998). Cached sufficient statistics for efficient machine learning with large datasets. *Journal for Artificial Intelligence Research*, 8:67–91.

[Steeg, 1997] Steeg, E. W. (1997). *Automated motif discovery in protein structure prediction.* PhD thesis, University of Toronto.

[Tarjan, 1983] Tarjan, R. E. (1983). *Data structures and network algorithms.* Society for Industrial and Applied Mathematics.

[West, 1996] West, D. B. (1996). *Introduction to Graph Theory.* Prentice Hall.

Feature selection for unbalanced class distribution and Naive Bayes

Dunja Mladenić
Department of Intelligent Systems
J.Stefan Institute
Jamova 39, 1000 Ljubljana, Slovenia
Dunja.Mladenic@ijs.si

Marko Grobelnik
Department of Intelligent Systems
J.Stefan Institute
Jamova 39, 1000 Ljubljana, Slovenia
Marko.Grobelnik@ijs.si

Abstract

This paper describes an approach to feature subset selection that takes into account problem specifics and learning algorithm characteristics. It is developed for the Naive Bayesian classifier applied on text data, since it combines well with the addressed learning problems. We focus on domains with many features that also have a highly unbalanced class distribution and asymmetric misclassification costs given only implicitly in the problem. By asymmetric misclassification costs we mean that one of the class values is the target class value for which we want to get predictions and we prefer false positive over false negative. Our example problem is automatic document categorization using machine learning, where we want to identify documents relevant for the selected category. Usually, only about 1%-10% of examples belong to the selected category. Our experimental comparison of eleven feature scoring measures show that considering domain and algorithm characteristics significantly improves the results of classification.

1 Introduction

In propositional learning a problem domain is given by a set of examples, where each example is described with a class value and a vector of feature values. Features used to describe examples are not necessarily all relevant and beneficial for inductive learning. Additionally, a high number of features may slow down the induction process while giving similar results as obtained with a much smaller feature subset. Feature subset selection is commonly used when learning on text data, since most text domains are characterized by several tens of thousands of features. There is a growing interest in the usage of machine learning on text data. It is especially stimulated by the intensive growth of the World Wide Web that can be seen as a widely accessible, large, distributed source of text data. The problem of automatic document categorization is well known in information retrieval and usually tested on publicly available data bases (eg. Reuters, MEDLINE). Here we use machine learning for document categorization using one of the existing Web hierarchies named Yahoo (Filo and Yang, 1997). In this way, current situation on the Web captured in Web hierarchy can be used for automatic document categorization.

Section 2 gives description of feature subset selection as used in machine learning and in text-learning. Section 2.1 describes several known and some new feature scoring measures applied on text data. Data characteristics and classification algorithm are described in Section 3. Experimental comparison of the tested measures on real-world data is given in Section 4. The results are discussed in Section 5.

2 Feature subset selection approaches

According to John et al. (John et al., 1994) there are two main approaches to feature subset selection used in machine learning: filtering and wrapper. In the filtering approach a feature subset is selected independently of the learning method that will use the selected features. The idea of the wrapper approach is to select feature subset using the evaluation function based on the same algorithm that will be used for learning. This can result in a rather time consuming process. In information retrieval and also in text-learning the whole process of feature subset selection is simplified with the assumption of feature independence. In this way the solution quality is traded for the time needed to find a solution, justified by the large number of features usually present in text domains.

2.1 Feature selection on text data

The usual way of learning on text defines a feature for each word that occurred in the training documents. This can easily result in several tens of thousands of features. Here we use the extended representation that defines a feature for each word sequence containing up to 5 consecutive words (Mladenić and Grobelnik, 1998). Methods for feature subset selection that are used on text are very simple compared to the methods developed in machine learning. Basically, some evaluation function that is applied to a single feature is used. All the features are independently evaluated, a score is assigned to each of them and the features are sorted according to the assigned score. Then, a predefined number of the best features is taken to form the solution feature subset.

Scoring of individual features can be performed using some of the measures used in machine learning for instance, *Information gain* used in decision tree induction (Quinlan, 1993). In our comparison eleven feature scoring measures were included. Information gain was included as the well known measure successfully used in some text-learning experiments. *Expected cross entropy* used in text-classification experiments (Koller and Sahami, 1997) is similar to Information gain. The difference is that instead of calculating average over all possible feature values, only the value denoting that word occurred in a document is considered. Our experiments show that this means an important difference in the resulting performance. *Mutual information* used in text-classification experiments (Yang and Pedersen, 1997) is similar to *Cross entropy for text* with the latter additionally taking into account word probability. These two measures and a very simple frequency measure proposed in (Yang and Pedersen, 1997) were reported to work well on text data. This third measure is calculated either as the number of documents that contain word W referred to as document frequency $DF(W)$ or as the number of occurrences of word W referred to as *Term frequency* $TF(W)$. This measure requires the stop words removal. We use the second definition: $Freq(W) = TF(W)$. Inspired by the way Cross entropy for text is derived from Information gain, we propose *Weight of evidence for text* that is based on the average absolute weight of evidence used in machine learning (Kononenko, 1995). *Odds ratio* is commonly used in information retrieval, where the problem is to rank out documents according to their relevance for the positive class value using occurrence of different words as features (van Rijsbergen, Harper and Porter, 1981). Our experiments show that this measure is especially suitable to be used in a combination with the Naive Bayesian classifier for our kind of problems. We propose four variants of *Odds ratio*, to test if the results are sensitive to some modifications in the formula. As a baseline method we used random scoring method defined to score each word by a random number. Table 1 contains formulas of the used scoring measures.

3 Domain and algorithm characteristics

We perform experiments on five domains defined from the Yahoo hierarchy as described in (Mladenić, 1998). Each domain is given as a classification hierarchy of text documents, with the more general categories closer to the root of the hierarchy. Each category is denoted by keywords, describing category content. More specific category is named by adding a keyword to the name of the more general category that is one level higher in the hierarchy. Each document is represented here as a feature vector, where a feature represents word or word sequence. Features are generated using an algorithm (Mladenić and Grobelnik, 1998) similar to the Apriori algorithm used for association rule generation. Five domains with the following characteristics are used in our experiments. *'Entertainment'* having 8,081 class values (nodes in the hierarchy), 30,998 features (selected word sequences) and 79,011 examples (actual Web documents). *'Arts and Humanities'* having 3,085 class values, 11,473 features and 27,765 examples. *'Computers and Internet'* having 2,652 class values, 7,631 features and 23,105 examples. *'Education'* having 349 class values, 3,215 features and 5,406 examples. *'References'* having 129 class values, 923 features and 1,995 examples. In order to learn from the class hierarchy and handle a large number of class values we induce a binary classifier for each class value (each of the hierarchy nodes, leaf or non-leaf) by collecting word probabilities from all the documents in and below the node (see (Mladenić, 1998), (Mladenić, 1998a) for more information). These documents are positive examples while all the other documents in the hierarchy are used as negative. This means that the most classifiers are induced from highly unbalanced class distribution with only about 1%-10% of posi-

$InfGain(W) =$	$P(W)\sum_i P(C_i\|W)\log\frac{P(C_i\|W)}{P(C_i)} + P(\overline{W})\sum_i P(C_i\|\overline{W})\log\frac{P(C_i\|\overline{W})}{P(C_i)}$
$CrossEntropyTxt(W) =$	$P(W)\sum_i P(C_i\|W)\log\frac{P(C_i\|W)}{P(C_i)}$
$MutualInfoTxt(W) =$	$\sum_i P(C_i)\log\frac{P(W\|C_i)}{P(W)}$
$Freq(W) =$	$TF(W)$
$WeightOfEvidTxt(W) =$	$\sum_i P(C_i)\times P(W)\times \|\log\frac{P(C_i\|W)(1-P(C_i))}{P(C_i)(1-P(C_i\|W))}\|$
$OddsRatio(W) =$	$\log\frac{P(W\|pos)(1-P(W\|neg))}{(1-P(W\|pos))P(W\|neg)}$
$WeightedOddsRatio(W) =$	$P(W)\times OddsRatio(W)$
$LogProbRatio(W) =$	$\log\frac{P(W\|pos)}{P(W\|neg)}$
$ExpProbDiff(W) =$	$e^{P(W\|pos)-P(W\|neg)}$
$CondOddsRatio(W) =$	$0.1\times\log\frac{P(W\|neg)(1-P(W\|pos))}{(1-P(W\|neg))P(W\|pos)}$ if $P(W\|neg)-P(W\|pos)>0.9$ and, otherwise equals $OddsRatio(W)$

Table 1: Formulas of the used feature scoring measures. Where $P(W)$ is the probability that word W occurred, $\overline{W}$ means that word doesn't occur, $P(C_i)$ in the probability of the i-th class value, $P(C_i|W)$ is the conditional probability of the i-th class value given that word W occurred, $P(W|C_i)$ is the conditional probability of word occurrence given the i-th class value, $P(W|pos)$ is the conditional probability of word W occurring given the class value 'positive', $P(W|neg)$ is the conditional probability of word W occurring given the class value 'negative', $TF(W)$ is term frequency (the number of times word W occurred).

tive examples. Since each classifier competes with the other classifiers, it is important that a classifier identifies documents belonging to its category. Thus we say that our problem has asymmetric misclassification costs given only implicitly in the problem. By asymmetric misclassification costs we mean that one of the class values (positive) is the target class value for which we want to get predictions and we prefer false positive over false negative. Problem with similar characteristics addressed in (Mladenić, 1998b) is predicting relevant/interesting documents on the Web, based on the clicked hyperlinks (that can be used by a personal browsing assistant).

Experiments are performed using the Naive Bayesian classifier base on the multinomial event model as suggested in (McCallum and Nigam, 1998). Notice that the product goes over all word sequences that occur in the representation of document *Doc*.

$$P(C|Doc) = \frac{P(C)\Pi_{W_j\in Doc}P(W_j|C)^{TF(W_j,Doc)}}{\sum_i P(C_i)\Pi_{W_l\in Doc}P(W_l|C_i)^{TF(W_l,Doc)}}$$

Where $P(W_j|C)$ is the conditional probability here estimated using Laplace probability estimate, $TF(W_j, Doc)$ is the frequency of word W_j in document *Doc*. Notice that using word sequences instead of only single words means even stronger violation of the feature independence assumption used in the Naive Bayesian classifier.

4 Experimental results

In our experiments we compare different feature scoring measures and observe the influence of the number of selected features to the system performance. Since we have a set of classifiers, the number of selected features is determined relatively to the classifier category size expressed by the number of features in positive examples. We refer to this relative number of features as *Vector size*. In this way, a classifier for a larger category is using more features than a classifier for some smaller category, while both classifying the same testing example. Reported results are averaged over 5 repetitions using hold-out testing on independent set of 500 (300 for the two smaller domains) randomly selected testing examples. In order to enable operational usage of the system on larger domains we include the pruning mechanisms described in (Grobelnik and Mladenić, 1998). Result is speed up of the classification process, since for each document classification, not all but only promising categories are considered (85%-95% of all categories are pruned).

To evaluate the results we use Precision, Recall and F_2-measure as commonly used evaluation measures for text data (Lewis, 1995). $F-measure$ is a combination of Precision P and Recall R commonly used in information retrieval $F_\beta = \frac{(1+\beta^2)P\times R}{\beta^2 P+R}$. The relative importance of each is expressed with the value of parameter β. We report average Precision and Re-

Dom. name	Scoring measure	Average on keyword assignment F1-measure	F2-measure	Precision	Recall
Ent.	**Odds ratio**	**0.48** ± 0.006	**0.59** ± 0.007	**0.44**± 0.006	**0.80** ± 0.006
	Weight of evidence for text	**0.48** ± 0.002	0.52 ± 0.004	0.74 ± 0.003	0.58 ± 0.003
	Term frequency	0.39 ± 0.003	0.49 ± 0.12	0.41± 0.006	0.71 ± 0.010
	Cross entropy Txt	0.29 ± 0.007	0.39 ± 0.007	0.35± 0.003	0.69 ± 0.007
	Mutual information Txt	0.25 ± 0.005	0.27 ± 0.006	0.57± 0.007	0.38 ± 0.007
	Information gain	0.27 ± 0.008	0.22 ± 0.004	0.86± 0.005	0.21 ± 0.006
	Random	0.002± 0.001	0.002± 0.001	0.99± 0.006	0.001± 0.007
Arts.	**Odds ratio**	0.46 ± 0.003	**0.59** ± 0.005	**0.40**± 0.002	**0.83** ± 0.006
	Term frequency	**0.47** ± 0.007	**0.58** ± 0.008	**0.48**± 0.003	**0.77** ± 0.009
	Weight of evidence Txt	0.50 ± 0.012	0.56 ± 0.012	0.70 ± 0.001	0.62 ± 0.012
	Cross entropy Txt	0.32 ± 0.003	0.44 ± 0.004	0.33± 0.004	0.75 ± 0.008
	Mutual information Txt	0.31 ± 0.005	0.35 ± 0.004	0.56± 0.007	0.46 ± 0.006
	Information gain	0.25 ± 0.006	0.21 ± 0.005	0.94± 0.002	0.20 ± 0.004
	Random	0.0051± 0.001	0.001± 0.001	0.99± 0.001	0.001± 0.001
Comp.	**Odds ratio**	0.46 ± 0.006	**0.60** ± 0.006	**0.40**± 0.007	**0.84** ± 0.005
	Term frequency	**0.48** ± 0.008	**0.58** ± 0.007	**0.50**± 0.004	**0.74** ± 0.005
	Weight of evidence Txt	0.46 ± 0.002	0.51 ± 0.11	0.76± 0.007	0.56 ± 0.010
	Cross entropy Txt	0.37 ± 0.007	0.49 ± 0.008	0.35± 0.004	0.75 ± 0.007
	Mutual information Txt	0.36 ± 0.003	0.38 ± 0.003	0.62± 0.005	0.45 ± 0.005
	Information gain	0.21 ± 0.005	0.17 ± 0.005	0.94± 0.005	0.15 ± 0.005
	Random	0.01 ± 0.001	0.01 ± 0.001	0.99 ± 0.001	0.004± 0.001
Edu.	**Term frequency**	**0.48** ± 0.007	**0.55** ± 0.007	**0.57**± 0.010	**0.65** ± 0.010
	Odds ratio	0.33 ± 0.008	**0.48** ± 0.008	**0.36**± 0.010	**0.81** ± 0.005
	Mutual information Txt	0.40 ± 0.004	0.46 ± 0.007	0.48± 0.010	0.59 ± 0.010
	Cross entropy Txt	0.32 ± 0.009	0.46 ± 0.007	0.28± 0.010	0.82 ± 0.006
	Weight of evidence Txt	0.30 ± 0.007	0.34 ± 0.006	0.69± 0.007	0.40 ± 0.005
	Information gain	0.13 ± 0.007	0.11 ± 0.006	0.98± 0.002	0.11 ± 0.006
	Random	0.01 ± 0.002	0.01 ± 0.002	0.99± 0.001	0.003± 0.002
Ref.	**Odds ratio**	**0.53** ± 0.006	**0.64** ± 0.006	**0.51**± 0.007	**0.81** ± 0.008
	Cross entropy Txt	0.52 ± 0.008	**0.60** ± 0.010	**0.62**± 0.003	**0.71** ± 0.010
	Mutual information Txt	0.52 ± 0.010	0.55 ± 0.010	0.73± 0.010	0.60 ± 0.020
	Term frequency	0.50 ± 0.010	0.53 ± 0.010	0.78± 0.005	0.57 ± 0.010
	Weight of evidence Txt	0.20 ± 0.008	0.22 ± 0.010	0.80± 0.009	0.31 ± 0.010
	Information gain	0.25 ± 0.007	0.22 ± 0.007	0.99± 0.002	0.21 ± 0.006
	Random	0.07 ± 0.006	0.06 ± 0.005	0.99± 0.001	0.05 ± 0.005

Table 2: Comparison of feature scoring measures for the problem of keyword prediction on five domains formed from the Yahoo hierarchy. For each domain, the compared feature scoring measures are sorted according to their performance in F2-measure. The values of F1-measure, Precision and Recall are given for better understanding. We give averages with standard errors calculated over 5 runs.

call per document calculated for the fixed probability threshold (experimentally set to 0.95 (Grobelnik and Mladenić, 1998)). Precision can be seen as the classification accuracy calculated only for positive examples, while Recall is the proportion of positive examples the system recognized as positive (values in [0..1]). If testing example is originally assigned to several categories, all these categories are taken as correct and compared to the set of predicted categories. We perform this comparison in two ways: (1) by taking into account proximity to the correct category using keywords assigned to each category (keyword prediction) and (2) by counting only prediction of the correct category (category prediction).

Additional to Precision and Recall we report F_2-measure that is a combination of the two, commonly used when we care more about Recall than about Precision. Tables 2 and 3 give results of the comparison (1) and (2) respectively. We observe performance (F2-measure) for the best performing number of selected features that is in most cases vector size 1 (meaning select as many features as there are features that occur in positive examples). To get an idea about the actual number of the used features, vector size 1 means in average over categories: on *'Entertainment'* 58 out of 30,998 features (0.2%), on *'Arts and Humanities'* 65 out of 11,473 features (0.7%), on *'Computers and Internet'* 42 out of 7,631 features (0.62%), on *'Education'*

Dom.	Scoring measure	Average on category prediction			
name		F1-measure	F2-measure	Precision	Recall
Ent.	**Odds ratio**	**0.29**± 0.002	**0.30** ± 0.003	**0.41** ± 0.004	**0.34** ± 0.003
	Term frequency	0.24± 0.003	0.27 ± 0.003	0.38 ± 0.003	0.34 ± 0.003
	Mutual information Txt	0.22± 0.004	0.23 ± 0.004	0.57 ± 0.006	0.29 ± 0.007
	Information gain	0.25± 0.002	0.20 ± 0.003	0.87 ± 0.002	0.17 ± 0.002
	Cross entropy Txt	0.15± 0.002	0.18 ± 0.002	0.29 ± 0.005	0.28 ± 0.005
	Weight of evidence Txt	0.14 ± 0.003	0.11 ± 0.002	0.67 ± 0.005	0.10 ± 0.003
	Random	0.001± 0.0001	0.001± 0.0002	0.99 ± 0.007	0.001±0.0002
Arts.	**Odds ratio**	**0.29**± 0.002	**0.32** ± 0.004	**0.36** ± 0.005	**0.38** ± 0.004
	Term frequency	0.28± 0.002	0.29 ± 0.003	0.43 ± 0.004	0.34 ± 0.003
	Mutual information Txt	0.24± 0.005	0.25 ± 0.005	0.56 ± 0.006	0.31 ± 0.007
	Cross entropy Txt	0.18± 0.002	0.22 ± 0.003	0.27 ± 0.005	0.32 ± 0.006
	Information gain	0.21± 0.002	0.17 ± 0.002	0.93 ± 0.003	0.15 ± 0.002
	Random	0.0012± 0.0001	0.001± 0.0003	0.99 ± 0.006	0.001±0.0002
	Weight of evidence Txt	0.11 ± 0.003	0.09 ± 0.002	0.55 ± 0.004	0.079± 0.002
Comp.	**Odds ratio**	**0.30**± 0.002	**0.33** ± 0.002	**0.36** ± 0.009	**0.57** ± 0.005
	Term frequency	0.27± 0.003	0.26 ± 0.002	0.45 ± 0.003	0.27 ± 0.003
	Mutual information Txt	0.25± 0.003	0.24 ± 0.004	0.60 ± 0.006	0.26 ± 0.006
	Cross entropy Txt	0.19± 0.005	0.21 ± 0.004	0.28 ± 0.004	0.27 ± 0.002
	Information gain	0.19± 0.007	0.14 ± 0.006	0.94 ± 0.004	0.12 ± 0.005
	Weight of evidence Txt	0.09± 0.002	0.07 ± 0.002	0.59 ± 0.010	0.06 ± 0.001
	Random	0.001± 0.0003	0.001± 0.0002	0.99 ± 0.001	0.001± 0.0002
Edu.	**Mutual information Txt**	**0.40**± 0.006	**0.45** ± 0.009	**0.52** ± 0.010	**0.53** ± 0.010
	Odds ratio	0.32± 0.005	**0.43** ± 0.005	**0.36** ± 0.009	**0.57** ± 0.010
	Term frequency	**0.40**± 0.010	**0.42** ± 0.010	**0.57** ± 0.010	**0.45** ± 0.020
	Weight of evidence Txt	0.05± 0.006	**0.42** ± 0.005	**0.53** ± 0.020	**0.04** ± 0.005
	Cross entropy Txt	0.2 ± 0.006	0.26 ± 0.004	0.23 ± 0.010	0.37 ± 0.005
	Information gain	0.09± 0.003	0.07 ± 0.002	0.97 ± 0.003	0.07 ± 0.002
	Random	0.01± 0.001	0 ± 0.001	0.99 ± 0.002	0.001± 0.001
Ref.	**Odds ratio**	**0.37**± 0.007	**0.42** ± 0.009	**0.46** ± 0.009	**0.51** ± 0.012
	Mutual information Txt	0.34± 0.005	0.32 ± 0.005	0.69 ± 0.015	0.32 ± 0.006
	Term frequency	0.28± 0.007	0.26 ± 0.070	0.72 ± 0.007	0.26 ± 0.007
	Cross entropy Txt	0.23± 0.005	0.22 ± 0.005	0.50 ± 0.003	0.23 ± 0.005
	Information gain	0.20± 0.003	0.16 ± 0.002	0.99 ± 0.002	0.14 ± 0.002
	Weight of evidence Txt	0.06± 0.007	0.05 ± 0.006	0.70 ± 0.011	0.05 ± 0.004
	Random	0.05± 0.006	0.04 ± 0.005	0.99 ± 0.001	0.04 ± 0.004

Table 3: Comparison of feature scoring measures for the problem of category prediction on five domains formed from the Yahoo hierarchy. For each domain, the compared feature scoring measures are sorted according to their performance in F2-measure. The values of F1-measure, Precision and Recall are given for better understanding. We give averages with standard errors calculated over 5 runs.

85 out of 3,198 features (2.7%), on *'References'* 49 out of 928 features (5.3%). Additionally to the value of F_2-measure, we give values of Precision, Recall and F_1-measure. F_1-measure is included to show how the same feature scoring measures would compare in case we would have a problem where Precision and Recall are equally important. As we can see from Tables 2 and 3, there would not be much difference, Odds ratio and Term frequency would remain the best.

On all domains Odds ratio is among the best performing measures (see Tables 2 and 3) and the best performance is achieved when only a small number of features is used. For instance, in Table 2 on *'Computers and Internet'* Odds ratio achieves F_2-measure of 0.60, Precision of 0.40 and Recall of 0.84, meaning that 40 % of document predicted positive are positive and that 84% of all positive documents are identified. This is consistent with the results reported in text-learning on the problem of predicting clicked hyperlinks from the set of visited Web documents (Mladenić, 1998b) where the feature selection based on Odds ratio achieved the best results. Similar observation regarding the number of features is reported on text categorization in (Yang and Pedersen, 1997), where the reduction of up to 90% in the number of features resulted in either an improvement or no loss in the system performance. Observation of standard error on all five domains confirms that the best performing measures are significantly better

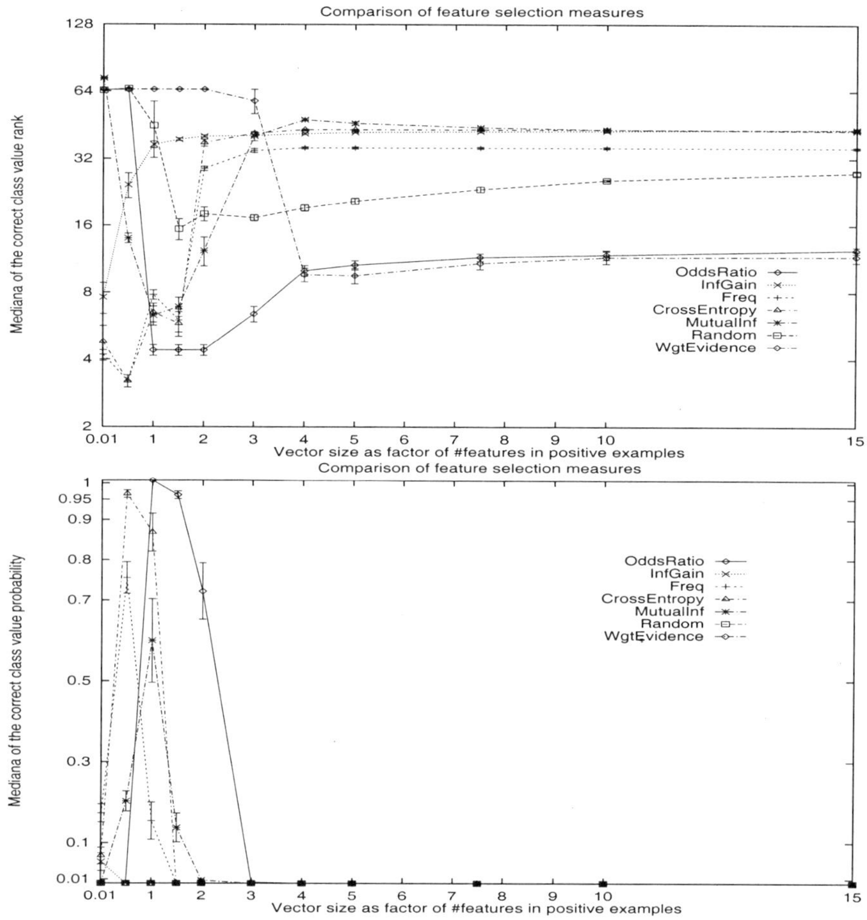

Figure 1: Comparison of (upper) the correct category rank (the lower the better) and (lower) probability for different feature scoring measures on domain *'Reference'*.

than the other tested measures.

Additionally, we report two non-standard but intuitive measures: rank and probability assigned to the correct category. For each testing example we observe a list of categories each assigned a probability as a result of consulting the corresponding subproblem classifier. Sorting categories according to that probability gives ranking that we use to get the rank of the correct category. If there are more correct categories, the one with the highest predicted probability is considered. To get summary results over the testing examples we give median rather than mean, since some of the testing examples are rather non-typical of their category, containing eg., a welcome page or only one sentence asking for language preference or an error message or a page giving redirection.

Rank and probability show that Odds ratio is again the best or one of the two best performing measures. Cross entropy for text and Term frequency achieved similar results as Odds ratio on two out of the five domains. Weight of evidence for text achieved on all domains good rank but low probability, while Information gain performed similar as Random. Tables with results of rank and probability are not included because of the space restrictions. They can be found in (Mladenić 1998). Standard errors confirm that the results are significant. Observation of the average number of considered categories during the classification shows that Odds ratio is considering about 3 times less categories than Cross entropy for text and about 2 times less categories than Term Frequency.

For illustration of the influence of the number of selected features we show graphs for domain *'Reference'*. Figure 1 gives median for the correct category rank and probability on domain *'Reference'*. It can be seen

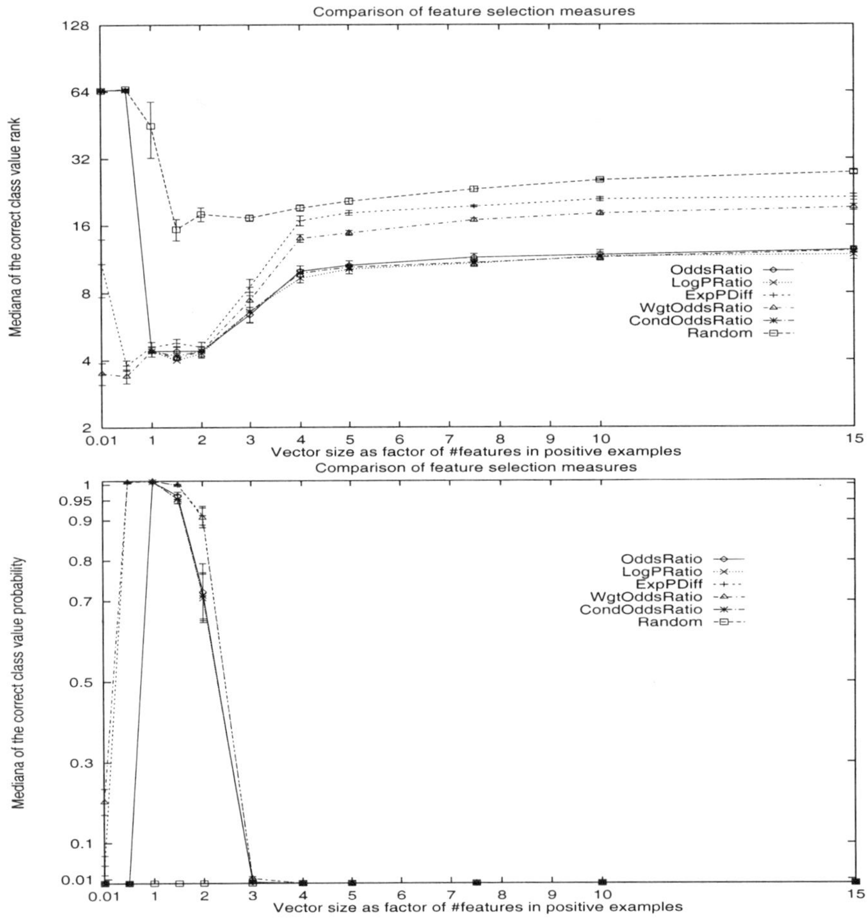

Figure 2: Comparison of Odds ratio and its variants on domain *'References'* defined from the Yahoo hierarchy. We give median of the correct category rank (left) and probability (right).

that the best performance in rank and probability is achieved by Odds ratio and Cross entropy for text using relatively small number of features (vector size 0.5-1.5). For instance, on *'References'* the mediana of the correct category rank is 3.8 the mediana of the correct category probability over 0.99, ie. the half of the testing examples are assigned rank up to 3.8 and probability > 0.99 for the correct category. For larger feature subsets the rank became insensitive to the additional features, while the probability is almost 0.

To show the efficiency of the used scoring measure we give in Figure 3 the influence of the relative number of selected features to the number of categories considered in classification. For Random and Information gain this number grows with the growing number of selected features (vector size). For the other measures, the number of considered categories is mostly stable when using more features (eg., using $\geq$ 50 features for domain *'Reference'*). The lowest number of categories is considered by Weight of evidence for text, but this measure did not achieve very good classification results. Odds ratio is the second best in the low number of considered categories and this is also one of the best performing measures. Cross entropy for text that is also among the best performing measures is the worst in the number of considered categories.

There is no significant difference in the performance between Odds ratio and any of its four variants we tested (for illustration, see Figure 2). This shows that the most important characteristics of Odds ratio are included in its variants. It also shows that we didn't get any significant improvement by including probability of word occurrence (Weighted Odds ratio) nor by including features characteristic for negative examples (Conditional Odds ratio).

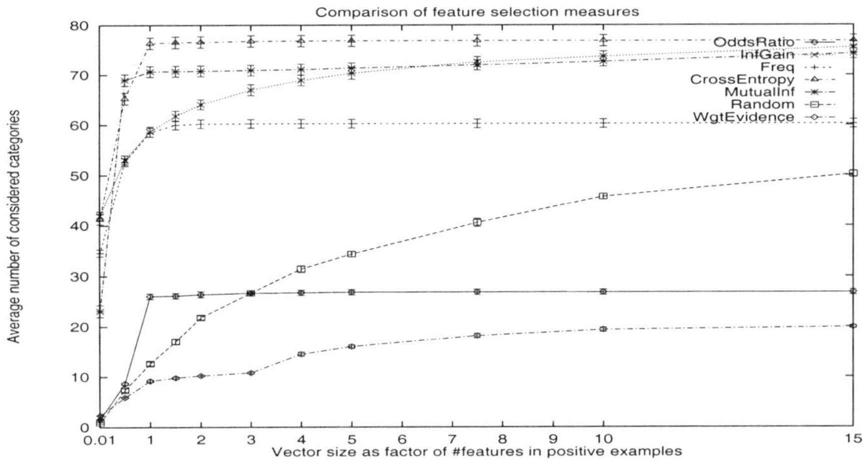

Figure 3: Comparison of the number of considered categories (the lower the better) for different feature scoring measures on domain *'Reference'*.

5 Discussion

In our experiments the best performing feature scoring measures are Odds ratio and its variants, while the worst are Random and Information gain. The other perform comparable or worse than Odds ratio and better than Information gain. A closer look to the highly scored features by Odds ratio and by Information gain explains the huge difference in their performance and poor performance of Information gain. It also indicates how important is to consider domain and algorithm characteristics.

5.1 Unbalanced class and feature value distribution

Yang and Pedersen (Yang and Pedersen, 1997) give experimental comparison of five measures for feature selection in text categorization on word-vectors representing documents. Their experiments confirm our observation that a rather small feature subset should be used since it gives either better or as good results as large feature subset or all the features. We also agree in the observation that a simple frequency of a feature (used after stop words removal and calculated either using term or document frequency) achieves very good results. Our results disagree in the performance of Information gain. Information gain was one of the best performing measures on problems addressed by Yang and Pedersen (Yang and Pedersen, 1997), while we found it performing similar as random on our domains. The reason for that we find in the difference in our domains and classification algorithms. We both use learning for document categorization but different approach to domain definition is used. Their domain is defined to include one class value for each category, while we split the problem into subproblems each corresponding to one category and having binary-valued class. The result of learning is in our case a set of specialized classifiers instead of one huge classifier including the union of features characteristic for different categories. The other important issue is the used classification algorithm. Yang and Pedersen (Yang an Pedersen, 1997) used k-Nearest Neighbor and Linear Least Square Fit mapping. The specific of the Naive Bayesian classifier we are using is that it considers only features that occur in a classification document. This means that highly scored features should be features that will probably occur in new documents.

From the formula for Information gain it can be seen that no difference between the class values or between the feature values is considered. Here we have unbalanced class distribution and also highly unbalanced feature value distribution. When calculating feature score we observe two values for each feature (word sequence): occurs or does not occur in a document. The prior probability that a word sequence occurs in a document $P(W)$ is rather small. Most of the features selected by Information gain are features with the majority feature value ($P(\overline{W})$ is high). If $P(\overline{W}) >> P(W)$ then the high value of Information gain in most cases means that the second part $P(\overline{W}) \sum_i P(C_i|\overline{W}) \log \frac{P(C_i|\overline{W})}{P(C_i)}$ of the Information gain formula is high. In other words, knowing that W does not occur in a document brings useful

Measure name	target class value	common features	using class value	using feature absence	perf.
Odds ratio	**Yes**	No	Yes	No	great
Weighted Odds ratio	**Yes**	**Yes**	Yes	No	great
Log. prob. ratio	**Yes**	No	Yes	No	great
Exp. prob. difference	**Yes**	No	Yes	No	great
Conditional Odds ratio	**Yes**	No	Yes	No	great
Cross entropy for text	No	**Yes**	Yes	**No**	good
Term frequency	No	**Yes**	No	No	good
Weight of evidence for text	No	Yes	Yes	No	mild
Mutual information for text	No	*No*	Yes	No	mild
Information gain	No	Yes	Yes	*Yes*	poor
Random	No	No	No	No	poor

Table 4: Comparison of feature scoring measures by their characteristics and performance (perf.) on our domains.

information about the class value. Intuitively, when classifying a new document, a better classification results are expected if the classification is based on words that occur in a document. It is possible that absence of some words in a document is very informative and this is taken into account by the new feature scoring measure we named Conditional Odds ratio. The problem is that the classification based mostly on the absence of words is usually harder and requires larger feature subset than the classification based on word occurrences. Cross entropy for text makes distinction between the feature values and achieves good results in our experiments. It equals Information gain calculated only for one of the feature values - W meaning word does occur. Odds ratio and its variants achieve better results than Cross entropy for text. They also ignore feature absence but additionally take into account that there is a target class value. While Odds ratio and its variants favor features characteristic for positive examples (high $P(W|'pos')$), the other tested measures make no distinction between the class values. Moreover, Information gain makes no distinction between the feature values (it is using feature absence). Since we have unbalanced class distribution with over 90% of examples having negative class value, most of the features are characteristic for negative examples. This means that most of the features highly scored by Information gain are either informative when they do not occur in a document or they are characteristic for negative class value (just the opposite of Odds ratio!).

In (Yang and Pedersen, 1997) the tested scoring measures are compared across several criteria: favoring common features, using class value, using feature absence and experimental performance. They conclude that the three measures (Frequency, Information gain and χ^2 statistics) achieving the best results on their domains (Reuters-22173, a subset of MEDLINE) all favor common features.

5.2 Conclusions

Table 4 gives characterization of the feature scoring measures compared in our experiments. We also observe whether the feature scoring measure makes difference between the class values, since this is important for our domains having one of the class values as the target class value. The best results are achieved by Odds ratio and its variants that assume the problem has binary-valued class and one of the class values is the target class value (asymmetric misclassification costs). Between these measures no significant difference in performance was observed. The next group of measures achieving good results all favor common features (Cross entropy for text, Term frequency, Weight of evidence for text). Mutual information for text differs from Cross entropy for text only in not favoring frequent features and achieves worse results. Information gain differs from Cross entropy for text only in using feature absence as well as feature presence and achieves poor results.

Our conclusion is that in general the most important characteristics of a good feature scoring measure for text are: favoring common features and considering domain and algorithm characteristics. For learning algorithms that make difference between feature presence and absence, such as the Naive Bayesian classifier used here, it is important that a scoring measure also makes this difference. For the domains with binary-valued class where one class value is the target class value, the most important characteristics of a good feature scoring measure is to make difference between the class values and favor features characteristic for the target class value. In this case, favoring common features is not an important issue. Namely, Weighted odds ratio that favors common features is not performing better than Odds ratio.

Instead of using a filtering approach to feature selection that ignores the learning algorithm or using the wrapper approach that uses the learning algorithm as a 'black-box', we suggest that domain and algorithm characteristics are studied in advance. We applied the Naive Bayesian classifier to the domains that have an unbalanced class and feature value distribution and asymmetric misclassification costs, where the minority class value is the target class value. Experimental comparison of different feature scoring measures used in feature selection shows that Odds ratio (and its variants) achieve the best results. Our classifier uses the same conditional probability as used in Odds ratio for scoring the features. In this way, the selected features are features expected to have the greatest influence to the posterior probability of class values returned by the Naive Bayesian classifier.

More precisely, let us consider domain and algorithm characteristics to see which features should be selected. In our case the majority class value is negative ($P(neg) > P(pos)$). If we want to identify the positive documents then the Naive Bayesian classifier should return $P(pos|Doc) > P(neg|Doc)$ for positive documents. This can be achieved only if $\Pi_{W_j \in Doc} P(W_j|pos)^{TF(W_j,Doc)} > \Pi_{W_j \in Doc} P(W_j|neg)^{TF(W_j,Doc)}$. At the same time, Odds ratio favors words that have $P(W_j|pos) > P(W_j|neg)$. Having many such words selected for learning means, that we have good chances to get the above product in the classifier higher for the positive than for the negative class value. Moreover, our experiments suggest that we should select as many best features as there are features (word sequences) that occur in the positive examples. Closer look to the features sorted according to Odds ratio show that this approximately means simply select all the features that occur in positive examples without performing any feature scoring. In general, we can conclude that on such problems with unbalanced class distribution and asymmetric misclassification costs, features characteristic for the positive examples should be selected.

References

Filo, D., Yang, J. (1997), Yahoo! Inc.

Grobelnik, M. & Mladenić, D. (1998), Efficient text categorization, *ECML-98 Workshop on Text Mining.*

John, G.H., Kohavi, R., Pfleger, K. (1994), Irrelevant Features and the Subset Selection Problem, *Proc. of the 11th International Conference on Machine Learning ICML94*, pp.121-129.

Koller, D., Sahami, M. (1997), Hierarchically classifying documents using very few words, *Proc. of the 14th International Conference on Machine Learning.*

Kononenko, I. (1995), On biases estimating multivalued attributes. *Proc. of the 14th International Joint Conference on Artificial Intelligence IJCAI-95.*

Lewis, D.D. (1995), Evaluating and optimizating autonomous text classification systems. *Proc. of the 18th Annual International ACM-SIGIR Conference on Research and Development in Information Retrieval.*

McCallum, A., Nigam, K. (1998), A comparison of event models for naive Bayes text classifiers. *AAAI-98 Workshop on Learning for Text Categorization.*

Mladenić, D. (1998), Machine Learning on non-homogeneous, distributed text data, *PhD thesis*, University of Ljubljana, Slovenia, October, 1998. http://www.cs.cmu.edu/~TextLearning/pww/PhD.html

Mladenić, D. (1998a), Turning Yahoo into an Automatic Web-Page Classifier. *Proc. of the 13th European Conference on Aritficial Intelligence ECAI'98.*

Mladenić, D. (1998b), Feature subset selection in text-learning, *Proc. of the 10th European Conference on Machine Learning ECML98.*

Mladenić, D., & Grobelnik, M. (1998), Word sequences as features in text-learning. *Proc. of the Seventh Electrotechnical and Computer Sc. Conference ERK'98*, pp.145-148, Slovenia: IEEE section.

Quinlan, J.R. (1993), Constructing Decision Tree in *C4.5: Programs for Machine Learning*, pp.17-26, Morgan Kaufman Publishers.

Pazzani, M., & Billsus, D. (1997), Learning and Revising User Profiles: The Identification of Interesting Web Sites. *Machine Learning, 27*, pp.313-331.

van Rijsbergen, C.J,. Harper, D.J., Porter, M.F. (1981), The selection of good search terms, *Information Processing & Management*, 17, pp.77-91.

Yang, Y., Pedersen, J.O. (1997), A Comparative Study on Feature Selection in Text Categorization, *Proc. of the 14th International Conference on Machine Learning ICML97*, pp.412-420.

Combining statistical learning with a knowledge–based approach — A case study in intensive care monitoring

Katharina Morik and **Peter Brockhausen** and **Thorsten Joachims**
Universität Dortmund, LS VIII
44221 Dortmund, Germany
{morik,brockhausen,joachims}@ls8.cs.uni-dortmund.de

Abstract

The paper describes a case study in combining different methods for acquiring medical knowledge. Given a huge amount of noisy, high dimensional numerical time series data describing patients in intensive care, the support vector machine is used to learn when and how to change the dose of which drug. Given medical knowledge about and expertise in clinical decision making, a first-order logic knowledge base about effects of therapeutical interventions has been built. As a preprocessing mechanism it uses another statistical method. The integration of numerical and knowledge-based procedures eases the task of validation in two ways. On one hand, the knowledge base is validated with respect to past patients' records. On the other hand, medical interventions that are recommended by learning results are justified by the knowledge base.

1 Introduction

In this paper, we want to present a challenging application of machine learning. The learning methods we use are already well known and theoretically well-founded. Why then should anybody be interested in our report on the application of these methods? Our principle point is that applications are a necessary precondition for the success of machine learning in several ways. On the one hand, practitioners who might want to apply machine learning benefit from scientific exploration of application fields. Well investigated application areas serve as points of reference so that experts of a field realize the impact of machine learning for their actual problems. The long way from learnability results to an application is made explicit step by step in the hope that these steps can easily be transferred to a similar practical problem. On the other hand, machine learning benefits from the challenge of true applications. Real world applications require many capabilities that can be ignored in learnability proofs or performance measurements with respect to a dataset library. First, detecting a suitable learning task in an application is one of the hardest problems when dealing with real-world applications. This task has been solved already for the datasets in, e.g. the UCI library. Second, another problem that is solved for the datasets in the libraries but demands much of the time when applying a learning algorithm to a new application is the feature selection or feature construction. Would there be more scientific interest in these topics if applications were of more concern [1]? Third, the use of background knowledge given by a domain expert determines our efforts in preparing the application. Can we easily write down what we have learned and is the learning algorithm able to make good use of it? Or do we have to find a clever way of how to encode the knowledge into our representation language? Fourth, the validation of machine learning results is an issue. When using a dataset of a library, accuracy of prediction is a suitable criterion. However, in real-world applications this criterion is one among others. Two other criteria are at least as decisive as is the accuracy, namely understandability and embeddedness.

By understandability, we denote how well an expert of the application domain can inspect the learning results in order to verify them. Most often, this demand restricts the representation for-

[1]The application field of knowledge discovery has raised the interest in feature selection and construction again, cf. (Liu and Motoda, 1998).

malism we can choose. Using a formalism which is close to the representation the expert is used to eases the verification by him or her. In addition, it restricts the size of the learning result. No expert has the time to inspect 10 or more pages of rules.

By embeddedness, we denote how well the learning algorithm can be integrated into the overall application system. This covers the use of already available data for learning as well as the use of learning results for processes of the application. The notions of pre- and post-processing are too much focused on the learning part of the application and, hence, simplify the issue of integrating several processes, among them possibly more than one learning algorithm. Again, the representation formalism for learning is constrained by the requirement of embeddedness. In contrast, the constraints regarding accuracy may even be weakened. In a sequence of (learning) processes, the low accuracy of one of them can be compensated by following (learning) processes[2].

Some of our arguments in favor of the scientific investigation of applications seem to underly the famous paper of Ross Quinlan (Quinlan, 1986). However, what received most of the attention was the ID3 algorithm. Also the subject of multistrategy learning issued by Ryszard Michalski (Michalski and Wnek, 1997) seems to point into the same direction. However, there are also good points against application-oriented publications, which we do not want to ignore. First, it is hard to show that the chosen modelling of the application is optimal. If the customer is happy with it – wouldn't he be even happier with another approach? All we can do about this, is to make our raw data publicly available in order to allow for the reproduceability and comparability of results. Second, readers do not learn from yet another application of the same kind. Hence, we have to characterize our application such that principled new points become clear. This is what we try next.

We have investigated whether machine learning could enhance on-line monitoring in intensive care medicine. Why is this a challenging application? There are three groups of reasons, namely the data situation, the task of monitoring, and the particular constraints given by the application. Let us consider one after the other.

DATA SITUATION In modern intensive care, each minute several hundreds of measurements of a patient are recorded at the bed-side. This gives us a very high dimensional space of data about a patient. However, this does not mean that for each patient, each vital sign is recorded properly. The values of some vital signs are recorded only once within an hour. Some other vital signs are recorded only for a subset of the patients. Hence, the overall high dimensional data space is sparse. Moreover, the data is noisy with respect to the point in time whenever the protocol is made by nurses and not automatically. The average time difference between intervention as charted and calculated hemodynamic effect is 12.34 minutes for catecholamines, vasodilators, and rapid infusions – opposed to an expected time lag of very few minutes. Even the automatic measurements can be noisy, for instance, if somebody touches the tube or moves the bed. To make it even worse, some highly relevant parameters are not recorded at all, for instance, why the patient needs intensive care. To summarize, we have masses of noisy, high dimensional, sparse time series of numerical data.

Medical experts explain the numerical data in qualitative terms of high abstraction. The background knowledge given by the expert covers functional models of the human body as well as expertise in the proper treatment of intensive care patients including effects of drugs and volume input. In the experts' reasoning, time becomes the relation between time intervals, abstracting away the exact duration of, e.g., an increasing heart rate and focusing on tendencies of other parameters (e.g., cardiac output) within overlapping time intervals. To summarize, we have complex qualitative background knowledge explaining both the patient's and the doctor's behavior.

MONITORING The task of monitoring can best be understood as time-critical decision support. The final goal is to enhance the quality of clinical practice. This means that imitating the actual interventions, i.e. the doctor's behavior, is not the goal. Actual behavior is influenced by the overall hospital situation, e.g., how long is the doctor on duty, how many patients require attention at the same time. The goal of decision support is to supply the best recommendation under all circumstances (Morris, 1998).

[2]In our robotics application, we conducted a sequence of learning runs, where the first achieved only 71% accuracy. Although exactly these results were the input to the following learning run, the results of the last run showed 94% accuracy. Moreover, the robot could, in fact, navigate using the learned rules!(Klingspor, 1998)

CONSTRAINTS The application area of intensive care constrains our work in three ways. First, on-line monitoring restricts the computational efforts. The system that supports decision making must analyze many parameters and output a recommendation for an intervention – if necessary – in short real time. Second, experiments are not possible. We can only test our algorithms based on what we observe as the results of one particular intervention. Whether another intervention would have been better cannot be determined. Third, it must be easy to validate the acquired rules of decision both, with respect to previously unseen patient records and by experts' inspections. To summarize, the overall system must work in real time, taking numerical data as input and deliver recommendations in an understandable way.

Now, that we have explained why we consider applications a relevant subject for machine learning and our intensive care application a challenging one, we can start to describe our case study. The paper is organized as follows. First, we describe our layout for learning and validation: the detection of learning tasks, the modelling of background knowledge, the selection of learning algorithms. Second, we describe the learning tasks which the support vector machine has solved and how the results were evaluated. Third, we describe our modelling of medical knowledge in a restricted first-order logic and how we used reasoning and multistrategy learning for its validation. We then use the validated knowledge base for justifying interventions proposed by the learning results of the support vector machine. This additional validation of learning results is of particular importance when putting learning results to good use in medicine. We conclude by summarizing where we are and indicating our next steps.

2 Layout for Learning and Validation

Clinical decision support aims at providing doctors and nurses with therapy guidelines directly at the bedside. This should enhance the quality of clinical care, since the guidelines sort out high value practices from those that have little or no value. The computerized protocol of care takes into account more aspects of the patient than a doctor can accommodate. It is not disturbed by circumstances or hospital constraints and it bridges the gap between low-level numerical measurements (the level of the equipment) and high-level qualitative principles (the level of medical reasoning). The system takes as input measurements of the patient as recorded at the bed-side. It outputs executable protocols of therapeutical interventions as a recommendation to the doctor. Such a decision support system has been developed and established at the LDS hospital of Salt Lake City for respiratory care (Morris, 1998). It is a knowledge-based system where the production rules have been acquired in about 25 person years. The system has been evaluated in several studies at diverse hospitals in more than 10 years. Our task is now to build such a decision support system for hemodynamic care. The question is: can we achieve equally good results using much less resources (i.e. person years) if we apply machine learning?

Looking again at the list of advantages of computer-assisted intensive care, we obtain a list of requirements for the system to be built. The system must ground its decisions in explicit medical methods. We do not aim at modelling the hemodynamic system, the cardiac processes of patients. Neither do we aim at modelling the actual doctors' behaviors. Instead, the knowledge base must represent a therapy protocol which can be applied to measurements of the patient. This reminds us of the early days of knowledge acquisition for expert systems. However, our task at hand goes beyond classical medical knowledge acquisition, since the system has to cope with high dimensional data in real time. Its task is on-line monitoring, not heuristic classification or cover and differentiate. Moreover, the data consists of time series. Time stamped data do not necessarily require sequence analysis methods. For an application, we have to determine whether points in time, time intervals and their relations, or curves of measurements offer an adequate representation. How do we handle the patient's history? How do we summarize the curves of measurements to abstract qualitative propositions? These questions point at the problem of finding an adequate representation. Two sets of requirements on the capabilities of the representation can be distinguished:

1. The representation must handle numerical data, valid in one point in time, and time series. For each point in time, it must classify whether and which therapy intervention is appropriate for the patient.
2. The representation must handle relations of time intervals, interrelations of diverse drugs and relations between different parameters of the patient. It has to derive expected effects of medical interventions from medical knowledge and compare expected outcome with actual outcome.

The requirements are conflicting. Whereas we know

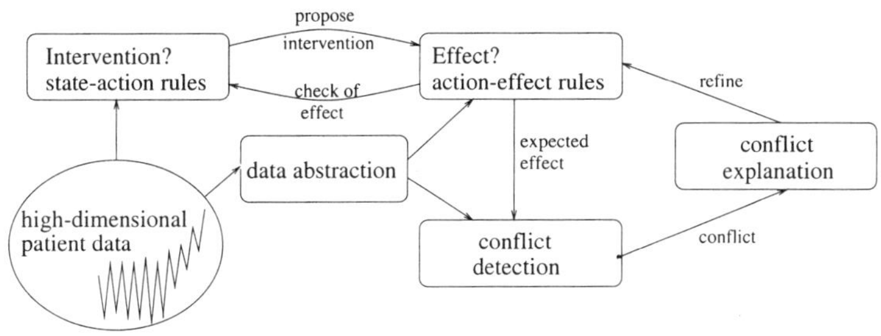

Figure 1: Overall architecture.

good formalisms for each of the sets, we are not aware of a representation that fulfills both sets of demands. Hence, we decided to break down the overall reasoning into several processes and find an appropriate representation for each of them, independently. The overall architecture is shown in Figure 1. The patients' measurements at one point in time are used in order to recommend an intervention. This corresponds to clinical practice where for each point in time a recommendation for optimal treatment is needed. Of course, one of the recommendations is to not change the current therapy. The recommendation of interventions constitutes a model of *doctors' behavior.* A recommended intervention is checked by calculating its expected effects on the basis of medical knowledge. Medical knowledge qualitatively describes a patient's state during a time interval and effects of drugs. It constitutes a model of the *patients' hemodynamical system.* The medical knowledge base uses relations between time intervals and their abstract characterizations. To this end, patients' measurements are abstracted with respect to their course over time. The abstraction mechanism handles curves of measurements. The integration of numerical and knowledge-based methods allows us to validate the processes carefully. On one hand, the qualitative assessment of a statistical prediction enhances the model of the doctor's behavior in order to obtain a model of best practice. On the other hand, the medical knowledge is validated with respect to past patients' data. In detail, the processes we have designed are:

data abstraction Given series of measurements of one vital sign of the patient, eliminate outliers and find level changes. This abstracts the measurements to qualitative propositions with respect to a time interval, e.g., within time point 12 and time point 63, the heart rate remained about equal, from time point 63 to time point 69 it was increasing.

state-action rules Given the numerical data describing vital signs of the patient and his or her current medication, find the appropriate intervention. An intervention is formalized as increasing, decreasing or not changing the dose of a drug. The decision is made every minute.

action-effect rules Given the state of a patient described in qualitative terms, medical knowledge about effects of substances, relations between different vital signs, interrelation between different substances, a sequence of interventions, and a current intervention, find the effects of the current intervention on the patient. The derivation of effects is made for each intervention.

conflict detection Given the expected effect of a medication for a patient and his or her actual state, find inconsistencies.

conflict explanation Given interventions with effects on the patient that follow the medical knowledge and those that are in conflict with medical knowledge, find characterizations which separate the two sets.

It is straightforward to determine appropriate representations now: state-action rules and data abstraction use numerical functions, the other modules use a restricted first-order logic. Knowing the representation class for each process we can detect learning tasks. Which process can be modelled using machine learning? Which learning algorithm is appropriate for the task? For learning state-action rules, we applied the support vector machine, because it is capable of handling high dimensional numerical data. Since the support vector machine is a binary classifier, we had to split the overall task of finding state-action rules into several particular learning tasks. For each drug, the support vector machine was trained on

16	demographic attributes	11	vital parameters
5	intensive care diagnoses	37	I/O parameters
6	continuously given drugs	10	drugs
14	breathing parameters	10	laboratory tests
9	derived parameters		

Figure 2: Attributes in the hemodynamic dataset.

two tasks, namely learning the direction of interventions and learning when to intervene. This work is described in section 3. A statistical method for data abstraction was readily available (Imhoff et al., 1997). Action-effect rules were not to be learned, since our medical expert, Michael Imhoff, provided us with the medical knowledge. Using the MOBAL system (Morik et al., 1993) it was extremely easy to write the according rules. The inference engine of MOBAL derives expected effects and compares them with actual effects. These are deductive inferences. However, the explanation of conflicts between prediction and actual outcome requires to investigate many hypotheses. For this task, we used the inductive logic programming tool RDT/DB (Morik and Brockhausen, 1997). Work on action-effect rules and validation is described in section 4.

Data Set. The data set was collected at the 16-bed intensive care unit (ICU) of the "Chirurgische Kliniken der Städtischen Kliniken Dortmund". It contains the data of 147 patients between January 1997 and October 1998. Measurements are taken every minute, amounting to 679,817 observations for which data from a Swan-Ganz catheter is available. There are 118 attributes forming 9 groups (cf. figure 2).

Some of the parameters (like the demographic attributes) are not time dependent. While especially the vital parameters are measured on a minute to minute basis, others occur only once per hour or less.

3 Learning State-Action Rules

3.1 Support Vector Machine

Support vector machines (see (Vapnik, 1998)) are based on the *Structural Risk Minimization* principle (Vapnik, 1998) from statistical learning theory. The idea of structural risk minimization is to find a hypothesis h for which we can guarantee the lowest true error. Vapnik connects the bounds on the true error with the margin of separating hyperplanes. In their basic form support vector machines find the hyperplane that separates the training data with maximum margin. Since we will be dealing with very unbalanced numbers of positive and negative examples in the following, we introduce cost factors C_+ and C_- to be able to adjust the cost of false positives vs. false negatives. Finding this hyperplane can be translated into the following optimization problem:

$$\text{Minimize:} \quad \frac{1}{2}||\vec{w}||^2 + C_+\sum_{i:y_i=1}\xi_i + C_-\sum_{j:y_j=-1}\xi_j \quad (1)$$

$$\text{subject to:} \quad \forall k : y_k[\vec{w}\cdot\vec{x_k} + b] \geq 1 - \xi_k \quad (2)$$

x_i is the feature vector of example i. y_i equals $+1$ (-1), if example i is in class $+$ $(-)$.

We solve this optimization problem in its dual formulation using SVM^{light} [3] (Joachims, 1999a), extended to handle unsymmetric cost-factors. It can efficiently handle problems with many thousand support vectors, converges fast, and has minimal memory requirements.

3.2 Learning the Direction of Interventions

The first question we asked ourselves was: Given that we know the doctor changed the dosage of some drug, can we learn when he increased the dosage and when he decreased the dosage based on the state of the patient? To learn such a function, we had to first find an appropriate representation describing the patient's state.

3.2.1 What is an Appropriate Representation of the Patient's State?

Our dataset contains 118 attributes, some real valued, some categorial. Which features should we use for learning? How can we represent them appropriately for the SVM?

Categorial attributes are broken down into a number of binary attributes, each taking the values $\{0,1\}$. Real valued parameters are either scaled so that all measurements lie in the interval [0..1], or they are normalized by empirical mean and variance.

$$norm(X) = \frac{X - mean(X)}{\sqrt{var(X)}} \quad (3)$$

We systematically evaluated a large number of plausible feature sets using a train/test scheme. The feature set with the best performance is given in figure 3.

[3] http://www-ai.cs.uni-dortmund.de/ svm_light

Vital Parameters	Continuously Given Drugs	Demographic Attributes
Diastolic Arterial Pressure	Dobutamin	Broca-Index
Systolic Arterial Pressure	Adrenalin	Age
Mean Arterial Pressure	Glyceroltrinitrat	Body Surface Area
Heart Rate	Noradrenalin	Ermergency Surgery?
Central Venous Pressure	Dopamin	
Diastolic Pulmonary Pressure	Nifedipin	
Systolic Pulmonary Pressure		
Mean Pulmonary Pressure		

Figure 3: The best feature set.

According to a doctor, these are actually the most important parameters of the patient. Only the attributes "Cardiac Output" and "Net I/O" are missing, since they are seldomly present. Moreover, "Cardiac Output" measurements are always a risk for the patient.

3.2.2 How much History is Necessary?

When making a decision about an intervention, it is (at least theoretically) possible to consider history in some form. We experimented with different ways of incorporating the history of the patient into the representation. We tried using only the measurements from one minute before the intervention (i. e. no history), using the last up to 10 minutes before the intervention, using averages of up to 60 minutes before the intervention, and combinations of both. We also tried incorporating the state of the patient at the previous intervention.

None of the approaches that use history gave significantly better results than just using the measurements from one minute before the intervention. This result is plausible and consistent with medical practice. According to doctors their decision to intervene is mostly based on the measurements they find after entering the patient's room. So short term history is ignored.

3.2.3 Prediction Performance

All experiments towards finding an appropriate representation were done on the training set. Using 10-fold cross validation on the training set we further optimized the parameters of the SVM (kernel and C). This lead to using linear SVMs for all drugs. The performance of the respective SVM on a previously untouched test set is given in figure 4.

To get an impression about how good these prediction accuracies are, we conducted an experiment with a doctor. On a subset of 40 test examples we asked an expert to do the same task as the SVM for Dobutamin, given the same information about the state of the patient. In a blind test the doctor predicted the same direction of dosage change as actually performed in 32 out of the 40 cases. On the same examples the SVM predicted the same direction of dosage change as actually performed in 34 cases, resulting in an essentially equivalent accuracy.

Drug	Accuracy	StdErr
Dobutamin	83.6%	2.5%
Adrenalin	81.3%	3.7%
Glyceroltrinitrat	85.5%	3.0%
Noradrenalin	86.0%	5.2%
Dopamin	84.0%	7.3%
Nifedipin	86.9%	7.0%

Figure 4: Accuracy in predicting the right direction of an intervention.

3.3 Learning when to Intervene

The previous experiment shows that SVMs can learn in how far drugs should be changed given the state the patient is in. In reality, the doctor also has to decide *when* to intervene or just keep a dosage constant. This leads to the following three class learning problem. Given the state of the patient, should the dosage of a drug be increased, decreased or kept constant? Knowing such a function is also a step towards deciding when to substitute one drug with another. Generating examples for this task from the data is difficult. The particular minute a dosage is changed depends to a large extent on external conditions (e.g. an emergency involving a different patient). So interventions can be delayed and the optimal minute an intervention *should* be performed is unknown. To make sure that we generate examples only when a doctor was closely monitoring the patient, we consider only those minutes where some drug was changed. This leads to 1319 training and 473 test examples.

For each drug we trained two binary SVMs. One is trained on the problem "increase dosage" vs. "lower or keep dosage equal", the other one is trained on the problem "lower dosage" vs. "increase or keep dosage equal". In order to better reflect the costs of inap-

Dobutamin	actual intervention up	equal	down
predicted up	**46**	32	3
predicted equal	50	**197**	54
predicted down	5	30	**56**

Adrenalin	actual intervention up	equal	down
predicted up	**23**	22	3
predicted equal	21	**310**	15
predicted down	4	34	**41**

Figure 5: Confusion matrices for predicting time and direction of Dobutamin and Adrenalin interventions.

Dobutamin	actual intervention up	equal	down
predicted up	**10 (9)**	12 (8)	0 (1)
predicted equal	7 (9)	**35 (31)**	9 (9)
predicted down	2 (1)	7 (15)	**13 (12)**

Adrenalin	actual intervention up	equal	down
predicted up	**4 (2)**	3 (1)	0 (0)
predicted equal	4 (6)	**65 (66)**	2 (2)
predicted down	1 (1)	8 (9)	**8 (8)**

Figure 6: Confusion matrices for predicting time and direction of Dobutamin and Adrenalin interventions in comparison to human performance.

propriate interventions, we use an SVM with a cost model. Lacking data for designing a more refined cost model, the cost-factors are chosen so that the potential total cost of the false positives equals the potential total cost of the false negatives. This means that the parameters C_+ and C_- of the SVM are chosen to obey the ratio

$$\frac{C_+}{C_-} = \frac{\text{number of negative training examples}}{\text{number of positive training examples}} \quad (4)$$

Figure 5 shows the test results for Dobutamin and Adrenalin. The confusion matrices give insight into the class distributions and the type of errors that occur. The diagonal contains the test cases, where the prediction of the SVM was the same as the actual intervention of the doctor. This accounts for 63% of the test cases for Dobutamin and for 79% of the test cases for Adrenalin. The SVM suggests the opposite intervention in about 1.5% for both drugs.

Again, we would like to put these numbers into relation with the performance of an expert when given the same information. For a subsample of 95 examples from the test set, we again asked a doctor to perform the same task as the SVM. The results for Dobutamin and Adrenalin are given in figure 6. The performance of the SVM on this subsample is followed by the performance of the human expert (in brackets). Both are well aligned. Again, the learned functions of the SVM are comparable in terms of accuracy with a human expert. This also holds for the other drugs.

4 Action-Effect Rules

Based on detailed information from our medical expert, Michael Imhoff, we have built a compact knowledge base modelling the effects of drugs. Not counting patients' records, the knowledge base consists of 39 rules and 88 facts. Figure 7 shows a typical rule from the knowledge base. The rule states that increasing the dose from D1 to D2 of a drug M leads to an increasing effect on the parameter V of a patient P. The time intervals in which a certain dose is given to the patient are immediate successors. The dose is changed significantly.

```
% Facts:
contains(dobutrex,dobutamin).
med_effect(dobutamin,1,10,hr,up).
med_effect(dobutamin,10,30,hr,up).
opposite(up,down).

% Rules:
intervention(P,T1,T2,M,D1) & intervention(P,T2,T3,M,D2) &
contains(M,S) &
med_effect(S,From1,To1,V,Dir) &
med_effect(S,From2,To2,V,Dir) &
ne(From1,From2) & gt(D2,D1) &
lt(D1,To1) & ge(D1,From1) & lt(D2,To2) & ge(D2,From2)
      → interv_effect(P,T2,T3,M,V,Dir).

% Patient Data:
level_change(pat460, 160, 168, hr, up)
intervention(pat460, 159, 190, dobutrex, 8)
```

Figure 7: Excerpt from the knowledge base.

4.1 Validating the Knowledge Base

In order to validate the knowledge base we applied it to the data of 148 patients. Part of an abstracted patient record is also shown in figure 7 for the time interval from the 160th minute to the 190th minute. Following an intervention, namely giving Dobutrex (= Dobutamin) in a dose of 8 units, a level change can be observed.

Overall, the patient data contain 8,200 interventions. 22,599 effects of the interventions were derived using forward chaining. In order to compare the predicted effects with the actual ones, we distinguish three types of conformity or contradiction. A predicted effect is

weakly conform with observed patient behavior, if no level change is observed, the patient's state remains stable;

strongly conform with observed patient behavior, if the observed level change has the same direction as is predicted by the rules;

contradictory with observed patient behavior, if a level change is observed into a direction opposite to the one predicted by the rules.

Note, that weak conformity is not in conflict with medical knowledge, but shows best therapeutical practice. Smooth medication keeps the patient's state stable and does not lead to oscillating reactions of the patient.

When matching the derived effects with the actual ones, the system detected:

weak conformity: 13,364 effects, i.e. 59.14%, took place in the restricted sense, that the patient's state remained stable.

strong conformity: 5,165 effects , i.e. 22.85%, took place in the sense, that increasing or decreasing effects of drugs on vital signs match corresponding level changes.

contradiction: 4,070 contradictions, i.e. 18.01% of the interventions, were detected. The observed level change of a vital sign went into the opposite direction of the knowledge-based prediction.

First, we started a knowledge revision process using concept formation using the methods of Stefan Wrobel (Wrobel, 1994). A concept is learned that separates successful rule applications (i.e. those, where the rules are not in conflict with the observations) from rule applications that lead to a contradiction. However, no clear separation could be found. Hence, we weakened the task to filtering out influential aspects. For learning, we chose 5,466 interventions with their effects being classified as conform (including the weak conformity described above) and as not conform. 11 predicates about the patient and the medications established the structured hypothesis space. Of all possible combinations, 121 hypotheses had to be tested. The findings were:

- The rule stating that a lowering a dose of a parameter increasing drug should lower the respective parameter is less reliable than the opposite rule.
- If combined with the age of the patient being around 55 years or the weight of the patient being small, the rule for effects of decreasing a medication is particularly unreliable.
- The weight of the patient alone has no impact on the reliability of action-effect rules.
- For elder patients (in the group of more than 65 years and in the group of more than 75 years), the weight is an influential feature.
- To our surprise, the amount of reducing or increasing the dose is not a relevant aspect for explaining contradictions, neither alone nor in combination with other features.

Relational learning did a good job in generating and testing many hypotheses. However, the learning results clearly indicate that the decisive features that would distinguish successful rule applications from not successful ones are not present in the data. The decisive features cannot even be formed from the available data using constructive induction! As is often the case, a negative result – even if it is well-based – is disappointing. It prevents us from inadequate revisions of the knowledge base, but it does not show us, how to effectively enhance the rules. When reporting our results to the medical expert, he assessed the ratio of 83.56 % correct predictions of effects very positively. Asked about possible missing data that could explain deviations, he indicated arhythmic heart beat as a decisive feature which is not present in the data. Also the missing values of cardiac output could possibly explain many deviations of observed from predicted effects.[4].

4.2 Using the Knowledge Base for Validating Interventions

As depicted in the overall architecture (cf. figure 1), we have chosen a design which allows us to use the action–effect rules in the knowledge base for validating predicted interventions. The underlying argument is that accuracy measures only reflect how well SVM's learning results fit actual behavior of the doctor. However, there are usually several different combinations of drugs that achieve the same goal of keeping the patient in a stable state: And indeed, different doctors, depending on their experience in the ICU, do use different mixtures and follow different strategies to reach this goal. For comparing treatment strategies,

[4]Note, that cardiac output is not measured for all patients, because of its potential harm to the patient.

	art.	hr.	same effect all param.	same behavior
Noradrenalin	436	428	424	420
Dobutamin	403	395	383	299
Dopamin	472	472	472	387
Adrenalin	407	406	393	374
Glyceroltrinitrat	437	388	380	342
Nifedipin	457	457	455	438

Figure 8: Accuracy and equivalence of decisions.

the real criterion is whether the recommendations have the same effect as the actual interventions. Therefore, we apply the action–effect rules from the knowledge base to both the proposed intervention of the SVM classifiers and to the intervention actually performed by the doctor. If the derived effects are equal, then the proposed decision of the SVM classifiers can be considered as "equivalent" to the intervention executed by the doctor.

The results of this comparison for 473 interventions are shown in figure 8. The right-most column indicates the accuracy, i.e. in how many cases the classification of SVM and doctor were identical (same behavior of SVM and doctor). The other columns state how often the SVM's intervention leads to the same effects as the intervention of the doctor. The first two columns show, how many of interventions had the same effect on arterial blood pressure or heart rate, respectively. The third column gives a more concise evaluation. Here it is stated, how many interventions recommended by the SVM had the same effects on all vital signs as the actual intervention. For instance, the SVM correctly classifies 299 test cases for Dobutamin (63%). If we compare the resulting effects of the predicted interventions concerning Dobutamin with the effects of the actual doctor's interventions, we find that in 383 cases (81%) the deduced effects will be equal. Thus, in 84 cases the recommendation of the SVM does not match the doctor's behavior, but the effects are the same, since the doctor has chosen an "equivalent" drug or combination of drugs. This example demonstrates the advantage of our approach for validating learning results in contrast to merely looking at accuracy rates.

5 Conclusions

We present an application of machine learning for patient monitoring in intensive care. This application involves high dimensional time series data, demanding high quality decision support under real time constraints. It requires the integration of numerical data and qualitative knowledge. The tasks of reasoning are abstraction, classification, and deductive inference. These properties make this case study a representative for a large number of applications in medicine and engineering. Consider, for instance, robot applications, where measurements of the sensors and actions are to be integrated. Abstracting the measurements allows for high-level plans that cover a variety of situations. The classification of appropriate actions constitutes the low-level planning routines of the robot. If the costs of an inappropriate action are high, its justification on the basis of general knowledge is necessary. For instance, automatic car driving should integrate the low-level perception and action with general knowledge about the traffic law.

This paper presents the necessary steps for solving this application as a whole. We identify how the application can be split up into manageable parts. We propose an overall architecture that integrates a number of task, organized both sequentially and in parallel. All tasks are embedded in a single system, while selecting the most appropriate technique and representation – including the difficult task of selecting and constructing appropriate features – for each task individually. A statistical method is used to detect level changes in the curve of a patient's vital sign. The SVM is chosen for learning state-action rules due to its ability to handle many features. Several feature sets including the history of the patient were tested. Surprisingly, best results were achieved if only the patients' data one minute before an intervention were considered. This corresponds to the actual routine of a doctor. We present first experimental results demonstrating a performance comparable to that of a human expert in terms of accuracy. Moreover, the learned classifications of possible interventions are justified by deriving expected effects. This evaluation of the SVM's learning results goes beyond accuracy measurements and is much more realistic.

For modelling medical knowledge in terms of action-effect rules we chose a first order logic representation using MOBAL. This allows a compact representation of medical knowledge with a small number of rules, fulfilling the real-world demand for a knowledge base to be understandable to humans and accessible for expert validation. In addition, the knowledge base directly serves as background knowledge for learning refined rules and for doing knowledge revision. Discussions with experts in intensive care showed that the knowledge base is, in fact, understandable. We presented our results at the 9'th international symposium on intensive care (Joachims, 1999b; Morik and Imhoff,

1999) and received positive feedback on our modelling approach as being in-line with both the structure of medical knowledge and it's use in decision making. Moreover, the consistency checking of MOBAL allows to automatically detect cases where the actual patient state differs from the predicted effect of an intervention. Experts find it very useful to discuss a rule in the light of selected contradictory cases. The knowledge base turns the classifications of the SVM into operational knowledge for monitoring patients. The overall system is designed such that it can be applied at the hospital.The systemexploits patients' data as given and outputs operational recommendations for interventions. Hence, embeddedness guided the design process.

Our next step is the validation of the system by a committee of medical experts in order to further evaluate its performance. In particular, the combinations of different drugs need to be validated. A comparison with a hemodynamic knowledge base that is currently developed at the LDS hospital at Salt Lake City is planned. The LDS knowledge base does not take the stream of measurements as input, but reads vital signs on demand. It cannot be applied to past data and be evaluated with respect to them, because there is no component for checking consistency. We plan to transfer the knowledge base into our system so that it can be tested on patients' data. The impact of a stream of data (our approach) as opposed to some selected points in time when a vital sign is read (the LDS approach) will be investigated carefully.

Acknowledgements

This work has been funded in part by the collaborative research action on "Complexity Reduction in Multivariate Data Structures" (DFG, SFB475). Many thanks to Michael Imhoff, who leads the intensive care section of the city hospital of Dortmund, runs the clinical information system there, and nevertheless found time to explain us medical knowledge and practice. We also thank Ursula Gather and Markus Bauer for offering us their tool for time series analysis. We thank Jörg-Uwe Kietz for fruitful discussions about advantages and disadvantages of dataset libraries.

References

Imhoff, M., Bauer, M., Gather, U., and Löhlein, D. (1997). Time Series Analysis in Intensive Care Medicine. *Applied Cardiopulmonary Pathophysiology*, 6:203 - 281.

Joachims, T. (1999a). Making large-Scale SVM Learning Practical. In Schölkopf, B., Burges, C., and Smola, A., editors, *Advances in Kernel Methods - Support Vector Learning*. MIT-Press.

Joachims, T. (1999b). Wissenserlangung aus grossen Datenbanken. In W.Kuckelt and K.Hankeln, editors, *9th Int. Symposium on Indensive Care*, Journal f. Anaesthesie und Intensivbehandlung, Lengerich, Berlin, Riga, Scottsdale (Az.), Wien, Zagreb. Pabstscience Publishers.

Klingspor, V. (1998). *Reaktives Planen mit gelernten Begriffen*. PhD thesis, Univ. Dortmund.

Liu, H. and Motoda, H. (1998). *Feature Extraction, Construction, and Selection: A Data Mining Perspective*. Kluwer.

Michalski, R. and Wnek, J. (1997). Guest Editors' Introduction. *Machine Learning*, 27(3):205–208.

Morik, K. and Brockhausen, P. (1997). A Multistrategy Approach to Relational Knowledge Discovery in Databases. *Machine Learning Journal*, 27(3):287–312.

Morik, K. and Imhoff, M. (1999). Vergleich medizinischen Wissens und des aus einer intensivmedizinischen Datenbank gewonnenen Wissens am Beispiel des haemodynamischen Monitorings. In W.Kuckelt and K.Hankeln, editors, *9th Int. Symposium on Indensive Care*, Journal f. Anaesthesie und Intensivbehandlung, Lengerich, Berlin, Riga, Scottsdale (Az.), Wien, Zagreb. Pabstscience Publishers.

Morik, K., Wrobel, S., Kietz, J.-U., and Emde, W. (1993). *Knowledge Acquisition and Machine Learning - Theory, Methods, and Applications*. Academic Press, London.

Morris, A. (1998). Algorithm-Based Decision Making. In M.J.Tobin, editor, *Principles and Practice of Intensive Care Monitoring*, chapter 77, pages 1355 - 1381. McGraw-Hill.

Quinlan, R. (1986). Induction of Decision Trees. *Machine Learning*, 1(1):81–106.

Vapnik, V. (1998). *Statistical Learning Theory*. Wiley.

Wrobel, S. (1994). *Concept Formation and Knowledge Revision*. Kluwer Academic Publishers, Dordrecht.

Policy invariance under reward transformations: Theory and application to reward shaping

Andrew Y. Ng, Daishi Harada, Stuart Russell
Computer Science Division
University of California, Berkeley
Berkeley CA 94720
{ang,daishi,russell}@cs.berkeley.edu

Abstract

This paper investigates conditions under which modifications to the reward function of a Markov decision process preserve the optimal policy. It is shown that, besides the positive linear transformation familiar from utility theory, one can add a reward for transitions between states that is expressible as the difference in value of an *arbitrary* potential function applied to those states. Furthermore, this is shown to be a necessary condition for invariance, in the sense that any other transformation may yield suboptimal policies unless further assumptions are made about the underlying MDP. These results shed light on the practice of *reward shaping*, a method used in reinforcement learning whereby additional training rewards are used to guide the learning agent. In particular, some well-known "bugs" in reward shaping procedures are shown to arise from non-potential-based rewards, and methods are given for constructing shaping potentials corresponding to distance-based and subgoal-based heuristics. We show that such potentials can lead to substantial reductions in learning time.

1 Introduction

In sequential decision problems, such as are studied in the dynamic programming and reinforcement learning literatures, the "task" is represented by the *reward function*. Given the reward function and a model of the domain, the optimal policy is determined. An elementary theoretical question that arises is this: What freedom do we have in specifying the reward function, such that the optimal policy remains unchanged?

In the field of utility theory, which studies primarily single-step decisions, the corresponding question for the utility function can be answered very simply. For single-step decisions without uncertainty, any monotonic transformation on utilities leaves the optimal decision unchanged; with uncertainty, only positive linear transformations are allowed [von Neumann and Morgenstern, 1944]. These results have important implications for designing evaluation functions in games, eliciting utility functions from humans, and many other areas.

To our knowledge, the question of policy invariance under reward function transformations has not been fully explored for sequential decision problems.[1] Policy-preserving transformations are important at least in these areas:

- The task of *structural estimation* of MDPs [Rust, 1994] involves recovering the model and reward function from observed optimal behavior. (See also the discussion of *inverse reinforcement learning* in [Russell, 1998].) Policy-preserving transformations determine the extent to which a reward function can be recovered.

- The practice of *reward shaping* in reinforcement learning consists of supplying additional rewards to a learning agent to guide its learning process, beyond those supplied by the underlying MDP. It is important to understand the impact of shaping on the learned policy.

[1] Some results are known for approximate invariance: if rewards are perturbed by at most ε, the new policy's value is within $2\varepsilon/(1-\gamma)$ of the original optimal policy [Singh and Yee, 1994, Williams and Baird, 1994].

This paper focuses primarily on reward shaping, which has the potential to be a very powerful technique for scaling up reinforcement learning methods to handle complex problems [Dorigo and Colombetti, 1994, Mataric, 1994, Randløv and Alstrøm, 1998]. (Similar ideas have arisen in the animal training literature; see [Saksida et al., 1997] for a discussion.) Often, a very simple pattern of extra rewards suffices to render straightforward an otherwise completely intractable problem.

To see why policy invariance is important in shaping, consider the following examples of bugs that can arise: [Randløv and Alstrøm, 1998] describes a system that learns to ride a simulated bicycle to a particular location. To speed up learning, they provided positive rewards whenever the agent made progress towards the goal. The agent learned to ride in tiny circles near the start state because no penalty was incurred for riding away from the goal. A similar problem occurred with a soccer-playing robot being trained by David Andre and Astro Teller (personal communication). Because possession in soccer is important, they provided a reward for touching the ball. The agent learned a policy whereby it remained next to the ball and "vibrated," touching the ball as frequently as possible. These policies are clearly not optimal for the original MDP.

These examples suggest that the shaping rewards must obey certain conditions if they are not to mislead the agent into learning suboptimal policies. The difficulty with positive-reward cycles leads one to consider rewards derived from a conservative potential—that is, the reward for executing a transition between two states is (essentially) the difference in the value of a potential function applied to each state. It turns out that not only is this a sufficient condition for guaranteeing policy invariance under reward transformations, but that, assuming no prior knowledge of the MDP, this is also a *necessary* condition for being able to make such a guarantee. Section 2 gives the definitions needed to state this claim precisely, and Section 3 states and proves the claim. Section 4 shows how to construct shaping potentials of various kinds and demonstrates their efficacy in speeding up learning on some simple domains. Finally, Section 5 connects our results to existing algorithms such as Advantage learning [Baird, 1994] and λ-policy iteration [Bertsekas and Tsitsiklis, 1996], and closes with discussion and future work.

2 Preliminaries

2.1 Definitions

In this section, we provide some of the definitions used throughout the paper, focusing on the case of finite-state Markov decision processes (MDPs). Shaping is of interest to us in both finite-state and infinite-state problems, but the underlying MDP theory for the infinite-state case is significantly more difficult, even in the absence of shaping. Nevertheless, our analysis and methodology are easily generalized from the finite to the infinite-state space case once the underlying MDP theory is laid out, and we will mention this again later; but for now, let us start our definitions with explicitly considering only finite-state domains.

A (finite-state) **Markov decision process (MDP)**, is a tuple $M = (S, A, T, \gamma, R)$, where: S is a finite set of **states**; $A = \{a_1, \dots, a_k\}$ is a set of $k \geq 2$ **actions**; $T = \{P_{sa}(\cdot) | s \in S, a \in A\}$ are the next-state **transition probabilities**, with $P_{sa}(s')$ giving the probability of transitioning to state s' upon taking action a in state s; $\gamma \in (0,1]$ is the **discount factor**; and R specifies the reward distributions. For simplicity, we will assume rewards are deterministic, in which case R is a bounded real function called the **reward function**. In the literature, reward functions are typically written $R : S \times A \mapsto \mathbb{R}$, with $R(s,a)$ being the reward received upon taking action a in state s. Though we will often write reward functions in this form, we will also allow a more general form, $R : S \times A \times S \mapsto \mathbb{R}$, with $R(s,a,s')$ being the reward received upon taking action a in state s and transitioning to state s'.

Given a fixed set of actions A, a **policy** over a set of states S is any function $\pi : S \mapsto A$. Note that policies are defined over states and not over MDPs, so the same policy may be applied to two different MDPs so long as the two MDPs use the same states and actions. Given any policy π over states S and any MDP $M = (S, A, T, \gamma, R)$ using the same states and actions, we may then define the **value function** V^π_M, which evaluated at any state s gives $V^\pi_M(s) = \mathrm{E}[r_1 + \gamma r_2 + \gamma^2 r_3 + \dots ; \pi, s]$, where r_i is the reward received on the ith step of executing the policy π from state s, and the expectation is over the state-transitions taken upon executing π. We then define the **optimal value function** to be $V^*_M(s) = \sup_\pi V^\pi_M(s)$, the Q**-function**, evaluated at any $s \in S, a \in A$ as

$$Q^\pi_M(s,a) = \mathrm{E}_{s' \sim P_{sa}(\cdot)}\left[R(s,a,s') + \gamma V^\pi_M(s')\right] \quad (1)$$

(where the notation $s' \sim P_{sa}(\cdot)$ means that s' is drawn according to the distribution $P_{sa}(\cdot)$), and the **optimal**

Q-function as $Q^*_M(s,a) = \sup_\pi Q^\pi_M(s,a)$. Finally, we define the **optimal policy** for an MDP M as $\pi^*_M(s) = \arg\max_{a\in A} Q^*_M(s,a)$. The optimal policy may not be unique, and we more generally say a policy π is optimal in M if $\pi(s) \in \arg\max_{a\in A} Q^*_M(s,a)$ for all $s \in S$. Lastly, when the context MDP is clear, we may also drop the M-subscript, and write V^π rather than V^π_M, etc.

We also need some (largely standard) regularity conditions so as to make sure all of the above definitions make sense. For undiscounted ($\gamma = 1$) MDPs, we assume that S contains a distinguished state s_0 called an **absorbing state**, so that the MDP "stops" after a transition into s_0, with no further rewards thereafter. Moreover, again for undiscounted MDPs, we assume all policies are **proper**, meaning that upon executing any policy starting from any state, we will with probability 1 eventually transition into s_0. Since this is really a condition on T, we will in this paper say the *transition probabilities* T are proper if this condition holds. Discounted MDPs have no corresponding absorbing state and are always infinite-horizon; note therefore that for them, we can write $S - \{s_0\} = S$.

The above were the standard regularity conditions needed for MDPs with *finite* state spaces (see, e.g. [Sutton and Barto, 1998]), which is the case which we had explicitly said we would focus on. For MDPs with infinite state spaces, more would be needed: for example, in the undiscounted case, the expectation in our definition of $V^\pi_M(s) = \mathrm{E}[r_1 + \gamma r_2 + \gamma^2 r_3 + \dots ; \pi, s]$ may not even exist.[2] These issues need to be properly addressed before we can even define things such as optimal policies, and excellent sources for this material include [Bertsekas, 1995, Hernández-Lerma, 1989, Bertsekas and Shreve, 1978]. But unfortunately, explaining the infinite $|S|$ case in full generality would require more measure theory than we wish to delve into here, and we only comment that, with the appropriate generalizations of the required regularity conditions on the MDP, all of our results are easily generalized to the infinite $|S|$ case. Throughout this paper, we will however continually draw links to how the results may be proved for infinite $|S|$, though we defer the more general proofs for infinite $|S|$ to the full paper. For now, we note only that for the infinite-state case, an important and useful condition is that the reinforcements are bounded in absolute value; this will be mentioned again later in the paper.

[2] This is in a similar sense to the "mean" of a Cauchy distribution not existing.

2.2 Shaping Rewards

In this section, we introduce our formal framework of shaping rewards. Intuitively, we are trying to learn a policy for some MDP $M = (S, A, T, \gamma, R)$, and we wish to help our learning algorithm by giving it additional "shaping" rewards which will hopefully guide it towards learning a good (or optimal) policy faster. To formalize this, we assume that, rather than running our reinforcement learning algorithm on $M = (S, A, T, \gamma, R)$, we will run it on some *transformed* MDP $M' = (S, A, T, \gamma, R')$, where $R' = R + F$ is the reward function in the transformed MDP, and $F : S \times A \times S \mapsto \mathbb{R}$ is a bounded real-valued function called the **shaping reward function**. (Similar to R, the domain of F for the undiscounted case should strictly be $S - \{s_0\} \times A \times S$, but we will not be overly pedantic about this point for now.) So, if in the original MDP M we would have received reward $R(s,a,s')$ for transitioning from s to s' on action a, then in the new MDP M' we would receive reward $R(s,a,s') + F(s,a,s')$ on the same event.

For any fixed MDP and assuming additive, memoryless shaping reward functions, this $R' = R + F$ is the most general possible form of shaping rewards.[3] Moreover, they cover a fairly large range of possible shaping rewards one might come up with. For example, to encourage moving towards a goal, a shaping-reward function that one might choose is $F(s,a,s') = r$ whenever s' is closer (in whatever appropriate sense) to the goal than s, and $F(s,a,s') = 0$ otherwise, where r is some positive reward. Or, to encourage taking action a_1 in some set of states S_0, one might set $F(s,a,s') = r$ whenever $a = a_1, s \in S_0$, and $F(s,a,s') = 0$ otherwise.

One elementary but important property of this form of reward transformation is that it can generally be *implemented*: In many reinforcement learning applications, we are not explicitly given M as a tuple (S, A, T, γ, R), but are allowed to learn about M only through taking actions in the MDP and by observing the resulting state transitions and rewards. Given such access to M, we can simulate having the same type of access to M' simply by taking actions

[3] In the full paper, we will consider an even more general, not necessarily additive, form: $R'(s,a,s') = F(r,s,a,s')$ for arbitrary F, and where $r = R(s,a,s')$ is the reward we would have received in the original MDP M. Under the appropriate conditions, it turns out that, if we are to give optimality guarantees similar to those we will give here, then the only additional freedom this gives us in choosing shaping rewards is it allows us to rescale rewards by any fixed positive factor. Since this does not add any interesting richness to F, we defer this result to the full paper.

in M, and then "pretending" we observed reward $R(s,a,s') + F(s,a,s')$ whenever we actually observed reward $R(s,a,s')$ in M. Naturally, the simple reason that this works is that M and M' use the same actions, states and transition probabilities. Thus, online/offline model-based/model-free algorithms that may be applied to M may in general be readily applied to M' in the same way.

Since we are learning a policy for M' in the hope of using it in M, the question at hand is thus the following: For what forms of shaping-reward functions F can we guarantee that $\pi^*_{M'}$, the optimal policy in M', will also be optimal in M? The next section will answer this to a fair degree of generality.

3 Main results

In practical applications, we often do not exactly know T a priori (and may or may not know $R(s,a,s')$). Our goal is therefore, given S and A (and possibly R), to come up with a shaping-reward function $F : S \times A \times S \mapsto \mathbb{R}$ that is "good" and so that $\pi^*_{M'}$ will be optimal in M. In this section, we will give a form for F under which we can guarantee $\pi^*_{M'}$ will be optimal in M. We also provide a weak converse showing that, without further knowledge of T and R, this is the only type of shaping function that can always give this guarantee.

First focusing on the undiscounted case ($\gamma = 1$), let us try to gain some intuition about what F might give rise to the shaping "bug" pointed out in the Introduction. On Randløv and Altrøm's bicycle task, when the agent was rewarded for riding towards the goal but not punished for riding away from it, it learned to ride in a tiny circle and thereby obtain positive reward whenever it happened to be moving towards the goal. More generally, if there is some sequence of states $s_1, s_2, \ldots, s_n$ such that the agent can travel through them in a cycle ($s_1 \to s_2 \to \cdots \to s_n \to s_1 \to \cdots$), and gain net positive shaping-reward by doing so ($F(s_1,a_1,s_2) + \cdots + F(s_{n-1},a_{n-1},s_n) + F(s_n,a_n,s_1) > 0$), then it seems that the agent may be "distracted" from whatever it really should be trying to do (such as ride towards the goal,) and instead try to repeatedly go round this cycle.

To address this difficulty with cycles, a form for F that immediately comes to mind is to let F be a *difference of potentials*: $F(s,a,s') = \Phi(s') - \Phi(s)$, where Φ is some function over states. This way, $F(s_1,a_1,s_2) + \cdots + F(s_{n-1},a_{n-1},s_n) + F(s_n,a_n,s_1) = 0$, and we have eliminated the problem of cycles that "distract" the agent. Are there other ways to choose F? And aside from cycles, are there any other problems with shaping that we need to address? It turns out that, without more prior knowledge about T and R, such potential-based shaping functions F are the only F that will guarantee consistency with the optimal policy in M. Moreover, this turns out to be essentially all we need in order to make this guarantee. This is made formal in the following theorem:

Theorem 1 *Let any S, A, γ, and any shaping reward function $F : S \times A \times S \mapsto \mathbb{R}$ be given. We say F is a* **potential-based** *shaping function if there exists a real-valued function $\Phi : S \mapsto \mathbb{R}$ such that for all $s \in S - \{s_0\}, a \in A, s' \in S$,*

$$F(s,a,s') = \gamma\Phi(s') - \Phi(s), \qquad (2)$$

(where $S - \{s_0\} = S$ if $\gamma < 1$). Then, that F is a potential-based shaping function is a necessary and sufficient condition for it to guarantee consistency with the optimal policy (when learning from $M' = (S,A,T,\gamma,R+F)$ rather than from $M = (S,A,T,\gamma,R)$), in the following sense:

- *(Sufficiency) If F is a potential-based shaping function, then every optimal policy in M' will also be an optimal policy in M (and vice versa).*
- *(Necessity) If F is not a potential-based shaping function (e.g. no such Φ exists satisfying Equation (2)), then there exist (proper) transition functions T and a reward function $R : S \times A \mapsto \mathbb{R}$, such that no optimal policy in M' is optimal in M.*

Also note the following: For the infinite-state case, if one were to choose some Φ to construct a potential-based shaping function, then for the formal results to go through, we really should demand that Φ be bounded, so that the shaping rewards F are also bounded (similar to the condition that R be bounded, in Section 2.1); this issue will be discussed again later. Note that for the finite-state case, this is a vacuous condition since Φ would, having a range of finite cardinality, automatically be bounded. Also, the necessity and sufficiency conditions above might seem a little more complicated than usual, and this is because there can be multiple optimal policies in M or in M'. Nevertheless, it should be clear that the quantifications used make this the strongest possible theorem of this form. The sufficiency condition says that so long as we use a potential-based F, then we are guaranteed any $\pi^*_{M'}$ we might be trying to learn will also be optimal in M. The necessity condition says that if we have no knowledge of T and R, then we must choose a potential-based F for learning in M', if we want to guarantee consistency with learning the optimal policy in M. (If we do have intimate knowledge of T, R, then the necessity condition does not say much, and it is possible that we might be able to use other shaping functions.)

The proof of necessity is given in Appendix A. Here, we only prove that Equation (2) is a sufficient condition: that if F is indeed of the form in (2), then we may guarantee that every optimal policy in M' will also be optimal in M. Again, we prove this result fully rigorously only for the case of finite $|S|$; the proof for infinite $|S|$ is nearly identical, but requires a little more care in justifying the use of the Bellman Equations.

Proof (of sufficiency): Let F be of the form given in (2). If $\gamma = 1$, then since replacing $\Phi(s)$ with $\Phi'(s) = \Phi(s) - k$ for any constant k would not change the shaping rewards F (which is a difference of these potentials), we may, by replacing $\Phi(s)$ with $\Phi(s) - \Phi(s_0)$ if necessary, assume without loss of generality that the Φ used to express F via (2) satisfies $\Phi(s_0) = 0$.

For the original MDP M, we know that its optimal Q-function Q^*_M satisfies the Bellman Equations (see e.g. [Sutton and Barto, 1998])

$$Q^*_M(s,a) = \mathrm{E}_{s' \sim P_{sa}(\cdot)}\left[R(s,a,s') + \gamma \max_{a' \in A} Q^*_M(s',a')\right]$$

Some simple algebraic manipulation then gives us

$$Q^*_M(s,a) - \Phi(s) = \mathrm{E}_{s'}\Big[R(s,a,s') + \gamma\Phi(s') - \Phi(s) + \gamma \max_{a' \in A}\left(Q^*_M(s',a') - \Phi(s')\right)\Big]$$

If we now define $\hat{Q}_{M'}(s,a) \triangleq Q^*_M(s,a) - \Phi(s)$ and substitute that and $F(s,a,s') = \gamma\Phi(s') - \Phi(s)$ back into the previous equation, we get

$$\begin{aligned}
&\hat{Q}_{M'}(s,a) \\
&= \mathrm{E}_{s'}\left[R(s,a,s') + F(s,a,s') + \gamma \max_{a' \in A} \hat{Q}_{M'}(s',a')\right] \\
&= \mathrm{E}_{s'}\left[R'(s,a,s') + \gamma \max_{a' \in A} \hat{Q}_{M'}(s',a')\right]
\end{aligned}$$

But this is exactly the Bellman equation for M'. For the undiscounted case, we moreover have $\hat{Q}_{M'}(s_0,a) = Q^*_M(s_0,a) - \Phi(s_0) = 0 - 0 = 0$. So, $\hat{Q}_{M'}(s,a)$ satisfies the Bellman equations for M', and must in fact be the unique optimal Q-function. Thus, $Q^*_{M'}(s,a) = \hat{Q}_{M'}(s,a) = Q^*_M(s,a) - \Phi(s)$, and the optimal policy for M' therefore satisfies

$$\begin{aligned}
\pi^*_{M'}(s) &\in \arg\max_{a \in A} Q^*_{M'}(s,a) \\
&= \arg\max_{a \in A} Q^*_M(s,a) - \Phi(s) \\
&= \arg\max_{a \in A} Q^*_M(s,a)
\end{aligned}$$

and is therefore also optimal in M. To show every optimal policy in M is also optimal in M', simply apply the same proof with the roles of M and M' interchanged (and using the shaping function $-F$). This completes the proof. □

Corollary 2 *Under the conditions of Theorem 1, suppose that F does indeed take the form $F(s,a,s') = \gamma\Phi(s') - \Phi(s)$. Suppose further that $\Phi(s_0) = 0$ if $\gamma = 1$. Then for all $s \in S$, $a \in A$,*

$$\begin{aligned}
Q^*_{M'}(s,a) &= Q^*_M(s,a) - \Phi(s), && (3) \\
V^*_{M'}(s) &= V^*_M(s) - \Phi(s). && (4)
\end{aligned}$$

Proof: (3) was proved in the sufficiency proof above; (4) follows immediately from the identity $V^*(s) = \max_{a \in A} Q^*(s,a)$. □

Remark 1 (Robustness and learning): Although we have not proved it here, the identities in Corollary 2 actually hold for arbitrary policies π, not just the optimal policy: $V^\pi_{M'}(s) = V^\pi_M(s) - \Phi(s)$ (and similarly for Q-functions). A consequence of this is that potential-based shaping is *robust* in the sense that near-optimal policies are also preserved; that is, if we learn a near optimal policy π in M' (say, $|V^\pi_{M'}(s) - V^*_{M'}(s)| < \varepsilon$) using potential-based shaping, then π will also be near-optimal in M ($|V^\pi_M(s) - V^*_M(s)| < \varepsilon$). (To see this, apply the identity we just pointed out to policies π and to $\pi^*_M = \pi^*_{M'}$, and subtract.)

Remark 2 (All policies optimal under Φ): To better understand why potential-based F preserve optimal policies, it is worth noting if we have an MDP M that has a potential-based *reinforcement function* $R(s,a,s') = \gamma\Phi(s') - \Phi(s)$, then *any* policy is optimal in M. Thus, potential-based shaping functions are indifferent to policies, in the sense that they give us no reason to prefer any policy over any other; at an intuitive level, this accounts for why they do not give us any reason to prefer any policy other than π^*_M when we switch from M to M'.

The Theorem suggests that we choose shaping rewards of the form $F(s,a,s') = \gamma\Phi(s') - \Phi(s)$. In applications,

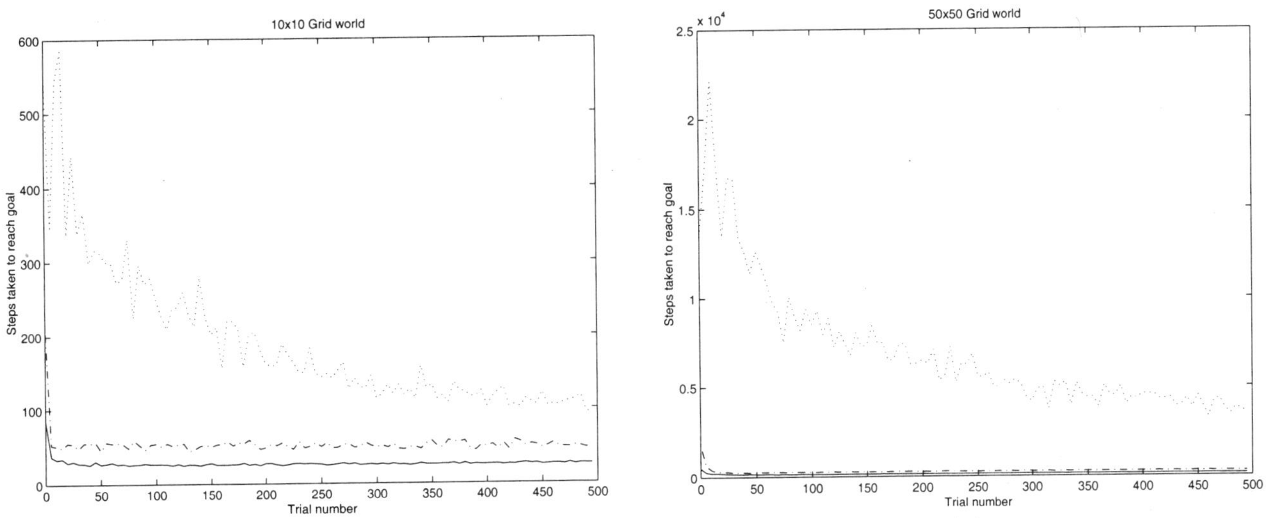

(a) (b)

Figure 1: (a) Experiment with 10x10 grid-world. Plot of steps taken to goal vs. trial number. Dot is no shaping, dot-dash is $\Phi = 0.5\Phi_0$, solid is $\Phi = \Phi_0$. (b) Experiment with 50x50 grid-world.

Φ should of course be chosen using expert knowledge about the domain. As to how one may do this, Corollary 2 suggests a particularly nice form for Φ, if we know enough about the domain to try choosing it as such. We see that if $\Phi(s) = V^*_M(s)$ (with $\Phi(s_0) = 0$ in the undiscounted case), then Equation (4) tells us that the value function in M' is $V^*_{M'}(s) \equiv 0$ — and this is a particularly easy value function to learn; even lacking a model of the world, all that would remain to be done would be to learn the non-zero Q-values. Though to avoid misconception, we also stress this is not the only way of choosing useful Φ, and that such shaping rewards can help significantly *even if Φ is far from* V^*_M (say in the sup-norm), such as by guiding exploration, etc., and we will see examples of this in the next section. But in any case, so long as we choose potential-based F, we have the guarantee that any (near-)optimal policy we learn in M' will also be (near-)optimal in M. Let us now turn our attention to some small experiments that demonstrate how potential-based shaping might be applied in practice.

4 Experiments

Much empirical work before us has convincingly justified the use of shaping [Mataric, 1994, Randløv and Alstrøm, 1998], and we will not bother to try to further justify its use. Here, our goal instead is to show how potential-style shaping functions fit into the picture, and to demonstrate how such shaping functions might be derived in practice.

Towards these goals, we chose for simplicity and clarity to use very simple grid-world domains to showcase the interesting aspects of potential-based shaping. The first domain was a shortest-path-to-goal 10x10 grid-world with start and goal states in opposite corners, no discounting, and a -1 per-step reinforcement. Actions are the 4 compass directions, and move 1 step in the intended direction 80% of the time and a random direction 20% of the time, and agent stays in the same place if it tries to walk off the grid. What might be a good shaping potential $\Phi(s)$? We had pointed out earlier that Equation (4) suggests $\Phi(s) = V^*_M(s)$ might be a good shaping potential. So let us now go through the type of reasoning that might suggest a crude estimate of V^*_M; by doing so, we hope to demonstrate how, with a little expert knowledge about distances and the location of the goal, similar reasoning may perhaps be used to similarly derive Φ for other minimum-cost-to-goal problems.

Upon trying to take a step towards the goal, we have an 80% chance of taking the desired step towards the goal, and a 20% chance of a random action. If we take a random action, then unless we are at the border of the gridworld, we are as likely to move towards as away from the goal. Hence, from most states, we would expect the optimal policy to make about 0.8 steps of (Manhattan distance) progress towards the goal per timestep, and a crude estimate of the expected number of steps needed to get to the goal from s would be MANHATTAN(s,GOAL)/0.8. Thus, we set

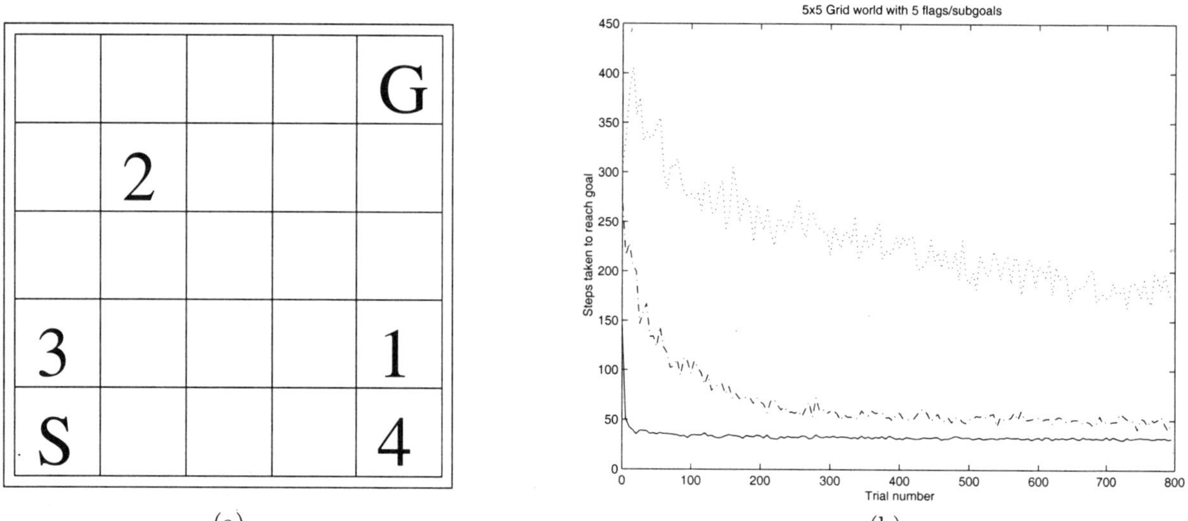

(a) (b)

Figure 2: (a) 5x5 grid-world with 5 subgoals (including goal state), which must be visited in order $1, 2, 3, 4, G$. (b) Experiment with 5x5 grid-world with subgoals. Plot of steps taken to goal vs. trial number. Dot is no shaping, dot-dash is $\Phi = \Phi_0$, solid is $\Phi = \Phi_1$.

our estimate of the value function and therefore $\Phi(s)$ to be $\Phi_0(s) = \hat{V}_M(s) = -\text{MANHATTAN}(s,\text{GOAL})/0.8$. This is what we used as our guess of a "good" shaping function. Also, as a shaping-reward that would be quite far (in the sup-norm) from $V^*_{M'}(s)$, we also tried using $\Phi(s) = 0.5\Phi_0(s)$. The results of this first experiment[4] are shown in Figure 1a. (All experiments reported in this section are averages over 40 independent runs.) As can be readily seen, using either of these shaping functions significantly helped speed up learning. Moreover, it is worth re-stressing that even though $0.5\Phi_0$ is quite far from V^*_M, it still significantly helped the initial stages of learning. For a larger 50x50 grid-world, the results become even more dramatic: Figure 1b shows the result of the same experiment repeated on the larger grid. The plots for Φ_0 and $0.5\Phi_0$ are so low in the graph that they can barely be seen; learning without shaping is clearly losing hopelessly to the potential-based shaping algorithm.

Reiterating, the goal of these experiments was not to try to justify shaping — that has been done far more convincingly by others. Instead, what we have demonstrated here is a style of some very simple reasoning that, by putting together a distance-to-goal heuristic, has enabled us to pick a sensible Φ that dramatically sped up learning.

Next, another class of problems for which a similar style of reasoning might work is domains where we can assign subgoals. Consider the grid-world in Figure 2a, where we start in the lower-left hand corner, and must pick up a set of "flags" in sequence before going to the final goal state. Actions and rewards are the same as in the previous grid-world, and the state-space is expanded to keep track of the collected flags. Since each flag is a subgoal, it is tempting to choose F so that we are rewarded for visiting the subgoals. Let us now see how a potential-function style of reasoning can indeed lead us to choose such an F, and how Equation (4) further suggests magnitudes for the subgoal rewards.

With knowledge of the subgoal locations and using reasoning analogous to that suggested earlier (0.8 steps of progress per timestep, etc.), we may estimate the expected number of timesteps, say t, needed to reach the goal. If we imagine that each subgoal is about equally hard to reach from the previous one, then having reached the n-th subgoal, we would still have about $((5-n)/5)t$ steps to go. A slightly more refined argument changes this to $((5-n-0.5)/5)t$ steps (where 0.5 comes from the "typical case" where we are halfway between the n-th and $n+1$-st subgoals), and so our first choice of $\Phi(s)$ is $\Phi_0(s) = -((5-n_s-0.5)/5)t$, where n_s denotes the number of subgoals we have achieved when we are at s. Using this form of shaping-reward function, we see that $\Phi(s) = \Phi_0(s)$ jumps by

[4] Using Sarsa [Sutton and Barto, 1998], 0.10-greedy exploration, learning rate 0.02. Experiments with Sarsa(λ) also gave analogous results showing shaping significantly speeding up learning.

$t/5$ whenever we reach any subgoal (other than the final goal state), and so the shaping reward function $F(s,a,s') = \Phi(s')-\Phi(s)$ is giving $t/5$ reward for reaching each of these subgoals. This is exactly what our intuition had suggested might be a good shaping reward. For comparison, we also carried out this experiment using a more fine-tuned shaping reward that, similar to the previous grid-world experiments, explicitly estimated the remaining time-to-goal for each state and constructed the corresponding $\Phi_1(s) = \hat{V}_M(s)$ potential function. The result of these experiments are shown in Figure 2b, and we see that using our first crude shaping function Φ_0 has allowed us to significantly speed up learning over not using shaping (and the fine-tuned Φ_1 unsurprisingly gave even better performance). When repeating this experiment on larger domains or with more subgoals, the results (not reported here) become even more dramatic.

5 Discussion and Conclusions

We have shown necessary and sufficient conditions for a shaping function F to leave optimal policies invariant. Here are two easy generalizations worth mentioning: Aside from guaranteeing consistency while trying to learn the optimal policy, it is easy to show (by an argument similar to Remark 1 in Section 3) that potential-based F also work when trying to learn a good policy from within a *restricted* class of policies, such as in the framework studied in [Kearns et al., 1999] (and which for example includes the task of finding the best weights for a neural network mapping from states to actions). Also, for Semi-Markov decision processes (SMDPs) where actions take varying amounts of time to complete, Equation (2) unsurprisingly generalizes to $F(s,a,s',\tau) = e^{-\beta\tau}\Phi(s') - \Phi(s)$, where τ is the time the action took to complete, and β is the discount rate.

Finally, the "$\gamma\Phi(s')-\Phi(s)$" form also seems on the surface reminiscent of terms in some of the equations used in Advantage learning [Baird, 1994] and λ-policy iteration [Bertsekas and Tsitsiklis, 1996]. At a very crude level, it turns out that each of them may be thought of as trying to modify Φ so to gain some computational or representational advantage. If we consider the problem of modifying Φ, then trying to learn a rough shaping function seems to lead quite naturally to an algorithm for multi-scale value-function approximation; and although it may initially seem unusual to try to *learn* a shaping function, it is the multiscale "rough vs. fine" approximation aspect that this leads to which makes it possibly powerful;[5] this will be the subject of future work.

In this paper, we have shown that potential-based shaping rewards $\gamma\Phi(s') - \Phi(s)$ leave (near-)optimal policies unchanged. Moreover, this was proved to be the only type of shaping that can guarantee such invariance unless we make further assumptions about the MDP. But just as some practitioners use discounting even on undiscounted problems (perhaps to improve convergence of algorithms), we believe that future experience with potential-style shaping rewards may also lead one to occasionally try shaping rewards that are inspired by potentials, but which are perhaps not strictly of the form we have given. For example, in analogy to using discounting even on undiscounted problems, it is conceivable that for certain problems, it may be easier for an expert to propose a potential Φ for an "undiscounted" shaping function $\Phi(s') - \Phi(s)$, even when $\gamma \neq 1$. Even though our theorem may no longer guarantee optimality in this case, such a shaping function may, purely from an engineering point of view, still be worth trying — judiciously and with care. In the same spirit, whereas our regularity conditions had demanded using bounded Φ, it is also plausible that some practitioners might want to try certain unbounded Φ. Naturally, if expert knowledge about the domain is available, then non-potential shaping functions might also be fully appropriate.

As guidelines for choosing shaping functions, we have suggested a distance-based heuristic and a subgoal-based heuristic for choosing potentials; because shaping is often crucial to making learning tractable, we believe the task of finding good shaping functions will be a problem of increasing importance.

Acknowledgments

A. Ng is supported by a Berkeley Fellowship. This work was also supported in part by ARO MURI grant DAAH04-96-1-0341, ONR grant N00014-97-1-0941, and NSF grant ECS-9873474.

References

[Baird, 1994] Baird, L. C. (1994). Reinforcement Learning in continuous time: Advantage updating.

[5] This also relates to the observation that something like a learned shaping reward seems to be operating psychologically—e.g., the capture of a piece in chess operates as a reward even though the underlying MDP has rewards only for checkmate.

In *Proceedings of the International Conference on Neural Networks.*

[Bertsekas, 1995] Bertsekas, D. P. (1995). *Dynamic Programming and Optimal Control, Volume II.* Athena Scientific.

[Bertsekas and Shreve, 1978] Bertsekas, D. P. and Shreve, S. E. (1978). *Stochastic Optimal Control: The Discrete Time Case.* Academic Press.

[Bertsekas and Tsitsiklis, 1996] Bertsekas, D. P. and Tsitsiklis, J. N. (1996). *Neuro-dynamic Programming.* Athena Scientific.

[Dorigo and Colombetti, 1994] Dorigo, M. and Colombetti, M. (1994). Robot shaping: Developing autonomous agents through learning. *Artificial Intelligence*, 71(2):321–370.

[Hernández-Lerma, 1989] Hernández-Lerma, O. (1989). *Adaptive Markov Control Processes.* Springer-Verlag.

[Kearns et al., 1999] Kearns, M., Mansour, Y., and Ng, A. Y. (1999). Approximate planning in large POMDPs via reusable trajectories. *(Preprint).*

[Mataric, 1994] Mataric, M. J. (1994). Reward functions for accelerated learning. In *Proceedings of the Eleventh International Conference on Machine Learning.* Morgan Kaufmann.

[Randløv and Alstrøm, 1998] Randløv, J. and Alstrøm, P. (1998). Learning to drive a bicycle using reinforcement learning and shaping. In *Proceedings of the Fifteenth International Conference on Machine Learning.* Morgan Kaufmann.

[Russell, 1998] Russell, S. (1998). Learning agents for uncertain environments (extended abstract). In *Proceedings of the Eleventh Annual ACM Workshop on Computational Learning Theory (COLT-98)*, Madison, Wisconsin. ACM Press.

[Rust, 1994] Rust, J. (1994). Do people behave according to Bellman's principal of optimality? Submitted to Journal of Economic Perspectives.

[Saksida et al., 1997] Saksida, L., Raymond, S., and Touretzky, D. (1997). Shaping robot behaviour using principles from instrumental conditioning. *Robotics and Autonomous Systems*, 22(3–4):231–249.

[Singh and Yee, 1994] Singh, S. and Yee, R. (1994). An upper bound on the loss from approximate optimal-value functions. *Machine Learning*, 16:227–233.

[Sutton and Barto, 1998] Sutton, R. S. and Barto, A. G. (1998). *Reinforcement Learning: An Introduction.* MIT Press.

[von Neumann and Morgenstern, 1944] von Neumann, J. and Morgenstern, O. (1944). *Theory of Games and Economic Behavior.* Princeton University Press, Princeton, New Jersey, first edition.

[Williams and Baird, 1994] Williams, R. J. and Baird, L. C. (1994). Tight performance bounds on greedy policies based on imperfect value functions. In *Proceedings of the Tenth Yale Workshop on Adaptive and Learning Systems.*

Appendix A: Proof of necessity

In this Appendix, we sketch the proof of the necessity part of Theorem 1. For brevity, we give the proof only for the case of $|A| = 2$; the generalization is obvious but more tedious. We begin with the following Lemma.

Lemma 3 *If there exists* $s \in S - \{s_0\}, s' \in S$ *and* $a, a' \in A$ *such that* $F(s,a,s') \neq F(s,a',s')$*, then there exists (proper) transition functions* T *and a reward function* R *such that no optimal policy in* M' *is optimal in* M*.*

Proof (Sketch, Lemma 3): Assume without loss of generality that $F(s,a,s') > F(s,a',s')$, and let $\Delta = F(s,a,s') - F(s,a',s') > 0$. In the undiscounted case, also assume for simplicity that $s \neq s'$. (When $\gamma = 1$, the proof for $s = s'$ is nearly the same, but having to ensure properness just makes it much more tedious.) We then construct M as follows: Let $P_{sa}(s') = P_{sa'}(s') = 1.0$, and let $R(s,a,s') = 0$ and $R(s,a',s') = \Delta/2$. Clearly $\pi^*_M(s) = a'$. On the other hand, since $R' = R + F$, we have $R'(s,a,s') = F(s,a,s')$ and $R'(s,a',s') = \Delta/2 + F(s,a',s') = F(s,a,s') - \Delta/2 < R'(s,a,s')$, and hence $\pi^*_{M'}(s) = a$. □

We are now ready to show the main necessity result.

Proof (of necessity). Assume F is not potential-based. We need to show we can construct T, R such that no optimal policy $\pi^*_{M'}$ in M' is also optimal in M. By Lemma 3, if $F(s,a,s')$ depends on a, we are done; hence we need only consider shaping functions

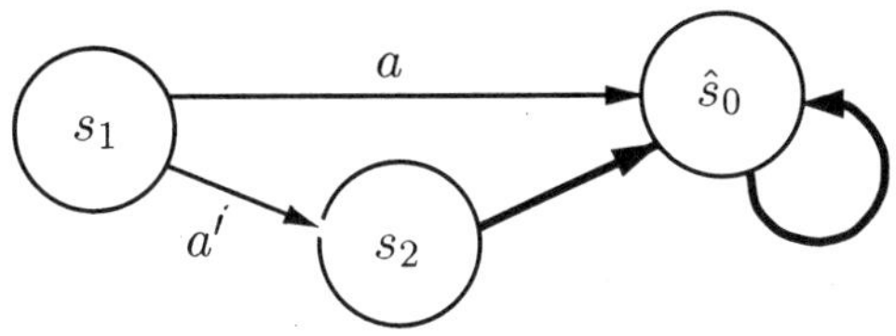

Figure 3: The unlabeled thick edges correspond to both actions. All edges have probability 1. The edge $(s_1, a, \hat{s}_0)$ carries a reward $\Delta/2$, and all other edges have zero reward.

of the form $F(s, a, s') = F(s, s')$ (which do not depend on a).

If $\gamma = 1$, let $\hat{s}_0 = s_0$ be the distinguished absorbing state; otherwise let $\hat{s}_0$ be some fixed state. Noting that constant offsets of the reward do not affect the optimal policy when $\gamma < 1$, we may, by replacing all $F(s, s')$ with $F(s, s') - F(\hat{s}_0, \hat{s}_0)$ if necessary, assume without loss of generality that $F(\hat{s}_0, \hat{s}_0) = 0$. Now define $\Phi(s) = -F(s, \hat{s}_0)$ for all s. By assumption of F not being potential-based, there exists s_1, s_2 such that $\gamma\Phi(s_2) - \Phi(s_1) \neq F(s_1, s_2)$ (let us assume $s_1, s_2, \hat{s}_0$ are distinct; the other cases are either impossible or handled similarly). We then construct M in the following way (still assuming $|A| = 2$). From state s_1, let $P_{s_1 a}(\hat{s}_0) = P_{s_1 a'}(s_2) = 1.0$, and from states s_2 and $\hat{s}_0$ let both actions a and a' lead to $\hat{s}_0$ with probability 1. Also define $\Delta = F(s_1, s_2) + \gamma F(s_2, \hat{s}_0) - F(s_1, \hat{s}_0)$ and let $R(s_1, a, \hat{s}_0) = \Delta/2$, $R(\cdot, \cdot, \cdot) = 0$ elsewhere. This model is illustrated in Figure 3. Then we have

$$\begin{aligned}
Q^*_M(s_1, a) &= \frac{\Delta}{2} \\
Q^*_M(s_1, a') &= 0 \\
Q^*_{M'}(s_1, a) &= \frac{\Delta}{2} + F(s_1, \hat{s}_0) \\
&= F(s_1, s_2) + \gamma F(s_2, \hat{s}_0) - \frac{\Delta}{2} \\
Q^*_{M'}(s_1, a') &= F(s_1, s_2) + \gamma F(s_2, \hat{s}_0),
\end{aligned}$$

where we have relied on the fact that $V^*_M(\hat{s}_0) = V^*_{M'}(\hat{s}_0) = 0$ by construction. Hence

$$\begin{aligned}
\pi^*_M(s_1) &= \begin{cases} a & \text{if } \Delta > 0, \\ a' & \text{otherwise} \end{cases} \\
\pi^*_{M'}(s_1) &= \begin{cases} a' & \text{if } \Delta > 0, \\ a & \text{otherwise} \end{cases}
\end{aligned}$$

□

Learning Discriminatory and Descriptive Rules by an Inductive Logic Programming System

Maziar Palhang
Artificial Intelligence Department
School of Computer Science and Engineering
The University of New South Wales
Sydney 2052, Australia
maziar@cse.unsw.edu.au

Arcot Sowmya
Artificial Intelligence Department
School of Computer Science and Engineering
The University of New South Wales
Sydney 2052, Australia
sowmya@cse.unsw.edu.au

Abstract

Machine learning techniques are often used to solve the knowledge acquisition problem. Inductive Logic Programming (ILP) is a new research area in Machine Learning, marked by the exploitation of background knowledge, and the use of first order logic to represent hypotheses. ILP systems are attractive for complex and real-world applications which also help to uncover the strengths and shortcomings of these systems. This paper first points out some shortcomings of some ILP systems. One is the discriminatory nature of rules created by them, when used in the area of object model learning. A model represented by such a discriminatory rule may cause an object to be falsely recognised. Further verification with a model containing all the necessary information about an object (a *descriptive model*) may solve this problem. In addition, rules generated by ILP systems are not exactly identical to a generalised graph which represents a model of a class of objects. A new ILP system, *TSFOIL*, that can **learn** both discriminatory and descriptive rules in two stages is introduced. The generated rules have also more similarity to a graph representation of object models. Experiments on a real world application are then reported which were conducted to show the shortcomings of discriminatory rules, and the advantage of using both kinds of rules.

1 Introduction

Machine Learning techniques are often used to address the knowledge acquisition problem. Inductive Logic Programming (ILP) is one of the new areas in Machine Learning. The exploitation of background knowledge, and the use of first order logic to represent hypotheses are two main advantages of ILP systems with respect to other learning systems. These factors make them attractive on real-world complex applications which also help to discover the strengths and shortcomings of these learning systems. So far there have been a few attempts to use them in such domains (Bratko and Muggleton, 1995; Srinivasan et al., 1997).

Constructing object models is one such complex problem. In our previous research (Palhang and Sowmya, 1997a; Palhang and Sowmya, 1997b), we used two ILP systems FOIL (Quinlan, 1990) and FFOIL (Quinlan, 1996) to learn object models. We found that the models learned by these systems have limitations in the area of object recognition. The reason is that the rules[1] learned by such systems are discriminatory in nature. That is, they keep the fewest possible relations in the rule such that it can discriminate an object from others. An object recognition system may encounter novel objects which the system has not been trained with, or an image may contain more than one object, some trained on earlier, others not (*clutter*). The objects may hide each other as well (*occlusion*). These effects along with shadows and noise may give rise to situations where the discriminatory features of an object seem to appear in the image, and the object is falsely recognised to be present (*false positive* effect). In addition, when an object is reported to exist in an image, one is interested in find-

[1]When the rules are used as object models, rules may be referred to as models as well.

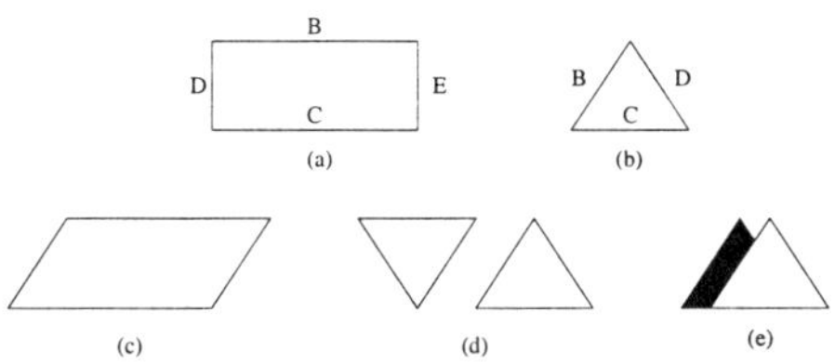

Figure 1: When a discriminatory learning system is used to learn models of shapes (a) and (b), the shapes (c), (d), and (e) are recognised as an instance of those two shapes as well.

ing the segments which belong to this object. This necessitates further tests to verify that the object is indeed present in an image, and to delineate its extent in the image. A partial remedy for these problems is to train the system again with cases that the system has wrongly classified. This may reduce the false positive effect. However, there may be a huge number of such cases. Another approach is to perform further tests with a model that contains complete information about the object. Such a model is called a *descriptive model.* The match with the descriptive model should be partial to be able to detect the parts of an object that are actually present in an image.

To illustrate the problem, assume that we are going to learn the models of a *rectangle*, and an *acute triangle*, as shown in Figs. 1(a) and (b). A discriminatory model learner may produce the following rules:

$$\begin{aligned} rectangle(A) &\ :-\ partof(A,B), parallel(B,C). \\ triangle(A) &\ :-\ partof(A,B), acute(B,C). \end{aligned}$$

If these rules are always applied to recognise rectangles and acute triangles there will not be any problem. However, if the system is faced with a parallelogram (Fig. 1(c)), it is recognised as both a rectangle *and* an acute triangle, and there is no way to pick one over the other. If the system is retrained and some examples of a parallelogram are considered as negative examples while it is learning either the rectangle or acute triangle concept, the system will come up with rules that can discriminate these shapes from parallelograms. Figures 1(d) and (e) display other situations where the system reports the existence of both shapes, though there are only acute triangles in these figures.

To attack these problems, we prefer the second approach, that is using descriptive models, since retraining is not necessary each time that a new falsely detected case is found. In the above example, descriptive rules could be:

$$\begin{aligned} rectangle(A) &\ :-\ partof(A,B), parallel(B,C), right\_angle(B,D), \\ &\qquad right\_angle(E,B), parallel(D,E), \\ &\qquad right\_angle(C,E), right\_angle(D,C), \\ &\qquad partof(A,C), partof(A,D), partof(A,E). \\ triangle(A) &\ :-\ partof(A,B), acute(B,C), acute(D,B), \\ &\qquad acute(C,D), right\_angle(D,C), partof(A,C), \\ &\qquad partof(A,D). \end{aligned}$$

These rules confirm that there is neither a rectangle, nor an acute triangle in Fig. 1(c), and there is no rectangle in Figs. 1(d) and (e).

To handle these issues, the idea of *two stage learning* of object models and *two stage recognition* of objects in images is proposed within a single system called *TSFOIL.* The TSFOIL system modifies and extends the search strategy within FOIL, such that after learning a discriminatory rule, the search is continued to find all other common relations among the instances which are covered by the discriminatory rule, in order to generate a complete descriptive rule. In the recognition phase, discriminatory models are first used to shortlist the possible objects in the image. Then, a partial match is performed with the descriptive rule to verify the match. The TSFOIL approach is a first step in making ILP systems more powerful to deal with complex applications like recognising objects in different images and contexts.

It is noteworthy to mention that object models are often better represented as graphs, where each node denotes a different part of an object. The rules generated by current ILP systems are not suitable for this purpose. The reason is that if the rule constructed by an ILP system is considered as a generalised graph of the graphs of the training instances, this graph may cover two graphs that are not exactly identical. Thus, the rule represents two objects which do not have completely similar structures. For example, let angles be considered directionally, that is line B is acute to line C if the angle that C should rotate in counterclockwise direction to reach B is less than 90°. Then the following rule:

$$\begin{aligned} shape(A) &\ :-\ partof(A,B), right\_angle(B,C), \\ &\qquad partof(A,D), obtuse(D,E). \end{aligned} \tag{1}$$

represents both the shapes in Fig. 2, because C and D may be instantiated to a same term. Moreover, the rule implicitly expresses that B, C, D, and E are four parts of A, whereas neither of the objects has four parts. TSFOIL takes these factors into account

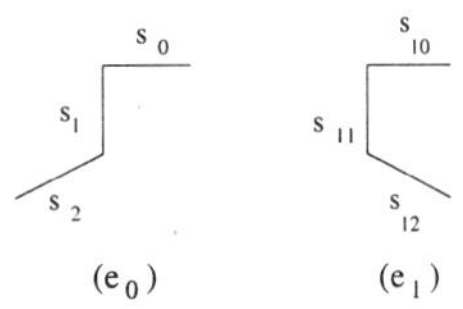

Figure 2: Two shapes with two different structures.

through a one-to-one mapping of variables to terms while constructing the rules.

In the next section, the TSFOIL algorithm is explained. Then, the experiments performed to show the performance of TSFOIL will be discussed. The paper then concludes with a discussion on the approach.

2 TSFOIL Algorithm

The TSFOIL algorithm is a modification of the FOIL algorithm (Quinlan, 1990; Cameron-Jones and Quinlan, 1994). Like FOIL, it has a major loop called a *covering loop* which is responsible for hypothesis construction. However, unlike FOIL, in each loop a pair of clauses, *discriminatory* and *descriptive*, are constructed which distinguish some of the positive instances from all the negative instances of the target concept. Those positive instances covered by the clauses are removed from the training set, and the loop is repeated until all the positive instances are covered.

Creation of this pair of clauses is performed in two stages using two *specialisation loops*. The first specialisation loop (FSL) is similar (but not identical) to the specialisation loop of FOIL, and constructs the discriminatory clause. This is achieved by evaluating all possible relations that can be added to the clause, and selecting the one which has the highest gain in each iteration of the loop. The gain is calculated by an information theoretic heuristic measure which causes an increase in the population of positive instances with respect to negative instances. Adding a relation to the definition being learned may lead to removal of some positive instances and some of the negative instances from the training set. The iteration stops when there are no more negative instances that may be removed from the training set.

The second specialisation loop (SSL) which creates the descriptive clause is exclusive to TSFOIL, and distinguishes it from FOIL. This loop is executed immediately after the first specialisation loop. Before entering the SSL, the discriminatory clause found so far

```
/* create a hypothesis */
-create a training set consisting of positive and
 negative instances of the target concept,
-initialise the head of the discriminatory clause to the target concept,
while there is any positive instance do
  /* create discriminatory rule */
  -copy the training set to the current training set,
  -initialise the discriminatory clause to the target concept,
  while there is any negative instance to be removed from the current
  training set do
    -evaluate all the relations possible to be added to the clause,
    -select the best relation and append it to the clause,
    -remove the tuples not covered by the clause and
     create a new training set
  endwhile
  /* create descriptive rule */
  -copy discriminatory clause to descriptive clause,
  repeat
    -find all the common relations using the current training set,
    if there is any common relation then
      -select one of the common relations and append it to the descrip-
      tive clause,
      -create a new training set,
    endif
  until there is not any common relation
  -include the discriminatory and descriptive clauses in the set of hy-
  potheses,
  -remove the positive instances covered by the discriminatory clause,
   and create a new training set
endwhile
```

Figure 3: TSFOIL algorithm.

is copied to a descriptive clause. All relations that are common to all positive instances covered by the discriminatory clause in each iteration are found, and one of them is selected and appended to the descriptive clause. The loop ends when there is no relation common to all the selected positive instances. Figure 3 displays the algorithm. During hypothesis construction, TSFOIL ensures that each variable is mapped only to one term. This mapping is called *super substitution.*

We have assumed so far that a common relation covers all of the positive instances covered by the discriminatory clause. However, in some situations the majority of instances might have a common relation, while a few instances lack it due to noise, or missing parts, or normal intra-concept variability. To handle such situations, TSFOIL accepts a relation as common if it covers a number of instances which is more than or equal to a threshold specified by the user. This threshold is called an *evidence level*, and its default value is 100, that is a common relation should cover 100% of the instances. The method used here is similar to the noise handling approach of FOIL, when it accepts a clause when it covers more than a threshold of positive instances.

In choosing common relations, priority is given to those which have higher coverage of the instances. For those relations which have the same coverage, the same criteria mentioned before are used. When those relations have been selected, the next set of relations

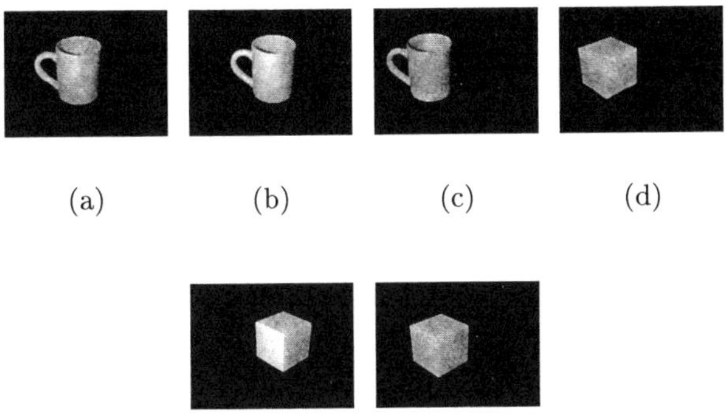

(a) (b) (c) (d)

(e) (f)

Figure 4: Sample images of objects used to learn their models by TSFOIL.

which has the next highest coverage and still above the threshold is taken into account. TSFOIL can be run in different modes. It can either create discriminatory or descriptive rules alone, or it may generate both together (default option).

The descriptive rule created by TSFOIL is not always the same as the relative least general generalisation (*rlgg*) clause (Plotkin, 1971) generated in a θ-subsumption lattice. A reason is that since one to one mapping of variables to terms is considered in TSFOIL, the clauses are not generated in the θ-subsumption lattice. As an example in Fig. 2 there is an ambiguity in representation of the common structure of objects $e0$ and $e1$. A common structure can be either of the following clauses:

$$shape(A) \quad :- \quad partof(A,B), partof(A,C), right\_angle(B,C).$$
$$shape(A) \quad :- \quad partof(A,B), partof(A,C), obtuse(B,C)$$

Any of these clauses is acceptable. TSFOIL creates only one of these clauses, depending on which one of the relations $right\_angle(B,C)$ or $obtuse(B,C)$ is optionally selected first. On the other hand, the *rlgg* contains both of these relations [2] (similar to the clause in 1), and does not correctly reflect the common structure of these two objects. An interesting property of descriptive rules of TSFOIL, is that each has a corresponding discriminatory rule that may be used to shortlist the possible matches for further testing on descriptive rules.

[2]Since cross product of the relations of $e0$ and $e1$ is used.

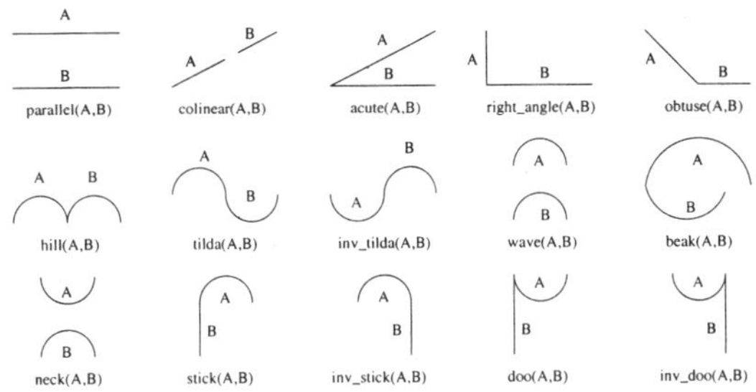

(a)

Relations between	Symbolic relations
two lines	$parallel(seg, seg)^*$ $colinear(seg, seg)^*$ $acute(seg, seg)$ $right\_angle(seg, seg)$ $obtuse(seg, seg)$ $near\_lines(seg, seg)^*$
two arcs	$hill(seg, seg)^*$ $tilda(seg, seg)^*$ $inv\_tilda(seg, seg)^*$ $wave(seg, seg)^*$ $beak(seg, seg)^*$ $neck(seg, seg)^*$ $near\_arcs(seg, seg)^*$
an arc and a line	$stick(seg, seg)(seg, seg)$ $inv\_stick(seg, seg)$ $doo(seg, seg)$ $inv\_doo(seg, seg)$ $near\_arc\_line(seg, seg)$

(b)

Figure 5: (a) Relations among the segments found by the system, and (b) their symbolic representation. Symmetric relations are marked with asterisks.

PROGOL (Muggleton, 1995) creates the most specific clause from one positive instance, and uses this as a guide to find a *discriminatory clause*, that covers a set of positive instances against a set of negative instances. TSFOIL, on the other hand, uses a FOIL-like discriminatory clause as the starting point and extends it to produce a descriptive clause.

3 Experiments

TSFOIL was used to learn the models of two kinds of objects: mug and cube. For each object, 150 images with the same view, but different displacement, were taken. From these images, 100 images of each object were used to train the system. Another 100 images, (50 of each), were used to test the learned models. Images were gray-level and have 320x240 pixels. Sample images are shown in Fig. 4. It is noteworthy to mention that no two images of an object are exactly

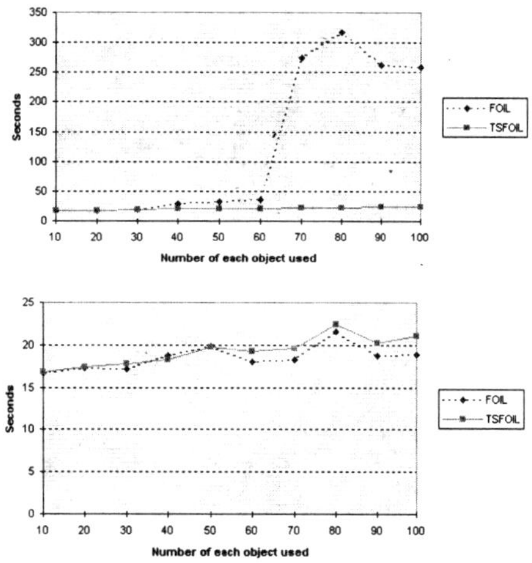

Figure 6: The times taken to learn models of of mug (top), and cube (bottom).

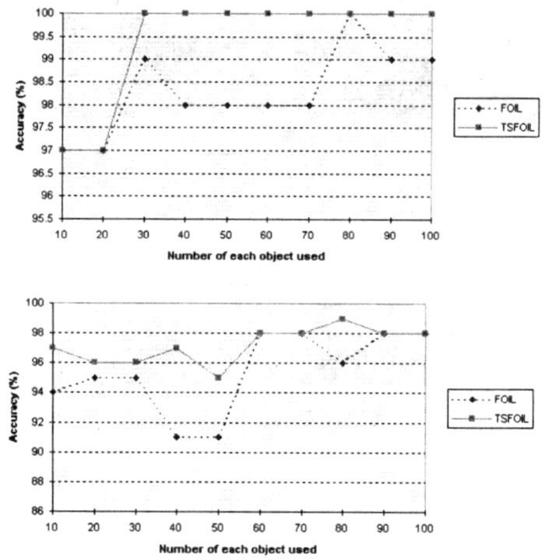

Figure 7: Recognition results on the test set for mug (top), and cube (bottom).

similar even if the images are taken at the same object pose, due to noise, lighting and imaging effects. Thus, we are not feeding the same image repeatedly to the learning system. The edges of these images were extracted using the Canny algorithm, and linked. The linked edges were segmented to straight and curved lines. The relations among these segments were found and represented symbolically. A repertoire of symbolic relations has been devised as shown in Fig. 5(a) and Fig. 5(b). The relations marked with $*$ are symmetric relations. Apart from these relations, there is another relation $partof(obj, seg)$ which represents the ownership of a segment to an object.

Two sets of experiments were performed. In the first set, the discriminatory models alone were tested. Ten experiments were conducted. First 10 images of the mug, and 10 images of the cube were used to learn their models, and the results were tested on the 100 image test set. Then, each time another 10 images of the mug, and another 10 images of the cube were added to the training set, and the experiment was repeated. This was continued until 100 images of each object were in the training set. The test set was always the same.

As seen in Fig. 6, the time taken to learn mug models for TSFOIL is considerably less than that of FOIL. In the case of the cube, the times are closer, while noting that the scale of the two charts are different. A reason that FOIL takes longer to learn mug models is that a mug often needs the relations between two arcs, such as *hill*, *tilda*, etc to be discriminated against cube. These relations are symmetric relations. While creating rules, FOIL checks different combinations of variables for each relation. When a symmetric relation is being checked that has a variable in common with the same relation which is already in the rule, such as checking $hill(C, D)$ while $hill(B, C)$ is already selected, the size of the training set grows considerably. This increase is due to instantiations of variable D to the same terms as those instantiated for B, plus other terms which may have *hill* relation with C. As representatives, the mug rules for training sets of 10, 60, and 70 images of each object are shown in Fig 8. When 70 images of each object were used, the third literal of the first rule has the mentioned condition, and has been selected. This causes the training set to expand, and learning time to increase considerably. TSFOIL was also faced with this situation as seen in Fig. 9, but because repetitive terms are not included in the tuples the learning time is much less than that of FOIL.

This situation does not occur for cube, and the small increase of learning time for TSFOIL is due to the overhead of checking that terms are not repeated for different variables. The accuracy measure defined below is used to evaluate the recognition results (Weiss and Kulikowski, 1991).

$$accuracy \quad = \quad \frac{(no.of\,TruePositives + no.of\,TrueNegatives)}{total\,no.\,of\,tests}$$

Figure 7 shows that rules created by both FOIL and TSFOIL have good accuracies, however, TSFOIL rules

$mug_{10}(A)$:− $partof(A,B), beak(B,C).$

$mug_{60}(A)$:− $partof(A,B), beak(B,C), wave(C,D).$

$mug_{70}(A)$:− $partof(A,B), hill(B,C), hill(C,D), stick(B,E), beak(B,F), inv\_doo(D,G).$

$mug_{70}(A)$ $partof(A,B), beak(B,C), wave(B,D).$

$cube_{10}(A)$:− $partof(A,B), parallel\_line(B,C), acute(D,B), obtuse(C,D).$

$cube_{60}(A)$:− $partof(A,B), parallel\_line(B,C), obtuse(B,D), acute(E,D), acute(C,F).$

$cube_{70}(A)$:− $partof(A,B), parallel\_line(B,C), obtuse(B,D), acute(E,D), acute(C,F).$

Figure 8: Rules created for *mug* and *cube* by FOIL when considering 10, 60, and 70 images of each object for training respectively. Indices under *mug* and *cube* names were not part of the rules, and have been added for clarity here.

$mug_{10}(A)$:− $partof(A,B), beak(B,C).$

$mug_{60}(A)$:− $partof(A,B), hill(B,C), hill(C,D), hill(B,E), hill(D,F).$

$mug_{70}(A)$:− $partof(A,B), hill(B,C), hill(C,D), hill(B,E), hill(D,F).$

$cube_{10}(A)$:− $partof(A,B), parallel\_line(B,C), acute(D,B), acute(B,E).$

$cube_{60}(A)$:− $partof(A,B), parallel\_line(B,C), obtuse(B,D), acute(E,D), acute(C,F).$

$cube_{70}(A)$:− $partof(A,B), parallel\_line(B,C), obtuse(B,D), acute(E,D), acute(C,F).$

Figure 9: Rules created for *mug* and *cube* by TSFOIL when considering 10, 60, and 70 images of each object for training respectively. Indices under *mug* and *cube* names were not part of the rules, and have been added for clarity here.

often performed better than those of FOIL. The recognition results were obtained by using the test options available in FOIL and TSFOIL. In these experiments, only discriminatory rules are considered, and matching is exact.

In the next set of experiments, we created both discriminatory and descriptive models of *mug* and *cube* when 100 images of each were used, to demonstrate the two stage recognition idea,. The models are shown in Fig. 10 for TSFOIL, and discriminatory rules of FOIL in Fig. 11. As seen, TSFOIL has produced both rules. The relations marked with $*$, and the relations after them have no relation with the segments in the first part of the descriptive rules. These relations either describe different parts of objects, and their connection to the other parts is broken due to imaging effects, or they are just noise. Usually these relations do not add many constraints among the segments, and they make partial matching difficult. Segments satisfying these relations may occur anywhere in the image, and unrelated segments are considered to be part of an object. Thus, we have not used these relations in the recognition phase, and removed them manually. This is not a problem of TSFOIL, which is doing its job very well. Further investigation is needed to add more constraints among segments while extracting features, and to assign weights to rules and relations for proper consideration of these relations.

In the case of our vision application, the removal of the above mentioned relations may be done automatically. To find the first relation for removal, the first *partof* relation which introduces a variable not already in the rule should be found (except the first *partof* relation at the beginning of the rule which links the rest of the rule with the head of the clause). In TSFOIL, when *partof* is the only common relation that is found (except at the beginning of the rule) the growing of the clause may be stopped.

In the same manner as learning, in the recognition phase the symbolic relations of an image was produced, but represented as Prolog facts. A Prolog program has been written that first checks the possibility of an object's presence in the image by matching the discriminatory models of objects. If a discriminatory model is matched, then a partial match with the descriptive rule is performed and the following simple quality of match (QM) measure is computed.

$$QM = \frac{Number\,of\,literals\,matched}{Total\,number\,of\,literals\,in\,the\,rule} \qquad (2)$$

Figures 12 and 13 illustrate 50 images used to test the system. Table 1 shows the recognition results for both TSFOIL and FOIL, based on rules learned using 100 images each of *cube* and *mug* in the learning phase. For TSFOIL, the table displays the quality of

```
mug(A)   :-  partof(A,B), hill(B,C), hill(C,D), stick(C,E), hill(B,F).
mug(A)   :-  partof(A,B), hill(B,C), hill(C,D), stick(C,E), hill(B,F), inv_stick(B,E), partof(A,C),
             partof(A,D), partof(A,E), partof(A,F), hill(C,B), hill(D,C), hill(F,B), stick(F,G),
             near_arc_line(H,G), partof(A,G), partof(A,H), partof(A,I)*, doo(I,J), partof(A,J),
             partof(A,K), inv_stick(K,L), partof(A,L), partof(A,M), near_arc_line(M,N),
             partof(A,N), partof(A,O), partof(A,P), partof(A,Q), partof(A,R), partof(A,S),
             partof(A,T), partof(A,U), partof(A,V), partof(A,W), partof(A,X), partof(A,Y).

cube(A)  :-  partof(A,B), parallel_line(B,C), obtuse(B,D), acute(E,D), acute(C,F).
cube(A)  :-  partof(A,B), parallel_line(B,C), obtuse(B,D), acute(E,D), acute(C,F), obtuse(F,G),
             partof(A,C), partof(A,D), partof(A,E), partof(A,F), partof(A,G),
             parallel_line(C,B), partof(A,H)*, obtuse(H,I), partof(A,I), partof(A,J),
             partof(A,K), partof(A,L), partof(A,M), partof(A,N), partof(A,O), partof(A,P).
```

Figure 10: The discriminatory and descriptive models of *mug* and *cube* when 100 images of each object were used for training.

```
mug(A)   :-  partof(A,B), hill(B,C), stick(C,D), inv_stick(E,D),
             beak(C,F), tilda(B,G).
mug(A)   :-  partof(A,B), hill(B,C), wave(B,D), tilda(B,E).

cube(A)  :-  partof(A,B), parallel_line(B,C), obtuse(B,D), acute(E,D),
             acute(C,F).
```

Figure 11: The discriminatory rules of *mug* and *cube* created by FOIL when considering 100 images of each object for training.

the match for the mug rule with 100% evidence level, mug rule with 90% evidence level, cube rule with 100% evidence level, and cube rule with 90% evidence level in order. If the discriminatory rule of each object was not satisfied, the program answered *no* to the query, otherwise it returned the quality of match for the corresponding rule. When more than one rule is satisfied for an object, the highest QM returned is taken into account. Prolog answers for matching FOIL rules are written in the right side of the table. Table 1 clearly demonstrate the inadequacy of using discriminatory rules alone, where satisfying such a rule does not properly reflect our confidence in the presence, the extent, or even the existence of an object in an image.

To explain the results, we look at the first ten images of Fig. 12 in more detail. Both discriminatory models of *mug* and *cube* created by FOIL and TSFOIL are not satisfied for images *a*, *b*, *i*, and *j*. As a result, the descriptive model is not checked further, and the search is stopped. Images *c* and *d* are recognised as *mug* and *cube* respectively. Another check with the descriptive rule verifies this match. These images are different from the test images used to measure the accuracies of the rules. Image *e* is recognised as *mug* by FOIL. The mug discriminatory rule of TSFOIL is also satisfied. A further partial match for the descriptive rule with evidence level 100% verifies that it is 100% *mug* as well. However, a further check with the descriptive rule with 90% evidence level shows that it is not completely similar to a mug. The reason is that when the evidence level is decreased, more relations are included in the rule, hence the rule constraints are increased. Image *f* is a special case where existence of shadows has produced a spurious situation so that discriminatory models recognise it as a cube. However, verification shows that it is not exactly so. Image *g* consists of a mug and a cube, and discriminatory rules of mug and cube are satisfied for them. Further verification with descriptive rules of mug shows that there is a mug in the image with 100% match. The descriptive rule of cube with 100% evidence level confirms the presence of a cube, but descriptive rule with 90% evidence level shows that it is not completely similar to the majority of cubes used to train the system. Finally, a mug is recognised in image *h* and descriptive rules help to find more segments belonging to this mug than the discriminatory rules of TSFOIL and FOIL do. The better accuracy of TSFOIL rules may also be noticed from Table 1, in cases where FOIL rules have wrongly reported the existence of an object, such as Fig. 12(u).

4 Conclusion

In this paper, shortcomings of rules created by current ILP systems were discussed. The rules created by these systems are discriminatory rules. Different effects such as noise, clutter, and occlusion, and novel objects which the system was not trained with may produce situations where discriminatory features of an object seem to appear in an image, and hence the recognition system reports the existence of the object in the image (*false positive* effect). Further checks are thus necessary to verify this match.

The approach of *two stage learning, and two stage recognition* is proposed, in which both discriminatory models and their corresponding descriptive models are learned by an integrated learning system, TSFOIL, designed and implemented by us. In the recognition phase, discriminatory models are matched first to shortlist the possible objects in an image. Then, a partial match with the descriptive models is carried out to verify the match.

Two stage recognition of objects is not completely a new idea in computer vision. Systems which incorporate hypothesise and verify methods (Jain et al., 1995), and those which apply indexing methods first (Rothwell, 1995) are two stage recognition systems as well. However in our method, what should be hypothesised or used as an index, and what should be verified are both *learned* in the integrated platform, *TSFOIL*, and are in logic form. The rules generated by TSFOIL are somewhat similar to graph-based descriptions. This is also pointed out in (Geibel and Wysotzki, 1997). This similarity sometimes enables faster learning within TSFOIL.

An exact match with the rules as in logic programming systems is not very effective in recognising objects in different environments. A combination of methods from evidential reasoning and inductive logic programming appears a very promising path to follow. In this work, it is addressed in part by partial matching with the descriptive rules, and adding an evidence level during the learning procedure. Implementing these new ideas demands further research, and provides a platform for future investigations.

References

Bratko, I. and Muggleton, S. (1995). Applications of inductive logic programming. *Communications of the ACM*, 38(11):65–70.

Cameron-Jones, R. M. and Quinlan, J. R. (1994). Efficient top-down induction of logic programs. *SIGART Bulletin*, 5(1):33–42.

Geibel, P. and Wysotzki, F. (1997). A logical framework for graph theoretical decision tree learning. In Lavrac, N. and Dzeroski, S., editors, *Proc. of the 7th International Workshop on Inductive Logic Programming (ILP-97)*, volume 1297 of *Lecture Notes in Artificial Intelligence*, pages 173–180, Prague, Czech Republic. Springer.

Jain, R., Kasturi, R., and Schunck, B. G. (1995). *Machine Vision.* Computer Science. McGraw-Hill.

Muggleton, S. (1995). Inverse entailment and Progol. *New Generation Computing*, 13:245–286.

Palhang, M. and Sowmya, A. (1997a). Automatic acquisition of object models by relational learning. In Leung, C., editor, *Visual Information Systems*, volume 1306 of *Lecture Notes on Computer Science*, pages 239–258. Springer.

Palhang, M. and Sowmya, A. (1997b). Classifying objects by a functional learning system. In *Proc. of the Second International Conference on Visual Information Systems (VISUAL'97)*, pages 29–36, San Diego, USA.

Plotkin, G. D. (1971). A further note on inductive generalisation. *Machine Intelligence*, 6:101–124.

Quinlan, J. R. (1990). Learning logical definitions from relations. *Machine Learning*, 5:239–266.

Quinlan, J. R. (1996). Learning first-order definitions of functions. *Journal of Artificial Intelligence Research (JAIR)*, 5:139–161. URL=http://www.cs.washington.edu/research/jair/home.html.

Rothwell, C. A. (1995). *Object Recognition through Invariant Indexing.* Oxford University Press.

Srinivasan, A., Muggleton, S. H., King, R. D., and Sternberg, M. J. E. (1997). The predictive toxicology evaluation challenge. In *Proc. of the 15th International Joint Conference on Artificial Intelligence (IJCAI'97)*, pages 4–9, Nagoya, Japan.

Weiss, S. M. and Kulikowski, C. A. (1991). *Computer Systems that Learn: classification and prediction methods from statistics, neural nets, machine learning, and expert systems.* Morgan Kaufmann.

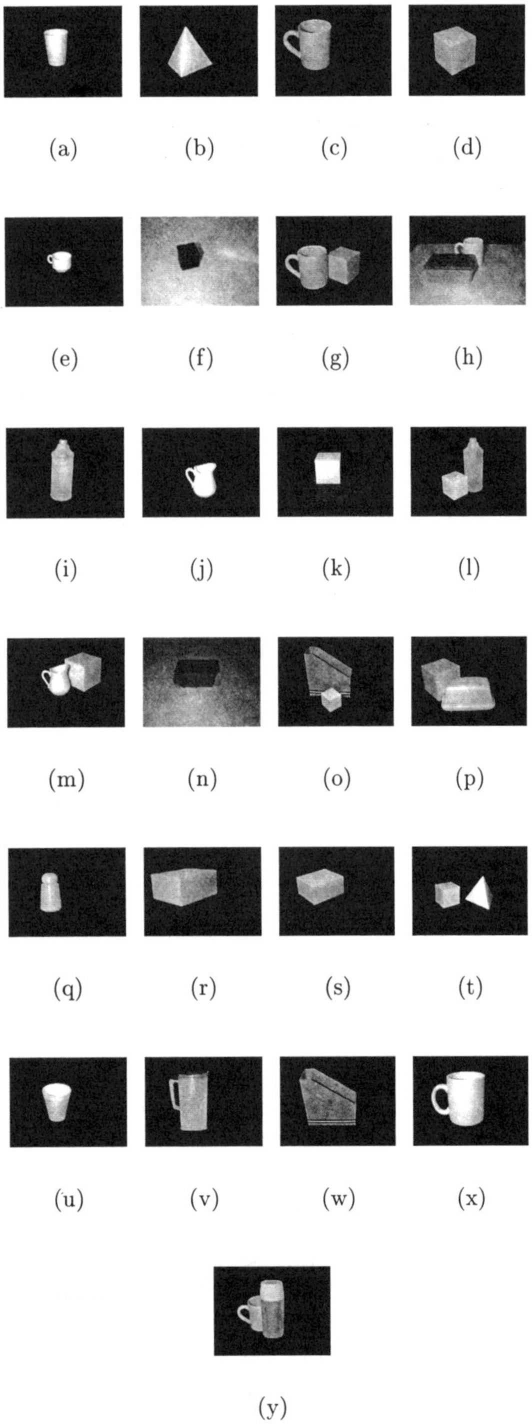

Figure 12: Images used to test the two stage recognition idea (I).

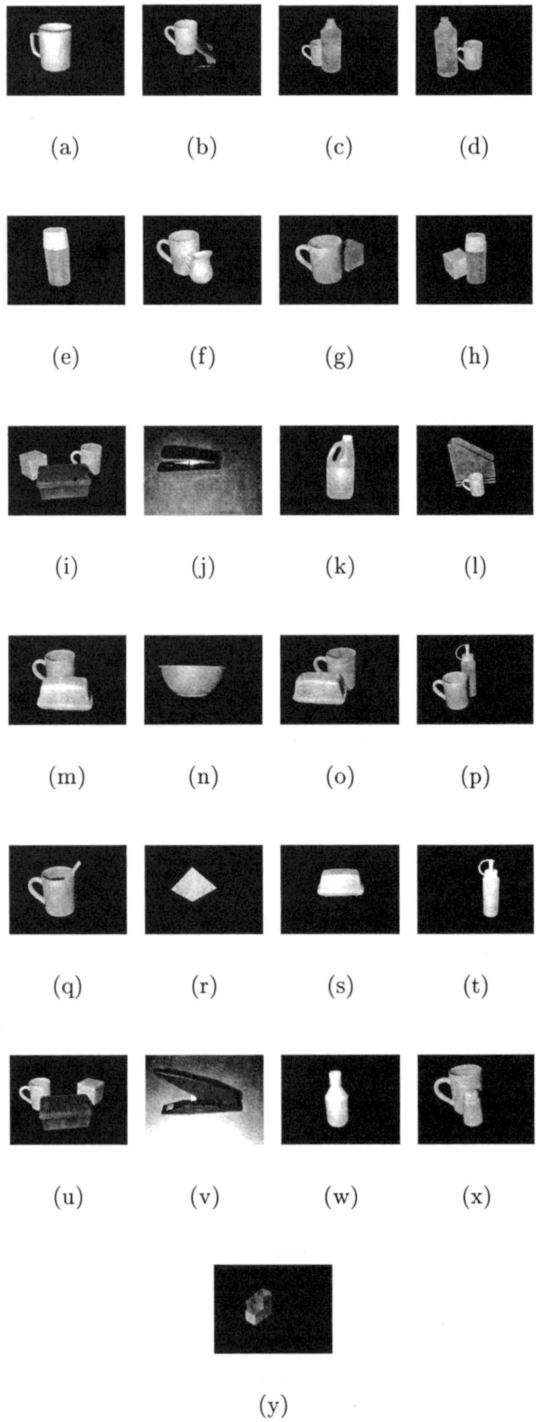

Figure 13: Images used to test two stage recognition idea (II).

Table 1: Recognition results of images of Figs. 12, and 13. Numbers represent QM, and *yes* and *no* are Prolog answers to queries. *mug*(90) and *cube*(90) means that the descriptive rule with evidence level 90% has been used to verify the match.

image	TSFOIL				FOIL	
	mug	mug (90)	cube	cube (90)	mug	cube
12(a)	no	no	no	no	no	no
12(b)	no	no	no	no	no	no
12(c)	100%	100%	no	no	yes	no
12(d)	no	no	100%	100%	no	yes
12(e)	100%	92%	no	no	yes	no
12(f)	no	no	91.7%	66.7%	no	yes
12(g)	100%	100%	100%	80%	yes	yes
12(h)	100%	100%	no	no	yes	no
12(i)	no	no	no	no	no	no
12(j)	no	no	no	no	yes	no
12(k)	no	no	no	no	no	no
12(l)	no	no	100%	100%	no	yes
12(m)	no	no	100%	85%	yes	yes
12(n)	no	no	no	no	no	no
12(o)	no	no	100%	95%	no	yes
12(p)	no	no	91.7%	75%	yes	yes
12(q)	no	no	no	no	no	no
12(r)	no	no	91.7%	85%	no	yes
12(s)	no	no	91.7%	90%	no	yes
12(t)	no	no	100%	90%	no	yes
12(u)	no	no	no	no	yes	no
12(v)	no	no	no	no	no	no
12(w)	no	no	no	no	no	no
12(x)	100%	96%	no	no	yes	no
12(y)	100%	96%	no	no	yes	no
13(a)	94.12%	92%	no	no	yes	no
13(b)	100%	100%	no	no	yes	no
13(c)	100%	100%	no	no	yes	no
13(d)	100%	100%	no	no	yes	no
13(e)	no	no	no	no	no	no
13(f)	100%	96%	no	no	yes	no
13(g)	100%	100%	no	no	yes	no
13(h)	no	no	100%	100%	no	yes
13(i)	100%	100%	91.7%	75%	yes	yes
13(j)	no	no	no	no	no	no
13(k)	no	no	no	no	yes	no
13(l)	100%	100%	no	no	yes	no
13(m)	100%	96%	no	no	yes	no
13(n)	no	no	no	no	no	no
13(o)	100%	100%	91.7%	80%	yes	yes
13(p)	100%	100%	no	no	yes	no
13(q)	100%	100%	no	no	yes	no
13(r)	no	no	no	no	no	no
13(s)	no	no	no	no	no	no
13(t)	100%	96%	no	no	yes	no
13(u)	100%	100%	100%	90%	yes	yes
13(v)	no	no	no	no	no	no
13(w)	no	no	no	no	no	no
13(x)	100%	96%	no	no	yes	no
13(y)	no	no	100%	75%	yes	yes

Simple DFA are Polynomially Probably Exactly Learnable from Simple Examples

Rajesh Parekh
Allstate Research and Planning Center
321 Middlefield Road
Menlo Park, CA 94025.
rpare@allstate.com

Vasant Honavar
Artificial Intelligence Research Laboratory
Department of Computer Science
Iowa State University
Ames, IA 50011-1040.
honavar@cs.iastate.edu

Abstract

Efficient learning of DFA is a challenging research problem in *grammatical inference.* Both exact and approximate (in the PAC sense) identifiability of DFA from examples is known to be hard. Pitt, in his seminal paper posed the following open research problem: "*Are DFA PAC-identifiable if examples are drawn from the uniform distribution, or some other known simple distribution?*" (Pitt, 1989). We demonstrate that the class of *simple* DFA (i.e., DFA whose canonical representations have logarithmic Kolmogorov complexity) is efficiently *probably exactly learnable* under the Solomonoff Levin *universal distribution* **m** (wherein an instance x with Kolmogorov complexity $K(x)$ is sampled with probability that is proportional to $2^{-K(x)}$). The *simple distribution independent learning theorem* states that a concept class is learnable under the universal distribution **m** *iff* it is learnable under the entire class of *simple distributions* provided the examples are drawn according to the universal distribution (Li & Vitányi, 1991). The class of simple distributions includes all *computable distributions.* Thus, it follows that the class of simple DFA is learnable under a sufficiently general class of distributions.

1 INTRODUCTION

DFAs are recognizers for *regular* languages which constitute the simplest class in the Chomsky hierarchy of formal languages (Chomsky, 1956). DFA induction from finite sets of labeled examples finds applications in several domains including *syntactic pattern recognition* (Fu, 1982), *intelligent autonomous agents* (Carmel & Markovitch, 1996), and *language acquisition* (Feldman *et al.*, 1990).

Exact learning of the target DFA is known to be a hard problem in that no efficient (polynomial time) algorithms are known that exactly learn a target DFA from an arbitrary set of labeled examples (Gold, 1978; Pitt & Warmuth, 1988). DFA learning can be made tractable if we assume that some additional information is available to the learner. Trakhtenbrot and Barzdin described a polynomial time algorithm for constructing the smallest DFA consistent with a *complete labeled sample* i.e., a sample that includes all labeled examples up to a particular length (Trakhtenbrot & Barzdin, 1973). Angluin showed that DFA can be exactly learned in polynomial time with the help of a *minimally adequate teacher* (MAT) capable of answering membership and equivalence queries. Oncina and García's *regular positive and negative inference* (RPNI) algorithm is guaranteed to identify a DFA that is consistent with a given sample S in time polynomial in the sum of the lengths of the examples in S (Oncina & García, 1992). Further, if S is a superset of a *characteristic set* (see section 2.1) for the target DFA then the DFA output by RPNI is guaranteed to be equivalent to the target (Oncina & García, 1992; Dupont, 1996b).

Even approximate learnability of DFA (in the *probably approximately correct* (PAC) sense (Valiant, 1984)) was proven to be a hard problem (see (Pitt & Warmuth, 1989; Kearns & Valiant, 1989)). The PAC model's requirement of learnability under all conceivable distributions is often considered too stringent for practical learning scenarios. Pitt's paper identified the following open research problem: "*Are DFA's PAC-identifiable if examples are drawn from the uni-*

form distribution, or some other known simple distribution?" (Pitt, 1989). Using a variant of Trakhtenbrot and Barzdin's algorithm (Trakhtenbrot & Barzdin, 1973), Lang empirically demonstrated that random DFAs are approximately learnable from a sparse uniform sample (Lang, 1992). However, exact identification of the target DFA was not possible even in the average case with a randomly drawn training sample.

Li and Vitányi proposed a model for PAC learning with *simple* examples called the *simple PAC* model wherein the class of underlying probability distributions is restricted to *simple* distributions. In this paper, we present a method for efficient PAC learning of DFA from simple examples and prove that the class of *simple* DFA is learnable under the simple PAC model. We demonstrate that for each DFA in the class of *simple* DFA there exists a polynomial sized characteristic set S_c of *simple examples.* Further, we show that a polynomial sized set of examples S drawn at random according to the *universal distribution* ($\mathbf{m}$) contains the characteristic set S_c with arbitrarily high probability. The RPNI algorithm on input S is thus guaranteed to return a canonical representation of the target DFA (with very high probability).

2 Preliminaries

Let Σ be a finite set of symbols called the *alphabet*; Σ^* be the set of strings over Σ; α, β, γ be strings in Σ^*; and $|\alpha|$ be the length of the string α. λ is a special string called the *null* string and has length 0. Given a string $\alpha = \beta\gamma$, β is the *prefix* of α and γ is the *suffix* of α. Let $Pref(\alpha)$ denote the set of all prefixes of α. A *language* L is a subset of Σ^*. The set $Pref(L) = \{\alpha \mid \alpha\beta \in L\}$ is the set of *prefixes* of the language and the set $L_\alpha = \{\beta \mid \alpha\beta \in L\}$ is the set of *tails* of α in L. The *standard order* of strings of the alphabet Σ is denoted by $<$. The standard enumeration of strings over $\Sigma = \{a, b\}$ is $\lambda, a, b, aa, ab, ba, bb, aaa, \ldots$ The set of *short prefixes* $S_p(L)$ of a language L is defined as $S_p(L) = \{\alpha \in Pref(L) \mid \nexists \beta \in \Sigma^*$ such that $L_\alpha = L_\beta$ and $\beta < \alpha\}$. The *kernel* $N(L)$ of a language L is defined as $N(L) = \{\lambda\} \cup \{\alpha a \mid \alpha \in S_p(L), a \in \Sigma, \alpha a \in Pref(L)\}$. Given two sets S_1 and S_2, let $S_1 \backslash S_2$ and $S_1 \oplus S_2$ denote the *set difference* and the *symmetric difference* respectively. Let ln and lg denote the log to the bases e and 2 respectively.

2.1 FINITE AUTOMATA

A *deterministic* finite state automaton (DFA) is a quintuple $A = (Q, \delta, \Sigma, q_0, F)$ where, Q is a finite set of states, Σ is the finite alphabet, $q_0 \in Q$ is the start state, $F \subseteq Q$ is the set of accepting states, and δ is the transition function: $Q \times \Sigma \longrightarrow Q$. A state $d_0 \in Q$ such that $\forall a \in \Sigma$, $\delta(d_0, a) = d_0$ is called a *dead* state. A state $q \in Q$ that is not dead is called a *live* state. The extension of δ to handle input strings is standard and is denoted by δ^*. The set of all strings accepted by A is its language, $L(A)$. The language $L(A)$ of a DFA is called a *regular language.*

Given any FSA A', there exists a minimum state DFA (also called the *canonical DFA*, A) such that $L(A) = L(A')$. Without loss of generality, we will assume that the target DFA being learned is a canonical DFA. Let N denote the number of states of A. It can be shown that any canonical DFA has at most one dead state (Hopcroft & Ullman, 1979). One can define a standard encoding of DFA as binary strings such that any DFA with N states is encoded as a string of length $O(N \lg N)$. A labeled example $(\alpha, c(\alpha))$ for A is such that $\alpha \in \Sigma^*$ and $c(\alpha) = +$ if $\alpha \in L(A)$ (i.e., α is a positive example) or $c(\alpha) = -$ if $\alpha \notin L(A)$ (i.e., α is a negative example). Let S^+ be a set of *positive* examples and S^- be a set *negative* examples of A. A is consistent with a *sample* $S = S^+ \cup S^-$ if it accepts all positive examples and rejects all negative examples. A set S^+ is said to be *structurally complete* with respect to a DFA A if S^+ covers each transition of A (except the transitions associated with the dead state d_0) and uses every element of the set of final states of A as an accepting state (Pao & Carr, 1978; Parekh & Honavar, 1993; Dupont *et al.*, 1994). It can be verified that a set $S^+ = \{b, aa, aaaa\}$ is structurally complete with respect to the DFA in Fig. 1.

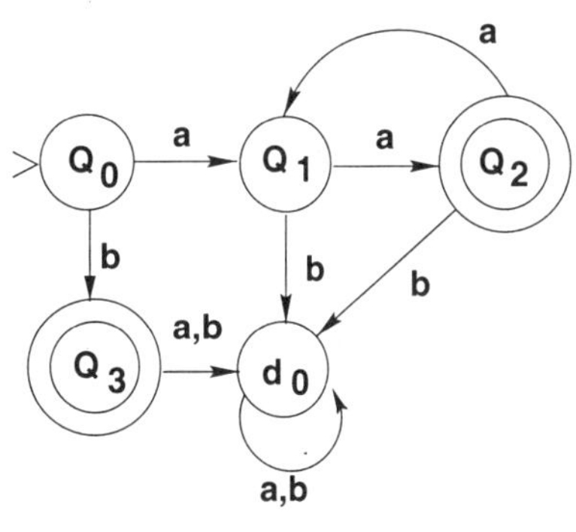

Figure 1: Deterministic Finite State Automaton.

A sample $S = S^+ \cup S^-$ is said to be *characteristic* with respect to a regular language L (with a canonical acceptor A) if it satisfies the following two conditions (Oncina & García, 1992):

- $\forall \alpha \in N(L)$, if $\alpha \in L$ then $\alpha \in S^+$ else $\exists \beta \in \Sigma^*$ such that $\alpha\beta \in S^+$.
- $\forall \alpha \in S_p(L), \forall \beta \in N(L)$, if $L_\alpha \neq L_\beta$ then $\exists \gamma \in \Sigma^*$ such that ($\alpha\gamma \in S^+$ and $\beta\gamma \in S^-$) or ($\beta\gamma \in S^+$ and $\alpha\gamma \in S^-$).

Intuitively, $S_p(L)$, the set of short prefixes of L is a *live complete* set with respect to A in that for each live state $q \in Q$, there is a string $\alpha \in S_p(L)$ such that $\delta^*(q_0, \alpha) = q$. The kernel $N(L)$ includes the set of short prefixes as a subset. Thus, $N(L)$ is also a live complete set with respect to A. Further, $N(L)$ covers every transition between each pair of live states of A. i.e., for all live states $q_i, q_j \in Q$, for all $a \in \Sigma$, if $\delta(q_i, a) = q_j$ then there exists a string $\beta \in N(L)$ such that $\beta = \alpha a$ and $\delta^*(q_0, \alpha) = q_i$. Thus, condition 1 above which identifies a suitably defined suffix $\beta \in \Sigma^*$ for each string $\alpha \in N(L)$ such that the augmented string $\alpha\beta \in L$ implies structural completeness with respect to A. Condition 2 implies that for any two distinct states of A there is a suffix γ that would correctly distinguish them. In other words, for any $q_i, q_j \in Q$ where $q_i \not\equiv q_j$, $\exists \gamma \in \Sigma^*$ such that $\delta^*(q_i, \gamma) \in F$ and $\delta^*(q_j, \gamma) \notin F$ or vice-versa. Given the language L corresponding to the DFA A in Fig. 1, the set of short prefixes is $S_p(L) = \{\lambda, a, b, aa\}$ and the kernel is $N(L) = \{\lambda, a, b, aa, aaa\}$. It can be easily verified that a set $S = S^+ \cup S^-$ where $S^+ = \{b, aa, aaaa\}$ and $S^- = \{\lambda, a, aaa, baa\}$ is a characteristic sample for L.

2.2 PROBABLY APPROXIMATELY CORRECT AND PROBABLY EXACTLY CORRECT LEARNING OF DFA

Let $\mathcal{X}$ denote the *sample space* defined as the set of all strings Σ^*. Let $x \subseteq \mathcal{X}$ denote a *concept*. For our purpose, x is a *regular language*. We identify the concept with the corresponding DFA and denote the class of all DFA as the *concept class* $\mathcal{C}$. The *representation* $\mathcal{R}$ that assigns a name to each DFA in $\mathcal{C}$ is defined as a function $\mathcal{R} : \mathcal{C} \longrightarrow \{0,1\}^*$. $\mathcal{R}$ is the set of standard encodings of the DFA in $\mathcal{C}$. Assume that there is an unknown and arbitrary but fixed distribution $\mathcal{D}$ according to which the examples of the target concept are drawn. In the context of learning DFA, $\mathcal{D}$ is restricted to a probability distribution on strings of Σ^* of length at most m.

Definition 1 *(due to (Pitt, 1989))*
DFAs are PAC-identifiable iff *there exists a (possibly randomized) algorithm $\mathcal{A}$ such that on input of any parameters ϵ and δ, for any DFA M of size N, for any number m, and for any probability distribution $\mathcal{D}$ on strings of Σ^* of length at most m, if $\mathcal{A}$ obtains labeled examples of M generated according to the distribution $\mathcal{D}$, then $\mathcal{A}$ produces a DFA M' such that with probability at least $1 - \delta$, the probability (with respect to distribution $\mathcal{D}$) of the set $\{\alpha \mid \alpha \in L(M) \oplus L(M')\}$ is at most ϵ ($0 < \epsilon < 1$ and $0 < \delta < 1$). For polynomial PAC-learnability, the run time of $\mathcal{A}$ (and hence the number of randomly generated examples obtained by $\mathcal{A}$) is required to be polynomial in N, m, $1/\epsilon$, $1/\delta$, and $|\Sigma|$.*

Definition 2 *DFAs are probably exactly learnable* iff *there exists an algorithm A such that on input of a parameter δ, for any DFA M of size N, for any number m, and for any probability distribution $\mathcal{D}$ on strings of Σ^* of length at most m, if $\mathcal{A}$ obtains labeled examples of M generated according to the distribution $\mathcal{D}$, then $\mathcal{A}$ produces a DFA M' such that with probability at least $1 - \delta$, M' is equivalent to M (i.e., $\Pr_{\mathcal{D}}(\{\alpha \mid \alpha \in L(M) \oplus L(M')\}) = 0$). For polynomial probably exact learnability, the run time of $\mathcal{A}$ is required to be polynomial in N, m, $1/\delta$ and $|\Sigma|$.*

2.3 KOLMOGOROV COMPLEXITY

Note that the definition of PAC learning requires that the concept class (in this case the class of DFA) must be learnable under any arbitrary (but fixed) probability distribution. This requirement is often considered too stringent in practical learning scenarios where it is not unreasonable to assume that a learner is first provided with *simple* and *representative* examples of the target concept. Intuitively, when we teach a child the rules of *multiplication* we are more likely to first give simple examples like 3×4 than examples like 1377×428. A *representative set* of examples is one that would enable the learner to identify the target concept exactly. For example, the characteristic set of a DFA would constitute a suitable representative set. The question now is whether we can formalize what simple examples mean. *Kolmogorov complexity* provides a machine independent notion of *simplicity* of objects. The Kolmogorov complexity of an object (represented by a binary string α) is the length of the shortest binary program that computes α. Objects that have regularity in their structure (i.e., objects that can be easily compressed) have low Kolmogorov complexity. For example, consider the string $s_1 = 010101...01 = (01)^{500}$. On a particular machine M, a program to compute this string would be "*Print*

01 500 times". On the other hand consider a totally random string s_2 that cannot be compressed. A program to compute s_2 on M would would have to explicitly specify the entire string s_2. The length of the program that computes s_1 is thus shorter than that of the program that computes s_2. Thus, we could argue that s_1 has lower Kolmogorov complexity than s_2 with respect to the machine M.

We will consider the *prefix* version of the Kolmogorov complexity that is measured with respect to prefix Turing machines and denoted by K. Consider a prefix Turing machine that implements the partial recursive function $\phi : \{0,1\}^* \stackrel{partial}{\longrightarrow} \{0,1\}^*$. For any string $\alpha \in \{0,1\}^*$, the Kolmogorov complexity of α relative to ϕ is defined as $K_\phi(\alpha) = min\{|\pi| \mid \phi(\pi) = \alpha\}$ where $\pi \in \{0,1\}^*$ is a program input to the Turing machine. Prefix Turing machines can be effectively enumerated and there exists a *Universal Turing Machine* (U) capable of simulating every prefix Turing machine. Assume that the universal Turing machine implements the partial function ψ. The *Optimality Theorem* for Kolmogorov Complexity guarantees that for any prefix Turing machine ϕ there exists a constant c_ϕ such that for any string α, $K_\psi(\alpha) \leq K_\phi(\alpha) + c_\phi$. Note that we use the name of the Turing Machine (say M) and the partial function it implements (say ϕ) interchangeably i.e., $K_\phi(\alpha) = K_M(\alpha)$. Further, by the *Invariance Theorem* it can be shown that for any two universal machines ψ_1 and ψ_2 there is a constant $\eta \in \mathcal{N}$ (where $\mathcal{N}$ is the set of natural numbers) such that for all strings α, $|K_{\psi_1}(\alpha) - K_{\psi_2}(\alpha)| \leq \eta$. Thus, we can fix a single universal Turing machine U and denote $K(\alpha) = K_U(\alpha)$. Note that there exists a Turing machine that computes the identity function $\chi : \{0,1\}^* \longrightarrow \{0,1\}^*$ where $\forall\alpha$, $\chi(\alpha) = \alpha$. Thus, it can be shown that the Kolmogorov complexity of an object is bounded by its length i.e., $K(\alpha) \leq |\alpha| + K(|\alpha|) + \eta$ where η is a constant independent of α.

2.4 UNIVERSAL DISTRIBUTION

The set of programs for a string α relative to a Turing machine M is defined as $PROG_M(\alpha) = \{\pi \mid M(\pi) = \alpha\}$. The algorithmic probability of α relative to M is defined as $\mathbf{m}_M(\alpha) = \Pr(PROG_M)$. The algorithmic probability of α with respect to the universal Turing machine U is denoted as $\mathbf{m}_U(\alpha) = \mathbf{m}(\alpha)$. $\mathbf{m}$ is known as the Solomonoff-Levin distribution. It is the universal enumerable probability distribution, in that, it multiplicatively dominates all enumerable probability distributions. Thus, for any enumerable probability distribution P there is a constant $c \in \mathcal{N}$ such that for all strings α, $c\,\mathbf{m}(\alpha) \geq P(\alpha)$. The *Coding Theorem* due independently to Schnorr, Levin, and Chaitin (Li & Vitányi, 1997) states that $\exists\eta \in \mathcal{N}$ such that $\forall\alpha$ $\mathbf{m}_M(\alpha) \leq 2^{\eta - K(\alpha)}$. Intuitively this means that if there are several programs for a string α on some machine M then there is a short program for α on the universal Turning machine (i.e., α has a low Kolmogorov complexity). By optimality of $\mathbf{m}$ it can be shown that: $\exists\eta \in \mathcal{N}$, such that $\forall\alpha \in \{0,1\}^*$, $2^{-K(\alpha)} \leq \mathbf{m}(\alpha) \leq 2^{\eta - K(\alpha)}$. We see that the universal distribution $\mathbf{m}$ assigns higher probability to simple objects (objects with low Kolmogorov complexity).

The interested reader is referred to (Li & Vitányi, 1997) for a thorough treatment of Kolmogorov complexity, universal distribution, and related topics.

3 The RPNI Algorithm

The *regular positive and negative inference* (RPNI) algorithm (Oncina & García, 1992) identifies a DFA consistent with a given set $S = S^+ \cup S^-$ of labeled examples in time polynomial in the sum of the lengths of the strings in S ($||S||$). Further, if S is a characteristic set for the target DFA then the algorithm is guaranteed to return a canonical representation of the target DFA. Given a labeled set of examples S, the algorithm constructs a *prefix tree automaton* (PTA) that accepts exactly the strings in S^+ and nothing else. The states of the PTA are numbered in the standard order of the shortest strings that lead to them from the start state. For instance, the PTA corresponding to the set $S = S^+ \cup S^-$ where $S^+ = \{b, aa, aaaa\}$ and $S^- = \{\lambda, a, aaa, baa\}$ is depicted in Fig. 2. The PTA is consistent with S and is treated as the initial hypothesis.

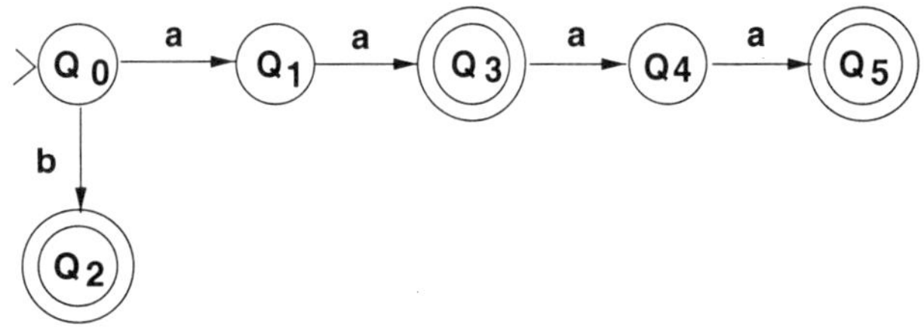

Figure 2: Prefix Tree Automaton.

A quadratic loop is used to find a more general hypothesis by systematically merging the states of the PTA in order (state 1 with state 0, state 2 with state 0, state 2 with state 1, and so on). The derived automaton obtained by merging two states is tested for consistency with the set S^-. If the derived automaton accepts any string from S^- then the merge is rejected and the remaining states are considered for merging in order. Otherwise, the derived automaton that is consistent with S^- is treated as the new hypothesis and the state merging continues with the states of the new hypothesis. For example, Fig. 3 depicts the derived automaton obtained by merging together the states 0 and 2 of the PTA. This derived automaton accepts the string $\lambda \in S^-$ and hence the merge is rejected.

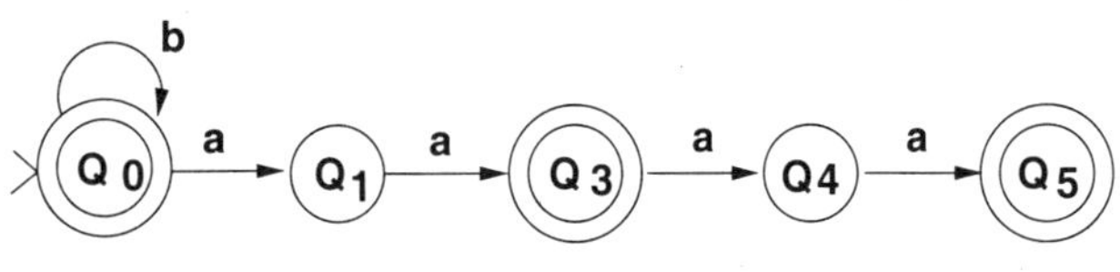

Figure 3: Derived Automaton Obtained by Merging the States 2 and 0 of the PTA.

The algorithm terminates when no further state merges result in a derived automaton that is consistent with S^-. The last consistent hypothesis is then returned as the learned DFA.

The interested reader is referred to (Dupont, 1996a) for a detailed exposition of the RPNI algorithm.

4 LEARNING SIMPLE DFA UNDER THE SIMPLE PAC MODEL

Li and Vitányi have proposed the simple PAC learning model where the class of probability distributions is restricted to *simple* distributions (Li & Vitányi, 1991). A distribution is simple if it is multiplicatively dominated by some enumerable distribution. Simple distributions include all computable distributions. Further, the *simple distribution independent learning theorem* due to Li and Vitanyí states that a concept class is learnable under universal distribution **m** *iff* it is learnable under the entire class of *simple distributions* provided the examples are drawn according to the universal distribution (Li & Vitányi, 1991). Thus, the simple PAC learning model is sufficiently general. Concept classes such as $\log n$*-term DNF* and *simple k-reversible DFA* are learnable under the simple PAC model whereas their PAC learnability in the standard sense is unknown (Li & Vitányi, 1991). We show that the class of *simple* DFA is polynomially learnable under the simple PAC learning model.

A simple DFA is one with low Kolmogorov complexity. More specifically, a DFA A with N states and a standard encoding (or canonical representation) r is simple if $K(r) = O(\lg N)$. For example, a DFA that accepts all strings of length N is a simple DFA. Note that this DFA contains a path for every string of length N and hence it has a path of Kolmogorov complexity N. In general, simple DFA might actually have very random paths. We saw in section 2.3 that a natural learning scenario would typically involve learning from a *simple* and *representative* set of examples for the target concept. We adopt Kolmogorov complexity as a measure of simplicity and define simple examples as those with low Kolmogorov complexity i.e., with Kolmogorov complexity $O(\lg N)$. Further, a characteristic set for the DFA A can be treated as its representative set. We demonstrate that for every simple DFA there exists a characteristic set of simple examples S_c.

Lemma 1 *For any N state simple DFA (with Kolmogorov complexity $O(\lg N)$) there exists a characteristic set of simple examples S_c such that the length of each string in this set is at most $2N - 1$.*

Proof: Consider the following enumeration of a characteristic set of examples for a DFA $A = (Q, \delta, \Sigma, q_0, F)$ with N states[1].

1. Fix an enumeration of the shortest paths (in standard order) from the state q_0 to each state in Q except the dead state. This is the set of short prefixes of A. There are at most N such paths and each path is of length at most $N - 1$.

2. Fix an enumeration of paths that includes each path identified above and its extension by each letter of the alphabet Σ. From the paths just enumerated retain only those that do not terminate in the dead state of A. This represents the kernel of A. There are at most $N(|\Sigma| + 1)$ such paths and each path is of length at most N.

3. Let the characteristic set be denoted by $S_c = S_c^+ \cup S_c^-$.

   (a) For each string α identified in step 2 above, determine the first suffix β in the standard enumeration of strings such that $\alpha\beta \in L(A)$. Since $|\alpha| \leq N$, and β is the shortest suffix in the standard order it is clear that $|\alpha\beta| \leq 2N - 1$. Each such $\alpha\beta$ is a member of S_c^+.

[1]Note that this enumeration strategy applies to any DFA and is not restricted to simple DFA alone.

(b) For each pair of strings (α, β) in order where α is a string identified in step 1, β is a string identified in step 2, and α and β lead to different states of A determine the first suffix γ in the standard enumeration of strings such that $\alpha\gamma \in L(A)$ and $\beta\gamma \notin L(A)$ or vice versa. Since $|\alpha| \leq N-1$, $|\beta| \leq N$, and γ is the shortest distinguishing suffix for the states represented by α and β it is clear that $|\alpha\gamma|, |\beta\gamma| \leq 2N-1$. The accepted string from among $\alpha\gamma$ and $\beta\gamma$ is a member of S_c^+ and the rejected string is a member of S_c^-.

Trivial upper bounds on the sizes of S_c^+ and S_c^- are $|S_c^+| \leq N^2(|\Sigma|+1)+N(|\Sigma|)$, $|S_c^-| \leq N^2(|\Sigma|+1)-N$. Thus, $|S_c| = \lceil(2N^2|\Sigma|+2N^2+N|\Sigma|-N)\rceil$ i.e., $|S_c| \leq kN^2$ where k is a constant . Further, the length of each string in S_c is less than $2N-1$.

The strings in S_c can be ordered in some way such that individual strings can be identified by an index of length at most $\lg(kN^2) = O(\lg N)$ bits. There exists a Turing machine M that implements the above algorithm for constructing the set S_c. M can take as input an encoding of a simple DFA of length $O(\lg N)$ bits and an index of length $O(\lg N)$ bits and output the corresponding string α belonging to S_c. Thus, $\forall \alpha \in S_c$,

$$\begin{aligned} K(\alpha) &\leq k_1 \lg N + k_2 \lg N \\ &= O(\lg N) \end{aligned}$$

This proves the lemma. □

Lemma 2 *Suppose a sample S is drawn according to* $\mathbf{m}$. *For $0 < \delta \leq 1$, if $|S| = O(N^k \lg(\frac{1}{\delta}))$ then with probability greater than $1-\delta$, $S_c \subseteq S$ where k is a constant.*

Proof: From lemma 1 we know that $\forall \alpha \in S_c$, $K(\alpha) = O(\lg N)$. Further, $|S_c| = O(N^2)$. By definition, $\mathbf{m}(\alpha) \geq 2^{-K(\alpha)}$. Thus, $\mathbf{m}(\alpha) \geq 2^{-k_1 \lg N}$ or equivalently $\mathbf{m}(\alpha) \geq N^{-k_1}$ where k_1 is a constant.
$\Pr(\alpha \in S_c$ is not sampled in one random draw$) \leq (1-N^{-k_1})$
$\Pr(\alpha \in S_c$ is not sampled in $|S|$ random draws $\leq (1-N^{-k_1})^{|S|}$
$\Pr($ some $\alpha \in S_c$ is not sampled in $|S|$ random draws $\leq |S_c|(1-N^{-k_1})^{|S|}$
$\Pr($ some $\alpha \in S_c$ is not sampled in $|S|$ random draws $\leq k_2 N^2 (1-N^{-k_1})^{|S|}$ since $|S_c| = O(N^2)$
$\Pr(S_c \not\subseteq S) \leq k_2 N^2 (1-N^{-k_1})^{|S|}$

We want this probability to be less than δ.

$$\begin{aligned} k_2 N^2 (1-N^{-k_1})^{|S|} &\leq \delta \\ k_2 N^2 (e^{-N^{-k_1}})^{|S|} &\leq \delta \\ (\text{ since } 1-x \leq e^{-x}) & \\ \ln(k_2) + \ln(N^2) - N^{-k_1}|S| &\leq \ln(\delta) \\ N^{k_1}(\ln(\frac{1}{\delta}) + \ln(k_2) + \ln(N^2)) &\leq |S| \\ O(N^k \lg(\frac{1}{\delta})) &= |S| \\ \text{where } k \text{ replaces } k_1 & \end{aligned}$$

Thus, $\Pr(S_c \subseteq S) \geq 1-\delta$. □

We now prove that the class of simple DFA is polynomially exactly learnable under $\mathbf{m}$.

Theorem 1 *For all N, the class $\mathcal{C}^{\leq N}$ of simple DFA whose canonical representations have at most N states is probably exactly learnable under the simple PAC model.*

Proof: Let A be a simple DFA with at most N states. Let S_c be a characteristic sample of A enumerated as described in lemma 1 above. Recall that the examples in S_c are simple (i.e., each example has Kolmogorov complexity $O(\lg N)$). Now consider the algorithm $\mathcal{A}$ in Fig. 4 that draws a sample S with the following properties:

1. $S = S^+ \cup S^-$ is a set of positive and negative examples corresponding to the target DFA A.
2. The examples in S are drawn at random according to the distribution $\mathbf{m}$.
3. $|S| = O(N^k \lg(\frac{1}{\delta}))$.

Algorithm $\mathcal{A}$

Input: $N, 0 < \delta \leq 1$
Output: A DFA M

begin
- Randomly draw a labeled sample S according to $\mathbf{m}$.
- Retain only those examples in S that have length at most $2N-1$.
- $M = RPNI(S)$
- **return** M

end

Figure 4: A Probably Exact Algorithm for Learning Simple DFA.

Lemma 1 showed that for every simple DFA A there exists a characteristic set of simple examples S_c where each example is of length at most $2N-1$. Lemma 2 showed that if a labeled sample S of size $O(N^k \lg(\frac{1}{\delta}))$ is randomly drawn according to $\mathbf{m}$ then with probability greater than $1-\delta$, $S_c \subseteq S$. The RPNI algorithm is guaranteed to return a canonical representation of the target DFA A if the set of examples S provided is a superset of a characteristic set S_c. Since the size of S is polynomial in N and $1/\delta$ and the length of each string in S is restricted to $2N-1$, the RPNI algorithm, and thus the algorithm $\mathcal{A}$ can be implemented to run in time polynomial in N and $1/\delta$. Thus, with probability greater than $1-\delta$, $\mathcal{A}$ is guaranteed to return a canonical representation of the target DFA A. This proves that the class $\mathcal{C}^{\leq N}$ of simple DFA whose canonical representations have at most N states is exactly learnable with probability greater than $1-\delta$. □

5 DISCUSSION

The problem of exactly learning the target DFA from an arbitrary set of labeled examples and the problem of approximating the target DFA from labeled examples under Valiant's PAC learning framework are both known to be hard problems. Thus, the question as to whether DFA are efficiently learnable under some restricted yet fairly general and practically useful classes of distributions was clearly of interest. In this paper, we have answered this question in the affirmative for the class of *simple* DFA by demonstrating that the class of simple DFA is polynomially learnable under the universal distribution $\mathbf{m}$ (the simple PAC learning model).

The class of simple distributions includes a large variety of probability distributions (including all computable distributions). It has been shown that a concept class is efficiently learnable under the universal distribution if and only if it is efficiently learnable under each simple distribution provided that sampling is done according to the universal distribution (Li & Vitányi, 1991). This raises the possibility of using sampling under the universal distribution to learn under all computable distributions. However, the universal distribution is not computable. Whether one can instead get by with a polynomially computable approximation of the universal distribution remains an open question. It is known that the universal distribution for the class of polynomially-time bounded simple distributions is computable in exponential time (Li & Vitányi, 1991). This opens up a number of interesting possibilities for learning under simple distributions.

Denis *et al* proposed a model of learning (known as the PACS model) where examples are drawn at random according to the universal distribution by a teacher that is knowledgeable about the target concept (Denis *et al.*, 1996). In this model examples that have low Kolmogorov complexity given a canonical representation (r) of the target concept (i.e., $K(x|r) = O(\lg N)$) are treated as *simple* examples. Further, the probability of drawing an example x is given by $\mathbf{m}_r(x) = 2^{-K(x|r)+O(1)}$. In related work we have shown that the entire class of DFA is efficiently learnable in the PACS model (Parekh & Honavar, 1997). Recently, Castro and Guijarro have independently shown that if a concept class is learnable under the PACS learning model then the set of *simple* concepts of that concept class are learnable under the simple PAC model (Castro & Guijarro, 1998). An analysis of the relationship between the PACS and simple PAC learning models and other popular models for learning in *helpful environments* such as learning from example based queries (Angluin, 1988), learning from polynomial teaching sets (Goldman & Mathias, 1993; Gold, 1978), and mistake bounded learning (Littlestone, 1988) appears in (Parekh & Honavar, 1999).

A related question of interest has to do with the nature of environments that can be modeled by simple distributions. In particular, if Kolmogorov complexity is an appropriate measure of the intrinsic complexity of objects in nature and if nature (or the teacher) has a propensity for simplicity, then it stands to reason that the examples presented to the learner by the environment are likely to be generated by a simple distribution. Against this background, empirical evaluation of the performance of the proposed algorithms using examples that come from natural domains is clearly of interest. Also of interest are investigation of other interesting and practically useful concept classes that might be learnable from simple examples.

References

Angluin, D. (1988). Queries and Concept Learning. *Machine Learning*, **2**(4), 319–342.

Carmel, D., & Markovitch, S. (1996). Learning Models of Intelligent Agents. *Pages 62–67 of: Proceedings of the AAAI-96 (vol. 1)*. AAAI Press/MIT Press.

Castro, J., & Guijarro, D. (1998). *Query, PACS and simple-PAC Learning*. Tech. rept. LSI-98-2-R. Universitat Polytéctica de Catalunya, Spain.

Chomsky, N. (1956). Three Models for the Description of Language. *PGIT*, **2**(3), 113–124.

Denis, F., D'Halluin, C., & Gilleron, R. (1996). PAC Learning with Simple Examples. *STACS'96 - Proceedings of the* 13th *Annual Symposium on the Theoretical Aspects of Computer Science*, 231–242.

Dupont, P. (1996a). Incremental Regular Inference. *Pages 222–237 of:* Miclet, L., & Higuera, C. (eds), *Proceedings of the Third ICGI-96, Lecture Notes in Artificial Intelligence 1147*. Montpellier, France: Springer.

Dupont, P. (1996b). *Utilisation et Apprentissage de Modèles de Language pour la Reconnaissance de la Parole Continue.* Ph.D. thesis, Ecole Normale Supérieure des Télécommunications, Paris, France.

Dupont, P., Miclet, L., & Vidal, E. (1994). What is the Search Space of the Regular Inference? *Pages 25–37 of: Proceedings of the Second International Colloquium on Grammatical Inference (ICGI'94).*

Feldman, J. A., Lakoff, G., Stolcke, A., & Weber, S. H. (1990). *Miniature Language Acquisition: A Touchtone for Cognitive Science.* Tech. rept. TR-90-009. International Computer Science Institute, Berkeley, CA.

Fu, K. (1982). *Syntactic Pattern Recognition and Applications.* Prentice Hall, N.J.

Gold, E. (1978). Complexity of Automaton Identification from Given Data. *Information and Control*, **37**(3), 302–320.

Goldman, S., & Mathias, H. (1993). Teaching a Smarter Learner. *Pages 67–76 of: Proceedings of the Workshop on Computational Learning Theory (COLT'93).* A. C. M. Press.

Hopcroft, J., & Ullman, J. (1979). *Introduction to Automata Theory, Languages, and Computation.* Addison Wesley.

Kearns, M., & Valiant, L. G. (1989). Cryptographic Limitations on Learning Boolean Formulae and Finite Automata. *Pages 433–444 of: Proceedings of the* 21st *Annual ACM Symposium on Theory of Computing.* ACM, New York.

Lang, K. (1992). Random DFA's can be approximately learned from sparse uniform sample. *Pages 45–52 of: Proceedings of the 5th ACM workshop on Computational Learning Theory.*

Li, M., & Vitányi, P. (1991). Learning Simple Concepts under Simple Distributions. *SIAM Journal of Computing*, **20**(5), 911–935.

Li, M., & Vitányi, P. (1997). *An Introduction to Kolmogorov Complexity and its Applications,* 2nd *edition.* New York: Springer Verlag.

Littlestone, N. (1988). Learning Quickly When Irrelevant Attributes Abound: A New Linear-Threshold Algorithm. *Machine Learning*, **2**, 285–318.

Oncina, J., & García, P. (1992). Inferring Regular Languages in Polynomial Update Time. *Pages 49–61 of:* Pérez, N. *et al* (ed), *Pattern Recognition and Image Analysis.* World Scientific.

Pao, T., & Carr, J. (1978). A Solution of the Syntactic Induction-Inference Problem for Regular Languages. *Computer Languages*, **3**, 53–64.

Parekh, R., & Honavar, V. (1993). Efficient Learning of Regular Languages using Teacher Supplied Positive Examples and Learner Generated Queries. *Pages 195–203 of: Proceedings of the Fifth UNB Conference on AI.*

Parekh, R., & Honavar, V. (1997). Learning DFA from Simple Examples. *Pages 116–131 of: Proceedings of the Eighth International Workshop on Algorithmic Learning Theory (ALT'97), Lecture Notes in Artificial Intelligence 1316.* Sendai, Japan: Springer. Also presented at the *Workshop on Grammar Inference, Automata Induction, and Language Acquisition* (ICML'97), Nashville, TN. July 12, 1997.

Parekh, R., & Honavar, V. (1999). *On the Relationship Between Models for Learning in Helpful Environments.* (Submitted for review).

Pitt, L. (1989). Inductive Inference, DFAs and Computational Complexity. *Pages 18–44 of: Analogical and Inductive Inference, Lecture Notes in Artificial Intelligence 397.* Springer-Verlag.

Pitt, L., & Warmuth, M. K. (1988). Reductions among prediction problems: on the difficulty of predicting automata. *Pages 60–69 of: Proceedings of the* 3rd *I.E.E.E. Conference on Structure in Complexity Theory.*

Pitt, L., & Warmuth, M. K. (1989). The minimum consistency DFA problem cannot be approximated within any polynomial. *Pages 421–432 of:*

Proceedings of the 21st ACM Symposium on the Theory of Computing. ACM.

Trakhtenbrot, B., & Barzdin, Ya. (1973). *Finite Automata: Behavior and Synthesis.* Amsterdam: North Holland Publishing Company.

Valiant, L. (1984). A Theory of the Learnable. *Communications of the ACM*, **27**, 1134–1142.

Learning Policies with External Memory

Leonid Peshkin
Computer Science Dept.
Brown University, Box 1910
Providence, RI, 02912-1910
ldp@cs.brown.edu

Nicolas Meuleau
Computer Science Dept.
Brown University
nm@cs.brown.edu

Leslie Pack Kaelbling
Computer Science Dept.
Brown University
lpk@cs.brown.edu

Abstract

In order for an agent to perform well in partially observable domains, it is usually necessary for actions to depend on the history of observations. In this paper, we explore a *stigmergic* approach, in which the agent's actions include the ability to set and clear bits in an external memory, and the external memory is included as part of the input to the agent. In this case, we need to learn a reactive policy in a highly non-Markovian domain. We explore two algorithms: SARSA(λ), which has had empirical success in partially observable domains, and VAPS, a new algorithm due to Baird and Moore, with convergence guarantees in partially observable domains. We compare the performance of these two algorithms on benchmark problems.

1 Introduction

A reinforcement-learning agent must learn a mapping from a stream of observations of the world to a stream of actions. In completely observable domains, it is sufficient to look only at the last observation, so the agent can learn a "memoryless" mapping from observations to actions [16]. In general, however, the agent's actions may have to depend on the history of previous observations.

Previous Work There have been many approaches to learning to behave in partially observable domains. They fall roughly into three classes: optimal memoryless, finite memory, and model-based.

The first strategy is to search for the best possible memoryless policy. In many partially observable domains, memoryless policies can actually perform fairly well. Basic reinforcement-learning techniques, such as Q-learning [25], often perform poorly in partially observable domains, due to a very strong Markov assumption. Littman showed [10] that finding the optimal memoryless policy is NP-Hard. However, Loch and Singh [11] effectively demonstrated that techniques, such as SARSA(λ), that are more oriented toward optimizing total reward, rather than Bellman residual, often perform very well. In addition, Jaakkola, Jordan, and Singh [7] have developed an algorithm for finding stochastic memoryless policies, which can perform significantly better than deterministic ones [20].

One class of finite memory methods are the finite-horizon memory methods, which can choose actions based on a finite window of previous observations. For many problems this can be quite effective [12, 18]. More generally, we may use a finite-size memory, which can possibly be infinite-horizon (the systems remembers only a finite number of events, but these events can be arbitrarily far in the past). Wiering and Schmidhuber [26] proposed such an approach, learning a policy that is a finite sequence of memoryless policies.

Another class of approaches assumes complete knowledge of the underlying process, modeled as a *partially observable Markov decision process* (POMDP). Given a model, it is possible to attempt optimal solution [8], or to search for approximations in a variety of ways [5, 4, 6, 13]. These methods can, in principle, be coupled with techniques, such as variations of the Baum-Welch algorithm [17], for learning the model to yield model-based reinforcement-learning systems.

Stigmergy In this paper, we pursue an approach based on *stigmergy*. The term is defined in the Ox-

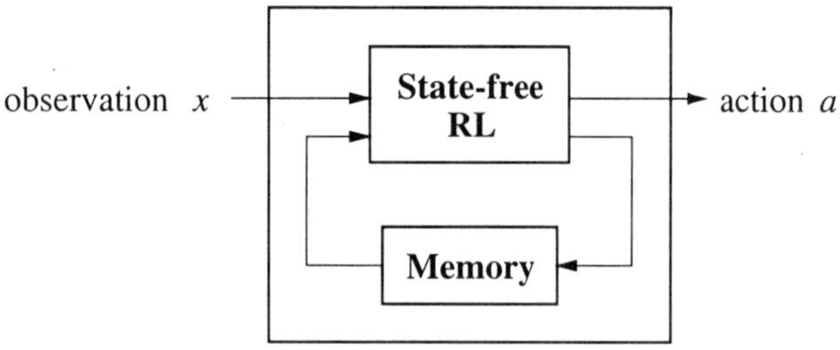

Figure 1: The architecture of a stigmergic policy.

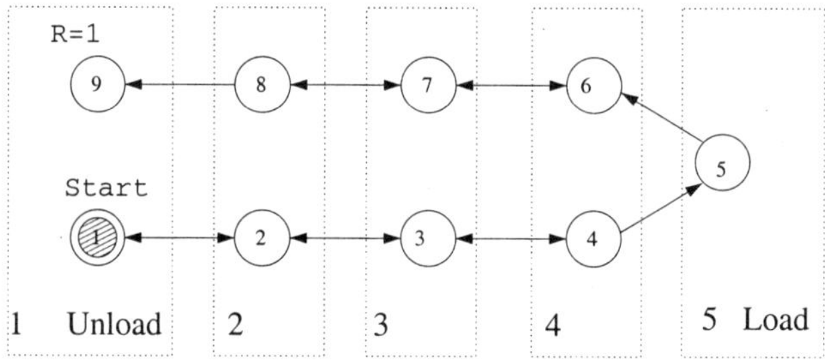

Figure 2: The state-transition diagram of the load-unload problem; aliased states are grouped by dashed boxes.

ford English Dictionary [19] as "The process by which the results of an insect's activity act as a stimulus to further activity," and is used in the mobile robotics literature [2] to describe activity in which an agent's changes to the world affect its future behavior, usually in a useful way.

One form of stigmergy is the use of external memory devices. We are all familiar with practices such as making grocery lists, tying a string around a finger, or putting a book by the door at home so you will remember to take it to work. In each case, an agent needs to remember something about the past and does so by modifying its external perceptions in such a way that a memoryless policy will perform well.

We can apply this approach to the general problem of learning to behave in partially observable environments. Figure 1 shows the architectural idea. We think of the agent as having two components: one is a set of memory bits; the other is a reinforcement-learning agent. The reinforcement-learning agent has as input the observation that comes from the environment, augmented by the memory bits. Its output consists of the original actions in the environment, augmented by actions that change the state of the memory. If there are sufficient memory bits, then the optimal memoryless policy for the internal agent will cause the entire agent to behave optimally in its partially observable domain.

Consider, for instance, the load-unload problem represented in Figure 2. In this problem, the agent is a cart that must drive from an *Unload* location to a *load* location, and then back to *unload.* This problem is a simple MDP with a one-bit hidden variable that makes it non-Markov (the agent cannot see whether it is loaded or not). It can be solved using a one-bit external memory: we set the bit when we make the *Unload* observation, and we go right as long as it is set to this value and we do not make the *Load* observation. When we do make the *Load* observation, we clear the bit and we go left as long as it stays at value 0, until we reach state 9, getting a reward.

There are two alternatives for designing an architecture with external memory:

- Either we *augment* the action space with actions that change the content of one of the memory bits (adds L new actions if there are L memory bits); changing the state of the memory may require multiple steps.
- Or we *compose* the action space with the set of all possible values for the memory (the size of the action space is then multiplied by 2^L, if there are L bits of memory). In this case, changing the external memory is an instantaneous action that can be done at each time step in parallel with a primitive action, and hence we can reproduce the optimal policy of the load-unload problem, without taking additional steps.

Complexity considerations usually lead us to take the first option. It introduces a bias, since we have to lose at least one time-step each time we want to change the content of the memory. However, it can be fixed in most algorithms by not discounting memory-setting actions.

The external-memory architecture has been pursued in the context of classifier systems [3] and in the context of reinforcement learning by Littman [10] and by Martín [15]. Littman's work was model-based; it assumed that the model was completely known and did a branch-and-bound search in policy space. Martín worked in the model-free reinforcement-learning domain; his algorithms were very successful at finding good policies for very complex domains, including some simulated visual search and block-stacking tasks. However, he made a number of strong assumptions and restrictions: task domains are strictly goal-oriented; it is assumed that there is a deterministic policy that achieves the goal within some specified number of steps from every initial state; and there is no desire for optimality in path length.

This work We were inspired by the success of Martín's algorithm on a set of difficult problems, but concerned about its restrictions and a number of details of the algorithm that seemed relatively *ad hoc*. At the same time, Baird and Moore's work on VAPS [1], a general method for gradient descent in reinforcement learning, appealed to us on theoretical grounds. This paper is the result of attempting to apply VAPS algorithms to stigmergic policies, and understanding how it relates to Martín's algorithm. In this process, we have derived a much simpler version of VAPS for the case of highly non-Markovian domains: we calculate the same gradient as VAPS, but with much less computational effort.

In the next section, we present the relevant learning algorithms. Then we describe a set of experimental domains and discuss the relative performance of the algorithms.

2 Algorithms

We begin by describing the most familiar of the algorithms, SARSA(λ). We then describe the VAPS algorithm in some detail, followed by our simplified version.

2.1 SARSA(λ)

SARSA is an on-policy temporal-difference control learning algorithm [23]. Given an experience in the world, characterized by starting state x, action a, reward r, resulting state x' and next action a', the update rule for SARSA(0) is

$$Q(x,a) \leftarrow Q(x,a) + \alpha[r + \gamma Q(x',a') - Q(x,a)]\,. \quad (1)$$

It differs from the classical Q-learning algorithm [24] in that, rather than using the maximum Q-value from the resulting state as an estimate of that state's value, it uses the Q-value of the resulting state and the action that was actually chosen in that state. Thus, the values learned are sensitive to the policy being executed.

In truly Markov domains, Q-learning is usually the algorithm of choice; policy-sensitivity is often seen as a liability, because it makes issues of exploration more complicated. However, in non-Markov domains, policy-sensitivity is actually an asset. Because observations do not uniquely correspond to underlying states, the value of a policy depends on the distribution of underlying states given a particular observation. But this distribution generally depends on the policy. So, the value of a state, given a policy, can only be evaluated *while executing that policy.* In fact, Q-learning can be shown to fail to converge on very simple non-Markov domains [22]. Note that, when SARSA is used in a non-Markovian environment, the symbols x and x' in equation (1) represent observations, which usually can correspond to several states.

The SARSA algorithm can be augmented with an eligibility trace, to yield the SARSA(λ) algorithm (a detailed exposition is given by Sutton and Barto [23].) With the parameter λ set to 0, SARSA(λ) is just SARSA. With λ set to 1, it is a pure Monte Carlo method, in which, at the end of every trial, each state-action pair is adjusted toward the cumulative reward received on this trial after the state-action pair occurred. Pure Monte-Carlo algorithms make no attempt at satisfying Bellman equations relating the values of subsequent states; in partially observable domains, it is often impossible to satisfy the Bellman equation, making Monte-Carlo a reasonable choice. SARSA(λ) describes a useful class of algorithms, then, with appropriate choice of λ depending on the problem. Thus, SARSA(λ) with a large value of λ seems like the most appropriate of the conventional reinforcement-learning algorithms for solving partially-observable problems.

2.2 VAPS

Baird and Moore have derived, from first principles, a class of stochastic gradient-descent algorithms for reinforcement learning. At the most abstract level, we seek to minimize some measure of the expected cost of our policy; we can describe this high-level criterion as

$$B = \sum_{T=0}^{\infty} \sum_{\tilde{s} \in \tilde{S}_T} \Pr(\tilde{s})\varepsilon(\tilde{s}) \enspace ,$$

where $\tilde{S}_T$ is the set of all possible experience sequences that terminate at time T. That is,

$$\tilde{s} = \langle x_0, u_0, r_0, ..., x_t, u_t, r_t, ..., x_T, u_T, r_T \rangle \enspace ,$$

where x_t, u_t, and r_t are the observation, action, and reward at step t of the sequence, and x_T is an observation associated with a terminal state. The loss incurred by a sequence $\tilde{s}$ is $\varepsilon(\tilde{s})$. We restrict our attention to time-separable loss functions, which can be written as

$$\varepsilon(\tilde{s}) = \sum_{t=0}^{T} e(\text{trunc}(\tilde{s}, t)) , \qquad \text{for all } \tilde{s} \in \tilde{S}_T ,$$

where $e(s)$ is an instantaneous error function associated with each (finite) sequence prefix $s = \langle x_0, u_0, r_0, ..., x_t, u_t, r_t \rangle$ (x_t being any observation, not necessarily a terminal one), and $\text{trunc}(\tilde{s}, t)$ representing the sequence $\tilde{s}$ truncated after time t. For instance, an error measure closely related to Q-learning is the squared Bellman residual:

$$e_{\text{QL}}(s) = \frac{1}{2} \sum_{x} \Pr(x_t = x \mid x_{t-1}, u_{t-1}) \\ [r_{t-1} + \max_{u} \gamma Q(x, u) - Q(x_{t-1}, u_{t-1})]^2 .$$

The SARSA version of the algorithm uses the following error measure:

$$e_{\text{SARSA}}(s) = \\ \frac{1}{2} \sum_{x} \Pr(x_t = x \mid x_{t-1}, u_{t-1}) \sum_{u} \Pr(u_t = u \mid x_t) \\ [r_{t-1} + \gamma Q(x, u) - Q(x_{t-1}, u_{t-1})]^2 .$$

Note that we average over all possible actions u_t according to their probability of being chosen by the policy instead of picking the one that maximizes Q-values as in e_{QL}. Baird and Moore also consider a kind of policy search, which is analogous to REINFORCE [27]:

$$e_{\text{policy}}(s) = b - \gamma^t r_t ,$$

where b is any constant. This immediate error is summed over all time t, leading to a summation of all discounted immediate rewards $\gamma^t r_t$. In order to obtain the good properties of both criteria, they construct a final criterion that is a linear combination of the previous two:

$$e = (1 - \beta) e_{\text{SARSA}} + \beta e_{\text{policy}} .$$

This criterion combines Value And Policy Search and is, hence, called VAPS. We will refer to it as VAPS(β), for different values of β.

Baird and Moore show that the gradient of the global error with respect to weight k can be written as:

$$\frac{\partial}{\partial w_k} B = \sum_{t=0}^{\infty} \sum_{s \in S_t} \Pr(s) \\ \left[\frac{\partial}{\partial w_k} e(s) + e(s) \sum_{j=1}^{t} \frac{\partial}{\partial w_k} \ln \Pr(u_{j-1} | x_{j-1}) \right] ,$$

where S_t is the set of all experience prefixes of length t. Technically, it is necessary that $\Pr(u^t = u \mid x_t = x) > 0$ for all (x, u) (otherwise, some zero probability trajectories may have a non-zero contribution to the gradient of B [9]). In this work we use the Boltzmann law for picking actions, which guarantees this property (see section 2.3).

It is possible to perform stochastic gradient descent of the "error" B, by repeating several trials of interaction with the process. Each experimental trial of length T provides one sample of $s \in S_t$ for each $t \leq T$. Of course, these samples are not independent, but it does not matter since we are summing them and not multiplying them. We are thus using stochastic approximation to estimate the expectation over $s \in S_t$ in the above equation. During each trial, the weights are kept constant and the approximate gradients of the error at each time t,

$$\frac{\partial}{\partial w_k} e(s) + e(s) \sum_{j=1}^{t} \frac{\partial}{\partial w_k} \ln \Pr(u_{j-1} | x_{j-1}) ,$$

are accumulated. Weights are updated at the end of each trial, using the sum of these immediate gradients. An incremental implementation of the algorithm can be obtained by using, at every step t, the following update rules:

$$\Delta T_{k,t} = \frac{\partial}{\partial w_k} \ln \Pr(u_{t-1} | x_{t-1}) ,$$

$$\Delta w_k = -\alpha \left[\frac{\partial}{\partial w_k} e(\tilde{s}_t) + e(\tilde{s}_t) T_{k,t} \right] ,$$

where s_t represents the experience prefix $\langle x_0, u_0, r_0, \ldots, x_t, u_t, r_t \rangle$, i.e., the history at time t. Note that the "exploration trace" $T_{k,t}$ is independent of the immediate error e used. It only depends on the way the output $\Pr(u_t = u | x_t)$ varies with the weights w_k, i.e., on the representation chosen for the policy.

The gradient of the immediate error e with respect to the weight w_k is easy to calculate. For instance, in the case of the SARSA variant of the algorithm we have:

$$\frac{\partial}{\partial w_k} e_{\text{SARSA}}(s) = \\ \sum_{x} \Pr(x_t = x \mid x_{t-1}, u_{t-1}) \sum_{u} \Pr(u_t = u \mid x_t) \cdot \\ [r_{t-1} + \gamma Q(x, u) - Q(x_{t-1}, u_{t-1})] \\ \left[\gamma \frac{\partial}{\partial w_k} Q(x, u) - \frac{\partial}{\partial w_k} Q(x_{t-1}, u_{t-1}) \right] .$$

Once more, we descend this gradient by stochastic approximation: the averaging over x_t and u_t is replaced

$w_k = Q(x, u)$
$T_{k,t}$: trace initial values 0

by a sampling of these quantities. However, since these variables appear twice in the equation and they are not just added, we have to sample both x_t and u_t independently two times in order to avoid any bias in the estimation of the gradient. It is not realistic to satisfy this requirement in a truly on-line situation, since the only way to get a new observation is by actually *performing* the action. Note that for the case $\beta = 1$ we do not need the second sample, so the VAPS(1) algorithm is effective in the on-line case.

In the case of policy search we have: $\frac{\partial}{\partial w_k} e_{\text{policy}}(s) = 0$, for all w_k. This may seem strange; but for policy search, the important thing is the state occupations, which enter into the weight updates through the trace.

2.3 VAPS(1)

In this section, we explore a special case of VAPS, in which the Q-values are stored in a look-up table. That is, there is one weight $w_k = Q(x, u)$ for each state-action pair. Note that it is not necessary to use the VAPS sequence-based gradient in a look-up table implementation of QL or SARSA, as long as it is confined to a Markovian environment. However, it makes sense to use it in the context of POMDPs. Under this hypothesis, the exploration trace $T_{k,t}$ associated with each parameter $Q(x, u)$ will be written $T_{x,u,t}$.

We will also focus on a very popular rule for randomly selecting actions as a function of their Q-value, namely the Boltzmann law:

$$Pr(u_t = u | x_t = x) = \frac{e^{Q(x,u)/c}}{\sum_{u'} e^{Q(x,u')/c}} ,$$

where c is a temperature parameter.[1] Under this rule we get:

$$\frac{\partial \ln \Pr(u_t = u | x_t = x)}{\partial Q(x', u')} = \begin{cases} 0 & \text{if } x' \neq x, \\ -\Pr(u_t = u' | x_t = x)/c & \text{if } x' = x \text{ and } u' \neq u, \\ [1 - \Pr(u_t = u | x_t = x)]/c & \text{if } x' = x \text{ and } u' = u. \end{cases}$$

In this case, and if we add the hypothesis that the problem is an achievement task, i.e., the reward is always 0 except when we reach an absorbing goal state, the exploration trace $T_{x,u,t}$ takes a very simple form:

$$\begin{aligned} T_{x,u,t} &= \tfrac{1}{c}\left[N^t_{x,u} - N^t_x \Pr(u_t = u | x_t = x)\right] \\ &= \tfrac{1}{c}\left[N^t_{x,u} - E[N^t_{x,u}]\right] , \end{aligned} \qquad (2)$$

where $N^t_{x,u}$ is the number of times that action u has been executed in state x at time t, N^t_x is the number of times that state x has been visited at time t, and $E[N^t_{x,u}]$ represents the expected number of times we should have performed action u in state x, knowing our exploration policy and our previous history.

As a result of equation (2), VAPS using e_{policy} as immediate error, look-up tables and Boltzmann exploration reduces to a very simple algorithm. At each time-step where the current trial does not complete, we just increment the counter $N^t_{x,u}$ of the current state-action pair. When the trial completes, this trace is used to update all the Q-values, as described above.

It is interesting to try to understand the properties and implications of this simple rule. First, a direct consequence is that when something surprising happens, the algorithm adjusts the unlikely actions more than the likely ones. In other words, this simple procedure is very intuitive, since it assigns credit to state-action pairs proportional to the deviation from the expected behaviour. Note that SARSA(λ) is not capable of such a discrimination. This difference in behaviour is illustrated in the simulation results.

A second interesting property is that the Q-value updates tend to 0 as the length of the trial tends to infinity. This also makes sense, since the longer the trial, the less the final information received (the final reward) is relevant in evaluating each particular action. Alternatively, we could say that when too many actions have been performed, there is no reason to attribute the final result more to one of them than to others. Finally, unlike with Baird and Moore's version of the Boltzmann law, the sum of the updates to the Q-values on every step is 0. This makes it more likely that the weights will stay bounded.

3 Experiments

Domains We have experimented with SARSA and VAPS on five simple problems. Two are illustrative problems previously used in the reinforcement-learning literature; two others are instances of load-unload with different parameters; and the fifth is a variant of load-unload designed by us in an attempt to demonstrate a situation in which VAPS might outperform SARSA. The five problems are :

[1] Note that Baird and Moore use an unusual version of the Boltzmann law, with $1+e^x$ in place of e^x in both the numerator and the denominator. We have found that it complicates the mathematics and worsens the performance, so we will use the standard Boltzmann law throughout.

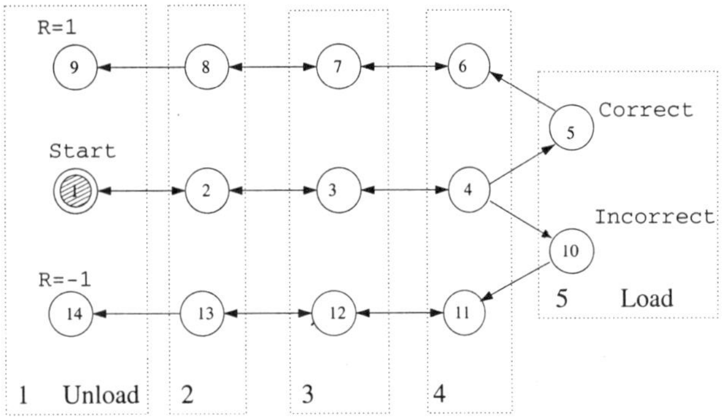

Figure 3: The state-transition diagram of the load-unload problem with two loading locations; aliased states are grouped by dashed boxes.

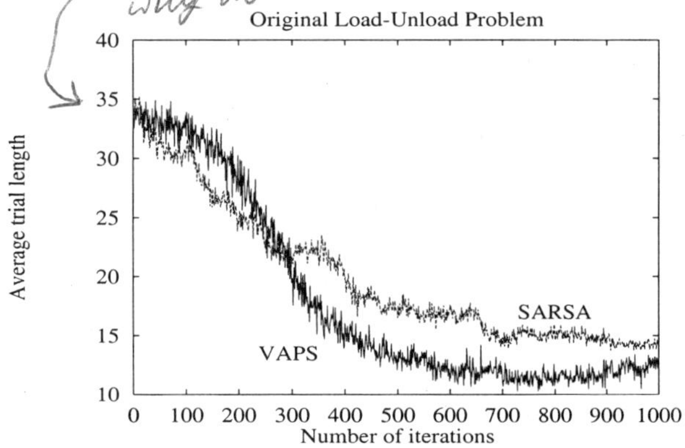

Figure 4: Learning curves for VAPS and SARSA on the load-unload problem (one loading location).

- Baird and Moore's problem [1], designed to illustrate the behavior of VAPS,
- McCallum's 11-state maze [12], which has only 6 observations.
- The load-unload problem, as described above, in which there are three locations (the loading location, the unloading location, and one intermediate one),
- A five-location load-unload problem (fig. 2), and
- A variant of the load-unload problem where a second loading location has been added, and the agent is punished instead of rewarded if it gets loaded at the wrong location. The state space is shown in figure 3; states contained in a box are observationally indistinguishable to the agent. The idea here is that there is a single action that, if chosen, ruins the agent's long-term prospects. If this action is chosen due to exploration, then SARSA(λ) will punish all of the action choices along the chain but VAPS will punish only that action.

All these domains have a single starting state, except McCallum's problem, where the starting state is chosen uniformly at random.

Algorithmic Details For each problem, we ran two algorithms: VAPS(1) and SARSA(1). The optimal policy for Baird's problem is memoryless, so the algorithms were applied directly in that case. For the other problems, we augmented the input space with an additional memory bit, and added two actions: one for setting the bit and one for clearing it.

The Q-functions were represented in a table, with one weight for each observation-action pair. The learning rate is determined by a parameter, α_0; the actual learning rate has an added factor that decays to 0 over time: $\alpha = \alpha_0 + \frac{1}{10N}$, where N is trial number. The temperature was also decayed in an *ad hoc* way, from $c_{\max}$ down to $c_{\min}$ with an increment of

$$\delta c = \left(\frac{c_{min}}{c_{max}}\right)^{1/(N-1)}$$

on each trial. In order to guarantee convergence of SARSA in MDPs, it is necessary to decay the temperature in a way that is dependent on the Q-values themselves [21]; in the POMDP setting it is much less clear what the correct decay strategy is. In any case, we have found that the empirical performance of the algorithm is not particularly sensitive to the temperature. The parameter b in the immidiate error e_{policy} of VAPS was always set to 0.

Experimental Protocol Each learning algorithm was executed for K runs; each run consisted of N trials, which began at the start state and executed until a terminal state was reached or M steps were taken. If the run was terminated at M steps, it was given a terminal reward of -1; M was chosen, in each case, to be 4 times the length of the optimal solution. At the beginning of each run, the weights were randomly reinitialized to small values.

Results It was easy to make both algorithms work well on the first three problems: Baird's, McCallum's and small load-unload. The algorithms typically converged in fewer than 100 runs to an optimal policy. One thing to note here is that our version of VAPS, using the true Boltzmann exploration distribution rather

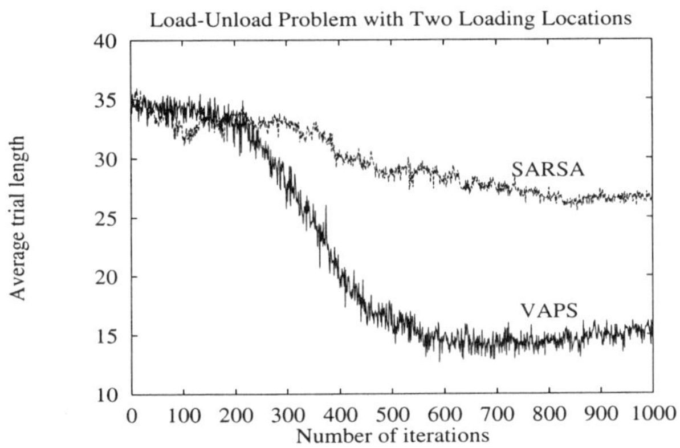

Figure 5: Learning curves for VAPS and SARSA on the load-unload problem with two loading locations.

than the one described by Baird and Moore, seems to perform significantly better than the original, according to results in their paper.

Things were somewhat more complex with the last two problems (5 location load-unload with one or two loading locations). We experimented with parameters over a broad range and determined the following:

- VAPS requires a value of β equal or very nearly equal to 1; these problems are highly non-Markovian, so the Bellman error is not at all useful as a criterion.
- For similar reasons, $\lambda = 1$ is best for SARSA(λ).
- Exploration was simplified by setting ϵ to 0; empirically, $c_{max} = 1.0$ and $c_{min} = 0.2$ worked well for VAPS in both problems, and $c_{max} = 0.2$, $c_{min} = 0.1$ worked well for SARSA(λ).
- A base learning rate of $\alpha_0 = 0.5$ worked well for both algorithms in both domains.

Figures 4 and 5 show learning curves for both algorithms, averaged over 50 runs, on the load-unload problem with one or two loading locations. Each run consisted of 1,000 trials. The vertical axis shows the number of steps required to reach the goal, with the terminated trials considered to have taken M steps.

On the original load-unload problem, the algorithms perform essentially equivalently. Most runs of the algorithm converge to the optimal trial length of 9 and stay there; occasionally, however it reaches 9 and then diverges. This can probably be avoided by decreasing the learning rate more steeply. When we add the second loading location, however, there is a significant difference. VAPS(1) consistently converges to a near-optimal policy, but SARSA(1) does not. The idea is that sometimes, even when the policy is pretty good, the agent is going to pick up the wrong load due to exploration and get punished for it. SARSA will punish all the state-action pairs equally; VAPS(1) will punish the bad state-action pair more due to the different principle of credit assignment.

4 Conclusion

As Martín and Littman showed, small POMDPs can be solved effectively using stigmergic policies. Learning reactive policies in highly non-Markovian domains is not yet well-understood. We have seen that the VAPS algorithm, somewhat modified, can solve a collection of small POMDPs, and that although SARSA(λ) performs well on some POMDPs, it is possible to construct cases on which it fails. In a generalization of this work, we applied the VAPS algorithm to the problem of learning general finite-state controllers (which encompass external-memory policies) for POMDPs [14].

Acknowledgments

This work was supported in part by DARPA/Rome Labs Planning Initiative grant F30602-95-1-0020.

References

[1] Leemon C. Baird and Andrew W. Moore. Gradient descent for general reinforcement learning. In *Advances in Neural Information Processing Systems 11*. The MIT Press, 1999.

[2] R. Beckers, Owen E. Holland, and J. L. Deneubourg. From local actions to global tasks: Stigmergy and collective robotics. In *Artificial Life IV*, Cambridge, Massachusetts, 1994. The MIT Press.

[3] L.B. Booker, D.E. Goldberg, and J.H. Holland. Classifier systems and genetic algorithms. *Artificial Intelligence*, 40, 1989.

[4] E.A. Hansen. *Finite-Memory Control of Partially Observable Systems*. PhD thesis, Department of Computer Science, University of Massachusetts at Amherst, 1998.

[5] E.A. Hansen. Solving POMDPs by searching in policy space. In *Proceedings of the Eighth Con-*

ference on Uncertainty in Artificial Intelligence, pages 211–219, Madison, WI, 1998.

[6] Milos Hauskrecht. *Planning and Control in Stochastic Domains with Imperfect Information.* PhD thesis, Massachusetts Institute of Technology, Cambridge, Massachusetts, 1998.

[7] T. Jaakkola, S. Singh, and M.R. Jordan. Reinforcement learning algorithm for partially observable Markov problems. In *Advances in Neural Information Processing Systems, 7.* The MIT Press, Cambridge, MA, 1994.

[8] Leslie Pack Kaelbling, Michael L. Littman, and Anthony R. Cassandra. Planning and acting in partially observable stochastic domains. *Artificial Intelligence*, 101, 1998.

[9] L.P. Kaelbling, K.E. Kim, N. Meuleau, and L. Peshkin. Searching for finite-state POMDP controllers. Technical Report CS-99-06, Brown University, 1999.

[10] Michael L. Littman. Memoryless policies: Theoretical limitations and practical results. In *From Animals to Animats 3*, Brighton, UK, 1994.

[11] John Loch and Satinder Singh. Using eligibility traces to find the best memoryless policy in partially observable Markov decision processes. In *Proceedings of the Fifteenth International Conference on Machine Learning*, Madison, Wisconsin, 1998.

[12] Andrew Kachites McCallum. *Reinforcement Learning with Selective Perception and Hidden State.* PhD thesis, University of Rochester, Rochester, New York, 1995.

[13] N. Meuleau, K.E. Kim, A.R. Cassandra, and L.P. Kaelbling. Solving POMDPs by searching the space of finite policies. *Fifteenth Conference on Uncertainty in Artificial Intelligence*, Submitted, 1999.

[14] N. Meuleau, L. Peshkin, K.E. Kim, and L.P. Kaelbling. Learning finite-state controllers for partially observable environments. *Fifteenth Conference on Uncertainty in Artificial Intelligence*, Submitted, 1999.

[15] Mario Martín. *Reinforcement Learning for Embedded Agents facing Complex Tasks.* PhD thesis, Universitat Politecnica de Catalunya, Barcelona, Spain, 1998.

[16] Martin L. Puterman. *Markov Decision Processes.* John Wiley & Sons, New York, 1994.

[17] L. R. Rabiner. A tutorial on hidden Markov models and selected applications in speech recognition. *Proceedings of the IEEE*, 77(2):257–286, 1989.

[18] Mark B. Ring. *Continual Learning in Reinforcement Environments.* PhD thesis, University of Texas at Austin, Austin, Texas, August 1994.

[19] John Simpson and Edmund Weiner, editors. *Oxford English Dictionary.* Oxford University Press, second edition, 1989.

[20] S. Singh, T. Jaakkola, and M.R. Jordan. Learning without state-estimation in partially observable Markovian decision processes. In *Machine Learning: Proceedings of the Eleventh International Conference.* 1994.

[21] Satinder Singh, Tommi Jaakkola, Michael L. Littman, and Csaba Szepesvari. Convergence results for single-step on-policy reinforcement-learning algorithms. *Machine Learning*, to appear.

[22] Satinder Pal Singh, Tommi Jaakkola, and Michael I. Jordan. Model-free reinforcement learning for non-Markovian decision problems. In *Machine Learning: Proceedings of the Eleventh International Conference*, pages 284–292, San Francisco, California, 1994. Morgan Kaufmann.

[23] Richard S. Sutton and Andrew G. Barto. *Reinforcement Learning: An Introduction.* The MIT Press, Cambridge, Massachusetts, 1998.

[24] C. J. C. H. Watkins. *Learning from Delayed Rewards.* PhD thesis, King's College, Cambridge, 1989.

[25] C. J. C. H. Watkins and P. Dayan. Q-learning. *Machine Learning*, 8(3):279–292, 1992.

[26] Marco Wiering and Juergen Schmidhuber. HQ-learning. *Adaptive Behavior*, 6(2), 1997.

[27] Ronald J. Williams. A class of gradient-estimating algorithms for reinforcement learning in neural networks. In *Proceedings of the IEEE First International Conference on Neural Networks*, San Diego, California, 1987.

Noise-Tolerant Recursive Best-First Induction

Uroš Pompe

School of Computer Science & Engineering
The University of New South Wales
Sydney 2052, Australia
puros@cse.unsw.edu.au

and

Faculty of Computer and Information Science
University of Ljubljana
Tržaška c. 25, 1000 Ljubljana, Slovenia
puros@fri.uni-lj.si

Abstract

Rarely can an inductive logic programming (ILP) system expect that the training information provided is perfect. This paper addresses the case where training examples contain errors in either class or arguments. The problem is analysed from the perspective of a general-to-specific rule learner. The impact of noise on the coverage of clauses and their refinements is determined. We show that for a cost function with certain properties, the cost of a refinement is unlikely to be less than the cost of a refined clause, when the latter is consistent over the noiseless data. We exploit this property to introduce noise-tolerant recursive best-first search in our ILP system CLIP. The algorithm combines ideas of both pre- and post-pruning. Experimental results on the KRK domain show that CLIP's performance is comparable or superior to some of the state-of-the-art first-rule learning systems. With a sufficient number of training examples learning is not affected when up to 30% of examples are randomly classified. The learning time increases almost linearly with the number of training examples.

1 INTRODUCTION

When applying machine learning (ML) algorithms in practice, we can rarely expect that the training information provided is perfect. In particular, training examples can often contain noise, i.e. random errors. This was soon realised throughout different branches of ML, including inductive logic programming (ILP) and the propositional rule learning community. Early algorithms like the AQ family (Michalski, Mozetič, Hong & Lavrač, 1986), CN2 (Clark & Niblett, 1989), and FOIL (Quinlan, 1990) included mechanisms to cope with this problem based on ideas of post-pruning and pre-pruning (using a statistical test or MDL based measure), respectively. The problem with the former approach is complexity, since we need to build over-complex descriptions to realize that a simple one would suffice. The weakness of the latter is that we are making decisions without actually seeing what is lying ahead. The approach is sometimes based on a tradeoff between the predictive capability of the rule and its complexity. We can only approximate the latter, so such stopping criteria are either too weak, too strong, or problem dependent at best.

Recently, there has been an increase of interest in rule learning algorithms, based on the ideas from *Reduced Error Pruning* (REP) (Brunk & Pazzani, 1991). Systems like Grow (Cohen, 1993), RIPPER (Cohen, 1995), TDP, and I-REP (Fürnkranz, 1997) all improve on the original idea by stopping overfitting earlier, or interleaving the overfitting and pruning phase. They avoid to some extent the efficiency pitfalls of post-pruning while not relying on any explicit form of rule complexity measure.

In this paper, we will present an algorithm that integrates the learning and pruning phase even more tightly, within a search procedure building a single rule. The algorithm is implemented in our ILP system CLIP. In the next section, we will present a short overview of its features. In Section 3, we will show the impact that either classification, or argument noise have on the coverage of clauses and introduce a family of cost functions with certain property. Section 4 contains the description of the search algorithm. Evaluation and discussion are presented in Section 5 and Section 6 contains the conclusions.

2 AN OVERVIEW OF CLIP

In this paper, we will sometimes rely on concepts and results from logic programming theory; see (Lloyd, 1987) for details. The details of the CLIP system, presented in this section, can be found in (Pompe, 1999a; Pompe, 1999b). We will denote empty clauses (value false) with $\square$ and empty theories (value true) with $\blacksquare$.

Let B be a normal logic program called *background knowledge*. Given a set of positive and negative training examples $E = E^+ \cup E^-$, the learning task in CLIP is to find a hypothesis H, such that, together with B, H can prove every positive example ($\forall e \in E^+ : B \wedge H \vdash_r e$) and none of the negative ones ($\forall e \in E^- : B \wedge H \not\vdash_r e$), where $\vdash_r$ is a time bounded resolution operator. The set E^+ is obtained by computing the least Herbrand model of a *range restricted* logic program. E^- is given as a set of ground queries.

2.1 SEARCH ALGORITHM

The form of H is controlled by *mode declarations*, in a similar manner to Progol (Muggleton, 1995). CLIP performs a general to specific search over the set of clauses L_d that can appear in L_H, where d denotes the maximum length of an acceptable clause. The search starts with $\square$ which is then gradually extended using the refinement operator $\rho_d : L_d \to 2^{L_d}$. The latter on each step collects all the extensions of a clause with a single literal such that the resulting clauses still conform to mode declarations.

A tree shaped search space, induced by the refinement operator, is explored using *recursive best-first induction* (RBFI)(Pompe, 1999b; Pompe, 1999a), a search algorithm based on Korf's RBFS (Korf, 1993). It performs a complete, space efficient, best-first minimization of a clause cost function $f(C)$, where the latter depends on the *size* of C and its coverage over the training set E. The coverage $Cov(C, E)$ represents a subset of E where each example can be proved using C and B. RBFI recursively descends the refinement tree in the best-first manner, collecting on the way all the consistent clauses. Search stops when candidate hypothesis H_c becomes complete, or the whole refinement tree has been explored. During the search, RBFI disregards all clauses whose coverage is a subset of the coverage of H_c.

At the end, H_c might contain redundant clauses. CLIP tries to greedily minimize the number of clauses that are necessary to maintain the coverage of H_c. We will denote this "*least redundant*" hypothesis with H_{lr}.

2.2 COST FUNCTIONS

Among several possibilities, there are two cost functions that are of interest to this paper. Let p and n represent the number of positive and negative examples in $Cov(C, E)$, respectively. Let s be the number of literals in the body of C. Then, *average information cost* (per unit of size) is given by

$$f_{ai}(C) = -\frac{p}{s} \cdot \left(\log_2 \frac{p}{p+n} - \log_2 \frac{|E^+|}{|E|} \right) \quad . \tag{1}$$

The other cost function of interest is based on Progol's clause evaluation function and is given by

$$f_p(C) = -(p - n - s) \quad . \tag{2}$$

Note that if we look at both costs as a function of p, n, and s, then they satisfy the following three conditions:

$$\frac{\partial f}{\partial p} < 0, \quad \frac{\partial f}{\partial n} > 0, \quad \frac{\partial f}{\partial s} > 0 \quad . \tag{3}$$

3 NOISE AND REFINEMENTS

In the rest of this paper, we will concentrate on the problem where E contains random errors. The errors in E can appear either in the class of an example or in the values of its arguments. We will use E' to denote the original training set E corrupted with noise of either kind.

3.1 CLASSIFICATION NOISE

Let $c : E \to \{\square, \blacksquare\}$ denote the *classification function* that determines the sign of an example. Let c' denote its noisy variant, where with probability β, the result is reversed. Note that this does not alter the coverage of any clause C ($Cov(C, E) = Cov(C, E')$), only the distribution of signs changes. Now suppose C is a consistent clause over E and let c' change its distribution of signs to covering p' positive and n' negative examples over E' (Figure 1). What is then the probability $Pr(i, j)$ that some refinement C_1 of C will have noisy distribution of signs equal to $\langle i, j \rangle$, where i is the number of positive and j is the number of negative examples covered? Let $p = p' + n'$ be the number of examples, covered by C and let $N_{ij} = \binom{p'}{i}\binom{n'}{j}$ and $N_r = \binom{p}{i+j}$ be the number of subsets with sign distribution $\langle i, j \rangle$, and the number of all subsets of the size $r = i + j$, respectively. Then the probability of sign distribution $\langle i, j \rangle$ is $Pr(i, j) = N_{ij}/N_r$. Of course, there may be many refinements of C, that cover $r = i + j$ examples. Suppose that they cover k different subsets of

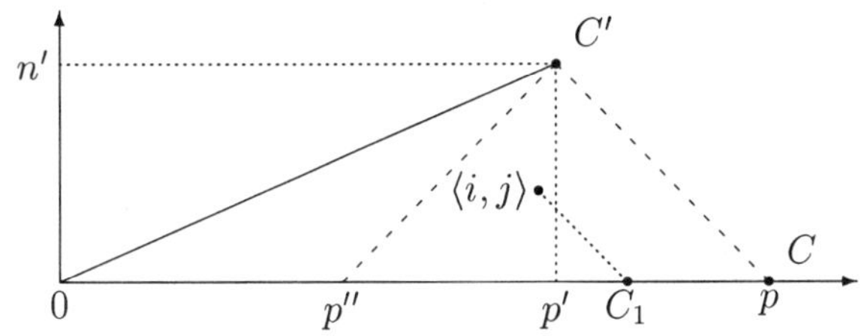

Figure 1: Introduction of Class Noise.

$Cov(C, E)$. Then, the probability $Pr_k(i,j)$ that any of the subcoverages will, after the introduction of noise, have sign distribution $\langle i,j\rangle$ is

$$Pr_k(i,j) = 1 - \frac{\binom{N_r - N_{ij}}{k}}{\binom{N_r}{k}} \quad . \tag{4}$$

The term $\binom{N_r - N_{ij}}{k}$ represents the number of ways k subsets can be selected out of the set of subsets of p examples, where the latter have the sign distribution different than $\langle i,j\rangle$. The term $\binom{N_r}{k}$ counts the number of selections of k different subsets of size r, out of p examples.

Now suppose that the cost function $f(C)$ is of the form $g(h(p,n), s)$, where function $h(p,n)$ satisfies the first two of the conditions in (3). We say that f is an *unbiased linear separator* if $h(p-l, n-l) \geq h(p,n)$ for all $l \geq 0$. If we assume that cost $f(C)$ increases with size s and that all the refinements of consistent clause C have size strictly greater than C, then we can see that after the introduction of noise, the cost of the refinements can be strictly lower only when they fall into triangle $\Delta p'C'p''$ (Figure 1), excluding edge $p''C'$, where p'' equals to $p' - n'$. Fortunately, the probability of this happening rapidly decreases with increasing number of covered examples p, except for the point $\langle p', n'-1\rangle$, where it equals $\frac{k}{p}\beta$. However, if f is able to compensate for this point (which (2) does), then we can say that the probability of a refinement having lower cost than the refined clause, which is consistent over noise-free training set, is very low. Note, that (2) is an unbiased linear separator while (1) is not. Also note that the probability of a refinement, falling into the critical region, increases slowly with the number of refinements with different coverage (k).

To understand better the difference between behaviour of a cost function, which is an unbiased linear separator and a function that is not, Figure 2 shows contour plots for several cost functions evaluated over an example coverage plane. Solid lines connect point with the same cost value. All figures are plotted over the same range (with initial distribution of examples 158 positive, 292 negative). On sub-figure (a), we can see that f_p clearly separates points on lower right corner, which, according to equation (4), have very low probability of being reached by chance when classification noise is present in data set and the current refined clause is actually a consistent clause in the noiseless case. Sub-figure (b) suggests, that the same holds for f_{ai}, even more, it indicates that f_{ai} leaves even less space to chance, but this is only the case because the initial distribution of examples was chose in a way so that negative class was the default ($\frac{1}{3}$ positive, $\frac{2}{3}$ negative). Sub-figure (c) shows the case with reverse example distribution. Now we can see that the cost function can quite likely make a mistake in preferring a refinement of clause, which is consistent over the noiseless data, simply because such such refinement is a very accurate clause, which unfortunately can be statistically less significant with coverage outside the low probability triangle from Figure 1.

3.2 NOISE IN ARGUMENTS

What happens if arguments of training examples are with probability α selected uniformly from the set of possible values? In this case, the coverage of clauses might be different ($Cov(C,E) \neq Cov(C,E')$). Let X represent the instance space and let D_X be a distribution over it. The problem of learning with noise in arguments can then be seen as a problem of learning with a changed distribution D'_X and noisy classification function c'. Note however, that with increasing number of arguments, almost every training example gets a chance of being corrupted. The changes in coverage also depend on B so it is hard to predict what the difference between c and c' truly is; for instance, it need not be evenly distributed over the instance space.

4 THE LEARNING ALGORITHM

Based on the results from the previous section we introduced changes in the search and final hypothesis selection algorithms in CLIP. The adapted version of RBFI is shown in Algorithm 4.1. Compared to the noiseless version, an additional argument is introduced ($M_{\max}$), which represents the maximum cost of an acceptable clause. Otherwise, it can be viewed as a function, although the reader should note that it modifies the global variable H_c (the current hypothesis), which is initialized to an empty set. The function returns ■ if at least one acceptable clause has been found during

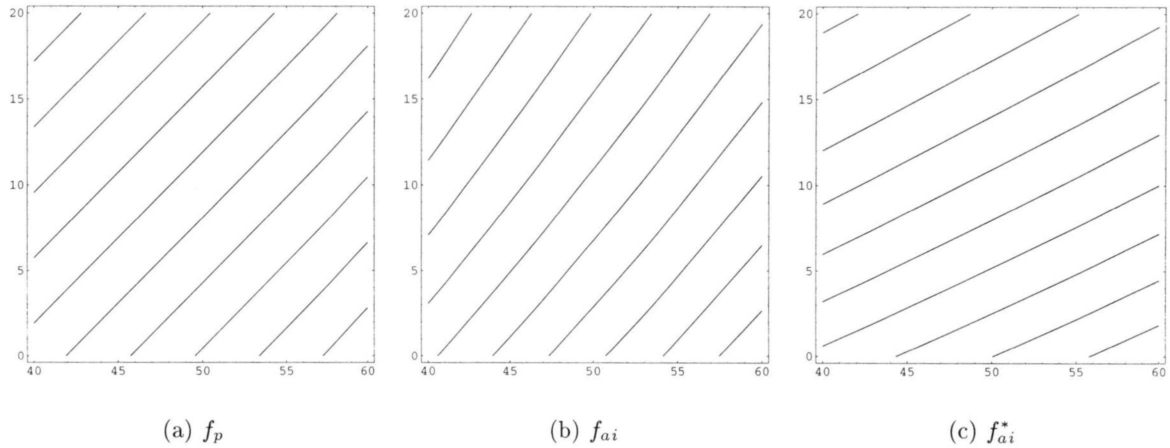

Figure 2: Contour Plot for Different Cost Functions.

its invocation, and $\square$ otherwise.

On each call, the algorithm checks whether the current clause is at least weakly consistent, i.e. when its accuracy is greater than or equal to $1 - \beta$ (line 12). The accuracy of a clause is measured on the training set alone as no hold-out set is used as in the case of REP family of algorithms. The fact about the weak consistency is remembered for future reference in local variable *wc*. If C is not weakly consistent, then the bound on the cost of an acceptable refinement remains the same, otherwise it is lowered to the cost of C if possible (line 14). This is achieved with function *NewBound*, which returns the lower of the second and third argument, if the first one is $\blacksquare$, and $M_{\max}$ otherwise. The pre-pruning effect is achieved by changing the refinement operator ρ_d (line 11) so that it additionally eliminates from further investigation all the refinements that have no *potential* of having lower cost than $M_{\max}$. These are basically clauses which, even if they become consistent with further refinements while still covering all the positive examples from the current coverage, their cost would no drop below $M_{\max}$. If the current clause is weakly consistent then RBFI ensures that all its refinements will be explored before returning (line 24) by raising the cost of the next best clause. And finally, if C is only weakly consistent then it is added to the candidate hypothesis (H_c) only if no better refinements were found (lines 17 and 30).

As in the noiseless case, function $f(\cdot)$ computes the static cost value of a clause. Either of the functions (2) or (1) can be used for this. Stored cost value of a clause is denoted with F. It represents either the static cost value or the lowest cost value of its refinements, that exceed the current search bound M. This enables RBFI to perform the search in a similar way to RBFS (see (Pompe, 1999a; Korf, 1993) for details). The resulting search algorithm retains the properties of the search in the noise free case (polynomial space consumption, completeness, ...).

4.1 AN ADAPTATION OF THE FINAL HYPOTHESIS SELECTION

To accommodate the possibility of inconsistent H_c, the final selection algorithm was changed so that clauses were greedily added to H_{lr} (starting with an empty hypothesis $\blacksquare$) as long as their accuracy on the set of examples not covered by H_{lr} was high enough $(1 - \beta)$. On each step, the remaining clause are sorted in decreasing order of their accuracy on the uncovered set and the most accurate clause is added to H_{lr}. In addition, we introduced an alternative hypothesis selection algorithm where clauses were added greedily using a different criterion. We denote this hypothesis with H_{mc} and refer to it as the "*most compressive*." Initially, it is an empty set $\blacksquare$. On each step, clauses are now sorted in decreasing order according to how well they compress the uncovered training set. Compression is measured as the difference between the number of positive examples covered and the sum of the number of negative covered examples and the number of literals in a clause. The most compressive clause is then added to H_{mc} and its covered examples are removed from the uncovered set of training examples. The process is repeated until there are no clauses with positive compression left in H_c.

Algorithm 4.1 Noise Tolerant Recursive Best-First Induction

Input: Local training set E_l
Current clause C
Current cost bound M
The greatest cost of an acceptable clause $M_{\max}$

Output: ■: At least one (weak?) consistent clause was found
□: otherwise

```
1:  function RBFI(E_l, C, M, M_max)
2:  begin
3:    if f(C) > M then F(C) = f(C); return □;
4:    if Consistent(C) then
5:      if f(C) ≥ M_max then F(C) = ∞; return □;
6:      else
7:        H_c = H_c ∪ {C}
8:        if Complete(H_c) then exit ;
9:        else F(C) = ∞; return ■;
10:     endif
11:   endif
12:   if WeakConsistent(C) ∧ f(C) < M_max then wc = ■ ;
13:   else wc = □ ;
14:   M'_max = NewBound(wc, f(C), M_max) ;
15:   R = ρ(C, M, M'_max)
16:   if |R| = 0 then
17:     if wc then goto 7 ;
18:     else F(C) = ∞; return □;
19:   for C_i ∈ R do
20:     if f(C) < F(C) then F(C_i) = max(F(C), f(C_i))
21:     else F(C_i) = f(C_i)
22:   ff = □ ; sort R in increasing order of F(C_i), C_i ∈ R
23:   while F(C_1) ≤ M ∧ F(C_1) < ∞ do
24:     if RBFI(Cov(H_c ∪ C_1, E_l), C_1,
            NewBound(wc, ∞, min(F(C_2), M)), M'_max) then
25:       ff = ■; R = Prune(H_c, R);
26:       if |R| = 0 then F(C) = ∞; return ■;
27:     endif
28:     insert C_1 sorted in R
29:   endwhile
30:   if ¬ff ∧ wc then goto 7 ;
31:   F(C) = F(C_1) ;
32:   return ff ;
33: end
```

5 EVALUATION

To evaluate CLIP's noise resistance we performed a series of experiments on the well known King-Rook-King chess endgame domain (Muggleton, Bain, Hayes-Michie & Michie, 1989). The goal is to determine when a position of the white king, white rook, and black king on a chess board is an illegal white-to-move position. The position is represented by the predicate $illegal(WKf, WKr, WRf, WRr, BKf, BKr)$, where $\{WK, WR, BK\}f$ and $\{WK, WR, BK\}r$ are files and ranks of all the pieces, respectively. Background knowledge consists of equality (matching between variables), order ($less(X, Y)$), and adjacency ($adj(X, Y)$). The latter two relations are represented by two background predicates each, for both files and ranks. We used 5 sets of 100 training examples from (Džeroski, 1991), with noise incrementally added in class, arguments, and both. The noise model used in (Džeroski, 1991) differs from ours, presented above. If γ is the level of noise then with probability γ the class of an example is selected randomly. This makes, on KRK domain, a noise level γ approximately equivalent to a noise level 2β in our model. In terms of γ, the noise levels were 5%, 10%, 15%, 20%, 30%, 50%, and 80%. Generated hypotheses were tested on the set of 5000 noiseless examples. The training and test data used make some of our experiments directly comparable to those in (Džeroski, 1991; Kovačič, 1994), and to some extent to those in (Ali & Pazzani, 1996; Fürnkranz, 1997).

The training data was also incomplete since the whole training set (500 examples) contained only one negative example of a legal position, where the white king was standing in line between the white rook and black king and was not positioned next to the latter. Therefore, it was only possible to learn an approximate solution (99.8% accurate), shown on Figure 3.

```
illegal(A,B,A,B,_,_).
illegal(A,B,_,_,A,B).
illegal(A,B,_,_,A,F) :- adj_rank(B,F).
illegal(A,B,_,_,E,B) :- adj_file(A,E).
illegal(A,B,_,_,E,F) :- adj_file(A,E),
                        adj_rank(B,F).
illegal(_,_,_,D,_,D).
illegal(_,_,C,_,C,_).
```

Figure 3: An Approximation of the Target Hypothesis

We were trying to establish how settings of different parameters affect the success of learning. Therefore, we exhaustively varied the maximum length of a clause ($d \in \{3, 4\}$), the noise level $\beta \in \{20\%, 30\%, 40\%\}$), cost function ($f_{ai}$, f_p), and hypothesis selection (H_{lr}, H_{mc}). In addition, we checked how the performance of CLIP is influenced by the number of training examples.

5.1 SMALL NUMBER OF TRAINING EXAMPLES

The initial set of experiments was performed on 5 original training sets. Table 2 shows the average classification results of the learned hypotheses, measured over the set of 5000 noiseless examples. For reference, in Table 1 the results obtained on the same training/test sets for the ILP systems mFOIL and MILP are listed. The figures are taken from (Džeroski, 1991) and (Kovačič, 1994), respectively.[1] We should point out that the results for mFOIL are the best results obtained by varying the parameter m in *m-estimate.* First, we should stress that some of the clauses had

[1]Experiments with MILP on the data with 80% of noise introduced were not performed, hence the missing values in table 2.

Table 1: Learning Results for mFOIL and MILP

Noise (γ)	*mFOIL*	*MILP*
0%	95.6	96.7
5% (na)	91.9	93.9
10%	84.6	87.1
15%	80.1	83.9
20%	76.5	79.1
30%	74.0	77.7
50%	68.6	73.6
80%	66.3	–
5% (nb)	89.6	91.7
10%	80.8	81.6
15%	76.6	78.7
20%	74.7	75.2
30%	69.7	70.4
50%	66.3	59.7
80%	61.7	–
5% (nc)	94.3	94.3
10%	92.0	92.0
15%	90.0	92.0
20%	88.4	88.7
30%	86.0	84.1
50%	79.2	75.7
80%	65.0	–

Table 2: Classification Accuracy, $|E| = 100$, $d = 3$, $\beta = 20\%$

Noise (γ)	f_{ai}		f_p	
	H_{lr}	H_{mc}	H_{lr}	H_{mc}
0%	96.9 ± 1.5	96.7 ± 1.3	97.7 ± 0.8	96.7 ± 1.3
5% (na)	93.9 ± 3.7	95.2 ± 1.3	93.6 ± 4.1	95.0 ± 1.5
10%	85.5 ± 6.0	84.1 ± 7.8	85.5 ± 6.0	84.1 ± 7.8
15%	82.8 ± 6.3	83.3 ± 8.0	84.4 ± 6.6	83.3 ± 8.0
20%	79.8 ± 8.5	78.9 ± 7.8	81.0 ± 8.0	79.3 ± 7.7
30%	76.7 ± 5.3	76.5 ± 5.5	77.1 ± 5.5	76.5 ± 5.5
50%	70.4 ± 3.4	70.7 ± 2.6	70.9 ± 2.8	70.9 ± 2.7
80%	66.4 ± 1.4	66.4 ± 2.9	66.4 ± 1.4	66.4 ± 2.9
5% (nb)	92.0 ± 2.3	93.8 ± 1.0	91.7 ± 2.7	93.5 ± 0.9
10%	80.3 ± 5.1	81.2 ± 5.7	81.1 ± 4.4	82.6 ± 5.9
15%	78.2 ± 1.8	79.2 ± 3.2	78.2 ± 1.8	79.2 ± 3.2
20%	77.7 ± 3.1	77.4 ± 3.3	79.1 ± 2.0	78.2 ± 2.4
30%	75.2 ± 4.0	75.3 ± 4.0	74.8 ± 4.4	74.9 ± 4.4
50%	70.5 ± 2.6	69.4 ± 3.7	70.5 ± 2.6	69.9 ± 3.0
80%	64.6 ± 6.1	63.6 ± 7.4	62.1 ± 8.4	62.4 ± 8.3
5% (nc)	95.3 ± 1.4	95.4 ± 1.2	96.0 ± 1.9	95.3 ± 1.3
10%	93.6 ± 2.8	93.8 ± 2.5	94.3 ± 3.4	93.7 ± 2.5
15%	94.0 ± 1.9	93.8 ± 2.5	94.7 ± 2.7	93.7 ± 2.5
20%	91.9 ± 3.5	91.1 ± 4.4	92.0 ± 3.1	91.1 ± 4.3
30%	87.9 ± 5.0	89.3 ± 4.2	88.0 ± 4.8	89.3 ± 4.2
50%	78.4 ± 7.0	82.5 ± 5.4	79.1 ± 6.8	82.5 ± 5.4
80%	66.8 ± 5.8	67.9 ± 5.4	67.8 ± 5.8	68.3 ± 5.1

very weak statistical support in the training sets. In some cases, specific examples were not even present in the training set; otherwise, some of the clauses covered from 1 to 3 examples. These clauses were the main reason that first, CLIP was not able to reach the top classification accuracy (in noiseless case), and second, that performance of the induced hypotheses dropped even for small amounts of noise, a well known problem of small disjuncts (Holte, Acker & Porter, 1989). We can note that CLIP performed better when using f_p instead of f_{ai} (measured by the performance of H_{lr}), though the differences were not significant. We also compared the performance of H_{lr} and H_{mc} (when f_p was used) and again the differences in the classification accuracy were not significant. H_{mc} performed slightly better with higher degree of classification noise but did not perform as well with argument noise. It also achieved better classification results with noise in both class and arguments but none of the differences were significant (with confidence level down to 80%).

The hypotheses produced with H_{mc} were smaller on average. Additional comparison revealed that the classification accuracy decreases almost linearly with the level of classification noise while it dropped more rapidly at first but then leveled out with noise in arguments and both class and arguments. Running times exhibited similar behaviour. They ranged from 0.01 to 0.7 seconds on an PII 400MHz, depending on the noise level. Learning with f_{ai} was a bit slower than learning with f_p. With classification noise, learning time grew linearly while with noise in arguments, it suddenly jumped when noise was introduced but then stayed at that level throughout the rest of the experiments. Learning behaviour in the presence of combined noise was somewhere in between these two extremes.

Compared to mFOIL and MILP, even the lowest classification accuracy in Table 2 is mostly higher than the results obtained by either of them, irrespective of the kind of noise. Both mFOIL and MILP have more user settable parameters. The former expects, in addition to the value of m in m-estimate, a significance threshold that is used in the stopping criterion. The latter has several parameters that control its stochastic search for consistent clauses. Table 2 suggest that CLIP achieves comparable or better results than both algorithms on the KRK domain while requiring fewer parameter settings. The testing set was chosen independently of the training sets and since the CLIP requires fewer parameter settings, it can be reasoned that it is a better algorithm, at least for learning on the presented domain (Scheffer & Herbrich, 1997).

5.2 SUFFICIENT NUMBER OF TRAINING EXAMPLES

As we have established in the previous section, 100 training examples are barely enough to support even the approximation of the target hypothesis (Figure 3). To get a better impression of CLIP's noise resisting ability when it is given a sufficient number of training examples, we combined the original 5 training sets and performed 10-fold cross validation on the resulting set. The number of training examples was increased to 450. The difference with the standard testing procedure was that we estimated the accuracy of the induced hypotheses over the independent set of 5000 noiseless examples and not on the set that was left out during the learning. The variation of learning parameters was identical to the settings in the previous section.

As expected, CLIP performed significantly better with a larger training set. Analysis of the results in Table 3 shows that H_{mc} almost always performed bet-

Table 3: Classification Accuracy, $|E| = 450$, $d = 3$, $\beta = 30\%$

Noise (γ)	f_{ai}		f_p	
	H_{lr}	H_{mc}	H_{lr}	H_{mc}
0%	99.8 ± 0.0	99.8 ± 0.0	99.8 ± 0.0	99.8 ± 0.0
5% (na)	99.8 ± 0.0	99.8 ± 0.0	99.8 ± 0.0	99.8 ± 0.0
10%	99.7 ± 0.3	99.7 ± 0.2	99.1 ± 0.6	**99.7 ± 0.2**
15%	97.8 ± 3.1	99.2 ± 1.4	97.7 ± 3.2	99.2 ± 1.6
20%	91.7 ± 2.4	93.8 ± 2.7	91.8 ± 2.4	93.8 ± 2.8
30%	83.5 ± 3.3	85.1 ± 3.3	83.0 ± 3.9	85.2 ± 3.3
50%	75.9 ± 1.6	74.7 ± 1.5	76.1 ± 1.8	74.4 ± 1.6
80%	70.3 ± 1.0	68.0 ± 1.5	**70.1 ± 0.8**	67.9 ± 1.5
5% (nb)	99.6 ± 0.3	99.8 ± 0.0	99.6 ± 0.3	99.8 ± 0.0
10%	91.9 ± 3.1	**96.6 ± 2.6**	91.6 ± 2.6	**96.6 ± 2.4**
15%	92.5 ± 2.9	95.0 ± 1.7	92.2 ± 3.0	94.6 ± 1.6
20%	78.9 ± 5.3	**82.5 ± 4.9**	79.2 ± 5.2	**82.5 ± 4.9**
30%	76.5 ± 2.8	77.9 ± 3.3	76.9 ± 2.5	78.1 ± 3.3
50%	76.0 ± 2.0	77.7 ± 2.2	76.5 ± 1.9	78.1 ± 2.6
80%	67.7 ± 3.1	67.7 ± 4.1	67.8 ± 3.3	67.7 ± 4.1
5% (nc)	99.8 ± 0.0	99.8 ± 0.0	99.8 ± 0.0	99.8 ± 0.0
10%	99.8 ± 0.0	99.8 ± 0.0	99.8 ± 0.0	99.8 ± 0.0
15%	99.8 ± 0.0	99.8 ± 0.0	99.8 ± 0.0	99.8 ± 0.0
20%	99.7 ± 0.2	99.8 ± 0.0	99.7 ± 0.2	99.8 ± 0.0
30%	98.4 ± 0.9	**99.6 ± 0.5**	98.6 ± 0.9	**99.7 ± 0.4**
50%	93.9 ± 0.8	**96.3 ± 1.1**	93.8 ± 0.8	**96.2 ± 0.9**
80%	76.3 ± 3.1	**79.2 ± 2.4**	76.2 ± 3.1	**79.1 ± 2.4**

ter than H_{lr}. With bold numbers are shown results where H_{mc} achieved significantly better results than H_{lr} with 99% confidence level. On the remaining data sets, where H_{mc} clearly performs better, the significance of the differences is mostly above 88%. The difference increases with greater levels of noise, except for the most noisy data sets (50%, 80%), where in the case of noise in arguments H_{lr} is significantly better (96% confidence level for f_p and 88% for f_{ai}). The reason for better behaviour of H_{mc} compared to H_{lr} is, in our opinion, that when selecting the former, statistical significance of clauses is also taken into account since between two clauses with identical accuracy, the one with higher coverage is preferred. In the case of H_{lr} only accuracy of clauses determines the order of inclusion, which might introduce accurate, but clauses with low coverage into the hypothesis.

Next we can establish that the differences in performance disappear when f_p or f_{ai} is used during learning. This is a consequence of the fact that on this domain, the distribution of signs in the training sets does not "break" the f_{ai} estimate. Also, with increased number of training examples the distance between the clauses (that is, the difference in the coverage of the examples) increases, especially between relevant and irrelevant clauses. The latter do not generalise well over the increased training set which further increases the distance. This brings many of them well out of danger of being mistakenly selected as better refinements of the target clause. Learning times increased almost linearly and ranged from 0.04 to 2.2 seconds for f_p and 0.04 to 6.6 seconds for f_{ai}.

Ultimately, the stopping condition depends on the setting of the expected rate of classification errors in the training set (β), or the minimum allowed classification accuracy of an acceptable clause. In Figure 4, we show how the various settings of beta influence the classifi-

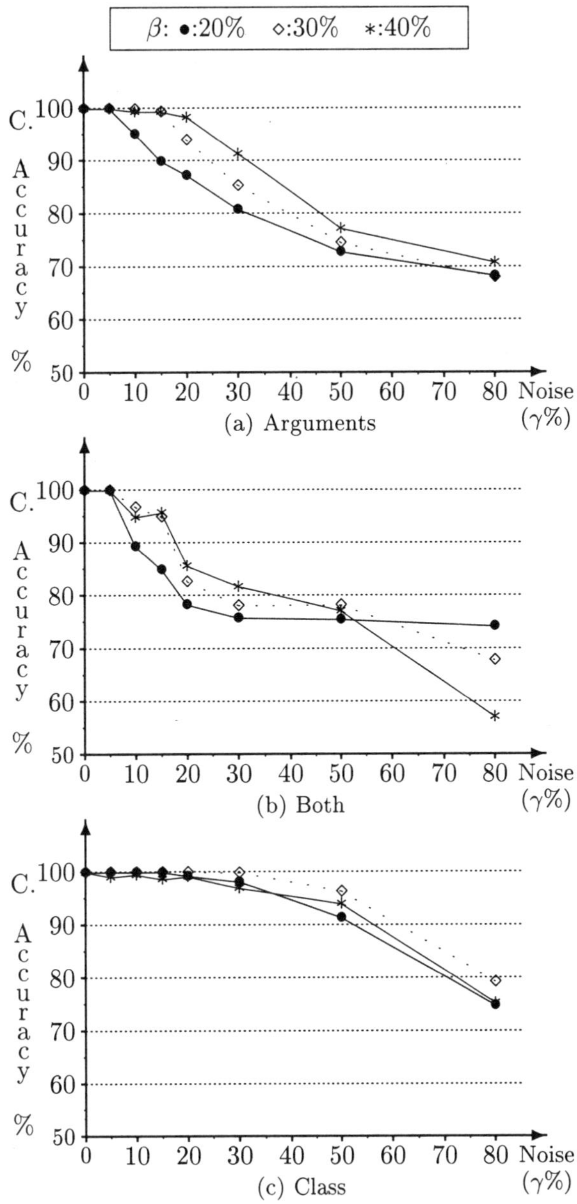

Figure 4: The Influence of Various Settings of β; (H_{mc}, $|E| = 450$, $d = 3$).

cation accuracy of H_{mc}, for different kinds of noise introduced. We can see that with increasing level of noise, hypotheses obtained with increasing values of β become more accurate, with a few exceptions, relative to the hypotheses obtained with lower settings of the minimal clause accuracy. The exceptions are associated with very large levels of noise (50% and 80%), applied to class and both class and arguments. We should emphasize that these levels are close to pure random data, where good and stable results were not expected. What is encouraging is that learning performance is not reduced in most cases, even when the actual noise level is well below the expected noise level β. This suggests that at least on the KRK domain, it is sufficient to overestimate (even significantly) the data noise level to obtain reasonably accurate results.

In the experiments mentioned so far, the allowed clause length tightly matched the length of the longest correct clause from Figure 3. With d increased to 4, the classification accuracy of the hypotheses produced did not change significantly, while learning time, when using f_{ai}, increased a lot (but it is within bounds mentioned above). In Figure 5, typical behaviour is

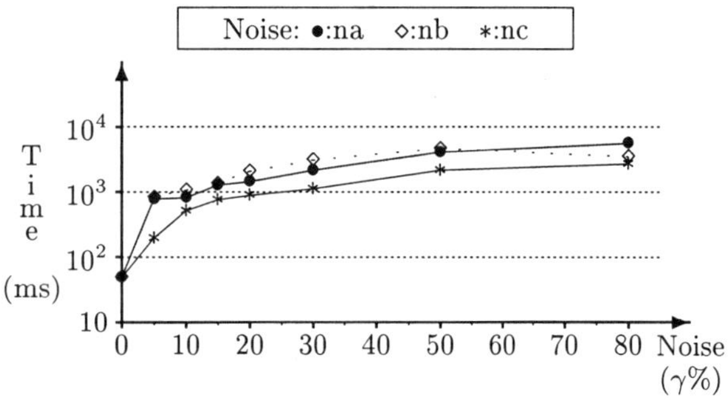

Figure 5: The Learning Time Dependency on the Noise Level, $|E| = 450$, $d = 4$, $\beta = 30\%$, f_{ai}.

shown. For noise in arguments and both class and arguments, the learning time increases significantly even when small amounts of noise are introduced, but the growth is quickly slowed down, so with higher amounts of noise, the learning time does not increase as dramatically any longer. The jump is even less noticable when the maximum clause length is more tight ($d = 3$).

Figure 6 show how the learning time increases with the number of learning examples. The results are shown for different kinds of noise introduced, with the use of f_p and smaller clause length. Both scales on the figure are logarithmic. Graph suggests almost linear increase of computation time with the increased training set size on this domain.

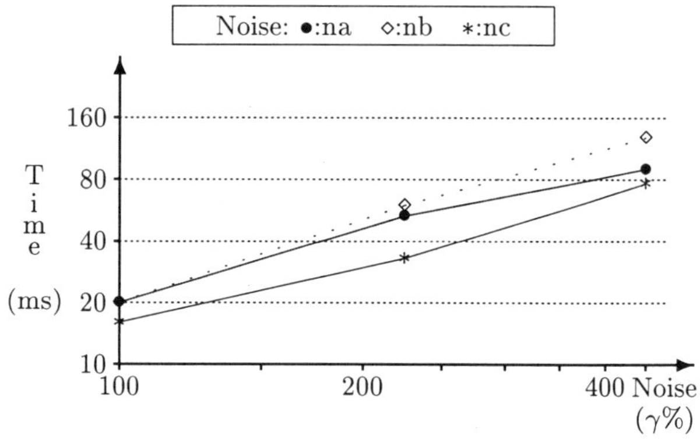

Figure 6: The Learning Time Dependency on the Training Set Size, $d = 3$, $\gamma = 20\%$, f_p.

5.3 DISCUSSION

Results, reported in (Ali & Pazzani, 1996; Fürnkranz, 1997; McCreath & Sharma, 1998), of some of the state-of-the-art rule learning algorithms capable of noise handling on the KRK domain are not directly comparable to ours. The number of training examples and the noise model are sometimes slightly different. Also, they are obtained on different training/test sets. Nevertheless, a comparison suggests that the performance of CLIP on KRK is on par or better to that of HYDRA (Ali & Pazzani, 1993), IREP, TDP and FOSSIL (Fürnkranz, 1997), Grow (Cohen, 1993), and LIME (McCreath & Sharma, 1998), with the exception of learning with small number of examples, where TDP appears to perform better.

Complexity-wise, CLIP represents an improvement over the ideas behind TDP, and IREP and its derivatives IREP* and RIPPER (Cohen, 1995). Although learning time can significantly increase with the number of learning examples, this is mainly due to an inefficient stopping criterion. The reader should note that CLIP was originally designed with different goals in mind. Its search strategy is complete in a sense that it will always find a complete hypothesis, if such a hypothesis exists in the current search space. Unfortunately, this sometime prevents CLIP from stopping searching earlier since it tries to covered a few of the remaining uncovered examples. If we disregard this weakness then we can see RBFI truly improves on IREP's ideas. The latter immediately post-prunes a clause when it is learned, before it attempts to learn clauses covering the remaining training set. In CLIP, pruning is actually incorporated in the learning phase itself. As soon as it encounters an acceptable clause, this fact is remembered and further refinements are more strongly pruned (pre-pruning). However, the search does not terminate immediately, since CLIP tries to find a refinement that improves the cost of the currently remembered clause. If no such clause exists, then search backtracks to the remembered clause (post-pruning), otherwise, the remembered clause is dropped in favor of the one that makes the improvement. In our experiments CLIP exhibits sub-quadratic behaviour, as measured by log-log analysis (Cameron-Jones, 1996) and shown in Figure 6.

There are a couple of areas where the current implementation of search falls short of the possibilities of the proposed noise handling framework. In particular, the detection of an acceptable clause and better refinements should be offset by the size of the space explored so far. In domains with much richer background knowledge (much larger search space), it is very likely that after a lot of search, very accurate clauses are more a matter of chance than the result of a true underlying relationship; the behaviour noticed in (Quinlan & Cameron-Jones, 1995). The same holds for very dense refinement spaces, where each clause has many refinements covering most of the coverage subsets. Another area where there is still room for improvement is the selection of the final hypothesis from H_c. Our greedy selection algorithms sometimes missed the proposed correct clause for reasons that require further investigation.

6 CONCLUSIONS

Efficient and effective noise handling is an important property of any machine learning system that is intended to be used on real-world, large-scale data sets. In this paper, we have presented a property of linear separability, that a cost function must satisfy, so that it becomes highly unlikely that refinements of the correct clause will have lower cost than that clause when evaluated over noisy training sets. The result relies only on the assumption that the class of any training example can be corrupted with certain probability. The framework avoids the pitfalls of MDL based approaches, which often rely upon an appropriate encoding scheme. To some extent, the framework is also applicable to handling noise in arguments but further investigation is necessary.

Based on this property, we adapted our recursive best-first search algorithm RBFI, which is incorporated in our learning system CLIP, to handle noisy training data better. The enhanced algorithm retains all the properties of the noiseless version (best-first search, polynomial memory requirements). Preliminary results on the KRK domain show that CLIP is very competitive to some of the state-of-the-art learning systems capable of noisy handling like mFOIL, MILP, HYDRA, IREP, TDP, FOSSIL, Grow, and LIME. Complexity wise, the idea presents an improvement over IREP and RIPPER (assuming efficient stopping criterion) but more thorough investigation is necessary.

Where CLIP is still lacking is better selection of final hypothesis and estimation of probability that an acceptable clause (or better refinement) has been found by chance. This, together with more extensive evaluation over a larger set of noisy domains, represents the core of our future work.

Acknowledgements

The author is grateful to Ross Quinlan for discussions and/or comments. My gratitude extends also to three anonymous reviewers for their valuable comments and suggestions. This work was supported by Australian Research Council. In part, it was funded by the Slovenian Ministry of Science and Technology and by the European Community Project ILP2 (ESPRIT IV, 20237). It represents a part of authors PhD thesis.

References

Ali, K. M. & Pazzani, M. J. (1993). Hydra: A noise-tolerant relational concept learning algorithm. In *Proceedings of the* 13th *International Joint Conference on Artificial Intelligence*, (pp. 1064–1070)., Chambery, France.

Ali, K. M. & Pazzani, M. J. (1996). Error reduction through learning multiple descriptions. *Machine Learning*, *24*(3), 173–202.

Brunk, C. & Pazzani, M. J. (1991). An inverstigation of noise-tolerant relational concept learning algorithms. In *Proceedings of the 8th International Workshop on Machine Learning*, (pp. 389–393)., Evanston, IL. Morgan Kaufman Publishers, Inc.

Cameron-Jones, R. (1996). The complexity of batch approaches to reduced error rule set induction. In *Proceedings of the 4th Pacific Rim International Conference on Artificial Intelligence*, (pp. 348–359)., Cairns, Australia. Springer Verlag.

Clark, P. & Niblett, T. (1989). The cn2 induction algorithm. *Machine Learning*, *3*(4), 261–283.

Cohen, W. W. (1993). Efficient pruning methods for separate-and-conquer rule learning systems. In *Proceedings of the* 13th *International Joint Conference on Artificial Intelligence*, volume 2, (pp. 988–994)., Chambery, France.

Cohen, W. W. (1995). Fast effective rule induction. In *Proceedings of the 12th International Conference on Machine Learning*, (pp. 115–123)., Lake Tahoe, CA. Morgan Kaufman Publishers, Inc.

Džeroski, S. (1991). Handling noise in inductive logic programming. Master's thesis, University of Ljubljana, Faculty of electrical engineering and computer science, Ljubljana, Slovenia.

Fürnkranz, J. (1997). Pruning algorithms for rule learning. *Machine Learning*, *27*(2), 139–172.

Holte, R. C., Acker, L. E., & Porter, B. W. (1989). Concept learning and the problem of small disjuncts. In *Proceedings of the Eleventh International Joint Coference on Artificial Intelligence*, volume 1, (pp. 813–818)., Detroit, Michigan. Morgan Kaufman Publishers, Inc.

Korf, R. E. (1993). Linear-space best-first search. *Artificial Ingelligence*, *62*, 41–78.

Kovačič, M. (1994). Milp-a stochastic approach to inductive logic programming. In Wrobel, S. (Ed.), *Proceedings of the Fourth International Workshop on Inductive Logic Programming*, (pp. 123–138).,.Bad Honnef/Bonn, Germany.

Lloyd, J. W. (1987). *Foundations of Logic Programming* (second ed.). Berlin, Germany: Springer Verlag.

McCreath, E. & Sharma, A. (1998). Lime: A system for learning relations. Technical report, School of Computer Science and Engineering, The University of New South Wales.

Michalski, R. S., Mozetič, I., Hong, J., & Lavrač, N. (1986). The multi-purpose incremental learning system aq15 and its testing application to three medical domains. In *Proceedings of the 5th National Conference on Artificial Intelligence*, (pp. 1041–1045)., Philadelphia, PA.

Muggleton, S. (1995). Inverse entailment and progol. *New Generation Computing*, *13*, 245–286.

Muggleton, S., Bain, M., Hayes-Michie, J., & Michie, D. (1989). An experimental comparison of human and machine learning formalisms. In *Proceedings fo the 6th International Workshop on Machine Learning (ML-89)*, (pp. 113–118). Morgan Kaufman Publishers, Inc.

Pompe, U. (1999a). *Inductive constraint-logic programming*. PhD thesis, University of Ljubljana, Faculty of Computer and Information Science, Ljubljana, Slovenia. (in Slovene).

Pompe, U. (1999b). Recursive best-first induction. Technical report, AI dept., CSE, The University of New South Wales.

Quinlan, J. R. (1990). Learning logical definitions from relations. *Machine Learning*, *5*, 239–266.

Quinlan, J. R. & Cameron-Jones, R. (1995). Oversearching and layered search in empirical learning. In *Proceedings of the Fourteenth International Joint Conference on Artificial Intelligence*, volume 2, (pp. 1019–1024)., Montreal, Quebec, Canada.

Scheffer, T. & Herbrich, R. (1997). Unbiased assessment of learning algorithms. In *Proceedings of the Fifteenth International Joint Conference on Artificial Intelligence*, volume 2, (pp. 798–803)., Nagoya, Japan. Morgan Kaufman Publishers, Inc.

Implicit Imitation in Multiagent Reinforcement Learning

Bob Price and Craig Boutilier
Department of Computer Science
University of British Columbia
Vancouver, B.C., Canada V6T 1Z4
{price,cebly}@cs.ubc.ca

Abstract

Imitation is actively being studied as an effective means of learning in multi-agent environments. It allows an agent to learn how to act well (perhaps optimally) by passively observing the actions of cooperative teachers or other more experienced agents its environment. We propose a straightforward imitation mechanism called *model extraction* that can be integrated easily into standard model-based reinforcement learning algorithms. Roughly, by observing a mentor with similar capabilities, an agent can extract information about its own capabilities in unvisited parts of state space. The extracted information can accelerate learning dramatically. We illustrate the benefits of model extraction by integrating it with prioritized sweeping, and demonstrating improved performance and convergence through observation of single and multiple mentors. Though we make some stringent assumptions regarding observability, possible interactions and common abilities, we briefly comment on extensions of the model that relax these.

1 Introduction

The application of reinforcement learning (RL) to multi-agent systems offers unique opportunities and challenges. When agents are viewed as independently trying to achieve their own ends, interesting issues in the interaction of agent policies [12] must be resolved (e.g., by appeal to equilibrium concepts). However, the possibility that agents may coordinate their policies for mutual gain [22] or distribute their search for optimal policies (and communicate partial results to one another) [13] offers intriguing possibilities for accelerating RL and enhancing agent performance.

Another way in which individual agent performance can be improved is by having a novice agent learn reasonable behavior from an expert *mentor*. This type of learning can be brought about through explicit *teaching* or demonstration [1, 11, 25], by sharing of privileged information [13] or through a more elaborate psychological theory of *imitation* [2]. In imitation, the agent's own exploration is used to ground its observations of other agent's behaviors in its own capabilities and resolve any ambiguities in observations arising from partial observability and noise. A common thread in all of this work is the use of a mentor to guide the *exploration* of the observer. Guidance is typically achieved through some form of explicit communication between mentor and observer. A less direct form of teaching involves an observer extracting information from a mentor without the mentor making an explicit attempt to demonstrate a specific behavior of interest [15].

In this paper we develop a model of *implicit imitation* through observation of a mentor. Roughly, an agent observes the state transitions induced by the mentor's actions. Assuming that it has actions similar to the (unknown) action taken by the mentor, the agent can use this information to update its value function. In addition, a mentor can provide hints to the observer about the parts of the state space on which it may be worth focusing attention. The observer's attention to an area might take the form of additional exploration of the area or additional computation brought to bear on the agent's prior beliefs about the area. We derive a new technique, *model extraction*, that is independent of any specific RL algorithm, though it is best suited for use with model-based methods. We illustrate its effectiveness empirically by incorporating it into prioritized sweeping.

Our model has several advantages over more direct forms of imitation and teaching. It does not require any agent to explicitly play the role of mentor or teacher. Observers learn simply by watching the behavior of other agents (mentors); if a mentor shares certain subtasks with the observer, the observed behavior can be incorporated (indirectly) by the observer. This is important because there will be many situations in which an observer can learn from a mentor that is unwilling or unable to alter its behavior to teach the observer, or even communicate information to it. For example, common communication protocols may be unavailable to agents designed by different developers (e.g., Internet agents); agents may be competing; or there may simply be no incentive for one agent to provide information to another.[1] Because an agent learns by observation, it can exploit the existence of multiple mentors, essentially distributing its search. The observer is also not constrained to directly imitate the mentor and can decide whether such imitation is worthwhile. Finally, we do not assume that the observer knows the actual actions taken by the mentor, or that the mentor shares a reward function (or goals) with the mentor. While we make some strict assumptions in this paper, the model can be generalized in interesting ways, as we describe below. Many of these generalizations are the subject of ongoing research.

We present the basic model and assumptions underlying model extraction in Section 2. We develop the model extraction algorithm and demonstrate a simple mechanism to focus the agent's updating mechanism on promising areas of the state space in Section 3, and illustrate the performance of the algorithm empirically in Section 4. We conclude in Section 5 with remarks on related work and a discussion of current and future research, especially with respect to the relaxation of certain modeling assumptions.

2 Model and Assumptions

Our model assumes that we have some number of agents acting to achieve their own objectives in a common environment. To keep the notation simple, we present the model using two agents only: a *mentor* m and an *observer* o. The observer is a reinforcement learner that can observe aspects of the mentor's behavior. The extension to multiple agents should be viewed as adding further (potential) mentors to the system, since we consider the RL problem facing a single observer.[2]

The agents act to control a *multiagent Markov decision process (MMDP)*, in which the agents select actions independently, and their *joint actions* determine stochastic state transitions.[3] In order to focus on imitation without getting into issues of strategic reasoning (e.g., game theoretic concepts like equilibria), we assume that the agents' actions are noninteracting; that is, each agent can ignore the behavior of the other in predicting the effect of its own actions on the system and the reward it receives. To do this, we factor the MMDP into two standard (single-agent) MDPs $M_o = \langle S_o, A_o, \Pr_o, R_o \rangle$ and $M_m = \langle S_m, A_m, \Pr_m, R_m \rangle$ pertaining to the observer and mentor, respectively. Here, for $i \in \{o, m\}$, S_i is the state space for agent i, A_i its set of actions, $\Pr_i(t|s,a)$ the stochastic state transition function and $R_i(s)$ its reward function (defined over S_i). For instance, in a grid world, we might assume that the mentor and observer can each move without affecting the other's ability to move or impact the reward it receives by occupying certain grid cells.

If the observer is to learn by observing the mentor, there must be some relationship between the space of potential behaviors they can implement. We make two especially strong assumptions in this regard. First, the agents have identical state spaces; i.e., $S = S_m = S_o$. Second, the observer has (at least) the same capabilities as the mentor; i.e., $A_m \subseteq A_o$ and $\Pr_m(t|s,a) = \Pr_o(t|s,a)$ for any a they have in common. These assumptions make our description of the imitation task somewhat simpler, but can be relaxed. The essential feature is that there be some analogical mapping between state transitions so that the observations of the mentor can be recast in terms the observer understands [19] (see Section 5). Our formulation makes this mapping trivial. However, we do not assume that the reward functions R_o and R_m are related in any specific way.

Initially, the observer will not know the transition model $\Pr_o$; but we assume it knows its reward function R_o. While in typical RL models, the learner does not know R_o, prior knowledge of R_o is consistent with the interpretation of RL as automatic programming: the agent designer can often provide predicates to evaluate the quality of a situation in advance, but cannot provide a model of the state dynamics. To learn from the mentor, the observer must be able to observe certain aspects of its behavior. Unless it communicates its policy or selected actions to the observer, the actual actions taken by the mentor will be unknown to the observer. All it can see is the effects of an action. For instance, in a noisy grid world, the mentor may attempt to move north but actually move east: the observer sees only the actual state transition, not the intended transition or actual action attempted. Therefore, we assume the observer can see the specific state transitions $s \rightarrow t$ taken by the mentor. The mentor's state is thus fully observable to the observer. This, too, is a strong assumption—we indicate ways in which it can be relaxed in Section 5.

3 Model Extraction and Implicit Imitation

The observer's problem is to determine an optimal course of action that maximizes expected value, where its value function is given by the Bellman equation:

$$V(s) = R_o(s) + \gamma \max_{a \in A_o} \left\{ \sum_{t \in S} \Pr_o(t|s,a) V(t) \right\} \quad (1)$$

We assume here a discounted infinite horizon context with discount factor γ. For the present, we also assume that the agent's actions do not influence the agent's reward structure, but this assumption will later be relaxed.

[1] For reasons of consistency, we use the term "mentor" to describe any agent from which an observer can learn, even if the mentor is an unwilling participant.

[2] This is not to say that the other "mentors" cannot be learners or even imitators themselves.

[3] MMDPs could be viewed as a form of *stochastic game* [20]; since Shapley's original formulation involved the zero-zum assumption, we use different terminology to avoid confusion.

In an RL context, our observer has access to transition samples of the form $\langle s, a, t\rangle$ (recall that it knows $R_o(s)$). An optimal policy can be determined by directly learning a Q-function $Q(s, a)$ [24], or using model-based methods that estimate the model $\Pr_o$ and solve (generally, asynchronously and incrementally) Equation 1 (e.g., prioritized sweeping [17]). There is a limited scope in which observations of the mentor's state trajectories can influence this computation. Since the observer already knows its reward function, its observations of the mentor cannot influence its reward model. Observations could be used to update its estimate of its own transition model $\Pr_o$, or the order in which to apply Bellman backups to its own estimated value function. We consider both forms of influence in this section. Two other possible (direct) influences are not explored here: the observer could attempt to infer the best action to perform in state s based on the mentor's trajectory; or the observer could use the observations to directly compute the value function, or constraints on the value function for states it has not visited [23].

In Section 3.1, we describe the model extraction algorithm in the context of model-based RL. However, in Section 3.2, we indicate how the same ideas can be incorporated into model-free algorithms such as Q-learning.

3.1 Model Extraction in General Terms

If a mentor is "expert" at achieving its objectives, we can assume it is executing a *stationary, deterministic* policy π_m, with $\pi_m(s)$ denoting its action choice at state s. Behavior π induces a Markov chain $\Pr_m(t|s) = \Pr_m(t|s, \pi_m(s))$ over S. By observing mentor transitions, the observer can construct an estimate $\widehat{\Pr}_m$ of this chain: $\widehat{\Pr}_m(t|s)$ can simply be estimated by the relative observed frequency of mentor transitions $s \rightarrow t$ (w.r.t. all transitions taken from s).

Since $A_m \subseteq A_o$, the observer knows that there is some action $a \in A_o$ that is the same as $\pi_m(s)$; that is, there exists an action a such that $\Pr_o(t|s, a) \approx \widehat{\Pr}_m(t|s)$. Unfortunately, since the observer does not know its own transition model—it has only estimates—and cannot observe the mentor's actions directly, it does not know the identity of this action $\pi_m(s)$. However, the mere fact that there *exists some action* with estimated transition probabilities $\Pr_m(\cdot|s)$ can be used to good effect by the observer in value function estimation. Since $A_m \subseteq A_o$, $V(s)$ can be given by the following *augmented Bellman equation*:

$$V(s) = R_o(s) + \gamma \max\left\{\max_{a\in A_o}\left\{\sum_{t\in S}\Pr_o(t|s,a)V(t)\right\}, \sum_{t\in S}\Pr_m(t|s)V(t)\right\} \tag{2}$$

This is the usual Bellman equation (1) with an extra term added, the second summation, denoting the expected value of duplicating the mentor's action $\pi_m(s)$. Since this (unknown) action is identical to one of the observer's actions, the term is redundant and the augmented value equation is valid. Of course, the observer using the augmented backup operation must rely on estimates of these quantities. If the observer's exploration policy ensures that each state is visited infinitely often, the estimates of the Pr_o terms will converge to their true values. The mentor's policy is not under the observer's control. However, if the mentor's policy is ergodic over state space S, then these terms too will converge to their true values. If the mentor's policy restricts it to a subset of states $S' \subseteq S$ (those forming the basis of its Markov chain), these estimates will converge correctly with respect to S' if the chain is ergodic, and states in $S - S'$ will remain unvisited. An observer can apply the augmented equation only for those states visited by the mentor. In either of these cases, the use Equation (2) does not impact the usual convergence results for RL algorithms.

Our primary interest, however, is the behavior of the system during the initial stages of learning when the advantage of a knowledgeable mentor can make the most difference to an observer. Assuming that the mentor is pursuing a greedy policy, there will be many states for which the observer has much more accurate estimates of $\Pr_m(t|s)$ than it does for $\Pr_o(t|s, a)$ for any specific a. Since the observer is learning, it must explore both state space (causing less frequent visits to s) and action space (thus spreading its experience at s over all actions a), generally ensuring that the sample size upon which $\Pr_m$ is based is greater than that for $\Pr_o$ for any specific action. Apart from being more accurate, the use of $\Pr_m(t|s)$ can often give more informed value estimates at state s, since prior action models are generally "flat" or uniform, and only become distinguishable at a given state when the observer has sufficient experience at state s.

When the mentor's Markov chain is not ergodic, or even if the mixing rate is sufficiently low, the mentor may visit a certain state s relatively infrequently. A state that is rarely (or never) visited by the mentor may provide a very misleading estimate—based on the small sample or the prior for the mentor's chain—of the value of the mentor's (unknown) action at s; and since the mentor's policy is not under the control of the observer, this misleading value may persist for an extended period. This stems in part from the fact that we use maximization to combine values based on the estimates of the mentor's chain and the observer's action models, and in part because we use mean values (estimated probabilities) based on observed samples. The augmented Bellman equation does not consider the reliability of the information sources.

To overcome this, we have incorporated an estimate of model confidence into our augmented backups. For the mentor's Markov chain and the observer's action transitions, we assume a Dirichlet prior over the parameters of each of these multinomial distributions [7]. These reflect the observer's initial uncertainty about the possible transition probabilities. From sample counts of mentor and observer transitions, we update these distributions. With this information, we could attempt to perform an optimal Bayesian estimation of the value function; but when the sample counts are small (and normal approximations are not appropriate), there is no simple, closed form expression for the resultant distributions over values. We therefore employ an approximate method for combining information sources inspired by Kaelbling's interval estimation method [9].

We first compute the observer's optimal action a_o^* using a simple max over the mean value of the state given each possible action (The usual method). With the benefit of the Dirichlet distributions, we then construct a lower bound v_o^- on the value of the state to the observer using the model derived from its own behavior—this is the lower bound of a suitable confidence interval over the expected value of that state. A second lower bound v_m^- is constructed using the model based on observations of the mentor. If $v_m^- < v_o^-$, then either the mentor-inspired model has, in fact, a lower expected value (within a specified degree of confidence) and uses a nonoptimal action (from the observer's perspective), or the mentor-inspired model has lower confidence. In either case, we reject the information provided by the mentor and use the model derived from the observer's observations of itself. Using Tchebycheff's inequality, we can choose a confidence level even though the Dirichlet distributions for small sample counts are highly non-normal.

We note that the reasoning above holds even if the mentor is implementing a (stationary) stochastic policy (since the expected value of stochastic policy for a fully-observable MDP cannot be greater than that of an optimal deterministic policy). While the "direction" offered by a mentor implementing a deterministic policy tends to be more *focussed*, empirically we have found that mentors offer *broader* guidance in moderately stochastic environments or when they implement stochastic policies, since they tend to visit more of the state space. We note that the extension to multiple mentors is straightforward—each mentor model can be incorporated into the augmented Bellman equation without difficulty.

Though the model has assumed no action costs (i.e., rewards that depend only on the state), we can use more general reward functions (e.g., where reward has the form $R(s,a)$). The difficulty lies in backing up action costs when the mentor's chosen action is unknown. We use a simple heuristic method to find the action of the observer that is "closest" to that of the mentor (given current transition probability estimates) and then construct an estimate of the value of the state using the information derived from mentor transitions based on this action. Let $\kappa(s)$ denote that observer's action at state s that is "closest" to the action executed by the mentor at state s. This is defined as the action whose observed transition distribution has minimum Kullback-Leibler distance from the mentor's observed transition distribution:

$$\kappa(s) = \mathrm{argmin_a} \left\{ -\sum_{\mathrm{t}} \mathrm{Pr_o(t|s,a)} \log \mathrm{Pr_m(t|s)} \right\} \quad (3)$$

The augmented Bellman equation 2 can be rewritten using the κ function as follows:

$$\begin{aligned} V(s) \;=\; \max \Bigg\{ & \max_{a \in A_o} \left\{ R_o(s,a) + \gamma \sum_{t \in S} \mathrm{Pr}_o(t|s,a) V(t) \right\}, \\ & R_o(s,\kappa(s)) + \gamma \sum_{t \in S} \mathrm{Pr}_m(t|s) V(t) \Bigg\} \end{aligned}$$

We note that Bayesian methods could be used could be used to estimate action costs in the mentor's chain as well.

Our *model extraction algorithm* requires that: (a) the observer maintain an estimate $\widehat{\mathrm{Pr}}_m(t|s)$ of the Markov chain induced by the mentor's policy—this estimate is updated with every observed transition; and (b) that all backups performed to estimate its value function use the augmented backup Equation 2 with confidence testing.[4]

A second way in which an observer can exploit its observations of the mentor is to focus attention on the states visited by the mentor. In a model-based approach, the specific *focusing mechanism* we adopt requires the observer to perform a (possibly augmented) Bellman backup at state s whenever the mentor transitions out of s. This has three effects. If the mentor tends to visit interesting regions of space (e.g., if it shares a certain positive or negative reward structure with the observer in state s), the observer's attention is drawn there. More importantly, this focus of attention directs computational effort toward parts of state space where the estimated model $\widehat{\mathrm{Pr}}_m(t|s)$ changes, hence where the estimated value of one of the observer's actions may change. In addition, computation is focused where the model is likely more accurate (as discussed above).

3.2 Model Extraction in Specific RL Algorithms

Model extraction and the focusing mechanism described above can be integrated into model-based RL algorithms with relative ease. In the experiments described in the next section, *prioritized sweeping* is used [17]. Roughly, prioritized sweeping works by maintaining an estimated transition model $\widehat{Pr}$ and reward model $\widehat{R}$. Whenever an experience tuple $\langle s,a,r,t \rangle$ is sampled, the estimated model at state s can change; a Bellman backup is done at s to incorporate the revised model and some (usually fixed) number of additional backups are performed at selected states.

[4] Of course, these backups are implemented using estimated models $\widehat{\mathrm{Pr}}_o(t|s,a)$ and $\widehat{\mathrm{Pr}}_m(t|s)$.

States are selected using a *priority* that estimates the potential change in their values based on the changes precipitated by earlier backups (see [17] for details). Essentially, computational resources (backups) are focused on those states that can most "benefit" from those backups.

Incorporating our ideas into prioritized sweeping simply requires the following changes:

(a) With each transition $\langle s, a, t\rangle$ the observer takes, the estimated model $\widehat{\Pr}_o(t|s,a)$ is updated and an *augmented backup* (Equation 2) is performed at state s. Augmented backups are then performed at a fixed number of states using the usual priority queue implementation.

(b) With each observed mentor transition $\langle s, t\rangle$, the estimated model $\widehat{\Pr}_m(t|s)$ is updated and an augmented backup is performed at s. Augmented backups are then performed at a fixed number of states using the usual priority queue implementation.

The fact that augmented backups are used instead of standard Bellman backups implements model extraction, while the requirement that backups be performed at observed transitions (in addition to experienced transitions) incorporates our focusing mechanism. We can view this RL algorithm as embodying a form of *implicit imitation*. The observer is not forced to "follow" or otherwise mimic the actions of the mentor directly. But it does back up value information along the mentor's trajectory as if it had. Ultimately, the observer must move to those states to discover which actions are to be used; but in the meantime, important value information is being propagated that can guide its exploration (we discuss exploration in more detail below).

We note that the usual convergence results hold for prioritized sweeping (and other algorithms such as certainty equivalence) when model extraction is used. As the models converge, the augmentation of the Bellman equation becomes irrelevant. During initial phases of training, however, it can induce different exploratory and computational behavior in the observer, and in many instances faster convergence. In particular, as we will see below, this implicit imitation often causes the learner to obtain higher accumulated reward during the initial stages of learning.

While model extraction fits naturally with model-based RL methods, some of these ideas can be readily incorporated into model-free algorithms like Q-learning. For example, the observer could augment its Q-function with a "fictitious" action a_m—the action used by the mentor—and update the Q-values of a_m using mentor transitions (imposing its own R). When updating the Q-values of its own actions, the value of any state s would be estimated using the maximum Q-values of all actions, including a_m.

3.3 Action Selection

Exploration is a key part of any RL algorithm, and here we adopt ε-greedy action selection, using a decaying exploration rate ε over time. The following remarks apply equally well to other pseudo-greedy methods such as Boltzmann exploration.

When selecting an action at state s, greedy action selection requires that we choose the action with highest expected value (i.e., the a that maximizes $\sum_t \widehat{Pr}_o(t|s,a)V(t)$). When the mentor's policy dictates an especially appealing action at state s, it may well be that $\sum_t \widehat{Pr}_m(t|s)V(t)$ is greater than the value of any known action, in which case the observer is better off trying to duplicate the action of the mentor. Unfortunately, this action is unknown. Again, we define the "greedy action" for the observer to be that action a whose estimated distribution $\widehat{Pr}_o(t|s,a)$ has minimum Kullback-Leibler distance from $\widehat{Pr}_m(t|s)$. This proves especially effective early in training when value estimates based on actions with small samples vary widely, while confidence in the mentor's model is much higher.[5]

4 Empirical Validation

The following empirical tests report on the incorporation of model extraction and our focusing mechanism with prioritized sweeping. These results illustrate the types of problems and scenarios in which implicit imitation of this form can provide advantages to an RL agent. In each of the experiments, an expert "mentor" is introduced into the experiment to serve as a model for an "observer" agent. In each case, the mentor is following an ϵ-greedy policy with a very small ϵ (on the order of 0.01). This tends to cause the mentor's trajectories to lie within a "cluster" surrounding optimal trajectories (and reflect good if not optimal policies). Even with this (and environment stochasticity), mentors generally do not "cover" the entire state space so confidence testing is important.

In all of these experiments, prioritized sweeping is used with a fixed number of backups per observed or experienced sample.[6] ε-greedy exploration is used with decaying ε. Observer agents are given uniform Dirichlet priors. Observer agents are compared to control agents that do not benefit from a mentor's experience, but are otherwise identical (implementing prioritized sweeping with similar parameters and exploration policies). The tests are all performed on stochastic grid-world domains, since these make it clear

[5] It is easy to construct cases where the action a closest to the mentor's a_m has lower expected value than action b, while the expected value of a_m is greater than that of b. In such a case, it often makes sense to view a as a better (greedy) action than b. However, we recognize that, ultimately, confidence factors should be incorporated into such judgments as well, so that mentor models with relatively small sample sizes are not given such priority.

[6] Generally, the number of backups was set to be roughly equal to the length of the optimal "noise-free" path.

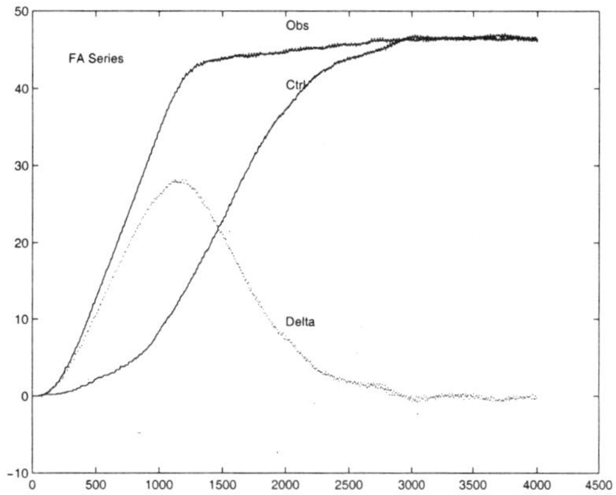

Figure 1: Basic Observer and Control Agent Comparisons

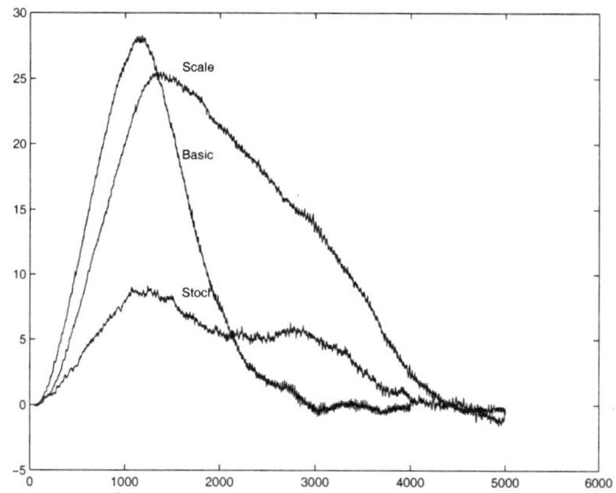

Figure 2: Influence of Domain Size and Noise

to what extent the observer's and mentor's optimal policies overlap (or fail to). We assume an eight-connectivity between cells so that any state in the grid has 9 neighbors including itself, but agent's use only the North, South, East and West actions. We focus primarily on whether imitation improves performance during learning, since the learner will converge to an optimal policy whether it uses imitation or not.

First we show a typical profile of an observer using model extraction (with an expert mentor) vs. a control agent which does not. Both agents attempt to learn a policy that maximizes discounted return on a 10x10 grid world. They start in the upper-left corner and seek a goal with value 1.0 in the lower corner. Upon reaching the goal, the agents are restarted at the top. Actions are noisy, resulting in an unintended transition 10% of the time. The discount factor is 0.9. In Figure 1 we plot the cumulative number of goals obtained over the previous 1000 time steps for the observer "Obs" and control "Ctrl" (results are averaged over 10 runs). The observer is able to quickly incorporate a policy learned from the mentor into its value estimates. This results in a steeper learning curve. In contrast, the control agent slowly explores the space to build a model first. The "Delta" curve shows the difference in performance between the agents. Both agents converge to the same optimal value function.

The next experiment illustrates the sensitivity of imitation to the size of the state space and action noise level. In Figure 2 we plot the delta curves for the "Basic" scenario just described, the "Scale" scenario in which the state space size is increased 69% 13x13, and the "Stoch" scenario in which the noise level is increased to 40% (results are averaged over 10 runs). The difference between the observer and the non-imitating prioritized sweeping agent increases with the state space size. This reflects Whitehead's observation for grid worlds that exploration needs can increase quickly with state space size, but that the optimal path length increases only linearly [25]. Here we see that the guidance of the mentor can help more in larger state spaces.

Increasing the noise reduces the observer's ability to act upon the information received from the mentor and therefore erodes its advantage over the control agent. We note, however, that the benefit of imitation degrades gracefully with increased noise and is present even at this relatively extreme noise level.

Sometimes the observer's prior beliefs about the transition probabilities of the mentor can mislead the observer and cause it to generate inappropriate values. The confidence mechanism proposed in the previous section can prevent the observer from being fooled by misleading priors on the mentor's transition probabilities. This experiment is based on the scenario illustrated in Figure 3. Again the agent's task is to navigate from the top-left corner to the bottom-right corner of a 10x10 grid in order to attain a reward of +1. We have created a pathological scenario in which islands of high value (+5) are enclosed by obstacles. Since the observer's priors reflect eight-connectivity and are uniform, the high-valued cell in the middle of each island are believed to be reachable from the states diagonally adjacent with some small prior probability. In reality, however, the agent's action set precludes this and the agent will therefore never be able to realize this value. The four islands in this scenario thus create a fairly large region in the center of the space with a high value which could potentially trap an observer.

To test, the confidence mechanism, the mentor follows a path around the outside of the obstacles so that its path cannot lead the observer out of the trap. The combination of a high initial exploration rate and the ability of prioritized sweeping to spread value across large distances then virtually guarantees that the observer will be "lead" to the trap. Given this scenario, we ran two observer agents and a control. The first observer used a confidence interval with width given by 5σ which according to the Tchebycheff rule should cover approximately 96 percent of an arbitrary distribution. The second observer was given a 0σ

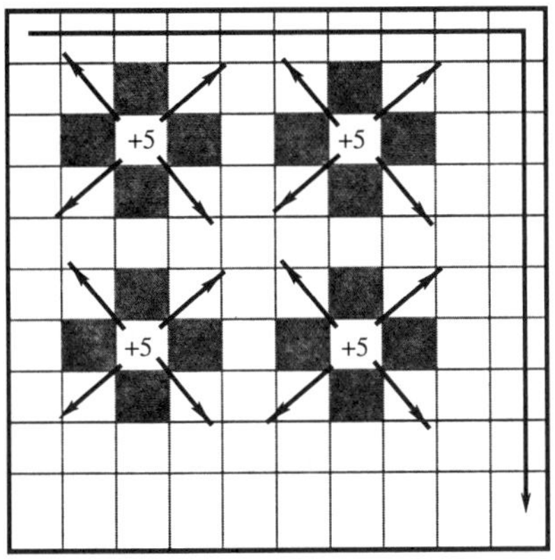

Figure 3: An Environment with Misleading Priors

Figure 5: A complex maze

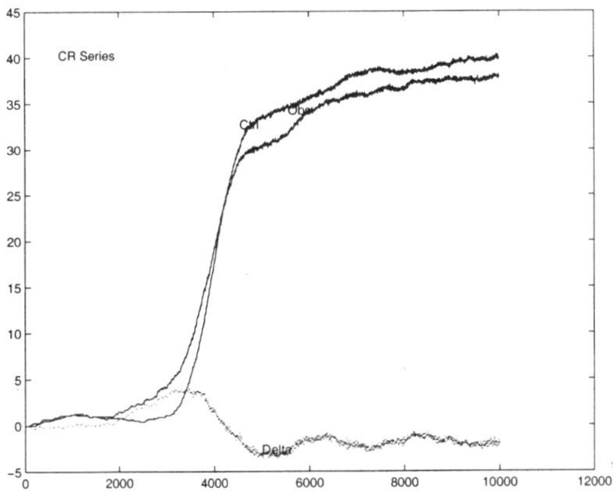

Figure 4: Misleading priors may degrade performance

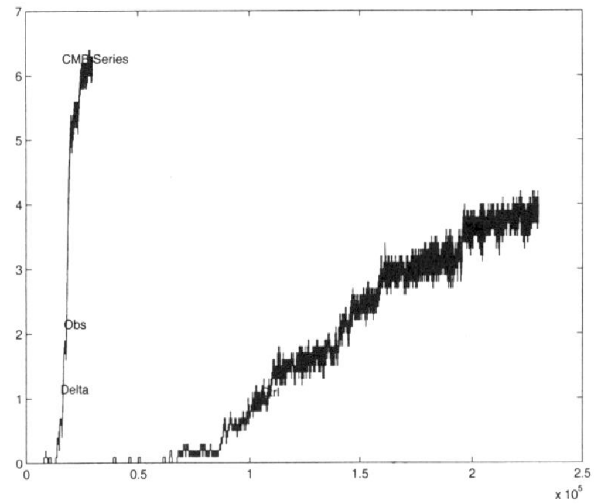

Figure 6: Imitation in a complex space

interval which effectively disables confidence testing. The observer with no confidence testing consistently became stuck. Examination of the value function revealed consistent peaks within the trap region and observation of the agent showed that it was stuck in the trap. The observer with confidence testing consistently escapes the trap. Observation of its value function over time shows that the trap forms, but fades away as the observer gains enough experience to throw out erroneous priors. In Figure 4, the performance of the observer with confidence testing is shown with the performance of the control agent (results are averaged over 10 runs). We see that the observer's performance is only slightly degraded from that of the unaugmented control agent even in this pathological case.

The next experiment demonstrates how the potential gains of imitation can increase with the (qualitative) difficulty of the problem. In the "maze" scenario we introduce obstacles in order to increase the difficulty of the learning problem. The maze is set on a 25x25 grid (Figure 5) with 286 obstacles complicating the agent's journey from the top-left to the bottom-right corner. The only solution takes the form of a snaking 133-step path, with distracting paths (up to length 22) branching off from the solution path necessitating frequent backtracking. The discount factor is 0.98. With 10% noise, the optimal goal-attainment rate is about 6 goals per 1000 steps.

From the graph in Figure 6 (with results averaged over 10 runs), we see that the control agent takes on the order of 150,000 steps to build a decent value function that reliably leads to the goal. At this point, it is only achieving 4 goals per 1000 steps on average as its exploration rate is still reasonably high (unfortunately, decreasing exploration more quickly does not lead to faster value function formation). The imitation agent is able to take advantage of the mentor's expertise to build a reliable value function in about 20,000 steps. Since the control agent has been unable to reach the goal at all in the first 20,000 steps, the delta between the control and the imitator is simply equal to the imitator's performance. The imitator can quickly achieve the optimal 6 goals per 1000 steps as its exploration rate decays much more quickly.

The augmented backup rule does not require that the reward

Figure 7: A maze with a perilous shortcut

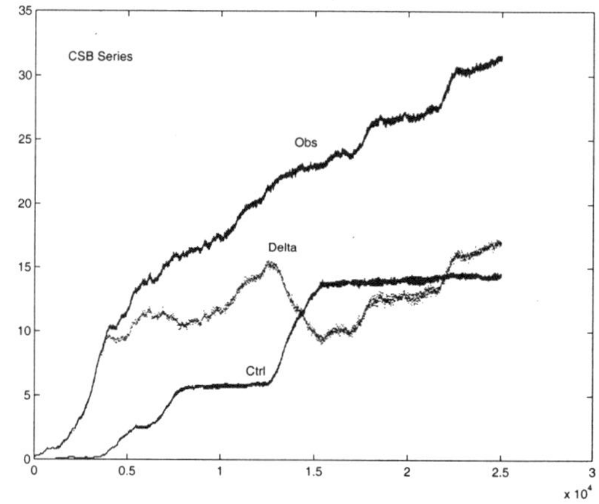

Figure 8: Transfer with non-identical rewards

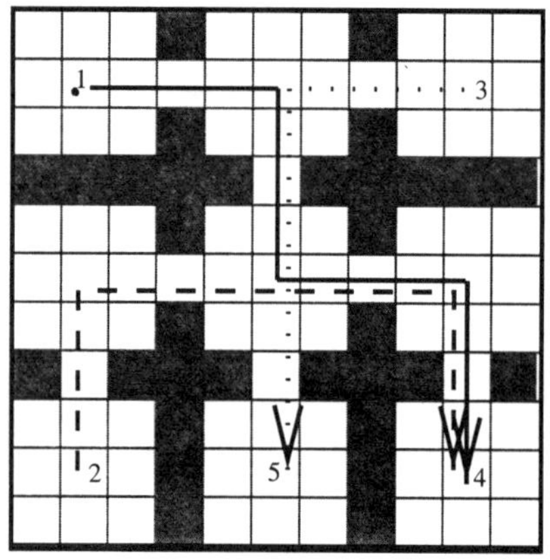

Figure 9: Multiple mentors scenario

structure of the mentor and observer be identical. There are many useful scenarios, where rewards are dissimilar but induce value functions and policies that share some structure. In this experiment, we demonstrate one interesting scenario in which it is comparatively easy to find a suboptimal solution, but difficult to find the optimal solution. Once the observer finds this suboptimal path, however, the observer agent is able to exploit its observations of the mentor to see that there is a shortcut that significantly shortens the path to the goal. The structure of the scenario can be seen in Figure 7. The suboptimal solution lies on the path from 1 around the scenic route at 2 to the goal at 3. The mentor takes the vertical path from 4 to 5 through the shortcut. To discourage the use of the shortcut by novice agents, it is lined with cells (marked "*") that jump back to the start state. It is therefore difficult for a novice agent executing many random exploratory moves to make it all the way to the end of the shortcut and obtain the value which would reinforce its future use. Both the observer and control therefore generally find the scenic route first.

In Figure 8, the performance (goals per 1000 steps) of the control and observer are compared (averaged over 10 runs), indicating the value of these observations. Observations show that the observer and control agent take about the same time on average to find the long scenic route to the goal, however, the observer instantly recognizes the shortcut and jumps to almost double the goal rate. This experiment shows that mentors can improve observer policies even when the observer's goals are not on the mentor's path.

The final experiment illustrates how model extraction can be readily extended so that the observer can extract models from multiple mentors and exploit the most valuable parts of each. In Figure 9, the learner must move from start location 1 to goal location 4. Two expert agents with different start and goal states serve as potential mentors. One mentor repeatedly moves from location 3 to location 5 along the dotted line, while a second mentor departs from location 2 and ends at location 4 along the dashed line. In this experiment, the observer must combine the information from the examples provided by the two mentors with independent exploration of its own in order to solve the problem.

In Figure 10, we see that the observer successfully pulls together these information sources in order to learn much more quickly than the control agent (results are averaged over 10 runs).

Though we have not explored this empirically, "negative" transfer can also be accommodated in our framework. Naturally, one might want an observer to learn about "negative" rewards. A mentor which is unsuccessful and ends up in a particularly bad state (from the observer's point of view) may nonetheless be profitable to study.

5 Concluding Remarks

5.1 Related Work

Imitation is a common strategy for information transfer in natural agents, from the octopus [8] to the primate, with many forms of imitation occurring in (and across) other

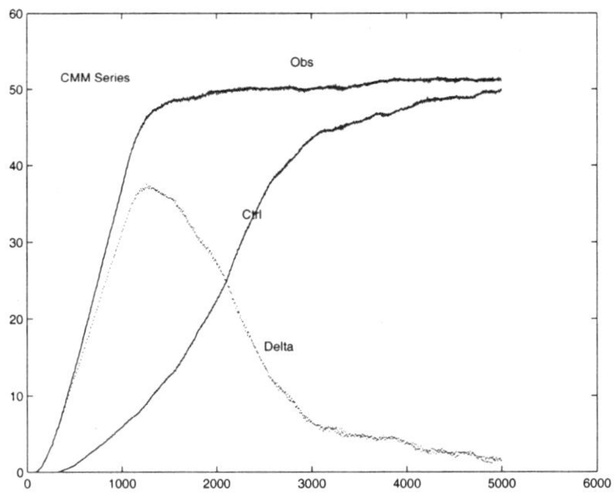

Figure 10: Learning from multiple mentors

species. Human imitation has been studied in contexts as varied as motor development and language acquisition [21]. Many researchers have considered imitation to be an important means of enhancing learning in multiagent systems [2, 4, 5, 13], and many interesting ideas have been pursued in the literature on imitation and teaching.

Much of this work relies on the observer *sharing* a common or similar (possibly perceptual) state with the mentor. In physical systems (e.g., mobile robots) this is often achieved by forcing the observer to follow the mentor [4, 5] or arranging for communication to occur when agents are in close proximity [13]. This can be viewed as ensuring both full observability of the mentor's state and resolving the "state analogy" problem. This approach is useful when partial observability is at issue, though it can be plagued by synchronization and alignment problems [3]. More principled approaches to partial observability should incorporate POMDP models (see below). The "action analogy" problem is addressed formally in [19], where an algebraic formulation of the implications of different abilities on the part of the mentor and observer is provided. We discuss this further below, but at present it is not clear how to use the specific formulation of [19] with RL.

Much work on imitation requires that the mentor directly communicate its intended action or reward, or provide some other feedback to the observer [4, 13, 25], or that complete state, reward and action information is directly accessible [11]. Research on explicit *teaching* or *demonstration* of behaviors includes work focused on abstract domains [11, 25] and on specific robotics tasks [1, 10, 16], where behaviors are learned by replicating observed human behaviors. This work relies on a cooperative relationship between the mentor and observer; in contrast, our model makes no such assumption. The middle ground—where a mentor must decide whether (and how) to facilitate the learning of another agent—should prove to be an interesting research topic. Tan [22] explores multiagent RL where agents share reward information and pool their perceptions—the focus is on accelerating learning. Knowledge transfer occurs through direct communication. While not imitation or teaching, this type of transfer could enhance imitative capabilities.

Work on "learning apprentices" [15, 18] can be seen as a form of learning by observation as well. The goal is to observe a human "mentor" and extract convenient rules of behavior to recommend to the mentor. This work differs from ours in that the observer is not attempting to solve its own decision problem, but is simply trying to improve the abilities of the mentor. Finally, some work has been done on using knowledge of other agent's decisions to place partial order constraints on the value function over states [23].

5.2 Possible Extensions of the Model

For our model to be more widely applied, a number of restrictive assumptions must be relaxed. We are currently exploring some of these. Though our agents have different reward structures, we have assumed that they have common state and action spaces. While requiring that the observer have the same abilities as the mentor is crucial to the simple augmented Bellman equation presented, it is often unrealistic. We are currently extending our algorithms to deal with agents with differing abilities, using methods that allow an observer to reason about how it can approximate a given mentor *trajectory* (rather than a specific action), and methods for reasoning about the similarity of the observer's actions to the observed mentor transition distribution at a given state. Preliminary work in model-free settings has shown remarkable transfer even when the mentor and observer have rather different actions at their disposal. We are also exploring the use of analogical mappings between state spaces to relax the assumption that the agents have a common state space. See [19] for more on such mappings.

We must also allow for partially observable models, especially with respect to the observer obtaining information about the true state (and trajectories) of the mentor. Our model can easily be extended to allow partial observability and we are currently tackling extensions of our model extraction algorithm in this framework. We hope to provide a principled approach to devising strategies that facilitate learning in this framework (in contrast to heuristics such as explicit following).

A more challenging extension would be the application of model extraction to models that allow interactions between the observer and the mentor. If both are self-interested, a game-theoretic model will be required to account for their strategic reasoning. An observer may need to account for the possibility of deception on the part of the mentor. Even in cooperative settings, issues such as coordination must be resolved. On the other hand, new opportunities for facilitation emerge (e.g., the mentor may alter the environment so that the observer can learn more readily, or learn in a risk-free environment).

Under the current modeling assumptions, other extensions of the algorithm can be explored. We are currently extending our explicit confidence measures in order to address reasoning about mentors with different abilities than the observer. More sophisticated exploration techniques [6, 14] can also exploit confidence factors such as these. Finally, we hope to explore generalization and value function approximation methods within this framework.

5.3 Summary

We have described a formal and principled approach to imitation called model extraction. For stochastic problems in which explicit forms of communication are not possible, the underlying model-based framework combined with model extraction provides an alternative to other imitation and learning-by-observation systems. We have shown model extraction to offer significant transfer capability on several test problems, where it proves to be robust in the face of noise, capable of integrating subskills from multiple mentors, and to provide benefits that increase with the difficulty of the problem. Our initial assumptions are somewhat restrictive—the observer and mentor have similar state and action spaces, for instance—but we are pursuing techniques that relax these.

Since model-extraction is a simple addition to model-based reinforcement learning we expect to be able to generalize the technique to many of the domains to which model-based techniques have been applied. Given its compact form and principled framework, we expect model extraction will be a sound basis on which to build a variety of algorithms for implicit forms of imitation.

Acknowledgements Thanks to the anonymous referees for their suggestions. Bob also thanks Gord McCalla for his early support of research into imitation. This research was supported by NSERC Research Grant OGP0121843, and IRIS Phase-III Project BAC.

References

[1] C. G. Atkeson and S. Schaal. Robot learning from demonstration. *ICML-97*, 1997.

[2] Paul Bakker and Yasuo Kuniyoshi. Robot see, robot do : An overview of robot imitation. *AISB96 Workshop on Learning in Robots and Animals*, pages 3–11, 1996.

[3] Aude Billard and Kerstin Dautenhahn. Grounding communication in autonomous robots: an experimental study. *Robotics and Autonomous Systems, Special Issue on Scientific Methods in Mobile Robotics, M. Recce and U. Nehmzow (eds.)*, 1-2(24):71–81, 1998.

[4] Aude Billard and Gillian Hayes. Learning to communicate through imitation in autonomous robots. *ICANN 97*, pages 763–68, 1997.

[5] Kerstin Dautenhahn. Getting to know each other – artificial social intelligence for autonomous robots. *Robotics and Autonomous Systems*, 16:333–356, 1995.

[6] R. Dearden, N. Friedman, and S. Russell. Bayesian Q-learning. In *AAAI-98*, pages 761–68. AAAI Press, 1998.

[7] M. H. Degroot. *Probability and Statistics*. Addison-Wesley, New York, 1986.

[8] G. Fiorito and P. Scotto. Observational learning in octopus vulgaris. *Science*, 256:545–47, 1992.

[9] Leslie Pack Kaelbling. *Learning in Embedded Systems*. MIT Press, Cambridge, 1993.

[10] Yasuo Kuniyoshi, Masayuki Inaba, and Hirochika Inoue. Learning by watching: Extracting reusable task knowledge from visual observation of human performance. *IEEE Transactions on Robotics and Automation*, 10(6):799–822, 1994.

[11] Long-Ji Lin. Self-improving reactive agents based on reinforcement learning, planning and teaching. *Machine Learning*, 8:293, 1992.

[12] Michael L. Littman. Markov games as a framework for multi-agent reinforcement learning. In *Proceedings of the Eleventh International Conference on Machine Learning*, pages 157–163, New Brunswick, NJ, 1994.

[13] Maja J. Mataric. Using communication to reduce locality in distributed multi-agent learning. *Journal of Experimental and Theoretical Artificial Intel.*, 10(3):357–369, 1998.

[14] Nicolas Meuleau and Paul Bourgine. Exploration of multi-state environments: Local measures and back-propagation of uncertainty. *Machine Learning*, 1998. to appear.

[15] T. M. Mitchell, S. Mahadevan, and L. Steinberg. LEAP: A learning apprentice for VLSI design. *IJCAI-85*, pages 573–580, 1985.

[16] H. Miyamoto, F. Gandolfo, H. Gomi, S. Schaal, Y. Koike, R. Osu, E. Nakano, Y. Wada, and M. Kawato. A kendama learning robot based on a dynamic optimization theory. *IEEE Int. Workshop on Robot and Human Comm.*, 1995.

[17] Andrew W. Moore and Christopher G. Atkeson. Prioritized sweeping: Reinforcement learning with less data and less real time. *Machine Learning*, 13, 1993.

[18] Hiroshi Motoda and Kenichi Yoshida. Machine learning techniques to make computers easier to use. *Artificial Intelligence*, 103(1-2):295–321, 1998.

[19] Chrystopher Nehaniv and Kerstin Dautenhahn. Mapping between dissimilar bodies: Affordances and the algebraic foundations of imitation. In *Proc. European Workshop on Learning Robots*, Edinburgh, 1998.

[20] L. S. Shapley. Stochastic games. *Proc. National Academy of Sciences*, 39:327–332, 1953.

[21] Gisela E. Speidel and Keith E. Nelson. *A Fresh Look at Imitation in Language Learning*, pages 1–19. Springer-Verlag, London, UK, 1989.

[22] Ming Tan. Multi-agent reinforcement learning: Independent vs. cooperative agents. *ICML-93*, pages 330–37, 1993.

[23] Paul E. Utgoff and Jeffrey A. Clouse. Two kinds of training information for evaluation function learning. *Proceedings of Ninth National Conference on Artificial Intelligence*, pages 596–600, 1991.

[24] C. J. C. H. Watkins and P. Dayan. Q-learning. *Machine Learning*, 8:279–292, 1992.

[25] Steven D. Whitehead. Complexity analysis of cooperative mechanisms in reinforcement learning. *AAAI-91*, pages 607–613, 1991.

Using Reinforcement Learning to Spider the Web Efficiently

Jason Rennie[†‡]
jrennie@justresearch.com

[†]School of Computer Science
Carnegie Mellon University
Pittsburgh, PA 15213

Andrew Kachites McCallum[‡†]
mccallum@justresearch.com

[‡]Just Research
4616 Henry Street
Pittsburgh, PA 15213

Abstract

Consider the task of exploring the Web in order to find pages of a particular kind or on a particular topic. This task arises in the construction of search engines and Web knowledge bases. This paper argues that the creation of efficient web spiders is best framed and solved by reinforcement learning, a branch of machine learning that concerns itself with optimal sequential decision making. One strength of reinforcement learning is that it provides a formalism for measuring the utility of actions that give benefit only in the future. We present an algorithm for learning a value function that maps hyperlinks to future discounted reward using a naive Bayes text classifier. Experiments on two real-world spidering tasks show a three-fold improvement in spidering efficiency over traditional breadth-first search, and up to a two-fold improvement over reinforcement learning with immediate reward only.

1 INTRODUCTION

Spiders are agents that explore the hyperlink graph of the Web, often for the purpose of finding documents with which to populate a search engine. As information extraction techniques improve, spiders are also becoming vital elements in the automated creation of Web-based knowledge bases.

Extensive spidering is the key to obtaining high coverage by the major Web search engines, such as AltaVista and HotBot. Since the goal of these general-purpose search engines is to provide search capabilities over the Web as a whole, they aim to find as many distinct web pages as possible. Such a goal lends itself to strategies like breadth-first search. If, on the other hand, the task is to find pages of a particular kind or on a particular topic (as is the case for the increasingly popular class of domain-specific search engines), then an intelligent spider should try to avoid hyperlinks that lead to off-topic areas, and concentrate on links that lead to documents of interest. Similarly, if the goal is to locate documents for use in populating a topic-specific knowledge base, much effort would be wasted by following every hyperlink that is found.

This paper describes our research in efficient, topic-directed web spidering. We argue that the creation of efficient web spiders is best framed and solved by reinforcement learning, a branch of machine learning that concerns itself with optimal sequential decision making. One strength of reinforcement learning is that it provides a formalism for measuring the utility of actions that give no immediate benefit, but do give benefit in the future. Reinforcement learning agents represent this delayed benefit by learning a mapping from each available action to a scalar value indicating the sum of future discounted rewards expected from executing that action. The "discount" makes later rewards less valuable than sooner rewards, thus encouraging efficiency.

In our current reinforcement learning spider, we learn a mapping from the text in the neighborhood of a hyperlink to the expected (discounted) number of relevant pages that can be found as a result of following that hyperlink. The mapping from the text to a scalar is performed by casting regression as classification [Torgo and Gama, 1997]. Specifically, we discretize the scalar values into a finite number of bins, and use naive Bayes to classify the text into a corresponding finite number of classes; the value assigned to a particular hyperlink is a weighted average of the values of the top-ranked bins.

Our research in efficient spidering is part of a larger project that has created Cora, a domain-specific search engine that indexes computer science research papers [McCallum *et al.*, 1999]. We have spidered computer science departments and labs, so far finding over 50,000 research papers in postscript format. Each of these papers is converted to plain text, then run through a specially-trained hidden Markov model to automatically find the title, authors, abstract, references, etc. Forward and backward references between papers are resolved. Finally, all this information is made available in a searchable, public web interface at *www.cora.justresearch.com.*

In Cora efficient spidering is a significant concern. The majority of the pages in many computer science department web sites do not contain links to research papers, but instead are about courses, homework, schedules and admissions information. Avoiding whole branches and neighborhoods of departmental web graphs can significantly improve efficiency and increase the number of research papers found given a finite amount of crawling time.

Our work is also driven by the WebKB project [Craven *et al.*, 1998]. Here the focus is on automatically populating a knowledge base with information that is available on the World Wide Web. The system is given an ontology consisting of object classes and relations of interest (*e.g.* company, location, CEO, is-located-in, is-officer-of), and also a training set consisting of labeled instances of these classes and relations (*e.g.* web pages labeled by class, and web page pairs labeled by relation). The system then aims to extract automatically new instances of these classes and relations from the Web. Before the system can extract such instances, it must locate the web documents containing the appropriate information. This is where spidering becomes important. By spidering efficiently we can increase the size of the attainable knowledge base in the face of ubiquitous limitations of time, computation and network-bandwidth. In this paper we spider to locate the Web page listing the chief executive officers of a company.

We report on experiments performed on data sets taken from both the Cora and WebKB domains. Our experiments show that reinforcement learning is a highly effective framework for the spidering problem. In both cases, reinforcement learning outperforms traditional spidering with breadth-first search by a factor of three or more. For both data sets, we find that explicitly modeling future reward provides significant benefit. The nature of the benefit depends somewhat on the context. In the case of Cora, where there are many reward-providing documents in each spidering run, modeling future reward provides benefit in the first half of the run only—before many hyperlinks leading to immediate reward have been discovered. In our WebKB task, however, each spidering run contains only a single reward document (as in common reinforcement-learning "goals of achievement"), and thus many decisions must be made based on future reward. As a result, our approach that explicitly models and predicts future reward can find the desired documents more efficiently. In our WebKB experiments, modeling future reward increases efficiency by a factor of two or more.

2 REINFORCEMENT LEARNING

The term "reinforcement learning" refers to a framework for learning optimal decision making from rewards or punishment [Kaelbling *et al.*, 1996]. It differs from supervised learning in that the learner is never told the correct action for a particular state, but is simply told how good or bad the selected action was, expressed in the form of a scalar "reward."

A task is defined by a set of states, $s \in \mathcal{S}$, a set of actions, $a \in \mathcal{A}$, a state-action transition function, $T : \mathcal{S} \times \mathcal{A} \to \mathcal{S}$, and a reward function, $R : \mathcal{S} \times \mathcal{A} \to \Re$. At each time step, the learner (also called the *agent*) selects an action, and then as a result is given a reward and its new state. The goal of reinforcement learning is to learn a *policy*, a mapping from states to actions, $\pi : \mathcal{S} \to \mathcal{A}$, that maximizes the sum of its reward over time. We use the infinite-horizon discounted model where reward over time is a geometrically discounted sum in which the discount, $0 \leq \gamma < 1$, devalues rewards received in the future. Accordingly, when following policy π, we can define the *value* of each state to be:

$$V^{\pi}(s) = \sum_{t=0}^{\infty} \gamma^t r_t, \qquad (1)$$

where r_t is the reward received t time steps after starting in state s and following policy π. The optimal policy, written $\pi^\star$, is the one that maximizes the value, $V^{\pi}(s)$, for all states s.

In order to learn the optimal policy, we learn its value function, $V^\star$, and its more specific correlate, called Q.

Let $Q^\star(s,a)$ be the value of selecting action a from state s, and thereafter following the optimal policy. This is expressed as:

$$Q^\star(s,a) = R(s,a) + \gamma V^\star(T(s,a)). \qquad (2)$$

We can now define the optimal policy in terms of Q by selecting from each state the action with the highest expected future reward: $\pi^\star(s) = \arg\max_a Q^\star(s,a)$. The seminal work by Bellman [1957] shows that the optimal policy can be found straightforwardly by dynamic programming.

2.1 SPIDERING AS REINFORCEMENT LEARNING

As an aid to understanding how reinforcement learning relates to spidering, consider the common reinforcement learning task of a mouse exploring a maze to find several pieces of cheese. The agent receives immediate reward for finding each piece of cheese, and has actions for moving among the grid squares of the maze. The state is both the position of the mouse and the locations of the cheese pieces remaining to be consumed (since the cheese can only be consumed and provide reward once). Note that the agent only receives immediate reward for finding a maze square containing cheese, but that in order to act optimally it must choose actions considering future rewards as well.

In the spidering task, the on-topic documents are immediate rewards, like the pieces of cheese. An action is following a particular hyperlink. The state is the set of on-topic documents remaining to be found, and the set of hyperlinks that have been discovered. The state does not include the current "position" (last page visited) of the agent since a crawler can jump to any known URL next. The number of available actions is large and dynamic, in that it depends on which documents the spider has visited so far. It is as if the mouse can leap to any square, as long as it has already visited a bordering square. The key feature of topic-specific spidering that makes reinforcement learning the proper framework is that the environment presents situations with delayed reward.

2.2 PRACTICAL APPROXIMATIONS

The problem now is how to apply reinforcement learning to spidering in such a way that it can be practically solved. Unfortunately, the state space is huge and difficult to generalize. It encapsulates not only the on-topic documents remaining to be found, but also the set of hyperlinks that are available as actions. It is not immediately apparent how one would construct a metric to compare different states. The action space can also be large: the number of distinct hyperlinks within the Web that we are considering.

We need to make some simplifying assumptions in order to make the problem tractable and to aid generalization. Note, however, that by first defining the exact solution in terms of the optimal policy, and making our assumptions explicit, we will better understand what inaccuracies we have introduced, and how to select areas of future work that will improve performance further. We make simplifying assumptions that: (1) disregard state and (2) capture the relevant distinctions between the actions using only the words in the "neighborhood"[1] of the corresponding hyperlink. By disregarding state, we generalize across all states and can determine a single Q-value for each action; by assigning a set of words to each hyperlink we can generalize across different hyperlinks by comparing the text around them.

Thus our Q function becomes a mapping from a "bag-of-words" to a scalar (discounted sum of future reward). Learning to perform efficient spidering then involves only two remaining sub-problems: (1) obtaining training data consisting of bag-of-words/Q-value pairs, and (2) learning a mapping using the training data. These are each described in the following two subsections.

2.3 OBTAINING TRAINING DATA AND CALCULATING Q-VALUES

There are several choices for how to gather training data. Although the agent could learn from experience on-line, we currently train the agent off-line, using collections of already-found documents and hyperlinks. For these training sets, we know the state transition functions, T, and the reward functions, R. With this knowledge, we can obtain bag-of-words/Q-value pairs and use these to estimate the Q-function for an unexplored portion of the Web.

Recall that the Q-value of a hyperlink is the discounted sum of rewards received by following the optimal policy after traversing the hyperlink in question. When calculating Q-values for tasks with a single goal and single reward, dynamic programming produces for

[1]Text that is related to the hyperlink in question, for example, the unordered list of words in the anchor, headers, and page title associated with the hyperlink.

each hyperlink a value equal to the reward, discounted by its distance to the goal. This calculation can be done directly without running full dynamic programming.

When there are many rewards, however, the process is more complicated. Rather than trying to fully represent the exponentially-sized state space and applying dynamic programming, we again aim to calculate the optimal sequence directly and set the Q-value to the discounted sum of this sequence. We calculate the optimal sequence directly by maintaining a "fringe" of hyperlinks available from all the pages in the sequence so far, and greedily traversing to the reward closest to the fringe. Initially, the fringe only contains the hyperlink whose Q-value we are currently calculating. Choosing among the fringe represents the fact that a spider is not required to select a hyperlink from among a last page visited, but can choose among any of the hyperlinks of which it is aware (*i.e.* the fringe). Note furthermore that the fringe in this calculation is based only on the pages reachable from the initial hyperlink; in practice at testing time, the agent will have already explored other hyperlinks, and will be able to "jump" to any of these.

To see why a greedy search is reasonable, consider assigning Q-values to two hyperlinks, A and B. A yields a reward of 1; B yields a reward of 0 and reveals a gold mine of hyperlinks, each of which gives a reward of 1. Imagine a spider that had only these two hyperlinks as possible actions. If it follows B first, its sequence of rewards would be $\{0, 1, 1, \ldots, 1\}$. Otherwise the rewards would be $\{1, 0, 1, \ldots, 1\}$. Since we value efficiency, A is the better choice. In fact, unlike many RL domains where moving towards immediate reward can take the agent further from a gold mine, here all alternative actions are available without futher cost, and it is always best to first follow a hyperlink that yields immediate reward. Thus, we choose a γ that mandates this policy (given a perfect Q-function predictor), $\gamma = 0.5$. This causes nearer rewards[2] to be more valuable and makes greedy search an appropriate way to determine an optimal action sequence.

2.4 MAPPING TEXT TO Q-VALUES

Given that we have calculated Q-values for hyperlinks in our training data, next we must learn a generalized value function that maps hyperlinks to scalar values. The mapping should be efficient, and should generalize to future, unseen hyperlinks.

We represent the value function using a collection of naive Bayes text classifiers, performing the mapping by casting this regression problem as classification [Torgo and Gama, 1997]. We discretize the discounted sum of future reward values of our training data into bins, place the text in the neighborhood of the hyperlinks into the bin corresponding to their Q-values, and use the hyperlinks' neighborhood text as training documents for a naive Bayes text classifier. For each new hyperlink that we find, naive Bayes yields a probabilistic class membership for each bin based on the neighborhood text for that hyperlink. The Q-value associated with each bin is set to the average of the Q-values associated with the training hyperlinks assigned to that bin. Then the value of a new hyperlink is estimated by taking a weighted average of each bin's Q-value, using the probabilistic class memberships as weights. This gives us a method for using naive Bayes as a function approximator.

We next introduce the naive Bayes text classifier. Approaching the task of text classification from a Bayesian learning framework, we assume that text data is generated by a parametric model, and use training data to calculate maximum a posteriori estimates of the model parameters. Equipped with these estimates, we classify new test documents using Bayes' rule to turn the generative model around and calculate the posterior probability that each class would have generated the test document in question. Classification is then the simple matter of selecting the most probable class given the document's words.

The classifier parameterizes each class separately with a document frequency and with word frequencies. Each class, c_j, has a document frequency relative to all other classes, written $\mathrm{P}(c_j)$. Each class is modeled by a multinomial over words. That is, for every word, w_t, in the vocabulary, V, $\mathrm{P}(w_t|c_j)$ indicates the frequency that the classifier expects word w_t to occur in documents in class c_j.

We represent a document, d_i, as an unordered collection of its words. To classify a new document with this model we make the naive Bayes assumption: the words in the document occur independently of each other given the class of the document, (and furthermore independently of position). Using this assumption, classification becomes straightforward. We calculate the probability of each class given the evidence of the document, $\mathrm{P}(c_j|d_i)$, and select the class for which this expression is the maximum. We write $w_{d_{ik}}$ for the

[2]Those obtainable through a shorter sequence of actions.

kth word in document d_i. We expand $P(c_j|d_i)$ with an application of Bayes' rule, and then make use of the word independence assumption:

$$\begin{aligned} P(c_j|d_i) &\propto P(c_j)P(d_i|c_j) \\ &\approx P(c_j)\prod_{k=1}^{|d_i|} P(w_{d_{ik}}|c_j). \end{aligned} \quad (3)$$

Learning these parameters ($P(c_j)$ and $P(w_t|c_j)$) for classification is accomplished using a set of labeled training documents, $\mathcal{D}$. To estimate the word probability parameters, $P(w_t|c_j)$, we count over all word occurrences for class c_j the frequency that w_t occurs in documents from that class. We supplement this with Laplace 'smoothing' that primes each estimate with a count of one to avoid probabilities of zero. Define $N(w_t, d_i)$ to be the count of the number of times word w_t occurs in document d_i, and define $P(c_j|d_i) \in \{0, 1\}$, as given by the document's class label. Then, the estimate of the probability of word w_t in class c_j is:

$$P(w_t|c_j) = \frac{1 + \sum_{d_i \in \mathcal{D}} N(w_t, d_i)P(c_j|d_i)}{|V| + \sum_{s=1}^{|V|} \sum_{d_i \in \mathcal{D}} N(w_s, d_i)P(c_j|d_i)}. \quad (4)$$

The class frequency parameters are set in the same way, where $|\mathcal{C}|$ indicates the number of classes:

$$P(c_j) = \frac{1 + \sum_{d_i \in \mathcal{D}} P(c_j|d_i)}{|\mathcal{C}| + |\mathcal{D}|}. \quad (5)$$

Empirically, when given a large number of training documents, naive Bayes does a good job of classifying text documents [Lewis, 1998]. More complete presentations of naive Bayes for text classification are provided by Mitchell [1997] and McCallum and Nigam [1998].

3 EXPERIMENTAL SETUP

In August 1998 we completely mapped the documents and hyperlinks of the web sites of computer science departments at Brown University, Cornell University, University of Pittsburgh and University of Texas. This comprises our Cora data set; it includes 53,012 documents and 592,216 hyperlinks. The 2,263 target pages (for which a reward of 1 is given) are computer science research papers. They are identified with very high precision by a hand-coded algorithm that checks for abstract and reference sections. In this dataset we define a hyperlink's neighborhood text to be two bags-of-words with separate vocabularies: (1) the full text of the page on which the hyperlink is located, and (2) the anchor text of the hyperlink and portions of the URL.

Our WebKB data set includes 6,643 web pages, the complete web sites of 26 companies. These companies were selected randomly from a pool of over 1000 companies in a WebKB knowledge base. Here, the target page is one that includes information about officers and directors of the company. One such page was located by hand for each company, thus giving us a total of 26 target pages. In this data set we define neighborhood text as four bags-of-words with separate vocabularies: (1) headers and title words, (2) the anchor text of the hyperlink, (3) directories and filenames in the URL of the hyperlink, and (4) a small set of words immediately before and after the hyperlink.

One should note that our choices of neighborhood text were hand selected and were not learned in any way. In ongoing work we are performing experiments to compare different "neighborhood text" representations on both data sets.

An advantage of choosing these two data sets is that they have extremely different properties. For Cora, the task is to find a large number of target pages in a single spidering run, and many rewards may be found connected to the same web page. Thus accurately identifying immediate rewards is very important. Each WebKB graph, on the other hand, contains only a single target page. In order to locate this single reward, the spider must traverse a path of hyperlinks. Along this path, the spider must compare the Q-values of many hyperlinks; thus, distinguishing future reward is very important.

For each experiment that we describe, we perform a series of runs, one for each department or company in the data set. The spider is trained using data from all other departments or companies and is tested on the Web of the remaining one. For comparison, we also present the results of two spiders that use no form of learning. The Breadth-First spider follows hyperlinks in the order it finds them using a FIFO action queue. The Optimal spider has full knowledge of the spidering graph and always follows the path to the nearest reward.

The RL Immediate spider uses binary classification for regression. One bin includes all hyperlinks with a Q-value of 1 (those hyperlinks that point directly at target pages). The second bin includes all other hyperlinks. If our Q-value approximator were perfect, this spider would perform breadth-first search until it found a hyperlink that points directly to a target page. Note, however, that probabilistic classification provides intermediate values for text that could be in either class. This is a weaker form of regression for representing future reward than a multi-binned classifier; the estimated value of a future reward hyperlink will only be high if it shares features with immediate-reward hyperlinks.

The RL Future spider uses future reward as described in section 2.3, and performs regression by classifying into three or more bins—one or more for varying amounts of future reward. We experimented with between three and five bins. For example, our four-bin classifier maps immediate-reward ($Q = 1$) hyperlinks into one bin, hyperlinks with $1 > Q \geq \gamma$ into a second bin, hyperlinks with $\gamma > Q \geq \gamma^2$ into a third bin, and all remaining hyperlinks ($\gamma^2 > Q$) into a fourth bin.

The main difference between RL Immediate and RL Future is that RL Future has one or more bins for representing future reward hyperlinks. For example, in our three-bin RL Future spider, the second bin represents hyperlinks that point to a web page with immediate-reward hyperlinks. On the other hand, RL Immediate only distinguishes immediate-reward hyperlinks from all other hyperlinks.

4 RESULTS

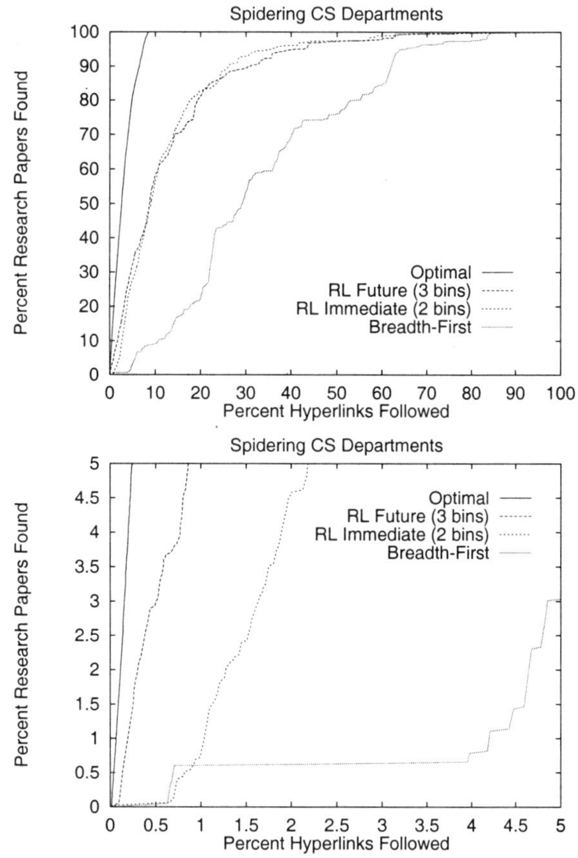

Figure 1: **(Top)** A comparison of spiders on the Cora dataset with results averaged over the four departments. The reinforcement learning spiders retrieve three-quarters of the research papers in one-third the page expansions that Breadth-First requires. Note that the spider with future reward knowledge performs particularly well in the early stages, when such knowledge is most important. **(Bottom)** A closeup near the origin of (Top).

Figure 1 (Top) shows results from our different spiders on the Cora data set. Notice that at all times during their progress, the reinforcement learning spiders have found more research papers than Breadth-first. One measure of performance is the number of hyperlinks followed before 75% of the research papers are found. Reinforcement learning performs significantly more efficiently, requiring exploration of only 16% of the hyperlinks; in comparison Breadth-first requires 48%. This represents a factor of three increase in spidering efficiency.

Note also that the RL Future spider performs better than the RL Immediate spider in the beginning, when future reward must be used to correctly select among alternative branches, none of which give immediate reward. RL Future locates up to 40% of the target documents more quickly. This early period is important because many applications of spidering require that only a sample of all target pages are retrieved. Figure 1 (Bottom) shows a closeup of the early part of the run. On average RL Future takes significantly less than half the time as RL Immediate to find the first 28 (5%) of the papers—efficiently avoiding an average of 700 extra page downloads that are performed by RL Immediate.

In Figure 1, after the first 40% of the papers are found, the RL Immediate spider performs slightly better than the RL Future spider. This is because the system has uncovered many links that will give immediate reward if followed, and the RL Immediate spider recognizes them more accurately. On average, RL Immediate is able to identify immediate reward links with 95% precision, while three-bin RL Future only achieves 88% precision. We believe this drop in precision is due to the added difficultly of classifying hyperlinks into

Table 1: Spidering performance on WebKB data.

SPIDER	PCT LINKS FOLLOWED
Optimal	3%
RL Future (4 bins)	13%
RL Future (3 bins)	22%
RL Future (5 bins)	27%
RL Immediate	27%
Breadth-First	38%

three classes instead of only two. In ongoing work we are investigating techniques for improving classification with the larger number of bins required for regression with future reward. We believe that through appropriate selection of neighborhood text and other improvements to the naive Bayes classifier, we can create a spider that overcomes this tradeoff and always outperforms the RL Immediate spider.

We now turn to the WebKB data set, where reward is much more sparse, and we expect future reward to be more important. Table 1 shows the results of different spiders on the WebKB data. As hoped, a spider that uses distinctions among future reward achieves the best results by far. On average, the four-bin RL Future spider is able to locate the officer page after traversing only 13% of the hyperlinks within the company. This is twice as efficient as RL Immediate, which follows an average of 27% of the hyperlinks before locating the target page. In further contrast, Breadth-First follows an average of 38% of the hyperlinks before finding each officers page.

Note also that the four-bin classifier performs better than the three-bin. There is a tradeoff, however, between the flexibility of the classifier-regressor and classification accuracy. Experiments with a five-bin classifier result in worse performance—roughly equivalent to the RL Immediate spider, following an average of 27% of available hyperlinks before locating the target page. Better features and other methods for improving classifier accuracy (such as shrinkage [McCallum *et al.*, 1998]) should allow the more sensitive multi-bin classifier to work better.

In order to provide a window into successful four-bin classification for the value function, Table 2 shows the ten most predictive words per class (ranked by weighted log-odds ratio) for the four-bin RL Future spider[3] The column at the top ("immediate") refers to the class containing immediate rewards; the column at the bottom ("other") refers to the class representing the least amount of reward. The parenthesized label indicates in which part of the hyperlink neighborhood each word was found[4].

Table 2: Most predictive words for RL Future (4 bins)

$Q = 1$ IMMEDIATE	
board (url)	corpinfo (url)
information (url)	executive (link)
directors (link)	team (link)
beckman (url)	board (link)
anrpt (url)	management (link)
$1 < Q \leq 0.5$ TWO-STEP	
aboutbb (url)	corp (url)
bb (link)	inc (head)
annual (url)	annual (head)
about (link)	report (head)
nbsp (near)	inside (url)
$0.5 < Q \leq 0.25$ THREE-STEP	
applications (url)	siteindex (url)
aerial (head)	employment (url)
burr (head)	position (head)
brown (head)	open (head)
sales (url)	administration (head)
$0.25 < Q \leq 0$ OTHER	
clp (url)	and (near)
elk (url)	region (head)
doc (url)	to (near)
elk (head)	nbsp (near)
datasheet (url)	sl (url)

Note that predictive words in the "immediate" class are directly relevant to a page that lists officers and directors of a company. We can induce from the "two-step" class that annual reports and "about" pages commonly include hyperlinks to a listing of company officers. The "three-step" class includes words concerning employment and product releases. It is common to include a link to the annual report on such pages.

[3] "aerial," "beckman," "burr," and "brown" are company names in our data.

[4] "Url" refers to text in the URL. "Head" indicates header and title words. "Link" refers to anchor text. "Near" indicates text found shortly before or after the hyperlink.

5 RELATED WORK

Several other studies have also researched spidering, but without a framework defining optimal behavior. ARACHNID [Menczer, 1997] is a system that uses a collection of agents for finding information on the Web. Each agent competes for limited computational resources, procreating and mutating proportionally to its success in finding relevant documents. Information gathering experiments are demonstrated on the Encyclopedia Britannica Propaidia tree and synthetic data. By contrast, our spider has roots in optimal decision theory, and searches unstructured pages from the real Web.

Cho *et al.* [1998] introduce a heuristic metric, PageRank, for valuing a web page based on its linkage properties. They show that PageRank is an effective spidering metric for locating pages with high PageRank counts or back link counts. However, these metrics perform poorly when the task is to locate pages that are relevant to a particular topic or query. Our research focuses on exactly that aspect: creating a framework to locate web documents that are related to a particular topic.

Additionally, there are systems that use reinforcement learning for non-spidering Web tasks. WebWatcher [Joachims *et al.*, 1997] is a browsing assistant that helps a user find information by recommending which hyperlinks to choose. It thus restricts its action space to only hyperlinks from the current page. WebWatcher uses a combination of supervised and reinforcement learning to learn the value of each word on a hyperlink. Our work is not user-centric and strives to find a method for learning an optimal decision policy for locating relevant documents when hyperlink selection is unlimited.

Laser [Boyan *et al.*, 1996] is a search engine that automatically optimizes a number of parameters to achieve improved retrieval performance. The CMU CS Web is used as the test bed and evaluation is based on the user's selection of links presented by Laser. The work finds that incorporating HTML markup into the TFIDF weighting scheme improves retrieval performance. Utilizing such markup may also be effective for further improving spidering performance.

6 CONCLUSIONS

Our results provide strong evidence that reinforcement learning is an excellent framework within which to perform Web spidering. Experimental results on two data sets show a three-fold improvement in spidering efficiency over traditional breadth-first search. We find that modeling future reward is particularly important when reward is sparse. This occurs in two important problem classes: (1) when the spider is trying to locate one or a proportionately small number of target pages in a large web graph (*e.g.* WebKB), or (2), when the spider is in the first half of a run in which there are many target pages (*e.g.* Cora). In these cases, explicitly modeling future reward provides a two-fold increase in efficiency.

Several areas of future work have already been mentioned. In particular, we are currently improving the classifier accuracy so that RL-Future out-performs the immediate spider even in cases with dense immediate rewards. Additionally, we plan to investigate other value function criteria that relax some of our current assumptions.

Acknowledgements

We thank Kamal Nigam, Kristie Seymore and Mark Craven for their insightful discussions and their feedback on earlier drafts.

References

[Bellman, 1957] R. E. Bellman. *Dynamic Programming.* Princeton University Press, Princeton, NJ, 1957.

[Boyan *et al.*, 1996] Justin Boyan, Dayne Freitag, and Thorsten Joachims. A machine learning architecture for optimizing web search engines. In *AAAI workshop on Internet-Based Information Systems*, 1996.

[Cho *et al.*, 1998] Junhoo Cho, Hector Garcia-Molina, and Lawrence Page. Efficient crawling through URL ordering. In *Computer Networks and ISDN Systems (WWW7)*, volume 30, 1998.

[Craven *et al.*, 1998] Mark Craven, Dan DiPasquo, Dayne Freitag, Andrew McCallum, Tom Mitchell, Kamal Nigam, and Sean Slattery. Learning to extract symbolic knowledge from the world wide web. In *Proceedings of 15th National Conference on Artificial Intelligence (AAAI-98)*, 1998.

[Joachims *et al.*, 1997] T. Joachims, D. Freitag, and T. Mitchell. Webwatcher: A tour guide for the World Wide Web. In *Proceedings of IJCAI-97*, 1997.

[Kaelbling *et al.*, 1996] Leslie Pack Kaelbling, Michael L. Littman, and Andrew W. Moore. Reinforcement learning: A survey. *Journal of Artificial Intelligence Research*, pages 237–285, May 1996.

[Lewis, 1998] David D. Lewis. Naive (Bayes) at forty: The independence assumption in information retrieval. In *ECML-98*, 1998.

[McCallum and Nigam, 1998] Andrew McCallum and Kamal Nigam. A comparison of event models for naive Bayes text classification. In *AAAI-98 Workshop on Learning for Text Categorization*, 1998. http://www.cs.cmu.edu/~mccallum.

[McCallum *et al.*, 1998] Andrew McCallum, Ronald Rosenfeld, Tom Mitchell, and Andrew Ng. Improving text clasification by shrinkage in a hierarchy of classes. In *ICML-98*, pages 359–367, 1998.

[McCallum *et al.*, 1999] Andrew McCallum, Kamal Nigam, Jason Rennie, and Kristie Seymore. Building domain-specific search engines with machine learning techniques. In *AAAI-99 Spring Symposium on Intelligent Agents in Cyberspace*, 1999. http://www.cs.cmu.edu/~mccallum.

[Menczer, 1997] Filippo Menczer. ARACHNID: Adaptive retrieval agents choosing heuristic neighborhoods for information discovery. In *ICML '97*, 1997.

[Mitchell, 1997] Tom M. Mitchell. *Machine Learning.* McGraw-Hill, New York, 1997.

[Torgo and Gama, 1997] Luis Torgo and Joao Gama. Regression using classification algorithms. *Intelligent Data Analysis*, 1(4), 1997.

Attribute dependencies, understandability and split selection in tree based models

Marko Robnik - Šikonja and Igor Kononenko
University of Ljubljana,
Faculty of Computer and Information Science,
Tržaška 25, 1001 Ljubljana, Slovenia,
Marko.Robnik@fri.uni-lj.si Igor.Kononenko@fri.uni-lj.si

Abstract

The attributes' interdependencies have strong effect on understandability of tree based models. If strong dependencies between the attributes are not recognized and these attributes are not used as splits near the root of the tree this causes node replications in lower levels of the tree, blurs the description of dependencies and also might cause drop of accuracy. If Relief family of algorithms which is capable of estimating the attributes' dependencies is used for split selectors we can partly overcome the problem. However, typically we still want to optimize accuracy of the tree and therefore use accuracy as the split selector measure near the fringe of the tree. We present a technique which helps us select a split criterion during tree growing based on some theoretical properties of Relief's estimate. We support our claims with empirical results.

1 Introduction

The problem of estimating the quality of attributes (features) is an important issue in machine learning and has received much attention in the literature. There are several measures for estimating the attribute's quality. If the target concept is a discrete variable (classification problem) these are e.g., information gain (Hunt et al., 1966), Gini index (Breiman et al., 1984), distance measure (Mantaras, 1989), j-measure (Smyth and Goodman, 1990), Relief (Kira and Rendell, 1992), ReliefF (Kononenko, 1994), MDL (Kononenko, 1995), Contextual Merit (Hong, 1997), and also χ^2 and G statistics are used. If the target concept is presented as a real valued function (continuous class, regression problem) then the estimation heuristics are e.g., the mean squared and the mean absolute error (Breiman et al., 1984) and RReliefF (Robnik Šikonja and Kononenko, 1997). There are several important tasks in the process of machine learning, e.g., feature selection, constructive induction, decision and regression tree building, which contain attribute estimation procedure as their (crucial) ingredient.

Most of the heuristic measures for estimating the quality of the attributes assume the independence of the attributes and indeed the experimental results (Kononenko et al., 1997) indicate that this myopia has no or only marginal effect on the majority of real world problems. However when we face a new problem it is unreasonable to try only these restricted measures unless we know in advance that there are no strong conditional dependencies between the attributes. Relief algorithms (Relief, ReliefF and RReliefF) do not make this assumption and are non-myopic in this sense. They are aware of the contextual information, efficient and can correctly estimate the quality of attributes in problems with strong dependencies between the attributes as well. While Relief algorithms have commonly been viewed as a feature selection methods that are applied in a preprocessing step before the model is learned (Kira and Rendell, 1992) and are one of the most successful preprocessing algorithms to date (Wettschereck et al., 1997; Dietterich, 1997), they are actually general feature estimators and have been used successfully in a variety of settings: to select splits in the building phase of decision tree learning (Kononenko et al., 1997), to select splits and guide the constructive induction in learning of the regression trees (Robnik Šikonja and Kononenko, 1997), as attribute weighting method in instance based learning (Wettschereck et al., 1997), and also in inductive logic programming (Pompe and Kononenko, 1995).

Decision and regression trees are popular description languages for representing knowledge in machine learning. While constructing a tree, a learning algorithm at each interior node selects a splitting rule (a feature) which divides the problem space into two separate subspaces. To select the appropriate splitting rule the learning algorithm has to evaluate several possibilities and decide which would partition the given (sub)problem most appropriately. The estimation of the quality of splitting rules seems to be of principal importance.

The focus of this paper is on the effect the attributes' interdependencies have on the understandability of decision and regression trees. Impurity based measures try to select as pure splits as possible i.e., separate instances with different class values into different subtrees. Strong dependencies between the attributes are not properly detected by these measures, therefore dependent attributes are not selected as splits near the root of the tree which would guarantee compact representation of dependencies. Instead they are selected in subsequent levels of the tree, mostly near the fringe (if at all) which causes node replication, blurs the description of dependencies and also might cause drop of accuracy.

One possible solution to this is to use multivariate splits (Brodley and Utgoff, 1995) but this can be computationally expensive. Another solution to this problem is to use non-myopic attribute estimator as split selection heuristics. ReliefF was used for that purpose within a decision trees learning system (Kononenko et al., 1997) and achieved significantly better results in terms of accuracy and complexity of decision trees in domains with highly dependent features compared to impurity based measures. It achieved the same performance in domains with independent features. RReliefF was used as split selector in regression tree learning system and also achieved better results in terms of error and complexity of the tree compared to the mean squared error (Robnik Šikonja and Kononenko, 1997). The tree structure chosen by Relief algorithms is closer to human partition of the problem and improves on the understandability and extracted knowledge (Kononenko et al., 1997; Dalaka et al., 1999).

Additional difficulty lies in the fact that if we want to improve accuracy we have to take into consideration that test nodes closer to the leaves of the tree should be chosen to maximize accuracy on the training set. This effect was investigated by (Brodley, 1995; Lubinsky, 1995) and showed empirically that this can improve classification accuracy, however the authors were working with myopic split selection measures and could not detect and address the effect the attribute dependencies have on the structure of the tree.

In this paper we are trying to look at both problems from the same point of view and to suggest some heuristic measures which would help us to automate the selection of the appropriate split.

In the next Section we describe the problem of attribute dependencies, explain how Relief algorithms detect these dependencies and establish relation between Relief's estimations and myopic measures. Section 3 describes how these relation can be used to determine when to switch from Relief to accuracy as split selection measure, and Section 4 describes empirical evaluation of our method. The last Section summarizes and gives guidelines for further work.

2 Attribute dependencies

When we are talking about attribute dependencies in this paper we have in mind the conditional dependencies (conditioned upon class values). Let us illustrate by three examples defined in Boolean space.

1. Let class value be defined as XOR (parity) of two attributes $C = X_1 \oplus X_2$. Knowing the values of the class and one of the attribute we have all the information about the other attribute, while the knowledge of the class value alone does not contain any information about the attributes' values. In this case we can say that X_1 and X_2 are (maximally) conditionally dependent.

2. Let class value be defined as conjunction of two attributes $C = X_1 \wedge X_2$. The knowledge about the class and one of the attributes is sometimes enough to determine the value of the other attribute (e.g., if $C = 0$ and $X_1 = 1$, the value of X_2 must be 0) but not always (e.g., if $C = 0$ and $X_1 = 0$, the value of X_2 is still undetermined), while the class value alone contains even less information (e.g., if $C = 0$ we cannot determine the values of X_1 and X_2). We can say that X_1 and X_2 are somehow conditionally dependent.

3. Let class be an arbitrary non-constant Boolean function, both values of the attributes are equiprobable ($P(X_1 = 1) = P(X_2 = 1) = 0.5$) and attributes are defined as $P(X_1 = 1|C = 1) = p$, $P(X_1 = 1|C = 0) = 1 - p$ and $P(X_2 = 1|C = 1) = q$, $P(X_2 = 1|C = 0) = 1 - q$. Each attribute contains some knowledge about the class value, but they contain this knowledge independently from each other. The knowledge of the class value conveys certain information about values of each of attribute, but this information does not increase even if we know the value of one of the attributes. So in this case we can say that X_1 and X_2 are conditionally independent. Another example of conditional independence are random attributes.

Relief algorithms estimate the quality of attributes in problems with strong dependencies between the attributes. How do they do that? The basic Relief algorithm (Kira and Rendell, 1992) is presented on Figure 1 and shortly described below.

The key idea is to estimate the quality of attributes according to how well their values distinguish between the instances that are near to each other. For that purpose, given a randomly selected instance R (line 3), Relief searches for its two nearest neighbors: one from the same class, called *nearest hit* H, and the other from a different class, called *nearest miss* M (line 4). It updates the quality estimation $W[A]$ for all the attributes A depending on their values for R, M, and H (lines 5 and 6). If the values of attribute A at instances R and H are different then attribute A separates two instances of the same class which is not desirable so we add negative update to the quality estimation $W[A]$. If the values of attribute A at instances R and M are different then attribute A separates two instances with different class values which is desirable so we add positive update to the quality estimation $W[A]$. The process is repeated for m times, where m is a user-defined parameter. Function $diff(Attribute, Instance1, Instance2)$ calculates the difference between the values of Attribute for two instances. For discrete attributes it was originally defined as:

$$diff(A, I_1, I_2) = \begin{cases} 0 & ; value(A, I_1) = value(A, I_2) \\ 1 & ; otherwise \end{cases} \qquad (1)$$

and for continuous attributes as:

$$diff(A, I_1, I_2) = \frac{|value(A, I_1) - value(A, I_2)|}{max(A) - min(A)} \qquad (2)$$

The function $diff$ is used also for calculating the distance between instances to find the nearest neighbors. The total distance is the sum of distances over all attributes.

Relief's estimate $W[A]$ of the quality of attribute A is an approximation of the following difference of probabilities (Kononenko, 1994):

$$W[A] =$$
$$P(\text{diff. value of A}|\text{nearest inst. from diff. class})$$
$$-P(\text{diff. value of A}|\text{nearest inst. from same class}) \qquad (3)$$

The original Relief can deal with discrete and continuous attributes. However, it can not deal with incomplete data and is limited to two-class problems. Its extension which solves these and some other problems is called ReliefF (Kononenko, 1994). One of the differences interesting for our paper is that ReliefF uses several nearest neighbors in the approximation of probabilities. The adaptation of ReliefF for regressional problems (continuous class) is called RReliefF (Robnik Šikonja and Kononenko, 1997).

The estimations of Relief algorithms are strongly related to impurity functions (Kononenko, 1994). As this relation is the basis for this paper we will repeat it below. When the number of nearest neighbors increases i.e., when we eliminate the requirement that the selected instance is the nearest, the Equation (3) becomes

$$\begin{aligned} W'[A] &= P(\text{different value of A}|\text{different class}) \\ &- P(\text{different value of A}|\text{same class}) \end{aligned} \qquad (4)$$

If we rewrite

$$P_{eqval} = P(\text{equal value of A})$$

$$P_{samecl} = P(\text{same class})$$

$$P_{samecl|eqval} = P(\text{same class}|\text{equal value of A})$$

we obtain using Bayes' rule:

$$W'[A] = \frac{P_{samecl|eqval} P_{eqval}}{P_{samecl}} - \frac{(1 - P_{samecl|eqval}) P_{eqval}}{1 - P_{samecl}}$$

For sampling with replacement in strict sense the following equalities hold:

$$P_{samecl} = \sum_C P(C)^2$$

$$P_{samecl|eqval} = \sum_V \left(\frac{P(V)^2}{\sum_V P(V)^2} \times \sum_C P(C|V)^2 \right)$$

Using the above equalities we obtain:

$$W'[A] = \frac{P_{eqval} \times Ginigain'(A)}{P_{samecl}(1 - P_{samecl})} \qquad (5)$$

where

$$\begin{aligned} Ginigain'(A) &= \sum_V \left(\frac{P(V)^2}{\sum_V P(V)^2} \times \sum_C P(C|V)^2 \right) \\ &- \sum_C P(C)^2 \end{aligned} \qquad (6)$$

is highly correlated with the Gini-index gain (Breiman et al., 1984) for classes C and values V of attribute A. The difference is that instead of factor

$$\frac{P(V)^2}{\sum_V P(V)^2}$$

the Gini-index gain uses

$$\frac{P(V)}{\sum_V P(V)} = P(V)$$

Algorithm Relief
Input: for each training instance a vector of attribute values and the class value
Output: the vector W of estimations of the qualities of attributes

```
set all weights W[A] := 0.0;
for i := 1 to m do begin
    randomly select an instance R;
    find nearest hit H and nearest miss M;
    for A := 1 to #all_attributes do
        W[A] := W[A] - diff(A,R,H)/m + diff(A,R,M)/m;
end;
```

Figure 1: Pseudo code of the basic Relief algorithm

Equation (5) (which we call myopic ReliefF), shows strong correlation of Relief's weights with the Gini-index gain. The probability $\sum_V P(V)^2$ that two instances have the same value of attribute A in Eq. (5) is a kind of normalization factor for multi-valued attributes. Impurity functions tend to overestimate multi-valued attributes and various normalization heuristics are needed to avoid this tendency (e.g. gain ratio (Quinlan, 1986), distance measure (Mantaras, 1989), and binarization of attributes (Cestnik et al., 1987)). Equation (5) shows that Relief exhibits an implicit normalization effect. Another deficiency of Gini-index gain is that its values tend to decrease with the increasing number of classes. Denominator which is constant factor in Equation (5) for a given attribute again serves as a kind of normalization and therefore Relief's estimates do not exhibit such strange behavior as Gini-index gain does. This normalization effect remains even if Equation (5) is used as (myopic) attribute estimator what was empirically confirmed in (Kononenko, 1995).

The above derivation eliminated the "nearest instance" condition from the probabilities. If we put it back we can interpret Relief's estimates as the average over local estimates in smaller parts of the instance space. This enables Relief to take into account the context of other attributes, i.e. the conditional dependencies between attributes given the class value which can be detected in the context of locality. From the global point of view, these dependencies are hidden due to the effect of averaging over all training instances, and exactly this makes impurity functions myopic. Impurity functions use correlation between the attribute and the class disregarding the context of other attributes. This is the same as using the global point of view and disregarding the local peculiarities. We illustrate this in Figure 2 which shows dependency of ReliefF's estimate to number of nearest neighbors taken into account. The estimates are for a parity domain with two informative and 10 random attributes and 200 examples. The dotted line shows how the ReliefF's estimate of one of informative attributes is becoming more and more myopic with increasing number of nearest neighbors and how it eventually becomes indistinguishable from random attribute (Note that it is indistinguishable for all myopic estimators).

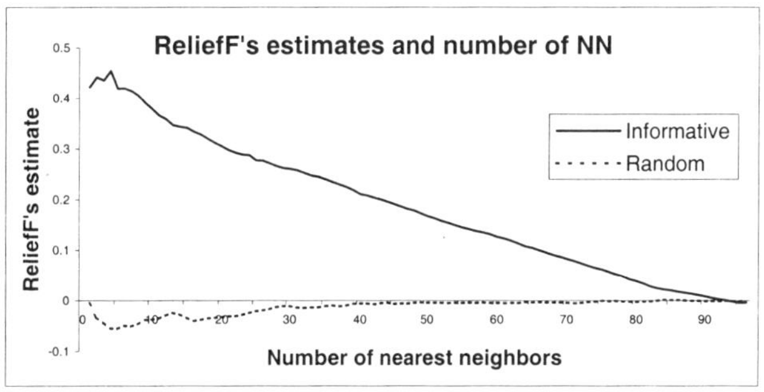

Figure 2: ReliefF's estimates of informative attribute are deteriorating with increasing number of nearest neighbors in parity domain.

3 Global vs. local view, switching estimators

In the process of building a (decision, regression) tree using Relief as the attribute selection heuristics we use all important dependent attributes in the upper part of the tree and come to a point where there are no more dependencies, i.e., the local view becomes the global view. This is the point when there are no more hidden dependencies and we should start optimizing the tree for accuracy. How can we detect this point? We argue that it can be detected by measuring the correlation between the global estimate (Equation (5)) and the average over local estimates (Relief's weights, Equation (3)) for various attributes.

The (linear) correlation coefficient $\rho_{x,y}$ between two vectors of observations x and y is defined as

$$\rho_{x,y} = \frac{\frac{1}{N}\sum_{i=1}^{N}(x_i - \mu_x)(y_i - \mu_y)}{\sigma_x \sigma_y} \qquad (7)$$

where $-1 \leq \rho_{x,y} \leq 1$. This is a well known statistical measure which measures the degree of linear relationship between the x_i and y_i values. In our case x_i is the ReliefF's estimate of i-th attribute and y_i is the estimate of the i-th attribute by another estimator.

Accuracy as attribute estimator has some major drawbacks (Brodley, 1995) in terms of the structure of the tree but once we have extracted the dependencies it can be very useful if we want to optimize the tree for accuracy. If we classify with the majority class the accuracy as the attribute estimator it is defined as

$$Acc = \sum_{V} P(V) \max_{C} P(C|V) \qquad (8)$$

If we want to compute the accuracy for a binary split of a multivalued attribute we group the attribute's values into two groups (left and right) and use the group probabilities in Equation 8.

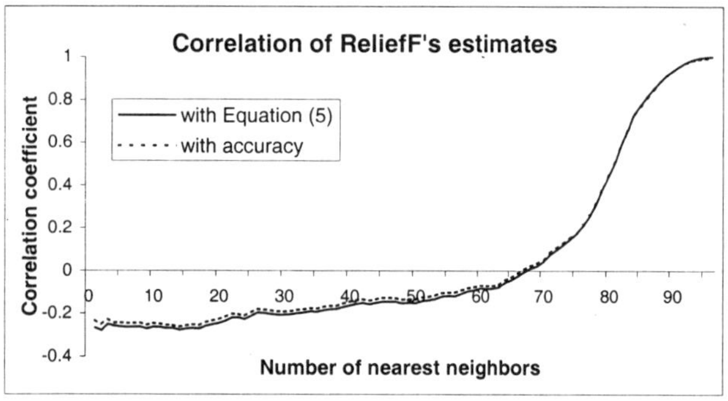

Figure 3: Correlation between ReliefF and Myopic Relief and ReliefF and accuracy in parity domain.

Figure 3 shows the correlation coefficient between the ReliefF's estimate and Equation (5)(solid line) and ReliefF's estimate and accuracy (dotted line) varying over the number of nearest neighbors taken into account for ReliefF's estimates. As before the estimates are for a parity domain with two informative and 10 random attributes and 200 examples. We see that the correlation coefficients are very similar and as it is indicative in other domains as well this leads to further simplification of our heuristic for selecting split criteria: by monitoring the correlation coefficient between ReliefF's estimate and accuracy we determine when there are no more dependencies in a local subspace (tree node). When the correlation coefficient is high enough (e.g., ≥ 0.8) we switch to accuracy optimization and select Equation (8) as the split selector measure in the subtree of a current node.

4 Empirical evaluation

Some recent studies e.g., (Dietterich, 1998; Rassmusen, 1996), have pointed out that the assumption of independence of training sets is violated in k-fold cross-validated paired Student's t-test, however (Dietterich, 1998) observes that this test is very powerful and has only somewhat elevated probability of Type I error. As most of the datasets we are using contain relatively small number of instances and 10-fold cross-validation is economical with the data we have selected 10-fold cross-validated paired Student's t-test for computing the significance of the differences. The significance of the differences were computed at 0.05 level. As we are comparing over several datasets we are also using Bonferroni adjustment (see e.g., (Salzberg, 1997)).

4.1 Decision trees

We have developed a learning system which builds binary decision trees by splitting training examples based on the values of attributes. The attribute in each node is selected according to the estimates of the attributes' quality. These estimates are computed on the subset of the examples that reach current node.

We run our system with three different estimators: ReliefF alone, accuracy alone, and combined ReliefF and accuracy (depending on the threshold for the correlation coefficient, which was set to 0.8). All other parameters for growing and pruning the tree were the same and set to their default values. We used two stopping criteria, namely the minimal number of cases in the leaf (=5) or the minimal purity of a leaf (97% of cases are from the same class) and postpruned the tree with the m-estimate ($m = 2$).

The datasets used are mostly from UCI (Murphy and Aha, 1995), those which are not are shortly described below. Their characteristics are described in Table 1.

Parity-2: Parity problem with two significant binary attributes and 10 random binary attributes. 5% of randomly selected instances were labeled with wrong class.

Parity-3: Same as Parity-2 except that there were three significant attributes for the parity relation which makes the problem harder.

KRK1: The problem of legality of King-Rook-King chess endgame positions. The attributes describe the rel-

Table 1: Some numerical characteristics of categorical datasets used in our experiments (number of classes, number of all, discrete and continuous attributes, number of instances, the percentage of majority class and the class entropy (in bits)).

domain	#class	#atts.	#disc.	#cont.	#inst.	maj.class (%)	entropy
Credit	2	15	9	6	690	56	0.85
Diabetes	2	8	0	8	768	65	0.93
Glass	7	9	0	9	214	36	2.18
Heart	2	13	6	7	270	56	0.99
Iris	3	4	0	4	150	33	1.59
KRK1	2	18	18	0	1000	67	0.92
KRK2	2	6	0	6	1000	67	0.92
LED	10	7	7	0	1000	11	3.33
Lymphography	4	18	18	0	148	55	1.28
Parity-2	2	12	12	0	200	54	0.99
Parity-3	2	13	13	0	200	54	0.99
Primary	22	17	17	0	339	25	3.89
Promoter	2	35	35	0	106	59	1.00
Rheumatic	6	32	11	21	355	66	1.73
Soya	15	35	35	0	630	15	3.62
Tic-tac-toe	2	9	9	0	958	65	0.93
Vote	2	16	16	0	435	61	0.96

evant relations between pieces, such as "same_rank" and "adjacent_file".

KRK2: Same as KRK1 except that the only available attributes are the coordinates of pieces.

For each domain we collected the results as the average of 10 fold cross-validation. We present results in Table 2. Besides the accuracy we included also the number of leaves in the tree as a measure of complexity of the tree.

There are 7 datasets where ReliefF is significantly more accurate than accuracy (KRK1, KRK2, Parity-3, Primary, Rheumatic, Soya, Tic-tac-toe). The combined approach was significantly better than accuracy alone in 6 datasets (KRK2, Parity-3, Primary, Rheumatic, Soya, Tic-tac-toe). There were no significant differences in accuracy between ReliefF and combined approach. Accuracy was never significantly better than the other two methods. The significance of the differences are summarized in Table 3.

The combined approach produced the trees which are on average slightly larger than those produced solely by ReliefF and slightly smaller than those produced solely by the accuracy.

Visual inspection of the trees confirmed that mostly the splitting criteria was switched when there were no more dependencies between the attributes. In average 37% of splits at the bottom of the trees were selected by the accuracy.

Table 3: Number of significant differences in favor of the estimators in the first column over the estimators in the first row.

estimator	ReliefF	accuracy	combination
ReliefF	-	7	0
accuracy	0	-	0
combination	0	6	-

We also experimented with the correlation threshold and it turned out that the switching method is quite robust against this parameter. By setting this parameter in the interval from 0.7 to 0.95 we get very similar results. Above 0.95 there are very few nodes selected by accuracy and below 0.7 there are majority of nodes selected by the accuracy.

What can we conclude from the above experiments? Although in average 37% of splits at the bottom of the tree were selected by the accuracy this switch did not not help ReliefF in improving the score in accuracy. Comparing that with significant improvement which was observed when switching from gain ratio to accuracy (Brodley, 1995; Lubinsky, 1995) it seems that ReliefF does not need such switch as its self-normalization factors (see Equation (5)) and locality of estimates already take that into account.

To confirm this hypothesis we built this switching criterion into our regression tree learning system CORE (Rob-

Table 2: Accuracy and complexity of the decision tree produced with RReliefF, accuracy and combination as the split selectors.

	ReliefF		accuracy		combination	
domain	#leaves	acc.	#leaves	acc.	#leaves	acc.
Credit	30	0.84	37	0.82	32	0.84
Diabetes	78	0.72	103	0.69	81	0.72
Glass	26	0.66	26	0.70	28	0.67
Heart	21	0.74	23	0.75	21	0.77
Iris	5	0.95	5	0.93	4	0.93
KRK1	11	0.99	6	0.91	11	0.92
KRK2	100	0.72	167	0.60	108	0.70
LED	31	0.73	31	0.71	31	0.71
Lymphography	14	0.74	12	0.72	14	0.72
Parity-2	4	0.96	16	0.91	4	0.96
Parity-3	8	0.95	12	0.58	8	0.95
Primary	48	0.42	6	0.28	45	0.42
Promoter	9	0.72	9	0.77	9	0.75
Rheumatic	53	0.65	55	0.56	53	0.65
Soya	37	0.92	46	0.87	38	0.92
Tic-tac-toe	43	0.94	29	0.82	41	0.94
Vote	6	0.96	2	0.96	6	0.96

nik Šikonja, 1997) and test it with two different models in the leaves of the tree (mean prediction value and linear models). This extended definition of the accuracy puts Relief's abilities to a much harder test than in decision trees where the model in the leaf is a majority class.

4.2 Regression trees

Similarly to decision trees we have built the correlation based switching criterion into our regression tree learning system CORE (Robnik Šikonja, 1997) which uses regressional version of ReliefF called RReliefF (Robnik Šikonja and Kononenko, 1997) or Mean Squared Error (MSE) as the attribute estimator. In the leaves of the tree we used two different predictors to forecast the function value: mean prediction value of the training instances in the leaf or linear model which fits the instances in the leaf computed with singular value decomposition method (Press et al., 1988). MSE estimate of the attribute A is minimum over all possible splits of attribute A of the weighted mean squared error of the predictor ϕ:

$$MSE(\phi,A) = \min_{split\ of\ A} p_L \cdot R_{t_L}(\phi) + p_R \cdot R_{t_R}(\phi), \quad (9)$$

where t_L and t_R are the subsets of cases that go left and right, respectively, by the split based on A, and p_L and p_R are the proportions of cases that go left and right. $R_t(\phi)$ is the mean squared error of the predictor ϕ compared to real prediction values c_i of instances x_i in the subset t :

$$R_t(\phi) = \frac{1}{N_t}\sum_{i=1}^{N_t}(c_i - \phi(x_i))^2. \quad (10)$$

$\phi(x_i)$ is the value predicted by ϕ.

MSE is used as attribute estimator and as the success criterion (counterpart of accuracy in decision trees). Previous study (Robnik Šikonja and Kononenko, 1997) already compared RReliefF and MSE on regression trees and it turned out that on the problems which contain dependent attributes RReliefF produced smaller trees with significantly lower error, while on problems without strong dependencies RReliefF and MSE produce comparable trees.

We run our system with three different estimators: ReliefF alone, accuracy alone, and combined ReliefF and accuracy (with the correlation coefficient set to 0.8). All other parameters for growing and pruning the tree were the same and set to their default values. We used the minimal number of instances in the leaf (=5) as the stopping criterion and postpruned the tree with the m-estimate ($m = 2$).

We ran our system on the artificial data sets and on data sets with continuous prediction value from UCI (Murphy and Aha, 1995). Artificial data sets used were:

Fraction is floating point generalization of the parity concepts of order $I = \{2,3\}$. Each domain contains continuous attributes with values from 0 to 1. The predicted value is the fractional part of the sum of I important attributes: $C = \sum_{j=1}^{I} A_j - \lfloor \sum_{j=1}^{I} A_j \rfloor$

Modulo-8 is integer generalization of the parity of order $I = \{2,3\}$. Value of each attribute is an integer value in the range 0-7. Half of the attributes are treated as discrete and half as continuous; each continuous attribute is exact match of one of the discrete attributes. The predicted value is the sum of the I important attributes by modulo 8: $C = (\sum_{j=1}^{I} A_j) \bmod 8$.

ParityC is continuously randomized parity of order $I = \{2,3\}$. Each data set consists of discrete, Boolean attributes. The I informative attributes define parity concept: if their parity bit is 0, the predicted value is set to a random number between 0 and 0.5, otherwise the predicted value is randomly chosen to be between 0.5 and 1.

Linear presents simple linear dependency with 4 important attributes: $f = A_1 - 2A_2 + 3A_3 - 3A_4$. The attributes are continuous with values chosen randomly between 0 and 1.

Cosinus is non-linear dependency with cosine multiplied by the linear combination of two attributes: $f = \cos(4\pi A_1) \cdot (-2A_2 + 3A_3)$. The attributes are continuous with values from 0 to 1.

Altogether there were 8 artificial data sets, each consisting of 10 attributes - 2 or 3 important, the rest are random, and containing 1000 examples. UCI datasets used were:

Abalone: predicting the age of the abalone, 1 nominal and 7 continuous attributes, 4177 instances.

Autompg: city-cycle fuel consumption, 1 nominal, 6 continuous attributes 398 instances.

Autoprice: prices of the vehicles, 10 nominal , 15 continuous attributes, 201 instances.

Cpu: relative CPU performance, 6 continuous attributes, 209 instances.

Housing: housing values in Boston area, 1 nominal, 12 continuous attributes, 506 instances.

Servo: rise time of a servo mechanism, 2 nominal, 2 integer attributes, 167 instances.

Wisconsin: time to recur in Wisconsin breast cancer database, 32 continuous attributes, 198 instances.

For each experiment we collected the results as the average of 10 fold cross-validation. In Table 4 we give relative mean squared error:

$$RE_t(\phi) = \frac{R_t(\phi)}{R_t(\mu)} \tag{11}$$

ϕ is the evaluated predictor (regression tree) and μ is a predictor which always returns the mean of the training instances. Sensible predictors have $RE(\phi) < 1$. Besides the relative error we included also the number of leaves in the tree as a measure of complexity of the tree. The significance of the differences were computed by a two-sided paired Student's t-test at a 0.05 level using the Bonferroni adjustment and are presented in Table 5.

With linear models in the leaves there are 5 datasets where RReliefF has significantly lower error than MSE (Abalone, Fraction-3, Parity-2, Parity-3, and Wisconsin). The combined approach is significantly better than MSE in 4 datasets (Abalone, Fraction-3, Parity-2, and Parity-3). There are no significant differences in accuracy between RReliefF and combined approach. MSE never produces significantly lower error than the other two methods. With mean prediction value in the leaves we obtained similar results. Both RReliefF and the combined approach have significantly lower error than MSE in 4 datasets (Fraction-2, Fraction-3, Modulo8-2, and Parity-3)

Table 5: Number of significant differences in RE in favor of the estimators in the first column over the estimators in the first row.

estimator	RReliefF	MSE	combination
	linear models in leaves		
RReliefF	-	5	0
MSE	0	-	0
combination	0	4	-
	mean prediction value in leaves		
RReliefF	-	4	0
MSE	0	-	0
combination	0	4	-

When the switching criterion was used on average 25% and 36% of the splits at the bottom of the trees were selected by the MSE with linear models and mean prediction value, respectively.

We consider the above results as a confirmation of our hypothesis that (R)ReliefF does not need such a switch as it is already self-normalizing.

Table 4: RE and complexity of the regression trees produced with RReliefF, MSE and combination as the split selectors.

	linear models in leaves						mean prediction value in leaves					
	RReliefF		MSE		combination		RReliefF		MSE		combination	
domain	#leaf	RE	#leaf	RE	#leaf	RE	#leaf	RE	#leaf	RE	#leaf	RE
Abalone	133	0.62	170	0.80	141	0.66	186	0.58	166	0.56	191	0.60
Autompg	7	0.14	7	0.17	7	0.14	13	0.21	11	0.22	13	0.23
Autoprice	4	0.20	2	0.14	3	0.20	8	0.26	5	0.14	9	0.25
Cosinus	25	0.11	15	0.05	23	0.06	53	0.30	46	0.22	49	0.29
CPU	3	0.14	3	0.16	3	0.14	6	0.30	6	0.29	6	0.30
Fraction-2	22	0.35	20	0.52	21	0.58	40	0.29	107	1.12	48	0.49
Fraction-3	52	0.88	63	2.06	43	1.15	96	0.91	152	1.73	99	0.98
Housing	7	0.23	7	0.19	7	0.24	16	0.28	14	0.22	16	0.27
Linear	1	0.00	1	0.00	1	0.00	27	0.18	29	0.19	28	0.17
Modulo8-2	21	0.00	10	0.00	16	0.00	40	0.04	115	0.96	37	0.05
Modulo8-3	94	1.49	66	1.18	93	1.50	113	1.40	148	1.70	113	1.40
ParityC-2	4	0.27	48	0.35	4	0.27	4	0.27	48	0.35	4	0.27
ParityC-3	8	0.27	103	0.50	8	0.27	8	0.27	103	0.50	8	0.27
Servo	4	0.22	6	0.21	4	0.22	4	0.22	4	0.23	4	0.23
Wisconsin	14	1.35	10	2.06	16	1.52	29	1.51	25	1.85	32	1.76

5 Conclusions

We present a method for switching the split criterion from ReliefF to accuracy in the process of building the decision tree and from RReliefF to MSE in the process of building regression tree. Our method is based on theoretical properties of Relief estimations. It allows ReliefF (RReliefF) to recognize dependencies between the attributes and use them near the root of the tree which guarantees their compact representation and switch to accuracy (error) optimization when there are no more such dependencies.

Contrary to impurity based methods which produce significant lower error when combined with the error optimization near the fringe of the tree (Brodley, 1995; Lubinsky, 1995) it seems that ReliefF does not need this switch as its self-normalization factors in Equation (5) and global view combined with local estimations already contains it. However this hypothesis needs a further theoretical study.

Acknowledgments

The results in this paper are part of the first author's work on PhD thesis at University of Ljubljana, Faculty of Computer and Information Science. Both authors were supported by Slovenian Ministry of Science and Technology.

References

Breiman, L., Friedman, J. H., Olshen, R. A., and Stone, C. J. (1984). *Classification and regression trees*. Wadsworth Inc., Belmont, California.

Brodley, C. E. (1995). Automatic selection of split criterion during tree growing based on node location. In *Proceedings of the XII International Conference on Machine Learning*. Morgan Kaufmann.

Brodley, C. E. and Utgoff, P. E. (1995). Multivariate decision trees. *Machine Learning*, 19(1):45–77.

Cestnik, B., Kononenko, I., and Bratko, I. (1987). Assistant 86: A knowledge-elicitation tool for sophisticated users. In Bratko, I. and Lavrač, N., editors, *Progress in Machine Learning, Proceedings of EWSL 87*, Wilmslow. Sigma Press.

Dalaka, A., Kompare, B., Robnik Šikonja, M., and Sgardelis, S. (1999). Modeling by artificial intelligence tools the effects of environmental conditions on apparent photosynthesis of stipa bromoides. (submitted).

Dietterich, T. G. (1997). Machine learning research: Four current directions. *AI Magazine*, 18(4):97–136.

Dietterich, T. G. (1998). Approximate statistical tests for comparing supervised classification learning algorithms. *Neural Computation*, 10(7):1895–1924.

Hong, S. J. (1997). Use of contextual information for feature ranking and discretization. *IEEE transactions on knowledge and data engineering*, 9(5):718–730.

Hunt, E., Martin, J., and Stone, P. (1966). *Experiments in Induction*. Academic Press, New York.

Kira, K. and Rendell, L. A. (1992). A practical approach to feature selection. In D.Sleeman and P.Edwards, editors, *Proceedings of International Conference on Machine Learning*, pages 249–256. Morgan Kaufmann.

Kononenko, I. (1994). Estimating attributes: analysis and extensions of Relief. In De Raedt, L. and Bergadano, F., editors, *Machine Learning: ECML-94*, pages 171–182. Springer Verlag.

Kononenko, I. (1995). On biases in estimating multivalued attributes. In *Proceedings of the International Joint Conference on Aartificial Intelligence IJCAI'95*, pages 1034–1040. Morgan Kaufmann.

Kononenko, I., Šimec, E., and Robnik-Šikonja, M. (1997). Overcoming the myopia of inductive learning algorithms with RELIEFF. *Applied Intelligence*, 7:39–55.

Lubinsky, D. J. (1995). Increasing the performance and consistency of classification trees by using the accuracy criterion at the leaves. In *Proceedings of the XII International Conference on Machine Learning*. Morgan Kaufmann.

Mantaras, R. (1989). ID3 revisited: A distance based criterion for attribute selection. In *Proceedings of Int. Symp. Methodologies for Intelligent Systems*, Charlotte, North Carolina, USA.

Murphy, P. and Aha, D. (1995). UCI repository of machine learning databases. (http://www.ics.uci.edu/ mlearn/-MLRepository.html).

Pompe, U. and Kononenko, I. (1995). Linear space induction in first order logic with ReliefF. In Della Riccia, G., Kruse, R., and Viertl, R., editors, *Mathematical and Statistical Methods in Artificial Intelligenc, CISM Courses and Lectures No.363*. Springer Verlag.

Press, W. H., Teukolsky, S. A., Vetterling, W. T., and Flannery, B. P. (1988). *Numerical recipes in C*. Cambridge University Press.

Quinlan, J. R. (1986). Induction of decision trees. *Machine Learning*, 1(1):81–106.

Rassmusen, C. E. (1996). *Evaluation of Gaussian processes and other methods for non-linear regression*. PhD thesis, University of Toronto, Department of Computer Science.

Robnik Šikonja, M. (1997). CORE - a system that predicts continuous variables. In *Proceedings of Electrotehnical and Computer Science Conference*, pages B145–148, Portorož, Slovenia.

Robnik Šikonja, M. and Kononenko, I. (1997). An adaptation of Relief for attribute estimation in regression. In Fisher, D., editor, *Machine Learning: Proceedings of the Fourteenth International Conference (ICML'97)*, pages 296–304. Morgan Kaufmann Publishers.

Salzberg, S. L. (1997). On comparing classifiers: Pitfalls to avoid and a recommended approach. *Data Mining and Knowledge Discovery*, 1:317–328.

Smyth, P. and Goodman, R. (1990). Rule induction using information theory. In Piatetsky-Shapiro, G. and Frawley, W., editors, *Knowledge Discovery in Databases*. MIT Press.

Wettschereck, D., Aha, D. W., and Mohri, T. (1997). A review and empirical evaluation of feature weighting methods for a class of lazy learning algorithms. *Artificial Intelligence Review*, 11:273–314.

+ve and -ve examples

GA-based Learning of Context-Free Grammars using Tabular Representations

Yasubumi Sakakibara
Dept. of Information Sciences
Tokyo Denki University
Saitama 350-0394, Japan
yasu@j.dendai.ac.jp

Mitsuhiro Kondo
Dept. of Information Sciences
Tokyo Denki University
Saitama 350-0394, Japan

Abstract

We propose a new algorithm for learning context-free grammars from a finite sample of positive and negative examples using genetic algorithms. The problem of learning context-free grammars from examples has two aspects: determining the grammatical structure (topology) of the unknown grammar and identifying nonterminals in the grammar. To solve these problems efficiently, we propose a new hypothesis representation method which uses a table similar with the parse table used in the efficient parsing algorithm for context-free grammars like Cocke-Younger-Kasami algorithm. By employing this representation method, the problem of learning context-free grammars from examples can be reduced to the partitioning problem of nonterminals. Then we use genetic algorithms for solving this partitioning problem. We also demonstrate some experimental results using this algorithm.

1 INTRODUCTION

Inductive learning of formal languages, often called *grammatical inference*, is an active research area in machine learning and computational learning theory (Sakakibara, 1997). Especially, the problems of learning finite automata from positive and negative examples have been widely and well studied. Inductive learning of formal languages inherently contains computationally hard problems. For example, identification of minimum-state finite automata from positive and negative examples is known as NP-hard (Gold, 1978). Nevertheless, one advantage in learning finite automata is that once we construct a so-called prefix-tree automaton for the positive examples (that is, a specific deterministic finite automaton which exactly accepts the positive examples), the learning problem can be reduced to the problem of merging states in the prefix-tree automaton. In (Dupont, 1994), the genetic algorithm is applied to solve the partitioning problem for the set of states in the prefix-tree automaton.

In this paper, we study the problem of inductively learning context-free grammars from positive and negative examples. This is more difficult learning problem than learning finite automata. The hardness reason is that the problem of learning context-free grammars from examples has two specific aspects: determining the grammatical structure (topology) of the unknown grammar, and identifying nonterminals in the grammar. The first problem is especially hard because the number of all possible grammatical structures to be considered for a given positive example becomes exponential of the length of the positive example. Thus, the hypothesis space of context-free grammars is very large (too large) to search a correct context-free grammar consistent with the given examples. It has been shown in (Sakakibara, 1992) that if information on the grammatical structure of the unknown context-free grammar to be learned is available for the learning algorithm, there exists an efficient algorithm for learning context-free grammars from only positive examples.

To overcome the hardness of learning context-free grammars from examples without structural information available, we propose a new hypothesis representation method using a table which is similar with the parse table used in the Cocke-Younger-Kasami parsing algorithm (CYK algorithm) for context-free grammars of Chomsky normal form. By employing this representation method, the problem of learning context-free grammars from examples can be reduced to the partitioning problem of nonterminals. This hypothesis representation method for CFGs corresponds to the prefix-tree automaton. Then we use genetic algorithms for solving this partitioning problem. We also demonstrate some experimental results using this algorithm.

2 TABULAR METHOD FOR REPRESENTING HYPOTHESES

A *context-free grammar* (CFG) is defined by a quadruple $G = (N, \Sigma, P, S)$, where N is an alphabet of *nonterminal symbols*, Σ is an alphabet of *terminal symbols* such that $N \cap \Sigma = \emptyset$, P is a finite set of production rules of the form $A \rightarrow \alpha$ for $A \in N$ and $\alpha \in (N \cup \Sigma)^*$, and S is a special nonterminal called the *start symbol*.

A *derivation* is a rewriting of a string in $(N \cup \Sigma)^*$ using the production rules of the CFG G. In each step of the derivation, a nonterminal from the current string is chosen and replaced with the right-hand side of a production rule for that nonterminal. This replacement process is repeated until the string consists of terminal symbols only. If a derivation begins with a nonterminal A and derive a string $\alpha \in (N \cup \Sigma)^*$, we denote $A \Rightarrow \alpha$.

The *language generated* by a CFG G is denoted $L(G)$, that is, $L(G) = \{w \mid S \Rightarrow w, w \in \Sigma^*\}$. Two CFGs G and G' are said to be *equivalent* if and only if $L(G) = L(G')$.

A CFG $G = (N, \Sigma, P, S)$ is in *Chomsky normal form* if each production rule is of the form $A \rightarrow BC$ or $A \rightarrow a$ where $A, B \in N$ and $a \in \Sigma$.

In the following, we fix a terminal alphabet Σ, and without loss of generality, we only consider context-free grammars without any ϵ-production rules and any useless production rules where an ϵ-production rule is of the form $A \rightarrow \epsilon$ (where ϵ means the empty string of length 0) and a production rule $A \rightarrow \alpha$ is *useless* if there is no derivation $S \Rightarrow \beta A \gamma \rightarrow \beta \alpha \gamma \Rightarrow w$ for any $\beta, \gamma \in (N \cup \Sigma)^*$ and any $w \in \Sigma^*$.

For learning context-free grammars or context-free languages, we usually use CFGs themselves for representing hypotheses. However, the hypothesis space of CFGs is very large (too large) to search a correct CFG consistent with the given examples. This is because the problem of learning CFGs from examples has two specific aspects:

1. determining the grammatical structure (topology) of the unknown grammar, and
2. identifying nonterminals in the grammar.

The first problem is especially hard. For example, assume that a given positive example is a string "*aabb*". All possible grammatical structures for this string are shown in Figure 1 when we consider the Chomsky normal form of CFGs.

Thus, the number of all possible grammatical structures to be considered for a string of length n becomes exponential of n. In order to solve this hardness, we propose a new representation method using a table

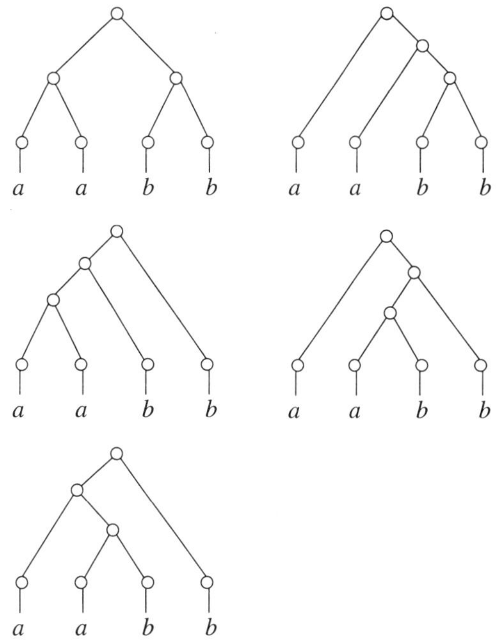

Figure 1: All possible grammatical structures for the string "*aabb*".

which is similar with the parse table used in the Cocke-Younger-Kasami parsing algorithm (CYK algorithm) (Aho & Ullman, 1972) for CFGs of Chomsky normal form.

First we introduce the tabular parsing method of the CYK algorithm, and next we propose a tabular representation method which efficiently represents an exponential number of possible grammatical structures for learning CFGs. The CYK algorithm is a polynomial time algorithm to solve the parsing (membership) problem of CFGs using "dynamic programming". The CYK algorithm assumes Chomsky normal form of CFGs, and the essence of the algorithm is the construction of a triangular *parse table* T. Given a CFG $G = (N, \Sigma, P, S)$ and the input string $w = a_1 a_2 \cdots a_n$ in Σ^* to be parsed according to G, each element of T, denoted $t_{i,j}$, for $1 \leq i \leq n$ and $1 \leq j \leq n - i + 1$, will have a value which is a subset of N. The interpretation of T is that a nonterminal A will be in $t_{i,j}$ if and only if $A \Rightarrow a_i a_{i+1} \cdots a_{i+j-1}$, that is, A derives the substring of w beginning at position i and of length j. To determine whether the string w is in $L(G)$, the algorithm computes the parse table T and look to see whether S is in entry $t_{1,n}$.

In the first step of constructing the parse table, the CYK algorithm sets $t_{i,1} = \{A \mid A \rightarrow a_i \text{ is in } P\}$. In the second step, it assumes that $t_{i,j'}$ has been computed for $1 \leq i \leq n$ and $1 \leq j' < j$, and it computes $t_{i,j}$ by examining the nonterminals in the following pairs of entries:

$$(t_{i,1}, t_{i+1,j-1}),\ (t_{i,2}, t_{i+2,j-2}),\ \ldots,\ (t_{i,j-1}, t_{i+j-1,1})$$

and if B is in $t_{i,k}$ and C is in $t_{i+k,j-k}$ for some k $(1 \leq k < j)$ and the production $A \rightarrow BC$ is in P, adding A to $t_{i,j}$.

For example, we consider a simple CFG $G = (N, \Sigma, P, S)$ of Chomsky normal form where $N = \{S, A\}$, $\Sigma = \{a, b\}$ and

$$P = \{\ S \rightarrow AA,\ \ S \rightarrow AS,\ \ S \rightarrow b,\ \ A \rightarrow SA,\ \ A \rightarrow a\ \}.$$

This CFG generates a string "*abaaa*", that is, $S \Rightarrow abaaa$, and the parse table T for "*abaab*" becomes as follows:

5	*S*, *A*				
4	*S*, *A*	*S*, *A*			
3	*S*, *A*	*S*	*S*, *A*		
2	*S*	*A*	*S*	*S*	
$j = 1$	*A*	*S*	*A*	*A*	*A*
	$i = 1$	2	3	4	5
	(*a*	*b*	*a*	*a*	*a*)

Figure 2: The parse table T of G for "*abaaa*".

The above parse table can efficiently store all possible parse trees of G for *abaaa*.

Now we propose a representation method using this parse table for efficiently representing hypotheses of CFGs. Given a positive example $w = a_1 a_2 \cdots a_n$, the *tabular representation* for w is the triangular table $T(w)$ where each element, denoted $t_{i,j}$, for $1 \leq i \leq n$ and $2 \leq j \leq n - i + 1$, contains the set $\{X_{i,j,k_1}, \ldots, X_{i,j,k_{j-1}}\}$ of $j - 1$ distinct nonterminals. For $j = 1$, $t_{i,1}$ is the singleton set $\{X_{i,1,1}\}$. (See Figure 3.) The *primitive* CFG $G(T(w)) = (N, \Sigma, P, S)$ derived from the tabular representation $T(w)$ is defined to be as follows:

$$N = \{X_{i,j,k} \mid 1 \leq i \leq n, 1 \leq j \leq n - i + 1, 1 \leq k < j\}$$

$$P = \{X_{i,j,k} \rightarrow X_{i,k,l_1} X_{i+k,j-k,l_2} \mid 1 \leq i \leq n, 1 \leq j \leq n - i + 1, 1 \leq k < j, 1 \leq l_1 < k, 1 \leq l_2 < j - k\}$$
$$\cup \{X_{i,1,1} \rightarrow a_i \mid 1 \leq i \leq n\}$$
$$\cup \{S \rightarrow X_{1,n,k} \mid 1 \leq k \leq n - 1\}$$

Thus for each nonterminal $X_{i,j,k}$ at entry $t_{i,j}$, we have the production rules $X_{i,j,k} \rightarrow X_{i,k,l_1} X_{i+k,j-k,l_2}$ with the right-hand sides of the nonterminals at entries $t_{i,k}$ and $t_{i+k,j-k}$. The number of nonterminals contained in $G(T(w))$ is at most n^3 and the size (the number

n	$\{X_{1,n,1}, \cdots, X_{1,n,n-1}\}$			
$n-1$	$\{X_{1,n-1,1}, \cdots, X_{1,n-1,n-2}\}$	$\{X_{2,n-1,1}, \cdots, X_{2,n-1,n-2}\}$		
$\vdots$	$\vdots$	$\vdots$	$\ddots$	
2	$\{X_{1,2,1}\}$	$\{X_{2,2,1}\}$	$\cdots$	
$j = 1$	$\{X_{1,1,1}\}$	$\{X_{2,1,1}\}$	$\cdots$	$\{X_{n,1,1}\}$
	$i = 1$	2	$\cdots$	n

Figure 3: The tabular representation for w.

4	$X_{1,4,1}, X_{1,4,2}, X_{1,4,3}$			
3	$X_{1,3,1}, X_{1,3,2}$	$X_{2,3,1}, X_{2,3,2}$		
2	$X_{1,2,1}$	$X_{2,2,1}$	$X_{3,2,1}$	
$j = 1$	$X_{1,1,1}$	$X_{2,1,1}$	$X_{3,1,1}$	$X_{4,1,1}$
	$i = 1$	2	3	4
	a	*a*	*b*	*b*

$$
\begin{aligned}
P = \{\ & S \rightarrow X_{1,4,1}, & & S \rightarrow X_{1,4,2}, \\
& S \rightarrow X_{1,4,3}, \\
& X_{1,4,1} \rightarrow X_{1,1,1} X_{2,3,1}, & & X_{1,4,1} \rightarrow X_{1,1,1} X_{2,3,2}, \\
& X_{1,4,2} \rightarrow X_{1,2,1} X_{3,2,1}, & & X_{1,4,3} \rightarrow X_{1,3,1} X_{4,1,1}, \\
& X_{1,4,3} \rightarrow X_{1,3,2} X_{4,1,1}, & & X_{1,3,1} \rightarrow X_{1,1,1} X_{2,2,1}, \\
& X_{1,3,2} \rightarrow X_{1,2,1} X_{3,1,1}, & & X_{2,3,1} \rightarrow X_{2,1,1} X_{3,2,1}, \\
& X_{2,3,2} \rightarrow X_{2,2,1} X_{4,1,1}, & & X_{1,2,1} \rightarrow X_{1,1,1} X_{2,1,1}, \\
& X_{2,2,1} \rightarrow X_{2,1,1} X_{3,1,1}, & & X_{3,2,1} \rightarrow X_{3,1,1} X_{4,1,1}, \\
& X_{1,1,1} \rightarrow a, & & X_{2,1,1} \rightarrow a, \\
& X_{3,1,1} \rightarrow b, & & X_{4,1,1} \rightarrow b\ \}
\end{aligned}
$$

Figure 4: The tabular representation $T(aabb)$ and the derived primitive CFG $G(T(aabb))$.

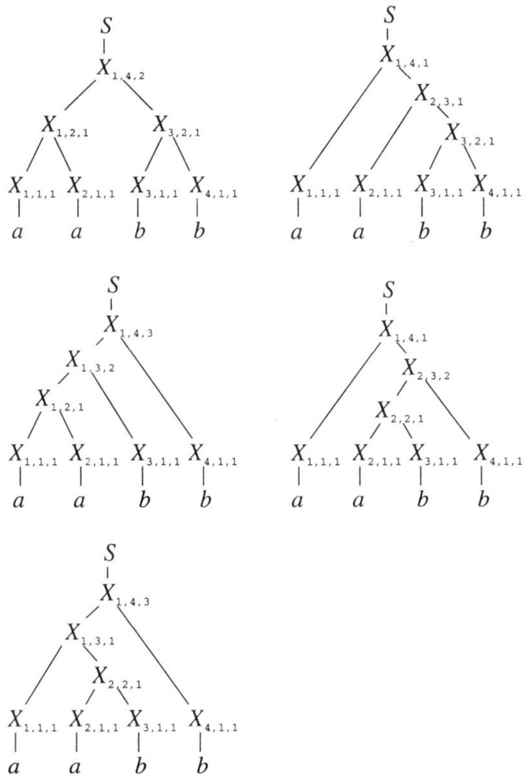

Figure 5: All possible parse trees of $G(T(aabb))$ for "*aabb*"

of production rules) of the primitive CFG $G(T(w))$ is very roughly $O(n^5)$, that is, polynomial of n.

This primitive CFG $G(T(w))$ only generates the string w but can generate all possible grammatical structures on w. For example, when a positive example "*aabb*" is given, the tabular representation $T(aabb)$ and the primitive CFG $G(T(aabb))$ become as shown in Figure 4.

While the size of $G(T(aabb))$ is polynomial of the length of the given example, this CFG $G(T(aabb))$ can generate all possible grammatical structures for *aabb* as shown in Figure 5.

3 LEARNING ALGORITHM USING GENETIC ALGORITHM

As we have seen in the previous section, the parsing is a process that given a CFG G, constructs a parse table for a string w and sees whether $w \in L(G)$. The learning is completely a reverse process that given a sample of positive examples w and negative examples, constructs the tabular representation $T(w)$ for w, merges the nonterminals in $G(T(w))$ to be consistent with the sample and produces a CFG.

We assume the unknown (target) CFG, denoted G_*, to be learned. A *positive example* of G_* is a string in $L(G_*)$ and a *negative example* of G_* is a string not in $L(G_*)$. A *representative sample* of G_* is defined to be a finite subset of $L(G_*)$ that exercises every production rule in G_*, that is, every production is used at least once to generate the subset.

A *partition* of some set X is a set of pairwise disjoint nonempty subsets of X whose union is X. If π is a partition of X, then for any element $x \in X$ there is a unique element of π containing x, which we denote $K(x, \pi)$ and call the *block* of π containing x. Let $G = (N, \Sigma, P, S)$ be a CFG and π be a partition of the set N of nonterminals. The CFG $G/\pi = (N', \Sigma, P', S')$ induced by π from G is defined as follows:

$$
\begin{aligned}
N' &= \pi \quad \text{(the set of blocks of } \pi\text{)},\\
P' &= \{K(A,\pi) \to K(B,\pi)\ K(C,\pi) \\
&\qquad\qquad \mid A \to BC \in P\}\\
&\quad \cup \{K(A,\pi) \to a \mid A \to a \in P\},\\
S' &= K(S,\pi).
\end{aligned}
$$

Our learning algorithm for CFGs will be designed as follows: Given positive examples w, we first construct the tabular representation $T(w)$ and the primitive CFG $G(T(w))$, and second we merge distinct nonterminals to be consistent with the given positive and negative examples and minimize the number of nonterminals in $G(T(w))$. Then, we use the genetic algorithm to solve the partitioning problem for the set of nonterminals $\{X_{i,j,k} \mid 1 \leq i \leq n, 1 \leq j \leq n-i+1, 1 \leq k < j\}$. This partitioning problem contains the problem of finding minimum-state finite automata consistent with the given examples and hence it is NP-hard. Therefore, it is reasonable to use the genetic algorithm for solving the computationally hard problem of partitioning nonterminals. The figure 6 illustrates our scenario.

Now we assume that a finite sample U of positive and negative examples which contains a representative sample of the unknown CFG G_* is given. Let U_+ denote the set of positive examples in U and U_- denote the set of negative examples. The learning algorithm TBL for CFGs is described as follows:

The Learning Algorithm TBL:

1. Construct the tabular representation $T(w)$ for each positive example w in U_+;
2. Derive the primitive CFG $G(T(w))$ for each w in U_+;
3. Take the union of those primitive CFGs, that is,

$$G(T(U_+)) = \bigcup_{w \in U_+} G(T(w))$$

Given a positive example "*abaaa*"

⇓ **construct the tabular representation** $T(abaaa)$

STEP 1:

5	$X_{1,5,1}$, $X_{1,5,2}$, $X_{1,5,3}$, $X_{1,5,4}$				
4	$X_{1,4,1}$, $X_{1,4,2}$, $X_{1,4,3}$	$X_{2,4,1}$, $X_{2,4,2}$, $X_{2,4,3}$			
3	$X_{1,3,1}$, $X_{1,3,2}$	$X_{2,3,1}$, $X_{2,3,2}$	$X_{3,3,1}$, $X_{3,3,2}$		
2	$X_{1,2,1}$	$X_{2,2,1}$	$X_{3,2,1}$	$X_{4,2,1}$	
$j = 1$	$X_{1,1,1}$	$X_{2,1,1}$	$X_{3,1,1}$	$X_{4,1,1}$	$X_{5,1,1}$
	$i = 1$	2	3	4	5
	(a	b	a	a	a)

⇓ **merge nonterminals**

STEP 2:

5	S, A				
4	S, A	S, A			
3	S, A	S	S, A		
2	S	A	S	S	
$j = 1$	A	S	A	A	A
	$i = 1$	2	3	4	5
	(a	b	a	a	a)

⇓

STEP 3:

$$P = \{ \; S \to AA, \quad S \to AS, \quad S \to b, \quad A \to SA, \quad A \to a \; \}$$

Figure 6: The tabular representation $T(abaaa)$, merging nonterminals, and the resulting CFG.

4. Find a smallest partition π_s such that $G(T(U_+))/\pi_s$ is consistent with U, that is, consistent with the positive examples U_+ and the negative examples U_-;
5. Output the resulting CFG $G(T(U_+))/\pi_s$.

We employ the genetic algorithm (GA) to solve the partitioning problem for the set of nonterminals in the primitive CFGs. The genetic algorithm is a parallel search technique in which a set, namely the *population*, of potential solutions, called *individuals* is progressively updated through a *selection mechanism* and *genetic operations*, that is, the *crossover* and the *mutation*. Each individual is coded as a fixed length string, called a *chromosome*.

Starting from a randomly generated initial population, each individual is evaluated by the *fitness function* to be optimized. The population of the next generation is obtained in three steps. Firstly, a random selection with repetitions is performed, usually on the whole population. The probability of a given individual to be selected is obtained from the ratio between its fitness value and the average fitness value computed over the whole population. Secondly, at a given *crossover rate* pairs are selected from this temporary population. Each pairs of *parents* give rise to two children which are constructed by taking alternative subparts from their parent chromosomes. After the crossover operation, the parents are replaced by their children in the temporary population. Thirdly, some individuals are selected at a given *mutation rate*. One position in the associated chromosome of each selected individual is randomly chosen and the corresponding value is replaced. The final population of the next generation is made of the individuals obtained after fitness proportionate reproduction, crossover and mutation. This process is iterated until some termination criterion is satisfied.

Genetic algorithms have been well studied for the partitioning problems (Michalewicz, 1996) and we take a successful approach by Von Laszewski (von Laszewski, 1991) for partitioning n elements into k categories (blocks). This approach encodes partitions using *group-number encoding*, that is, partitions are represented as strings of integer number of length n,

$$(i_1, i_2, \ldots, i_n)$$

where the j-th integer $i_j \in \{1, \ldots, k\}$ indicates the group number assigned to element j. This representation is supported by specific GA operators called "intelligent structural operators": structural crossover and structural mutation.

structural crossover: the mechanism is explained by the following example. Assume that there are two selected parents (strings of length 12)

$p_1 = (112341232253)$ and $p_2 = (112423122335)$.

These strings decode the following partitions:

$$\begin{array}{l} p_1 \;:\; \{1,2,6\},\ \{3,7,9,10\},\ \{4,8,12\},\ \{5\},\ \{11\} \\ p_2 \;:\; \{1,2,7\},\ \{3,5,8,9\},\ \{6,10,11\},\ \{4\},\ \{12\} \end{array}$$

First, a random block is selected, say block #2. This block is copied (introduced) from p_1 into p_2:

$$p_2' = (112423222235)$$

and the resulting partition is:

$$p_2' \;:\; \{1,2\},\ \{3,5,7,8,9,10\},\ \{6,11\},\ \{4\},\ \{12\}$$

structural mutation: it replaces a single component of a string by some random number. Thus, a parent

$$p_2' = (112423222235)$$

may produce the following offspring (the number on position 9 is replaced):

$$p_2'' = (112423225235)$$

$$p_2'' \;:\; \{1,2\},\ \{3,5,7,8,10\},\ \{6,11\},\ \{4\},\ \{9,12\}$$

In addition to those operators, we introduce a specific mutation operator that deletes a randomly selected element with small probability. The deletion operator randomly selects a single component (position) of a string and replaces it to the special number (say, -1) indicating that the element at the position is deleted. This deletion operator contributes to deleting unnecessary nonterminals in a CFG $G(T(w))$.

Finally, we define the fitness function f from individuals to real numbers $[0,1]$ between 0 and 1. Let p be an individual and π_p be a partition which p encodes for the set of nonterminals in the CFG $G(T(U_+))$. Let U_+ be the given positive examples and U_- be the given negative examples. The fitness function f is defined as follows:

$$f_1(p) = \frac{|\{w \in U_+ \mid w \in G(T(U_+))/\pi_p\}|}{|U_+|}$$

$$f_2(p) = \frac{1}{|\pi_p|}$$

$$f(p) = \begin{cases} 0 & \text{if some } w \text{ in } U_- \text{ is generated by } G(T(U_+))/\pi_p \\ \frac{C_1 \times f_1(p) + C_2 \times f_2(p)}{C_1 + C_2} & \text{otherwise} \end{cases}$$

where C_1, C_2 are some constants.

This fitness function f tries to find a CFG consistent with both of the given positive and negative examples. Especially, the penalty for a CFG which accepts any negative example is huge, it discards all those individuals. Among the CFGs consistent with the positive and negative examples, we follow the "Occam razor" to choose the best ones. That is, we look for a CFG, consistent with the positive and negative examples, which moreover contains the minimal number of nonterminals.

4 EXPERIMENTAL RESULTS

We had two experiments for learning two context-free languages using our learning algorithm TBL.

4.1 EXPERIMENT 1

The unknown (target) context-free language is $\{a^m b^m c^n \mid m, n \geq 1\}$ over $\Sigma = \{a, b, c\}$. This context-free language is especially important to see the performance of the learning algorithm because it contains all typical grammatical structures specific to the CFG: branch structure ($A \rightarrow BC$), parenthesis (paired) structure ($A \rightarrow aBb$), and iteration structure ($A \rightarrow aA$).

We gave all positive examples of length up to 10 and all negative examples of length up to 20. The learning algorithm TBL outputs the following correct CFG $G = (N, \Sigma, P, S)$ as the best individual in the population of size 100 after 2000 iterations:

$$\begin{array}{rcl} N &=& \{\langle 1\rangle, \langle 2\rangle, \langle 3\rangle, \langle 104\rangle, \langle 113\rangle, \langle 121\rangle, \langle 148\rangle\}, \\ P &=& \{\ S \rightarrow \langle 104\rangle, \\ && \langle 104\rangle \rightarrow \langle 148\rangle\ \langle 121\rangle,\quad \langle 104\rangle \rightarrow \langle 148\rangle\ \langle 3\rangle, \\ && \langle 148\rangle \rightarrow \langle 113\rangle\ \langle 2\rangle,\quad \langle 148\rangle \rightarrow \langle 1\rangle\ \langle 2\rangle, \\ && \langle 113\rangle \rightarrow \langle 1\rangle\ \langle 148\rangle, \\ && \langle 121\rangle \rightarrow \langle 3\rangle\ \langle 121\rangle,\quad \langle 121\rangle \rightarrow \langle 3\rangle\ \langle 3\rangle, \\ && \langle 1\rangle \rightarrow a,\ \ \langle 2\rangle \rightarrow b,\ \ \langle 3\rangle \rightarrow c \quad \}. \end{array}$$

4.2 EXPERIMENT 2

The unknown context-free language is $\{ac^m \mid m \geq 1\} \cup \{bc^m \mid m \geq 1\}$ over $\Sigma = \{a, b, c\}$. This is the union of two languages.

We gave all positive examples of length up to 6 and all negative examples of length up to 12. The learning algorithm TBL outputs the following correct CFG $G = (N, \Sigma, P, S)$ as the best individual in the population of size 20 after 1000 iterations:

$$\begin{array}{rcl} N &=& \{\langle 1\rangle, \langle 2\rangle, \langle 3\rangle, \langle 112\rangle, \langle 113\rangle\}, \\ P &=& \{\ S \rightarrow \langle 113\rangle, \end{array}$$

$$\begin{array}{ll} \langle 113\rangle \rightarrow \langle 1\rangle\ \langle 112\rangle, & \langle 113\rangle \rightarrow \langle 2\rangle\ \langle 112\rangle, \\ \langle 113\rangle \rightarrow \langle 1\rangle\ \langle 3\rangle, & \langle 113\rangle \rightarrow \langle 2\rangle\ \langle 3\rangle, \\ \langle 112\rangle \rightarrow \langle 112\rangle\ \langle 3\rangle, & \langle 112\rangle \rightarrow \langle 3\rangle\ \langle 3\rangle, \\ \langle 1\rangle \rightarrow a,\ \ \langle 2\rangle \rightarrow b, & \langle 3\rangle \rightarrow c \qquad \}. \end{array}$$

5 CONCLUDING REMARKS

We have proposed a new hypothesis representation method, called the tabular representation, based on the parse table for learning CFGs examples. The problem of learning CFGs is reduced to the partitioning problem of nonterminals, and we have used the genetic algorithm for solving the partitioning problem.

We are now working on more experiments and more heavy experiments. Our future works are comparisons with other practical learning methods for inductive learning of grammars and rules, and investigations of theoretical analyses for the tabular representation methods for learning CFGs from examples. For example, when we construct a primitive CFG from a tabular representation $T(w)$, we assume the following condition: if there are two production rules $A \rightarrow CD$ and $B \rightarrow EF$ such that $C \Rightarrow v$, $E \Rightarrow v$ and $D \Rightarrow w$, $F \Rightarrow w$ for $v, w \in \Sigma^*$, then A and B must be equal, that is, they must be the same nonterminal. It is interesting to see whether this condition could not reduce the generative power of CFGs, that is, whether there exists the normal form of CFGs which satisfies this condition.

Acknowledgements

This work was supported in part by "The TDU Foundation for Advancement of Research" No. Q97J-07.

References

Aho, A. V. & Ullman. J. D. (1972). *The Theory of Parsing, Translation and Compiling, Vol. I: Parsing.* Prentice Hall.

Dupont. P. (1994). Regular grammatical inference from positive and negative samples by genetic search: the GIG method. *Proceedings of Second International Colloquium on Grammatical Inference (ICGI-94)* (LNAI 862), 236–245. Springer-Verlag.

Gold. E. M. (1978). Complexity of automaton identification from given data. *Information and Control* **37**:302–320.

Michalewicz. Z. (1996). *Genetic Algorithms + Data Structures = Evolution Programs.* Springer-Verlag.

von Laszewski, G., (1991). Intelligent structural operators for the k-way graph partitioning problem. *Proceedings of Fourth International Conference on Genetic Algorithms*, 45–52. CA: Morgan Kaufmann.

Sakakibara. Y. (1992). Efficient learning of context-free grammars from positive structural examples. *Information and Computation* **97**:23–60.

Sakakibara. Y. (1997). Recent Advances of Grammatical Inference. *Theoretical Computer Science* **185**:15–45.

Expected Error Analysis for Model Selection

Tobias Scheffer
Technische Universität Berlin
FR 5-8, Franklinstr. 28/29
10587 Berlin, Germany
scheffer@cs.tu-berlin.de

Thorsten Joachims
Universität Dortmund
LS VIII, Baroper Str. 301
44221 Dortmund, Germany
joachims@ls8.cs.uni-dortmund.de

Abstract

In order to select a good hypothesis language (or *model*) from a collection of possible models, one has to assess the generalization performance of the hypothesis which is returned by a learner that is bound to use that model. This paper deals with a new and very efficient way of assessing this generalization performance. We present a new analysis which characterizes the expected generalization error of the hypothesis with least training error in terms of the distribution of error rates of the hypotheses in the model. This distribution can be estimated very efficiently from the data which immediately leads to an efficient model selection algorithm. The analysis predicts learning curves with a very high precision and thus contributes to a better understanding of why and when over-fitting occurs. We present empirical studies (controlled experiments on Boolean decision trees and a large-scale text categorization problem) which show that the model selection algorithm leads to error rates which are often as low as those obtained by 10-fold cross validation (sometimes even lower). However, the algorithm is much more efficient (because the learner does not have to be invoked at all) and thus solves model selection problems with as many as thousand relevant attributes and 12,000 examples.

1 Introduction

Consider the following situation: In order to solve a learning problem we need to choose a hypothesis language from a set of possible languages (or models) – decision trees of variable depth perhaps, or a neural network with a variable number of hidden neurons. Our goal is to select the model which gives us the highest generalization performance. If we choose too simple a model (a tree of depth one say) even the best hypothesis in that model is likely to incur both a high error on the training data and a high true error. On the other hand, if we choose too rich a model (*e.g.,* a neural network with a hundred hidden units) our hypothesis might be poor due to over-fitting. The task of choosing a model such that the error of the hypothesis returned by a learner (which uses this model) is low is referred to as *model selection.* Approaches to model selection fall into the categories hold-out testing, complexity penalization, and Bayesian learning. See [17] or [7] for a more detailed overview.

Hold-out testing algorithms stratify the potential hypothesis language H into subsets ("models") $H_1, H_2, \ldots \subset H$. Starting with the smallest model, the learning algorithm returns one hypothesis from each model. The hold-out set (which has not been used for learning) is then used to obtain an estimate of the expected generalization error; the model with the lowest estimate is selected and the learner is invoked for this model with the whole sample. In order to minimize the variance of the estimate the idea of n-fold cross validation, *e.g.,* [10, 19], and bootstrapping [5] is to average many error measurements which are generated on re-sampled data sets. For many applications, n-fold cross validation works quite well, but it does not scale well for very large-scale problems as the learner has to be invoked about at least once for each model (*e.g.,* [8]).

Complexity penalization based methods minimize a demerit criterion which consists of the empirical error of the hypothesis and an additional term that penalizes the complexity of the model which the hypothesis came from. Effectively, complexity penalization algorithms try to reconstruct the learning curve (*i.e.*, the dependency between model index and generalization error) from only the empirical error rate and some measure of the model complexity. Unfortunately, the learning curve can exhibit various shapes [18] and therefore no single complexity penalization scheme can perform well for all model selection problems. For each complexity penalization algorithm one can construct a pair of model selection problems such that the algorithm performs well for one problem and fails (*i.e.*, incurs an additional error λ that does not vanish when the sample size grows) for the other one [7]. Therefore, all practical learners which conduct complexity penalization (*e.g.*, the Support Vector Machine [20], decision tree pruning algorithms [9], neural weight decay algorithms [3]) possess a regularization parameter that can be adapted for the given problem (*e.g.*, by cross validation).

Bayesian learners [1] focus on the posterior probability of a function f having generated the sample S: $P(f|S)$. Under certain ideal conditions, one can, under high computational effort, derive the Bayes hypothesis from $P(f|S)$ which is guaranteed to have the least generalization error. The Bayes hypothesis is a weighted majority (where $P(f|S)$ defines the weights) over all hypotheses. Usually, the posterior is used for less expensive heuristics such as MAP (the *maximum a posteriori* hypothesis maximizes the chance of having generated the data) or MDL [11] (the MDL hypotheses minimizes the description length required for the data by compressing it to a hypothesis and the exceptions to the hypothesis in the data). Using Bayes' rule, the posterior $P(f|S)$ works out to $P(S|f)P(f)/P(S)$. $P(S)$ is constant for a problem (sometimes, $P(S)$ can be derived from $P(S|f)$ and $P(f)$), and $P(S|f)$ can usually be determined. However, the prior distribution $P(f)$ is assumed to be known in advance – which is indeed a very strong assumption. The general belief is that Bayesian learners are fairly robust against some degree of misalignment between the actual and the assumed $P(f)$ (this setting is referred to as robust Bayesian analysis [2]). The No-Free-Lunch Theorems [23] explain that Bayesian learners perform better than randomly guessing only if the actual and the assumed prior are "not completely unaligned".

This paper's scope. Suppose that we have to solve some learning problem for which two possible models are available. Model H_1 contains just one single hypothesis h_1 while model H_2 contains two hypotheses, h_{21} and h_{22}. All three hypotheses incur (unknown) generalization errors. When we draw a sample, each hypothesis exhibits an empirical error which is an *unbiased* estimate of its true error. Unbiased means that the expected empirical error of each hypothesis is just its generalization error. The relation between true and empirical error is known: the empirical error is governed by the binomial distribution with the true error as its mean value. Now suppose that we minimize the empirical error in H_2; let h_2^* be the hypothesis in H_2 with the least empirical error (H_1 contains only one hypothesis, so minimizing the empirical error in H_1 is trivial). When both hypotheses in H_2 incur equal empirical errors, we draw one at random. Unfortunately, the empirical error of h_2^* is not an unbiased estimate of its true error. Why is that? With a chance of almost $\frac{1}{2}$, the empirical error of each hypothesis is an optimistic estimate of its true error, and with a chance of almost $\frac{1}{2}$ it is a pessimistic estimate. An optimistically assessed hypothesis has a greater chance of being selected as h_2^* than a pessimistically assessed one. In return, the empirical error of h_2^* is, on average, optimistically biased. So, what should we do when the empirical error of h_2^* is less than the empirical error of h_1? The empirical error of h_1 is unbiased while the empirical error of h_2^* (which is lower) is known to be optimistic. Here, the question is how strong this bias is. In this paper, we present an answer to this question. We will see that the expected error of the hypothesis which minimizes the empirical error in model H_2 depends on the distribution of error values in that model. The distribution of error values of all hypotheses in H_2 contains (at most) two occurring error values; however, the true error rates are unknown. But we can estimate the distribution of true error rates by recording the distribution of empirical error rates in H_2. The distribution of empirical error values in H_2 is, in this case, very simple because only (at most) two distinct values occur which can be observed. When these two error values are known, this suffices to determine an estimate of the expected generalization error of h_2^*. The most interesting aspect of our solution is that no learning has to be conducted in order to determine the error of the hypothesis that would be the result of learning.

2 Preliminaries

In this paper, we focus on classification learning from labeled examples where the target criterion is the expected zero-one loss.

Instances. We assume that there is a set of *instances*

X and a finite set of *class labels* Y. A classification problem is defined by an unknown distribution $D_{XY} = D_{Y|X}D_X$ over labeled instances $(X \times Y)$, which we want to approximate as closely as possible. Sometimes, when this is more convenient, we speak of target functions. Note that target distributions can "emulate" target functions ($D_{Y|X}(y|x) = 1$ iff $y = f(x)$, 0 otherwise).

Hypotheses and Error. A *hypothesis* $h : X \to Y$ is a mapping from instances to class labels. The *true (or generalization) error of a hypothesis*, with respect to the (unknown) distribution D_{XY} is $E_D(h) = \int_{(x,y)\in X\times Y} \ell(h(x), y) dD_{XY}(x, y)$, where ℓ is the zero-one loss function. Let the *sample* S be a sequence of m labeled instances drawn *independently and identically distributed* according to D_{XY}. We then define the *empirical or observed error* as $E_S(h) = \frac{1}{m}\sum_{(x,y)\in S} \ell(h(x), y)$.

Hypothesis Language and Model. We assume the existence of a given hypothesis language H which may be infinite and may even have an infinite VC-dimension. A *stratification* of the hypothesis language is a finite sequence of models $\langle H_1, \ldots, H_m\rangle$, $H_i \subseteq H$. We do not assume the models to be properly nested, but we require the models H_i to be *finite* subsets of H.

Learner. A *learner* takes as input a sample S and a model H_i and determines the set $H_i^*(S) = \{h \in H_i : E_S(h) = \min_{h'\in H_i}(E_S(h'))\}$ of hypotheses with least empirical error. There is at least one such hypothesis. If there is more than one, we assume that the learner draws one at random under uniform distribution.

Notations. We generally write probability distributions and densities in the form $P_{\{x\}}(f(x) = y)$ where the subscript x indicates that x is a random variable. The distribution of x should become clear in the given context. $P_{\{x\}}(f(x) = y)$ refers to the chance of drawing an x such that $f(x) = y$. Similarly, we write $\mathbf{E}_{\{x\}}(f(x))$ for the expectation of $f(x)$ over all x (again, the distribution of x becomes clear in the context). We write the binomial distribution as $B[p, n](x)$, denoting the probability of making x mistakes on n trials when the chance of a mistake is p.

3 Expected Error Analysis

Let us look at a model H_i and a target distribution D_{XY}. The target D_{XY} defines an error $E_D(h)$ for each hypothesis $h \in H_i$. These error values define a distribution of error values in H_i, which we write as $P_{\{h\}}(E_D(h)|H_i, D_{XY})$ and which is the "prior" in our analysis. (Here, "prior" means prior to observing the sample and minimizing the empirical error.) $P_{\{h\}}(E_D(h) = e_D|H_i, D_{XY})$ is the chance of drawing a hypothesis h from H_i (when drawing under uniform distribution) which incurs an error of e_D.

Suppose that H_i contains two hypotheses (as an easy example). The prior $P_{\{h\}}(E_D(h)|H_i, D_{XY})$ tells us which error values occur in H_i. There are either two values with a chance of $\frac{1}{2}$ or one value with a chance of 1 (if both hypotheses have equal errors). Let us invent names h_1 and h_2 for the hypotheses and let $E_D(h_1)$ and $E_D(h_2)$ be the two occurring true error values. When we will draw a sample S, the hypotheses will show empirical error values of $E_S(h_1)$ and $E_S(h_2)$, respectively. The empirical errors on the sample S of size m are distributed according to $B[E_D(h_1), m]$ and $B[E_D(h_2), m]$, where B is the binomial distribution. (Each example is classified correctly or wrongly, the chance of a wrong answer being $E_D(h_1)$ and $E_D(h_2)$, respectively. This results in a binomial distribution.) Let us now select the hypothesis with the smaller empirical error, call it h_L. The chance that h_L has a particular error value e_D is now no longer $P_{\{h\}}(E_D(h) = e_D|H_i, D_{XY})$, because h_L is not a randomly drawn hypothesis. It is, instead, the hypothesis which minimizes the empirical error. The expected true error of h_L is likely to be greater than its empirical error (which is optimistically biased) but less than the error of a randomly drawn hypothesis. But precisely what is the expected error of h_L? Our analysis characterizes the expected error of h_L (the distribution of error values of h_L is our "posterior") in terms of the prior $P_{\{h\}}(E_D(h)|H_i, D_{XY})$. And, as we will see, the prior can be estimated from a sample S by recording $P_{\{h\}}(E_S(h)|H_i, S)$, the empirical counterpart of $P_{\{h\}}(E_D(h)|H_i, D_{XY})$. This is the principle idea of the expected error analysis which we will discuss in the following.

Since the prior tells us how many hypotheses incur which error values, we can assign names h_1 through $h_{|H_i|}$ to the occurring error values $E_D(h_1)$ through $E_D(h_{|H_i|})$. If, for example, $P_{\{h_i\}}(E_D(h) = 0|H_i, D_{XY})$ equals $\frac{2}{|H_i|}$, we know that there are exactly two hypotheses with true error of zero. Although we do not know *which* hypotheses these are, we can name them, for instance, h_1 and h_2. Now we can claim that $E_D(h_1) = E_D(h_2) = 0$. But note that assigning hypothesis names to the known error values is only a notational "trick" that will make life easier for us during the main proof; we do not actually know (and our derivation does not exploit) *which* individual hypothesis incurs a particular error value. Now the following happens. On a sample S of size m, each hypothesis incurs an empirical error which is binomially distributed: $P_S(E_S(h) = e_S|E_D(h), m) = B[E_D(h), m](e_S)$. The learner first determines the set $H_i^*(S)$ of hypotheses with least empirical error. Then the learner returns a hypothesis h_L from $H_i^*(S)$ (the set of hypotheses with least empirical error), breaking ties by drawing randomly under uniform distribution. Assume that the sample size m is fixed and given *a priori*. By contrast, the sample S itself is a random variable, distributed according to $(D_{XY})^m$. This implies that $H_i^*(S)$ is a random variable (as it depends on S) and so is h_L; h_L is drawn randomly from $H_i^*(S)$. This leads us to the posterior distribution $P_{\{S,h_L\}}(E_D(h_L) = e_D|H_i, D_{XY}, m, h_L \in H_i^*(S))$ which is the chance of drawing a sample S (of fixed size m) and, consequently, a hypothesis h_L from $H_i^*(S)$, such that the true error of h_L is e_D. The principle difference between the prior and posterior distribution is that the prior gives the distribution of error values of hypotheses which are drawn uniformly from H_i, whereas the posterior gives the distribution of error values for hypotheses which have been generated by an error minimization process. Knowing the posterior $P_{\{S,h_L\}}(E_D(h_L) = e_D|H_i, D_{XY}, m, h_L \in H_i^*(S))$ we can easily derive the expectation $\mathbf{E}_{\{S,h_L\}}(E_D(h_L)|H_i, D_{XY}, m, h_L \in H_i^*(S))$. It is the expected true error of h_L (the hypothesis returned by the learner) using model H_i and a sample of size m. This expectation is a natural (and often used [21, 19]) measure of the quality of a model and will serve as the model selection criterion in our study.

We quantify the expected true error of h_L, $\mathbf{E}_{\{S,h_L\}}(E_D(h_L)|H_i, D_{XY}, m, h_L \in H_i^*(S))$ in Theorem 1. The crucial part of the proof is how to determine the minimum error e_S and the number of hypotheses $|H_i^*(S)|$ which achieve this error. The idea is that we can determine the chance that $H_i^*(S)$ is a particular subset H^* by factorizing the least error e_S and calculating the chances that each hypothesis in H^* has an empirical error of e_S and each hypothesis outside incurs a strictly greater error. This, however, imposes another difficulty. We know that the empirical error of a hypothesis is distributed binomially, given the true error. But here we have to determine the chance of *several hypotheses* incurring a certain empirical error e_S. Unfortunately, this probability cannot be determined unless we assume the empirical errors of distinct hypotheses to be independent (in reality, the empirical errors are somewhat dependent because they are measured on the same sample). The empirical error rates depend on the corresponding true error rates and are not identically distributed. We do not make any assumptions on the true error rates. This independence assumption is often made implicitly; for instance, the calculation of p-values which is required to compare n-fold cross validation results (the p-value gives the chance that one learner does better than another learner for some problem, given the cross validation results) is based on the assumptions that the hold-out errors are independent estimates.

Assumption 1 (Independence Assumption) *The empirical errors $E_S(h)$ of hypotheses $h \in H$ are independent given the corresponding true errors $E_D(h)$. $P(E_S(h_1), \ldots, E_S(h_{|H_i|})|H_i,\ D_{XY},\ m,\ E_D(h_1), \ldots, E_D(h_{|H_i|})) = \prod_{j=1}^{|H_i|} P(E_S(h_j)|H_i, D_{XY}, m, E_D(h_j))$.*

Theorem 1 (Expected error of an empirical error minimizing hypothesis) *For a distribution D_{XY} of labeled instances and a finite model H_i let $E_D(h)$ be the true error of each hypothesis $h \in H$. Let m be the fixed sample size. Let h_L be a hypothesis which is drawn uniformly from the set $H_i^*(S)$ of hypotheses in H_i with least empirical error with respect to a sample S, drawn according to $(D_{XY})^m$. Then, under the independence assumption, the expected error of h_L is*

$$
\begin{aligned}
&\mathbf{E}_{\{S,h_L\}}(E_D(h_L)|H_i, D_{XY}, m, h_L \in H_i^*(S)) \\
&= \sum_{j=1}^{|H_i|} E_D(h_j) \sum_{e_S} B[E_D(h_j), m](e_S) \sum_{m=1}^{|H_i|} \frac{1}{n} \qquad (1) \\
&\quad \sum_{\substack{H^* \subseteq H_i \setminus \{h_j\} \\ |H^*| = n-1}} \prod_{h^* \in H^*} P_{\{S\}}(E_S(h^*) = e_S|E_D(h^*), m) \\
&\quad \prod_{h \in H \setminus \{h_j\} \setminus H^*} P_{\{S\}}(E_S(h) > e_S|E_D(h), m)
\end{aligned}
$$

The proof is given in Appendix A. Equation 1 can, in principle, be evaluated, given the distribution of true error values $P_{\{h\}}(E_D(h)|H_i, D_{XY})$, $|H_i|$, and the sample size m. Later in this Section, we will see how the prior $P_{\{h\}}(E_D(h)|H_i, D_{XY})$ can be estimated efficiently when only H_i and a sample are known. We then have a means of estimating the expected generalization error of a hypothesis which minimizes the empirical error without actually having to invoke a learner. A straightforward implementation of Theorem 1 would run in time exponential in $|H_i|$ which is clearly unacceptable. Therefore, we make the technical assumption that removing one single hypothesis from H_i does not considerably alter the distribution of error values.

Assumption 2 *We assume that* $P(|H^*| = n | h_i \in H^*, E_S(h_i) = e_{min}, H_i, m, D_{XY}) = P(|H^*| = n | h_j \in H^*, E_S(h_j) = e_{min}, H_i, m, D_{XY})$.

Assumption 2 means that the chance of the set of hypotheses with least empirical error being of size m when it is known that a hypothesis h_i with empirical error e_{min} belongs to this set is not dependent on *which* hypothesis with empirical error e_{min} is known to be in this set. This is always true when H_i is "large". This assumption is reasonable in all practical cases as $|H_i|$ grows doubly exponential for Boolean functions and at least singly exponential for languages such as monomials.

Theorem 2 (Efficient evaluation of Theorem 1) *For a distribution D_{XY} of labeled instances and a finite model H_i, let $E_D(h)$ be the true error of each hypothesis $h \in H$. Under assumptions* 1 *and* 2, *the expected error of the hypothesis h_L returned by the learner given an* i.i.d. *sample S drawn according to D_{XY} is*

$$\mathbf{E}_{\{S,h_L\}}(E_D(h_L)|H_i, m, D_{XY}, h_L \in H_i^*(S)) = \frac{\int e_D P_{\{h\}}(E_D(h) = e_D|H_i, D_{XY})}{\int P_{\{h\}}(E_D(h) = e_D|H_i, D_{XY})} \frac{dP_{\{S\}}(h_{eD} \in H_i^*(S)|H_i, m, E_D(h_{e_D}))}{dP_{\{S\}}(h_{e_D} \in H_i^*(S)|H_i, m, E_D(h_{e_D}))} \quad (2)$$

where

$$P_{\{S\}}(h_{eD} \in H_i^*(S)|H_i, m, E_D(h_{e_D})) = \sum_{e_S} B[e_D, m](e_S) \prod_{e'_D} \left(\sum_{e \geq e_S} B[e'_D, m](e) \right)^{f(e_D, e'_D)} \quad (3)$$

$$f(e_D, e'_D) = \begin{cases} |H_i| P_{\{h\}}(E_D(h) = e'_D|H_i, D_{XY}) & \text{iff } e_D \neq e'_D \\ |H_i| P_{\{h\}}(E_D(h) = e'_D|H_i, D_{XY}) - 1 & \text{iff } e_D = e'_D \end{cases}$$

and h_{eD} is an arbitrary hypothesis with true error $E_D(h_{eD}) = e_D$.

The proof can be found in Appendix B. Note that the only input to Theorem 2 are the error prior, $|H_i|$, and m. Theorem 2 (which effectively replaces Theorem 1) solves the primary complexity problem by removing the product over all subsets of H_i from Equation 2. A careful implementation of the formula (see the full paper [17] for details) now runs in $O(m^2)$.

Estimating $P_{\{h\}}(E_D(h)|H_i, D_{XY})$. As $P_{\{h\}}(E_D(h)|H_i, D_{XY})$ depends on D_{XY}, it cannot be determined exactly. All information on D_{XY} which we can access is contained in S. We can use S to measure $P_{\{h\}}(E_S(h)|H_i, S)$, which will serve as an estimate of $P_{\{h\}}(E_D(h)|H_i, D_{XY})$. As m grows, $P_{\{h\}}(E_S(h)|H_i, S)$ converges towards $P_{\{h\}}(E_D(h)|H_i, D_{XY})$; so it is a consistent estimate and for a reasonably large S we can hope to obtain a good estimate of $P_{\{h\}}(E_D(h)|H_i, D_{XY})$. In fact, the experiments presented in the following sections show that even samples of size 50 allow for fairly accurate estimates. Note that this is a one-dimensional distribution only; the dimensionality does not increase when H_i grows. $P_{\{h\}}(E_S(h)|H_i, S)$ can be estimated by drawing a small number of hypotheses uniformly from H_i and recording the empirical error values.

Algorithm. We now have an efficient model selection algorithm: For each model (a) record $P_{\{h\}}(E_S(h)|H_i, S)$ by drawing a small number of hypotheses and use it as an estimate of $P_{\{h\}}(E_D(h)|H_i, D_{XY})$, (b) use Theorem 2 to determine the expected generalization error. (c) Select the model with the lowest estimated expected generalization error. Copies of the implementation can be obtained from the authors upon request.

4 What is Over-Fitting?

A learning curve is a function which maps a model index i to the error of the hypothesis which is generated by a given learner on model H_i for a given learning problem. Often, the error increases for large models which is generally referred to as over-fitting. This is frequently considered to be due to the high hypothesis complexity in models with high indeces. However, over-fitting does not necessarily occur in all settings. Boosting algorithms have often exhibited a complementary behavior [14]; experiments by Schaffer [13] support the view that whether over-fitting occurs at all is a property of the problem.

Using Chernoff bounds, one can guarantee that (with high probability) the difference between true and empirical error of *no* hypothesis in some model H_i exceeds a certain threshold. This immediately leads to worst-case error bounds. This is the way that PAC and VC theory argue. The empirical error is binomially distributed, so even a poor hypothesis has a small chance (depending on the sample size) of exhibiting a low empirical error. When H_i grows, the chance of *some* hypothesis in H_i having a large difference between true and empirical error grows steeply. Therefore, given two hypotheses with equal empirical error which come from distinct models, PAC theory gives better guarantees for the one which comes from the smaller model. But just because *there is* a hypothesis with a large difference between true and empirical error does not mean that the expected error of the returned hypothesis is (absolutely) high. In fact, from our expected error analysis we can derive that, when the prior distribution of error values in the model remains constant, the expected error of the returned hypothesis *converges from above* as H_i grows.

Let us look at the expected error of the returned hypothesis h_L when the model size, $|H_i|$, approaches infinity and $P_{\{h\}}(E_D(h)|H_i, D_{XY})$ stays constant.

Theorem 3 *When* $P_{\{h\}}(E_D(h)|H_i, D_{XY})$ *is constant, the expected error of a randomly drawn empirical minimizer* h_L *converges as* $|H_i|$ *grows.*

$$\lim_{|H_i|\to\infty} \mathbf{E}_{\{S,h_L\}}(E_D(h_L)|H_i, m, D_{XY}, h_L \in H_i^*(S)) \quad (4)$$
$$= \frac{\int_{e_D} e_D \times (1-e_D)^m dP_{\{h\}}(E_D(h) = e_D|H_i, D_{XY})}{\int_{e_D} (1-e_D)^m dP_{\{h\}}(E_D(h) = e_D|H_i, D_{XY})}$$

The proof can be found in [17]. Note that Theorem 3 is subject to the assumption that $P_{\{h\}}(E_D(h)|H_i, D_{XY})$ remains fixed while H_i grows. Let us now study how $P_{\{h\}}(E_D(h)|H_i, D_{XY})$ actually behaves when we want to learn Boolean functions under uniform distribution of the Boolean instances. In this case, the prior can be determined analytically. When the target function uses attributes x_1 through x_n and the model H_i consists of hypotheses over attributes x_1 through x_i, then the prior is a certain binomial distribution depending on i and n (function and hypothesis must agree on all possible $2^{\max\{i,n\}}$ instances which can be distinguished by target function or hypothesis). By plugging the exact prior into Theorem 1 we can determine the learning curve analytically. Figure 1 shows some prior distributions of error values $P_{\{h,D_{XY}\}}(E_D(h)|H_i)$ (D_{XY} is now a random variable as we draw Boolean functions at random) for various models when the target function is over three attributes. Note that models H_1 through H_3 have identical error priors; the increase in the model size leads to a decrease in error. When irrelevant attributes are added (models H_4 through H_6) the tails of the distribution become skinnier – intuitively, the concentration of really good (and really bad) hypotheses decreases and more hypotheses incur an error of close to $\frac{1}{2}$. This causes the learning curve to rise; Figures 2 and 3 show some predicted learning curves (for various sample sizes) and compare them to learning curves measured in a simulation (the predicted curves are the ones labeled "predicted learning curve, exact prior"). The "simulation" curve shows the error measured in an experiment, averaged over 200 randomly drawn target functions. The deviation originates from three sources: The simulation curve is only measured in an experiment and hence subject to some inaccuracy, the independence assumption 1 on the empirical error causes a modest bias, and the simplification 2 on which the implementation is based incurs a very small error. However, the learning curve is still predicted very accurately. While PAC theory predicts learning curves very poorly for non worst-case problems, our analysis incorporates a joint property of the hypothesis language and the problem – namely $P_{\{h\}}(E_D(h)|H_i, D_{XY})$ – and is therefore able to explain learning curves with high accuracy.

5 Experiments

In our experiments, we study the accuracy and variance of the predicted error (in comparison to 10-fold cross validation).

Learning Boolean decision trees. In this set of experiments, we used randomly drawn Boolean functions as targets. Figures 2 and 3 compare some predicted learning curves (where the prior has been estimated from the sample) to the average of 200 learning curves measured empirically. As we expected, the quality of

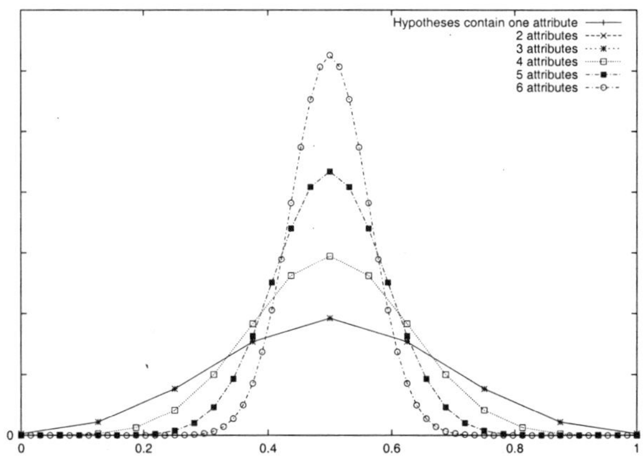

Figure 1 (horizontral axis: error rate; vertical axis: frequency of hypotheses in H_i which incur that error rate): Various shapes of $P_{\{h,D_{XY}\}}(E_D(h)|H_i, D_{XY})$ curves for models which consist of i Boolean attributes when the target function is a randomly drawn function over attributes x_1, x_2, x_3.

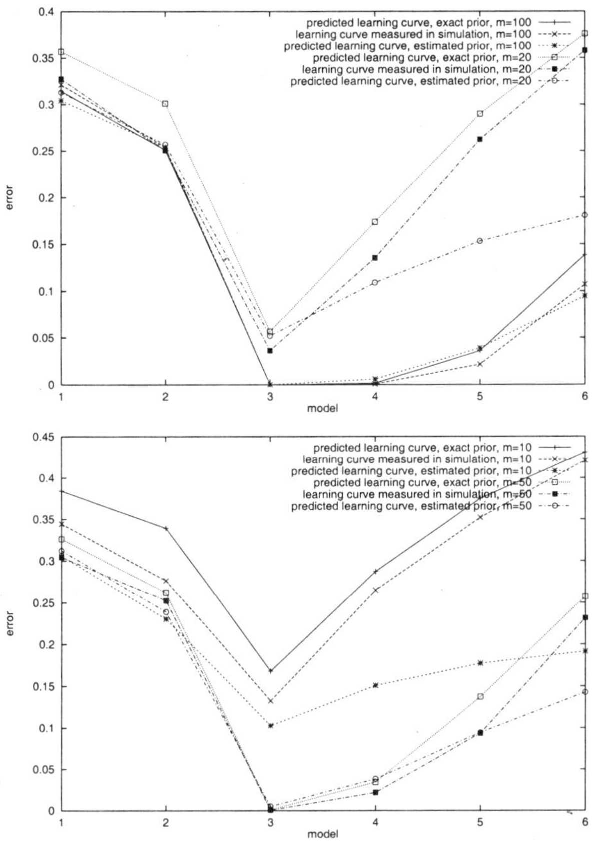

Figures 2 and 3: Averaged learning curves for 200 randomly drawn Boolean target functions. The target functions have 3 attributes (X-axis: number of attributes i in the model).

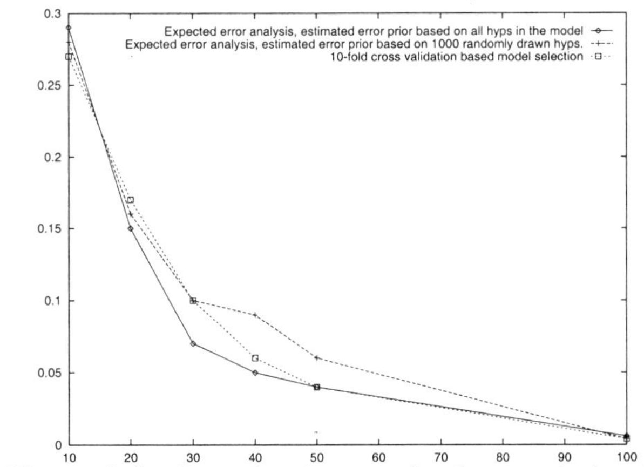

Figure 4 (horizontal axis: sample size, vertical axis: error): True error of hypothesis returned by model selection based learning. Average over 200 randomly drawn target functions with i attributes (i distributed uniformly).

the prediction depends crucially on how well the prior has been estimated. Sample sizes of 10 and 20 lead to unsatisfactory results; when the sample size is 50, the estimated curve approaches the measured curve and for $m = 100$ the predicted curve is a fair estimate of the measured curve. We now want to compare this means of error estimation to 10-fold cross validation. We use the following setting: First, the depth of the target tree is drawn uniformly between 2 and 6 attributes, the target tree is then determined at random with the chosen number of attributes. Next the sample is drawn. We then compare a 10-fold cross validation based model selection algorithm to expected error analysis based model selection. In both cases, models H_1 through H_6 are available where H_i contains all decision trees over i attributes. The cross validation based algorithm uses the averaged hold-out errors to select a model while the expected error analysis based algorithm makes a decision on grounds of the predicted generalization error for each model. After the model is selected, a learner is invoked which uses the whole sample and the true error of the resulting hypothesis is determined. The true error can be determined because the target function is known (but unknown to the learner). Figure 4 shows the results; each point is averaged over 200 randomly drawn target functions. The resulting error decreases, of course, with growing sample size. For a sample size of 30, expected error analysis does significantly better than 10-fold cross validation (p-value is .002); for $m = 40$ cross validation does better than the expected error analysis when the prior is only estimated by drawing 1000 hypotheses. The error rate achieved by expected error analysis as at least comparable to cross validation based model selection. The principle advantage of our expected error analysis is that the estimate is obtained in an extremely efficient manner since no learning has to be done.

Scaling up: text categorization. Now we want to demonstrate that the expected error analysis easily scales up to large learning problems with as many as thousand relevant attributes. Text categorization is the problem of mapping texts to semantic categories. Interesting applications of this are classification of newspaper articles and classification of web pages. Documents are represented as a vector of the word stems occurring in them (*i.e.*, the word ordering is ignored). We used the Reuters-21578 corpus of newspaper articles. It contains roughly 12,000 documents with 10,000 features and we used the ten most frequent categories. Experiments by Joachims [6] have shown that decision trees learned on this corpus are highly unbalanced. So we decided to use 2-DL (decision lists with two literals per conjunction) [12] as hypothesis language. Training was done with a very efficient greedy learner (based on the coverage approach) using an inverse indexing technique to determine empirical errors quickly. Assessing a model by means of the expected error analysis requires approximately 2 minutes on a PC while running hold-out testing for one fixed model and one category takes about 2-3 hours. As we wanted to compare the predicted error rates to cross validation error rates, we had to settle for a small number of models. Initial experiments indicated that almost all attributes are relevant. So we used 7 models where H_i contains decision lists with monomials that cover at least $1, 10, 20, 30, 50, 70$, and 100 examples, respectively. The parameter which is adapted here influences the model by only allowing monomials which are supported by a certain sample size. One could think of this number of examples which have to be covered by each monomial as a pruning threshold which is adapted. We refer the reader to the full paper for a more detailed discussion of the experimental settings. Figure 5 shows the predicted error rates and the error rates estimated by one-fold cross validation, averaged over the ten most frequent categories. The predicted values are subject to a pessimistic bias of .03 (which we already observed in the previous experiments), but the shapes of the learning curves are fairly similar. By means of the expected error analysis we can obtain a fair error estimate for a large number of models while hold-out testing (or even cross validation) is unfeasible for all but an extremely small number of models.

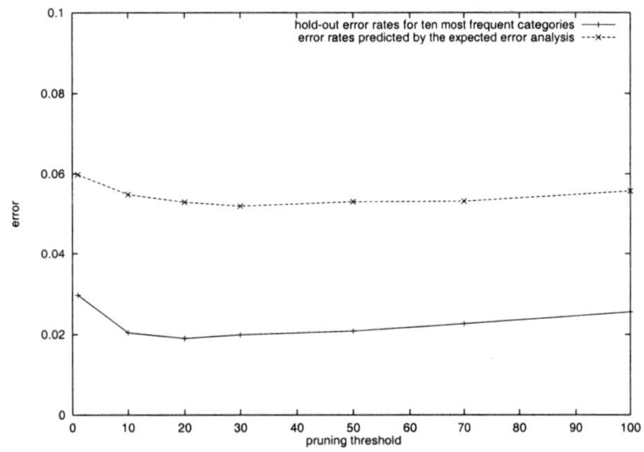

Figure 5: Learning curves (one-fold cross validation and expected error analysis for the text categorization problem), averaged over 10 categories.

6 Discussion

Many attempts have been made to find an efficient means of assessing models. The potential benefit of analyzing $P_{\{S\}}(E_D(h_L)|H_i, D_{XY}, m, L)$ has been discussed by Wolpert [22]. Scheffer and Joachims [15, 16] have found a solution which is based on two independence assumptions, one of which is rather strong. Domingos [4] presented a solution which is based on several very strong assumption (*e.g.,* it is assumed that the hypotheses which are contained in one model have equal true errors[1]). In this paper, we presented a very general solution for finite models which is only based on the relatively mild assumption that the empirical error rates of distinct hypotheses are independent given the corresponding true error rates (and no assumption is made on the true error rates). We presented experiments which showed that, when the prior distribution of error values $P_{\{h\}}(E_D(h)|H_i, D_{XY})$ is known (as is the case when the target is a Boolean function and the instances are uniformly distributed), our analysis predicts and thus explains learning curves with a very high precision. When the error prior is estimated from the sample, the error estimate is poor when the sample is too small to estimate the error distribution of h well. In our experiments estimates become reasonably accurate for sample sizes of 50 or above. We observed a small pessimistic bias which is caused by Assumption 1, but this bias was almost independent of the model. Note that an almost constant bias does not hurt too much when one wants to know which of several hypotheses is the best one (as opposed to when one wants to know the precise error of a particular hypothesis). Therefore, for the Boolean decision tree problem, the expected error analysis based model selection algorithm performed at least as good as 10-fold cross validation (even for small samples). However, the expected error analysis is much more efficient than cross validation, because no learning has to be done. Therefore it can be applied to large scale problems (such as text categorization or knowledge discovery in databases) with many (tens of) thousands of relevant attributes and many (tens of) thousands of examples.

A Proof of Theorem 1

Proof. The expected error $\mathbf{E}_{\{S,h_L\}}(E_D(h_L)|H_i, D_{XY}, m, h_L \in H_i^*(S))$ is the average over all errors $E_D(h_j)$ weighted by the chance that h_j is selected by the learner. $\mathbf{E}_{\{S,h_L\}}(E_D(h_L)|H_i, D_{XY}, m, h_L \in H_i^*(S)) = \sum_{j=1}^{|H_i|} E_D(h_j)\ P_{\{S,h_L\}}(h_L = h_j|H_i, D_{XY}, m, h_L \in H_i^*(S))$. The chance of a hypothesis being selected which is not

[1]We have been reported that Domingos eliminated this particular assumption in a new, not yet published paper.

in $H_i^*(S)$ (the set of minimum error hypotheses) is zero (Equation 5). We now factorize the number of minimum error hypotheses n (Equation 6). The chance of h_j being chosen as h_L when h_j is a minimum error hypothesis is $\frac{1}{n}$ (Equation 7). Now we factorize the empirical error e_S of h_j.

$$
\begin{aligned}
& P_{\{S,h_L\}}(h_L = h_j | H_i, D_{XY}, m, h_L \in H_i^*(S)) \qquad (5)\\
&= P_{\{S,h_L\}}(h_L{=}h_j | H_i, D_{XY}, m, h_j{\in} H_i^*(S), \\
&\quad h_L{\in} H_i^*(S)) P_{\{S,h_L\}}(h_j{\in} H_i^*(S) | H_i, D_{XY}, m) \\
&= \sum_{n=1}^{|H_i|} P_{\{S,h_L\}}(h_L = h_j | h_j \in H_i^*(S), |H_i^*(S)| = n, \\
&\quad H_i, D_{XY}, m, h_L \in H_i^*(S)) \\
&\quad P_{\{S\}}(h_j \in H_i^*(S), |H_i^*(S)| = n | H_i, D_{XY}, m) \qquad (6)\\
&= \sum_{n=1}^{|H_i|} \frac{1}{n} P_{\{S\}}(h_j \in H_i^*(S), |H_i^*(S)| = n | \\
&\quad H_i, D_{XY}, m) \qquad (7)\\
&= \sum_{e_S} P_{\{S\}}(E_S(h_j) = e_S | E_D(h_j), H_i, m) \\
&\quad \sum_{n=1}^{|H_i|} \frac{1}{n} P_{\{S\}}(h_j \in H_i^*(S), | \\
&\quad H_i^*(S)| = n | E_S(h_i) = e_S, H_i, D_{XY}, m) \qquad (8)
\end{aligned}
$$

The empirical error (given the true error is binomially distributed, so $P_{\{S\}}(E_S(h_j) = e_S | E_D(h_j), H_i, m)$ in Equation 8 equals $B[E_D(h_j), m](e_S)$. Now we need to determine the unknown term $P_{\{S\}}(h_j \in H_i^*(S), |H_i^*(S)| = n | E_S(h_i) = e_S, H_i, D_{XY}, m)$. In Equation 9, we factorize all possible $H_i^*(S)$ of size n. When the hypotheses in $H_i^*(S)$ incur an empirical error of e_S, all other hypotheses have to incur a strictly higher error (according to the definition of $H_i^*(S)$. In Equation 10, we exploit the independence assumption to resolve the quantifiers.

$$
\begin{aligned}
& P(h_j \in H_i^*(S), |H_i^*(S)| = n | E_S(h_j) = e_S, H_i, D_{XY}, m) \qquad (9)\\
&= \sum_{\substack{H^* \subseteq H_i \\ |H^*| = n}} P(\forall h^* {\in} H^*{:} E_S(h^*) {=} e_S, \forall h {\in} H_i \backslash H^*{:} E_S(h) {>} e_S | \\
&\qquad E_S(h_j) {=} e_S, E_D(h), E_D(h^*), m) \\
&= \sum_{\substack{H^* \subseteq H_i \\ |H^*| = n}} \prod_{h^* \in H^*} P(E_S(h^*) = e_S | E_S(h_j) = e_S, E_D(h^*), m) \\
&\qquad \prod_{h \in H \backslash H^*} P(E_S(h) > e_S | E_S(h_j) = e_S, E_D(h), m) \qquad (10)\\
&= \sum_{\substack{H^* \subseteq H_i \backslash \{h_j\}, \\ |H^*| = n-1}} \prod_{h^* \in H^*} B[E_D(h^*), m](e_S) \\
&\qquad \prod_{h \in H_i \backslash \{h_i\} \backslash H^*} \sum_{e > e_S} B[E_D(h^*), m](e) \qquad (11)
\end{aligned}
$$

This completes the proof. ∎

B Proof of Theorem 2

Remember that the learner draws a hypothesis from $H_i^*(S)$ under uniform distribution and that assigning error values to individual hypothesis names was a notational trick in the first place. This means, if $E_D(h_i) = E_D(h_j)$ then $P_{\{S\}}(h_L = h_i | H_i, m) = P_{\{S\}}(h_L = h_j | H_i, m)$. Let h_{e_D} be an arbitrary hypothesis with $E_D(h_{e_D}) = e_D$. Then,

$$
\begin{aligned}
& \mathbf{E}_{\{S,h_L\}}(E_D(h_L) | H_i, m, D_{XY}, h_L \in H_i^*(S)) \qquad (12)\\
&= \int_{e_D} e_D dP_{\{h\}}(E_D(h) = e_D | H_i, D_{XY}) \\
&\quad P_{\{S,h_L\}}(h_L = h_{e_D} | H_i, D_{XY}, m, h_L \in H_i^*(S))
\end{aligned}
$$

Now we have to take care of $P_{\{S,h_L\}}(h_L = h_{eD} | H_i, D_{XY}, m, h_L \in H_i^*(S))$. We insert Equation 8 into Equation 12.

$$
\begin{aligned}
& \mathbf{E}_{\{S,h_L\}}(E_D(h_L) | H_i, m, D_{XY}, h_L \in H_i^*(S)) \\
&= \int_{e_D} e_D dP_{\{h\}}(E_D(h) = e_D | H_i, D_{XY}) \\
&\quad \sum_{e_{min}} \left(\sum_{n=1}^{|H_i|} \frac{1}{n} P_{\{S\}}(|H_i^*(S)| = n | h_{e_D} \in H_i^*(S), \right. \\
&\qquad \left. E_S(h) = e_{min}, H_i, D_{XY}, m) \right) \\
&\quad P(h_{e_D} \in H_i^*(S) | E_S(h_{e_D}) = e_{min}, H_i, m) \\
&\quad B[e_D, m](e_{min}) \qquad (13)
\end{aligned}
$$

Exploiting assumption 2 we can claim that

$$
\begin{aligned}
const &= \sum_{n=1}^{|H_i|} \frac{1}{n} P(|H_i^*(S)| = n | h \in H_i^*(S), \\
&\quad E_S(h) = e_{min}, H_i, D_{XY}, m) \qquad (14)
\end{aligned}
$$

is constant for all hypotheses h. $P_{\{S,h_L\}}(E_D(h_L) | H_i, m, D_{XY}, h_L \in H_i^*(S))$ should integrate to 1. This fixes the scaling factor *const* to

$$
\begin{aligned}
const = 1 / \Big(& \sum_{e_{min}} B[e_D, m](e_{min}) \qquad (15)\\
& P(h_{e_D} \in H_i^*(S) | E_S(h_{e_D}) = e_{min}, H_i, m) \Big).
\end{aligned}
$$

This proves Equation 2. Now we will focus on Equation 3. Equation 16 follows from the straightforward observation that h_{e_D} is in $H_i^*(S)$ iff h_{e_D} incurs an empirical error of e_S and all other h_j incur at least an error of e_S. Note that this equation exploits assumption 1. In Equation 17, we group all hypotheses with equal true error e'_D into one factor and take this factor to the number of hypotheses with that error. One hypothesis (h_{e_D}) has already been assigned an empirical error and is thus not included in the product.

$$P_{\{S\}}(h_{eD} \in H_i^*(S)|H_i, m, E_D(h_{e_D})) \quad (16)$$

$$= \sum_{e_S} B[e_D, m](e_S) \prod_{\substack{j=1 \\ h_j \neq h_{e_D}}}^{|H_i|} \left(\sum_{e \geq e_S} B[E_D(h_j), m](e) \right)$$

$$= \sum_{e_S} B[e_D, m](e_S) \prod_{e'_D} \left(\sum_{e \geq e_S} B[e'_D, m](e) \right)^{|\{h: h \in H \setminus \{h_{e_D}\}, E_D(h) = e'_D\}|} \quad (17)$$

Now Equations 13, 15, and 17 can be rewritten as Equation 3. This completes the proof. ∎

ACKNOWLEDGMENT

We would like to thank Uschi Sondhauss and Fritz Wysotzki for discussions about earlier versions of this paper. This work was partially supported by grants WY 20/1-2 of the German Research Council (DFG), the DFG collaborative research center SFB 475, and an Ernst-von-Siemens fellowship held by Tobias Scheffer.

References

[1] J. Berger. *Statistical Decision Theory and Bayesian Analysis.* Springer-Verlag, 1985.

[2] J. Berger. An overview of robust Bayesian analysis. Technical Report 93-53C, Department of Statistics, Purdue University, 1993.

[3] Y. Le Cun, J. Denker, and S. Solla. Optimal brain damage. In *NIPS-89*, pages 598–605, 1989.

[4] P. Domingos. A process-oriented heuristic for model selection. In *ICML-98*, pages 127–135, 1998.

[5] B. Efron. Bootstrap methods: another look at the jacknife. *Annals of Statistics*, 7(1):1–26, 1979.

[6] T. Joachims. Text categorization with support vector machines. In *Proceedings of the European Conference on Machine Learning*, 1998.

[7] M. Kearns, Y. Mansour, A. Ng, and D. Ron. An experimental and theoretical comparison of model selection methods. *Machine Learning Journal*, 27:7–50, 1997.

[8] R. Kohavi and G. John. Wrappers for feature subset selection. *Artificial Intelligence*, 97(1-2):245–271, 1997.

[9] J. Mingers. An empirical comparison of selection measures for decision-tree induction. *Machine Learning*, 3:319–342, 1989.

[10] C. Mosier. Problems and designs of cross validation. *Educational and Psychological Measurement*, 11:5–11, 1951.

[11] J. Rissanen. Minimum-description-length principle. *Ann. Statist.*, 6:461–464, 1985.

[12] R. L. Rivest. Learning decision lists. *Machine Learning*, 2(2):229–246, 1987.

[13] C. Schaffer. Overfitting avoidance as bias. *Machine Learning*, 10:153–178, 1993.

[14] R. Schapire, Y. Freund, P. Bartlett, and W. Lee. Boosting the margin: A new explanation for the effectiveness of voting methods. In *ICML-97*, pages 322–330, 1997.

[15] T. Scheffer and T. Joachims. Estimating the expected error of empirical minimizers for model selection (abstract). AAAI-98, 1998.

[16] T. Scheffer and T. Joachims. Estimating the expected error of empirical minimizers for model selection. Technical Report TR 98-9, Technische Universitaet Berlin, 1998.

[17] T. Scheffer and T. Joachims. Expected error analysis for model selection. Preprint, TU Berlin, 1999. Available at http:ki.cs.tu-berlin.de/ scheffer.

[18] D. Schuurmans, L. Ungar, and D. Foster. Characterizing the generalization performance of model selection strategies. In *ICML-97*, pages 340–348, 1997.

[19] G. Toussaint. Bibliography on estimation of misclassification. *IEEE Transactions on Information Theory IT20*, 4:472–479, 1974.

[20] V. Vapnik. *Statistical Learning Theory.* Wiley, 1998.

[21] W. Wapnik and A. Tscherwonenkis. *Theorie der Zeichenerkennung.* Akademie Verlag, Berlin, 1979.

[22] D. H. Wolpert. The relationship between PAC, the statistical physics framework, the Bayesian framework, and the VC framework. In *The Mathematics of Generalization*, pages 117–214, 1995.

[23] David Wolpert. On the connection between in-sample testing and generalization error. *Complex Systems*, 6(1):47, 1992.

Distributed Value Functions

Jeff Schneider
Carnegie Mellon University
Pittsburgh, PA 15213
Jeff.Schneider@cs.cmu.edu

Weng-Keen Wong
Carnegie Mellon University
Pittsburgh, PA 15213
wkw@cs.cmu.edu

Andrew Moore
Carnegie Mellon University
Pittsburgh, PA 15213
awm@cs.cmu.edu

Martin Riedmiller
University of Karlsruhe
D-76128 Karlsruhe, FRG
riedml@ira.uka.de

Abstract

Many interesting problems, such as power grids, network switches, and traffic flow, that are candidates for solving with reinforcement learning (RL), also have properties that make distributed solutions desirable. We propose an algorithm for distributed reinforcement learning based on distributing the representation of the value function across nodes. Each node in the system only has the ability to sense state locally, choose actions locally, and receive reward locally (the goal of the system is to maximize the sum of the rewards over all nodes and over all time). However each node is allowed to give its neighbors the current estimate of its value function for the states it passes through. We present a value function learning rule, using that information, that allows each node to learn a value function that is an estimate of a weighted sum of future rewards for all the nodes in the network. With this representation, each node can choose actions to improve the performance of the overall system.

We demonstrate our algorithm on the distributed control of a simulated power grid. We compare it against other methods including: use of a global reward signal, nodes that act locally with no communication, and nodes that share rewards (but not value function) information with each other. Our results show that the distributed value function algorithm outperforms the others, and we conclude with an analysis of what problems are best suited for distributed value functions and the new research directions opened up by this work.

1 Introduction

Many interesting problems that are candidates for solving with Reinforcement Learning (RL), also have properties that make distributed solutions desirable. Whenever the state and/or action space is large, a distributed approach to performing the computation is desirable because it makes computational speedups from coarse-grain parallelism possible. In many systems access to sensors and actuators is inherently distributed, thus making a distributed solution method an attractive alternative to implementing a global high bandwidth communication network. Potential applications include control of power grids (or any other distribution of a resource such as water, gas, etc.), automobile traffic control, electronic network routing, and control of robot teams. Fig. 1 provides an intuitive sense of the kinds of applications we envision for our algorithms.

1.1 Related Work

Reinforcement learning and dynamic programming-based methods for optimal control are fairly well understood [14, 4]. By contrast distributed reinforcement learning is a much less mature concept because it is harder to formulate and analyze theoretically. One approach is to assume restricted interaction between the nodes. For example, if the transfer function is such that the dynamics of the local state depend only on the local state and the local control, and the value function can be trivially split into components depending only on local states and controls, then the solution to optimally controlling the entire system is just the composite solution created by solving the individual parts. Of course making that assumption eliminates almost all interesting problems.

A completely segregated approach can be taken with the additional allowance that the choice of controls by one node may restrict the space of controls available to another [12]. The resulting algorithm requires some global information, but does provide a provably optimal solution. Distributed elevator control has been addressed with reinforcement learning [7] . That work has shared, global state and cost information, but the agents act independently., Other work provides a similar framework, but in the context of competing rather than cooperating agents [9]. Homogeneous agents that seek to learn similar value functions can improve learning speed and performance by exchanging learned policies and sensing [15] .

Weiss proposes a "bucket brigade" scheme for credit assignment among cooperating reinforcement learning agents[17]. Rather than each agent acting locally and independently, they communicate globally in an auction to arbitrate which subset of agents will be allowed to "take over the global controls" in each state. Similarly, there are approaches where different behaviors are learned for a system and they are combined with the idea of choosing actions that will accomplish all goals [1]. Similarly, economic models can form the basis of credit assignment methods [3].

Packet routing is a domain for which completely distributed approaches have been taken [5, 6, 13]. In this problem, each node must make a decision about which neighboring node to rout each packet to. The global state space is the list of all packets in the system, their current locations, and their destinations. Each node, however, only has that information for the packets in its own queue. The global cost function is the the average length of time it takes to send packets in the network, but each node only stores and computes the length of time it will take to send packets from itself. As part of the routing algorithm, nodes periodically ask their neighbors how long they predict it will take them to deliver a packet if it is routed through them. Empirical studies have been promising but have also shown problems with ringing, instability, and adapting to changing load conditions.

2 Distributed Value Functions

In the description of our method, we refer to the sample problem diagrammed in fig. 1. The job of the distribution network is to minimize a cost function based on providing resources to the customers. The figure shows the nodes in a chain, but we make no assumptions on the connectivity of the graph. This problem could easily be written as a global reinforcement learning problem with, states X that represent flow rates and resource levels, actions A that represent changes in flow rates, and rewards (or penalties) R that represent satisfaction of customer requests and costs incurred in doing so. A distributed formulation of the problem makes the following changes:

- **State space.** Each node, i, observes some of the flows and resource levels (presumably those it can sense locally), which are represented by X_i. It may be the case that some state variables are observable by more than one, or even all nodes.
- **Action space.** Each node, i, has the ability to choose some of the flow control actions, called A_i. We assume that each action variable from the global formulation is chosen by exactly one node in the distributed formulation.
- **Rewards.** Each node, i, receives a reward presumably based on the satisfaction of its own customers, called R_i. We assume that the sum of the reward functions in the distributed case is equal to the global reward function in the global case ($R = \sum_i R_i$), and that the overall goal in the distributed formulation is to optimize that sum over time.

2.1 Global RL Formulation

The usual approach to solving the resource distribution problem with globally available states, actions, and rewards leads to a Bellman equation:

$$V(x) = \max_{a \in A}(R(x,a) + \gamma \sum_{x' \in X} p(x'|a,x)V(x')) \quad (1)$$

where V is the value function and γ is a temporal discount factor. This equation may be solved using many methods including many reinforcement learning variants. The result is the optimal value function which also represents the expected discounted sum of future rewards under the optimal policy:

$$V^*(x) = E(\sum_{t=0}^{\infty} \gamma^t R(x_t, a_t)) \quad (2)$$

Once obtained, the value function may be used to generate optimal control decisions by finding the action, a, that gives the maximum in eq. 1.

2.2 A Distributed RL Formulation

The main purpose of this paper is to introduce and evaluate four algorithms for distributed RL (DRL). In this section we describe each of them. The first two are common in the literature in various forms, while the last two are new.

We start by assuming that each action variable is chosen by a particular node and the reward function is broken up into a sum where each term is received at one node. For simplicity we continue to assume the state is globally observable. The question of local state

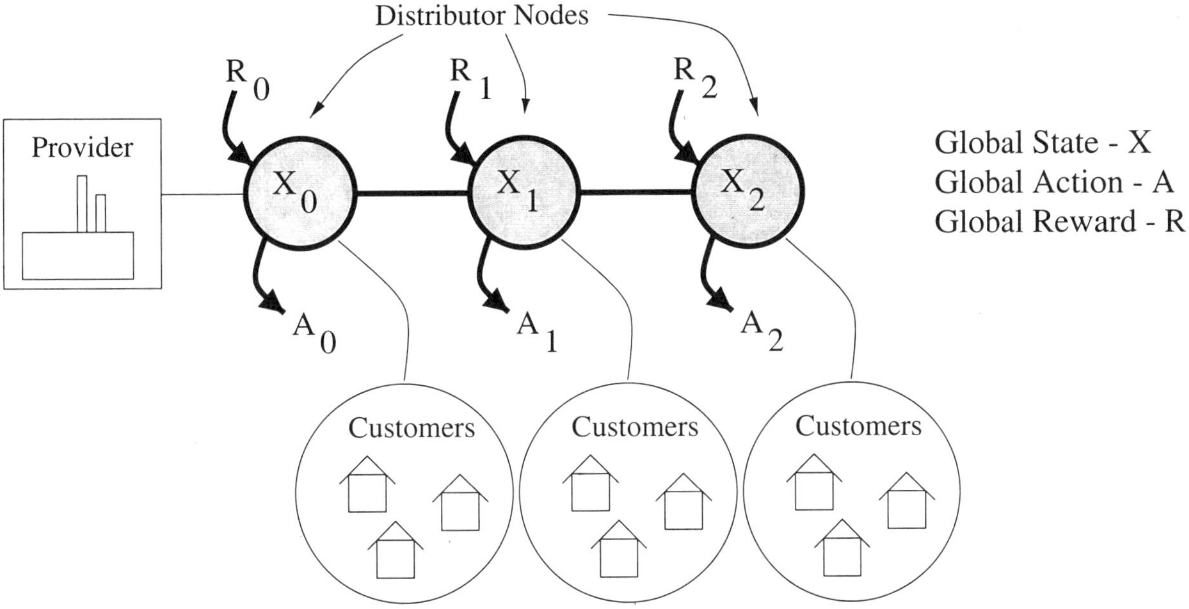

Figure 1: A sample resource distribution network. The shaded circles have a dual meaning in this figure. They represent 1) physical distribution centers in a network with resource providers and customers, and 2) logical nodes in the distributed RL formulation of the problem. They are the points at which state is sensed, actions are taken, and rewards are received.

observability will be addressed later. Our approach is to define a value function for each node, $V_i(x)$, that will be computed and used to choose that node's actions.

2.2.1 Global reward DRL

A first step toward distributed RL (DRL) is to have each node sense, act, and learn locally, but base learning and control decisions on a global reward signal. That results in a Bellman equation of the form:

$$V_i(x) = \max_{a \in A_i}(R(X,A) + \gamma \sum_{x' \in X} p(x'|a,x)V(x')) \quad (3)$$

where A_i represents only the action variables available for node i to choose. The unknown action choices of the other nodes will affect the probabilities in the transfer function, $p()$. X and A refer to the combined global state and action spaces, and R is the single, global reward that is distributed to all nodes. Unfortunately, the probability on the right-hand side of eq. 3 isn't well defined for node i. It depends on what policy the neighboring nodes are following and would be very hard to estimate. An alternative is the Q-learning formulation, which will be described later. Without addressing the issue of how/if a simultaneous solution to the set of these equations can be found, we observe that once it is found, the value function retains its meaning as the expected discounted sum of future rewards under the resulting policy:

$$V_i(x) = E(\sum_{t=0}^{\infty} \gamma^t R(X_t, A_t)) \quad (4)$$

Each node is attempting to learn the same value function ($V_i^* = V^*$), but is hindered by its lack of knowledge about what actions the other nodes will take (and by having only local state available, which will be addressed later). This method is not fully distributed, though, since it depends on the global broadcast of a reward signal.

2.2.2 Local DRL

A naive, but fully distributed, formulation is one where each node acts only to optimize its own rewards and does not communicate with its neighbors. That results in a Bellman-like equation of the form:

$$V_i(x) = \max_{a \in A_i}(R_i(x,a) + \gamma \sum_{x' \in X} p(x'|a,x)V(x')) \quad (5)$$

Rather than assuming a global reward function that is computed (probably based on information transmitted in from each node's sensors to a central location) and broadcast to all nodes, we use a local signal available at each node. It is assumed that this reward function can be computed directly from a node's own local sensors and actions. Again, without addressing the issue of how/if a simultaneous solution to the set of these equations can be found, we observe that the value function retains its meaning as the expected discounted sum of future rewards under the resulting policy:

$$V_i(x) = E(\sum_{t=0}^{\infty} \gamma^t R_i(x_t, a_t)) \qquad (6)$$

The catch is that the composite policy is no longer guaranteed to be optimal for the overall system. It is easy to see an example of this in terms of the example in fig. 1. Suppose the provider does not offer enough to satisfy all customers and the penalty for depriving the node 2 customers is greater than that for depriving the node 0 customers. If the resource must flow through the distribution nodes from 0 to 1 to 2, node 0 will act to satisfy its own customers even at the greater expense of starving the others further down. Note that the result is bad even if the penalties are equal, but quadratic.

2.2.3 Distributed reward DRL

One way to have nodes communicate and act to help each other out is to have neighbors exchange information about the immediate rewards they receive. If each considers a weighted average of its local rewards and those of its neighbors we get the following equation for each node's value function:

$$V_i(x) = \max_{a \in A_i}(\sum_j f(i,j) R_j(x, a_j) + \gamma \sum_{x' \in X} p(x'|a, x) V_i(x')) \qquad (7)$$

where $f(i,j)$ is a weighting function that determines how strongly node i will weight the immediate rewards of node j in its average. It is assumed that $f(i,j)$ will be zero for all pairs of nodes that are not neighbors, and that $f(i,i)$ will be non-zero. The equation contains the variable a_j, which is the action to be chosen by node j. We do not assume that node i will get to see this action choice, but that node j will report the resulting reward, R_j.

We might hope that this will result in less greedy behavior because if everyone cares about themselves and their neighbors, then good will might propagate throughout the network. If we consider a system with discrete states and the value function is represented in a table, we can see that a solution takes the form:

$$V_i(x) = E(\sum_{t=0}^{\infty} \gamma^t \sum_j f(i,j) R_j(x_t, a_{j,t})) \qquad (8)$$

A node that uses this value function to make its policy decisions will act to improve the long term rewards of its neighbors and will make tradeoffs according to the weights given by $f(i,j)$. Unfortunately, it will still not help its non-neighbors, because, as we see in eq. 8, node i still does not have any component of rewards other than its immediate neighbors. Reusing the previous example, node 0 will still act to starve node 2's customers.

2.2.4 Distributed value function DRL

Nodes can act to assist non-neighbors if the value function equation is updated to have the nodes exchange information not about their immediate rewards, but about their value functions:

$$V_i(x) = \max_{a \in A_i}(R_i(x, a) + \gamma \sum_j f(i,j) \sum_{x' \in X} p(x'|a, x) V_j(x')) \qquad (9)$$

At this point we have changed the Bellman equation to the point where we can not say much about what properties a solution would have. In a deterministic system such as the example below, we can write a solution in the following form:

$$V_i(x) = \sum_j f'(i,j) R_j(x_t, a_{j,t}) \qquad (10)$$

One thing to note is that the weights in the average for eq. 10, $f'(i,j)$, are no longer equal to the weights in eq. 9 as they were previously between eqs. 7 and 8. Pairs of nodes that have zero weight in the former equation, may receive non-zero weights in the latter. In that case, nodes can act to help their non-neighbors as well.

In order to see how weighting of non-neighbors occurs consider a system organized as a 3 node chain where each node uses a simple average of itself and its neighbors. We remove the max from eq. 9 by assuming the nodes already implement a fixed, optimal policy. We further simplify by assuming we have a system with only one state, thereby making it stateless (we'll fix that later). The three value function equations (with the sums in eq. 9 expanded) are:

$$V_0(x) = R_0(x, a) + \gamma(0.50V_0(x) + 0.50V_1(x) + 0.00V_2(x)) \qquad (11)$$
$$V_1(x) = R_1(x, a) + \gamma(0.33V_0(x) + 0.33V_1(x) + 0.33V_2(x))$$
$$V_2(x) = R_2(x, a) + \gamma(0.00V_0(x) + 0.50V_1(x) + 0.50V_2(x))$$

Because there is only one state, the transition probabilities and the expected value on the right hand side of eq. 9 are reduced to a single term. The solution to these equations (with $\gamma = 0.9$) is:

$$\begin{aligned} V_0(x) &= 4.0R_0(x,a) + 3.9R_1(x,a) + 2.1R_2(x,a) \quad (12) \\ V_1(x) &= 2.6R_0(x,a) + 4.8R_1(x,a) + 2.6R_2(x,a) \\ V_2(x) &= 2.1R_0(x,a) + 3.9R_1(x,a) + 4.0R_2(x,a) \end{aligned}$$

These equations match eq. 10 with different coefficients for $f'(i,j)$ as mentioned before. Most importantly, we see that the value function for node 0 now includes a positive weight on the rewards received by node 2 even though those two nodes never communicate directly, which was the original intent of this algorithm. In the real case where there are numerous states, eq. 12 becomes a matrix of equations, one for each node-state pair, and the weighted sum of next states returns to each equation. The solution to that set of equations is still just a matter of linear algebra, but the resulting weights on the rewards depend on the transition probabilities between the states.

With this formulation we have effectively created a distributed representation of the value functions over the nodes. Each node is trying to learn a weighted sum of its own expected future rewards and those of the other nodes in the network. If we have chosen our weighting function well (more on this later), we could sum the value functions over all the nodes and the result would be an expected future weighted sum of rewards over all the nodes just as in the global RL approach. However, this is accomplished with access only to local rewards and communication of value function information only between immediate neighbors.

2.3 Local state and the use of Q-Learning

In the previous section, we based our discussions on the use of global state information available at all nodes. In order to have a fully distributed method, it is necessary to also have local state. Intuitively, this is easiest to think about in terms of function approximation. In the case of traditional, global reinforcement learning work, the use of function approximators to represent the value function has become common. Its main purpose is to handle state spaces that are too large to be stored in tabular form, and to speed up learning through generalization in large state spaces. In some cases, the convergence proofs for reinforcement learning have been extended to the use of function approximation [8, 2]. In the case of local state for distributed RL, we can think of it exactly as value function approximation where each node has chosen differing sets of features (their own locally observable state) to be used by their function approximators. Based on that intuition, we speculate that these convergence results may extend to our algorithms, but answering that question is future work. Additionally, the question of how good the chosen function approximator is for a particular problem remains important.

There is a practical problem introduced by the use of local state variables. All of the equations in our derivation have been written strictly in terms of the value function. At first glance, it might seem that this will lead to the use of a kind of value iteration coupled with the learning of system models to solve the problem ([10, 11], for example). This can't be done easily, though, because the use of local state means neighbors can't use state as a common language with which to communicate. It isn't possible for one node to ask another *"If I am in state x and choose action a, what state will that put you in, and what action will you choose?"* because neither of them has any representation of the other's states and actions.

Despite this problem, reward and value functions are a universal language. Constructing a Q-learning [16] algorithm to solve the problem only requires nodes to communicate in these terms. A Q-learning rule that each node can implement to learn the value function in eq. 9 is:

$$\begin{aligned} Q_i(x_i,a_i) &\leftarrow (1-\alpha)Q_i(x_i,a_i) + \quad (13) \\ &\quad\ \alpha(R_i(x_i,a_i) + \gamma \sum_j f(i,j)V_j(x'_j)) \\ V_i(x_i) &\leftarrow \max_{a\in A_i} Q_i(x_i,a) \end{aligned}$$

Each node performs the updates specified by these equations online. Because the learning is done online (it can also be done off-line using a trace) as the system actually passes through various states, there is no need for neighbors to specify to each other what state or action they've been in or taken. It is only necessary for them to transmit their current estimated value of the state they land in at each iteration.

3 Experimental Results

We tested our algorithm on a simulated power grid problem. We use a D.C. formulation because it simplifies the simulation and keeps the number of state variables smaller. Simulation of a real A.C. power grid requires the use of complex, rather than real, variables. Our simulation uses variable resistors as a means of controlling power flow. Historically, this hasn't been possible in real power grids, but new devices are being developed that will allow it. Our system has the following components (again, refer to fig. 1):

Providers. These are the power generation facilities and are treated as fixed voltage sources.

Customers. These represent cities, which have a desired voltage (or a desired power requirement based on a fixed resistance load).

Distributors. The distributors represent both physical entities and the *nodes* of our distributed RL formulation. This is where the intelligent control decisions must be made. The variables of the control problem are as follows:

Local actions. Each node makes a choice for each power line connected to it. It can request that the resistance on that line be doubled, halved, or left the same. Lines that go between distributors and providers, or distributors and cities, are controlled by the distributor. Any line that goes between two distributor nodes will get two requests on how its resistance should change. The arbitration scheme shown below determines the actual change in resistance. The resistors have 6 possible values and attempts to increase them beyond their maximum value, or decrease them below their minimum value result in them staying the same.

Node 1 request	Node 2 request		
	Halve	Same	Double
Halve	Halve	Halve	Same
Same	Halve	Same	Double
Double	Same	Double	Double

Local state. A distributor receives state information for each line it has depending on what its connected to:

distributor-distributor: 1) Whether the neighboring voltage is higher or not (2 states), 2) whether the neighboring voltage increased, lowered, or remained the same from the last iteration (3 states), 3) whether the resistor is at its minimum, maximum, or in between (3 states). There are 18 possible states total.

distributor-city: The same as for distributors except that item 2 is whether or not the city needs more voltage. There are 12 possible states total.

distributor-provider: Only items 1 and 3. There are 6 possible states total.

The complete local state space for a node is the cross product of the states for each line it is attached to. For example, a node that connects to one city, one provider, and one other node will sense one of 1296 possible states.

Local reward. The local reward received by each node is based solely on the satisfaction of its local customers (the city it is directly attached to). If the voltage available to them is below the desired level, the node receives a penalty equal to the difference between the two, otherwise the reward signal is zero. Note that this can be a problem when some distributors are connected only to other distributors, but not to any customers. They will have no local reward to base their decisions and learning on. We will see the effects of this in the experiments.

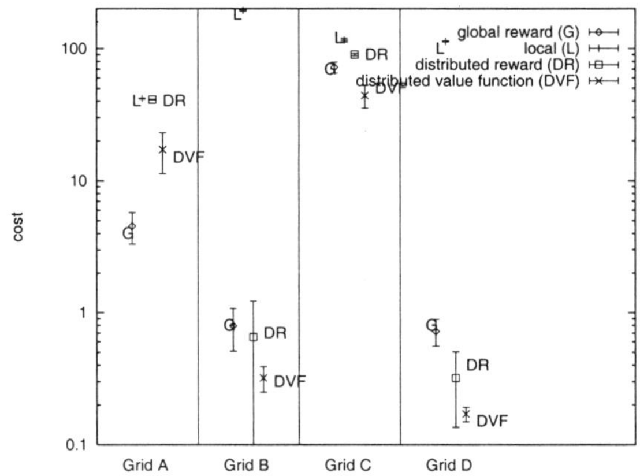

Figure 3: Graph of results on a log scale showing cumulative cost over 60000 iterations in policy evaluation mode.

We ran each distributed RL algorithm on each of the power grids shown in fig. 2. Note that it was not practical to run the traditional global RL method because even the smallest grid has hundreds of millions of states. For each run there were 60000 learning steps, followed by an evaluation phase which did not learn and followed its policy 95% of the time and chose randomly the other 5%. We used $\gamma = 0.95$. $\alpha = 0.1$ initially and is decayed. The exploration rate is started at 1.0 and stays there for the first 30000 steps, then decays. For the distributed reward and distributed value function cases, $f(i,j)$ is chosen to compute a simple average of the node and its neighbors. During the trials, an initial random setting of all the resistors is chosen. The system operates for 300 steps, and then the resistors are changed to new random settings. This loop continues throughout the learning and evaluation phases.

Fig. 3 and table 3 summarize the experimental results. They show average cost (negative reward) per step during the evaluation phase along with their confidence intervals. These are averages over 10 trials and each took about 45 minutes on a 400MHz Pentium II.

The results show distributed value function performing best in every case except grid A. On grid A, global reward is best. We speculate that this is because there are only two cities, and thus only two sources of re-

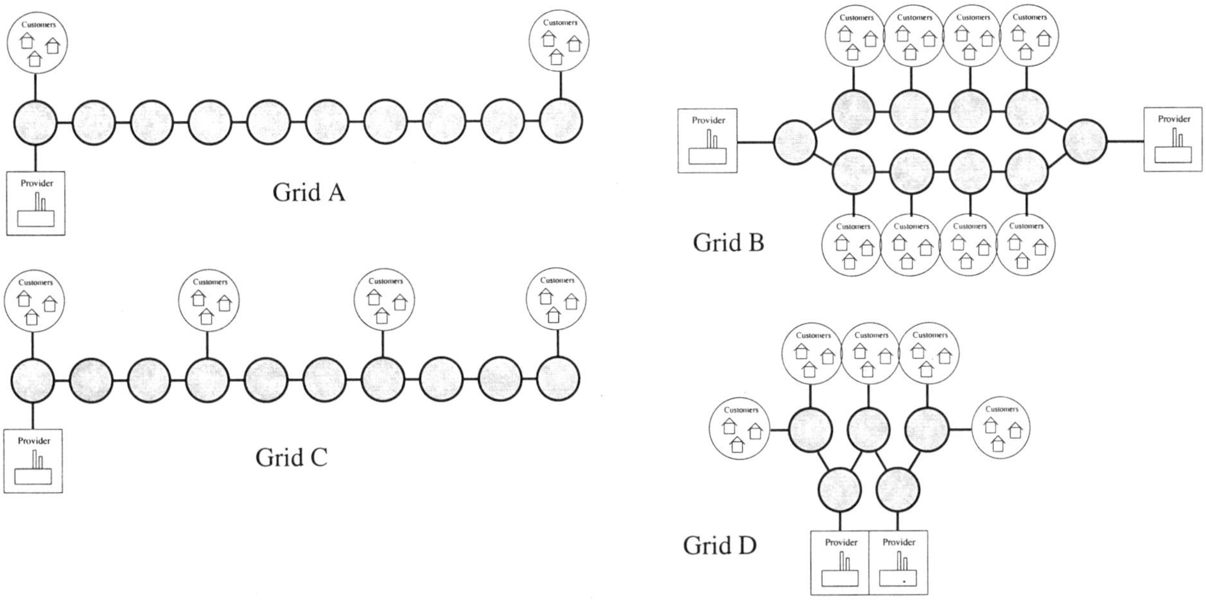

Figure 2: The 4 power grids used in the experiments.

Algorithm	**Grid A**			**Grid B**		
	Rank	Avg cost	95% C.I.	Rank	Avg cost	95% C.I.
Global reward	1	4.55	±1.22	3	0.79	±0.28
Local	4	41.67	±0.39	4	193.33	±3.22
Dist. reward	3	41.00	±0.30	2	0.65	±0.57
Dist. value fn	2	17.17	±5.87	1	0.32	±0.07
	Grid C			**Grid D**		
Global reward	2	72.33	±6.82	3	0.72	±0.17
Local	4	115.50	±3.97	4	113.00	±1.07
Dist. reward	3	90.00	±1.78	2	0.32	±0.19
Dist. value fn	1	44.00	±8.75	1	0.17	±0.02

Table 1: Average reward per step in policy evaluation mode for the 4 DRL algorithms on 4 different power grids.

ward. Lumping them together into a global reward signal doesn't hide as much information as in the other cases. Local DRL performs poorly everywhere, which shows that locally greedy approaches aren't sufficient to solve this problem. The fact that distributed reward performs reasonably, but not as well as distributed value function indicates that it is necessary to consider more than the rewards of immediate neighbors. Local DRL and distributed reward both suffer when there are nodes without cities attached (or in the latter case when no neighboring distributors have cities attached), because they have no source of local reward.

4 Conclusions and Future Work

In summary, we have presented a general algorithm for distributed reinforcement learning that allows nodes to work toward the benefit of other nodes across the system, while only requiring communication with immediate neighbors. Our results show this algorithm performing well on a power grid control application.

A remaining question is how to choose $f(i,j)$ in order to get the best result. In the derivation, we observed that the different algorithms result in similar looking solutions (eqs. 4, 6, 8 and 10). The only difference is in the effective weighting function $f'(i,j)$. Local and global reward offer one specific function each, while distributed reward and distributed value function offer a class of functions depending on the chosen $f(i,j)$. Distributed value function can imitate global reward (using a fully connected graph with uniform weights) and local (zero weights on all neighbors), but it can not imitate distributed reward. Although we did not find any here, there may be cases where distributed reward performs best.

Another question is whether, and under what conditions, the solution to eq. 9 yields an optimal or near-optimal policy for the entire system. It is obvious that it does not for some choices of $f(i,j)$. It might if the graph of nodes is fully connected and all nodes weight all others equally (the global reward case), but this is uninteresting practically because it requires full communication between all nodes. Possible future work is to put bounds on the suboptimality for specific weightings.

An interesting extension to this method is the case where the neighbor relation and the weighting function, $f(i,j)$, change dynamically. In a simple case the structure of the grid may change during the learning process due to external causes. In a more sophisticated version, nodes may have actions that allow them to change who their neighbors are. That could be appropriate when the nodes are mobile agents traveling around occasionally encountering each other, or choosing to work together in teams.

References

[1] M. Asada, E. Uchibe, S. Noda, S. Tawaratsumida, and K. Hosoda. Coordination of multiple behaviors acquired by vision-based reinforcement learning. In *Proceedings of the International Conference on Intelligent Robots and Systems (IROS 94)*, pages 917–924, 1994.

[2] L. Baird. Residual Algorithms: Reinforcement Learning with Function Approximation. In *Machine Learning: Proceedings of the Twelfth International Conference.* Morgan Kaufman, 1995.

[3] E. Baum. *Manifesto for an Evolutionary Economics of Intelligence*, pages 285–344. Springer-Verlag, 1998.

[4] D. Bertsekas. *Dynamic Programming and Optimal Control.* Athena Scientific, 1995.

[5] J. Boyan and M. Littman. Packet routing in dynamically changing networks: A reinforcement learning approach. In *Neural Information Processing Systems*, volume 6, 1994.

[6] S. Choi and D. Yeung. Predictive q-routing: A memory-based reinforcement learning approach to adaptive traffic control. In *Neural Information Processing Systems 8*, 1996.

[7] R. Crites and A. Barto. Improving elevator performance using reinforcement learning. In *Neural Information Processing Systems 8*, 1996.

[8] G. Gordon. Stable function approximation in dynamic programming. In *The 12th International Conference on Machine Learning*, 1995.

[9] M. Littman. Markov games as a framework for multi-agent reinforcement learning. In *Proceedings of the Eleventh International Conference on Machine Learning*, pages 157–163, 1994.

[10] J. Schneider. Exploiting model uncertainty estimates for safe dynamic control learning. In *Neural Information Processing Systems 9*, 1996.

[11] J. Schneider, J. Boyan, and A. Moore. Value function based production scheduling. In *International Conference on Machine Learning*, 1998.

[12] S. Singh and D. Cohn. How to dynamically merge markov decision processes. In *Neural Information Processing Systems*, volume 10, 1998.

[13] D. Subramanian, P. Druschel, and J. Chen. Ants and reinforcement learning: A case study in routing dynamic networks. In *Proceedings of IJCAI-97*, 1997.

[14] R. Sutton and A. Barto. *Reinforcement Learning: An Introduction.* MIT Press, 1998.

[15] M. Tan. Multi-agent reinforcement learning: independent vs. cooperative agents. In *Proceedings of the Tenth International Workshop on Machine Learning*, pages 330–337, 1993.

[16] C. Watkins. *Learning from Delayed Rewards.* PhD thesis, Cambridge University, 1989.

[17] G. Weiss. Distributed reinforcement learning. *Robotics and Autonomous Systems*, 15:135–142, 1995.

Feature Engineering for Text Classification

Sam Scott
Cognitive Science Department
Institute for Interdisciplinary Studies
Carleton University
Ottawa, ON, K1S 5B6 (Canada)
sscott2@chat.carleton.ca

Stan Matwin
School of Information Technology and Engineering
University of Ottawa
Ottawa, ON, K1N 6N5 (Canada)
stan@site.uottawa.ca

Abstract

Most research in text classification to date has used a "bag of words" representation in which each feature corresponds to a single word. This paper examines some alternative ways to represent text based on syntactic and semantic relationships between words (phrases, synonyms and hypernyms). We describe the new representations and try to justify our hypothesis that they could improve the performance of a rule-based learner. The representations are evaluated using the RIPPER learning algorithm on the Reuters-21578 and DigiTrad test corpora. On their own the new representations are not found to produce significant performance improvements. We also try combining classifiers based on different representations using a majority voting technique, and this improves performance on both test collections. In our opinion, more sophisticated Natural Language Processing techniques need to be developed before better text representations can be produced for classification.

1. INTRODUCTION

Text classification is the task of automatically placing pre-defined labels on previously unseen documents. Used in document indexing, e-mail filtering, web browsing, and personal information agents, text classification is an active and important area of research where machine learning and information retrieval (IR) intersect. New feature selection techniques [Yang and Pederson, 1997; Ng et al., 1997] and learning algorithms [Joachims, 1998; Lam and Ho, 1998; McCallum et al., 1998] have produced good results on a number of standard test collections. But the vast majority of this work uses a simple "bag of words" representation of text in which each feature corresponds to a single word or stem. The aim of this paper is to examine some alternative ways to represent text for classification. We look at new representations based on syntactic and semantic relationships between words, and evaluate these new representations using a rule-based learner on two major document collections.

In the sections that follow, we first motivate and describe our feature engineering techniques, and then describe extensive experiments on 8 automatically-generated representations based on words, phrases, synonyms and hypernyms. In no case do we find that the new representations on their own produce a significant performance improvement, although combining classifiers based on different representations does produce some benefit. In our opinion, more sophisticated Natural Language Processing (NLP) techniques need to be developed before better text representations can be produced. In the short term, research into new algorithms based on combining classifiers probably holds the most promise.

2. A QUICK LOOK AT RIPPER

Before moving on to discuss the new text representations, we need to quickly introduce the learning algorithm we used. RIPPER was developed by William Cohen [1995a] based on repeated application of Furnkranz and Widmer's [1994] IREP algorithm followed by two new global optimization procedures. Like other rule-based learners, RIPPER grows rules in a greedy fashion guided by an information gain heuristic. It is comparable in accuracy to similar algorithms such as c4.5rules, but is significantly more efficient [Cohen 1995a]. This efficiency combined with RIPPER's implementation of set-valued features [Cohen, 1996b] allows learning in much larger feature spaces than would be possible with c4.5rules.

RIPPER has already been applied to a number of standard problems in text classification with quite promising results [Cohen, 1996a; Cohen and Singer, 1996]. It is important to emphasize that RIPPER is a rule-based machine learning system that has made its mark in a field dominated by purely statistical algorithms such as Naive Bayes, Widrow-Hoff, or k-Nearest Neighbor. The high-dimensionality of most representations of text has in the past lead researchers away from rule- or tree-based learning systems. This makes RIPPER interesting since most conclusions about the effectiveness of various representations have been drawn in a context that may not apply to a rule-based learner.

3. THE BAG OF WORDS[1]

The type of representation that dominates the text classification literature is known as the "bag of words". For most bag of words representations, each feature corresponds to a single word found in the training corpus, usually with case and punctuation removed. Infrequent and frequent words are often filtered out of the original text, and sometimes words appearing in a list of *stop words* are removed (stop words are functional or connective words that are assumed to have no information content). When the feature values are binary, a document is represented as one corner of a unit hypercube in a high-dimensional space (typically tens of thousands of dimensions.)

In addition to the removal of frequent, infrequent, and stop words, there is often some attempt to make the features more statistically independent. The most common way achieve this is to remove suffixes from words using a *stemming* algorithm such as the one developed by Lovins [1968]. Stemming has the effect of mapping several morphological forms of words to a common feature. For example the words "learner", "learning", and "learned" would all map to the common stem "learn", and this latter string would be placed in the feature set rather than the former three.

Stemming, filtering and stop-word removal are so widely regarded as useful that they are almost always used in text classification experiments. However, there is reason to doubt the universality of their effectiveness [Riloff, 1995]. The chief advantage of infrequent word removal is reduction of feature set size, but since the number of word features in our experiments did not pose a problem for RIPPER, we did not use this technique. The chief historical advantage of stop-word and frequent word removal is reduction of file size, but since this was not a concern, we chose not to use these techniques either. As for stemming, the advantages and disadvantages were less clear, so both stemmed and unstemmed representations were explored.

4. PHRASE-BASED REPRESENTATIONS

A very basic observation about bag of words representations is that a great deal of the information from the original document is discarded. Paragraph, sentence and word order is disrupted, and syntactic structures are broken. The end result is that the text is rendered incoherent to humans in order to make it coherent to a machine learning algorithm. The goal of using phrases as features is to attempt to preserve some of the information left out of the bag of words.

The observation that words alone do not always represent true atomic units of meaning is not new. David Lewis undertook a major study of the use of noun phrases for statistical classification as part of his Ph.D. thesis [Lewis, 1992b]. He reviewed the existing IR literature on the use of syntactic phrases and found that most studies had not been able to demonstrate much improvement over word-based indexing. To try to explain these results, Lewis suggested that previous work fared poorly because phrase-based representations: a) contain a high number of terms, b) have an uneven distribution of feature values, c) contain many redundant features, and d) contain a lot of noise. All these characteristics pose theoretical problems for Bayesian classification. Lewis attempted to correct these problems by using a clustering algorithm to group phrase features into meta-features, but the new representation did not produce any improvement either [Lewis, 1992a; 1992b].

Despite the negative results obtained by this research, there was still reason to believe that in some cases phrase-based representations might improve the performance of rule-based learners. For example, the phrase "machine learning" has a highly specific meaning that is separate and distinct from the words "machine" and "learning". In a situation where the classes to be learned include, say, *Artificial Intelligence*, *Machine Tools* and *Education*, it is conceivable that the phrase "machine learning" would yield a high information gain for *Artificial Intelligence*, even though the individual words yield a low gain. In this case, a potentially powerful rule such as

"machine" & "learning" → *Artificial Intelligence*

might never be learned. The greedy search heuristic would prevent the addition of either individual word to the empty rule. But if the feature set included two-word phrases, then the rule

"machine learning" → *Artificial Intelligence*

could be learned more easily. Statistical algorithms like naïve Bayes are immune to this sort of worry, as they always work with all available features.

The main problem in converting to a bag of phrases is the huge potential increase in the number of features. If there are n unique words, there are potentially n^k unique sequences of length k. This number is bounded above by the size of the corpus, but typically the number of unique phrases is still at least an order of magnitude higher than n. In order to keep the task tractable, some technique must be used to keep the size of the feature set down. (Note

[1] Strictly speaking, the text representation described in this section should be called a "set" of words rather than a bag, since we do not make use of any word frequency information.

that this issue is distinct from the issue of data set size that motivates stop word removal.) Cohen [1995b; 1995c] attempted to solve the problem using FLIPPER, a first-order version of RIPPER, to learn in a feature space that included phrase-defining predicates. This technique did not produce an improvement, but the result is not as strong as it could be because the argument about the greedy search heuristic employed by RIPPER also applies to FLIPPER [Scott, 1998]. Only a representation that includes phrases as atomic features can overcome this problem.

The only way to avoid the ballooning feature space while still retaining phrases as atomic features is to employ a selection strategy. Luckily, not all sequences of words are equally meaningful. For example the sentence "The quick brown fox jumps over the lazy dogs," contains a number of potentially useful phrases such as "brown fox", "quick brown fox", and "lazy dogs" in addition to a larger number of word sequences that are probably not useful for classification ("the quick", "fox jumps", "over the", and so on.) So the new phrase-based representation should be amenable to an aggressive selection strategy aimed at weeding out the word sequences that are least likely to be useful. We now present two techniques for performing this task.

4.1 NOUN PHRASE EXTRACTION

Motivated by the observation that phrases indicating the objects and subjects of a text are likely to be the most useful, the first technique selects only those word sequences that are recognized as noun phrases. For instance if the system encounters our example sentence, it should recognize that "quick brown fox" is a noun phrase while "the quick" and "over the" are not. Importantly, it should also recognize that "brown fox" and "fox" are valid noun phrases as well. There is no a priori way to determine which of these phrases will yield the highest information gain. This is an important difference from Lewis [1992a; 1992b] who used a bracketing technique that was biased towards the longest phrases, and specifically excluded single word phrases ("quick brown fox" would be extracted but not "brown fox" or "fox".)

Extracting noun phrases from a document requires two separate algorithms. The first is a tagging algorithm to assign part of speech tags (*noun*, *verb*, *preposition*, etc.) to the individual words, and the second is an algorithm to group the tagged words into noun phrases. Eric Brill's rule-based part of speech tagger [Brill, 1992; 1994] is used in its default configuration to assign the part of speech tags, and grouping is done with a simple regular expression. The two algorithms together are referred to as the Noun Phrase Extractor (NoPE).[2] For our purposes a *noun phrase* is defined as a sequence of nouns or adjectives terminating in a noun. In regular expression form this is represented as:

$$NP = \{A, N\}^* N.$$

This definition is applied at every possible point in a text to look for matching phrases. Complex noun phrases such as "the quick brown fox that got away" will be missed, but NoPE does accomplish its stated task: the number of word sequences is reduced by selecting many of those that represent the objects or subjects of discussion.

4.2 KEY PHRASE EXTRACTION

In addition to NoPE's use of linguistic knowledge for phrase selection, we also tried a non-linguistic method for achieving the same goal. The Extractor system developed by Peter Turney [1999] tries to extract the most meaningful phrases from a document without using any part of speech information. The algorithm used by Extractor is itself the result of learning phase, during which it was trained to assign keyphrases to a document so as to mimic the choices a human would make. Assuming the task is performed well, Extractor's keyphrases should be highly meaningful, unambiguous, and indicative of the content of the document – the very properties desired in the choice of phrase features for classification. Turney compared the performance of Extractor to other keyphrase extraction algorithms and found that Extractor's choices matched human choices better than the other algorithms on a number of test corpora.

4.3 CONSTRUCTING THE REPRESENTATIONS

Both NoPE and Extractor were used in the same way to generate a phrase-based representation. First phrases were extracted from every document in the corpus and assembled into a global list. Part of speech tags were removed from the words if necessary, and stemming and further feature selection was performed on this list. (In the case of stemming, each word of the phrase was replaced by its stem.) The resulting list was used as the set of features for classification, and a final pass assembled feature vectors based on this set.

5. HYPERNYM REPRESENTATIONS

The bag of words representation also ignores semantic relationships between words. In particular, potentially useful information about synonymy and hypernymy is not

[2] Links to all the tools and data referred to in this work can be found on the National Research Council of Canada web site - http://ai.iit.nrc.ca/II_public/Classification/resources.html.

directly used. ("Hypernym" linguistic term for the "is a" relationship – a knife is a weapon, therefore "weapon" is a hypernym of "knife".) A rule-based learner could be aided by a feature engineering method that mapped words with low information gain to common hypernyms that yield a higher information gain. We used this observation previously to build a new text representation that produced significant increases in accuracy on some small data sets [Scott and Matwin, 1998]. The current research builds on the preliminary work by applying a similar technique to much larger data sets.

5.1 WORDNET

The feature engineering methods described here rely on the use of WordNet, a large on-line thesaurus that contains information about synonymy and hypernymy [Miller, 1990; Fellbaum, 1998]. Figure 1 shows an idealized piece of the WordNet hierarchy. The nodes in WordNet are referred to as "synsets". Each synset represents a particular meaning, or "sense", shared by a group of words and phrases. Each word or phrase in the synset is a synonym of the others with respect to that particular sense, and a word or phrase with more than one sense will appear in more than one synset. Arcs between the nodes represent the hypernym relation.

We know of only one previously published attempt to make use of WordNet for text classification. Rodríguez et al. [1997] used WordNet with linear discriminant learning algorithms to produce better classification performance on the Reuters-22173 data set.[3] They were able to take advantage of the fact that Reuters topic headings often correspond to words appearing in the text of the documents. They compiled a list of all the topic headings and looked up these words in WordNet to find synonyms. This list of synonyms was then used to bias the learning algorithm for each topic by increasing the initial weights of the features corresponding to the synonyms of that topic. This entire process was done by hand and took advantage of the researchers' a priori knowledge of the Reuters domain. No change of representation was involved, and the use of WordNet was limited to the synonymy relation only.

Some researches have also applied WordNet to retrieval tasks. Sharon Flank [1998] reported good results using many of the WordNet semantic relations, including hypernymy, to expand short descriptions of pictures for retrieval. Ellen Voorhees looked at the possibility of using WordNet for document indexing [Voorhees, 1993] and query expansion [Voorhees, 1994]. The latter work found that when the queries were expanded or converted to synsets manually, some retrieval tasks were improved significantly. But automatic expansion posed problems due to the difficulty of choosing the correct sense for a word in a given context – a problem known in the NLP community as "word sense disambiguation".

WordNet's organization of synsets into parts of speech allows for some partial disambiguation, but each part of speech can still contain many different senses for each word. The problem of automatic disambiguation has been tackled by a number of researchers (see Ide and Véronis [1998] for a summary of recent work) but its difficulty has hampered past attempts to use WordNet in the IR community. Often, the problem is solved by manually selecting the correct sense, but this method was not practically possible in the current work. The changes of representation discussed in this section proceed on the idea that in the presence of a large amount of training data, the problem of disambiguation can be partially sidestepped.

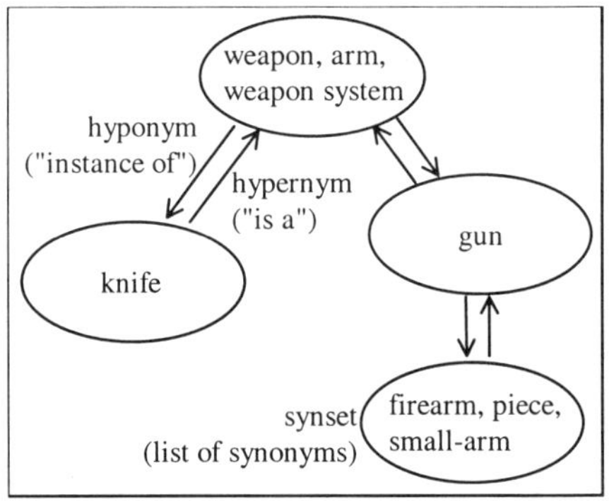

Figure 1: A piece of the WordNet semantic hierarchy (idealized model.)

5.2 CONSTRUCTING THE REPRESENTATIONS

If every word could be correctly disambiguated, a function similar to stemming could be performed in which synonymous words were mapped to the same meta-feature. The difference is that the mapping would be semantically rather than morphologically based. To extend this idea, the hypernym links could also be followed through the semantic network to generalize by mapping to the hypernym senses of each word. For instance, in the preliminary work a class of documents was learned using both a word-based and a hypernym-based representation. The hypernym "weapon" often appeared in the rules learned using the hypernym-based representation, but the words mapping to the "weapon" synset never appeared in the rules learned using the word-based representation. It seems the individual words that were instances of the concept "weapon" did not yield enough information gain on their own to be selected. But when they were all mapped via WordNet to the appropriate meta-feature, RIPPER was able to make use of them and the resulting hypotheses were significantly more accurate [Scott, 1998; Scott and Matwin, 1998].

[3] Reuters-22173 is an earlier version of Reuters-21578.

This benefit was obtained without any automatic word sense disambiguation. Including all synsets produced a noisy feature space that contained a few highly informative features. For instance, even though "knife" mapped to hypernyms other than "weapon", the "weapon" hypernym was still included and available for classification.

Following on these observations, no disambiguation was attempted in the current work either. Instead all senses returned by WordNet were judged equally likely to be correct, and all of them were included in the feature set. Synsets were identified by tagging the documents, then looking up all noun and verb hypernyms in WordNet and assembling a list of all synsets occurring in the output. A second pass converted documents to feature vectors based on this new representation. This process was influenced by the value of a parameter h that controlled the "height of generalization". This parameter was used to limit the number of steps upward through the hypernym hierarchy for each word. At height $h=0$ only the synsets that contained the words in the corpus were included (i.e. synonyms). At height $h>0$ the same synsets were included as well as all the hypernym synsets that appeared up to h steps above them in the hypernym hierarchy. The best value of h for a given task presumably depends on such characteristics of the text as vocabulary, and similarity and breadth of topics.

6. METHODOLOGY

6.1 TEST COLLECTIONS

The two data sets used for this study were the Reuters-21578 corpus of newswire stories, and a corpus of folk song lyrics called The Digital Tradition, (DigiTrad) [Greenhaus, 1996]. Reuters is well established and has been used as the basis of much recent text classification work [Joachims, 1998; Lam and Ho, 1998]. Like other researchers, we used the "ModApte" testing/training split for these experiments, which results in 9603 training documents and 3299 testing documents, each assigned to 0 or more of the 90 topic labels.

DigiTrad was first introduced for text classification research by Scott and Matwin [1998]. Most folk songs in the DigiTrad collection have been assigned one or more keywords from a fixed list, thus defining a classification task. We used the "DT100" testing/training split [Scott, 1998] which results in 4333 training and 2166 testing documents, each assigned 0 or more of the 33 keyword labels. (Only those keywords represented by 100 or more examples in the entire collection were used.) Some statistics for the two data sets are shown in table 1. In this table, "balance" shows the percentage of positive classifications, "words" shows the total number of words in the corpora, and "vocab" shows the number of unique words.

Not all types of text are equally difficult to classify, and the collections chosen for this research represent two opposite extremes. Reuters consists of articles written as a source of factual information. The writing style tends to be direct and to the point, and uses a restricted vocabulary to aid quick comprehension. It has been observed that the topic headings in Reuters tend to consist of words that appear frequently in the text, and this observation has been exploited to help improve classification accuracy [Rodríguez et al., 97]. DigiTrad, where the texts make heavy use of metaphoric, rhyming, unusual and archaic language, is a good example of the opposite extreme. The texts are far less succinct and the vocabulary is much less restricted, a difference demonstrated by the comparatively large vocabulary reported in table 1. Consequently, the DigiTrad classes should be harder to automatically classify than Reuters.

Table 1: Some Statistics for the Two Test Collections

	Reuters-21578		**DigiTrad**	
	Train	**Test**	**Train**	**Test**
Docs.	9603	3299	4333	2166
Classes	90	90	33	33
Balance	1.1	1.3	4.1	4.2
Words	1257993	399179	1161244	576156
Vocab.	27940	16907	43301	29415

6.2 EVALUATION METHODS

In order to compare the current work with that of other recent studies, we used the micro-averaged breakeven point of precision and recall instead of the more traditional statistic of average cross-validated accuracy. The breakeven point is uncommon in the machine learning literature, but is the measurement of choice in the IR literature. For the benefit of readers unfamiliar with the latter, we briefly describe the technique here. Parallel discussions can be found in a number of places, such as [Lewis, 1992b].

Text classification tasks are unlike normal machine learning problems in two respects: examples can be given multiple class labels, meaning separate binary classifiers must be trained for each; and the positive examples of each class are usually in a very small minority (see the "balance" statistics in table 1). These two characteristics combined mean that a plain accuracy statistic is not adequate to evaluate performance. To deal with the unbalanced nature of the classes, precision and recall are used instead of accuracy. Precision is the proportion of examples labeled positive by the system that were truly positive, and recall is the proportion of truly positive examples labeled positive by the system. Sometimes these statistics are combined using a weighted averaging technique called the F-measure [Lewis, 1995]. Figure 2 shows how to compute precision, recall, and the F-measure from a confusion matrix.

A process called micro-averaging is used to deal with the multiple classifiers in a given task. The confusion matrices for each class are added component-wise to yield an aggregate matrix for the entire task, and then the precision and recall statistics are computed from this matrix. This component-wise addition is made possible by treating each matrix as representing a binary classification into either a *positive* or *negative* class. The 2×2 matrix resulting from this addition represents the overall picture for all classes.

Most learning algorithms contain parameters that can be varied, often with the effect of trading off precision against recall. (In RIPPER the *loss ratio* parameter adjusts the relative weight of false positive and false negative errors in a binary task.) To obtain a single number representing the performance of the system, the learning task is repeated for various values of these parameters. Each run yields micro-averaged precision and recall statistics that are interpolated (or extrapolated if necessary) to yield the hypothetical point at which precision and recall are equal. This is the *micro-averaged breakeven point*.

		Hypothesis	
		+ve	-ve
Correct Class	+ve	a	b
	-ve	c	d

$$\text{Accuracy} = \frac{a}{a+b+c+d}$$

$$\text{Precision (P)} = \frac{a}{a+c} \qquad \text{Recall (R)} = \frac{a}{a+b}$$

$$\text{F-measure } (F_\beta) = \frac{(\beta^2+1)PR}{\beta^2 P + R}$$

Figure 2: How to compute precision, recall, and the F-measure from a confusion matrix.

6.3 EXPERIMENTAL DESIGN

Experiments were performed on each test collection using 8 different representations. Table 2 summarizes these representations and shows the number of features in each. (Note the acronyms for each representation that will be used from here on.) We used stemmed and unstemmed versions of each of the bag of words, noun phrase and keyphrase representations, and tried two versions of the hypernym representation corresponding to $h=0$ and $h=1$. Stemming was performed using the Lovins stemmer [Lovins, 1968]. Feature selection was used only for the noun phrase representations (NP and NP_S), because the number of features originally identified by NoPE was too high (well over 100 000 in both cases). In this case all phrases appearing fewer than 4 times in the corpus were discarded. Feature values were binary in order take advantage of the speed of RIPPER's set-valued features.

Table 2: Number of Features in Each Representation

Name	Description	# of Features	
		Reuter	DigiTrad
BW	bag of words	27940	43301
BW_S	stemmed words	18590	28996
NP	noun phrases	21427	14204
NP_S	stemmed NP	20061	12457
KP	keyphrases	23110	15287
KP_S	stemmed KP	22122	14264
H_0	hypernym (h=0)	13385	18646
H_1	hypernym (h=1)	15393	21044

In the preliminary hypernym work, where the test collections were much smaller, we used values for h ranging from 0 to 9. We were restricted to low h values for the current work, due to the fact that the representations became less sparse at higher values for h. Since much of RIPPER's speed on text classification tasks derives from its sparse vector representation, this understandably caused a significant slowdown in performance.

Default options were used for RIPPER with two exceptions. The first was the enabling of negative tests, allowing the algorithm to use both the "$\in$" and "$\notin$" operation on set valued features. This option was found to marginally improve performance in initial trials. Secondly, the *loss ratio* parameter was varied to try to bracket the micro-averaged breakeven points on each task. The values used were {0.5, 1, 2, 4} for Reuters and {0.25, 0.5, 1, 2} for DigiTrad. Only those classes with 10 or more example documents (60 of the 90 Reuters classes and all of the DigiTrad classes) were classified using RIPPER. The rest were submitted to a default classifier that always returned a negative answer.

7. RESULTS AND DISCUSSION

Table 3 summarizes the micro-averaged breakeven points obtained using RIPPER on each representation. Figure 3 shows sample precision/recall graphs for the BW and NP representations. At a first glance, it is clear that the prediction about the relative difficulty of DigiTrad and Reuters was correct. DigiTrad results are consistently less than half as good as Reuters. The results for Reuters can also be compared to recent work by Joachims [1998] to show that RIPPER outperforms the naïve Bayes, Rocchio, and c4.5 algorithms using bag of words, and does about as well as k-Nearest Neighbour. We also now know that new machine learning algorithms such as Combined Support Vector Machines [Joachims, 1998] and Generalized Instance Set [Lam and Ho, 1998] can improve this performance to a breakeven of approximately 0.86 on Reuters. But the main point of comparison for the current study is between the representations based on words (BW and BW_S) and the other representations. Unfortunately, none of the new representations performed significantly better than the bag of words.

Table 3: Performance for Each Representation

	Micro-averaged b.e.[4]	
	Reuters	**DigiTrad**
BW	.821	.359
BW_S	.810	.360
NP	.827	.357
NP_S	.819	.356
KP	.817	.288[e]
KP_S	.816	.297[e]
H_0	.741[e]	.283
H_1	.734[e]	.281

7.1 PERFORMANCE OF PHRASE-BASED REPRESENTATIONS

The performance of the phrase-based representations (NP, NP_S, KP, and KPS) supports the conclusions of most past research – that phrases do not add much classification power. It seems that even in a learning paradigm based on greedy search, grouping words into phrases does not make the domain significantly more learnable. Recalling our discussion of the example phrase "machine learning", it seems that the situation in which a phrase is more informative than its component words simply does not arise often enough to impact the micro-averaged precision and recall. This being said, there were some small benefits from the use of the NP representation on Reuters. First, RIPPER obtained a slightly higher breakeven point using less complex hypotheses than with BW – approximately 1 fewer rule for every second hypothesis, with the same number of clauses per rule (see Scott [1998] for more details). Second, the phrase representations reduced the number of features almost as much as stemming (see table 2) without the negative effects on performance (see table 3).

Our results with phrase based features are confirmed in recent work by Fürnkranz [1998] who used RIPPER with n-gram features (word sequences of length $\leq n$) on Reuters and found only a very slight improvement with 2-grams and no improvement with longer sequences. Fürnkranz et al. [1998] also tried linguistic phrases with RIPPER in other text domains and found improvements in precision, but only at low recall levels. In contrast, recent work by Mladenić and Grobelnik [1998] found a more significant overall performance improvement using n-gram features with naïve Bayes for hierarchical classification of web documents. Unfortunately, the latter study has too many points of difference to make a useful comparison to the results presented here.

[4] A superscript "e" indicates an extrapolated rather than interpolated point.

7.2 PERFORMANCE OF HYPERNYM REPRESENTATIONS

The results from the hypernym representations were the most disappointing. Preliminary work had shown significant improvements on some classes in the DigiTrad domain, and the hope was that this would generalize to the entire corpus. But the representations used in this study were informationally poorer than in the preliminary work: h values were kept low and the features were binary rather than real-valued density measurements. The former factor may have excluded many valuable hypernyms, and the latter may have removed too much information for RIPPER to pick the meaningful senses out of all the noise.

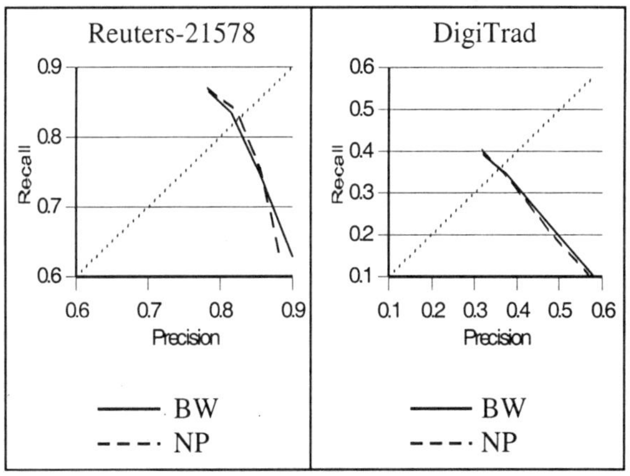

Figure 3: Sample precision and recall graphs for Reuters and DigiTrad. The dotted line is the breakeven point.

8. FURTHER EXPERIMENTS

8.1 COMBINATIONS OF FEATURE SETS

The only improvement over BW in the above work was the result for NP on Reuters. The improvement was only slight, but it seemed natural to keep going to see if we could improve it further. The obvious thing to do was to try a union of NP and BW features (denoted NP_W). It seemed quite conceivable that in the selection process for the NP features, some valuable non-noun single words were screened out, and that providing RIPPER with a union of noun phrases and non-noun single words could improve performance any further. To form the NP_W representation, the NP representation was combined with all words from BW that appeared in the corpus 4 times or more. This resulted in a set of 24733 features. We then performed the standard 4 runs with RIPPER, varying the loss ratio parameter each time, and found the micro-averaged breakeven point to be 0.823 – falling between the breakeven points of BW and NP.

8.2 COMBINATIONS OF CLASSIFIERS

The final round of experiments evaluated combinations of classifiers based on different representations. Dietterich [1997] pointed out that any set of high-quality classifiers that make at least partially uncorrelated errors could be expected to produce higher performance when combined with a simple majority vote. He also pointed out that due to the potential for the formation of differently shaped decision boundaries in the feature space, almost any pair of classifiers trained in slightly different conditions can be expected to make partially uncorrelated errors. We felt that the new text representations were probably producing enough variation in the feature space that the majority vote technique should improve RIPPER's predictions when combining hypotheses formed using the different representations. Furthermore, the majority vote technique can easily be applied to text classification, since every decision made by the system is binary, regardless of the number of classes involved,.

We experimented with combinations of 3 and 5 classifiers in which a class label was assigned only if the majority of classifiers predicted that it should be. The best results for 3 and 5 classifiers on each test collection are reported in table 4 and compared to the best results using a single classifier. Note that performance is improved in all cases and that the Reuters result is comparable to, though still not quite as high as the best reported results of Joachims [1998] and Lam and Ho [1998].

Table 4: Best results for combining classifiers

	Reuters		DigiTrad	
#	reps.	b.e.	reps.	b.e.
1	NP	.827	BW_S	.360
3	BW, NP, NP_S	.845	BW, BW_S, NP	.404[e]
5	BW, NP, NP_S, KP, KP_S	.849	BW, BW_S, NP, KP_S, KP	.422[e]

9. CONCLUSIONS AND FUTURE DIRECTIONS

Lewis and Sparck Jones [1996] wrote that statistical techniques for classification and retrieval have "picked some of the low-hanging fruit off the tree." They believe that significant advances must be made before NLP techniques can be used to improve text classification. The results of our work strengthen their general conclusions by showing that simple NLP-based representations do not improve the performance of symbolic learners. In particular we believe that it is probably not worth pursuing simple phrase-based representations any further. But it may be worth the effort, in domains like DigiTrad, to try to find a way to make hypernym representations more tractable for RIPPER. This will probably involve integrating a partial word-sense disambiguation algorithm in the feature formation step to produce a sparser representation and allow higher values for the h parameter. We also found evidence that alternative representations could serve as the basis for combining classifiers to produce better results. Indeed it is worth pointing out that one of the only published results that beats our own for Reuters is itself based on combinations of classifiers [Joachims, 1998]. Future work in this area, possibly using other types of learning algorithms, may be well worth the effort.

Finally, we have some concerns over the use of micro-averaged breakeven point in the IR literature. Research could be conducted to try to define a more nuanced evaluation technique. For instance, Provost and Fawcett's [1997] ROC curves provide a slightly more sensitive measurement that can be adapted to show the convex hull of precision and recall, providing a more informative picture of performance than the single breakeven point. This is feasible in our setting, since the loss ratio parameter can be varied to provide points from which the ROC curve can be interpolated. The micro-averaging step of the analysis should also be critically evaluated, since many of the subtle details of performance can get lost in such an aggressive statistical move. Future work should look into defining new performance measurements that do not suffer these shortcomings.

Acknowledgements

Sam Scott acknowledges the generous support of the National Research Council of Canada's Interactive Information Group, and both authors acknowledge the support of the Canada's Natural Sciences and Engineering Research Council.

References

Brill, Eric. 1992. A simple rule-based part of speech tagger. *Proceedings of the Third Conference on Applied Natural Language Processing*. ACL. 152-155.

Brill, Eric. 1994. Some advances in rule-based part of speech tagging. *AAAI-94*. 722-727.

Cohen, William W. 1995. Fast effective rule induction. *ICML-95*. 115-123.

Cohen, William W. 1995. Learning to classify English text with ILP methods. *Proceedings of the 5th International Workshop on Inductive Logic Programming*. 3-24.

Cohen, William W. 1995. Text categorization and relational learning. *ICML-95*. 124-132.

Cohen, William W. 1996. Learning rules that classify e-mail. *Proceedings of the 1996 AAAI Spring Symposium on Machine Learning in Information Access*. (www.parc.xerox.com/istl/projects/mlia)

Cohen, William W. 1996. Learning trees and rules with set-valued features. *AAAI-96*. 709-716.

Cohen, William W. and Singer, Yoram. 1996. Context-sensitive learning methods for text categorization. *SIGIR-96*. 307-316.

Dietterich, Thomas G. 1997. Machine learning research: four current directions. *Artificial Intelligence Magazine*. Winter, 1997. 97-136.

Fellbaum, Christiane (ed.). 1998. *WordNet: An Electronic Lexical Database*. MIT Press.

Fürnkranz, Johannes. 1998. A study using *n*-gram features for text categorization. Technical Report OEFAI-TR-98-30, Austrian Institute for Artificial Intelligence.

Fürnkranz, Johannes; Mitchell, Tom; and Riloff, Ellen. 1998. A case study in using linguistic phrases for text categorization on the www. *Proceedings of the AAAI/ICML-98 Workshop on Text Categorization.*

Fürnkranz, Johannes and Widmer, Gerhard. 1994. Incremental Reduced Error Pruning. *ICML-94*. 70-77.

Flank, Sharon. 1998. A layered approach to NLP-based information retrieval. *COLING-ACL'98*. 397-403.

Greenhaus, Dick. 1996. *About the Digital Tradition*. www.mudcat.org/DigiTrad-blurb.html. (DigiTrad itself can be found in Reuters-style SGML format on the NRC web page referenced in footnote 2 of the main text.)

Ide, Nancy and Véronis, Jean. 1998. Introduction to the special issue on word sense disambiguation: the state of the art. *Computational Linguistics*, 24(1). March, 1998. 1-40.

Joachims, Thorsten. 1998. Text categorization with support vector machines: learning with many relevant features. *ECML-98*. 137-142.

Lam, Wai and Ho, Chao Yang. 1998. Using a generalized instance set for automatic text categorization. *SIGIR-98*. 81-89.

Lewis, David D. 1992a. An evaluation of phrasal and clustered representations on a Text Categorization Task. *SIGIR-92*. 37-50.

Lewis, David D. 1992b. *Representation and Learning in Information Retrieval*. Ph.D. thesis, University of Massachusetts at Amherst. Technical Report 91-93. February, 1992.

Lewis, David D. 1995. Evaluating and optimizing autonomous text classification systems. *SIGIR-95*. 246-254.

Lewis, David D. and Sparck Jones, Karen. 1996. Natural language processing for information retrieval. *Communications of the ACM*, 39(1). January, 1996. 92-101.

Lovins, J. B. 1968. Development of a stemming algorithm. *Mechanical Translation and Computational Linguistics*, 11. 22-31.

McCallum, Andrew; Rosenfeld, Ronald; Mitchell, Tom; and Ng, Andrew Y. 1998. Improving text classification by shrinkage in a hierarchy of classes. *ICML-98*. 359-367.

Miller, George A. 1990. WordNet: an on-line lexical database. *International Journal of Lexicography*, 3(4). 235-244.

Mladenić, Dunja, and Grobelnik, Marko. Word sequences as features in text-learning. *ERK-98*.

Ng, Hwee Tou; Goh, Wei Booh; and Low, Kok Leong. 1997. Feature selection, perceptron learning, and a usability case study for text categorization. *SIGIR-97*. 67-73.

Provost, Foster and Fawcett, Tom. 1997. Analysis and visualization of classifier performance: comparison under imprecise class and cost distributions. *KDD-97*. (www.croftj.net/~fawcett/ROCCH)

Riloff, Ellen. 1995. Little words can make a big difference for text classification. *SIGIR-95*. 130-136.

Rodríguez, Manuel de Buenaga; Gômez-Hidalgo, José María; and Díaz-Agudo, Belén. 1997. Using WordNet to complement training information in text categorization. *RANLP-97*. 150-157.

Scott, Sam. 1998. *Feature Engineering for a Symbolic Approach to Text Classification*. Masters Thesis, University of Ottawa Computer Science Department. Technical report TR-98-09. (http://ai.iit.nrc.ca/II_public/Classification/abstract.html)

Scott, Sam and Matwin, Stan. 1998. Text classification using WordNet hypernyms. *Usage of WordNet in Natural Language Processing Systems: Proceedings of the Workshop*. 45-51. (www.ai.sri.com/~harabagi/coling-acl98/acl_work/acl_work.html)

Turney, Peter D. 1999. Learning to extract keyphrases from text. National Research Council of Canada, Institute for Information Technology, Technical Report ERB-1057.

Voorhees, Ellen M. 1993. Using WordNet to disambiguate word senses for text retrieval. *SIGIR-93*. 171-180.

Voorhees, Ellen M. 1994. Query expansion using lexical-semantic relations. *SIGIR-94*. 61-69.

Yang, Yiming and Pederson, Jan O. 1997. A comparative study on feature selection in text categorization. *ICML-97*. 412-42

Feature Selection as a Preprocessing Step for Hierarchical Clustering

Luis Talavera
Dept. Llenguatges i Sistemes Informàtics
Universitat Politècnica de Catalunya
Campus Nord, Mòdul C6, Jordi Girona 1-3
08034 Barcelona, Spain
talavera@lsi.upc.es

Abstract

Although feature selection is a central problem in inductive learning as suggested by the growing amount of research in this area, most of the work has been carried out under the supervised learning paradigm, paying little attention to unsupervised learning tasks and, particularly, clustering tasks. In this paper, we analyze the particular benefits that feature selection may provide in hierarchical clustering tasks and explore the power of feature selection methods applied as a preprocessing step under the proposed dimensions. Instead of only predicting class labels, the focus is on a more general inference tasks over all the features. Empirical results suggest that feature selection as preprocessing only provides limited improvements in the performance task. In addition, they raise the problem of the notion of irrelevance in unsupervised settings.

1 INTRODUCTION

Inductive learning systems are a powerful approach for automatically extracting useful information from data or for assisting humans in this process. Data mining problems or WWW information are examples of sources of large volumes of data involving many features and objects. A problem related to this sort of data is the presence of a large number of features that might tend to decrease the effectiveness of learning algorithms, especially if most of these features appear to be irrelevant with regard to the learning task. In fact, feature selection is a central problem in inductive learning as suggested by the growing amount of research in this area (Blum & Langley, 1997; Dash & Liu, 1997; Kohavi & John, 1997).

Clustering is a form of unsupervised learning used to discover useful patterns in data. Particularly, hierarchical clustering methods construct a tree-structured clustering where sibling clusters partition the observations covered by their parent. Hierarchical structuring provides a view of data at several levels of abstraction, yet flexibly allowing different flat partitions to be extracted during data analysis. Although clustering construction might benefit from feature selection similarly to supervised learning approaches, most of the work concerning feature selection has been carried out under the supervised paradigm, paying little attention to unsupervised learning tasks. Only few proposals exist concerning this problem, and to our knowledge only two works (Dash, Liu, & Yao, 1997; Devaney & Ram, 1997) have explored preprocessing mechanisms of feature selection.

In this paper we present a study of unsupervised methods of feature selection applied as a preprocessing step. We discuss the particular benefits that feature selection may provide in hierarchical clustering tasks remarking the particular nature of this sort of classifiers. This discussion raises three different dimensions for evaluating feature selection, namely, irrelevant features, efficiency in the performance task and comprehensibility. We implement several feature selection mechanisms and evaluate them in terms of the these dimensions.

2 FEATURE SELECTION IN HIERARCHICAL CLUSTERING

Typically, the primary goal of feature selection is intended to make inductive learning algorithms more robust (i.e. to maintain a good performance) in the face of irrelevant features. In supervised learning, the typical performance task is the prediction of class labels over unseen instances. As unsupervised approaches, hierarchical clustering systems are not restricted to predict a single class label. As remarked by several authors, unsupervised learning systems can support a *flexible prediction* task aimed to support prediction over all the features (Fisher, 1987; Langley, 1995). Because of this multiple inference task, the presence of irrelevant features may be even more harmful in unsupervised systems. On the other hand, unsupervised learning may focus in *description* tasks, rather than in prediction. In such a case, we can view feature selection as a means of simplification of concept descriptions that may provide a more readable interpretation of the domain, without necessarily taking into account accuracy concerns.

Additionally, there is an important factor related to the organization of the knowledge base in hierarchical clusterers. Commonly, hierarchical clusterings are *polythetic* classifiers, that is, they divide objects based on their values along multiple features. Particularly, they tend to use the full set of features at each node to decide how to classify a new object. Note that, while in *monothetic* classifiers such as decision trees, a redundant feature adds one additional test when classifying a new observation, in polythetic classifiers it adds a test for each node in the classification path.

Taking into account these issues, we can summarize three benefits that the hierarchical clustering task may obtain from incorporating feature selection mechanisms. The first two are concerned with predictive performance tasks, and the last one with descriptive tasks:

- *Irrelevant features.* The set of features used in an inductive learning task is a powerful representational bias that determines the performance a learning system. When faced with a lot of irrelevant features, the performance of inductive learning systems tends to degrade. In hierarchical clustering systems, the loss of performance may be even more important, since they must perform a more general inference task than supervised systems.

- *Efficiency in the performance task.* The number of features may also influence a performance task such as prediction. Since the decision of how to classify a new instance has to be made along several nodes in the tree that, in turn, contain all the features, the number of features present in the data directly influences the complexity of the prediction task. Selecting an appropriate subset of features may reduce this complexity without degrading accuracy.

  Comprehensibility of the results. With the exception of logic-based approaches which select features by using the dropping conditions rule, clustering systems usually make use of all the available features at each node of the hierarchy. Reducing the number of features used in the clustering process allow to provide shorter cluster descriptions to the user. Short descriptions tend to be more readable and, hence more comprehensible. Comprehensibility has been recognized as a specially important concern in clustering (Michalski & Stepp, 1983).

3 PREPROCESSING FEATURES IN CLUSTERING

In this paper, our concern is in exploring the application of unsupervised feature selection methods as a preprocessing step. This is a typical approach in the supervised paradigm where a subset of features is selected before learning proceeds. Under this framework, we can expect to improve the performance of hierarchical clustering algorithms under the three dimensions outlined in the previous section.

We consider appropriate to differentiate between *feedback* and *blind* methods of feature selection. Feedback methods use information from running the clustering algorithm to estimate performance of a subset of features, while blind methods rely on some previous assumptions about which are the most relevant features, usually reflected in some metric. This distinction is similar to the one of *filter* and *wrapper* methods (Kohavi & John, 1997).

Feedback methods are relatively easy to implement. For instance, we can estimate accuracy on the training set itself, although this could lead to overestimate the performance of the algorithm. In the same way, one can implement a *hold-out* approach (Weiss & Kulikowski, 1991) and divide the training set into two subsets, one effectively for training, and the second for validation. We train the algorithm with different feature subsets and use the validation set to estimate performance over each subset. An alternative approach, very popular in implementations of the wrapper approach in supervised learning, is to use *cross-validation* over the training set to obtain a more conservative estimate.

The problem in unsupervised learning lies in how to implement blind methods. Supervised approaches typically use metrics that estimate the predictive power of each feature as regards the class label. There are lots of metrics to compute the discrimination power of a feature among the existing classes but, in unsupervised environments, there is no class label present in data, so we need to develop an alternative method. A solution could be to resort to some metric used in clustering algorithms since it should promote predictive clusterings. The category utility metric used in Fisher's COBWEB (Fisher, 1987) is one of these metrics and it is defined as follows:

$$\frac{\sum_k P(C_k) \sum_i \sum_j [P(A_i = V_{ij} \mid C_k)^2 - P(A_i = V_{ij})^2]}{n} \quad (1)$$

This metric estimates the predictive ability of a given cluster C_k in a partition of n clusters, for inferring any feature value V_{ij} given the base rate accuracy that we could get without forming any cluster and represented by $P(A_i = V_{ij})$. The formulation is analogous to that of attribute selection measures for decision trees, which in turn, measure the predictive ability of a feature with respect to class label prediction. However, even though the measure is oriented towards unsupervised tasks, it makes use of class information. Of course, these classes are not predefined labels over the instances in the data set, but the clusters that the algorithm forms during the learning process. But the problem is that, considering feature selection as a preprocessing step, there is no cluster formed, so there is not class information available.

Generally, metrics designed to guide clustering have to evaluate several alternative partitionings and, therefore, they tend to use the class information. If we focus on the definition of the unsupervised performance task of predicting all the features in the data, we can consider that relevant features are those that have a higher predictive ability for inferring the value of other features. Fisher has proposed a measure of *feature dependence* to characterize the domains in which clustering is applied (Fisher, 1987). The formulation is very similar to that presented for the category utility metric. Let us define the expected number of feature values that can be correctly predicted for a feature A_M given knowledge of the value V_{ij_i} for a feature A_i as

$$E(A_M, A_i) = \sum_{j_M} P(A_M = V_{j_M} \mid A_i = V_{ij_i})^2 \quad (2)$$

Further, let us define the expected number of feature values than can be predicted with no knowledge for a feature A_M, i.e., the base rate, as:

$$E(A_M) = \sum_{j_M} P(A_M = V_{Mj_M})^2 \quad (3)$$

Intuitively, a feature is relevant if knowing its value allows to improve the prediction of the value of other features. Removing those features that have a little contribution in predicting other features, should allow to maintain the original accuracy in a flexible prediction task. This contribution can be modeled as the dependency of a feature A_M on another feature A_i with the expression:

$$\sum_{j_i} P(A_i = V_{j_i}) E(A_M, A_i) - E(A_M) \quad (4)$$

that measures the increase in the expected number of feature values that can be predicted given knowledge of the value of A_i, weighting the importance of individual values. Since this metric does not make use of any class information, it is a good candidate to perform feature selection as a preprocessing step.

4 EMPIRICAL EVALUATION

In order to obtain some insight of the abilities of the different approaches to feature selection as a preprocessing step for hierarchical clustering, we performed two sort of experiments on several data sets from the UCI Repository. The first uses the typically used LED data set containing 17 irrelevant features. In the second, we use other standard datasets to obtain a wider view of the performance of each method.

The experimental settings were as follows. Our implementation is based on COBWEB (Fisher, 1987), since it is a well-known and widely used clustering system. COBWEB is a hierarchical clustering system that constructs a tree from a sequence of observations. The system follows a strict *incremental* scheme, that is, it learns from each observation in the sequence without reprocessing previously encountered observations. An observation is assumed to be a vector of nominal values V_{ij} along different features A_i. COBWEB employs *probabilistic concept* descriptions to represent the learned knowledge. In this sort of representation, in a cluster C_k, each feature value has an associated conditional probability $P(A_i = V_{ij} \mid C_k)$ reflecting the proportion of observations in C_k with the value V_{ij} along the feature A_i.

Given an observation and a current hierarchical clustering, COBWEB categorizes the observation by sorting it through the hierarchy from the root node down to the leaves. At each level, the learning algorithm evaluates the quality of the new clustering resulting from placing the observation in each of the existing clusters, and the quality resulting from creating a new cluster covering the new observation. In addition, the algorithm considers two more actions that can restructure the hierarchy in order to improve its quality. *Merging* attempts to combine the two sibling clusters which were identified as the two best hosts for the new observation; *splitting* can replace the best host and promote its children to the next higher level. The option that yields the high quality score is selected and the procedure is recursed, considering the best host as the root in the recursive call. The recursion ends when a leaf containing only the new observation is created. In order to choose among the four available operators, the *category utility* metric that we have previously defined is used.

We designed two preprocessing procedures, covering both the feedback and blind approaches. The performance task considered is the flexible prediction task previously discussed, which is measured as the average accuracy over all of the features present in the data. This accuracy is computed for each instance by repeatedly masking out one feature and then using the cluster hierarchy to classify the instance and predict the masked value. Final accuracy is obtained by averaging the accuracy obtained for each individual feature. The predicted value always corresponds to the one found in the reached leaf.

Our implementation of the blind method is based on an *ordering* scheme. Under this strategy, a weight is individually computed for each feature and features are ordered according to these weights. From this ordered list, the k features with the highest weights can be selected. Instead of directly choosing a value for k, we can define a *feature selection threshold* τ defined between 0 and 1. Specifically, for a given set of n features $\{A_1, A_2, \ldots, A_n\}$ and a given τ value, we remove the features in the set

$$\{A \mid weight(A) < \tau \cdot Max\{weight(A_i) \mid i = 1, \ldots, n\}\}$$

As a weighting function, the feature dependency measure described above is used. In the experiments, we used the usual proportions of 2/3 of instances for training and 1/3 for testing. All the results are averages over 30 independent runs using random splits.

As a feedback method we implemented a hold-out approach that divided the data set into 40% for training, 40% for validation and 20% for testing. Given the high dependency of feedback methods to the amount of data used for validation and the fact that they use a smaller training set, we opted for reducing the amount of data for testing. The search into the feature space was carried out by using a classical greedy stepwise approach that adds or removes one feature at each decision point and chooses the state that most improves accuracy. Two popular variations of this technique were implemented (Doak, 1992). In the *forward selection approach (FS)*, the search starts with an empty feature set and at each step adds the feature that produces a higher accuracy improvement. Similarly, *backward elimination (BE)* initially selects the full feature set, and removes a feature at each step. Again, results are averages over 30 runs.

In addition, we measured the improvements of the preprocessing step for the two other dimensions related to the performance task, efficiency in prediction and comprehensibility. We measured prediction efficiency empirically by recording the number of *feature tests* needed to classify an instance when making a prediction. For instance, if there are n features, for a given instance, the COBWEB algorithm first evaluates the utility of making an independent cluster and performs n tests to compute the category utility metric. Other operators such as evaluating the utility of incorporating the instance to an existing cluster among k different clusters, need $k{\cdot}n$ tests. The sum of all these tests averaged for all the predictions made, is used as an indicator of the complexity of making predictions. Finally, comprehensibility is evaluated simply by looking at the average number of features per node. We assume that shorter descriptions are more readable, and thus, more comprehensible.

4.1 IRRELEVANT FEATURES

In our first experiment, we used the LED data set containing 24 features, from which 17 contain randomly assigned values and, thus, are deemed as irrelevant. We used the data set generator from the UCI Repository to generate 600 instances. We generated instances without noise, as opposed to the traditional use of this data set so that not additional influencing factors were introduced. Table 1 shows the results obtained with feedback based methods. The results for the plain algorithm without feature selection are computed by us-

Table 1: Results for the LED dataset with irrelevant features (feedback methods).

Method	Accuracy	Tests	Features/Node
None	59.16 ± 1.07	350.91 ± 8.41	24.00 ± 0.00
FS	61.73 ± 2.17	460.22 ± 215.96	6.50 ± 1.83
BE	70.41 ± 1.65	375.16 ± 18.29	22.37 ± 0.96

Table 2: Results for the LED dataset with irrelevant features (blind method).

τ	Accuracy	Tests	Features/Node
0.00	71.06 ± 1.47	403.15 ± 5.85	24.00 ± 0.00
0.10	62.05 ± 0.71	547.45 ± 57.62	7.00 ± 0.37
0.20	61.36 ± 0.78	498.24 ± 29.83	6.10 ± 0.40
0.30	60.96 ± 0.73	537.50 ± 37.22	5.30 ± 0.47
0.40	60.76 ± 0.67	557.37 ± 26.74	4.83 ± 0.38
0.50	59.30 ± 1.01	529.92 ± 92.89	3.40 ± 0.50

ing only the training and test sets, but not the validation set in order to get a baseline accuracy. Results seem to suggest two trends. First, the FS method selects a significantly lower amount of features than BE, but at the expense of diminishing accuracy. This could be due to the greedy nature of both techniques that makes FS more sensitive to local maxima. Note that BE starts with the full feature set, so it is a much more conservative method. On the other hand, it appears that in order to get high accuracies, most of the features are needed. However, since none of the methods select an intermediate number of features, we cannot determine if it is possible to obtain a better balance between the number of features and accuracy.

An interesting result is that feature selection does not improve efficiency in the prediction task, rather, it degrades it. Curiously, FS selects a small number of features but augments the number of tests in a 30% over the plain COBWEB. The reason is that COBWEB organizes the cluster hierarchy in a different manner with the reduced feature set, generating a larger number of nodes. Note that in a polythetic hierarchical classifier, the complexity is not only dependent on the number of features per node, but also on the topology of the hierarchy. A deeper study is needed in order to get further insight into this issue. Finally, as regards comprehensibility, it appears that we have to trade simplicity for accuracy, which is a result widely observed in supervised tasks.

Table 2 shows the results for the blind method. The first relevant result observed is the good performance of the plain algorithm that, in fact, clearly outperforms the results obtained with feature selection. We think that this could be explained by the fact that when evaluating feedback methods we used only 200 instances for training, since 200 have to be used for validation. Now training is done with 400 instances, and these results are probably reflecting that the clustering algorithm may reach good performance when facing irrelevant features at the expense of using a larger training set. Moreover, this result appears to confirm that most –if not all– of the features are needed in order to get high accuracies as we noted when discussing the previous results. Blind feature selection appears to perform poorly, due to the highly restrictive selection performed. In addition, and similarly to feedback methods, feature selection does not improve efficiency and comprehensibility is improved but with a significant accuracy loss.

However, it can be observed that, by using a $\tau = 0.10$, the preprocessing step tends to select 7 features, which is exactly the number of relevant features in this data set. So we ran an additional experiment but this time measuring the final accuracy of predicting the class label. Since the data contains no noise, without irrelevant features, the accuracy achieved is of 100%. We observed that the 7 features selected by the blind method provided the same accuracy over class labels. Therefore, it seems that the method is selecting the correct set of features, so where is the problem?

A more detailed look into one of the runs provides further insight into these results. Without feature selection, the accuracy for the 7 relevant features was 83.00% and for the irrelevant ones, 63.47%. Using a

Table 3: Results for the UCI data sets (feedback methods).

Dataset	Method	Accuracy	Tests	Features/Node
zoo	None	85.49 ± 2.14	155.46 ± 7.68	16.00 ± 0.00
	FS	83.51 ± 2.74	123.07 ± 37.60	5.90 ± 1.65
	BE	85.91 ± 2.31	158.35 ± 28.27	12.70 ± 1.88
soybean small	None	85.56 ± 2.26	259.70 ± 18.11	35.00 ± 0.00
	FS	85.06 ± 1.84	56.83 ± 14.92	5.47 ± 1.59
	BE	86.12 ± 1.71	149.60 ± 30.67	16.00 ± 2.99
soybean large	None	82.57 ± 1.14	452.49 ± 21.05	35.00 ± 0.00
	FS	80.40 ± 2.32	314.55 ± 101.70	9.77 ± 3.18
	BE	84.61 ± 1.22	473.20 ± 35.17	32.03 ± 1.67
mushroom	None	78.66 ± 0.47	358.56 ± 5.17	22.00 ± 0.00
	FS	78.72 ± 0.67	348.01 ± 144.23	8.70 ± 2.05
	BE	78.50 ± 0.49	351.20 ± 24.91	19.30 ± 1.34

$\tau = 0.10$ value, the preprocessing step selected only the 7 relevant features obtaining accuracies of 89.86% and 50.94% for relevant and irrelevant features respectively. This suggests that the problem lies in the definition of irrelevance. For this dataset, irrelevant features are defined as regards to their inability to predict the class label. Clearly randomly generated values will tend to be irrelevant for this task. However, when considering a flexible prediction task, these features are also included in the performance measurement, that is, they also have to be predicted accurately. By generating uniform distributions of random values, we prevent these features of being useful for predicting labels, but they can still be useful for predicting other irrelevant features, and thus, be useful under our definition of the unsupervised performance task. In fact, these counterintuitive results are a byproduct of the philosophy underlying the formulation of the category utility measure, i.e., maximize the overall prediction ability of the cluster hierarchy for *any* feature.

One could think that what we really want to measure is only performance over the relevant features –7 in the case of LEDs– and that the feature selection measure performs well. However, if such knowledge is available, there is no need to use the remaining features and the feature selection process renders useless. A solution could be to use the feature selection step to select not only the features used in the clustering process, but also the features to be included in the prediction task, although this solution would probably need the intervention of the user. In sum, the problem of defining the notion of relevance in flexible prediction is an open problem and deserves further investigation beyond the scope of this work.

4.2 UCI DATASETS

In our second set of experiments we used several data sets from the UCI Repository. These data sets are not known to contain explicitly irrelevant features. Nevertheless, it is possible that for the clustering task some features could be redundant. Table 3 shows the results for feedback methods. We can observe the same trends pointed out for the previous results as regards the FS and BE methods. Again, FS appears to get stuck at local maxima, giving small feature sets but with an accuracy loss. The BE methods performs fairly good, but the number of removed features is very small with the exception of the soybean small data set. However, this data set contains 14 features that take the same value for all the instances that are consistently detected by our feature selection methods, being the additional reduction of features very low. The mushroom data set is an exception in that all the methods seem to achieve similar accuracy. Results are much better for this data set, obtaining a reduction of the 60% of features. The larger size of the mushroom dataset suggests that the problem with the FS method is that the training and validation sets of the other data sets are too small to obtain good performance estimates. However, results could be also dependent on the structure of the data. As regards efficiency, no important improvements are achieved in either case. Comprehensibility is again improved by using the FS method, although the amount of accuracy that must be sacrificed to achieve this improvement is doubtful, given the contradictory results of the different data sets.

We also run our implementation of the blind method giving the results shown in Table 4. Similarly to feed-

Table 4: Results for the UCI data sets (blind method).

Dataset	τ	Accuracy	Tests	Features/Node
zoo	0.00	86.45 ± 1.75	193.17 ± 8.79	16.00 ± 0.00
	0.10	87.15 ± 1.91	174.99 ± 8.01	14.00 ± 0.26
	0.20	86.64 ± 1.80	182.77 ± 17.24	13.37 ± 0.67
	0.30	86.19 ± 2.03	178.76 ± 21.31	11.60 ± 0.89
	0.40	84.44 ± 2.54	145.15 ± 28.20	8.70 ± 1.44
	0.50	83.47 ± 2.38	125.89 ± 20.22	5.90 ± 1.06
	0.60	82.82 ± 2.53	118.00 ± 12.79	5.03 ± 0.18
soybean small	0.00	86.65 ± 1.48	332.52 ± 19.67	35.00 ± 0.00
	0.10	86.53 ± 1.70	190.27 ± 9.76	20.20 ± 0.66
	0.20	86.44 ± 1.50	153.96 ± 9.66	16.17 ± 0.75
	0.30	86.46 ± 1.33	138.93 ± 10.23	14.63 ± 0.67
	0.40	86.10 ± 0.88	122.67 ± 7.62	12.53 ± 0.94
	0.50	85.73 ± 1.30	111.43 ± 8.23	10.93 ± 0.52
	0.60	85.15 ± 1.21	91.44 ± 11.13	8.57 ± 1.01
soybean large	0.00	84.65 ± 1.12	523.19 ± 18.25	35.00 ± 0.00
	0.10	84.57 ± 1.24	502.81 ± 18.11	33.67 ± 0.55
	0.20	84.77 ± 0.90	461.02 ± 23.29	31.17 ± 0.59
	0.30	84.69 ± 0.87	447.25 ± 31.92	30.07 ± 1.78
	0.40	83.74 ± 1.13	390.73 ± 25.55	24.33 ± 1.47
	0.50	83.44 ± 1.05	412.81 ± 29.20	21.93 ± 0.37
	0.60	83.15 ± 1.36	508.90 ± 125.56	20.40 ± 0.77
mushroom	0.00	78.67 ± 0.52	400.08 ± 4.91	22.00 ± 0.00
	0.10	78.69 ± 0.53	353.47 ± 12.67	19.47 ± 0.63
	0.20	78.63 ± 0.54	309.46 ± 3.76	17.00 ± 0.00
	0.30	78.64 ± 0.55	299.37 ± 13.45	16.43 ± 0.68
	0.40	78.66 ± 0.51	270.33 ± 6.10	14.83 ± 0.38
	0.50	79.08 ± 0.46	357.75 ± 126.62	11.07 ± 0.83
	0.60	78.10 ± 0.84	609.04 ± 80.63	7.17 ± 0.99

back methods, the mushroom data set arises as a special case. The rest of results indicate that the blind method can maintain the performance by removing a small fraction of the set of features. We can observe that the number of features to obtain good accuracies for each data set is very similar to that obtained with feedback methods. In the case of the mushroom data set we obtain particularly good results and the blind method seems to obtain good accuracy with a similar amount of reduction than the feedback methods. Again, it remains to be seen if these results are a byproduct of the data set structure or of the number of training instances that could influence the probability estimates.

As regards to the ability of feedback and blind methods, in general, we can say that both methods perform similarly. This is an interesting result, since feedback methods are computationally expensive, because they have to repeatedly build clusterings and perform multiple classifications in order to evaluate performance. At first, feedback methods are more sensitive to the amount of training data, but also, we have to take into account the reliability of the probability estimates used by the blind method.

5 RELATED WORK

Few works have addressed the problem of feature selection. Gennari (1991) investigated a feature selection mechanism embedded in CLASSIT, a descendant of COBWEB, and made some preliminary experiments. However, his research differs from this work in that we focus in feature selection as preprocessing and that our evaluation is not done by measuring accuracy over class labels. Two works that follow the preprocessing view are Dash, Liu and Yao (1997) and Devaney and

Ram (1997), but again, evaluation is performed over class labels. In sum, our work is novel in two aspects. First, we make a specific study of methods to be applied before learning, which pose additional problems due to the absence of hypothesis about the domain. Secondly, we focus in a multiple inference task that have been proposed for unsupervised learning systems instead of class label prediction.

6 CONCLUDING REMARKS

We have addressed the problem of unsupervised feature selection as a preprocessing step. Particularly, we focused in hierarchical clustering tasks in the context of the performance task of predicting any missing feature. We discussed the benefits of feature selection for these tasks given their specific nature and proposed two dimensions to evaluate feature selection beyond predictive accuracy, namely, efficiency in prediction and comprehensibility.

Feature selection methods have been divided into feedback and blind methods, depending on their use of the clustering algorithm to estimate performance. Experiments running implementations of both approaches have shown that unsupervised feature selection as a preprocessing step has a limited impact in the three evaluation dimensions mentioned above. As regards comprehensibility, it appears that we have to trade accuracy for simplicity with the implemented feature selection methods.

Our approaches could be adapted to different clustering algorithms since they are preprocessing steps independent of the subsequent learning process. Feedback-based methods are particularly easy to adapt, since they use the induction algorithm to evaluate feature subsets. As regards the dependency measure, we think that the underlying assumptions involved in its definition should hold for other algorithms than COBWEB, although this issue deserves further research. At first sight, it appears doubtful the extension of these approaches to other performance tasks than flexible prediction. We can assume that partitions offering high predictive power over all the features are also 'good' partitions for description purposes. The results with the LED data set seem to suggest that the dependency measure is able to detect irrelevant features from the point of view of discovering the 'correct' classes. We plan to develop future work on these topics.

Our results, have also highlighted interesting questions about what have to be deemed as irrelevant in clustering in the context of a multiple prediction task. Experiments have shown that features considered irrelevant for supervised tasks, become relevant in unsupervised ones, since these features may help to predict other theoretically irrelevant features. In addition, we have seen that the metric used to implement a blind method worked fairly well when compared with expensive feedback methods. This could be an indicator that other dependency-based measures not involving class labels (e.g. mutual information between features) could be good candidates to implement metrics for the blind approach. Further research should study and develop additional and improved measures for this problem.

We think that unsupervised feature selection is a quite difficult task, and that applied as a preprocessing step becomes even harder, because of the complete absence of information. As an alternative approach, we are investigating unsupervised feature selection methods applied as a post-processing step that make use of the information provided by the cluster hierarchy built (Talavera, 1999). Note that this allows to use different blind metrics since we can label the formed clusters to get the class information needed for some of these metrics. Additionally, we are working in dynamic feature selection methods, that select and modify feature sets during the learning process. Future work will compare these methods and evaluate the limitations and strengths of all these approaches.

References

Blum, A. L., & Langley, P. (1997). Selection of relevant features and examples in machine learning. *Artificial Intelligence*, *97*, 245-271.

Dash, M., & Liu, H. (1997). Feature selection for classification. *Intelligent Data Analysis*, *1*(3).

Dash, M., Liu, H., & Yao, J. (1997). Dimensionality reduction for unsupervised data. In *Ninth IEEE International Conference on Tools with AI, ICTAI'97*.

Devaney, M., & Ram, A. (1997). Efficient feature selection in conceptual clustering. In *Machine Learning: Proceedings of the Fourteenth International Conference.* Nashville, TN.

Doak, J. (1992). *An evaluation of feature-selection methods and their application to computer security* (Tech. Rep. No. CSE-92-18). Dept. of Computer Science, University of California at Davis.

Fisher, D. H. (1987). Knowledge acquisition via incremental conceptual clustering. *Machine Learning*, *2*, 139-172.

Gennari, J. H. (1991). Concept formation and attention. In *Proceedings of the Seventh Annual Conference of the Cognitive Science Society* (p. 724-728). Irvine,CA: Lawrence Erlbaum Associates.

Kohavi, R., & John, G. H. (1997). Wrappers for feature subset selection. *Artificial Intelligence*, *97*, 273-324.

Langley, P. (1995). *Elements of machine learning.* San Francisco, CA: Morgan Kaufmann.

Michalski, R. S., & Stepp, R. E. (1983). Learning from observation: Conceptual clustering. In R. S. Michalski, J. G. Carbonell, & T. M. Mitchell (Eds.), *Machine learning: An artificial intelligence approach* (p. 331-363). San Mateo, CA: Morgan Kauffmann.

Talavera, L. (1999). Feature selection as retrospective pruning in hierarchical clustering. In *Third International Symposium on Intelligent Data Analysis, IDA99.* Amsterdam, The Netherlands: Springer Verlag. (To appear.)

Weiss, S. M., & Kulikowski, C. A. (1991). *Computer systems that learn.* San Francisco, CA: Morgan Kaufmann.

OPT-KD: An Algorithm for Optimizing Kd-Trees

Improving Nearest Neighbor...

Douglas A. Talbert
Department of Computer Science
Vanderbilt University
Nashville, TN 37235
dat@vuse.vanderbilt.edu

Douglas H. Fisher
Department of Computer Science
Vanderbilt University
Nashville, TN 37235
dfisher@vuse.vanderbilt.edu

Abstract

We present OPT-KD, an algorithm that uses previously seen queries to optimize kd-trees for nearest-neighbor searching. First, common query patterns are extracted from a population of queries. These patterns are then used to build customized search trees for the data. The learned trees are used in conjunction with a pattern classifier to improve search efficiency by directing new queries to one of the pattern-specific trees when appropriate. We focus on a nutritional domain, but OPT-KD is relevant to any application in which customized nearest-neighbor searches are advantageous.

1 INTRODUCTION

Kd-trees (Friedman, Bentley & Finkel, 1977; Bentley, 1980; Moore, 1991) support efficient nearest-neighbor searches. They are commonly used within larger algorithms to assist with tasks such as instance-based reasoning (Dasarathy, 1991; Deng & Moore, 1995; Wettschereck, Aha & Mohri, 1997).

This paper describes OPT-KD, a kd-tree optimization algorithm that learns and adapts to user search patterns. We use OPT-KD to construct customized kd-trees for a diet management tool, but the method is relevant to any task for which customized nearest-neighbor searches are advantageous.

In our domain, the search space is defined by continuously-valued variables called *nutrients* (*e.g.*, protein content, vitamin-A content). A search of the space of *food instances* returns the m (user-specified) instances closest to a user-specified point. (A *food instance* is a particular serving size of a food substance.)

OPT-KD's initial tree is a "standard" kd-tree (Friedman, *et. al.*, 1977) that is optimized *without* respect to a given query population. In domains like ours, however, users have specific needs and goals and could benefit from a search strategy that adapts to fit a user's need.

The next section describes the nutrition database. Sections 3 explains the "standard" kd-tree algorithm and how it behaves in this domain. Section 4 describes how OPT-KD learns a set of attributes that are of interest to a user and uses them to build a kd-tree. Section 5 explains to OPT-KD can scale up this technique to improve search for multiple attribute sets. This is followed by discussion of related and future work.

2 NUTRITION DATA

OPT-KD is not domain specific, but it is helpful to ground discussion with a specific domain. Our data set was constructed using the United States Department of Agriculture's Nutrient Database for Standard Reference (USDA, 1998), which describes 5,976 foods using 56 nutritional components. Examples of these components include protein, fat, vitamin A, calcium, and individual amino acids.

The USDA database describes each food in terms of nutrients per 100 grams. Relational tables can be used to convert those values to the appropriate values for a range of common serving sizes. Speed is more of a concern for us than space. Thus, rather than compute serving size specific information during search, our database is flattened into nutrients per serving size for each food. This results in a database with 11,697 food instances.

Differing scales and missing values are common difficulties in real-world databases. Many nutrients are on different scales. There can be multiple orders of magnitude in differences of the ranges. Unaddressed, this would affect the utility of our distance measure. Moreover, not every food instance has a value for all the components we included. In fact, over 20% of all values are missing. Some nutrients, like protein and fat, have no missing values. Other components, such as alcohol and caffeine, have hardly any values, but most have missing value percentages ranging from 5% to 25%.

3 KD-TREES

Kd-trees are binary trees that organize a k-dimensional data set with the intention of reducing search costs for nearest neighbors. Internal nodes represent splits using a threshold along a given attribute, and leaves contain lists of instances that number below a user-specified maximum.

Figure 1 shows a simple kd-tree on the following data points: (-10, 5) (-5,3) (0,1) (3,2) (4,12) (8,14)

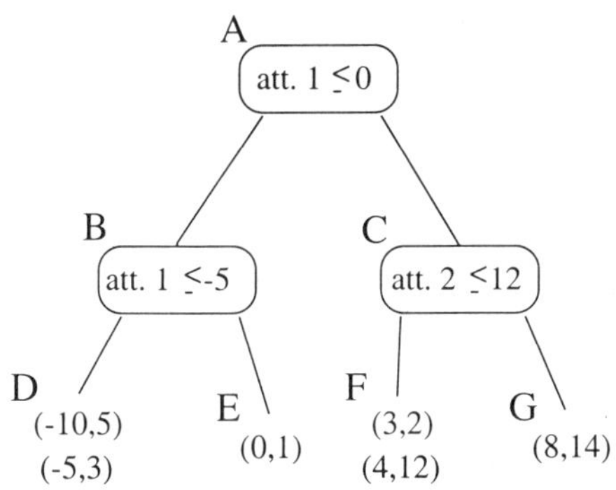

Figure 1: A Simple Kd-tree

3.1 KD-TREE SEARCHES

A kd-tree search begins with the specification of a query and a neighborhood size. A query is an ordered set of values, one value for each variable (*e.g.*, nutrient) describing the data. For example, a query using the tree in Figure 1 might request the 2 neighbors nearest to the point `(-7, 4)`.

The algorithm maintains two lists to help in the search. One list keeps track of the appropriate number of nearest neighbors along with their distances from the query. The other list keeps track of the geometric boundaries of the current node. These boundaries are defined by the split point values at all of the node's ancestors. For the tree in Figure 1, the bounds on the root, node A, are $(-\infty < att_1 < \infty, -\infty < att_2 < \infty)$ and the bounds for node F are $(0 < att_1 < \infty, -\infty < att_2 \leq 12)$. All data points that lie within the bounds of a node are in the subtree of that node.

The list of nearest neighbors is initialized to contain the necessary number of instance slots with all the associated distances set to ∞.

The query instance is passed to a node. If that node is not a leaf, the query is compared to the node's split point and the appropriate child is identified. The boundaries list is updated, and the recursive call to the child is made. If the node is a leaf, the algorithm computes the distance of each datum at the leaf to the query instance and compares this distance to the farthest distance in the list of neighbors. The list of closest neighbors thus far is updated whenever a closer element is found.

Our example begins as follows:

Initial boundaries list:	$(-\infty < att_1 < \infty,$ $-\infty < att_2 < \infty)$
Initial neighbor list:	$(null, \infty; null, \infty)$

The query starts at the root, passes through node B, and reaches a leaf at node D. After searching D's data, the nearest neighbor list is (`(-10, 5)`, 3.16; `(-5, 3)`, 2.24).

After a node has been completely searched, the algorithm uses the boundary information to decide if it is done searching. If all the boundaries are a least as far away from the query as the farthest near neighbor, the algorithm can stop because every point outside that boundary is too far away to be of interest, and every point inside that boundary has already been examined. This is the "ball-within-bounds" test (Friedman, *et. al.*, 1977).

In our example, the farther neighbor is 3.16 units away, but according to the current boundary conditions, ($-\infty < att_1 \leq -5, -\infty < att_2 < \infty$), there is a boundary only 2 units from our query. So, we are not done.

The algorithm backtracks to the previous node and checks to see if the other child needs to be searched. The boundaries of the unexamined child are compared to the distance to the most distant near neighbor. If the space defined by the bounds of that node intersects the region of space within d units of the query, the node needs to be searched because there could be a closer value within that node's subtree. This is the "bounds-overlaps-ball" test (Friedman, ıet. al., 1977).

In our example, the boundary for the unexplored child, node E, are $(-5 < att_1 \leq 0, -\infty < att_2 < \infty)$. We have a neighbor farther away than the boundary, $att_1 = 5$. Therefore, we search the node, but do not find any items close enough to update the neighbor list. E's bounds do not completely enclose the area containing possible near neighbors. So, we continue our search.

Since all of B's children have now been searched, the check to see if we can quit is performed again. The current boundaries are $(-\infty < att_1 \leq 0, -\infty < att_2 < \infty)$. All of those boundaries are more than 3.16 units from our query. Thus, our search stops here and returns the current list of neighbors.

By only searching those nodes closest to the query, *search cost* is reduced. Search cost is related to the number of nodes examined but can be defined more precisely. The fundamental operation during a kd-tree search is checking the distance from the query instance to a point along a single dimension. This operation occurs once at each examined split point, and, if there are N variables in the query instance and M instances in a leaf, it occurs $N * M$ times during a leaf search. "Ball-within-bounds" check perform this operation as many as $2 * N$ times, where N is the number of variables in the query, and in the "bounds-overlaps-ball" check it can occur $3 * N$ times. Unlike a simple node count, this measure allows us to accurately compare search cost between queries of different sizes.

3.2 KD-TREE CONSTRUCTION

A kd-tree is a k-dimensional generalization of a 1-dimensional binary search tree. A well-balanced binary search tree partitions the data at each node at the median value and places half the items in the left subtree and the other half in the right subtree. This process reduces the search space by half at each step.

A kd-tree learning algorithm (Friedman, *et. al.*, 1977) can use any of the k-dimensions to partition the data. At each node, the algorithm partitions the data by the median of the dimension with the greatest range. By splitting the "longest" dimension at a node, this technique tries to keep each node's geometric region as compact as possible.

The user specifies the number of elements allowed in a leaf node. The algorithm uses this threshold to decide when to stop partitioning a node.

The tree is Figure 1 was constructed in this manner. Recall that the points covered by this tree were (-10,5) (-5,3) (0,1) (3,2) (4,12) (8,14).

Attribute 1, with a range of [-10, 8], has a broader spread than attribute 2. Thus, its median value, 0, is chosen as the first split point. The instances are then partitioned, and the process repeats until leaves smaller than the specified threshold are formed. Our example allows leaves of size two or smaller.

3.3 KD-TREES AND THE NUTRITION DATA

There are characteristics of our data and task that forced us to adapt the basic algorithms described above.

3.3.1 Search Issues

The most important difference in task definition is that we are not interested in finding nearest neighbors across all dimensions, but in finding nearest neighbors only in terms of queried attribute values. For example, a user may only be interested in the nearest neighbors of protein (8 grams) and fat (2 grams). Henceforth, a query is a list of values along a subset of the dimensions.

As seen above, the key to efficient searching in a kd-tree is the ability to check the relationship of the query to the boundaries of the current node. The utility of these checks and, hence, the cost of searches in our domain, is affected by the small queries we expect. A query that only has values for a few nutrients might not have a value for some of the attributes used to partition the data. When this happens, boundary conditions become impossible to check. Our modified algorithm handles this situation by not allowing the "ball-within-bounds" check to be executed when such a boundary condition exists, and by forcing the search to visit both children of any node split along an unqueried attribute.

Missing values also affect search. We do not compute the distance from a query to a food instance when the food instance does not have a value for one of the queried nutrients. In this case, we currently ignore that food instance.

3.3.2 Construction Issues

In organizing our food database, we use the same construction algorithm described above for 56 dimensions. As in searching, aspects of our data cause some problems here. The differing scales of the nutrients are easily handled through normalization. We divide each value along a dimension by that dimension's standard deviation.

Instances missing a value for a split attribute are placed in the left subtree. The only queries for which such an instance can be a nearest neighbor are ones that are not defined along that split attribute. Such a query is guaranteed to visit each subtree formed by that split.

Moreover, missing values reduce the informativeness of a split. Median partitioning maximizes the information provided by a binary choice (Friedman, *et. al.*, 1977), but information can only be gained about those instances with a known value. Thus, OPT-KD uses an additional term that weights attribute selection by the percentage of known values.

Experiments with this estimate of "information amount" demonstrated its usefulness and are shown in Table 1. (Standard deviations are in parentheses.) The kd-tree for these tests had a maximum leaf size of 10 instances, and each search looked for 10 neighbors. The "unweighted" tree size was 3335 nodes, and the "weighted" tree size was 3425 nodes.

Table 1: Cost-Related Effects of Consider Missing Values During Attribute Selection

Query size	Search cost unweighted tree	Search cost weighted tree
5	12398.26 (4061.01)	12883.66 (4265.27)
10	18371.58 (11957.07)	16924.95 (9507.32)
20	27422.96 (22959.47)	23993.18 (20903.56)

3.3.3 Kd-Tree Performance in the Nutrition Domain

Table 2 shows the results of testing our default kd-tree in a variety of situations. (Standard deviations of the costs are in parentheses.)

For our purposes, the important aspect of these tests is that they demonstrate that searches using smaller numbers of dimensions use the default tree less efficiently. Section 3.1 explained that much of the cost is linear with respect to the size of the query. The cost, however, does not decrease linearly with query size. For example, a query of size 2 searching for 10 neighbors costs nearly as much as a query of size 5

Table 2: Kd-Tree Performance in the Nutrition Domain

Query size	Number of neighbors	Cost
20	50	44619.03 (24211.78)
20	10	23993.18 (20903.56)
20	5	21869.26 (16196.75)
15	50	31518.44 (20161.12)
15	10	23209.49 (16825.73)
15	5	16825.46 (12710.29)
10	50	28453.45 (15775.88)
10	10	16924.95 (9507.32)
10	5	14596.12 (8729.54)
5	50	16751.02 (6642.84)
5	10	12883.66 (4265.27)
5	5	11469.27 (3659.43)
2	50	12362.59 (2258.54)
2	10	11448.41 (2828.83)
2	5	10546.84 (10546.84)

searching for 10 neighbors. For smaller queries, there are fewer single dimension comparisons that have to be performed at the leaves, but more subtrees have to be searched as well.

4 OPTIMIZING FOR A SINGLE TYPE OF QUERY

We assume that a user's queries will tend to follow a discernable pattern or set of patterns. This assumption is fundamental because if the user only makes random queries, there is nothing to learn. Beyond that, however, we believe it is a reasonable assumption because each person's health, lifestyle, and preferences will dictate non-random nutritional interests.

4.1 LEARNING A USER'S INTERESTS

In our domain, we don't know what nutrients a user will be interested in. Thus, OPT-KD learns a user's interests from the queries.

OPT-KD begins by counting how frequently different nutrients are jointly queried. The user can specify how frequently a set must occur to be considered interesting. By computing the maximal sets of nutrients that surpass this threshold, OPT-KD can identify a user's interests.

Frequent set identification is well-understood in the

Table 3: Optimizing a Single Tree

	Default tree	Optimized tree
Experiment 1		
random	13695.33 (6012.13)	13208.30 (7385.26)
patt. 1	18867.36 (5434.91)	1388.47 (800.23)
patt. 2	24327.56 (6248.89)	1483.05 (1761.38)
patt. 3	21980 (6281.19)	1410.71 (1457.12)
Experiment 2		
random	12833.32 (2741.15)	14794.67 (8693.88)
patt. 1	26371.54 (5675.54)	1164.94 (417.21)
patt. 2	18630.27 (4563.01)	1387.32 (867.36)
patt. 3	20063.89 (6015.64)	1245.43 (916.21)
Experiment 3		
random	12601.96 (5292.79)	12014.24 (5653.56)
patt. 1	12915.39 (6163.92)	986.35 (399.09)
patt. 2	22998.19 (1948.77)	479.2 (138.23)
patt. 3	13418.71 (5318.70)	809.43 (350.14)
Experiment 4		
random	12102.26 (4626.98)	13309.30 (6666.78)
patt. 1	29024.04 (5494.31)	1228.57 (882.08)
patt. 2	30265.29 (2624.71)	4463.94 (3288.74)
patt. 3	25321.11 (7995.24)	972.44 (662.87)
Experiment 5		
random	13096.68 (3927.95)	11894.61 (4665.72)
patt. 1	7672.20 (2549.95)	651.81 (337.42)
patt. 2	7708.21 (1668.92)	709.08 (312.02)
patt. 3	9364.56 (2837.18)	859.84 (463.68)

context of association rule learning (Agrawal, Imielinski & Swami, 1993). We implemented the level-by-level efficient counting algorithm described in (Agrawal & Srikant, 1994).

4.2 BUILDING A OPTIMIZED KD-TREE

KD-OPT optimizes a kd-tree by limiting the set of attributes used for splitting to the set that was used during querying. This reduces the number of unhelpful splits in which a query must examine both subtrees, and it increases the likelihood that the "ball-within-bounds" test can be performed.

4.3 EXPERIMENTS

To test OPT-KD's ability to learn a user's interests and optimize a kd-tree to serve those interests, we simulated a user who was primarily interested in a single set of nutrients. We selected three random food instances and four random nutrients for which each instance had a value. The nutritional content of the food instances for those four nutrients served as models for our user's queries. A fourth query model, representing a random query, was included in our user simulation. These random queries could contain values from any attribute not just the set selected for the patterns.

Each model was equally likely to serve as the basis for each of our 100 simulated queries. Therefore, approximately 75% of the queries used the nutrients our "user" was interested in. OPT-KD used its frequent set algorithm to learn this set. It then built a new kd-tree optimized for that nutrient set.

100 more simulated queries were executed, and the costs were compared. Table 3 shows the results of OPT-KD interacting with five simulated users.

In the experiments of this section and the next, when a non-random model was chosen, the nutrient values were generated based on narrow, Gaussian distributions centered on the model's values. Furthermore, for all the tests, OPT-KD allowed a maximum leaf size of 10.

These experiments show that OPT-KD significantly reduces query cost for a specific set of attributes with no adverse effects on the average cost of a random query (across all five experiments). While the speed-up for query instances matching the training pattern is not too surprising, the extent of the improvement coupled with the small impact on the average query cost for other patterns provides a tremendous reduction in average case performance even though worst case performance may have been worsened.

5 CUSTOMIZING FOR MULTIPLE TYPES OF QUERIES

In our nutrition domain, a user may not be interested in only a single set of attributes. Thus OPT-KD must be able to learn multiple "interesting" attribute sets and optimize search for those sets.

5.1 LEARNING MULTIPLE ATTRIBUTE SETS

The number of attribute sets OPT-KD identifies as interesting depends only upon the queries and the user-specified threshold of the necessary frequency with which the attribute set must appear. The algorithm is the same whether it is learning a single set or multiple sets. That is, given a population of queries, OPT-KD identifies frequent sets of attributes that cooccur during queries, and for each of these frequent sets, OPT-KD builds a customized tree.

5.2 SEARCHING WITH MULTIPLE TREES

Each discovered frequent attribute set then iss part of a classifier that processes each query as it is entered and directs it the appropriate kd-tree. This decision is made by comparing the query to each learned attribute set. A query "matches" a frequent set if the query is a subset of the frequent set's attributes. If a query does not match any of the frequent sets, the default kd-tree is used.

5.3 EXPERIMENTS

The experiments are identical to the single tree experiments except that each experiment generated a different number of frequent attribute sets from which query patterns were derived. Five experiments were run randomly generating a number of frequent attribute sets. Experiment 1 generated 2 attribute sets, each one having 3 query patterns for a total of 6 query patterns plus 1 random query. Experiment 2 generated 3 attribute sets, each with 3 query patterns, and so on.

For brevity, OPT-KD's performance in learning multiple trees is summarized in Table 4. For all these experiments our frequent set threshold was equal to 0.1.

Table 4: Summary of Multiple Tree Experiments

	Default tree	Customized tree
random	12425.27 (3907.22)	10672.13 (3649.30)
patterned	18483.95 (5560.94)	1646.90 (1461.65)

The summary accurately reflects the general behavior of the algorithm. Some patterns did not improve nearly as much as the averages would imply. For example, one pattern only improved by about 70%, from 10,723 to 3,038, but there were also cases where remarkable improvements occurred. One pattern's average cost decreased from 18,467 to 681.

These experiments reinforce the utility of optimizing a kd-tree when patterns can be learned and show OPT-KD can scale up the single attribute set technique to improve search efficiency across a number of different types of queries.

6 RELATED WORK

OPT-KD can be characterized as an unsupervised user profile learning technique. Intelligent agents (Meas, 1994) for automated user profiling have received much attention lately, especially in regard to the World Wide Wide. For example, the SYSKILL & WEBERT system (Pazzani & Billsus, 1997). learns to classify web pages as interesting or uninteresting according to how a user has classified previous web pages, and similar to OPT-KD's idea that each specific pattern needs a separate tree, SYSKILL & WEBERT learns a different user profile for each subject. So, each user has multiple profiles.

Two other interesting Web agents are WebWatcher (Armstrong, Freitag, Joachims & Mitchell, 1995) and LETIZIA (Lieberman, 1995). Both of these systems learn by watching user behavior as they browse the Web. WebWatcher tries to learn how a user performs tasks, and Letizia attempts to infer preferences from behavior (*e.g.*, saving a page implies that user likes it).

Machine learning has been also been applied to diet management in the CAMPER system (Marling, Petot & Sterling, 1998). This system combines case-based reasoning techniques with a rule-based reasoning technique to use information about an individual's nutritional needs and personal preferences to suggest a daily menu for that person.

7 FUTURE WORK

OPT-KD currently uses very simple adaptive strategies that weight attributes, that discover frequent sets of attributes, and that customize trees by simply excluding attributes.

Alternative algorithms for biasing a tree toward a particular pattern need to be explored. A more information intensive algorithm that analyzes the interactions between attribute values distributions in the data and value distributions in the queries might be helpful, but our experiments with split selection measures analogous to those used in decision tree induction (for example) do not yield improvement over simply excluding non-queried attributes and splitting on the longest range. We continue to explore these measures and experimental designs that might better highlight their advantage.

More complex pattern definitions might be used to profile users. For example, one could use a quantitative association rule algorithm (Srikant & Agrawal, 1996) to include numeric values as part of the query patterns, or one could go a step further and model an estimation of the query distribution for each dimension using a Maximum Entropy approach (Theil, 1984).

Long term maintenance of a tool such as ours was not examined here. After the initial construction is completed, several issues remain to be addressed, such as how do we decide when to prune a customized tree from the user profile and how can we best update existing customized indices. These and other issues of incremental learning and concept drift are extremely relevant.

Finally, ommitting instances with missing values along a queried attribute may be too harsh. Rather, methods that computed worst and best case distances are probably preferred in our domain and others.

Acknowledgements

We thank the reviewers for their comments and suggestions.

References

Agrawal, R., Imielinski, T. & Swami, A. (1993). Mining association rules between sets of items in large databases. In *Proceedings of the ACM SIGMOD Conference on Management of Data* Washington, DC: ACM Press.

Agrawal, R. & Srikant, R. (1994). Fast algorithms for mining association rules. In *Proceedings of the 20th International Conference on Very Large Databases* Santiago, Chile: Morgan Kaufmann.

Armstrong, R., Freitag, D., Joachims, T. & Mitchell, T. (1995). WebWatcher: A learning apprentice for the World Wide Web. In *Working Notes of the AAAI Spring Symposium Series on Information Gathering from Distributed Heterogeneous Environments.* Palo Alto, CA: AAAI Press.

Bentley, J. L. (1980). Multidimensional divide and conquer. *Communications of the ACM*, 23:214–229.

Dasarathy, B. V. (Ed.) (1991). *Nearest neighbor (NN) norms: NN pattern classification techniques.* Los Alamitos, CA: IEEE Computer Society Press.

Deng, K. and Moore, A. W. (1995). Multiresolution instance-based learning. In *IJCAI-95.* San Mateo, CA: Morgan Kaufmann.

Friedman, J. H., Bentley, J. L., & Finkel, R. A. (1977). An algorithm for finding best matches in logarithmic expected time. *ACM Transactions on Mathematical Software*, 3:209–226.

Lieberman, H. (1995) Letizia: An agent that assists web browsing. in *Proceedings of the International Joint Conference on Artificial Intelligence.* Montreal.

Maes, P. (1994) Agents that reduce work and overhead load. *Communications of the ACM*, 37(7):31–40.

Marling, C., Petot, G., & Sterling, L. (1998). A CBR/RBR hybrid for designing nutritional menus. In *Multimodal Reasoning: Papers from the 1998 AAAI Spring Symposium.* (Freuder, G. ed.) Menlo Park, CA: AAAI Press.

Moore, A. & Lee, M. S. (1998). Cached sufficient statistics for efficient machine learning with large datasets. *Journal of Artificial Intelligence Research*, 8:67–91.

Pazzani, M. & Billsus, D. (1997). Learning and revising user profiles: the identification of interesting web sites. *Machine Learning*, 27:313–331.

Srikant, R. & Agrawal, R. (1996). Mining quantitative association rules in large relational tables. In *Proceedings of the ACM SIGMOD Conference* Montreal, Canada: ACM Press.

Theil, H. & Fiebig, D. G. (1984). *Exploiting Continuity: Maximum Entropy Estimation of Continuous Distributions.* Cambridge, MA: Ballinger Publishing.

U.S. Dept. of Agriculture, Agricultural Research Service, (1998). USDA Nutrient Database for Standard Reference, Release 12. Nutrient Data Laboratory Home Page, http://www.nal.usda.gov/fnic/foodcomp.

Wettschereck, D., Aha, D. W. & Mohri, T. (1997) A review and empirical evaluation of feature weighting methods for a class of lazy learning algorithms. *Artificial Intelligence Review* 11: 273–314.

Goal: minimise cost of annotations for semantic content
method: active learning: Human annotates examples which the machine is least certain about.

Active Learning for Natural Language Parsing and Information Extraction

Cynthia A. Thompson
CSLI, Ventura Hall
Stanford University
Stanford, CA 94305
cthomp@csli.stanford.edu

Mary Elaine Califf
Dept. of Applied Computer Science
Illinois State University
Normal, IL 61790
mecalif@ilstu.edu

Raymond J. Mooney
Dept. of Computer Sciences
University of Texas
Austin, TX 78712
mooney@cs.utexas.edu

Abstract

In natural language acquisition, it is difficult to gather the annotated data needed for supervised learning; however, unannotated data is fairly plentiful. Active learning methods attempt to select for annotation and training only the most informative examples, and therefore are potentially very useful in natural language applications. However, existing results for active learning have only considered standard classification tasks. To reduce annotation effort while maintaining accuracy, we apply active learning to two non-classification tasks in natural language processing: semantic parsing and information extraction. We show that active learning can significantly reduce the number of annotated examples required to achieve a given level of performance for these complex tasks.

1 INTRODUCTION

Active learning is an emerging area in machine learning that explores methods that, rather than relying on a benevolent teacher or random sampling, actively participate in the collection of training examples. The primary goal of active learning is to reduce the number of supervised training examples needed to achieve a given level of performance. Active learning systems may construct their own examples, request certain types of examples, or determine which of a set of unsupervised examples are most usefully labeled. The last approach, *selective sampling* (Cohn, Atlas, & Ladner, 1994), is particularly attractive in natural-language learning, since there is an abundance of text, and we would like to annotate only the most informative sentences. For many language learning tasks, annotation is particularly time-consuming since it requires specifying a complex output rather than just a category label, so reducing the number of training examples required can greatly increase the utility of learning.

An increasing number of researchers are successfully applying machine learning to natural language processing (see Brill and Mooney (1997) for an overview). However, only a few have utilized active learning, and those have addressed two particular tasks: part of speech tagging (Dagan & Engelson, 1995) and text categorization (Lewis & Catlett, 1994; Liere & Tadepalli, 1997). Both of these are fundamentally classification tasks, while the tasks we address, semantic parsing and information extraction, are not. Many language learning tasks require annotating natural language text with a complex output, such as a parse tree, semantic representation, or filled template. However, the application of active learning to tasks requiring such complex outputs has not been well studied. Our research shows how active learning methods can be applied to such problems and demonstrates that it can significantly decrease annotation costs for important and realistic natural-language tasks.

The remainder of this paper is organized as follows. Section 2 presents background on active learning, and Section 3 introduces the two language-learning systems to which we apply active learning. Sections 4 and 5 describe the application of active learning to parser acquisition together with experimental results. Sections 6 and 7 describe the application of active learning to learning information extraction rules and present experimental results for this task. Section 8 suggests directions for future research. Finally, Section 9 describes some related research, and Section 10 presents our conclusions.

2 BACKGROUND ON ACTIVE LEARNING

Because of the relative ease of obtaining on-line text, we focus on selective sampling methods of active learning. In this case, learning begins with a small pool of annotated examples and a large pool of unannotated examples, and the learner attempts to choose the most informative additional examples for annotation. Existing work in the area has emphasized two approaches, *certainty-based* methods (Lewis & Catlett, 1994), and *committee-based* methods (Freund, Seung, Shamir, & Tishby, 1997; Liere & Tadepalli, 1997; Dagan & Engelson, 1995; Cohn et al., 1994).

In the certainty-based paradigm, a system is trained on a small number of annotated examples to learn an initial classifier. Next, the system examines unannotated examples, and attaches certainties to the predicted annotation of those examples. The k examples with the lowest certainties are then presented to the user for annotation and retraining. Many methods for attaching certainties have been used, but they typically attempt to estimate the probability that a classifier consistent with the prior training data will classify a new example correctly.

In the committee-based paradigm, a diverse committee of classifiers is created, again from a small number of annotated examples. Next, each committee member attempts to label additional examples. The examples whose annotation results in the most disagreement amongst the committee members are presented to the user for annotation and retraining. A diverse committee, consistent with the prior training data, will produce the highest disagreement on examples whose label is most uncertain with respect to the possible classifiers that could be obtained by training on that data.

Figure 1 presents abstract pseudocode for both certainty-based and committee-based selective sampling. In an ideal situation, the batch size, k, would be set to one to make the most intelligent decisions in future choices, but for efficiency reasons in retraining batch learning algorithms, it is frequently set higher. Results on a number of classification tasks have demonstrated that this general approach is effective in reducing the need for labeled examples (see citations above). Our current work has explored certainty-based approaches, although committee-based approaches for our tasks of learning parsers and information extraction rules is a topic for future research.

```
Apply the learner to n bootstrap examples, creating
   one classifier or a committee of them.
Until there are no more examples or the annotator
   is unwilling to label more examples, do:
      Use most recently learned classifier/committee
         to annotate each unlabeled instance.
      Find the k instances with the lowest annotation
         certainty/most disagreement amongst
         committee members.
      Annotate these instances.
      Train the learner on the bootstrap examples
         and all examples annotated to this point.
```

Figure 1: Selective Sampling Algorithm

3 NATURAL LANGUAGE LEARNING SYSTEMS

3.1 PARSER ACQUISITION

CHILL is a system that, given a set of training sentences each paired with a meaning representation, learns a parser that maps sentences into this semantic form (Zelle & Mooney, 1996). It uses *inductive logic programming* (ILP) methods (Muggleton, 1992; Lavrač & Džeroski, 1994) to learn a deterministic shift-reduce parser written in Prolog. CHILL solves the parser acquisition problem by learning rules to control the step by step actions of an initial, overly-general parsing shell. While the initial training examples are sentence/representation pairs, the examples given to the ILP system are positive and negative examples of states of the parser in which a particular operator should or should not be applied. These examples are automatically constructed by determining what sequence of operator applications (e.g., shift and reduce) leads to the correct parse. However, the overall learning task for which user feedback is provided is not a classification task.

This paper will focus on one application in which CHILL has been tested, learning an interface to a geographical database. In this domain, CHILL learns parsers that map natural-language questions directly into Prolog queries that can be executed to produce an answer. Following are two sample queries for a database on U.S. geography paired with their corresponding Prolog query:

What is the capital of the state with the biggest population?

```
answer(C, (capital(S,C), largest(P,
    (state(S), population(S,P))))).
```

What state is Texarkana located in?

```
answer(S, (state(S),
   eq(C,cityid(texarkana,_)),
   loc(C,S))).
```

Given a sufficient corpus of such sentence/representation pairs, CHILL is able to learn a parser that correctly parses many novel sentences into logical queries.

3.2 INFORMATION EXTRACTION

We have also developed a system, RAPIER, that learns rules for information extraction (IE) (Califf, 1998). The goal of an IE system is to find specific pieces of information in a natural-language document. The specification of the information to be extracted generally takes the form of a template with a list of slots to be filled with substrings from the document (Lehnert & Sundheim, 1991). IE is particularly useful for obtaining a structured database from unstructured documents and is being used for a growing number of Web and Internet applications.

RAPIER is a bottom-up relational learner, and acquires rules in the form of a sequence of patterns that identify relevant phrases in the document. The patterns are similar to regular expressions that include constraints on the words, part-of-speech tags, and semantic classes of the extracted phrase and its surrounding context; however, in the results in this paper, we use the simplest version of the system which only makes use of words. We have found that part-of-speech tags may be useful in some domains, but that words alone provide most of the power.

Like semantic parsing, IE is not a classification task; although, like parsing in CHILL, it can be mapped to a series of classification subproblems (Freitag, 1998; Bennett, Aone, & Lovell, 1997). However, RAPIER does not approach the problem in this manner, and in any case, the example annotations provided by the user are in the form of filled templates, not class labels.

In our active learning research, we have focused on one of the three tasks on which RAPIER has been extensively tested, that of extracting information about computer-related jobs from netnews postings. Figure 2 shows an example with part of the corresponding filled template. The task is to extract information for 17 slots appropriate for the development of a jobs database. The slots vary in their applicability to different postings. Relatively few postings provide salary information, while most provide information about the job's location. A number of the slots may have more than one filler; for example, there are slots for the platform(s) and language(s) that the prospective employee will use.

4 ACTIVE LEARNING FOR SEMANTIC PARSING

Applying certainty-based sample selection to both of these systems requires determining the certainty of a complete annotation of a potential new training example, despite the fact that individual learned rules perform only part of the overall annotation task. Therefore, our general approach is to compute certainties for each individual decision made during the processing of an example, and combine these to obtain an overall certainty for an example. Since both systems learn rules with no explicit uncertainty parameters, simple metrics based on coverage of training examples are used to assign certainties to rule-based decisions.

In CHILL, this approach is complicated slightly by the fact that the current learned parser may get stuck, and not even complete a parse for a potential new training example. This can happen because a control rule learned for an operator may be overly specific, preventing its correct application, or because an operator required for parsing the sentence may not have been needed for any of the training examples, so the parser does not even include it. If a sentence cannot be parsed, its annotation is obviously very uncertain and it is therefore a good candidate for selection. However, there are often more unparsable sentences than the batch size (k), so we must distinguish between them. This is done by counting the maximum number of sequential operators successfully applied while attempting to parse the sentence and dividing by the number of words in the sentence to give an estimate of how close the parser came to completing a parse. The sentences with a lower value for this metric are preferred for annotation.

If the number of unparsable examples is less than k, then the remaining examples selected for annotation are chosen from the parsable ones. A certainty for each parse, and thus each potential training example, is obtained by considering the sequence of operators applied to produce it. Recall that the control rules for each operator are induced from positive and negative examples of the contexts in which the operator should be applied. As a simple approximation, the number

Posting from Newsgroup

```
Telecommunications. SOLARIS Systems Administrator. 38-44K.
Immediate need

Leading telecommunications firm in need of an energetic
individual to fill the following position in the Atlanta office:

        SOLARIS SYSTEMS ADMINISTRATOR
        Salary: 38-44K with full benefits
        Location: Atlanta Georgia, no relocation assistance provided
```

Filled Template

```
computer_science_job
title: SOLARIS Systems Administrator
salary: 38-44K
state: Georgia
city: Atlanta
platform: SOLARIS
area: telecommunications
```

Figure 2: Sample Message and Filled Template

of examples used to induce the specific control rule used to select an operator is used as a measure of the certainty of that parsing decision. We believe this is a reasonable certainty measure in rule learning, since, as shown by Holte, Acker, and Porter (1989), *small disjuncts* (rules that correctly classify few examples) are more error prone than large ones. We then average this certainty over all operators used in the parse of the sentence to obtain the metric used to rank the example.

To increase the diversity of examples included in a given batch, we do not include sentences that vary only in known names for database constants (e.g., city names) from already chosen examples, nor sentences that contain a subset of the words present in an already chosen sentence.

5 EXPERIMENTAL RESULTS: SEMANTIC PARSING

For the experimental results in this paper, we use the following general methodology. For each trial, a random set of test examples is used and the system is trained on subsets of the remaining examples. First, n bootstrap examples are randomly selected from the training examples, then in each step of active learning, the best k examples of the remaining training examples are selected and added to the training set. The result of learning on this set is evaluated after each round. When comparing to random sampling, the k examples in each round are chosen randomly.

The initial corpus used for evaluating parser acquisition contains 250 questions about U.S. geography, paired with Prolog queries. This domain was chosen due to the availability of an existing hand-build natural language interface to a simple geography database containing about 800 facts. The original interface, *Geobase*, was supplied with Turbo Prolog 2.0 (Borland International, 1988). The questions were collected from uninformed undergraduates and mapped into logical form by an expert. Examples from the corpus were given in Section 3.1. The parser that is learned from the training data is used to process the test examples, the resulting queries submitted to the database, the answers compared to those generated by the correct representation, and the percentage of correct answers recorded.

In tests on this data, test examples were chosen independently for 10 trials with $n = 25$ bootstrap examples and a batch size of $k = 25$. The results are shown in Figure 3, where CHILL refers to random sampling, CHILL+Active refers to sample selection, and *Geobase* refers to the hand-built benchmark. Initially, the advantage of sample selection is small, since there

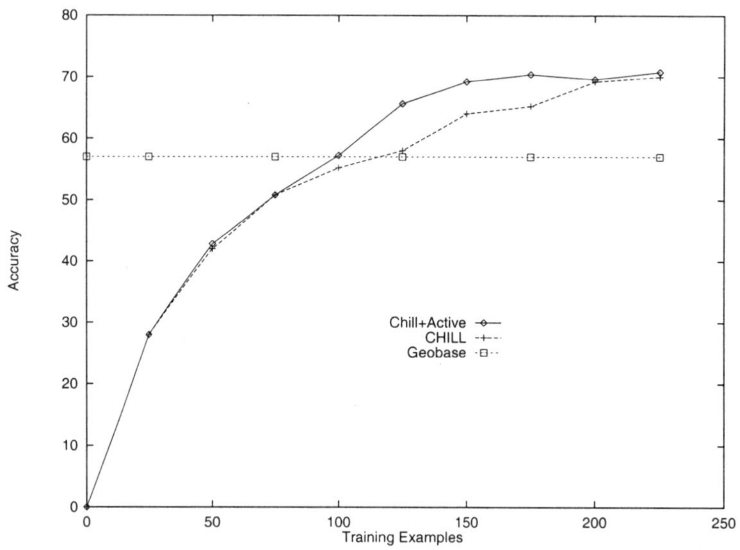

Figure 3: Parser Acquisition Results for Geography Corpus

is insufficient information to make an intelligent choice of examples; but after 100 examples, the advantage becomes clear. Eventually, the training set becomes exhausted, the active learner has no choice in picking the remaining examples, and both approaches use the full training set and converge to the same performance. However, the number of examples required to reach this level is significantly reduced when using active learning. To get within 5% of the final accuracy requires 125 selected examples but 175 random examples, a savings of 29%. Also, to surpass the performance of *Geobase* requires under 100 selected examples versus 125 random examples, a savings of 20%. According to a t-test, the differences between active and random choice at 125 and 175 training examples are statistically significant at the .05 level or better.

We also ran experiments on a larger, more diverse corpus of geography queries, where additional examples were collected from undergraduate students in an introductory AI course. The set of questions in the previous experiments was collected from students in introductory German, with no instructions on the complexity of queries desired. The AI students tended to ask more complex and diverse queries: their task was to give 5 interesting questions and the associated logical form for a homework assignment. There were 221 new sentences, for a total of 471. This data was split into 425 training sentences and 46 test sentences, for 10 random splits. For this corpus, we used $n = 50$ and $k = 25$. The results are shown in Figure 4. Here, the savings with active learning is about 150 examples to reach an accuracy close to the maximum, or about a 35% annotation savings. The curve for selective sampling does not reach 425 examples because of our elimination of sentences that vary only in database names and those that contain a subset of the words present in an already chosen sentence. Obviously this is a more difficult corpus, but active learning is still able to choose examples that allow significant savings in annotation cost.

6 ACTIVE LEARNING FOR INFORMATION EXTRACTION

A similar approach to certainty-based sample selection was used with RAPIER. A simple notion of the certainty of an individual extraction rule is based on its coverage of the training data: $pos - 5 \cdot neg$, where pos is the number of correct fillers generated by the rule and neg is the number of incorrect ones. Again, "small disjuncts" that account for few examples are deemed less certain. Also, since RAPIER, unlike CHILL, prunes rules to prevent overfitting, they may generate spurious fillers for the training data; therefore, a significant penalty is included for such errors.

Given this notion of rule certainty, RAPIER determines the certainty of a filled slot for an example being evaluated for annotation certainty. In the case where a single rule finds a filler for a slot, the certainty for the slot is the certainty of the rule that filled it. However, when more than one slot-filler is found, the certainty of the slot is defined as the minimum of the certainties

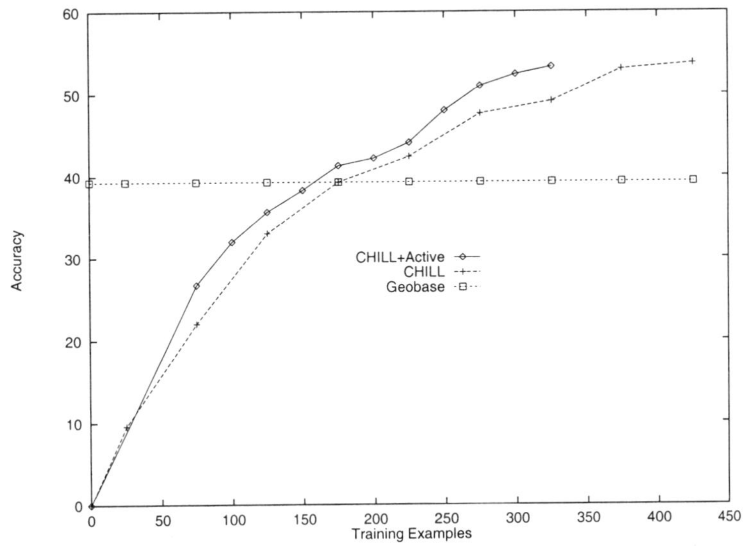

Figure 4: Parser Acquisition Results for a Larger Geography Corpus

of the rules that produced these fillers. The minimum is chosen since we want to focus attention on the least certain rules and find examples that either confirm or deny them.

A final consideration is determining the certainty of an empty slot. In some tasks, some slots are empty a large percentage of the time. For example, in the jobs domain, the salary is present less than half the time. On the other hand, some slots are always (or almost always) filled, and the absence of fillers for such slots should decrease confidence in an example's labeling. Consequently, we record the number of times a slot appears in the training data with no fillers and use that count as the confidence of the slot when no filler for it is found. Once the confidence of each slot has been determined, the confidence of an example is found by summing the confidence of all slots.

In order to allow for the more desirable option of actively selecting a single example at a time ($k = 1$), an incremental version of RAPIER was created. This version still requires remembering all of the training examples but reuses and updates existing rules as new examples are added. The resulting system can incrementally incorporate new training examples reasonably efficiently, allowing each chosen example to immediately effect the result and therefore the choice of the next example.

7 EXPERIMENTAL RESULTS: INFORMATION EXTRACTION

The computer-related job-posting corpus used to test active learning in RAPIER consists of 300 postings to the local newsgroup `austin.jobs`, as illustrated in Figure 2. Training and test sets were generated using 10-fold cross-validation, and learning curves generated by training on randomly or actively selected subsets of the training data for each trial. For active learning, there were $n = 10$ bootstrap examples and subsequent examples were selected one at a time from the remaining 260 examples.

In information extraction, the standard measurements of performance are precision (the percentage of items that the system extracted which should have been extracted) and recall (the percentage of items that the system should have extracted which it did extract). In order to combine these measurements to simplify comparisons, it is common to use F-measure: $F = (2 \cdot precision \cdot recall)/(precision + recall)$. It is possible to weight the F-measure to prefer recall or precision, but we weight them equally. For the active learning results, we measured performance at 10-example intervals. The results for random sampling are measured less frequently.

Figure 5 shows the results, where RAPIER uses random sampling and RAPIER+Active uses selective sampling. From 30 examples on, RAPIER+Active consistently outperforms RAPIER. The difference between the curves is not large, but does represent a large re-

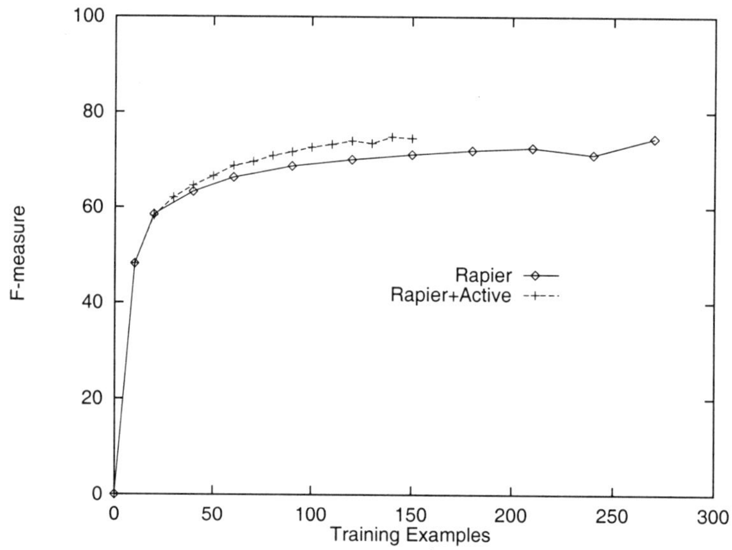

Figure 5: Information Extraction Results for Job Postings

duction in the number of examples required to achieve a given level of performance. At 150 examples, the average F-measure is 74.56, exactly the same as the average F-measure with 270 random examples. This represents a savings of 120 examples, or 44%. The differences in performance at 120 and 150 examples are significant at the 0.01 level according to a two-tailed paired t-test. The curve with selective sampling does not go all the way to 270 examples, because once the performance of 270 randomly chosen examples is reached, the information available in the data set has been exploited, and the curve will just level off as the less useful examples are added.

8 FUTURE WORK

Experiments on additional semantic parsing and information extraction corpora are needed to test the ability of this approach to reduce annotation costs in a variety of domains. It would also be interesting to explore active learning for other natural language processing problems such as syntactic parsing, word-sense disambiguation, and machine translation.

Our current results have involved a certainty-based approach; however, proponents of committee-based approaches have convincing arguments for their theoretical advantages. Our initial attempts at adapting committee-based approaches to our systems were not very successful; however, additional research on this topic is indicated. One critical problem is obtaining diverse committees that properly sample the version space (Cohn et al., 1994).

Although they seem to work quite well, the certainty metrics used in both CHILL and RAPIER are quite simple and somewhat *ad hoc*. A more principled approach based on learning probabilistic models of parsing and information extraction could perhaps result in better estimates of certainty and therefore improved sample selection.

Finally, a more intelligent method for choosing batch sizes is needed. From initial informal experiments with CHILL, we have observed that the optimal batch size seems to vary with the total amount of training data. At first, small batches are most beneficial, but later in learning, larger batches seem better. However, converting CHILL to an incremental version as done with RAPIER might sidestep this issue and allow efficient learning at one step increments.

9 RELATED WORK

Cohn et al. (1994) were among the first to discuss certainty-based active learning methods in detail. They focus on a neural network approach to actively searching a version-space of concepts. Liere and Tadepalli (1997) apply active learning with committees to the problem of text categorization. They show improvements with active learning similar to those that we obtain, but use a committee of Winnow-based learners on a traditional classification task. Dagan and Engelson (1995) also apply committee-based learning to part-of-speech tagging. In their work, a committee of hidden Markov models is used to select examples for annotation. Lewis and Catlett (1994) use *heterogeneous* certainty-based methods, in which a simple classifier is used to select examples that are then annotated and presented to a more powerful classifier. Again, their methods are applied to text classification.

One other researcher has recently applied active learning to information extraction. Soderland's (1999) WHISK system uses an unusual form of selective sampling. Rather than using certainties or committees, WHISK divides the pool of unannotated instances into three classes: 1) those covered by an existing rule, 2) those that are near misses of a rule, and 3) those not covered by any rule. The system then randomly selects a set of new examples from each of the three classes and adds them to the training set. Soderland shows that this method significantly improves performance in a management succession domain; however, it is unclear how more traditional sample selection methods would perform by comparison.

10 CONCLUSIONS

Active learning is a new area of machine learning that has been almost exclusively applied to classification tasks. We have demonstrated its successful application to two more complex natural language processing tasks, semantic parsing and information extraction. The wealth of unannotated natural language data, along with the difficulty of annotating such data, make selective sampling a potentially invaluable technique for natural language learning. Our results on realistic corpora for semantic parsing and information extraction indicate that example savings as high as 44% can be achieved by employing active sample selection using only simple certainty measures for predictions on unannotated data. Improved sample selection methods and applications to other important language problems hold the promise of continued progress in using machine learning to construct effective natural language processing systems.

Acknowledgements

This research was supported by the National Science Foundation under grant IRI-9704943.

References

Bennett, S., Aone, C., & Lovell, C. (1997). Learning to tag multilingual texts through observation. In *Proceedings of the Second Conference on Empirical Methods in Natural Language Processing*, pp. 109–116.

Borland International (1988). *Turbo Prolog 2.0 Reference Guide.* Borland International, Scotts Valley, CA.

Brill, E., & Mooney, R. (1997). An overview of empirical natural language processing. *AI Magazine, 18*(4), 13–24.

Califf, M. E. (1998). *Relational Learning Techniques for Natural Language Information Extraction.* Ph.D. thesis, Department of Computer Sciences, University of Texas, Austin, TX. Also appears as Artificial Intelligence Laboratory Technical Report AI 98-276 (see http://www.cs.utexas.edu/users/ai-lab).

Cohn, D., Atlas, L., & Ladner, R. (1994). Improving generalization with active learning. *Machine Learning, 15*(2), 201–221.

Dagan, I., & Engelson, S. P. (1995). Committee-based sampling for training probabilistic classifiers. In *Proceedings of the Twelfth International Conference on Machine Learning*, pp. 150–157 San Francisco, CA. Morgan Kaufman.

Freitag, D. (1998). Multi-strategy learning for information extraction. In *Proceedings of the Fifteenth International Conference on Machine Learning*, pp. 161–169.

Freund, Y., Seung, H. S., Shamir, E., & Tishby, N. (1997). Selective sampling using the query by committee algorithm. *Machine Learning, 28*, 133–168.

Holte, R. C., Acker, L., & Porter, B. (1989). Concept learning and the problem of small disjuncts. In *Proceedings of the Eleventh International Joint Conference on Artificial Intelligence*, pp. 813–818 Detroit, MI.

Lavrač, N., & Džeroski, S. (1994). *Inductive Logic Programming: Techniques and Applications.* Ellis Horwood.

Lehnert, W., & Sundheim, B. (1991). A performance evaluation of text-analysis technologies. *AI Magazine, 12*(3), 81–94.

Lewis, D. D., & Catlett, J. (1994). Heterogeneous uncertainty sampling for supervised learning. In

Proceedings of the Eleventh International Conference on Machine Learning, pp. 148–156 San Francisco, CA. Morgan Kaufman.

Liere, R., & Tadepalli, P. (1997). Active learning with committees for text categorization. In *Proceedings of the Fourteenth National Conference on Artificial Intelligence*, pp. 591–596 Providence, RI.

Muggleton, S. H. (Ed.). (1992). *Inductive Logic Programming.* Academic Press, New York, NY.

Soderland, S. (1999). Learning information extraction rules for semi-structured and free text. *Machine Learning, 34*, 233–272.

Zelle, J. M., & Mooney, R. J. (1996). Learning to parse database queries using inductive logic programming. In *Proceedings of the Thirteenth National Conference on Artificial Intelligence* Portland, OR.

Monte Carlo Hidden Markov Models: Learning Non-Parametric Models of Partially Observable Stochastic Processes

BAUM-WELCH EM alg.
see also CONDENSATION alg; work of CALDER? at BIRKBECK

Use density trees to represent data

Sebastian Thrun **John C. Langford** **Dieter Fox**

Robot Learning Laboratory, School of Computer Science
Carnegie Mellon University
5000 Forbes Ave., Pittsburgh, PA 15213
{thrun,jcl,dfox}@cs.cmu.edu

Abstract

We present a learning algorithm for non-parametric hidden Markov models with continuous state and observation spaces. All necessary probability densities are approximated using samples, along with density trees generated from such samples. A Monte Carlo version of Baum-Welch (EM) is employed to learn models from data. Regularization during learning is achieved using an exponential shrinking technique. The shrinkage factor, which determines the effective capacity of the learning algorithm, is annealed down over multiple iterations of Baum-Welch, and early stopping is applied to select the right model. Once trained, Monte Carlo HMMs can be run in an any-time fashion. We prove that under mild assumptions, Monte Carlo Hidden Markov Models converge to a local maximum in likelihood space, just like conventional HMMs. In addition, we provide empirical results obtained in a gesture recognition domain.

1 Introduction

Hidden Markov models (HMMs) [27] have been applied successfully to a large range of temporal signal processing problems, for tasks such as modeling, filtering, classification and prediction of partially observable time sequences, stochastic environments. Hidden Markov models are often the method of choice in areas such as speech recognition [27, 33], natural language processing [3], robotics [21, 29], biological sequence analysis [11, 16], and time series analysis [10].

We present a new hidden Markov model, called *Monte-Carlo Hidden Markov Models (MCHMMs)*. MCHMMs use samples and non-parametric density trees to represent probability distributions. This makes it possible to learn non-parametric hidden Markov models with continuous state and observation spaces. Since continuous state spaces are sufficiently rich to overfit any data set, our approach uses shrinkage as a mechanism for regularization. The shrinkage factor, which determines the effective capacity of the HMM, is annealed down over multiple iterations of EM, and early stopping is applied for model selection.

MCHMMs possess the following four characteristics, which distinguishes them from the traditional HMM approach [27]:

1. **Real-valued spaces.** Both the state space and the observation space of MCHMMs are continuous. This is important in domains where the true state and observation space of the environment is continuous. The importance of continuous-valued spaces has been recognized by several authors, which have proposed real-valued extensions using parametric models such as Gaussians and neural networks [2, 8, 9, 13, 17].

2. **Non-parametric.** Most existing HMM models rely on parametric densities, defined by a small set of parameters (discrete distributions included). This is clearly appropriate when one has reason to believe that the parametric model is correct. In practice, however, one might lack such strong prior knowledge. MCHMMs learn non-parametric models of partially observable stochastic systems. Such non-parametric methods can fit much larger sets of functions, hence provide additional flexibility.

3. **Built-in complexity control.** MCHMMs make it possible to control the complexity of the state space during learning. In contrast, the complexity of discrete HMMs is determined by the number of states, which has to be determined in advance, before training. Multiple training runs may thus be necessary to determine the right number of states.

4. **Resource adaptive.** Finally, after training MCHMMs

can be used in an *any-time* fashion. Any-time algorithms can generate an estimate at *any* time; the more time available, however, the better the answer [4, 34]. The any-time property is directly inherited from sampling-based methods, as the number of samples can be controlled on-line.

This paper presents MCHMMs. It describes a sample-based learning algorithm that extends Baum-Welch to MCHMMs. We also give theoretical results that prove (with probability one) convergence of the learning algorithm to a local maximum in likelihood space. This result, whose proof is only outlined here (see [32] for all proofs), extends the well-known convergence result for discrete HMMs to the real-valued, non-parametric case. We also present empirical results obtained in a gesture recognition domain, which seek to provide the first evidence of the usefulness of MCHMMs in practice.

2 Generalized Hidden Markov Models

This section introduces the necessary notation to extend HMMs to continuous state and observation spaces. It follows the excellent deposition of [27], with continuous density replacing discrete distributions throughout. For convergence, we assume all event spaces and random variables (e.g., state, observations) are measurable. Unless otherwise specified, all probability density functions are Lipschitz (implying continuity) and non-zero over some compact interval.

A *generalized HMM* (in short: GHMM) is a partially observable, time-invariant Markov chain with continuous state and observation spaces and discrete time. At each time $t \geq 1$, the HMM's state is denoted x_t. Initially, at time $t = 1$, the state of the HMM is selected randomly according to the density π. State transitions are governed by a conditional probability density, denoted $\mu(x' \mid x)$ and called *state transition density*.

In HMMs (and thus in GHMMs), the state cannot be observed directly. Instead, only a probabilistic projection of the state is observable. Let b_t denote a measurable random variable that models the observation at time t. Observations are generated according to a probability density conditioned on the state of the HMM (called the *observation density*), denoted $\nu(b \mid x)$. A generalized HMM is uniquely defined trough three densities: $\lambda = \{\pi, \mu, \nu\}$.

Putting computational considerations aside for the moment, knowledge of λ is sufficient to tackle a variety of interesting practical problems, such as computing distributions over states and observations at arbitrary points in time, generating representative example trajectories in state and observation space, determining the likelihood of example trajectories under an HMM, and classifying data sequences generated by mixtures of labeled HMMs. Algorithms for these problems are described in detail in [27]; they are easily transferred from the finite to the continuous case.

In practice, the densities λ are often unknown and have to be estimated from data. The data, denoted d, is a sequence of observations[1], denoted

$$d = \{O_1, O_2, \ldots, O_T\}. \tag{1}$$

Here O_t denotes the observation at time t. The total number of observations in d is T.

The well-known Baum-Welch algorithm [1, 20, 27] provides a computationally efficient and elegant approach for learning π, μ, and ν. Baum-Welch begins with an initial model, denoted $\lambda^{(0)}$. It iterates two steps, an E-step and an M-step (see also [6]). In the n-th E-step, distributions for the various state variables x_t are computed under a fixed model $\lambda^{(n)}$ (with $n \geq 0$). The n-th M-step uses these distributions to derive a new, improved model $\lambda^{(n+1)}$.

In the E-step, distributions are computed for the state variables x_t conditioned on a fixed model λ and the data d. Recall from [27] that in the discrete case,

$$\alpha_t^{(n)}(x) = Pr(x_t = x \mid O_1, \ldots, O_t, \lambda^{(n)}) \tag{2}$$

$$\beta_t^{(n)}(x) = Pr(O_{t+1}, \ldots, O_T \mid x_t = x, \lambda^{(n)}) \tag{3}$$

$$\gamma_t^{(n)}(x) = Pr(x_t = x \mid d, \lambda^{(n)}) \tag{4}$$

$$\xi_t^{(n)}(x, x') = Pr(x_t = x, x_{t+1} = x' \mid d, \lambda^{(n)}) \tag{5}$$

The continuous case is analogous; however, here α and β are densities (and thus may be larger than 1). Following [27], these densities are computed incrementally; α is computed forward in time, and β backwards in time (for which reason this algorithm is often referred to as the *forward-backward algorithm*). Initially,

$$\alpha_0^{(n)}(x) = \pi^{(n)}(x) \quad \text{and} \quad \beta_T^{(n)}(x) = 1 \tag{6}$$

and for all other α_t and β_t:

$$\alpha_t^{(n)}(x) = \int \alpha_{t-1}^{(n)}(x')\, \mu^{(n)}(x \mid x')\, \nu^{(n)}(O_t \mid x)\, dx' \tag{7}$$

$$\beta_t^{(n)}(x) = \int \beta_{t+1}^{(n)}(x')\, \mu^{(n)}(x' \mid x)\, \nu^{(n)}(O_{t+1} \mid x')\, dx' \tag{8}$$

Bayes rule governs the conditional density over the state space at time t:

$$\gamma_t^{(n)}(x) = \frac{\alpha_t^{(n)}(x)\, \beta_t^{(n)}(x)}{\int \alpha_t^{(n)}(x')\, \beta_t^{(n)}(x')\, dx'} \tag{9}$$

[1]For simplicity of the presentation, we only present the case in which the data consist of a single sequence. The extension to multiple sequences is straightforward but requires additional notation.

Similarly, the state transition densities $\xi^{(n)}$ are computed as

$$\xi_t^{(n)}(x, x') = \frac{\alpha_t^{(n)}(x)\ \mu^{(n)}(x' \mid x)\ \nu^{(n)}(O_{t+1} \mid x')\ \beta_{t+1}^{(n)}(x')}{\int\int \alpha_t^{(n)}(\bar{x})\ \mu^{(n)}(\bar{x}' \mid \bar{x})\ \nu^{(n)}(O_{t+1} \mid \bar{x}')\ \beta_{t+1}^{(n)}(\bar{x}')\ d\bar{x}\ d\bar{x}'} \quad (10)$$

This computation is completely analogous to the finite case, replacing conditional probabilities by conditional densities.

The M-step uses $\gamma_t^{(n)}(x)$ and $\xi_t^{(n)}(x, x')$ to compute a new model $\lambda^{(n+1)}$, using the maximum likelihood estimator:

$$\pi^{(n+1)}(x) = \gamma_0^{(n)}(x) \quad (11)$$

$$\mu^{(n+1)}(x' \mid x) = \frac{\sum_{t=1}^{T-1} \xi_t^{(n)}(x, x')}{\sum_{t=1}^{T-1} \gamma_t^{(n)}(x)} \quad (12)$$

$$\nu^{(n+1)}(b \mid x) = \frac{\sum_{t=1}^{T} I_{O_t=b}\ \gamma_t^{(n)}(x)}{\sum_{t=1}^{T} \gamma_t^{(n)}(x)} \quad (13)$$

Here I_{cond} denotes an indicator variable that is 1 if the condition *cond* is true, and 0 otherwise. A straightforward result is the convergence of GHMMs.

Theorem 1. (GHMM Convergence Theorem) *Under the assumptions above, the GHMM learning algorithm does not decrease the likelihood of the observation sequence with probability 1. With probability 1, it does not improve the likelihood if, and only if a local maximum or a saddle point has been reached.*

The full proof can be found in [32]. Our proof is a direct extension of a result by Juang [13], who has shown convergence to local maxima for HMMs with a finite number of states and continuous observations, where the observation densities are a mixture of log concave or ellipsoidal symmetrical densities. The convergence of GHMMs follows from the fact that any continuous and Lipschitz density can be approximated by mixtures of Gaussians, hence by a sequence of HMMs that meet Juang's assumptions.

3 Sampling and Density Trees

3.1 Sampling

MCHMMs use samples to approximate all densities (models, posteriors, conditional and joint densities). Sample sets are (finite) sets of values, annotated by numerical probabilities [18, 23]. More specifically, let f be a probability density function, and let N denote a positive number (the cardinality of a sample set). A *sample set* is a set

$$X = \{\langle x_1, p_{x_1}\rangle \ldots, \langle x_N, p_{x_N}\rangle\} \quad (14)$$

where for all n with $1 \leq n \leq N$: $x_n \in \mathrm{dom}(f)$, $p_{x_n} \in [0,1]$, and $\sum_{n=1}^{N} p_{x_n} = 1$. Sample sets can be thought of as discrete probability distributions over the event space $\{x_1, \ldots, x_N\}$, defined through the p-values [23, 26] For reasons that will become clear below, p-values are often referred to as *importance factors* [28].

A *sampling method* is a method that approximates f through samples. We will call a sampling method *asymptotically consistent* if for $N \to \infty$, X converges to f with probability 1 when integrated over the system of half-open Borel sets:

$$\lim_{N\to\infty} \sum_{(x,p_x)\in X} I_{x_0 \leq x < x_1}\ p_x = \int_{x_0}^{x_1} f(x)\ dx \quad (15)$$

Sampling can be applied to approximate any probability density f [31].

We will distinguish two methods for sampling, both of which are asymptotically consistent:

1. **Likelihood-weighted sampling.** When f is available explicitly, we will directly sample from f (e.g., using rejection sampling [31]). In likelihood-weighted sampling, all p-values are $1/N$. The concentration of the resulting sample set will be proportional to the density f, i.e., the larger the measure of f over a region A, the more samples will be in A (in expectation).

2. **Importance sampling.** In some cases, however, likelihood-weighted sampling cannot be applied. This is the case, for example, when approximating $\alpha_t^{(n)}(x)$, which is a recursive product of convolved densities and other densities conditioned on observations (c.f., (7)). Instead of sampling directly from f, importance sampling [28] samples from a different distribution g that has the property $f(x) > 0 \Longrightarrow g(x) > 0$. The difference between f and g is accounted by the p-values, which are defined as follows:

$$\bar{p}_{x_n} = f(x_n)/g(x_n) \quad (16)$$

$$p_{x_n} = \frac{\bar{p}_{x_n}}{\sum_{n=1}^{N} \bar{p}_{x_n}} \quad (17)$$

Importance sampling [28] has been studied extensively in the statistics literature (see for example [31]). The reader may notice that likelihood-weighted sampling is a special case of importance sampling (with $f \equiv g$).

Figure 1a shows a sample set drawn by likelihood-weighted sampling from a distribution that resembles the shape of a sine wave. All probabilities p_x of the sample set shown there are the same, and the samples are concentrated in a small region of the $\Re^2$.

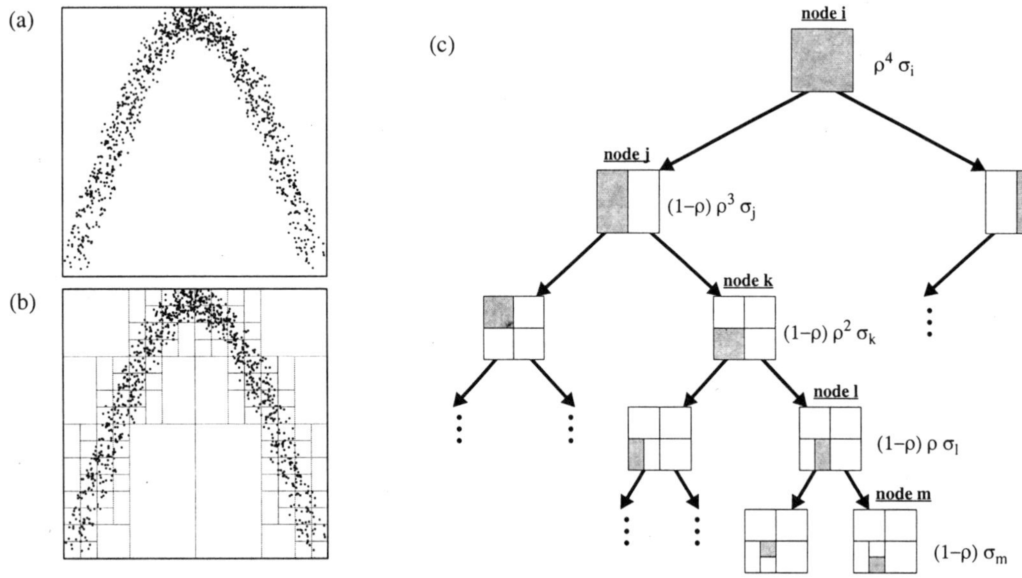

Figure 1: (a) Data set (b) partitioned by a density tree. (c) Density tree with shrinkage for complexity control. Each branch cuts the area under a node into two equally-sized, rectangular halves, shown in grey. The density of each node is an exponentially weighted mixture of densities of the nodes along the path to the leaf. The ρ-terms describe the mixture coefficients for this example.

Both sampling methods can equally be applied to *sample from a sample set* (often referred to as *resampling* [28]). Let X be a sample set. Likelihood-weighted sampling draws samples from X according to the (discrete) probability distribution induced by their p_x-values. Each sample is then assigned the same probability $(1/N)$. Importance sampling draws samples x from X according to some other density g, and assigns $\frac{p_x}{g(x)}$ to the new sample's p-value. Sampling from sample sets plays an important role in the Monte Carlo HMM algorithm described below.

A straightforward but important result is the following:

Theorem 2. *Likelihood-weighted sampling converges (in the sense of (15) with probability one to f as $N \longrightarrow \infty$, at a rate of $1/\sqrt{N}$. Importance sampling also converges with probability one to f at the same asymptotic rate if $\frac{f(x)}{g(x)} < \infty$.*

The proof, which is given in detail for likelihood-weighted sampling in [32], follows directly from a result in [31], pg. 33. For the importance sampler, the variance of the error depends on the "mismatch" between f and g.

3.2 Particle Filters

Armed with the definition of sample sets and procedures for generating them, we can now devise a sample-based algorithm for tracking the state of a dynamical system: *particle filters* [26]. Variants of this algorithm, which have become popular in recent years, can be found in the literature under names such as *survival of the fittest* [14], *condensation algorithm* [12], or, in the context of mobile robotics, *Monte Carlo localization* [5, 7].

Particle filters assume that the model λ is known. They approximate the distributions of α_t using sampling/importance resampling:

1. **Initialization:** Generate N samples of π (e.g., using likelihood-weighted sampling).
2. **For each** $t = 1, \ldots$ **do:**
   (a) Generate N samples $\langle x', p_{x'} \rangle$ from the sample set representing α_{t-1} using likelihood-weighted sampling.
   (b) For each sample $\langle x', p_{x'} \rangle$, generate a random x from $\mu(x \mid x')$ using likelihood-weighted sampling.
   (c) Set p_x to a value proportional to $\nu(O_t \mid x)$, where O_t is the t-th observation in the data set.

Particle filters have successfully been applied to state estimation problems in computer vision [12] and robotics [5, 7]. In MCHMMs, this algorithm is used to approximate the distributions of α_t and β_t.

3.3 Density Trees

While sample sets are sufficient to approximate continuous-valued distributions, they differ from those in that they are *discrete*. This is problematic if one wants to combine densities represented through different sample sets. For example, according to Equation (9), γ_t is the normalized product of two densities, α_t and β_t, each of which represented by its own sample set. Unfortunately, with probability one, none of the samples in α_t and β_t are identical, and thus it is *not* straightforward how to obtain an approximation of their product.

MCHMMs solve this problem by transforming sample sets into (non-parametric) density trees [15, 22, 25], which effectively "generalize" discrete distributions (samples) to continuous distributions. Each node in a density tree is annotated with a hyper-rectangular subspace of $\text{dom}(f)$, denoted V (or V_i for the i-th node). Initially, all samples are assigned to the root node, which covers the entire domain of f. The tree is grown by splitting each node i whenever the following two conditions are fulfilled:

1. At least $\sqrt{N}$ samples $\langle x, p_x \rangle \in X$ fall into V_i.
2. Its depth, i.e., its distance from the root node, does not exceed $\lfloor \frac{1}{4} \log_2 N \rfloor$.

If a node is split, its hyper-rectangle v is divided into two equally sized hyper-rectangles along its longest dimension, as illustrated in Figure 1c. Figure 1b shows a density tree generated for the sample set shown in Figure 1a.

Let f be a density function, X a sample drawn from this density, and for all $x \in \text{dom}(f)$ let $i(x)$ denote the leaf whose region V_i contains x. Furthermore, let $\hat{\sigma}_i$ denote the relative frequency of samples in the i-th node weighted by their respective p_x values:

$$\hat{\sigma}_i \quad = \quad \sum_{\langle x, p_x \rangle \in X} I_{x \in V_i} \, p_x \tag{18}$$

Hence the density function of a tree, denoted $\hat{f}$, is defined as follows:

$$\hat{f}(x) \quad = \quad \frac{\hat{\sigma}_{i(x)}}{|V_{i(x)}|} \qquad (\forall x \in \text{dom}(f)) \tag{19}$$

The numerator of (19) describes the weighted relative frequency that a sample falls into the interval of the node $i(x)$. The denominator is the size of the interval, which is necessary to transform a relative frequency into a density over the interval $V_{i(x)}$. The density function $\hat{f}(x)$ can be equally defined for *internal nodes* (non-leaf nodes). This will be important below, where estimates at different levels of the tree are mixed for regularization.

In [32] we prove the following important convergence result:

Theorem 3. *With probability one, density trees converge to f as $N \rightarrow \infty$.*

The proof exploits the fact that our splitting rule ensures that (1) the depth of the tree grows without bounds and (2) the number of samples in each leaf also grows without bound as $N \rightarrow \infty$. The convergence then follows from the fact that f is Lipschitz.[2]

3.4 Regularization Through Shrinkage and Annealing

The continuous nature of the state space in GHMMs (and hence in MCHMMs), makes it possible to overfit *any* data set, no matter how large. This is because GHMMs are rich enough to assign a different state to each observation in the training data (of which there are only finitely many), making it essentially impossible to generalize beyond sequences other than the ones presented during training. A similar problem arises in conventional HMMs, if they are given more states than there are training examples. In GHMMs the problem is inherent, due to the topology of continuous spaces. Thus, some kind of regularization is needed to prevent overfitting from happening.

Our approach to regularization is based on *shrinkage* [30]. Shrinkage is a well-known statistical technique for "lumping together" different estimates from different data sources. In a remarkable result by Stein [30], shrinking estimators were proven to yield uniformly better solutions over unbiased maximum-likelihood estimators in multivariate Gaussian estimation problems. *Shrinkage trees* were introduced by McCallum [19]. Instead of using the density estimates at the leafs of a tree, shrinkage trees mix those densities with densities obtained further up in the tree. These internal densities are less specific to the region covered by a leaf node; however, their estimates are usually obtained from more data, making them less susceptible to variance in the data.

Figure 1c shows an example using shrinkage with an exponential factor, parameterized by ρ (with $0 \leq \rho \leq 1$). Here each node in the tree, with the exception of the root node, weighs its own density estimate by $(1 - \rho)$, and mixes it with the density estimate from its parent using the weighting factor ρ. As a result, every node along the path contributes to the density estimate at the leaf; however, its influence decays exponentially with the distance from the leaf node. Obviously, the value of ρ determines the amount of shrinkage. If $\rho = 1$, only the root node is consulted,

[2] The termination conditions for growing trees where chosen to facilitate the derivation of Theorem 3. In practice, these conditions can be overly restrictive, as they often require large sample sets to grow reasonable-sized trees. Our actual implementation sidesteps these conditions, and trees are grown all the way to the end. While the convergence results reported here are not applicable any longer, our implementation yielded much better performance specifically when small sample sets were used (e.g., 100 samples).

Model Initialization: Initialize $\lambda = \{\pi, \mu, \nu\}$ by three randomly drawn sets of samples of the appropriate dimension. Generate density trees from these samples. Set $\rho = 1$, and chose an initial sample set size $N > 0$.

E-step:

1. Computation of α_0 (c.f., (6)). Generate N samples from the tree representing π using likelihood-weighted sampling.
2. Computation of α_t (c.f., (7)). For each t with $1 < t \leq T$ do:
   (a) Generate N samples $\langle x', p_{x'} \rangle$ from the sample set representing α_{t-1} using likelihood-weighted sampling.
   (b) For each sample $\langle x', p_{x'} \rangle$, generate the conditional density $\mu(x \mid x')$ using the tree-version of μ. Sample a single x from this tree, using likelihood-weighted sampling.
   (c) Set p_x to a value proportional to $\nu(O_t \mid x)$, where O_t is the t-th observation in the data set. This density value is obtained using the tree representing ν.
   (d) Generate a tree from the new sample set.
3. Computation of β_T (c.f., (6)). Generate N uniformly distributed samples.
4. Computation of β_t (c.f., (8)). For each t with $T > t \geq 1$ do:
   (a) Generate N samples $\langle x', p_{x'} \rangle$ from the sample set representing β_{t+1} using likelihood-weighted sampling.
   (b) For each sample $\langle x', p_{x'} \rangle$, generate the conditional density $\mu(x' \mid x)$ using the tree-version of μ. Sample a single x from this tree, using likelihood-weighted sampling.
   (c) Set p_x to a value proportional $\nu(O_{t+1} \mid x')$, where O_{t+1} is the $t+1$-th observation in the data set. This density value is obtained using the tree representing ν.
   (d) Generate a tree from the new sample set.
5. Computation of γ_t (c.f., (9)). For each t with $1 \leq t \leq T$ do:
   (a) Generate $N/2$ sample from α_t by likelihood weighted sampling, and assign to each sample x an importance factor p_x proportional to $\beta_t(x)$, using the tree approximation of β_t.
   (b) Generate $N/2$ sample from β_t by likelihood weighted sampling and assign to each sample x an importance factor p_x proportional to $\alpha_t(x)$, using the tree approximation of α_t.

M-step:

1. Estimation of the new state transition density μ (c.f., (12)): Pick N random times $t \in \{1, \dots, T-1\}$ and generate samples $\langle x, p_x \rangle$ and $\langle x', p_{x'} \rangle$ from γ_t, and γ_{t+1}, respectively, by likelihood-weighted sampling. Add $\langle (x, x'), N^{-1} \rangle$ into the sample set representing μ. Generate a tree from the sample set. When using $\mu(x' \mid x)$, condition the tree on x.
2. Estimation of the new observation density ν (c.f., (13)): Pick N random $t \in \{1, \dots, T\}$ and generate a sample $\langle x, p_x \rangle$ from γ_t by likelihood-weighted sampling. Add $\langle (x, O_t), N^{-1} \rangle$ into the sample set representing ν. Generate a tree from the sample set. When using $\nu(b \mid x)$, condition the tree on x.
3. Estimation of the new initial state distribution π (c.f., (11)): Copy the sample set γ_0 into π. Generate a tree from the sample set.

Annealing: Set $\rho \leftarrow \rho\bar{\rho}$. Stop when the likelihood of an independent cross-validation set is at its maximum.

Sample set size: $N \longleftarrow \eta N$, for some $\eta > 1$.

Table 1: The MCHMM algorithm.

hence, the probability density induced by the tree is uniform over its domain. If $\rho = 0$, on the other hand, there is no shrinkage and only the estimates in the leaf nodes determine the shape of the density function. For intermediate values of ρ, estimates along the entire path are combined.

Since the optimal value of ρ is problem-specific—de facto it depends on the nature of the (unobservable) state space—our approach uses annealing and cross validation to determine the best value for ρ. More specifically,

$$\rho^{(n)} = \bar{\rho}^{\,n-1} \tag{20}$$

where $\bar{\rho} < 1$ is a constant (e.g., 0.9) and n denotes the iteration counter of the Baum-Welch algorithm (starting at 1). Thus, ρ starts with $\rho^{(0)} = 1$, for which nothing can be learned, since every density is uniform. The parameter ρ is then annealed towards zero in an exponential fashion. Cross validation (early stopping) is applied to determine when to stop training.

4 Monte Carlo HMMs

We are now ready to present the main algorithm of this paper, along with the main theoretical result: The Monte Carlo algorithm for GHMMs, called *Monte Carlo hidden Markov models* (in short *MCHMM*). An MCHMM is a computational instantiation of a GHMM that represents all densities through samples and trees.

The learning algorithm for MCHMMs is depicted in Table 1. MCHMMs use both sample-based and tree representations during learning. In a nutshell,

- **E-step.** Particle filters are applied for forward and

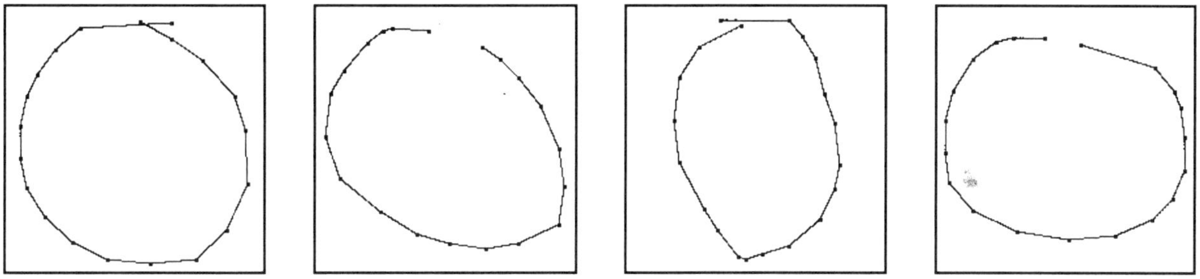

Figure 2: Examples of gestures. The first two gestures were drawn counterclockwise; whereas the other two were drawn clockwise. The MCHMM learning task is to differentiate them.

backward projection (c.f., Section 3.2 and Equations (7) and (8)), using the tree approximations of π, μ and ν.

Forward and backward densities are multiplied (c.f., Equation (9)) by multiplying the importance factors of one of the sample sets (e.g., α_t) with their density values under the tree induced from the other sample set (e.g., β_t). This "trick" overcomes the problem discussed in the beginning of Section 3.3, namely that with probability 1 no two samples in the sets representing α_t and β_t are the same. Its asymptotic correctness follows from the convergence results for sampling and density trees, and the convergence of importance sampling [28, 31].

- **M-step.** The new model $\lambda = \{\pi, \mu, \nu\}$ is obtained by generating samples from the initial state distribution (in the case of π), distributions of pairs of consecutive states (in the case of μ), and distributions of states paired with the corresponding observations (in the case of ν). Trees are then induced from these sample sets.

  The trees of μ and ν represent joint distributions, not conditional distribution. Hence, when using these trees they are conditioned on a state x (c.f., Equations (12) and (13)).

For regularization, MCHMMs use annealing and cross-validation to determine the best shrinkage factor. To ensure convergence, the number of samples N is increased over time.

The convergence of MCHMMs is guaranteed by the following important theorem:

Theorem 4 (MCHMM Convergence Theorem). *Under the assumptions stated above, any strictly monotonically increasing schedule of N's will cause an MCHMM to converge to a local maximum of the corresponding GHMM with probability 1.*

We omit the lengthy proof, which can be found in [32].

Once an MCHMM has been trained, it suffices to memorize only the tree-based version of the model $\lambda = \{\pi, \mu, \nu\}$; all sample sets can be discarded. Problems such as state tracking, prediction, analysis and discrimination can then typically be solved using particle filters (or variants/extensions thereof). By adapting the sample set size on-line, these methods can be implemented as *any-time* algorithms [4, 34] that adapt their computational complexity to the available resources. In addition, sampling in a likelihood-weighted manner places computation where needed: at regions with high likelihood. These properties make MCHMMs attractive for real-time tracking and control [7].

5 Experimental Results

This section reports experimental results, obtained for MCHMMs applied to two problems: an artificial one which was chosen for demonstration purposes, and a gesture recognition problem. The results are primarily intended to illustrate MCHMMs in the finite sample case. Comparisons with existing HMM methods is beyond the scope of this paper.

The artificial data set consists of multiple oscillatory sequences. Observations are 10-dimensional and governed by

$$O_t = \begin{cases} \langle 0.25 + \varepsilon_{t,1}, 0.25 + \varepsilon_{t,2}, 0.25 + \varepsilon_{t,3}, \\ \quad \ldots, 0.25 + \varepsilon_{t,10} \rangle & \text{if } t \text{ odd} \\ \langle 0.75 + \varepsilon_{t,1}, 0.75 + \varepsilon_{t,2}, 0.75 + \varepsilon_{t,3}, \\ \quad \ldots, 0.75 + \varepsilon_{t,10} \rangle & \text{if } t \text{ even} \end{cases}$$

where $\varepsilon_{t,i}$ (with $1 \leq t \leq 20$ and $1 \leq i \leq 10$) are independent and identically distributed noise variables with zero-centered triangular distribution over $[-0.15; 0.15]$. To test the discriminatory accuracy of the learned model, we also generated a second, similar data set (using other inde-

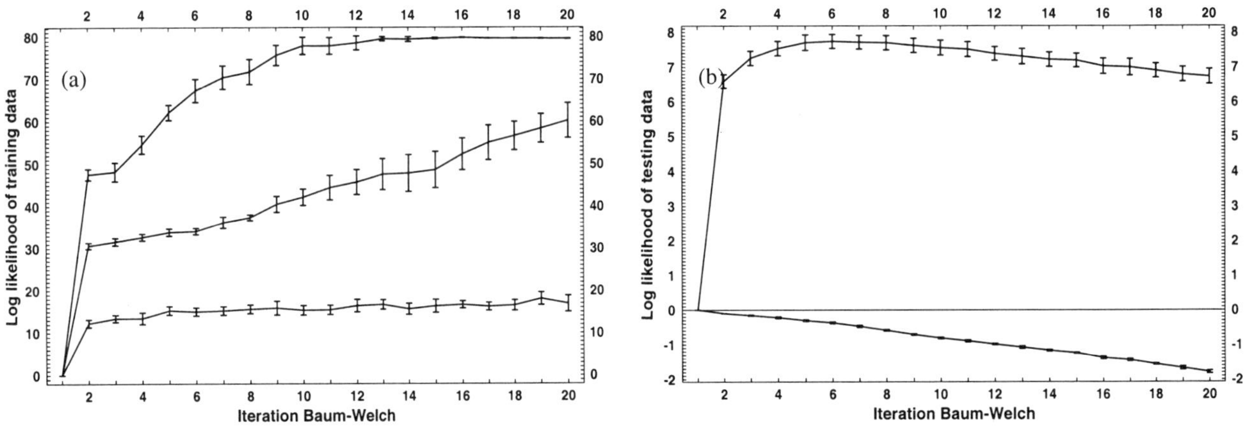

Figure 3: Log likelihood as a function of the iteration of EM, for the synthetic data set. **(a) Training**: Top curve: 1000 samples for all densities. Middle curve: 1000 samples for μ and ν, 100 samples for α, β, γ, and π. Bottom curve: 100 samples for μ and ν, 10 samples for α, β, γ, and π. **(b) Testing**: The top curve shows the log likelihood of "positive" training data (same orientation as used for training), whereas the bottom curve shows the log likelihood for the "negative" class (opposite orientation as used for training). Each result is averaged over 10 independent experiments; 95% confidence bars are also shown.

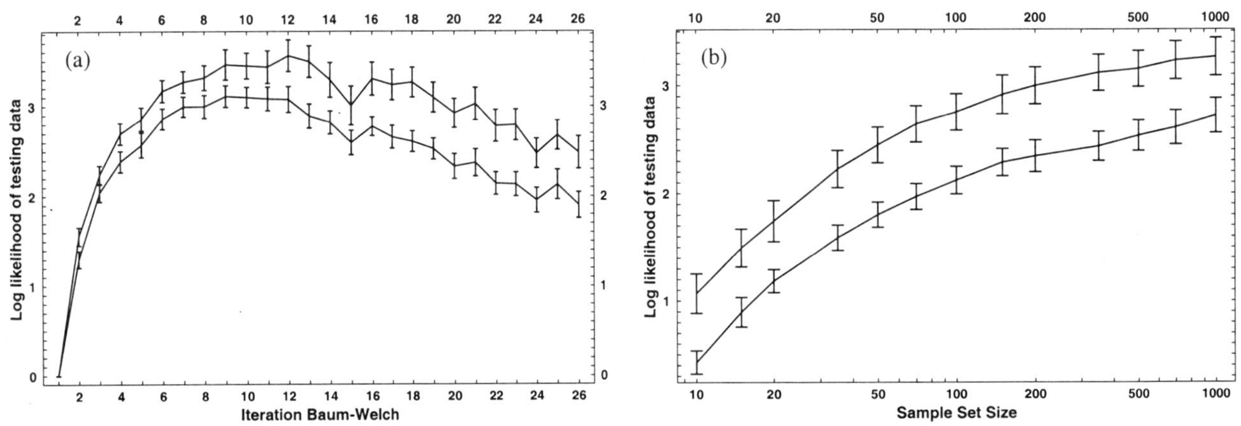

Figure 4: (a) Log likelihood for the gesture data base obtained for independent testing data. The top curve shows the log likelihood of gestures drawn in same same way as the training gesture, whereas the bottom curve shows the log likelihood of gestures drawn in opposite direction. (b) Trade-off between sample set size and log likelihood, for the gesture data set. The more samples are available, the higher the likelihood, and hence the more accurate the results. However, even extremely small sample sets yield reasonable discrimination.

pendent noise variables ε):

$$O_t = \begin{cases} \langle 0.25 + \varepsilon_{t,1}, 0.75 + \varepsilon_{t,2}, 0.25 + \varepsilon_{t,3}, \\ \quad \ldots, 0.75 + \varepsilon_{t,10} \rangle & \text{if } t \text{ odd} \\ \\ \langle 0.75 + \varepsilon_{t,1}, 0.25 + \varepsilon_{t,25}, 0.75 + \varepsilon_{t,3}, \\ \quad \ldots, 0.25 + \varepsilon_{t,10} \rangle & \text{if } t \text{ even} \end{cases}$$

The second data set consisted of a collection of hand-drawn gestures. Figure 2 shows examples. Once drawn, all gestures in our data base look quite similar. However, some of the gestures were drawn clockwise, whereas others were drawn counterclockwise. Here we are interested in discriminating clockwise from counterclockwise gestures. Notice that this problem is more difficult then the artificial one, as the observations alone (stripped of their temporal order) are insufficient for discrimination; instead, the MCHMM has to learn a meaningful model of the internal state.

Figures 3 shows results obtained for the first dataset. Shown in both figures are curves that characterize the log likelihood (notice that the log likelihood is unbounded for continuous distributions). Figure 3a illustrates that the log likelihood of the *training set* increases monotonically over multiple iterations of EM (Baum-Welch), for different experimental conditions described in the figure caption. Figure 3b shows testing results. The upper curve depicts the log likelihood for a set of random sequences that are generated from the same model as the training sequences. The bottom curve depicts the log likelihood for independently generated sequences using the other model, for which the MCHMM was not trained. In both cases, only a single data set (of length 20) was used for training, and testing was performed using 20 data sets generated independently. The initial shrinkage factor was $\rho = 1$, which was annealed down at the rate $\bar{\rho} = 0.9$. Figure 3b shows the effect of overfitting: the testing likelihood increases first, but then levels off (approx. iteration 6) and decreases. Using early stopping, we obtained 100% generalization accuracy in all experiments, even if as few as $N = 10$ samples were used.

Figure 4a shows the corresponding testing result for the more difficult gesture recognition problem. These results were obtained using a single gesture for training only, and using 50 gestures for testing. The top curve depicts the log likelihood for gestures drawn in the same direction as the training gesture, whereas the bottom curve shows the log likelihood for gestures drawn in the opposite direction. As easily noticed in Figure 4a, the difference between classes is smaller than in Figure 3b—which comes at no surprise—yet the likelihood of the "correct" class is still a factor of 4 to 5 larger than that of the opposite class. Figure 4a also shows the effect of annealing. The best shrinkage value is obtained after 12 iterations, where $\rho = 0.28$. As in the previous case, cross-validation using a single gesture performs well. On average, the classification accuracy when using cross-validation for early stopping is 86.0%. This rate is remarkably high, given that only a single gesture per class was used for training.

Figure 4b illustrates the trade-off between computation and accuracy empirically for the gesture data base. Shown there is the log likelihood of the testing data as a function of the sample set size N. Notice that the horizontal axis is logarithmic. All of these points are generated using a model λ obtained using early stopping. The sample set size was generated *after* training, to investigate the effect of computational limitations on the on-line performance of the MCHMM. As in Figure 4a, the top curve in Figure 4b depicts the log likelihood of gestures drawn in the same direction as the training data, whereas the bottom curve shows the log likelihood of gestures drawn in opposite direction. The result in Figure 4b illustrates that the likelihood (and hence the accuracy) of both data sets increases with the sample set size. This is not surprising, as the accuracy of the approximations increases with the sample set size. In addition, Figure 4b suggests that the distance between clockwise and counterclockwise gestures is approximately constant in log likelihood space (hence it grows in likelihood space). This illustrates that better results are achieved with larger sample sets. In our experiments, however, even small sample sets yielded good discrimination (after training with larger sample sets). For example, we observed on average 16% classification error with $N = 10$ samples.

For the gesture data base, one iteration of EM (using the settings described in the caption of Figure 3a) took the following time:

sample set size for μ, ν	sample set size for $\alpha, \beta, \gamma, \pi$	training time (in seconds)
100	100	0.852
1000	100	1.53
100	1000	10.36
1000	1000	18.38

After training, processing a single gesture (which involves running the particle filter on two different MCHMMs) took the following time:

sample set size for α	running time (in seconds)
10	0.00242
100	0.0242
1000	0.260

These numbers were obtained on a low-end PC (equipped with a 266Mhz Pentium II). The latter numbers illustrate that after learning, the processing of a gesture is several orders of magnitude faster than the hand motion involved in gesture generation.

6 Conclusion

We have presented Monte Carlo Hidden Markov Models (MCHMMs), a new algorithm for hidden Markov model learning. MCHMMs extend HMMs to real-valued state and observation spaces and non-parametric models. They represent all densities by samples, which are transformed into probability density functions using density trees. Because the continuous state spaces are rich enough to fit (and overfit!) arbitrary data sets, our approach uses shrinkage to reduce its complexity. The shrinkage parameter is gradually annealed down over time, and cross-validation (early stopping) is used for model selection (regularization).

In this paper, MCHMMs have been shown to converge to local maxima in likelihood space for a large non-parametric class of probability density functions. Empirical results, carried out in an artificial and a gesture recognition domain, demonstrate that our approach generalizes well even when trained with extremely scarce data. Additional experiments characterize the natural trade-off between sample set size and accuracy, illustrating that good results may be achieved even from extremely small sample sets. Additional results described in [32] illustrate the effect of *smoothing* in the forward/backward project step.

The choice of density trees for representing densities in

MCHMMs is somewhat ad hoc. In principle, a range of methods could be applied, such as Gaussian kernels. The trade-offs involved in choosing the right density model are currently poorly understood and therefore warrant future research.

Acknowledgement

The authors gratefully acknowledge inspiring discussions with Frank Dellaert, Nir Friedman, Daphne Koller, and Larry Wasserman.

This research is sponsored in part by NSF (CAREER Award IIS-9876136) and DARPA via TACOM (contract number DAAE07-98-C-L032), and Rome Labs (contract number F30602-98-2-0137), which is gratefully acknowledged. The views and conclusions contained in this document are those of the authors and should not be interpreted as necessarily representing official policies or endorsements, either expressed or implied, of NSF, DARPA, TACOM, Rome Labs, or the United States Government.

References

[1] L.E. Baum and T. Petrie. Statistical inference for probabilistic functions of finite state markov chains. *Annals of Mathematical Statistics*, 37, 1966.

[2] T. Briegel and V. Tresp. A Monte Carlo generalized EM-type algorithm for state and parameter estimation in nonlinear state space models. *NIPS-98*.

[3] E. Charniak. *Statistical Language Learning*. MIT Press, 1993.

[4] T. L. Dean and M. Boddy. An analysis of time-dependent planning. *AAAI-92*.

[5] F. Dellaert, D. Fox, W. Burgard, and S. Thrun. Monte Carlo Localization For Mobile Robots *ICRA-99*.

[6] A.P. Dempster, A.N. Laird, and D.B. Rubin. Maximum likelihood from incomplete data via the em algorithm. *Journal of the Royal Statistical Society, Series B*, 39(1), 1977.

[7] D. Fox, W. Burgard, F. Dellaert, and S. Thrun. Monte Carlo Localization: Efficient position estimation for mobile robots. *AAAI-99*.

[8] Z. Ghahramani and S. Roweis. Learning nonlinear stochastic dynamics using the generalized EM algorithm. *NIPS-98*.

[9] N. Gordon. Novel approach to nonlinear/non-gaussian bayesian state estimation. *IEE Proceedings (F)*, 140(2), 1993.

[10] B. Hannaford and P. Lee. Hidden markov model analysis of force torque information in telemanipulation. *International Journal of Robotics Research*, 10(5), 1991.

[11] J. Henderson, S. Salzberg, and K. Fasman. Finding genes in human DNA with a hidden Markov model. *ISMB-96*.

[12] M. Isard and A. Blake. Condensation: conditional density propagation for visual tracking. *International Journal of Computer Vision*, 1998.

[13] B.H. Juang. Maximum likelihood estimation for mixture multivariate stochastic observations of markov chains. *AT&T Technical Journal*, 64(6), 1985.

[14] K. Kanazawa, D. Koller, and S.J. Russell. Stochastic simulation algorithms for dynamic probabilistic networks. *UAI-95*.

[15] D. Koller and R. Fratkina. Using learning for approximation in stochastic processes. *ICML-98*.

[16] A. Krogh, I.S. Mian, and D. Haussler. A hidden markov model that finds genes in e. coli dna. *Nucleic Acids Research*, 22, 1994.

[17] L.A. Liporace. Maximum likelihood estimation for multivariate observations of markov sources. *IEEE Transactions in Information Theory*, 28(5), 1982.

[18] J. Liu and R. Chen. Sequential monte carlo methods for dynamic systems. *Journal of the American Statistical Association*, 93, 1998.

[19] A. McCallum, R. Rosenfeld, T. Mitchell, and A.Y. Ng. Improving text classification by shrinkage in a hierarchy of classes. *ICML-98*.

[20] G.J. McLachlan and T. Krishnan. *The EM Algorithm and Extensions*. Wiley, 1997.

[21] M. Meilă and M.I. Jordan. Learning fine motion by markov mixture of experts. *NIPS-96*.

[22] A.W. Moore, J. Schneider, and K. Deng. Efficient locally weighted polynomial regression predictions. *ICML-97*.

[23] R.M. Neal. Probabilistic inference using markov chain monte carlo methods. TR CRG-TR-93-1, University of Toronto, 1993.

[24] R.M. Neal and G.E. Hinton. A view of the EM algorithm that justifies incremental, sparse, and other variants. In *Learning in Graphical Models*. Kluwer, 1998.

[25] S. M. Omohundro. Bumptrees for Efficient Function, Constraint, and Classification Learning. *NIPS-91*.

[26] M. Pitt and N. Shephard. Filtering via simulation: auxiliary particle filter. *Journal of the American Statistical Association*, 1999.

[27] L. R. Rabiner. A tutorial on hidden markov models and selected applications in speech recognition. In *Proceedings of the IEEE*, 1989.

[28] D.B. Rubin. Using the SIR algorithm to simulate posterior distributions. In *Bayesian Statistics 3*. Oxford University Press, 1988.

[29] H Shatkay and L. Kaelbling. Learning topological maps with weak local odometric information. *IJCAI-97*.

[30] C. Stein. Inadmissibility of the usual estimator for the mean of a multivariate normal distribution. In *Proceedings of the Third Berkeley Symposium on Mathematical Statistics and Probability 1*, 1995.

[31] M.A. Tanner. *Tools for Statistical Inference*. 2nd ed., Springer, 1993.

[32] S. Thrun and J. Langford. Monte carlo hidden markov models. TR CMU-CS-98-179, Carnegie Mellon University, 1997.

[33] A. Waibel and K.-F. Lee, editors. *Readings in Speech Recognition*. Morgan Kaufmann, 1990.

[34] S. Zilberstein and S. Russell. Approximate reasoning using anytime algorithms. In *Imprecise and Approximate Computation*. Kluwer, 1995.

Approximation Via Value Unification

Paul E. Utgoff
David J. Stracuzzi
Department of Computer Science
University of Massachusetts
Amherst, MA 01003
{utgoff|stracudj}@cs.umass.edu

Abstract

Numerical function approximation over a Boolean domain is a classical problem with wide application to data modeling tasks and various forms of learning. A great many function approximation algorithms have been devised over the years. Because the goal is to produce an approximating function that has low expected error, algorithms are typically guided by error reduction. This guiding force, to reduce error, can bias the algorithm in a detrimental manner. We illustrate this bias, and then propose an alternative approach based on a notion of value unification.

1 Introduction

Suppose that we are given a batch of N labeled training points, each of the form $(\mathbf{b}, v(\mathbf{b}))$. The point $\mathbf{b}$ is represented as a vector of d Boolean variables. The real value $v(\mathbf{b})$ is the target value for point $\mathbf{b}$, which means that it is the ideal value for the approximator to return, noise in the measurement of $v()$ notwithstanding. Our problem is to find a good approximation $\hat{v}$ such that the desired error measure is minimized. A commonly used error measure is mean-squared error $\frac{1}{N}\sum_{j=1}^{N}(\hat{v}(\mathbf{b}_j) - v(\mathbf{b}_j))^2$. Furthermore, we desire a $\hat{v}$ that has low error for any set of $(\mathbf{b}, v(\mathbf{b}))$ points that could be drawn from the same distribution as the training points.

It is common to map non-Boolean variables to Boolean. For example, a discrete variable of k values can be mapped to k Boolean variables. For a given discrete value, the corresponding Boolean variable is set to `true`, and the others for that discrete variable are set to `false`. Similarly, a continuous variable can be partitioned into k intervals, ahd hence k Boolean variables. For a given real value, the Boolean variable corresponding to the interval in which the value falls is set to `true`, and the others for that continuous variable are set to `false`. We do not revisit these mapping procedures here, and consider the problem in Boolean form.

2 Regression Tree Induction as Approximation

One method of function approximation is to form a tree-structured regression, known as a *regression tree* (Breiman, Friedman, Olshen & Stone, 1984). The domain $\mathbf{b}$ is partitioned recursively into a finite set of blocks, and for each block a constant value, e.g. the mean, is fixed as the value of the approximation $\hat{v}$ for every point in that block. The partition represents a piece-wise constant function.

How is the partition determined? A common approach is to split any block in which the variance of the $v()$ values therein is too large, as measured by exceeding a user specified threshold. Variance is equivalent to the mean squared error when approximating by the mean of the sample, so this is the same as minimizing error. A split is accomplished by enumerating the possible tests, and selecting a test for which the average error in the resulting blocks would be minimized. For our purposes, each Boolean variable b_i can serve as a binary test. Let L be the instances in one block, and R be the instances in the other block. Then the assessment of the test is $\frac{|L|\sigma_L^2+|R|\sigma_R^2}{|L|+|R|}$. A test (Boolean variable) with the lowest value of this metric is selected and installed at the decision node, and each of the two resulting blocks is partitioned recursively until each block is of sufficiently low error (variance). In the extreme, every block will contain a single training point, but typically there is a useful amount of generalization, producing fuller blocks and a smaller tree.

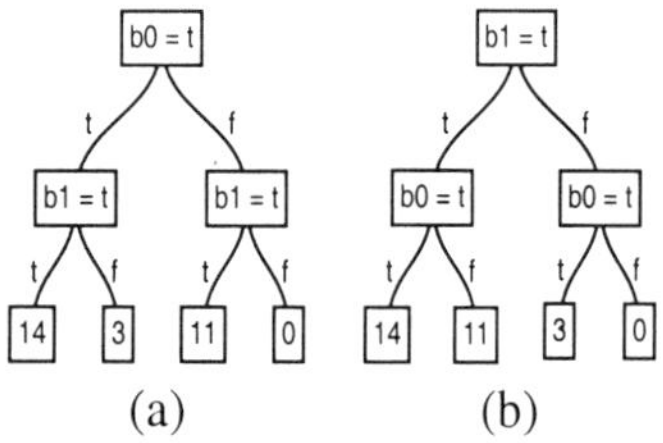

Figure 1: The Two Possible Regression Trees

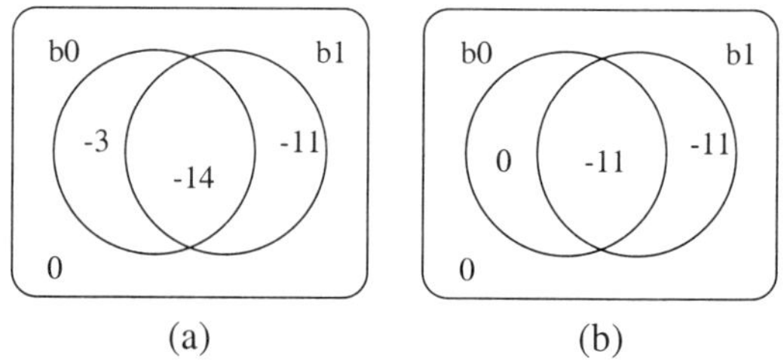

Figure 2: Unification of Values

3 Bias of Error Reduction

Consider a simple approximation task for instances of two Boolean variables. Suppose that the target function is $v(\mathbf{b}) = 3b_0 + 11b_1$, and that we have been given all four possible instances for training. Because $v()$ does not include any second degree terms, these two Boolean variables make independent contributions to the value of the function. We should not expect either variable to be preferred for the purpose of building a regression tree. However, a regression tree inducer guided by error (variance) reduction will prefer to test b_1 at the root. As shown in Figure 1, testing b_0 at the root groups 14 with 3 in one block, and 11 with 0 in the other. However, testing b_1 at the root groups 14 with 11 in one block, and 3 with 0 in the other, which produces lower expected error. So, although we happen to know in this case that either test is equally good, we see that the test selection metric is biased to favor one over the other. This bias is misleading.

4 Value Unification

Let us examine this same simple function approximation problem from a different point of view. Figure 2(a) depicts the target function v as a Venn diagram, where each value shown is the error with respect to $\hat{v}$, which is initially the 0 function. A set contains those instances for which the corresponding Boolean variable is `true`. Suppose that we could infer the $3b_0$ component of the target function. Then the error function would change to that of Figure 2(b). The point that is in the b_0 set but not the b_1 set now has error 0, and the error for the point that is in both the b_0 set and the b_1 set now has error -11. Originally, there were four different values, but now there are two. A unification of values has occurred, making the remaining approximation problem simpler. Notice that if we had instead first inferred the $11b_1$ component of the target function, a different but equally useful unification would have occurred.

These observations suggest that an induction process based on value unification is possible, and that it would be biased differently from one based on error reduction. The variance reduction bias first groups instances by target value, and then finds a test to facilitate that grouping. This can be very misleading because instances can have similar values for different reasons. In contrast, the unification bias seeks to account for the reasons that an instance has the value it does. For example, one instance may have value 20 because of evaluation $10b_7 + 10b_9$, whereas another instance may have value 20 because of different feature contributions $5b_3 + 9b_5 + 6b_8$. Attempting to group these two instances because they each evaluate to 20 is misguided.

5 Comparison of Biases in Regression Tree Induction

In this section we digress briefly from our quest to formulate a function approximation algorithm driven primarily by value unification instead of primarily by error reduction. For discussion purposes, we fashion a regression tree algorithm that is driven by value unification. Then we consider how different such a mechanism is from classification tree induction.

For regression tree induction we do not need to unify any values, but we can be guided by the same goal. By substituting a new test selection metric into the same splitting mechanism described above, we can reduce the total number of distinct values observed. Let $u(T)$ be the number of distinct $f(\mathbf{b})$ values in T, where T is a set of training points. Define the test selection metric to be $u(L) + u(R)$, where as before L and R are the two blocks of the partition. A test is good to the extent that it separates instances into blocks with small value sets. Note that for regression tree induction, it is not necessary to unify the values of the blocks since they are handled independently, but the motivation is the same.

It is instructive to examine two regression trees for a single small problem. Figure 3 shows a typical example in which partitioning based on error reduction, called *error_tree*, does a poor job of grouping values, and hence capturing the regularity in the data. Notice that error_tree sends four of six values down the left branch and another four of six val-

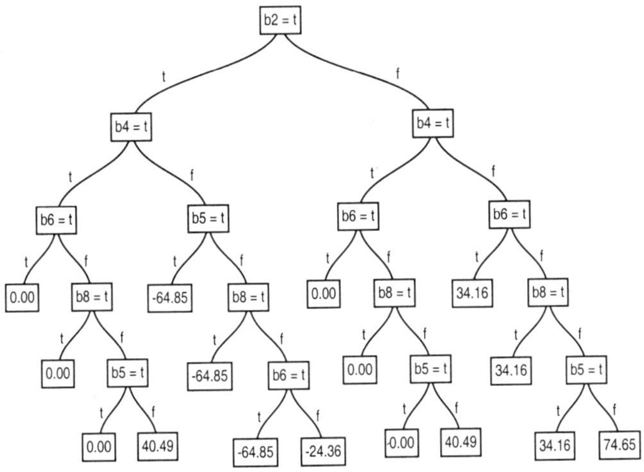

Figure 3: Regression Tree Using Variance Metric

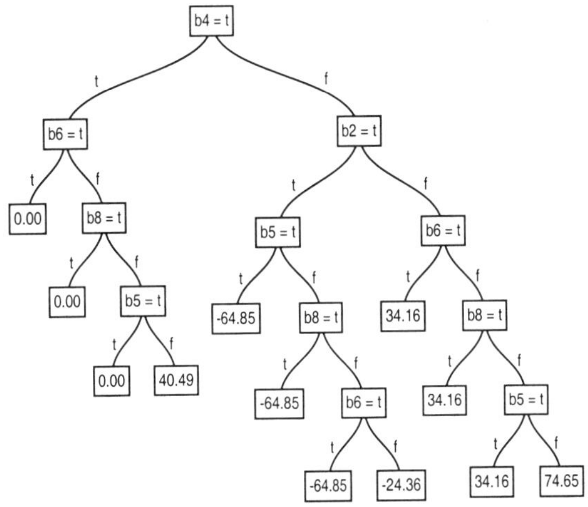

Figure 4: Regression Tree Using Unification Metric

ues to the right, causing much duplication of subproblems and replication of subtrees. Figure 4 shows the tree built for the same problem using the unification metric, called *unify_tree*. Two of the six possible values are sent down the left branch, and the remaining four are sent down the right branch, eliminating duplication in the subproblems. The FRINGE algorithm (Pagallo & Haussler, 1990) would be able to shrink either of these trees by constructing conjunctive tests. Nevertheless, one should not count on FRINGE to overcome a bad bias in every case.

How do these two test selection metrics compare in practice? We could measure error on independent training and testing sets, but here we simply look at the number of leaves, assuming that a smaller tree does a better job of finding the regularity in the data. Table 1 shows tree size for four different algorithms under several combinations of 'number of binary variables' and 'number of features in the target function'. Two classification tree inducers ITI (Utgoff, Berkman & Clouse, 1997) and C4.5 (Quinlan, 1993) are included. For those, the numeric target value for each instance is treated as a non-numeric class label. The tree sizes shown in the table are computed by averaging the number of leaves for 100 artificial problems.

Based on these runs, unify_tree builds smaller trees than error_tree. This suggests that grouping instances by numeric closeness of target value does not offer an advantage, and may be detrimental. ITI finds still smaller trees, suggesting that its test selection metric, a form of Kolmogorov-Smirnoff distance (Friedman, 1977; Utgoff & Clouse, 1996), is better. It might be fruitful to pursue this digression a little further, but the purpose here was to illustrate that an error reduction approach to regression tree induction has a bias, and that it is not favorable to the induction processes, as measured by tree size.

#vars	#features	unify_tree	error_tree	iti	c4.5
10	10	151.77	165.71	145.88	290.68
10	20	557.82	626.68	553.43	1105.27
15	10	608.60	654.90	519.76	968.07
20	10	1310.05	1497.64	1167.71	1833.42
25	10	2204.29	2617.21	2040.40	2696.58

Table 1: Tree Induction Measurements

6 Feature Construction Guided by Value Unification

Let us return to the problem of designing an algorithm that fits the set of N training points. The algorithm is to be guided primarily by unification of values. To motivate the algorithm that is presented below, consider first what happens when a feature and its coefficient are appended to a function. This provides a sense of how the myriad values come into being, which will be useful for trying to reverse the process. Given the data points, we will want to be able to determine a set of features and coefficients that would produce them.

Define the function approximator of no features to have value 0 for all points, giving $v(\mathbf{b}) = 0$. This function has a one element value set $\{0\}$. Now define a feature $f_0(\mathbf{b})$ to evaluate to 1 for any point in which variable b_0 is `true`, and to evaluate to 0 otherwise. Define c_0, $c_0 \neq 0$, to be its coefficient, giving $v(\mathbf{b}) = c_0 f_0(\mathbf{b})$. This function v has a two element value set $\{0, c_0\}$. The data points covered by feature $f_0(\mathbf{b})$ evaluate to c_0, and the remaining points evaluate to 0. A feature makes a non-zero contribution to the value of each instance that it covers.

For the sake of discussion, and following our earlier example, let $c_0 = 3$. Add a new feature $f_1(\mathbf{b})$ that covers exactly those points for which variable b_1 is `true`, and define its coefficient $c_1 = 11$. Our function is now $v(\mathbf{b}) = 3f_0(\mathbf{b}) + 11f_1(\mathbf{b})$, which has value set $\{0, 3, 11, 14\}$. An instance that is covered by a feature has a non-zero value. That is not true in general, because the sum of a set of coefficients could be zero, but the discussion will be simpler if for now we assume that no covered instance evaluates to 0.

6.1 Top Level

We can construct an algorithm that attempts to reproduce the features and their coefficients that define the target function v. The reproduction $\hat{v}$ may not be exact, making it an approximator of v. Our approach, embodied in an algorithm called *VU*, is to identify the coefficient-feature pairs sequentially, searching in the general-to-specific direction in the space of features, as defined by the sets of instances covered. For example, the most general feature is the one that covers all possible instances in instance space.

Consider the top level of the algorithm:

1. Receive N training points $(\mathbf{b}, v(\mathbf{b}))$ in d variables.
2. For each training point, initialize its error to $0 - v$.
3. Initialize $\hat{v} = 0$.
4. While some instance has non-zero error:
   (a) Find the next feature.
   (b) Find the feature's coefficient.
   (c) Append the term to the definition of $\hat{v}$.
   (d) For each instance covered by the new feature, add the coefficient to its error.

This looks very much like an error-reduction procedure, and it is. To unify values is to reduce error. However, the algorithm is not grouping instances by size of error, nor is it trying to reduce error for all instances simultaneously. Instead, it is unifying values by extracting coefficient-feature pairs one at a time. When one does this successfully, the size of the value set of the adjusted instance values is reduced. Ultimately, all adjusted instance values (the instance error values) reach 0.

Watch how the algorithm works for the following training instances of two variables. The operations of finding the next feature and its coefficient are treated as black boxes for the moment.

b_0	b_1	$v(\mathbf{b})$	error
1	1	14	-14
1	0	3	-3
0	1	11	-11
0	0	0	0

At this point, we have $\hat{v}(\mathbf{b}) = 0$. Now the feature $f_0(\mathbf{b})$ and its coefficient 3 are found. The new term is added to the approximator, giving $\hat{v}(\mathbf{b}) = 3f_0(\mathbf{b})$, and the error values are adjusted, giving:

b_0	b_1	$v(\mathbf{b})$	error
1	1	14	-11
1	0	3	0
0	1	11	-11
0	0	0	0

The unification of values is taking place on the error values. The size of the value set has been reduced from 4 to 2. One more iteration of the top level would finish the process by unifying all error values to 0, with $\hat{v}(\mathbf{b}) = 3f_0(\mathbf{b}) + 11f_1(\mathbf{b})$.

6.2 Finding A Feature

The procedure for finding the next most general feature is implemented as best-first search, but in practice it amounts to hill-climbing. The `open` list is initialized with the most general feature, which covers all instances. A feature that covers an instance with error (unified) 0 can be specialized. Indeed, that is desirable because it means that a more specialized feature will not alter the value of an instance that currently has error 0.

The metric for the best-first search is the number of training instances covered by the feature that have error 0, and the search prefers nodes with lower values of the metric. The search terminates when any of three conditions is met:

1. the fewest-true-values instance (`true` values for exactly those variables tested in the feature cover definition) is present in the training instances,
2. the metric value for the best feature on the `open` list is 0 (no instances with 0 error are covered),
3. the metric value for the best feature on the `closed` list is not greater than the best feature on the `open` list (no progress in minizing the number of covered 0 error instances).

Until the search terminates, the best feature is removed from `open` and placed onto `closed`, and the successors of that currently best feature are inserted into the `open` list.

A successor is generated by copying the feature definition, and then conjoining a missing variable to it. For example, the most general feature is 1 because it evaluates to 1 regardless of the values of the variables in an instance. A specialization of the most general feature is b_0 because it evaluates to 1 for just those instances in which b_0 is `true`, and to 0 otherwise. If a successor feature covers no instances, it is discarded immediately without putting it onto the `open` list.

6.3 Finding a Feature's Coefficient

The VU algorithm finds features one at a time, and in general-to-specific order. For this reason, it is essential to pay attention to whether the fewest-true-values instance covered by the feature is present in the training instances. Consider the instance in which all variables are `false`. No specialized feature can cover this instance. To choose a coefficient that does not unify this instance with 0 will produce a permanent error. So, in this case, the coefficient can be extracted directly from the training instance.

When the fewest-true-values instance for a feature is not present in the data, how does one find a coefficient? We could choose a value that would most reduce the size of the resulting value set. This would be most obviously in keeping with the principle of value unification. However, this measure is sometimes ambiguous. A second possibility is to choose a value that unifies the largest number of instances with 0. Either of these approaches works well, but neither is foolproof. A third approach follows from the reasoning above about wanting to handle fewest-true-values instances. Find a fewest-true-values training instance from those covered by the feature, and use its weight as the coefficient. This approach may not be foolproof either, but we have not yet observed it to make an error. It unifies the values as we would like, so it achieves our purpose.

6.4 Illustration

Here is a trace of the VU algorithm for a small approximation task in which there are $d = 8$ Boolean variables, giving $2^d = 256$ possible points $\mathbf{b}$. The target function consists of the three indicated features, making eight possible v values. The 100 training instances were drawn at random with replacement.

A feature definition is depicted as a string of '.'s and '1's. A dot means that the variable value is not relevant to the value of the feature, whereas a one means that it is relevant. The feature depicted by all dots is the most general feature. A feature evaluates to 0 if any of the tested variables (indicated by a '1' in the string) is `false`, and 1 otherwise. The `open` and `closed` lists are summarized by showing the metric value (number of training instances covered with 0 error) for up to the five best features on the list. The word 'quality' refers to metric value.

```
Using 8 variables
Using 3 features in target
Using 100 training instances

Target
   3.00 ....11..
   4.00 11......
   5.00 .1..1...

Closed:
Open:    61

Expand  ........
  Child .......1 quality    34
  Child ......1. quality    35
  Child .....1.. quality    16 <-- best
  Child ....1... quality    21
  Child ...1.... quality    33
  Child ..1..... quality    31
  Child .1...... quality    16 <-- best
  Child 1....... quality    21

Closed: 61
Open:    16 16 21 21 31 ...

Expand  .....1..
  Child .....1.1 quality     8
  Child .....11. quality    12
  Child ....11.. quality     0 <-- best
  Child ...1.1.. quality     6
  Child ..1..1.. quality    11
  Child .1...1.. quality     6
  Child 1....1.. quality     3

Closed: 16 61
Open:    0 3 6 6 8 ...

Weight 3.00 from hamming dist 0 instance
Append  ....11.. to approx with weight 3.00

Closed:
Open:    75

Expand  ........
  Child .......1 quality    39
  Child ......1. quality    42
  Child .....1.. quality    30
  Child ....1... quality    35
  Child ...1.... quality    40
  Child ..1..... quality    38
  Child .1...... quality    16 <-- best
  Child 1....... quality    25

Closed: 75
Open:    16 25 30 35 38 ...

Expand  .1......
  Child .1.....1 quality     8
```

```
  Child .1....1. quality    8
  Child .1...1.. quality    6
  Child .1..1... quality    0 <-- best
  Child .1.1.... quality    5
  Child .11..... quality    7
  Child 11...... quality    0 <-- best

Closed: 16 75
Open:   0 0 5 6 7 ...

Weight 5.00 from hamming dist 1 instance
Append .1..1... to approx with weight 5.00

Closed:
Open:   82

Expand ........
  Child .......1 quality   40
  Child ......1. quality   45
  Child .....1.. quality   34
  Child ....1... quality   42
  Child ...1.... quality   41
  Child ..1..... quality   43
  Child .1...... quality   23 <-- best
  Child 1....... quality   25

Closed: 82
Open:   23 25 34 40 41 ...

Expand .1......
  Child .1.....1 quality    9
  Child .1....1. quality   11
  Child .1...1.. quality   10
  Child .1..1... quality    7
  Child .1.1.... quality    6
  Child .11..... quality   12
  Child 11...... quality    0 <-- best

Closed: 23 82
Open:   0 6 7 9 10 ...

Weight 4.00 from hamming dist 0 instance
Append 11...... to approx with weight 4.00

Approximator:
   4.00 11......
   5.00 .1..1...
   3.00 ....11..
```

6.5 Sample Size for Training

How many training instances are needed for the VU algorithm? One must sample the instance space adequately so that the features can be extracted from the data. The VU approach to feature construction depends on the ability to discriminate instances that should be covered by a feature from those that should not. Thus the problem of finding a feature is one of concept learning, and the algorithm for finding a feature definition conducts a general-to-specific search (Mitchell, 1982), with non-zero values denoting positive instances, and zero-values denoting negative instances. Concept learning occurs for each feature, and is embedded in the larger VU process of inducing a function approximator. Because the features are found one at a time, we have a sequence of concept learning problems. Upon learning finding a feature definition (learning a concept), the outer process finds a coefficient and adjusts the instance values.

We can apply sample complexity results for concept learning to the VU approach to approximator induction. We have here a sequence of concepts to be learned, so a small extension is required. Ehrenfeucht, Haussler, Kearns, & Valiant (1988) provide a lower bound m on the sample size that is based on three parameters: the size of the hypothesis space $|H|$, the acceptable misclassification rate ε, and the probability δ of failing to induce a concept with misclassification rate at most ε. For a target function of one feature, the size of the hypothesis space $|H|$ is 2^d, where d is the number of Boolean variables. The lower bound can be computed directly. For two features, we have two concept learning problems. One might say that the one oroginal sample will suffice for each problem, but it is important to keep in mind that one is rolling a $\frac{1}{\delta}$-sided die for each feature (concept) to be found. Because δ is the probability of failure, $1-\delta$ is the probability of success. We need a μ such that $(1-\mu)^k = (1-\delta)$, where k is the number of features in the target function. Rearrangement of terms gives $\mu = 1-(1-\delta)^{\frac{1}{k}}$. Use μ in place of δ when computing the sample size for the sequence of concept learning problems. The effect is to increase the sample size. We do not know ahead of time how many features are in the target function. We could attempt to estimate k, but it is fruitless to consider a uniform distribution of possible functions to be approximated (Rao, Gordon & Spears, 1995).

The VU algorithm fails when the training instances are not sufficient to enable it to paint the feature boundaries. Our remedy is to increase the sample size, but we would like to make the algorithm robust to this condition.

6.6 Feature Cancellation

The VU algorithm will also fail when an instance has 0 error because it is covered by features whose coefficients sum to 0. The best-first search for a feature that excludes all instances with error 0 eventually degenerates into producing features that cover individual instances. Work is underway to remove this limitation.

6.7 Computational Efficiency

The algorithm can be implemented efficiently. The number of instances that are covered by a feature and have 0 error can be computed in a single sweep over the instances. In terms of sweeps over the instances, the VU algorithm requires $O(d^2)$ sweeps per feature to be found.

6.8 Empirical Evaluation

We have only tested this particular algorithm on artificial target functions of the same form used by the approximator itself. More work is needed to see whether other kinds of targets have any important differences. We have varied the value of d, the distribution of coefficient values for the target features, the distribution over the number of bits to set in a features, the number of features in the target concept, and the number of training instances. We have not tested the algorithm on 'real' problems, nor have we investigated issues relating to noise and overfitting.

Regarding noise, we expect that small amounts of noise in the function value can be tolerated by relaxing the test for unified values. Instead of requiring true equality, we can treat similar values as equal. For instances that are outliers by virtue of large errors, either in the variable values or the function value, we expect that the algorithm would construct a very specialized feature to cover each outlying instance. Such features could be discarded afterward, constituting a form of pruning. We have not done any experimentation regarding noise, so these thoughts are speculative.

6.9 Other Approximator Inducers

Table 2: Target Function

```
Target:
   5.00 .1.....1.....1..11..
   3.00 .......11.11.....1..
   2.00 .11........1.......1
   4.00 ....1.......1..11...
   1.00 .1..............11..
   5.00 ...........1......11.
   1.00 .....1.......1......
   4.00 ................1..1.
   3.00 ....1............1..
   5.00 ...........1.1......
```

A great many methods have been devised for approximating functions, most of which are guided primarily by error minimization. Value unification provides a different avenue for finding regularity in the data. We decided to test an artificial neural network inducer (Rumelhart & McClelland, 1986) on the target function shown in Table 2. The target function has $d = 20$ Boolean variables and $k = 10$ features, and $10,000$ training instances were generated at random with replacement. The artificial neural network had 20 input units, 10 sigmoid threshold hidden units, and 1 unthresholded output unit. Such an architecture is sufficient for representing the target function because a hidden unit can represent a set cover feature, and the output unit can represent a linear combination of the feature values.

Counting a network output as correct if it is within 5% of the target output, and letting backprop run for 320 epochs produces a network that is 'correct' for 9,501 of the 10,000 examples. Allowing the training to continue for 20,000 epochs improves accuracy only slightly. Each 100 epochs takes about 1 minute of cpu. For some purposes, 95% accuracy may be sufficient, but it is clear that the network is not finding all the regularity in the data. In contrast, VU finds an exact solution in 9 cpu seconds.

This is just one problem, but it is another kind of indication that one may not find regularity when striving too hard to reduce all error at one time. A more systematic set of comparisons is needed.

6.10 Compactness of Overlapping Features

The VU algorithm produces a compact representation in the form of overlapping features. This offers considerable economy compared to a regression tree. For example, for the target function in Table 2, a regression tree based on the unification metric contains 879 leaves, versus 10 features for VU. The regression tree algorithm (unify_tree) requires 15 seconds to construct the tree, versus 9 seconds for VU to find its approximation. Regression trees based on the input variables, whatever the metric, partition the space into disjoint regions.

7 Summary

Our work presents three ideas. The first is that algorithms that are driven primarily by error reduction can be led into missing regularities in the data that would facilitate function approximation. Second, it is beneficial to try to group instances that have similar values for similar reasons. Finally, it is possible to fashion algorithms that are driven primarily by value unification, and only secondarily by error reduction. In particular we presented the novel VU algorithm that uses value unification to identify useful overlapping features.

Acknowledgments

This work was supported by National Science Foundation Grant IRI-9711239. We are indebted to Gang Ding, who produced the neural network results. We thank David Jensen, Doina Precup, Amy McGovern, and Yanfeng Lu for providing helpful comments.

References

Breiman, L., Friedman, J. H., Olshen, R. A., & Stone, C. J. (1984). *Classification and regression trees*. Belmont, CA: Wadsworth International Group.

Ehrenfeucht, A., Haussler, D., Kearns, M., & Valiant, L. (1988). A general lower bound on the number of examples needed for learning. *Proceedings of the 1988 Workshop on Computational Learning Theory* (pp. 110-120). San Mateo, CA: Morgan Kaufmann.

Friedman, J. H. (1977). A recursive partitioning decision rule for nonparametric classification. *IEEE Transactions on Computers, C-26*, 404-408.

Mitchell, T. M. (1982). Generalization as search. *Artificial Intelligence, 18*, 203-226.

Pagallo, G., & Haussler, D. (1990). Boolean feature discovery in empirical learning. *Machine Learning, 5*, 71-99.

Quinlan, J. R. (1993). *C4.5: Programs for machine learning*. San Mateo, CA: Morgan Kaufmann.

Rao, R.B., Gordon, D. , & Spears, W. (1995). For every generalization action, is there really an equal and opposite reaction? Analysis of the Conservation Law for Generalization Performance. *Machine Learning: Proceedings of the Twelfth International Conference* (pp. 115-121). Tahoe City, CA: Morgan Kaufmann.

Rumelhart, D. E., & McClelland, J. L. (1986). *Parallel distributed processing*. Cambridge, MA: MIT Press.

Utgoff, P. E., Berkman, N. C., & Clouse, J. A. (1997). Decision tree induction based on efficient tree restructuring. *Machine Learning, 29*, 5-44.

Utgoff, P. E., & Clouse, J. A. (1996). *A Kolmogorov-Smirnoff metric for decision tree induction*, (Technical Report 96-3), Amherst, MA: University of Massachusetts, Department of Computer Science.

Model Selection in Unsupervised Learning With Applications To Document Clustering

Shivakumar Vaithyanathan shiv@almaden.ibm.com
Byron Dom dom@almaden.ibm.com

IBM Almaden Research Center
650 Harry Rd.
Jose, CA 95120

Abstract

This paper addresses the problem of model structure determination in unsupervised learning. In contrast to previous work, we define the problem of model selection to be determining both the optimal number of clusters and the optimal feature set. We formulate this problem in a Bayesian statistical estimation framework, proposing a general expression for an objective function, the maximization of which will be taken to correspond to the optimal model structure. By making assumptions about the generative model, we derive a closed-form expression for the document clustering problem. We then provide heuristics that find the optimum (or at least a sub-optimum) of this objective function in terms of the feature sets and the number of clusters. We finally evaluate our objective function and optimization algorithm by extensive experimentation and comparison against an expert-judged, non-trivial, data-set. We find that there is good agreement between the clusters produced using our objective function/algorithm and the expert-judged classes. We also show that our approach compares favorably with others present in the literature.

1.0 Introduction

Unsupervised learning is an attempt to determine the intrinsic structure in data and is often cast as one of finding clusters in the data-set. Clustering is an important tool in the analysis of data with applications in several domains such as psychology, humanities, clinical diagnosis, pattern recognition, information retrieval etc. Several traditional approaches to clustering have been proposed in literature and the reader is referred to the following survey[JAIN88].

Clustering (at least when carried out in the context of or by using density estimation) is a special case of the problem of model selection, a byproduct of which is the determination of the number of adjustable model parameters. Postulating too few parameters leads to a poor fit whereas too many parameters can lead to overfitting thus distorting the density of the underlying data [RISSANEN92]. Model selection in clustering applications has proven to be particularly challenging as the notion of "optimality" is difficult to characterize. This difficulty notwithstanding several recent efforts have emerged [KONTKANEN96, SMYTH96] in this area. These efforts have primarily addressed model selection from the point of view of estimating the number of clusters. One aspect that has been ignored, however, is that of clustering in different feature spaces. It is easy to see, especially in applications where the number of features is very large, that the various choices of feature subsets will reveal different structures underlying the data - and therefore, potentially, different numbers of clusters. In essence we argue that it is the interplay between the feature subset and the number of clusters that provides the appropriate view of the data.

In this paper we tackle the problem of model selection in clustering and in contrast to previous efforts we define the problem of model selection as selecting both the number of clusters *and* the feature subset. This broader definition creates new problems, however, - specifically, how do we compare two models existing in different feature spaces ? We need a mechanism that can be used to compare different model structures ("model structure" is formally defined in section 2). Towards this end we propose a unified objective function whose arguments include the feature space and number of clusters. We derive this objective function in the next section using a Bayesian approach. In section 3 we apply our approach to the document clustering problem and derive a closed form for our objective function by making certain assumptions about the document generation model. This is followed in section 4 by the description of a heuristic for initial feature selection, to prune the search space, based on distributional clustering of terms. Section 5 describes the experimental setup and our approach to validate the proposed models and algorithms based on comparison against ground truth. Section 6 reports and discusses the results of our experiments and finally section 7 provides directions for future work.

2.0 MODEL SELECTION IN CLUSTERING

Model selection approaches in clustering have primarily concentrated on the problem of determining the number of components/clusters. These attempts include Bayesian approaches [KONTKANEN96], MDL based approaches [RISSANEN92] and cross-validation techniques [SMYTH96]. As noticed in [SMYTH96, page 14, last paragraph] however, the optimal number of clusters is dependent on the feature space in which the clustering is performed. In [DEVANEY97] a preliminary investigation of *feature selection* in the context of concept clustering, using COBWEB, revealed that a reduction in the number of features improved the quality of the results. Another application of feature selection in clustering is in the context of content-based image retrieval [DY99]. In this application feature selection is used to provide a finer-grained distinction between images of a particular class. Besides these, practitioners in other applications, such as document clustering, that encounter very large feature space, have resorted to comparatively ad hoc procedures to prune the feature space. Given these important applications it seems an obvious extension to include feature selection as a part of model structure determination in unsupervised learning. In the next sections we derive a generalized objective function for model selection in unsupervised learning that includes determining both the number features and the number of components.

2.1 A BAYESIAN APPROACH TO MODEL SELECTION FOR CLUSTERING

Let D be a data-set consisting of "patterns"[1] $\{d_1, d_2, ..., d_n\}$ We will assume that the patterns are represented in some feature space T that has a cardinality M. The particular unsupervised learning problem we address is that of clustering D into groups (clusters) such that the likelihood of D described by a certain probability model, is maximized. In the most common formulation of the cluttering problem this can be written as finding $\hat{\Omega}$ and $\hat{\xi}$ such that

(1) $$(\hat{\Omega}, \hat{\xi}) = \arg\max_{\Omega,\xi} P(D^T|\Omega, \xi)$$

where:

D^T indicates the representation[2] of the data in feature space T. It will be implicitly assumed that T consists of the complete set of features.

Ω is the structure of the model

ξ is the set of all parameter vectors

The model structure Ω consists of the number of clusters, the partitioning of the feature set - to be explained below - and (in the case of "hard" clustering) the assignment of patterns to clusters. Parts of Ω such as the number of clusters, are usually fixed. If not, some *regularization* criterion is needed (more on this below.) The maximization of equation (1) constitutes a maximum-likelihood estimate of the model structure Ω and the parameter vector ξ, which can be accomplished using several techniques - the most popular being the EM algorithm [DEMPSTER77].

We assume that the feature space T consists of two sets U and N, where N is a set of noise features and U is a set of useful features. The feature-selection problem for clustering will thus be defined as one of identifying the optimal partition of T *for a given number of clusters*[3]. Note that there are a total of 2^M possible partitions.

Assumption 1 The feature sets represented by *U* and *N* are (conditionally) independent

$$P(D^T|\Omega, \xi) = P(D^N \mid \Omega, \xi)\, P(D^U \mid \Omega, \xi)$$

where:

D^N indicates data represented in the noise feature space

D^U indicates data represented in useful feature space

Using assumption 1 we can rewrite equation (1) as below

(2) $$(\hat{\Omega}, \hat{\xi}) = \arg\max_{\Omega,\xi}\{P(D^N \mid \Omega, \xi)\, P(D^U \mid \Omega, \xi)\}$$

Assumption 2 Data {d₁, d₂, d₃ .... d$_v$} is i.i.d (independent and identically distributed)

$$P(D^N \mid \Omega, \xi)\, P(D^U \mid \Omega, \xi) = \prod_{i=1}^{v} p(d_i^N \mid \xi^N)\, p(d_i^U \mid \xi^U_{k(i)})$$

where:

v is the number of patterns in D

ξ_k^U is the parameter vector for the cluster k. It only applies to features in U

$p(d_i^U)$ is the probability of pattern i given the parameter vector ξ_k^U based on the assumption of some distribution - also called likelihood function.

[1] The term "patterns" is used here to refer to the objects to be clustered. For example, the patterns we cluster can be documents

[2] This representation is usually a reduced representation constituting a loss of information from the complete representation.

[3] We will revisit the issue of determining the number of clusters in the next section.

$k(i)$ is the cluster to which pattern i is assigned

$p(d_i^U)$ is the probability of the pattern i given the parameter vector ξ^N

Restricting our attention to hard clustering (i.e. every data-point is a member of one and only one cluster) and using assumption 2 we can write

$$(\hat{\Omega}, \hat{\xi}) = \arg\max\left\{\prod_{i=1}^{v} p(d_i^N \mid \xi^N) \cdot p(d_i^U \mid \xi_{k(i)}^U)\right\} \quad (3)$$

Note that while the explicit dependence on Ω has been removed in this notation, it is implicit in $k(i)$ and the partition of T into N and U. Equation (3) can be rewritten as

$$(\hat{\Omega}, \hat{\xi}) = \arg\max\left\{\prod_{i=1}^{v} p(d_i^N \mid \xi^N) \cdot \prod_{k=1}^{K}\prod_{j\in D_k} p(d_j^U \mid \xi_k^U)\right\} \quad (4)$$

where: K is the number of clusters and the notation "$j \in D_k$" denotes that document j is assigned to cluster k.

Unfortunately, the objective function, represented in equation (4) is not regularized[4] and attempts to optimize it directly may result in the set N becoming empty - resulting in overfitting. To overcome this problem we use the "marginal or integrated likelihood" [BERNARDO94] whose negative logarithm is also called "stochastic complexity" [RISSANEN89].

Assumption 3. All parameter vectors are independent.

$$\pi(\xi) = \pi(\xi^N) \cdot \prod_{k=1}^{K} \pi(\xi_k^U)$$

The marginal likelihood, using assumption 3, can be written as

$$p(D^T|\Omega) = \int_{\Xi^N}\left[\prod_{i=1}^{v} p(d_i^N|\xi^N)\right]\pi(\xi^N)d\xi^N \times \prod_{k=1}^{K}\int_{\Xi^N}\left[\prod_{i\in D_k} p(d_i^U|\xi_k^U)\right]\pi(\xi_k^U)d\xi_k^U \quad (5)$$

where:

$\pi(\xi^N)$ prior distribution over the noise-feature parameters

$\pi(\xi^U)$ prior distribution over the useful-feature parameters

Ξ^N, Ξ^U integral limits appropriate to the particular parameter spaces. These will be omitted to simplify the notation

Note that for a fixed number of clusters (K), as we increase the cardinality of the set U, the model complexity increases and similarly for a fixed U the model complexity increases with increasing K. The reader is referred to [BISHOP96] for a lucid explanation of the use of marginal likelihoods for regularization.

2.2 Search Space For The Model Selection Problem

The formulation shown in equation (5) leads to a search problem that can be computationally very expensive. Consider a data-set consisting of 10,000 features where we are interested in finding between 5 and 10 clusters. Then the total number of cluster-pattern-feature partitions that we have to evaluate (in principle) is equal to $\Sigma_{j=5}^{10} v^j \times 2^{10000}$. We can avoid explicitly evaluating all the v^j pattern-to-cluster partitions by using the EM algorithm, but some heuristic is clearly required to drastically reduce the number of feature partitions. In section 3, for the particular problem of document clustering that we address, we provide heuristics that allow the pruning of this search space.

2.3 Approximations to Marginal Likelihood/Stochastic Complexity

The objective function of equation (5) is still general in the sense that functional forms for the distributions $p(d^N|\xi^N)$, $\pi(\xi^N)$, $p(d^U|\xi_k^U)$ and $\pi(\xi_k^U)$ have not been specified. In Section 3.1 we specify forms for these and use them to derive a closed-form expression for equation (5). If closed-form solutions for the integrals in equation (5) are not available, however, one can hope to optimize it directly by using computationally expensive *Markov Chain Monte Carlo* (MCMC) simulations. Fortunately, well-studied asymptotic approximations are available. A good overview of some of these approximations is available in [CHICKERING97], while the information-theoretic approximations can be understood from [RISSANEN89]. We will briefly consider the BIC approximation [SCHWARZ78] to equation (5), which is identical to the original asymptotic approximation of Minimum Description Length (MDL) [RISANNEN78, RISANNEN83][5]. Applying this approximation to equation (5) and simplifying we obtain

[4] This *lack of regularization* essentially means that since there is no penalization for more complex models, resulting in the choice of the most complex model.

[5] We take a moment to note that this speicific asymptotic analysis should not be mistaken as constituting the entire domain of MDL. For a lucid explanation of the several facets of MDL the interested reader is referred to [BARRON98

$$P(D \mid \Omega) = \sum_i \log p(d_i^N \mid \widetilde{\xi^N}) - \frac{|\xi^N|}{2} \log v + \sum_k \left(\sum_{i \in D_k} \log p(d_i^U | \widetilde{\xi_k^U}) - \frac{|\xi_k^U|}{2} \log v_k \right) \quad (6)$$

where:

$\lvert\xi^N\rvert$	number of free parameters in the "noise features"
$\lvert\xi_k^U\rvert$	number of free parameters in the "useful" features
v_k	number of patterns in the kth cluster
$\widetilde{\xi_k^U}, \widetilde{\xi^N}$	are the maximum likelihood estimates for ξ^N and ξ_k^U respectively

The BIC/MDL approximations are based on an asymptotic analysis, i.e., as $v \to \infty$. For applications such as document clustering where the number of features is large, potentially larger than the number of documents, such approximations can lead to problems.

3.0 DOCUMENT CLUSTERING

Document clustering is an important problem that was proposed more than 30 years ago [SALTON68]. Recent interest in document clustering has emerged due to the availability of large volumes of online text [CUTTING92]. Document clustering algorithms typically start by representing the document as a "bag-of-words" in a vector representation, called the vector-space model, and the clustering algorithms perform operations on these vectors. The words/tokens[6], henceforth referred to as features, in this vector-space representation can number as high as few tens of thousands or more. Each token is provided a weight in the document vector and several possible weighting schemes exist in literature [SINGHAL96]. Although feature selection in supervised text classification has been well studied we are not aware of any formal methods applied to feature selection in document clustering. Most attempts have been based on stop-word removal and simple frequency based truncations [SAHAMI98]. Other dimensionality reduction approaches involve feature extraction based on projection techniques such as LSI [DEERWESTER90]. Once the dimensionality has been reduced, the documents are then clustered into an *arbitrary* number of clusters. In most uses of document clustering this number is determined by the particular application - e.g., not more than 10 clusters can be shown on a computer screen.

3.1 Multinomial Models

Several models of text generation have been studied in literature [CHURCH95]. In the context of supervised and partially supervised learning, however, multinomial models have been particularly popular. Evidence of the success of these models is available in the literature[NIGAM98, LEWIS98]. For our present paper we too have chosen *multinomial* models for $p(d_i^U \mid \xi_k^U)$ and $p(d_i^N \mid \xi^N)$ using term counts as the feature representation. Due to this choice, another parameter indicating the probability of the N and U split is introduced into our analysis. This is equivalent to assuming a generation model where the number of noise and useful terms for each document is determined by a probability θ^S and then the terms in a document are "drawn" with a probability (θ^n or θ_k^u) that is independent of any of the other terms in the document including other instances of the same term[7].

Consider the second term in equation (5). For documents modeled using a multinomial distribution we can write

$$p(d_i^U \mid \theta_k^U) = \binom{t_i^U}{\{t_{i,u} | u \in U\}} \prod_{u \in U} (\theta_k^u)^{t_{i,u}} \quad (7)$$

where $\binom{....}{\{...\}}$ is the multinomial coefficient, $t_{i,u}$ is the number of occurrences of the feature (term) u in pattern i, t_i^U is the total number of all features (terms) in the pattern (document) and is computed as $\sum_u t_{i,u}$.

Similarly, in the first term in (5) we can substitute

as
$$p(d_i^N \mid \theta^N) = \binom{t_i^N}{\{t_{i,n} | n \in N\}} \prod_{n \in N} (\theta^n)^{t_{i,n}} \quad (8)$$

where t_i^N and $t_{i,n}$ are the corresponding counts for noise features.

The split probability is modeled as a Binomial distribution and written as below (9)

$$P(S \mid \widetilde{\theta^S}) = \binom{t^N + t^U}{t^N} (\theta^S)^{t^N} (1 - \theta^S)^{t^U}$$

where: $\binom{n}{k} = \frac{n!}{k!(n-k)!}$ Substituting equations (7), (8) and (9) into (5) and simplifying we get:

$$P(D \mid \Omega) = \binom{t^N + t^U}{t^N} \int [(\theta^S)^{t^N} (1 - \theta^S)^{t^U}] \pi(\theta^S) d\theta^S \cdot \left[\prod_{k=1}^{K} \prod_{i \in D_k} \binom{t_i^U}{\{t_{i,u} | u \in U\}} \right] \int \left[\prod_{u \in U} (\theta_k^u)^{t_{i,u}} \right] \pi(\theta_k^U) d\theta_k^U \cdot \left[\prod_{j=1}^{v} \binom{t_j^N}{\{t_{j,n} | n \in N\}} \right] \int \left[\prod_{n \in N} (\theta^n)^{t_{j,n}} \right] \pi(\theta^N) d\theta^N \quad (10)$$

---

[6] In some applications linguistically extracted higher order features such as "noun phrases" are used.

[7] Note that this is a special case of the so-called "Naive Bayes" independence assumption

note that we still need to choose a form for the prior distribution of the parameters. Since both the noise and the useful features are represented using the same functional form - multinomial - we will choose identical forms for the priors of both parameter sets. The Beta family is *conjugate* to the Binomial family [BERNARDO94] and therefore we choose the Dirichlet distribution (multiple Beta) as the form of the prior for both $\pi(\theta_k^U)$ and $\pi(\theta^N)$ [8] and the Beta distribution for $\pi(\theta^S)$. Substituting the Dirichlet and the Beta form for the prior into equation (10) and simplifying provides us with the following final form of the marginal likelihood for the entire data-set

$$P(D \mid \Omega) = \left[\frac{\Gamma(\gamma_a + \gamma_b)}{\Gamma(\gamma_a)\Gamma(\gamma_b)} \frac{\Gamma(t^N + \gamma_a)\Gamma(t^U + \gamma_b)}{\Gamma(t^U + t^N + \gamma_a + \gamma_b)} \right] \left[\frac{\Gamma(\beta)}{\Gamma(\beta + t^N)} \prod_{n \in N} \frac{\Gamma(\beta_n + t^n)}{\Gamma(\beta_n)} \right] \left[\frac{\Gamma(\sigma)}{\Gamma(\sigma + v)} \prod_{k=1}^{K} \frac{\Gamma(\sigma_k + |D_k|)}{\Gamma(|D_k|)} \right] \cdot \left[\prod_{k=1}^{K} \frac{\Gamma(\alpha)}{\Gamma(\alpha + t^{U(k)})} \prod_{u \in U} \frac{\Gamma(\alpha_u + t_k^u)}{\Gamma(\alpha_u)} \right] \quad (11)$$

where β_n and α_u are the hyper-parameters of the Dirichlet prior for noise and useful features respectively, $\beta = \sum_{n \in N} \beta_n$, $\alpha = \sum_{u \in U} \alpha_u$, $\sigma = \sum_{k=1} \sigma_k$an $\Gamma()$ is the "gamma" function. Further, γ_a, γ_b are the hyper parameters of the Beta prior for the split probability, $|D_k|$ is the number of documents in cluster k and $t^{U(k)}$ is computed as $\sum_{i \in D_k} t_i^U$.

Equation (11) contains the final form that is used in all our computations and evaluations in the remainder of the paper. The results reported for our evaluation will be Negative Log Marginal Likelihood (NLML) - which is the negative of the log of the value obtained using equation (11)[9]. One other issue that needs to be discussed is the setting of the hyper-parameter values. For the experiments we report here, a uniform Dirichlet ("uniform prior") was used - i.e. all values of β_i, α_i, γ_a and $\gamma_b$are set equal to 1. Other forms of non-informative Dirichlet priors are discussed in [CHICKERING97].

4.0 Feature Subset Selection Algorithm For Document Clustering

In the previous section we derived an objective function that can be used to evaluate feature subsets in unsupervised learning. In this and the remaining sections we will apply and evaluate this objective function to document clustering. In particular we will be concerned only with the final form derived in equation (11). As noted in Section 2.1, for a feature-set of size M there are a total of 2^M partitions. This number can be enormous for even small corpii and it would clearly be computationally infeasible to search through all possible partitions to find the optimal subset of features[10]. We therefore propose a heuristic method to obtain a subset of words/tokens that can be used as features in the bag-of-words model to cluster documents.

4.1 Content-Bearing, Function And Topical Terms

It is well accepted in both information retrieval and computational linguistics literature that words can be broadly divided into content-bearing and function words. Intuitively, we can see that a good feature subset for document clustering, should consist primarily of content-bearing terms. Our task of feature subset selection can therefore be redefined as one of identifying content-bearing terms for the corpus under consideration[11]. More importantly, our goal is to identify topical terms - i.e., terms that are indicative of the topics underlying the corpus.

Identifying content-bearing and topical terms, is an active research area and there are several published efforts addressing this topic much of it concentrating on using parametric methods to model terms - see [CHURCH95] for an overview of current approaches. For our purposes we are less concerned with modeling the exact distribution of each individual term as we are with simply identifying groups of terms that are topical. In the next section we describe a distributional clustering scheme based on a simple non-parametric density estimation algorithm, to identify such topical terms.

4.2 Distributional Clustering For Feature Subset Selection

The use of distributional clustering (DC) in text processing and computational linguistics is not new. Apparently first proposed by Pereira et al [PEREIRA93] for the purposes of clustering nouns based on their association with verbs, it has since been used for feature -selection in supervised text classification [BAKER98] and clustering images in video sequences [IYENGAR98]. For our purposes we are interested in clustering words based on their distributions over the documents. The hypothesis being that function terms, content-bearing and topical terms have different distributions over the

[8] A conjugate prior is a prior that yields a posterior that is identical to the form of the prior. Note that in our computations we do not necessarily need a conjugate form for the priorbut need a functional form that provides aclosed-form solution.

[9] Note that log of equation (11) will be a negative number and therefore NLML will be positive. Further since we are trying to maximize (11), smaller values of NLML are better.

[10] The number of clusters is assumed to be fixed.

[11] Indeed, popular frequency-based approaches can be viewed as crude attempts to identify content-bearing terms.

documents. Previous attempts at capturing these distributions have achieved reasonable success modeling individual tokens as mixtures of Poisson distributions. If we hypothesize that topical terms (terms indicative of underlying topics) follow similar distributions, then clustering terms can help in identifying groups of topical terms. In effect, distributional clustering helps reduce the search space for feature selection from 2^M to 2^C, where C is the number of clusters produced by the DC algorithm. Note that the terms in a cluster do not necessarily have any semantic relationship - they simply have similar distributions across the documents.

Instead of using computationally expensive Poisson mixtures for each token, we rely on a simple non-parametric density estimation scheme. Following the suggestions in [KATZ95], we compute the following histogram for each token. The first bin consists of the number of documents with zero occurrences of the token, the second bin is the number of documents consisting of a single occurrence of the token and the third bin is the number of documents that contain two or more occurrences of the term.

To cluster the histograms generated we need a measure of similarity. For this we use relative entropy or the K-L distance $\Delta(. \parallel .)$. For two terms (1 and 2) with probability distributions $p_1(.)$ and $p_2(.)$, this is given by [COVER91]:

$$\Delta(p_1(t) \parallel p_2(t)) \equiv \sum_t p_1(t) \log \frac{p_1(t)}{p_2(t)} \quad (12)$$

Note that this is non-symmetric with respect to p_1 and p_2

We use this in a k-means style algorithm for distributional clustering. In that procedure the histograms are normalized to sum to one and the sum in Equation (12) is taken over the three bins corresponding to counts of 0,1, and ≥ 2. The distance between two individual term distributions is never actually computed, however. Rather, during the assignment-to-clusters step of k-means we compute $\Delta(p_w \parallel p_{c_k})$ (where p_w is the normalized histogram for term w and $p_{c_k}(t)$ is the centroid of cluster k) and the term w is assigned to the cluster for which this is minimum. The reader is referred to [PEREIRA93] and [IYENGAR98] for further details on distributional clustering.

5.0 EXPERIMENTAL SETUP

To evaluate our models and algorithms we have performed extensive tests and compared them against ground truth. The corpus used for our evaluations was the AP Reuters Newswire articles from the TREC collection. A total of 8235 documents, from the routing track, existing in 25 classes were used for our experiments[12]. About 450 documents existed in multiple classes. To simplify matters we disregarded multiple assignments and retained each document as only a member of a single class. These known assignments of the documents into the 25 classes will be used as our *ground truth* against which we will compare the results of our proposed models and algorithms. This comparison will be performed using a mutual information measure which is described below. Our evaluations have two main goals:

1. Validate the models proposed in section 2
2. Compare the distributional-clustering-based feature-selection schemes described in section 4 against existing heuristics for creating the bag-of-words model. These heuristics will include:
   a. Simple stop-word and frequency based approaches [SAHAMI98].
   b. Dimensionality reduction techniques using projections, such as LSI and Random Projections

5.1 Mutual Information As An Evaluation Measure Of Clustering

As mentioned in the previous section, *we verify our algorithms and models* on a standard test collection. We propose to do this by comparing our clustering results against pre-classified text. The assignment of the documents to the different classes, in the pre-classified text, will be treated as the gold standard against which we will compare all our results. *To ensure a fair comparison we force all clustering algorithms to produce the same number of clusters.* We use exactly as many clusters as there are classes in the pre-classified text. The mutual information measure $I(G;K)$ itself can be computed as:

$$I(G;K) = \Sigma_i \Sigma_j p(G_i,K_j) \log \frac{p(G_i,K_j)}{p(G_i)p(K_j)} = H(G) - H(G|K)$$

where:

$p(G_i,K_j)$	is the joint probability of class i and cluster$j$
$p(G_i)$	is the (marginal) probability of class
$p(K_j)$	is the (marginal) probability of cluster

$H(G) = -\Sigma_i p(G_i) \log P(G_i)$ is the entropy of the *marginal class distribution* $\{P(G_i)\}$

$H(G|K) = -\Sigma_i \Sigma_j p(G_i,K_j)\, p(G_i|K_j)$ is the conditional entropy

This *mutual information (MI)* is a measure of how much information the cluster of a document contains about its class; of how useful the cluster is as a predictor of the class. In coding-theoretic terms it is the average number of bits that can be saved in encoding (compressing) the class ids if the encoder and the decoder have free access to the *cluster ids*, but only the encoder has access to the

[12] The list of these documents is available from the authors upon request.

class ids. MI, its properties and related definitions are discussed at length in [COVER91].

As far as we know, the only other formal attempt at comparing document clusters, using pre-classified, text as a gold standard, is reported in [SAHAMI98]. A fundamental difference between that effort and ours is that their evaluation was done by first labeling each of the clusters (detemined using the clustering algorithm) as one of the classes based on a majority vote for each cluster. The documents in the clusters were then assigned the label of the cluster and the percentage error between pre-labeled classes and the new classes was used as a gold standard. We prefer MI as with the scheme outlined in [SAHAMI98] it is possible for multiple clusters to be labeled as the same class. In passing we note that a scheme similar to ours was used in [BRADLEY98].

6.0 RESULTS AND DISCUSSIONS

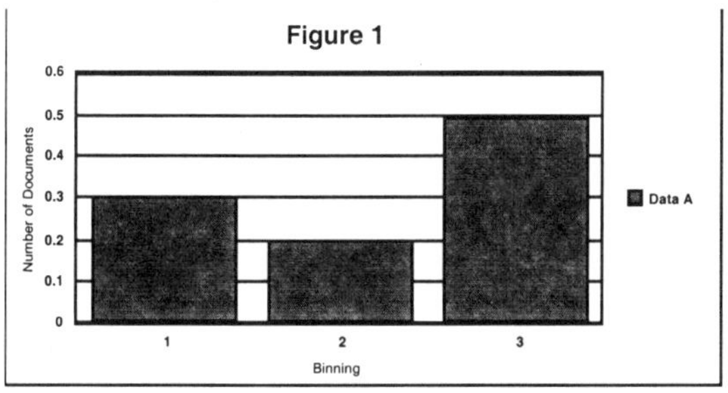

Two of the main results of our paper are an objective function (equation (5) and equation (11)) for doing model selection in clustering and a scheme (described in Section 4) for generating candidate feature sets based on distributional clustering. Appropriate combinations of these candidate feature sets were also used as feature sets. In this section we present the results of an experimental evaluation of these components, starting with distributional clustering.

6.1 Results of Distributional Clustering

After tokenizing the documents and discarding terms that appeared in less than 3 documents we were left with 32450 tokens. The results for 3 different numbers of distributional clusters (3, 4 and 5) are presented in Table 1. For each of these we chose the best of 20 runs corresponding to different random starting clusters. The reported results were best in the sense of lowest error[13] as measured by the K-L distance (equation (12)) from the cluster centroids. Each of these sets includes one cluster that consists of

high-frequency words and upon examination were found to contain primarily *function* words. These were eliminated from further consideration. Figure 1 shows the centroid of a typical high-frequency function-words cluster. The remaining non-function-word clusters were used as feature sets for the clustering algorithm. Based on the results of the individual feature sets, some of the candidate feature sets were then eliminated from further consideration. Only combinations of feature sets that produced good results were used for further document clustering runs. The results of these experiments are reported in the next section.

Number of Clusters	Number of Elements In Each Cluster
3	{273} {28671} {3506}
4	{92} {5038} {26201}{1119}
5	{53} {1725} {386}{24383} {5903}

Table 1 Results of Distributional Clustering

6.2 Finding the Optimum Features and Document Clusters for a Fixed Number of Clusters

We now apply the objective function derived in section 2 to the feature subsets selected by DC. To make use of (11) we need a clustering algorithm to partition the data-set. A popular choice in the literature for probabilistic clustering is the EM algorithm. We experimented with both the conventional EM algorithm and a hard-thresholded version of the E-M algorithm called "Classification" EM (CEM).. To initialize CEM/EM we used the k-means algorithm, a popular choice in document clustering[14]. Other techniques for initializing the CEM/EM algorithm are discussed in [MEILA98]. K-means was run using a cosine similarity measure and initialized by randomly perturbing the centroid of the entire data-set to obtain the starting cluster centroids. The feature vectors used in the k-means algorithm were generated using the pivoted normal weighting suggested in [SINGHAL96][15]. The CEM algorithm directly maximizes the likelihood. This means that the classification step in the CEM algorithm uses multinomial distributions (one per cluster) with parameter vectors $\{\theta_k^U\}$estimated using Laplace's Rule of Succession. A complete description of the EM algorithm

[13] We found that the results of the distributional clustering algorithms were remarkably stable and most of the runs converged to the same solution.

[14] Note that, at least in theory, it is possible for the k-means initialization to produce a better MI than the (k-means+EM/CEM). Since the difference in MI before and after EM is marginal, we have chosen to ignore this difference

[15] We tried several weighting schemes: simple frequency counts, tf-idf, normalized tf-idf etc. and found that the pivoted normal weighting scheme gave us the best results.

in the context of text clustering using multinomial models is provided in [NIGAM98].

Table 2 shows the results of document clustering using the feature subsets selected by the different numbers and combinations of distributional clusters. The feature subsets are coded as FSXP where X indicates the number of clusters in the distributional clustering and P indicates the combination number (explained below). For computational reasons we restricted our attention to the CEM algorithm. All results reported are averages over 3 runs of the k-means+CEM combination with different initialization for the k-means algorithm. For clarity, the MI (explained in Section 4) numbers reported are normalized such the largest theoretically possible number is 1.0, which would correspond to having perfectly captured the manually assigned categories.

Feature Set	Number of Useful Features	NLML k-means +CEM X 10^7	MI
FS31	28671	2.8770	0.4000
FS32	3506	2.7025	0.6087
FS31-2	32177	2.7110	0.6000
FS41	5038	2.7957	0.5950
FS42	26201	2.9268	0.2400
FS43	1119	2.7322	0.5925
FS41-3	6157	**2.6566**	**0.6134**
FS51	1725	2.7815	0.5882
FS52	386	2.7985	0.5147
FS53	24383	2.9534	0.0748
FS54	5903	2.8473	0.5589
FS51-2	2111	2.6836	0.5904
FS51-4	7628	2.6966	0.6010
FS52-4	6289	2.7205	0.5897
FS51-2-4	8014	2.6572	0.6073
NF	32450	2.9645	0.5787
CSW	31957	2.7216	0.5973

Table 2 Negative Log Marginal Likelihood and Mutual Information

To evaluate the performance of k-means+CEM we also ran experiments using the feature-selection heuristics available in literature. The clustering algorithm used in conjunction with these feature-selection heuristics is k-means[16]. The following are compared with distributional clustering (DC).

1. Removal of the top 20% of the most frequent terms (FBTop20).
2. Removal of the top 40% of the most frequent terms[17] (FBTop40).
3. Removal of top 40% of the most frequent terms and removal of all tokens that do not appear in at least 10 documents. (FBTop40Bot10).
4. LSI projected space. Clustering in an LSI-style subspace spanned by the first 165 singular vectors[18] was performed using a Euclidean k-means algorithm.
5. No feature selection (NF). All terms were used.
6. Common stop words removed (CSW).

Feature Set	Number of Useful Features	MI
LSI	31957 (165)	0.569
FBTop20	32,433	0.5864
FBTop40	32,417	0.5846
FBTop40Bot10	15,416	0.602
DC	6,157	0.612
NF	32,450	0.5777
CSW	31,957	0.5995

Table 3: Results of Alternative Feature Selection Schemes[19]

Experiments comparing EM and CEM were also run and only marginal differences were observed in the results.

6.3 Optimizing for the Number of Clusters

In the previous section we fixed the number of clusters at 25 and evaluated the performance of several feature subsets. Since none of our feature subsets provided us

[16] Agglomerative clustering algorithms [WILLET88] are the other variety of document clustering algorithms that are popular - but compuationally very expensive. We therefore have compared only with k-means.

[17] We used these heuristics because the numbers reported in the literature for frequency-based truncations vary dramatically.

[18] With random projections the MI obtained was very low. We are therefore investigating this no further.

[19] Note that the MI results for NF, CSW and DC are different between tables 2 and 3. This difference is due to the fact that the results reported in table 4 is the result of only k-means

with an exact match with the ground truth, we assume that we have not found the optimal feature-space for 25 clusters. To understand further the properties of equation (11) we ran experiments by fixing the feature-space and varying the number of clusters. For computational reasons we have limited our evaluation to three feature subsets that provided the highest mutual information - FS3-2, FS41-3 and FS51-2-4. The plot of NLML for different number of clusters is shown in Figure 2.

6.4 Discussion

The first striking result is the consistency between the MI and NLML shown in Figure 3. The trend is clearly visible in that as the NLML increases, MI decreases. This trend is more apparent at higher NLML indicating that bad clusterings are more easily detected by NLML while as the solution improves the differences are more subtle. The best results for the NLML and MI are printed in bold. *Note that the best value of NLML and MI co-incide*. This is a powerful result as this means that our choice of feature sub-set, based on NLML, would be that feature sub-set that gave us the best MI. Given the assumptions made in deriving equation (11) this consistency, and the final choice, is very encouraging as

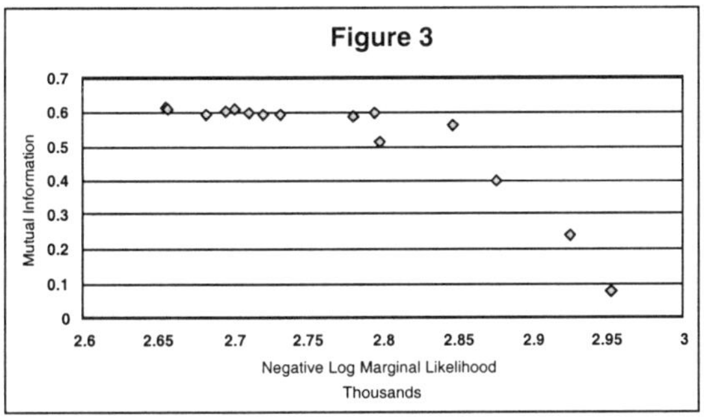

it gives us confidence in the objective function for future research and applications.

The second striking result is that, with the 6157 features corresponding to our best MI, we are able to get a performance (in comparison against the gold standard) that is better than that obtained by the complete feature-set of 32450 words and better than using 31497 words after stop-word removal. This suggests that our heuristic scheme based on distributional clustering is capable of finding reasonable feature subsets. Effectively, we have reduced our feature-set size to about 1/5 of its original size and in return gained accuracy. To understand the relationships between the feature-sets that provided us with good MI we studied the feature subsets FS32, FS41-3 and FS51-2-4. About 95% of FS32 overlaps with FS41-3 and similarly about 95% of FS41-3 overlaps with FS51-2-4. This strongly suggests that, for the corpus under consideration, a core group of features are needed for good clustering.

In Figure 3 it is pleasing to note that the form of the NLML plots, as the number of clusters increases, is in accordance with other studies of model selection in unsupervised learning - see [KONTKANEN96] and [CHICKERING96] for example. Feature set FS32 indicates a higher number of clusters (around 130) while both FS41-3 and FS51-2-4 reveal an optimal structure around 40 clusters. Also, FS51-2-4 starts increasing more steeply than FS41-3.

Our results in table 3 suggest that the feature selection scheme based on the distributional clustering is performing adequately. However, this, in our opinion, can be improved considerably. Some of the arbitrariness involving DC needs to addressed. We are working on extensions to the scheme described here.

6.5 Anecdotal Evidence

Our final analysis of the results involved examining the individual clusters and understanding the results obtained - i.e., look at the individual clusters for both anomalies and consistencies. For clarity, we are reporting analysis only for the clusters obtained using feature subset FS41-3[20]. We first identified those classes that were clearly recognized by the clustering. To be considered as identified, a class must have at least 70% of its documents in a single cluster. 12 classes were marked as identified[21]. Besides these 12 classes, 7 other classes that has more than 50% of their documents in a single cluster and the remaining documents peppered among different clusters. None of the other clusters had any significant portion of these 7 classes. For lack of space we do not report detailed results. The reader is referred to [VAITHYANATHAN99] for more information. The documents in the 6 remaining classes had significant percentages in different clusters and this is of interest. An example of such a class is "Antitrust Cases Pending". We found that the documents of this class were clustered along with documents from "Acquisitons" and "Patent Infringement Lawsuits". Similarly, about 20% of the documents from "Legal Repercussions of Agrochemical Use" were clustered along with "Patent Infringement Lawsuits" while about 22% of the documents from the class "Marketing of Agrochemicals" was clustered along with "Measures to Control Agrochemicals".

It is reassuring to note that even though our clustering did not recover the exact structure of the expert judged classes - the ovelaps and the results suggest that the overall clustering is qualitatively acceptable. A point to remember here is that we have, in restricting ourselves to hard clustering, limited every document to be a member of a single cluster. Using the soft version of EM, some of these overlaps should be recoverable and this is an area

---

[20] In general we noticed that all subsets that gave us high MI/NLML values behave approximately the same.

[21] A complete listing of all the classes is available from http://nist.trec.gov

of further investigation. Further, we are presently analyzing the relationships between the structure discovered by the *optimal number of clusters* and that of the expert judged classes and these results will be reported in a subsequent paper. Finally, it should be pointed out that the manual labeling does not necessarily capture the optimal structure of the document collection, but rather the labeler's opinion about what it should be. This will also be assessed in a subsequent paper.

7.0 CONCLUSIONS AND FUTURE WORK

In this paper we have attacked the problem of model structure determination in clustering. The main contribution of the paper is an objective function (based on a Bayesian estimation scheme) that treats optimal model selection as choosing both the number of clusters *and* the feature subset. An important and novel aspect of our development of this objective function is a formal notion that forms a basis for doing feature selection in unsupervised learning. We then derive a closed-form solution of this objective function for the document clustering problem by making assumptions about the generation model. In order to make feasible the optimization problem associated with this objective function, we introduce a distributional-clustering heuristic for identifying good candidate feature subsets. Both the objective function and the feature selection scheme have been tested on real data. The main conclusions from the experiments are:

1. There is a high consistency between our objective function and good clusterings of documents for the real data we have examined.
2. Our heuristic distributional clustering scheme, proposed in Section 3, does a reasonable job of identifying good feature subsets.
3. For the document clustering problem we addressed, the number of features required to cluster the documents is much smaller than the total number of features, at least for the data set we studied.
4. From our experiments we conclude that the difference between the hard-thresholded version of the EM algorithm and the soft version is very minor - at least for the very high-dimensional sparse data encountered in document clustering.

The work presented here has suggested several lines of investigation, which we plan to pursue. We would like to apply the objective function proposed in equation (5) to various other problems - especially applications involving continuous distributions (for which applications already exist in literature as evidenced by the work in [DY99]). Further, there is also a need for more powerful search algorithms that can efficiently search this space of feature-cluster combinations.

From a document clustering perspective we intend to thoroughly investigate the performance of our models on other data sets - including several noisy ones - on the web for example. Second, our assumptions in deriving equation (11) notwithstanding, the complete feature space we used may be insufficient for the clustering we attempt. An important area for future study, therefore, is the inclusion of higher order features such as phrases. Another obvious area for further study is the development and use of other feature selection and extraction algorithms. More importantly, these need to be studied from the point of view of not just document clustering, but generating a topic hierarchy. From a machine learning standpoint it would be interesting to evaluate other functional forms for the likelihood function and the priors, including varying the values of the hyper parameters of the Dirchilet prior we used.

8.0 References

[BAKER98] Baker, D., McCallum, A., Distributional Clustering of Words for Text Classification, SIGIR 1998.

[BARRON98]Barron, A.; Rissanen, J.; Bin, Yu,The minimum description length principle in coding and modeling, IEEE Transactions on Information Theory, 44(6), Oct, 1998, pp. 2743-2760

[BERNARDO94] Bernardo, J. M. and Smith, A. F. M., Bayesian Theory, Wiley, 1994.

[BISHOP96] Bishop, C. M., Neural Networks For Pattern Recognition, Oxford University Press, 1996.

[BRADLEY98] Bradley, P., Fayyad, U.,Reina, C., Scaling Clustering Algorithms to Large Databases, KDD, 1998.

[CHICKERING97] Chickering, D. M. and Heckerman, D., Efficient Approximations for the Marginal Likelihood of Bayesian Networks with Hidden Variables, Microsoft Research Technical Report, MSR-TR-96-08, 1997.

[CHURCH95] Church, K.W., and Gale, W.A., Poisson Mixtures, Natural Language Engineering, 12,163-190, 1995.

[COVER91] Cover, T.M. and Thomas, J.A. Elements of Information Theory. Wiley-Interscience. 1991.

[CUTTING92] Cutting, D. R., D. R. Karger, J. O. Pedersen and J. W. Tukey., Scatter/Gather: A Cluster-based Approach to Browsing Large Document Collections, SIGIR, 1992.

[DEERWESTER90] Deerwester, S.; Dumais, S. T., Furnas, G.W., Indexing by Latent Semantic Analysis, JASIS, 1990.

[DUDA73] Duda, R and Hart, P., Pattern Classification and Scene Analysis. Wiley, New York, 1973.

[DEMPSTER77] Dempster, A., Laird, N. and Rubin, D., Maximum Likelihood from Incomplete Data Via the

(EM) Algorithm, Journal Of The Royal Statistical Society, 39, pp 1-38, 1977.

[DEVANEY97] Devaney, M., Ram, A., Efficient Feature Selection in Conceptual Clustering, ICML, 1997.

[DY99] Dy, J.G., et al, SPIE Storage and Retrieval for Image and Video Databases VII, 1999.

[FELDMAN95] Feldman, R., Dagan, I., Knowledge Discovery in Textual Databases (KDT). KDD, 1995.

[IYENGAR98] Iyengar, G., Clustering images using relative entropy for efficient retrieval, VLDB, 1998.

[JAIN88] Jain, A.K. and Dubes, R.C. Algorithms for clustering data. Prentice-Hall, New Jersey, 1988.

[KATZ96] Katz, S.M. , Distribution of content words and phrases in text and language modeling, Natural Language Engineering, 2-1, pp15-60, 1996.

[KONTKANEN96] Kontkanen, P.T., Myllymaki, P.J., and Tirri, H.R., Comparing Bayesian Model Class Selection Criteria by Discrete Finite Mixtures, Proceedings of the ISIS'96 Conference, 367-374, 1996.

[LEWIS98] Lewis, D.D., Naive (Bayes) at Forty: The Independence Assumption in Information Retrieval, ECML, 1998.

[MEILA98] Meila, M., Heckerman, D., An Experimental Comparison of Several Clustering and Initialization Methods, Microsoft Research Technical Report, MSR-TR-98-06.

[NIGAM98] Nigam, K., McCallum, A., Thrun, S. and Mitchell, T., Learning to Classify Text from Labeled and Unlabeled Documents, AAAI, 1998.

[PEREIRA93] Pereira, F.C.N., Tishby, Z.N., and Lee, L., Distributional clustering of English words, ACL, 1993.

[RISSANEN78] Rissanen, J., Modelling by shortest data description, Automatica, 14, pp.465-471,1978

[RISSANEN83] Rissanen, J., A Universal Prior for Integers and Estimation by Minimum Description Length, The Annals of Statistics,2(11),pp.211-222, 1983

[RISSANEN89] Rissanen, J., Stochastic Complexity in Statistical Inquiry. World Scientific, 1989.

[RISSANEN92] Rissanen, J., Ristad E., Unsupervised classification with stochastic complexity. The US/Japan Conference on the Frontiers of Statistical Modeling,1992.

[SAHAMI98] Sahami, M., Yusufali, S., and Baldonado, M. Q. W., SONIA: A Service for Organizing Networked Information Autonomously. Digital Libraries, 1998.

[SALTON68] Salton, G. Automatic Information Organization and Retrieval, McGraw-Hill, New York, 1968.

[SCHWARZ78] Schwarz, G., Estimating the Dimension of A Model, Annals of Statistics, 6, pp 461-464, 1978.

[SINGHAL96] Singhal A., Buckley C., Mitra M., Pivoted Document Length Normalization, SIGIR, 1996.

[SMYTH96] Smyth, P., Clustering using Monte Carlo cross-validation, Knowledge Discovery in Databases, 1996.

[VAITHYANATHAN99] Vaithyanathan, S. and Dom, B. Model Selection in Unsupervised Learning with Applications to Document Clustering. IBM Research Report RJ-10137 (95012) Dec. 14, 1999.

[WILLET88] Willet, P Recent Trends in Hierarchical Document Clustering: A Critical Review, Information Processing Management, 1988.

Machine-Learning Applications of Algorithmic Randomness

Volodya Vovk, Alex Gammerman, Craig Saunders
Computer Learning Research Centre and Department of Computer Science
Royal Holloway, University of London, Egham, Surrey TW20 0EX, England
{vovk,alex,craig}@dcs.rhbnc.ac.uk

Abstract

Most machine learning algorithms share the following drawback: they only output bare predictions but not the confidence in those predictions. In the 1960s algorithmic information theory supplied universal measures of confidence but these are, unfortunately, non-computable. In this paper we combine the ideas of algorithmic information theory with the theory of Support Vector machines to obtain practicable approximations to universal measures of confidence. We show that in some standard problems of pattern recognition our approximations work well.

1 INTRODUCTION

Two important differences of most modern methods of machine learning (such as statistical learning theory, see Vapnik [21], 1998, or PAC theory) from classical statistical methods are that:

- machine learning methods produce bare predictions, without estimating confidence in those predictions (unlike, eg, prediction of future observations in traditional statistics (Guttman [5], 1970));
- many machine learning methods are designed to work (and their performance is analysed) under the general iid assumption (unlike the classical parametric statistics) and they are able to deal with extremely high-dimensional hypothesis spaces; cf Vapnik [21] (1998).

In this paper we will further develop the approach of Gammerman et al [4] (1998) and Saunders et al [17] (1999), where the goal is to obtain confidences for predictions under the general iid assumption in high-dimensional situations. Figure 1 demonstrates the desirability of confidences. The main contribution of this paper is embedding the approaches of Gammerman et al [4] (1998) and Saunders et al [17] (1999) into a general scheme based on the notion of algorithmic randomness.

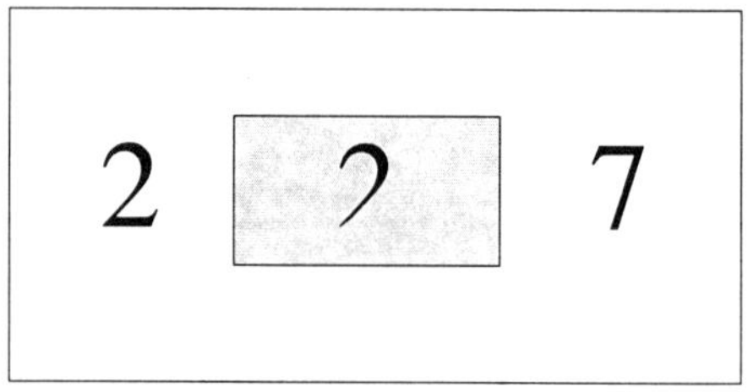

Figure 1: If the training set only contains clear 2s and 7s, we would like to attach much lower confidence to the middle image than to the right and left ones

As will become clear later, the problem of assigning confidences to predictions is closely connected to the problem of defining random sequences. The latter problem was solved by Kolmogorov [8] (1965), who based his definition on the existence of the Universal Turing Machine (though it became clear that Kolmogorov's definition does solve the problem of defining random sequences only after Martin-Löf's paper [15], 1966); Kolmogorov's definition moved the notion of randomness from the grey area surrounding probability theory and statistics to mathematical computer science.

Kolmogorov believed his notion of randomness to be a suitable basis for *applications* of probability. Unfortunately, the fate of this idea was different from Kolmogorov's 1933 axioms (Kolmogorov [7], 1933), which are universally accepted as the basis for the *theory* of probability. The algorithmic notion of randomness has mainly remained of a purely mathematical interest and has not become the leading paradigm in statistics or machine learning. Some of the reasons why this happened are:

- algorithmic measures of randomness are non-computable;
- little work has been done on computable approximations to Kolmogorov's randomness (one of the exceptions is Longpré [14], 1992);
- the algorithmic theory of randomness has been mainly concerned with the case of binary sequences, which is far too restrictive for any practical applications.

Remark 1 It is interesting that the situation with the notion of Kolmogorov complexity is somewhat different, despite the fact that the notions of Kolmogorov complexity and randomness are extremely closely connected[1]: despite being non-computable, Kolmogorov complexity inspired the MDL and MML principles [16, 26] (and their generalization, Complexity Approximation Principle [24]), which have many practical applications. (It should be noted, however, that algorithmic randomness has been used in the discussions of the MDL principle; see Li and Vitanyi [13], 1997, and [12], 1995.)

The main advantage of Kolmogorov's notion of randomness in comparison with the earlier definitions (eg, von Mises's) is that it is applicable to finite sequences and that it provides degrees of randomness; this is its crucial feature which makes practical applications possible. Later Kolmogorov's definition was developed by, among others, Martin-Löf [15] (1966), Levin [11] (1973) and Gács [2] (1980).

The main goal of this paper is to study computable approximations to algorithmic randomness and to apply those approximations to some benchmark datasets. The main technical tool will be Vapnik's [21] (1998) theory of Support Vector machines, but in principle it is possible to find useful approximations based on other techniques, such as ridge regression (see, eg, Saunders et al [18], 1998). The approach of the algorithmic theory of randomness, as presented in this paper, provides a unified view of the results in Gammerman et al [4] (1998) and Saunders et al [17] (1999).

For excellent reviews of algorithmic information theory, see V'yugin [25] (1994) and Li and Vitanyi [13] (1997).

2 ALGORITHMIC THEORY OF RANDOMNESS

Typically we will be interested in randomness of a sequence $z = (z_1, \ldots, z_n)$ of elements $z_i \in Z$ of some *sample space* Z. (In the traditional algorithmic information theory $z_i \in \{0, 1\}$; in our typical applications z is a sequence

$$(x_1, y_1), \ldots, (x_l, y_l), (x_{l+1}, y_{l+1}), \ldots, (x_{l+k}, y_{l+k})$$

containing the training classified examples and the test examples with their provisional classifications; l is the number of training examples and k is the number of test examples.) We will assume that Z is equipped with some computability structure which allows us to speak of, say, computable functions on Z (but we do not assume that Z is, say, discrete).

We will consider two kinds of randomness deficiency, which we call Martin-Löf deficiency (this is a universal version of the standard statistical notion of p-values) and Levin deficiency (which is close to being a universal version of Bayes factors). Let $\mathcal{P} = \mathcal{P}_1, \mathcal{P}_2, \ldots$ be a sequence of statistical models such that, for every $n = 1, 2, \ldots$, $\mathcal{P}_n$ is a set of probability distributions in Z^n. In this paper we will only be interested in specific $\mathcal{P}$ (namely, the iid models and exchangeability models) which are computable, and our definitions of randomness deficiency will only make intuitive sense for computable $\mathcal{P}$.

We say that a function $t : Z^* \to \overline{\mathbb{N}}$ (where $\overline{\mathbb{N}}$ is the set $\mathbb{N} = \{0, 1, \ldots\}$ of nonnegative integers extended by adding the infinity ∞) is a *Martin-Löf test for $\mathcal{P}$-randomness* if

1. for all $n \in \mathbb{N}$ and $m \in \mathbb{N}$ and all $P \in \mathcal{P}_n$,
$$P\{z \in Z^n : t(z) \geq m\} \leq 2^{-m};$$
2. t is semicomputable from below, in the sense that there exists a computable sequence of computable functions $t_i : Z^* \to \mathbb{N}$, $i = 1, 2, \ldots$, such that $t(z) = \sup_i t_i(z)$ for all $z \in Z^*$.

Intuitively, a test for randomness is a device for finding unusual features in the data $z \in Z^n$. Item 1 says that

[1] For example, one of the definitions of randomness deficiency of a finite binary sequence is the length of this sequence minus its Kolmogorov complexity.

the amount of unusual features is measured in bits (and every extra bit halves the amount of sequences exhibiting the unusual features); item 2 says that the device should be implementable on a computer (we are interested in universal tests for randomness, which find **all** unusual features in our data; therefore, our tests for randomness are allowed to work forever, all the time finding new regularities in the data; technically, they are only required to be semicomputable from below rather than computable).

A useful modification of the previous definition is where item 1 is strengthened as follows. We say that a function $t : Z^* \to \overline{\mathbb{Z}}$ (where $\overline{\mathbb{Z}}$ is the set of all integers $\mathbb{Z}$ extended by adding the infinity ∞) is a *Levin test for $\mathcal{P}$-randomness* if

1. for all $n \in \mathbb{N}$ and all $P \in \mathcal{P}_n$,

$$\int_{Z^n} 2^{t(z)} P(dz) \leq 1;$$

2. t is semicomputable from below.

(To see that item 1 of this definition implies item 1 of the previous definition, apply Markov's inequality.)

We will say that a Martin-Löf test for $\mathcal{P}$-randomness T is *universal* if it is largest to within an additive constant, in the sense that for any other Martin-Löf test for $\mathcal{P}$-randomness t there exists a constant C such that, for all $z \in Z^*$, $T(z) \geq t(z) - C$. Analogously, a largest to within an additive constant Levin test for $\mathcal{P}$-randomness will also be called *universal.*

Lemma 1 (Kolmogorov, Martin-Löf, Levin) *If $\mathcal{P}$ is computable, there exist a universal Martin-Löf test for $\mathcal{P}$-randomness and a universal Levin test for $\mathcal{P}$-randomness.*

For every computable $\mathcal{P}$ we will fix some universal Martin-Löf test for $\mathcal{P}$-randomness $d_{\mathcal{P}}^{\mathrm{ML}}$ and some universal Levin test for $\mathcal{P}$-randomness $d_{\mathcal{P}}^{\mathrm{L}}$; the value $d_{\mathcal{P}}^{\mathrm{ML}}(z)$ will be called the *Martin-Löf $\mathcal{P}$-randomness deficiency* of z and the value $d_{\mathcal{P}}^{\mathrm{L}}(z)$ will be called the *Levin $\mathcal{P}$-randomness deficiency* of z.

The standard notions of the algorithmic theory of randomness use the "logarithmic scale" (in which randomness deficiency is defined to within an additive constant). In applications, it is often more convenient to use the "direct scale". Now we will reformulate some of the previous definitions in the "direct scale".

We say that a function $t : Z^* \to [0, 1]$ is a *p-value function wr to $\mathcal{P}$* if

1. for all $n \in \mathbb{N}$, all $r \in [0, 1]$ and all $P \in \mathcal{P}_n$,

$$P\{z \in Z^n : t(z) \leq r\} \leq r;$$

2. t is semicomputable from above, in the sense that there exists a computable sequence of computable functions $t_i : Z^* \to [0, 1]$, $i = 1, 2, \ldots$, such that $t(z) = \inf_i t_i(z)$ for all $z \in Z^*$.

This definition is practically equivalent to the standard statistical notion: in practice, item 2 is completely irrelevant, since the p-value functions of any interest in applications of statistics are always computable.

Notice that:

- if t is a Martin-Löf test for $\mathcal{P}$-randomness, 2^{-t} is a p-value function wr to $\mathcal{P}$;
- if t is a p-value function wr to $\mathcal{P}$, $\lfloor -\log t \rfloor$ (in this paper, log always stands for the base 2 logarithm) is a Martin-Löf test for $\mathcal{P}$-randomness.

We will call the function $2^{-d_{\mathcal{P}}^{\mathrm{ML}}}$ the *Martin-Löf $\mathcal{P}$-randomness level*; this function is a smallest, to within a constant factor, p-value function wr to $\mathcal{P}$.

We say that a function $t : Z^* \to [0, \infty]$ is a *$\mathcal{P}$-lottery* if

1. for all $n \in \mathbb{N}$ and all $P \in \mathcal{P}_n$,

$$\int_{Z^n} t(z) P(dz) \leq 1;$$

2. t is semicomputable from below.

The connection with the notion of Levin test of $\mathcal{P}$-randomness is obvious. We will call the function $2^{-d_{\mathcal{P}}^{\mathrm{L}}}$ the *Levin $\mathcal{P}$-randomness level*; the inverse $2^{d_{\mathcal{P}}^{\mathrm{L}}}$ of this function is a largest, to within a constant factor, $\mathcal{P}$-lottery.

Remark 2 The difference between Martin-Löf and Levin randomness levels is analogous to the difference between Bayes factors and p-values. The latter is discussed in, eg, Schervish [19] (Section 4.6.2) and Vovk [23]. It is always possible (though not advisable in practice) to use Levin randomness level as Martin-Löf randomness level.

Since randomness deficiencies are defined to within an additive constant and randomness levels are defined to within a constant factor, the following notation will turn out to be very useful: $=^+$, $\leq^+$ and $\geq^+$ stand for the equality and inequalities to within an additive constant; $=^\times$, $\leq^\times$ and $\geq^\times$ stand for the equality and inequalities to within a constant factor.

It turns out that Levin and Martin-Löf deficiencies are closely connected (cf the relation between plain and prefix complexity (3.4) in Li and Vitanyi [13], 1997):

Theorem 1 *For any computable $\mathcal{P}$ and z ranging over Z^*,*

$$d_{\mathcal{P}}^{\mathrm{ML}}(z) =^+ d_{\mathcal{P}}^{\mathrm{L}}(z \mid d_{\mathcal{P}}^{\mathrm{ML}}(z)).$$

(This theorem involves "conditional" variants of randomness deficiency; such variants are defined in a natural way.) This immediately implies

Corollary 1 *Levin and Martin-Löf randomness deficiency coincide to within* log.

Remark 3 Our definition of randomness is not the only possible: we can define "uniform randomness deficiency" and define, eg, the iid deficiency as the minimum of the deficiencies over all iid measures. The difference is not big when the sample space Z is compact; this follows from the following elaboration of Levin's [11] (1973) result: for any compact class $\mathcal{P}$ of probability measures,

$$d_{\mathcal{P}}^{\mathrm{L}}(x) =^+ \inf_{P \in \mathcal{P}} d_P^{\mathrm{L}}(x) \qquad (1)$$

and

$$d_{\mathcal{P}}^{\mathrm{ML}}(x) =^+ \inf_{P \in \mathcal{P}} d_P^{\mathrm{ML}}(x). \qquad (2)$$

However, in applications $\mathcal{P}$ is often not compact (although it is always "constructively closed"). It is an important problem to study whether (1) and (2) hold true for the iid distributions; intuitively, we would expect that a sequence is iid random if and only if it is random wr to some iid distribution.

3 THE IDEAL PREDICTION IN THE IID CASE

In this paper we will be mostly interested in $\mathcal{P} = (\mathcal{P}_1, \mathcal{P}_2, \ldots)$ for which $\mathcal{P}_n$ is the set of all distributions P^n, P ranging over all probability distributions in Z. This $\mathcal{P}$ will be called the *iid model* and $\mathcal{P}$-randomness deficiency will be called *iid deficiency* and denoted d_{iid} (with upper index ML or L). From this point on we will be mainly interested in the iid deficiency and we will also use the less awkward expression "randomness deficiency" in place of "iid deficiency" (retaining the lower index "iid" in d_{iid}). This terminology agrees with that accepted in nonparametric statistics (see, eg, Fraser [1], 1957).

Remark 4 An important alternative to the iid model is the stationarity model. In this paper, however, we will restrict our attention to the iid assumption, which is more widely used in machine learning.

Suppose for a minute that the randomness deficiency (either Martin-Löf or Levin) is computable. Then our prediction problem will become trivial (if we accept the iid assumption and ignore computation time). Assuming we have training set $(x_1, y_1), \ldots, (x_l, y_l)$ and test set $x_{l+1}, \ldots, x_{l+k}$ and our goal is to predict the classifications $y_{l+1}, \ldots, y_{l+k}$ for $x_{l+1}, \ldots, x_{l+k}$, we can act as follows:

1. Consider all possible values $Y_1, \ldots, Y_k$ for labels $y_{l+1}, \ldots, y_{l+k}$ and compute (in practice, approximate from above) the randomness level of every possible completion

$$(x_1, y_1), \ldots, (x_l, y_l), (x_{l+1}, Y_1), \ldots, (x_{l+k}, Y_k).$$

2. Predict the set $Y_1, \ldots, Y_k$ corresponding to the completion with the largest randomness level.
3. Output as the *confidence* in this prediction one minus the second largest randomness level.
4. Output as the *credibility* the randomness level of the output prediction $Y_1, \ldots, Y_k$ (ie, the largest randomness level for all possible predictions).

To understand the intuition behind confidence, let us tentatively choose a conventional "significance level" such as 1%. If the confidence in our prediction exceeds 99% and the prediction is wrong, the actual data sequence belongs to an *a priori* chosen set of probability less than 1% (namely, the set of all data sequences with randomness level less than 1%).

Intuitively, low credibility means that either the training set is non-random or the test examples are not representative of the training set (say, in the training set we have images of digits and in the test set we have those of letters).

Remark 5 A common belief in algorithmic information theory is that terms of order $O(\log n)$ are not important in inequalities between complexities or randomness deficiencies for sequences of length n. It is interesting that, under our approach to prediction under the iid assumption, randomness deficiency of the order of magnitude $\log n$ becomes the best we can realistically hope for in the problem of pattern recognition with one unclassified example. Indeed, suppose we have a training set

$$(x_1, y_1), \ldots, (x_l, y_l), \quad y_i \in \{-1, 1\}$$

and a new unclassified example x_{l+1}; we want to predict the label $y_{l+1} \in \{-1, 1\}$ of x_{l+1}. **Claim:** *If the true sample*

$$(x_1, y_1), \ldots, (x_l, y_l), (x_{l+1}, y_{l+1})$$

is random, the maximum randomness deficiency of the wrong sample

$$(x_1, y_1), \ldots, (x_l, y_l), (x_{l+1}, -y_{l+1})$$

is $\log(l+1)$ *(as usual, up to an additive constant).* To see why this is true, notice that if the true sample is random with respect to some iid distribution P^n, the wrong sample will have randomness deficiency at most $\log(l+1)$ wr to P^n corrupted by changing the label of every example with probability $1/(l+1)$. It is easy to see that this upper bound, $\log(l+1)$, is precise: if there is a very simple algorithm for finding y_i from x_i, the last example will be the "strangest" one in the wrong sample, and so the randomness deficiency of the wrong sample will jump to $\log(l+1)$.

4 PERMUTATION DEFICIENCY

In this section we consider a fundamental lower bound on randomness deficiency, which we call permutation deficiency. In practice we will only be able to find a lower bound on the randomness deficiency of some sequence z by first finding a lower bound L on the permutation deficiency of z and then using L as a lower bound on the randomness deficiency of z. We will see that the difference between permutation deficiency and randomness deficiency can be quite big, and it remains an open problem whether one can find easily computable and natural lower bounds for randomness deficiency that are not simultaneously lower bounds for permutation deficiency.

First we will define the exchangeability model (which is very popular in the foundations of Bayesian statistics; see, eg, Schervish [19], 1995). We say that a measure P on a product set Z^n is *exchangeable* if the distribution of the vector $z_1 \ldots z_n$ under P equals the distribution of the vector $z_{\pi(1)} \ldots z_{\pi(z)}$ for any permutation π on the set $\{1, \ldots, n\}$ (here $z_1, \ldots, z_n$ are the coordinate random variables). The *exchangeability model* is defined to be the sequence $\mathcal{P}_1, \mathcal{P}_2, \ldots$ of the following statistical models: every $\mathcal{P}_n$ is the set of all exchangeable distributions on Z^n. The $\mathcal{P}$-randomness deficiency, where $\mathcal{P}$ is the exchangeability model, will be called the *permutation deficiency.* The following theorem will give a more explicit representation of permutation deficiency, but before we can state it we will need several definitions. A *bag* is a set to each element of which is assigned a nonnegative integer called its *arity* (intuitively, how many times this element occurs in the bag). The *size* $|b|$ of a bag b is the sum of the arities of its elements. The *configuration* of a sequence $z = z_1 \ldots z_n$ is the bag which consists of all distinct elements in z, the arity of each element being the number of times it occurs in the sequence. For any sequence z, $\mathrm{conf}(z)$ stands for the configuration of z and $\Xi(z)$ stands for the set of all sequences of the same length and with the same configuration as z. If K is prefix complexity and C is plain Kolmogorov complexity (see Li and Vitanyi [13], 1997), the Martin-Löf and Levin deficiency of randomness of an element z of a set A can be defined as

$$d_A^{\mathrm{ML}}(z) = \log|A| - C(z \mid A), \; d_A^{\mathrm{L}}(z) = \log|A| - K(z \mid A),$$

respectively.

Theorem 2 *If z ranges over Z^*, $d_{\mathrm{exch}}^{\mathrm{ML}}(z) =^+ d_{\Xi(z)}^{\mathrm{ML}}(z)$ and $d_{\mathrm{exch}}^{\mathrm{L}}(z) =^+ d_{\Xi(z)}^{\mathrm{L}}(z)$.*

This theorem shows that Kolmogorov's [9] (1968) "Bernoulli sequences" are exactly the sequences with a small permutation deficiency in the binary case.

To establish a relation between randomness deficiency and permutation deficiency we will use the notion of randomness deficiency of a bag. Let $\mathcal{P}$ be the iid model. We will say that a test for $\mathcal{P}$-randomness (either Martin-Löf or Levin) is *bag-invariant* if it takes the same value for any two sequences with the same configuration. There exists a universal bag-invariant test which will be called *randomness deficiency* (for bags) and denoted $d_{\mathrm{iid}}(\mathrm{conf}(z))$ with a suitable upper index.

The following theorem generalizes Theorem 1 in Vovk [22] (1986):

Theorem 3 *The randomness deficiency of a sequence equals the sum of its permutation deficiency and the randomness deficiency of its configuration:*

$$d_{\mathrm{iid}}^{\mathrm{L}}(z) =^+ d_{\mathrm{iid}}^{\mathrm{L}}(\mathrm{conf}(z)) + d_{\mathrm{exch}}^{\mathrm{L}}\left(z \mid d_{\mathrm{iid}}^{\mathrm{L}}(\mathrm{conf}(z))\right).$$

Theorem 2 in Vovk [22] (1986) gives a simple characterization of Levin randomness deficiency for bags in terms of prefix complexity in the binary case. That result shows that in the binary case the randomness deficiency of bags of size n is at most $\log n$. Unfortunately, in the case of infinite sample space the randomness deficiency of bags of size n can be as large as n:

Theorem 4 *If the sample space is constructively infinite (meaning that it contains an infinite computable sequence of distinct elements),*

$$\sup_{|b|=n} d_{\mathrm{iid}}^{\mathrm{ML}}(b) \geq^{+} \sup_{|b|=n} d_{\mathrm{iid}}^{\mathrm{L}}(b) \geq^{+} n \log e - \frac{1}{2} \log n,$$

where n ranges over the positive integers and b ranges over the bags.

Remark 6 Kolmogorov ([9], 1968) believed that, in the binary case, Bernoulli sequences should be defined as sequences with small permutation deficiency rather than sequences with small randomness deficiency. Note [22] (Vovk, 1986) was written in an attempt to understand the difference between Kolmogorov's definition and the definition accepted in this paper. The main result of [22] is that, in the binary case, these two definitions are close but different.

Remark 7 In the case of infinite sequences, de Finetti's theorem (see, eg, Schervish [19], 1995) says that the two models of iid and exchangeability are equivalent; therefore, for the infinite sequences, $d_{\mathrm{iid}} =^{+} d_{\mathrm{exch}}$. There are finite variants of de Finetti's theorem (see, eg, Schervish [19], 1995, Theorem 1.70 due to Diaconis and Freedman); similarly to the results of Vovk [22] (1986) (but contrary to Theorems 3 and 4 above) they say that the iid and exchangeability models are close.

5 PRACTICABLE APPROXIMATIONS

Let us concentrate on the problem of pattern recognition, in which the set Y of possible labels is $\{-1, 1\}$, and the case where $k = 1$ (there is only one test example). Following Vapnik [21] (1998), we consider the quadratic optimization problem

$$\Phi(w, \xi) = \frac{1}{2}(w \cdot w) + C \left(\sum_{i=1}^{l+1} \xi_i \right) \to \min \qquad (3)$$

$$\left(w \in H,\ \xi = (\xi_1, \ldots, \xi_{l+1}) \in \mathbb{R}^{l+1}\right),$$

where C is an *a priori* fixed positive constant, subject to the constraints

$$y_i \left((w \cdot F(x_i)) + b \right) \geq 1 - \xi_i, \quad i = 1, \ldots, l+1, \qquad (4)$$

$$\xi_i \geq 0, \quad i = 1, \ldots, l+1, \qquad (5)$$

where F is some (typically non-linear) transformation applied to the data and taking values in a Hilbert space H.

Using Lagrange multipliers α_i corresponding to constraints (4) we can approximate from below both d^{ML} and d^{L}. The latter was done in Gammerman et al [4] (1998) and the former was done in the recent paper Saunders et al [17] (1999). The approach of Gammerman et al [4] (1998) suffered from the "distortion phenomenon" (see Subsection 8.2 of that paper); the solution suggested (implicitly) in [4] was to use the function

$$p(z_1, \ldots, z_{l+1}) = \frac{f(\alpha_1) + \cdots + f(\alpha_{l+1})}{f(\alpha_{l+1})(l+1)}, \qquad (6)$$

where f is some monotonic non-decreasing function with $f(0) = 0$, as an upper bound for the Levin permutation level. The specific function $f(\alpha)$ suggested in Gammerman et al [4] (1998) was $f(\alpha) = \operatorname{sign} \alpha$ (that is, $f(0) = 0$ and $f(\alpha) = 1$ when $\alpha > 0$). The results reported in [4] correspond to using the SV method for prediction and using function (6) for estimating confidence and credibility. Those results are reproduced here as Figure 2. In that figure (and in the figures below) it is easy to identify two clusters; one of the clusters contains those examples which are support vectors in both "pictures" (in the terminology of Gammerman et al [4]; in other words, which are support vectors and remain support vectors when the classification of the last example is changed), and the other cluster contains those examples which are support vectors in only one "picture".

Those experiments and all experiments described in this paper are done for a simple pattern recognition problem of identifying handwritten digits using a database of US postal data of 9300 digits, where each digit is a 16×16 vector (cf LeCun et al [10], 1990). The experiments are conducted for a subset of these data (a training set of 400 examples and 100 test sets of 1 example each), and include a construction of two-class classifier to separate digit "2" from digit "7". The constant C in (3) was set to ∞ (we felt that this way we would obtain good approximations to randomness deficiency); therefore, we actually solved the quadratic optimization problem

$$\frac{1}{2}(w \cdot w) \to \min \quad \left(w \in H,\ \xi = (\xi_1, \ldots, \xi_{l+1}) \in \mathbb{R}^{l+1}\right),$$

subject to the constraints

$$y_i \left((w \cdot F(x_i)) + b \right) \geq 1, \quad i = 1, \ldots, l+1. \qquad (7)$$

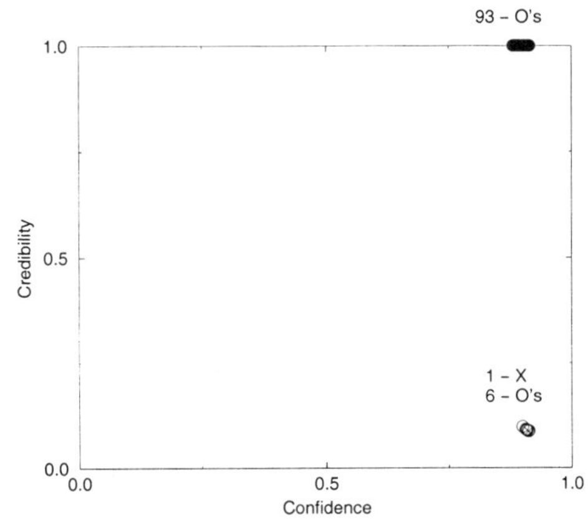

Cluster	**1**	**2**
Average confidence	0.902	0.910
Average credibility	1	0.091

Figure 2: Experimental results for SV predictions and for confidences and credibilities corresponding to $f(\alpha) = \operatorname{sign} \alpha$; characteristics of the two clusters (which can be identified by their average credibility); the correctly predicted examples are marked with O and the errors with X

Using results of preliminary experiments we chose as F in (7) a function implicitly given by the polynomial (of degree 3) kernel $K(x, x') = (x \cdot x')^3/256$.

The "distortion phenomenon" leads to much poorer predictive performance (ie, the number of mistakes made) for the "pure" algorithm of Gammerman et al [4] (1998) (corresponding to $f(\alpha) = \operatorname{sign} \alpha$); see Figure 3. The predictive performance, confidences and credibilities corresponding to the functions $f(\alpha) = \alpha$ and $f(\alpha) = \alpha^2$ are shown in Figures 4 and 5.

Remark 8 In the spirit of Remark 5, it is instructive to compare our approximations to randomness deficiency (typical order of magnitude $\log(l+1)$, assuming there is only one example to be classified) with the usual results of statistical learning theory (see, eg, Vapnik [21], 1998, Chapters 4 and 10) and PAC theory (see, eg, Haussler et al [6], 1994). Say, Vapnik's ([21], Theorem 10.5; Theorems 10.6 and 10.7 are of a similar form) denominator $l+1$ in

$$\text{prob(error)} \leq \frac{\mathbf{E}\mathcal{K}_{l+1}}{l+1}$$

corresponds to our $\log(l+1)$ (when the "direct scale" is used). Of course, the advantage of our approach

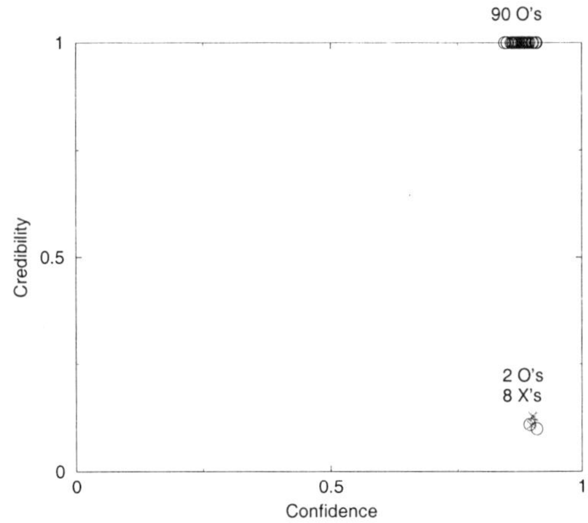

Cluster	**1**	**2**
Average confidence	0.899	0.900
Average credibility	1	0.120

Figure 3: Experimental results for $f(\alpha) = \operatorname{sign} \alpha$

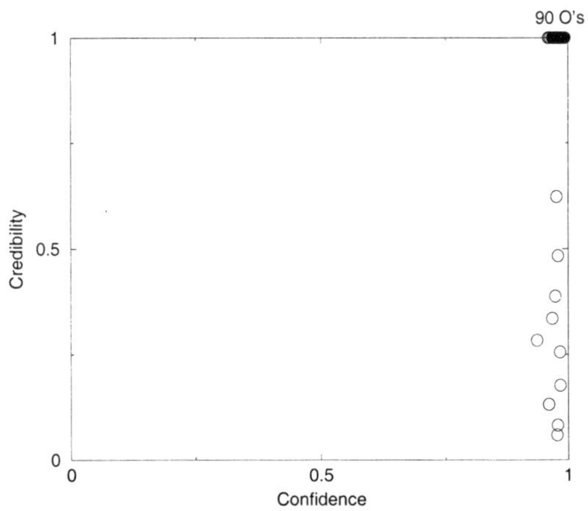

Cluster	**1**	**2**
Average confidence	0.993	0.980
Average credibility	1	0.282

Figure 4: Experimental results for $f(\alpha) = \alpha$

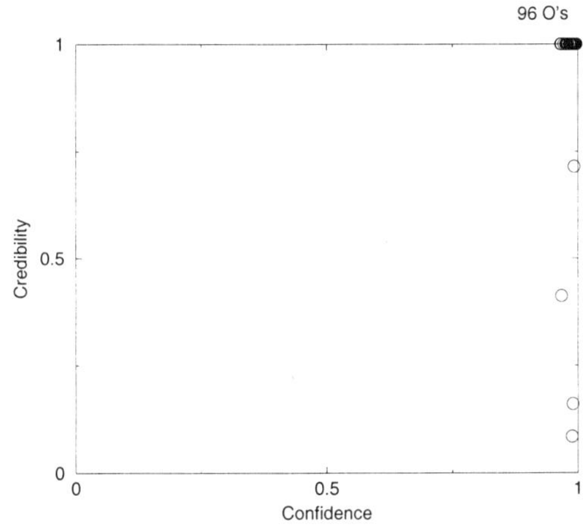

Cluster	**1**	**2**
Average confidence	0.997	0.990
Average credibility	1	0.343

Figure 5: Experimental results for $f(\alpha) = \alpha^2$

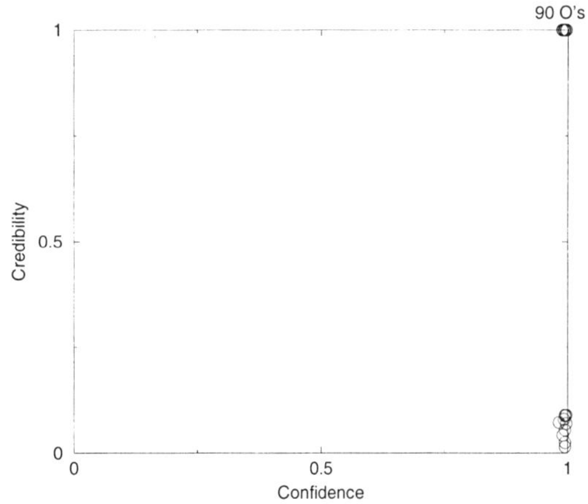

Cluster	**1**	**2**
Average confidence	0.998	0.996
Average credibility	1	0.063

Figure 6: Experimental results for Martin-Löf randomness level

is that our measures of credibility and confidence are applicable to individual examples and not just describe the results of hypothetical repetitions of the prediction task.

Our preliminary studies show that in the problem of regression lotteries are very convenient, but in the problems of pattern recognition considered in this paper it is not clear which function f to choose in (6). Our solution is to use the following p-value function p as an upper bound for the Martin-Löf permutation level (and, *a forteriori*, randomness level): arrange all Lagrange multipliers α_i in decreasing order and define $p(z_1 \dots z_n)$ to be the rank of α_{l+1} divided by $l + 1$. The results for this approach (which is also described in Saunders et al [17], 1999) are given in Figure 6.

6 SOME IMPOSSIBILITY RESULTS

6.1 ON-LINE PREDICTION

Another interesting application of the algorithmic theory of randomness is the following explanation why the bulk of work in machine learning under the general iid assumption (such as statistical learning theory and PAC theory) has been done in the batch setting. (The on-line setting has also been very popular, eg, in the theory of prediction with expert advice, but it uses different assumptions.) The algorithmic theory of randomness implies that on-line prediction under the iid assumption is impossible, at least at random moments in time. We will say that $n \in \mathbb{N}$ is "locally random" if n is a random element of the set

$$A(n) = \left\{2^{\lfloor \log n \rfloor}, \dots, 2^{\lfloor \log n \rfloor + 1} - 1\right\};$$

formally, the *local randomness deficiency* of n is $d^{\mathrm{ML}}_{A(n)}(n)$, or $d^{\mathrm{L}}_{A(n)}(n)$. Analogously to Martin-Löf and Levin randomness deficiencies defined above, we can define randomness deficiencies for infinite data sequences in Z^∞. The next theorem formalizes the impossibility of on-line prediction under the iid assumption at random time (notice that it is possible to predict at time n with $K(n) \ll n$: this situation differs little from the batch setting, where n is given in advance).

Theorem 5 *Let $(x_1, y_1), \dots, (x_n, y_n)$, $y_i \in \{-1, 1\}$, range over all finite data sequences (with the first $l = n - 1$ elements interpreted as the training set and (x_n, y_n) interpreted as the test example) and ζ range over all continuations of the sequence*

$$(x_1, y_1), \dots, (x_{n-1}, y_{n-1}), (x_n, -y_n) \tag{8}$$

(the test example is classified wrongly). Then

$$\inf_\zeta d^{\mathrm{L}}_{\mathrm{iid}}(\zeta) \leq^+ d^{\mathrm{L}}_{\mathrm{iid}}\left((x_1, y_1), (x_2, y_2), \dots, (x_n, y_n)\right) + d^{\mathrm{L}}_{A(n)}(n). \tag{9}$$

(It is clear that a similar inequality holds for Martin-Löf deficiency as well.) Inequality (9) shows that we cannot exclude the wrong classification if the data sequence is random and the time n is also random: the wrong sequence (8) also has a random continuation.

6.2 DENSITY ESTIMATION

According to Vapnik [20] (1995) (see also Vapnik [21], 1998) there are three main problems of statistical learning theory: pattern recognition; regression estimation; density estimation. As we have seen earlier, the problem of pattern recognition can be efficiently solved for typical real-world data sets, in the sense that we can obtain measures of confidence and credibility which are valid under the iid assumption (without need of any other assumptions) and which work well in practice. On the other hand, in typical high-dimensional cases the problem of density estimation can only be solved under assumptions essentially stronger than the iid assumption. To see why, assume that the unlabelled examples x_i are taken from some discrete space X, that $y_i \in \{-1, 1\}$, and we are asked to estimate the probability that $y_{l+1} = 1$. If all unlabelled examples in the training and test sets are distinct (which is typical when the number of attributes is big as compared to the number of examples), no non-trivial estimate (such as an interval containing neither 0 nor 1) of this probability is possible. Indeed, if the full sample $(x_1, y_1), \ldots, (x_{l+1}, y_{l+1})$ is random wr to an iid distribution P, it will also be random wr to a distribution P^* randomly generated by the following stochastic process: for all $c \in X$, $P^*(x = c) = P(x = c)$ and $P^*(y \mid x = c)$ is concentrated on $y = -1$ or $y = 1$, the latter with probability $P(y = 1 \mid x = c)$ and the former with probability $P(y = -1 \mid x = c)$. Of course, density estimation becomes possible when additional assumptions are made. In low-dimensional situations, informative confidence intervals for density estimation are obtained in, eg, Gammerman and Thatcher [3] (1992).

6.3 REGRESSION

There are several possible understanding of the term "regression". One understanding is "regression estimation": we assume that the examples (x_i, y_i) are generated by some iid distribution, and our goal is to estimate the conditional expectation of y_{l+1} given x_{l+1} (we are assuming that there is only one test example). This problem coincides with that of density estimation when $y_i \in \{-1, 1\}$, and so, according to the previous subsection, is infeasible when our only assumption is iid.

If "regression" is understood as estimating y_{l+1} when $y_i \in \mathbb{R}$ are not restricted to a finite set like $\{-1, 1\}$, the problem of regression can be efficiently solved under the iid assumption in high-dimensional cases (work in progress).

There is one more popular statement of the regression (and pattern recognition) problem, where only y_i are generated stochastically given x_i; x_i themselves are not generated stochastically and are just given constants. It is easy to see that in this case even pattern recognition (and *a forteriori* regression) is impossible without making additional assumptions.

7 CONCLUSION

This paper answers the question why one should want to use the algorithmic theory of randomness: in practice, we still use "non-algorithmic" notions such as p-values or lotteries. As we have shown, using the algorithmic theory of randomness we can ask (and answer) questions about relationships between

- universal p-values and universal lotteries (Martin-Löf vs Levin randomness level);
- exchangeability and randomness.

The second item raises the open question (already mentioned): is it possible to make use of the randomness deficiency of the configuration (which can, according to Theorem 4, be quite big)?

Besides the "positive" results discussed in the previous paragraph, the algorithmic theory of randomness also allows us to prove impossibility of prediction in certain situations; as shown in the previous section, such important problems as density estimation in high-dimensional spaces, regression estimation in high-dimensional spaces, and on-line prediction (where it is required that valid measures of confidence are output at every step) cannot be solved if our only assumption is iid.

Acknowledgements

The referees' insightful comments helped us to improve the presentation. We thank EPSRC for providing financial support through grants GR/L35812 ("Support Vector and Bayesian learning algorithms"), GR/M14937 ("Predictive complexity: recursion-theoretic variants") and GR/M16856 ("Comparison of Support Vector Machine and Minimum Message Length methods for induction and prediction").

References

[1] D A S Fraser. *Nonparametric methods in statistics.* Wiley, New York, 1957.

[2] Peter Gács. Exact expressions for some randomness tests. *Z Math Logik Grundl Math*, 26:385–394, 1980.

[3] Alex Gammerman and A R Thatcher. Bayesian diagnostic probabilities without assuming independence of symptoms. *Yearbook of Medical Informatics*, pages 323–330, 1992.

[4] Alex Gammerman, Vladimir Vapnik, and Volodya Vovk. Learning by transduction. In *Proceedings of the Fourteenth Conference on Uncertainty in Artificial Intelligence*, pages 148–156, San Francisco, CA, 1998. Morgan Kaufmann.

[5] Irwin Guttman. *Statistical tolerance regions: classical and Bayesian.* Griffin, London, 1970.

[6] David Haussler, Nick Littlestone, and Manfred K Warmuth. Predicting $\{0, 1\}$-functions on randomly drawn points. *Information and Computation*, 115:248–292, 1994.

[7] Andrei N Kolmogorov. *Grundbegriffe der Wahrscheinlichkeitsrechnung.* Springer, Berlin, 1933.

[8] Andrei N Kolmogorov. Three approaches to the quantitative definition of information. *Problems Inform Transmission*, 1:1–7, 1965.

[9] Andrei N Kolmogorov. Logical basis for information theory and probability theory. *IEEE Trans Inform Theory*, IT-14:662–664, 1968.

[10] Y LeCun, B Boser, J S Denker, D Henderson, R E Howard, W Hubbard, and L J Jackel. Handwritten digit recognition with back-propagation network. *Advances in Neural Information Processing Systems*, pages 396–404, 1990.

[11] Leonid A Levin. On the notion of a random sequence. *Soviet Mathematics Doklady*, 14:1413, 1973.

[12] Ming Li and Paul Vitányi. Computational machine learning in theory and praxis. In J van Leeuwen, editor, *Computer Science Today, Recent Trends and Developments*, volume 1000 of *Lecture Notes in Computer Science*, pages 518–535. Springer, 1995.

[13] Ming Li and Paul Vitányi. *An introduction to Kolmogorov complexity and its applications.* Springer, New York, 2nd edition, 1997.

[14] L Longpré. Resource-bounded Kolmogorov complexity and statistical tests. In O Watanabe, editor, *Kolmogorov Complexity and Computational Complexity*, pages 66–84. Springer, 1992.

[15] Per Martin-Löf. The definition of random sequences. *Information and Control*, 9:602–619, 1966.

[16] Jorma Rissanen. Stochastic complexity (with discussion). *J R Statist Soc B*, 49:223–239 and 252–265, 1987.

[17] Craig Saunders, Alex Gammerman, and Volodya Vovk. Transduction with confidence and credibility. In *Proceedings of IJCAI'99.* To appear.

[18] Craig Saunders, Alex Gammerman, and Volodya Vovk. Ridge regression learning algorithm in dual variables. In J Shavlik, editor, *Machine Learning, Proceedings of the Fifteenth International Conference*, pages 515–521, San Francisco, CA, 1998. Morgan Kaufmann.

[19] Mark J Schervish. *Theory of statistics.* Springer, New York, 1995.

[20] Vladimir N Vapnik. *The nature of statistical learning theory.* Springer, New York, 1995.

[21] Vladimir N Vapnik. *Statistical learning theory.* Wiley, New York, 1998.

[22] Volodya Vovk. On the concept of the Bernoulli property. *Russ Math Surv*, 41:247–248, 1986.

[23] Volodya Vovk. A logic of probability, with application to the foundations of statistics (with discussion). *J R Statist Soc* B, 55:317–351, 1993.

[24] Volodya Vovk and Alex Gammerman. Complexity Approximation Principle. *The Computer Journal*, 1999. To appear.

[25] Vladimir V V'yugin. Algorithmic entropy (complexity) of finite objects and its applications to defining randomness and amount of information. *Selecta Mathematica Sovietica*, 13:357–389, 1994.

[26] Chris S Wallace and P R Freeman. Estimation and inference by compact coding (with discussion). *J R Statist Soc* B, 49:240–265, 1987.

Common problems with other methods:

Domain & tool knowledge
Deal with only one channel
Data hungry / Accuracy / Incomprehensible

Learning Comprehensible Descriptions of Multivariate Time Series

How to find / choose PEPs? Learning them may be hard. Ask experts.

Mohammed Waleed Kadous
School of Computer Science & Engineering
University of New South Wales
Sydney, NSW 2052, Australia
waleed@cse.unsw.edu.au

Abstract

Supervised classification is one of the most active areas of machine learning research. Most work has focused on classification in static domains, where an instantaneous snapshot of attributes is meaningful. In many domains, attributes are not static; in fact, it is the way they vary temporally that can make classification possible. Examples of such domains include speech recognition, gesture recognition and electrocardiograph classification. While it is possible to use ad hoc, domain-specific techniques for "flattening" the time series to a learner-friendly representation, this fails to take into account both the special problems and special heuristics applicable to temporal data and often results in unreadable concept descriptions. Though traditional time series techniques can sometimes produce accurate classifiers, few can provide comprehensible descriptions. We propose a general architecture for classification and description of multivariate time series. It employs event primitives to analyse the training data and extract events. These events are clustered, creating prototypical events which are used as the basis for creating more accurate and comprehensible classifiers. A minimal implementation of this architecture, called TClass, is applied to two domains, one real and one artificial and compared against a naïve approach. TClass shows great promise, particularly in comprehensibility, but also in accuracy.

Keywords: machine learning, classification, temporal classification, gesture recognition, time series.

1 INTRODUCTION

One prominent area of machine learning research is supervised classification and in particular, attribute-value learning. Attribute-value learners typically assume that each training instance is defined by a set of attributes, that for the purposes of the learner, do not change. In many domains however, it is this change in attributes over time that makes classification possible. Examples of such domains include recognition of gestures, medical signal analysis, robot sensor analysis and mining in temporal databases.

To make the distinction clear, consider the speech recognition task, where an audio signal representing a word must be classified. The audio signal consists of 22 spectral frequency coefficients, updated 50 times a second. Looking at the values of the coefficients at a single instant of time is not very useful for classification; rather, classification can only be performed by looking at the changes of these coefficients over time.

It is possible to extract features from time series, then apply a conventional learner. There are several drawbacks to such an approach. Firstly, the techniques tend to be ad hoc, domain-specific and labour-intensive; the current work arises from the author's frustrating experiences trying to do this for the sign recognition task [Kadous, 1995]. Secondly, there are special heuristics applicable to temporal domains that are difficult to capture by such a conversion process (for example, different parts of the instance being slightly stretched or delayed in time). Thirdly, descriptions built using these extracted features can be hard to understand.

A description of the problem, followed by two examples of temporal classification tasks are given. A general architecture is proposed for the classification and description of multivariate time series. An implemen-

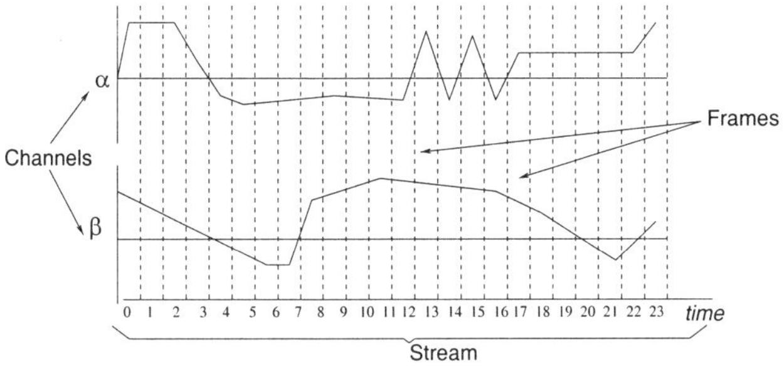

Figure 1: The relationship between channels, frames and streams.

tation of the system, called TClass, is presented; as is its application to the two temporal classification tasks.

1.1 PROBLEM DESCRIPTION

As with conventional supervised classification, the input consists of a set of training instances and associated class labels. In this case however, the instances are streams. Each stream consists of a sequence of frames. Each frame represents an instant of time of the stream, and consists of a set of measurements or values from different sources, termed channels. The number of frames need not be fixed. Figure 1 illustrates the relationship between these terms. Each stream is also labelled with its class[1].

Our main goals in this work are: to produce a classifier with a low error rate, and to produce descriptions which are comprehensible to a human.

2 EXAMPLE LEARNING TASKS

Because of the novelty of classification in temporal domains, standard datasets, such as those used in static classification, are not easy to find. For this reason, we have had to use one artificial domain and one natural domain where we collected the data ourselves. We discuss these domains first to give a practical example of typical temporal classification problems.

2.1 CYLINDER-BELL-FUNNEL

The artificial cylinder-bell-funnel task was originally proposed by Saito [Saito, 1994], and further worked on by Manganaris [Manganaris, 1997]. The task is to classify a stream as one of three classes, cylinder (c), bell (b) or funnel (f). Samples are generated as follows:

$$\begin{aligned} c(t) &= (6+\eta)\cdot\chi_{[a,b]}(t)+\epsilon(t) \\ b(t) &= (6+\eta)\cdot\chi_{[a,b]}(t)\cdot(t-a)/(b-a)+\epsilon(t) \\ f(t) &= (6+\eta)\cdot\chi_{[a,b]}(t)\cdot(b-t)/(b-a)+\epsilon(t) \\ \chi_{[a,b]} &= \begin{cases} 0 & t<a, \\ 1 & a\le t\le b \\ 0 & t>b \end{cases} \end{aligned}$$

where η and $\epsilon(t)$ are drawn from a standard normal distribution $N(0,1)$, a is an integer drawn uniformly from $[16,32]$ and $b-a$ is an integer drawn uniformly from $[32,96]$. See figure 2 (right hand side) for some instances of each class. The cylinder class is characterised by a plateau from time a to b, the bell class by a gradual increase from a to b followed by a sudden decline and the funnel class by a sudden increase at a and a gradual decrease until b. Although univariate (i.e., only has one channel) and of a fixed length (128 frames), the CBF task attempts to characterise some of the typical properties of temporal domains. Firstly, there is random amplitude variation as a result of the η in the equation. Secondly, there is random noise (represented by the $\epsilon(t)$). Thirdly, there is significant temporal variation in both the start of events (since a can vary from 16 to 32) and the duration of events (since $b-a$ can vary from 32 to 96).

The left-hand side of figure 2 shows the rules generated by our system and discussed in the rest of this paper.

2.2 AUSLAN SIGN RECOGNITION

The goal for this learning task is to classify a subset of Auslan (Australian sign language, the language of the Australian Deaf community) signs. Instances of the signs were collected using an instrumented glove[2]. The domain consists of eight channels: x (left/right), y (up/down), and z (away/towards the body) position, wrist roll (whether the palm is facing up or down), thumb, fore, middle and ring finger bend. This information is updated approximately 23 times a second. Thus each frame consists of the value of these eight channels at an instant in time. The signs were collected one at a time starting and ending at a fixed

[1]It is also possible to conceive of a more complex learning task, where each stream has a sequence of class labels. However, for the rest of this paper, we will only consider single class labels.

[2]A Nintendo PowerGlove was used to collect the data. It is highly sensitive to noise, suffers low temporal and value resolution, is sensitive to environmental factors, only captures information from one hand and has no sensor on the little finger. Newer equipment has been procured which should significantly improve the quality of the data, and consequently classification.

Rule 7:
local max at time 31
local min at time 116
-> class cyl

Rule 1:
increases from time 28 to 52
local max at time 48
local max at time 67
-> class bell

Rule 12:
decreases from time 34 to 48
flat from 2 to 26
local max at time 61
-> class funnel

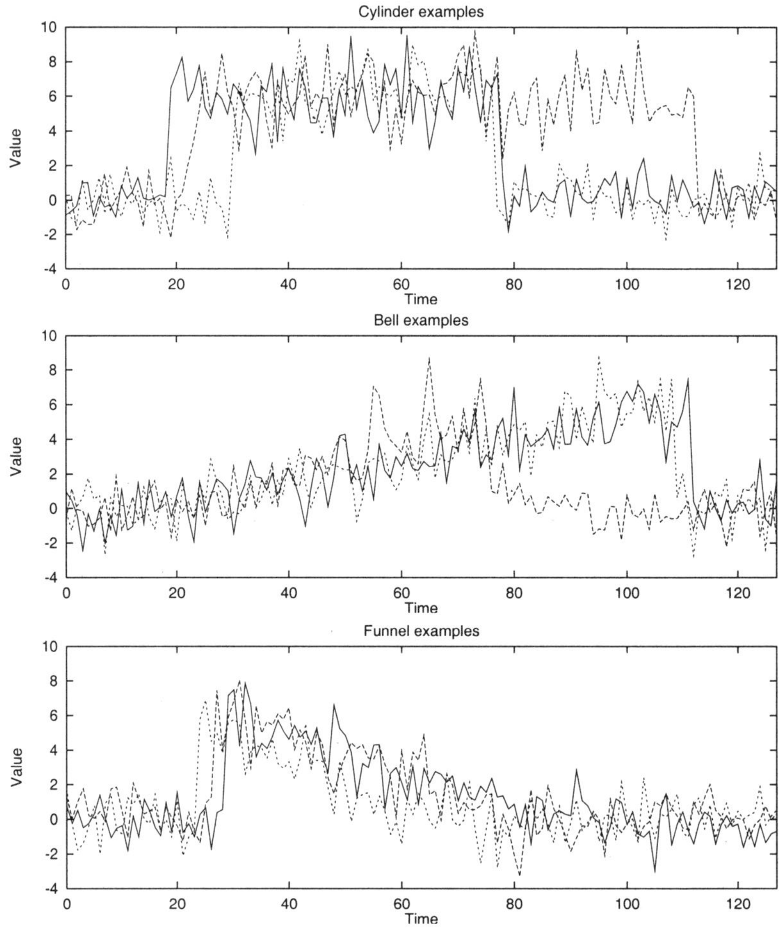

Figure 2: Selected rules produced by TClass in the CBF task and some instances of each class.

2322
v (end dir) **COME,** *SE* **COME**. Translucent sign. Evidently from the sign BECKON. [ASL, BSL] ***A one-handed sign in which the X handshape, palm up, hand away, is held in neutral space and moved left and towards.***

91
n (end dir, redu) **THANKS**. *v (end dir, redu)* **THANK,** *SE* **THANK**. Opaque sign. 'Thank you' is sometimes produced as a blend of THANK + YOU (i.e., as THANK ending in the G handshape directed at one's interlocutor). ***A one-handed sign in which the B handshape, palm towards, hand up, is placed on the chin and moved away with stress.***

Rule 6:
z: global maximum is 0.070312
[hand goes far away from body]
z: increases from time 10 to 30
[hand moving to far position shown]
fore: flat from 0 to 5 with value 0.72
[initially finger is fully bent]
-> class come

Rule 7:
y: local maximum at time 38
[i.e. touching chin as shown]
z: decreases from time 11 to 31
[hand is pulled towards body]
fore: flat from time 3 to 41 with value 0.02
[forefinger kept straight for most of sign]
-> class thank

Figure 3: Selected rules produced by TClass and the corresponding definitions from the Auslan Dictionary [Johnston, 1989].

Table 1: The training set for the BR task.

Stream	c	Class
1	FFFTTTFFFFFF	Red
2	FFFTFFFTFFTTTT	Blue
3	FFTFFTFFFFFFTTT	Blue
4	FFFFTTTTFFFFF	Red
5	FFFTTTFFFF	Red
6	FFTTFFFTFFTTT	Blue

point (a closed fist at the side of the body). The average number of frames per sign was 51, but varied from 30 frames up to 102 frames.

Figure 3 shows two signs from the Auslan domain. The top part shows the gloss (dictionary definition) of the sign from the Auslan dictionary [Johnston, 1989]. The lower part shows some of the rules extracted by TClass.

3 ARCHITECTURE AND IMPLEMENTATION

We propose a general architecture for temporal classification problems as shown in figure 4. To explain concisely, we will use a simple illustrative domain, the Blues and Reds (BR) task. This domain has single channel (c), which can only have two possible values: true (T) or false (F). There are two possible classes for each stream, Blue or Red. A sample training set is shown in table 1. As can be seen, streams vary in length from 10 frames to 15 frames.

The data is processed in two ways: global feature calculation and event extraction. Global feature calculation extracts various features the stream as a whole. Typical global features include global maxima, global minima, means of each channel and the duration of the stream. For many temporal domains, these global features provide a good "first cut" representation for classification[3].

In the BR task, a simple global feature is the ratio of time that the channel c is true to the overall duration of the stream. The results of applying this to the data of table 1 are shown in column 2 of table 3.

Event extraction is applied by using a set of parametrised event primitives (PEPs). PEPs represent particular types of "events" that are expected to occur in the domain (the best PEPs are typically domain-specific). Each PEP is defined by:

- A tuple of parameters $p = (p_1, ..., p_k)$, which describe a particular parametrised event. Let P_1 represent the range of the parameter p_1. Let P be the space of possible parameter values, i.e., $P = P_1 \times P_2 \times ... \times P_k$. P will be referred to as the *parameter space.*
- A *finding function* f which takes a stream s and returns a set of parametrised events e, such that $e \subseteq P$.

A key characteristic of a PEP is that it should explicitly represent the temporal characteristics of the events as parameters; thus representing time in a way that facilitates learning.

Table 2: TrueRun PEP applied to the BR training set.

Stream	Events found
1	$\{(3,3)\}$
2	$\{(3,1),(6,1),(9,4)\}$
3	$\{(2,1),(5,1),(12,3)\}$
4	$\{(4,4)\}$
5	$\{(3,3)\}$
6	$\{(2,2),(6,1),(9,3)\}$

One simple PEP we could use with the BR task is to finds runs of T values, and returns a tuple (t, d) where t is the time the run starts and d is the duration of the run. The finding function would be given a stream and return all pairs (t, d). The results of applying this PEP to the BR training data is shown in table 2. We shall term this PEP the TrueRun PEP.

Since each PEP is described in terms of a set of parameters, clustering can be performed in the parameter space of each PEP. For example, if the data from table 2 is plotted (as in figure 5) we can cluster it as shown. Typically, rather than hand-clustering, some clustering algorithm would be used.

Each cluster then forms the basis of a synthetic event attribute. For each stream, the value of the synthetic event attribute is true only if it has an event belonging to that cluster. More generally, a confidence metric of cluster membership is used, rather than just a true/false value.

Once we have these clusters, the training data can be re-attributed with these synthetic event attributes. Applying this to the BR data, we get the results shown in columns 3, 4 and 5 of table 3.

The data from the global and event processing streams

[3]For example, in the large Auslan domain, 30 per cent accuracy can be obtained using only the maxima and minima of the x, y and z channels.

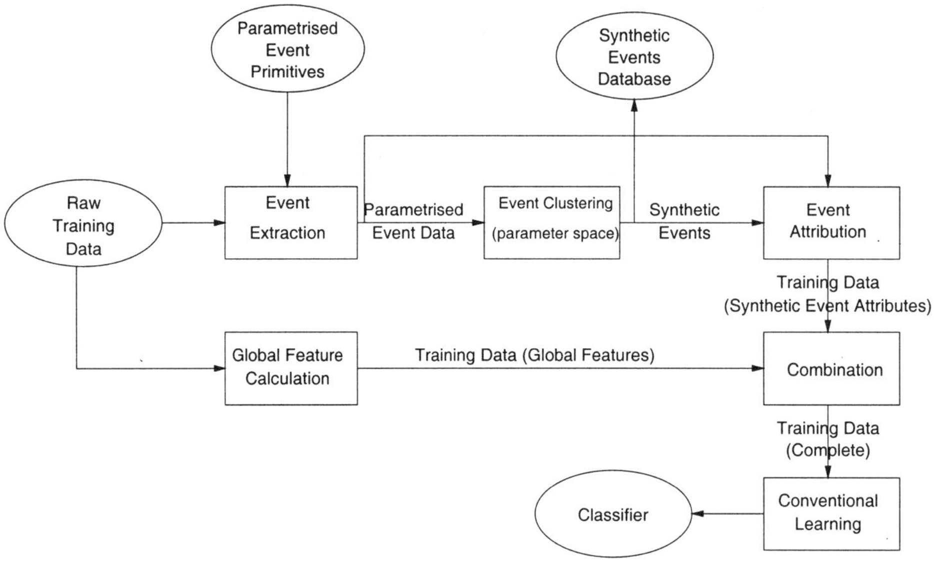

Figure 4: General architecture for training.

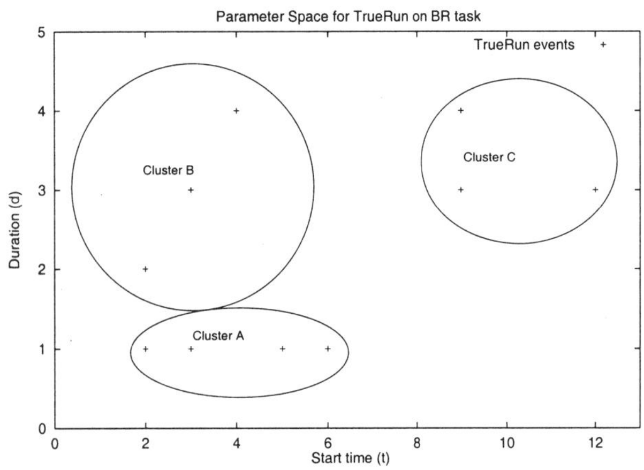

Figure 5: TrueRun parameter space and clustering for BR task.

Table 3: Global and event attributes for the BR task.

Stream	Globals	Event Attributes		
	True ratio	A	B	C
1	0.25	No	Yes	No
2	0.46	Yes	No	Yes
3	0.33	Yes	No	Yes
4	0.31	No	Yes	No
5	0.30	No	Yes	No
6	0.50	No	No	Yes

are recombined, in a format suitable for processing by an attribute-value learner. The result of applying `c4.5rules` [Quinlan, 1993] on the BR data in table 3 are shown in figure 6 (left side). Furthermore, if there is some way to produce a prototype from the clusters (for instance, by finding the centroid of the cluster), we can substitute the prototype's description to produce a descriptive rule[4] (as shown on the right hand side of figure 6). It should also be pointed out that because of the way C4.5 operates, the rule for Blue is discriminant (i.e., how to tell it from Red), rather than characteristic (giving the defining characteristics of Blue).

3.1 IMPLEMENTATION

An instance of the above architecture, called TClass, has been implemented. This implementation is designed in an object-oriented manner to allow different PEPs, global feature calculators, clustering algorithms and learners to be substituted.

Currently, the following global feature calculators are available: mean, median, mode, maximum value and minimum value for a channel. These can be applied to any channel.

Similarly, the PEPs implemented are:

- Increasing (an extended period with significant

[4]Such a rule is not suited for classification, it is only for description.

```
Rule 1:                              Rule 1: (post processed)
        clusterC = Yes                       true run starting at 10 duration 3
        -> class blue   [63.0%]              -> class blue
Default class: red                   Default class: red
```

Figure 6: Rules produced by applying `c4.5rules` to table 3.

positive gradient) and Decreasing (an extended period with significant negative gradient). These both return four parameters: start time, duration, average value of the channel, and average gradient.

- Flat (no perceptible change in gradient). This returns three parameters: the start time, average value and duration.
- Localmax and Localmin[5]. These both return two parameters: time of the maximum/minimum, and the value.

All of these have some simple heuristics for dealing with noise. For instance the local maximum applies a smoothing filter first to reduce noise before locating maxima.

Currently, TClass uses k-means clustering, with all values normalised by standard deviation. The confidence metric used for cluster membership is distance to the cluster's centroid. The learner can either be a naïve Bayes learner[6] or C4.5 [Quinlan, 1993] with the default parameters.

Empirically, it was found that the k-means clustering algorithm did not perform well when all of the events from different classes were clustered simultaneously. Thus a slight modification was made to the architecture; the basic architecture was replicated from the event clustering stage onwards on a per-class basis, as shown in figure 7. Event clustering is now performed only on events coming from instances of the same class. These clusters are then used to extract the synthetic events as before. All training instances are then attributed[7] with these synthetic events, creating a set of synthetic event attributes. These class-specific synthetic event attributes are combined with the class-independent global features, creating a set of features that are used by the learner to induce a classifier. Because one such classifier is constructed per class, if there are n classes, there are n classifiers induced.

To classify an unseen instance, event extraction and global feature calculation are applied. For each class, the instance is then attributed with that class' synthetic events, thus generating the synthetic event attributes required by the classifier associated with that class. The instance is then classified by each classifier. In this way, n classifications will be made. The most common classification is then taken as the final prediction.

4 EXPERIMENTAL RESULTS

4.1 ERROR RATE

TClass was applied to both the Auslan and CBF tasks to get some idea of its accuracy compared with other techniques. Unfortunately, there is no central repository for temporal classification datasets (unlike conventional classification). This limits how rigorously the accuracy of TClass can be evaluated.

For the CBF task, all five PEPs were applied to the only channel. The global mean was the only global feature used. 266 instances of each class were generated. For ease of comparison with previous results, 10-fold cross validation was used.

For the Auslan task, all five PEPs were applied to the x, y and z channels. Increasing, Decreasing and Flat were applied to the remaining rotation and finger bend channels. The mean was calculated for each channel, as were the global maximum and minimum for the x, y, and z channels. Two tests were done, one with a small dataset consisting of 10 signs, and the other with a larger dataset with 95 signs. To simplify comparison with previously published results, 5-fold cross-validation was performed.

A naïve segmentation approach to feature extraction was used to allow comparison to TClass's performance. Each channel was divided into 10 segments along the

[5] Note the distinction between a global maximum (over the whole signal) and a local maximum (a peak relative to the points surrounding it).

[6] Laplace correction [Domingos and Pazzani, 1997] and equal frequency discretisation into 5 bins [Dougherty et al., 1995] for continuous values were used.

[7] In this context, attribution occurs by finding the event from the instance that most closely matches the synthetic event. The distance between the synthetic event and the closest match is used as the synthetic event attribute.

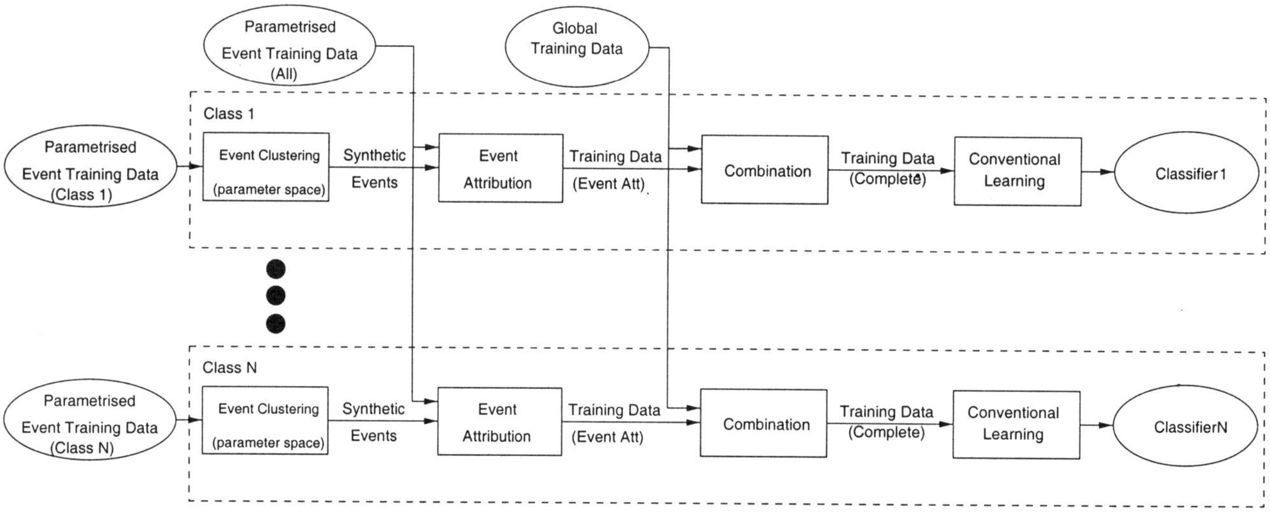

Figure 7: Approach used in implementing to simplify clustering task. Classifier 1 through to Classifier N are voted to make a final classification.

time axis. The mean for each segment was computed and used as a feature. This created 10 features for the CBF task and 80 for the Auslan task. The same global features used with TClass were also combined with the segment features before being processed with the learners.

Two learning algorithms were compared: naïve Bayes and C4.5. The error rates of these experiments are shown in table 4.

Table 4 shows some interesting patterns. Firstly, the "segment" approach to feature extraction performs surprisingly well, especially in the small Auslan task where there is no significant difference[8] between it and the TClass approach. At 2.4 per cent error it outperforms the best known published results for the CBF task, including complex approaches involving local discriminant bases using wavelets (3.75 per cent) [Saito, 1994] and trend episode analysis (2.98 per cent) [Manganaris, 1997] but is beaten by TClass's 1.9 per cent error rate.

TClass has a better error rate overall compared to the naïve segmentation technique, regardless of the underlying learner.

Learner performance is consistent with previous results [Domingos and Pazzani, 1997]; in that in the Auslan task, which is characterised by few data (only 16 instances to train on per class), many classes and many attributes, naïve Bayes outperforms C4.5. On the other hand, in a domain with many data (240 training instances per class), few channels and few classes, such as the CBF task, C4.5 outperforms naïve Bayes.

The author had previously attempted both the small and large Auslan tasks using domain-specific, labour intensive, ad hoc feature extraction and iterative analysis of the errors to guide the inclusion of additional features, followed by feature selection and a nearest neighbour classifier [Kadous, 1995]. TClass exceeds the performance of this approach for the small Auslan task (2.5 per cent error rate vs 8.0 per cent error rate), but lags behind in the large Auslan task (24.0 per cent error rate vs 17.0 per cent error rate). Considering the PEPs are generic, this is hardly surprising.

It is also interesting to note the positive impact of using an ensemble of classifiers based on class. For example, in the large Auslan task, with TClass features and naïve Bayes learning, the average error rate of an individual class classifier was 36.1 per cent, whereas the combined classifier had an error rate of 24.0 per cent. Similarly in the CBF task, the average error rate of individual class classifiers was 5.6 per cent, compared with the error rate of the combined classifier of was 1.9 per cent.

4.2 COMPREHENSIBILITY

An important advantage of TClass over other techniques is that it produces comprehensible results. For

[8] All significance statements are based on a paired t-test at the 99 per cent confidence level.

Table 4: Error rates expressed as percentages (mean ± std error of the mean) on the learning tasks.

Features/Learner	Small Auslan	Large Auslan	CBF
TClass/Naïve Bayes	2.50 ± 0.79	24.00 ± 1.09	3.67 ± 0.61
Segments/Naïve Bayes	3.00 ± 1.46	29.58 ± 1.10	6.20 ± 0.67
TClass/C4.5	14.00 ± 2.03	40.37 ± 0.83	1.90 ± 0.57
Segment/C4.5	18.00 ± 2.67	53.37 ± 1.18	2.41 ± 0.48

instance, after combining the outputs of synthetic events from the clusterer and `c4.5rules`, we can produce rules that may be useful for understanding what the learner is doing.

Selected rules produced by TClass for the CBF task (see figure 2) capture some essential characteristics of each class. Because C4.5 is designed for discrimination, not characterisation, the rules should be interpreted with this in mind. For instance, it is unlikely that anything except a cylinder class will have both a maximum early in the signal and a minimum towards the end of the signal. But this does not define the cylinder class, only how it is different from the others classes.

Because matching is based on confidences, one event may actually "register" (i.e., produce a non-zero confidence) with multiple synthetic features. For instances, for the bell class, if there was a local maximum at time 55, it would match, with a certain confidence, the local maximum at time 48 *and* the local maximum at time 61. Even a maximum at time 80 would match both of these events, but with less confidence.

For the Auslan domain, selected rules found for two signs are shown against the glosses from the Auslan Dictionary [Johnston, 1989] in figure 3. Comments in square braces explain the connection between the rule and the gloss. As can be seen, some of the key characteristics of each sign are identified. For example, the identifying features for the come sign are that the hand travels far from the body (as indicated by the maximum z), there is a sudden movement of the hand away from the body early on in the sign and that the finger is initially fully bent. For the thank sign, the detected features are that there is a local maximum on channel y about midway through the sign (corresponding to the point in time where the hand touches the chin), that there is a pulling of the hand towards the body before the chin is touched, and that the forefinger remains straight for most of the sign. The comprehensibility of descriptions on both tasks is to the author's knowledge, novel. HMMs and other techniques have not been used to create comprehensible descriptions to the author's knowledge.

5 RELATED WORK

The best developed technique for temporal classification is the hidden Markov model (see [Rabiner and Juang, 1986] for more details). HMMs have proved themselves to be very useful for speech recognition, and are the basis of most commercial systems. Despite this, they do suffer some serious drawbacks for general use. Firstly, the structure of the HMM – similar to that of a finite state machine – needs to be specified *a priori*. The structure selected can have a critical effect on performance. Secondly, extracting comprehensible rules from HMMs is not at all easy. Thirdly, even making some very strong assumptions about the probability model, there are frequently hundreds or thousands of parameters per HMM. As a result, many training instances are required to learn effectively. None of these three problems is of primary importance in the speech recognition domain[9].

A recent development has been dynamic Bayes networks (DBNs) – a superset of HMMs – for temporal classification tasks. DBNs augment HMMs by allowing for more complex representations of the state space. Zweig and Russell, for example, were able to obtain higher accuracy than conventional hidden Markov models [Zweig and Russell, 1998] on a speech recognition task. The structure of the dynamic Bayes network was informed by physiological models of the vocal system, and while this is feasible for speech recognition, it may not be for other tasks. Friedman et al [Friedman et al., 1998] explore some techniques for learning DBN structure; these techniques are still primitive.

[9] It is difficult to compare the current work with HMMs in an objective manner, since it is not clear what states and transitions are appropriate for the domains used in this work. Furthermore, because of the noise levels in the data and the small number of instances per class in the Auslan domain, we found in preliminary experiments that in many cases a simple 3-state (54 parameter) HMM did not converge.

Another technique that has gained some use is recurrent neural networks (RNNs) ([Bengio, 1996] has a good discussion of their application to temporal classification). This method utilises a normal feed-forward neural network, but introduces a "context layer" that is fed back to the hidden layer one timestep later. The context layer allows for retention of some state information. RNNs suffer from many of the same problems as HMMs: incomprehensibility, many parameters need to be set with little guidance from theory, and slow learning. In addition, they do not work well for longer sequences of observations [Bengio, 1996].

Some work has also been completed on signals with high-level event sequence descriptions. Rather than representing temporal information as a time-sampled signal, as in this work, temporal information is represented as a set of timestamped events with parameters. This is a higher level of temporal abstraction than is used in this work, but is applicable to many problems, for example network traffic analysis [Mannila et al., 1995] or network failure analysis [Oates et al., 1998]. In such cases, researchers look for sequences of events that cause particular phenomena.

Several temporal expert systems have also been developed. Shahar [Shahar and Musen, 1995] suggests an expert system architecture for knowledge-based temporal abstraction in medical domains. This is extended to a framework for temporal abstraction in his later work [Shahar, 1997]. This framework is more extensive than the one presented here, but has a different focus; which is for building of expert systems. It seems overly complicated for learning purposes. Paliouras [Paliouras, 1997] shows how to automatically refine parameters in an existing temporal expert system, and applies this technique to the analysis of whale songs.

Recently machine learning approaches have showed some promise. Manganaris [Manganaris, 1997] developed a system for supervised classification of univariate (not multivariate, as in this work) signals using piecewise polynomial modelling, and applied it to space shuttle data as well as artificial datasets. Keogh and Pazzani [Keogh and Pazzani, 1998] developed a technique for agglomerative clustering of univariate time series based on enhancing the time series with a line segment representation. By using delay portraits (looking at the relationship between a channel at time t and time $t-n$), Rosenstein and Cohen [Rosenstein and Cohen, 1998] improve the reliability of robot sensor readings. Das et al [Das et al., 1998] extracts simple rules from univariate datasets.

6 CONCLUSIONS & FUTURE WORK

6.1 CONCLUSIONS

The general architecture proposed improves both accuracy and comprehensibility by taking advantage of the special properties and dealing with the specific problems of temporal classification. An implementation of this architecture, called TClass, is applied to several learning tasks. It proved to be more accurate than a naïve approach, competitive with hand-crafted solutions and in some cases showed better performance than complex feature extraction techniques, while still providing useful descriptions of learnt concepts.

6.2 FUTURE WORK

The PEPs presented are simple and do not identify domain-specific features. Surprisingly, they perform relatively well. It is possible improve performance by designing multi-channel PEPs (for example, rather than treat x, y and z separately, a PEP could treat them as a single unit). Furthermore, the PEP design did make use of a useful property of temporal domains: correlated events on different channels.

The classifiers used here do not use feature subset selection at all. Previous research [John et al., 1994] shows that learners may benefit significantly from feature selection, especially in cases like this one where so many features are generated by event clustering.

The descriptions produced could be significantly improved over those generated by C4.5, since C4.5 is designed to tell classes apart; as a result, it does not always produce characteristic descriptions, rather it prefers discriminant ones [Quinlan, 1998]. While this is appropriate for a tree, it is not necessarily appropriate for building intuitive descriptions of temporal classes. Future work will focus on alternative learning algorithms for producing comprehensible descriptions.

Acknowledgements

Thanks to The Creator for giving me the ability to do this work. Secondarily, my sincere thanks go to Michael Harries for assistance in many forms; Claude Sammut for sparing me time when it was very valuable to him; Ross Quinlan for many suggestions; my wonderful family; and to Hoi Shan Chong for helping me stay calm and stable.

References

[Bengio, 1996] Bengio, Y. (1996). *Neural Networks for Speech and Sequence Recognition.* International Thomson Publishing Inc.

[Danyluk, 1998] Danyluk, A. (1998). Predicting the future: AI approaches to time-series problems. Technical Report WS-98-07, AAAI Press.

[Das et al., 1998] Das, G., Lin, K.-I., Mannila, H., Renganathan, G., and Smyth, P. (1998). Rule discovery from time series. In *Proceedings of the Fourth International Conference on Knowledge Discovery and Data Mining (KDD-98).* AAAI Press.

[Domingos and Pazzani, 1997] Domingos, P. and Pazzani, M. (1997). On the optimality of the simple bayesian classifier under zero-one loss. *Machine Learning*, 29:103–130.

[Dougherty et al., 1995] Dougherty, J., Kohavi, R., and Sahami, M. (1995). Supervised and unsupervised discretization of continuous features. In *Machine Learning: Proceedings of the 12th International Conference on Machine Learning*, pages 194–202. Morgan-Kaufmann.

[Friedman et al., 1998] Friedman, N., Murphy, K., and Russell, S. (1998). Learning the structure of dynamic probabilistic networks. In *Proceeding Uncertainty in Artificial Intelligence Conference 1998 (UAI-98).* AAAI Press.

[John et al., 1994] John, G. H., Kohavi, R., and Pfleger, K. (1994). Irrelevant features and the subset selection problem. In *Proceedings of the International Conference on Machile Learning 1994*, pages 121–129.

[Johnston, 1989] Johnston, T. (1989). *Auslan Dictionary: a Dictionary of the Sign Language of the Australian Deaf Community.* Deafness Resources Australia Ltd.

[Kadous, 1995] Kadous, M. W. (1995). GRASP: Recognition of Australian sign language using instrumented gloves. Master's thesis, School of Computer Science and Engineering, University of New South Wales.

[Keogh and Pazzani, 1998] Keogh, E. J. and Pazzani, M. J. (1998). An enhanced representation of time series which allows fast and accurate classification, clustering and relevance feedback. In [Danyluk, 1998], pages 44–51.

[Manganaris, 1997] Manganaris, S. (December 1997). *Supervised Classification with Temporal Data.* PhD thesis, Computer Science Department, School of Engineering, Vanderbilt University.

[Mannila et al., 1995] Mannila, H., Toivonen, H., and Verkamo, A. I. (1995). Discovering frequent episodes in sequences. In *Proceedings of the First International Conference on Knowledge Discovery and Data Mining (KDD-95)*, pages 210–215.

[Oates et al., 1998] Oates, T., Jensen, D., and Cohen, P. R. (1998). Discovering rules for clustering and predicting asynchronous events. In [Danyluk, 1998], pages 73–79.

[Paliouras, 1997] Paliouras, G. (1997). *Refinement of Temporal Constraints in an Event Recognition System using Small Datasets.* PhD thesis, University of Manchester.

[Quinlan, 1993] Quinlan, J. R. (1993). *C4.5: Programs for Machine Learning.* Morgan Kaufmann.

[Quinlan, 1998] Quinlan, J. R. (1998). Personal discussion.

[Rabiner and Juang, 1986] Rabiner, L. R. and Juang, B. H. (1986). An introduction to hidden markov models. *IEEE Magazine on Accoustics, Speech and Signal Processing*, 3(1):4–16.

[Rosenstein and Cohen, 1998] Rosenstein, M. T. and Cohen, P. R. (1998). Concepts from time series. In *AAAI '98: Fifteenth National Conference on Artificial Intelligence*, pages 739–745. AAAI, AAAI Press.

[Saito, 1994] Saito, N. (1994). *Local feature extraction and its application using a library of bases.* PhD thesis, Yale University.

[Shahar, 1997] Shahar, Y. (1997). A framework for knowledge-based temporal abstraction. *Artificial Intelligence*, 90(1-2):79–133.

[Shahar and Musen, 1995] Shahar, Y. and Musen, M. A. (1995). Knowledge-based temporal abstraction in clinical domains. Technical report, Stanford University.

[Zweig and Russell, 1998] Zweig, G. and Russell, S. (1998). Speech recognition with dynamic Bayesian networks. In *Fifteenth National Conference on Artificial Intelligence (AAAI'98)*, pages 173–180. AAAI Press.

Hierarchical Optimization of Policy-Coupled Semi-Markov Decision Processes

Gang Wang Sridhar Mahadevan
Department of Computer Science and Engineering
Michigan State University
East Lansing, MI 48823, USA
(wanggan1, mahadeva)@cse.msu.edu

Abstract

One general strategy for approximately solving large Markov decision processes is "divide-and-conquer": the original problem is decomposed into sub-problems which interact with each other, but yet can be solved independently by taking into account the nature of the interaction. In this paper we focus on a class of "policy-coupled" semi-Markov decision processes (SMDPs), which arise in many nonstationary real-world multi-agent tasks, such as manufacturing and robotics. The nature of the interaction among sub-problems (agents) is more subtle than that studied previously: the components of a sub-SMDP, namely the available states and actions, transition probabilities and rewards, depend on the policies used in solving the "neighboring" sub-SMDPs. This "strongly-coupled" interaction among sub-problems causes the approach of solving each sub-SMDP in parallel to fail. We present a novel approach whereby many variants of each sub-SMDP are solved, explicitly taking into account the different modes of interaction, and a dynamic merging algorithm is used to combine the base level policies. We present detailed experimental results for a 12-machine transfer line, a large real-world manufacturing task. We show that the hierarchical approach is not only much faster than a "flat" algorithm, but also outperforms two well-known heuristics for running transfer lines used in many factories.

1 INTRODUCTION

Increasingly, many aspects of autonomous agents, including sensing, planning, learning, and acting are being studied using the framework of Markov decision processes (MDPs) [17]. Unlike classical methods for solving MDPs, reinforcement learning (RL) [23] is a framework for solving MDPs without any prior knowledge of the underlying state dynamics or rewards. In the RL framework, agents learn policies for acting in dynamic uncertain environments through a trial-and-error process. Although RL has had a large number of successes in recent years, a fundamental problem is that many current techniques don't scale well to larger problems.

We can categorize approaches for scaling RL into two general classes. The first approach is to construct simpler MDPs by defining temporally abstract actions, which are really policies over primitive actions. Among the various *abstraction* approaches proposed to address the scaling issue are macro-based models called "options"[24], hierarchical finite-state machine models called "HAMs" [15], and the "MAXQ" method [5].

A second general strategy for scaling RL is to decompose the original intractably large MDP. Some examples of research taking the *decomposition* approach are Dean and Lin [4], Meuleau et al. [13], Parr [14] and Singh [20]. These approaches to MDP decomposition rely more on the specific characteristics of a problem and try to "divide and conquer" the original problem. Some of them try to divide the original MDP using "boundary" states (e.g. complete or partial decoupling of navigation problems [14]), others allow subprocesses to directly affect each other through the available action set [13]. However, the coupling between the smaller MDPs in previous studies typically is "weak", allowing the divide-and-conquer approach to be successful (e.g. [4]).

In this paper we generalize the second approach to a class of "policy-coupled" semi-Markov decision processes (SMDPs), which arise in many multi-agent domains. Although our work focuses on manufacturing given its practical importance [7, 18], examples of policy-decomposable SMDPs can be found in other multi-agent domains (e.g. robots playing soccer, two elevator systems, each of which serves half the floors etc.). The nature of the interaction is more subtle than problems previously considered: the components of each sub-SMDP, i.e. states, actions, transition probabilities and rewards, depend on policies used to solve "neighboring" sub-SMDPs. This interaction defeats the approach of solving each sub-SMDP in parallel. Yet, by analyzing the character of this interaction, we present a novel hierarchical approach that approximately solves the overall SMDP by explicitly taking into account the nature of interactions between the sub-SMDPs. Our approach is based on using an average reward SMDP Q-learning algorithm called SMART [12] for solving many variants of the constituent sub-SMDPs, and then uses a second level "dynamic merging" approach to combine these base policies into a final policy for solving the overall problem.

In Section 2, we introduce the framework of SMDPs. In Section 3, we provide an informal characterization of different ways of decomposing SMDPs, including previous work as well as the particular decomposition of SMDPs we study. In Section 4, we describe the transfer line problem in the manufacturing domain, and show how particular characteristics of this problem make it suitable for our method. Section 5 presents our hierarchical algorithm. Section 6 presents detailed experimental results of our hierarchical method applied to a large 12-machine transfer line problem, and compares it to the "flat" reinforcement learning algorithm. Section 7 summarizes the paper.

2 SEMI-MARKOV DECISION PROCESSES

We first introduce the framework of semi-Markov decision processes [17]. We also sketch an average-reward reinforcement learning algorithm for solving an SMDP, which does not assume any underlying knowledge about the transition probabilities or rewards.

A semi-Markov decision process (SMDP) is defined as a five tuple (S, A, P, R, F), where S is a set of states, A is a set of actions, P is a set of state and action dependent transition probabilities, R is a reward function, and F is a function giving probability of transition times for each state-action pair. SMDPs generalize MDPs in several ways, principally through allowing actions to be history dependent and by modeling the transition time distribution of each action.

More specifically, $P_{xy}(a)$ denotes the probability that action a will cause the system to transition from state $x \in S$ to $y \in S$. This transition probability function describes the transitions at decision epochs only, whereas the *natural process* describes the state trajectory at all times. F is a function where $F(t \mid s, a)$ is the probability that the next decision epoch occurs within t time units, after action a is executed in state s. From F, and P, we can compute Q by

$$Q(t, y \mid x, a) = P(y \mid x, a)F(t \mid x, a)$$

where Q denotes the probability that the system will be in state y for the next decision epoch, at or before t time units after choosing action a in state s, at the last decision epoch. Q can be used to calculate the expected transition time between decision epochs.

In general, the reward function for SMDPs consists of a fixed reward $k(x, a)$, resulting from an action a taken in state x, and an additional reward that is accumulated at *rate* $c(y, x, a)$ for the time the natural process remains in state y between the decision epochs. Note that the natural process may change state several times between decision epochs, and therefore, the rate at which the rewards are accumulated between decision epochs may vary.

Formally, the expected reward between two decision epochs, given that the system is in state x, and action a is chosen at the first decision epoch, may be expressed as

$$r(x, a) = k(x, a) + E_x^a \left\{ \int_0^\tau c(W_t, x, a) dt \right\} \quad (1)$$

where τ is the transition time to the second decision epoch, and W_t denotes the state of the natural process.

We have previously demonstrated a model-free average-reward algorithm (SMART) for finding gain-optimal policies for SMDPs [12]. This algorithm estimates the action value function $R^\pi(x, a)$, which is the average-adjusted sum of rewards received for the non-stationary policy of doing action a once, and then subsequently following a stationary policy π. $R^\pi(x, a)$ can be defined as

$$R^{\pi}(x,a) = r(x,a) - \rho^{\pi}\tau(x,a) + \sum_{y \in S} P_{xy}(a) \max_{b} R^{\pi}(y,b) \quad (2)$$

The temporal difference between the action-values of the current state and the actual next state is used to update the action values. In this case, the expected transition time $\tau(x,a)$ is replaced by the actual transition time, and the expected reward is replaced by the actual immediate reward. Therefore, the action values are updated as follows: [1]

$$R(x,a) \overset{\alpha}{\leftarrow} \left(r_{imm}(x,a) - \rho\tau + \max_{b} R(y,b) \right) \quad (3)$$

where $r_{imm}(x,a)$ is the actual cumulative reward earned between decision epochs due to taking action a in state x, ρ is the average reward, and α is a learning rate parameter. Note that ρ is actually the reward rate, and it is estimated by taking the ratio of the total reward so far, to the total simulation time.

3 A TAXONOMY OF METHODS FOR DECOMPOSING SMDPs

We now provide an informal characterization of different ways of decomposing SMDPs, including those studied in past work, and relate them to the problem class studied in our paper.

As mentioned earlier, there have been several prior methods proposed for decomposing MDPs (e.g. [4], [9], [13], [14], [20]). However, most of these focus on a specific class of MDP problems where the state space of the original problem can be divided into subsets to create smaller subproblems. In this paper we would like to broaden the concept of decomposition, where not only the state space but also other components of an SMDP, such as the action set and on a higher level, the policies for each subproblem, can be used to decompose the original problem.

First, we introduce the following concept. We term a problem $\mathcal{P}$ *SMDP-decomposable* if it satisfies the following criteria:

1. It can be described by a semi-Markov decision process.
2. It can be divided into several associated subproblems, $\mathcal{P}_1, \mathcal{P}_2, \ldots \mathcal{P}_m$, such that:
3. Each $\mathcal{P}_i$ can be further described by a semi-Markov decision process (denoted by $\mathcal{M}_i = (S_i, A_i, P_i, R_i, F_i)$), if for each of the other subproblems $\mathcal{P}_j, j \neq i$, actions are chosen using a fixed policy $\pi_j : S_j \rightarrow A_j$.

Note that the notion of SMDP-decomposable [2] is abstractly defined, and focuses mainly on how each sub-SMDP affects each other. It doesn't specify how the original problem is decomposed to get an equivalent set of subproblems so we can utilize the solution of these subproblems to get a solution to the overall problem. As a matter of fact, for the division of the original problem to be meaningful, we have to redefine the state space, action space, state/action transition probabilities and most importantly, reward function for each subproblem. In table 1, we give various examples of SMDP-decomposable problems, classified by the nature of the interaction among sub-problems.

Navigation problems, such as the one in table 1, are typical of the class of problems suitable for *state decomposition*. In such problems, the original state space can be simply divided into subsets, each one resulting in a smaller subproblem (which are coupled by interface states, as marked by "x" in table 1). By "guessing" or "successively approximating" the expected state value of the optimal policy of the original problem ([4]) and then solving the respective subproblems, the overall policy can be constructed hierarchically from the base-level policy. In most cases of state decomposition, the internal components of each sub-SMDP, such as the available action set for each state and the transition probabilities, inherit their values from the original problem, and remain the same during the problem solving process.

For problems approached using *action decomposition*, sub-SMDPs are coupled by the action set, such as in the air campaign planning problem [13], and the "composite" MDPs studied by Singh [20]. In problems of this category, the decision to apply a resource to a given task (e.g. an action taken in one sub-SMDP) influences the availability of that resource (action set) for other tasks. On the other hand, the transition probabilities of particular actions in one sub-SMDP are not affected by policies used to solve other sub-SMDPs. In this kind of decomposition, it is not only the state space, but also the action set through which the constituent sub-MDPs affect each other.

Finally, for problems solvable through *policy decompo-*

[1] We use the notation $y \overset{\alpha}{\leftarrow} x$ as an abbreviation for the stochastic approximation update rule $y \leftarrow (1-\alpha)y + \alpha x$.

[2] In the remaining part of this paper, we view MDPs as a special case of SMDPs

State Decomposition

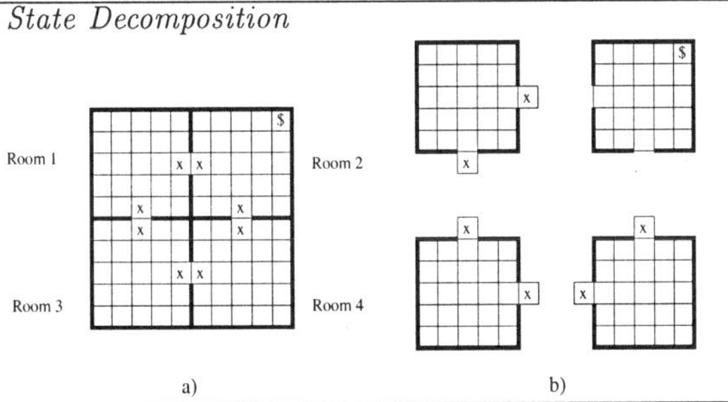

An example is a navigation problem of getting to state \$. In part b) the reward functions for all sub-SMDPs except room 2 are redefined (positive reward at "x"), but other components (e.g. actions) remain unchanged. See [4], [14], [16].

Action Decomposition

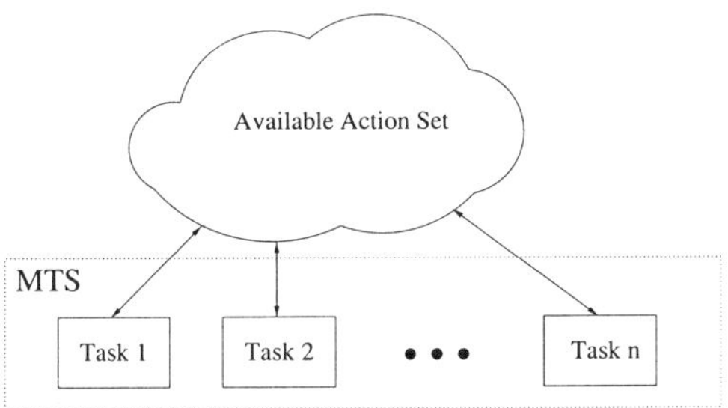

An example is the air campaign planning problem [13]. Here, the sub-SMDPs are also coupled by the set of available actions. Another example is the "factorial" composite MDP studied in [20] where the action set of the composite MDP is a proper subset of the cross product of the component action spaces.

Policy Decomposition

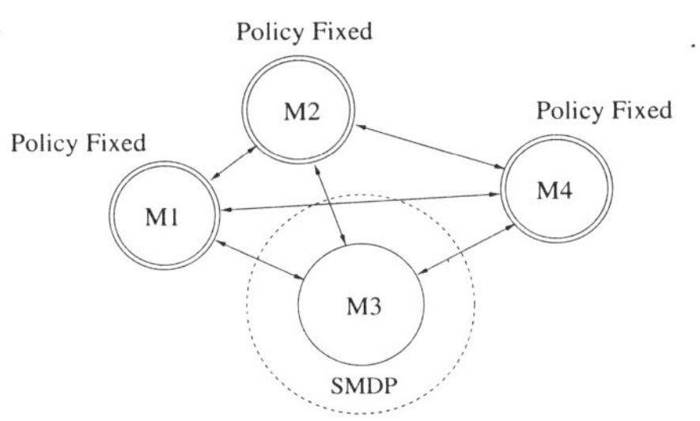

An example is the transfer line problem, where sub-SMPDs "strongly" interact, influencing each other's available states, actions, rewards, and transition probabilities. This problem will be discussed in detail in the next section.

Table 1: Different ways of decomposing SMDPs based on how the sub-problems interact with each other.

sition, states, actions, transition probabilities and rewards all may change when other sub-SMDPs change their policies. This makes for a more complicated coupling and therefore, requires a tricker way in approaching them.

When we examine the coupling of sub-SMDPs generated from the original problem $\mathcal{P}$, the most "weakly" coupled case occurs when the internal components of the sub-SMDP, such as the states, action sets and transition probabilities, inherit their values from the original SMDP. The coupling becomes stronger as more and more components of the sub-SMDPs are subject to change due to changes in other sub-SMDPs. Policy decomposition problems could possibly constitute the "strongest" coupling among sub-SMDPs.

In the following section we will introduce a real world instance of policy decomposition, namely the transfer line problem. In section 4 we will discuss our approach to solving this problem.

4 STOCHASTIC MODEL OF A TRANSFER LINE

The manufacturing problem we study is a discrete-part system consisting of a serial combination of distinct machines, whose overall goal is to satisfy target demand while minimizing work-in-process inventory [8]. The machines age as they are used, and are subject to breakdown and consequently need repair. Periodic maintenance can avoid unnecessary and costly repair. Transfer lines are a well-known model of factories (in particular, assembly plants) where product buffers are placed in between machines to reduce the effect of a breakdown of one machine on the overall production process. Since it is intractable to analytically compute an optimal control policy for transfer lines with more than 2 machines [8], some heuristic control methods have to be employed, such as KANBAN [1] and constant work-in-progress(CONWIP) [21]. A key disadvantage of these heuristics is that they only address the problem of minimizing work-in-process inventory. However, in reality, many other costs need to be considered, including the cost of production of parts, and the repair and preventive maintenance costs. It is all these factors that we'd like to optimize as well through solving the policy-coupled semi-Markov decision process model.

We will analyze transfer lines from the simplest case, a single machine under a fixed configuration, to the much more complicated case of multiple machines.

4.1 Single Machine Transfer Line

Before introducing transfer lines, let's briefly examine an SMDP model of a single machine (see figure 1). At each decision epoch, the single machine's action space set is $A_M = \{producing, maintenance, idling\}$. If it chooses *producing*, the machine takes supply materials from the upstream buffer and works on it until it is done and sends it to the downstream buffer. All raw materials are supplied at a *supply rate*, while all finished product in the buffer are removed from it at a *demand rate*. The action of *producing* increments a machine's running time, which when accumulated to a certain level, will lead (with high probability) to a *failure*. When the machine fails, it needs to be repaired. The failure, repair and maintenance times are all stochastic variables modeled by some distributions.

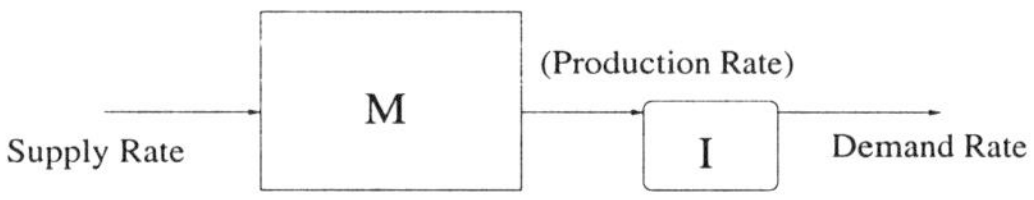

Figure 1: A single machine (M) and its inventory (I) is modeled as a semi-Markov decision process, with non-constant time actions such as "produce" or "maintain". The SMDP process is parameterized by the supply and demand rate.

If described as a SMDP, the state space S_M for a single machine transfer line can be described by a vector $< t, l >$, where t denotes the running time of the machine since last maintenance or repair; and l denotes the inventory size right after the machine. Since time is a continuous variable, for simplicity in this paper we coarsely discretize this value into intervals to turn the state space into a finite one.

The reward function R_M of the machine can be characterized by $r(x, a)$ as specified in the previous section, where $k(x, a)$ provides a fixed lump-sum reward (or cost) for each type of action (for example, a positive reward for producing, a negative cost for maintenance, and zero for idling). There is a continuous rate-cost for items that are stored in buffers. Failure and repair results in a fixed cost. These are all included in the function $c(W_t, x, a)$ in equation 1. Given a fixed demand rate and supply rate, the machine's state/action transition probabilities, $P_{xy}(a)$, for all states x and y and action a, can be specified.

Therefore, it is appropriate to say that a single machine SMDP model $\mathcal{M}$ is parameterized by three kinds of parameters: $(r^s_M, conf_M, r^d_M)$. Here r^s_M is a supply rate for machine M, r^d_M is its demand rate, and $conf_M$ includes various parameters for M's configuration such as machine failure time, repair time, producing time, buffer size, unit product reward, repair and failure cost, and finally unit cost for inventory buffer. Fortunately, these configuration parameters are fixed, and we may take them as constants for single and multiple machine transfer lines.

4.2 Transfer Line with Multiple Machines

A transfer line [8] models an assembly line operation in many factories, where a sequence of machines (or operations) is needed to make finished parts (see figure 2).

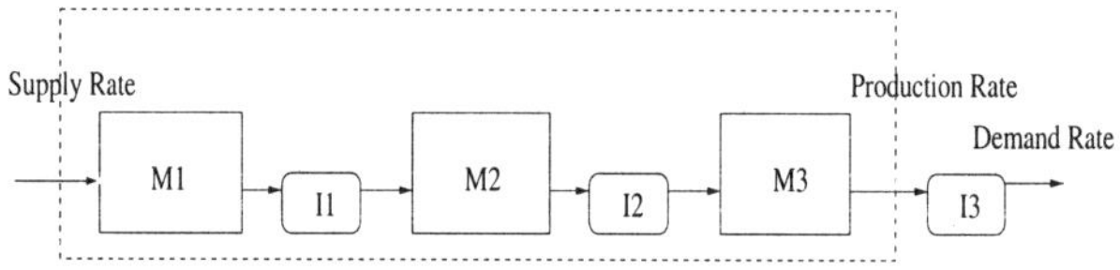

Figure 2: A transfer line with multiple machines can be viewed as a very large semi-Markov decision process, parameterized by supply and demand rate at its input and output.

The action space is the union of the expanded individual machine action spaces: $A_T = A'_{M1} \cup A'_{M2} \cup \ldots A'_{Mn}$, where A'_{Mi} is the labeled action for machine i. Considering the other machines' natural processes, when one machine is at a decision epoch, the state space of the whole transfer line is actually bigger than the cross product of the individual machine state spaces. Therefore, although the entire transfer line can still be described by a semi-Markov decision process, the state space is actually larger than the cross product of individual machine state spaces, and completely intractable.

However, if we look at the processes in a transfer line closely, we can see that the upstream machine's production rate is the downstream machine's supply rate; and the downstream machine's production rate is the upstream machine's demand rate. For example, in the transfer line of figure 3, for machine 3, the only factor among all the machines upstream that can influence it is machine 2's production rate. At the same time, since machine 3 is the last machine lined up in the transfer line, the machine's demand rate is exactly the demand rate of the whole transfer line. Therefore, we can decompose the overall "flat" semi-Markov decision process into n smaller semi-Markov decision processes which are sequentially coupled with each other. In this problem, the "contacting point" between the sub-SMDPs is each machine's production rate.

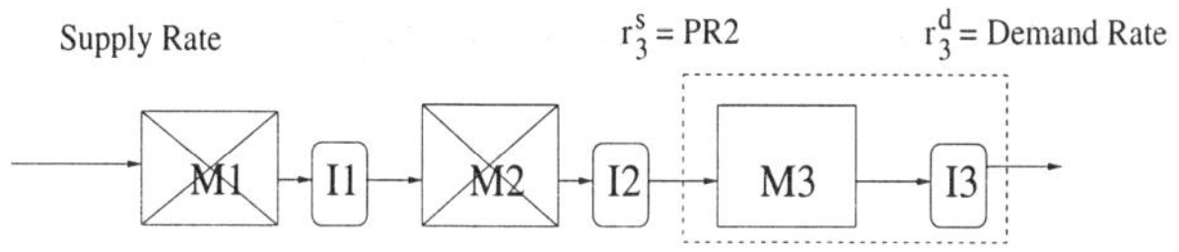

Figure 3: The overall SMDP model of a transfer line can be decomposed into a set of strongly-coupled, but significantly smaller single machine SMDPs. Here $PR2$ is production rate of machine 2. Machine 1 and machine 2 are operated with fixed policies, which makes machine 3 modelable as a semi-Markov decision process, with supply rate as $PR2$ and demand rate the demand rate of the whole transfer line.

Since each machine's production rate directly affects its neighboring machine's SMDPs, the internal dynamic character make the SMDPs more strongly coupled than that studied previously. This characteristic requires us to solve the problem in a hierarchical way, as described in the next section, and provides a much faster and better approach than "flat" optimization.

5 THE HIERARCHICAL OPTIMIZATION ALGORITHM

We now describe a hierarchical two-phase optimization algorithm, which combines an offline reinforcement learning algorithm for solving many variants of the constituent sub-SMDPs, and an online merging algorithm which dynamically recombines the learned policies.

Once the original problem is decomposed into coupled SMDPs, there are two ways to approximately solve this problem. One is to individually and simultaneously learn policies for every machine on-line by independently running n copies of the reinforcement learning algorithms together. We refer to this below as the *flat-SMART* algorithm [3]. However, for individual machine indexed i in a transfer line, its semi-Markov decision process is dependent on the machine's supply rate and demand rate, in other words, it depends on the production rate of machine $i-1$ and machine $i+1$. Therefore, if the production rates of the machine upstream and downstream are changing, the semi-Markov decision process of machine i will also vary accordingly. This makes on-line learning of an individual machine's policy in a transfer line extremely difficult and slow.

We already know that the overall semi-Markov decision process of the whole transfer line can be subdivided into a sequence of semi-Markov decision processes coupled by the actual production rates. Therefore, instead of training each machine *in-situ* while it is part of the transfer line, we train each machine in isolation using SMART for a variety of different boundary conditions, in particular, supply rates of parts coming in, and target demand rates of parts consumed by machines down the line. Once each machine is trained individually, we then optimize the transfer line as a whole, where instead of selecting each action for operating a machine, we dynamically choose between different *policies*. This algorithm is summarized in Figure 4.

This algorithm bear some similarities with other previous work. Parr [14] creates "policy caches" for subtasks before they are combined to make optimal or near optimal policies for the overall problem. In Dean and Lin's work [4], for each subproblem, a new policy is computed based on the estimation of the "boundary states" values. However, both of these systems assume that the overall problem can be divided simply by the state set, which is impossible in the transfer line problem.

- *Off-line Reinforcement Learning* $(S_{min}, S_{max}, D_{min}, D_{max}, \theta)$

  For $(s = S_{min}; s \leq S_{max}; s = s + \theta)$
      For $(d = D_{min}; d \leq D_{max}; d = d + \theta)$
          {
          Run SMART algorithm on a single machine transfer line with supply/demand rate as s/d.
          Store the obtained policy as $\Pi(s, d)$.
          } /* See Figure 6 for an example */

- *On-line Dynamic Merging* (τ)
  For each machine i in parallel, with time interval τ:
      {
      Observe over τ s_i = production rate of machine $i-1$;
      Observe over τ d_i = production rate of machine $i+1$;
      Set $\pi = \Pi(s_i, d_i)$;
      Run policy π for time τ;
      }

Figure 4: A two-phase hierarchical algorithm for optimizing a policy-decomposable transfer line SMDP.

Note we have two levels of control: the lower one is a reinforcement learning level of learning control of

[3]The SMART algorithm is a modified Q-learning method for average-reward SMDPs and is described in Section 3.

the individual machine actions. The higher level is an abstract dynamic policy merging step based on the observed supply and demand rates from machines upstream and downstream. We will refer to this technique as *hierarchical-SMART* below.

6 EXPERIMENTAL RESULTS

In this section we present detailed experimental results of the hierarchical SMART algorithm for optimization of transfer lines. We compare the performance of our algorithm to standard industrial heuristics, in particular KANBAN and CONWIP. We also compare the benefits of hierarchical decomposition with a "flat" optimization algorithm.

For the results described below, we used the following parameters. The unit (rate) cost for a single product on inventory is 2.0, the cost of failure is 40.0, and the maintenance cost is 5.0. For each product, a reward of 10 is received if it is "sold". Each machine has a failure time modeled as a normal distribution with mean of 10.0 and standard deviation of 2.0. Repair time, after each failure, is exponentially distributed with mean of 10.0. The time for maintenance is also exponentially distributed with mean of 2.0. The time to produce a product is lognormally distributed with mean of 1.0. We emphasize that our approach does not depend on the distributional or cost model, and we have conducted experiments with other cost and distributional models also.

6.1 "FLAT" OPTIMIZATION OF A 3-MACHINE LINE

We begin by comparing SMART on a three machine transfer line problem with the KANBAN and CONWIP heuristic methods. Note that this is a non-hierarchical approach, where each machine is trained while it is part of the overall transfer line. Figure 5 compares the average reward and average inventory size for the policy learned by SMART with that produced by the CONWIP and KANBAN heuristics. Each graph shows the result over 50,000 time units. In this experiment, the inventory buffer size for each machine in KANBAN is 10, and the total work-in-progress inventory in CONWIP is 11. The supply/demand rate is infinite/0.6. The results are averaged over 10 separate runs. Clearly, the average reward of the policy learned by SMART is significantly better than that achieved by CONWIP or KANBAN. This improvement is partly due to the fact that the latter heuristics do not incorporate a maintenance policy

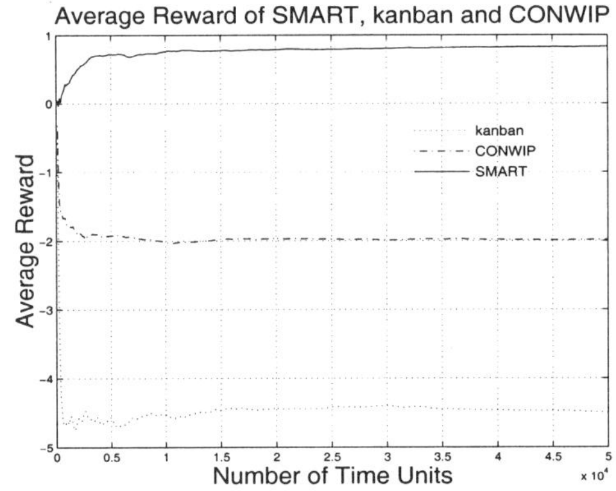

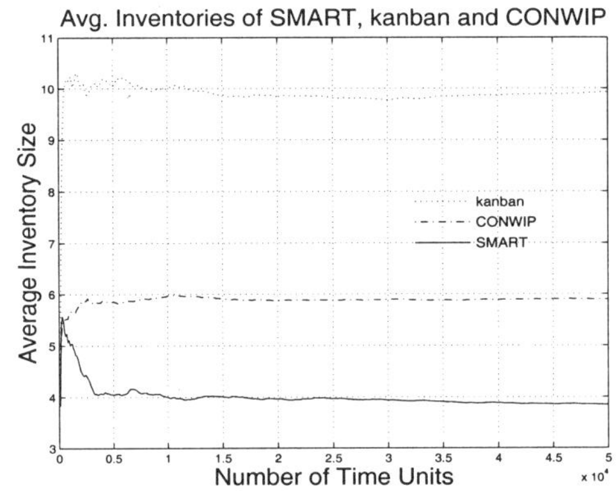

Figure 5: Comparing the average reward and inventory size learned by SMART for a three-machine transfer line with that produced by the KANBAN and CONWIP heuristics.

to minimize repair costs. Also, the policy learned by SMART also achieves a significant reduction in inventory size over KANBAN and CONWIP.

6.2 HIERARCHICAL OPTIMIZATION OF A LARGE 12-MACHINE LINE

We now turn to hierarchical optimization, where we divide the whole optimization process into two phases: an offline training phase and an online merging phase.

6.2.1 Offline Training

First, a "typical" machine is trained in isolation with different supply/demand rates. For each supply/demand rate combination, we ran SMART for 100,000 time units. The results are shown in Figure 6. Note that KANBAN performs poorly, when support rate is higher than demand rate, because it tends to fill inventory space. In such cases, SMART does a much better job at balancing the production rate along with supply and demand rate to get a higher average reward

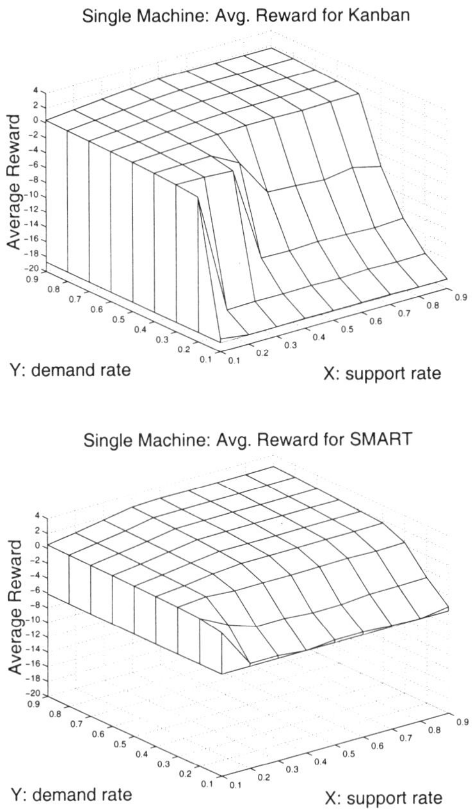

Figure 6: Average reward of KANBAN and SMART on variants of the sub-SMDPs created by varying the supply/demand rates.

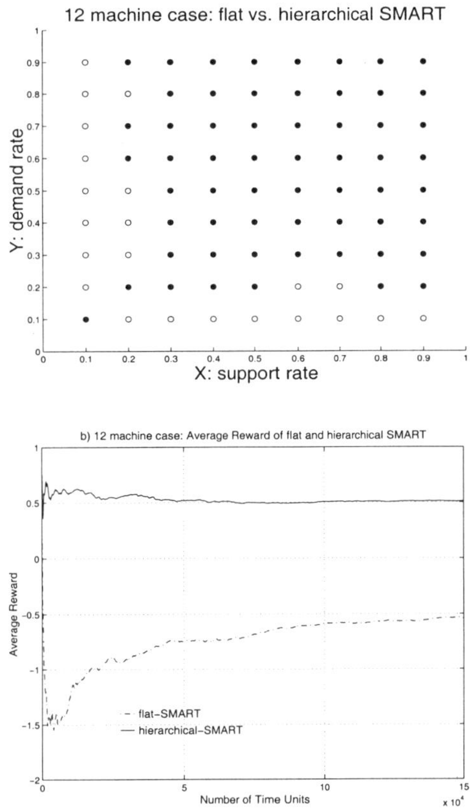

Figure 7: a) Comparison of average reward of hierarchical-SMART versus flat-SMART for a 12 machine transfer line. The solid dot means that hierarchical-SMART outperformed the flat-SMART approach. b) Average reward plot for the 12 machine transfer line for flat-SMART and hierarchical-SMART.

policy.

6.2.2 Online Merging

After training, we reinsert each machine into the line, and use the dynamic merging algorithm described in Figure 4 to compute the policy for the whole transfer line. Here, each machine is operated by selecting from one of the previously learned policies, according to its observed supply/demand rate. In this set of experiments, each machine keeps track of its supply and demand rate for the last 20 events and chooses the closest policy. For a big transfer line with 12 machines, figure 7 (a) compares the average reward of the policy learned by the hierarchical-SMART algorithm versus the flat-SMART approach, averaging over 5 runs for each approach. Figure 7 (b) is the result from a single run for both flat and hierarchical SMART. The supply/demand rate is 0.7/0.7. This experiment shows that on a larger scale optimization problem, the hierarchical SMART method results a dramatic improvement over the "flat" approach.

6.3 Transfer Line with "Bottle-neck" Machine

Here, we explore the question of what would happen if in our transfer line one machine breaks down more frequently than others. Obviously this machine cannot be treated the same as the others. Using the algorithm presented in the previous section, we train this bottle-neck machine and the "typical" machine separately, and then merge the policies as before.

In this experiment, for the bottle-neck machine in the middle of the transfer line, the mean failure time is at 3.0, instead of 10.0 time units. Figure 8 plots the average of 5 runs for each approach. From the result we can see that it is better to train the failure-prone machine separately before the policy merging step is applied. One possible consequence of this approach is that if each sub-SMDP in a policy-decomposable SMDP is very different from each other, each of them

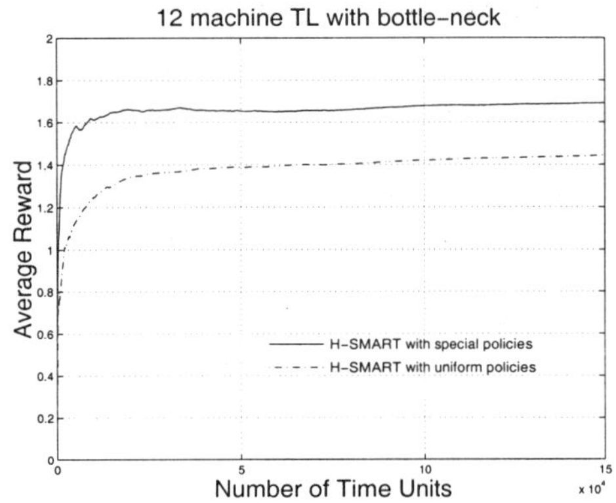

Figure 8: 12 machine transfer line with bottle-neck machine indexed 6. Ignoring and special-treating the bottle-neck machine have different results as shown in this picture.

has to be trained separately, which adds considerable computation/simulation time before the online merging phase can be used.

6.4 Varying the Temporal Intervals for Policy Merging

We also show that varying the timing interval for the abstract-level control using the policy merging step in H-SMART affects its performance. Figure 9 shows the average reward of the policy learned by H-SMART on a 12-machine transfer line with different τ values. The figure shows the average over 5 different runs for each timing interval, ranging from 10 time-events to 60 time-events. We see here clearly the more frequently we observe the demand/supply rate for each machine, the more precisely we estimate the configuration for that machine and therefore, the better the performance of hierarchical-SMART.

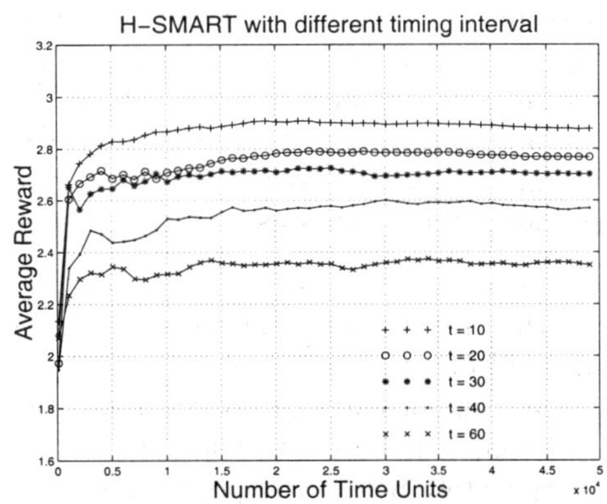

Figure 9: H-SMART with different τ values on 12 machine transfer line.

7 CONCLUSIONS AND FUTURE WORK

In this paper we proposed a novel algorithm for solving large SMDPs, which are policy-decomposable: the original SMDP can be decomposed into simpler sub-SMDPs, which strongly interact. That is, the components (states, actions, rewards, transition probabilities) for a particular sub-SMDP depend on the policies used to solve "neighboring" sub-SMDPs. We described a general algorithm (hierarchical-SMART) to optimize a real-world instance of policy-decomposable SDMPs from manufacturing, namely a transfer line. The hierarchical-SMART algorithm uses an average-reward SMDP Q-learning method to solve many variants of the individual sub-SMDPs, taking into account the modes of interaction among them, and then uses a dynamic policy merging strategy at the abstract level to compute a policy for the entire transfer line. The experimental results showed that this approach is superior to well-established heuristics for operating transfer lines, as well as to using a "flat" approach of learning to control each machine in parallel.

Many issues remain unexplored in this research. There are many other examples of policy-coupled SMDPs in manufacturing, such as jobshops and flowshops, which are possibly even more challenging than transfer lines. As another example, consider the RoboSoccer task where different agents learn in a non-stationary environment to play soccer. If we view each agent as a sub-SMDP, then the various sub-SMDPS are clearly policy-coupled: each agent can be trained to reliably play a certain "role" only when all the other agents use fixed policies. In fact, recent work has employed training sessions of this type, e.g. see Stone [22]. Another issue that remains to be investigated is policy-coupled SMDPs with deeper abstraction hierarchies, such as in MAXQ [5]. The taxonomy of decomposition methods that we proposed is somewhat intuitive. Clearly, a more formal characterization would be useful. Finally, a general algorithm for solving arbitrary forms (or even special classes) of policy-coupled SMDPs would be a significant step forward.

Acknowledgement

This research is supported in part by an NSF CAREER Award Grant No. IRI-9501852, and by a Michigan State University (MSU) AURIG grant.

References

[1] Berkley, B. J. 1992. "A review of the KANBAN production control research literature" in *Production and Operations Management 1(4)*, 393-411.

[2] Bonvik, A. M. Couch, C. Gershwin, S. 1996. "A Comparison of Production-Line Control Mechanism". Accepted for *International Journal of Production Research.*

[3] Crites, R. Barto, A. 1996. "Improving elevator performance using reinforcement learning" in *Neural Information Processing System (NIPS).*

[4] Dean, T. Lin, S.H. 1995. "Decomposition Techniques for Planning in Stochastic Domains", in *Proceedings of IJCAI'95*, Montreal, 1995.

[5] Dietterich, T. G. 1998. "The MAXQ method for hierarchical reinforcement learning". Proceedings of 1998 International Conference on Machine Learning.

[6] Gershwin, S., Caramanis, M., Murray, P. 1988. "Simulation Experience with a Hierarchical Scheduling Policy for a Simple Manufacturing System", in *Proceedings of the 27th IEEE Conference on Decision and Control*, Austin, Texas.

[7] Gershwin, S. 1987. "A Hierarchical Framework for Manufacturing System Scheduling: A Two-Machine Example." in *Proceedings of the 26th IEEE Conference on Decision and Control*, Los Angeles, CA.

[8] Gershwin, S. 1994. *Manufacturing System Engineering.* Prentice Hall.

[9] Kaelbling, L. P., 1993. "Hierarchical Reinforcement Learning: Preliminary Results," in *Proceedings of the Tenth International Conference on Machine Learning*, 1993.

[10] Law, A. Kelton, W. 1991. *Simulation Modeling and Analysis.* New York, USA: McGraw-Hill.

[11] Mahadevan, S. 1996. "Average Reward Reinforcement Learning: Foundations, Algorithms, and Empirical Results" in *Machine Learning.*, 22, 159-195.

[12] Mahadevan, S., Marchalleck, N., Das, T., and Gosavi, A. 1997. "Self-improving factory simulation using continuous-time average reward reinforcement learning" in *Proceedings of the Fourteenth International Machine Learning Conference.*, D. Fisher (editor), Morgan Kaufmann. 202-210.

[13] Meuleau, N., Hauskrecht, M., Kim, K, Peshkin, L., Kaelbling, L., Dean, T., Boutilier, C. 1998. "Solving Very Large Weakly Coupled Markov Decision Processes", in *Proceedings of the Conference on Uncertainty in AI*, 1998.

[14] Parr, R. 1998. "Flexible Decomposition Algorithms for Weakly Coupled Markov Decision Problems" in *Proceedings of the Conference on Uncertainty in AI*, 1998.

[15] Parr, R. and Russell, S. 1998. "Reinforcement Learning with hierarchies of machines" in *Advances in Neural Information Processing Systems (NIPS).*

[16] Precup, D., Sutton, R. S. 1997. "Multi-time models for temporally abstract planning", in *Advances in Neural Information Processing Systems 10: Proceedings of the 1997 Conference*, Denver, Colorado. MIT Press.

[17] Puterman, M. L. 1994. *Markov Decision Processes: Discrete Stochastic Dynamic Programming.* Wiley Series in Probability and Mathematical Statistics. John Wiley & Sons, Inc.

[18] Sethi, S., and Zhang, Q. 1994. *Hierarchical Decision Making in Stochastic Manufacturing Systems.*, Birkhauser.

[19] Singh, S. Bertsekas D. 1996. "Reinforcement Learning for Dynamic Channel Allocation in Cellular Telephone Systems" in *Neural Information Processing Systems (NIPS)*, 1996.

[20] Singh S, Cohn D. 1998, "How to Dynamically Merge Markov Decision Processes", In NIPS 11.

[21] Spearman, M. L., D. L. Woodruff, and W. J. Hopp. 1990. "CONWIP: a pull alternative to KANBAN" in *International Journal of Production Research 28(5)*, 879-894.

[22] Stone, P., "Layered Learning for Multi-Agent Systems", Ph.D. thesis, Carnegie Mellon University, December 1998.

[23] Sutton, R., Barto, A. 1998. *Reinforcement Learning: An Introduction*, MIT Press, Cambridge, MA. A Bradford Book.

[24] Sutton, R., Precup, D., and Singh, S. 1998, "Intra-option Learning about Temporally Abstract Actions", Proceedings of the 15th International Conference on Machine Learning (IMLC-98), pp. 556-564.

Large Margin Trees for Induction and Transduction

Donghui Wu
Dept of Math. Sciences
Rensselaer Polytechnic Inst.
Troy, NY 12180, USA
wud2@rpi.edu

Kristin P. Bennett
Dept of Math. Sciences
Rensselaer Polytechnic Inst.
Troy, NY 12180, USA
bennek@rpi.edu

Nello Cristianini
Dept of Engineering Math.
University of Bristol
Bristol BS8 1TR, UK
nello.cristianini@
bristol.ac.uk

John Shawe-Taylor
Dept of Computer Science
Royal Holloway
Univ. of London, Egham
Surrey TW20 0EX, UK
jst@dcs.rhbnc.ac.uk

Abstract

The problem of controlling the capacity of decision trees is considered for the case where the decision nodes implement linear threshold functions. In addition to the standard early stopping and pruning procedures, we implement a strategy based on the margins of the decision boundaries at the nodes. The approach is motivated by bounds on generalization error obtained in terms of the margins of the individual classifiers. Experimental results are given which demonstrate that considerable advantage can be derived from using the margin information. The same strategy is applied to the problem of transduction, where the positions of the test points are revealed to the training algorithm. This information is used to generate an alternative training criterion motivated by transductive theory. In the transductive case, the results are not as encouraging, suggesting that little, if any, consistent advantage is culled from using the unlabelled data in the proposed fashion. This conclusion does not contradict theoretical results, but leaves open the theoretical and practical question of whether more effective use can be made of the additional information.

1 INTRODUCTION

Perceptron Decision Trees (PDT) are decision trees in which each internal node is associated with a hyperplane in general position in the input space. Given their high flexibility, a feature that they share with more standard decision trees, they tend to overfit the data if their complexity is not somehow kept under control. The standard approach to controlling their complexity is to limit their size, with early stopping or pruning procedures. In this paper we use their margin (namely, the minimum distance between the decision boundaries and the training points) to control their capacity both in an inductive and in a transductive situation. Transduction has been proposed by Vapnik [11] as an alternative form of inference, which skips the inductive step of generating a hypothesis, but directly infers the labels on a given test set from the training data. In this paper we examine methods for incorporating capacity-control using margins into PDT for both inductive and transductive inference. We demonstrate that by incorporating margin maximization using relatively minor algorithmic changes, into an existing PDT algorithm, generalization can be greatly enhanced.

For the inductive case, the theoretical motivations behind the use of the margin lie in the Data-Dependent Structural Risk Minimization [7]: the scale of the cover used in VC theory to provide a bound on the generalization error depends on the margins and hence the hierarchy of classes is chosen in response to the data. For the transductive case where the consistent hyperplane with maximal margin on both the training and test points is selected, similar bounds can be obtained more directly by defining a hierarchy of classes of hyperplanes derived from their margins on the training and test points. The bounds obtained are qualitatively similar, so that the question of what advantage can be obtained using this method remains open. The ramification of this theory is also quite intuitive – decisions with wider margins are better. The two trees in Figure 1 have the same number of decisions, and training accuracy, but the right tree has a smaller probability of future error since it has wider margins.

The algorithms described here are greedy procedures aimed at producing large margin trees. We propose

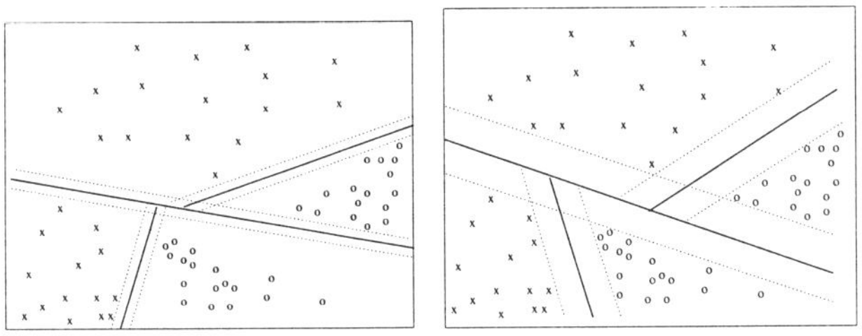

Figure 1: Small Margin versus Large Margin Decision Trees

three such algorithms for induction: FAT, MOC1 and MOC2, and one for transduction MTT, comparing their performance with that of OC1 [4], one of the best known PDT learning systems. Practically, these algorithms were implemented by either modifying the splitting criterion within the basic OC1 algorithm (MOC1, MOC2, and MTT) or by post-processing the OC1 output (FAT). All three large-margin inductive systems and the transductive system outperform OC1 on most of the real world data-sets we have used, indicating that overfitting in PDTs can be efficiently combatted by enlarging the margin of the decision boundaries on the training data. In this case, it does not much matter how the large margin bias is enforced: the quite different approaches of MOC1, MOC2, FAT, and MTT all work. The important thing seems to be to enforce the large margin.

We report preliminary experiments with real world datasets comparing transductive and inductive inference. Our first experiment on average case transductive behavior is consistent with what already was observed in a similar experiment on transduction using support vector machines [2], namely that the use of working set information rarely hurts and sometimes helps the generalization. In a second experiment we look at the difference between transduction and induction on a single task that would seemingly favor transduction, our results are less conclusive. Both the margin based algorithms outperform OC1 but the transductive approach is not consistently better than the margin-based inductive approach.

2 PERCEPTRON DECISION TREES

PDTs are decision trees in which each internal node is associated with a hyperplane in general position in the input space. The space is so partitioned into different (polytopic) regions which are then assigned to classes. It is useful to formally define the class of functions computed by PDTs as a special case of Generalized Decision Trees functions:

Definition 2.1 Generalized Decision Trees (GDT). *Given a space* X *and a set of boolean functions* $\mathcal{F} = \{f : X \to \{0,1\}\}$, *the class* $\mathrm{GDT}(\mathcal{F})$ *of Generalized Decision Trees over* $\mathcal{F}$ *are functions which can be implemented using a binary tree where each internal node is labelled with an element of* $\mathcal{F}$, *and each leaf is labelled with either 1 or 0.*

To evaluate a particular tree T on input $x \in X$, all the boolean functions associated to the nodes are assigned the same argument $x \in X$, which is the argument of $T(x)$. The values assumed by them determine a unique path from the root to a leaf: at each internal node the left (respectively right) edge to a child is taken if the output of the function associated to that internal node is 0 (respectively 1). This path is known as the *evaluation path*. The value of the function $T(x)$ is the value associated to the leaf reached. We say that input x reaches a node of the tree, if that node is on the evaluation path for x. We will also call *nodes* the internal nodes of a tree, *leaves* the external ones.

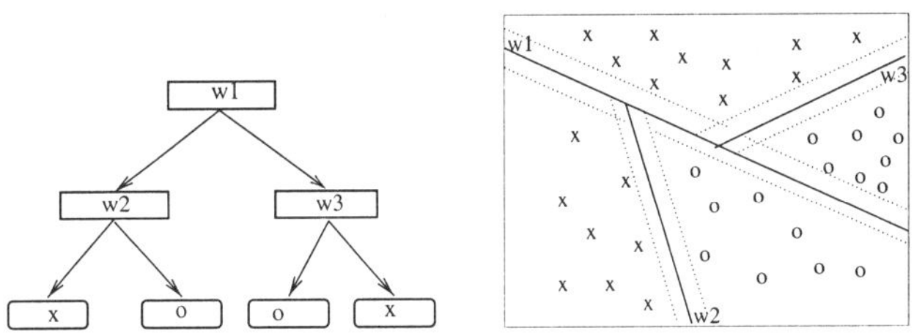

Figure 2: A Perceptron Decision Tree and the way it splits the input space

Definition 2.2 *Given* $X = R^n$, *a* Perceptron Decision Tree (PDT) *is a GDT over*

$$\mathcal{F}_{\mathrm{PDT}} = \{f_w : f_w(x) = 1 \Leftrightarrow w^T x > 0,\ w \in R^{n+1}\}$$

where we have assumed that the inputs have been augmented with a coordinate of constant value, hence implementing a thresholded perceptron.

PDTs are generally induced by means of a TopDown growth procedure, which starts from the root node and greedily chooses a perceptron which maximizes some cost function, usually a measure of the "impurity" of the subsamples implicitly defined by the split. See for example the algorithm C4.5[5]. This maximization is usually hard to perform, and sometimes replaced by randomized (sub)optimization. The subsamples are then mapped to the two children nodes. The procedure is then recursively applied to the nodes, and the tree is grown until some stopping criterion is met. Such a tree is then used as a starting point for a "BottomUp" search, performing a pruning of the tree. This implies eliminating the nodes which are redundant, or which are unable to "pay for themselves" in terms of the cost function. Generally pruning an overfitting tree produces better classifiers than those obtained with early stopping, since it makes it possible to check if promising directions were in fact worth exploring, and if locally good solutions were on the contrary a dead-end. So, while the standard "TopDown" algorithm is an extremely greedy procedure, with the introduction of pruning it can be possible to look-ahead: this allows for discovery of more hidden structure.

3 GENERALIZATION ANALYSIS FOR INDUCTION USING PDTS

The theory of generalization for large margin classifiers relies on data-dependent structural risk minimisation [7] in the sense that the hierarchy of the hyperplanes is determined by their margin on the training data. The same approach can be applied to decisions trees with large margin decision nodes. The following theorem holds [8, 1]

Theorem 3.1 *[8, 1] Suppose we are able to classify an m sample of labelled examples using a perceptron decision tree and suppose that the tree obtained contained K decision nodes with margins γ_i at node i, then we can bound the generalization error with probability greater than $1-\delta$ to be less than*

$$\frac{130R^2}{m}\left(D'\log(4em)\log(4m)+\log\frac{(4m)^{K+1}\binom{2K}{K}}{(K+1)\delta}\right)$$

where $D' = \sum_{i=1}^{K}\frac{1}{\gamma_i^2}$ and R is a bound on the norm of the training examples.

This result gives an upper bound on generalization error for consistent trees. It is a decreasing function of the margins and number of points and increasing function of the number of decisions. Empirical study have shown that just minimizing the number of decision nodes does not produce the best tree [4]. Margins play a significant factor, so PDT algorithms should incorporate margin maximization.

4 DESCRIPTION OF THE INDUCTIVE ALGORITHMS

In this section we examine three different approaches for incorporating margin maximization for inference within PDT. The first two approaches incorporate margin maximization into the splitting criterion or impurity measure used to construct the tree. The last approach maximizes margins in a post-processing phase. More extensive description of these algorithms can also be found in [1].

We started with one of the best known PDT learning systems, OC1 of Murthy, Kasif and Salzberg, which is freely available over the Internet[4]. It is a randomized algorithm which performs a randomized hill-climbing search for learning the perceptrons, and builds the tree TopDown. Starting from the root node, the system chooses the hyperplane which minimizes a predefined "impurity" measure (e.g. information gain, Gini index, or the Twoing Rule). The system is greedy because at each stage it chooses the best split available, and randomized because such a best split is not obtained by means of exhaustive search but with a randomized hill-climbing process. In our experiments the twoing rule is used as the "impurity" measure in OC1.

The standard twoing rule is

$$\text{TwoingValue} = \frac{|T_L|}{|n|}\frac{|T_R|}{|n|}\left(\sum_{i=1}^{k}\left|\frac{|L_i|}{|L_L|}-\frac{|R_i|}{|R_R|}\right|\right)^2$$

where $n = |T_L| + |T_R|$

k - number of classes,

$|T_L|$ - number of instances on the left of the split

$|T_R|$ - number of instances on the right of the split

$|L_i|$ - number of instances in category i on the left of the split

$|R_i|$ - number of instances in category i on the right of the split.

This is a goodness measure rather than an impurity one, and OC1 attempts to maximize it at each split during the growth via minimizing 1/TwoingValue.

4.1 DESCRIPTION OF ALGORITHM MOC1

MOC1 (Margin_OC1) is a variation of OC1, which modifies the objective function of OC1 to consider the size of the margin. The underlying philosophy is to find a separating plane with a tradeoff between decision impurity and the size of margin at each node. MOC1 attempts to minimize the impurity function and maximize the margin during induction process.

The MOC1 algorithm minimizes the following objective function:

$$(1 - \lambda) * OC1\_Objective + C * \frac{1}{current\_margin}$$

where

- $OC1\_Objective$ is the impurity measure of OC1, in this study, the twoing rule is used as impurity measure.

- $current\_margin$ is the distance between two nearest points on the different sides of the current separating hyperplane.

- λ is a scalar weight, $\lambda \in [0, 1]$.

- $C = \lambda * log10(\text{no\_of\_points\_at\_current\_node})$.

λ determines how much the large margin is weighted in selecting the split. Tuning λ could improve the performance. When determining the weight of the margin, we also take the number of points at the current node into consideration. The idea is that a constant weight of margin for all nodes is not good. The weight should be able to adapt to the position of current node and size of training examples at the current node. Since we are not particularly interested in finding the tree with highest possible accuracy, but rather demonstrating that large margins can improve the generalization, we did not tune the λ for each dataset to achieve the highest possible accuracy. We set $\lambda = .05$ for all datasets in all of the experiments. In other words, the results of MOC1 presented below are not the best results possible.

4.2 DESCRIPTION OF ALGORITHM MOC2

MOC2 uses a modified twoing rule, which directly incorporates the idea of large margin to the impurity measure. Unlike MOC1, MOC2 uses a soft margin. It treats points falling within the margin and outside of the margin differently. Only the impurity measure is altered. The rest is same as in the standard OC1 algorithm.

The modified twoing rule

$$TwoingValue = \frac{|MT_L|}{n} * \frac{|MT_R|}{n} * \sum_{i=1}^{k} \left| \frac{|L_i|}{|T_L|} - \frac{|R_i|}{|T_R|} \right| * \sum_{i=1}^{k} \left| \frac{|ML_i|}{|MT_L|} - \frac{|MR_i|}{|MT_R|} \right|$$

where $n = |T_L| + |T_R|$ - total number of instances at current node

k - number of classes, for two class problems

$|T_L|$ - number of instances on the left of the split, i.e. $w^T x \geq 0$

$|T_R|$ - number of instances on the right of the split i.e. $w^T x < 0$

$|L_i|$ - number of instances in category i on the left of the split

$|R_i|$ - number of instances in category i on the right of the split

$|MT_L|$ - number of instances on the left of the split, $w^T x \geq 1$

$|MT_R|$ - number of instances on the right of the split $w^T x \leq -1$

$|ML_i|$ - number of instances in category i with $w^T x \geq 1$

$|MR_i|$ - number of instances in category i with $w^T x \leq -1$.

In the modified twoing rule, our goal is, at each node, to find a split with fewer points falling within the margin (in between $-1 < w^T x < 1$), with high accuracy outside the margin and good overall accuracy. Here again, we try to achieve a balance of classification accuracy and size of margin. By doing this, we want to push apart the two classes from the separating hyperplane as far as possible while maintaining a reasonable good classification accuracy, hence, improve the generalization of the induced decision tree. The advantage of MOC2 is that there are no free parameters to tune.

4.3 DESCRIPTION OF ALGORITHM FAT

The algorithm FAT first described in [8] uses the tree produced by OC1 as a starting point, and maximizes its margins at each decision. This involves finding - for each node - the hyperplane which performs *the same* split as performed by the OC1 tree but with the maximal margin. This can be done by considering the subsample reaching each node as perfectly divided into two parts, and feeding the data accordingly relabelled to an algorithm which finds the optimal separating hyperplane - separating hyperplane with maximal margin in this now linearly separable data. The optimal separating hyperplanes are then placed in the corresponding decision nodes and the new tree is tested on the same test data. Note that, the PDT produced by FAT will have the same tree structure and training accuracy as the original PDT constructed by OC1. They will only differ on test accuracy. We use the Support Vector Machine (SVM) algorithm [10] to find the optimal separating hyperplane. To conform with the definition of a PDT, no kernel is used in the SVM, the optimal separating hyperplane is constructed in the input space.

Algorithm for FAT

1. Construct a decision tree using OC1, call it OC1-PDT.
2. Starting from root of OC1-PDT, traverses through all the non-leaf nodes. At each node,
   - Relabel the points at this node with $\omega^T x \geq 0$ as class *right*, the other points at this node as class *left*.
   - Find the perceptron (optimal separating hyperplane) $f(x) = {\omega^*}^T x$, which separates class *right* and class *left* perfectly with maximal margin.
   - replace the original perceptron with the new one.
3. Output the FAT-PDT.

5 EXPERIMENTS WITH INDUCTION

This first set of experiments deal with the predictive power of large margin PDTs in a induction setting. As described in the previous section, the first two algorithms, MOC1 and MOC2, have different impurity measures which take into consideration the margins. the other one, FAT, accepts input a PDT constructed using OC1 and outputs a large margin version of the same tree. All three algorithms work for multi-class data. The three systems have been compared with OC1 on 10 benchmarking datasets. The results confirm the predictions of the theoretical model, clearly indicating that the generalization is improved by enlarging the margin.

The datasets we have used for the study are 6 datasets used in the original OC1 paper[4], and 4 other datasets, which are publicly available in the UCI data repository [12]. The datasets studied in [4] are *Dim*, *Bright*, *Wisconsin Breast Cancer*, *Pima Indians Diabetes*, *Boston Housing* and *Iris*. The four additional datasets are *Bupa*, *Sonar*, *Heart* and *Wisconsin Breast Cancer Prognosis*. The datasets differ greatly from subjects, sizes and number of attributes, the subjects of datasets range from medical to astronomical, sizes from 150 to 4192, number of attributes from 4 to 60. For details of these datasets see [4, 12]. For each dataset, a single run of 10-fold cross-validation is carried out. The relevant quantity, in this experiment, is the difference in the test accuracy between PDTs with arbitrary margins constructed by OC1 and the PDTs with large margins on the same data.

We used 10-fold cross-validation to measure the learning ability of the algorithms against OC1, and to test the difference between the means of our algorithms and OC1, a paired t-test is used (p value). All p-values with significance .25 or less/.75 or greater are reported.

Table 1: Ten-fold Cross-Validation Accuracy Means of OC1, FAT, MOC1 and MOC2

Dataset	OC1 $\bar{x}$	FAT $\bar{x}$ (p)	MOC1 $\bar{x}$ (p)	MOC2 $\bar{x}$ (p)	BEST
Bright	98.46	98.62 (*.05*)	**98.94** (*.10*)	98.82 (*.10*)	MOC1
Bupa	65.22	66.09 (*.10*)	68.41 (*.20*)	**70.14** (*.04*)	MOC2
Cancer	95.89	**96.48** (*.05*)	95.60	95.89	FAT
Dim	94.82	94.92 (*.20*)	95.23 (*.09*)	94.90	MOC1
Heart	73.40	76.43 (*.12*)	75.76 (*.21*)	**77.78** (*.10*)	MOC2
Housing	81.03	**83.20** (*.05*)	82.02	80.23	FAT
Iris	95.33	96.00 (*.17*)	95.33	96.00	FAT
Pima	71.09	71.48 (*.04*)	**73.18** (*.08*)	72.53 (*.23*)	MOC1
Prognosis	78.91	74.15 (*.96*)	78.23	**79.59**	MOC2
Sonar	67.79	**74.04** (*.01*)	72.12 (*.19*)	73.21 (*.16*)	FAT

Of the 10-fold cross-validation results of the 10 datasets, FAT has higher mean than that of OC1 on 9 datasets, and all of them are significantly higher; MOC1 has higher mean than that of OC1 on 7 datasets, and 6 of them are significantly higher; MOC2 has higher mean than that of OC1 on 8 datasets and 5 of them are significantly higher. OC1 has equal or higher means only on 3 datasets, on *Cancer* dataset, MOC1 has a slightly smaller mean than that of OC1, MOC2 has the same mean as that of OC1; on *Housing* dataset, MOC2 has slightly smaller mean than that of OC1; on *Prognosis* dataset, FAT has a significantly smaller mean than that of OC1, MOC1 also has a slightly smaller mean but the difference is not significant. Overall, comparing to MOC1, MOC2 or FAT, on only one dataset, OC1 has significantly higher mean that of FAT. Of the classifiers with highest mean, FAT produced four, MOC1 and MOC2 each produced three, and OC1 produced none.

6 TRANSDUCTION IN DECISION TREES

In the standard, inductive, model of supervised learning, one has to find a function f in a set H using information from a training set. Of course, the larger the set H the more information is needed in order to solve the problem. The function f so found is then used to label a test set. This problem can be considerably easier if the location of the test points is known a priori. In transduction we have fixed a hypothesis space H of functions $f(x, \alpha)$, and are given simultaneously a training set of labelled points $(x_1, y_1), ..., (x_\ell, y_\ell)$ and a test set of unlabelled points $x_{\ell+1}, ..., x_{\ell+k}$. In essence, the hypothesis space is effective reduced since functions that label the test data identically are equivalent.

Theorem 3.1 can be adapted to the transduction case. In both theorems the role of the VC dimension can be played by a quantity which depends both on the tree size and on the margin at each decision node [1]. In the appendix, we prove that the minimization of such quantity, calculated with respect to the overall set, minimizes a bound on the risk of error on the unlabelled test/working set. Specifically we show :

Theorem 6.1 *Consider the problem of transduction on an input space X with hypothesis class PDTs. Suppose we have a set of $\ell + k$ inputs points, a random ℓ of which are labelled. Suppose we are able to classify the labelled examples using a perceptron decision tree T and suppose that the tree obtained contained K decision nodes with margins γ_i at node i, then we can bound the generalization error with probability greater than $1 - \delta$ to be less than*

$$\epsilon(T, \delta) \leq \frac{1}{\ell}\left[\sum_{i=1}^{K} \frac{R^2}{\gamma_i^2} \log_2 \frac{em_i\gamma_i^2}{R^2} + \ln \frac{2S_K 8^K \ell}{\delta}\right],$$

where $R = \max_j \|x_j\|$ and m_i is the number of training and test points reaching node i.

Unfortunately the upper bound on generalization so obtained is not much tighter than the bound for induction, so we cannot necessarily predict great performance increases based on this type of approach. We propose an algorithm, MTT, that directly acts on such a quantity. The algorithm is identical to MOC1 except that the margin is calculated based on both the training and working set data. Note that FAT and MOC2 cannot be so simply generalized to transduction. Since FAT makes no changes in the training set accuracy, using both labelled and unlabelled data to choose the final margins would produce no changes of classification on the unlabelled data. For MOC2, the modified twoing rule would have to be changed to include information about unlabelled data, and how best to do this is an open question.

Very few attempts have been made to actually implement transduction into a practical algorithm. We believe this is the first attempt to do so within decision trees. Our computational results are roughly consistent with a transductive support vector machine approach [2] that found that using testing set information (without labels) rarely hurt and sometimes helped generalization when compared to the inductive version of SVM.

7 DESCRIPTION OF TRANSDUCTIVE ALGORITHM: MTT

MTT (Margin Tree Transduction) a variation of MOC1 which which directly incorporates the size of the margin with respect to both the testing and training data. The idea is to find a separating hyperplane which is a good trade-off between training accuracy and large overall margin, also with respect to the unlabelled points. MTT further develops the idea of enlarging the margins of decision trees by using mixture of labelled training data and unlabelled test data to induce the decision trees. MTT has the same objective function of MOC1, the only difference is the calculation of current_overall_margin. In MOC1, the current_margin is calculated using the labelled training points falling upon current node; but in MTT, the current_margin is calculated using both labelled training data and unlabelled test data falling upon current node.

The new cost function is:

$$(1-\lambda) * OC1\_Objective + C * \frac{1}{\textbf{current\_overall\_margin}}$$

8 EXPERIMENT WITH TRANSDUCTION

First we repeated the 10-fold cross-validation experiment described in Section 4 using MTT. The results are shown in Table 2. The third and fourth columns compare MOC1 and MTT with OC1. The fifth column indicates the difference in accuracy between MTT and

MOC1 and the corresponding paired t-test significance level at 0.25 significance level in either direction.

In comparison with OC1, MTT performed well, once again reemphasizing the importance of incorporating margin-based capacity control. MTT performed as good or better than OC1 on eight of the ten dataset without any tuning of the λ parameter in MTT. OC1 only performed better on the prognosis dataset which also caused difficulties for FAT and MOC1 in the previous experiment.

The benefits for transduction are less clear. The transductive algorithm, MTT, performed better than the inductive MOC1 algorithm on 8 of the 10 datasets, but the differences were not usually statistically significant. MTT did particularly poor on the prognosis dataset. These results exhibit a similar trend as those reported for a transductive support vector machine [2], the transductive algorithm worked about the same as the inductive algorithm and better on a few datasets. But the level of significance reported here is even lower. The SVM approach used an exact algorithm to find a global minimum solution for a single linear decision. MTT/OC1 is using an inexact heuristic approach to find locally good solutions for multiple decisions and then performs pruning. Small changes in objectives and data cause much more variance in OC1, MTT, and MOC1 than the SVM approach. Also in MTT, we are growing the tree with transduction and pruning it using only training data. We only have weak evidence that transduction as implemented here can improve generalization. But this by no means eliminates the possibility that the additional information in transductive inference cannot be effective exploited in PDT.

8.1 TRANSDUCTION ON HEART DISEASE DATA

Vapnik [11] speculates that the advantages of transduction could be more apparent in cases where there is a shift in the distribution between training and test data. An example of this situation comes from a hospital testing environment, as application of diagnostic testing may be slightly different in different hospitals, and an artificial diagnostic system should be able to adapt to each hospital's specific methods of measuring data. One such database that allows us to examine this hypothesis is formed by the four heart disease datasets from UCI machine learning repository, which have diagnostic data from four different hospitals. By training on one hospital's results and testing on the rest, we can assess the robustness of the algorithm across the changes of the hospital.

Table 2: 10-fold cross-validation accuracy means of OC1, MOC1 and MTT

Dataset	OC1 $\bar{x}$	MOC1 $\bar{x}$ (*p*)	MTT $\bar{x}$ (*p*)	MTT-MOC1 (*p*)	Best
Bright	98.46	98.94 (*.10*)	**99.07** (*.01*)	0.13	MTT
Bupa	65.22	**68.41** (*.20*)	67.83 (*.24*)	-0.58	MOC1
Cancer	**95.89**	95.60	95.75	0.15	OC1
Dim	94.82	**95.23** (*.09*)	95.01	-0.22 (*.78*)	MOC1
Heart	73.40	75.76 (*.21*)	**77.44** (*.15*)	1.68 (*.18*)	MTT
Housing	81.03	82.02	**82.81** (*.16*)	0.79	MTT
Iris	95.33	95.33	95.33	0.00	Tie
Pima	71.09	73.18 (*.08*)	**73.70** (*.02*)	0.52	MTT
Prognosis	**78.91**	78.23	73.47	-4.76 (*.89*)	OC1
Sonar	67.79	72.12 (*.19*)	**77.21** (*.01*)	5.09 (*.07*)	MTT

The four heart disease datasets from UCI repository are Cleveland, Switzerland, Hungarian and Long Beach, Virginia(VA). We use only the first 11 attributes of the commonly used 13 attributes, because the remaining two attributes are frequently missing within three of the datasets. The original 5 classes (0,1,2,3,4) are transformed into two classes: negative ($0 \rightarrow -1$), positive ($1, 2, 3, 4 \rightarrow 1$). We only use those points without missing values, the resulting four datasets are: i) Cleveland (303/164/139), of total 303 points, 164 points labelled as negative class, 139 points labelled as positive class; ii) Hungarian (94/27/67); iii) Switzerland (46/1/45); iv) Virginia (87/14/73). In terms of distribution, the four datasets are quite different. Due to the extremely skewed class distribution (1 vs. 45) of Switzerland, we did not train on Switzerland, and only used it as test data. As in the previous experiments, we set $\lambda = .05$ for both MOC1 and MTT. Again we purposely did not tune the λ for the best performance, to keep the experiment more objective.

For OC1 and MOC1 we trained on one dataset, fixed the tree and then tested on the other three datasets. For MTT, we trained using one dataset as labelled training data and one testing dataset as as unlabelled working data, and then reported the accuracy on the working data. MTT constructed a new tree for each testing set. Table 3 summarizes the testing accuracy when trained on the Cleveland data and tested on the others. Table 4 summarizes the results for the Hungarian data. Table 5 lists the results for the Virginia data. Since the Switzerland data has only one negative example (without missing values), we did not train on it.

Table 3: Induction and Transduction Results When Trained on Cleveland

Algorithm	Hungarian	Switzerland	Virginia
OC1	77.66	69.57	80.46
MOC1	75.53	95.65	86.21
MTT	76.60	95.65	86.21

Table 4: Induction and Transduction Results When Trained on Hungarian

Algorithm	Cleveland	Switzerland	Virginia
OC1	60.73	28.26	37.93
MOC1	70.63	95.65	82.76
MTT	73.27	97.83	81.61

Table 5: Induction and Transduction Results when Trained on Virginia

Algorithm	Cleveland	Hungarian	Switzerland
OC1	59.41	37.23	76.09
MOC1	62.71	44.44	97.83
MTT	69.64	71.28	97.83

The results clearly indicate that large margin trees generalize much better on the heart disease data. Of eight of the nine test cases, MOC1 and MTT achieved higher testing accuracy than OC1. Comparing MOC1 and MTT, we found that MTT did better than MOC1 on five cases, and did as well as well MOC1 on three case, and did worse than MOC1 only on one case. The experiment results suggest that in cases of few training data and/or skewed distribution, MOC1 and MTT have a great advantage over OC1. Table 5 indicates that, when training on the small and skewed Virginia data(87/14/73), MTT showed a major advantage over MOC1.

9 CONCLUSIONS

We have studied the effect of enlarging the margin of Perceptron Decision Trees in the standard inductive setting and in the setting of transduction. In the first case we have provided clear evidence of an advantage in controlling capacity by means of the margin, by comparing the performance of our algorithms with a standard PDT learner, OC1. All three large-margin inductive systems outperform OC1 on most of the real world data-sets we have used, indicating that overfitting in PDTs can be efficiently combatted by enlarging the margin of the decision boundaries on the training data. In this case, it doesn't much matter how the large margin bias is enforced: the quite different approaches of MOC1, MOC2 and FAT all work. The important thing seems to be to enforce the large margin.

In the transductive setting, however, the results are still preliminary but they do not give any clear indication either in favour or against this approach. The algorithm MTT does not show a clear advantage over MOC1, its direct analogue, though it still works better than OC1. The avoidance of the cost of performing data-dependent structural risk minimisation where the estimation of the margin on the training set is used to predict the margin on the test set, appears to have been offset by the smaller margins observed in practice on the larger sets. We conjecture that using the approach adopted here, the advantage of transduction will be largest for relatively smaller additional test sets.

It is however possible that a different technique will work: transduction can cause great changes in the decision tree structure, and the pruning strategy we used does not take this into consideration. The entire decision tree construction process needs to be rethought for the case of transduction: how much unlabelled data to use, what is an appropriate splitting criterion and how to do pruning in order to exploit the data, what kind of data will be improved by transduction. All these issues are important open problems.

We believe that combining the approach used here with soft margin results [9] may be the way forward. In this way the margin observed on the labelled data points can be retained, but a cost will be associated with any unlabelled points falling inside this band. Optimising the criterion over the whole dataset, we expect that there can be a significant advantage derived from the unlabelled data which may be carried forward to performance on further unseen data.

References

[1] Bennett K., Cristianini N., Shawe-Taylor J., Wu D. (1999). Enlarging the Margin in Perceptron

Decision Trees, submitted to Machine Learning.

[2] Bennett K., Demiriz A. (1998). Semi-Supervised Support Vector Machines, to appear in *Advances in Neural Information Processing Systems 11.*

[3] David A. McAllester, (1998) Some PAC-Bayesian Theorems, Proceedings of the Eleventh Conference on Computational Learning Theory, New York: ACM Press, pp. 230–234.

[4] Murthy S.K., Kasif S., & Salzberg S. (1994). A System for Induction of Oblique Decision Trees, Journal of Artificial Intelligence Research, 2 , pp. 1-32.

[5] Quinlan J.R. (1993). *C4.5: Programs for Machine Learning*, Morgan Kaufmann.

[6] Quinlan,J.R, & Rivest, R. (1989). Learning Decision Trees Using the Minimum Description Lenght Principle, Information and Computation 80, 227-248.

[7] Shawe-Taylor, J., Bartlett, P. L., Williamson, R.C., & Anthony M. (1996). Structural Risk Minimization over Data-Dependent Hierarchies, NeuroCOLT Technical Report NC-TR-96-053, IEEE Transactions on Information Theory, 44 (5) 1926–1940.

[8] Shawe-Taylor, J. and Cristianini, N. (1998) Data Dependent Structural Risk Minimization for Perceptron Decision Trees, Proceedings of the Eleventh Conference on Neural Information Processing Systems, NIPS'97. Advances in Neural Information Processing Systems 10 Michael I. Jordan, Michael J. Kearns, and Sara A. Solla (eds.) Cambridge, MA: MIT Press, pp. 336–342.

[9] Shawe-Taylor, J. and Cristianini, N. (1999) Margin Distribution Bounds on Generalization, to appear in the Proceedings of EuroCOLT'99.

[10] Vapnik, V.(1995). *The Nature of Statistical Learning Theory*, Springer-Verlag, New York.

[11] Vapnik V.(1998), *Statistical Learning Theory*, Wiley Interscience, New York

[12] University of California, Irvine – Machine Learning Repository, http://www.ics.uci.edu/~mlearn/

A APPENDIX

A.1 BACKGROUND RESULTS

We will require the following result bounding the generalization error of a classifier in terms of a prior placed on the set of possible hypotheses. The trick with transduction is that we know the performance of the classifiers on all the training and test points before we begin the training process and so we can make a suitable choice of prior over the finite set of possible hypotheses.

Theorem A.1 *[3] Suppose we have a set of $\ell + k$ inputs points, a random subset of size ℓ of which are labelled. Suppose H is a finite set of hypotheses with a probability distribution P assigning non-zero probability to every concept. Then the probability that $h \in H$ which is consistent with the labelled points has error greater than ϵ is bounded by*

$$\epsilon(h) \leq \frac{\ln \frac{1}{P(h)} + \ln \frac{1}{\delta}}{\ell}.$$

Using this theorem we now prove a template proposition for our application.

Proposition A.2 *Let $H = \sum_{i=1}^{M} H_i$ be a partition into finite subsets of a countable set of hypothesis. Further assume that for each H_k there has been defined a (1-1) mapping*

$$n : H_k \longrightarrow \mathbb{N}^{k+1}.$$

Suppose we have a set of $\ell + k$ inputs points, ℓ of which are labelled. Then with probability $1 - \delta$, if $h \in H_k$ is consistent with the labelled points then it has error bounded by

$$\epsilon(h, \delta) = \frac{1}{\ell}\left(\sum_{i=1}^{k} \lfloor \log_2(n_i(h)) \rfloor + \ln \frac{N_k 4^k M}{\delta}\right),$$

where $N_k = \max_{h \in H_k}(n_0(h))$.

Proof: We apply Theorem ?? once for each hypothesis class H_k, $k = 1, \ldots, M$ using $\delta' = \delta/M$ in each case. For the application of the theorem to H_k we define a probability distribution over the hypotheses, by assigning a weight to each hypothesis in such a way that the sum of the weights is less than 1. Hypothesis $h \in H_k$ is assigned weight

$$w(h) = \frac{1}{4^k N_k} \prod_{i=1}^{k} \exp(-\lfloor \log_2 n_i(h) \rfloor).$$

Plugging this value into Theorem ?? gives the required bound. Hence, it remains to show that

$$\sum_{h \in H_k} w(h) \leq 1.$$

Claim: The following sum is bounded as follows

$$\sum_{i=1}^{\infty} \exp(-\lfloor \log_2(i) \rfloor) \leq 4.$$

The following sequence of inequalities establishes the claim

$$\begin{aligned}\sum_{i=1}^{\infty} \exp(-\lfloor \log_2(i) \rfloor) &\leq \sum_{j=0}^{\infty} 2^j \exp(-j) \\ &\leq \sum_{j=0}^{\infty} \left(\frac{2}{e}\right)^j = \frac{1}{1-2/e} \\ &< 4.\end{aligned}$$

We now consider the sum

$$\begin{aligned}\sum_{h \in H_k} w(h) &= \sum_{h \in H_k} \frac{1}{4^k N_k} \prod_{i=1}^{k} \exp(-\lfloor \log_2(n_i(h)) \rfloor) \\ &\leq \sum_{j=1}^{N_k} \sum_{n \in \mathbb{N}^k} \frac{1}{4^k N_k} \prod_{i=1}^{k} \exp(-\lfloor \log_2(n_i) \rfloor) \\ &\leq \sum_{j=1}^{N_k} \sum_{n \in \mathbb{N}^{k-1}} \frac{1}{4^{k-1} N_k} \prod_{i=1}^{k-1} \exp(-\lfloor \log_2(n_i) \rfloor) \\ &\leq \sum_{j=1}^{N_k} \frac{1}{N_k} = 1.\end{aligned}$$

where we have used the fact that the mapping n is (1-1) and used the claim k times. ∎

A.2 TRANSDUCTIVE INFERENCE

Transduction is concerned with learning in the situation where the learning algorithm is given access to the test data before it proposes a classification function. This contrasts with more traditional learning where the test data is used to evaluate the hypothesis once it has been returned by the algorithm. We give a more formal definition in the next section and then describe the strategy we adopt to analyse this problem.

A.2.1 GROWTH FUNCTION OF GENERALIZED DECISION TREEs

We start by giving a bound on the number of different tree architectures that have a given number of computational nodes. Then we provide a bound on the growth function of GDTs.

Definition: a *k-DT skeleton* is a binary tree having exactly k nodes, without any association of features to the nodes, nor of classes to the leaves.

Lemma A.3 *[6] The number of leaf-labelled k-DT skeletons is:*

$$2^{k+1} S_k = \frac{2^{k+1}}{k+1}\binom{2k}{k}.$$

A.3 TRANSDUCTIVE PDTS

In order to apply our approach to analysing transduction to the PDT situation, we must perform the partitioning of the set of trees and then define a suitable (1-1) mapping n, before applying Proposition ??.

Proof of Theorem 6.1: We partition H into subsets according to the number K of computational nodes. This number cannot exceed the number of labelled examples and so $M = \ell$. For a fixed number of computational nodes $n_0(h)$ will be a numbering of the $S_{K+1}2^{K+1}$ labelled tree skeletons, and hence $N_K = S_{K+1}2^{K+1}$. Finally, for each skeleton, we fix an ordering of the nodes such that a parent appears before its children. Now inductively for each node i, we order the maximal margin hyperplanes than can be placed on the data reaching that node (determined by the hyperplanes already chosen for the ancestor nodes). The ordering is chosen to be compatible with the margins, that is the smaller the margin the higher the index $n_i(T)$ chosen. Now clearly, $n(T) = (n_0(T), n_1(T), \ldots, n_K(T))$ is a (1-1) mapping from K node trees to $\mathbb{N}^{K+1}$. Applying Proposition ??, we have

$$\epsilon(T,\delta) = \frac{1}{\ell}\left(\sum_{i=1}^{K} \lfloor \log_2(n_i(T)) \rfloor + \ln \frac{2 S_K 8^K \ell}{\delta}\right).$$

Finally, observe that the number of hyperplanes with margin larger than γ_i on m_i points is bounded by

$$\left(\frac{e m_i \gamma_i^2}{R^2}\right)^{R^2/\gamma_i^2},$$

since the VC dimension of γ_i margin hyperplanes is bounded by R^2/γ_i^2, the bound resulting from an application of Sauer's lemma. This therefore gives a bound on $n_i(T)$ of

$$n_i(T) \leq \left(\frac{e m_i \gamma_i^2}{R^2}\right)^{R^2/\gamma_i^2},$$

and substituting in the formula gives the result. ∎

Sparse data; not uniform time intervals.

A Region-Based Learning Approach to Discovering Temporal Structures in Data

Wei Zhang
The Boeing Company
P.O. Box 3707, MS 7L-66
Seattle, WA 98124-2207
wei.zhang@boeing.com

Abstract

This paper proposes a new approach to discovering temporal structures in event-sequence data. Methods for learning temporal regions are developed for solving problems with irregularly distributed events and finding temporal dependency relations in a large time horizon. The preliminary experimental study shows that this approach has worked successfully in finding temporal relations from data.

1 INTRODUCTION

Many problems in the real world involve sequences of events over time. Data are in the form of multivariate, discrete-valued time series. The task is to discover structures or patterns in event sequences so they can be applied as a model to predict future events. Often conducting such analysis is very challenging. The hypothesis space can be huge even when only a fairly small time horizon of event dependency is considered. This space grows dramatically fast when the time horizon increases.

A typical problem, arising from the manufacturing domain, is to analyze alarm events over time. Today, increasingly factories are applying advanced manufacturing technologies in production processes, leading to the use of automated processes. Such a process is often encoded with hundreds of different types of alarms where some of alarms, usually called *critical* alarms, represent serious problems so a process has to avoid and others provide *informational* or *warning* signals to help detect potential serious problems to occur. Discovering correlations and patterns in alarm occurrence can help find problems in operation, better understand alarm conditions and effect, and possibly predict severe future problems.

Most event sequence problems in the real world are considered as in a sort of *sparse*, *irregularly distributed* data structure. Events occur rarely at each time step, and they are not uniformly distributed over time. For example, in manufacturing alarms are often recorded by seconds, but there are particularly only several dozens or hundreds of alarm occurrences daily.

Recently, a lot of research has been conducted for the analysis of event sequences. Methods and algorithms are being developed for solving problems with various properties. For example, Mannila et al (1995) developed approaches to discovering event patterns in the form of *episodes* to analyze telecommunication network alarms. Agrawal et al (1995) focus on mining sequential patterns for sales transaction databases, methods are developed to find *maximal sequences* that have a minimal user-specified level of *support.* Oates et al (1997) developed MEDD and MSDD algorithms based on exhaustive search to detect temporal dependency in the forms of *partially instantiated events* and *multiple event streams.* Howe and Somlo (1997) take a state-space modeling approach to learning *state transition diagrams* for predicting future events.

The limitations of these approaches in general are that they do not consider analyzing event correlations in a large time horizon and finding event temporal relationship specified with time conditions. To be specific, none of these methods are good for discovering a rule like "If event A occurs now and event B occurred about 15 seconds ago then event C will occur in about 1 hour afterward". To discover such a rule, firstly, a method must be able to *efficiently* search event dependency relationship in several thousand time steps apart. Secondly, it must be able to come up with time conditions on event dependency, not just simply telling the "before" and "after" relationship. Thirdly, because often significant correlations rarely exist on a rigid time condition, say exactly x seconds apart, for practical use a method must be developed in a way that temporal relations on a *range* of time can be revealed. For example, in the above example, we use term *about* in describing time conditions, "about 15 seconds" could be described as "between 14 and 16 seconds". Developing relations in a form of *temporal regions* not only is important for finding significant correlations, but also makes a method *robust* so that important relations may be found even when there is noise in time data. In real world applications, it is common that time data collected are not perfectly accurate. Noise can be developed by either manual recording or automated systems. When multiple clocks or timers are applied, they may not exactly agree with each other and be synchronized ideally.

In this paper, we propose a *temporal region-based learning* approach to discovering temporal relations for the general family of problems with sparse, irregularly distributed event occurrences. The idea applied in the approach is very simple: It relies on data to extract *minimal temporal regions* and then test them to select those of significant correlations. The key contribution of the paper is introducing metrics for assessing temporal-region conditions. An algorithm is presented to show how such a discovery process can be implemented efficiently.

This paper is organized as follows. The next section reviews the approaches that have been developed for different types of problems. The third section introduces the temporal region-based learning approach. After then, the paper presents an empirical study on this approach, followed by discussions and concluding remarks.

2 BACKGROUND: PROBLEM TYPES

Approaches being developed to event-sequence analysis can be basically grouped into three classes based on the types of problems they are trying to solve: *time-omitted sequences*, *uniform sequences*, and *generic sequences*.

Time-omitted Sequences: This class of problems considers *temporal partial relations* on event sequences while the time condition on event occurrences is ignored. A sequence can be described as a linked list as Figure 1 shows where a "→" represents a precedence relation. Mannila et al's episode framework falls into this family, and so Agrawal et al's maximal sequences framework as well as Howe and Somlo's state transition diagrams. Since the problems are not represented in time-specific scales so these methods in general are able to handle irregularly-distributed events and long time horizons (not necessarily long sequences). Sometimes these methods are extended and applied to develop time-specific dependency conditions (maybe because of unfortunately no better solutions available). In this situation, efforts of human-engineering would be enormous. Often extensive "windowing" pre-processing tasks must be conducted to *shape* problems into some forms such that rules with meaningful explanation of time conditions can be developed. Some methods for time windowing are suggested in (Srikant & Agrawal, 1996; Mannila et al., 1995).

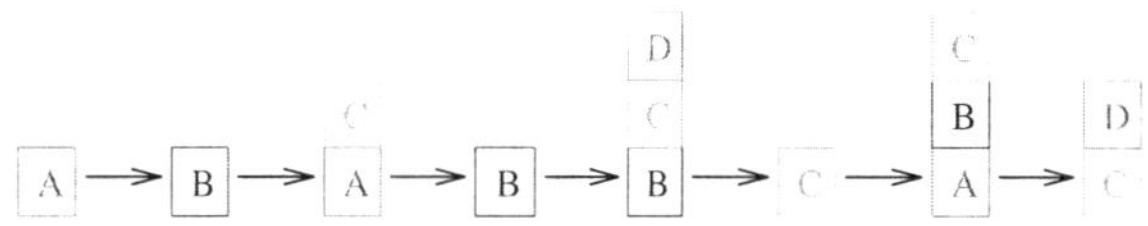

Figure 1: An Example Using Time-Omitted Sequence Representation

```
Time:       0         50         100        150        200
---------------------------------------------------------

Event A:    N Y N Y N N N N N N N N Y N N N N N N N N
Event B:    N N N Y Y N Y N N N N N Y N N N N N N N N
Event C:    N N N Y N N Y N N N Y N Y N N N N N N N Y
Event D:    N N N N N N Y N N N N N N N N N N N N N Y
```

Figure 2: A Uniform Table Representation

Uniform Sequences: When events are distributed quite uniformly over time, the most convenient and straight-forward method is to apply tables to represent sequences, one record recorded at each time step. An important issue in here is how to deal with the *granularity* of data in order to accomplish an analysis efficiently. This considers the tradeoff between applying a fine-scale representation with complete information but maybe a huge dataset or applying a coarse-scale representation for efficient processing but with incomplete information. Sometimes events which are not quite uniformly distributed in a fine scale may be quite uniform in a coarse scale. Sometimes solutions on a coarse scale may be satisfactory. However, in gen-

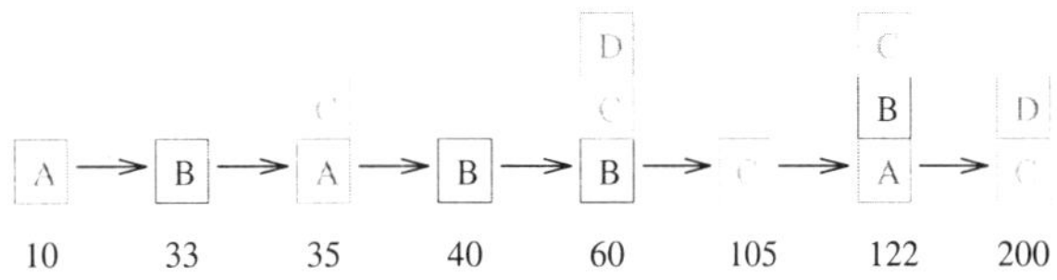

Figure 3: Generic Sequence Representation For the Same Example.

eral, using uniform tables is an inefficient approach to solving the irregularly-distributed problems. Figure 2 shows how an intermediate scale is applied to represent the example of Figure 1 in a table. Here data are grouped in every 10 time steps.

Oates et al's Multi-Stream Dependency Detection (MSDD) is an approach in this family. One important character of this representation is that event non-occurrence (Ns in Figure 2) information can be taken care so that rules like "If no event occurred in the past 30 time steps, then event A occurs now" can be discovered. This type of rules can be useful in many real-world problems. Furthermore, the method can also be applied with multi-valued variables.

Generic Sequences: This considers generic sequence problems including all event sequence information where events may be sparsely and unevenly distributed over time. We can use a linked list plus time as Figure 3 shows to represent a problem. Although many methods may be applied to solve the problems, we would like to offer a *direct* approach that in general is much simpler and easier to apply for solving the problems. Therefore, much of manual data-engineering efforts can be avoided and problems can be solved efficiently.

3 METHODS

3.1 MINIMAL TEMPORAL REGIONS

A *temporal region feature* is a feature defined as a condition for a *target* event type, where a condition is represented as an event type associated with a period of time in the form of $E[a, b]$. Here, E is the name of an event and a and b are the start and end time of a region in which an event of E occurs. This condition-target pair can be written in the form of *rules*

$$E_C[a, b] \Rightarrow E_T,$$

which says that an event of E_T occurs if an event of E_C occurs in the past $[a, b]$ time steps ($0 \leq a \leq b$).

While there exists infinite number of temporal regions for a pair of events, our idea is to only look at rules with *minimal temporal regions* with respect to data. Let S be a given sequence of events where each event records two pieces of information, the name of the event and the time this event occurs. For all pair of events of types E_C and E_T where the E_C event occurs no later than the E_T event, we can compute the *lag* between them and obtain a set of lag values S_{lag} in $\Re$. For any subset s' of S_{lag}, we can define its *minimal temporal region*, which is the smallest time interval that covers all the values in the subset, $[min(s'), max(s')]$. The complete set of minimal temporal regions for $E_C \Rightarrow E_T$ for a given sequence is comprised of all different minimal temporal regions. Therefore, there are a total of $\binom{k+1}{2}$ minimal temporal regions for a lag set S_{lag} of size k ($k = |S_{lag}|$).

For example, for the sequence in Figure 3, the lag set for rule $C \Rightarrow A$ is $\{0, 17, 62, 87\}$. This results in 10 minimal temporal regions: [0,0], [0,17], [0,62], [0,87], [17,17], [17,62], [17,87], [62,62], [62,87], and [87,87].

Use of minimal temporal regions implies applying a bias for smaller regions. When there are two *concepts* explaining a set of cases, we prefer the more *specific* concept. Notice that here we do not have explicit *negative* examples for preventing concepts from going more *general*. In this situation, use of the bias for more specific concepts is essential. Similar ideas have been applied in many other machine learning methods. Particularly for event sequences, rules with smaller regions help for prediction of time of future event occurrences.

This paper develops an approach to searching from all minimal temporal regions to find those with statistically significant correlations. There are several nice properties of this approach.

1. Minimal temporal regions are independent with time horizon. The factors determining the number of minimal temporal regions are the lags computed based on event occurrence time.

2. This approach works for problems with irregularly distributed events. Minimal temporal regions are flexible so they can well represent irregular distribution of events.

3. It also works with noisy data. Region-based methods are robust in finding important relationships even when there are some noise in time recording.

3.2 METRICS

Now let us turn the attention to the problem of evaluating temporal regions. We develop the following six metrics for assessing them to find important relations.

1. **Prediction Accuracy** (ACCP): This computes the percentage of cases that a target event occurs in the time region over all cases that a condition event occurs. For example, ACCP for rule $C[0, 87] \Rightarrow A$ is 80%. There are 5 C occurrences and four times that at least one A occurs within a period of 87 time steps of a C occurrence, which are C at 35, 60, 105, and 122 respectively. Event C at 200 does not follow an A occurrence.

2. **Recall Accuracy** (ACCR): This computes the same metric in the opposite temporal direction. It is the percentage of cases that a condition event occurred in the time region before over all cases that a target event occurs. This value is 66.7% for the same rule.

3. **Prediction Bonus** (BNSP): Sometimes target events may occur multiple times in a given time region. This metric provides a score for additional occurrences of target events. Let *FwdCnt* be the number of cases satisfying a rule where only one time is counted at most for each condition event occurrence (this is the count used in ACCR computation), and let *AllCnt* be the count for all cases satisfying the rule which include multiple occurrences of target events. We compute the bonus as $1 - FwdCnt/AllCnt$. For $C[0, 87] \Rightarrow A$, *AllCnt* is 5 and *FwdCnt* is 4 (Note C at 35 follows two A occurrences, at 35 and 122 respectively). So this bonus is 20%.

4. **Recall Bonus** (BNSR): Similarly, we define *BwdCnt* by considering at most one case for each target event occurrence. This bonus is defined as $1 - BwdCnt/AllCnt$.

5. **Range** (RNG): Apparently, both ACCP and ACCR reward larger regions, their values increase monotonously as a temporal region gets bigger. It is important to have metrics rewarding smaller regions. RNG is the one. We employ a procedure (see the algorithm later) that allows users to define a lag scope in searching temporal relations, which is specified by a minimal lag `MinLag` and a maximal lag `MaxLag`. RNG is defined as $1 - \text{INTV}(r)/(\texttt{MaxLag} - \texttt{MinLag} + 1)$, where $\text{INTV}(r)$ is the region size of rule r.

6. **Coverage** (COV): This metric computes the rate of cases covered by a rule over all cases covered by the same rule but with the full search scope defined by `MinLag` and `MaxLag`. We denote the latter as *AllCntScp*. Then COV is *AllCnt*/*AllCntScp*.

In summary, both ACCP and BNSP assess the predicting power of events. These are important for model learning and any *forward* relation discovery. Prediction bonus helps for finding structures with multiple occurrences. On the other hand, both ACCR and BNSR are important for causal analysis and diagnosis. They are used for finding reasons for occurrences of events. RNG is important to ensure to find regions that describe the key structures of data (We will explain this later). COV is important for finding regions with large coverage of cases over all cases in the search scope. Finally, it is important to note that for different purposes of analysis, one should apply different weight settings for these metrics.

4 EXPERIMENTAL STUDY

To understand how this method performs in discovering temporal structures from data, we did a series of experiments. This paper presents a study of using this method for model discovery. We first describe the testbed problems for this study.

4.1 DATA SETS

The testbed is composed of three synthetic data sets which vary in the size of problems. The size is measured by the number of event types and the number of *direct* temporal dependency relations defined in the underlying data models. We define models as *directed acyclic graphs* (DAGs) for consideration of the causal nature of generic problems. Therefore, a model does not contain any recursive relations like $A \Rightarrow A$ or $A \Rightarrow B \Rightarrow A$. Direct temporal relations are those describing direct effect, while the complete set of temporal relations contains both direct ones as well as *transitive* relations. Transitive relations are those that can be derived from direct relations. For example, If $A \Rightarrow B$ and $B \Rightarrow C$, then $A \Rightarrow C$ is a transitive relation.

The first set contains problems with 15 event types and 18 direct temporal relations, abbreviated as `M15-18`. Described in this notation, the second set is `M30-36`, and the third set is `M60-72`. Each set contains 10 models.

Each direct temporal relation is a rule which contains the information about the names of both condition event and target event as well the start and the end time (both are integer) of the temporal lag between the two events. We form two types of direct temporal rela-

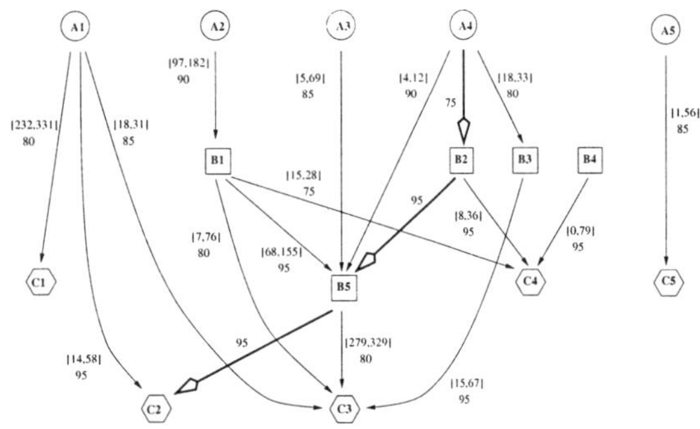

Figure 4: An Example of Forward Temporal Models

tions. One is *generic* temporal relations specified with both start and end time for temporal lags. The other is *associations*, which is the type of relations describing an occurrence of an event may result in an occurrence of another event at the *exact* same time (both start and end lag time are 0). The association problem has been studied in many literatures (Agrawal, Mannila, Srikant, Toivonen, & Verkamo, 1996). Among all direct relations, we assign 10% as associations. For the other relations (generic), we control the start lag time of two events between 0 and 500 in the exponential distribution using $exp(-x/250)$ and control the lag range (the differences between the start time and the end time) between 0 and 100 in the exponential distribution using $exp(-x/50)$ (when the start time is 0, it is controlled between 1 and 100). Forming the two types of relations is attempted to mimic some real manufacturing problem. We are interested in applying a single temporal learning procedure to solve both association and temporal-relation problems at the same time.

In addition, we also introduce some stochastic characteristics of event occurrences. We assign a probability for each temporal relation. The value is selected from the set of percentage values $\{75, 80, 85, 90, 95\}$. This attempts to represent the noise in a real data collection environment.

Figure 4 shows a `M15-18` model generated by the above method except the lag ranges applying the uniform distribution. The 15 types of events are grouped into three classes `A`, `B`, and `C` to mimic the three classes of manufacturing alarms—informational, warning, and critical respectively. Among 18 direct temporal relations, three are associations ($A_4 \Rightarrow B_2$, $B_2 \Rightarrow B_5$, and $B_5 \Rightarrow C_2$) and the rest are generic. A generic relation is described with a region condition in the form of $[a, b]$. Both types of relations are described with probabilities.

After models are developed, we generate event-sequence data by simulation. The simulation process follows the rules defined in the models. To get initial events, we apply the following simple procedure. At each time step, there is 0.001 chance that one new event, called a *seed*, can be generated without having a parent event. The type of a seed is selected uniformly from the set of event types.

4.2 ALGORITHM

The key purpose of this study is to find if learning methods based on minimal temporal regions and metrics developed above can be applied to effectively uncover the underlying models by observing the simulation data. Because a learning algorithm never sees the models, we cannot let it run to come up with a set of solutions and evaluate the performance on the best one. To be fair, we must evaluate the performance on whatever the solutions that an algorithm are coming up with. Therefore, providing more solutions may not be a good idea. Our procedure is aimed at developing models that can match the underlying models most closely.

Table 1 shows the *Best Region-Rules* algorithm developed for finding a set of the *best* rules. The learning procedure is a *data-driven* process. The BESTREGIONRULES procedure reads through the events from input sequence. Every time when it reads a new event, the program combines the event with all event that has been processed earlier and then call the ADDLAG procedure for each combination if the lag of the two events is within the search scope defined by the minimal and maximal lags. Note here the ADDLAG procedure is called twice if two events occur at the same time ($d = 0$). In this situation, the method works to find event associations.

ADDLAG creates and maintains a set of rules each in the form of $E_{cond} \Rightarrow E_{tar}$. Under each rule, it maintains an ordered lag set where each member of the set is a lag value associated with a list of case indices. We use the condition-event occurrence time of a case as the index value. These provide the information needed for computing all counts and accordingly the six types of metric values.

PRINTBESTRULES goes through all rules. For each rule, it selects the best region based on the score function, which is the weighted sum of metric values using input weights W. This selected best region rule must have a score larger or equal to a given minimal score v.

Table 1: Best Region-Rules Algorithm

```
procedure BestRegionRules(S, M1, M2, W, v)
inputs:
    S         // Event sequence in (e1, t1), (e2, t2), ..., (en, tn)
    M1        // Minimal Lag, default = 0
    M2        // Maximal Lag
    W         // Weights of a score function
    v         // Minimal score

if (S not empty)
    Push(L, Pop(S))             // Move first element of S to L
while (S not empty) do
    e := Pop(S)
    for all e' ∈ L
        let t be time of e and t' be time of e'
        let d = t − t'
        if (M1 ≤ d ≤ M2)
            let E and E' be the name of events e and e'
            AddLag(E, E', d, t')
            if (d = 0) AddLag(E', E, d, t')
    Push(L, e)
end while
PrintBestRules(W, v)
end procedure

procedure AddLag(E_tar, E_cond, d, t)
inputs:
    E_tar     // Name of a target event
    E_cond    // Name of a condition event
    d         // Lag between the two events
    t         // E_cond time, used as the index for the case

r := FindRule(E_tar, E_cond, R)   // R maintains a list of rules
if (r = NIL)                      // if this rule does not exist
    r := MakeRule(E_tar, E_cond)
    AddRule(r, R)                 // add the rule into R
SubAddLag(d, t, r)                // add the lag and index into r
end procedure
```

Table 2: Comparison of the Learned Models and the Underlying Models

SET		Match	Near M.	Reg Ovlp	Term M.	UnM	Fit Score
1	Min	4.00	0.00	1.00	0.0	0.00	0.511
	1Q	11.25	1.25	2.00	0.0	0.00	0.774
	Md	12.50	2.00	3.00	0.0	0.00	0.819
	Mn	11.50	2.10	3.50	0.2	0.70	0.776
	3Q	13.00	2.75	3.75	0.0	1.75	0.833
	Max	14.00	4.00	8.00	2.0	2.00	0.889
2	Min	17.00	2.00	1.0	0.0	1.00	0.653
	1Q	22.25	5.00	3.0	0.0	2.00	0.799
	Md	23.50	6.00	3.0	0.0	2.00	0.823
	Mn	23.40	5.90	4.2	0.2	2.30	0.803
	3Q	25.50	7.75	4.0	0.0	2.75	0.832
	Max	28.00	9.00	11.0	1.0	4.00	0.885
3	Min	34.00	12.00	3.00	0.00	1.00	0.684
	1Q	38.75	13.00	4.25	0.00	6.25	0.738
	Md	42.00	15.00	7.00	0.00	8.50	0.752
	Mn	40.90	15.50	6.70	0.30	8.60	0.753
	3Q	42.75	15.75	8.75	0.75	11.75	0.779
	Max	46.00	23.00	11.00	1.00	14.00	0.830

4.3 RESULTS

4.3.1 Model Discovery

For model discovery, we do not need to apply the metrics on recall. We set weight 0 for AccR and BnsR and 1 for all other four metrics. We set the minimal-score parameter 140, the minimal lag 0 and the maximal lag 600. For all model in the three sets, simulation was conducted with 2000 events.

After learning was completed, we compared the learned models with the underlying models. For all direct temporal dependency in a underlying model, we find the rule in the corresponding learned model (same condition and target event, there is at most one such rule because the algorithm only prints the best region). If both rules have at least 80% region overlapping with each other and the prediction accuracy of the learned rule is close to the probability assigned in the underlying rule with difference no bigger than 0.1 then we say the two rules *match*. Otherwise, if they both have at least 50% region overlapping with each other and the probability difference is no bigger than 0.25, we say they are *"near-match"*. Otherwise, we say the two rules *"region-overlap"* if there is at least at one point covered by the both rules. If the two rules do not overlap, then we say they are *"term-match"*. Both region-overlap and term-match require the probability difference no bigger than 0.40. If we do not find the rule with the same condition and target names in the learned model, then we say this relation in the underlying model is *unmatch* to the learned model.

After this assessment, we computed a *fitness* function for all model. For each relation in a underlying model, we gave 1 point for a match, 0.75 point for a near-match, 0.25 point for a region-overlap, 0.1 point for a term-match, and 0 for unmatch. The fitness score is the sum of all the points divided by the number of relations in the underlying model.

Table 2 shows the performance assessed by these six measures. We separate problems from three different sets from the smallest `M15-18` models (Set 1) to the largest `M60-72` models (Set 3). Each set shows six statistics `Min`, `1st Qu`, `Median`, `Mean`, `3rd Qu`, and `Max` on the six measures.

The table concludes that learning was well performed on all three sets of problems. The match rate is high, in average it is about 60%. For the rest of the relations, most are near-match. One interesting finding from this table is that the median-sized problems seem slightly easier to learn than the other two. It is easy to understand why larger-sized problems are more difficult—

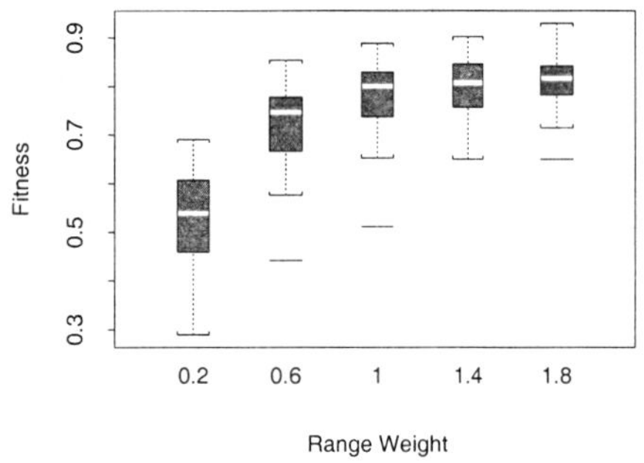

Figure 5: The Effect of the RNG Weight on Problems of Exponential-Distributed Lag Ranges

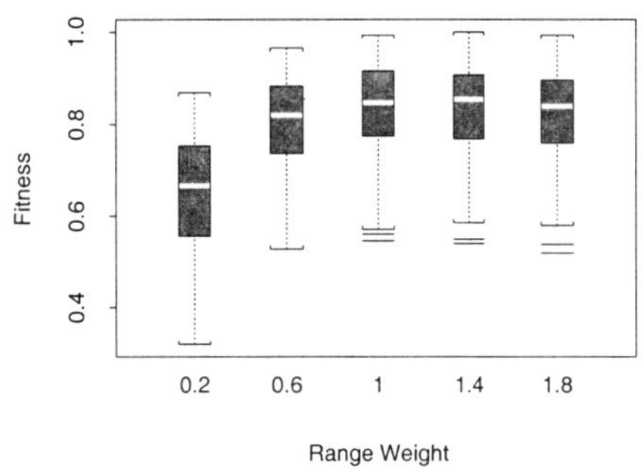

Figure 6: The Effect of the RNG Weight on Problems of Uniformly-Distributed Lag Ranges

they need more time to learn. To explain why small problems are maybe more difficult to learn, we suspect this is due to the sensitivity of small models: only a couple of mistakes may make a big difference.

4.3.2 The RNG Parameter

Next we conducted an experiment to understand the impact of the weight on RNG. On the same learning setting, we vary this weight using the values 0.2, 0.6, 1, 1.4, and 1.8 respectively. Figure 5 shows the boxplots for these five settings respectively. Here the three data sets are grouped together. It shows clearly that 0.2 is a bad choice and setting the weight in between 1 and 1.8 in general is good while 1.8 comes up with the best result. We can see that if we don't set this weight properly, the algorithm is not able to find the key structures in data.

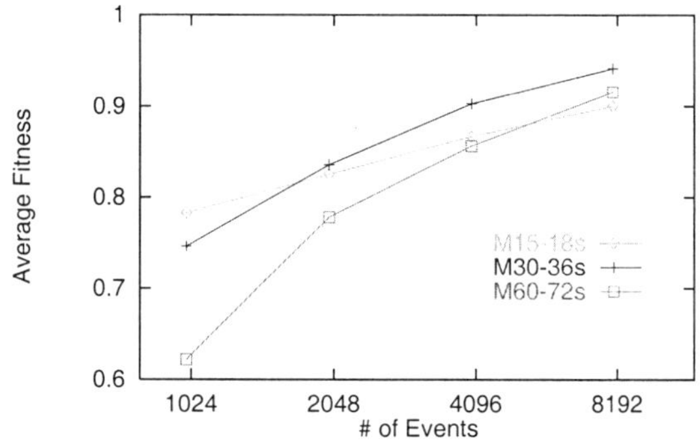

Figure 7: Amount of Data for Simulation and Learning

It is important to notice that selection of the RNG weight depends on the distribution of the lag range in the underlying model. Figure 6 shows the result of the same experiment on a different set of testbed problems where the lag ranges are generated according to the uniform distribution. Similarly, the plot combines the results on simulation of 30 models of the three different sizes. In this case, setting RNG at 1 seems perform slightly better than setting at both 1.4 and 1.8.

Nonetheless, an important observation is that in all the cases there is a wide range of RNG values that can be selected to come up with similar, good results. A more close examination found that they actually come up with the same region rules for most of event pairs. Thus, it is not difficult to find and determine an appropriate setting for this parameter.

4.3.3 Amount of Data and Learning Time

Another experiment we conducted is to test the amount of data required for model learning. Intuitively, a big model needs more simulation data. Figure 7 shows the experimental results. This time learning is conducted on the setting of the RNG weight at 1.8. We see with more data the average model fitness increases. Furthermore, this plot shows more evidence on the difficulty of learning small-sized problems. This in general suggests that for problems of size `M15-18` the most gain of learning can be obtained by simulation in up to about 1000 events. But for `M30-36` problems it is worth to train up to 8000 events, and for larger-sized problems longer training is encouraged.

For the interest of time complexity, we also observed the CPU time for each model simulation. For most of `M30-36` and `M60-72` problems, it takes 25 minutes or less on a Sun Ultra-1 for an 8000 event simulation. Learning on `M15-18` problems takes longer time because it generates much more lag values for each rule (pair of event types) despite of having fewer number of rules. Simply put, the key factors for the time complexity is the number of events and the search scope parameters `MinLag` and `MaxLag`. Considering the scope parameters being set constantly, in the case when the number of lag values is fairly small, which can be resulted from a small search scope or some underlying data-model structures, the CPU time basically grows linearly with the number of events. Otherwise, in the worse case the time can grow quadratically with the number of events. For a given event sequence, increasing the search scope in general results in a quadratical growth of the CPU time. Therefore, when there is a need to search through a very large scope, it is suggested to divide it into several regions and then search through them one by one. Performance loss that may occur at region boundaries can be handled by using overlapping regions.

5 DISCUSSIONS AND FUTURE WORK

These experiments showed the temporal region-based method developed in this paper can be successfully applied to uncover the underlying models of data. However, the study is preliminary. Several important aspects should be examined, this can lead to many interesting future work.

In essence this learning procedure is developed for finding significant statistical correlations between events. Our effort is to observe these correlations to find event dependency and key structures of data or underlying models. This follows an important question: What is the difference between correlations and event dependency relationship? To understand this, we characterize three types of correlations: (a) direct temporal dependencies, (b) transitive temporal relations, and (c) parallel correlations. We have explained type (a) and type (b) relations. Parallel correlations are the other correlations that do not fall into these two camps. While this paper has paid attention only on the type (a) relations, our experience has told that both of the other two types are just as important as the former. They can provide crucial information for discovery and refinement of models and knowledge. Developing methods that can analyze and synthesize different types of correlations is an interesting research problem.

We also noticed some pitfall in our algorithm. Clearly, BESTREGIONRULES is not guaranteed to find all large correlations. It is even not guaranteed to find all direct temporal dependencies. It finds only one, the best relation for each pair of events. The following shows an example how this algorithm may miss to find a direct dependency relation. Suppose we have three direct temporal relations: (1) $A[1,1]0.9 \Rightarrow B$, (2) $A[2,2]0.8 \Rightarrow C$, and (3) $B[3,3]0.9 \Rightarrow C$. (1) and (3) develop the transitive relation $A[4,4]0.81 \Rightarrow C$ which may be selected by learning as opposed to the relation (2) because the latter has a slightly smaller probability (0.8 compared with 0.81).

While BESTREGIONRULES is just a simple realization of the temporal-relation search principle introduced in the paper—a principle that suggests ways to use and evaluate temporal regions, use of this principle can go far beyond this. It can be applied and incorporated to other learning procedures such as decision trees or neural networks to deal with more complicated temporal data structures. Most simply, we can employ the temporal region methods to extract useful features for these learning methods.

Development of transitive temporal relations can be related to the *temporal difference* (TD) learning methodology by Sutton (1988). TD learns to predict the long-term future for Markov problems. Learning based on temporal difference provides an efficient approach to developing long-term transitive temporal relations. Of course, TD was developed for problems in a much simpler setting.

Another technical area that has addressed many similar issues is *probabilistic networks* (Heckerman, Geiger, & Chickering, 1995). It will be interesting to investigate whether the similar ideas based on the Bayesian theory for causal analysis can be applied in the problems with temporal conditions.

Also, it is interesting to formalize this analysis process using the *inductive logic programming* methodology (Muggleton & Raedt, 1994). A part of problems in discovering rules in the form of $E_C[a,b] \Rightarrow E_T$ can be solved by several existing ILP systems, although their computational complexity may not be appealing. Nonetheless, despite of its theoretical value, in practical problem-solving ILP can help combine ground event facts and existing domain knowledge to improve the process of knowledge/model discovery and refinement.

6 CONCLUDING REMARKS

This paper has introduced a new approach to discovering temporal structures in event-sequence data. Methods for learning temporal regions are developed to solve problems with irregularly distributed events and find temporal dependency relations in a large time horizon. The experimental study showed that this approach has worked successfully in finding temporal relations from data.

While the experiments reported in the paper refers to a set of simulated models, the motivation of this development is completely driven by real-world industrial problems. This temporal analysis method (including the earlier versions) has been applied in real Boeing problems for almost one year. In most cases, it is applied for finding and understanding the conditions and reasons of event occurrences. While reporting a real-world application should be much more interesting, the purpose of this report is only limited to justify the validity of this analysis method. Real problems often do not provide well-defined underlying data models. A practical analysis would involve many other issues with knowledge discovery and refinement. Reporting such a work exceeds the scope of this paper.

Research in this area is continuing. This paper presented a part of work at the Boeing research organization for solving industrial time-series problems. A large part of our current effort has been focused on discrete-valued problems—We are developing a suite of tools called *Event Time-Series Rules* `ETSRules` for dealing with various practical challenges. The purpose of the research is to develop methods that can be practically applied in industry to help solve a wide spectrum of problems from prediction and knowledge discovery to causal understanding and decision making using massive amount of data collected during business processes.

Acknowledgements

The author thanks colleagues Kathryn Soucy, Dragos Margineantu, Kathryn Chalfan, Rod Tjoelker, Roman Fresnedo, and Ying Zhang for the valuable discussions and helps received during this work. The author gratefully acknowledges the support of this research by both MC&T and MR&D organizations of The Boeing Company.

References

Agrawal, R., Mannila, H., Srikant, R., Toivonen, H., & Verkamo, A. I. (1996). Fast discovery of association-rules. In Fayyad, U. M., Piatetsky-Shapiro, G., Smyth, P., & Uthrumsamy, R. (Eds.), *Advances in Knowledge Discovery and Data Mining*, chap. 12, pp. 307–328. AAAI/MIT.

Agrawal, R., & Srikant, R. (1995). Mining sequential patterns. In *Proceedings of the Eleventh International Conference on Data Engineering.* IEEE Press.

Heckerman, D., Geiger, D., & Chickering, D. M. (1995). Learning bayesian networks. *Machine Learning, 20*, 197–243.

Howe, A., & Somlo, G. (1997). Modeling discrete event sequences as state transition diagrams. In *Proceedings of the Second Conference on Intelligent Data Analysis.*

Mannila, H., Toivonen, H., & Verkamo, A. I. (1995). Discovering frequent episode in sequences. In *Proceedings of the First International Conference of Knowledge Discovery in Databases and Data Mining.* AAAI Press.

Muggleton, S., & Raedt, L. D. (1994). Inductive logic programming: Theory and methods. *Journal of Logic Programming, 19*(20), 629–679.

Oates, T., Schmill, M. D., Jensen, D., & Cohen, P. R. (1997). A family of algorithms for finding temporal structure in data. In *Proceedings of the Sixth Internationl Workshop on Artificial Intellegence and Statistics.*

Srikant, R., & Agrawal, R. (1996). Mining sequential patterns: generalizations and performance improvements. In *Proceedings of the Fifth International Conference on Extending Database Technology.*

Sutton, R. S. (1988). Learning to predict by the method of temporal difference. *Machine Learning, 3*(1), 9–44.

Lazy Bayesian Rules: A Lazy Semi-Naive Bayesian Learning Technique Competitive to Boosting Decision Trees

Zijian Zheng, Geoffrey I. Webb, Kai Ming Ting
School of Computing and Mathematics
Deakin University
Victoria 3217 Australia
{zijian,webb,kmting}@deakin.edu.au

Abstract

LBR is a lazy semi-naive Bayesian classifier learning technique, designed to alleviate the attribute interdependence problem of naive Bayesian classification. To classify a test example, it creates a conjunctive rule that selects a most appropriate subset of training examples and induces a local naive Bayesian classifier using this subset. LBR can significantly improve the performance of the naive Bayesian classifier. A bias and variance analysis of LBR reveals that it significantly reduces the bias of naive Bayesian classification at a cost of a slight increase in variance. It is interesting to compare this lazy technique with boosting and bagging, two well-known state-of-the-art non-lazy learning techniques. Empirical comparison of LBR with boosting decision trees on discrete valued data shows that LBR has, on average, significantly lower variance and higher bias. As a result of the interaction of these effects, the average prediction error of LBR over a range of learning tasks is at a level directly comparable to boosting. LBR provides a very competitive discrete valued learning technique where error minimization is the primary concern. It is very efficient when a single classifier is to be applied to classify few cases, such as in a typical incremental learning scenario.

1 INTRODUCTION

Among the commonly used and well studied classifier learning techniques, the simple and computationally efficient naive Bayesian classifier (Duda & Hart, 1973; Kononenko, 1990; Langley & Sage, 1994) has been shown in many domains to be surprisingly accurate compared to alternatives including decision tree learning, rule learning, neural networks, and instance-based learning (Cestnik, Kononenko, & Bratko, 1987; Kononenko, 1990; Domingos & Pazzani, 1996). Naive Bayesian classification is based on Bayes' theorem and an assumption that all attributes are mutually independent within each class. This technique predicts that a test example with a vector of attribute values $V = \langle v_1, v_2, \cdots, v_n \rangle$ belongs to the class C_i that maximizes the posterior probability $P(C_i|V) \propto P(C_i) \prod_j P(v_j|C_i)$, where $P(C_i)$ is the prior probability of class C_i, and $P(v_j|C_i)$ is the conditional probability that v_j occurs in class C_i examples. The prior probability and conditional probabilities are usually directly estimated from frequency counts over a given training set.

The attribute independence assumption makes the application of Bayes' theorem to classification practical in many domains. Domingos & Pazzani (1996) argue that the naive Bayesian classifier is optimal even when the independence assumption is violated, so long as the ranks of the conditional probabilities of classes given an example are correct. However, previous research has shown that semi-naive techniques and Bayesian networks that explicitly adjust the naive strategy to allow for violations of the independence assumption, can improve upon the prediction accuracy of the naive Bayesian classifier in many domains (Friedman & Goldszmidt, 1996; Kohavi, 1996; Kononenko, 1991; Langley, 1993; Langley & Sage, 1994; Pazzani, 1998; Sahami, 1996; Singh, & Provan, 1996; Webb & Pazzani, 1998). This suggests that the ranks of conditional probabilities are frequently not correct.

To tackle this problem, the naive Bayesian tree learner, NBTREE (Kohavi, 1996), combines naive Bayesian classification and decision tree learning (Breiman, Friedman, Olshen & Stone, 1984; Quinlan, 1993). It uses a tree structure to split the instance space into sub-spaces defined by the paths of the tree. It generates one naive Bayesian classifier in each sub-space. The decision nodes of these trees contain the univariate tests of conventional decision trees. Each leaf of a naive Bayesian tree contains a local naive Bayesian classifier that does not consider attributes involved in tests on the path leading to the leaf, and is used to classify examples that reach this leaf. It has been shown that NBTREE frequently achieves higher accuracy than either a naive Bayesian classifier or a decision tree learner (Kohavi, 1996).

Although NBTREE can alleviate the attribute interdependence problem of naive Bayesian classification to some extent, NBTREE suffers from the replication and fragmentation problems (Pagallo & Haussler, 1990) as well as the small disjunct problem (Holte, Acker, & Porter, 1989; Ting, 1994) due to the tree structure. To solve these problems and further improve the performance of naive Bayesian classification, we previously proposed a lazy Bayesian rule (LBR) learning technique (Zheng & Webb, 1998). LBR can be thought of as applying lazy learning techniques (Aha, 1997) to naive Bayesian tree induction. At classification time, for each test example, LBR builds a most appropriate rule with a conjunction of conditions as its antecedent and a local naive Bayesian classifier as its consequent. Our experimental results (Zheng & Webb, 1998) have shown that LBR is, on average, more accurate than a naive Bayesian classifier, C4.5 (Quinlan, 1993), our implementation (Zheng & Webb, 1998) of NBTREE (Kohavi, 1996), a constructive Bayesian classifier that eliminates attributes and constructs new attributes using Cartesian products of existing nominal attributes (Pazzani, 1998), a selective naive Bayesian classifier (Langley & Sage, 1994), and a lazy decision tree learning algorithm (Friedman, Kohavi & Yun, 1996).

While these comparisons with directly related algorithms reveal good performance, it is interesting to hold a new contender up against the state-of-the-art. Recent studies have shown that committee learning techniques, notably boosting and bagging, achieve very low prediction error, especially for decision tree learning (Bauer & Kohavi, 1999; Breiman, 1996; Freund & Schapire, 1997; Quinlan, 1996; Schapire, Freund, Bartlett & Lee, 1997). These techniques generate multiple models to form a committee by repeated application of a single base learning algorithm. At classification time, the committee members vote to make the final decision. Here, we compare LBR with boosting and bagging decision trees, as previous research showed that they achieve very high average accuracy (Bauer & Kohavi, 1999; Quinlan, 1996). It is interesting to note that boosting naive Bayes is not very effective (Ting & Zheng, 1999) as boosting requires that the base learner be sensitive to variations in the training set while naive Bayes is very stable across training samples, resulting in low variance but high bias.

The following section describes the algorithms used in this paper, LBR, AdaBoost, and bagging. Section 3 contains empirical studies. We first carry out extensions to our previous analysis of LBR (Zheng & Webb, 1998), and then compare LBR to AdaBoost and bagging. We will show that LBR can significantly reduce the bias of naive Bayesian classification at a cost of a slight increase in variance. Furthermore, LBR has, on average, significantly lower variance and higher bias than AdaBoost with decision trees. As a result of the interaction of these effects, the average prediction error of LBR over a range of learning tasks is at a level directly comparable to AdaBoost. Finally, Section 4 summarizes our findings.

2 THE LBR, ADABOOST, AND BAGGING ALGORITHMS

We describe the LBR algorithm in the following subsection. Sub-sections 2.2 and 2.3 present short descriptions of AdaBoost and bagging respectively. Readers are referred to elsewhere for more detailed descriptions of these two algorithms (Freund & Schapire, 1997; Breiman, 1996). The empirical studies in this paper also involve two other algorithms: a naive Bayesian classifier, NB, and a decision tree learner, C4.5. NB was described briefly in Section 1. More detail is available elsewhere (Duda & Hart, 1973; Kononenko, 1990; Langley & Sage, 1994). In our implementation of NB, when the probability of an attribute value conditional on a class is estimated from a training set, the m-estimate (Cestnik, 1990) with m = 2 is used. When the probability of a class is estimated, the Laplace estimate (Cestnik, 1990) is used. We assume that readers are familiar with C4.5, since it is widely used. A complete description of C4.5 is given by Quinlan (1993).

2.1 LBR

LBR uses lazy learning to alleviate the attribute interdependence problem of naive Bayesian classification, as well as to avoid the replication, fragmentation, and small disjunct problems from which NBTREE (Kohavi, 1996) may suffer. It retains all training examples until classification time. Before classifying a test example, LBR generates a rule (called a *Bayesian rule*) that is most appropriate to the test example. This contrasts with creating a model at training time, such as NBTREE's single tree, that is, on average, most appropriate to all examples. The antecedent of a Bayesian rule is a conjunction of attribute-value pairs (conditions) each of the form 'attribute = value'. The current version of LBR can only deal directly with discrete valued attributes. Numeric attributes are discretized as a pre-process. The consequent of a Bayesian rule is a local naive Bayesian classifier created from *local training examples* that satisfy the antecedent of the rule.

Table 1: The Lazy Bayesian Rule learning algorithm

```
LBR(Att, D, E_test)
  INPUT: Att: a set of attributes,
         D: a set of training cases described
            using Att and classes,
         E_test: a test case described using Att.
  OUTPUT: a predicted class for E_test.
LocalNB = a NB classifier trained using Att on D
Errors = errors of LocalNB estimated using N-CV on D
Cond = true
REPEAT
  TempErrors_best = the number of cases in D + 1
  FOR each attribute A in Att whose value v_A on
      E_test is not missing DO
    D_subset = cases in D with A = v_A
    TempNB = a NB classifier trained using
             Att - {A} on D_subset
    TempErrors = errors of TempNB estimated using
                 N-CV on D_subset + the portion
                 of Errors in D - D_subset
    IF ((TempErrors < TempErrors_best) AND
       (TempErrors is significantly lower than Errors))
    THEN
       TempNB_best = TempNB
       TempErrors_best = TempErrors
       A_best = A
  IF (an A_best is found)
  THEN
     Cond = Cond ∧ (A_best = v_Abest)
     LocalNB = TempNB_best
     D = D_subset corresponding to A_best
     Att = Att - {A_best}
     Errors = errors of LocalNB estimated using
              N-CV on D
UNTIL (no A_best is found)
classify E_test using LocalNB
RETURN the class
```

This local naive Bayesian classifier uses only those attributes that do not appear in the rule's antecedent.

Table 1 outlines the LBR algorithm. During the generation of a Bayesian rule, only attribute-value pairs that utilize attribute values of the test example are considered. The objective is to grow the antecedent of a Bayesian rule that ultimately decreases the errors of the local naive Bayesian classifier in the consequent of the rule. The antecedent of the Bayesian rule defines a sub-space of the instance space to which the test example belongs, selecting a subset of the available training instances. All instances in this sub-space have the attribute-values specified in the antecedent. In consequence, these attributes are removed from the local naive Bayesian classifier.

For each test example, LBR uses a greedy search to generate a Bayesian rule with an antecedent that matches the test example. The growth of the rule starts from a special Bayesian rule whose antecedent is *true*. The rule's local naive Bayesian classifier is trained on the entire training set using all attributes. This classifier is identical to a conventional naive Bayesian classifier. At each step of the greedy search, LBR tries to select and add, to the antecedent of the current Bayesian rule, the best attribute-value pair ($A_i = v_{A_i}$) where v_{A_i} is the value of A_i on the test example. During this search, those attributes are ignored that are already included in the antecedent of the current rule or whose value on the test example is missing. The objective is to determine whether including this attribute-value pair into the Bayesian rule can significantly improve the estimated accuracy. This search method is similar to forward selection which has been used for relevant attribute subset selection (John, Kohavi & Pfleger, 1994).

The utility of adding each possible $A_i = v_{A_i}$ to the current rule is evaluated as follows. A subset of examples D_{subset} that satisfies $A_i = v_{A_i}$ is identified from the current local training set D, and is used to train a temporary naive Bayesian classifier using all attributes other than A_i that do not occur in the antecedent of the current Bayesian rule. The error of this classifier on D_{subset} is estimated by N-fold cross-validation (N-CV).[1] This estimate together with an N-CV estimate of the errors of the local naive Bayesian classifier of the current Bayesian rule on $D - D_{subset}$ are used to assess the value of adding $A_i = v_{A_i}$ to the current Bayesian rule.[2] If this measure is lower than the estimated errors of the local naive Bayesian classifier on D at a significance level better than 0.05 using a one-tailed pairwise sign-test, this attribute-value pair becomes a candidate condition to be added to the current Bayesian rule. The sign-test is used to control the likelihood of adding conditions that reduce error by chance. After evaluating all possible conditions, the candidate condition with the lowest error estimate is added to the antecedent of the current Bayesian rule.

Training cases that do not satisfy the antecedent of the rule are then discarded, and the above process repeated. This continues until no more candidate conditions are found. This happens when no damaging attribute inter-dependencies exist for the local naive Bayesian classifier, or the local training set is too small

[1] We use N-CV because N-CV errors are more reliable estimates of true errors than re-substitution errors (Breiman, Friedman, Olshen & Stone, 1984) and N-CV on a naive Bayesian classifier is computationally efficient.

[2] Here we evaluate the utility of each attribute-value pair on the whole local training set, D. Since different attribute-value pairs cover different subsets of D, estimated errors for different attribute-value pairs on their corresponding subsets of training examples, D_{subset}, are not comparable.

to further reduce the instance sub-space by specializing the antecedent of the Bayesian rule. In such cases, further growing the Bayesian rule would not significantly reduce its errors. Finally, the local naive Bayesian classifier of this Bayesian rule is used to classify the test example under consideration.

2.2 ADABOOST

Boosting (Freund & Schapire, 1997) is a general framework for improving a base learning algorithm. During training, it sequentially builds different classifiers to form a committee by adaptively modifying the distribution of the training set based on the performance of previously created classifiers. The objective is to make the generation of the next classifier concentrate on the training examples misclassified by the previous classifiers.

Our implementation of AdaBoost uses C4.5 (Quinlan, 1993) as the base learner. Given a training set D consisting of m instances and a specified number of trials T, AdaBoost builds T pruned trees over T trials by repeatedly invoking C4.5. Let $w_t(x)$ denotes the weight of instance x in D at trial t. At the first trial, each instance has weight 1, that is, $w_1(x) = 1$ for each x. At trial t, decision tree H_t is built using D under the distribution w_t. The training error ϵ_t of H_t is then calculated by summing up the weights of the instances that H_t misclassifies and dividing by m. For the next trial, the weight $w_{t+1}(x)$ is set to $w_t(x)/2\epsilon_t$ if H_t incorrectly classifies x, and $w_t(x)/2(1-\epsilon_t)$ otherwise. If $w_{t+1}(x) < 10^{-8}$, set it to 10^{-8} to solve the numerical underflow problem (Bauer & Kohavi, 1999). These weights are then renormalized so that they sum to m.

Following the example of Bauer & Kohavi (1999), when ϵ_t is greater than 0.5, $w_t(x)$ is re-initialized to allow the boosting process to continue. Following Webb (forthcoming), we also reweight examples to continue boosting if ϵ_t reaches zero. This allows the possibility that more than one committee member with zero error will be derived, enabling these to vote against each other (with very large but finite weight) and giving other committee members a casting vote in case of a draw between committee members with zero resubstitution error. We employ Webb's (forthcoming) reweighting scheme in these contexts, setting $w_t(x)$ to random values from the continuous Poisson distribution, generated by:

$$Poisson() = -log\left(\frac{Random(1\ldots999)}{1000}\right), \quad (1)$$

where $Random(min\ldots max)$ returns a random integer value between min and max inclusive. After values are assigned using this random process, the vector of weights is normalized to sum to the size of the training set. Then, the boosting process continues to build the next tree. Note that any tree with $\epsilon_t > 0.5$ is discarded and this trial is repeated with the re-initialized instance weights, while a tree with $\epsilon_t = 0$ is accepted by the committee.

At the classification stage, for each test example, all decision trees in the committee perform weighted voting to make the prediction. The vote of decision tree H_t is worth $\log(1/\beta_t)$ units, where $\beta_t = \epsilon_t/(1-\epsilon_t)$.

This implementation of AdaBoost is very similar to that of Bauer & Kohavi (1999). The only difference is that Bauer & Kohavi (1999) halt induction and treat H_t as having infinite weight if $\epsilon_t = 0$, and use the bootstrap sampling method to re-initialize the weights when $\epsilon_t > 0.5$, whereas our implementation sets $\beta_t = 10^{-10}$ when $\epsilon_t = 0$, and re-initializes the weights using the continuous Poisson distribution in both situations. The continuous Poisson distribution is chosen because our experiments show that this weight re-initialization method has a small advantage over the bootstrap sampling method.

2.3 BAGGING

Like boosting, bagging (Breiman, 1996) generates committees by changing the distribution of the training set. However, for bagging, the change of the instance distribution is stochastic. The primary idea is to generate a committee of classifiers with each induced from a bootstrap sample of the original training set. Given a committee size T and a training set D consisting of m instances, bagging generates T bootstrap samples with each being created by uniformly sampling m instances from D with replacement. It then applies C4.5 to build one decision tree from each bootstrap sample. All decision trees in the committee vote with equal weight to classify a test example.

3 EVALUATION

In this section, we analyze the behavior of LBR using the bias and variance decomposition to gain insight into how it improves the performance of its base learning algorithm. Then we compare LBR with boosting and bagging. Section 3.1 describes the bias and variance decomposition. Section 3.2 illustrates the experimental domains and methods used in this paper. The following two subsections present the results of the analysis with LBR, and the comparison with boosting and bagging. Section 3.5 gives a comparison in terms of compute time.

3.1 BIAS AND VARIANCE

Bias and *variance* analyses can provide useful insights into the generalization performance of a learning algorithm. Bias is a measure of error due to the central tendency and variance is a measure of error due to disagreements between the classifiers formed by an algorithm across a distribution of training sets. Among several definitions of bias and variance, in this study we adopt Kohavi & Wolpert's (1996) definitions that decompose error into intrinsic noise (optimal Bayes error), squared bias, and variance. Due to the difficulty of estimating the intrinsic noise in practical experiments with real domains, we follow Kohavi & Wolpert's (1996) strategy of generating a bias term that includes both intrinsic noise and squared bias. The values are calculated directly from the performance of each classifier on each test case in the experiments described below.

3.2 EXPERIMENTAL DOMAINS AND METHODS

This study uses the same twenty-nine natural domains used in previous studies of LBR (Zheng & Webb, 1998). These cover a wide variety of domains from the UCI machine learning repository (Blake, Keogh & Merz, 1998). This test suite includes all the twenty-eight domains used by Domingos & Pazzani (1996) for studying naive Bayesian classification, as well as the Tic-Tac-Toe domain. The last domain was chosen for previous research because it contains inter-dependent attributes and its target concept is known.

We employ the bias/variance estimation process developed by Webb (forthcoming). For each domain ten three-fold cross-validations (Breiman, Friedman, Olshen & Stone, 1984) are carried out for each algorithm. All the algorithms are run with their default option settings on the same training and test set partitions in every domain. Only the error rate on the test set is reported. An error (or bias, or variance) rate reported in the following subsections is an average over the 30 runs for an algorithm.

Since the current implementation of LBR and NB can only deal with discrete valued attributes, numeric attributes are discretized as a pre-process in the experiments using an entropy-based discretization method (Fayyad & Irani, 1993) for all learning algorithms. In other words, the algorithms are being compared on performance when learning from discrete valued data. For each pair of training set and test set, both training set and test set are discretized by using cut points found from the training set alone.

3.3 BIAS AND VARIANCE ANALYSIS FOR LBR

LBR is designed to improve the performance of the naive Bayesian classifier NB. A bias and variance decomposition of LBR's performance provides interesting

Table 2: Error rates (%) of LBR, NB, C4.5, AdaBoost, and bagging

Domain	LBR	NB	C4.5	AdaBoost	bagging
Annealing	2.8	3.0	10.4	7.8	8.9
Audiology	28.0	28.4	23.7	19.4	21.5
Breast(W)	2.6	2.6	5.1	3.8	4.4
KR-KP	2.7	12.5	0.8	0.5	0.7
Credit(A)	14.4	14.5	14.5	15.9	14.3
Echocar.	30.8	30.8	36.2	33.9	35.1
Glass	34.1	34.0	35.8	33.1	32.8
Heart(C)	17.6	17.6	24.0	22.3	20.7
Hepatitis	14.7	14.7	21.0	17.7	18.9
Horse	20.3	21.0	17.0	21.3	16.8
HouseVote	6.7	9.9	5.1	4.9	4.6
Hypo	1.5	1.8	1.3	1.2	1.2
Iris	6.6	6.6	7.5	7.5	7.1
Labor	10.7	10.7	19.5	18.2	18.6
LED 24	39.7	39.5	36.9	36.4	31.8
Liver	36.2	36.2	35.7	36.0	36.0
LungC.	49.7	49.4	59.4	55.0	61.3
Lympho	18.5	18.3	23.6	17.7	20.7
Pima	25.1	25.2	25.5	27.0	25.0
Postop.	35.9	36.0	29.9	39.7	31.1
P.Tumor	52.4	52.4	61.0	58.4	57.8
Promoters	10.7	10.7	26.3	8.4	17.2
Solar	17.1	19.1	15.7	17.0	15.9
Sonar	25.4	26.5	32.1	22.1	24.9
Soybean	7.0	9.8	10.3	6.9	8.2
Splice	4.3	4.5	6.5	4.7	5.5
TicTacToe	19.1	29.5	16.5	1.3	9.3
Wine	2.5	2.5	11.8	4.7	8.9
Zoology	6.2	6.2	8.5	6.2	8.4
mean	18.7	19.8	21.4	18.9	19.6
e.r. mean		1.12	1.21	.93	1.07
w/t/l		4/11/14	10/0/19	13/1/15	14/0/15
p. of wtl		.0304	.1360	.8506	1.0000

e.r. mean: geometric mean of error ratios.

insights into how it achieves this effect.

Table 2 presents the error rates of LBR and NB (results for C4.5, AdaBoost, and bagging are discussed in the following section). The penultimate row shows the geometric mean error ratio of NB over LBR. Geometric rather than arithmetic mean is used as it is more appropriate for averaging ratio values. The last row in the table shows the numbers of wins, ties, and losses between the error rates of NB against those of LBR in the 29 domains, and the significance level of a two-tailed pairwise sign-test on this win/tie/loss outcome. We consider the comparison significant if the sign-test reveals a probability of less than 0.05 that the observed result or more extreme should be obtained by chance. To illustrate the impact to bias and variance of applying LBR's semi-naive Bayesian approach in place of NB's naive Bayesian approach, Figure 1 presents a bar chart that shows for each domain the decrease in error due to bias reduction and increase in error due

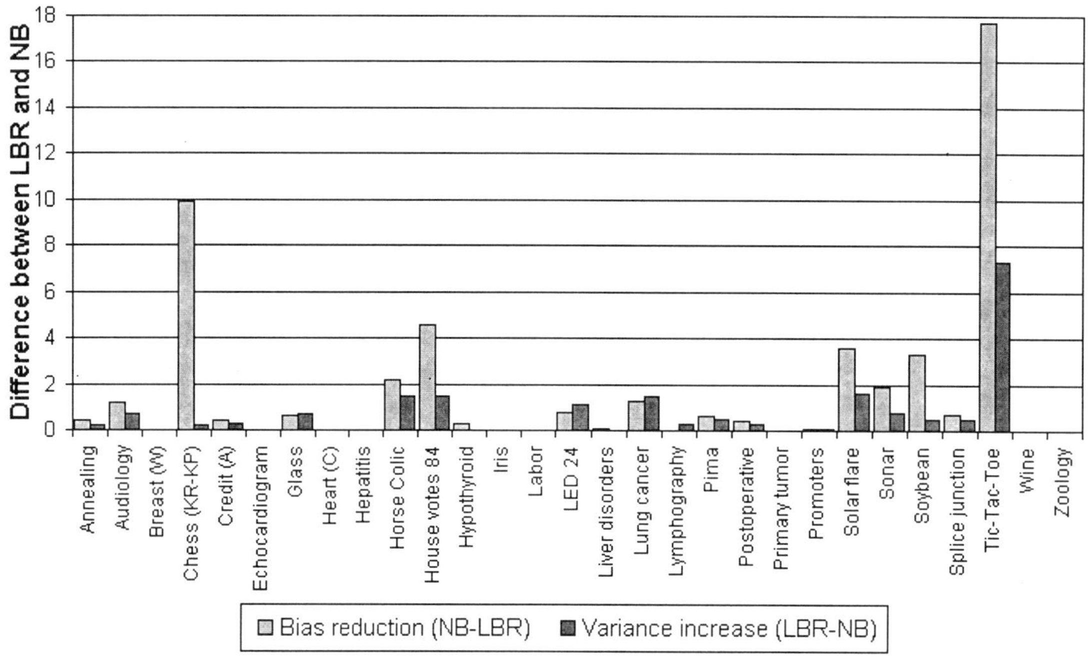

Figure 1: Bias and variance comparison between LBR and NB

to increased variance. Figure 2 summarizes this result across all domains by displaying the average error of all algorithms decomposed into average bias and variance.

It is apparent that LBR outperforms NB in terms of average error rate, error ratio, and w/t/l record. The relative error reduction of LBR over NB is 12%. The sign-test shows that LBR obtains lower error rates significantly more often than the reverse in comparison to NB.

It is also apparent that the effect of LBR is to substantially reduce the bias of naive Bayes. Figure 1 shows that LBR does not obtain higher bias than NB in any of the experimental domains. However, LBR never reduces the variance of NB. The reason is that introducing rules reduces the instance space and the number of training instances. This is very likely to increase the variance. The bias term strongly dominates the error of NB and hence the bias reduction usually outweighs the variance increase. This accounts for LBR's lower error in most domains.

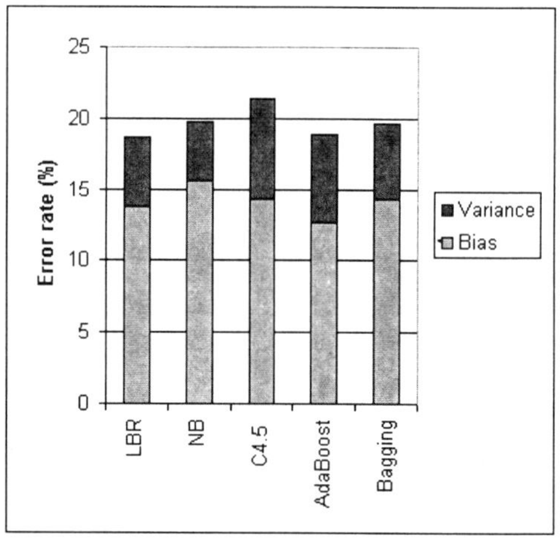

Figure 2: Error rate with bias and variance decomposition

3.4 COMPARING LBR WITH C4.5, ADABOOST, AND BAGGING

We turn now to a comparison of LBR against boosting and bagging decision trees. As C4.5 is the base learning algorithm used in the committee techniques, its performance is also considered.

We use AdaBoost and bagging with 100 trees in our experiments since it has been shown that increasing the committee size usually further improves the performance, especially with AdaBoost (Schapire, Freund, Bartlett & Lee, 1997). The results of C4.5, AdaBoost and bagging are provided in Table 2 and Figure 2.

The relative error reduction of LBR over C4.5 is 21%. Although the sign-test fails to show that LBR is significantly better than C4.5, LBR has lower error rates than C4.5 almost twice as often as the reverse. Also, LBR has lower bias and variance than C4.5 on average.

Note that, despite the discretization of numeric attributes, the results of AdaBoost and bagging reported here are either comparable to or better than earlier published results (Bauer & Kohavi, 1999; Breiman, 1996; Quinlan, 1996) since we use a higher value of T. With reference to their base learning algorithm C4.5, AdaBoost reduces bias from 14.3% to 12.7%, and variance from 7.1% to 6.2%. Bagging has the same bias as C4.5, but reduces variance from 7.1% to 5.3%. Note also that we have repeated the experiments with committees of size 10 and that the results are less favorable to boosting and bagging than the results reported here. For example, the average error rate of AdaBoost with 10 trees is 20.2%, substantially higher than that of AdaBoost with 100 trees (18.9%). With 10 trees, the average error of bagging is 20.3% compared to 19.6% with 100 trees.

Comparing LBR with AdaBoost and bagging, we have the following observations.

- LBR has lower average error than either AdaBoost or bagging. In terms of geometric mean error ratio, AdaBoost has lower error than LBR by 7%. However, when the geometric mean *accuracy* ratio is calculated, it shows that AdaBoost has lower accuracy than LBR by 1%. This seemingly incompatible outcome results from AdaBoost's tendency to better performance where error is low (and hence accuracy is high) while LBR tends to perform well in the reverse context. AdaBoost wins in 13 domains, loses in 15 domains and draws in 1 domain. All this indicates that LBR is very competitive to AdaBoost.

  The geometric mean error ratio indicates the bagging has 7% higher average error than LBR. Bagging wins in 14 domains and loses in 15 domains.
- LBR has lower average variance than either AdaBoost or bagging—4.9% compared to 6.2% for AdaBoost and 5.3% for bagging. The frequency with which LBR achieves lower variance is significant at the 0.05 level with respect to AdaBoost but not bagging.
- LBR has higher average bias than AdaBoost (13.8% versus 12.7%), but lower average bias than bagging (13.8% versus 14.3%). The frequency with which LBR has higher bias is significant at the 0.05 level with respect to AdaBoost but not bagging.

Since C4.5 can deal directly with numeric attributes, it might impede C4.5 to carry out discretization as a pre-process when running C4.5. This also applies for AdaBoost and bagging with C4.5. In an additional experiment, with exactly the same experimental method, C4.5, AdaBoost, and bagging were run without discretization. The average error rates of C4.5, AdaBoost, and bagging without discretization in these 29 domains using the same training and test set partitions are 21.3%, 17.9%, and 18.6% respectively. These are slightly lower than the corresponding values with discretization. The accuracy of C4.5 without discretization is also worse than that of LBR, with 1.18 as the geometric mean error ratio and 11/1/18 as the win/tie/loss record of the former over the latter. AdaBoost without discretization shows a slight advantage over LBR. The win/tie/loss record of AdaBoost without discretization over LBR is 16/1/12 in the 29 domains. This difference is not significant at the level 0.05 using a two-tailed pairwise sign-test ($p = .572$). The geometric mean error ratio of AdaBoost without discretization over LBR is 0.86. While this seems a big advantage to AdaBoost, the geometric mean accuracy ratio of AdaBoost without discretization over LBR is only 1.006, a very slight advantage to AdaBoost. As discussed in the context of AdaBoost with discretization, this results from AdaBoost's tendency to better performance where error is low (and hence accuracy is high) and LBR's tendency to perform well in the reverse context. The geometric mean error ratio and the win/tie/loss record of bagging without discretization over LBR are 1.004 and 14/1/14 respectively, suggesting that bagging even without discretization has no advantage over LBR on average. On the other hand, these results suggest that the performance of LBR might be further improved by carrying out discretization during the generation of Bayesian rules instead of pre-processing or by employing techniques for handling undiscretized numeric values such as those proposed by John & Langley (1995).

3.5 COMPUTATION TIME

In this section, we discuss LBR's computational profile and compare its computation time with that of AdaBoost with 100 decision trees. Since AdaBoost and bagging have similar execution times, the result of the latter is omitted.

Lazy learners have very different computation time profiles to eager learners that generate an explicit model at training time. If we consider the total computation time for learning from a given training set and classifying objects in a given test set, the computation time of an eager learner is strongly dominated by the requirements for learning a model from the training set. The computation associated with applying the model to classify test objects is usually relatively trivial. In particular, the computational profile is relatively insensitive to the number of objects to be classified. The total compute time will differ little irrespective of whether one or 1000 objects are to be classified. In contrast, lazy learners delay computation to classification time and the amount of computation is dependent on the number of objects to be classified.

The major computational overhead in LBR is the evaluation of each potential addition of a condition to the antecedent of the rule being constructed. This requires N-fold cross-validation of the resulting local naive Bayesian classifier. As N-fold cross-validation of a naive Bayesian classifier can be implemented very efficiently, the computational requirements for classifying a single test case are reasonable. However, lazy learning requires that the same process is repeated for each test example, and the cumulative computation for a large test set can be substantial. The computational overhead can be substantially reduced by caching useful information. In the current implementation of LBR, the evaluation function values of attribute-value pairs that have been examined are retained from one test example to the next. This avoids re-calculation of the evaluation function values of the same attribute-value pairs when classifying test examples that appear later in the test set, thus reducing the entire execution time. Our experiment shows that caching this information reduces the execution time of LBR by 96% on average on the 29 datasets used in the experiment. This is because the evaluation of attribute-value pairs for different test examples are often repeated, including repeated generation of identical rules for different test examples. LBR could be made even more efficient by caching further information such as local classifiers and indices for training examples in different stages of the growth of rules. Of course, this would increase memory requirements.

Table 3 shows the execution time (in seconds) of LBR and AdaBoost, running on a Sun UltraSPARC 2 computer. AdaBoost uses more time than LBR in 24 domains. Although, in terms of mean execution time over the 29 domains, LBR is about five time slower than AdaBoost, this is dominated by 5 domains in which AdaBoost is much faster than LBR. In these 5 domains, large numbers of test instances contribute to the long execution in LBR. For example, in the Splice junction domain, the test set size used in the current experiment is 1059. When we change the experiment from three-fold cross-validation to ten-fold cross-validation (the test set size is reduced to 318), the execution time of LBR reduces from 266.30 seconds to 180.39 seconds, while AdaBoost's execution time increases from 40.20 seconds to 46.37 seconds. This suggests that the test set size has a great effect on the execution time of LBR, and has a very little effect on the execution time of AdaBoost.

When interpreting the results in Table 3 it should be noted that they relate to contexts, created by three-fold cross-validation, in which two thirds of the available data are used for training and one third for testing. The results would better favor LBR if the proportion of data used for testing was decreased and better favor AdaBoost if this proportion was increased.

Table 3: Compute time (in seconds) of LBR, and AdaBoost

Domain	AdaBoost	LBR
Annealing	6.74	3.84
Audiology	8.50	21.75
Breast(W)	1.65	0.35
KR-KP	31.10	388.74
Credit(A)	3.67	1.30
Echocar.	0.41	0.02
Glass	1.22	0.16
Heart(C)	1.44	0.20
Hepatitis	1.09	0.09
Horse	4.25	0.77
HouseVote	1.44	0.86
Hypo	13.29	54.14
Iris	0.22	0.01
Labor	0.31	0.01
LED 24	2.98	0.97
Liver	0.64	0.16
LungC.	0.61	0.15
Lympho	1.02	0.12
Pima	2.90	0.64
Postop.	0.48	0.03
P.Tumor	6.43	1.42
Promoters	1.13	0.10
Solar	5.06	2.92
Sonar	2.88	1.30
Soybean	8.95	55.50
Splice	40.20	266.30
TicTacToe	3.52	1.94
Wine	0.54	0.04
Zoology	0.45	0.03
mean	5.28	27.72
e.r. mean		1.34
w/t/l		24/0/5
p. of wtl		.0004

4 CONCLUSIONS

This paper evaluates the Lazy Bayesian Rule learning algorithm. This algorithm seeks to overcome the attribute interdependence problem of the naive Bayesian classifier by forming a customized naive Bayesian classifier for each case to be classified. This customized naive Bayesian classifier is formed by selecting a subset of the available training examples that appear most relevant to classifying the current test example. In practice this often builds a more accurate naive Bayesian classifier for the test example than the naive Bayesian classifier trained using all training examples.

This paper shows that the lazy Bayesian rule induction algorithm is an effective technique for improving upon the naive Bayesian classifier. We show that this effect is achieved by significantly and substantially reducing the bias of naive Bayesian classification, though this is achieved at the cost of a slight increase in variance.

Current implementation constraints, notably that it accepts only discrete attributes and is restricted to antecedent conditions of the form 'attribute = value', suggest that there is room to further improve the performance of the basic lazy Bayesian rule induction algorithm described in this paper. This is a promising direction for future research.

We also show that the prediction error of LBR for discrete valued data is very competitive to state-of-the-art non-lazy techniques. Due to the use of lazy learning, the computation profile of the technique is dominated by the number of cases to be classified. In consequence, it is very efficient when there are only a small number of test cases for each training set, as is the case in contexts where incremental learning is traditionally employed.

Acknowledgments

The authors are grateful to J. Ross Quinlan for providing C4.5. Many thanks to the anonymous reviewers for their very valuable comments.

References

Aha, D.W. (ed.) (1997) *Lazy Learning.* Dordrecht: Kluwer Academic.

Bauer, E. & Kohavi, R. (1999) An empirical comparison of voting classification algorithms: Bagging, boosting, and variants. To appear in *Machine Learning.*

Blake, C., Keogh, E. & Merz, C.J. (1998) UCI Repository of Machine Learning Databases [http://www.ics.uci.edu/~mlearn/MLRepository.html]. Irvine, CA: University of California, Department of Information and Computer Science.

Cestnik, B., Kononenko, I., & Bratko, I. (1987) ASSISTANT 86: A knowledge-elicitation tool for sophisticated users. In *Proc. 2nd European Working Session on Learning*, 31-45, Wilmslow, UK: Sigma Press.

Breiman, L., Friedman, J.H., Olshen, R.A., & Stone, C.J. (1984) *Classification and Regression Trees.* Wadsworth, Belmont.

Breiman, L. (1996) Bagging predictors. *Machine Learning*, 24: 123-140.

Cestnik, B. (1990) Estimating probabilities: A crucial task in machine learning. In *Proc. European Conf. on Artificial Intelligence*, 147-149.

Domingos, P. & Pazzani, M. (1996) Beyond independence: Conditions for the optimality of the simple Bayesian classifier. In *Proc. 13th Intl. Conf. on Machine Learning*, pp. 105-112,. San Francisco, CA: Morgan Kaufmann.

Duda, R.O. & Hart, P.E. (1973) *Pattern Classification and Scene Analysis.* New York: John Wiley.

Fayyad, U.M. & Irani, K.B. (1993) Multi-interval discretization of continuous-valued attributes for classification learning. In *Proc. 13th Intl. Joint Conf. on Artificial Intelligence*, 1022-1027, San Mateo, CA: Morgan Kaufmann.

Freund, Y. & Schapire, R. E. (1997) A decision-theoretic generalization of on-line learning and an application to boosting. *Journal of Computer and System Sciences*, 55(1): 119-139.

Friedman, J., Kohavi, R., & Yun, Y. (1996) Lazy decision trees. In *Proc. 13th Natl. Conf. on Artificial Intelligence*, 717-724, Menlo Park, CA: AAAI Press.

Friedman, N. & Goldszmidt, M. (1996) Building classifiers using Bayesian networks. In *Proc. 13th Natl. Conf. on Artificial Intelligence*, 1277-1284, Menlo Park, CA: AAAI Press.

Holte, R.C., Acker, L.E., & Porter, B.W. (1989) Concept learning and the problem of small disjuncts. In *Proc. 11th Intl. Joint Conf. on Artificial Intelligence*, 813-818, San Mateo, CA: Morgan Kaufmann.

John, G., Kohavi, R., Pfleger, K. (1994) Irrelevant features and the subset selection problem. In *Proc. 11th Intl. Conf. on Machine Learning*, 121-129, San Mateo, CA: Morgan Kaufmann.

John, G. & Langley, P. (1995) Estimating continuous distributions in Bayesian classifiers. In *Proc. 11th Conf. on Uncertainty in Artificial Intelligence*, 338-345, San Mateo, CA: Morgan Kaufmann.

Kohavi, R. (1996) Scaling up the accuracy of naive-Bayes classifiers: A decision-tree hybrid. In *Proc. 2nd Intl. Conf. on Knowledge Discovery and Data Mining*, 202-207, Menlo Park, CA: AAAI Press.

Kohavi, R. & Wolpert, D. (1996) Bias plus variance decomposition for zero-one loss functions. In *Proc. 13th Intl. Conf. on Machine Learning*, 275–283, Morgan Kaufmann.

Kononenko, I. (1990) Comparison of inductive and naive Bayesian learning approaches to automatic knowledge acquisition. In B. Wielinga *et al.* (Eds.), *Current Trends in Knowledge Acquisition.* Amsterdam: IOS Press.

Kononenko, I. (1991) Semi-naive Bayesian classifier. In *Proc. of European Conf. on Artificial Intelligence*, 206-219.

Langley, P. (1993) Induction of recursive Bayesian classifiers. In *Proc. European Conf. on Machine Learning*, 153-164, Berlin: Springer-Verlag.

Langley, P. & Sage, S. (1994) Induction of selective Bayesian classifiers. In *Proc. 10th Conf. on Uncertainty in Artificial Intelligence*, 339-406, Seattle, WA: Morgan Kaufmann.

Pagallo, G. & Haussler, D. (1990) Boolean feature discovery in empirical learning. *Machine Learning*, 5: 71-100.

Pazzani, M.J. (1998) Constructive inductive of Cartesian product attributes, In Liu, H, & Motoda, H. (eds.) *Feature Extraction, Construction and Selection - A Data Mining Perspective*, 341-354, Boston, MA: Kluwer Academic.

Quinlan, J.R. (1993) *C4.5: Programs for Machine Learning*, San Mateo, CA: Morgan Kaufmann.

Quinlan, J.R. (1996) Bagging, boosting, and C4.5. In *Proc. 13th Natl. Conf. on Artificial Intelligence*, 725-730, Menlo Park, CA: AAAI Press.

Sahami, M. (1996) Learning limited dependence Bayesian classifiers. In *Proc. 2nd Intl. Conf. on Knowledge Discovery and Data Mining*, 334-338, Menlo Park, CA: AAAI Press.

Schapire, R.E., Freund, Y., Bartlett, P., & Lee, W.S. (1997) Boosting the margin: A new explanation for the effectiveness of voting methods. In *Proc. 14th Intl. Conf. on Machine Learning*, 322-330, Morgan Kaufmann.

Singh, M. & Provan, G.M. (1996) Efficient learning of selective Bayesian network classifiers. In *Proc. 13th Intl. Conf. on Machine Learning*, 453-461, San Francisco, CA: Morgan Kaufmann.

Ting, K.M. (1994) The problem of small disjuncts: Its remedy in decision trees. In *Proc. 10th Canadian Conf. on Artificial Intelligence*, 91-97, Canadian Soc. for Comp. Studies of Intelligence.

Ting, K.M. & Zheng, Z. (1999) Improving the performance of boosting for naive Bayesian classification. In *Proc. 3rd Pacific-Asia Conf. on Knowledge Discovery and Data Mining*, Berlin: Springer-Verlag.

Webb, G. (forthcoming) MultiBoosting: A technique for combining boosting and bagging. Accepted for publication in *Machine Learning.*

Webb, G.I. & Pazzani, M.J. (1998) Adjusted probability naive Bayesian induction. In *Proc. 11th Australian Joint Conf. on Artificial Intelligence*, Berlin: Springer-Verlag.

Zheng, Z. & Webb, G.I, (1998) *Lazy Bayesian rules*, Deakin University Computing Technical Report TR C98-17 (Available at "http://www3.cm.deakin.edu.au/~zijian/Papers/lbr-tr-c98-17.ps.gz").

A Hybrid Lazy-Eager Approach to Reducing the Computation and Memory Requirements of Local Parametric Learning Algorithms

Yuanhui Zhou and Carla Brodley
School of Electrical and Computer Engineering
Purdue University
West Lafayette, IN 47907
yuanhui,brodley@ecn.purdue.edu

Abstract

Locally weighted regression has been successfully applied to many complex regression problems. Its potential drawbacks are its high prediction time and storage requirements. This paper presents a new kind of local parametric learning algorithm that combines the strengths of lazy and eager learning in order to address these drawbacks. Unlike conventional locally weighted regression, which defers processing of training data until a query needs to be answered, our approach analyzes the training data to discover local regions in which the data can be fit well by a linear regression model. For each such local region, our method replaces the training data with the local linear regression model, which shortens the prediction time and reduces the memory requirements. An empirical evaluation of the algorithm on nine datasets, illustrated that our approach significantly reduces prediction time and storage requirements without impacting prediction accuracy.

1 INTRODUCTION

Locally weighted regression (LWR) is a nonparametric learning approach to estimating nonlinear functions (Atkeson et al., 1997; Cleveland, 1979; Friedman, 1984; Hastie and Loader, 1993). Unlike global regression, also called global parametric learning (Schaal, to appear), which sets up a single global model to fit all of the training data, local regression attempts to fit the training data only in a region around the location of the query point. Locally weighted regression belongs to the class of lazy learning algorithms that exhibit three characteristics that distinguish them from eager learning algorithms (Aha, 1997). First, they defer processing of their inputs until they receive a request for answering a query. This usually involves storing the training data in memory. Next, they reply to information requests by finding relevant data points that are near to the query in instance space. Finally, they do not retain the constructed answer or any intermediate results.

Compared with global regression, locally weighted regression has several advantages. Firstly, locally weighted learning does not require choosing a general function for the entire data set. It only considers the data points near the query point that can be fit by a simple model, such as a linear, quadratic or spline model. Because few data are needed for learning, the learning efficiency is improved greatly (Atkeson et al., 1997). Secondly, locally weighted regression can solve the problem of negative interference (Atkeson et al., 1997), which means forgetting of useful knowledge when learning from new data. Thirdly, local regression can adapt well to complex problems (Deng and Moore, 1995).

Although local regression has many attractive characteristics, it has computation and storage costs that are typically greater than that of global regression; local regression algorithms have a lower computational cost than global regression algorithms during training, but the time to answer a query is far greater (Atkeson et al., 1997). Unlike global regression, local regression does nothing until a query is made, at which point it uses data near the query point to create a corresponding model. This requires examining all of the data for each prediction, which has a cost proportional to the size of the training data for every query. In addition, local regression requires more storage space than global regression because it must retain all of the training data.

The goal of this research is to solve the computation and storage problems of LWR. This paper presents a new local parameter learning algorithm which combines the ideas of lazy learning and eager learning to address these shortcomings. Unlike conventional local learning which defers processing of training data until a query needs to be answered, our approach analyzes the training data to discover the local regions in which the data can be fit well by a linear regression model. For each such local region, our method replaces the training data with a local linear regression model. Therefore, unlike conventional local learning, which stores all the training data for prediction, we replace portions of our training data with linear models, greatly reducing the memory requirement.

The remainder of this paper is organized as follows. Section 2 briefly reviews LWR. Section 3 discusses some existing approaches to solving the high computational and storage cost of local learning. Section 4 presents a new local parameter learning algorithm–ALPL. Section 5 presents an experimental evaluation of the approach on benchmark ML data sets and on the network resource-CPU time prediction task, which motivated this research. Section 6 provides an overview of other hybrid lazy-eager learning approaches. Section 7 draws conclusions about the new approach and also points out some of the work for the future.

2 LOCALLY WEIGHTED REGRESSION

For a set of n observations $(X_i, Y_i), i = 1, 2, ..., n$, a standard global linear model expresses the relationship between the independent variable X and dependent variable Y as: $X^T\beta = Y$, where the dimensionality of X is $n \times (d+1)$, n is the number of data points, and $d+1$ is the dimensionality of X_i plus one. The goal is to estimate the parameters $\hat{\beta}$, that minimize the criterion: $\sum_{i=1}^{n}(Y_i - \hat{\beta}X_i)^2$. We can calculate $\hat{\beta}$ using $\hat{\beta} = (X^TX)^{-1}X^TY$.

Locally weighted linear regression differs from global linear regression in that it only considers data near the query point X_q, rather than all of the data. Each data point's contribution to the local model is proportional to its distance to the query point. The exact weight is computed by a chosen kernel function $K(.)$. A commonly used weighting function is Gaussian, $K(d) = exp(-d^2/h)$, where d is the distance of the query point to a data point and h is the bandwidth, which is a parameter that determines how quickly weights decline in value as one gets further away from the query. Given a kernel function, the fitting criterion for LWR becomes:

$$min \sum_{i=1}^{n}(Y_i - \hat{\beta}X_i)^2 K(d(X_i, X_q), h)$$

Computing the distance $d(X_i, X_q)$ between each point X_i and the query point X_q requires that we define a distance function. In our implementation of LWR we use the Euclidean distance function. We can rewrite this fitting criterion as: $min(Y - X\hat{\beta})^T W (Y - X\hat{\beta})$, where $W = diag(K(d(X_i, X_q), h))_{n\times n}$. The solution $\hat{\beta} = (\hat{\beta}_0, \hat{\beta}_1, ..., \hat{\beta}_d)^T$ can be expressed as $\hat{\beta} = (X^TWX)^{-1}X^TWY$.

In summary, to apply locally weighted regression one must choose the bandwidth, the kernel function, the distance function (to measure the distance of the query point to all other points), the parametric family that is fitted locally, and the fitting criterion used to fit the local model.

3 EXISTING APPROACHES TO IMPROVING THE EFFICIENCY OF LOCALLY WEIGHTED LEARNING

Local weighted learning has been applied successfully to many complex problems (Atkeson et al., 1997). A recent focus of research addresses their prohibitive computational and storage cost. One solution is the instance pruning approach in which only a portion of the data points are used for prediction. There are two basic approaches to instance pruning. The incremental approach begins with the empty subset, and only adds a new instance if it fulfills some criterion (Aha, 1992). The decremental approach begins with the entire training set, and then searches for instances to remove (Aha, 1992; Wilson, 1997). One challenge of instance pruning is in determining which data should be discarded such that as little information as possible is lost. Our approach can be viewed as a decremental approach. But rather than discard instances, for some regions, we replace the data of the region with a weighted linear model. The remaining data that cannot be fit well by local region linear models are retained.

A different solution is based on a multiresolution search of an augmented kd-tree (Deng and Moore, 1995; Moore et al., 1997). Before making any predictions, this approach performs some quick computation of weighted X^TX, X^TY and Y^TY, which is independent of potential queries, of the chosen weighting functions and kernel width. To answer a query, this approach does not need to span all the training data because it cuts off a computation at a node when it spots that all the nodes below it have near-identical weights given the current query, kernel width and weighting function. As such, it can make fast predictions with arbitrary local weighting functions, arbitrary kernel widths and arbitrary queries. Moreover, for the majority of the queries, it never needs to inspect any individual data points. Although this approach provides an elegant solution to reducing computation time, it needs to store all training data and therefore does not solve the problem of high storage requirements.

Regression trees (Breiman et al., 1984; Quinlan, 1993) provide a solution to both the time and space drawback of LWR. Regression trees are a special type of decision tree that deal with prediction of a continuous variable, rather than a discrete variable. It performs prediction by means of an efficient recursive partitioning algorithm. The leaf nodes can either be a constant or a linear regression model. The choice of the test at each internal node of the tree is usually guided by a least squares error criterion. Splitting continues until fewer than a minimum number of cases are covered by a node, or until all cases within the node have an identical value of y. The pruning process is similar to that of decision tree. If the mean squared error of a subtree is larger than that of its root, it replaces the subtree with a leaf node. The difference between our approach and regression trees lies in that our approach is a bottom-up approach, while regression trees are a top-down approach which begin with the entire data set. A second difference is that in our approach the margins between local regions are soft, meaning that regions can overlap. When a query point falls into more than one region the resulting prediction is the aggregate over all of the regions into which it falls.

4 ADAPTIVE LOCAL PARAMETER LEARNING (ALPL)

Our approach combines the strengths of lazy and eager regression algorithms. During training, the basic idea is to divide the input space into local regions and then for each local region, learn a simple model. If our method judges that the model fits the data in the region well, we replace the data with the model. Regions for which we cannot find an accurate model, retain the original data. The boundary of a region is defined by its radius, which is calculated to be the maximum distance of any point from the center point in the region. Note that we permit the regions to overlap. Before describing how such regions are found, we describe how queries are handled.

To answer a query, we first find the local regions that contain the query point. The resulting prediction is the average of the predictions made by these regions. For regions that have a model, we use the model for prediction. For regions that do not have a model we use a lazy learning algorithm to make the prediction. In Section 5 we assess the impact of using a 1-NN, k-NN and LWR as the lazy learning component of our approach. Figure 1 illustrates the effect of overlapping regions. The true model is shown by the parabola in each figure. On the left hand side we show the traditional approach to LWR, which uses a single local model to form a prediction. The value for the query point is predicted by a single local linear regression model. On the right hand side, we show the case where the query point falls into two local regions (the regions are not explicitly shown in the figure). Each local region has its own linear regression model (shown by the two straight lines). The resulting prediction is the unweighted average of both local parametric models' predictions. Note that in this case, overlapping regions result in a lower prediction error.

The goal of our approach is to reduce the computation and storage requirements of local learning methods. To this end, ALPL searches for a small set of local regions, each of which can be fit well by a simple model (in our current implementation we consider only linear models). The information that must be stored for each local parametric model is the location of the center point for the region, the radius of the region and $\hat{\beta}$, the parameters of the model. Because the space to store this information is less than the space required to store three data points we achieve a substantial saving in storage space. In Section 5 we present experiments that show that on average the space reduction is 72% for the datasets studied.

To find the local regions and set up the corresponding linear models, ALPL begins with one randomly selected center point and all of the data. Then it searches for the value of the bandwidth and the number of data points to retain in the local region such that the mean

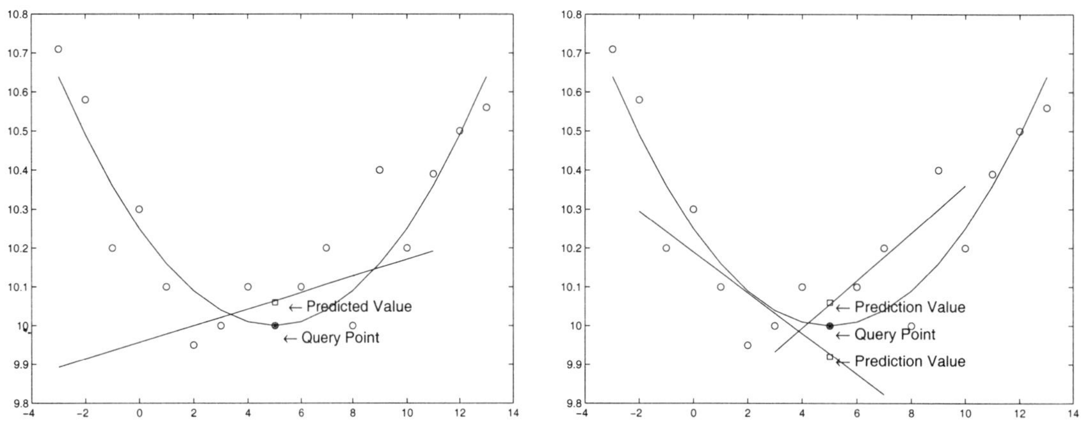

Figure 1: The Averaging Effect of Overlapping Regions

square error of the local region is minimized as measured by the data in the region. In our implementation we use a Kernel function $K(d) = exp(-d^2/h)$, which is a *Gaussian kernel* that is commonly applied in locally weighted learning (Cleveland and Loader, 1994).

To set the parameters of each local parametric model and decide whether to replace the data points in the local region with a local parametric model, we evaluate each candidate model using the mean-squared error as computed by a leave-one-out cross validation over the local region. We store the local parametric model if the MSE of the best model is less than a threshold, ϵ_{MSE} (how this value is chosen is explained below). This procedure is run ten times with different randomly chosen starting center points. For computational efficiency, if during this search, we obtain a local parametric model with MSE less than ϵ_{MSE} we halt the search and store the model. We have run an experiment comparing running all ten iterations to halting when we find a good model and find that it makes little difference with respect to the accuracy of ALPL. We continue the random selection of center points until one of two conditions is met: 1) all points are covered by at least one of local regions or 2) after ten runs we were unable to find a local parametric model with an MSE below our threshold, we retain the remaining uncovered data and halt the search.

Pseudo code of the algorithm is given in Figure 2. The algorithm continues to add local parametric models as long as we can find one with mean squared error below the threshold ϵ_{MSE} and data exists that is not covered by any local parametric model. When ALPL is finished with its training phase, we discard the data that is covered by at least one stored local parametric model.

In choosing the number of regions and the size of each region we would like our procedure to avoid overfitting the data. Too many regions results in overfitting, while too few regions, each of which covers a large percentage of the data, may overgeneralize. Our search begins with number of data points, D set to D_{max} and continues to D_{min}, where D_{min} is set to be the number of features describing the data, and is the minimum number of data points for which a regression is defined. In our current implementation D_{max} is set to be 1/5 of the training data, but it could be larger or smaller and future work will examine the impact of this choice. Our search starts with D set to be D_{max} in order to bias the search toward finding large regions.

To select the value of the bandwidth h, we perform a search for the value of h inside of the search for the value for D. The value of the bandwidth influences the quality of a local model because different h will cause different weights for each data point during the regression. There are several ways to adaptively change the value of h (Cleveland, 1979). In our implementation we explicitly search for the value of h that minimizes the MSE as measured by a leave-one-out cross-validation. Our method searches in the range h_{max} to h_{min}. In our current implementation h_{max} is set to be 1000, and is decremented in steps of size 100, then of size 10 once $h \leq 100$.

The final parameter required by our algorithm is the threshold that we use to determine whether to retain a particular model for a local region. This threshold ϵ_{MSE} is set for each dataset, by examining how it performs on a two-fold cross validation. Currently we per-

1. Repeat
2. $M_{best} \leftarrow NULL$; $MSE(M_{best}) \leftarrow$ infinity
3. for $i = 1$ to max-iterations
4. randomly select a new center point from points not contained in any local region
5. for $D = D_{max}$ to D_{min}
6. for $h = h_{max}$ to h_{min}
7. Fit a model $M_{D,h}$
8. Calculate $MSE(M_{D,h})$
9. if $MSE(M_{D,h}) < MSE(M_{best})$ then $M_{best} \leftarrow M_{D,h}$
10. if $MSE(M_{best}) < \epsilon_{MSE}$ store model M_{best}, break (goto Step 2)
11. end
12. end
13. end
14. Until $MSE(M_{best}) > \epsilon_{MSE}$ or out of data
15. Discard data covered by models and retain remaining data

Figure 2: Pseudo Code of ALPL

form experiments for ten values of ϵ_{MSE}. The range is computed by examining the average mean absolute error (MAE) of 3-NN by a two-fold cross-validation over the training data. The range then becomes MAE(3-NN),...,MAE(3-NN)/10. This is a fairly coarse search and in the immediate future we will address whether our results can be improved by a more fine-grained search. In Section 5 we show how different choices for ϵ_{MSE} impact performance.

5 EMPIRICAL EVALUATION

In this section we evaluate the behavior of ALPL. We compare ALPL to k nearest neighbor and locally weighted linear regression on several UCI benchmark machine learning datasets and on the CPU resource prediction time dataset, which provided the original motivation for this research.

5.1 EXPERIMENTAL METHOD

To evaluate our ALPL, we choose six regression (Housing, Auto-mpg, Servo, Machine CPU, Abalone and Network) and three classification data sets (Breast, Pima and Liver). For each classification task, we transform the two-class prediction problem into a regression problem. We map the first class to a value of 1, and the second class to a value of -1. During prediction, the class assigned to the query is determined by whether the predicted value is closer to 1 or -1.

For each experiment we performed a 10-fold cross-validation giving the same splits to each algorithm. Descriptions of the UCI data sets can be found at their web site.[1].

The goal of the network resource task is to predict the CPU time for a given run on the basis of software specific run-time input. Our motivation for studying this task is we are working to create a network accessible, on-demand network based computing system (Kapadia and Fortes, 1998). A demand-based computing system can be characterized by its ability to make automatic cost/performance tradeoff decisions at run time. These decisions are based on run-specific resource usage, of which one resource is the CPU. Because in most cases it is impossible to obtain analytical expressions that describe the relationship between the runtime input and the corresponding CPU usage, it is necessary to learn this relationship for each tool. Resource prediction must deal with short term variations in the performance of the computer system, which can occur due to unpredictable events such as a file server or a network router becoming overloaded. The learning algorithm must be able to quickly tailor its predictions to such short term variation without being unduly affected by them in the longer term. Moreover, because prediction must occur in real time, it is necessary to ensure that the time required to make a prediction is bounded. ALPL was developed with these objectives in mind. Currently, ALPL does not use a bound on prediction time to help tailor its training process, as the average prediction time on a Sun ULTRA-1 Sparc 5.6 is less than 0.04 seconds for the

[1] http://www.ics.uci.edu/mlearn/MLRepository.html

Network data. In the future, we plan to extend ALPL to allow it to adapt to changes in the underlying concept, a key factor to its future success in a demand-based computing environment.

In this paper we present results for only one software tool – a simulation tool, T-Suprem3, which is a commercial package that simulates the processing steps used to manufacture silicon devices. T-Suprem3 is used routinely in classes at Purdue University and therefore we have amassed a sufficient amount of historical data to make running an experiment possible. We are currently in the process of collecting data for other software packages available in our demand-based computing environment. The feature vector for T-Suprem3 was selected by a domain expert and is comprised of a subset of the inputs to the software (number of grid points, total diffusion time, cumulative epitaxial growth, minimum implant energy, number of deposit steps, number of etch steps, and number of implant steps.) We have 2000 runs, whose CPU times range from 1 to 730 seconds (although 99 percent of the runs took less than 30 seconds).

To assess how ALPL performs we compared it to k-nearest neighbor and locally weighted regression. We include three variants of ALPL, each with a different lazy learning approach to answering queries in regions for which there is no stored model. Specifically we compare

1-NN, 3-NN, 10-NN: Select the k (1, 3, 10) nearest data points to the query and take the unweighted average (for continuous) or the unweighted vote (for discrete prediction tasks).

LWR: Locally weighted regression in which the number of data points for regression and the value of bandwidth are changed adaptively so that it fits the data points well. We used a Gaussian kernel function $K = e^{-d^2/h}$ and query-based local bandwidth selection (Atkeson et al., 1997). To search for the bandwidth, we performed a cross-validation search over the training data for the value that minimized the MSE.

ALPL-none: ALPL, but all data points are incorporated into the linear regression models even though the $nMSE_i$ is not below the threshold ϵ_{MSE}.

ALPL-k-NN: ALPL using k NN for regions that do not have a local parametric model. We use $k = 1$ here.

ALPL-LWR: ALPL using LWR for regions that do not have a local parametric model. The same parameters for the lazy part of ALPL-LWR were used as for LWR alone.

5.2 COMPARING MSE, COMPUTATION TIME AND STORAGE REQUIREMENTS

Our goal in creating ALPL was to reduce the computation and storage time of LWR. In Table 1 we report the CPU time to answer a query for each method averaged across the ten-fold cross validation. From the table we can observe that overall ALPL-none and ALPL-k-NN takes significantly less time than each of the other methods. Note that for some of the datasets, ALPL-LWR requires more time than k-NN. Of all methods, LWR required the most time. This is because, like k-NN, it must examine each instance and then it must calculate a linear regression around the query point. For the network data, the average time required to make a prediction for ALPL-k-NN is 0.012. The reader may be wondering whether all of the savings in prediction time comes at too high a price of training time. The maximum training time for any dataset was five hours. However, we conjecture that since this time is tied directly to our parameter search, it can probably be significantly reduced without a large hit in accuracy.

In Table 2 we show the storage requirements of each method averaged across the ten-fold cross-validation. For the lazy learning methods we report the number of instances, which is equal to the size of the training data (90% of the total data). For the ALPL methods we report the number of models stored and the number of training instances retained. Recall that the space required to store a model, which is defined by $\hat{\beta}$, its center point and its radius, is less than the space required to store three data points. ALPL-none, replaces all of the data with models, whereas ALPL-k-NN and ALPL-LWR only replace the data in regions where the model has a MSE lower than a set threshold. Therefore in the table we report both the number of models and the number of instances retained for both ALPL-k-NN and ALPL-LWR. The counts are the same as the only difference between the two methods is how queries are handled when they fall outside of any of the local regions. If we multiply the number of models by three and add the number of instances for ALPL-k-NN for the Network data we obtain more than an order of magnitude reduction in space (140.8 versus 1800). A side benefit of the storage savings of ALPL is that

Table 1: Average CPU Time per Prediction in Seconds

	1-NN	3-NN	10-NN	LWR	ALPL None	ALPL k-NN	ALPL LWR
Network	0.780	0.840	1.090	6.890	0.016	0.013	0.033
Abalone	1.680	1.990	2.010	5.180	0.011	0.013	0.027
Breast	0.340	0.360	0.430	4.460	0.026	0.026	0.028
Servo	0.048	0.058	0.064	1.750	0.006	0.007	0.007
Auto-mpg	0.165	0.173	0.212	3.320	0.028	0.029	0.033
Housing	0.375	0.391	0.422	3.870	0.034	0.027	0.170
CPU	0.078	0.084	0.102	9.020	0.013	0.031	1.330
Pima	0.368	0.397	0.461	8.340	0.021	0.024	0.025
Liver	0.126	0.138	0.168	8.720	0.019	0.022	0.650

Table 2: Storage Requirements

	k-NN,LWR Instances	ALPL None Models	ALPL k-NN and LWR Models	ALPL k-NN and LWR Instances
Network	1800	23.3	18.3	85.9
Abalone	3600	94.6	89.1	129.0
Breast	659	36.3	35.5	13.2
Servo	147	10.8	9.7	6.3
Auto-mpg	350	44.2	42.2	14.4
Housing	456	33.0	24.5	65.5
CPU	186	8.4	4.0	106.0
Pima	628	36.5	35.8	14.0
Liver	317	40.5	37.3	25.0

Table 3: Mean Absolute Error of Prediction

	1-NN	3-NN	10-NN	LWR	ALPL None	ALPL k-NN	ALPL LWR
Network	1.78	**1.63**	1.78	2.21	2.32	1.86	1.87
Abalone	2.07	1.69	**1.57**	1.82	2.01	1.64	1.99
Breast	**0.03**	**0.03**	0.04	0.04	0.06	0.04	0.04
Servo	0.65	0.52	0.77	0.57	0.46	**0.44**	**0.44**
Auto-mpg	3.43	**2.74**	2.83	3.17	3.34	2.93	3.79
Housing	6.45	6.50	6.39	4.37	3.91	**3.67**	4.73
CPU	42.00	**34.80**	43.10	44.80	35.70	40.50	44.30
Pima	0.29	0.28	0.31	0.32	0.26	**0.24**	0.26
Liver	**0.35**	0.37	0.37	0.38	0.36	0.37	0.37

by replacing data in local regions by linear models, we may obtain a summary of the data that is interpretable by a human. Although at present time, we have not explicitly evaluated this contribution.

To determine whether our time and storage savings came at the price of lower prediction accuracy, Table 3 reports the mean of the absolute error of each of the seven algorithms averaged across the ten-fold cross validation. We show the minimum error in boldface type. We omit the sample standard deviation from the table due to space limitation, but we note that in many cases these differences in error are not large. The first thing we note is that in six of the nine datasets, the most accurate method is *k*-NN, and in the other three cases the most accurate method is ALPL-*k*-NN. Indeed for all nine data sets ALPL-*k*-NN achieves equal or lower error rate than ALPL-LWR and in seven of the nine cases it outperforms ALPL-none. *k*-NN applies a locally constant function for prediction, whereas LWR and ALPL apply a locally linear function for prediction. Which performs better for a given dataset depends on the data distribution. A locally constant function performs better than locally linear function when the data distribution is planar. On the other hand, locally linear functions are better when the data distribution is nonuniform or the regression function has substantial curvature (Hastie and Loader, 1993).

Comparing ALPL-LWR to LWR we see that in six of the nine cases, ALPL-LWR achieves an equal or lower error rate than LWR. For LWR the prediction error depends heavily on the distribution of points near the query. If it is located between two "regions", then it may not be easy to find a linear parametric model that fits the query point well. We conjecture that in the cases where ALPL-LWR outperforms LWR, the difference is due to the benefits in allowing overlapping regions. This means that the prediction value of a query can be the average of several models. In the future we will design experiments to assess the impact of overlapping regions by looking at those query points that LWR predicts incorrectly, but ALPL-LWR predicts correctly.

5.3 THE IMPACT OF PARAMETER ϵ_{MSE} ON PERFORMANCE

To determine the influence of the parameter ϵ_{MSE} on the prediction performance, we took an in-depth look at its impact on error, prediction time, instances pruned and the average size of the local regions. We present experiments for the Network dataset (the other datasets showed similar trends) applying ALPL-*1*-NN. In Figures 3 and 4 each graph shows the value of ϵ_{MSE} on the horizontal axis. The left hand plot in Figure 3 shows the absolute error on the vertical axis. We observe that too large a value of ϵ_{MSE} causes the error to rise. We conjecture that the rise is due to the size of the local regions, which grow as the value of ϵ_{MSE} increases (see the plot on the right hand side of Figure 4). Whereas too small a value of ϵ_{MSE} appears to cause overfitting as the size of the regions is relatively small, but the error is large. An exception to this trend is for very low values of ϵ_{MSE}. When we set the threshold to be 0, ALPL-*k*-NN becomes a *k*-NN classifier which is more accurate for this domain than ALPL-*k*-NN. Note that other datasets did not exhibit this dip for very low values.

In the right hand plot in Figure 3 we show how prediction time is effected by changes to ϵ_{MSE}. Clearly as we increase the value of the threshold we accept more models and store fewer instances (as shown in the left hand plot in Figure 4) which reduces prediction time.

6 RELATED WORK

In this section we highlight three other approaches to combining lazy and eager learning and their relationship to ALPL. Quinlan (1993) introduced a method for combining instance-based learning and model-based learning together for numeric prediction. The composite method uses the model to adjust the predictions of each neighbor in the instance based approach; by using the model to predict the difference between the query point and the neighbor and adjusting the prediction by this difference. The similarity of this approach to ALPL is that they both combine ideas from lazy and eager learning for prediction. A key difference is that ALPL only uses a model if it fits the data in the corresponding region well, otherwise it applies the lazy (instance-based) learning approach to answer the query.

Domingos (1996) introduced an algorithm that integrates instance-based and rule-based induction learning together for discrete classification problems. It has a very similar result to ALPL; after learning each region is either covered by a rule or by data. Regions are permitted to overlap. A key difference between this approach and ALPL is that ALPL replaces instances with linear parametric models, whereas Domingos' approach replaces instances with DNF rules for discrete classification.

Weiss and Indurkhya (1995) developed a rule-based learning method for numeric prediction. This ap-

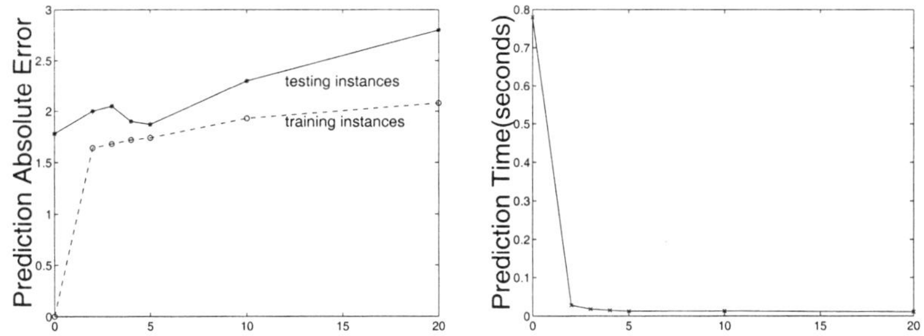

Figure 3: Effect of ϵ_{MSE} on the Error and Prediction Time

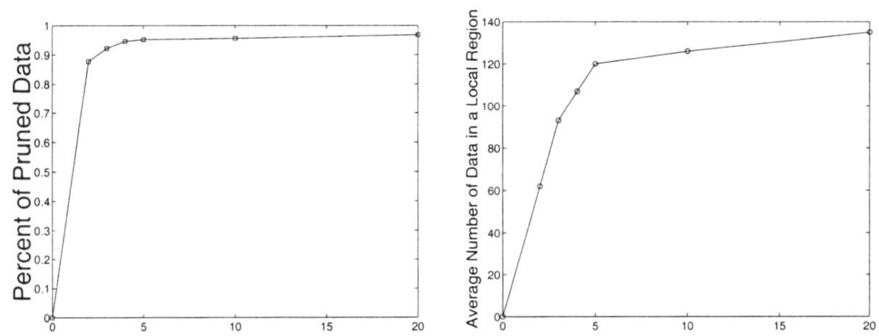

Figure 4: Effect of ϵ_{MSE} on the Percent of Data that are Pruned and the Size of Local Regions

proach first discretizes the output of training data using a variant of k-means clustering on the output value. This transforms the numeric prediction problem into a discrete classification problem, allowing them to utilize a rule-covering method to learn a set of rules for each class. A similarity to ALPL is that the instance space is partitioned into several small overlapping regions. In each region all of the data belong to the same class. However, Weiss and Indurkhya's approach belongs to the class of eager learning algorithms, whereas ALPL is a hybrid eager/lazy learning approach.

7 CONCLUSION

In this paper we have presented a supervised learning algorithm that combines the strengths of lazy and eager learning. Our goal was to reduce the computation and storage time of local learning methods, while retaining the benefit of their ability to fit any function well. Unlike conventional locally weighted regression, which defers processing of the training data until a query needs to be answered, our approach analyzes the training data to discover local regions in which the data can be fit well by a linear regression model. For each such local region, our method replaces the training data with the local linear regression model for prediction. An empirical evaluation of the algorithm on nine datasets, illustrated that our approach significantly reduces prediction time and storage requirements without impacting prediction accuracy significantly.

Although the results are strong, there are several places in which we would like to improve our approach and expand our comparisons. First, in the current implementation, the center point of each local region is randomly selected from the training data that is not covered by any local region. Because the selection is random we must run this process n times (n= 10 in the experiments presented in the paper). This can take a fairly long time to train. We plan to apply some ideas from unsupervised clustering to help us select good starting center points. Second, we would also like to explore our choices for D_{max} and h_{max} the maximum choices for the number of data in the region and the bandwidth respectively.

A troubling aspect of our experiments is that LWR did not perform as well as k-NN. We conjecture that this is due to our choice of kernel function and method for choosing the bandwidth. In future experiments we will implement various methods from the literature to try to optimize LWR's performance, thereby gaining a harder performance standard against which to measure ALPL's prediction performance. Finally, in the near future we plan to compare our approach to the recent work on efficient locally weighted polynomial regression prediction (Moore et al., 1997), to regression trees (Breiman, et al., 1984) and to instance pruning methods (Wilson and Martinez, to appear).

Acknowledgments

We thank our anonymous reviewers for their many suggestions. We would like to thank Nirav Kapadia and José A. B. Fortes for their suggestions and for providing the Network CPU data. This research was supported by the National Science Foundation under grant number IIS-9733573.

References

Aha, D. (1992). Tolerating noisy, irrelevant and novel attributes in instance-based learning algorithms, *International Journal of Man-Machine Studies*, Vol 36, pp 267-287.

Aha, D. (1997). Lazy learning, *Artificial Intelligence Review*, 11:7-10.

Atkeson, C. G., Moore, A. W. and Schaal, S. (1997). Locally weighted learning, *Artificial Intelligence Review*, 11:75-113.

Breiman, L., Friedman, J. H., Olshen, R. A., and Stone, C. J. (1984). *Classification and Regression Trees*, Belmont, California, Wadsworth.

Cleveland, W. S. (1979). Robust locally weighted regression and smoothing scatter plots, *Journal of American Statistical Association*, Vol 74, pp 829-836.

Cleveland, W. S. and Loader, C. (1994). Smoothing by local regression: Principles and methods, T.R. 95.3, AT &T Bell Labs, Statistics Department, Murray Hill, NJ.

Deng, K. and Moore, A. W. (1995). Multiresolution instance-based learning, *International Joint Conference on Artificial Intelligence*, August 20-25, 1995, Montreal, Canada.

Domingos, P. (1996). Unifying instance-based and rule-based induction, *Machine Learning*, Vol 24, No 2, pp 141-168, Kluwer Academic Publishers.

Friedman, J. H. (1984). A variable span smoother, *T.R. LCS5.* Statistics Department, Stanford.

Hastie, T. and Loader, C. (1993). Local regression: Automatic kernel carpentry, *Statistics Science*, Vol 8, pp 120-143.

Kapadia, N. H. and Fortes, A. B. (1998). On the design of a demand-based network-computing system: The Purdue university network-computing hubs, *Seventh IEEE International Symposium on High Performance Distributed Computing*, pp 71-88, July 1998, Chicago, Illinois.

Moore, A. W., Schneider, J. and Deng.K (1997). Efficient locally weighted polynomial regression prediction, *Proceedings of the Fourteenth International Conference on Machine Learning*, pp 236-244, July 8-12, 1997, Nashville, Tennessee, USA.

Quinlan, J. R. (1993). Combining instance-based and model-based learning, *Proceedings of the Tenth International Conference on Machine Learning*, pp 236–243, June 27-29, 1993, Amherst, MA USA.

Schaal, S. (to appear). Nonparametric regression for learning nonlinear transformations, In Ritter, H, Holland, O and Mohl, B (eds.) *Prerational Intelligence in Strategies, High-Level Process and Collective Behavior*, Kluwer Academic Press.

Weiss, S. and Indurkhya, N. (1995). Rule-based machine learning methods for functional prediction, *Journal of Artificial Intelligence Research*, Vol 3, pp 383-403.

Wilson, D. and Martinez, T. (1997). Instance pruning techniques, *Proceedings of the Fourteenth International Conference on Machine Learning*, pp 404-411, July 8-12, 1997, Nashville, TN, USA.

Wilson. D. and Martinez, T. (to appear) Reduction techniques for exemplar-based learning algorithms, *Machine Learning*.

INVITED PAPERS

How to understand the web? web standards

SHOE, XML, RTF, ...

1/ Make it look like a KB

2/ query the KB

Real problem: REPRESENTATION

two kinds of info system: 1/ search engines, ... 2/ Databases

we don't know how to handle information from diverse sources.

Traditional deduction eg in a RDB

On the web: lacks common nomenclature. How to translate?

example domains: kids' GAMES N.A. BIRDS

- use informal names & descriptions
- use techniques of information retrieval
- use probabilistic reasoning to identify

$$SIM(doc_i, doc_j) = \sum_{t \in T_{ij}} wt(t, doc_i) . wt(t, doc_j)$$

T_{ij} set of terms

wt(t, d) large if t frequent in d
rare in corpus searched for d.

normalise: $0 \le SIM(d, d') \le 1$

WHIRL [Cohen, SIGMOD 98]

like prolog, but a query returns a list of scored substitutions

eg companies: top500(X), hiTech(Y), X ~ Y

Note: use similarity (~) since different sites use different names.

eg finding text contents: name(X), paragraph(Y), X ~ Y

X ~ Y iff Y contains a term or terms like X.

wrapper: a program which extracts text from HTML

WHIRL can be used to interpret wrappers/rank wrappers.

ML driven by choices of representations

Q Michie: WORDNET db

Q Metrics A There are other metrics

implementation of WHIRL:

modified A* search; inverted indices

size of search space depends on nos. of partial matches (~)

What Can We Learn From the Web?

William W. Cohen
AT&T Labs–Research
Shannon Laboratory 180 Park Avenue
Florham Park, NJ 07932-0971 USA
wcohen@research.att.com

Abstract

It would nice if the Web were more like a knowledge base—that is, if information on the Web were understandable to computers. Unfortunately, information on the Web is hard to represent with the usual knowledge base formalisms: problems include terminological differences across sites, and the frequent combination of structured information with unstructured textual descriptions. The primary focus of my research in the last few years has been WHIRL, an "information representation language" that is designed to address these problems. WHIRL allows information to be represented using a combination of formally structured facts and informal textual descriptions. Incorporating ideas from both AI and statistical information retrieval, WHIRL generalizes both logical deduction and ranked retrieval of documents. Below I will describe informally my motivations in developing WHIRL; introduce the WHIRL representation language; and then disuss some issues of interest to the machine learning community.

1 INTRODUCTION

In a recent paper, Craven *et al* [1998] note that "although your workstation can currently *retrieve* 200 million Web pages, it currently *understands* none of these". In response to this problem, there has been substantial recent research on extracting information from the Web and then storing this information (either actually or conceptually) in a knowledge base that can be queried by a user. This research has included, for example, work on extracting database relations from tabular, database-like Web pages [Hammer *et al.*, 1997; Kushmerick *et al.*, 1997; Muslea *et al.*, 1998]; work on classifying Web pages into a predefined taxonomy [Nigam *et al.*, 1998; Craven *et al.*, 1998]; and work on efficiently collecting from the Web the information needed to answer a specific query [Levy *et al.*, 1996; Ambite and Knoblock, 1998]. A number of systems have also been constructed that implement some solution to all of these subproblems, thus providing a database-like interface to a portion of the Web [Levy *et al.*, 1996; Knoblock *et al.*, 1998; Lacroix *et al.*, 1998; Mecca *et al.*, 1998; Tomasic *et al.*, 1997].

For the last several years I've been working on this problem—how can we make the Web look more like a knowledge base?—from a somewhat different perspective than most other researchers in the area. To motivate my approach, let me start with another question: why isn't there *already* a part of the Web that looks like a knowledge base? or conversely, why are there no existing knowledge bases that have the same loosely distributed architecture seen in the Web?

To make this a bit more precise, consider the following two desiderata for a "Web-like knowledge base":

1. Facts about the world can be asserted by different people at different Web sites.
2. New facts can be deduced by combining assertions stored at different sites, and maintained by different people.

An an example, the assertion "AT&T has a machine learning research group" might be stored on one site, perhaps a site concerned entirely with information relating to machine learning, while a second site containing business-related information might store the assertion "AT&T is a publicly traded company". From these facts one would like to draw the modest conclusion that AT&T is both publicly traded *and* conducts research in machine learning—doubtless a fact of great interest to any wise investor.

These requirements for a "Web-like knowledge base" are minimal ones: they ask only that information can be distributed across multiple sites (which is the main point of the Web) and that information can be combined in some way to derive new facts (which is the main point of a knowledge base). However, knowledge bases that are "Web-like" by this definition seem to be rare; to my knowledge, none exist. This is perhaps surprising, for such a distributed knowledge base would clearly be useful in many contexts; and while many of the research problems mentioned above are interesting in their own right, it is not clear that any of them would be encountered in building such a knowledge base "from the ground up" (rather than trying to convert the Web *post facto* into a knowledge base).

I believe that the main problems in building a widely distributed "Web-like" knowledge base are terminological ones. To build such a knowledge base, the contributing parties need to agree on a single formal ontology. For instance, if the formal version of the example given above is as follows:

site 1:	*hasResearchGroup(att, machineLearning)*
site 2:	*publiclyTraded(att)*
$\therefore$	*hasResearchGroup(att, machineLearning)* $\wedge$ *publiclyTraded(att)*

then site 1 and site 2 must agree on at least some large set of company identifiers (like *att*). The example also suggests agreement on some non-trivial vocabulary of technical terms (like *machineLearning*). In practise, this sort of agreement is very difficult to reach.[1] Even in the unlikely case that agreement can be reached, adding to the knowledge base is now much more difficult for a human knowledge engineer, as it requires knowing the shared ontology—and the difficulty of learning this ontology increases with the size of the distributed knowledge base.

The difficulty of adding information to a "Web-like knowledge base" should be contrasted with the situation on the Web itself, to which any information can be added, anywhere. This extensibility has doubtless been a major reason for the Web's growth; on the other hand, the Web is so easily extensible only because there are no formal semantics to worry about.

[1]For example, consider technical terms. Whenever I find myself facing a forced choice of keywords to attach to one of my papers, I invariably find that I don't agree with any of them.

2 REPRESENTING KNOWLEDGE WITH INFORMAL TEXT

To summarize, I believe the fundamental difficulty in constructing a Web-like knowledge base is *not* figuring out how to translate existing Web sites into a conventional knowledge base. Instead, I believe the real problem is devising a formalism that could be used to represent and reason with information derived from loosely-coupled, widely-distributed information sources, like those found on the Web.

To address this problem, I have implemented a new scheme for representing knowledge called WHIRL.[2] The primary goal of WHIRL is to support deduction, while making only minimal requirements regarding formal vocabulary. This is done by allowing the represented information to include *informal* vocabulary—by which I mean unstructured natural-language text. For instance, the assertions in the example above might be represented with these WHIRL "facts":

hasResearchGroup("AT&T Labs–Research",
"learning—especially
reinforcement learning,
learning theory, and
learning applied to text").
publiclyTraded("AT&T").

In order to approximate deduction using "facts" like these, WHIRL makes heavy use of certain *similarity* metrics for text that have been developed by the statistical information retrieval community—specifically, the vector space model of similarity [Salton, 1989]. For instance, in order to find a publicly traded company that has a research group in machine learning, one might use the similarity operator "$\sim$" in the following query:

$$\text{?- } hasResearchGroup(Company1, Topic) \wedge Topic \sim \text{"machine learning"} \wedge publiclyTraded(Company2) \wedge Company1 \sim Company2. \quad (1)$$

Informally, Query 1 asks for two similar company names *Company1* and *Company2*, such that *Company1* conducts research on a topic similar to "machine learning", and *Company2* is publicly traded.

In WHIRL, the similarity predicate is a "soft" pred-

[2]For Word-based Heterogeneous Information Representation Language.

icate: it does not evaluate to *true* or *false*, but to a real-valued score somewhere between one and zero. In evaluating an answer to a query, similarity scores are combined like independent probabilities. Thus a high-scoring answer to this query would bind the variables *Company1* and *Company2* to pieces of text that are highly similar to each other, and bind *Topic* to some piece of text highly similar to the string "machine learning". The query above thus approximates the conventional logical query

?- *hasResearchGroup(X,machineLearning)* ∧
publiclyTraded(X).

but requires far less shared formal vocabulary: the different Web sites still need to agree on the predicates used, but can use informal text for company names (like "AT&T" or "AT&T Labs–Research") and technical terms.

The extensions to Prolog implemented in WHIRL—a built-in data-type for text, and an associated built-in similarity predicate—allow representations that are conceptually quite different from those traditionally used in knowledge base and database systems. Traditional knowledge bases model *entities* and the *relations* between them. In WHIRL, formal designators for entities (like *att*) can be replaced by informal textual names for these entities (like "*AT&T Labs-Research*"), leading to a knowledge base potentially without *any* formal entities. In the same way, predicates can be reified and replaced with appropriate textual descriptions, as is suggested by the treatment of *machineLearning*. This avoids the step of adopting a formal vocabulary for entities, and reduces the number of predicates in an ontology. The disadvantage of WHIRL's approach, of course, is that queries can only be approximately answered.

WHIRL has a number of nice technical properties. To answer a query, the WHIRL interpreter returns the K highest-scoring answers (substitutions), in descending order by score, where K is fixed by the user. As one special case, if the knowledge base is a single unary predicate p and a query like

?- *p(X)* ∧ *X*∼ *"four-star hotels in Ljubljana"*

is given, then the output of WHIRL is the K elements of p that are most similar to the query text "four-star hotels in Ljubljana". This is precisely the output of a statistical information retrieval engine given this query (assuming it has indexed exactly the documents in p).

Another interesting special case arises when the textual descriptions in the knowledge base are all only one word long, *e.g.*, when all texts are a single artificial term, like *machineLearning*. In WHIRL, the similarity of two texts X and Y depends on the number and importance of the terms shared by X and Y; and if all texts contain only a single term, every similarity predicate will be scored as either one (if the terms are the same) or zero. Thus in this "degenerate" case WHIRL coincides with an ordinary logic (specifically, a subset of Prolog.)

A final nice property of WHIRL is that, by borrowing indexing methods from information retrieval and search techniques from AI, WHIRL can be implemented quite efficiently [Cohen, 1998a]. Furthermore, the off-the-shelf similarity metrics taken from information retrieval prove to do quite well at matching entity names, and hence the answers given by WHIRL, at least for simple queries, are surprisingly accurate [Cohen, 1998a].

3 APPLICATIONS OF WHIRL

3.1 QUERY-ANSWERING SYSTEMS FOR THE WEB

Above I proposed WHIRL as a solution to a fundamental question—how to represent knowledge in a Web-like knowledge base. To validate this use of WHIRL, I used it to implement a number of Web-based query-answering systems: systems that extract information from the Web, represent it in a WHIRL knowledge base, and then allow the user to query this information [Cohen, 1998b; Cohen, 1998c].

Although it is perhaps difficult to measure quantitatively, I think that using WHIRL instead of a conventional knowledge base made it much easier to build these systems. If nothing else, the amount of terminology that needs to be translated to a common framework is vastly reduced—from hundreds of thousands of entity names and categories to a handful of predicates.

WHIRL also makes the job of extracting data from Web pages easier, since WHIRL is less sensitive to exactly what text is extracted. In the query-answering systems, I implemented, it was usually possible to use very simple, easy-to-program, *approximate* extraction routines[Cohen, 1998c]. As an example of this, consider the second argument of the WHIRL fact for *hasResearchGroup* above. Using this data in a conventional database might well require extracting the initial word "learning" from the text "learning—especially reinforcement learning ... applied to text";

subtopicOf("inductive logic programming", "machine learning")
subtopicOf("reinforcement learning", "machine learning")
subtopicOf("on-line learning", "machine learning")
⋮
subtopicOf("logic programming", "knowledge representation")
subtopicOf("description logics", "knowledge representation")
subtopicOf("non-monotonic reasoning", "knowledge representation")
⋮

Table 1: Subtopics of various areas of artificial intelligence

using WHIRL, this extraction step can be omitted.

More recently, I have explored using WHIRL itself as a language for extracting data from Web pages [Cohen, 1999]. The main advantage of this approach is that WHIRL makes it possible to implement extraction programs that rely in part on the content, rather than the format, of the page. For instance, in extracting a list of publicly traded companies from a Web page, a traditional extraction routine might go to some specified position on the page, look for the next unordered list (<*ul*>) HTML element, and extract each list item (<*li*>) element that follows. An extraction routine written in WHIRL might look anywhere on the page for an unordered list such that most[3] associated list items contain a piece of text X similar to some known company name Y.

These sorts of heuristics could either be used directly, as robust extraction routines for specific pages; or indirectly, as a means of proposing extraction routines (encoded in a more conventional language) for a user to either accept or reject. To date, I have only explored indirect use of these heuristics. Using them directly is perhaps a more exciting possibility, as providing a single, uniform tool for both extraction and representation would link WHIRL much more closely to the Web.

3.2 SIMILARITY REASONING AND NEAREST-NEIGHBOUR CLASSIFICATION

To return to the example given in the introduction, suppose that the facts associated with the predicate *hasResearchGroup* are expressed in terms of fairly narrow subtopics, and suppose also that we have obtained (from the Web or elsewhere) another set of facts of the form *subtopicOf(subtopic,topic)*, as shown in Table 1. If we'd like to find out what broad research topics are currently in vogue we might use this query:

researchInTopic(Place, Topic) ←
  hasResearchGroup(Place,Subtopic1) ∧
  subtopicOf(Subtopic2, Topic) ∧
  Subtopic1∼*Subtopic2.*

?- *researchInTopic(P, T).*

Here a similarity test on subtopics is used to circumvent the problem that subtopic descriptions may vary from site to site, and the temporary predicate *researchInTopic* is used to discard the subtopics—which I assume here are not of interest to the user—from the final answer, which will be a list of ⟨*Place, Topic*⟩ pairs.

This query has an interesting property: it is possible for WHIRL to return a *correct* answer on the basis of an *incorrect* pairing of subtopics. For example, suppose that the fact

hasResearchGroup("University of Maryland",
"inductive inference")

is in the knowledge base, but the true fact

subtopicOf("inductive inference", "machine learning")

is, for whatever reason, not part of the predicate *subtopicOf*. WHIRL will still be able to deduce the fact

researchInTopic("University of Maryland",
"machine learning"),

albeit with a low score, based on the similarity of the texts "inductive inference" and "inductive logic programming".

The process of associating a broad category (*e.g.*, "machine learning") with an object (the text "inductive

[3]Here "most" is implemented using a "soft" version of a universal quantifier [Cohen, 1999].

inference") based on similarity to another object with a known category ("inductive logic programming") is highly reminiscent of nearest-neighbour classification. In fact, one can easily implement a sort of nearest-neighbour classifier with WHIRL: given facts of the form *train*($inst_i$,$class_i$) associating each training instance $inst_i$ with its class $class_i$, one can find a class *Class* of a new instance $inst_*$ by first asserting the fact *test*($inst_*$), and then finding the top-scoring answer to the WHIRL query

predictClass(Class) ←
  test(X) ∧ *train(Y,Class)* ∧ $X \sim Y$.

?- *predictClass(C)*

If one unravels the actions of the WHIRL interpreter on this sort of query, it turns out to implement a variant of a vector space distance-weighted K-NN method investigated by Yang and Chute [1994].

With Haym Hirsh, I evaluated WHIRL's performance on this sort of query [Cohen and Hirsh, 1998]. In brief, performance is quite good: WHIRL's generalization accuracy on benchmark problems was slightly better than the closely related Yang and Chute method, and substantially better than classifiers like C4.5 [Quinlan, 1994] that are not designed for text. The indexing techniques used by WHIRL also mean that classification is fairly fast. As a rough measure of efficiency, we measured the time needed to learn a model, and then classify the test data. For the larger benchmark problems, WHIRL was up to 60 times faster than RIPPER [Cohen, 1995], and up to 500 times faster than the tree version of C4.5.

It should be emphasized that WHIRL was not intended to be a nearest-neighbour learning system. The goal of WHIRL was to implement fast, robust reasoning about the similarity of fragments of text, an ability that I deemed important in a Web-like knowledge representation system. Nearest-neighbour classification is simply one special type of similarity reasoning—but a type of reasoning that is well-studied, and hence relatively easy to evaluate systematically.

The nearest-neighbour reasoning performed by WHIRL is also of interest because in the Web-based query-answering systems I implemented, many of the information sources *are* incomplete; thus behavior of the type described above is quite common. In answering moderately complex queries, this behavior often occurs simply as a side-effect of the similarity matching. For instance, given the knowledge base described above, a user who wishes to invest in a publicly traded company with a machine learning research group might issue the query:

goodInvestment(Company2) ←
  hasResearchGroup(Company1,Subtopic1) ∧
  subtopicOf(Subtopic2, "machine learning") ∧
  Subtopic1∼*Subtopic2* ∧
  publiclyTraded(Company2) ∧
  Company1∼*Company2*.

?- *goodInvestment(C)*.

It may be that in answering this query WHIRL inductively "fills in" missing entries in the *subtopicOf* predicate, the *publiclyTraded* predicate, or both, or neither. In any case this behavior is completely transparent to both the user and the system designer; the only evidence it has occurred is the lower score given to certain answers.

4 WHIRL AND LEARNING

As machine learning researchers, when we hear about a new field or new idea, we are used to asking "what can learning contribute?" Unlike a traditional IR search engine, the logical queries issued to a query-answering system based on WHIRL tend to have many regularities. (For instance, one could imagine a setting in which many user queries would be similar to Query 1 above, but with "machine learning" replaced by some other text.) Also, WHIRL's scheme for representing information involves giving a numeric weight to each word that appears anywhere in the knowledge base, and thus, a typical knowledge base will have literally thousands of parameters. Hence it is clear that learning could potentially improve the quality of the inferences made by WHIRL. In fact, when I began this work, I expected that some sort of learning would be absolutely necessary in WHIRL, and it was surprising to me that WHIRL could make nontrivial inferences accurately without any sort of problem-specific tuning. However, most of the work I have done to date involves relatively simple WHIRL programs, and I still believe that techniques for explicitly parameterizing WHIRL programs, and then tuning these parameters, will be important for solving more difficult problems.

I also believe that many of the ideas used in WHIRL can be used to leverage research in machine learning. One possibility is to use WHIRL as the underlying reasoning component in a learning system, analogous to the use of Prolog in inductive logic programming systems. The potential value of using WHIRL rather than a traditional logic is that it can be used to encode a broader spectrum of background knowledge—from formal to informal. It is also sometimes the case that very simple WHIRL programs can be accurate classifiers, as is illustrated by the nearest-neighbour classifier of Section 3.2.

More generally, WHIRL suggests new ways for incorporating many types of background knowledge into a learning problem. Use of appropriate background knowledge is absolutely crucial in any learning problem—if nothing else, background knowledge guides the initial step of choosing a set of useful features. Ideally, one would like to be able to easily exploit the vast amounts of knowledge that is available on the Web in formulating and solving a new learning problem. To some extent this can be done now, and indeed is being done. (As one example of this from my own work, testing a proposed inductive approach to the task of collaborative movie recommendation required extracting from the Web information about thousands of movies [Basu *et al.*, 1998]. Another excellent example of how knowledge from the Web can be exploited—although in a problem-solving context, not a learning context—is provided by the crossword puzzle solving system PROVERB [Keim *et al.*, 1999].)

WHIRL offers a new perspective on the task of collecting and incorporating background information. Furthermore, although collecting background information is often viewed as separate from the task of learning, I would argue that this task is fundamentally different if the end consumer of the information is a learning program—as opposed to, say, a query-answering system. In query-answering, WHIRL's cheap, flexible, and approximate information-gathering has a cost, as WHIRL can only approximate the answers to certain logical queries. However, the robustness of learning methods to noise in their inputs makes it quite reasonable to use WHIRL-like approximate methods to collect background information. Thus WHIRL may point the way toward systems that learn more effectively, by using the Web as background knowledge.

Acknowledgements

I thank the numerous colleagues that have contributed to my work, including: Haym Hirsh, Alon Levy, Alex Borgida, Edith Cohen, Jaewoo Kang, David Lewis, Fernando Pereira, Yoram Singer, Amit Singhal, Divesh Srinivasan, and Dan Suciu. I am also grateful to Sašo Džeroski for comments on a draft of this paper.

References

(Ambite and Knoblock, 1998) Jose Luis Ambite and Craig A. Knoblock. Flexible and scalable query planning in distributed and heterogeneous environents. In *Proceedings of the Fourth International Conference on Artificial Intelligence Planning Systems (AIPS-98)*, Pittsburgh, PA, 1998.

(Basu *et al.*, 1998) Chumki Basu, Haym Hirsh, and William Cohen. Recommendation as classification: Combining social and content-based information in recommendation. In *Proceedings of the Fifteenth National Conference on Artificial Intelligence (AAAI-98)*, Madison, WI, 1998.

(Cohen and Hirsh, 1998) William W. Cohen and Haym Hirsh. Joins that generalize: Text categorization using WHIRL. In *Proceedings of the Fourth International Conference on Knowledge Discovery and Data Mining*, pages 169–173, New York, NY, 1998.

(Cohen, 1995) William W. Cohen. Fast effective rule induction. In *Machine Learning: Proceedings of the Twelfth International Conference*, Lake Tahoe, California, 1995. Morgan Kaufmann.

(Cohen, 1998a) William W. Cohen. Integration of heterogeneous databases without common domains using queries based on textual similarity. In *Proceedings of ACM SIGMOD-98*, Seattle, WA, 1998.

(Cohen, 1998b) William W. Cohen. Providing database-like access to the web using queries based on textual similarity. In *Proceedings of ACM SIGMOD-98*, Seattle, WA, 1998.

(Cohen, 1998c) William W. Cohen. A Web-based information system that reasons with structured collections of text. In *Proceedings of Autonomous Agents-98*, St. Paul, MN, 1998.

(Cohen, 1999) William W. Cohen. Recognizing structure in web pages using similarity queries. In *Proceedings of the Sixteenth National Conference on Artificial Intelligence (AAAI-99)*, Orlando, FL, 1999.

(Craven *et al.*, 1998) M. Craven, D. DiPasquo, D. Freitag, A. McCallum, T. Mitchell, K. Nigam, and S. Slattery. Learning to extract symbolic knowledge from the world wide web. In *Proceedings of the Fifteenth National Conference on Artificial Intelligence (AAAI-98)*, Madison, WI, 1998.

(Hammer *et al.*, 1997) J. Hammer, H. Garcia-Molina, J. Cho, and A. Crespo. Extracting semistructured information from the Web. In Dan Suciu, editor, *Proceedings of the Workshop on Management of Semistructured Data*, Tucson, Arizona, May 1997. Available on-line from http://www.research.att.com/~suciu/workshop-papers.html.

(Keim *et al.*, 1999) Greg A. Keim, Noam Shazeer, Michael L. Littman, Sushant Agarwal, Catherine M. Cheves, Joseph Fitzgerald, Jason Grosland, Fan Jiang, Shannon Polland, and Karl Weinmeister. PROVERB: the probabilistic cruciverbalist. Technical Report CS-1999-02, Duke University, 1999.

(Knoblock *et al.*, 1998) Craig A. Knoblock, Steven Minton, Jose Luis Ambite, Naveen Ashish, Pragnesh Jay Modi, Ion Muslea, Andrew G. Philpot, and Sheila Tejada. Modeling web sources for information integration. In *Proceedings of the Fifteenth National Conference on Artificial Intelligence (AAAI-98)*, Madison, WI, 1998.

(Kushmerick *et al.*, 1997) Nicholas Kushmerick, Daniel S. Weld, and Robert Doorenbos. Wrapper induction for information extraction. In *Proceedings of the 15th International Joint Conference on Artificial Intelligence*, Osaka, Japan, 1997.

(Lacroix *et al.*, 1998) Zoe Lacroix, Arnaud Sahuguet, and Raman Chandrasekar. User-oriented smart-cache for the web: what you seek is what you get. In *Proceedings of the 1998 ACM SIGMOD*, June 1998.

(Levy *et al.*, 1996) Alon Y. Levy, Anand Rajaraman, and Joann J. Ordille. Querying heterogeneous information sources using source descriptions. In *Proceedings of the 22nd International Conference on Very Large Databases (VLDB-96)*, Bombay, India, September 1996.

(Mecca *et al.*, 1998) Giansalvatore Mecca, Paolo Atzeni, Alessandro Masci, Paolo Merialdo, and Giuseppe Sindoni. The ARANEUS web-base management system. In *Proceedings of the 1998 ACM SIGMOD*, June 1998.

(Muslea *et al.*, 1998) Ion Muslea, Steven Minton, and Craig Knoblock. Wrapper induction for semistructured, web-based information sources. In *Proceedings of the Conference on Automated Learning and Discovery (CONALD)*, 1998.

(Nigam *et al.*, 1998) K. Nigam, A. McCallum, S. Thrun, and T. Mitchell. Learning to classify text from labeled and unlabeled documents. In *Proceedings of the Fifteenth National Conference on Artificial Intelligence (AAAI-98)*, Madison, WI, 1998.

(Quinlan, 1994) J. Ross Quinlan. *C4.5: programs for machine learning*. Morgan Kaufmann, 1994.

(Salton, 1989) Gerard Salton, editor. *Automatic Text Processing*. Addison Welsley, Reading, Massachusetts, 1989.

(Tomasic *et al.*, 1997) Anthony Tomasic, Remy Amouroux, Philippe Bonnet, and Olga Kapitskaia. The distributed information search component (Disco) and the World Wide Web. In *Proceedings of the 1997 ACM SIGMOD*, May 1997.

(Yang and Chute, 1994) Y. Yang and C.G. Chute. An example-based mapping method for text classification and retrieval. *ACM Transactions on Information Systems*, 12(3), 1994.

ACT-R and Learning (Extended Abstract)

John R. Anderson
Department of Psychology
Carnegie Mellon University
Pittsburgh, PA 15213
ja+@cmu.edu

ACT-R (Anderson & Lebiere, 1998) is a unified theory of cognition that tries to satisfy Newell's constraints on a theory of mind. In addition it tries to be faithful to the detailed empirical literature on human cognition in tasks ranging from searching simple visual arrays to designing scientific experiments. ACT-R is embodied as a computer simulation program which can perform the same laboratory tasks as human subjects.

The basic control cycle in the ACT-R architecture involves (1) selecting a production rule relevant to the current goal; (2) executing the actions associated with that rule which can include retrieval of information from a declarative memory; and (c) updating the goal with the results of the actions and retrievals. In addition to symbolic learning of new productions and declarative information, critical learning in the ACT-R theory involves a subsymbolic tuning of the parameters that govern selection among productions and access to declarative information.

The basic thesis is that human intelligence depends of the subsymbolic tuning of knowledge to the statistical structure of environment. This will be illustrated in two domains. The first domain is human memory where we will describe the statistical patterns by which information repeats in the environment (Schooler & Anderson, 1998). ACT-R's subsymbolic learning mechanisms enable it to order the availability of information to reflect the probability that the information is relevant to the current processing. To illustrate the impact of these learning mechanisms, Christian Lebiere's (Lebiere, 1998) simulation of cognitive arithmetic will be described. This simulation captures the impact of the practice of the basic arithmetic facts over the first 20 years of life.

The second domain will concern selection of problem-solving operators. Marsha Lovett's research (Lovett, 1998) will be described showing how operator selection is sensitive to both the features of the current problem and the past history of success of the operators. ACT-R's subsymbolic mechanisms for learning utility of different production rules will be described. This includes a credit-assignment policy where all productions that apply to a particular goal receive equal credit for the outcome when that goal is resolved. Psychological data will be presented to evaluate this credit-assignment policy.

References

Anderson, J. R. & Lebiere, C. (1998). *The atomic components of thought.* Mahwah, NJ: Erlbaum.

Schooler, L. J. & Anderson, J. R. (1997). The role of process in the rational analysis of memory. *Cognitive Psychology, 32,* 219-250.

Lebiere, C. (1998). The dynamics of cognition: An ACT-R model of cognitive arithmetic. Ph.D., Dissertation. *CMU Computer Science Department, Technical Report* CMU-CS-98-186. Pittsburgh, PA.

Lovett, M. C. (1998). Choice. In J. R. Anderson and C. Lebiere (Eds.) *The atomic components of thought,* pp. 255-296. Mahwah, NJ: Erlbaum.

Some Elements of Machine Learning (Extended Abstract)

J. R. Quinlan
School of Computer Science and Engineering
UNSW
Sydney Australia 2052
quinlan@cse.unsw.edu.au

1 INTRODUCTION

This talk will revisit some important elements of ML lore, focusing on the design of classifier-learning systems. Within ML, the key desiderata for such systems have been predictive accuracy and interpretability. Although Provost, Fawcett and Kohavi (1998) have shown that accuracy alone is a poor metric for comparing learning systems, it is still important in most real-world applications. The quest for intelligibility, stressed from earliest days by Michie, Michalski and others, is now crucial for those data-mining applications whose main objective is insight. Scalability is also vital if the learning system is to be capable of analyzing the burgeoning numbers of instances and attributes in commercial and scientific databases.

The design of classifier-learning systems is guided by several perceived truths, including:

- Learning involves generalization.
- Most ML models are structures (exceptions being Naive Bayes and some instance-based models).
- A model is an element in a lattice of possible models, so search is unavoidable.
- General-to-specific and specific-to-general search are both important – most systems will use both.
- Similar instances probably belong to the same class (the *similarity assumption*).
- Learned models should not blindly maximize accuracy on the training data, but should balance resubstitution accuracy against generality, simplicity, interpretability, and search parsimony.
- Error can be decomposed into components arising from bias and variance, thereby helping to understand the behavior of learning systems.

We might all accept these, but that does not mean that their consequences and possibilities have been thoroughly explored. I would like to illustrate this with four mini-topics relevant to the design of classifier-learning systems: creating structure, removing excessive structure, using search effectively, and finding an appropriate tradeoff between accuracy and complexity.

2 STRUCTURED MODELS

Two commonly-used approaches used in ML are *divide-and-conquer*, which produces tree-structured models, and *cover*, which generally yields sequence models such as rulesets and Horn Clause programs. Both divide-and-conquer and cover can transform any parametric model class into a structured model class, reducing its bias but at the same time increasing its variance.

In propositional learning, model components such as leaves or rules are associated with contiguous regions in the instance space, and can thus be justified under the similarity assumption. But "closeness" in the instance space is not the only way to measure similarity; two instances can also be regarded as similar if they are mapped to the same output by some function. For example, consider the application of divide-and-conquer to Naive Bayes. Whereas Kohavi's (1996) NBTree generates a tree-structured model based on the familiar regional partition of the instance space, an alternative divides the instances on the basis of the class predicted by the current Naive Bayes model.

3 RIGHT-SIZING MODELS

The downside of structured models is their potential to overfit the training data. In ML we generally accept that it is better to construct a model and then post-process the structure to remove unhelpful parts. The methods used to decide whether structure is warranted can be grouped into

- syntactic heuristics such as MML/MDL, cost-complexity pruning, and structural risk minimization, and
- non-syntactic heuristics such as cross-validation, reduced error pruning, and pessimistic pruning.

MML/MDL is appealing – it has a firm basis in theory, does not require construction of additional models, uses all the training data, and avoids strong assumptions. However its performance depends critically on the way in which the conceptual messages are encoded. For example, MDL fares poorly in evaluations conducted by Kearns, Mansour, Ng, and Ron (1997). Wallace, the founder of MML, has questioned the coding approach used by Kearns et al and shows that an alternative scheme produces much better results.

4 COMPUTATION-INTENSIVE LEARNING

Structured models imply vast model spaces, so early ML algorithms used greedy heuristics in order to make the search tractable. As cycles have become exponentially cheaper, researchers have experimented with more thorough search. The results have been rather unexpected – theories have been found that are both simpler and fit the data better, but predictive accuracy has often suffered. Examples are provided by Webb's (1993) work with finding optimal rules, and Cameron-Jones' and my (1995) experiments varying the amount of search. (In hindsight, we might have expected this, since the phenomenon of overtraining is well-known in Neural Networks.)

Domingos (1998) has recently developed a "process-oriented" approach that relates true error rate directly to search complexity, much as MML/MDL relates it to theory complexity. An ideal formalism would take into account resubstitution error, theory complexity, and search complexity.

5 BOOSTING

Freund and Schapire's (1996) *boosting* has been acclaimed by ML researchers and statisticians alike. All empirical studies have found that boosting usually increases predictive accuracy, often dramatically.

On the other hand, boosted classifiers can become totally opaque. For instance, it is possible to construct a single decision tree that is exactly equivalent to a boosted sequence of trees, but the single tree can become enormous even when the sequence is as short as three.

Is there a middle ground? I will discuss a fledgling technique for using boosting to improve the predictive accuracy of a rule-based classifier without increasing its complexity. A more ambitious goal would be to find a comprehensible approximation to a boosted classifier.

6 LOOKING AHEAD

ML is a mature field with unique features that distinguish it from related disciplines such as Statistics. My list of its most valuable assets includes:

- A head start in relational learning (one decade at least).
- A substantial body of theory (eg, PAC-learnability, weak learnability, identification in the limit).
- Links between theory and system development (eg, boosting).
- An understanding of search and heuristics (a legacy of ML's roots in AI).
- A lack of hang-ups about optimality.

If I were given one wish regarding future directions in ML, it would be that we pay more attention to interpretability. For example, I would like to see:

- A model of interpretability (or, alternatively, of opacity).
- Approaches for constructing understandable approximations to complex models.
- Ways of reformulating models to improve their intelligibility.

Acknowledgements

Thanks to Sašo Džeroski and Ivan Bratko for comments on a draft of this abstract.

References

Domingos, P. (1998) A process-oriented heuristic for model selection. *Proceedings ICML'98*, 127-135. San Francisco: Morgan Kaufmann.

Freund, Y., and Schapire, R.E. (1997) A decision-theoretic generalization of on-line learning and an application to boosting. *Journal of Computer and System Sciences, 55*, 119-139.

Kearns, M., Mansour, Y., Ng, A.Y., and Ron, D. (1997) An experimental and theoretical comparison of model selection methods. *Machine Learning, 27*, 1, 7-50.

Kohavi, R. (1996) Scaling up the accuracy of naive-Bayes classifiers: a decision-tree hybrid. *Proceedings KDD-96.*

Provost, F., Fawcett, T., and Kohavi, R. (1998) The case against accuracy estimation for comparing induction algorithms. *Proceedings ICML'98*, 445-453. San Francisco: Morgan Kaufmann.

Quinlan, J.R., and Cameron-Jones, R.M. (1995) Oversearchinhg and layered search in empirical learning. *Proceedings IJCAI'95*, 1019-1024. San Francisco: Morgan Kaufmann.

Webb, G. (1993) Systematic search for categorical attribute-value data-driven machine learning. *Proceedings 6th Australian Joint Conference on Artificial Intelligence*, 342-347. Singapore: World Scientific.

Index

Large DB: see p 398   USDA nutrient DB.

Choosing discrete repn. of continuous data which minimises complexity: see
FAYYAD & IRANI 1993   refs: p 122

Nonparametric statistics: p. 453
D.A.S. FRASER   Wiley, New York 1957.

EM algorithm: p442
DEMPSTER, LAIRD & RUBIN
J. Royal Statistical Society 39 1-38 (1977)

Survey of clustering algorithms
A.K. JAIN & R.C. DUBES
Algorithms for Clustering Data. Prentice-Hall 1988

L.A. RABINER (p. 114)
A tutorial on Hidden Markov Models and Selected Applications in Speech Recognition
Proc IEEE 77(2) 257-285 (1989)

R.E. SCHAPIRE & Y. SINGER (p. 133)
Improved boosting algorithms using confidence-rated predictions
Proc 11th COLT p. 80-91 (1998)   to appear in ML